OXFORD HISTORY OF MODERN EUROPE

General Editors

LORD BULLOCK *and* SIR WILLIAM DEAKIN

Praise for THE TRIUMPH OF THE DARK

'A terrifically good read . . . a definitive account, the distillation of a lifetime's dedicated scholarship . . . No short review can do justice to the book's riches.'

Piers Brendon, *The Independent*

'A gigantic work of synthesis . . . a staggering achievement.'

Alex Danchev, *Literary Review*

'Magisterial . . . a magnificent work of scholarship, narrative, and authoritative historical judgment.'

Richard J. Evans, *The New Republic*

'A remarkable achievement of conscientious scholarship.'

Vernon Bogdanor, *New Statesman*

'Magisterial . . . Anyone who works on the 1930s will be permanently in Steiner's debt . . . Zara Steiner's account of this troubled decade is fuller and richer than any yet published.'

Richard Overy, *Times Literary Supplement*

'A modern classic . . . magnificent . . . Authoritative and absorbing, Steiner's volume will stand the test of time.'

Joe Maiolo, *BBC History Magazine*

'One of those masterpieces of exact scholarship, conceived on a vast scale, which will remain the standard work on the subject for many years.'

Jonathan Sumption, *The Spectator*

'A landmark event . . . Steiner's two volumes will undoubtedly become a standard work of reference for the two decades between the world wars . . . a triumph . . . a magnificent achievement . . . A distillation of a lifetime of fine scholarship, this is an invaluable account of one dimension of these complex and fateful years.'

Britain and the World

'A superbly wrought history and a major contribution to the field. It is a mammoth work filled to the brim with prodigious scholarship'

Patrick Porter, *History Today*

'Definitive . . . the most thorough, wide-ranging and carefully argued narrative available on the tumultuous decade that ended in world war. Every historian of the period will stand in Steiner's debt.'

Richard Overy, *Wall Street Journal*

'Zara Steiner has written a beautifully crafted and persistently intelligent survey of Europe's descent in the 1930s into war and barbarism.'

Harold James, *International Affairs*

THE TRIUMPH OF THE DARK

EUROPEAN INTERNATIONAL HISTORY 1933–1939

ZARA STEINER

UNIVERSITY PRESS

Great Clarendon Street, Oxford, OX2 6DP,
United Kingdom

Oxford University Press is a department of the University of Oxford.
It furthers the University's objective of excellence in research, scholarship,
and education by publishing worldwide. Oxford is a registered trade mark of
Oxford University Press in the UK and in certain other countries

First Edition published in 2011
First published in paperback 2013

Published in the United States of America by Oxford University Press
198 Madison Avenue, New York, NY 10016, United States of America

British Library Cataloguing in Publication Data
Data available

ISBN 978–0–19–967609–5

Printed and bound by
CPI Group (UK) Ltd, Croydon, CR0 4YY

The manufacturer's authorised representative in the EU for product safety is
Oxford University Press España S.A. of El Parque Empresarial San Fernando de Henares, Avenida de Castilla, 2 – 28830 Madrid (www.oup.es/en or product.safety@oup.com).
OUP España S.A. also acts as importer into Spain of products made by the manufacturer.

To George — the alpha and omega

CONTENTS

List of Maps ix
List of Tables x
List of Abbreviations xii

Prologue 1

Part I. Retreat from Internationalism, 1933–1938

1. Brown Dawn: The Rise of Hitler and the Death of Disarmament, 1933–1934 9
2. Uncertain Embraces: The European Powers and Nazi Germany, 1934–1935 62
3. The Assault on Versailles and Locarno: Ethiopia and the Remilitarization of the Rhineland 100
4. The Remnants of Internationalism, 1936–1938 167
5. The Spanish Cockpit, 1936–1937 181
6. 'Loaded Pause': Rearmament and Appeasement, 1936–1937 252
7. Illusions of Neutrality: Eastern Europe, 1936–1938 359
8. Whither the Soviet Union? Moscow and the West, 1936–1938 414
9. Thunder from the East: The Sino-Japanese Conflict and the European Powers, 1933–1938 474
10. Hitler Moves: Austria and Czechoslovakia, 1938 552
11. The Munich Settlement 610

Part II. The Road to Hitler's War, 1938–1939

12. The Fog of Peace: Strategic Choices after Munich 671
13. Black Sun: Aggression and Deterrence 727
14. Darkening Skies: Peace Talking and War Planning in Britain and France 765
15. Unleashing the Dogs of War 832
16. Red Clouds: The Soviet Union and the Nazi–Soviet Pact, 1939 867

17. Escape from War or Persecution? The Smaller Powers and the Jews 923
18. The Nightmare of the Dark: The Decisions for War 995
CONCLUSION 1036
EPILOGUE 1058
APPENDICES 1068
A. Statistical Tables 1068
B. Prime Ministers and Foreign Ministers of Selected European Powers 1073
C. Chronology of International Events, 1933–1941 1077

GENERAL BIBLIOGRAPHY 1082

INDEX 1117

LIST OF MAPS

1. Germany: Territorial Acquisitions and Frontier Changes 1935 – March 1939 11
2. Hoare–Laval Proposals, 1935 Based on map from Martin Gilbert, *Recent History Atlas, 1860–1960* (London, 1977), 51 124
3. The Rhineland Demilitarized Zone 1935 143
4. Spain during the Spanish Civil War 182
5. Eastern Europe, 1933–1938 361
6. East Asia 1931–1939 475
7. Potential Soviet Aerial Support for Czechoslovakia, September 1938 Based on map provided by Col. David M. Glantz (ret.) 620
8. Soviet Military Mobilization, September 1938 Based on map provided by Col. David M. Glantz (ret.) 621
9. The Dismemberment of Czechoslovakia, 1938–1939 688
10. The British Empire in the 1930s 796
11. The French Empire in the 1930s Based on map from Robert Aldrich, *Greater France: A History of Overseas Expansion* (Basingstoke, 1996) 797
12. Distribution of British Troops, 1 January 1938 Based on map from Brian Bond, *British Military Policy between the Two World Wars* (Oxford, 1980) 801
13. The Free City of Danzig, 1919–1939 840
14. The Nazi–Soviet Pact, 23 August 1939 Based on map from Martin Gilbert, *Recent History Atlas, 1860–1960* (London, 1977), 62 911
15. Europe on the Eve of War, 1939 Adapted from Michael Jabara Carley, *1939: The Alliance that Never Was and the Coming of World War II* (Chicago, 1999) 994

LIST OF TABLES

1.1 Defence Requirement Committee (DRC), 1934 52
3.1 British and Italian Fleet Strengths during the Ethiopian Crisis 114
5.1 German Trade with Spain, 1932–1939 197
5.2 Spain's Market Share of German Pyrites Imports, 1932–1940 198
5.3 Italian War Material and Forces Sent to Spain, July 1936 – March 1939 220
5.4 Soviet War Material Sent to Spain by mid-May 1937 231
5.5 Soviet Planes Sent to Spain by June 1937 231
6.1 German Production Increases in the Four-Year Plan 257
6.2 French Military Expenditure, 1932–1937 273
6.3 German Military Expenditure, 1933–1938 331
6.4 Comparison of Annual Expenditure on the Three Services in Britain, 1933–1939 345
7.1 Germany's Share of East European Trade 374
7.2 Changes in the Direction of German Trade, 1929 and 1938 374
7.3 Disengagement of Germany from Trade with Western Powers, 1928–1938 375
7.4 British and German Exports as a Percentage of the Total Imports of the Nordic Countries, 1929–1939 388
7.5 British and German Shares of the Export Trade of the Baltic States, 1920–1938 388
7.6 British and German Shares of the Import Trade of the Baltic States, 1920–1938 389
8.1 Soviet Budget Outlays, Total and on Defence, 1928/29–1940 441
8.2 Gross Production of Soviet Armaments Industries, 1932–1937 442
8.3 Soviet Weapons Procurement, 1933–1936 442
8.4 State Budget Appropriations to NKVM–NKO in the First and Second Five-Year Plans 446
8.5 Soviet–German Trade, 1932–1940 448
9.1 Arms and Munitions to China up until 1937 (in pounds sterling) 519
9.2 Japanese Oil Imports 537
10.1 German Air Strength, 1936–1939 598
10.2 Comparison of Air Strengths, Munich Crisis 608
11.1 British Chiefs of Staff Assessment of Soviet Mobilization Strength—European Theatre Only 622
11.2 French Superiority by the Fifth Day of Mobilization, September 1938 625

12.1 Military Spending as Percentage of National Income, 1933–1941 676
12.2 Emigration from Germany, 1933–1938 678
12.3 Exports from British Colonies to Germany, Selected Commodities, 1925–1931 and 1932–1938 703
13.1 Value of German Trade with Eastern Europe, 1928, 1933–1939 731
13.2 Foreign Share of German Imports Immediately before the War 732
14.1 British Aircraft Deliveries, 1939–1940 773
14.2 French Military Expenditure, 1936–1939 779
14.3 Percentage of Gross National Product Devoted to Military Expenditure (Great Britain, Germany, France, 1935–1940) 779
14.4 British Defence Expenditure as Percentage of National Income, 1933–1939 779
14.5 Value of Imports to Britain—Analysis by Country Source 799
14.6 Percentage Represented by France's Trade with the Colonies 806
15.1 German Army Expansion, 1936–1939 835
15.2 German Production of Aircraft and Ammunition, 1937–1939 835
15.3 The Future of German Ammunition Production (as Presented to Hitler, July 1939) 836
16.1 Personnel of the Soviet Regular Armed Forces 871
16.2 Ships Entering Service with the Soviet Navy, 1930–1941 872
16.3 Soviet Tank and Armament Production and Procurement, 1930–1940: Alternative Figures 874
16.4 The Number of Weapons in Military Procurement, 1930–1940 875
16.5 Soviet Raw Material Deliveries to Germany under the Nazi–Soviet Pact, 1939–1941 916
17.1 Main Countries of Jewish Immigration in 1937 974
17.2 Main Countries of Jewish Immigration, January–June 1938 975
17.3 Distribution of Jewish Emigrants in 1938 976
17.4 German Jewish Immigrants into Palestine, 1933–1939 977
18.1 German and Polish Forces in September 1939 1020
18.2 German, Polish, and Soviet Losses in September 1939 1029
A-1 US$ Conversion Tables, 1929–1941 1068
A-2 German Output of Modern Bombers and Fighters, 1936–1939 1069
A-3 German Aircraft Production, 1934–1939 1070
A-4 Comparative Strengths of the Principal Naval Powers before September 1939 1071
A-5 Major Soviet Exports to Germany, 1939–1941 1071
A-6 Major German Exports to Soviet Union, 1938–1941 1072

LIST OF ABBREVIATIONS

AA	*Auswäntiges Amt* (German Foreign Ministry)
APD	*Association pour la paix par le droit* (Association for Peace through Law)
ARP	air raid precaution
ASDIC	underwater sound detection apparatus
BCEN	Banque Commerciale pour l'Europe du Nord (Commercial Bank for Northern Europe)
BEF	British Expeditionary Force
CAB	Cabinet Office
CCP	Chinese Communist Party
CER	Chinese Eastern Railway
CGT	*Confédération Générale du Travail* (General Confederation of Labour)
CID	Committee of Imperial Defence
CNT	*Confederación Nacional de Trabajo* (National Confederation of Labour)
Comintern	Communist International
COS	Chiefs of Staff
CP	Confidential Print
CPDN	*Comité Permanent de la Défense Nationale* (Permanent Committee of National Defence)
CSDN	*Conseil Supérieure de la Défense Nationale* (Supreme Council of National Defence)
CTV	*Corpo di Truppe Volontarie* (Corps of Volunteer Troops)
Deuxième Bureau	*Deuxième Bureau de l'État-major général* (Second Bureau of the General Staff)
DBFP	*Documents on British Foreign Policy*
DCR	*Division Cuirassée de Réserve* (Reserve Armoured Division)
DDF	*Documents Diplomatiques Français* (French Diplomatic Documents)
DDI	*Documenti diplomatici italiani* (Italian Diplomatic Documents)
DGFP	*Documents on German Foreign Policy*
DRC	Defence Requirements Committee
DVP	*Dokumenty vaeshnei politiki SSSR* (Documents on foreign policy, USSR)

EFO	Economic and Financial Organization
FBI	Federation of British Industries
FRUS	*Foreign Relations of the United States*
GK	God Krizisa: dokumenti i materiali (Year of Crisis: documents and materials)
GRU	*Glavnoye Razvedyvatel'noye Upravleniye* (Main Intelligence Directorate)
Hansard	Official Report of Parliamentary Debates (Commons and House of Lords)
HISMA	*Compañía Hispano-Marroquí de Transportes Limitada* (Spanish-Moroccan Transport Comany Limited)
IIC	Industrial Intelligence Centre
ILO	International Labour Organization
IPC	International Peace Campaign
JONS	*Juntas de Ofensiva Nacional-Sindicalista* (Unions of the National-Syndicalist Offensive)
KdP	*Karpatendeutsche Partei* (Party of Carpathian Germans)
KMT	*Kuomintang*
KPD	*Kommunistische Partei Deutschlands* (Communist Party of Germany)
LICP	*Ligue internationale des combattants de la paix* (International League of Combattants for Peace)
LNU	League of Nations Union
MAE	Ministère des affaires étrangères, Paris
NARKOMINDEL	People's Commissariat of Foreign Affairs
NIC	Non-Intervention Committee
NID	Naval Intelligence Division
NKVD	*Narodnyy komissariat vnutrennikh del* (People's Commissariat for Internal Affairs)
NSB	*Nationaal-socialistische Beweging in Nederland* (Dutch National Socialist Movement)
NSDAP	*Nationalsozialistische Deutsche Arbeiterpartei* (National Socialist German Workers' Party)
OKH	*Oberkommando des Heeres* (High Command of the Army)
OKW	*Oberkommando der Wehrmacht* (High Command of the Armed Forces)
PCE	*Partido Comunista de España* (Communist Party of Spain)
PCF	*Parti Communiste Français* (French Communist Party)
PMC	Permanent Mandates Commission
POUM	*Partido Obrero Unificación Marxista* (Workers' Party of Marxist Unification)
PPU	Peace Pledge Union
PRO	Public Record Office (Kew)
PSUC	*Partido Socialista Unificado de Cataluña* (Unified Socialist Party of Catalonia)
Quai d'Orsay	French Ministry of Foreign Affairs
RAF	Royal Air Force

RI	Reichgruppe Industrie
ROWAK	*Rohstoffe- und Waren-Einkaufsgesellschaft* (Purchasing company for raw materials and goods)
RUP	*Rassemblement universel pour la paix* (Universal Association for Peace)
SA	*Sturmabteilung* (Storm-troopers)
SdP	*Sudetendeutsche Partei* (Party of Sudeten Germans)
SGDN	*Secrétariat Général de la Défense Nationale* (Secretariat-General for National Defence)
SIS	Secret Intelligence Service (Britain)
SS	*Schutzstaffel* (Protective Squads)
TASS	*Telegratnoe agentstvo Sovetskogo Soiuza* (Telegraph Agency of the Soviet Union)
VNV	*Vlaamsch Nationaal Verbond* (Flemish Nationalist Union)
WHO	World Health Organization
Wilhelmstrasse	German Foreign Ministry

PROLOGUE

It is with good reason that the 1930s have been called the dark decade. The events in themselves give grounds for despair. The knowledge that there was no light at the end of the tunnel but only more and greater catastrophes to come makes it difficult to keep any historical distance from the mistakes and errors of judgement that mark these years. This is a time with few heroes, two evil Titans, and an assortment of villains, and knaves. I have not enjoyed their company. Those statesmen who tried to do what they thought was best for their countries won only temporary reprieves from the impending disaster of war. Only a few, and not always the deserving, succeeded in escaping the consequences of the turmoils of the 1930s.

I found it impossible to write this book without being conscious of what was to follow. The longer I have worked on this period, the more convinced I have become that though initial and terminal dates are useful and necessary, they distort and falsify the historical record. They are, at best, only bookmarks. This is the second of a two-volume study. I have argued in the first volume, *The Lights that Failed: European International History, 1919–1933*, that any study of the inter-war years should start with the Great War, for it was the impact of that long and uniquely destructive European struggle that set the scene for all that followed. I chose to conclude that book with a discussion of the 'hinge years', 1929 to 1933, which witnessed the breakdown of the fragile reconstruction that followed the war's conclusion. I tried to show how the spreading economic depression exposed the fissures that ran through the international system and the structures of the European states, both old and new, forced to deal with the multiple problems created by the global 'Great Depression'. This concluding section is the necessary introduction to the present volume, which begins in 1933, a date that is both conventional and misleading.

In retrospect, Hitler's assumption of power marked a new chapter in German and European history but for most Europeans, as well as for many Germans, it was but part of a continuing story. The past was very much alive in contemporary memory. The shadow of the Great War still hung over the continent; many of those leaders who will feature in this book fought in that war and carried its psychological and physical scars. Few people over forty years of age remained untouched by its human and material costs. The 'never again' syndrome that so deeply marked French and British policies in the 1930s had its roots in the war's huge casualty figures. In Germany, the memory of wartime privations explains in large measure the fears of an older generation when faced with the possibility of war in 1938. Much of the diplomacy of the 1930s still addressed the issues raised by the peace treaties of 1919. Hitler brilliantly exploited the principle of 'self-determination' while the rivalries created in the redrawing of Eastern Europe exercised a baneful influence on the behaviour of statesmen right up to and after the outbreak of war. The more recent and, for some, still ongoing world depression remained an ever-present backdrop for the governments of the thirties. The prolonged and unusually severe economic crisis affected the daily life of large numbers of people not only in Europe but in other continents as well. Its long-lasting consequences went far beyond its original causes. There were exceptions, the Soviet Union was the most obvious, but the Great Depression left its mark on Great Powers and the small states, in the East as well as in the West. In these respects, as well as in other ways explored in subsequent chapters, there are continuities between the 1920s and 1930s which are all too easily obscured when Hitler takes centre stage.

The ending date for this volume, 1939 and the outbreak of war, is again obvious but even more unsatisfactory and inconclusive. The very brief epilogue, covering 1939–1941, marks only a stage, albeit a defining one, in the history of the conflict. For what began in September 1939 as a struggle between four European states (in fact, a war between Germany and Poland) became a continental and global war which ended the era of European predominance and called into question the very concept of Europe as something more than a geographic expression. Despite the voices of many Cassandras, neither of these possibilities were actually foreseen in 1939. For Europeans, the roots and consequences of the events covered by this volume go far beyond its calendar years.

This book records both the continuities and changes that took place in Western and Eastern Europe. It has a different focus to that of its predecessor. There is a central figure; in a surprisingly short time, Hitler dominates the scene. No European government could ignore his presence and the revival of German power associated with his leadership. Almost every chapter in this study reflects this reality. Whereas my previous book recounted the attempts to reconstruct Europe after the Great War, this one concentrates on the people and events that led to the outbreak of a new war. The first part of this book records not the reconstruction but the collapse of the international political and economic systems and the policies of those prepared to destroy them by force or to maintain them, by peaceful means, if possible. The last section sets out to explain why Hitler launched a war that he was not ready to fight, and why the British and French, neither of whom ever wanted to go to war again, elected to mobilize their populations for a new call to arms. I have tried, moreover, to suggest why men and women responded to this call despite the deep-seated and widespread reluctance to repeat the experiences of 1914–1918. In a more summary way, a penultimate chapter looks at the seemingly successful attempts of the smaller nations to flee from involvement in war and examines the reasons why the remaining Jews of the Greater Reich were denied even the possibility of flight. The final darkness was still to come.

I have tried to write 'international history' and not restrict my narrative to the exchanges between foreign ministries. This becomes harder for the thirties than for the twenties because the international canvas shrinks and the political relations between the states take precedence over all other aspects of inter-state behaviour. The enfeeblement of the League of Nations accelerated the retreat from multilateralism at every level. The Ethiopian crisis and the Rhineland reoccupation of 1935 affected the small states as well as the Great Powers. The former turned their backs on Geneva and sought in neutrality the defence of their independence which the League promised but could not deliver. The summit meetings of September 1939 had little in common with Lloyd George's conference diplomacy or the Locarno tea parties. Geneva was now irrelevant to any attempted management of international affairs. The concepts of 'collective security' and 'disarmament' lingered on well beyond their expiry date. By the end of the 1930s, bi-lateral treaties, alliances, and arms races dominate the scene. There could not be a real revival of the 'old diplomacy'; its basis had been permanently eroded by the Great War. But diplomatic practices returned to many of their pre-1914 forms. A few statesmen moved the pieces around the diplomatic chess-boards; their populations followed. The emergence of mass electorates, particularly in those few democracies that still survived, may have set limits on what elected leaders could do, but elsewhere dictators and autocrats could use the new techniques of propaganda and indoctrination, as well as violence, to ensure agreement, loyalty, and support. The balance between the nation-state and the international community moved decisively in the national direction. This was a time when few, if any governments, were prepared to interfere with the 'domestic affairs' of other nations, no matter how evil the abuse of power or the extent of the suffering inflicted. The purges in the Soviet Union and the Nazi persecution of the Jews were domestic matters. The political weakening of the League of Nations naturally affected its humanitarian work. Its impotence in the face of the refugee crisis of the thirties is just one example, if the most tragic, of the League's retreat. The vocabularies of the chancelleries reflected the return to pre-war practices; rearmament, arms races, and alliances were the common diplomatic currency of 1939.

As always in a book of this kind, one tries to find the balance between the discussion of domestic and foreign affairs while fully recognizing their inter-dependence. Less attention has been paid here to international economic questions; reparations had vanished although war debts were still on the American agenda. The limited attempts at currency stabilization and tariff reform hardly dented the almost universal movement into exclusively domestically determined policies. For the most part, I have concentrated on the influence of financial and economic questions on the behaviour of the ruling élites in determining foreign and strategic policy options. Some, it is true, were concerned mainly with economic recovery and attention was focused on domestic rather than foreign affairs. For others, however, when faced with the imminence of war, questions of finance and trade were seen as critical both for rearmament and the choice of diplomatic options. Even Hitler, who had no patience with the economic constraints on the preparations for war, had to consider their importance when launching his attack in September 1939. Far more attention has been given in this volume to the role of ideology and the uses made of the press and radio to enlist mass support. Ideological differences became central both to civil strife and to inter-state conflicts. As previously, I have dealt with Eastern Europe as well as the Soviet Union, sometimes separately and at other points as part of the larger European picture. Europe was still a unit though splitting apart.

In various places, but above all, in the Conclusion, I have tried to say something about the balance between systemic and domestic factors in shaping the course of European international history while always conscious of their continual interaction. There are two chapters that cut across the chronological approach followed in this account, one on the Spanish Civil War and the other on the Sino-Japanese conflict. It is my argument that the special ideological resonances of the former reached far beyond the conflict in Spain and are still heard in present-day accounts of this internally generated civil war. Historical myths can acquire realities of their own. The undeclared war in the Far East was a regional affair that had special importance for the Soviet Union and for Britain and its Empire. It was in this region, far more than in Europe, that the Anglo-American connection entered the global strategic scene. Too often, the attention focused on the 1939–1941 period in the Far East fails to underline the interconnections between the conflicts in East and West. I would have liked to include a chapter on European imperialism and international relations that would have picked up some of the themes which are only sketched in my first volume and discussed intermittently in this second work. More attention could have been paid to the British Commonwealth and Empire as well as to the far from negligible empires of the other European powers. This would have allowed further discussion of the Middle East where for the first years of the war, more Commonwealth and imperial troops were engaged than those from Britain. I have explained my decision not to include a separate chapter on the United States without denying that the Germans, as well as the British and French, believed that American intervention would spell the difference between victory and defeat. At least until 1938, the United States was a case of the 'dog that did not bark' and, is consequently, more fairly treated as part of the general narrative. I have tried throughout to concentrate on what the decision-makers thought they were doing, however difficult the problem of decipherment, rather than reviewing what successive generations of historians have said about their behaviour. I have referred to the most important of these historiographic debates, some of which have already lost their relevancy, where I have felt they have actually contributed to the understanding of the twisted road to war.

I am deeply indebted to the impressively massive and continually growing list of scholars who have dealt with the 1930s. The chapter bibliographies can give only a hint of the vast available literature. There are good reasons why so many of the new studies of this period are multi-authored volumes. Even with the willing help of the many authors I have consulted, I have found it almost impossible to walk through the dense forest of the secondary material. Too often, I have succumbed to the temptation of going back to the archives, only to find that the material could not be incorporated without expanding an already long account to impossible lengths. I can only hope that some of what I have found will give life and substance to my arguments. The temptation to follow the paper trail has sometimes been overwhelming. I look back with envy at my very first book which was based almost entirely on primary sources.

I can only thank in a general way the large number of people in at least eight countries who have assisted me, either by answering questions or by calling my attention to books, articles, and sources that would have escaped my attention. Some have willingly translated documents in languages in which I have no competence. Those who have spent time in foreign archives on my behalf have been named in the body of the book. I would like to mention specifically a few people without whom this book would never have seen the light of day.

The three anonymous readers of the original manuscript covering both books have agreed to be named. Professors Sally Marks, David Reynolds, and Jonathan Steinberg each gave the kind of detailed critique that no author has the right to expect. I can only hope that, despite dealing with a stubborn and often resistant writer, they will not feel that their extensive labours were in vain. I would also like to thank one of my former Ph.D. students, Dr Andrew Webster, now teaching at Murdoch University in Perth, Australia, who, through the miracle of email, has managed to keep me afloat throughout the writing of this volume. Dr Peter Jackson, of the University of Wales at Aberystwyth, has repeatedly come to my rescue even with regard to subjects that were only of marginal interest to him. Professor Keith Neilson, of the Royal Military College of Canada at Kingston, has saved me from errors of both fact and interpretation. He is in no way responsible for those that remain. To all these men and women, named and unnamed, I want to offer my sincere and heartfelt thanks. I plead guilty, before publication, for any material that has been used without attribution or permission. I can only plead that this was not conscious plagiarism.

Since my retirement, I realize how fortunate I have been to have had so many research students who have kept me at the coal-face of current research. I miss their presence, but am much gratified by the number of their theses that have become books and are cited in the chapter bibliographies. Like so many others, I have found librarians and archivists unfailingly helpful. To the list found in my first volume, I would like to add Professor O. A. Rzheshevsky formerly of the Institute of Universal History, Russian Academy of Sciences, Moscow, Professor Dr Serban Papacostea, director of the Institutul de Istorie 'Nicolae Iorga' in Bucharest, and the Deutsches Tagebucharchiv for permission to use the archives under their respective direction. Editors at OUP have shown exemplary patience with this work. Kay Clement took on the heavy burden of copy-editing the whole manuscript. I also want to thank Jo Wallace-Hadrill for preparing the electronic version of this book and helping with the proof-reading of the final manuscript. I have previously thanked the foundations that funded much of the research in Britain and abroad for both these books. I want to acknowledge again the support I received from the Leverhulme Trust, the Nuffield Foundation Small Grants Scheme, the John D. and Catherine T. MacArthur Foundation, and the John Simon Guggenheim Memorial Foundation. Dr Tom Neuhaus found time from work on his Ph.D. thesis to unravel the mysteries of my computer files and to help prepare the final manuscript for publication. Thanks are due to Jonathan Dwerryhouse without whose care and computer skills, this manuscript would have never emerged from the hands of it technophobic author. My greatest debt is acknowledged elsewhere.

PART I

Retreat from Internationalism, 1933–1938

'Men do make their own history, but they do not make it as they please, not under conditions of their own choosing, but rather under circumstances which they find before them, under given and imposed conditions.'

Karl Marx, Eighteenth Brumaire of Louis Bonaparte

1

Brown Dawn: The Rise of Hitler and the Death of Disarmament, 1933–1934

At the start of 1933, the international system was in disarray. The League of Nations had been badly damaged by its mishandling of the Manchurian crisis and by the prolonged disarmament discussions being held in Geneva. Much had been expected from the World Disarmament Conference of 1932; the failure of the statesmen to make any progress was a severe blow to popular expectations. The on-going depression had shattered the fragile, international financial and trading structure and led to a general retreat from co-operation between the states. Countries adopted domestic remedies to shore up damaged economies and engaged in 'beggar-thy-neighbour' policies. Britain, long the champion of liberal internationalism, and the United States abandoned gold and turned inward in the search for solutions to their problems. The World Economic Conference of 1933 had been a disaster. Bilateral and competitive bloc agreements replaced the multilateral arrangements of the previous decade. The political repercussions of the depression were felt in both Western and Eastern Europe, and throughout the world. Particularly in Eastern Europe, governments turned to centralizing and interventionist policies. Many countries introduced state-assisted or directed economic measures, strengthening the power of the state. Political, economic, ethnic, and religious tensions at home spilled over to magnify enmities between neighbouring countries. In the Baltic, Central Europe, and in the Balkans, where new or more authoritarian governments had been established, neo-fascist and extreme right-wing movements, some financed by Rome or Berlin, became increasingly popular and influential. Though copying the slogans, uniforms, and techniques of mobilization from movements in Italy and Germany, they had their own programmes and genuine sources of native support. The danger to the ruling conservative élites came from the extreme right rather than from the Communists, whose parties were outlawed in many countries, and whose appeal was limited in states with large peasant populations, who hated the very idea of collectivization.

Threatened governments copied the nationalist rhetoric of the extremists, and adopted the same anti-Semitic, anti-Bolshevik, and anti-democratic platforms as their far right rivals. Almost everywhere in Europe, changes were taking place which made public life more dangerous and threatening to the existing international order. Its fragility presented many opportunities for new assaults on the status quo. And on 30 January 1933, Hitler was sworn in as Chancellor of Germany. The twisted and tortuous road to Europe's war stretched out far ahead, but the first steps had already been taken.

I

It is with Hitler and Hitler's intentions that any student of European international history must start. The abundance of German documentary sources provides a treasure trove of information for historians and in contrast to Soviet/Russian practice, they were rapidly made available to researchers. The flood of books on Nazi Germany began early, yet studies of Hitler and the Third Reich continue to flow. How could this basically banal and crude Austrian, hardly distinguishable from so many other post-war politicians, have succeeded in a politically sophisticated, highly industrialized, and culturally advanced nation? The Weimar experiment, whatever its faults and failures, offered a rich menu of possibilities: too rich, perhaps, for the constrained circumstances within which it had to operate. The multi-causal story of the demise of Weimar Germany and the rise of Hitler has been explored in depth. Historians point to the burden of defeat and the Treaty of Versailles, the failure to create a deep-rooted legitimacy of its own, the weakness of the country's economic recovery, and the crushing experience of inflation and depression as the key contributing factors to the collapse of the Weimar Republic. Well before Hitler's 1930 electoral breakthrough, the basic structure of the state had fractured and the electorate had begun to desert the Weimar parties. The disasters of the years 1929 to 1932—the exceptionally severe depression, the introduction of presidential government, and demise of parliamentary politics, the divisive effects of the unpopular deflationary measures—produced that 'disintegration of power' and created the political vacuum which brought the old anti-republican conservative élite into office. It was at their invitation that Hitler became chancellor. His selection was not an inevitable result of the death of Weimar. He was appointed, however, because he headed a mass party, which though past its peak of popularity, could provide the popular backing that the anti-republican élite so badly needed. The rewarding 'working towards the Führer' thesis put forward by Ian Kershaw in his biography of Hitler to explain his rise should not shift

Map 1. Germany: Territorial Acquisitions and Frontier Changes 1935 – March 1939

attention from Hitler's extraordinary talents. He had come from nowhere to make his mark in German politics even before the onset of the depression. His unusual combination of political skills and the exceptional situation in Germany after 1929 provided the openings for their full display. Charisma, oratory, political cunning, and the singularity of a 'vision' that reflected and enhanced the fears, anxieties, resentments, and desires of millions of Germans explain, in part, Hitler's ability to mobilize the disillusioned and disaffected in every class throughout Germany. Without Hitler, there could have been no Nazi party. The same was not true of Stalin and the Communist party.

The search for the sources of Hitler's popularity continues to the present day. Much has been written about the 'real Hitler' but little settled. What is indisputable is that a great number, though not a majority, of Germans supported him and that their numbers swelled after 1933, despite individual hostility to some of his methods and the acknowledged failure of the regime to keep many of its promises. German loyalty to Hitler remained constant even when the country faced defeat and destruction. Coercion and terror were certainly part of the story. So were the Nazi propaganda and indoctrination campaigns, both brilliantly executed. The techniques of mass mobilization, employing the latest technology, undoubtedly enhanced the sense of unity and collective strength while a series of foreign policy triumphs confirmed the links between leader and people. Hitler was fortunate in his timing. The depression had already reached its nadir in Germany, and recovery had begun. Whatever the economic difficulties of the early Hitler years, life was better for the majority than during the depression. Early rearmament put the unemployed back to work. The international scene, too, provided opportunities for risk-taking; Hitler's boldness paid high domestic dividends. In a surprisingly short time, he had restored German self-respect and pride in nation.

What were Hitler's objectives? Did he have in mind some form of foreign policy 'programme', open or concealed, which won such overwhelming support? The old 'intentionalist–functionalist debate' has lost much of its intensity. It is no longer argued, as some 'intentionalists' claimed, that Hitler was the head of a monolithic power structure, or that he had a coherent programme of aggression to be implemented stage by stage, according to some pre-arranged timetable. Nor has the extreme version of the functionalist (or structuralist) case survived. Few today believe that Hitler was a pure opportunist or that much of his foreign policy was 'domestic policy projected outwards' without any defined objectives in mind. Though most contemporary historians start from a Hitler-centric view of Nazi foreign policy, it is generally agreed that both approaches, Hitler's 'intentions' and 'impersonal structures', are required for any understanding of the 1930s.[1] Hitler's ideological goals shaped the course of Nazi foreign policy; he actively intervened in its management and determined its ultimate direction. Nonetheless, the achievement of his long-term objectives were subject to structural forces that led to changes and adjustments in his actions. Hitler was an opportunist who knew where he was going. Given the highly developed administrative structure and polycratic nature of the German government, and Hitler's active encouragement of competition among his subordinates, it was inevitable that there should be inconsistencies and confusions in German diplomacy. Hitler's periods of inaction and even physical withdrawal from Berlin left ministers free to pursue their own programmes, often simultaneously and in opposition to each other. Hitler disliked dealing with the details of policy and was lazy about paperwork. Much was done without his personal authorization and even without his knowledge. There was a 'war against all' in Berlin, but when major issues had to be decided and conflicts resolved, Hitler moved decisively and imposed his authority. He was always master in his own house.

Hitler was aware of the limitations on his freedom of action, some arising from the financial and economic weaknesses of the Reich, and others from the need to satisfy the competitive claims of élites and agencies, both military and civilian, whose co-operation was essential for the achievement of his objectives. Moreover, Germany was hardly in a position to press Hitler's claims to a hegemonic position in Europe in the face of objections from other great powers. Moves on the diplomatic chess-board and their timing depended on external circumstances over which Hitler had no, or only limited, control. The country had no strategic, military, or economic advantage that allowed Hitler to prejudge the outcome of his actions. Germany's comparative weakness was the basic cause of the arguments between Hitler and his advisers in 1938 and 1939. The dictator's range of options diminished after the Munich conference in the face of the hardening Anglo-French attitude. He took risks but not without calculation.

Throughout the pre-war years, there was a constant interplay between Hitler's fixed objectives and the structural factors that determined how they were to be achieved. The twists and changes in German diplomacy never involved the abandonment of Hitler's long-term goals and the ideological presumptions upon which they were based. Were these goals specifically defined or were they merely 'ideological metaphors'? Are we not dealing with the age-old 'struggle for the mastery of Europe', old wine poured into newly labelled bottles? It is the underlying thesis of this book that Hitler's ultimate purposes had a concrete meaning and that

[1] Ian Kershaw, *The Nazi Dictatorship: Problems and Perspectives of Interpretation* (London, 1993, 2000), 108–130.

they found their fruition in an unimaginable war and the destruction of European Jewry. Hitler's basic ideas were common currency in pre-war Vienna and post-war Munich, but he was able to translate them into an achievable reality hardly imagined even by their begetters. Using the Social Darwinian terminology of the 1890s, the stock-in-trade of so many politicians, Hitler argued that countries were engaged in a perpetual struggle for self-preservation and survival. As states were forced to provide the sustenance for their expanding populations and the available room for expansion was limited, struggle was endemic in the world system. Germany needed land, not people, and land could only be won through war. The nation would have to be taught 'that we can be saved only by fighting and that every other thought must give way to this', Hitler told his army and navy commanders on 3 February 1933.[2] In the end, victory in war was the ultimate test of men and nations. Both in *Mein Kampf* (1925) and in the *Zweites Buch* (1928, but only published in 1961) Hitler wrote that the required lands would have to be wrested from the Soviet Union. He rejected any return to Germany's 1914 borders or the fulfilment of the annexationist goals of Wilhelmine Germany. Colonial pickings outside of Europe would hardly serve his purpose. Most of the many references to the 'conquest of living space in the East and its ruthless Germanization' are found in speeches to military officers and party chiefs. Hitler cultivated, for domestic as well as foreign purposes, a public image that could have made him a candidate for the Nobel peace prize. In some respects, as became clear in September 1938, he may have succeeded too well for he felt it necessary after Munich to launch a press campaign to make the German people 'war-worthy'.

Hitler warned in *Mein Kampf* that Germany would 'either be a world power, or cease to be'. The phrase, so familiar to historians of the Great War, took on a new racial meaning in Hitler's hands that was central to the theme of *Lebensraum* ('living space'). Only the acquisition of an empire in the East would enable Germany to fulfil its historic mission to lay the foundation of an Aryan world order. Hitler purposely avoided disclosing his apocalyptic vision for the future, unwilling to frighten his more conservative followers and the wider public he wished to enlist. As a result, the outbreak of war came as an unwelcome shock to many Germans. It may be true that relatively few Germans grasped in 1939 what a racial war entailed. Yet Hitler's Jew-hatred and quest for racial purity was at the heart of his imperial ambitions. The paranoiac obsession with 'the Jewish question' found expression in its most virulent

[2] Comments by Hitler to meeting of leading generals, 3 February 1933, in J. Noakes and G. Pridham (eds.), *Nazism, 1919–1945: A Documentary Reader*, Vol. 3: *Foreign Policy, War and Racial Extermination* (Exeter, 1998), no. 472.

form in Hitler's earliest writings and public speeches. His first recorded written statement about the 'Jewish question' was in a letter sent to Adolf Gemlich, dated 16 September 1919. Asserting that Jewry was a race and not a religion, Hitler went on to say that the final aim of anti-Semitism based on reason 'must unshakeably be the removal of the Jews altogether'.[3] It proved to be a lifetime sickness. In the last paragraph of the *Political Testament* written just before his suicide in the Berlin bunker, the 'man of destiny' charged 'the leaders of the nation and those under them to scrupulous observance of the laws of race and to merciless opposition to the universal poisoner of all peoples, international Jewry'.[4] There was nothing startling about Hitler's anti-Semitism. Suspicion, dislike, and hatred of the Jews were common currency in Europe before, during, and after the Great War. The influx of Jews from the East and the visible role of Jews in Communist and radical parties had already produced anti-Semitism of an unprecedented virulence in Germany during the chaotic post-war period. Anti-Semitic sentiments and attacks on Jews were far more numerous in other European nations. However widespread and well-nourished Hitler's obsession with the Jews may appear, he was able to recast traditional Jew-hatred into terms that strongly attracted many of his original followers. He preached that the Jew posed a special danger to the 'blood value' of the German people, a danger increased by the past policies of earlier governments. The triumph of the Aryans depended on the elimination of the Jewish 'parasites' at home and the struggle, as he wrote in *Mein Kampf*, had to be carried on beyond Germany's borders. In the conclusion to the *Zweites Buch*, Hitler argued that the Jewish people, incapable of creating a territorial state, fed on the creative power of others. They sought the 'denationalization' and the 'promiscuous bastardization of other peoples'. The Jewish challenge was a world-wide attempt ('Juda is a world plague') to bring about 'bloody Bolshevization' and 'world dominion over mankind'. Anti-Semitism and anti-Marxism were integrally linked in Hitler's rhetoric; he repeatedly used the term 'Jewish Bolshevism'. When necessary, however, he could also treat them as separate entities depending on the nature of his audience. Because he endowed Jews with powers they had never possessed, his belief in a Jewish world conspiracy was real and extended beyond Europe to the United States. In the *Zweites Buch*, he had called attention to the American threat and its challenge to the global significance of Europe. Subsequently, particularly in the face of the outraged American reaction to *Kristallnacht*, the 'international Jewish question' came to be

[3] Ian Kershaw, *Hitler: 1889–1936: Hubris* (London, 1998), 125.

[4] Werner Maser, *Hitlers Briefe und Notizen* (Düsseldorf, 1973), 355–375.

understood in the Third Reich as synonymous with America. Roosevelt was seen as the tool of Jewish capital and the United States as the fulcrum of the Jewish world conspiracy for the ruination of Germany. After 1938, Jew-dominated America joined the ranks of Germany's 'hate inspired enemies'.[5]

Just as Hitler played down his intention to lead the German people to war, so he disguised his obsession with the Jews and distanced himself from the violent anti-Semitic outrages of the party activists. Hitler rarely reverted in public, before 1941, to the crude anti-Semitic language of his early years. There were relatively few speeches between 1933 and 1939 devoted solely to 'the Jewish question', and most of these were addressed to the party faithful. At the Nuremberg party rally in September 1935, Hitler took to the podium to justify the introduction of the 'Nuremberg laws'. In this instance, he emphasized the legality of the state's campaign to isolate the Jews and called on the party and nation to maintain discipline and avoid 'individual acts against Jews'. Though his sympathies lay with the extremists, it was not yet time to publicly show his hand. During the next two years, he made only occasional public references to the 'Jewish problem' and gave no major speech on the subject. There was, of course, no reason to push forward the radicalization of the Jewish question. By 1936, Nazi anti-Semitic legislation and the isolation of the Jews were generally acceptable to most Germans, even those who did not actively participate in anti-Jewish activities or take part in the dissemination of the official view. It was not until September 1937, again at a party rally, that Hitler, linking the Jews with the Bolsheviks, gave vent to his raw Jew-hatred. He stood behind, though again without any public identification, the vicious propaganda campaign and waves of physical attacks on Jews in the summer of 1938, culminating in the *Kristallnacht* pogrom on 9–10 November. The nationwide attacks on individual Jews, the destruction of property, and the burning of synagogues had Hitler's personal approval. On the eve of the horrors, at a party reception held in Munich, Hitler conferred with Goebbels. Goebbels noted in his diary: 'Huge amount going on. I explain the matter to the Führer. He decides; let the demonstrations continue. Pull back the police. The Jews should for once get to feel the anger of the people. That's right.'[6] Hitler made no reference to these events, either privately or publicly but they appear to have made a deep impact on him. *Kristallnacht* revived not only the deeply imbedded urge

[5] Adam Tooze, *The Wages of Destruction: The Making and Breaking of the Nazi Economy* (London, 2006), 282.

[6] Elke Fröhlich (ed.), *Tagebücher von Joseph Goebbels*, Teil 1, Vol. 6 (Munich, 1993), 180 (entry for 9 November 1938).

to rid Germany of its Jews, but his belief in the Jewish world conspiracy to destroy Germany. In Hitler's speech to the Reichstag on 30 January 1939, the sixth anniversary of his take-over of power, the connections between world Jewry, the opposition of Britain and the United States to German expansion in the East, and the beginning of another war were explicitly drawn. The democratic powers were threatened with an 'all-out struggle' if they blocked Germany's export drive or march to the East. The Jews were threatened that: 'if international finance Jewry inside and outside Europe should succeed in plunging the nations once more into a world war, the result will be not the Bolshevization of the earth and thereby the victory of Jewry, but the annihilation of the Jewish race in Europe'.[7] The German public was so conditioned by the anti-Jewish character of the Nazi regime that Hitler's reference to the fate of the Jews, though picked out for special notice in a number of German papers, evoked neither enthusiasm nor condemnation. The way had been prepared for acquiescence in, if not approval of, the next step. In 1941 and repeatedly during 1942, Hitler would refer back to his prophetic words, knowing that the 'Final Solution' to the Jewish problem had been found.

Clear about his ultimate goals, Hitler was unsure about how to achieve them. In the early 1920s, he thought in terms of a war of revenge against France that would put an end to its hegemonic position in Europe. He wrote in *Mein Kampf* of the close links between Germany and Italy and of his hopes for an alliance with Britain. The partnership with Rome took on new importance with the triumph of Italian Fascism. The two ideologically sympathetic nations could create, he wrote, the nucleus of a new Europe that would stem the triumph of Jewish–Marxist–Bolshevism in state after state. The question of *Anschluss* could be solved, and the Italians persuaded to abandon their opposition. If Italy was to be Germany's first friend, Hitler believed that Britain, too, could play a special part in furthering his foreign policy aims. He assumed that as Germany would be engaged on eastward expansion for many years to come, there was no reason for either Britain or Italy 'to keep up the enmity of the World War'. Though in *Mein Kampf*, Hitler recognized Britain's historic association with the balance of power and its wish 'to prevent any one continental power in Europe from attaining a position of world importance', his reading of the mistakes made by the leaders of Wilhelmine Germany convinced him that he could enlist British backing for German ambitions in the East. As

[7] Max Domarus, *Hitler: Reden und Proklamationen, 1932–1945: Kommentiert von einem deutschen Zeitgenossen*, Vol. II (Munich, 1965), 1058.

long as expansion was confined to the continent and did not threaten British maritime and imperial interests, he assumed, mistakenly, that there was no reason for Anglo-German conflict, and that he could enlist the British as allies. Until 1937, if not later, the Führer took care not to initiate an overseas policy that would provoke British hostility. In return for a free hand in the East, Hitler was prepared to underwrite the British Empire. In the *Zweites Buch,* he wrote of his hopes that Britain would join Germany in the war against America, in order to preserve its global position. Whatever his ideas, and these were vague, about German world dominion and the future struggle against Britain and the United States, the latter being the ultimate adversary, his immediate objectives were concentrated on the continent and the inevitable 'showdown with Russia'. *Lebensraum* may have had a metaphysical meaning but it was also something concrete that could not be achieved without a war against Bolshevik Russia, an enemy already weakened by the triumph of the Judeo-Bolsheviks over its Germanic inhabitants who had made the country so powerful in the past. Hitler made a concerted effort to secure British friendship and continued along this path even when the offers produced less than he hoped. The often muffled or ambivalent British response encouraged illusions that his tactics might prove successful. If during 1937 he came to doubt whether Britain would accept a free hand for Germany in Eastern Europe, he still did not abandon the quest for an arrangement or at the least, an assurance of future neutrality. Even when determined on war, he went through the motions of offering the British a bribe in return for their desertion of Poland.

Hitler's view of France changed with his perceptions of its strength. Throughout the 1920s, as the strongest military power in Western Europe, he portrayed France as Germany's most immediate enemy. By 1931, he was moving away from this position and considered whether France might not be convinced to abandon her 'policy of encirclement'. In a now discredited interview with Richard Breiting, the editor of the *Leipziger Neueste Nachrichten,* Hitler is supposed to have said that once he took power he would approach both Britain and France, counting on their understanding of his need to lead a crusade against Bolshevism. During his first year in office, he sought an arrangement with Paris on the basis of French recognition of German rearmament and when these moves failed, worked through London to secure French acceptance of a post-Versailles treaty arrangement favourable to Germany. Trying to avoid direct confrontation during the period of German weakness, he tried to isolate France diplomatically, forcing Paris to choose between unilateral action and acquiescence in German rearmament. Early success, and the French failures to respond militarily to German provocation, increased Hitler's confidence.

The Rhineland re-occupation confirmed his belief that despite its numerically superior army, France would never act without Britain.

II

Whereas, in retrospect, it is clear that Hitler's appointment as chancellor of Germany on 30 January 1933 was a decisive change in German and European politics, this was not so obvious to contemporaries. Few Germans were in any doubt about Hitler's message or the Nazi tactics used to win support and crush opposition but much of the Nazi programme, apart from its anti-Semitic and anti-Bolshevik message, was clothed in generalities. The violence in the streets and the clashes between the various paramilitary groups had become a common, and almost acceptable, feature of German political life. Hitler's public speeches during the electoral campaign leading up to the 5 November 1932 elections were mainly attacks on the Papen government. The rhetoric was anti-Weimar and anti-Marxist, but without specific content. Against the background of the seemingly endless depression, despair and apathy spread throughout the Reich along with considerable bitterness about the impotence of the Republic and all the parties associated with it. Though, in the November election, the Nazis had lost both votes and seats in the Reichstag and appeared to have passed their peak, they still were the largest party (196 seats) in the Reichstag. The Communists, too, made gains, and with a total of a hundred seats were not far behind the shrinking but still second-largest party, the Social Democratic party (SPD). The decisive political moves were not in the Reichstag but in manoeuvrings behind the scenes. Neither Franz von Papen (1 June 1932 – 3 December 1932) nor his successor as chancellor, General Kurt von Schleicher (3 December 1932 – 30 January 1933), though each tried, was able to convince Hitler to join their respective governments. As the economic scene improved, Schleicher prepared a massive job-creation programme and a 'winter aid scheme' in a bid for public support, but he lacked a viable political base in the Reichstag. With the Nazi party in considerable internal difficulty and losing voters, Schleicher made a new bid for Nazi support, offering Gregor Strasser, Hitler's main party organizer, the vice-chancellorship. Hitler kept his nerve, imposed his authority on Strasser and those willing to compromise, and continued to demand the chancellorship. Schleicher's possible success stirred his enemies to action. President Hindenburg's entourage, including his son, Oskar, and ex-chancellor Papen, conspired to bring Schleicher down. Assured of presidential support, Papen and his circle, convinced that they could box Hitler in and render him harmless, agreed to pay his price for participation in their anti-republican government: the chancellorship and two key cabinet posts. Hitler was sworn in on the morning of 30 January.

Whatever Papen may have thought about the future, the Nazis and their supporters were triumphant. Joseph Goebbels, Hitler's chief propagandist, seized the opportunity to mount that night a torch-lit parade of SA and SS men, along with right-wing veterans' associations. The actual number of marchers and onlookers is disputed, but Goebbels succeeded in creating an atmosphere of victory and triumph. Many Berliners were caught up in the excitement. Similar parades took place throughout Germany. The response of the nation, whether in the capital or in the provinces, was far more mixed than these public demonstrations suggest: hostility, alarm, fear, apathy and indifference, and a belief that the Hitler regime, like its predecessors, would be short-lived. Horace Rumbold, the well-informed British ambassador in Berlin, reported that people throughout the country 'took the news phlegmatically'.[8] In the weeks leading to yet another election on 5 March which had been demanded by Hitler as part of the price for collaboration, the new chancellor stressed his intention to stamp out Marxism and to free Germany from the threat of Communism. The Communists remained relatively inactive in the face of widespread SA and police violence. The party leadership believed that the new government, the final gasp of 'monopoly capitalism', would last but a few months, and that its collapse would be followed by the 'German October'. Communists were instructed to keep their heads down and prepare for the time of revolution. If some Social Democrats and members of the Reichsbanner, their paramilitary force, wanted to take action, the SPD spokesmen, demoralized by their earlier loss of influence and seats and unwilling to join the Communists on the latter's terms, opted instead for a legalistic defence of the party's position. Even among Germany's Jews, representing less than 1% of the total population, opinions varied as to the threat posed by Hitler's appointment and the likely durability of the new government. As most Jews felt that they were Germans (nowhere in Europe were the Jews more assimilated), few took alarm. The majority assumed that the advent of Hitler would make no difference to their assured place in the Reich. The emergency decrees and the pre-election campaign of Nazi terror were recognized as warning signals, but it was only in the aftermath of the Reichstag fire on the night of 27–28 February that real alarm began to spread in Jewish circles.

The Reichstag fire, set by a Dutchman named Marinus van der Lubbe but blamed by the Nazis on the Communists, was the pretext for a massive campaign of violence against individual Communists, and for

[8] Quoted in Kershaw, *Hitler*, 432.

the issue of a presidential decree to protect Germany from an alleged Communist conspiracy. The decree created a permanent state of emergency and abolished the rights (freedom of expression, freedom of the press, freedom of assembly and association) guaranteed by the Weimar constitution. Extended and extensive powers were given to the police. To avoid a political backlash, the propaganda campaign against the Communists was intensified, and though the party was not actually outlawed—because supporters might then vote for the Social Democrats instead—individual Communists were treated as criminals. There was no likelihood that any Communist would be allowed to take his Reichstag seat. Despite the intimidation and acts of terrorism, the Nazis secured only 43.9% of the total vote. Even with their Nationalist allies, the total vote (51.9%) fell far short of the two-thirds majority in the Reichstag required to amend the constitution. The violence was further accelerated; the left was crushed; the Reichstag's rules amended, and the Catholic Centre party, pressed by the papal authorities, agreed to support the long planned 'Law for the Alleviation of the People's and the Reich's Misery', otherwise known as the 'Enabling Law'. At the Kroll Opera House, the temporary home of the Reichstag, with SA and SS men lining the walls, the Enabling Act was ratified by a large majority of those present with only the Social Democrats voting against it. The government could now pass budgets and promulgate laws for four years without parliamentary approval. Hitler could dispense with the Reichstag, rid himself of his 'gentlemen riders', and institute the first phase of his 'political revolution'. The diplomatic despatches record the waves of violence, the boycotts of Jewish businesses, the dismissal of Jewish civil servants and judges, and the 'burning of un-German literature' that followed.

Hitler's appointment as chancellor of Germany came as a surprise to foreign observers. Most diplomats in Berlin tended to underestimate Hitler and were contemptuous of the 'third or fourth rate men' whom they regarded as Hitler's rivals. Diplomats had recorded with disgust, rather than alarm, the Nazi party's raucous behaviour in the Reichstag and the violence in the streets after their 1930 electoral breakthrough. In the autumn of 1932, both André François-Poncet and Horace Rumbold, the highly experienced French and British ambassadors in Berlin, commenting on the loss of over two million votes in the November election, reported that the Nazi movement had passed its peak. François-Poncet predicted the probable fall of Schleicher but did not believe a government headed by Hitler possible. Political commentators, representing a wide political spectrum, wrote Hitler off as a spent force. 'Adolf Hitler; a stubby little Austrian with a flabby handshake, shifty brown eyes, and a Charlie Chaplin moustache', the *Daily Herald* reported, just after Hitler's appointment. 'What sort of man is this to lead a great nation?'[9] If there was general surprise, there was little sense of panic. Prime Minister Édouard Daladier assured the members of the Senate committee on the army on 16 February 1933 that there would be no change in France's German policy and suggested that the change of government might be advantageous for France. 'France has no reason to lose her calm', François-Poncet concluded his long despatch explaining the background to the formation of the new cabinet. 'She must await the actions of the new masters of the Reich.'[10] Rumbold, too, while alerting the Foreign Office to the dangers implicit in National Socialism, advocated a 'wait and see' policy. 'The Hitler experiment had to be made sometime or other', he wrote to his son, 'and we shall now see what it will bring forth'.[11] Both ambassadors expected that the Hitlerites would benefit at the expense of the Nationalists, but neither anticipated a radical change in German policy. The presence of the well-respected Konstantin von Neurath as foreign minister in the new cabinet was in itself a guarantee of continuity in foreign affairs. Many in London and Paris continued to view the new chancellor as a transitory figure, a demagogue whose moment would pass. The first French edition of *Mein Kampf* was only published in 1934 and few French politicians read German.[12] Extracts from the book were quoted in the Chamber of Deputies and *Le Temps* ran a series of articles on the so-called 'Bible' of the new Germany in 1933. The contents of François-Poncet's early Hitler despatches suggest that if the ambassador was familiar with the book, he did not treat its contents with any seriousness until some years later.

As in France, few in Britain grasped the significance of Hitler's triumph or had much understanding of Hitler's racial dogmas and future goals. Rumbold was outraged by the brutal behaviour of the new rulers and the attacks on Jews in March and April 1933. In his very first meeting with Hitler, the ambassador, who never doubted that the German leader was the source of the anti-Jewish campaigns, warned the chancellor of their negative effects on British attitudes toward Germany. While regularly commenting on Nazi anti-Semitism and anti-Bolshevism, however, Rumbold took little notice of the underlying ideology of the new movement. Even if *Mein Kampf* was read—there was one copy of the original version at the Foreign Office, which was temporarily lost during 1933, but the shortened English translation,

[9] Gordon Beckles, 'Hitler, the Clown who wants to Play Statesman', *Daily Herald*, 31 January 1933.

[10] *DDF*, 1st ser., Vol. II, No. 253.

[11] Quoted in M. Gilbert, *Sir Horace Rumbold* (London, 1973), 367.

[12] Jean-Baptiste Duroselle, *La décadence, 1932–1939*, 2nd edn. (Paris, 1979), 61.

purged of the most offensive paragraphs, was available—it would have been difficult to take its message seriously. It was not until 23 April 1933 that Rumbold called attention to Hitler's long-term goals as outlined in this 'blood and thunder book'. In a 5,000 word report later referred to as the '*Mein Kampf* despatch', the ambassador picked out the *Lebensraum* sections for special attention without fully grasping its central position in Hitler's thinking. Rumbold stressed the German leader's declared intention to restore the German nation 'by force of arms'. In the months before his retirement in the summer of 1933, he repeatedly warned that Hitlerism would lead to war and dismissed Hitler's propaganda as a camouflage for his real and unchangeable long-term goals. The '*Mein Kampf* despatch' made a considerable impact on its Foreign Office readers. It was circulated to the cabinet and seen by the prime minister. There was, however, considerable uncertainty over how to respond to Rumbold's gloomy assessment. A few, like the permanent under-secretary at the Foreign Office, Sir Robert Vansittart, for whom the Nazi revolution 'had altered everything', concluded that 'if we wish to avoid the disaster for which Hitlerism is working, we must keep as close as possible to the USA, to France, if possible also to Italy'. Whereas Fascism presented no real threat to Britain, and Russia had proved too 'incompetent a country' to be really dangerous, 'Germany is an exceedingly competent country, and she is visibly prepared for external aggression'.[13] Others in the Foreign Office, like Owen O'Malley, head of the Southern Department, argued that the British 'should not allow ourselves to be prejudiced by a revolution just because it has substituted a dictatorship for a parliamentary regime'.[14] Strongly Francophobe, O'Malley favoured conciliating Germany through treaty revision, while nonetheless warning Hitler that the excesses of the Nazi regime would alienate his neighbours and bring about the encirclement that would frustrate his aims. Orme Sargent, head of the Central Department that handled German affairs, still hoped for the eventual moderation of the German regime and recommended the 'wait and see' policy that was subsequently followed.

It was not that the message in *Mein Kampf* was ignored but that officials hardly knew what to make of it. In the summer of 1933, in reply to queries from the Foreign Office about the state of Russo–German relations, William Strang, writing from Moscow, quoted directly from Hitler's book: 'We have finished with the pre-war policies of colonies and trade, and are going over to the land policy

[13] Minute by Vansittart, 9 July 1933, The National Archives: Public Record Office, TNA: PRO, FO 371/16726, C 5963/319/18.

[14] Memo by O'Malley, 28 September 1933, in author's possession.

of the future. When we talk of new lands in Europe, we are bound to think first of Russia and her border states.'[15] Yet the counsellor of the British embassy felt unable to give any predictions as to the future of Russo-German relations except to warn that the German attitude would be decisive. Expansion into Russia was associated not with Hitler but with nationalists like Hugenberg or ideologues like Alfred Rosenberg. At the end of 1933, the Foreign Office was still uncertain of how to deal with Hitler. 'We cannot regard him [Hitler] solely as the author of *Mein Kampf*, for in such case we should logically be bound to the policy of a "preventive" war', the new ambassador to Berlin, Eric Phipps, wrote on 21 November 1933, 'nor can we afford to ignore him. Would it not, therefore, be advisable soon to bind that damnably dynamic man?'[16]

In Paris, political opinions ranged from those very few who favoured an immediate preventive war to those prepared to open immediate negotiations with Hitler while it was still possible. There were as many different views of Nazi Germany on the right of the political spectrum as on the left. Various scenarios were considered by successive cabinets but none of them was effectively pursued. It is clear that French intelligence kept the government well informed about the Nazi menace. It had followed German military activity obsessively since 1919 and long been preoccupied with the Reich's superior war-making potential. The *Deuxième Bureau*, the chief French intelligence office, was convinced that Germany was determined to rebuild its military power to launch a new bid for European hegemony. The dramatic rise of the Nazi party to power created great disquiet at the *Deuxième Bureau*. An army intelligence report of May 1932 emphasized that: 'the principal element of the Hitlerian conception of foreign policy is an extreme hatred of France, which is regarded as the hereditary and mortal enemy of Germany'.[17] Military attaché General Renondeau in Berlin was more specific. 'If Hitler becomes Chancellor', he warned, 'Germany will be transformed into one huge military barracks.'[18] After Hitler's seizure of power, Renondeau wrote that 'the government which now controls the destiny of the Reich has made no secret of the fact that its first priority upon taking power will be the building of the largest military force possible in

[15] *DBFP*, 2nd ser., Vol. VII, No. 532.

[16] Quoted in Gaynor Johnson, *Our Man in Berlin: The Diary of Sir Eric Phipps, 1933–1937* (Basingstoke 2007), 31.

[17] SHD-DAT, 7N 2623, 'Attitude du Parti National-Socialiste à l'égard de la France', 4 May 1932; quoted in Peter Jackson, *France and the Nazi Menace: Intelligence and Policy Making, 1933–1939* (Oxford and New York, 2000), 56–57.

[18] SHD-DAT, 7N 2588, 'Service du travail obligatoire', 24 February 1932; quoted in Jackson, *France and the Nazi Menace*, 57.

the shortest space of time possible.'[19] The intelligence services did not take long to turn up new evidence of rearmament and signs of possible collusion between Nazi Germany and Fascist Italy. These essentially accurate appreciations of the long-term intentions of the Nazi government were unfortunately combined with false assessments of the actual imminence of the German threat. Conspicuously lacking from these early analyses was any systematic consideration of the formidable economic and financial restraints on Hitler's ambitions. Throughout the 1920s, the *Deuxième Bureau* had tended towards 'worst case' assessments that exaggerated the military threats from Germany and Italy. This proclivity continued into the 1930s, with military analysts minimizing the structural weaknesses in the German economy. The intelligence assessment of the Nazi threat was embraced by the French military establishment. General Weygand rightly warned Prime Minister Daladier that the German demand at the World Disarmament Conference for equality of armaments was a trap. 'In reality there will be no equality, but a very pronounced superiority for Germany given the military culture of this nation and the intensive efforts already undertaken to prepare the German armaments industry for rearmament.'[20]

Such warnings produced no decisive action. Daladier gave an impression of resolve, but behind his image as the 'bull of the Vaucluse' (the journalist 'Pertinax' commented that Daladier's horns were in fact those of a snail) he was a reflective but indecisive and irresolute politician. His foreign minister, Joseph Paul-Boncour, was ideologically committed to disarmament and internationalism despite the rise of Hitler. Neither man was unduly alarmed by the changes in Germany. Having served in the trenches, they found it difficult to contemplate the idea of French rearmament and a new war. All the major French parties were focused on domestic issues, most notably the continuing effects of the depression. For the government's foreign policy, this meant pressure to seek *rapprochement* with Germany and the rejection of military demands for large-scale rearmament. Massive expenditure on armaments was completely at odds with the prevailing politics of disarmament and deflation. Less than one week after the advent of the Nazis, 638 million francs were slashed from the national defence budget by the Daladier government, on top of the 1.6 billion francs that had been cut in 1932. Between 1931 and 1934, military spending was cut by more than 25% overall.[21]

[19] SHD-DAT, 7N 2591, 'L'Armée allemande de l'avenir', 7 March 1933; quoted in Jackson, *France and the Nazi Menace*, 58.

[20] SHD-DAT, Fonds Weygand, 1K 130–131, 'Note sur les négociations avec l'Allemagne', 22 December 1933; quoted in Jackson, *France and the Nazi Menace*, 64.

[21] Figures from Jackson, *France and the Nazi Menace*, 67.

The military's warnings were dismissed by their political masters. With civil–military relations at a low point in any case, the constantly exaggerated estimates of German military power since 1919 inspired disbelief in their credibility. François-Poncet, considered the chief diplomatic expert on Germany, counselled caution and moderation. As late as 1936, when specifically referring to *Mein Kampf*, he wavered between believing that it was an accurate account of Hitler's proposed course of action, and the hope that the years in power had sobered the chancellor and that these earlier views could be dismissed as irrelevant to his present thinking. After his first meeting with Hitler on 8 April 1933, the ambassador reported on Hitler's assurances that the German 'government is sincerely and deeply pacifist', and thought that Hitler genuinely favoured an arrangement with France. François-Poncet was not naïve. 'The pacifism of Hitler is relative, temporary and conditional', he warned his superiors. 'It would seem better not to nourish illusions in this regard.'[22] He repeatedly argued, however, that it was better to strike a bargain with Hitler while the Nazi regime was weak than to face a rearmed Germany freed from all international restraints. The ambassador's more hopeful reports on Nazi intentions combined with Hitler's conciliatory overtures to France during the spring and early summer of 1933 made it possible to dismiss the pessimistic military scenarios. The anti-militarist mood of the electorate left little room for a decisive foreign policy and reinforced the tendency to wait on future events. However accurate the intelligence reaching France's policymakers, they were in no mood or position to act upon it.

The muted and hesitant response to Hitler's consolidation of power, in part the result of his self-portrayal as a 'man of peace', was not confined to the western democracies. The Italian press was enthusiastic about the new chancellor and saw in his appointment a welcome death-blow to the old liberal parliamentary system and an end to the Versailles treaty structure. The Italian ambassador in Berlin, Vittorio Cerruti, surprised, as were most of his colleagues, by Hitler's appointment, showed little enthusiasm for the new chancellor and was cautious in his despatches to Rome. The more admiring Guiseppe Renzetti remained Mussolini's chief private contact with Hitler and Göring and reported directly to the Duce. Dino Grandi, foreign minister since September 1929, had been cool about the Nazi approaches to Mussolini before1933 and worried about the implications for Italy of a revitalized Germany. Italo Balbo, chief of the air force, respected German strength but not the Nazis. Most of Mussolini's recent biographers have stressed his mixed feelings about Hitler's success. While pleased to have Hitler in power and basking in his open admiration, there was an element of jealousy in Mussolini's reactions and a desire to

[22] *DDF*, 1st ser., Vol. III, Nos. 251, 259, and 314.

distinguish between the two movements, with the emphasis on the priority of the Fascist model. In January 1933, Mussolini expressed the hope that the Nazi presence in the cabinet would make Hitler more 'realistic' in his politics. The German elections of 5 March and the 'freeing' of Hitler left the Duce somewhat uneasy. Mussolini, who had anti-Semitic prejudices of his own, read *Mein Kampf* with mixed feelings. He feared that the Nazi propaganda campaign would provoke international censure and disliked the possible anti-Latin direction of German racial doctrines. He warned Hitler against the latter's 'egregious anti-Semitism' and feared that Fascism would be tarred with the 'crude' National Socialist brush. There was also a possible clash of interests with Germany over Austria. Early in 1933, he indirectly cautioned Hitler not to raise the issue of *Anschluss,* and was considerably exercised by the Nazi agitation in Austria against Chancellor Dollfuss, whom he considered a personal friend. But whatever his worries, he was flattered by Hitler's admiration and respect. The new German chancellor had launched a successful anti-Bolshevik and anti-democratic movement along Fascist lines, and openly acknowledged his debt to Mussolini's example. The latter took obvious pride in his 'patronage' of the Nazi revolution and rapidly recognized that the German threat to the Versailles system opened up new possibilities for Italian expansion. Along with Grandi, he believed that Italy could become the 'determining weight' between Hitler's Germany on one side and France and Britain on the other, and reap the benefits of such a position.

The Soviets were taken by surprise by Hitler's appointment. During the last months of the Weimar Republic, the Communists were still fighting the Social Democrats as well as the *Stahlhelm* and Nazis. In Moscow, the Politburo debated whether a Nazi victory would prove a greater threat to the Versailles powers than to the Soviet Union. The arguments ceased after the November 1932 elections, only to be resumed in January. There was a strong pro-German element in the Politburo and among the senior Soviet officers; it included among others, Molotov, Rykov, Voroshilov, and Tukhachevsky. A week before Hitler took power, Molotov told the Soviet of the People's Commissars of the USSR that the Soviet Union's relations with other powers were developing in a normal way: 'A special place in these relations is devoted to Germany. Among all the countries with which we have diplomatic relations, those with Germany were and remain strong economic ties. This did not happen by chance. This stems from the interests of both countries.'[23] Military contacts with the Germans

[23] Quoted in Sergei Gorlov, *Sovershenno Sekretno: Alians Moskva-Berlin, 1920–1933 gg (Voenno–politichiskie otnoshenia SSSR–Germania)*, 295–296. Subsequently cited by translated English title: *Top Secret: The Moscow–Berlin Alliance, 1920–1933. Military–Political Relations, USSR–Germany* (Moscow 2001).

had been strengthened during Schleicher's chancellorship, and Tukhachevsky had attended the autumn manoeuvres in Germany at the former's invitation. Despite Hitler's accession, conversations held with the newly appointed German military attaché in Moscow in April 1933 suggest that the Soviets were still hoping that these contacts would remain in place. It was hardly surprising that French counter-intelligence concentrated on the possibility of a Nazi–Soviet alignment.

In fact, there should have been few doubts in the Politburo about Hitler's ambitions in the East. Litvinov read *Mein Kampf* and it was brought to Stalin's attention. But few, with the probable exception of Litvinov, took the real measure of the new chancellor or believed in the reality of his *Lebensraum* dreams. Like their capitalist counterparts, though with less reason, the Soviets ignored Hitler's ideological goals. They tried instead to reassure themselves that though the Nazis were fiercely anti-Bolshevik at home, German policy towards the Soviet Union would remain unchanged. Again like western diplomats, the Russians took comfort from Neurath's continuation in office, believing that he would restrain the anti-Soviet Papen, distrusted more than Hitler because of his attempts to create an anti-Soviet bloc at the Lausanne conference in 1932. Assurances from Neurath and Göring encouraged these illusions, as did an exaggerated view of the influence of the military and commercial interests in Germany well disposed to the old Rapallo connection. In practice, the Soviets remained strangely passive in the face of the destruction of the *Kommunistische Partei Deutschlands* (KPD) and responded slowly to the harassment of Soviet nationals working in Germany. Such inaction may have stemmed from self-deception and an inflated estimate of the strength of the German proletariat, or from Moscow's preoccupation with Russia's long-term interests. The Soviets waited on events. Ratification on 5 May of the Moscow protocol extending the Berlin Pact of Non-Aggression and Neutrality, which the Russians attributed mainly to Hitler's hope to disrupt the Franco–Soviet *rapprochement*, did not calm Soviet anxieties, particularly at a time when internal difficulties arising from the famine and collectivization programme and the possibility of a war in the Far East preoccupied the Politburo. The Four-Power Pact suggested by Mussolini in April 1933, was seen in Moscow as the possible basis for the capitalist anti-Soviet front that never ceased to haunt the Soviet leadership.

A German military delegation visited the USSR in May. It was well received by senior officers and allowed to see various weapons, aviation, chemical, and tractor factories, as well as the hydro-electric station on the Dnieper. Nonetheless, the Soviets called a halt to the joint chemical experiments at 'Tomka' and revoked a decision to send young German officers to the tank school at Kazan. The memorandum from the Reich economics minister, Hugenberg, prepared for the World Economic Conference in mid-June, called for a return of Germany's lost colonies and for 'new territories at the expense of the USSR'. The Soviets lodged a formal protest in Berlin. In the summer of 1933, in the face of cooling relations on both sides, all three German military training schools in the Soviet Union were closed and military visits cancelled. The trade figures were already plummeting from their pre-Hitler high.

There is little evidence of what Stalin was thinking. His touch with regard to foreign policy was less sure than in domestic affairs and he may have preferred to keep silent. He might have wanted to nourish the Rapallo link but had to acknowledge the extreme anti-Soviet direction of Hitler's policies. On 30 April the Russians warmly received Colonel Miedzinski, the editor of a semi-official Polish paper, who came from Warsaw as Piłsudski's personal envoy to assure the Russians that Poland would not join Germany in an anti-Soviet front. Another public sign of Soviet unease was an article, published in *Pravda* on 10 May 1933, 'The Revision of Versailles' by Karl Radek, an old-time Polish conspirator and negotiator for Lenin, currently in charge of foreign affairs in Stalin's personal secretariat. Radek identified revision with the victory of Fascism and warned that 'the international proletariat—the enemy of the Versailles peace—cannot be on the side of those imperialist forces which seek to bring about a new division of the world in the conflagration of a new imperialist war'.[24] This suggestion that the Soviet Union might align itself with the status quo nations was only a feeler. The arrest of the Soviet TASS (Telegraph Agency of the Soviet Union) and *Izvestia* journalists arriving in Germany to report on the trial of the Bolsheviks accused of setting fire to the Reichstag led to the recall of journalists from both countries. The matter was not resolved until the end of October when the Soviet correspondents were given permission to attend the Leipzig trial. The Russians moved uneasily, unwilling to shut the door on future *Reichswehr*–Red Army contacts and unsure of the value of the difficult *rapprochement* with France as a counter-weight.

III

For Hitler, the first priority was the establishment of the Nazi regime. It was only when the state became stronger and its people properly educated that an active foreign policy was possible. It was essential to concentrate on short-term objectives and to avoid any discussion of longer-term aims that would alienate some at home and alarm Germany's neighbours. As both the *Reichswehr* and the *Auswärtiges Amt*

[24] Karl Radek, 'The Revision of Versailles', *Pravda*, 10 May 1933.

were united in their rejection of the 'unjust treaty', and in their hopes to see Germany re-established as a great power, they were not unduly disturbed by the Nazi seizure of power. With Hitler anxious to preserve an appearance of normality to soothe foreign apprehensions, the professionals were given a free hand at Geneva. For the military chiefs, rearmament was the key to great power status. From the time the second armaments programme was adopted in early 1932, the *Reichswehr* leaders were determined on full rearmament with or without an international agreement. No disarmament convention would be allowed to interfere with the re-militarization of Germany. Pleased that Hitler would back their efforts, they looked forward to a period of fruitful co-operation in which they would set the rearmament agenda. The position of the diplomats was more complicated. Both von Neurath and state secretary Bülow had inherited the older nationalist and economic-imperialist aims of the Wilhelmine era. They tended to ignore or discount the 'wilder ideas' of the Nazis and were convinced that the movement could be disciplined and 'tamed'. Even the future state secretary, Ernst von Weizsäcker, who had strong doubts about the National Socialists, thought that the revolution would take a more conservative turn. In the summer of 1933, returning from Oslo, he encouraged the Wilhelmstrasse diplomats to join the Nazi party. Seven had already joined before 1933; by 1937 a third of the ninety-two senior officials had become members, many undoubtedly for purely careerist reasons. A very small number of diplomats had to be relieved of their posts on political grounds and fewer still, the ambassador in Washington being the outstanding example, left the service on grounds of conscience.

Hitler's concentration on home politics and emphasis on short-term goals encouraged the old élites to think that they could preserve their influence and even convert the new chancellor to their own views. They saw themselves as a conservative force in Nazi Germany, and a guarantee of continuity and respectability. Their support would allow Hitler to present himself as a man of moderation and peace, thwarted by the French in his efforts to create a disarmed Europe. Already during his first year in power, Hitler demonstrated his striking ability to take initiatives that would win public acclaim at home without provoking foreign retaliation, while Germany was without the means to defend herself. There were small but unsettling incidents that worried the French and Poles. In late February, members of the SA and *Stahlhelm* were incorporated into the German police and given small arms. In early March, an SA detachment occupied some old army barracks in Kehl, located in the demilitarized zone across the Rhine from Strasbourg, provoking strong and successful representations from France. Nazi activity in Danzig at the same time, and the denunciation of the Polish harbour police agreement by the Danzig government, resulted in Polish reinforcements of their garrison at Westerplatte. The subsequent crisis fuelled rumours of Polish or Franco-Polish plans for a preventive war already circulating in the chancelleries of Europe. The possibility was canvassed in Warsaw and Paris but dismissed by the French as politically impossible. Rumours continued to circulate during the summer and autumn of 1933. It seems highly probable that the Westerplatte affair, like Piłsudski's hints and soundings, were intended to underline Poland's capacity for independent action and was a warning to the French as much as to the Germans. It was not without effect. A sense of unease may explain Hitler's caution in March and April, and his first approaches to the Poles at the start of May.

French worries about the new Hitler government gave point, too, to a new campaign for a Franco-Italian agreement. Early in the year, with the diplomatic rumour mills working overtime, there were reports from Belgrade of a forthcoming Italian invasion and Italian talk of a French preventive strike. The French had already decided to send Senator Henry de Jouvenel (an unusual political appointment in the closed French career diplomatic service) to Rome in January 1933 for six months, with a mandate to settle outstanding issues with Mussolini. But Mussolini's price proved higher than was expected. He was less interested in bilateral exchanges than in some kind of 'political *entente*' dealing with general European matters. The Duce spoke to Jouvenel, on 3 March, of future changes in the Polish Corridor, revision of the Hungarian frontiers, an Italian presence in Albania to guarantee Italian security in the Adriatic, and the preservation of the independence of Austria. 'The time is over', Jouvenel reported, 'when Mussolini's ambition can be satisfied by a few palm trees in Libya'.[25] Whatever their distaste for Mussolini's sweeping programme, the French were not prepared to allow the conversations to lapse.

The British were trying to keep the initiative at the Geneva disarmament talks. The 35-year-old Anthony Eden, a relatively unknown though highly ambitious parliamentary under-secretary at the Foreign Office, was appointed to handle disarmament questions to ease the burden on an unwell and increasingly apathetic Sir John Simon. Together with General A. C. Temperley, the War Office representative, and Alexander Cadogan of the Foreign Office, both old Geneva hands, Eden put together a new disarmament package, modest and balanced in its provisions, which the cabinet was persuaded to accept. Eden managed to induce the unenthusiastic prime minister to come to Geneva to

[25] *DDF*, 2nd ser., Vol. I, No. 288; cited in William I. Shorrock, *From Ally to Enemy: The Enigma of Fascist Italy in French Diplomacy, 1920–1940* (Kent, OH, 1988), 71.

present the draft personally to the conference. The 'MacDonald plan', as it was commonly called, began with an agreement of all the signatories to consult together in case of a breach of the peace. In the second part of the draft, following French precedents, the British proposed the standardization of all continental forces on the basis of short-term service (eight months) with armed police and paramilitary forces counted in the totals. Germany and Poland were each to have forces of 200,000 men. France would have 200,000 troops in metropolitan France and another 200,000 outside it; Italy 200,000 metropolitan and 50,000 outside forces. Qualitative limits were set on land guns and tanks. Pending an examination of the abolition of all military and naval aviation, except those needed for 'police bombing' (a concession to the British who used planes for imperial policing in the Middle East), the major powers were to have 500 aircraft each but Germany none. The London Treaty's naval limitations were to be extended to cover France and Italy, with the latter permitted one additional battleship. Planned for a duration of five years after which a new convention would be negotiated, provision was made for a permanent disarmament commission, though inspection and supervision would occur only if a violation of the convention was suspected. The somewhat naïve British proposal, launched on 16 March by MacDonald in a rambling speech, was intended to give Britain the chance to renew its role as European arbiter at minimal cost. At least, there was something new and concrete on the disarmament table. Eden, eager for success and over-optimistic, knew that neither MacDonald nor Simon, for whom he had little liking or respect, was enthusiastic about the proposal. He was more than annoyed when the two men agreed to go to Rome to discuss Mussolini's new initiative, the offer on 18 March of a 'Four-Power Pact', diverting attention from the Geneva talks. The best that could be achieved before the meetings were adjourned for the Easter recess, was the adoption of the draft agreement as a basis for discussion with rights reserved for future amendment.

Was Mussolini's initiative an example of the Duce's 'pseudo-pacifism' as he sought to initiate a more active policy, either in the Danubian basin or in Ethiopia where General de Bono had been sent at the end of 1932 to assess the local situation and prepare a plan of intervention? Or had Hitler's accession to power alerted the Italian leaders to the possibility of recruiting a useful supporter in Italy's quest for great power status? The source of the pact lay partly in the Duce's desire to prevent a French preemptive war (hardly a real possibility) while encouraging Berlin to slow down the pace of German rearmament in order to reduce the threat of *Anschluss*. Anxious to put Rome at the centre of European politics, Mussolini was as yet unwilling to commit Italy too far in any one direction. Some form of four-power condominium, based on an Italian–British directorate, was safer than any bilateral arrangement and far better than a useless League engagement. Article 2 of Mussolini's proposed pact called for the four powers, in accordance with the Covenant and within the framework of the League, to reaffirm the principle that the peace treaties should be revised where conditions might lead to conflict. Article 3 provided that if the Disarmament Conference led to partial results, the Germans' claim to equality of rights would be recognized. Implementation of equality would be by stages. Similar rules would be applied to the other disarmed ex-enemy powers. The four signatories would follow a common policy in both political and non-political matters and in extra-European and colonial questions, the latter provision dropped at British insistence.

The reaction to the proposed pact ranged from cool to hostile. Mussolini thought that Britain would accept Italian assistance in stabilizing the European equilibrium. MacDonald's March visit to Rome was a success; the British prime minister was impressed by Mussolini and by what he saw of Fascist Italy. After suggesting a few changes, MacDonald was prepared to put the proposal to the cabinet. He quoted with approval Mussolini's comment that 'all treaties were holy but none were eternal'. But the cabinet demanded substantial revisions and when the Commons debated the question, on 23 March and 13 April 1933, a surge of anti-German and pro-League feeling doomed hopes that the Mussolini draft would be quickly accepted. The March election violence in Germany provoked a chorus of disapproval from both sides of the Commons. Clement Attlee's condemnation of Nazi actions was followed by a speech from Winston Churchill who, abandoning his earlier support for the revision of the Polish Corridor, defended the prolongation of Germany's unarmed state. Austen Chamberlain, the ex-foreign secretary, identified the new spirit of German nationalism with the worst of 'All-Prussian Imperialism'. There was now an 'added savagery, a racial pride. Are you going to discuss revision with a Government like that? Are you going to discuss with such a Government the Polish Corridor?'[26] MacDonald and Simon had to respond to this abrupt change in parliamentary sentiment.

From the first, the *Quai d'Orsay* saw little in Mussolini's draft to attract French support, and considerable danger to its eastern alliances. Daladier and Paul-Boncour were quick to register their opposition but Jouvenel, an ambassador picked for his Italophile sympathies, demanded a more positive reaction, hoping that by appeasing Mussolini the way

[26] *Hansard*, HC Deb, 23 March 1933 and 13 April 1933, Vol. 276, Cols. 2739–2747, 2755–2759, 2786–2799.

would be opened for negotiations *à deux*. The *Quai d'Orsay* modified the revisionist tone of the draft and enlarged the League role. Mussolini had already told Jouvenel of his hopes to focus German revisionist ambitions on the Polish Corridor and to seek an adjustment of Hungary's borders, to its advantage. Aloisi, the secretary-general at the Foreign Ministry, noted in his journal that Mussolini's guiding motto was, 'let us avoid above all that the little nations make the great ones fight among themselves'.[27] From late March until the pact was initialled on 7 June, the *Quai d'Orsay* was subjected to criticism at home, and to mounting pressure from Poland and the Little Entente nations. Józef Beck's previously announced visits to Paris and Prague were temporarily postponed. In response, the French succeeded in their efforts to reduce the new agreement to 'an elaborate nullity'. The German Foreign Ministry opposed the pact from the start, for it fell far short of their objectives, but Italian backing for German claims to equality of arms was proving useful in Geneva, and Neurath was anxious that the Austrian question should not drive Italy into the French embrace. By the time the French were finished emasculating the pact, there was little left to satisfy even the minimal German requirements. Hitler was more sympathetic and supported by Blomberg overcame the diplomats' objections. Neither man believed that anything concrete would come out of the new agreement, but there were advantages in adopting the draft and avoiding a blow-up in Geneva that would call attention to German rearmament.

Despite all the reservations which showed that none of the governments thought that Mussolini's proposal would break the deadlock in Geneva, the Four-Power Pact was initialled on 7 June 1933 and to Mussolini's great pleasure, signed on 15 July. It was never ratified. Little had been accomplished despite Italian claims of a diplomatic triumph. Mussolini's willingness to accept the French changes betrayed his anxiety to show something concrete for all his efforts. The French, however, gained nothing from this diplomatic detour and were disappointed in their hopes for a bilateral agreement with Italy. When the disarmament talks resumed, Italy continued to act as mediator between Germany and the western powers. No Franco–Italian action was taken in the Danube. In September 1933, the French revived a form of the economic 'Tardieu plan', calling for an economic pact based on an economic union between Austria, Yugoslavia, Romania, and Czechoslovakia. A series of bilateral accords would be followed by a separate convention signed by the non-Danubian countries (France, Italy, Britain, Poland, and possibly Germany) who would agree to assist the Danubian states economically but respect their territorial and political

[27] Quoted in Shorrock, *From Ally to Enemy*, 75.

independence. This suited neither Mussolini, who wanted some form of Austro-Hungarian union with a privileged economic position for Italy, that France would recognize, nor did it suit the Czech prime minister, Edvard Beneš, who wanted to tie Mussolini down to a guarantee of Austrian independence, and then to make the Little Entente powers the economic centre of the Danube region with underwriting from France and Italy.

The discussions of the Four-Power Pact and the economic proposals only confirmed Little Entente suspicions that the French were willing to pay for Italian support against Germany by making concessions in the Danube region. Warned that the Daladier cabinet would fall and an unsympathetic government of the right replace it, Beneš recruited his Little Entente partners to provide grudging support for the French revised draft. The Poles remained adamant in their opposition. In their view, the French action, which would direct revisionist ambitions towards Poland, had further diminished the value of the Franco-Polish alliance. These differences also soured relations between Warsaw and Prague, burying the idea canvassed by Beneš of a 'pact of perpetual friendship'. Partly for fear of French desertion, the Poles looked to Berlin. Believing that Hitler, as a non-Prussian with strong anti-Soviet sympathies, might break with the traditions of his Weimar predecessors, Piłsudski considered the moment favourable for diplomatic soundings. Well-established in the chancellor's chair, Hitler was ready to make his own entry into foreign affairs. At Polish urging, on 2 May, Hitler received the Polish envoy. A joint public communiqué stated his intention of maintaining German policy toward Poland within the framework of the existing treaties, while privately he gave assurances of his hopes for German–Polish co-operation against the USSR. During the summer, Hitler, with a political understanding in mind, was prepared to meet Polish economic requirements even at the expense of German commercial interests and against the advice of the traditionally anti-Polish Wilhelmstrasse. These first exchanges between the Poles and Germans represented only one side of the Polish coin. Almost simultaneously, the Poles sent their envoy to Moscow to assure the Russians that Poland would not ally with Germany in any aggressive action against the Soviet Union.

The Soviets, fearing a conflict in the Far East and the formation of an anti-Soviet front in Europe, were re-appraising their own situation. In late June, Stalin actually served as one of the pallbearers at the funeral of Klara Zetkin, one of the former leaders of the KPD, who had fled to Moscow. This unusual mark of respect to a German comrade was an indication of the apprehension felt in Moscow about Hitler's intentions. Radek's *Pravda* article in May was followed by his long visit to Poland in

July, with offers of a free hand in Lithuania and suggestions, aired in the Soviet press, of a preventive war to join Danzig and East Prussia to Poland. The Poles were not tempted. As the Russians suspected, they were already engaged in secret talks with Hitler. The spectre of a German–Polish–Japanese combination (intelligence links were established between Poland and Japan in 1920) loomed on the Russian horizon. The Russians looked to France. The Soviet military authorities had sought out the French after the conclusion of the November 1932 non-aggression pact between the two countries. In early July 1933, Litvinov visited Paris and Herriot returned the visit at the very end of August. A mission headed by Pierre Cot, the minister of air, heralded the beginning of some form of air co-operation. It may have been at this time that Cot's ties with the Bolsheviks began. Neither Daladier nor Paul-Boncour were ready for such a move and were lukewarm in their response to the Soviet offers. Daladier was considering direct negotiations with Germany; Paul-Boncour, taking advantage of the temporary anti-German mood in London, looked to a joint policy with the British. The Russians, unsure of the French, pursued other options. A much delayed non-aggression pact with Italy was signed on 2 September 1933. Litvinov sought to smooth relations with the British after the March Metro-Vickers affair when employees of the firm, British and Russian, were accused of espionage activities. Concern for relations with Britain led to the commutation of the sentences passed on the British engineers and their subsequent deportation. Litvinov visited Washington in November to solicit recognition of the USSR and to win American backing in the Far East. Hitler's policies were forcing the Soviets to buttress their position.

IV

The Four-Power Pact was only a diversion; the main diplomatic activity was in Geneva where the British disarmament proposal was still on the table. The first reading of the MacDonald plan began on 30 April and continued until 8 June. The Germans were already in a strong diplomatic position, having won, thanks to British efforts, recognition of their claim to 'equality of rights' in the Five-Power Declaration of 11 December 1932. The British proposal hardly suited the *Reichswehr*, even though Germany would have doubled its military strength, gained new equipment, and enjoyed a reduction in the French predominance of weapons. Nor, understandably, did it please the French military and naval authorities, who opposed the increase in the number of German troops, the cuts in French armaments, and the new naval arrangements, all to take place without an adequate supervision regime. Anxious to avoid an open confrontation with General Weygand, the *Conseil Supérieur de la Défense Nationale* (CSDN), the epicentre of the defence establishment, was by-passed. Paul-Boncour, while opposing the plan, wanted to avoid alienating Britain, the United States, or Belgium, each of which had distanced itself from France on security questions. The French choice to take up Mussolini's 'Four-Power Pact' offer was in part taken to avoid making decisions at Geneva. The tense international situation strengthened support for the Daladier government, but no radical rethinking of France's disarmament policy followed. The French concentrated on linking any arms reduction scheme with the creation of an effective control system. The diplomatic duel with Germany continued, with each side anxious to lay the blame for failure in the disarmament talks on the other. The first round went to the French who insisted that the delegates take up the question of standardizing armies and not, as the Germans proposed, the question of material which would have meant French disarmament. Nadolny, the German delegate, took an entirely negative line and progress was blocked. Tempers were hardly improved by Nadolny's loose statements to journalists and public comments by Blomberg and von Neurath claiming the right to rearm, outside the League system if not within it. With everyone's nerves on edge, Neurath and Blomberg considered leaving the conference and Neurath asked Hitler to make a public statement. Despite his intransigence, Nadolny had taken fright at Germany's isolation and in Munich on 14 May told an angry Hitler that the British proposals should be accepted.

Two days later, on the eve of Hitler's pre-announced speech, President Roosevelt addressed an appeal to the heads of the states represented at Geneva and recommended accepting the MacDonald plan as a first step towards a disarmament convention. He proposed that all countries sign a non-aggression pact and forego any increase in arms spending until the agreement was signed. The British and French, who had discussed disarmament with the president in their pre-World Economic Conference talks in Washington, were bitterly disappointed. They had hoped for a positive offer of American co-operation in support of combined action against an aggressor. The president, in the course of his message, attacked 'offensive weapons', war planes, heavy artillery, and tanks, all of which were still denied to the Germans. It was a clumsy, if well-intentioned move though it hardly deserved MacDonald's acid response. 'The whole thing is depressing and shows the unsatisfactory nature of Ameri[can] Diplomacy', the British prime minister minuted. 'They cannot keep out of the limelight; they are always prone to do things on their own in the middle of negotiations.'[28] Roosevelt's message gave Hitler an unexpected opportunity to stress Germany's ardent desire for peace and willingness to accept the British proposal.

Hitler's speech on 17 May 1933 was a triumph. Using the Reichstag to address a world audience, the first of a series of such actions, he portrayed Germany as a disarmed and peace-loving country sinned against by the framers of the Treaty of Versailles. 'Our boundless love for and loyalty to our own national traditions makes us respect the national claims of others', he said, 'and makes us desire from the bottom of our hearts to live with them in peace and friendship. We therefore have no use for the idea of Germanization.' Hitler offered to accept the British plan as the basis for discussion and welcomed both Mussolini's and Roosevelt's proposals. He told his audience that Germany would accept a transitional period of five years but only if at the end of the period it would 'be put on a footing of equality with other states'. If the majority at Geneva tried to dictate terms to Germany, he warned, the German people would leave the League of Nations.[29] The *Friedensrede* was published in several languages and was generally welcomed. Only a minority in Britain, one of Hitler's main targets, questioned his sincerity. Cabinet ministers were relieved by the chancellor's public avowal of peaceful intentions. Having been sufficiently alarmed by recent reports of German rearmament to have considered an Anglo-French-American warning to Berlin, ministers could now return to a policy of temporization, causing further anguish in Paris.

François-Poncet stressed the emptiness of Hitler's speech but concluded that now was the time to begin negotiations with the Germans. The *Quai d'Orsay*, anxious that France should not be isolated, was prepared to proceed with the MacDonald plan. Daladier shifted his emphasis from a pact of mutual assistance to the promotion of a system of supervision and controls. Under consideration since March, the new French proposals only received cabinet approval at the start of May and were announced at Geneva on 23 May. At a meeting of the French, British, and American representatives in Paris on 8 June when Daladier disclosed its details, he pointedly asked what would happen if the new convention was violated. Neither the American, Norman Davis, nor Anthony Eden stressed the point in reports to their respective governments, probably because they took for granted a negative reply. The answer was crucial for French acceptance of the MacDonald proposals. The new Daladier amendments included a two-phased convention lasting ten years. During phase one, armies would be standardized and

[28] *DBFP*, 2nd ser. Vol. V, No. 150.

[29] John Wheeler-Bennett (ed.). *Documents on International Affairs* (London, 1933), 196–208.

some restrictions placed on the construction of heavy armaments and tanks. A system of periodic and automatic inspection would be created. The actual destruction of surplus material or its transfer to the League of Nations would take place only during the second phase. Once again, in a different form, the French were asking for guarantees that neither the Americans nor the British were prepared to offer. The French amendments were still on the table when, because of the forthcoming World Economic Conference scheduled to open on 12 June, the meetings were abruptly adjourned until 16 October. It was another episode in the more or less deliberate policy of postponement in view of fundamental disagreements. Arthur Henderson, president of the Disarmament Conference, was instructed to continue his efforts to reconcile the different points of view through private talks in the interval.

The summer of 1933 was not a happy time in Europe. Hitler was in full control of Germany and taking a more active part in foreign matters. The Germans had launched a major anti-Dollfuss propaganda campaign in Austria and the Austrian Nazis were harassing the chancellor in Vienna. In response to Austrian counter-measures, Hitler imposed a prohibitive visa tax on Germans visiting Austria, seriously disrupting the country's tourist trade and an important source of income. At the end of July, Dollfuss appealed first to Britain and then to Italy for assistance. The World Economic Conference (12 June – 27 July 1933) ended with governments seeking national solutions to financial and economic problems regardless of their international impact.[30] The blow to economic internationalism did not augur well for progress at Geneva, where hopes for success were at a low ebb. The Germans were determined to rearm. The French did not want to make reductions in their armaments relative to Germany at a time when the *Deuxième Bureau* was reporting the increasing intensity of German illegal rearmament. The British had welcomed the adjournment because they found themselves in a minority over their unwillingness to consider proposed schemes for aerial disarmament. The cabinet feared, too, that when the details of the MacDonald plan were discussed, they would lose the support at home that they hoped to gain by taking the initiative in Geneva. The Italians, already increasing their defence expenditure year by year, were not interested in general disarmament though they hoped Germany would accept a disarmament convention. Litvinov's far more radical disarmament proposals were received with general suspicion. Confidence in multilateral diplomacy and international conferences plummeted.

[30] See the discussion in Zara Steiner, *The Lights that Failed: European International History 1919–1933* (Oxford and New York, 2005), chapter 12.

During the summer holidays, the diplomats resorted to private negotiations. Henderson, shunned by the representatives of all the major states during the economic conference in London, spent the rest of July visiting European capitals. His cool if not hostile reception in Paris confirmed his view, shared in this instance with MacDonald, that France was the main culprit in the unsuccessful quest for agreement. Henderson found little response in Rome; Mussolini's attention was focused on securing signatures to his Four-Power Pact. The visit to Germany, where Henderson was received by Hitler, seemed more encouraging. Despite objections to the French proposal of a 'probationary period' and German insistence on returning to the original British draft, he left satisfied by Hitler's assurances that Germany was not rearming and encouraged by the Führer's support for the MacDonald terms. Hitler also responded favourably to Daladier's suggestion, forwarded by Henderson, that the two leaders might meet, insisting only on extensive preparations before the encounter took place. Hitler's willingness to approach France was a response, in part, to fears about French efforts to enlist British and American support for a League investigation of German rearmament. There were German public speeches in favour of a Franco–German *rapprochement*. Fernand de Brinon, the Germanophile French journalist, and Joachim von Ribbentrop, the rising Nazi careerist with access to Hitler, were asked to bring about a meeting between Hitler and Daladier. Apart from the Saar, which was German, Hitler assured Brinon that Germany had no wish for war or for any territorial acquisitions, and was anxious for an arrangement with France.

Daladier was not unsympathetic to these feelers. 'No one contests Germany's right to its existence as a great nation', he told the Radical party congress at Vichy on 8 October 1933, 'No one seeks to humiliate Germany.'[31] There was a strong temptation to conclude some kind of treaty with the Germans. Dependent on socialist backing and faced with an unbalanced budget, Daladier's Radical government could not possibly consider preventive war or massive rearmament. Even General Weygand, who argued that only military action would stop German rearmament, would not contemplate French mobilization without British support. The new effort to enlist Anglo-American backing for sanctions was, at best, a dubious gamble and may well have been a gesture for domestic consumption. With evidence that Germany was rearming and the French margin of superiority under future threat, there were reasons to believe that France should make the best bargain possible with Hitler while there was still something about which to bargain. Movements in

[31] Quoted in Maurice Vaïsse, *Sécurité d'abord: la politique française en matière de désarmement, 9 décembre 1930 – 7 avril 1934* (Paris, 1981), 448.

this direction would immensely improve relations with London. In the end, however, the French premier drew back and no meeting with Hitler took place. Daladier was a politician above all and kept a close watch on his supporters. Though his radical-socialist backers favoured disarmament and cuts in military spending, they were not prepared for an exclusive arrangement with Gemany. Tardieu and his colleagues were already campaigning to alert the public to the dangers of a rearmed Germany. Direct exchanges with Hitler would have implied a revolution in French diplomacy well beyond Daladier's reach. Instead, faced with the German challenge, French diplomacy became even more defensive and hesitant. The differences between the politicians, diplomats, and service chiefs in Paris precluded positive action and, indeed, postponed any action at all. On 5 September, Mussolini approached Charles de Chambrun, the new French ambassador in Rome, with suggestions intended to forward the Rome–Paris *rapprochement*. The Duce agreed to the French plan for disarmament by stages and the implementation of a permanent and automatic supervision system. He insisted in return that the Germans be given rights to defensive arms, including aircraft, in the first stage of the new convention. Chambrun urged rapid acceptance but French officials remained suspicious and hostile. In late September, the French foreign minister turned a similarly deaf ear to offers from Neurath and Goebbels who had come to Geneva where the technicians were dealing with the question of armaments and a mutual security pact. The *Quai d'Orsay* clung to the Geneva talks and the *entente* with Britain but despite talk about joint action, there was no improvement in Anglo-French relations.

The weakness of the French position was compounded by Britain's continuing search for a disarmament formula that Hitler would accept. This could only be done at the expense of France. For a brief time, while Simon was off on a summer sea cruise to regain his health, Vansittart and Eden sought ways to reassure the French in order to secure their adhesion to Britain's disarmament plan. They tried to enlist Mussolini to join a three-power protest against Nazi activities in Austria. The Italian leader preferred unilateral action and secured his own assurances from Hitler. The British cabinet would not sanction plans to use revelations that Germany was planning a major air rearmament programme as the basis for a three-power *démarche* at Berlin and insisted, instead, that Britain should act alone. Nor would the cabinet agree to examine a French dossier on the rearmament of the *Reichswehr* preparatory to a joint enquiry at Berlin. The idea, welcomed by Eden and Sir William Tyrrell, the British ambassador in Paris, was quickly buried. At Anglo-French and Anglo-French-American meetings in Paris just before the disarmament talks were resumed, Daladier agreed to some of the British draft terms but demanded 'guarantees of execution' which neither London nor Washington would consider.

When the general commission of the Disarmament Conference recommenced its sessions in October, the situation looked less bleak for the French, who had won Mussolini's backing for their amendments to the British draft. The Germans found themselves on the defensive when the British rejected their demands for large quantities of forbidden weapons in the first stage of disarmament and were further angered by German attempts to reject the trial period entirely. Neurath feared that the talks would collapse and the blame placed on Germany. More importantly, Hitler was not yet ready to abandon the talks, alienating both the British and the Italians. Counting on the divisions between the western powers, he accepted Neurath's advice to continue the talks. Negotiations proved short-lived.

What brought about the change in policy that led to Germany's departure from the conference and from the League of Nations on 14 October? The starting point was news that the British were considering a new convention in collaboration with President Roosevelt that would reject the German demand for samples of weapons and, while vetoing sanctions, might invoke a provision of the League Covenant against violations of the convention. Bismarck's report, misrepresenting the American position, conveyed the essence of the Foreign Office attempt to bridge the gap between Paris and Berlin. Germany would be compelled to forego new weapons during the first four-year period of the convention in return for a French agreement to disarm. With this news in hand, the Germans decided on 4 October not to negotiate on any new plan that forced them to compromise. To avoid the blame for disrupting the conference, Blomberg suggested a return to the 'original question'. Germany should demand the disarmament of the other states and threaten to leave the conference and League if they did not either disarm or grant Germany equality of rights. Following the German departure, Hitler expected to repeat his success of the previous May with a speech to the Reichstag that would rally domestic and world opinion to the German cause. Forewarned of Hitler's intentions by German officials in London, a shocked Simon went to Geneva warning that he would reply with a 'frank and full pronouncement' to any such German statement. The meeting between Nadolny and Simon proved decisive for Berlin; the British would not accept German rearmament in the first stage. Other major powers still wanted to avoid a German withdrawal and Simon was prevailed upon to soften his message. Before reading his much reworked statement on 14 October, Simon 'made P.-B. [Paul-Boncour] purple with rage', according to Anthony Eden, 'by going to sit ostentatiously on the opposite side of room to whisper to German [sic] (God knows what about!) and holding up business for this'.[32]

The German decision had been taken already. Nadolny, ordered back to Berlin the day before Simon spoke, argued the case against withdrawal but Hitler wanted no further delays. He would follow up the German announcement, to be made immediately after Simon's statement, with his own radio address. The Reichstag and Land parliaments would be dissolved and fresh elections held to show the world that the German people 'identified itself with the peace policy of the Reich government'. The Berlin announcement was made at midday; the Führer addressed the nation in the evening. This was the first of Hitler's 'Saturday surprises' that were to so disorient the chancelleries of Europe. While making friendly references to Daladier and France, 'our ancient, but glorious, opponent' (Hitler had discounted a preventive war but the risk remained) and declaring that 'only a madman would consider the possibility of war between the two states', the chancellor avoided any reference to the question of German rearmament. He spoke instead of the failure of other powers to fulfil their obligations under the Versailles Treaty, leaving Germany insecure and inadequately armed with defensive weapons. As the disarmament conference was determined to keep Germany in a position of inferiority and would deny its equality of rights, it would leave the conference and the League to escape 'an irremediable situation'.[33] A German plebiscite, held on 12 November, one day after the fifteenth anniversary of the 1918 armistice, produced a 95% vote for Hitler.

The German announcement was received abroad with stupefaction and, at first, with anger. The French rightly felt that their warnings had been fully justified and Paul-Boncour enjoyed a brief moment of self-satisfaction. The British felt that Simon had been badly used and his speech just a pretext for the German action, as indeed it was. The Americans and Italians were incensed; the Russians warned that Germany was preparing for war. There was, however, no closing of the ranks, no demonstration of unity, and no action taken. On the contrary, Hitler's challenge exposed the weakness of the French position and the unwillingness of any state or states to move against him. The Geneva powers did nothing. There was not even a formal protest in Berlin. General von Blomberg placed his forces on alert on 25 October in anticipation of combined action by France, Poland, Czechoslovakia, and Belgium, but Hitler was right and the war scare faded. The French wanted the conference to proceed without Germany along the lines

[32] David Dutton, *Anthony Eden: A Life and Reputation* (London, 1997).
[33] Wheeler-Bennett, *Documents on International Affairs*, 291.

proposed in the amended British draft convention but this was opposed first by the Italians and Americans and then by the British. The General Commission adjourned on 16 October 1933 initially for ten days and subsequently until 29 May 1934 when the Disarmament Conference began its last futile plenary session.

Hitler drew his own lessons from this propaganda victory at a time when Germany was weak and isolated. On 17 October, he told his cabinet that the 'critical moment' had passed and Germany had nothing to fear. The way was open for unrestricted rearmament and the implementation of more audacious plans. The *Reichswehr* had secured its goal but Hitler had orchestrated the score, and the officers and diplomats followed their conductor. Hitler's domestic position was considerably strengthened by the withdrawal from Geneva and the plebiscite. He could now prepare to take up the fight against Ernst Röhm, the leader of the *Sturmabteilung* (SA) and his followers who might possibly challenge his political position. He knew that the *Reichswehr* was equally anxious to dispose of its most powerful rival. The 'man of peace' was intent on speeding up rearmament while considering how to smooth the way for the future use of Germany's still limited military strength. The Defence Ministry swung into action. In December it was agreed to create a 21 division peacetime army of 300,000 men within four years. Orders were given that the build-up should begin on 1 April 1934. The *Reichswehr* looked forward to the introduction of conscription and a one-year period of service to ensure the rapid tripling of the existing army. The 'second armaments programme' was judged inadequate for an army which the *Reichswehr* leaders, though not Hitler, wanted to fight defensive wars on several fronts. General Beck, the conservative chief of staff, thought in terms of a long-term build-up. Without any deep appreciation of the broader strategic and economic parameters of the tasks ahead, his opposition to Hitler's demands for speed in the spring of 1934 was based on the knowledge that a modern army needed extensive training and armament in depth before it moved. At this juncture, he was more concerned with the reconstruction of the army than with the future uses to which it might be put.

Hitler's attention was focused on political goals. Immediately after the German withdrawal from the Disarmament Conference, he launched a foreign 'peace offensive'. Attention shifted away from Geneva to the chancelleries of Europe. Business was conducted in the old-fashioned way, the exchange of notes, diplomatic visits to foreign capitals, and bilateral negotiations. The very question of Geneva's role in any future disarmament scheme became a subject for debate. The high hopes connected with the opening of the Disarmament Conference had been replaced now by a sense of deep disappointment. Admittedly, the German withdrawal did not put an end to the pursuit of an arms agreement. For the British cabinet, at least, it had become even more essential to find a way to bring the Germans back into the disarmament fold. Irritation with the French mounted as the possibility of an arrangement with Berlin receded. But as with the other links in the internationalist chain of the 1920s, the quest for disarmament was a failed effort that only increased the sense of disillusion among its former enthusiasts and those who had supported it in the face of public pressure.

V

Hitler seized the initiative. On 24 October, he received the new British ambassador, Sir Eric Phipps, and outlined his terms for a disarmament convention. Germany would accept a short-term (twelve months' service) army of 300,000 men with no 'offensive' but unlimited 'defensive' weapons, if the 'highly armed states', that is France, Poland, and Czechoslovakia, were subject to a standstill in armaments. Hitler spoke of the dangers of Russian competition and, while disclaiming any wish to alter the Polish Corridor by force, referred to 'certain possibilities of expansion in Eastern Europe'. This approach was followed by an offer of substantial air and sea rearmament for Britain and the suggestion of joint Anglo-Italian pressure on France. By these means, Hitler initiated the campaign for the British alliance first canvassed in *Mein Kampf*. The highly capable, lucid, and somewhat contemptuous Phipps was shaken by his interview with 'so unbalanced a being' but given 'the notorious disinclination of any power to embark on sanctions', he pressed the Foreign Office to respond to Hitler's overtures.[34] On 9 December, Phipps (the negotiations were known in Berlin as 'Das Schema Phipps') was instructed to tell the chancellor that his demands were excessive. The British were not prepared to renew negotiations on Hitler's terms, but they wanted a convention and were ready to convince the French that even a bad bargain was better than no bargain at all. It was widely believed that the Labour candidate had won a by-election in East Fulham on 25 October 1933, just days after Germany's departure from the Disarmament Conference, by standing on a peace platform. This reading of the results has been subsequently questioned, but at the time the Conservative party leader, Stanley Baldwin, was appalled by the outcome and later confided that 'it was a nightmare' because of its apparent demonstration of the strength of anti-rearmament feeling. The public was not told but the cabinet was seriously shaken when an analysis of the German demands disclosed

[34] *DBFP*, 2nd ser., Vol. V, No. 489 and Vol. VI, No. 81.

that Germany's existing productive capacity had been underestimated. It was less the size of the army that raised alarm than reports of Germany's expanded aircraft production. Still intent on convincing the French to compromise, the British played for time. The Foreign Office worked out a new formula, if only to show Britain's good intentions, and the service departments revised the terms. A modified version of the MacDonald plan was intended to meet some, though not all (Germany was still not to have military aircraft), of Hitler's demands. To gain French acceptance, the British offered automatic supervision but no guarantees beyond a consultative pact.

In Paris, cabinet attention was focused on budgetary matters. Four cabinets in 1932 followed by three more in 1933 failed to deal with the country's budgetary deficits. After the fall of the relatively long-lasting Daladier cabinet (January to October 1933), came the governments of Sarraut (26 October to 23 November) and Chautemps (26 November 1933 to 27 January 1934), none of which had any success. With government revenues declining, ministers were either unable or unwilling to raise taxes or to cut expenditure drastically enough to balance the books. Still trying to support the gold value of the franc but unable to marshal backing for draconian deflationary policies, finance ministers covered their budgetary deficits by borrowing, and pushing up interest rates, producing a sharp drop in public confidence. While Radical ministers were implementing some of the financial policies favoured by the right, they were dependent on the parties of the left, which, without any agreed alternative programme, could bring the government down. Pressure for radical change was weak, experimentation was discouraged, and unorthodox programmes ruled out. These Radical-led ministries, relying on Socialist support, nonetheless retained the backing of the rural voters and much of the urban middle class. Numerous and often violent demonstrations by disaffected interest groups, officials, small businessmen, shopkeepers, and peasants were indicative of the widespread public disaffection. On the right, together with the growing popularity of the extra-parliamentary 'Leagues', more conventional politicians like Tardieu returned to the idea of a strengthened executive to end the period of political paralysis. The end result was disunion at the centre of French politics, and a succession of ministries composed of essentially the same men with basically the same policies, often holding the same positions in successive cabinets: Bonnet at the Finance Ministry, Paul-Boncour at the *Quai d'Orsay*, Daladier at the War Ministry, and Pierre Cot at the Ministry of Air. The ministerial merry-go-round of 1932 and 1933 would continue into 1934. Naturally the dismal political situation affected the government's foreign and defence policies. Paul-Boncour, a man increasingly given to empty rhetoric, clung to a League solution when most other statesmen were looking elsewhere. Psychologically as well as physically, Boncour moved between Paris and Geneva. Daladier at defence, well informed about the needs of the army and anxious to modernize and mechanize its forces, engaged in a bitter struggle with General Weygand, the chief of staff, over the one-year service term and the defence estimates. Weygand, politically on the far right, had no patience with the Cartel governments and cultivated the opposition. Meanwhile, the army was left in its unreformed state. Much of the blame rested with Daladier. It was hardly surprising that one of the first things he did as war minister in the Popular Front government in 1936 was to commission a staff study to show what he was doing to promote the national defence. By that time, the damage inflicted during 1933–1934 was all too apparent.

While intent on separating London and Paris and isolating the French, Hitler also renewed his peace overtures to Daladier. Soon after the November 1933 plebiscite, Hitler again approached Fernand de Brinon and François-Poncet. In an interview published in *Le Matin* on 16 November, he publicly proclaimed his hopes for an accord with France. Responding to Hitler's overtures and to Phipps's proddings, François-Poncet urged his government to act. 'Time did not work for us', he warned the *Quai d'Orsay*, it was necessary to tie Hitler down before it was too late.[35] In a speech to the Reichstag at the end of January 1934, Hitler again made a personal appeal to Daladier (in power from 30 January to 9 February 1934) as old soldiers who should take the lead after the efforts of the 'cold politicians' and 'professional diplomats' had failed. It was difficult for the French to do nothing. The British were determined to bring Hitler back to the negotiating table. Mussolini, in one of his fiercely anti-League moods, favoured the immediate granting of equality of rights to Germany as the necessary price for an arms limitation treaty. The Belgians, who in December 1933, had voted a major appropriation to reinforce and modernize their army, urged the French to open bilateral talks with the Germans 'in the silence and peace of the chancelleries'. In December, Paul Hymans came to Paris to press his case for a French initiative at Berlin.

The *Quai d'Orsay* made a symbolic gesture. After lengthy exchanges between François-Poncet and Neurath, the French produced an *aide-memoire* on 1 January 1934 rejecting German demands for rearmament but demonstrating France's willingness to disarm. The first phase of the new programme would have created parity between German and French metropolitan forces. It would bring an end to German rearmament and prohibit manufacture of war materials, denied to other countries.

[35] *DDF*, 1st ser., Vol. V, No. 94.

In return, France would reduce its existing air force by 50% (this was part of air minister Cot's planned reorganization) and would propose qualitative limitations on authorized weapons. As was no doubt intended, the Germans rejected the French proposal. There followed a futile but elaborate diplomatic game with each side seeking to avoid a break in the talks but neither willing to yield any point of substance. On the French side, it was a brilliantly planned exercise that achieved no purpose. The Germans simply proceeded with their rearmament plans. The British were irritated and the Belgians annoyed by the *Quai d'Orsay's* tactics. The French message ending the charade was sent to Berlin on 13 February not by Paul-Boncour but by Louis Barthou, the new foreign minister in the Doumergue cabinet. By this time, the modified British proposal was on the negotiating table and Anthony Eden was sent on a tour of the major European capitals to survey the political landscape. His trip was postponed because of a political crisis in France that appeared to threaten the life of the Republic.

The crisis was set off by Serge Stavisky, a crooked financier with friends in the highest places. When his shady operations became known, he fled Paris and, pursued by the police, committed suicide in January 1934. The radical right made the most of their opportunity; Stavisky was of central European Jewish origins and his connections with Chautemps and the other leading Radicals made him a natural target. It was suggested that Stavisky's 'suicide' was staged in order to avoid embarrassing revelations. Such was the power of the ultra-right that Chautemps was forced to resign. Daladier, the so-called 'Robespierre of Radicalism' was called to the premiership only to be driven out as the result of further fall-out from the Stavisky affair. His sacking of the Paris Prefect of Police, Jean Chiappe, infuriated the right who claimed it was all a Communist plot. On 6 February, various mainly right-wing organizations called on their members to demonstrate against the premier. Some 100,000 people converged on the Place de la Concorde, preparing to attack the reassembled Chamber of Deputies. An undisciplined crew of disparate groups and individuals, with different grievances and no single leader or goal in mind, clashed with the police assembled to protect the Chamber. Fourteen people and one policeman were killed and scores of people wounded. Despite a vote of confidence from the terrified deputies, Daladier was forced to resign and was replaced by Gaston Doumergue, a colourless ex-president of the Republic who reassembled the radical and right-wing forces of Poincaré's former coalition in an attempt to form a government of national unity. It included six former prime ministers and eight ex-foreign ministers. The venerable 78-year-old Marshal Pétain took the War Ministry and the septuagenarian Louis Barthou, a senator enjoying semi-retirement, entered the *Quai d'Orsay* as foreign minister. The Communists, still wedded to the war against the Socialists, unexpectedly joined the general strike called by the *Confédération Générale du Travail* (CGT), the socialist trade union federation, for 12 February. Demonstrations were held throughout France. In Paris, the Socialists and Communists marched separately but then converged. This fleeting moment of left-wing unity became the symbolic starting point of the Popular Front.

Under these circumstances, foreign affairs were put on the back burner. Barthou brought a breath of fresh air to the *Quai d'Orsay*. The old political veteran (he had entered public life in 1889) was endowed with enormous energy, both physical and intellectual. He was a prodigious worker and an attentive listener. Known for his sharp tongue, he was willing to speak out without concern for consequences. A man of wit and charm, with a somewhat scandalous reputation, Barthou had lost his only son in the Great War and had served Poincaré at the time of the Ruhr occupation. Few were more alert to the dangers of German revisionism. For him, as he told contemporaries, 1934 had the smell of 1914. Yet he loathed the idea of another war and had shown already considerable sympathy with the ideas of the late Aristide Briand and that denigrated leader's vision of a European federation of nations. Barthou's most recent biographer has concluded that the new foreign minister was neither a hawk nor a dove.[36] Sceptical about German professions of good faith and opposed to a policy of concessions to Berlin, he nonetheless believed that the only solution to the problem of French security would be found in a reconciled Europe. If Barthou was no clearer on how this could be achieved than any of his predecessors, he proved willing to initiate more adventuresome policies.

During the second half of February and March 1934, Eden tried to sell the British compromise plan of 29 January. The French, as might have been expected, objected to the proposals for immediate German rearmament and French disarmament in the absence of any security proposals. The Germans, for their part, disliked the ten-year duration of the convention, the denial of aircraft for two years, and the insistence on Germany's return to the League of Nations. Eden returned from his foreign visits impressed with Hitler, whom he thought to be 'sincere' in desiring a disarmament convention, but doubtful about the intentions of his entourage. Any agreement, Eden believed, would have to meet German demands for defensive aircraft. Hitler's conditions became part of the negotiating package. The British accepted that Germany should have an army of 300,000 men and a 'defensive' air force about

[36] Robert Young, *Power and Pleasure: Louis Barthou and the Third French Republic* (Montreal and London, 1991), 211–222.

half the size of the French. Hitler agreed to place restrictions on the SS and SA to emphasize their supposedly non-military character. All forces would be subject to the system of controls. Hitler insisted that the question of Germany's return to the League of Nations should be separated from the disarmament issue and subject to a prior solution of the question of armaments and equality of rights. During his visit to Paris on 1 March, Eden informed the French of Hitler's proposed amendments and pressed for an answer to the British memorandum. The French, stressing internal preoccupations, refused to be rushed. Eden returned home convinced that the whole security question would have to be addressed if there was to be any chance of the French swallowing what was clearly an unpalatable pill. The British desire for French acceptance of German rearmament co-existed with anxieties that the Germans were building a new air force that could threaten Britain. In February 1934, the Foreign Office noted the German Air Ministry's acknowledgements of infringements of the Treaty of Versailles, and its new estimates of German military aircraft both in existence and under construction. Modest increases in the British air estimates were debated on 8 March. In reply to an attack by Churchill, who demanded numerical equality in the air with Germany, Stanley Baldwin, the deputy prime minister, told the House of Commons that, if an air convention was concluded, 'this Government will see to it that in air strength and air power this country shall no longer be in a position inferior to any country within striking distance of our shores'.[37] The subject was reviewed at the Foreign Office during March. Officials concluded that 'vital British interests will require a certain rearmament on our part in order to defend them against the threat of Germany's growing military and aeronautical strength'.[38] British security was at stake. But the cabinet, the chiefs of staff, as well as dominion representatives who were consulted, were unanimously opposed to any form of continental commitment to France.

The Defence Requirements Committee, created in November 1933 to consider deficiencies in imperial defence (its members were Sir Maurice Hankey, the cabinet secretary, Sir Robert Vansittart from the Foreign Office, Sir Warren Fisher from the Treasury and the three chiefs of staff), presented its report to the cabinet on 28 February 1934. There were two main areas of contention in its deliberations. The first was over which presented the greater threat, Germany or Japan. The chiefs of staff, particularly the Admiralty, supported by the cabinet secretary, the highly influential Hankey, opted for Japan but the

[37] *Hansard*, HC Deb, 8 March 1934, Vol. 286, Col. 2126.
[38] *DBFP*, 2nd ser., Vol. VI, No.363.

final result was a compromise (the language brokered by Hankey) with the views of Vansittart and Fisher who stressed the primacy of the German threat. Germany was designated 'the ultimate potential enemy against whom our "long-range" defence policy must be directed', but the more immediate danger came from Japan. The second area of contention was over how to divide the defence funding. In the five-year expansion programme recommended to cover the 'worst deficiencies' of the three services, the committee again compromised. The Far East was designated the first 'contingency' and Germany the second. The largest share of the estimated total appropriation, £71.3 million for the first five years, was to go to the army (£40 million) to build up an expeditionary force (although the army high command was ambivalent about its suggested continental role) and to repair its home and imperial defences. The navy would be given £21 million and the RAF £10.3 million to allow completion of the 52-squadron programme of 1932. The navy's deficiency scheme was largely endorsed.[39] The cabinet, after discussing the report, referred it to the ministerial committee on disarmament in May, where its conclusions were contested by the chancellor of the exchequer, Neville Chamberlain. Faced with such large and unwelcome figures, Chamberlain, by dint of his arrogant self-assurance and overriding concern with financial prudence, succeeded in overturning its conclusions and imposing his own strategic vision on the cabinet. He convinced his ministerial colleagues to cut overall appropriations to £50.3 million and to increase the amount given to the RAF (£20 million) at the expense of the navy (£13 million) and army (£20 million). Germany was the greater threat but could be held in check through the existence of a 'deterrent force' of aircraft 'of a size and efficiency calculated to inspire respect in the mind of a possible enemy', rather than a large army expeditionary force.[40] Meanwhile an effort should be made to come to terms with Japan without alienating the United States and permitting cuts in the naval estimates. The consequence of the chancellor's intervention was to block the chiefs of staff's balanced approach to rearmament and made air defence the crucial deterrent to deal with immediate and long-term threats.

[39] TNA: PRO, CAB 24/247, CP 64(34), 5 March 1934.

[40] See Brian McKercher's argument in Brian McKercher, 'Deterrence and the European Balance of Power: The Field Force and British Grand Strategy, 1934–1938', *English Historical Review*, 123: 500 (2008), 98–131; 'Note by the Chancellor of the Exchequer on the Report of the Defence Requirements Committee', DC (M) (32) 120, 20 June 1934, TNA: PRO, CAB 27/511, quoted in Keith Neilson, 'The Defence Requirements Sub-Committee, British Strategic Foreign Policy, Neville Chamberlain and the Path to Appeasement', *English Historical Review*, 118: 477 (2003), 675.

Table 1.1 Defence Requirements Committee (DRC), 1934 (£ million)

	Original	Revised by Chamberlain, 1935
Army	40	20
Navy	21	13
RAF	10.3	20

The French government deliberated over their reply to the British proposals for recognizing German rearmament, as the *Quai d'Orsay* and Foreign Office engaged in a game of 'hide and seek' over the question of security guarantees. In the meantime, the Germans made their own effort to secure French consent to a German army of 300,000 men and recognition of its right to defensive weapons. On 4 March Ribbentrop made a private visit to Barthou and pleaded the cause of Franco–German *rapprochement*. 'The words are of peace', the foreign minister replied as he vetoed talks with Hitler, 'but the activity is of war'.[41] When the French interim reply to the British duly came on 19 March, it was distinctly cool. Any possibility of a more positive French reaction was diminished with the publication in late March of the German military estimates for 1934 showing an increase of 356 million RM over the 1932–1933 figures. Air expenditure alone rose from seventy-nine million RM in 1932–1933 to 210 million RM in 1934, but there was little agreement within the French cabinet over what to do. Doumergue, installed in the *Quai d'Orsay* with rooms just above those of Barthou, stood for the maintenance of the peace treaties and a strong stand against German rearmament. Barthou spoke of continuing the more conciliatory line of Paul-Boncour and still wanted to work with the British. Tardieu and Herriot opposed conciliating Germany but were divided over what to do with regard to the Soviet Union. Pierre Laval, furious at not getting the *Quai d'Orsay*, was the only minister fully prepared to play the card of Franco-German reconciliation. The military chiefs, who with the creation of the new cabinet re-emerged as a major force in deciding policy, demanded an immediate reversal of the reduction in army numbers and an increase in defence appropriations. Pétain, Weygand, and Denain, the air minister, using information derived from intelligence sources, painted a black picture of rapid German rearmament which made the proposed disarmament convention not only harmful but positively dangerous. Denain knew that France still enjoyed

[41] Vaïsse, *Sécurité d'abord*, 554.

a quantitative edge over Germany in planes but argued that the Germans enjoyed a decisive qualitative and industrial advantage. On 16 April, as the French prepared their response to the British proposals, the German government, while agreeing to negotiate on the basis of the British plan, demanded immediate possession of the means of aerial defence. By offering concessions to Britain, it hoped to put the onus of obstruction on France. The French analysis of the German position was far more accurate than that of the British, but they failed to convince the latter of the substance of their case. Mussolini, too, whatever his uneasiness about German rearmament, believed that the key question was not to prevent German rearmament but 'to avoid having it take place independent of all rules and all controls'. His own proposals recognized the German right to rearm and conceded its demands for defensive weapons while recommending that all armed countries should keep the arms they had. While this was more acceptable to the *Quai d'Orsay* than the British proposals, there was no move towards Rome. Mussolini summed up the situation on 17 March when he claimed that, while relations between the two countries had improved during the last months, 'truth obliges me to add that none of the large or small problems at issue over the last fifteen years has been resolved'.[42] The Belgian cabinet, too, added its voice to those wanting Hitler to return to Geneva. The question of disarmament became a central issue in the political battles in Brussels. When Barthou visited Brussels on 27 March as part of his general diplomatic fence-mending exercise, foreign minister Hymans claimed to have convinced him to abandon the idea of force and to work for a convention of accord. When faced with the French *non possumus*, however, the Belgian foreign minister drew back, unwilling to actually break ranks with France.

The French sent their answer to London on 17 April: 'France must put at the forefront of its preoccupations the conditions of its own security. Its wish for peace should not be confused with the abdication of its defence'.[43] It had come down to the competing views of Barthou and Doumergue: the foreign minister favoured negotiations, the prime minister wanted to break them off. François-Poncet returned to Paris to convince his chief that it was better to have a limited agreement with Berlin, and Germany rearming under surveillance, than a rupture that would give the Germans total freedom. The foreign minister was outvoted and threatened to resign, but was persuaded to stay lest the cabinet fall and the country face a new political crisis. The final communication was drafted by Doumergue but edited and amended by Barthou. The reasons for the foreign minister's subsequent reversal on

[42] Shorrock, *From Ally to Enemy*, 85.

[43] *DDF*, 1st ser., Vol. VI, No. 104.

policy and his subsequent public defence of the French position are still open to speculative argument. He may have been undecided before opting for an open anti-German line or, given the political circumstances, he may have been genuinely reluctant to pull the Doumergue government down. The *Figaro* headline encapsulated the French stand: 'France says no.' The Doumergue ministry enjoyed an unusual moment of self-confidence and a real sense of liberation. The game of pretence, with London as well as Berlin, was over. With good reason, French exasperation with London had mounted steadily during 1933. Britain's unwillingness to call public attention to German rearmament and the negative response to French demands for sanctions created considerable ill-will even at the Anglophile *Quai d'Orsay*.

These hostile feelings were fully reciprocated in London. The British felt, at the time and later, that the French had squandered a unique opportunity to strike a bargain with the Germans. The cabinet assumed Hitler would keep his word. Ministers twisted and turned on the security issue but would not yield to the French demand for a British pledge to stand by France in the event of German aggression. Barthou put the case clearly to the British chargé d'affaires when handing him the French reply. 'England need only say "If Germany attacks France I shall be at your side".'[44] It was a statement that no British government was prepared to make. It was firmly believed in London that alliances would increase the danger of war and Britain would be dragged into continental conflicts arising from problems in which it had limited interest. However discouraged, the British were reluctant to accept the fact that their initiative was dead. The knowledge that Germany was rearming, and would rearm faster if nothing was done, convinced them to continue the search for an agreement. By the beginning of May, however, with the service chiefs impatient to deal with the DRC recommendations, the cabinet had to find a way of ending the Geneva talks. It was decided not to re-open the question of security. If the French raised the subject, the British might re-affirm Locarno but it had to be made clear 'that we are unable to enter into any further commitments of that character'.[45] When Hymans asked on 17 May for a 'preventive guarantee' making the invasion of Belgium an automatic signal for British intervention, the cabinet judged the moment 'inopportune'. It was claimed that the French, involved in their own proposed 'eastern pact' proposals would not favour tripartite talks. The British showed no inclination to convince them. There was, during a discussion of the Eastern Locarno proposal in the Commons on 13 July, an 'unobtrusive'

44 *DDF*, 1st ser., Vol. VI, No. 105.
45 TNA: PRO, CAB 24/249, CP 132(34), 9 May 1934.

reaffirmation of Britain's interest in the integrity of Belgium but no pledge to defend Belgian territory.

VI

Most statesmen accepted by the spring of 1934 that they had reached the end of the Geneva disarmament road. It was felt necessary to give the Disarmament Conference a decent burial. Too much effort and public attention had been focused on the talks to abandon the scheduled summer session. At the same time, it was feared that continued discussions with no results would serve only to further discredit the League. After a seven months interval, the general conference reconvened on 29 May in an atmosphere of total gloom. Litvinov's recommendation that the conference stay in permanent session underlined the hopelessness of the disarmament cause. On 11 June, the Conference adjourned *sine die.* The Bureau of the Disarmament Conference continued to meet periodically until February 1935. It did little more than record the signs of preparations for the next war. The quest for peace through disarmament that began with the fourth of President Wilson's Fourteen Points and Article 8 of the Covenant sent out the wrong public signals and encouraged false expectations. It was due to the small powers that the League took up the preparations for a World Disarmament Conference in 1925. Thereafter, the pressure came from the weak, disarmed, or threatened states but above all from private individuals who wanted neither war nor armament bills. Statesmen, whatever their own reservations about the wisdom of disarmament, encouraged their citizens to think that a reduction of arms was possible and that the banning or reduction of weapons would promote peace. The governments of France and Britain, the main League providers of security, became hostages to confused but loudly articulated public expectations. Discussions continued despite their futility. By the time the World Disarmament Conference met, the question of arms had become the new battleground between France and Germany. Even when Hitler rose to power few were prepared to expose the myth of disarmament at a time when each major state was preparing to rearm. The British blamed the French for obstructing progress but offered nothing to offset the concessions that they thought should be made to Germany. The French found themselves unwilling to accept German rearmament but unable to prevent it. As a consequence, Hitler emerged from his first serious diplomatic contest with most of the battle honours. Unable to secure a disarmament convention that would allow Germany to rearm publicly, he torpedoed the Geneva talks and left the League. No common front against Germany emerged. Instead the British took the lead in pursuing the phantom of renewed discussions on Hitler's terms. While the German rearmament programme was put into high gear, Hitler could watch from the sidelines as the other states fell to quarrelling over the proper response to Germany's new course. All the participants in the disarmament talks knew that Germany was rearming. The League's efforts at disarmament failed in the most public way and to its singular discredit. Europe's statesmen could hardly have been shocked for they were Cassandras well before the Disarmament Conference opened. Talks continued, outside of Geneva, because popular disapproval and budgetary considerations ruled out the alternative. They went on, too, because the Great War cast a large shadow and few wanted to think of a new war. The exceptions included the ex-combatant, Adolf Hitler, and it was he who appeared in the clothes of the peace-maker.

Primary sources are in the General Bibliography. Starred items have been read after completion of the manuscript.

General Books

Evans, R. J., *The Coming of the Third Reich* (London, 2003).
—— *The Third Reich in Power* (London, 2005).
—— *The Third Reich at War* (London, 2008).
Hildebrand, K., *The Foreign Policy of the Third Reich* (London, 1973).
Hillgruber, A., *Deutschlands Rolle in der Vorgeschichte der beiden Weltkriege* (Göttingen, 1967), republished in English as *Germany and the Two World Wars* (Cambridge, MA, and London, 1981).
—— *Endlich genug über Nationalsozialismus und Zweiten Weltkrieg? Forschungsstand und Literatur* (Düsseldorf, 1982).
—— *Zweierlei Untergang: Die Zerschlagung des Deutschen Reiches und das Ende des europäischen Judentums* (Berlin, 1986).
Jäckel, E., *Hitlers Weltanschauung: Entwurf einer Herrschaft*, rev. 4th edn. (Stuttgart, 1991).
Jacobsen, H.-A., *Nationalsozialistische Außenpolitik, 1933–1938* (Frankfurt am Main and Berlin, 1968).
Militärgeschichtliches Forschungsamt (ed.), *Germany and the Second World War*, English translations from the German volumes: *Ursachen und Voraussetzungen der deutschen Kriegspolitik* (1979)/Vol. 1 *The Build-up of German Aggression*, ed. Wilhelm Deist, Manfred Messerschmidt, Hans-Erich Volkmann, and Wolfram Wette (Oxford, 1990); *Die Errichtung der Hegemonie auf dem europäischen Kontinent* (1979)/Vol. 2 *Germany's Initial Conquests in Europe*, ed. Klaus A. Maier, Ernest Rohde, Bernd Stegemann, Hans Umbreit (Oxford, 1991); *Der Mittelmeerraum und Südosteuropa* (1984)/Vol. 3 *The Mediterranean, South-East Europe and North Africa, 1939–1941*, ed. Gerhard Schreiber, Bernd Stegemann, and Detlef Vogel (Oxford, 1995).

PANAYI, P. (ed.), *Weimar and Nazi Germany: Continuities and Discontinuities* (Harlow and New York, 2001). See G. T. Waddington.
RICH, N., *Hitler's War Aims*, Vol. 1: *Ideology, the Nazi State and the Course of Expansion* (New York, 1973).
SCHREIBER, G., *Hitler-Interpretationen, 1923–1983: Ergebnisse, Methoden und Probleme der Forschung* (Darmstadt, 1984).
STOAKES, G., *Hitler and the Quest for World Dominion* (Leamington Spa, 1986).
TURNER, H. A., *German Big Business and the Rise of Hitler* (New York, 1985).
—— *Hitler's Thirty Days in Power: January 1933* (London, 1996).
WÄCHTER, D. (ed.), *Von Stresemann zu Hitler: Deutschland 1928 bis 1933 im Spiegel der Berichte des englischen Botschafters Sir Horace Rumbold* (Frankfurt and New York, 1997).
WEINBERG, G. L., *The Foreign Policy of Hitler's Germany*, Vol. 1: *Diplomatic Revolution in Europe, 1933–1936* (Chicago, 1970), Vol. 2: *Starting World War Two, 1937–1939* (Chicago and London, 1980).
—— *A World At Arms: A Global History of World War II* (Cambridge, 1994).

Hopes, Dreams, and Realities, 1933–1934

Books

BESSEL, R. (ed.), *Fascist Italy and Nazi Germany: Comparisons and Contrasts* (Cambridge, 1993). Especially articles by M. Knox and M. Geyer.
BLOCH, C., *Hitler und die europäischen Mächte, 1933–1934: Kontinuität oder Bruch?* (Frankfurt am Main, 1966).
BRACHER, K., FUNKE, M., and JACOBSEN, H. (eds.), *Nationalsozialistische Diktatur, 1933–1945: eine Bilanz* (Düsseldorf, 1983).
—— *Deutschland, 1933–1945: neue Studien zur nationalsozialistischen Herrschaft*, 2 vols. (Düsseldorf and Bonn, 1992–1993).
BROSZAT, M., *The Hitler State* (London, 1981).
DEIST, W., *Militär, Staat und Gesellschaft* (Munich, 1991).
DÜLFFER, J., *Weimar, Hitler und die Marine: Reichspolitik und Flottenbau, 1920–1939* (Düsseldorf, 1973).
GEYER, M., *Aufrüstung oder Sicherheit: die Reichswehr in der Krise der Machtpolitik, 1924–1936* (Wiesbaden, 1980).
GRIESWELLE, D., *Propaganda der Friedlosigkeit: eine Studie zu Hitlers Rhetorik, 1920–1933* (Stuttgart, 1972).
HAMANN, B., *Hitlers Wien: Lehrjahre eines Diktators* (Munich, 1997).
KERSHAW, I., *Popular Opinion and Political Dissent in the Third Reich: Bavaria, 1933–1945* (Oxford, 1983).
—— *The Nazi Dictatorship: Problems and Perspectives of Interpretation*, 3rd edn. (London, 1993).
—— and LEWIN, M. (eds.), *Stalinism and Nazism: Dictatorships in Comparison* (Cambridge, 1997).
KNOX, M., *Common Destiny: Dictatorship, Foreign Policy, and War in Fascist Italy and Nazi Germany* (Cambridge, 2000).
MASER, W., *Adolf Hitler: Legende-Mythos-Wirklichkeit* (Munich, 1971).

MICHALKA, W. (ed.), *Der Zweite Weltkrieg: Analysen, Grundzüge, Forschungsbilanz* (Munich and Zurich, 1990). Unusually rich collection of articles, both general and specific.

MOSSE, G. L., *The Crisis of German Ideology: Intellectual Origins of the Third Reich* (New York, 1964).

NOLTE, E., *The Three Faces of Fascism* (London, 1965).

O'NEILL, R., *The German Army and the Nazi Party, 1933–1939* (London, 1968).

RAUSCHNING, H., *Die Revolution des Nihilismus: Kulisse und Wirklichkeit im Dritten Reich* (Zurich, 1938). There is an English version available as *Germany's Revolution of Destruction* (trans. E. W. Dickes) (London, 1939).

SCHULZ, G., *Von Brüning zu Hitler: der Wandel des politischen Systems in Deutschland, 1930–1933* (Berlin, 1992).

SMITH, W. D., *The Ideological Origins of Nazi Imperialism* (New York and Oxford, 1986).

STERN, J. P., *Hitler: The Führer and the People*, rev. edn. (London, 1990).

Articles

BRACHER, K., 'Das Anfangsstadium der Hitlerschen Außenpolitik', *Vierteljahrshefte für Zeitgeschichte*, 5 (1957).

DEIST, W., 'The Road to Ideological War: Germany, 1918–1945', in Murray, W., Knox, M., and Bernstein, A. (eds.), *Making of Strategy: Rulers, States and War* (Cambridge and New York, 1994).

DÜLFFER, J., 'Zum "Decision-Making Process" in der deutschen Außenpolitik 1933–1939', in Funke, M. (ed.), *Hitler, Deutschland und die Mächte* (Düsseldorf, 1976).

HILDEBRAND, K., 'Monokratie oder Polykratie? Hitlers Herrschaft und das Dritte Reich', in Hirschfeld, G. and Kettenacker, L. (eds.), *Der Führerstaat: Mythos und Realität. Studien zur Struktur und Politik des Dritten Reiches* (Stuttgart, 1981).

KETTENACKER, L., 'Sozialpsychologische Aspekte der Führer-Herrschaft', in Hirschfeld, G. and Kettenacker, L. (eds.), *Der Führerstaat: Mythos und Realität. Studien zur Struktur und Politik des Dritten Reiches* (Stuttgart, 1981).

KNOX, M., 'Conquest, Foreign and Domestic, in Fascist Italy and Nazi Germany', *Journal of Modern History*, 56: 1 (1984).

MAIER, C. S., 'The Economics of Fascism and Nazism', in Maier, C. S. (ed.), *In Search of Political Stability: Explanations in Historical Political Economy* (Cambridge, 1987).

MOMMSEN, H., 'Hitlers Stellung im nationalsozialistischen Herrschaftssystem', in Hirschfeld, G. and Kettenacker, L. (eds.), *Der Führerstaat: Mythos und Realität. Studien zur Struktur und Politik des Dritten Reiches* (Stuttgart, 1981).

OVERY, R., 'Misjudging Hitler: A. J. P. Taylor and the Third Reich', in Martel, G. (ed.), *The Origins of the Second World War Reconsidered: A. J. P. Taylor and the Historians*, 2nd edn. (London, 1999).

SCHÖLLGEN, G., 'Das Problem einer Hitler-Biographie: Überlegungen anhand neuerer Darstellungen des Falles Hitler', in Bracher, K.-D., Funke, M., and

Jacobsen, H.-A. (eds.), *Nationalsozialistische Diktatur, 1933–1945: eine Bilanz* (Düsseldorf, 1983).

Trevor-Roper, H., 'Hitlers Kriegsziele', *Vierteljahrshefte für Zeitgeschichte*, 8 (1960).

—— 'The Mind of Adolf Hitler', introduction to *Hitler's Table Talk, 1941–1944*, 3rd edn. (London, 2000).

Hitler and the Great Power Response

For bibliographic references to disarmament and the World Disarmament Conference, 1933–1934, see Zara Steiner, *The Lights that Failed* (Oxford, 2005), 796–799.

Books

Bariéty, J., Valentin, J., and Guth, A. (eds.), *La France et l'Allemagne entre les deux guerres mondiales: actes du colloque tenu en Sorbonne (Paris IV), 15–17 janvier Nancy 1987* (Nancy, 1987). Especially the chapters by Bariéty, Droz, and Prost.

—— and Poidevin, R., *Les relations franco-allemandes, 1815–1975* (Paris, 1977). Especially the chapter by Bariéty.

Budrass, L., *Flugzeugindustrie und Luftrüstung in Deutschland, 1918–1945* (Düsseldorf, 1998).

Cannistraro, P. V. and Sullivan, B. R., *Il Duce's other Woman: The Untold Story of Margherita Sarfatti, Mussolini's Jewish Mistress* (New York, 1993).

Clarke, J. C., *Russia and Italy against Hitler: The Bolshevik–Fascist Rapprochement of the 1930s* (New York and London, 1991).

De Felice, R., *Mussolini e Hitler: i rapporti segreti, 1922–1933, con documenti inediti* (Florence, 1975).

Granzow, B., *A Mirror of Nazism: British Opinion and the Emergence of Hitler 1929–1933* (London, 1964).

Jackson, P., *France and the Nazi Menace: Intelligence and Policy Making, 1933–1939* (Oxford, 2000).

Kindermann, G., *Hitlers Niederlage in Österreich: bewaffneter NS-Putsch, Kanzlermord, und Österreichs Abwehrsieg von 1934* (Hamburg, 1984).

Kuhn, A., *Hitlers außenpolitisches Programm: Enstehung und Entwicklung, 1919–1939* (Stuttgart, 1970).

Micaud, C., *The French Right and Nazi Germany, 1933–1936: A Study of Public Opinion* (New York, 1972).

Müller, K., *Das Heer und Hitler: Armee und nationalsozialistisches Regime, 1933–1940* (Stuttgart, 1969).

Nadolny, S., *Abrüstungsdiplomatie, 1932–1933: Deutschland auf der Genfer Konferenz im Übergang von Weimar zu Hitler* (Munich, 1978).

Petersen, J., *Hitler–Mussolini: die Entstehung der Achse Berlin-Rom, 1933–1936* (Tübingen, 1973).

Robertson, E. M., *Mussolini as Empire Builder: Europe and Africa, 1932–1936* (London and New York, 1977).

SALEWSKI, M., *Die deutsche Seekriegsleitung, 1935–1945*, vol. 1: *1935–1941* (Frankfurt am Main, 1970).

SCHLEUNES, K. A., *The Twisted Road to Auschwitz: Nazi Policy toward German Jews, 1933–1939* (Urbana, IL, 1970).

SCOTT, W. E., *Alliance against Hitler: The Origins of the Franco-Soviet Pact* (Durham, NC, 1963).

SHORROCK, W. I., *From Ally to Enemy: The Enigma of Fascist Italy in French Diplomacy, 1920–1940* (Kent, OH, 1988).

TOOZE, A., *The Wages of Destruction: The Making and Breaking of the Nazi Economy* (London and New York, 2006).

VAÏSSE, M., *Sécurité d'abord: la politique française en matière de désarmement, 9 décembre 1930–17 avril 1934* (Paris, 1981).

WANDYCZ, P., *The Twilight of French Eastern Alliances, 1926–1936: French–Czechoslovak–Polish Relations from Locarno to the Remilitarization of the Rhineland* (Princeton, NJ, 1988).

WARK, W. K., *The Ultimate Enemy: British Intelligence and Nazi Germany, 1933–1939* (London, Ithaca, NY, and Oxford, 1985).

WOLLSTEIN, G., *Vom Weimarer Revisionismus zu Hitler: das Deutsche Reich und die Großmächte in der Anfangsphase der nationalsozialistischen Herrschaft in Deutschland* (Bonn, 1973).

YOUNG, R. J., *In Command of France: French Foreign Policy and Military Planning, 1933–1940* (Cambridge, MA, 1978).

Articles

BARIÉTY, J. and BLOCH, C., 'Une tentative de réconciliation franco-allemande et son échec, 1932–1933', *Revue d'Histoire moderne et contemporaine*, 15 (1968).

CANNISTRARO, P. V. and WYNOT, E. D. JR., 'On the Dynamics of Anti-Communism as a Function of Fascist Foreign Policy, 1933–1943', *Politico*, 38 (1973).

DÜLFFER, J., 'Determinants of German Naval Policy, 1929–1939', in Militärgeschichtliches Forschungsamt (ed.), *Germany and the Second World War*, vol. 1: *The Build-up of Military Aggression*, ed. Wilhelm Deist (Oxford, 1990).

HASLAM, J., 'The Comintern and the Origins of the Popular Front, 1934–1935', *Historical Journal*, 22: 3 (1979).

HÖRLING, H., 'L'opinion française face à l'avènement d'Hitler au pouvoir, première partie', *Francia*, 3 (1975).

—— 'L'opinion française face à l'avènement d'Hitler au pouvoir, deuxième partie', *Francia*, 4 (1976).

JACKSON, P., 'French Intelligence and Hitler's Rise to Power', *Historical Journal*, 41: 2 (1998).

JERVIS, R., 'Perceiving and Coping with Threat', in Jervis, R., Lebow, R. N., and Stein, J. G. (eds.), *Psychology and Deterrence* (London, 1985).

MCKERCHER, B. J. C., 'Deterrence and the European Balance of Power: The Field Force and British Grand Strategy, 1934–1938', *English Historical Review*, 123: 500 (2008).

RADICE, L., 'The Eastern Pact, 1933–1935: A Last Attempt at European Co-operation', *The Slavonic and Eastern European Review*, 55: 1 (1977).

SOUCY, R. J., 'French Press Reactions to Hitler's First Two Years in Power', *Contemporary European History*, 7: 1 (1998).

SULLIVAN, B. R., 'From Little Brother to Senior Partner: Fascist Italian Perceptions of the Nazis and of Hitler's Regime', in Alexander, M. S. (ed.), *Knowing your Friends: Intelligence inside Alliances and Coalitions from 1914 to the Cold War* (London, 1998).

TÜRKES, M., 'The Balkan Pact and its Immediate Implications for the Balkan States', *Middle Eastern Studies*, 30: 1 (1994).

TURNER, A., 'Austen Chamberlain, *The Times* and the Question of Revision of the Treaty of Versailles in 1933', *European History Quarterly*, 18: 1 (1988).

2

Uncertain Embraces: The European Powers and Nazi Germany, 1934–1935

I

The New Year opened with Hitler breaking from Weimar's traditional foreign policy: a ten-year German–Polish non-aggression treaty was signed on 26 January 1934. The treaty, called a 'declaration', contained no recognition of the existing borders but imposed an unrestricted neutrality obligation on both countries, which allowed aggression against other states.[1] From Hitler's point of view, a *rapprochement* with Warsaw improved the German position. It covered its exposed eastern flank while the country was still vulnerable. It weakened the Franco-Polish alliance, notwithstanding Polish assurances to France to the contrary. It could be used to assure Britain as well as others that Germany was a peaceful nation, willing to conclude bilateral pacts of non-aggression rather than make alliances that lead to war. Most usefully, the declaration proved a way to block the conclusion of an Eastern Locarno, as was discussed between France and the Soviet Union at the end of 1933 and again in the spring and summer of 1934. From Hitler's first approaches to Warsaw in May 1933 until the conclusion of the agreement, the German leader claimed that he had no wish to Germanize other people and was more than willing to abandon the use of force. Most probably he had not yet decided what role Poland would play in the fulfilment of his eastern ambitions and whether it would be accomplice or victim. It was important to ensure that Poland did not participate in any kind of eastern multi-national security pact that would weaken Hitler's negotiating hand. Relations in Danzig improved during the summer and the press war between the two states ceased in the autumn. Neither the German diplomats nor the army

[1] See R. Ahmann, *Nichtangriffspakte: Entwicklung und operative Nutzung in Europa 1922–1939. Mit einem Ausblick auf die Renaissance des Nichtangriffsvertrages nach dem Zweiten Weltkrieg* (Baden-Baden, 1988), 310–322.

chiefs abandoned their hopes for future territorial changes at Poland's expense. The Wilhelmstrasse, traditionally hostile to Warsaw, backed Hitler's move, believing, correctly, that it was a temporary expedient measure that suited a time of military and diplomatic weakness. The diplomats feared only that Hitler would prove over-hasty and unduly provocative while they prepared the step-by-step revision of Versailles they favoured. Hitler had different ideas. His actions in the East and the demand for a faster rearmament schedule suggested a more adventure-some foreign policy than either his military or diplomatic advisers thought prudent but they accepted, with only some murmurs of dissent, the changed priorities in Poland.

Behind Piłsudski's support for the settlement with Germany were uncertainties about the value of the Franco-Polish alliance. The French decision in December 1932 to accept the German demand for 'equality of rights' at the Disarmament Conference, taken without consulting Warsaw, was compounded by Paul-Boncour's willingness to discuss territorial revision with the Italians in the spring of 1933. Polish opposition to Mussolini's Four-Power Pact and anger at the weak French response to Hitler's withdrawal from the Disarmament Conference made some form of countermove imperative. Immediately after the German departure from Geneva, Piłsudski demanded a report on the state of German armaments and sought an exchange of views with the French general staff. He used private channels to put two key questions to Paris. If Germany attacked Poland, would France respond with general mobilization? Would the French, in such a case, concentrate all their forces on the German frontier? The questions were apparently answered in the negative. The French would promise only material aid, collaboration between the general staffs, and political support for Warsaw. There would be no French assistance should Poland launch a preventive war. Piłsudski could hardly have been surprised by such a response. Doubtful about the prospects of a firm French line towards German rearmament or about their future military support for Poland, he drew his own conclusions about the limited value of the French alliance and decided to capitalize on the *détente* with Berlin. Somewhat reassured by the non-Prussian composition of the Nazi regime and hopeful that German attention would be shifted from Poland, he was prepared to take a positive view of Hitler's rearmament programme in return for a normalization of relations based on the territorial status quo.

In early November, Józef Lipski, the newly appointed Polish minister in Berlin, was instructed to see what price Hitler would offer if Poland refrained from taking new defence measures. If offered a non-aggression pact, the Führer should be told that his proposals would be seriously considered. At a meeting between Hitler and Lipski on 15 November, Hitler denied any aggressive designs against either Poland or France and excluded the use of war for the settlement of disputes. His statement, at Lipski's request, was made public as an official communiqué. It was enough to elicit an uneasy response from the Polish public and to create a diplomatic *frisson* in Paris and Prague. Rumours of possible German overtures to Warsaw and Prague for non-aggression pacts were thick on the ground in the autumn of 1933. François-Poncet, writing from Berlin, warned that Hitler was trying to break up the Polish–French alliance. On 27 November, the Germans proposed a written declaration of non-aggression; three weeks were to elapse before the Poles responded. In the interval, Piłsudski again sounded out the French. Laroche, the French minister in Warsaw, wanted a clear and strong statement of support for Poland and urged Paul-Boncour to come himself. The *Quai d'Orsay*, however, failed to make any gesture to steady their ally. Paul-Boncour's passivity was an error if the French wanted to reassure the Poles.

Beneš was more perceptive. He made much of his loyalty to France and Czechoslovakia's correct behaviour towards Poland. His government had reacted to the disruption of the Disarmament Conference by strengthening its civil–military co-ordinating machinery and instituting a major defence programme. The frontier fortifications along the German–Czechoslovak border were reinforced and the first tanks rolled off the Škoda assembly lines in 1933–1934. But the first Czech line of defence was to look to Paris and to seek an understanding with the Poles. Arriving for a three-day visit to Paris on 14 December, Beneš sought to stiffen Paul-Boncour's opposition to German rearmament. Always inclined to over-optimism, the Czech foreign minister declared himself satisfied with the concurrence of French and Czechoslovak views; non-aggression pacts should be concluded only under the aegis of the League of Nations. It was during this Paris visit that Beneš met with the Polish minister and told him that he was ready, 'at any moment, even tomorrow, to open appropriate talks with the Polish government in order to give a constant and unchangeable form to our relations'.[2] When Piłsudski had sought a *rapprochement* with Prague a year earlier, the Czechoslovak reaction was cool. It was now the turn of Czechoslovakia to do the soliciting with equally negative results. At a meeting between Beck and Beneš in Geneva on 20 January, during a session of the League Council, neither man was honest with the other. Whether

[2] Quoted in Piotr Wandycz, *The Twilight of French Eastern Alliances, 1926–1936: French–Czechoslovak–Polish Relations from Locarno to the Remilitarization of the Rhineland* (Princeton, NJ, 1988), 316.

Beneš actually knew about the German offer to Warsaw is still an open question, but he spoke only of general staff collaboration and did not actually offer a military alliance. Beck only discussed Poland's foreign policy aims in the most general terms. As Piotr Wandycz has concluded, the encounter only proved 'that the ways of Polish and Czechoslovak diplomacy were virtually irreconcilable'.[3] Their uneasy relationship was likely to develop only in one direction—by becoming more strained and antagonistic. Common ties with France had never been strong enough to bridge their mutual antipathies while different geographic orientations reinforced their separate order of priorities.

On 9 January, Piłsudski gave his assent to the new German–Polish declaration. He believed it would strengthen Poland's security position for the short-term, if not for the ten-year period of the agreement, and would enlarge the country's freedom of action. The declaration gave the Polish leaders far greater confidence and partly assuaged the thirst for great power status. In Piłsudski's view, the declaration reduced Poland's dependence on France without creating new obligations towards Germany. The Franco-Polish alliance remained untouched but, as the marshal explained to Laroche, it now applied only to a direct German attack on France. Despite rumours to the contrary, no territorial questions were raised. The declaration did raise problems about Poland's relations with the Soviet Union, with whom Poland had concluded a non-aggression pact in 1933. Yet Piłsudski was not unduly worried by Hitler's hopes to enlist Poland in an anti-Communist crusade, an approach made more explicit in 1935. He remained committed to his old policy of balancing between Berlin and Moscow, hoping to maintain a free hand in dealing with his two antagonistic neighbours but still believing that Russia posed the greater threat to Poland's safety. For the *Quai d'Orsay*, the German–Polish declaration was an unexpected check, despite Piłsudski's claims that the Franco-Polish alliance was not affected and that Poland retained her complete freedom of action. Not only did the French diplomats resent the Polish failure to consult and inform them but they believed that Poland's new 'freedom' was achieved at French expense. Military co-operation between the two countries continued but the Poles now claimed that equality of status so long denied them. The French were more shaken than their official statements disclosed; the public reaction would have been stronger had the country not been caught up in its domestic turmoils. Joseph Paul-Boncour was implicated in the Stavisky scandal and had little time for foreign affairs. It was not until Louis Barthou took over the *Quai d'Orsay* in February 1934 in the new Doumergue cabinet that there would be a

[3] Ibid., 323.

positive response to the new situation. The Prague reaction was more immediate and stronger though there had never been any Polish commitment to Czechoslovakia with regard to Germany. Czech–Polish military contacts continued, but the Czechs felt that the new agreement left them in a weaker military position. In private conversations with British and Soviet diplomats, Beneš lashed out at Piłsudski and Beck, his anger increasing as an anti-Czech campaign was launched in Warsaw in the government-sponsored and right-wing press. The Czechs were accused of maltreating Poles in Teschen, an old story given a new importance. The press war reached its height during February–March 1934. There were further domestic complications. Since early 1933, the Hlinka populist party in Slovakia had become increasingly vocal and extremist in its nationalism. Whereas Hlinka frowned on cultivating Polish connections, the younger Slovak nationalists had no such reservations. It is hardly surprising that there were those in Prague who felt that their country was the first victim of Poland's swollen head.

The Polish–German declaration of 26 January was followed by Beck travelling to Moscow. The conversations between 13 and 15 February, if outwardly friendly, were unproductive and served only to convince Litvinov that Poland could not be enlisted in any political or military *entente* against Germany. It was agreed that the Polish–Soviet non-aggression treaty should be prolonged and that legations in both countries should be raised to embassy rank. The question of co-operation in the Baltic was not explored. The new Polish agreement created problems in Moscow where there was still hope of a *détente* with Germany, with Warsaw as the possible bait. A few days before the Polish–German declaration was signed, Karl Radek, in charge of foreign affairs in Stalin's personal secretariat, told German journalists in Moscow, 'We shall do nothing that could commit us for a long term. Nothing will happen that could permanently block our way to a common policy with Germany . . . My love for Poland is certainly not greater than for National Socialist Germany. With us there is no anti-German group.'[4] At the XVII Party Congress that opened on 26 January, Stalin still appeared uncertain, making veiled threats against Germany but warning against undue optimism about the Franco-Soviet negotiations. He was not fully committed to any course. In late March 1934, Litvinov offered the Germans a Baltic pact, once more testing the Rapallo waters. The German rejection of this proposal proved to be a turning point in Soviet–German relations. On the German side it signalled Hitler's intention to safeguard his new freedom of action in the East. For Stalin,

[4] Quoted in Jonathan Haslam, *The Soviet Union and the Struggle for Collective Security in Europe, 1933–1939* (Basingstoke, 1984), 31–32.

still hoping to change Hitler's course, the German rejection of the protocol made it necessary to pursue the French alignment.

During the rest of 1934, Russia moved closer to France but only after prolonged and interrupted negotiations and continuing hesitations on both sides. The Soviets wanted the backing of a major European power but remained distrustful of all the capitalist states. New Soviet–French talks had begun on 20 October 1933, in response to Germany's withdrawal from Geneva. Both sides, however, acted with great caution. The French had no intention of being dragged into Soviet quarrels with the Japanese in the Far East, a major Soviet concern. Nor had the Cartel government ruled out the bilateral arrangements which Hitler sought in the months after the Geneva walkout. However unsympathetic Paul-Boncour may have been to the German option, he was not ready to embrace the Russians as part of an alternative package. In November, he drew back from the idea of a mutual assistance pact and suggested a more limited form of commercial and political agreement. The Russians were equally uncertain about future moves. It was mainly the fear of a Franco-German agreement and their own altercations with the Germans that led to the exchanges of views in Paris. On 12 December, the *Politburo* agreed to a resolution in favour of collective security and instructed the Narkomindel to propose a multilateral assistance pact with France and Poland but also embracing Belgium, Czechoslovakia, the three Baltic countries, and Finland. It was decided, too, that the Soviet Union should join the League of Nations. Careful to cover their tracks, the Soviets wanted it made clear that it was France who had initiated the idea of a regional agreement. Faced with the new Soviet proposals, Alexis Léger, the *Quai d'Orsay's* secretary general, dragged his feet. The talks lapsed either because of divisions between the pro-Soviet and pro-German forces in the French cabinet, as the Russians believed, or because of strong opposition from key officials in the *Quai d'Orsay*, who enjoyed considerable influence at a time when Paul-Boncour was politically embarrassed.

There were signs, too, that the smaller states were starting to take the measure of the new fluidity in European arrangements. Hitler's accession to power increased fears about existing territorial boundaries in central and south-east Europe. The Four-Power Pact signed in June 1933 raised apprehensions that a 'Great Power Directorate' would try to revise the peace treaties without regard to the interests of the smaller states. An annual Balkan Conference had been initiated in 1929 but some of the Balkan leaders felt the need for closer co-operation. A Treaty of Friendship and Arbitration was signed between Turkey and Romania in October 1933. The Greek government, in one of its more anti-Italian phases, began to sing the praises of the Little Entente, impressed by the Romanians' stand against Mussolini's Four-Power Pact. In early November 1933, the fourth Balkan Conference met at the University of Saloniki and despite Bulgarian reservations, delegates agreed to recommend a Balkan Pact to their respective governments. Only the Bulgarians dragged their feet, demanding special treatment and protection for the Bulgarian nationals living elsewhere. On 9 February 1934, the representatives of Greece, Romania, Turkey, and Yugoslavia publicly announced the conclusion of a Balkan Pact, guaranteeing the security of their respective frontiers against any aggressor. Due to Soviet insistence (the Turks promptly communicated its terms to Moscow in accordance with their treaty obligations) the guarantee was restricted to the Balkan frontiers. Bulgaria, though invited to join, remained outside the new grouping. On 5 June, two identical military conventions were signed between Turkey and Yugoslavia and between Turkey and Romania. The new agreements meant that if Bulgaria attacked any one of the signatories in association with Italy, the other parties would take up arms against both aggressors. Greece was not a party to the military conventions; it feared being drawn into a conflict with Italy in which Greece had no interest. The admittedly weak, anti-revisionist Balkan Pact was a regional arrangement to defend the territorial status quo and to support efforts to outlaw war as a means of settling disputes. It was directed only against Balkan revisionism and was aimed primarily at Bulgaria and Italy. Though there were still hopes that Bulgaria might join at a later date, by isolating Bulgaria the Balkan Pact made any easy collaboration between Sofia and Rome more difficult. No provision was made for the possibility of an attack by a non-Balkan state acting on its own. The Greeks, due to Venizelos, declared that they would not take up arms against any Great Power, a barely concealed reference to Italy. The new grouping was viewed with distaste by the Bulgarians and by both the Italians and the Germans, though the Balkan Pact was not anti-German and all the states in the region were actively engaged in developing their economic ties with Berlin. The British were cool, preferring bilateral relations with each of the Balkan states and doubtful about any grouping that excluded Bulgaria. The French were sympathetic but stood aside, relying on their links with the Little Entente countries and talks with the Soviet Union to preserve their position as defenders of the status quo against Germany. The most important feature of the Balkan Pact was its negotiation by the anti-revisionist Balkan states. It remained to be seen whether it would lead to any common action.

If Italy was the pivotal revisionist power in the Balkans, Mussolini's own ambitions were obviously affected by Hitler's diplomatic moves in 1934. The Duce had been considerably upset by the German departure from the Disarmament Conference, for it meant the collapse of his Four-Power Pact. His efforts to mediate between Germany and France by recognizing the former's right to rearm without requiring the French to disarm had failed to produce concrete results. An unrestrained and rearmed Germany posed a serious threat to Italian interests in Austria and to Mussolini's claims to a dominant role in the Danubian basin. Mussolini, moreover, was already planning an attack on Ethiopia sometime during 1935 and needed to avoid any German move towards *Anschluss*. As a sizeable army and substantial quantities of equipment would have to be sent to East Africa, the Italians would be in no position to defend their continental borders. Hitler's reassurances in December 1933 failed to calm the Duce. Many in the Italian ruling élite, including Pietro Badoglio, nominally head of the combined chiefs of staff, were highly alarmed about a Nazified Austria on Italy's northern frontier which, at the very least, might lead to German economic domination of south-eastern Europe. With his eye on Ethiopia, Mussolini had to be sure that Hitler was not planning a *coup* in Vienna. Yet even with regard to Austria, he preferred direct dealing with Berlin and his own pressure on the diminutive Christian Social Chancellor of Austria, Engelbert Dollfuss, to joint representations with France and Britain. There were talks in Rome with the French ambassador about a common stand against *Anschluss* and collaboration in the building of a Danubian 'common market', but there was no real basis for common action. As against a mutual interest in preserving Austrian independence was French unhappiness about Mussolini's insistence on a privileged position as protector of Austria and the Dollfuss regime. Dollfuss's brutal elimination of the Vienna Socialists on 12–14 February 1934, encouraged by Mussolini, aroused considerable criticism and opposition in Paris to any financial assistance for the Viennese government. Franco-Italian economic and commercial competition continued in the Danube. On 17 March, the Rome Protocols pledging Italy, Austria, and Hungary to joint consultation and economic co-operation were signed. The Little Entente leaders complained to the French of a move that not only confirmed Mussolini's intention to act as Austria's protector but would create an Italian-dominated regional system rivalling their own. The rivalry between the Italians and the Little Entente would complicate the French wooing of Mussolini.

II

The new French foreign minister, Louis Barthou, sought to extricate France from the situation in which it found itself in early 1934. The Germans were rearming; the Italian agreement was proving elusive; and

Poland was embarked upon an autonomist course. The only French policy that made logical sense after the rejection of the British disarmament proposals on 17 April 1934 would have been a major rearmament effort. Instead Weygand continued to pursue a defensive strategy while the government reduced the armaments credits and failed to produce a plan of industrial mobilization. Financial considerations and British pressure for disarmament favoured inaction. The diplomats had to find an alternative to the British attempt to appease Germany on the armaments front. Barthou's private doubts about the note of 17 April, which rejected any compromise with Germany, were publicly disguised but his subsequent actions suggest that he was prepared to break with the passive policies of his predecessor, Paul-Boncour. The new foreign minister shared the prevailing cabinet view that not much could be expected from Britain. When he went, somewhat reluctantly, to Geneva at the end of May to hear John Simon woo the Germans and blame the French for the impasse in the disarmament talks, Barthou responded with an ironic and aggressive speech reminding Simon of what Britain was demanding from France. Only the intervention of the Belgian foreign minister and Barthou's soothing charm kept the irate Englishman from leaving Geneva in high indignation. But Simon, while admitting that the do-nothing policy was only encouraging the Germans along the road of rearmament, offered no alternative to London's rejected proposals.

Instead Barthou rapidly took up the task of repairing France's damaged diplomatic bridges. His first visit on 27 March 1934 had been to Belgium. He met the new King Leopold III and spoke with Prime Minister Charles de Broqueville and Paul Hymans, the foreign minister. Franco-Belgian relations remained unsettled. The military convention of 7 September 1920 was in some respects remarkably imprecise, most of its provisions dealing with the occupation of the Rhineland and provisions for a common response to a German mobilization. The decision reached in 1931 to subordinate the agreement to the League and the Locarno treaties formally still left open fundamental questions about Belgium's obligations to France. Pétain's provocative statements in 1930 and again in 1933 that, in case of war with Germany, French troops would march into Belgium with or without Belgian permission, did not improve matters. Further attempts made to clarify the situation during 1933 and 1934 showed only how deep was the gulf between the two governments. The French rejection of the British disarmament formula in April, coming after Barthou's visit to Brussels and in clear contradiction to Hymans's advice, left the Belgians in a difficult situation. Faced with German rearmament and its withdrawal from the League of Nations, they could not afford to offend France by denouncing the military agreement. At the same time, they did not want to be involved in any Franco-German quarrel in central Europe where no Belgian interests were at stake. In May, Belgian diplomats went off to London to seek the unambiguous British commitment which Simon refused to give. There was no easy solution to the Belgian security dilemma.

Barthou next travelled to Warsaw and Prague in April. Józef Beck pointedly failed to meet him at the railway station, reproducing exactly the circumstances of Beck's own trip to Paris in September 1933. It was the first time a French foreign minister had visited Warsaw and Barthou went well briefed. Though the Warsaw visit was a personal success for the Frenchman, little concrete was accomplished. Piłsudski remained highly critical of French attitudes towards German rearmament: 'You will give in again', he told Barthou,[5] and made clear his intention of developing the new links with Hitler. Both Piłsudski and Beck touched on their continuing suspicion of the Soviet Union and rehearsed their many grievances with regard to French behaviour. Barthou was assured, however, that the pact with Germany had done nothing to weaken Poland's alliance with France and he, in turn, both in private and in public, acknowledged Poland's Great Power status and signalled its importance to the security of Eastern Europe. Beck was flattered by Barthou's wooing and the Polish crowds cheered the French foreign minister, but there was no diminution in the level of suspicion between Warsaw and Paris. Not unexpectedly, Barthou had a far easier time in Prague. Beneš was already a close personal friend and the French visitor increased his circle of admirers, charming all whom he met in the capital. There were some differences over Austria as Beneš stressed the need for a tripartite arrangement—France, Czechoslovakia, and Italy—if Austria and Hungary were to be saved from German domination. It may be, too, that Beneš aired his highly critical views of Piłsudski's new course but these were already well-known in Paris. Complaints about the state of commercial relations between the two countries (Czechoslovakia was suffering from a negative balance of payments with France) were not serious enough to disturb the basically harmonious relations between the governments.

Barthou and the *Quai d'Orsay* wanted more than the restoration of the old alliances in Eastern Europe. There were two possibilities that would complement each other and strengthen France's diplomatic position. The first was an 'Eastern Locarno' pact—to match the 1925 Locarno treaty that guaranteed the sanctity and inviolability of Germany's western borders—in which each power would assist its neighbour if attacked by another signatory, assurances buttressed by

[5] Wandycz, *The Twilight of French Eastern Alliances*, 348.

an agreement with the Soviet Union. The proposed regional agreement could be extended to include Germany, enhancing French security but also making the pact acceptable to Britain. In this first part of Barthou's diplomatic strategy, the key was clearly going to be the Soviet Union. While there were signs of a new wind blowing out of Moscow, notably the unexpectedly co-operative attitude of the Communists in both Paris and Vienna during the recent political crises, these were still only tentative. Opinion in France was sharply divided over the question of relations with Moscow. The Communist party wanted an alliance but only gradually moderated its criticism of Barthou. The Socialists welcomed *rapprochement* with the Soviet Union but maintained their loyalty to the principles of collective security and opposed alliances that would split Europe into camps. The Radicals, who occupied the crucial middle ground in French politics at this time, were both publicly and privately divided. Some shared the fears of the 'realistic right', that without such an accord the Soviets would strike a bargain with the Germans. Others looked, with the Socialists, to Geneva. At the far end of the spectrum, the extreme right, whether royalist or fascist, strongly opposed the alliance and repeatedly denounced Barthou's policies in the columns of *Le Matin* and *L'Action Française*.

On 20 April 1934, Barthou, who, like Briand, never allowed his ideological preferences to interfere with the definition of national interests, informed the Soviets that he intended to take up the languishing Franco-Soviet talks, in abeyance since January. Eight days later, the *Quai d'Orsay* produced a new formula in which Germany would be included together with the Soviet Union, Poland, and Czechoslovakia in a mutual assistance treaty. A separate Franco-Soviet Pact would be linked to the new treaty. The terms of the new agreements were settled in early June. The Soviet Union would assume the same obligations towards France as if she were a signatory of Locarno while France would act as the guarantor of the multilateral pact. The Doumergue cabinet approved the pact on 5 June with Laval, who still favoured an accommodation with the Germans, the sole opponent. It was mainly to safeguard the interests of their Eastern European allies that the French insisted the USSR should join the League of Nations before the multilateral assistance pact was negotiated. Barthou nonetheless faced strong opposition from the Poles, annoyed by the apparent French unwillingness to treat them as an equal partner and preferring to place their confidence in their newly created bilateral non-aggression pacts. An Eastern Pact ran counter to almost all Polish hopes of regaining her position as France's most important ally. It conflicted, too, with Warsaw's continuing illusions of creating its own regional system extending from the Baltic to Romania. Under the French scheme, the Poles would be subjected to a Franco-Soviet regime, a totally unacceptable prospect. The Germans, too, had little interest in an Eastern Locarno and launched a diplomatic offensive in Paris and Moscow to block the initiative. Litvinov found the Czechs and Romanians more sympathetic. He was able to secure *de jure* recognition from each in an exchange of notes on 9 June 1934. The Prague government was later to follow the French example in concluding a mutual assistance pact with the USSR. The Romanians held back because of the continuing conflict over Bessarabia. The *Quai d'Orsay* insisted on a mutual assistance pact that would include their Eastern European allies but not, due to Polish objections, the Baltic states. The Soviets, who doubted whether the Germans would join, continued to fight unsuccessfully for the inclusion of the Baltic right up until the conclusion of the Franco-Soviet alliance in 1935.

The demand for Soviet membership in the League was still being debated in Moscow when, on 30 June, the 'Night of the Long Knives', Hitler settled, with the help of the *Reichswehr* and SS, the fate of Ernst Röhm and the SA. Under Röhm's leadership, the SA had retained its identity as an independent and separate military–political force. It was not only that Röhm's ambitions to set up a 'separate state' with a 'people's militia' and 'control of the police force' threatened Hitler's exclusive domination of German domestic affairs, but they also aroused the enmity of the army and SS. The arrogance, violent actions, and daily disturbances of Röhm's large band of followers set off a mass of protests at a time when the National Socialists were already facing considerable public criticism. Supported by the *Reichswehr* generals and the SS leaders, Hitler decided to act. Göring and Himmler put together the details of a 'SA plot'; Hitler personally confronted Röhm and the SS leaders at Bad Wiessee, a small town in Bavaria where they had assembled for a meeting with the Führer who obviously sanctioned their subsequent murders. Hitler's forces took advantage of the killings to slaughter indiscriminately other so-called critics of the regime, including ex-chancellor Schleicher, two generals, and the head of Catholic Action. Brüning escaped by fleeing the country. While some in the West were shocked by this brutal disregard of all legal processes, most people in Germany applauded Hitler's decisive action, so different from that of his dithering predecessors in checking the SA threat to public order. In a remarkably adroit speech to the Reichstag, reviewing the events of 30 June, Hitler defended the murders by emphasizing Röhm's homosexuality and the moral laxness of the SA, and stressing the need to protect order and security against anyone who would threaten them. The SS, Hitler's élite praetorian guard, had disposed of its chief rival and now had undisputed authority over the police. The action was also a victory for the *Reichswehr* but it gave the army no policy clout. On Hindenburg's death on 2 August, Hitler abolished the separate office of Reich president and became 'Führer and Reich Chancellor'. Thereafter, all officers, soldiers, ministers, and civil servants were required to take a personal oath to Adolf Hitler. The army was now at Hitler's feet. The new order was celebrated at the party congress at Nuremberg in December, commemorated by Leni Riefenstahl's brilliantly re-worked film, *Triumph of the Will*.

Observers in London and Moscow misread the significance of the Röhm 'putsch'. British officials saw the June action as a success for the right and the *Reichswehr*, and spoke of a 'return to the Rapallo line'. The Russians, too, believed the move heralded the re-emergence of their old allies, the army and big business, and optimistically anticipated a new German crisis that would end the Hitler regime. These illusions encouraged Litvinov's opponents, including Marshal Voroshilov, the commissar of defence, but not Nikolai Krestinsky, the deputy commissar of foreign affairs, to oppose the French connection. The 'spirit of unalloyed optimism' persisted in Moscow until the attempted Austrian Nazi *coup* of 25 July and the assassination of Chancellor Dollfuss, discussed below, put an end to Soviet hopes that Hitler was on his way out. On the day after the abortive Austrian *coup*, Litvinov finally told the French that the Soviet Union would join the League if properly invited and promised a permanent seat on the Council. The Soviet Union needed a defence against Germany and the French proposal was the only one on the table. A sudden deterioration in relations with Japan in the summer of 1934 provided an additional reason for joining the League, for it might provide some protection in the case of a Pacific war. Stalin, doubtful about the proposed Eastern Locarno, might well have preferred a more restricted arrangement both for European and Far Eastern purposes.

The events in Germany and Austria brought the Italians into line but the Poles, Belgians, Portuguese, and Swiss did their best to block the Soviet entry into the League. Nevertheless, on 18 September 1934 the Russians were admitted to the League and took their seat on the League Council. There was, however, no immediate French diplomatic follow-up. Polish and German objections to the Eastern Pact stayed Barthou's hand: a security pact without either country diminished its value to France. It is still an open question whether, given this effective Polish and German veto, Barthou would have opted for an alliance with Moscow. Léger and others at the *Quai d'Orsay* retained their doubts about the wisdom of a Soviet treaty and counselled caution. Nor was the *Politburo* ready for such an alternative. Litvinov was instructed in September not to hasten an initiative for a pact without Germany and

Poland. The Germans sent out mixed signals. Count von der Schulenburg, the new German ambassador in Moscow, suggested a trade pact that would facilitate an improvement in political as well as economic relations between the two countries. In Berlin, however, Hitler's reception of Jacob Surits, a Jew newly appointed as *polpred* (ambassador) in Berlin, was one of the briefest in recent memory. Few in Moscow could have seriously believed in a possible revival of Rapallo but this did not make the French alliance more attractive.

The other possibility, given the objections of both Germany and Poland to an eastern security pact, which made its conclusion highly problematical, was to pursue a 'Mediterranean Locarno' in co-operation with Fascist Italy. Briand, whom Barthou much admired, had thought along similar lines but proved unable to bring the idea to a successful conclusion. All through the spring of 1934, Barthou worked on this southern wing of his 'great design' to contain German revisionism. While this approach was complicated by the opposition from the Little Entente, the strains in the Mussolini–Hitler relationship assisted Barthou's endeavours. On 15–16 June, Hitler and Mussolini met in Venice. It was an unsatisfactory encounter. Hitler insisted on the replacement of Dollfuss and an early election to give the Austrian Nazis the representation in the government that they deserved. The Duce viewed Hitler's promise of close consultation on economic questions as little more than a further step towards establishing the German presence in Vienna. Mussolini had already decided on an attack upon Ethiopia—he gave permission for operational planning to proceed for an attack in 1935—and needed to guard his northern borders. As an African adventure would require large numbers of Italian troops and equipment, Mussolini had to take seriously warnings from his advisers about the extreme danger of a two-front war in Europe. The abortive putsch in Vienna on 25 July 1934 left Mussolini angry and suspicious. Though seemingly an independent action, Italian military intelligence confirmed that the *coup* had been orchestrated by Berlin and that Hitler was behind it.[6] The killing of Dollfuss, a friend as well as a political protégé, was regarded by Mussolini as a personal affront administered by the Führer. The Austrian chancellor was to have met the Duce at Riccione on the day of his murder; his wife was already there. Mussolini reacted by moving a few local units to the Austrian frontier as a political gesture. A distinct if temporary chill set in between Rome and Berlin. Hitler

[6] See the evidence for Hitler's role and the pre-planning of the putsch in Germany in Gerhard L. Weinberg, 'German Foreign Policy and Austria', in id., *Germany, Hitler and World War II* (Cambridge, 1995), 95–108 and Gerhard L. Weinberg, *The Foreign Policy of Hitler's Germany: Diplomatic Revolution in Europe, 1933–1936* (Chicago, 1970), 98–105.

knew that he had to alter his tactics if he was to achieve the desired understanding with Mussolini. He had exaggerated the power of the Austrian *Nationalsozialistische deutsche Arbeiterpartei* (NSDAP) and overlooked its divisions; he had also underestimated the effects of the planned *coup* on Italy and France. The Austrian NSDAP was now reined in and the organization separated from that in Germany. Papen, who had somehow escaped the shootings of 30 June, was sent to Vienna with fresh instructions. Hitler, acting in accord with Neurath, his foreign minister, was prepared to wait for *Anschluss*.

The *Quai d'Orsay* would have liked a League of Nations guarantee of Austrian independence or joint action with the British and Italians in Geneva. They were forced to accept instead, due to British reluctance to give approval to Italy's unilateral action, a more limited demonstration of three-power co-operation. On 27 September, in a joint declaration, the British, French, and Italians reaffirmed their 17 February pledge of mutual consultation with regard to policies designed to maintain Austrian independence. Fearful of antagonizing Czechoslovakia and Yugoslavia, the French could go no further towards Rome. Each of France's allies opposed Italian dominion over Vienna. Barthou was both indignant and shaken by the murder of Dollfuss. Nevertheless, there were renewed Franco-Italian approaches. At Geneva, Barthou and Aloisi worked closely together in support of the Soviet Union's entry into the League and in framing the declaration of support for Austrian independence. In Rome, Mussolini told Chambrun that he looked forward to a visit from Barthou and suggested that a start might be made on resolving a number of long-standing Franco-Italian problems, specifically those concerning Tunisia and Libya. Barthou wished to avoid discussing armaments and any military issues that might provoke Belgrade and hoped rather to focus on Austrian independence and North Africa. The talks in Rome were difficult but not unpromising. Contrary to Barthou's hopes, Mussolini insisted that armaments be discussed first before turning to the negotiating list: central Europe, the rectification of the Libyan frontier, the status of the Italians in Tunisia and the general treaty that the *Quai d'Orsay* wanted. Within a few days, however, the Italians switched the focus of the talks to Ethiopia, explaining that Italy would modify both its Libyan and Tunisian demands 'in exchange for the development of her influence' in Ethiopia, without prejudice to French interests in her possession of Djibouti.[7] With an agenda set but no positive response given to these Ethiopian feelers, Barthou set the date for his visit to Rome on 4–11 November 1934. He now tried to reconcile Yugoslavia to the possibility

[7] *DDF*, 1st ser., Vol. VII, Nos. 265, 290.

of Franco-Italian friendship, inviting King Alexander to come to France on 9 October, and planning to greet the king personally when he arrived at Marseilles. The French security services were warned of possible threats to the king's life from exiled Croatian separatists but they nonetheless committed a series of security blunders. Almost as soon as the king and Barthou settled themselves in the first car, a man opened fire on the sovereign. In the pandemonium that followed, Barthou appears to have been shot in the arm by a stray police bullet. Unknown to him, a humeral artery was severed. By the time he was taken to hospital it was too late.

III

It would be Pierre Laval who succeeded Barthou at the *Quai d'Orsay*; he pledged himself to continue the policies of his deceased predecessor. He was to remain as foreign minister or prime minister for fifteen tumultuous months (October 1934 to January 1936). The contrast in the personalities of the two men could not have been greater. Barthou, once he determined on a course of action, pursued it openly and with energy and vigour. He inspired confidence and trust among both his officials and foreigners. Laval, by contrast, was highly secretive and confided in no one. Though able, highly intelligent, and ambitious, even his supporters thought him devious and cunning. A quick and skilled negotiator, he played for high stakes, pursuing private policies that were often at variance with his public declarations. Laval was soon at odds with his secretary-general, Alexis Léger. The new foreign minister had little time for the experienced diplomat's cautious and carefully prepared plans. Relations between the two men deteriorated during the Italian negotiations of 1935 to the point where Léger threatened resignation. But then, as on later occasions, the secretary-general was persuaded to stay at his post: Laval found that Léger's reputation for personal integrity provided a useful corrective for the mistrust he himself often aroused, including in domestic political circles.

Though he spoke of the continuity of French foreign policy, Laval had long been a proponent of talks with Germany and, as the Kremlin anticipated, showed little liking for the alliance with Moscow. One of his first tasks, however, was to follow up Barthou's efforts in Rome. While he had to postpone Barthou's scheduled trip to the Italian capital in early November, Laval remained determined to reach a settlement with Mussolini that would involve Italy in joint action, should Germany unilaterally reject the disarmament provisions of the Treaty of Versailles or renew its pressure against Austria. Such an agreement would encourage the Germans to be more accommodating and open the way to a more general European settlement that would include both Italy and Germany. Laval was quick to limit the anti-Italian sentiments created by the Marseilles assassination. The judicial investigation placed the major share of the blame on terrorists operating in Hungary, though it was highly probable that the assassins had the moral, if not the actual, support of the Croatian Ustaša leaders and were backed by Italian military intelligence. The Little Entente governments were not so easily placated; the Yugoslavs demanded the extradition of the two Ustaša leaders living in Italy and relations with Rome were badly shaken. The early Franco-Italian discussions in Rome went well nonetheless, with the main sticking point not the colonial questions in North Africa but the French concern over the hostile Italo-Yugoslav relations. During the last week of 1934, Mussolini, exercised over German interest in Yugoslavia, offered to join the Little Entente nations to defend Austrian independence in co-operation with the League. Belgrade reluctantly agreed to a French formula for an Italo-Yugoslav treaty and Laval's visit to Rome was set for 4–7 January 1935.

In Rome, as the negotiations with Paris continued, the Italians now concentrated on Ethiopia. They wanted a formula specifying French disinterest in the country and demanded larger territorial concessions in Africa. Despite Italian pressure, Laval said nothing about Ethiopia and just before he left for Rome told the French representative in Addis Ababa to reassure Haile Selassie about the French attitude. Laval clearly intended to keep his Ethiopian cards well concealed. He left Paris without any detailed briefing from his advisers, some of whom were concerned about the Italian price for an accord. Laval's approach to the forthcoming talks was encapsulated by his comment to a gathering of journalists in Rome: 'Diplomacy, what is that? You offer something; your opponent offers something else. And you end by making a deal; it's no more difficult than that.'[8] During the visit, Suvich and Aloisi for Italy and Chambrun and Léger for France were in constant negotiations, but the real breakthrough came in a private meeting of Mussolini and Laval with no one else present. The key question about the bargain struck between the two leaders on the night of 6–7 January is what was said about Ethiopia. The published agreement, which contained a pledge of support for Austria and concerted action should Germany resort to unilateral rearmament, included a three-part agreement on Africa. France secured its position in Tunisia but ceded some 44,000 square miles of territory on Italy's southern Libyan frontier, and some 309 square miles of territory to the Italian colony of Eritrea.

[8] William I. Shorrock, *From Ally to Enemy: The Enigma of Fascist Italy in French Diplomacy, 1920–1940* (Kent, OH, 1988), 109.

The agreement was received with some amazement. The terms appeared as a great diplomatic triumph for France. Laval boasted that he had come away 'with the Duce's shirt and studs'. Mussolini had yielded to France the future of 100,000 Italians in Tunis, and received 'half a dozen palm trees in one place and a strip of desert which did not even contain a sheep in another', as the Duce himself explained to Eden in June 1935.[9] The real point of the bargain, however, was the secret protocol noting that France 'does not look in Abyssinia for the satisfaction of any interest other than those economic interests relating to the traffic of the Djibouti–Addis Ababa Railway'.[10] Laval insisted to the end of his life that he had conceded nothing more than French 'economic disinterest'. Evidence from various sources, including from Laval himself in his comments to Eden in June 1935 and at the Pétain trial of 1945, confirm that Mussolini was offered a 'free hand' in Abyssinia. In a note dated 30 December 1935, Léger wrote that when the expression 'free hand' was raised in the course of the Mussolini–Laval conversation, the latter had commented that 'I myself consider these words in such a way that they could not be put to any improper use.' Mussolini's tone was cheerful but clearly serious as he replied that 'he did not have pacific intentions with regard to Ethiopia'.[11] While none of these references or the exchange of private and secret letters between Mussolini and Laval in 1935–1936 settles the question of Laval's real intentions, it seems highly probable that the French premier was not explicitly sanctioning an Italian military adventure, but gave ample reason for Mussolini to believe that he would not be opposed over Ethiopia. The Italian record of part of the conversations notes that when Mussolini raised the question of Ethiopia and reminded Laval 'of the importance to us of the "*désistement*" in Abyssinia', Laval replied that he had 'understood perfectly the Italian concept and that, apart from economic interests which France wishes to safeguard, his country did not intend to hinder Italian penetration of Abyssinia'.[12] As with the exchanges between Briand and Stresemann at Thoiry in September 1926, personal diplomacy created as many problems as it solved. Chambrun, a professional diplomat, carefully distinguished at the time between the last minute Mussolini–Laval accord and the official Franco-Italian agreement. The latter was warmly received in the French Chamber of Deputies. Having been assured that the agreements in no way compromised the sovereignty and independence of Ethiopia, the huge vote in favour of ratification was 555 to 9.

[9] Ibid., 111. [10] Ibid.

[11] Quoted in Jean-Paul Cointet, *Pierre Laval* (Paris, 1993), 155–156.

[12] *DDI*, 7th ser., Vol. XVI, No. 399.

The military, too, welcomed the arrangement. In the spring of 1935, the *Deuxième Bureau* predicted that Hitler's ambitions in central Europe and the Balkans would absorb his attention for several years but if, as they assumed, he intended to move southwards and eastwards, he would first strengthen his western defences by a move into the Rhineland. While not anticipating a German attack on the western powers until 1939, France needed an alternative way of defending her eastern allies. Jean Fabry, Laval's war minister in the new cabinet formed in January 1935 to 'save the franc', enthusiastically supported the proposed talks in Rome. Fabry, a *mutilé de guerre*, was known for his Germanophobic and anti-Bolshevik views. Faced with the extreme reluctance of the Chamber of Deputies to sanction military spending when cuts on expenditure were the order of the day, co-operation with the Italians was highly welcome. The French would be able to withdraw soldiers from the Franco-Italian border and from Tunis and Algiers, while at the same time strengthening the barrier to German expansionism. For the moment, the French military leaders were delighted when Mussolini, on 11 January 1935, suggested talks, and in February, it was agreed to open discussions between the intelligence branches of the two countries' general staffs. Military talks with the Italians were scheduled for March or April. It is most likely, however, that the Franco-Italian military agreements that followed, like the Laval–Mussolini accord itself, were conceived in Rome as short-term expedients. Mussolini concluded them to reassure his senior advisors. Support from France and Britain would keep Hitler out of Austria while he was engaged in Ethiopia. When pressure was placed on the connection as a result of Italian moves in Ethiopia and British opposition, it was all too easy for the Duce to discard them.

Laval thought that he had made a good bargain. It was his intention to use his success with Mussolini to make it easier to deal with Germany. In stark contrast to his policy towards Fascist Italy, Laval was far less energetic in following up Barthou's line to Moscow. He had little liking for the projected mutual assistance pact. The *Quai d'Orsay*, nevertheless, refused to accept Polish reservations on the Eastern Pact as a final rejection, and did everything possible to meet Beck's objections, still hoping for a broader eastern agreement. When Litvinov and Laval met in Geneva on 21 November 1934, the Russian had found the latter reluctant to accept a mutual obligation to refrain from political agreements with Germany without the consent of the other party. Pressed by the Soviets and the Little Entente representatives, Laval finally agreed to a protocol—'colloquially described here [Geneva] as a promise not to betray each other during the forthcoming political manoeuvring'[13]—

[13] Nicholas Rostow, *Anglo-French Relations, 1934–36* (London, 1984), 65.

stating that neither signatory would conclude any accord compromising the Eastern Pact with any future member of it, and would keep the other powers informed of any such negotiations. The *Politburo* sanctioned the conversations with France because they feared a Franco-German settlement. There was still considerable scepticism in Moscow about Litvinov's policies and Laval's future intentions. In his speech to the seventh Congress of Soviets on 28 January 1935, Molotov went out of his way to keep the door to Berlin open. Between the end of February and the beginning of April, the Franco-Soviet negotiations barely moved at all.

The transition from Barthou to Laval marked a distinct change in French policy. For the former, the Eastern Pact was a 'countervailing force in Eastern Europe to deter German revisionism'.[14] The pieces of Barthou's 'grand design' fit together. Laval had scant interest in the Soviet Union and little concern for central Europe. His chief interest was to secure a compromise with Germany, a policy that had the added advantage of appealing to the British, who were still convinced that an arrangement with Nazi Germany over rearmament was both desirable and attainable. If there were doubts in London about Laval's sincerity, there was a greater consensus of views between the two foreign ministries than had existed under Barthou.

IV

Hitler's established position in Germany and his diplomatic initiatives convinced British ministers that it was essential to bring the Germans into an arms limitation convention before it was too late. Barthou was warned when he first sought British backing for his Eastern Pact that France would have to accept the legalization of German rearmament and include Germany in any eastern arrangement in exchange. It was, as Simon said, 'recognizing the inevitable and getting such terms as we can while we recognize it'.[15] The foreign secretary hoped that the recognition of German rearmament would lead to a German return to Geneva and an arms limitation accord. It was the 'great task' Simon set himself for 1935. In December 1934, when Simon met Laval, he was pleased to find the foreign minister amenable to a 'general settlement' with Germany, including French acceptance of German rearmament. In return, the British foreign secretary pledged his backing for a Franco-Italian *rapprochement*, Italian participation in a formal guarantee of Austrian independence, and

[14] Lisanne Radice, 'The Eastern Pact, 1933–1935: A Last Attempt at European Co-operation', *Slavonic and East European Review*, 55: 1 (1977), 53.
[15] TNA: PRO, CAB 27/572, 29 November 1934.

an Eastern Pact in which Germany would participate. Though some questioned whether the Laval–Mussolini accords had produced a real *rapprochement* between Italy and France, most officials accepted Vansittart's view of the treaty.

Do not look this gift horse too sternly in the mouth. (I know all about his teeth). We have wanted it for long, and now we have got it, and it is a long stride in the right direction . . . [L]ots of good *ménages* have not been founded on sentiment, and have survived without the spur of necessity so patent here. We must welcome the necessity since we cannot have it otherwise—unfortunately. And we must do all we can to preserve this unromantic combination.[16]

Without any input of their own, the British could congratulate themselves on the strengthening of French security and the possibility of a more stable central and Eastern Europe. They accepted the agreement in ignorance of its secret aspects regarding Ethiopia. It was soon clear, however, that the British had no wish to encourage Mussolini's ambitions in East Africa. Dino Grandi, exiled as ambassador to London in the summer of 1932 after disputes with Mussolini, was directed to open talks with Simon and Vansittart. He was warned not to reveal the details of Italy's military planning, but to indicate that Mussolini expected British 'sympathy' when he was forced to deal with the intransigent Ethiopians in an effective manner. Grandi's attempt to secure British approval for an arms embargo against Ethiopia, and his demand that the British offer no political support to Addis Ababa in its conflicts with Rome, served only to increase British scepticism about Italy's peaceful intentions. Reports of significant shipments of Italian troops and materials to East Africa in mid-February highlighted Foreign Office suspicions. Early in March, the Admiralty strengthened its naval presence in the eastern Mediterranean.

Both in Paris and in London, attention was primarily focused on German rearmament. On 31 January, Laval and Prime Minister Pierre-Étienne Flandin arrived in London. In preparing for the meeting, the British cabinet rejected Foreign Office recommendations for 'putting teeth into Locarno'. The French were warned not to raise the question of general staff talks. With a British general election looming, there was no wish to revive memories of the pre-1914 Anglo-French military conversations. But Flandin and Laval had to be offered something if they were to reverse the policies of their predecessors and agree to German rearmament. The French felt themselves to be particularly vulnerable, for the 'lean years' caused by the low birth-rate during the Great War would begin in the autumn of 1935 and continue until 1940. Only about

[16] Shorrock, *From Ally to Enemy*, 116.

120,000 recruits, half the usual intake, would be conscripted annually. The Flandin ministry was already considering extending the term of service from one to two years to compensate for the lack of men. It should be remembered, too, that France was in poor financial straits in 1935, the nadir year of the French depression and so extremely anxious to avoid fuelling an arms race. As so often when the British and French met, the former had a positive negotiating programme in mind to which the French felt they had to respond. It was in no sense a 'positive' programme for France. As often happened, a proposal that served British interests was presented to the French as 'good for everyone'. It was, nonetheless, a French-inspired suggestion for a mutual guarantee against air attack that became the basis of the new approach to Berlin. In the London Declaration of 3 February 1935, the British and French governments agreed that the Versailles limitations on German armed strength (Part V of the treaty) should be abolished, and a new arms agreement recognizing German rearmament negotiated. Germany would return to the League of Nations, participate in an East European collective security pact, and adhere to a guarantee of Austrian independence. There would be a new treaty, in addition to Locarno, pledging air support from Britain, France, Germany, and Belgium should any signatory be attacked by one of the others. Britain would make separate arrangements with Italy. This communiqué remained the basis of British policy towards Germany for the next twelve months. In London, it was, from the first, a futile and illusory policy based on a dangerous misreading of Hitler's intentions. The 'air pact', in particular, held out the false hope of increased security without an extension of Britain's continental obligations. The French had fewer illusions about Germany, but clung to the hope that the new negotiations might lead the British to offer something more than the Locarno guarantees. In fact, Flandin and Laval were offered almost nothing.

The German leader was flushed with the rich propaganda gift that had fallen into his lap with the return of the Saar territory to Germany, through a plebiscite held on 13 January 1935. The vote was an overwhelming triumph for Hitler: just under 91% of the Saar's electorate voted for a return to Germany. It was always likely that a majority would favour a return to Germany, especially the Saar Catholics, who, due to the intense efforts of their priests, looked to Hitler as a leader who would rescue them from the imagined spectre of Bolshevism. In his first 'little step' towards Germany, Laval had abandoned support for those opposing reunion with Germany and had encouraged a settlement of conflicting Franco-German claims. Direct negotiations between the two governments settled the question of German payments for the mines. The goodwill generated by the accord was intended by Laval to pave the way for a Franco-German agreement, a possibility that Hitler would consider only if France yielded on the armaments question. Hitler milked the triumph but typically spoke in peaceable terms for international consumption. 'Following the completion of your return', he told the Saarlanders, the German Reich 'had no further territorial demands to make of France'.[17] He was quick to test the solidarity of the new '*entente*'. On 3 February, he rejected the French-proposed Eastern Pact and warned both the British and French ambassadors that he would not suffer the Rhineland demilitarized zone for long. On 14 February came the suggestion of opening bilateral talks with Britain. As proof of German sincerity, Berlin would be prepared to use its 'aerial forces' as a deterrent against disturbances of the peace. By these means, the Führer hoped to separate Britain from France while indirectly announcing the existence of Germany's air force. The British willingly took the bait. There was strong pressure from the Admiralty, apprehensive about Japan and the outcome of the forthcoming international naval conference in London, to sound out the Germans, preparatory to the naval meetings. The publication of the British White Paper on 4 March explaining the need for new defence estimates, identified Germany as the chief danger to British security, but emphasized that the purpose of the estimates was 'the establishment of peace on a permanent footing'. Publication produced a diplomatic 'cold' in Berlin and a delay in an arranged meeting by Simon with the irate Hitler, but did not deflect either side from their intended purpose. The British cabinet was insistent on the need to avoid an arms race that would upset economic recovery, and place the government in opposition to the main currents of public sentiment. Stanley Baldwin, who was soon to succeed the ailing MacDonald as prime minister, while publicly declaring that rearmament was 'a horrible thing' and 'a terrible conclusion', knew that new defence measures were essential. The March White Paper was prepared in order to convince the electorate that the maintenance of peace depended on the repair of the country's defensive capacity.

The German leader was not unduly worried. 'Again some time had been won', he commented. 'Those ruling England *must* get used to dealing with us only on an equal footing.'[18] On 9 March, the military attachés in Berlin were officially informed of the *Luftwaffe*'s existence. In his comments to the assembled representatives, Göring almost doubled the numbers of aircraft actually at Germany's disposal in 1935. On 16 March, one day after the French Chamber of Deputies approved the re-establishment of two-year military service, Hitler announced the

[17] Quoted in Ian Kershaw, *Hitler, 1889–1936: Hubris* (London, 1998), 547.
[18] Ibid., 549.

introduction of compulsory military service and the increase of the army to thirty-six divisions (an army of 550,000 men). Neurath made a similar announcement to the assembled diplomats and press corps. Special editions of newspapers were put out in Germany announcing the move, and excited crowds gathered outside the Reich Chancellery cheering Hitler. 'Today's creation of a conscript army in open defiance of Versailles will greatly enhance his domestic position', commented the American journalist William Shirer in Berlin, 'for there are few Germans, regardless of how much they hate the Nazis, who will not support it wholeheartedly. The great majority will like the way he has thumbed his nose at Versailles, which they all resented.'[19] The German people were indeed unprepared for Hitler's action, but reacted enthusiastically when it was realized that there would be no retaliatory action on the part of the western powers.

Hitler had taken the decision without consulting either his military leaders or relevant ministers and ignored their subsequent protests. Military leaders had long recognized that the expansion of the army was impossible without conscription. The announcement was the signal to all three services that they could take the wraps off their rearmament plans. There were divisions over the tempo of expansion, as Hitler desired to push ahead much more quickly than his commanders thought possible. Despite problems of personnel and equipment, and the absence of any longer-term plans, the army build-up was rapidly accelerated. By the autumn of 1935, the *Wehrmacht* (new military designations were introduced in the summer) numbered 400,000 men, a vast increase over the 1933 army. Because Germany lacked the material basis for such a rapid expansion, planning became increasingly provisional and *ad hoc.* Both for operational and economic reasons, the build-up focused general staff attention on the demilitarized Rhineland zone. If Germany were to defend itself against a French attack (highly improbable given Locarno), the army would have to quickly establish a line along the Rhine. On the false assumption that the French army enjoyed a high degree of mobility, army leaders feared that German troops stationed east of the zone would not reach the areas of action in time to contain the French thrust. Though a favourable international situation and domestic politics would ultimately determine Hitler's action in March 1936, he knew he could count on the support of the army for what it believed was a high-risk action.

The *Luftwaffe* had 2,500 aircraft of which only 800 could be used in combat. This was not the force of 1,200 first-line planes claimed

[19] William Shirer, *Berlin Diary: The Journal of a Foreign Correspondent, 1934–1941* (London, 1941), 34.

by Hitler, but the German achievement by the spring of 1935 was nonetheless an impressive one. The Reich Aviation Ministry under Göring's control was only established in 1933, and the *Luftwaffe*'s industrial substructure had to be fashioned from a very small base. Protected by Göring's close relationship with Hitler, the youngest service moved ahead despite army and navy efforts to regain control over their respective air units. There were problems of recruitment and training as well as serious technical difficulties in developing a strategic bomber which could be used as a deterrent during the critical period of rearmament until Germany could successfully fight a two-front war against France and Poland. This 'risk *Luftwaffe*' (the term borrowed from Tirpitz's pre-1914 fleet) would raise the stakes for any conceivable enemy and reduce the danger of a preventive strike. The *Luftwaffe* leaders soon realized that the bomber could be used in a variety of ways—for instance 'to attack the enemy's sources of strength' and its 'will to resist'—that went far beyond either its deterrent function or co-operative action with the army and navy, but such operations were still only a remote possibility even as late as 1936 when work on the four-engine strategic bomber had to be dropped from the general development programme.

Foreigners were anticipating a German move since the Saar plebiscite but few expected blatant violations of the Versailles and Locarno treaties. Hopes that the Nazi regime would enjoy only a temporary life had to be abandoned. There were increasing fears that Hitler would embark on new assaults on the existing international regime; the German economic recovery would allow him to pursue a more aggressive economic and military policy beyond the German borders. Hitler's dramatic announcement on 16 March had an immediate effect on the Italians and French, but the British refused to call off Simon's visit to Germany or to join in a collective protest. Unwilling to leave the country in its exposed state, yet deeply reluctant to engage in an arms race that could prove electorally disastrous, ministers refused to abandon their search for an agreement with Germany. Hitler's announcement made no difference. Without consulting Paris, on 18 March, the British sent a formal note of protest at the German unilateral action. In the same note (to the surprise of the German diplomats) the Reich government was asked whether it was still interested in a meeting between Simon and Hitler. The meeting was re-scheduled for 25–26 March despite French and Italian objections. Eden, but not Simon was sent to Paris to meet with Laval and Suvich, the Italian ambassador in Paris, to calm their nerves and was instructed to proceed on to Moscow, Warsaw, Prague, and Vienna to settle the disturbed diplomatic waters.

When they finally took place, the Berlin talks between Hitler, Simon, and Eden were hardly encouraging and, for once, the British could not blame the French. The Führer was uncompromising. He insisted on a peacetime army of thirty-six divisions and announced (falsely) during the course of the talks, that Germany had reached air parity with Britain. Simon and Eden were sceptical but said nothing. He served notice that any German return to the League would depend on the rectification of the injustices of Versailles, and the German re-acquisition of colonies. He showed no inclination to co-operate in regional security arrangements and rejected participation in the Danubian and Eastern Pacts. Hitler's intention in seeking an understanding with London was to separate the entente powers. If Hitler's visitors showed little interest in tentative offers of an alliance, they were quick to follow up his offer to discuss naval armaments and limit German claims to 35% of the British navy. The Germans were invited to participate in preparations for the forthcoming London naval conference. Only the intervention of the British ambassadors in Paris and Rome resulted in a postponement of the Anglo-German naval conversations in London until after the Stresa talks were concluded. Robert Craigie, the main Foreign Office negotiator, and Sir Bolton Eyre-Monsell, the first lord of the Admiralty, were so anxious to proceed that they dismissed possible French and Italian objections to the bilateral talks as irrelevant to their negotiations. Simon was encouraged, too, by Hitler's declared interest in an air pact, and the Führer's suggestions for limitations on bombing, or even a prohibition of bombardment from the air.

The 'risk *Luftwaffe*' was intended as a weapon against France (much of whose air force was already obsolete) and Poland, yet it was Britain that showed the greatest alarm. As early as 1932, the fear of bombing and the possible destruction of London became a factor in the cabinet discussions of disarmament policies. During 1932–1933, despite strong Air Ministry objections, ministers searched for ways to eliminate or control the use of bombers so as to eliminate the risk of the 'knock-out blow'. As the Disarmament Conference faltered and public apprehension grew, cabinet committees turned their attention to Britain's air defences. In the summer of 1934, the cabinet agreed to a new air rearmament programme, providing for an air force for home defence of seventy-five squadrons instead of the fifty-two suggested by the Defence Requirements Committee earlier in the year. The new figures for front-line aircraft were intended to reassure the public and act as a deterrent against any enemy. On 30 July 1934, Baldwin, deputy prime minister in the National Government, who was highly sensitive to the bombing danger, defended the new estimates in the Commons on the grounds of absolute necessity. He reminded MPs, in what became one of his most quoted phrases, that 'since the day of the air, the old frontiers are gone. When you think of the defence of England you no longer think of the chalk cliffs of Dover; you think of the Rhine.'[20] The implications of his speech should have pointed in the direction of closer ties with France. This was not the case. The subsequent 'air panic' of November 1934 to May 1935, not unlike the naval panic of 1908–1909, concentrated ministerial attention on the creation of an air force that could match the estimated figures of future German production. Despite the Air Ministry's well-founded scepticism both about the necessity and the speed of the build-up, the government was publicly committed to achieving air parity in bombers with Germany, the definition and date still unclear.

V

Hitler's announcement and his continued interference in Austrian affairs at a time when Mussolini was preoccupied with the military build-up for an invasion of Ethiopia in the autumn, caused considerable anxiety in Rome, above all in Italian military circles. It is true that Hitler's assault on the Versailles settlement, though seen as threatening to Italian interests, was not without possible advantages for the future. As Mussolini harboured expansionist ambitions far beyond Ethiopia, Germany might become a willing partner in their fulfilment. For the moment, however, the Duce was faced with the possibility of a new *coup* attempt in Vienna while Italian troops were in East Africa and the British were hostile towards his ambitions in Ethiopia. On 30 March, Mussolini suggested a three-power meeting in Isola Bella near Stresa, to outline a common policy in areas of potential German disruption—Austria, Memel, Czechoslovakia, and the demilitarized zone of the Rhineland. The Germans took alarm at what looked like a combined front against Nazi Germany. Quite apart from Mussolini's intention to prevent German action in Austria, he hoped to use the Stresa meetings to sound out the British about Ethiopia. Warned by his naval chiefs of the extreme danger of a war in Ethiopia without an understanding with London, and prompted by Pompeo Aloisi, the *chef de cabinet* at the Foreign Ministry, Mussolini hoped to convince MacDonald and Simon that the Italian price for continuing co-operation against Germany was a free hand in Ethiopia.

Despite the beauty of the surroundings, the meetings held at the Palazzo Borromeo on the Isola Bella between 11 and 14 April were disputatious and unpleasant. Though the French and Italians had coordinated their diplomatic responses to the Hitler announcement, neither was prepared to 'encircle' Germany. Both Mussolini, delighted at being host, and Laval were prepared to respond to Hitler's challenge to

[20] *Hansard*, HC Deb, 30 July 1934, Vol. 292, Cols. 2339–2340.

Versailles and Locarno with strong words, but wanted to associate the British leaders with their rebuke. The real differences were between MacDonald and Simon, on the one hand, and Flandin and Laval on the other. In this debate, Mussolini took only a secondary role. The British leaders, intent on a general settlement in which Germany would join, and preparing for bilateral naval talks with Berlin, wanted to restrain the other two negotiators from any confrontation with Germany. 'We had to maintain a union for the time being with Italy and France until we knew more of Germany's intentions', MacDonald wrote in his diary. 'For the three of us to disagree would give Germany liberty to do what it likes. This may cost us something but they will get as little from me as is necessary and even that will be limited for I cannot get away from the fact that the French policy has been a logical cause of all this trouble.'[21] Any reader of the documents can only be struck by the sheer perversity of MacDonald's judgments of France at this time. In the desperate search for some sort of protection, the French wanted the League Council to condemn Germany and to consider the promise of economic and financial sanctions against any future unilateral repudiation of the treaties. The British leaders were still promoting some form of collective security under the League of Nations but refused to accept any new security commitments. Above all, they were determined to avoid coercing the Germans. It was the old Anglo-French battle over the application of sanctions. In Laval's mind, Italian support was no substitute for British backing but he hoped that a three-power agreement would soften the British opposition to commitments. He was mistaken.

Settling for a statement of solidarity that had little substance, the three governments agreed to pursue a common line at Geneva with regard to German violations of the peace and, in a joint declaration, to oppose 'by all practicable means, any unilateral repudiation of treaties which may endanger the peace of Europe'.[22] They would continue negotiations for security in Eastern Europe and an air pact in the West. The signatories also reaffirmed the principle of Austrian independence and recommended associating the central European governments with the Rome *procès-verbal* of January 1935 in regard to Austria. Beyond the joint protest by the French at a special session of the League's Council in April, none of the 'Stresa powers' was prepared for further action. The so-called 'Stresa front', as Hitler quickly discovered, was little more than a paper tiger. On 2 May, the ailing MacDonald, in his last month as prime minister before being replaced by Baldwin, dismissed Stresa as a sham. Simon, even more hesitant than usual, showed little enthusiasm

[21] MacDonald diary, 11 April, quoted in Rostow, *Anglo-French Relations*, 146.
[22] *DBFP*, 2nd ser., Vol. XII, No. 722.

for common action. As he believed that Germany's ambitions lay in Eastern Europe, an area in which Britain had no political interest, he was not averse to encouraging Hitler in that direction.

The Italians did raise the question of Ethiopia with the British at Stresa. British officials made clear that Britain would not sanction an attack on Ethiopia, which Simon and Vansittart believed would deter Mussolini from acting. Simon's speech at the League Assembly on 15 April, immediately following the Stresa meeting, should have removed any Italian doubts. Mussolini was not to be deterred. He ordered his naval chief of staff to plan for the possibility of war against both Germany and Britain. It was hardly surprising that there was high alarm among the Italian naval leaders. The strategic realities made a mockery of such plans. Given the vast numbers of troops and equipment earmarked for East Africa, the Italians would have been hard pressed to defend Austria against a Nazi takeover. Under such circumstances, Mussolini was prepared to follow up hints from Berlin that the Germans did not want war with Italy and might guarantee Austrian independence, at least, for the present. There was no way that the Duce would be deterred from his Ethiopian adventure.

Attention in London was focused on the forthcoming naval talks, welcomed even by those in the Foreign Office who were generally more suspicious of Germany than their political chiefs. Hitler, having already approved plans for Germany's new ship building programme, showed little interest in the forthcoming naval conference but a naval treaty with Britain was a prize worth winning. The French were neither consulted nor told about the subsequent conversations. In April 1935, the British, due to the work of the Naval Intelligence Division (NID), were well informed about the new German construction plans, including the building of a submarine fleet. Despite negative reactions in the Admiralty, the information did not alter its intention to go ahead with the talks. The Admiralty was anxious to exploit Hitler's willingness to impose a limit on the building plans of the commander-in-chief of the navy, Admiral Raeder, as quickly as possible. In a speech to the Reichstag on 21 May, Hitler balanced the announcements of the German rearmament plans and his rejection of the Eastern Pact with proposals for non-aggression pacts with all of Germany's neighbours (except Lithuania because of Memel), and promises of peaceful revision in the future. The concession of a 35% ratio was 'final and abiding', but he also held out the prospect of an armaments treaty abolishing heavy weapons and an offer to prohibit aerial bombardment outside the battle zone. If the rest of Europe rejected his terms, the Führer warned that he might have to use force to achieve them. Against this background, Ribbentrop, Hitler's successful diplomatic interloper, was sent to London where the Anglo-German talks began on 4 June. He immediately demanded, in such a peremptory fashion that Simon actually left the room, that the British accept the 35% relationship before any discussions could begin. Why did the cabinet, on Admiralty advice, accept the German terms almost without question, and without informing the other powers, including France, as the foreign secretary recommended? The Admiralty believed that a German navy limited to 35% was perfectly compatible with its plans for a future two-power standard and that the Germans were highly unlikely to reach this standard until 1942. It was argued that an agreement would provide an excellent opportunity to limit German strength and monitor future German naval building progress. Britain could pursue its naval objectives without worrying about a German naval threat. At a time when the British were refurbishing a number of the Royal Navy's capital ships, a programme not to be completed until 1939, and when the Admiralty knew of the Japanese intention to abandon the ratio system, there were definite advantages in controlling the rate of increase of the German fleet. It was even hoped that the Germans, once a bilateral treaty was agreed, would join future treaty rules for qualitative limitation and the exchange of information.[23] Neither the German ability to build up to 35% of British surface tonnage or up to 45% of its submarine tonnage (to be increased to 100% if Berlin judged it necessary for German security) posed a threat to British sea power. The strength of the navy, the most critical aspect of British overall strategy, would increasingly be dictated by the need to fulfil two tasks, the Defence Requirements sub-committee reported in November 1935.

> We should be able to send to the Far East a Fleet sufficient to provide 'cover' against the Japanese fleet; we should have sufficient additional forces behind the shield for the protection of our territory and mercantile marine against Japanese attack; at the same time we should be able to retain in European waters a force sufficient to act as a deterrent and to prevent the strongest European naval Power from obtaining control of our vital home terminal areas while we make the necessary redispositions.[24]

The new treaty would assist in the fulfilment of the requirements that would assure the maintenance of British naval security. In fact, the first token British fleet was only sent to the Far East at the very end of 1941. The British never considered the diplomatic price of the treaty; the failure to consult France, Britain's unilateral revision of the Treaty of

[23] Joseph A. Maiolo, *The Royal Navy and Nazi Germany, 1933–1939: A Study in Appeasement and the Origins of the Second World War* (Basingstoke, 1998), 32–35.

[24] TNA: PRO, CAB 24/259, CID Defence Requirements Subcommittee Report, November 1935.

Versailles, only increased the existing distrust between the two nations when any hope of restraining Nazi Germany depended on their co-operation. Nor could the British have guessed that the agreement would confirm Ribbentrop's 'spurious credentials as a diplomat', and launch him on his unfortunate ambassadorial career in London.

The Anglo-German naval agreement, signed on 18 June, served British interests but failed to promote their future hopes of a general settlement with Germany. The small German fleet posed no threat to the British, despite the latter's global interests as long as Hitler honoured the 1935 limits. The Admiralty believed that a costly arms race with Germany could be avoided while they built up a fleet that would maintain their global naval supremacy and their qualitative lead over other navies. The National Government—led since 7 June by Stanley Baldwin, with Sir Samuel Hoare replacing Simon as foreign secretary—was, nevertheless, naïve in thinking that the naval agreement would lead to an air pact and 'general settlement' with Germany. The search for agreements, interrupted but not stopped by the Ethiopian crisis, was met with evasive replies in Berlin. When Hitler was pressed on an air pact in December, the Führer was distinctly irritable: he would accept limits in shipbuilding but not on aircraft. At the same time, Hitler was mistaken in his belief that the new agreement would provide a springboard for a political agreement, if not an alliance, with Britain. Given his hopes for arrangements with London, German naval planning remained on a provisional basis. Rearmament depended more on the availability of resources and dockyards rather than on the fulfilment of the navy's more far-reaching strategic ambitions. The accepted tonnage under the new agreement was far greater than the existing capacity of the German shipyards, and there was little incentive to divert scarce resources to build new ones.

The French were severely shaken by the news of the treaty. It would serve as a constant reminder of British duplicity long after the immediate echoes of the announcement died. French observers knew that the Germans wanted to expand their fleet. What they had not expected was that the British government would acquiesce in their claim. In April, Laval had written that the scope of the German demands 'leaves no possibility of an accord'.[25] After the signature of the agreement, the chief conclusion drawn in Paris was that the Admiralty had been seduced by worthless Nazi pledges of good faith. Foreign Office officials discounted French indignation, using the specious Admiralty argument

[25] SHM, 1BB2, 193, 'Revendications allemandes en matière navale', Laval to Piétri, 18 April 1935; quoted in Peter Jackson, *France and the Nazi Menace: Intelligence and Policy Making, 1933–1939* (Oxford and New York, 2000), 138.

that the agreement would benefit France as much as Britain. In fact, the negative ramifications for France were substantial: the permitted German naval expansion meant the French goal of a two-power standard, able to deal with Germany and Italy combined, without British assistance, would no longer be sustainable. For his part, Mussolini treated the agreement as yet another example of British self-interest prevailing over collective co-operation, a useful propaganda tactic which he used repeatedly when tensions with Britain increased over Ethiopia during the summer of 1935.

VI

Laval proceeded straight from Stresa to Geneva for the special League session of 15–17 April 1935. The Russians and the Little Entente powers had been assured that a Franco-Soviet pact of mutual assistance would be concluded, regardless of what was decided at the Stresa conference. Prodded by the British, Laval and his officials sought to avoid any far-reaching commitments to Moscow. In addition to his personal dislike of a bilateral treaty with the Soviets, Laval was well aware of British opposition and the strong anti-Soviet sentiments of the Poles. Like his officials, he still hoped for some form of broader arrangement that would make the Soviet alliance unnecessary. The *Deuxième Bureau* stressed the risks of pushing Poland further towards Germany and gave priority on both political and military grounds to the Polish alliance. But Laval's efforts to resurrect the Eastern Pact, already emasculated to win British support, were proving fruitless. The Stresa meetings had intensified Little Entente and Balkan Pact apprehensions about French diplomacy. At home, sections of the Radical and Socialist parties were demanding a stiffer line towards Hitler. A treaty with the Soviet Union would win votes and strengthen his governing coalition. Laval, whatever his hesitations, felt he had to negotiate with Litvinov, but he proceeded with great caution. He fought off Litvinov's efforts to make mutual assistance immediate and prior to a decision of the League Council, and took pains to make French aid dependent on the League and Locarno procedures. At the last moment, Léger tried to further weaken the protocol by restricting the scope of automatic action, driving the furious Litvinov to cancel his projected trip to Paris. An acceptable compromise was reached. Mutual assistance was explicitly subordinated to a decision of the Council. The timing of the decision was left indefinite but both parties were obliged to hasten the Council's proceedings. If no decision was reached, assistance would still be given. To conform to Locarno, French action would depend on British and Italian approval. The pact, as the French intended, was restricted to Europe.

The Franco-Soviet pact was signed on 2 May 1935. Laval visited Moscow on 13 May and was welcomed by Stalin. The Soviet leader wanted a military alliance; Laval parried his request and proposed conversations between the respective chiefs of staff. Laval asked that the attacks of the PCF (French Communist Party) and *L'Humanité* on his government should cease and that the PCF end its opposition to the defence appropriations. He won from Stalin a statement approving 'the policy of national defence pursued by France in keeping her armed forces at the level needed for her security'.[26] But he won less than he thought. In Paris, the PCF continued to oppose the government's defence bills. Its subsequent alignment with the other left-wing parties during the summer of 1935, quite apart from increasing its own popularity, considerably strengthened the attacks on Laval's financial and economic policies. While the German danger was the source of both Litvinov's search for collective security agreements and the Popular Front tactics of the Comintern, the two programmes, while complementary, were not identical and did not always move in tandem. Nor was either course without enemies in Moscow. Barely a week after the Franco-Soviet pact was signed, and not long before Laval was expected in Moscow, Litvinov had a 'friendly conversation' with the German ambassador, suggesting that a non-aggression pact would 'lessen the significance of the Franco-Soviet pact'.[27] He may have anticipated the negative German reaction but the very fact that the offer was made suggests that the German door had not been shut. On his way to Moscow, Laval stopped in Warsaw to assure Beck that the new pact should not be seen as anti-German or as an expression of a pro-Soviet policy. When he again broke his homeward journey at Warsaw, in order to attend Piłsudski's funeral, he minimized the importance of the new pact in speaking to Göring, Hitler's special emissary. While warning of French disquiet at Germany's attitude and actions, Laval spoke of his strong desire of pursuing '*la politique de pacification*' between the two countries and outlined his idea for a multilateral pact. Hitler's Reichstag speech on 21 May signalling the end of any further negotiations over an Eastern Pact, and suggesting that the new Franco-Soviet agreement was incompatible with Locarno, did not encourage optimism about Laval's initiatives.

The Franco-Soviet pact was followed by a pact between Czechoslovakia and the Soviet Union, signed on 16 May and ratified during Beneš's visit to Moscow in early June. The agreement, in every other respect identical to the Franco-Soviet treaty, would only become

[26] Quoted in Haslam, *The Soviet Union and the Struggle for Collective Security in Europe*, 51.
[27] Ibid., 82.

operative if the French took action first. This restriction, insisted upon by the Czechs, was welcomed by the Soviets who had no wish to be dragged into quarrels, such as over Austria, in which their own interests were not directly engaged. Both sides shared hopes for a broader agreement that would include Poland and Germany. Pressed by Beneš over how the Soviet Union could assist Czechoslovakia, the Soviet war commissar was quoted as saying that the Soviets would cross Romania and Poland whether they had agreements or not. The Poles had little liking for either of the new treaties and did their best to dissuade Beneš from concluding the understanding. Given the latter's failure to interest the Poles in a bilateral treaty and his strong disapproval of the pro-German orientation of Polish diplomacy, Beneš felt free to ignore the objections from Warsaw. The new treaty with Moscow consequently further embittered Czechoslovak–Polish relations; co-operation between their military intelligence staffs ceased and a press war ensued. Without an Eastern Pact and wary of too great a dependence on the USSR, Beneš judged that the safety of Czechoslovakia depended on keeping in step with France. This task became increasingly difficult as the Ethiopian crisis accelerated, straining all the incomplete and highly fragile diplomatic combinations created during 1934–1935, and leaving Hitler free to continue his assault on the Locarno treaties.

VII

The speed with which Hitler consolidated his power within Germany was matched and aided by his ability to begin his long planned assault on the European status quo. Admittedly, he took power when the international order was already in disarray and when the events of 1928–1933 had weakened the global order and exposed the limits of international co-operation. Almost all the countries in Europe and beyond had turned to the pursuit of nationalist economic policies that took little note of their wider implications. The American financial retreat from Europe undercut the critical links that had fostered some degree of American involvement in European affairs. The United States, for the next few years, hardly entered into the strategic calculations of the European nations. The League's perceived failure to check the Japanese expansion into Manchuria and Japan's departure from the League of Nations was a blow both to the Washington and Geneva systems. And well before Hitler's appointment to the chancellorship of Germany, the disarmament talks were already faltering and few statesmen anticipated a successful outcome. Yet even allowing for the breakdown of the international regime, Hitler moved with a speed and a sense of ultimate purpose that clearly distinguished him from his predecessors. While still discussing disarmament, he sanctioned in the early summer of 1933 vastly increased military funding that went far beyond what any western power could even contemplate. The army and air force embarked on major rearmament programmes that made a mockery of Germany's continued presence at the Disarmament Conference. Once Hitler withdrew from the talks and from the League of Nations, the way was clear to attack the remaining Treaty restraints on Germany's freedom of diplomatic action. Such initiatives could only increase his popularity at home and quieten popular fears about the foundations of the German economic recovery.

The policy, however, was not without risks. During 1933–1934, a continuing fall in foreign exchange reserves revived talk of a necessary devaluation. Rising consumer demands and the rearmament programme fuelled import demands while exports were declining. In the summer of 1934, an unusually bad harvest and a severe foreign exchange crisis threatened to overwhelm the German economy.[28] Strict controls on the exchanges proved ineffective; devaluation was ruled out as being impractical and risky for a country with large foreign debts and minimal foreign exchange reserves. Hjalmar Schacht, Hitler's minister of economics and president of the Reichsbank, allied with the military authorities to block any cuts in rearmament. He responded to the crisis by introducing a comprehensive system of trade control, the New Plan, based on the strict regulations of imports, an expanded export subsidy scheme, and the increasing use of bilateral clearing agreements which saved on the use of scarce foreign exchange. On 14 June 1934, he announced a complete moratorium on all foreign debt repayments. He subsequently embarked on a high-risk policy that proved beneficial to the Reich by driving a wedge between the United States, Germany's chief creditor, and Britain. Schacht's aggressive strategy towards the Americans resulted in the cancellation of Germany's massive debt obligations to its private citizens. The American government had no means of retaliation. Its one effective weapon might have been the creation of a creditor bloc, but the Netherlands and Switzerland had already broken ranks in 1933 by signing bilateral agreements with the Reich and Schacht moved to splinter any possible Anglo-American action. The British agreed to negotiate a bilateral commercial agreement, the Anglo-German Payments Agreement of 1 November 1934, which allowed Germany to

[28] For this material see Adam Tooze, *The Wages of Destruction: The Making and Breaking of the Nazi Economy* (London, 2006), 79–88, 92–94; Neil Forbes, *Doing Business with the Nazis: Britain's Economic and Financial Relations with Germany, 1931–1939* (London and Portland, OR, 2000), 11–12, 97–128. For further discussion of these questions and the consequences of both the cancellation of the American debt and the proliferation of the clearing agreements, see pp. 373–374.

enjoy a favourable balance of trade in return for facilitating debt repayments of all kinds, including those due on the Dawes and Young loans. While 55% of Germany's sterling revenues were to be used for importing British goods and another 10% were to be set aside for repaying British creditors, the Reich was left with a substantial margin of 'free foreign exchange' for use outside the sterling zone. The default on the American debt was followed by a clash between Secretary of State Cordell Hull's multilateral trading system (Reciprocal Trade Agreements Act of 1934) and Schacht's strategy of bilateralism. The Germans withdrew from the trade agreement concluded with the Weimar Republic in 1923 and Hull stripped Germany of its most-favoured nation status and refused to negotiate a new tariff agreement under the Reciprocal Trade Agreements Act. There was a sharp contraction of American–German trade, which reached derisory levels by 1936. Trade with Britain, while not approaching early 1930s levels, increased, with the Germans enjoying a positive balance of exports over imports. Mainly due to Schacht's initiatives and the strict imposition of the new trading system, Germany survived the 1934 crisis. The measures taken laid the foundations for the management of the Nazi economy for years to come. With the recovery of the world economy and the new subsidy scheme, exports increased between June 1935 and the spring of 1938, permitting a steady increase in the volume of imports. Exports did not return to pre-Depression levels and the *Reichsbank* continued to operate with a small quantity of gold and foreign exchange, but an extraordinary volume of import and export business took place. By severely contracting some of its consumer industries, the Reich was able to fund the growth of its investment goods industries and all the sectors associated with the drive towards self-sufficiency. Economic recovery continued, as did the funding allotted to military spending.

Hitler's early successes owed a great deal to the divergent policies of Britain and France and their inability to agree on a common policy. In terms of their ultimate aims, more united the two countries than divided them. At some level, their leaders, whatever their personal inclinations, recognized their mutual dependence. Anxious to preserve the peace and some semblance of the international order, they recognized the dangers posed by a revived and rearmed Germany. Both countries were conscious of their weakness. The greater the threat, the more difficult it would become to act in isolation. Admittedly, this was not a partnership of equals as the British, somewhat tactlessly, reminded the *Quai d'Orsay*. But despite its current financial difficulties and political instability, France was an essential partner for Britain in Europe. Even those most critical of French policy knew that the frontier of British security lay on the Rhine. The difficulty was that each side was deeply suspicious of the other, suspicions reinforced by a long history of rivalry and antagonism and a reluctance to admit to their mutual dependence. The two countries started with different assumptions about the origins of the Great War and the reasons for the failure to reconstruct a more stable Europe. With Hitler in power, their respective geographic positions and exposure to the dangers of revisionism further complicated the task of working together. Faced with the growing threats from the aggressor powers, their immediate reaction was to blame each other rather than the aggressor for their failure to respond successfully. The failure 'to work in tandem was the dominant feature of Anglo-French relations'.[29] During 1935–1936, this failure gave Hitler the opportunities he needed to implement his plans to create the Third Reich of his dreams.

Books

Ahmann, R., *Nichtangriffspakte: Entwicklung und operative Nutzung in Europa 1922–1939: Mit einem Ausblick auf die Renaissance des Nichtangriffsvertrages nach dem Zweiten Weltkrieg* (Baden-Baden, 1988).

Alexander, M. S., *The Republic in Danger: General Maurice Gamelin and the Politics of French Defence, 1933–1940* (Cambridge, 1992).

Bell, C. M., *The Royal Navy, Sea-power and Strategy between the Wars* (Basingstoke, 2000).

Campus, E., *The Little Entente and the Balkan Alliance* (Bucharest, 1978).

Dreyfus, F. G. (ed.), *Les relations franco-allemandes 1933–1939* (Paris, 1976). See chapter by J. Bariéty.

Duroselle, J-B., *La décadence, 1932–1939* (Paris, 1979).

Gooch, J., *Mussolini and His Generals: The Armed Forces and Fascist Foreign Policy 1922–1940* (Cambridge, 2007).

Haslam, J., *The Soviet Union and the Struggle for Collective Security in Europe 1933–39* (Basingstoke, 1984).

Jackson, J., *The Politics of Depression in France, 1932–1936* (Cambridge, 1985).

Jackson, P., *France and the Nazi Menace: Intelligence and Policy Making, 1933–1939* (Oxford, 2000).

Jordan, N., *The Popular Front and Central Europe: The Dilemmas of French Impotence, 1918–1940* (Cambridge, 1992).

Kindermann, K., *Hitlers Niederlage in Österreich: Bewaffneter NS–Putsch, Kanzlermord, Österreichs Abwehrsieg 1934* (Hamburg, 1984).

Maiolo, J.A., *The Royal Navy and Nazi Germany, 1933–1939: A Study in Appeasement and the Origins of the Second World War* (Basingstoke, 1998).

Morewood, S., *The British Defence of Egypt 1935–1940: Conflict and Crisis in the Eastern Mediterranean* (Abingdon and New York, 2005).

[29] Richard Davis, *Anglo-French Relations before the Second World War: Appeasement and Crisis* (Basingstoke, 2007), 189.

Mühle, R. W., *Frankreich und Hitler: die französische Deutschland-und Außenpolitik, 1933–1935* (Paderborn, 1995).

Pauley, B. F., *Der Weg in den Nationalsozialismus* (Vienna, 1988).

Radice, L., *Prelude to Appeasement: East Central European Diplomacy in the Early 1930s* (New York, 1981).

Rostow, N., *Anglo-French Relations, 1934–1936* (London, 1984).

Tooze, A., *The Wages of Destruction: The Making and Breaking of the Nazi Economy* (London, 2006).

Wandycz, P., *The Twilight of French Eastern Alliances, 1926–1936: French–Czechoslovak–Polish Relations from Locarno to the Remilitarization of the Rhineland* (Princeton, 1988).

Weinberg, G. L., *The Foreign Policy of Hitler's Germany: Diplomatic Revolution in Europe 1933–1936* (Chicago, 1970).

—— *Germany, Hitler, and World War II* (Cambridge, 1995).

Articles and Chapters

Ahmann, R., '"Localizations of Conflicts" or "Indivisibility of Peace": The German and the Soviet Approaches towards Collective Security and East Central Europe, 1925–1939', in Ahmann, R., Birke, A. M., and Howard, M. (eds.), *The Quest for Stability: Problems of West European Security 1918–1957* (Oxford, 1993).

Bell, P. M. H., *France and Britain, 1900–1940: Entente and Estrangement* (London and New York, 1996), chapter 10.

Cairns, J. C., 'A Nation of Shopkeepers in Search of a Suitable France, 1919–1940', *American Historical Review*, 79: 3 (1974).

Cassels, A., 'Mussolini and the Myth of Rome', in Martel, G. (ed.), *The Origins of the Second World War Reconsidered: A. J. P. Taylor and the Historians*, 2nd edn. (London, 1999).

Gasiorowski, Z. J., 'The German Polish Non-Aggression Pact of 1934', *Journal of Central European Affairs*, 13 (1953).

D'Hoop, J.-M., 'Le problème du réarmement français jusqu'à mars 1936', in id., *La France et l'Allemagne, 1932–1936* (Paris, 1980).

Jackson, P., 'La perception des réarmements allemand et italien et la politique navale française de 1933 à 1939', *Revue Historique des Armées*, 44: 4 (2000).

Radice, L., 'The Eastern Pact, 1933–1935: A Last Attempt at European Co-operation', *Slavonic and East European Review*, 55: 1 (1977).

Scammell, C., 'The Royal Navy and the Strategic Origins of the Anglo–German Naval Agreement of 1935', *Journal of Strategic Studies*, 20 (1997).

Türkes, M., 'The Balkan Pact and its Immediate Implications for the Balkan States', *Middle Eastern Studies*, 30: 1 (1994).

Volkmann, H.-E., 'Polen im wirtschaftlichen Kalkül des Dritten Reiches, 1933–1939', in Michalka, W. (ed.), *Der Zweite Weltkrieg. Analysen, Grundzüge, Forschungsbilanz* (Munich, 1989).

Weinberg, G. L., 'German Foreign Policy and Austria', in id., *Germany, Hitler and World War II* (Cambridge, 1995).

3

The Assault on Versailles and Locarno: Ethiopia and the Remilitarization of the Rhineland

I

It was Mussolini's actions in Ethiopia that accelerated the unravelling of the existing security systems in Europe. What transformed this colonial war into a major European crisis was the existence of the League of Nations and the belief in collective security among politically significant sections of the public in Britain and France. Mussolini had made no secret of his ambitions in Ethiopia; his bitter childhood memories of the humiliating defeat at Adowa in 1896 when the Emperor Menelik administered a shattering blow to the Italians ('ten thousand dead and seventy-two canons lost') fed the appetite for revenge. The Ethiopian adventure was not, however, about revenge; it marked the beginning of a long-planned programme of imperial expansion. The 67-year-old General Emilio De Bono, restored to favour at the Ministry of Colonies after his trial for complicity in the Matteotti murder, had twice visited Eritrea, an Italian held territory bordering on Ethiopia, in 1932. Planning for an expedition began during 1933 and was accelerated in 1934. The time seemed auspicious for Italian action. An imperial adventure would detract attention from Italy's economic difficulties and revitalize Fascism with an injection of militant nationalism. It was important, too, to move before Germany made another bid for *Anschluss* after the failed *coup* and murder of Dollfuss in July 1934. Further delay brought no advantages. The diminutive but impressive Ethiopian ruler Haile Selassie had begun to modernize his wretchedly poor and backward state and there were signs that the emperor's authoritarian rule was slowly beginning to pull his country out of its feudal condition. Mussolini knew from intelligence intercepts that there were Ethiopian negotiations with the British over territorial changes. The Duce intensified the propaganda war against the 'uncivilized' Ethiopians and border conflicts multiplied in 1934. Haile Selassie responded by using what money he could to buy arms from whomsoever would sell. The Germans responded favourably and sent machine guns and rifles to Addis Ababa. They quickly sensed how a clash in East Africa could divide the European powers and bury the Stresa front.

On 5 December 1934, there was a clash between an Anglo-Ethiopian Border Commission and the Italians entrenched near Wal Wal, a dusty watering hole in the Ogaden desert, claimed by the Italians but well within Ethiopian territory. The British commissioners, faced with two opposing lines of troops, stepped back, unwilling to make an issue of what was a preliminary probe to test the diplomatic waters. The boundary commissioners retired but the Ethiopian and Italian troops were left menacing each other at the disputed wells. After a ten day stand-off, shots were fired; Italian planes and armoured cars appeared and the Ethiopians were forced to retreat. Further fighting broke out at other water-holes, though by 1 March a local cease-fire had been negotiated. The fact was that neither the Italians nor the Ethiopians were prepared to treat the Wal Wal incident as a frontier dispute. Haile Selassie, disregarding the conciliatory advice of the British minister in favour of the more radical course recommended by the influential American minister at his court, decided to appeal to the League of Nations. On 9 December, the conflict was brought to the League's notice, and in early January 1935, at the meeting of the League Council, the Ethiopians made their first request for intervention. It was a diplomatic gamble based on the emperor's well-justified belief that the Italians were determined on a military solution. The internationalization of the conflict, he reasoned, might force the Italians to forego an invasion and give the Great Powers time to negotiate the frontier issue.

Mussolini, in a secret and lengthy directive circulated on 30 December 1934, made clear his determination to secure a military solution to the Ethiopian question. He defined Italy's objectives as 'no other than the destruction of the Abyssinian armed forces and the total conquest of Ethiopia'.[1] He warned his ministers that Italy had to be ready to act by October 1935 in order to benefit from the existing advantageous diplomatic situation. Beyond that date, Germany might be strong enough to seize the initiative in Europe. 'The more rapid our military action, the less will be the danger of diplomatic complications', he wrote. 'No one will raise any difficulties in Europe if the conduct of military operations will result rapidly in a *fait accompli*. It will suffice to let England and France know that their interests will be safeguarded.'[2] Mussolini spent the next

[1] *DDI*, 7th ser., Vol. XVI, No. 358.

[2] Quoted in Renzo de Felice, *Mussolini il duce: Gli anni del consenso, 1929–1936* (Torino, 1996), 608.

ten months moving supplies and men through the Suez Canal to Eritrea and Italian Somaliland, while the diplomats debated whether Italy would invade Ethiopia and how the League of Nations should react if it did.

As the tight-lipped Laval and his party boarded the train to Rome on 4 January 1935, the Ethiopian telegram demanding League action was front-page news. The tough and clever French negotiator had his mind on Germany and paid little, if any, attention to this colonial dispute. Until the Wal Wal incident, Laval probably knew little about Ethiopia and was astonished to find that the country was a member of the League of Nations. What was later conceded to Mussolini in their private *tête-à-tête* was more than balanced by what Laval thought was obtained. Regardless of the interpretation of the latter's offer of a 'free hand', it seems improbable that he had not considered the possibility of some future Italian military action. Laval's purpose was to gain Italian backing for co-operation against Hitler. Even at the January Council meeting, Laval found it difficult to take the Ethiopian complaints seriously. It was only in mid-February that Italy's military preparations began to raise serious apprehensions. In the wake of the Laval–Mussolini accords and the high hopes raised at the War Ministry for a military agreement with Italy, the French wanted to avoid taking any role in this unfortunate affair. Laval had no wish to see the League of Nations involved or to associate France with Britain as mediators. The second Ethiopian appeal for help, this time under Articles 10 and 15 of the Covenant, was made on 17 March, the same day as the announcement of Germany's unilateral rearmament.

Encouraged by the impending completion of the Maginot fortifications and the prospect of air and land exchanges with Italy, the French army chiefs were enjoying a rare moment of self-confidence. With Italy as an ally, the French Alpine army could be reduced and there would be no further Italian air and land threat to the plans for reinforcements being brought from North Africa. For the first time in years, the French army could think in offensive terms. In the weeks before General Gamelin's visit to Rome in June 1935, at the invitation of the Italians, the French looked at a number of military contingencies including the possibility of a joint response to a German attack on France involving a major Italian thrust across the Tyrol into Bavaria while French forces, transported across north Italy by Italian railway into Carinthia, would move north-eastward into Bavaria. Not only would the major burden of offensive action in central Europe fall on the Italians but northern Italy would also provide the land bridge by which France could open up a second front and assist its eastern allies. Such military plans explain why the French high command was so enthusiastic about the Italian connection.

They relieved the pressure on one of France's vulnerable frontiers while giving substance to hopes of defending France by fighting outside its borders in conjunction with allies. Despite qualms about Italian technological backwardness and growing concern about the Ethiopian affair, the optimistic mood persisted until Mussolini actually invaded Ethiopia in October. Inexorably, Mussolini's determination to have his war, on the one hand, and British diplomacy, on the other, would pull the French into the 'Anglo-Italian crisis' and shatter the prospects opened by the summer's air and military exchanges with Italy.

The British Foreign Office was as averse as the *Quai d'Orsay* to making Ethiopia a major source of conflict with the Italians. The cabinet, intent on a general European agreement leading to Germany's return to the League of Nations, had no wish to enter into colonial quarrels in East Africa. The Italians were warned of British opposition to an attack on Ethiopia, both at the Stresa Conference (11–14 April) and in London, where Dino Grandi, the Italian ambassador, fruitlessly sought their acquiescence, if not backing, for Italian action. At Stresa, the Ethiopian issue was relegated to the back room and was discussed by the Italian and British African experts. The former warned that the Italian problems in Africa could not be settled by conciliation commissions and 'expatiated on the difficulties of Italy's colonial position'.[3] The British representative responded that it would be useless to hope, as the Italians suggested, that Britain would actively assist Italy to achieve her Ethiopian objectives. The foreign ministers did not discuss Ethiopia, and when Mussolini suggested that the three-power declaration opposing any unilateral repudiation of treaties, which might endanger the peace, should include the additional words 'in Europe' no one protested. Both Mussolini and Laval assumed that the British would not take active measures against any Italian action. Similarly, though Grandi made it perfectly clear in mid-May that Italy was considering major military operations against Ethiopia, the British foreign secretary was more concerned about Italian co-operation in Europe than with that small country's sovereignty. At the time and in the months that followed, Britain and France pressed Haile Selassie to make concessions to the Italians.

Mussolini pressed on with his war preparations. On 14 April, he ordered his naval chief of staff, Domenico Cavagnari, to plan for the possibility of war against Germany in defence of Austria, and against Britain in the Mediterranean. Not surprisingly, the diplomats and the service chiefs, Cavagnari above all, were highly alarmed. There was no

[3] C. J. Lowe and F. Marzari, *Italian Foreign Policy, 1870–1940* (London and Boston, MA, 1975), 262.

way that Italy could engage two enemies simultaneously, and the fledgling Italian fleet could hardly challenge Britain's naval supremacy. Nevertheless Dino Grandi was instructed to warn Simon that Italy would not accept Geneva's arbitration, and that 'our intention is absolutely firm not to permit our pursuit of Italy's colonial interests to be stopped by extraneous matters'.[4] Mussolini was not totally deaf to the importunings of his advisers. Both Cavagnari and Pompeo Aloisi, the *chef de cabinet* at the Foreign Ministry, believed that an Italian settlement with Germany would convince the British that they had to give the Italians a free hand in Ethiopia if they were not to lose Italy to the Germans. The final push towards Berlin came from intelligence reports in late April that Hitler had summoned the Austrian Nazis to Berlin and stressed his intention to incorporate Austria into a Greater Reich.[5] Mussolini moved to force Hitler 'to go public'. On 18 May, in a speech to the Chamber of Deputies, the Duce condemned Britain and France, who wished to 'nail us to the Brenner', and openly appealed to Hitler for an assurance that Austria would remain independent. Three days later, Hitler told the Reichstag deputies that Germany would not intervene in Austria's internal affairs and did not intend to annex Austria. Though Mussolini authorized further arms sales to Austria, he looked to an agreement with Berlin, hoping to relieve the pressure on Vienna but, more importantly, to speed up an alignment with Germany.

With hopes that the Germans would leave Austria alone and stop the deliveries of supplies to Ethiopia, Mussolini took a tougher line with both the French, demanding that Djibouti be closed as a transit point for Ethiopian arms, and with the British, whose offer of economic concessions in Ethiopia in return for a less bellicose stand was rejected. The British were increasingly concerned with the massive Italian build-up in East Africa. While refusing to negotiate directly with the Italians, they moved to defuse the situation through Geneva and proceeded in London to define their interests in Ethiopia. A committee was created under Sir John Maffey, the former governor-general of the Sudan, which concluded on 18 June that an Italian conquest of Ethiopia would not directly and immediately threaten any vital British interest.[6] A remote threat to British control of the Sudan and the upper waters of the Nile hardly warranted resistance. By the time the secret

[4] *DDI*, 8th ser., Vol. I, No. 60 (20 April 1935).

[5] Robert Mallett, *Mussolini and the Origins of the Second World War* (Basingstoke, 2003), 39.

[6] *DBFP*, 2nd ser., Vol. XIV, No. 313. The report was probably intercepted and relayed by the Italian agent, Secondo Constantini, a chancery servant in the British embassy in Rome with easy access to the ambassador's safe and to the British codes and ciphers. His brother, Francesco Constantini, a messenger at the embassy, also passed material to the Italians, though for over ten years he worked primarily for the Soviets, who obtained through him large amounts of secret diplomatic material.

report, its contents soon known to the Italians, was circulated to the cabinet on 16 August, public feeling had changed the context of the debate.

Neither the British nor the French wanted to become involved in Italy's African adventure. Both governments used their knowledge of the other's hesitations to reinforce their individual preference to do nothing that might lead to a clash with Rome. They continued to counsel compromise at Addis Ababa and worked together to delay action in Geneva. Neither would take the lead in Geneva or Rome, but blamed each other for doing nothing. As the storm clouds gathered during the summer of 1935, the League Council waited for the disputants to arbitrate their dispute while Britain and France pressed for an Italo–Ethiopian agreement at Ethiopian expense. Mussolini was cautioned against taking military action, but Italian troops and equipment continued to pour into Eritrea. On 25 May, the League Council agreed to a three-month delay; it would not meet again until 25 August. The delay was a bonus for Mussolini, with his eye on the October deadline. In early June, Stanley Baldwin replaced the almost senile Ramsay MacDonald as prime minister, and Sir Samuel Hoare took over the Foreign Office from the ineffective Simon. Anthony Eden, considered too young and too temperamental to be named foreign secretary, was made minister for League of Nations affairs with a seat in the cabinet. The changes in fact reinforced the government's decision to avoid confrontation with Italy. Eden had to parry Opposition demands for a more assertive policy, and a threat to close the Suez Canal if Mussolini persisted in his aggressive plans. It was unfortunate for the new League minister that the recent announcement of the Anglo-German naval agreement had poisoned relations between Paris and London. Pierre Laval, now premier as well as foreign minister, was in no mood for joint action. In their June meeting, Eden made no mention of a new British proposal, the so-called 'Zeila plan', that he intended to discuss with Mussolini in Rome after his Paris visit. On 24 June, he duly suggested to the Duce that the Ethiopians be given a corridor to the sea, ending at the port of Zeila in British Somaliland, and that the Italians be compensated with substantial territorial concessions in the Ogaden. An incandescent Duce rejected the offer and demanded control of all of Ethiopia. If war came, he threatened, Ethiopia would be wiped off the map. The unprepared Eden was shocked; his dealings with Mussolini convinced him that the Duce was 'a complete gangster', a view that he never abandoned. The British effort to 'buy off' Mussolini had failed. The French, naturally informed by the Italians, were put out by the lack of consultation and Britain's total indifference to their interests. The French-owned Djibouti–Addis Ababa railway and the port of Djibouti would lose business to Zeila, if developed.

In London, during the summer months, the powerful pro-League groups went into action. Their prestige was greatly enhanced by the publication of the results of the so-called 'peace ballot' on 27 June 1935, after a year-long publicity campaign. Whatever doubts the government had about the ballot and the scepticism, shared by Eden, with regard to the public's grasp of the issues involved, the results could not be brushed aside. About eleven and a half million people answered the questionnaire, amounting to more than half the total number of votes cast in the 1935 general election. Ten million voters favoured the use of economic and non-military measures to stop an aggressor. Six and three-quarter millions approved the use of military sanctions; four and three-quarter million people voted 'no' or abstained. Baldwin, who like most of his colleagues had no faith in the League as a coercive force, was nevertheless obliged to tell Viscount Cecil, the president of the League of Nations Union, that he believed in 'the vital character of the League of Nations as a fundamental element in the conduct of our foreign affairs'.[7] There were some counter-currents, mainly in imperialist circles and among those pacifists and socialists who believed that sanctions led to war. But the general mood in the country was strongly pro-League and pro-sanctions and Baldwin, always quick to adjust policies to the prevailing winds, responded accordingly. Public opinion was not only pro-League but anti-Italian. Feelings mounted as the military build-up in Eritrea continued. It was generally assumed that with the ending of the summer rains, Italy would embark on a war of conquest. The League of Nations Union mobilized its speakers and writers to excellent effect. Such formidable troublemakers as the feminist Sylvia Pankhurst led the anti-Fascist campaign, forming committees, bombarding the press, lobbying politicians and civil servants and rallying sympathetic audiences. Samuel Hoare—dubbed by F. E. Smith, the former lord chancellor and secretary of state for India, 'the last in a long line of maiden aunts'—warned the British ambassador in Rome, Sir Eric Drummond, that there was every sign of the country being swept with the same kind of movements that Gladstone had started over the Bulgarian atrocities in 1876 when he roused the country against the Turks. The image of the Italian bully and victimized Ethiopia blotted out the arguments of those who pointed to Ethiopia's uncivilized past and still backward condition (Simon had written the preface to a book by his wife exposing the horrors of slavery in Ethiopia) or who argued that a colonial war was not really a cause for League action. Imperial adventures of the Italian variety were simply no longer acceptable to many sections of the British electorate.

[7] Keith Middlemas and John Barnes, *Baldwin: A Biography* (London, 1969), 837.

After his acrimonious exchanges with Eden, Mussolini turned again to France. He had already been told on 11 June, in response to an appeal for a clarification of Laval's position, that though France would remain loyal to the Rome accords, the Italians should take no action incompatible with the principles of the League of Nations, and 'not create a situation in which our goodwill, large as it is, would inevitably be paralysed'.[8] In Rome, the Italophile French ambassador, Charles de Chambrun, seeing his diplomatic handiwork threatened by a conflict of no real interest to France, assured Suvich, the under-secretary at the Foreign Ministry, that Laval would do everything possible to assist the Italians and that the issue could be settled without League intervention and without an Italian resort to war. Laval was attracted by the proposals being hatched by Joseph Avenol, the devious French secretary general of the League of Nations, which would make Ethiopia appear as the aggressor nation, contemplating military action against the Italian colonies. Laval did not care much about the future of Ethiopia, but needed to defuse a situation that threatened to become an international problem which could only damage France's diplomatic position and cause difficulties with the native inhabitants of the French empire. Though usually impervious to public feeling, he was not entirely immune from such pressures at home. His government depended on the parties of the centre-right and on the acquiescence, if not the support, of the Radicals. Among the former there was considerable admiration for Mussolini and strong backing for an alliance with Rome, which would obviate the need for the Soviet treaty. Léon Daudet, the chief polemicist for the *Action Française*, saw no reason to compromise France's relations with Italy for the sake of the League of Nations, 'that detestable, saliva-slinging society'. There were some right-wing 'moderates' who felt that France had to associate herself with Britain, even if this meant supporting the League, but the real danger for Laval came from the divided Radical party. He needed to keep the loyalty of the Herriot Radicals if his government was to survive, and Herriot was one of the strongest advocates of the League of Nations. The ex-prime minister warned his cabinet colleagues in August 1935 that if the crisis made a choice between England and Italy necessary, 'I would not hesitate two seconds; I stand with GB. Nor do I want to abandon the SDN [League of Nations], the keystone of our security.'[9] The other wing of the Radical party led by Daladier, the Socialists and the Communists,

[8] *DDF*, 1st ser., Vol. XI, No. 311 (Laval to de Chambrun, 19 July).

[9] MAE, FN, Papiers Herriot, Vol. 34, 28 August 1935, quoted in William I. Shorrock, *From Ally to Enemy: The Enigma of Fascist Italy in French Diplomacy, 1920–1940* (Kent, OH, 1988), 147.

already re-grouping under the Popular Front banner, took up the pro-League and anti-Italian cause both inside and outside the Chamber. Laval's troubled diplomacy as well as his unpopular economic policies became the object of fierce attacks in the autumn of 1935.

While still hopeful of support from France, Mussolini faced an increasingly hostile Britain as tensions grew more acute during the summer months. In London, public feeling was forcing the government's hand. This is not to deny that British statesmen shared some of the same feelings about the League as their fellow countrymen, but past experience had made them wary of expecting positive results from Geneva, and they were highly sceptical of the claims made for its peace-keeping functions by the League's enthusiastic supporters. Ministers knew that the electorate expected their government to use the League's procedures and reluctantly turned their attention to the sanctions clause (Article 16) of the Covenant, while fervently hoping it would not be used. Whitehall was almost unanimous in its opposition to sanctions or to the closure of the Suez Canal, either of which would force Mussolini's hand. Already at the Council meeting in Geneva on 25 June, Eden had made a strong speech raising the possibility of sanctions if the Italians invaded Ethiopia. The Foreign Office increased its pressure on Laval to convince Mussolini to negotiate, and thus prevent him from attacking Ethiopia, 'seeing that Italy, strong and efficient in Europe, is now held to be a *sine qua non* of French security'.[10] There is little question that the British were trying to shift the responsibility of forcing Mussolini's hand on to the French. Laval had no wish to take on this task. On 1 August, Hoare, in a speech to the Commons, openly warned Mussolini against waging war in Africa. And yet, when Laval, Eden, and Aloisi met on 16 August, they worked out proposals for a disguised Italian protectorate over Ethiopia (despite its membership in the League as a sovereign state), under the auspices of the League. Mussolini found the offer totally unacceptable. Mussolini's intransigence was pushing the British and the even more reluctant French to some form of League action.

In Rome, Mussolini's chiefs of staff were warning of the disastrous consequences of an Anglo-Italian war. The Italian military establishment was adamant that Italy would be defeated; the timid King Victor Emmanuel III criticized Mussolini outright and implored him to avoid conflict. Mussolini had no intention of being cheated of his war. Infuriated by British obstruction, he refused efforts at negotiation and was prepared to risk an armed clash with Britain to conquer the whole of Ethiopia. His first line of defence was France. Franco-Italian air staff talks had taken place in mid-March, and in June, Badoglio and Gamelin,

[10] Shorrock, *From Ally to Enemy*, 145.

the two chiefs of staff, had agreed on military action in case of a German attack on Austria or on metropolitan France. There were no naval talks; the French *Marine* was far too concerned with the possible British reaction. Given Mussolini's belief that the French had every wish to maintain their close relations with Rome, he naturally looked to Laval to keep the British in check. The French faced the same dilemmas as the British. They would do all they could to satisfy Italian aspirations but Mussolini would have to come to the negotiating table. While Laval was opposed to League intervention, he had to face the possibility that sanctions would be considered. He could not turn his back on Geneva or put the *entente* with Britain under excessive strain. A past-master at finding *ad hoc* solutions to difficult situations, he pressed Mussolini to abandon the idea of an invasion by promising him the substance of his demands while simultaneously agreeing to co-operate with Britain at Geneva. In this delicate balancing act, there was the added difficulty of the pressure from the Italophile elements in Laval's cabinet, from the parties of the right and, above all, from the military. Should France become committed to sanctions, it would be difficult to find a way to save the country from the unfortunate European consequences of the Duce's African adventure.

Anglo-Italian tensions reached their peak in August. The British pressure on Laval to make Mussolini see reason intensified, as did efforts to get the French to commit themselves to support for Britain in case of a Mediterranean conflict. Laval approached Hoare on the eve of the latter's important speech to the League Assembly on 11 September. The two men agreed that only economic sanctions should be imposed if the League took action, and that these should be limited in scope and applied in stages. There was to be no blockade or closure of the Suez Canal. The French ambassador in London was instructed to enquire formally whether Britain would invoke sanctions immediately if any European state resorted to unprovoked aggression and, more specifically, to ask what Britain would do if Germany took advantage of the Ethiopian situation to realize its Austrian ambitions.[11] The French, using Britain's dependence on France's co-operation as the danger in Africa and the Mediterranean escalated, had raised the diplomatic temperature by drawing a direct connection between the Ethiopian situation and any future German challenge in Europe. It was a query repeated many times during the following months. It would never receive a positive answer.

[11] *DDF*, 2nd ser., Vol. XII, No. 132 (Laval to Corbin, 8 September); also No. 145 (Corbin to Laval, 10 September).

The London cabinet, supposedly committed since late August to the League procedures, decided that the British should do no more than the French to stop Italy. If the French stalled on sanctions, as many hoped, Britain could refuse to act alone without incurring the direct blame for failure. If sanctions were imposed, the cabinet believed it would become obvious that without the co-operation of non-members, that is, without the United States, they were bound to fail and would have to be abandoned. In either case, the government could claim they had supported the cause of collective security and satisfied the electorate. Whatever was done, there had to be 'collective action' which meant, in effect, Anglo-French action. Both countries hoped to use the other to avoid the imposition of sanctions.

No one in London or Paris expected assistance from Washington, though Haile Selassie had asked for American intervention and mediation. Both President Roosevelt and Secretary of State Cordell Hull were sympathetic to the emperor's plight, but they rejected his appeal, carefully avoiding the use of the 1928 Kellogg–Briand Pact prohibiting war, while still insisting on its binding nature. Strong anti-Mussolini sentiment in the United States was more than matched by the strength of the anti-war feeling provoked by the hearings of the Nye Committee in Washington. The committee's final report issued in early 1936 contained statistics showing the profits made by private corporations from the sales of armaments during the 1914–1918 war. The 'merchants of death', it was suggested, were responsible for pulling the United States into the European war. The Nye Committee proceedings gave added momentum to moves in Congress for the passage of a tough neutrality bill that would prevent a repetition of the previous disaster. On 23 August 1935, the bill was sent to Roosevelt for signature. It became mandatory for the president, on finding that a state of war existed, to prohibit the sale or export of 'arms, ammunition and implements of war' to all belligerents. Other goods were not subject to this prohibition. Hull tried to convince Congress to permit a discretionary embargo that would have given the president the power to block shipments of goods to an aggressor nation without forbidding trade to its victim. Anti-presidential as well as isolationist feeling defeated Hull's last-minute efforts and, on 31 August, Roosevelt signed the bill. The Neutrality Act was a powerful and popular expression of American isolationism. On 5 October, after Mussolini's invasion of Ethiopia, the president would invoke the Act, embargoing arms sales to both sides. Americans were warned that dealing with belligerents would be at their own risk. There were plenty of items not on the embargo list, including oil, enough to satisfy hungry American exporters. Mussolini was the main beneficiary. While the president called for a 'moral embargo', oil shipments to Italy tripled.

To the Geneva community, British policy in September seemed unusually decisive. On 11 September, Hoare, suffering from an attack of arthritis, hobbled to the podium and addressed the League of Nations Assembly. To his own surprise, his carefully planned speech, delivered in his usual precise manner, was listened to in complete silence and produced an extraordinary demonstration of approval when he finished. He told the overflowing audience what so many wanted to hear: 'The League stands and my country with it, for the collective maintenance of the Covenant in its entirety and particularly for steady and collective resistance to all acts of unprovoked aggression in whatever quarter such a danger to the peace of the world may arise.'[12] The carefully selected words were intended to warn the French that Britain would not act alone and would participate only in collective action. It was also the foreign secretary's answer to ambassador Corbin's query about action in Europe. Hoare was 'amazed at the universal acclamation' with which his words were received. The Assembly fastened on this unusual British espousal of the League and collective security. Assuming Britain would now take the lead at Geneva, almost all its members fell in line. It was a graphic demonstration of British influence. Two days later, Pierre Laval assured the Assembly that 'France's policy rests entirely on the League'.[13]

Words appeared to be backed by a demonstration of British naval strength. Four battleships and two battle-cruisers were sent to Gibraltar to join the Mediterranean fleet in an open display of British power. In late September, Sir Eric Drummond told Mussolini that 144 ships of war were cruising in what the Duce liked to call '*mare nostrum*'. But this exhibition of British firmness merely disguised the hesitations and ambiguities in the cabinet's position. Though prepared to caution Mussolini by a show of force, the British did not want to provoke him. The naval dispositions and military reinforcement of Egypt were meant to show support for the League, but were also intended to prevent Italian retaliation against British interests. In London, ministers and the chiefs of staff were worried whether these aims were compatible. Deterrence and defence might appear provocative to the Italians. The naval chiefs were perfectly confident that they could defeat the Italians, but the Admiralty, though not the regional commanders, feared that any loss of ships in the Mediterranean would weaken Britain's global position, above all in the Far East. Mussolini responded to the arrival of the British ships by sending two army divisions to Libya.

[12] League of Nations, *Official Journal*, Vol. 18 (Aug./Sep. 1937), 659.

[13] League of Nations, *Official Journal*, Special Supplement, No. 138 (1935), 65–66, cited in *Documents on International Affairs*, 1935, Vol. 1, 243.

He soon learned, thanks to the officials at the *Quai d'Orsay* and to his own agents at the British embassy in Rome, that these moves were far less menacing than they appeared. While the British cabinet concentrated on the possibility of a Fascist 'mad dog' act against the Royal Navy, its main purpose was to avoid it. Unwilling to take up Mussolini's offer to remove his divisions if the British withdrew its fleet from the Mediterranean, the British assured the Duce about the peaceful purpose of the fleet concentration. Hoare told Mussolini that Britain did not intend to humiliate Italy, and would not impose military sanctions nor close the Suez Canal. Armed with these assurances, Mussolini could calm the fears of the highly agitated General Badoglio as well as his naval advisers. While ordering the navy to plan for a Mediterranean and Red Sea war against the Royal Navy, Mussolini rightly suspected that the British were bluffing about their naval resolve. In Geneva, a committee of five initiated by Laval and Eden, and consisting of Britain, France, Poland, Spain, and Turkey, quickly produced a possible settlement just a week after Hoare's speech. Italian diplomats, alarmed at the militant mood in the Assembly, strongly recommended acceptance of the proffered 'international mandate' over Ethiopia and an Anglo-French promise of future territorial adjustments. Mussolini rejected the compromise. He was not going to step back now that Italian prestige and troops, some 250,000 men, were engaged.

II

On 3 October 1935, without any declaration of war, Italian forces invaded Ethiopia. The Council and the Assembly declared Italy in violation of Article 12 which stated that if any dispute between members might lead to a rupture, they should be submitted either to arbitration or to inquiry by the Council, with no resort to war permitted until three months after the award by the arbitrators or the report by the Council. Only Italy, Austria, Hungary, and Albania dissented. A committee of eighteen was created to supervise the application of Article 16. An embargo on arms and loans was to be imposed, and limited economic sanctions, banning all imports from Italy and prohibiting the export of rubber and metallic ores among other items, was to be introduced on 18 November. Cheeses and French *foie gras* appeared on the list, but iron, steel, coal, cotton and, critically, oil did not. The vote was fifty to four in condemnation of Italy with the same four states opposing. What Britain, France, and the Soviet Union had hoped to avoid had happened. A colonial conflict had become a challenge to the League of Nations, and the member states were committed to sanctions. To their own surprise, the British found themselves leading the League in its first application of Article 16. Laval had not wanted the 'Anglo-Italian crisis' but he could not dissociate France from Britain at Geneva. He was reluctantly prepared to answer Hoare's query of 24 September as to whether France would back Britain with naval support if Italy attacked its Mediterranean fleet or bases. France might promise such support, Laval responded, if Britain would support France in case the Germans moved westward. The French would try to use the Mediterranean crisis to secure that engagement on the Rhine which had eluded all previous governments. In its absence, Laval refused to offer the unequivocal assurances the British sought. Sir George Clerk, the British ambassador in Paris, saw Laval on 15 October and insisted that Britain 'expected' French support by air, land, and sea if attacked by Italy. The French foreign minister, not a man easily bullied, claimed that the British fleet in the Mediterranean was now so large that the Italians could claim that it went beyond League agreements for the enforcement of the Covenant. The growing danger of a confrontation with Italy heightened the tensions between London and Paris.

The Baldwin government's stand with regard to Italy was highly popular, not just with Liberal and Labour voters but with the vast majority of the electorate, which had declared its allegiance to collective security in the June 'peace ballot'. Beyond its public identification with the Geneva system, however, the cabinet remained uncertain about what this should involve and uneasy about its costs. The highly ambitious and personally engaged Anthony Eden represented the pro-sanctionist wing of the cabinet. He argued that Mussolini could be pushed about sufficiently to compel him to compromise. He rightly assumed that Italy would not attack Britain, and in any case believed the British fleet easily capable of handling the Italian navy. Eden's support for collective action did not mean opposition to conciliation and negotiations with Mussolini. His differences from Hoare, with whom, contrary to what is written in Eden's autobiography, he worked quite well, should not be exaggerated, though the minister for League affairs was more susceptible to the Geneva atmosphere, and was anxious to consolidate his public stand as a 'League man'. The service ministers, above all, the first lord of the Admiralty, represented the other end of the cabinet spectrum, apprehensive of an Italian attack and fearful of the long-range consequences of an armed conflict in the Mediterranean. They argued that the services were unprepared for war, and that the country was just about to embark on a five-year rearmament plan aimed at Germany and Japan. They expressed doubts about the reliability of France, and insisted on a specific promise of backing before any further action. Again and again, the admirals stressed Britain's vulnerability in the Mediterranean, the dangers in having to move naval forces from the

TABLE 3.1 British and Italian Fleet Strengths during the Ethiopian Crisis

	British Empire	Italy
Mediterranean		
Battleships	5	2 (excluding 2 undergoing refit and modernization)
Battle Cruisers	2 (at Gibraltar)	0
Aircraft Cruisers	2	0
8-inch Cruisers	5	7
6-inch Cruisers	10 (including 3 at Gibraltar)	10
Flotilla Leaders	0	18
Destroyers	54	65
Submarines	11	62
Red Sea		
8-inch Cruisers	1	0
6-inch Cruisers	2	2 (5.9-inch)
Flotilla Leaders	0	2
Destroyers	5	3
Submarines	0	4
Sloops	5	2

Source: Arthur Marder, 'The Royal Navy and the Ethiopian Crisis of 1935–36', *American Historical Review*, 75: 5 (1970), 1338.

Far East, and the anticipated Italian damage to the British fleet. The reality was quite different; the Italians posed no threat to the Royal Navy. The British had five battleships in the Mediterranean and the Italians two (two others were in dry docks).

The senior naval and military commanders in the Eastern Mediterranean were adamant that the existing British forces could have dealt with the Italians with little risk of incurring the losses feared by the chiefs of staff in London and without needing the assistance of the French. Local commanders were confident that the Italians could not mount a serious invasion of Egypt. Winston Churchill's verdict still stands: 'If ever there was an opportunity of striking a decisive blow in a generous cause with the minimum of risk, it was here and now.'[14]

In contrast to public perceptions, Baldwin seems to have been particularly indecisive during the summer and autumn of 1935. Without a

[14] Winston Churchill, *The Second World War*, Vol. 1, *The Gathering Storm* (London, 1948). See Steven Morewood, 'The Chiefs-of-Staff, the men on the spot, and the Italo-Abyssinian Emergency, 1935–6' in D. Richardson and G. Stone (eds.), *Decisions and Diplomacy. Essays in Twentieth-Century International History* (London, 1995) and an unpublished paper given to the British History International Group conference at Salford, England, September 2009. I am grateful to Dr Morewood for permission to use his paper.

consensus among his ministers, he appeared at a loss. His usually placid nature, which reinforced a reputation for solidity, was distinctly ruffled as Britain seemed to be drifting into confrontation with the Italians. It was Neville Chamberlain who, according to his own account, kept the cabinet on a steady course. 'So you see', he wrote to his sister Hilda on 25 August, 'I have been very active and though my name will not appear I have as usual greatly influenced policy and, which is almost as important in these delicate situations, method also.'[15] Chamberlain's own view, according to Leo Amery, the colonial secretary, was

> That we were bound to try out the League ... (in which he does not himself believe very much) for political reasons at home and that there was no question of our going beyond the mildest economic sanctions ... If things become too serious the French will run out first, and we could show that we had done our best.[16]

Chamberlain and Hoare were in fundamental agreement on current policy. Britain should continue to back the League while seeking a compromise that Mussolini would accept. But Foreign Office hopes that, if Mussolini were calmed, the so-called Stresa front could be resurrected, were already misplaced. Hoare, who enjoyed a considerable political reputation as a result of his long duel with Churchill over the 1935 India Act, was already a tired and sick man when he took over the Foreign Office. He was, moreover, a neophyte in the diplomatic world and leaned heavily on the advice of Robert Vansittart, his unusually assertive permanent under-secretary. Vansittart was preoccupied with the German danger and Britain's military unpreparedness and feared that sanctions would lead to war and drive Mussolini into Hitler's embrace. Though angered by Laval's temporizing tactics, he shared the latter's fears that disaster lay at the end of the Geneva road. Vansittart's pessimism owed much to his close contacts with the chiefs of staff, who saw no reason for incurring the risks of war for the sake of a League of Nations in which they did not believe. Many saw Mussolini as an anti-Bolshevik force. They had little interest in a colonial conflict in Africa. It was the Vansittart view that prevailed in Whitehall. The permanent under-secretary insisted that Laval, who was even more intent on finding a diplomatic solution to the Ethiopian clash than the British, should give Britain an unequivocal promise of support in case of an Italian 'mad-dog act' in the Mediterranean. Laval equivocated, attaching conditions to the French assurances and then escalating the crisis by trying to link the events in Ethiopia with future treaty violations in Europe.

15 NC 18/1/929, Chamberlain to Hilda, 25 August 1935.

16 Leo Amery, *My Political Life* (London, 1955), 174. Quoted in Richard Davis, *Anglo-French Relations before the Second World War: Appeasement and Crisis* (Basingstoke, 2001), 75.

In Ethiopia, the Italian columns moved southward without meeting any opposition. Adowa, emptied of Ethiopian troops, fell to the Italians on 6 October, honour was satisfied. De Bono, cautious by nature, and not at all anxious to do battle with the Ethiopians, took time to enjoy his triumph and showed no wish to push on with the campaign. If the Italians had completed their conquest with speed, as Mussolini suggested in his December memorandum, an international crisis might have been avoided. Instead, the Italian forces waited and the Duce beat the anti-British war drum while the service chiefs did their best to restrain him. Mussolini used the imposition of sanctions as a rallying cry to increase popular support for the Ethiopian campaign. As he had always despised the League, its condemnation of Italy on 11 October meant nothing to him, international chastisement simply made it impossible to accept anything less than total victory in Ethiopia. The problem was that victory did not come quickly and the Ethiopians were given time to assemble their forces and regroup. The subsequent months of delay meant that France became the mediator between London and Rome and the Anglo-French differences became as important and time-consuming as the Anglo-Italian conflict. Laval quickly assumed the role of 'honest broker'. With their fleet in the Mediterranean, the British appeared unusually dependent on French under-writing and Laval made full use of his enhanced position. Hoare and Eden were forced to deal with a man whom they disliked and distrusted; they both anticipated a French desertion at Britain's hour of need. The Baldwin government wanted firm and specific assurances; Laval temporized and avoided unequivocal commitments. Finally cornered into offering the pledge of military support demanded by London, on 18 October Laval gave way with ill-grace. The pledge of support was extracted only after a threat that a French refusal would imperil the Locarno agreements. 'We have had to get it out of the French with forceps and biceps,' Vansittart minuted, 'and if we hadn't had the latter we shouldn't have got it at all.'[17] The sharpness and acrimony of the exchanges between London and Paris coloured their relations well into 1936. Personal dislikes, particularly on the part of the British, and mutual suspicions shadowed the moments of co-operation even when both governments acknowledged the need for common action.

On the French side, Laval had coupled the pledge of support for Britain in case of an attack 'clearly brought about by application of provisions of [Article 16]', with demands for a reduction of Britain's naval forces in the Mediterranean, as the Italians were insisting. His effort to diffuse the Anglo-Italian situation only brought further rebukes

[17] *DBFP*, 2nd ser., Vol. XV, No. 115 (minute by Vansittart, 19 October 1935).

from London. The British Admiralty wanted access to the French naval bases at Toulon and Bizerta, and a promise to initiate air operations against targets in northern Italy from southern France, thereby diverting the Italian air threats to Malta and the Mediterranean fleet. On 26 October, the French agreed to the use of the ports and suggested talks between the two Admiralties. The French retreat was, in part, window-dressing. In the event of an Italian attack on British forces, France would delay a declaration of war until ready to fight, and would need British assistance to bring troops from North Africa to metropolitan France. This was hardly enough for the British navy. At the same time, French attempts to extend the joint staff talks to cover violations of the Covenant by force in Europe came to nothing. 'We are talking about Italy and will only talk about Italy', Vansittart said when the French raised the question on 31 October. 'Only a little resolution will be necessary to hold to such firm ground.'[18] The French did not have sufficient diplomatic clout to force the issue.

Whether Laval's renewed attempts to woo the Germans in October were a response to the difficulties with Britain and Italy, or part of his longer range strategy, remains an unanswered question. Though Laval knew that any settlement with Berlin would have to include Britain, a bilateral arrangement would provide a welcome response to the Anglo-German naval agreement and would boost French confidence. With the ratification of the Franco-Soviet pact in sight, it was essential to take the initiative before Hitler cashed in his diplomatic chips. On 18 October, Fernand de Brinon, again enlisted as Laval's personal emissary, was received by the Führer and conveyed the premier's hopes for a useful conversation with Germany. On 16 November Laval approached Roland Köster, the intelligent and far from servile German ambassador in Paris, proposing a 'diplomatic document' that 'would constitute a "preamble" to the negotiations on concrete questions, such as, for instance, the limitation of armaments and the Air Pact'.[19] A few days later, on 21 November, François-Poncet saw the Führer to 'reassure' him about the Franco-Soviet Pact, and to press again for the joint communiqué that Laval had suggested. Hitler insisted that the assistance pact was 'the equivalent of a military alliance exclusively directed against Germany'.[20] He would not consider either an air pact or an arms limitation agreement while the Ethiopian war continued. Well briefed on the forthcoming French elections, he wondered whether the next

[18] Quoted in George W. Baer, *Test Case: Italy, Ethiopia and the League of Nations* (Stanford, CA, 1976), 88.

[19] *DGFP*, Ser. C, Vol. IV, No. 415.

[20] *DGFP*, Ser. C, Vol. IV, No. 425.

government might share, or even wish to share, Laval's views with regard to Germany. The discussion lasted nearly two hours, and by its end, Hitler had effectively closed the door on the Laval initiative. There was, in any case, little enthusiasm either at the *Quai d'Orsay* or among the senior military officers for Laval's approach to Hitler. Gamelin continued to hope that France could emerge from the present crisis with its lines to Italy and Britain intact. He wanted the assistance of both in the forthcoming duel with Germany. He reacted with a combination of despair and disgust when Laval explained his strategy towards the Third Reich, during a meeting of the *Haut Comité Militaire*. After a sleepless night, the chief of the general staff, who had little respect for Laval, condemned the approach to Hitler as unrealistic and demeaning, and its perpetrators unfit to wear the mantle of Clemenceau and Poincaré. 'Perhaps one day we shall be able to arrive at an understanding with Germany; but let's do it with our heads held high once our defence equipment programme is completed.'[21]

The task of maintaining the link with Italy and the partnership with Britain was a difficult one. The French felt they had been bullied into the offer of support in the Mediterranean. What would France receive in return for the loss of the 'solid and definite' advantages derived from the friendship of Mussolini? Anglo-French military and air staff conversations were scheduled to begin on 9–10 December. By this time, the Baldwin government, under pressure to accept an oil sanction, was ready for a diplomatic bargain on Laval's terms. In anticipation of the military talks, the British chiefs of staff outlined their requirements which included a French attack on northern Italy and an engagement on the Tunisian border with Tripolitania. The actual instructions sent to the British negotiators in December were far more general. It was, of course, pure illusion to think that France, given the state of its armed forces and its fears about Germany, not to speak of Gamelin's wish to keep the Italian agreements intact, would attack Italy unless first attacked themselves. The British demands said more about their own reluctance to engage with the Italians and their deep distrust of France, than about their naval capabilities. The talks further exacerbated relations between the two countries and led to a mini press war as each side tried to blame the other for the lack of effective action. In London, the service heads reviewed, for the cabinet's benefit, the extent of Britain's vulnerability. Malta, where the fleet was sent from the exposed harbours at Alexandria,

[21] Maurice Gamelin, 'Réflexions... au sortir d'un Haut Comité Militaire', Fonds Gamelin, 1K 224 Carton 7, SHAT, quoted in Martin S. Alexander, *The Republic in Danger: General Maurice Gamelin and the Politics of French Defence, 1933–1940* (Cambridge, 1992), 76.

was open to air attack. Egypt, where the Wafd were demanding new constitutional and treaty changes, was menaced by the Italian military build-up in Libya. The barrage of anti-British broadcasts from the Italian radio station at Bari was stirring Arab nationalism, at least among the few who could understand literary Arabic. What appeared as defensive measures in London, it was feared, might easily set off the supposedly unstable Mussolini. Once British reinforcements were in place and the French pledge on the table, the cabinet was prepared to see what could be done in Geneva. Like the French, they preferred temporization to action.

After Laval's efforts to negotiate an Anglo-Italian *détente* failed, Britain made its own bid for a reduction in Anglo-Italian tension. Embittered by the British naval presence in the Mediterranean, Mussolini turned down piecemeal negotiations regarding Libya and Egypt, and demanded a discussion of the whole future balance of forces in the Mediterranean. Despite promptings from Laval and Aloisi, no further offers came from London. Vansittart was convinced that Laval was playing a double game, committing France to sanctions and support for Britain, but assuring Mussolini of a settlement favourable to Rome. The nervous and overstretched civil servant doubted whether the French would actually come to Britain's assistance in case of war. His dislike of Laval, fanned by Anglophile friends in the French embassy, only sharpened his anxiety to end the crisis and to avoid any discussion of extending sanctions. Hoare was less alarmist than Vansittart but just as anxious to find a way of getting Mussolini to stop the war and prevent the erosion of Anglo-French relations. The British played down the provocative character of the defensive measures they had taken. Haile Selassie was given no financial aid and though the embargo on arms to Ethiopia was lifted, only a small shipment of British guns and ammunition was actually sent. The Baldwin government, however, could not be seen offering any concessions to Italy that could be interpreted as a betrayal of the League. The articulate public was more anti-Italian than the government.

In Paris, Laval's left-wing critics accused the government of subverting the policies of collective security. The right-wing press, however, lashed out at Britain and defended Mussolini's policies and regime. If Mussolini fell, readers of *Le Figaro* were warned, Bolshevism would triumph in Italy. As for Laval, he believed that he was being asked to foot the bill for actions which would cost France the Rome agreements without any offer of compensation in Europe. At the *Quai d'Orsay*, Alexis Léger, the secretary general, and René Massigli, both hostile towards the Italians, were more concerned about the effects of the crisis on the Anglo-French *entente* than on France's relations with Italy.

According to Gamelin, by the end of 1935 Léger was deeply pessimistic about the future: 'If France commits herself definitely to Russia, [Germany] will reply by occupying the left bank of the Rhine; if Italy emerges weakened from her current difficulties that means *Anschluss*; if there is war between Britain and Italy and we come in, Germany is prepared to move against us. Only the closest understanding between France and Britain can keep the peace from now on.' Even this insurance policy, Léger added, was in doubt.[22] Laval continued his effort to broker an agreement in Rome. He was prepared to cede major portions of Ethiopia to Italy and establish a League mandate with Italian influence predominant for what remained of the country. In response to these promptings, Mussolini presented counter-proposals not fundamentally different but with the added demand that Ethiopia should be disarmed and that its suggested outlet to the sea, Assab, be placed under Italian control. Much of this negotiation was pure window-dressing and part of Mussolini's attempt to drive a wedge between France and Britain. Given the highly alarmist reports from his ambassador in London and the fears of his service chiefs about a war against Britain in the Mediterranean, Mussolini wanted assurances from Laval that he would restrain the Baldwin government. Reports of renewed Anglo-French negotiations in Geneva threw doubt on a favourable response from Paris.

In late October, despite British irritation with Laval, Sir Maurice Peterson, the British expert on East Africa affairs, was sent to Paris to confer with his French counter-part, René de Saint-Quentin. The two men put together a new negotiating package. When the details were discussed in London, it was feared that the new proposed partition of Ethiopia would raise a storm of protest in Britain. The discussions were put on hold until after the British general election on 14 November, the date selected by Baldwin in mid-October in the hope of capitalizing on public enthusiasm for the government's foreign policy. The Conservative victory was, in part, due to its manifesto pledge 'to uphold the Covenant and maintain and increase the efficiency of the League'. Whatever the reasoning, which so often reflected the confusion about what League action actually involved, there was almost universal support for the use of the 'whole collective force' of the League to end Italian aggression in Ethiopia. With the elections over, ministers were prepared to return to the negotiating table. The difficulty was the increasing demand for oil sanctions, both in Geneva and in London. The issue had been raised in Geneva as early as 2 November when the Canadian representative, acting on his own initiative, suggested that oil should be included in the list of omitted sanctions (the agreed sanctions

[22] Maurice Gamelin, *Servir*, Vol. II (Paris, 1946), 177.

came into operation on 18 November) to be imposed on Italy. The committee on sanctions solicited the views of member states. Countries which had supplied oil to Italy agreed to an embargo. The Americans, who were doing a handsome business selling non-embargoed goods, including oil to the Italians, were not deterred by presidential statements intended to discourage such trade. Though Mussolini had stockpiled large oil reserves, he became alarmed and responded by threatening Britain, and warning that he would leave the League of Nations should the oil embargo be imposed. The Duce appealed to the sympathetic Laval; the latter warned Hoare, who needed no such cautioning, that Mussolini would go to war if the oil embargo was implemented. From the Baldwin cabinet's point of view, a war with Italy was the wrong war in the wrong place, and at the wrong time. 'I will not have another war. *I will not*', the ailing George V wrote to Lloyd George. 'If there is another one and we are threatened with being brought into it, I will go to Trafalgar Square and wave a red flag myself sooner than allow this country to be brought in.'[23] The British sought to delay the discussions in Geneva but, refusing to take the initiative, turned to Laval for assistance.

In Paris, under extreme political pressure, Laval needed a solution to the crisis. With the implementation of sanctions, the Franco–Italian military conversations were adjourned and Gamelin watched the collapse of his recently fashioned strategic edifice. In mid-November, the *Quai d'Orsay* learned that the currently pugnacious General Badoglio would replace the ineffective De Bono in Ethiopia. Faced with a stalemate on the Ethiopian fronts and anxious for action before the oil sanctions debate, Mussolini had decided that De Bono would have to go.[24] Badoglio's appointment removed a friend of France from the locus of power in Rome. When the French Chamber of Deputies reassembled at the end of November after five months of vacation, Laval had to defend his deflationary decrees against the attacks from Socialists, Radicals, and Communists. He also faced Paul Reynaud, president of the Centre Republican party and an increasingly influential campaigner for devaluation. In such circumstances, Laval had to accept the scheduling of a debate over Ethiopia. Desperately needing a foreign policy success, the premier wanted British agreement to an Ethiopian solution before the issue of oil was debated in Geneva. Mussolini, alarmed by the possibility of an oil sanction, appealed to Laval who, backed by the equally anxious

[23] Quoted in Kenneth Rose, *King George V* (London, 1983), 387.

[24] Created a marshal as a consolation prize, the elderly De Bono faded from view and would not reappear on the historical stage until his fatal vote against Mussolini on 9 September 1943.

Hoare, managed to postpone the critical meeting of the Committee of Eighteen from 29 November until 12 December. Even then, the timetable for negotiations was short. Laval pushed hard for an immediate settlement.

Faced with warnings of the serious gaps in the system of imperial defence, the Baldwin cabinet endorsed the search for a settlement. Peterson was again sent to Paris and on 23 November discussions began on a new set of proposals presented by the Italian ambassador in Paris. Though the British suspected that Laval was doing 'the Italians' bargaining for them', they had to work with the French, as direct negotiations with Mussolini were impossible. Laval's first proposals were rejected as yielding too much to Rome, but Peterson and St. Quentin worked on a plan that would keep the talks alive. It involved an exchange, absent from the Laval draft, of parts of the Tigre, the Danakil excluding Aussa (which adjoined French Somaliland), and most of the Ogaden in return for the cession of a port (possibly Zeila) and corridor to the Abyssinians. There were indications that the Italians, with an eye on the Geneva clock, might be prepared to talk. Warned by Drummond that Mussolini still counted on French neutrality in the event of war, Hoare demanded that Mussolini be told that France would stand by Britain in case of an attack in the Mediterranean. Not trusting a French warning to the Italian ambassador in Paris, Laval was asked on 25 November to have the message issued directly to Mussolini. Five days later, it was learnt in London that no such message was sent. Vansittart found Laval's behaviour 'intolerable'. Laval, advised by his ambassador in Rome, preferred not to shake the Anglo-French stick while he was trying to court Mussolini. The demanded message was finally sent on 5 December. The British and French military authorities opened separate but parallel discussions to give substance to the theoretical agreements about implementing Article 16.

Convinced of Laval's unreliability, the British nevertheless believed that they needed his assistance. The forthcoming meeting of the Committee of Eighteen focused attention in both capitals on the need to find a diplomatic solution before the oil embargo was imposed. The renewed meetings of the experts in Paris in late November produced a plan, based on extensive Ethiopian concessions to Italy, that the British as well as the French believed Mussolini would accept. Laval wanted a high-level meeting to work out the terms of the offer, which would then be endorsed in Geneva and presented as the League's proposals. An urgent request from Léger on 28 November produced an agreement that Hoare, ordered by his doctors to have an immediate rest, would stop in the French capital in early December on his way to a holiday in Switzerland. Vansittart would accompany him and would remain in

Paris to settle any details. At a cabinet meeting held on 2 December, before Hoare left, it was decided that while in principle Britain would join in oil sanctions, and that military talks with the French should be extended to cover the two air forces, an attempt should be made to begin 'peace talks' with Mussolini. It was extraordinary that nothing was said in the cabinet of a detailed plan for settlement, nor was there any discussion of what such a settlement should contain. The foreign secretary was instructed to come back to the cabinet only 'if the peace talks did not offer any reasonable prospect of settlement', or if the military conversations showed that 'France was not willing to co-operate effectively'.[25] Contrary to what was claimed subsequently, Hoare went to Paris with the cabinet's approval. He was neither tricked by Laval nor misled by the over-anxious Vansittart. He went to reach a bargain with the French that would prove acceptable to the Italians.

This was the background to the well-known 'Hoare–Laval plan'. Laval, dressed in his usual black suit and white tie, seated his guests on his right and his advisors on his left. He painted a grim picture of the consequences of oil sanctions: an Italian attack against Britain, French involvement, and Hitler quietly waiting in the wings to see the results. Time was short. Hoare and Vansittart needed no prompting and quickly came to the point. Hoare asked if France would support Britain in the event of an Italian attack. French co-operation, Laval answered, would depend on the outcome of the present talks. He would, however, authorize the beginning of military staff talks. The discussion then shifted to the subject of the peace plans on which the officials had been working intermittently for six weeks. The proposals presented by Laval on 7 December, while not basically different from earlier recommendations, conceded more to Mussolini than any previous offer. Hard bargaining followed, and some points were left unsettled, but both sides appeared satisfied with the results. Hoare was persuaded to stay an extra day to conclude the negotiations. The Ethiopians were to give Italy all of Eastern Tigre already in Italian hands, and the Danagil and Ogaden regions, amounting to about two-thirds of Ethiopia. They were to receive in exchange a corridor through Eritrea to Assab, a port on the Red Sea—a 'corridor for camels', according to *The Times*. The Italians would be given extensive economic rights in south and south-west Abyssinia under League auspices. These accessions would nearly double the area of Italian Somaliland. The British cabinet approved the plan on 9 December and on the following day urged that Ethiopia be pressed to accept it, and instructed Eden, who while very uneasy about proposals which ceded so much to Mussolini, advised acceptance, to support the peace plan at Geneva. Blocking Laval's attempt to force the emperor's

[25] TNA: PRO, CAB 23/82, 50 (25)2.

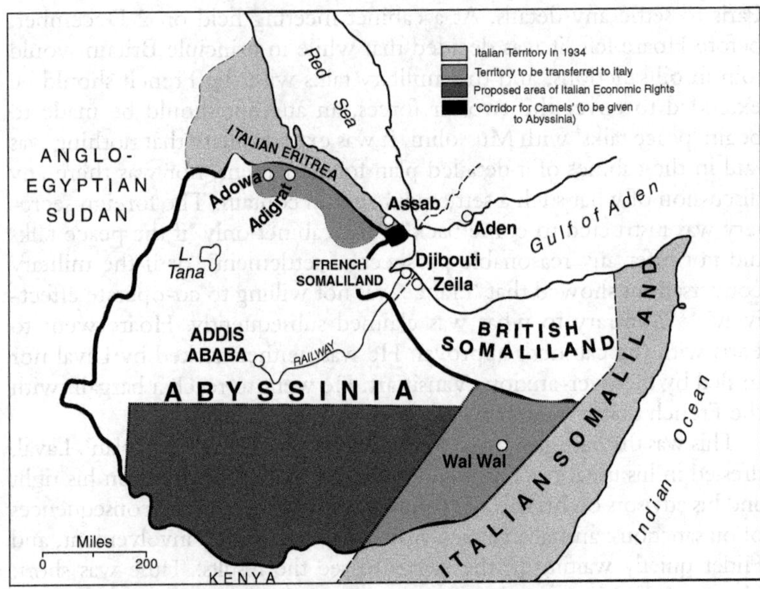

Map 2. Hoare–Laval Proposals, 1935

hand by giving prior notification to Mussolini, the cabinet authorized telegrams to be sent to Rome and Addis Ababa simultaneously. Haile Selassie was cautioned to give the proposals 'careful and favourable consideration . . . and on no account to reject them lightly'.[26]

The final bargaining took place between Laval and Vansittart, who was still in Paris. The well satisfied Laval believed that he had scored a diplomatic *coup*. He was confident that Mussolini would accept the proposed solution and that in the face of Anglo-French co-operation, the Ethiopians, but more importantly the League states, would accept the settlement. At the French Council of Ministers on 10 December, Herriot was the main objector, but made little impression on his fellow ministers. Chambrun was instructed to warn Mussolini, with whom Laval had been in daily contact, that Laval had gone as far as he could with the British, and that if this proposal was rejected he would cease his conciliatory efforts. According to Aloisi, Mussolini was willing to 'interrupt the war', take the territorial offer, and wait before finishing the job. Other Italian diplomats were more doubtful. Meanwhile Mussolini's son, Vittorio, was enjoying the sensation of dropping bombs on Ethiopian tents and horsemen.

[26] Quoted in R. A. C. Parker, 'Great Britain, France and the Ethiopian Crisis, 1935–1936', *English Historical Review*, 89: 351 (1974), 322.

The immediate problems for the British cabinet began on 9 December, when the details of the Hoare–Laval plan, probably leaked by an unsympathetic *Quai d'Orsay* official (possibly Pierre Comert, chief of the press services, or even Léger himself), were published by André Géraud ('Pertinax') in *L'Echo de Paris* and Geneviève Tabouis in *L'Oeuvre*. Due to an impromptu press conference held by Hoare at the British embassy, the London and New York papers published fairly accurate accounts on the same day. There was an immediate and strongly hostile reaction, both in the House of Commons and in the national press. On the afternoon of the following day, with the full text of the agreement published, Baldwin had to face MPs. Unable to satisfy his listeners with a series of evasions, he called on the faithful to put their trust in him. It was the growing chorus of opposition among his own backbenchers that led him to desert Hoare in order to convince the public of the cabinet's ignorance of the whole affair. Eden, after an embarrassed performance in the Commons, scurried off to Geneva to attend the session of the Committee of Eighteen, called to discuss the projected oil embargo, only to be met with an equally heavy barrage of criticism from its non-French members. During the next nine days, opposition to the 'policy of scuttle' spread through the ranks of the Conservative party. Baldwin and Chamberlain knew that most of their backbenchers were in revolt. Critical motions signed by government supporters and hostile speeches in the Foreign Affairs Committee left the cabinet in no doubt about the strength of parliamentary feeling. 'Nothing could be worse than our position', Chamberlain wrote in his diary. 'Our whole prestige in foreign affairs at home and abroad has tumbled to pieces like a house of cards. If we had to fight the election all over again, we should probably be beaten.'[27] On 16 December, Hoare, who had a blackout while ice-skating and suffered a broken nose, returned from Switzerland, already warned of the growing political storm. The bruised foreign secretary was ordered to bed. Chamberlain was sent to explain that the cabinet doubted whether they could continue to support the peace proposals in the face of the public reaction against it. On 18 December, the prime minister referred gloomily to a 'worse situation in the House of Commons than he had ever known', and the cabinet decided both to jettison the plan and sacrifice Hoare.[28] The absent foreign secretary was told either to recant or resign. Deserted by his

[27] Neville Chamberlain, *The Neville Chamberlain Diary Letters*, Vol. IV, *The Downing Street Years, 1934–1940*, ed. Robert Self (Aldershot, 2005), 166 (15 December 1935).

[28] R. A. C. Parker, *Chamberlain and Appeasement: British Policy and the Coming of the Second World War* (New York, 1993), 55.

colleagues, Hoare resigned that evening. The Hoare–Laval plan was dead.

'What a pity', Pompeo Aloisi, wrote in his diary. In Italy, sanctions were causing prices to rise. By January 1936, as compared with the previous year, Italian exports had dropped by nearly half and imports by well over a third. Yet it was highly doubtful that Mussolini would have accepted the offer, even as the basis for further negotiation, unless the whole of the Ethiopian empire was put on the table. In any case, Baldwin's announcement that the Hoare–Laval offer was 'completely and absolutely dead', buried the possibility of a political compromise. Laval made desperate but unsuccessful attempts to induce the Duce to act, despite the British disavowal. He won some breathing space at Geneva where, by proposing in the Committee of Eighteen that the peace plan should be examined, he convinced the overwhelmingly pro-sanctionist membership to postpone further consideration of the oil embargo. Eden went along with Laval and then returned home to help inter the battered plan. The dropping of the Hoare–Laval pact was one of the very few inter-war examples of the government in London giving way to public pressure, at least as it was filtered through parliament. Baldwin tried to contain the political damage by appointing Anthony Eden, lucky not to have been more directly involved in the Paris negotiations, to take Hoare's place. Though Eden was more pro-League than some of his ministerial colleagues, he was far less resolute than the public assumed or his autobiography suggests. By this quick and adroit move, Baldwin, ever the master politician, restored unity within the party and demonstrated its support for collective security, without introducing any radical alteration in Britain's diplomacy. Vansittart was left in place despite rumours that he would be sent abroad. His personal relations with Eden were never good and this was not to be a harmonious team. Churning out endless (if wonderfully quotable) minutes and memoranda, some quite impressive, but others woolly, and many far too long, Vansittart was soon to suffer a diminution of influence in the highest quarters.

The cabinet expected that Eden would continue the Hoare–Vansittart line, and was not disappointed. The new foreign secretary tried to postpone a decision on the imposition of oil sanctions, questioned their effectiveness, and underlined the possible military consequences of their imposition. It was not until 22 January 1936 that the Committee of Eighteen met again to discuss the oil embargo, and then only to appoint a sub-committee to enquire into its practicality. These delaying tactics were fully acceptable to Laval as well as to Mussolini. There was some optimism in London that the campaign in Ethiopia would go on and the current sanctions policy would force Mussolini to compromise.

In mid-December, the Ethiopian forces launched a counter-attack to contain the Italian invasion in the north, and prepared for an invasion of Italian Somaliland where the enemy's forces were weak. Within a few weeks, this counter-campaign began to falter; Badoglio, using bombers and poison gas (used before against 'primitive people' by France and Spain, but never on such a scale) sprayed from aircraft, halted the advance and went on to the offensive. Until February, when Badoglio routed the Ethiopian armies, the British military authorities remained optimistic. With no visible signs of Italian action against Britain, anxieties about a 'mad-dog attack' subsided. The public debate over the oil embargo continued, but on a reduced scale. Domestic news took the headlines. King George V took ill over Christmas and died on 20 January. There would be a state funeral and a new king.

The collapse of the Hoare–Laval agreement was a personal setback to Laval but did not produce any major change in French policy. The French premier was vilified in the British press as the real author of the abortive diplomatic sell-out to Mussolini. This was, of course, a travesty of the truth. Time, however, was running out for Laval. The failure of his peace efforts did not endear him to Mussolini. Well-founded French intelligence reports of an Italo-German *rapprochement* boded ill for the continuing hopes to keep Italy on France's side. The British, anxious to dissociate themselves from the French leader, took umbrage at French approaches to Hitler, while launching their own. These separate initiatives in the winter months confirmed Hitler's belief that neither country would actively defend international law. Laval's 549 decrees failed to produce a balanced budget and the government was again facing a financial and political crisis. The countryside was quiet but the cities seethed with discontent. The seemingly imperturbable leader nonetheless clung to office, surviving the critical autumn debate on the government's financial and economic policies. The right, whatever its doubts about some of Laval's policies, did not want to bring the left to power. The left, still divided despite the *rapprochement* of Radicals, Socialists, and Communists, failed to find any alternative economic programme on which they could agree. The focus on domestic affairs allowed Laval to survive the fierce attacks on the Hoare–Laval agreement. He was bitterly criticized during the Chamber debates on 27 and 28 December. A vote of no-confidence was defeated by 297 votes to 276, but more than one-third of the Radical party voted against the government. Herriot was constantly pressed to distance himself from Laval in anticipation of the spring elections. On 18 December, Daladier, the Radical most clearly associated with the Popular Front, replaced Herriot as chairman of the party. With no breakthrough on either the economic or diplomatic fronts, Laval could not keep the loyalty of the Radicals.

On 22 January 1936, four of the six Radical ministers, including Herriot, resigned. Without waiting for an adverse vote of confidence, Laval left office the next day. With only three months to go before the elections, Albert Sarraut, an indecisive figure on the right of the Radical party, formed a caretaker government whose main task was to maintain the status quo and prepare for the electoral campaign. The government continued to survive financially because the Bank of France agreed, in private, to rediscount Treasury bills which were now flooding the market. In February, Blum was beaten up by members of the Action Française. There was a massive protest march in Paris and the 'anti-Fascist' parties attracted large numbers of new supporters. It was a Sarraut interim cabinet that had the misfortune of being in power when Hitler marched into the Rhineland.

The British had as little confidence in the new French cabinet as in its predecessor. The difficulties in Paris only confirmed ministerial views that France was undependable, its leaders faithless, and its finances in a mess. In mid-February, as a last resort, the French Treasury was able to secure a short-term loan in London to stave off the monetary crisis. The 'pompous and pretentious' Flandin, a far less able version of Laval, replaced the latter at the *Quai d'Orsay*. He would try to continue his predecessor's policies but sought an improvement in relations with London. At first, this seemed possible as neither government wanted to proceed to oil sanctions, but the Italian military triumph changed the scenario. Badoglio's defeat of the Ethiopian armies in mid-February opened the way to Addis Ababa. Mussolini spoke confidently of victory within six weeks. Faced with a shortened time-table and the prospect of a massive blow to the prestige of his government and the League, Eden changed course and with Baldwin's assistance won cabinet consent to an oil embargo on 26 February. The British *volte-face* was hardly welcome news for the French, when Flandin was approached for support. Chambrun reported from Rome that oil sanctions could not stop an Italian victory in Ethiopia, but would prejudice the Franco-Italian military accords and force Italy out of the League of Nations. Official Italian speeches and press reports warned of a redefinition of Italy's obligations under the Locarno treaty. Chambrun urged Flandin to oppose the British initiative as he remained convinced that the Duce still favoured the French orientation, and would play the German card only if necessary. The *Quai d'Orsay*, too, believed that Mussolini was vacillating between Paris and Berlin.

In fact, Mussolini had made his choice. On 7 January 1936, the Duce, in conversation with Ulrich von Hassell, the highly capable German ambassador in Rome, had raised the possibility of a German–Austrian non-aggression pact that would 'in practice bring Austria in to Germany's wake, so that she could pursue no other foreign policy than one parallel with that of Germany'.[29] He told Hassell that he did not object to Austria becoming a *de facto* German satellite state as long as she maintained her independence. The Mussolini–Hassell conversation was only the latest step in the Italian–German *rapprochement* that had begun in the summer of 1935. Once the war against Ethiopia started in earnest, the Italians privately pressed their case for closer links between the two regimes. They were met with a favourable response, though coupled with warnings that German assistance to Italy would have to be circumspect in order not to cause problems with Britain. Schacht, among others, underlined the need for strict neutrality in order not to offend the British but, in a veiled way, offered the Italians an economic agreement and increased coal supplies in return for an understanding over Austria. Bernardo Attolico, the new Italian ambassador in Berlin (as well as officials in Rome), cautioned Mussolini in his reports on these meetings, to go carefully before compromising Austrian independence for an arrangement with Germany. Mussolini pushed ahead. The Hoare–Laval fiasco only strengthened his determination to proceed with the full conquest of Ethiopia, and with the agreement with Hitler. His declaration on 28 December that the January 1935 accords with Laval were now defunct underlined his new orientation. Hitler continued to temporize, waiting to see whether Mussolini's words would be matched by his deeds. Stresa was fresh in his memory. It was still possible that once Italy secured her victory in Africa, the Duce would be less amenable to a solution of the Austrian question and a settlement with Berlin. These considerations were not unconnected with Hitler's timing of the Rhineland *coup*. Mussolini, too, did not quite trust Hitler's intentions, for he authorized further clandestine shipments of arms to Austria in late 1935 and these continued well into 1936. Throughout 1936 and into 1937, the three armed services continued with preparations for war against Germany, though the naval staff no longer gave it priority over the war against Britain and/or France. There were further reasons for Mussolini's caution. In the belief that Britain would oppose his imperial ambitions in the Mediterranean, if his enterprise was to be achieved, the Germans still would have to be won over to an actively anti-British policy. Nor could Mussolini ignore Italian public opinion which, despite a massive anti-British propaganda campaign, remained pro-Austrian and even more strongly anti-German.

In Geneva on 2 March, Flandin refused to agree to the imposition of oil sanctions and suggested that Italy might be ready to discuss terms. While the British were prepared to back a new peace effort, Eden

[29] *DGFP*, Ser. C, Vol. IV, No. 485.

insisted on announcing British backing for the oil embargo. On the next day, Flandin reverted to Laval's device of linking collective security in Africa with similar British action in Europe. France would not support oil sanctions, he warned, unless assured of British support in the Rhineland. Eden, like Hoare, refused to be drawn, opposing any commitment to France and any linkage between the Ethiopian affair and the Rhineland. Flandin demanded to know whether Britain would be 'ready to support France, even alone, in the maintenance of the Demilitarized Zone' against Germany?[30] The British cabinet debated how best to answer without any discussion of Locarno, for ministers were considering a unilateral deal with Germany over the Rhineland. The problem was becoming more acute as the question of Hitler's next move in Europe was discussed in every European chancellery.

Hitler's march into the Rhineland on 7 March shifted European attention away from Ethiopia and onto Germany. Though Mussolini had been warned of the forthcoming move by Hassell, he was taken by surprise by the actual remilitarization. It was not until late April, with an Italian triumph in sight, that Ethiopia again became the main issue of Anglo-French debate. The League Committee of Thirteen had given up any further effort to force concessions from the Ethiopians to satisfy Mussolini. For the French, however, the prospect of the Rhineland fortifications and the fear of an Italian–German agreement made Italy of critical importance. Italian friendship would release army divisions from the Franco-Italian frontier. Flandin made one more effort before the 26 April – 3 May elections to secure a joint intervention in the Ethiopian affair, but Eden refused to co-operate. He was unwilling to accept that the Ethiopian campaign was almost over, and dismissed Flandin's warnings of an Italo-German understanding. On 5 May, Addis Ababa was occupied. Four days later Mussolini proclaimed the annexation of Ethiopia and the establishment of the Fascist Empire. From his Palazzo Venezia balcony, the Duce invoked the memory of ancient Rome. On 12 May, Pope Pius XI expressed the Vatican's satisfaction at the 'triumphal happiness of a great and good people' in an outcome which he saw as the prelude to 'a new European and world peace'.[31] On the same day, the Italian delegation left Geneva, but not the League.

Haile Selassie, after a difficult escape, arrived in Britain on 3 June. There were no high officials to greet him, but thousands lined his anticipated route to the Ethiopian embassy. Sanctions remained in place despite Eden's scepticism about their utility and the widespread feeling in London, as in Geneva, that it was time to bury the smelling

[30] *DBFP*, 2nd ser., Vol. XVI, Annexe to No. 20.

[31] *Il Giornale d'Italia*, 13 May 1936.

corpse. Chamberlain, undoubtedly the most influential man in the cabinet, and Baldwin's heir apparent, observed at a banquet on the evening of 10 June that the continuation or intensification of sanctions was 'the very midsummer of madness'.[32] A week later, the cabinet agreed to lift the sanctions. On 30 June, at the Assembly meeting, a dignified Haile Selassie, after reviewing the 'fearful tactics' used by the Italians against his country, rebuked the fifty-two member nations of the League, including 'the most powerful in the world', for failing Ethiopia, and the cause of all small nations that were the victims of aggression. The lifting of sanctions was a blow to collective security; to 'the very existence of the League; of the trust placed by states in international treaties'.[33] On 4 July, the League assembly voted to lift the sanctions against Italy.

The Hoare–Laval fiasco, and the subsequent withdrawal of sanctions, had repercussions throughout the Geneva community. The weakness of the League of Nations and the futility of Article 16 led many of the smaller nations to re-think their policies. Without withdrawing from the League, the Nordic states, along with the Netherlands, Spain, and Switzerland, declared in July 1936 that as long as the Covenant was applied 'so incompletely and inconsistently', they no longer felt obliged to participate in sanctions against an aggressor. In some countries, as in Norway, the return to a narrower concept of neutrality was accompanied by new rearmament measures. Finland, which had played an active role in Geneva, now looked for protection elsewhere, particularly to Sweden and the other Scandinavian countries, should there be a Great Power conflict in the Baltic. For Estonia and Latvia, the Ethiopian affair represented one more step in their retreat from the Geneva security system, that had begun with the Manchurian incident and the failure of the disarmament talks. In the case of Switzerland, Ethiopia proved to be the definitive moment in its diplomacy during the years leading up to the outbreak of war. Forced to chose between its obligations to the League of Nations, already modified to exclude Swiss military operations at the time of its joining, and its support for Italy, whose assistance was needed to help in maintaining an equilibrium in relations with Switzerland's largest neighbours, France and Germany, Berne chose the Italian option. Its opposition to the League sanctions regime not only exposed the limits of the League's punitive measures, but propelled Switzerland down a path that would lead, in 1938, to its exit from the

[32] 'The League and Sanctions: Mr Chamberlain's Conclusions', *The Times*, 10 January 1936, 10.

[33] Quoted in Thomas M. Coffey, *Lion by the Tail: The Story of the Italian–Ethiopian War* (London, 1974), 344.

League of Nations and its return to a position of 'integral', or absolute, neutrality in foreign relations. Poland had gone along with sanctions, despite considerable sympathy for Italy, which had always been a possible ally in south-eastern Europe, to keep in line with France. There was no love lost, however, between Warsaw and Geneva, and no trust in Laval, 'a little man' according to Beck, but preferable to the pro-Soviet Herriot. The Little Entente countries were particularly hard hit by the Hoare–Laval revelations. Though Beneš carefully concealed his feelings, he understood that the Anglo-French agreement set a dangerous precedent for carving up a weak country in order to secure a Great Power settlement. Titulescu, the foreign minister of Romania, was infuriated by Laval's devious diplomacy, for he had been at the forefront of the pro-sanctionist lobby at the League, and anxious to check Mussolini. A wave of Francophobia swept the foreign ministries at Bucharest and Belgrade. As the Little Entente economies, above all that of Yugoslavia, were particularly vulnerable to the sanctions imposed on Italy and no British or French steps were taken to assist them, the Hoare–Laval pact was considered an unpardonable 'sell-out', and France the main culprit in the Geneva fiasco. The final months of the crisis only confirmed Little Entente doubts about French reliability.

The Italian occupation upset the equilibrium in the eastern Mediterranean and resulted in changes in the positions of both Turkey and Egypt. The Turkish leaders, alarmed by the signs of Italian aggression and militarism, were able to negotiate a successful revision of the Straits Convention concluded at Lausanne in 1923. The British, recognizing the importance of Turkish goodwill in order to protect their lifelines to the Near and Middle East, abandoned their long-standing opposition to revision, and agreed to a new Straits regime, negotiated at Montreux in the summer of 1936, which met the Turkish demands. The Straits Commission was abolished and Turkey regained full sovereignty over the Straits and the right to fortify the Dardanelles. Merchant shipping was free to navigate the Straits but Turkey could close the Straits to warships in wartime or when it was threatened and could refuse transit for merchant ships belonging to countries at war with Turkey. Severe restrictions were imposed with regard to the number and tonnage of foreign warships passing through the Straits which could only stay in the Black Sea for up to three weeks. The Soviet Union would have preferred a convention handing control of the Straits to the Black Sea powers alone, but the Turks would not agree to this. To satisfy the Soviets, who had long sought to strengthen the security of their southern flank through a revision of the Lausanne agreement, the ships of the Black Sea powers were exempted from most of these restrictions and were permitted to send capital ships of any tonnage as well as submarines through the Straits. The Turkish control of the Straits, and their closure to military shipping in time of war, restricted the Royal Navy's freedom to strike at the Soviet Union but Moscow now depended for its extra security on Turkey's honest implementation of the agreement. At Montreux, the Turkish negotiators moved cautiously between the conflicting claims of the British and Russians, but tended to favour the British and laid the basis for a future *rapprochement* between the two countries.

The Italian action in Libya broke the deadlocked Anglo-Egyptian negotiations over a new treaty on the status of Egypt, formerly a British protectorate. The Wafd majority in Egypt sought full independence and control of the Sudan; the British wanted a treaty that would preserve, if mask, their rule and confirm their rights to control Egyptian foreign and defence policy. The invasion of Ethiopia changed the situation as the Egyptian nationalists took alarm at the increasing number of Italian troops moving through the Suez Canal and the massive reinforcements of Libya, fearing the occupation of the unarmed country lying between Libya and Ethopia. Needing British military and naval support, the nationalists approached London for a resumption of the treaty talks, offering a secret pledge of support in the event of an Anglo-Italian war. When, however, no British action followed and it appeared that London was only interested in a settlement with Mussolini without regard to Egyptian sovereignty, demands for the resumption of parliamentary government and a new treaty were accompanied by public rioting. The check in Abyssinia, the Arab revolt in Palestine in the summer of 1936, and potential Italian threats against British Somaliland, Kenya, and the Sudan convinced the British cabinet that they had to compromise over the issue of independence, though without sacrificing any military interest. In the new treaty, concluded on 26 August 1936, following extremely difficult negotiations, Britain recognized Egypt as a fully sovereign and independent state with the right to return Egyptian forces to Sudan, which was restored to condominium status. Limited British forces were to remain in peacetime, with the right of unlimited reinforcements in an international emergency or war. The British army and RAF were given special privileges in peacetime and in case of war or threat of war, the promise of unrestricted British reinforcements and provision of additional military facilities. Despite the achievement of independence, little was won in substantive terms, and British military forces remained in Egypt. The nationalists had won enough to prevent further revolts but relations between Cairo and London remained uneasy, not helped by the imperious attitude and behaviour of Sir Miles Lampson, the former High Commissioner and now British ambassador to Egypt.

The Ethiopian crisis had further European ramifications. In Moscow, the Hoare–Laval pact was a bombshell, and the subsequent collapse of 'collective security' a blow to Litvinov's position. It was only after much hesitation, because the Soviets had good political and economic reasons for cultivating Mussolini, that the commissar for foreign affairs had succeeded in convincing the *Politburo* to adopt a pro-sanctions policy though, in practice, the embargo was only partially applied. Stalin, mainly concerned with domestic matters, but fully aware of the threats from Germany and Japan, was exceedingly cautious about involvement in what he and Molotov saw as a struggle between the imperialist powers. There was a powerful anti-British current flowing in Moscow, which Whitehall's attitude towards the Franco-Soviet pact only intensified. It was mainly by portraying sanctions as a demonstration against colonialism in all its forms that Litvinov won his battle in the *Politburo*. He was left, however, in the awkward position of trying to support the League while maintaining his lines with Britain and France. The French Senate finally ratified the hard-won Franco-Soviet pact on 12 March. Like Hoare, Litvinov wanted the League of Nations publicly vindicated, but hoped that the Italians and Ethiopians could settle their differences without further League intervention. He certainly did not wish to take the lead in the Council, preferring to let the British and French set the pace rather than risk Soviet isolation. Throughout the crisis, Soviet attention was focused on Germany. It was, consequently, with some relief that the Soviets received the news of Haile Selassie's flight. They now assumed that sanctions would be lifted and the Council could concentrate on Germany. Litvinov tried to tie the ending of sanctions with an Italian promise to support the principle of collective security, and the League of Nations. It was far too late for such an initiative. In many ways, the whole Ethiopian episode was a defeat for the Soviets. Britain and France were hardly grateful for Litvinov's defence of the Covenant, which only complicated their dual policy. Worse still, anticipating a new crisis over the Rhineland, the Hoare–Laval revelations convinced Litvinov that neither Britain nor France would try to check Hitler, but would seek a settlement with Berlin instead. It was hardly surprising that the 'isolationists' in Moscow increased their influence at Litvinov's expense.

Italy's 'little colonial adventure' which pinned down substantial forces in Africa and cost far more than Italy could afford, irreparably damaged the League of Nations. If Mussolini's action in East Africa had taken place before 1914, it would have been dismissed as a successful, if ruthless, imperial war fought against a backward people. The Great War and the peace settlement, however, had altered the rules of international behaviour. Mussolini's successful challenge to the new conventions undercut the whole concept of collective security. No future Great Power conflict would be handled in Geneva; no state, whatever its size, would believe in the effectiveness of League-imposed sanctions. The real culprit was not really the League but Britain and France, for since its inception, the League's peacekeeping functions had always depended on Great Power co-operation and action. The fiasco in Geneva revealed the gap between the myth of the League and its reality to the discredit of the British and French leadership. The League of Nations remained active and, indeed, some of its non-political work benefitted from the increasing association of the Americans with its economic and social committees, but it had visibly failed to fulfil its chief functions. Collective action against aggressors, the settlement of inter-state disputes, and the promotion of disarmament, were at the core of the Covenant. The record was one of failure. The consequences were immediately felt during the Rhineland crisis.

This 'anachronistic imperial war' did more than reveal the weaknesses of the Geneva system. It affected the European balance of power and opened to question the British and French commitment to its maintenance. Mussolini's move towards Nazi Germany made, at the least, the creation of a common front against Hitler more difficult. The failure to act decisively, and the propensity to wait upon events, exposed the weakness of both the British and French governments in the face of aggression. For both countries, the problem of Germany was far more dangerous than an imperialist Italy, yet they could not disregard the League of Nations. Both attempted to follow a dual policy, the preservation of the Stresa front to contain Germany but also the maintenance of their public positions with support of the League of Nations. The marked divergence between these two policies became obvious in Britain with the leaking of the Hoare–Laval pact, when the whole public edifice collapsed.

The British might have acted alone. They could have enforced the closure of the Suez Canal which would have put Italian forces in Abyssinia on the defensive and dependent on accumulated supplies. In combination with oil sanctions, the aggressor could have been thwarted without any damage to Britain's Mediterranean or global position. But the Baldwin government did not want to act. It tried to straddle the fence, conciliating public opinion by supporting the League, and seeking an agreement with Mussolini. The Duce became convinced that the British (and French) Empire was on its last legs. He ordered his military to plan for the capture of Egypt, a possibility he attempted only in 1940. Doubtful about French support, Mussolini looked to Berlin to protect his back door. The Germans were incredulous at the revelations of the Hoare–Laval pact, having assumed initially that Mussolini's recklessness would have been checked by Britain. Hitler's respect for Mussolini increased, and he brought forward his plans to remilitarize the Rhineland. In August 1939, the German chancellor would remind his generals of Mussolini's resolution in 1935 in the face of British promises to uphold the League. Would Britain prove any more resolute over Poland?

At the time, the British blamed Laval and the French for their failure to check Mussolini. In fact, the cabinet majority had always preferred to come to an arrangement with Rome at Ethiopian expense. The French were equally maladroit in their *entente* diplomacy, asking for assurances from Britain that Laval knew London would not give in order to avoid taking a decisive stand. Laval accused the British of hiding behind the League and refusing to give France the support in Europe that would allow it to pursue a tougher line in Rome. But he too, even more than Hoare, was intent on maintaining the friendship with Italy which he believed to be crucial for France. Neither the British nor French governments showed much interest in Ethiopia. The former's main concern was the protection of its imperial position in Egypt and the Suez Canal. Despite the high alarm of the service chiefs in London, that position could have been easily maintained without surrendering to Mussolini. Not only were both governments indecisive in their policies, but each blamed the other for their failure to act. Both were particularly bitter about Laval's behaviour, and his behind-the-scenes contacts with Mussolini. Sir Horace Rumbold, the ex-ambassador to Germany, told the editor of *The Times* in December 1935 that 'the only white thing about Laval was his tie and even that was only washed occasionlly (*sic*)'.[34] While their respective policies actually pointed in the same direction, London and Paris failed to present a united front. Accusations of disloyalty and double-dealing on both sides proved a disastrous background for the trials to come. The Ethiopian crisis was one of the lowest points in Anglo-French relations during the whole of the 1930s.

III

While on both sides of the Channel ministers anticipated a move into the Rhineland, Hitler's action on 7 March 1936 took them by surprise. It was probably only in early February that Hitler decided to use the ratification of the Franco-Soviet pact as a justification for a German move. He had spoken earlier of his intention to move no later than the

[34] Quoted in Michael Dockrill, *British Establishment Perspectives on France, 1936–1940* (Basingstoke and New York, 1999), 27.

spring of 1937, and it was thought in London and Paris that he would wait until the *Wehrmacht* was better equipped, and in a strong enough position to march without anxiety. Germany was to host the Olympic Games in the summer of 1936; these were expected to give the regime world respectability and prestige. There were reports of serious strains in the economy, but these did not make a move into the Rhineland necessary. Why did Hitler speed up his timetable? He may have grown impatient; it was almost a year since the announcement of conscription, and the regime would benefit from a new success. A move into the Rhineland would provide a useful tonic for the masses. More important was the shift in the international balance in Germany's favour. Mussolini's war, with its attendant 'horrors', was engaging the world's attention and a bloodless *coup* on German soil would contrast favourably with the Italian action in Africa. The Italians had denounced their pact with France and the fissures in the Anglo-French partnership could not have escaped Hitler's attention. Under these circumstances, the remilitarization of the Rhineland would disrupt the entire Locarno structure. There were those in Hitler's immediate entourage who advised against the move. Neurath, however, acting on his own intelligence reports, advised his chief that France would not retaliate, and urged action. Hitler sought support from Mussolini before springing his surprise. The German ambassador was recalled from Rome and a diplomatic campaign planned to make sure that Italy would not co-operate with France and Britain against any German violation of the Locarno agreements. Already reassured by Hassell, Hitler was informed on 22 February that Italy would not participate in any 'action by Britain and France against Germany occasioned by an alleged breach by Germany of the Locarno treaty'.[35] Hitler used the debates in Paris over the ratification of the Franco-Soviet treaty, held during February, as an excuse. Aware of the weaknesses of the Sarraut government with its hundred-day mandate, and the strong opposition to the Soviet treaty inside the Chamber, the debates only confirmed the view of the *Auswärtiges Amt* that France would not fight unless actually attacked. They would have been even more confident had they known of the discussions at the highest levels of the French army.

The French knew that the remilitarization was on Hitler's calendar, yet neither the chiefs of staff nor the diplomats considered a military response to a German move in the Rhineland as either appropriate or possible. The bleak mood at the Rue Saint Dominique was, in part, a reaction to the Ethiopian crisis and the feared loss of the Italian connection. But it had more to do with the exaggerated view of German

[35] *DGFP*, Ser. C, Vol. IV, No. 579 (22 February 1936).

military preparedness, and the disastrous state of the French army and air force. The intelligence services overestimated Germany's military capability and the pacing of the German rearmament programme. To give weight to their counsels of caution as well as to highlight the need for greater funding, the French military chiefs further inflated the intelligence figures they were given. There was also a widely-held belief, shared by the British, that a dictatorial regime could and would efficiently mobilize the country's industrial capacity, already so much greater than that of France, to equip its armies. The intelligence services failed to identify the deficiencies in *matériel* that made the mobilization of a large German field force and air force virtually impossible. Without accurate information, they consistently adopted a 'worst case scenario' that overestimated the capacity of the German armaments industry. However, it was the dismal state of the French army and air force, and the unwillingness of successive governments to address their problems, that preoccupied the French chiefs of staff. 1935 represented the low point in interwar defence spending; a modest start was subsequently made on modernization. Two-year military service was reinstated, and the first orders given for the artillery, light tanks, anti-aircraft guns, and ammunition, which were so desperately needed. For years, what funds had been available had been channelled to completing the defensive fortifications of the Maginot Line, the only politically acceptable form of large-scale defence spending. The conflict between Laval's policies of 'sound finance' and the generals' hopes to re-equip their army bedevilled civil–military relations and soured the already troubled relationship between the military and their industrial suppliers. Doctrinal disunity and the inability of the army to agree on priorities and prototypes, quite apart from the absence of government guarantees and funding, discouraged the private investment needed for industrial expansion. Key firms such as Renault, the country's largest tank manufacturer, refused to accept the military's specifications and rejected ministerial demands that the company decentralize its operations for security purposes. Testimony before the Senate's army commission in March 1936, after the Rhineland remilitarization, revealed glaring weaknesses in the armaments chain, revelations that were to convince the military as well as politicians that key defence industries would have to be nationalized if rearmament was to become a practical proposition.

Despite expectations of a German move in the Rhineland, French military planning was curiously dilatory; no detailed plans were prepared for the eventuality. The general staff had already written off the demilitarized zone as a serious factor in French strategy, and the possibilities for mobile warfare created by aircraft, tanks, and personnel carriers had further reduced its strategic value. Gamelin had come to accept the move as inevitable. In his view, given the state of the French army and the reductions in defence allocations, any action against Germany would be dangerous, if not disastrous. The 'thinking man's general', Gamelin was, beneath a mask of outward calm, a deeply emotional man. He had never recovered fully from those days on the Marne when as Joffre's *chef de cabinet* he had faced the prospect of a German sweep through France. Given the financial parsimony of successive French governments, Gamelin did not believe that his antiquated army, despite its numerical margin, could successfully face a German attack in the west. The French mobilization plan adopted in January 1935 (Plan D *bis*), Gamelin's first after Weygand's retirement, showed that the army would not fight for the Rhineland, but would leave open its future options depending on the direction of the German attack and the ability of France to create a defensive coalition. After the remilitarization of the Rhineland, Gamelin expected Hitler to move eastwards in order to secure the resources needed for Germany's hegemonic war. France's best chance to avoid a conflict that would put her own security at risk was to open up a central European theatre. Whatever Gamelin's hopes in the latter direction, he never abandoned his assumption that, however inadequate the British contribution to the opening stages of a European war, close co-operation with Britain was central to French safety. In his post-war defence, *Servir,* he wrote, 'Whatever the significance of our relations with Italy, all that mattered compelled us to maintain solidarity with London. For us Italy was important; Britain was essential.'[36] There was no question of France responding alone to any German action in the Rhineland by an invasion of Germany, or using force to dislodge German troops from the demilitarized zone. Gamelin's main interest in the Rhineland was not to protect its demilitarized status but to use the German threat as a way to draw Britain into a three-power (Britain, Belgium, and France) military alliance to replace the militarily useless Locarno pact.

The *Quai d'Orsay*, for its part, had to consider the effects of an unopposed Rhineland *coup* on France's continental allies and friends; Belgium, Czechoslovakia, and Poland were of particular concern. To do nothing would undermine their confidence and expose French weakness. Flandin, above all, feared isolation. Memories of the aftermath of the Ruhr occupation ran deep. So did worries about the near exhaustion of the Treasury's reserves and the spectre of the forthcoming election. The franc was on the verge of collapse and the election campaign was one of the most bitter and divisive of the interwar period. In their numerous exchanges with the defence chiefs during February, the

[36] Gamelin, *Servir,* 174–175.

diplomats pressed for some form of military planning, not just as a response to any German move but, if possible, to discourage the Reich from engaging in the enterprise. The generals refused to contemplate any form of preventive action. Any occupation of the demilitarized zone would make France appear as the aggressor. Gamelin, and his views were shared by the majority of officers, dismissed any military demonstration as unrealistic and dangerous. Flandin's proposal of a preventive collective *démarche* in Berlin, followed by talks over the status of the demilitarized zone proved still-born, as were his efforts to open discussions with London and Berlin. On 27 February, the council of ministers agreed that in response to a flagrant violation of Article 42 or 43 of the Treaty of Versailles, France would take no isolated action, but act in agreement with her Locarno allies, presumably after a League of Nations Council decision in the French favour. At the same time, France reserved the right to take all preparatory measures, including military, in view of any collective action determined by the Council and Locarno guarantors. This decision, providing ample time for the Germans to consolidate their position, already revealed the weakness of the French response. The Belgians were informed of the decision on the same day. Eden was to be told at a later meeting. Any French action would require both Belgian and British backing. During 1936, France failed to get either.

On 6 March, the Belgians denounced the 1920 secret Franco-Belgian military convention, as a result of a combination of internal and external pressures. As the coalition government of the young and popular Paul van Zeeland, a French-speaking Catholic, looked forward to new Belgian elections in March, the question of military reform re-ignited all the traditional animosities and differences over France in this much-divided society. The dark international situation meant that the minister of defence, Albert Devèze, the intelligent and ardently Francophone Liberal leader, had delayed introducing his bill for the extension of national service (from eight to eighteen months) until the start of the New Year. Any question dealing with defence was bound to create controversy, for strategic matters had become both dramatized and politicized. The defence minister and the Walloon-dominated Liberal party embraced the idea of the integral defence of the borders and co-operation with France. The king and senior officers, supported by the Flemish-speaking areas, argued that Belgium should rely on its internal rivers and fortresses for defence, and be prepared to fight independently of France. The Walloons feared the French; the Flemish hated them. The arguments resuscitated long-held suspicions about the scope of the Franco-Belgian military agreement. Would not the new reforms, intended to ensure the 'integral defence of the frontier', mean an extension of the Maginot Line and the use of the Belgian army as the left wing of the French army, or worse still, as a weapon in defence of French interests in Eastern Europe? In late February, in a preliminary vote on the eighteen months service law, Socialists and Flemish Catholics combined with Flemish Nationalists and Communists to defeat the Devèze proposal. Suddenly the whole political future of the government was in doubt. The maintenance of the Franco-Belgian military agreement could destroy both the military reform programme and the ruling coalition. The debate took place against a background of rising and spreading Francophobia. Anti-Bolshevism ran deep among Catholic and middle-class Belgians and the Franco-Soviet pact fanned fears that France would drag Belgium into a war situation created by Moscow. The terror of being 'entangled in the wake of France in the dreadful cog-wheels of a war from which it ought to remain far removed', went far beyond anti-Bolshevism and embraced Walloons as well as Flemings.[37] The van Zeeland government decided that the military agreement had to go if the reform programme was to be implemented. The formal renunciation was announced to a cheering Chamber of Deputies in Brussels on 11 March. The Rhineland invasion made no difference. The only shared obligations linking Belgium and France were those arising from the Locarno agreements and the Covenant of the League of Nations. Faced with the decision of staying with France or opting for neutrality, Belgium chose neutrality. The effects of the choice would find their echoes in the events of 1940.

During February, the British too were considering the 'dangerous question' of the demilitarized zone, though no immediate German move was anticipated. Officials and military men, without minimizing the zone's strategic importance, argued that the maintenance of the status quo was impractical. The foreign secretary summarized his department's views on 14 February, when considering how to arrange future relations with Germany. Britain should not be forced either to fight for the zone, Eden advised, or to surrender it, without getting something from Germany in return. For the cabinet, the Rhineland issue was only part of a much broader debate over what should be done about the 'German danger'. During the autumn and winter months, different options were canvassed in the hope of bringing Hitler into a general settlement that would include an arms limitation agreement. Even Vansittart, the official most concerned with the German threat and the slow pace of British rearmament, believed that concessions would

[37] Quoted from the Walloon paper, *La Libre Belgique* in David Owen Kieft, *Belgium's Return to Neutrality: An Essay in the Frustrations of Small Power Diplomacy* (Oxford, 1972), 51.

have to be given until Britain was strong enough to discuss a general settlement with Berlin. There was little disagreement on the need for concessions until Britain rearmed, the only differences were over what should be offered to Hitler. Officials discussed the restitution of German colonies or the opening of export markets in central and south-eastern Europe. After first considering the reaffirmation of the Rhineland pledge as a necessary part of any general settlement, there was a change of opinion. As it became clear that Hitler would soon grab his prize, officials began to urge the use of the demilitarized zone as a 'bargaining chip'. The long and cumbersome internal consultation process in London was just about to begin, when the oil sanction question came to the surface. On 3 March, Flandin asked for an undertaking that Britain would fulfil her Locarno commitments alone, if Italy abandoned the security pact and demanded new British reassurances with regard to the demilitarized zone. As Eden needed a quick answer to get the oil embargo against Italy in place, it seemed imperative to provide an answer that would circumvent the highly unwelcome problem of Britain's obligations under Locarno. The cabinet, hurriedly assembled to consider Flandin's demands, accepted Eden's proposal to open immediate negotiations with Germany linking its acceptance of an Air Pact with the question of the demilitarized zone. Once agreement was reached with the Germans, the French would be drawn in and the question 'settled'. In other words, Britain would abandon its commitments with regard to the Rhineland, in an agreement negotiated behind France's back. On 6 March, Eden called in the German ambassador to suggest the beginning of 'serious discussions'. At the end of the conversation, Hoesch asked for an interview on the next morning.

Hitler achieved the full measure of surprise that he intended when the invasion took place on 7 March. He had managed the run-up to the Rhineland campaign with consummate skill. He consulted only a small number of advisers, probably Ribbentrop, Göring, and Goebbels, with whom he met at Garmisch where he went to open the Winter Olympics on 6 February, and with his military chiefs on returning to Berlin. Fritsch, summoned by the Führer on 12 February, wanted to be assured that there would be no risk of hostilities, but neither he nor War Minister Blomberg offered any objections to Hitler's proposals. A move into the Rhineland was essential for the next stage in their rearmament programme. The German ambassadors in Rome and Paris, alone of the diplomats abroad, knew what was being planned. In London, ambassador Hoesch, who was not a Nazi, was closely questioned at the Foreign Office, but he had not been told of the impending action until the last moment. The British, on the point of launching their Rhineland offer,

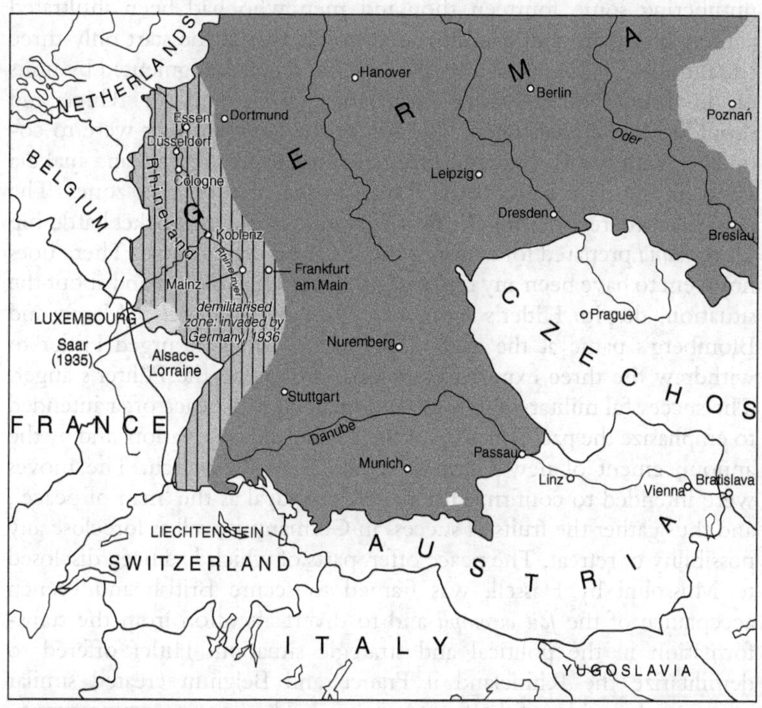

Map 3. The Rhineland Demilitarized Zone 1935

were caught off balance. Since mid-February, the Germans had appeared conciliatory and prepared for a bilateral pact. The *Quai d'Orsay* had been assured by their ambassador, François-Poncet, that Germany could not yet abandon the protection of the Locarno agreements, and that the general staff would dissuade Hitler from premature action. The *Auswärtiges Amt* took steps to silence press attacks on the Franco-Soviet treaty in February, and carefully avoided giving any indication of what Germany would do after ratification. On 21 February, Hitler received Bertrand de Jouvenel, stressing Germany's peaceful intentions and speaking of the absurdity of the traditional enmity between the two countries. On 3 March, with everything prepared for military action, the Germans responded negatively to François-Poncet's enquiry about specific proposals to improve Franco-German relations, citing the imminent signature of the Franco-Soviet pact as 'a great impediment'.

On Saturday morning, 7 March, 22,000 German forces entered the demilitarized zone. They were joined by paramilitary forces numbering some fourteen thousand men who had been infiltrated earlier. Blomberg and Fritsch issued orders that at the start only three battalions—3,000 men of a total of 30,000 regulars augmented by units of the Landespolizei—were to advance far beyond the Rhine and should retreat if challenged. The rest of the German units were to co-operate with the Reinforced Frontier Surveillance service and make a stand on the right bank of the Rhine in prepared defence zones. The navy was ordered to bring the fleet to readiness and the pocket battleship *Deutschland* prepared for action if the situation deteriorated. There does not seem to have been any real anxiety in the High Command about the situation, despite Hitler's momentary loss of nerve on 5 March and Blomberg's panic at the start of the affair, when he urged Hitler to withdraw the three exposed battalions, provoking the Führer's anger. The successful military *coup* was accompanied by a peace offer intended to emphasize the pacific nature of the Rhineland occupation, and by the announcement of new German elections on 29 March. The moves were intended to confirm Hitler's self-portrayal as the 'man of peace', and thus gather the fruits of success in Germany as well as foreclose any possibility of retreat. The peace offer, parts of which had been disclosed to Mussolini by Hassell, was framed to secure British and French acceptance of the *fait accompli* and to divert attention from the transformation in the political and strategic situation. Hitler offered to demilitarize the Rhineland if France and Belgium created similar zones on their sides of the frontier as well. The Locarno arrangements, without the Rhineland provisions, would be renewed in the form of twenty-five-year non-aggression pacts and might include the Netherlands. Hitler would agree, moreover, to a three-power air pact in the west and to non-aggression treaties with Germany's eastern neighbours, including Lithuania. To Mussolini's surprise and annoyance, the Führer suggested, in what was a later addition to the peace agenda, that Germany would return to the League of Nations if the problem of its association with the Versailles Treaty was negotiated, and German river and colonial claims settled. Ambassador Hoesch made excellent use of this offer to further Hitler's courtship campaign in London.

After frantic activity in Paris, French ministers decided to appeal to the Council of the League, in accordance with the Treaty of Locarno, but this was not 'to prejudice any other measures'. Gamelin was allowed to implement a series of steps toward *couverture* (the last stage before general mobilization) but not to call up the reserves. On the Sunday, the full cabinet met and agreed not to take any military measures, but to appeal to the League of Nations. 'Foreign reactions splendid', Goebbels wrote in his diary on 7 March. 'France will involve the League. Fine! It therefore will not act. That's the main thing. Nothing else matters.'[38] On that same Sunday evening, in a broadcast to the French people, Sarraut asserted that France would maintain the Locarno guarantee and that Strasbourg would not be left under German guns.[39] His resolute words fell flat. In a reference to Poincaré, the label 'Sarraut-la-guerre' made the rounds in Paris. As there is no formal record of the cabinet meetings during the first days of the crisis, and the memoir material is notoriously unreliable, it is difficult to know how much support there was for some form of military action under the League umbrella or, as Flandin suggested, for partial mobilization which he hoped would alarm the British and improve France's bargaining position. It was never suggested by the politicians, before the reoccupation, that France should use force to remove German troops from the Rhineland. Flandin, as a former finance minister, was aware of the state of the country's finances, and knew that mobilization would be both financially ruinous (the daily cost of *couverture* was estimated to be some thirty million francs) and politically disastrous. The German move provoked a serious financial crisis; only the anticipation of a peaceful settlement prevented a financial panic in Paris during the second week of March. At the *Quai d'Orsay*, the secretary general, Alexis Léger, and René Massigli, the assistant director of political affairs, were anxious that there should be some form of response. The press reaction was, on the contrary, remarkably calm, reflecting the mood of most of the French public. The Rhineland was not considered worth fighting over. Even those wanting to see Hitler punished, dismissed the idea of a military riposte. With commentators predicting a victory of the left in the May elections, there was no pressure from right or left for vigorous action. There was, in any case, no possibility that the army would move. The service chiefs were not even willing to discuss what could be done. France had no rapid deployment capacity in Europe. The army was purposely designed to hold the eastern defences during the six-stage, sixteen day mobilization period. It was only then that France could take the offensive. Gamelin would not consider occupying German soil without *couverture*, which required eight days and the call-up of large numbers of reservists. A mass army, lacking in arms and unable to move quickly, was not geared to action outside of a coalition. In addition, independent French action would have alienated Britain and most of the League of Nations states. It is true that the chiefs of

[38] Goebbels diary, 7 March, quoted in Stephen A. Schuker, 'France and the Remilitarization of the Rhineland, 1936', *French Historical Studies*, 14: 3 (1986), 310.

[39] Bonnefous, *Histoire politique*, Vol. 5, cited in Anthony Adamthwaite, *France and the Coming of the Second World War, 1936–1939* (London, 1977), 37.

staff somewhat overestimated the number of German troops the French would face, and ignored quite accurate intelligence reports that pointed to the weaknesses in the German organization and back-up. But Gamelin was convinced, rightly, that if challenged the Germans would fight, and he had no wish to engage his under-equipped and under-trained army against admittedly numerically inferior forces (at the start) defending their own territory, which he no longer considered to be strategically important for France. The moment of crisis thus found the army unwilling and unable to respond.

The cabinet agreed that France could not engage in '*action isolée*' but there were differences between Paris and London about the best policy to follow. A majority of ministers wanted to use the German occupation to secure from London those positive guarantees, backed by military conversations, that had so often eluded France's grasp. A small group, led by Georges Mandel and Sarraut, suggested joint punitive measures, if only to reassure France's eastern allies. Flandin, backed by Léger at the *Quai d'Orsay*, hoped that even the threat of military action might extract from London a British guarantee of French security. The French foreign minister had no illusions about the difficulty of his task. Eden's first reaction after condemning Hitler's *coup* was to call attention to the Führer's peace programme and to warn the French ambassador that nothing should be done to make the situation more difficult. If the French could be kept quiet, Eden was prepared to conclude with Germany 'as far-reaching and enduring a settlement as possible whilst Herr Hitler is still in the mood to do so'.[40] In the Commons on 9 March, Eden spoke of 'shaken confidence' in any engagements with Germany, and acknowledged Britain's obligations under Locarno, but he stressed, too, Britain's 'manifest duty to rebuild' confidence if peace was to be secured. In the afternoon debate on the 1936 Defence White Paper, Baldwin blamed both the French and the Germans for the failure to compromise, 'a historical cleavage which goes back to the partition of Charlemagne's empire', and reiterated Britain's desire 'to continue to try to bring France and Germany together in a friendship with ourselves'.[41] The British were prepared to balance the German propensity to break treaties with the French unwillingness to accept Britain's terms for negotiations with Berlin. The action of April 1934, when France had 'torpedoed' the British disarmament plan, was coming back to haunt Flandin. In London, the government's reaction was in keeping with the public mood. There were no League of Nations Union demonstrations,

[40] *DBFP*, 2nd ser., Vol. XVI, No. 48 (memorandum by Eden, 8 March 1936).
[41] *Hansard*, HC Deb, 9 March 1936, Vol. 309, Cols. 1817–1934.

protest marches, or demands for sanctions against Germany. The contrast with Ethiopia was striking.

The *Quai d'Orsay* knew that the Belgians would not favour a military response and would follow the British lead if a split occurred between London and Paris. Van Zeeland's preoccupation throughout the crisis was the preservation of Anglo-French unity and the avoidance of any provocative action that might disrupt it. 'It will be necessary to rebuild', the Belgian prime minister, echoing Baldwin's words, stated on 11 March when announcing the end of the Belgian–French military agreement. 'It will be necessary to reconstruct.'[42] The Belgian minister would broker the subsequent four-power talks in London, but his main interest was to secure a guarantee of Belgian security. Eden and Lord Halifax, the Lord Privy Seal, went off to Paris on 10 March, determined not to be towed in the French wake. Flandin, informed of Gamelin's objections even to the low-risk military strategies proposed (without enthusiasm) by General Georges, sought to convince the British that the Locarno powers acting in concert could force the Germans to withdraw without a resort to arms. Supported in this instance by van Zeeland, Flandin argued the case for adopting successive economic, financial, and military sanctions. The main divergence between the French and Belgians was the latter's willingness to accept a partial withdrawal of German troops as against Flandin's demand for complete withdrawal. Eden was taken aback by this unexpected demonstration of Franco-Belgian resolve. In fact, both Flandin and van Zeeland wanted to force the British into an offer of additional security guarantees as 'compensation'.

In the belief that the French wanted 'firm action', the British cabinet, which had unanimously favoured quick condemnation of the German move and the early opening of talks (that is, strong words but no retaliation) felt it had to find a way out of this difficult situation. The simplest way was blocked by Hitler when he rejected a not very hopeful British demand that he withdraw troops from the Rhineland as a gesture of conciliation. The Führer offered only to refrain from strengthening existing contingents and to promise not to move his troops closer to the frontier if Belgium and France followed suit. To impress his home audience as well as his foreign antagonists, the German reply was accompanied by warnings that the peace proposals would be withdrawn if either the troops or Germany were 'mistreated'. Flandin's hopes with regard to Britain were doomed to failure. Eden won the advantage of having the Locarno talks and the League's Council meetings held in London. The French foreign minister, conscious of the rising anti-French mood in London and fearful of the diplomatic consequences

[42] Quoted in Kieft, *Belgium's Return to Neutrality*, 60.

of any military move, was soon in retreat. Within a few days, he abandoned his efforts to secure British agreement to sanctions, and acknowledged this check to his hopes in private conversations with Baldwin and Chamberlain, the highly influential chancellor of the exchequer. Baldwin stressed Britain's military unpreparedness and the need for three years of peace. After 15 March, Flandin concentrated on securing compensation for the loss of the Rhineland by demanding extended guarantees. Van Zeeland again served as mediator between France and Britain, veering from one side to the other, supporting Flandin in matters of form, but agreeing with Eden on points of substance. Van Zeeland co-operated with Eden in convincing Flandin to abandon the demand for the complete German evacuation of the Rhineland, but joined with the French in demanding a revival of the Locarno agreements, stripped of their League procedures, but backed by tripartite military accords and staff talks.

On 19 March, after considerable effort on the part of both the Foreign Office and the French embassy, an agreement was reached that barely disguised the lack of consensus. The proposals, embodied in a 'White Paper', were given to Ribbentrop who, after some delay, had been sent to London to present the German case. The 'Text of Proposals' was intended, at least by the British, to win time, calm the French, and lay the basis for future talks with Germany. The Germans were invited to refrain from sending more troops to the Rhineland and to keep their paramilitary forces on a pre-*coup* basis. The Locarno powers suggested the creation of a new demilitarized zone, 20 kilometres deep, along the frontiers with France and Belgium, to accommodate an international force that would be sent with the permission of all the governments concerned. The Germans were requested, moreover, not to construct any forts, ground works or landing strips in the rest of the former zone. Germany and France should submit the Franco-Soviet pact to the International Court of Justice for a judgment on its compatibility with Locarno. There was no mention of punitive measures, as Flandin wanted, should Hitler refuse or if the tribunal's judgment went against Germany. Once these conditions were met, negotiations could start on revision of the Rhineland status, and on Hitler's peace proposals and a new mutual assistance pact. The French and Belgians secured assurances that if the 'effort of conciliation' failed, there would be immediate consultations between the Locarno powers, and Britain (and Italy) would come to the assistance of either government 'in respect of any measures which shall be jointly decided upon'. The Locarno guarantee against 'unprovoked aggression' was reaffirmed, and staff talks authorized to arrange the 'technical conditions' in which these obligations would be carried out. There was little possibility that

Hitler would accept these terms which, in fact, recognized the remilitarization. With Britain's proposed commitment to the defence of French and Belgian territory against unprovoked aggression, and the prospect of immediate staff talks in sight, Flandin and van Zeeland were prepared to accept the remilitarization of the Rhineland. The general public in all three countries was relieved and generally satisfied. Even Herriot, known for his antipathy towards Nazi Germany, thought that with the guarantee of British assistance, negotiations for an understanding with Hitler could start. The Italians refused to endorse the 'Text of Proposals', but they did not repudiate it. League Council members meeting in London condemned the German action as a 'threat to European security', and created a committee to recommend measures that would 'safeguard the peace of nations'. All present knew that with the passage of time, action would become increasingly difficult, and more improbable.

It was only with great difficulty that the British cabinet agreed to the opening of staff conversations. In separate notes to the French and Belgians, the Baldwin government insisted that the contacts between the General Staffs should not lead to any political understanding nor any obligations regarding the organization of national defence. Ministerial objections to the staff talks were taken up by the chiefs of staff, who were concerned both with the German reaction, and the fear that France would believe that Britain had given a moral commitment that would encourage French intransigence. Chamberlain congratulated himself on the successful outcome of the talks and the cabinet's acceptance of the proposals. Writing to his sister on 21 March, he told her that he had 'supplied most of the ideas and taken the lead all through . . . '.[43] On 26 March, Eden scored a great success in the Commons when he defended the resolutions of 19 March and claimed to have preserved both the peace and the Locarno agreements. He assured MPs: 'I am not prepared to be the first British Foreign Secretary to go back on a British signature. And yet our objective throughout this difficult period has been to seek a peaceful and agreed solution. It is the appeasement of Europe as a whole that we have constantly before us.'[44] The only critique of this involuted and false piece of diplomatic verbiage came from those in the Commons worried by the prospect of staff talks, though Eden minimized their importance. In the two sets of negotiations set in train by the Rhineland crisis, Eden had successfully circumvented the Franco-Belgian demand for a formal guarantee but

[43] Chamberlain papers, NC 18/1/952, Neville Chamberlain to Hilda Chamberlain, 21 March 1936.

[44] *Hansard*, HC Deb, 26 March 1936, Vol. 310, Cols. 1435–1549.

failed to move Hitler any closer to opening talks. Hoping to drag out the discussions and fearing that Britain might not restrain France again in a new crisis, if no offer was made, Hitler coupled his rejection of the 19 March 'White Paper' with counter-proposals sent on 31 March. This 'peace plan', intended mainly to soothe the London government, was constructed to take advantage of the fissures in the weak anti-German bloc. It was not markedly different from Hitler's previous offers, and totally ignored the League condemnation of the Rhineland action. Its main new feature was to set a deadline. By 1 August 1936, Germany, France, and Belgium would conclude a twenty-five-year non-aggression, or security, pact, guaranteed by Italy and Britain, and supplemented by an air pact. During the next four months, no German reinforcements would enter the Rhineland if France did not increase her forces in the frontier regions. Germany would accept any permanent military limitation of her western frontier, if France and Belgium accepted the same restrictions. There would follow non-aggression pacts with Czechoslovakia, Austria, and Lithuania. A novel suggestion was made for Franco–German agreements to monitor the teaching of history, in order to eradicate anything that might poison the two countries' relations. Earlier offers of future discussions on arms limitation, the humanization of aerial warfare, and German re-entry into the League were renewed. This long, elaborate list of *desiderata* offered nothing of real substance to would-be negotiators. They merely confirmed Germany's improved bargaining position.

As Ian Kershaw has noted, after the Rhineland success, Hitler 'was more than ever a believer in his own infallibility'.[45] He continued to do just as he pleased in the militarized zone and ignored all 'invitations' that would restrict his freedom of action. He had, after an intense and triumphant electioneering campaign, won the approval from 98.8% of the German electorate in the election held on 29 March. The popular euphoria at the news of the Rhineland remilitarization embraced all sections of the population. The 'election campaign' consisted of Hitler's triumphal procession through Germany. While fear and intimidation contributed to the staggering result, there is no doubt about Hitler's popularity. He had every reason for confidence. Not only was he sure of providential guidance, but neither the response of the Locarno powers nor the League's members suggested that he would be challenged in the future. The first forty-eight hours after the occupation may have been, as he later claimed, the most tense in his life, but thereafter he had little to fear. During the Council meetings in London, it became clear that there would be little pressure from League members for retribution.

[45] Ian Kershaw, *Hitler, 1889–1936, Hubris*, (London, 1998), 591.

Only the Czechs, Romanians, and Russians endorsed Flandin's early demands for condemnation and punishment, and both Beneš and Titulescu abandoned their efforts and backed the French attempt to co-ordinate policy with Britain when it became obvious that the moment for retaliation had passed. Titulescu organized an informal meeting of Little Entente and Balkan Entente representatives on 11 March, the day of the Council meeting, and informed the press that the five powers would back France 'absolutely and without reservation'. His announcement immediately brought denials from Belgrade, Athens, and Ankara. Józef Beck, while assuring the French of Polish loyalty to the alliance, joined the neutral powers (those that had not fought in the Great War) in opposing sanctions and made difficulties for the French-sponsored motion condemning Germany's action. The Italians remained non-committal, participating in the Locarno talks and holding out the possibility of an exchange of support for France in return for the ending of sanctions over Ethiopia. There was no promise of any participation in collective action. Nor was there any reaction from Washington when Flandin tried to get President Roosevelt to condemn the unilateral denunciation of treaties on moral grounds.[46]

With the German rejection of the White Paper, already much less than the French wanted, Flandin tried to extract some form of compensation from Britain. Eden artificially prolonged the so-called period of negotiation with Berlin to avoid the conversations promised to France and Belgium in the 'last resort'. The 'effort of conciliation' continued, nominally at least, until 1938. In mid-April 1936, French and Belgian officers came to London for staff talks, to be told that Britain would only have two infantry divisions available fourteen days after mobilization, but could give no guarantee that they would be sent either to France or Belgium. The British chiefs of staff would not discuss how or where their troops would be employed, nor would they permit any enlargement of the talks to consider the Belgian proposal of furnishing materials rather than men. On British insistence, the naval and air staff talks were mainly restricted to exchanges of information. The British agreed to maintain future contacts through their military attachés. One Foreign Office official described the talks as 'merely eye wash'. Flandin had won only the most modest concessions from Eden. The one concrete result of these spurious exchanges was the resumption of bilateral Franco-Belgian conversations and a plan, elaborated on 15 May, for a combined defence on the Meuse with forces concentrated on the Albert Canal running from Liège to Antwerp. For a few months, or at least until King Leopold III's strong defence of Belgium's 'policy of

[46] *FRUS,* 1936, I, p. 207.

independence' on 14 October, France's strategy of forward defence in the north made sense. The Belgian generals were highly sympathetic to the French and a period of close liaison followed. Even this brief honeymoon did not compensate for the lack of British participation. When in May, van Zeeland approached Eden, his good and close friend, to suggest bilateral staff talks, he was told the time was inappropriate.

It was hardly surprising that the reaction to the Rhineland remilitarization was so muted. The Third Reich was not Italy; it was a power to be feared and respected, whatever the moral disapproval of Hitler's methods. There was little possibility that the Council would endorse the Franco-Belgian demand for successive sanctions to secure a full or even partial restoration of the demilitarized zone. The British were unwilling to run the risk of war and were in no position to make a military contribution to any continental force. With sanctions against Italy still in place and Britain opposed to their termination, it was hardly likely that the Italians would fulfil their Locarno obligations. The countries not directly allied to France made clear their unwillingness to impose either an economic or financial embargo against Germany. The Poles and even the Romanians, despite Titulescu's efforts, opposed any action against Berlin. Göring threatened the Lithuanians and Czechs, and warned Denmark and the Netherlands, against joining an economic boycott. Germany's pivotal trading position in Europe, enhanced by the sanctions against Italy, ruled out the possibility of economic action. This alone predisposed almost all the Danubian states, Greece, and Turkey to keep a low profile. Yugoslavia, badly hit by its participation in the sanctions against Italy, looked to Germany to fill the resulting void. The neutral states felt they would seriously suffer if economic sanctions were imposed on the Reich. The Latin American countries too, looked to Germany to absorb the raw materials they could not sell elsewhere. Apart from Britain's commercial vulnerability (should the standstill agreements with Germany be revoked and the interest on German debts to the City left unpaid), exporters feared the shrinkage of the coal market if sanctions should be imposed. Litvinov's call on 27 March for collective action to avoid future treaty violations fell on deaf ears. Anti-Bolshevism and strong doubts about the Franco-Soviet treaty predisposed even those antipathetic to Nazism and Fascism to avoid any further diplomatic action.

Increasingly confident that France would follow Britain's lead, Hitler pressed on with his bid for Britain's friendship. His campaign had begun earlier with the unofficial visit to London of the duke of Saxe-Coburg-Gotha, a relation of the British monarch. During his visit he saw many of the leaders of the Conservative party and dined with Edward VIII. Much was expected in Berlin from the new monarch who rapidly became the object of German press attention. On 18 March, the London correspondent of the *Berliner Tageblatt* reported:

> The King is taking an extraordinarily active part in the whole affair; he has caused a number of important people in the Government to come and see him and has said to them: 'This is a nice way to start my reign'. The King won't hear of there being a danger of war. He is absolutely convinced that what must now be done is to get over the 'break of law' as quickly as possible and get on to the practical discussion of the Führer's and Chancellor's proposals.[47]

However unfounded were the German beliefs about the influence of the king, the latter's views reflected the views of most of the British cabinet.

Informed opinion in London, Paris, and Brussels was not impressed by Hitler's offer, yet Eden assured Hitler's emissary, Joachim von Ribbentrop, the former wine salesman soon to be 'rewarded' with the London embassy, that the proposals were 'deserving of careful study'. There was a distinct preference in London for informal negotiations with Berlin which excluded the French, until after their May 1936 elections. By that time, it was hoped, the crisis atmosphere would have diminished and an inexperienced Popular Front government might prove easier to manage. The main fear in London was that French intransigence would end the possibility of dialogue with Hitler. The British did try during the coming weeks, without success, to secure concessions on German fortifications in the Rhineland. Flandin responded to their failure by trying to force Eden to discuss sanctions should Hitler erect fortifications in the Rhineland zone. The French threatened not to negotiate with the Germans at all unless Britain would guarantee the Eastern European countries as compensation for their loss of French protection. On 8 April, Flandin, hoping to restore his personal credibility before the elections, produced his own peace plan, a 'sky-scraper of pacts and visions' according to Hitler, who promptly rejected it. The 9–10 April conversations at Geneva with regard to imposing oil sanctions against Italy were ill-tempered. Flandin made a last-minute attempt to again link the Ethiopian and Rhineland questions, only to find that Eden was in no mood to take up any of his proposals. The French foreign secretary knew that it was too late to insist. He agreed to a 'questionnaire' asking Hitler to explain the principles upon which Germany would agree to keep its international engagements. The futility of the exercise made it almost laughable. The French list of questions was pared down to avoid offending Hitler. When ambassador Phipps delivered the British questionnaire at Berlin

[47] *DGFP*, Ser. C, Vol. V, No. 147.

on 7 May, it was accompanied with an assurance of how deeply his government desired the opening of negotiations and with an offer to send a minister to facilitate them. The Führer did not bother to reply. On 14 May, rejecting a request to temporarily postpone the construction of fortifications in the Rhineland, he told Phipps that 'outsiders should mind their own business'. What followed during the next eighteen months was nothing more than a diplomatic farce of many equally tedious and unrewarding exchanges. No negotiations took place, but endless suggestions were made in London as to how to get talks started, while Hitler successfully stalled. Unwilling to allow the 'effort of conciliation' to lapse lest the 'guarantees' given France and Belgium come into effect, the British were reduced to asking whether or not to admit that their futile efforts had 'failed'.

In a characteristic move, at the end of April 1936, the British cabinet discussed the failures and the future of British policy. Baldwin, prompted by Chamberlain, decided to establish a cabinet committee on foreign policy to consider and report on future policy. After a first meeting, the committee adjourned and did not meet again until mid-July. During this period, there were divided counsels over what should be done in the Mediterranean, confusion over whether Mussolini and Hitler would come together, and indecision over what concessions could or should be given to Hitler while Britain rearmed. Baldwin told Eden 'he had "no idea" how to improve relations with Germany—that is your job'.[48] The foreign secretary was at a loss, indecisive and vacillating, believing his colleagues too concerned about alienating Germany, yet wanting talks with Hitler, unwilling to treat France as an equal in his dealings with Berlin, but fully aware of the dangers of France's weakening position. Eden played for time, finding it easier to take a stand on Ethiopia, where he had insisted on maintaining sanctions until July, than to suggest a positive solution to the 'German problem'. A formal Anglo-French-Belgian meeting on 23 July resulted in invitations to Germany and Italy to attend a five-power conference at an unspecified date, to discuss a western pact. On the 25 August, the British rejected a French claim that conciliation had broken down. If Hitler refused to make any concessions, apart from the renewed guarantee of French and Belgian territory, 'The British should decline to disinterest ourselves from the East and Centre of Europe.'[49] Even this modest offer of reassurance went beyond what the cabinet was willing to sanction. The new Blum Popular Front government that

[48] Quoted in Gaines Post, N., *Dilemmas of Appeasement: British Deterrence and Defense, 1934–1937* (Ithaca, NY, and London, 1993), 215.

[49] Quoted in Dockrill, *British Establishment Perspectives on France*, 42.

took office in May agreed to drop the idea of punitive measures against Germany for its actions in March. Nothing more was said either about imposing sanctions when Hitler began to build the 'west wall' fortifications or about the questionnaire that he had no intention of answering. The Germans continued to procrastinate over the proposed conference while preparing for the Olympic Games in August 1936, which would reveal the benefits of Nazism to the outside world. In contrast to his own Foreign Ministry's delaying tactics, on 24 August 1936, Hitler ordered the extension of compulsory military service to two years. No five-power conference was ever held. The British refused to admit that conciliation had collapsed.

IV

While the British and French continued to search for a way to make Hitler come to the negotiating table, Mussolini moved to refurbish his links with Hitler. The latter was much annoyed at the Italian participation in the London talks over the Rhineland. Though ambassador Grandi was instructed not to go beyond a moral note of censure against Germany, Italian fears that success in the Rhineland would again put the question of *Anschluss* on the table, together with Mussolini's hopes that sanctions would be lifted, explain the Italian presence at the talks. Impressed by his own importance, Mussolini equivocated, promising to support the German position but refusing to denounce the White Paper with the Rhineland terms. By default, the proposals did not carry the Italian endorsement, but there was no public statement in Germany's favour. The main thrust of Mussolini's diplomacy, nonetheless, was not towards Paris or London but towards Berlin. The appointment of the youthful Galeazzo Ciano (Mussolini's son-in-law) as head of the Consulta on 9 June 1936, and the subsequent dismissal of both Fulvio Suvich and Pompeo Aloisi, pointed to the downgrading of the professional diplomats, and to the clear German orientation of Italian diplomacy. Mussolini was dreaming of preparing his new colony for a future North African adventure that would link East Africa with Libya and threaten the Suez Canal. Unfortunately for his daydreams, the defeated Ethiopians proved recalcitrant; guerrilla war continued and little money was available for the colony's military development.

Mussolini followed up his earlier conversations with the Germans by warning Schuschnigg, the Austrian chancellor, that the Austrian problem had to be solved because it stood in the way of good Italian–German relations. In Vienna, Schuschnigg, a rather rigid figure who had a somewhat mystical belief in a greater Germany modelled on the Holy

Roman Empire, had been trying to strengthen his government by winning over the German Nationalists and preventing them from joining the Nazis. Unknown to him, the German ambassador, Franz von Papen, was already grooming the Austrian Nazis for their future political role, while warning them against any acts of terrorism. He was urging Schuschnigg to include in his cabinet the respectable representatives of the 'national opposition' (the umbrella group of all those Austrians favouring *Anschluss*) who were, in fact, strong supporters of Nazi Germany's claims on Austria. During informal talks between Papen and Schuschnigg in the summer of 1935, an agreement was concluded to restrain press attacks on each other. Political changes in Vienna delayed further contacts between the two men. Soon after the Italian invasion of Ethiopia, Schuschnigg loosened his ties with the Mussolini-backed Heimwehr, and in May dismissed the pro-Mussolini, but strongly anti-Nazi, vice chancellor, Ernst Rüdiger Starhemberg. Some months later, the Heimwehr was officially disbanded. Mussolini seemed unperturbed by the sacking of his protégé, for his eye was already on Berlin. Exchanges in the German capital in January 1936 indicated that Hitler was willing, if Italy did not rejoin the Stresa Front, to pursue a policy of benevolent neutrality toward Italy's 'African adventure'. The Italians, in turn, were willing to be more accommodating in Vienna. The German diplomats followed up Mussolini's hints, but serious negotiations were delayed until after the occupation of the Rhineland.

Talks were resumed in Vienna between Papen and Schuschnigg in the spring and summer of 1936 and proceeded rapidly to a successful conclusion. Mussolini impressed on the Austrian chancellor the urgent need to come to terms with Germany and was shown a draft of the final agreement. While affirming his interest in Austrian independence, the Duce argued it would be easier to help Austria if both Italy and Austria were on good terms with Germany. The Austro-German agreement was concluded on 11 July. In exchange for the recognition of its sovereignty, Austria acknowledged itself to be a 'German state' and promised to conduct its policies accordingly. A customs union and military talks were envisaged for the future. There was to be a general amnesty, an essential concession for the Austrian Nazis. A secret supplementary agreement provided that the 'national opposition' would be incorporated into the ruling *Vaterländische Front*. Seyss-Inquart, a cautious and clever lawyer with a penchant for intrigue, was appointed trustee of the 'nationals' and charged with the task of bringing the pro-*Anschluss* sympathizers into the government. Over 16,000 Austrian Nazis were pardoned and were free to operate within the Republic. The still banned Austrian NSDAP, divided into revolutionary and evolutionary factions, provided ample opportunities for intrigues in both Vienna and Berlin. Göring and Himmler, at first rivals, agreed to support an evolutionary approach to the Austrian question. It was their nominee, SS Gruppenführer Wilhelm Keppler, who was picked for the joint commission created to oversee the new agreement. He was subsequently appointed by Hitler to handle Austrian affairs. The Führer wanted no premature local embarrassment as he planned a gradual take-over of power in Austria, nor did he want any incidents that might endanger Germany's relations with Britain, and his developing friendship with Italy. He could afford to wait. Once deserted by Mussolini, Schuschnigg had no alternative (contacts with Prague yielded nothing concrete) but to conclude with Nazi Germany. He thought that the agreement would give Austria two years' breathing space and hoped that the Stresa front might be reconstituted during that time. The bilateral Austro-German agreement, signed during the same week that sanctions against Italy were lifted, was yet another blow to the whole concept of multilateral negotiations. Mussolini's interest in Austria rapidly diminished. His ambitions were centred on the Mediterranean where the partnership with Germany could pay higher dividends than support for a doomed Austria. On 1 November 1936, the Duce proclaimed the Rome–Berlin Axis, not yet an alliance, but a major step in that direction. A representative of the 'National Opposition', now in the Schuschnigg government, visited Berlin in November and concluded a secret agreement about press, cultural, and economic exchanges and, while reserving Austria's rights under the Rome Protocols, promised consultation with Germany in all other matters. Austria had moved out of Italy's sphere of influence and was, with Mussolini's agreement, being groomed for *Anschluss*.

With the remilitarization of the Rhineland, the *Wehrmacht* would no longer need to keep large numbers of troops on the French frontier and the Reich's industries could be organized for war without concern for the safety of the Rhine and Ruhr. Hitler moved slowly to reap the benefits of his new freedom; many in Germany believed that this was the time to take advantage of the improved world trade situation to improve the country's economic position and to capitalize on Hitler's successes. Hitler had other goals in mind. The inaction of France and Britain encouraged him to 'assume even greater risks, disregard cautious advice, and triumph by bluff until he could conquer by force'.[50] His confidence soared as his possible enemies avoided confrontation and sought reconciliation. It was time to prise open the weak Anglo-French *entente* and convince Britain, like Italy, to accept German expansion in Europe.

[50] Gerhard. L. Weinberg, *The Foreign Policy of Hitler's Germany: Diplomatic Revolution in Europe, 1933–36* (Chicago and London, 1970), 262.

The Rhineland militarization was a missed opportunity to check Hitler before Germany was rearmed. Yet there was no possibility that either France or Britain would consider fighting for the Rhineland. Their recent histories and domestic dispositions as well as the enfeebled state of the European order precluded any form of active response. In France, a caretaker government, facing a bitter and divisive election campaign and fearing that the franc might collapse at any moment, had neither the courage nor the will to reverse the strategic decisions made at the end of the previous decade. The country had already adopted a defensive strategy and the retreat from the eastern alliances had begun. The Rhineland had been written off before Hitler took power. The army, like the *Quai d'Orsay*, had long anticipated a German remilitarization, and preferred to use the Rhineland as a bargaining chip before Germany moved. The high command assumed, rightly, in March 1936, that the threat of military action would not be enough to stop the Germans and that France would have to be prepared to fight. The French had the troops needed to defeat the numerically inferior Germans, but there was no mobile force to send to the Rhineland, and full mobilization would be slow and costly. Gamelin told ministers that any idea of sending even a token force into the Rhineland was a chimera because the army was a 'static' force and 'no offensive action could be undertaken until the twelfth day'.[51] The exaggerated intelligence estimates of Germany's military power only justified the earlier decision not to move into western Germany. Flandin's attempt on 11 March to secure British backing for actions which he speciously claimed to be planning against Germany was mainly intended to provide an excuse for French passivity. His subsequent aim was to secure some form of British concession to France, preferably a defensive alliance, to compensate for the loss of the Rhineland. Later accusations that the French were held back from decisive action by the British have little justification. The overwhelming majority of the cabinet was only too pleased to follow the military's advice. The government was acting in accord with French public opinion. The parties of the right and left, as well as the trade unions and veterans' groups, opposed any action that carried the risk of war. The Socialists even denounced as provocative the government's decision to man the Maginot Line. The press was almost unanimous in its opposition to retaliatory action. The fierce political battles of the day did not extend to the Rhineland.

[51] Quoted in Adamthwaite, *France and the Coming of the Second World War*, 39. See the argument in Schuker, 'France and the Remilitarization of the Rhineland, 1936', 299–338.

The main British fear was a French action that would precipitate war. Eden demanded and secured a promise of prior consultation. Successive British governments had long sought to bring Germany back into the European concert. Hitler's actions, though prompting moves towards rearmament, did not check the search for an Anglo-German understanding. For months before the occupation, the cabinet and Foreign Office considered the practicality of using the Rhineland, in addition to other concessions, to secure Hitler's support for an air pact and general European agreement. The Germans moved before the British offer could be made. The Rhineland clauses were unpopular in London and the British had long opposed the French alliances in Eastern Europe. The failure of the Eastern Pact negotiations in 1934–1935 confirmed their view that it was impossible to conclude any kind of Eastern Locarno, and their judgement that it was more productive to deal with Germany alone. The Foreign Office had only grudgingly accepted the Franco-Soviet alliance (2 May 1935), which it felt would antagonize Germany and involve Britain in the affairs of Eastern Europe. Eden's line throughout the Rhineland crisis was to discourage French action and to seek 'as far reaching and enduring a settlement as possible whilst Herr Hitler is still in the mood to do so'.[52] There was a fleeting moment on 12 March when Eden, faced with the German refusal to make any concessions and under increased French pressure, considered sanctions, but no proposals were made. Even as Hitler gambled and won, there was no diminution of anti-French feeling in London, though there was some recognition of the importance of the sacrifice made by France. Public and parliamentary opinion backed the government's decision to avoid violence, reject sanctions, and seek a western settlement. Eden's declared intention to pursue an agreement with Hitler was warmly received in the Commons. Herr Hitler, after all, had only marched into his own back garden. The Dominions, anxious to lift the sanctions against Italy, were strongly opposed to any action against Germany, and looked to a general agreement based on Anglo-German co-operation. South Africa, in particular, opposed the commitments made to France and Belgium, but it was not alone.

The Ethiopian affair provided Hitler with a unique opportunity to disregard the whole Geneva system. Given the League's failure to prevent or check Mussolini's attack, he knew it was highly unlikely that it would move to action against Germany. The loss of confidence in collective action weakened the resolve of all but a few of the smaller powers, to move beyond condemnation. In exposing the League's weakness, Mussolini had played his part in assuring Hitler's success. If

[52] Quoted in David Carlton, *Anthony Eden: A Biography* (London, 1981), 79.

the latter was annoyed at Italy's participation in the Locarno discussions in London, he swallowed his temporary indignation to offer the carrots that would prevent any revival of the Stresa front. The French were anxious to repair the lines to Rome. Some 14 French divisions, about one-fifth of the army, that might have been concentrated on the Rhineland, had to be transferred to the Alps and Tunisia. The heightened apprehension in Paris that the balance of power had shifted to Germany made the British alliance more essential for French security. Yet the handling of the Ethiopian crisis had driven Britain and France apart and exacerbated the tensions in their relationship. The legacy of bitterness and distrust, built up during 1935 overshadowed the Rhineland crisis and the post-crisis discussions with Germany. There were good reasons why Hitler should anticipate exploiting the differences between the two countries.

Hitler's unopposed action was a crucial marker on the road to a European war. He had gambled and won. The German public, after a period of anxious waiting, were convinced that Hitler could deliver future victories without fighting. Fully backed at home, and without any fear of a military riposte from France, Hitler could move with renewed confidence. For France, the German militarization of the Rhineland, however anticipated, was a psychological as well as a strategic blow. The destruction of the Locarno treaties of 1925 left the eastern frontiers of France and Belgium dangerously exposed. France had shown that it was unable to make good its claims as the defender of the status quo and the provider of security in central and south-eastern Europe. 'If on 7 March you could not defend yourself, how will you defend us against an aggressor?', the Romanian foreign minister asked Flandin.[53] Once Germany fortified its western frontier (the fortifications had still to be completed in the autumn of 1938) the French could not launch an offensive into Germany in support of its allies. The exposure of French weakness shook the Little Entente; even Prague considered negotiations with Germany. The French hoped, it is true, right up to the conclusion of the Rome–Berlin Axis in November, that they could restore the links with Rome and build on the military collaboration of 1934 providing a land bridge to south-central Europe. There were tentative negotiations on the part of both parties in May, checked, much to the irritation of the French, by the British insistence on the retention of the sanctions. The one positive feature of the crisis for France was Britain's formal commitment to the defence of French and Belgian territory against unprovoked aggression, and the opening of the Anglo-French-Belgian staff talks. The British offer of two divisions was

[53] *DDF*, 2nd ser., Vol. VII, No. 5.

a meagre one and their continental role was left unsettled. Nonetheless, even a small mechanized force would assist the French. More to the point, the French could count on Britain's future rearmament and its essential contribution to the *guerre de longue durée* that they expected to fight. The *entente* had not only survived; it had been reinforced. The British had acknowledged their stake in French security.

The British did not suffer the same loss of prestige and influence as France but the crises of 1936 added little lustre to their position. Though the government recovered from the impact of the Hoare–Laval agreement, its claims to moral superiority had been compromised and its fidelity to the League of Nations opened to question. The countries in Eastern Europe were confirmed in their doubts about any assistance from London, either directly or through the League. The British did not believe in the 'indivisibility of peace' and continued to assume that what happened in Eastern Europe did not touch on their security concerns. Though Eden was far from optimistic about the chances of coming to an arrangement with Germany, the main thrust of his policies was the creation of a new international order based on reconciliation with Germany. Whether to 'gain time' for rearmament, as some intended, or because they believed that Hitler could be convinced, through timely concessions, to pursue a policy of peaceful change, ministers were determined to renew their efforts to come to terms with Germany. But Hitler kept the initiative, dragging out the talks and refusing to discuss concrete terms. Eden found it difficult to make any progress in the late summer of 1936, though the new French prime minister, Léon Blum, was intent on restoring good relations with Britain. It was an anxious and depressing time in London.

Books

ADAMTHWAITE, A., *France and the Coming of the Second World War, 1936–1939* (London, 1977).

ALEXANDER, M. S., *The Republic in Danger: General Maurice Gamelin and the Politics of French Defence, 1933–1940* (Cambridge, 1992).

BAER, G. W., *The Coming of the Italian–Ethiopian War* (Cambridge, 1967).

—— *Test Case: Italy, Ethiopia and the League of Nations* (Stanford, CA, 1976).

BARIÉTY, J., GUTH, A., and VALENTIN, J. M. (eds.), *La France et l'Allemagne entre les deux guerres mondiales: actes du colloque tenu en Sorbonne (Paris IV), 15–17 janvier 1987* (Nancy and Paris, 1987).

BELL, P. M. H., *France and Britain, 1900–1940* (London, 1996).

CHURCHILL, W., *The Second World War*, Vol. I: *The Gathering Storm* (Harmondsworth, [1948], 1985).

COLLOTTI, E., *Fascismo e politico di potenza: politica estera 1922–1939* (Florence, 2000).

Davis, R., *Anglo-French Relations before the Second World War: Appeasement and Crisis* (Basingstoke and New York, 2001).

Del Boca, A., *Gli Italiani in Africa Orientale, la conquista dell'Impero* (Milan, 1992).

Dockrill, M., *British Establishment Perspectives on France, 1936–1940* (Basingstoke and New York, 1999).

Dreifort, J., *Yvon Delbos at the Quai d'Orsay: French Foreign Policy during the Popular Front, 1936–1938* (Lawrence, KS, 1973).

Editions du Centre national de la recherche scientifique (ed.), *Les relations franco-britanniques de 1935 à 1939: communications présentées aux colloques franco-britanniques tenus à Londres (Imperial War Museum) du 18 au 21 octobre 1971, Paris (Comité d'histoire de la 2ème guerre mondiale) du 25 au 29 septembre 1972* (Paris, 1975).

Emmerson, J. T., *The Rhineland Crisis, 7 March 1936: A Study in Multilateral Diplomacy* (London, 1977).

La France et l'Allemagne, 1932–1936: communications présentées au colloques franco-allemand tenu à Paris (Palais de Luxembourg, salle Médicis) du 10 au 12 mars, 1977 (Paris, 1980).

Funke, M., *Sanktionen und Kanonen: Hitler, Mussolini und der internationale Abessinienkonflikt 1934–36* (Düsseldorf, 1970).

Gooch, J., *Mussolini and His Generals: The Armed Forces and Fascist Foreign Policy 1922–1940* (Cambridge, 2007).

Guillebaud, C. W., *The Economic Recovery of Germany from 1933 to the Incorporation of Austria in March 1938* (London, 1939).

Henke, J., *England in Hitlers politischem Kalkül, 1935–1939* (Boppard am Rhein, 1973).

Hildebrand, K., Manfrass, K., and Werner, K. F. (eds.), *Deutschland und Frankreich, 1936–1939* (Munich, 1981).

Hohne, H., *Die Zeit der Illusionen: Hitler und die Anfänge des Dritten Reiches, 1933–1936* (Düsseldorf, 1991).

Jackson, J., *The Politics of Depression in France, 1932–1936* (Cambridge, 1985).

Laurens, F. D., *France and the Italo-Ethiopian Crisis, 1935–1936* (The Hague and Paris, 1967).

Mallett, R., *The Italian Navy and Fascist Expansionism, 1935–1940* (London, 1998).

Michalka, W., *Ribbentrop und die Deutsche Weltpolitik, 1933–1940: außenpolitische Konzeptionen und Entscheidungsprozesse im Dritten Reich* (Munich, 1980).

Militärgeschichtliches Forschungsamt (ed.), *Germany and the Second World War*, vol. I: *The Build-up of German Aggression*, ed. Deist, W. et al. (Oxford, 1990).

—— *Germany and the Second World War*, Vol. III: *The Mediterranean, South-East Europe and North Africa, 1939–1941: From Italy's Declaration of Non-belligerence to the Entry of the United States into the War*, ed. Schreiber, G., Stegemann, B., and Vogel, D. (Oxford, 1995). See G. Schreiber.

Minniti, F., *Fino alla guerra: strategie e conflitto nella politica di potenza di Mussolini: 1923–1940* (Naples, 2000).

MOREWOOD, S., *The British Defence of Egypt 1933–1940: Conflict and Crisis in the Eastern Mediterranean* (Abingdon and New York, 2005).

PETZINA, D., *Autarkiepolitik im Dritten Reich: der Nationalsozialistische Vierjahresplan* (Stuttgart, 1968).

ROBERTSON, E. M., *Mussolini as Empire Builder: Europe and Africa 1932–1936* (London, 1977).

ROI, M. L., *Alternative to Appeasement: Sir Robert Vansittart and Alliance Diplomacy, 1934–1937* (Westport, CT, and London, 1997).

SALERNO, R., *Vital Crossroads: Mediterranean Origins of the Second World War, 1935–1940* (Ithaca, NY, 2002).

SALEWSKI, M., *Wehrmacht und Nationalsozialismus, 1933–1939* (Munich, 1978).

SHORROCK, W. I., *From Ally to Enemy: The Enigma of Fascist Italy in French Diplomacy, 1920–1940* (Kent, OH, 1988).

TAMKIN, N., *Turkey and the Soviet Union 1940–1945: Strategy, Diplomacy, and Intelligence in the Eastern Mediterranean* (Basingstoke, 2009).

THOMAS, M., *Britain, France and Appeasement: Anglo-French Relations in the Popular Front Era* (Oxford and New York, 1996).

WALEY, D., *British Public Opinion and the Abyssinian War, 1935–1936* (London, 1975).

WEINBERG, G. L., *The Foreign Policy of Hitler's Germany: Diplomatic Revolution in Europe, 1933–1936* (Chicago, IL, 1970).

YOUNG, R. J., *In Command of France: French Foreign Policy and Military Planning, 1933–1940* (Cambridge, MA, 1978).

Articles

ALEXANDER, M. S., 'French Military Intelligence Responds to the German Remilitarisation of the Rhineland, 1936—The Military Consequences for France at the End of Locarno', *Intelligence and National Security*, 22: 4 (2007).

CAIRNS, J. C., 'March 7, 1936 Again: The View from Paris', *International Journal*, 20 (1965).

COHEN, M. J., 'British Strategy in the Middle East in the Wake of the Abyssinian Crisis, 1936–39', in Cohen, M. J. and Kolinsky, M. (eds.), *Britain and the Middle East in the 1930s: Security Problems, 1935–1939* (Basingstoke, 1992).

DAVIS, R., 'Le débat sur "l'appeasement" britannique et français dans les années 30', *Revue d'Histoire Moderne et Contemporaine*, 45 (1998).

—— 'Mésentente cordiale: The Failure of the Anglo-French Alliance: Anglo-French Relations during the Ethiopian and Rhineland Crises', *European History Quarterly*, 23 (1993).

FUNKE, M., '7. März 1936: Fallstudie zum außenpolitischen Führungsstil Hitlers', in Michalka, W. (ed.), *Nazionalsozialistische Außenpolitik* (Darmstadt, 1978).

GOLDMAN, A. L., 'Sir Robert Vansittart's Search for Italian Cooperation Against Hitler, 1933–36', *Journal of Contemporary History*, 9: 3 (1974).

HILLGRUBER, A., 'England in Hitlers außenpolitischer Konzeption', in Hillgruber, A. (ed.), *Deutsche Grossmacht- und Weltpolitik im 19. und 20. Jahrhundert* (Düsseldorf, 1979).

JACKSON, P., 'La politisation du renseignement en France, 1933–1939', in Soutou, G.-H., Frémeaux, J., and Forcade, O. (eds.), *L'exploitation du renseignement en Europe et aux États-Unis des années 1930 aux années 1960* (Paris, 2001).

JORDAN, N., 'Maurice Gamelin, Italy and the Eastern Alliances', *Journal of Strategic Studies*, 14: 4 (1991).

KENT, P., 'Between Rome and London: Pius XI, the Catholic Church, and the Abyssinian Crisis, 1935–1936', *International History Review*, 11 (1989).

KNIPPING, F., 'Frankreich in Hitlers Außenpolitik, 1933–1939', in Funke, M. (ed.), *Hitler, Deutschland und die Mächte: Materialen zur Außenpolitik des Dritten Reiches* (Düsseldorf, 1976).

MALLETT, R., 'The Italian Naval High Command and the Mediterranean Crisis, January–October 1935', *Journal of Strategic Studies*, 22: 4 (1999).

—— 'Fascist Foreign Policy and Official Italian Views of Anthony Eden', *Historical Journal*, 43: 1 (2000).

MARDER, A., 'The Royal Navy and the Ethiopian Crisis of 1935–1936', *American Historical Review*, 75: 5 (1970).

MASSON, P., 'Les conversations militaires franco-britanniques (1935–1938)', in Editions du Centre national de la recherche scientifique (ed.), *Les Relations franco-britanniques de 1935 à 1939: communications présentées aux colloques franco-britanniques tenus à Londres (Imperial War Museum) du 18 au 21 octobre 1971, Paris (Comité d'histoire de la 2ème guerre mondiale) du 25 au 29 septembre 1972* (Paris, 1975).

MICHAELIS, M., 'Italy's Strategy in the Mediterranean, 1935–1939', in Cohen, M. J. and Kolinsky, M. (eds.), *Britain and the Middle East in the 1930s: Security Problems* (Basingstoke, 1992).

MICHALON, R. and VERNET, J., 'L'armée française et la crise du 7 mars 1936', in *La France et l'Allemagne, 1932–1936: communications présentées aux colloques franco-allemand tenu à Paris (Palais de Luxembourg, salle Médicis) du 10 au 12 mars, 1977* (Paris, 1980).

MOREWOOD, S., 'Protecting the Jugular Vein of Empire: The Suez Canal in British Defence Strategy, 1919–1941', *War and Society*, 10 (1992).

—— 'Anglo-Italian Rivalry in the Mediterranean and the Middle East, 1935–1940', in Boyce, R. W. D. and Robertson, E. M. (eds.), *Paths to War: New Essays on the Origins of the Second World War* (London, 1995).

—— 'The Chiefs-of-Staff, the "Men on the Spot" and the Italo–Abyssinian Emergency, 1935–1936', in Richardson, D. and Stone, G. (eds.), *Decisions and Diplomacy: Essays in Twentieth-Century International History* (London, 1989).

PANKHURST, R., 'The Italo-Ethiopian War and the League of Nations Sanctions, 1935–1936', *Genève-Afrique*, 13: 2 (1974).

PARKER, R. A. C., 'The First Capitulation: France and the Rhineland Crisis of 1936', *Word Politics*, 7 (1956).

—— 'Great Britain, France and the Ethiopian Crisis, 1935–1936', *English Historical Review*, 89: 351 (1974).

PEDRONCINI, G., 'La stratégie française et l'Italie de 1932 à 1939', in Duroselle, J.-B. and Serra, E. (eds.), *Italia e Francia dal 1919 al 1939* (Milan, 1981).

Post, G. Jr., 'The Machinery of British Policy in the Ethiopian Crisis', *International History Review*, 1: 4 (1979).

Quartararo, R., 'Imperial Defence in the Mediterranean on the Eve of the Ethiopian Crisis, July–October 1935', *Historical Journal*, 20: 1 (1975).

—— 'La crisi mediterranea del 1935–1936', *Storia Contemporanea*, 6: 4 (1975).

Reynolds, S., 'Britain, France and the Emerging Italian Threat, 1935–1938', in Alexander, M. S. and Philpott, W. J. (eds.), *Anglo-French Defence Relations between the Wars* (Basingstoke, 2002).

Robertson, E. M., 'Hitler and Sanctions: Mussolini and the Rhineland', *European Studies Review*, 7: 2 (1977).

Robertson, J. C., 'The Origins of the British Opposition to Mussolini over Ethiopia', *Journal of British Studies*, 9: 1 (1969).

—— 'Race as a Factor in Mussolini's Policy in Africa and Europe', *Journal of Contemporary History*, 23: 1 (1988).

Roi, M. L., 'A Completely Immoral and Cowardly Attitude: The British Foreign Office, American Neutrality and the Hoare–Laval Plan', *Canadian Journal of History*, 39: 2 (1994).

—— 'From the Stresa Front to the Triple Entente: Sir Robert Vansittart, the Abyssinian Crisis and the Containment of Germany', *Diplomacy and Statecraft*, 6: 1 (1995).

Sakwa, G., 'The Franco-Polish Alliance and the Remilitarization of the Rhineland', *Historical Journal*, 16: 1 (1973).

Salerno, R., 'Multilateral Strategy and Diplomacy: The Anglo-German Naval Agreement and the Mediterranean Crisis, 1935–1936', *Journal of Strategic Studies*, 17 (1994).

Sbacchi, A., 'Towards the Recognition of the Italian Empire, 1936–1937', *Revista di Studi Politici Internazionali*, 42: 1 (1975).

Schuker, S., 'France and the Remilitarization of the Rhineland, 1936', *French Historical Studies*, 14: 3 (1986).

Shore, Z., 'Hitler, Intelligence and the Decision to Remilitarise the Rhine', *Journal of Contemporary History*, 34: 1 (1999).

Strang, D. B., 'Imperial Dreams. The Mussolini-Laval Accords of January 1935', *Historical Journal*, 44: 3 (2001).

Sullivan, B. R., 'A Fleet in Being: The Rise and Fall of Italian Sea Power, 1861–1943', *International History Review*, 10: 1 (1988).

—— 'The Italian Armed Forces, 1918–1940', in Millett, A. R. and Murray, W. (eds.), *Military Effectiveness*, Vol. II: *The Interwar Period* (London and Boston, MA, 1988).

—— 'The Italian–Ethiopian War, October 1935 – November 1941: Causes, Conduct and Consequences', in Ion, A. H. and Errington, E. J. (eds.), *Great Powers and the Little Wars: The Limits of Power* (Westport, CT, 1993).

—— 'More than Meets the Eye: The Ethiopian War and the Origins of the Second World War', in Martel, G. (ed.), *The Origins of the Second World War Reconsidered: A. J. P. Taylor and the Historians*, 2nd edn. (London, 1999).

Thomas, M., 'Imperial Defence or Diversionary Attack? Anglo-French Strategic Planning in the Near East, 1936–1940', in Alexander, M. S.

and Philpott, W. J. (eds.), *Anglo-French Defence Relations between the Wars* (Basingstoke, 2002).

Vaïsse, M., 'La mission de Jouvenel à Rome', in Duroselle, J.-B. and Serra, E. (eds.), *Italia e Francia dal 1919 al 1939* (Milan, 1981).

Watt, D. C., 'German Plans for the Re-occupation of the Rhineland: A Note', *Journal of Contemporary History*, 1: 4 (1966).

Wrench, D. J., 'The Influence of Neville Chamberlain on Foreign and Defence Policy, 1932–1935', *RUSI Journal*, 125: 1 (1980).

Young, R. J., 'Soldiers and Diplomats: The French Embassy and Franco-Italian Relations, 1935–1936', *Journal of Strategic Studies*, 7 (1984).

—— 'French Military Intelligence and the Franco-Italian Alliance, 1933–1939', *Historical Journal*, 28: 1 (1985).

4

The Remnants of Internationalism, 1936–1938

The crises of 1935–1936 represented one further chapter in the dissolution of the mechanisms established in the 1920s to keep the peace. They affected far more than the foreign ministries of Europe and the diplomatic map. In those countries where open discussion was still possible, they brought foreign affairs to the forefront of the public political debate. There was a marked diminution of confidence in the Geneva system and a darkening of the general mood. One area where this manifested itself, and where the contrast with a decade earlier was the most marked of all, was the question of disarmament. With the indefinite adjournment of the World Disarmament Conference in June 1934, it appeared that the entire enterprise of disarmament had come to an end. It is true that naval disarmament lasted for some more months, until the unsatisfactory end of the second London naval conference, but the processes revolving around the League of Nations quickly dropped from the centre of public attention. The final defeat of Abyssinia in May 1936 hammered home the futility as well as the danger of imposing sanctions. In Britain, in particular, faith in the League's peacekeeping powers was severely shaken. Anti-French feeling rose to new heights as it was thought that French action might provoke the very conflict the British wished to avoid. In France, the Rhineland crisis saw no popular demand for sanctions to force the Germans out of the reoccupied zone. The meekness evinced at the meetings of the League Council, held in London, only confirmed French doubts about any recourse to Geneva. Elsewhere, not only did the Scandinavian states and Switzerland reject their obligations under Article 16 of the Covenant, but almost all the other smaller states demanded the article's modification without reaching any consensus as to what should replace its terms. Most of the smaller states remained in the League (Switzerland was one of the exceptions) and continued to press the cause of disarmament. They wanted a League that would promote compromise and conciliation rather than take coercive measures to keep the peace. It was a revealing and dispiriting sign of the times that governments adopting policies of 'independence', 'neutrality', or 'non-engagement' could count on broad popular support.

The pro-peace organizations were among the first to feel the impact of the changing mood. Neither in Britain nor France did such groups represent more than a small percentage of the electorate, yet because they were led by people of unusual charisma, energy, and prestige, with close connections to politically influential élites, they exercised influence well beyond their numbers. Above all they were able to conduct propaganda and educational campaigns that reached outside of London and Paris and roused significant support for their popular demonstrations. Though diplomats across Europe continually monitored public opinion in their host countries, it remained difficult to gauge public sentiment with any degree of accuracy. The changes in the memberships and programmes of the pacifist organizations are useful mainly as a barometer of shifts in mood. The older movements, such as the League of Nations Union (LNU) in Britain and the *Association pour la paix par le droit* (APD) and other League societies in France lost membership and influence. In both countries there was a turn to more absolute forms of pacifism. The Communist peace campaign, more significant in France than in Britain, further divided the peace movement, sapping efforts to mobilize support for collective security and driving some anti-Communists into the pro-appeasement camp. In contrast, the large National Government majority in parliament and Baldwin's careful handling of the rearmament issue during the 1935 election avoided the fierce political divisions found in France.

Membership figures for the LNU dropped in 1936 and 1937 as its leadership found it increasingly difficult to bridge or even paper over the gap between its pro- and anti-sanctions wings. Former supporters sought other alternatives more in keeping with their prevailing anxieties. Clifford Allen, a conscientious objector in the Great War and an enthusiastic activist for the LNU, began to campaign for 'peaceful change' as a means to avoid the divisive issue of military force. After attending the Nuremburg rally at Hitler's invitation in September 1936, he became a leading advocate of negotiations for a new 'all around peace settlement' and concessions to Germany that would promote Anglo-German friendship. LNU members were also attracted to the Peace Pledge Union (PPU), the most dynamic and most popular pacifist organization in Britain. Launched by Canon Dick Sheppard in May 1936, its original sponsors included Bertrand Russell, Aldous Huxley, Storm Jameson, Rose Macauley and, later, Vera Brittain. No subscription was required for membership, only a postcard renouncing war. Its simple message, humanitarian appeal, and high-profile supporters, as well as the use of the most modern propaganda techniques, proved a winning combination. By the end of 1936, it had some 118,000 members and for a time it seemed possible that it might become a true mass movement, or at least one with sufficient leverage to make its voice heard in the highest political circles. The LNU also lost support when one of its most important figures, Viscount Robert Cecil, who not only became co-president of the *Rassemblement universel pour la paix* (RUP), along with Pierre Cot, a prominent French Socialist politician, decided to launch a British section called the International Peace Campaign (IPC) early in 1936. The IPC proved to be a major rival to the LNU in attracting left-wing support for a common peace front. From the start the French Communists played a major role in the RUP; its Communist links, about which Cecil remained singularly naïve, blocked any form of amalgamation between the LNU and IPC as trade unionists, Catholics, and Conservatives defeated Cecil's efforts in this direction. The IPC thus continued as a separate organization (with a strong Stalinist wing) until 1940, standing on a collective security platform and running highly successful 'peace weeks'. The duplication of effort and of recruitment drives undermined the impact of the collective security message and indeed led to a polarization of attitudes.

Pro-peace groups divided into those supporting, for very different reasons, the conciliation and appeasement of Germany and those advocating rearmament and containment as the best means of meeting the German challenge. But it seems highly probable that, taken together, those favouring a more sympathetic attitude towards German claims for revision represented a majority of the articulate population. If the Peace Ballot had been held in the summer or autumn of 1936, the result might have been very different from that of 1935. In October 1936, Churchill, a backer of sanctions and a League of Nations 'strong enough to hold a potential aggressor in restraint by armed strength' before turning to the mitigation of 'just and real grievances', planned a great public meeting to rally cross-party support for rearmament.[1] Despite marshalling all the various small groups with which he was associated, along with supporters of rearmament from within the LNU and even from within the Trades Union Congress, it was a failure. Many of the pacifists present could not bring themselves to support war-like preparations. To compound matters, Edward VIII's romance with Wallis Simpson became public news only two days before the meeting was held; there was little room for coverage of any other domestic items.

The situation in France was different, but the results were similar. The political and ideological divisions leading up to the May 1936 elections, and the responses to the triumph of the Popular Front, went far deeper than any that existed in Britain. The questions of peace and war, rearmament and militarism, were fought out in the political arena.

[1] Quoted in R.A.C. Parker, *Churchill and Appeasement*, 107.

Such issues not only divided the parties on the right and the left but led to splits within the parties, as was the case with the Socialists. Though the Popular Front slogan 'Paix, pain, liberté' appealed to a wide circle of voters, the Spanish Civil War disrupted the consensus on the left and exposed the fault lines of the Blum coalition. Anti-war feeling ran deep; its adherents were highly vocal. The intellectual élites, the *lycée* teachers, the powerful veterans' groups, and the peasantry shared the common hostility to militarism and to extended spending on rearmament. The older forms of dissent, such as the APD's brand of pacifism with its optimistic belief in international law and respect for justice, were already being crowded out during the 'hinge years' of 1929–1933 and their number of supporters continued to shrink thereafter. The triple crises of Ethiopia, the Rhineland, and Spain exposed the fragility of its belief that nations would abide by the rules of law and that isolation and moral sanctions would be sufficient to maintain the peace. The Ligue internationale des combattants de la paix (LICP), founded by Victor Méric in 1930, was the largest and most active pacifist group in France. It attracted those who feared that the coming war with its new weapons of destruction would destroy civilization. Méric hoped to enrol all 'absolute pacifists', men and women who believed that peace was only 'possible and lasting by total and rapid disarmament without concerning oneself about the neighbour'.[2] The organization grew quickly, with a paid-up membership of about 20,000 (still small by British standards), as it sponsored highly successful and well-attended winter speaking tours across France. But the flowering of the LICP was a brief one. Membership began to level off from about 1934 to 1936 and then entered a period of decline. Its appeal was of a negative kind. The focus was on the enemy within, mainly the 'capitalists' who had led France into war, and there was little by way of a concrete programme. Members were urged to fight Fascism in France but not to join in any form of anti-Fascist activity abroad. At first sympathetic to the Popular Front, its leaders (Méric died in October 1933) became disillusioned with Blum and the Socialist party, which, they charged, had abandoned its belief in antimilitarism. The Spanish Civil War posed a real problem for these 'integral pacifists'. Some believed that while France should not intervene in Spain for fear of spreading the war, they were willing to join in France's defence with arms should it be directly attacked. Others remained faithful to the concepts of absolute pacifism. Such uncertainties undercut the influence of their public awareness campaigns.

[2] Quoted in Norman Ingram, *The Politics of Dissent: Pacifism in France, 1919–1939* (Oxford, 1991), 136.

The RUP, formed after the conclusion of the Franco-Soviet pact and in its origins very much the offspring of the Popular Front, represented one of the final efforts to save the League of Nations. Its slogan, 'Sauver la Société des Nations, c'est sauver la paix', gave some indication of its purpose. Its programme strongly resembled that of the LNU with its emphasis on collective security, disarmament, and strengthening the League mechanisms for resolving disputes that might lead to war. In its promotion both of collective security and resistance to aggressors, it attracted a wide variety of supporters: unions, cooperative associations, women's and youth movements. The Communists continued to play a major part in its development; it was very much part of the Moscow-led peace campaign. While many members of the RUP were not Communists, Paris became one of the centres of the European anti-Fascist movement and the RUP was its most important public voice. Spain again proved a critical divider: the RUP supported intervention and a military front to check aggressors, which pushed away the 'integral pacifists' who were more concerned with preserving the peace than facing the Fascist threat. Communist activities also adversely affected the women's peace organizations as doctrinaire leaders broke off from the main body of the international women's peace movement and, following the Stalinist line, became isolated both from the feminist and pacifist movements while leaving a trail of acrimony behind them.

The Geneva system was found wanting by many, but it had some life in it yet. It was not in fact true that disarmament was dead after June 1934. Arthur Henderson, president of the effectively defunct World Disarmament Conference, received the Nobel Peace Prize in 1934 for his efforts, vain as they had been. He died in October 1935, his hopes for the conference's resurrection unfulfilled. Its executive bureau met one last time in May 1937, only to urge that work continue and that the League Secretariat's disarmament section should carry out a survey of national policies for controlling the manufacture of and trade in arms. The collection and publication of information, in the shape of the annual *Armaments Year-Book* and *Statistical Year-Book of the Trade in Arms and Ammunition*, remained practically the only function of this tiny but dedicated staff. The fifteenth and final edition of the *Armaments Year-Book*, for 1939–1940, appeared in June 1940 and was the very last League publication under the long series heading of 'disarmament'. Cecil may have complained with some justice that all the data they contained were already public property but, despite the German absence, these annual reports were sometimes the only published source of information and remained essential for charting the changes taking place in national armaments levels. They are still an invaluable source for contemporary historians of the 1930s. Other efforts continued for more interventionist measures. A public wave of revulsion with the activities of the so-called 'merchants of death', the manufacturers of armaments and the financiers who profited from the arms trade, led to demands for the imposition of controls. The Nye committee hearings of 1934 in Washington and the report of the Royal Commission on the Manufacture of and Trade in Armaments in London (1935–1936) made major impacts on public attitudes in both countries.

Some reflection of this emerged in Geneva during September 1936, in the Assembly's Third Committee dealing with disarmament, which had not met since 1931 because of the summoning of the World Disarmament Conference. The following year, the smaller states led by the Scandinavian countries, Belgium, and Switzerland pressed for a renewal of the disarmament effort. It was both poignant and tragic that Christian Lange of Norway, winner of the 1921 Nobel Peace Prize and one of the most powerful voices speaking for disarmament at the very first Assembly in 1920, should again proclaim the need for states to take heed. Even while calling for disarmament, he lamented that 'the world was at present living in a state of war which was none the less real for not having been declared'.[3] He was followed to the podium by another old disarmament hand, Joseph Paul-Boncour of France, who agreed that disarmament was the League's 'most essential aim', provided 'it were matched with its necessary complement, the organization of mutual assistance and collective security'.[4] It was the same French argument made repeatedly since the days of the Geneva Protocol of 1924. The Assembly adopted the optimistic resolution 'that a first step should be taken towards the conclusion of a general convention for the reduction and limitation of armaments', but unsurprisingly no action followed during the ensuing year. The 1938 Assembly once again requested governments to respond to its call for action on the supervision of the manufacture and trade in arms, but nothing was done. Instead, the realities of the European situation could be tracked in the rising tempo of rearmament recorded in the annual arms year-books. Secretary General Joseph Avenol, in the middle of the Munich crisis, explained to the Council that he felt it better to postpone any further meetings on reconvening the all-but-forgotten World Disarmament Conference until 'a more propitious date'. Neither the genuine camaraderie generated among those engaged in the lengthy pursuit of disarmament, nor the expertise of the many technical advisers who set their minds to the question, nor the

[3] Lange to Third Committee, 23 September 1937, League of Nations, *Official Journal*, Special Supplement 172 (Geneva, 1937), 8–15.

[4] Paul-Boncour to Third Committee, 23 September 1937, League of Nations, *Official Journal*, Special Supplement 172 (Geneva, 1937), 8–15.

determined efforts of some of the smaller countries to exert leverage on the major powers through the forum of the League Assembly, could produce the compromises needed to achieve a workable disarmament agreement. National interest reigned supreme—and the national interest of the Great Powers was the paramount consideration in determining the outcomes of many years of deliberations in Geneva.

The League of Nations continued to function at another level and here the hopes of the idealists that the League would become a global community working for the greater good of the world's inhabitants were not without substance. This was not Woodrow Wilson's grand vision, nor even the more modest reality born during the 1920s, but an organization that was able to create a long-lasting international regime and to establish norms of state behaviour that, though repeatedly breached, became part of the international fabric. The very failure of the League's disarmament efforts shifted attention to the work of its technical and functional affiliates and sections. Some bodies, such as its Health Organization (HO) and the International Labour Organization (ILO), were semi-independent. Under the inspired leadership of Ludwik Rajchman, who led the Health Organization from 1921 to 1938, an élite network of biomedical and healthcare specialists not only pioneered the collecting and dissemination of information about the outbreak of specific diseases and the spread of epidemics but created laboratory-based programmes that established international standards for biological agents (antitoxins, vaccines, hormones, etc.). Laboratories in Copenhagen and London coordinated trials and evaluations of drugs around the world. Even in the late 1930s, the League, at its own expense, supplied sample standards to countries globally. The HO furnished assistance to governments creating public health and medical programmes, passing information from the more to the less developed countries both within and outside of Europe. A similar case can be made for the contributions of the ILO. Much of its work was technocratic, with emphasis on the collection of economic and labour statistics that became the basis for conventions on industrial and welfare legislation which states could choose to implement or not. Britain, for instance, refused to ratify the convention on the eight-hour day and other countries followed its example and delayed ratification. The ILO moved warily, avoiding investigations into questions that might raise national objections. It relied heavily on implementing measures that could be shown to be advantageous for workers and their employers. Both the HO and the ILO were able to build up long-lasting international networks of expertise. The lines between international and national action became more porous as governments found it useful to adopt standards that were created by acknowledged specialists.

This was equally true of the Social Section of the League, the only section headed by a woman and mostly staffed by women. Though its work was limited by the national priorities of member governments, it made considerable progress in such fights as that against the traffic in human beings. Its constant and close reviews of the world situation, reflected in the annual reports on human traffic by the Fifth Committee of the Assembly, contributed to the development of an institutional memory and the extension of the sphere of its responsibilities. The Advisory Committee on Trafficking employed strategies ranging from the introduction of legal instruments to the creation of enforcement mechanisms. The adoption of the Convention on the Suppression of Traffic of Women of Full Age in 1933 critically provided protection for women of all ages, not just those, as previously, under 21, and gave the League a legal base to campaign for the abolition of licensed houses of prostitution. Despite wariness in addressing the issue of state regulation of prostitution, the draft Convention for the Suppression of the Exploitation of the Prostitution of Others was introduced in 1937, though the war intervened before it could be adopted. Such measures clearly involved interference with the domestic affairs of member states, yet they indicated how domestic matters had become issues for international investigation and action. Action was necessarily limited; in such areas as child welfare, its work was restricted to the exchange of information and expertise. Implementation was possible because of the many contacts with national civil servants active in that area.

The largest and fastest growing section of the League was the Economic and Financial Organization (EFO), the collective name given to its various economic and financial agencies. In order to facilitate the coordination of the global economy, the EFO undertook pioneering work in the collection and dissemination of essential data, materials that remain among the most widely cited sources used to measure the performance of the inter-war world economy. From the outset, this section was the most proactive group within the League. As the section grew in size and status, it did more than gather and publish information on economic performance. The organization sought to advance international cooperation on a wide range of pressing economic and financial issues that engaged its attention. These included studies of the impact of clearing agreements, the utility of the gold standard, the good and bad effects of protectionism, the causes of the world depression, and the means by which another such slump might be averted. One of the great strengths of the Economic and Financial Organization was that, from 1927, the Americans participated in its work. Behind the scenes the EFO made important contributions to international monetary negotiations, including the 1936 Tripartite Stabilization Agreement negotiated between Britain, France, and the United States. There were setbacks. Efforts to promote a five-power conference in 1936 and 1937 to negotiate far-reaching financial and economic agreements that would cut through the extensive network of currency and trade controls failed to produce the desired results. It was not only that Germany and Italy refused to lower their tariffs, the British were strongly opposed to trade liberalization and the French were indifferent. The effort went nowhere, to the frustration of its dedicated officials. This was a star-studded cast. Those who served the EFO included three future Nobel Prize winners, the future head of the International Monetary Fund, Per Jacobson, and one of the architects of the European Union, Jean Monnet. Officials believed that given accurate information, statesmen would adopt rational policies to the benefit both of their own country and the international community. They were to be deeply disappointed in such hopes. After 1937, attempts were made to reform the EFO and to decouple it from the League; some of these ideas were incorporated into the Bruce Report of 22 August 1939. The report, which called attention to the League's social and economic work and urged its development and expansion through a new specialized organ, was shelved during the war but disinterred in 1944, when the Bretton Woods agreement established new independent economic and financial organizations.

Some of the work initiated by the League of Nations during the 1920s was continued right up to the outbreak of the war.[5] Other initiatives collapsed in the face of the new challenges provided by the actions of the authoritarian regimes, above all, by Nazi Germany. The League was committed to the implementation of the Versailles treaty clauses covering mandated territories and minority rights. The Permanent Mandates Commission (PMC) which met twice yearly in Geneva, was supported by a small permanent section of the League. Its last act was to send a report to the Council, scheduled to meet in September 1939, criticizing the British White Paper of May 1939 on Palestine. The PMC, which received and scrutinized the annual reports from the mandatory powers and examined and questioned the latter's representatives, consisted of very distinguished Council appointees, with the necessary experience to more than match the expertise of the colonial administrators. The latter came to have a healthy respect for their interrogators and did not easily dismiss their criticism. The PMC was dependent on material supplied by the mandatory powers and could not prevent them from distorting or withholding information. It had no coercive powers and could only report to the Council as a final sanction.

[5] See the discussion in Zara Steiner, *The Lights that Failed: European International History 1919–1933* (Oxford, 2005), chapter 7.

It could, however, approve or condemn actions, and publicize its views. Some nations were more sensitive to criticism than others but few liked to be publicly rebuked. As was intended, the mandate system served to legitimize this special form of colonial rule but also served to promote the governance of the mandate in the interest of the local inhabitants. Given the variety of the mandates and the practices of the different mandatory powers, it is difficult to draw up an overall balance sheet. 'The mandates system is better understood as a mechanism for generating publicity and norms', Professor Susan Pedersen has concluded, 'than as a system of governance'.[6] The PMC acquired a considerable amount of information, for its examination of the colonial administrators was thorough and painstaking. It was able to set norms of behaviour and provided legitimacy for those nations who came to Geneva and gave proof of their efforts to live up to what the Covenant called their 'sacred trust'. The Council, the last court of appeal, could not, and given its respect for the rights of the sovereign state, would not, compel any mandatory power to conform to the established rules. Nevertheless, the unsparing scrutiny of the mandatory powers' annual reports undoubtedly forced the administering powers to acknowledge the new rules of behaviour if not to meet them. In some cases, the right to petition created or encouraged a degree of political self-awareness that was to have long-range consequences. Within its very restricted limits, the PMC accomplished more than was expected.

The Minority Commission proved a frail instrument of protection during the turbulent 1930s. With the withdrawal of Germany from the League and the repudiation of the minorities treaty by Poland in 1934, the number of petitions to the Minority Commission fell dramatically from a peak of 204 in 1930–1931 to only 15 in 1936. A large number of the receivable petitions during the inter-war period came from the German minority in Poland between 1922 and 1930. Historians differ on the effectiveness of the system even within its restricted scope. There were severe limits on the jurisdiction of the Minority Commission, not only geographically (covering only those states, mainly in Eastern Europe, which had signed minority treaties), but with regard to what petitions the Minority Commission would accept. The system depended on the informal work of the Commission in settling issues through private negotiation with the 'offending' government. The few cases that actually came before the Council, for many were settled informally, generally failed because of the Council's predisposition to respect the full sovereignty of member states. The small minorities

6 Susan Pedersen, 'The Meaning of the Mandates System: An Argument', *Geschichte und Gesellschaft*, 32: 4 (2006), 560.

section of the Secretariat took its work seriously, collecting information, consulting with petitioners, and seeking to find solutions acceptable to 'offenders' who preferred to avoid the publicity involved in an appearance in front of the Council. Again, publicity was the only means of enforcing the minorities regime. Most of the states in Eastern Europe adopted quota systems for educational purposes and introduced discriminatory legislation against their Jewish populations. Nazi propaganda and activity in the multinational states revived nationalist sentiments among the German minority groups, and the Italians were particularly active in Yugoslavia. The League's loss of prestige in the mid-thirties meant the entire system lost a good deal of its efficacy. The hopes of the well-meaning but over-optimistic League officials that governments could be persuaded to accept new norms of behaviour towards their minority groups proved as illusory as the assumptions of the peacemakers that the establishment of democratic states would promote their peaceful assimilation.

The refugee regime suffered most from the weakening of the League, despite the progress made during the 1920s when the driving energy of Fridtjof Nansen and his hand-picked team created a special status for refugees and managed the resettlement of hundreds of thousands of displaced persons. It was not thought at the start of the 1930s that the refugee problem would continue to be of major international concern. In 1931, a new and autonomous Nansen International Office for Refugees was set up with a minute administrative budget. The advent of the Nazis raised the unhappy possibility of a new stream of refugees. The Spanish Civil War would send thousands in search of places of refuge. Before Germany left the League in October 1933, an agreement was reached whereby German refugees would not be placed under the Nansen Office but under the auspices of a separate organization only indirectly connected to the League. It was located in Lausanne to underline its separate existence. The new high commissioner for refugees was an American, James G. MacDonald, a former president of the Foreign Policy Association who had extensive contacts in the New York Jewish community. Because he did not have direct support from the League, MacDonald was even more dependent than Nansen on his private networks both for finance and assistance. Without League backing he found himself at a heavy disadvantage when dealing with national authorities. He discovered, moreover, that most countries were reluctant to admit new refugees and were, in fact, raising barriers to immigration. Despite these circumstances, the High Commission office managed to place almost two-thirds of the refugees leaving Germany between 1933 and 1935. Defeated in his efforts to arouse the international community to take any action in Berlin, MacDonald's resignation letter exposed the inadequacies of the existing system. He insisted that the refugee problem had to be tackled at its source; the League had to make direct representations to the Nazi authorities and not concern itself only with dealing with those forced to flee. MacDonald's letter was widely publicized but no government would consider his main recommendation of protests in Berlin. As he urged, however, the German refugee office was brought directly under the authority of the League. Its competence was narrowly defined as governments were unwilling to interfere in the domestic affairs of any state, least of all a powerful country like Germany. The depression and its after-effects, moreover, created strong domestic opposition to any influx of new emigrants. The international climate hardly favoured the resettlement of Jews. Anti-Semitism was virulent in parts of Eastern Europe and present in the West as well. The member states were careful to avoid appointing any new refugees' administrators who might follow in MacDonald's footsteps.

What emerges from this picture of the post-1935 League of Nations is an institution that no longer was perceived as meeting the chief aims of its founders. The primary focus of its activity was no longer the preservation and, ultimately, the enforcement of peace. That element of its work had by now been discredited, despite the arguments and anguish that debates about the League's powers and obligations continued to generate. Instead, it was mainly in its technical and social work that the League continued to operate, steadily expanding the boundaries of its welfare and economic interests and responsibilities. These were undoubtedly worthy tasks, which forged new types of transnational approaches and networks that would underlie much of the success experienced by the United Nations after 1945. Yet in recognizing these advances, one must not overlook the cheerless truth that during the later 1930s the League was perceived to be, and indeed simply was, a failure. A few individuals and governments would continue to call for reform and even to launch new initiatives. The smaller nations, and, indeed, Litvinov representing the Soviet Union, would try unsuccessfully to re-establish Geneva's position as part of the diplomatic network. The League was no longer at the hub of political negotiations, not even in the attenuated form of the Locarno era. As peace crumbled at the decade's end, few seriously believed that the League could provide the solution to the seemingly unstoppable descent into renewed war.

Less than five months after the German occupation of the Rhineland, the outbreak of the Spanish Civil War showed how irrelevant Geneva had become to European security affairs. In so far as this internal dispute came to involve other European nations, the focus of negotiation was in London where the Non-Intervention Committee held its meetings. While the conflict brought Paris and London together in their joint efforts to contain the Spanish war, the Germans and Italians found new grounds for cooperation and Hitler was provided with further opportunities for advancing his objectives without a major expenditure of men or material. The Soviet Union found itself isolated and Litvinov's efforts to build an anti-German front repeatedly frustrated. The ideological conflict, however erroneously perceived, created further difficulties in establishing the common front against the Axis powers, that might have provided an alternative to the search for an accommodation with Hitler.

Books

Barros, J. C., *Betrayal from Within: Joseph Avenol, Secretary-General of the League of Nations, 1933–1940* (New Haven, CT, 1969).

Callahan, M. D., *A Sacred Trust: The League of Nations and Africa, 1929–1946* (Brighton, 2004).

Ceadel, M., *Pacifism in Britain, 1914–1945: The Defining of a Faith* (Oxford, 1980).

—— *Thinking about Peace and War* (Oxford, 1987).

—— *Semi-detached Idealists: The British Peace Movement and International Relations, 1854–1945* (Oxford, 2000).

Fink, C., *Defending the Rights of Others: The Great Powers, the Jews, and International Minority Protection, 1878–1938* (Cambridge, 2004).

Ingram, N., *The Politics of Dissent: Pacifism in France, 1919–1939* (Oxford, 1991).

Iriye, A., *Global Community: The Role of International Organizations in the Making of the Contemporary World* (Berkeley, CA, 2002).

Kelen, E., *Peace in their Time: Men who Led us In and Out of War, 1914–1945* (New York, 1963).

Kuehl, W. F. and Dunn, L. K., *Keeping the Covenant: American Internationalists and the League of Nations, 1920–1939* (Kent, OH, 1997).

Mazower, M., *Dark Continent: Europe's Twentieth Century* (London, 1998).

Méouchy, N. and Sluglett, P., *The British and French Mandates in Comparative Perspectives/Les mandats français et anglais dans une perspective comparative* (Leiden, 2004).

Pienaar, S., *South Africa and International Relations between the Two World Wars: The League of Nations Dimension* (Johannesburg, 1987).

Scheuermann, M., *Minderheitenschutz contra Konfliktverhütung? Die Minderheitenpolitik des Völkerbundes in den zwanziger Jahren* (Marburg, 2000).

Skran, C. M., *Refugees in Inter-war Europe: The Emergence of a Regime* (New York and Oxford, 1995).

United Nations Library and Graduate Institute of International Studies (ed.), *The League of Nations in Retrospect: Proceedings of the Symposium* (Berlin and New York, 1983). See M. D. Dubin.

Veatch, R., *Canada and the League of Nations* (Toronto, 1975).

Weindling, P. (ed.), *International Health Organizations and Movements, 1918–1939* (Cambridge, 1995). See C. Miller and M. D. Dubin.

Articles and Chapters

CLAVIN, P., 'Europe and the League of Nations', in Gerwarth, R. (ed.), *Twisted Paths: Europe 1914–1945* (Oxford and New York, 2007).

—— and WESSELS, J.-W., 'Transnationalism and the League of Nations: Understanding the Work of its Economic and Financial Organization', *Contemporary European History*, 14: 4 (2005).

DUBIN, M. D., 'Transgovernmental Processes in the League of Nations', *International Organization*, 37: 3 (1983).

MAZOWER, M., 'Minorities and the League of Nations in Interwar Europe', *Daedalus*, 126 (1997).

MEARSHEIMER, J., 'The False Promise of International Institutions', *International Security*, 19: 3 (1994/1995).

METZGER, B., 'Towards an International Human Rights Regime during the Inter-War Years: The League of Nations' Combat of Traffic in Women and Children', in Grant, K., Levine, P. and Trentmann, F. (eds.), *Beyond Sovereignty: Britain, Empire and Transnationalism, c.1880–1950* (Basingstoke, 2007).

MILLER, C., 'Geneva—the Key to Equality: Inter-war Feminists and the League of Nations', *Women's History Review*, 3: 2 (1994).

PEDERSEN, S.,'The Meaning of the Mandates System: An Argument', *Geschichte und Gesellschaft*, 32: 4 (2006).

—— 'Review Essay: Back to the League of Nations', *The American Historical Review*, 112: 4 (2007).

SALERNO, R., 'Britain, France and the Emerging Italian Threat, 1935–1938', in Alexander, M. S. and Philpott, W. J. (eds.), *Anglo-French Defence Relations between the Wars* (Basingstoke, 2002).

STONE, D. R., 'Imperialism and Sovereignty: The League of Nations' Drive to Control the Global Arms Trade', *Journal of Contemporary History*, 35: 2 (2000).

WEBSTER, A., 'The Transnational Dream: Politicians, Diplomats and Soldiers in the League of Nations' Pursuit of International Disarmament, 1920–1930', *Contemporary European History*, 14: 4 (2005).

Theses

METZGER, B., 'The League of Nations and Human Rights: From Practice to Theory', Ph.D. thesis, University of Cambridge, 2001.

5

The Spanish Cockpit, 1936–1937

I

The assassination of José Calvo Sotelo, a leading monarchist, on the evening of 12 July 1936, by left-wing Socialists, was the signal to a small group of army leaders to launch their challenge to the Popular Front regime in Spain. The three key perpetrators, General Emilio Mola and his two fellow conspirators, generals Francisco Franco and José Sanjurjo, anticipated a quick victory and the rapid replacement of the Republican regime by a military junta. Instead of a swift *coup d'état*, the rebel generals found themselves engaged in a long and bloody civil war that did not end until April 1939, and which reverberated far beyond the country's borders. In a state where neither the Fascists nor the Communists had been of any serious political significance, Spain became a battleground for these contending ideologies. Germany and Italy backed the Nationalist forces while the Soviet Union, Mexico, and to a limited extent France, supplied the Republicans. The British and French governments supported a policy of non-intervention that successfully prevented the expansion of the conflict, but at the price of assuring Franco's victory. Since none of the countries involved wanted a general war, the struggle in 'the Spanish cockpit' was contained.[1] It remained, nevertheless, prominent on the diplomatic agenda until Hitler's assaults on the territorial status quo in 1938 focused attention on central Europe.

Within weeks of the attempted *coup*, the struggle became ideological. For contemporaries in Europe and in the Western hemisphere, the conflict seemed a battle between good and evil. Those supporting the Nationalist cause, which was rapidly identified directly with Franco personally, saw it as a crusade for order and stability against the forces of anarchy, Communism, and godlessness. Under this crusading banner, the *Caudillo* ('leader', Franco's choice of title), backed by the Church, insisted that the war had to be pursued to its bloody end until the

[1] The phrase comes from the title of a memoir of the civil war: Franz Borkenau, *The Spanish Cockpit: An Eye-witness Account of the Political and Social Conflicts of the Spanish Civil War* (London, 1937).

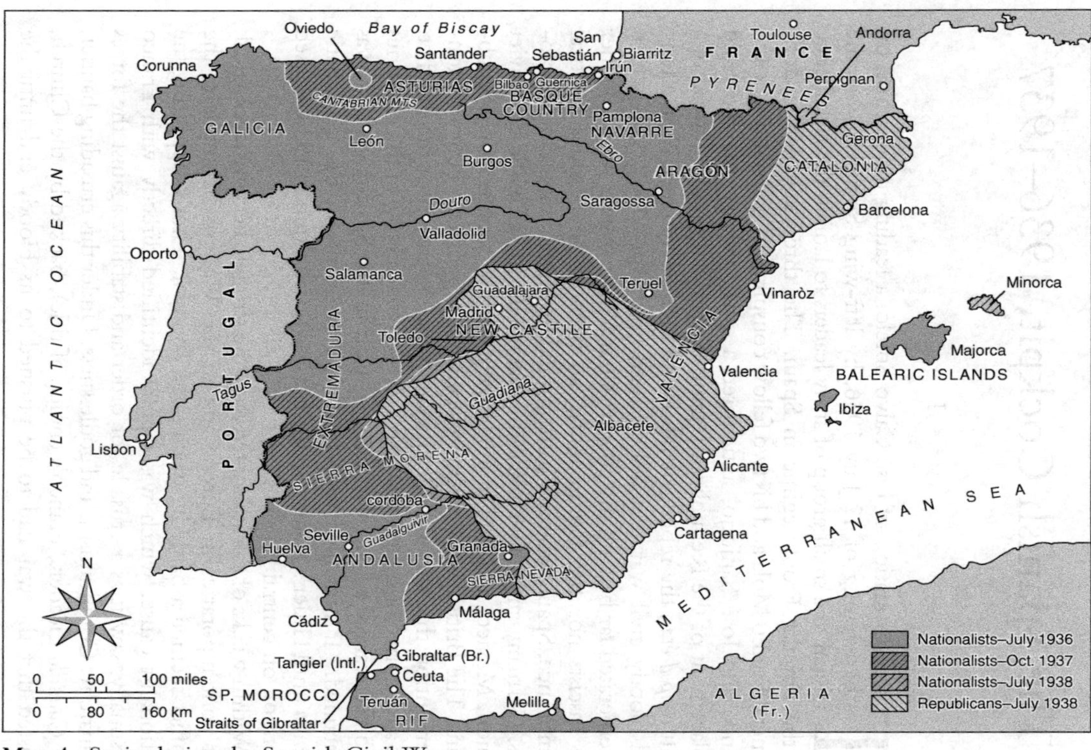

Map 4. Spain during the Spanish Civil War

evil-doers were annihilated. All attempts at mediation were disregarded. The intervention of the Soviet Union on the Republican side confirmed this Manichean image of the war, giving point to Fascist claims that only a Nationalist victory would avert the Bolshevik subversion of Spain and the contamination of the rest of Europe. Those who embraced the Republic's cause subscribed to an equally simplified version of the Spanish story. For much of the European and American left, and the term covered a wide spectrum of political opinion in 1936, the Republicans were fighting a war to maintain a democratic and progressive government against the forces of reaction, the landowners, industrialists, priests, and foreign exploiters. The involvement of Germany and Italy was the proof that Franco had made a bargain with the Fascist devil. For the Republic's supporters, the conflict was seen as a struggle between democracy and 'fascism', between 'right' and 'wrong'. Outside Spain, there was a uniquely charged emotional response to what was seen as the first real effort to fight the dictators. This image of the civil war continued to resonate down the century. '[I]t remains the only political cause which, even in retrospect', the British historian Eric Hobsbawm wrote in 1994, 'appears as pure and compelling as it did in 1936'.[2] Spain, indeed, became a 'cause', commemorated in verse, prose, and art. No earlier event in the inter-war period elicited this kind of response in so many different countries. Almost every well-known writer and artist was called upon to declare himself or herself for or against the Republic, and some indeed went to Spain to fight, the majority, but not all, on the anti-Franco side. The 'Spanish crusade', meaning the Nationalist cause, received the pope's blessing. The pictures and reports of bombings and executions heightened the sense of moral outrage. It was partly for this reason that later accounts of what actually happened in Spain, such as George Orwell's *Homage to Catalonia* (1938), angered or shocked so many pro-Republican readers. The coverage of the war contributed to its importance on both sides. Newsreels brought the scenes of battle to local cinemas; accounts of fighting were front-page news in New York and in Paris where domestic events generally commanded most attention. The modern combat cameraman came of age during 1936–1937. *Life* in the United States and *Picture Post* in Britain carried photographs from Spain, most famously those by Robert Capa. As the focus of public attention and debate, often fierce and emotional, the civil war's myths and realities became part of the contemporary climate of opinion. Mussolini saw in the Spanish war an opportunity to fashion the 'new Italy' and the 'new

[2] Eric Hobsbawm, *The Age of Extremes: The Short Twentieth Century, 1914–1991* (London, 1994), 160.

Italian'. 'There is only one way to create a warlike people', the Duce claimed, 'to have ever greater masses who have waged war and ever greater masses who want to go to war'.[3] If Hitler could not fully exploit the triumphs of his air aces and Condor Legion, while wearing the mask of non-intervention, he could use anti-Bolshevism to create an enhanced sense of unity without cost or danger to his still vulnerable country. In the western democracies, some supporters of the Republic deserted the peace movement and began to talk of rearmament. Many more saw the conflict as a necessary war to halt the rise of European Fascism. Others in liberal and left-wing circles, however, saw Spain as an object lesson in the horrors of modern warfare. The fact that atrocities were being committed in Spain, and not in some remote country, gave added point to current fears. The pictures of ravaged Guernica, and the reports of the bombing of Madrid and Barcelona, fed the fear of aerial bombardment, already so important a factor in British policy in Europe and in its rearmament programme. H. G. Wells's film, *Things to Come,* appeared on local screens in 1936 to warn of the disasters the next war would bring. Traditional pacifism, always stronger on the left than on the right, was strengthened rather than weakened by the events in Spain. Even where reports created sympathy for the Republic, they could reinforce the anti-war case. Dick Shepperd's Peace Pledge Union attracted many anti-Franco intellectuals to the pro-peace cause. Enthusiasm for the Republic did not reverse the anti-war currents so strong in France, particularly in the countryside, where half of France's population still lived. Two-thirds of the country's five million WWI veterans still living in 1938 were formally enrolled in veterans' associations, almost all of which stood on an anti-war platform. Members of right-wing parties, strong, partisan, and highly vocal in France, preferred to defeat the 'Reds' at home rather than join the anti-Bolshevik crusade in Spain.

Franco was well aware of the appeal of anti-Communism to rightist groups, and fully exploited foreign fears of a 'Red Spain' and the spread of Russian Bolshevism. The defenders of the Republic were labelled 'Communist', even before the Soviet Union sent aid or men. It was to gain assistance from Berlin and Rome that Franco waved the anti-red flag; it was a tactic, as was his offer to create a Fascist state. Anti-Bolshevism attracted support in Catholic and conservative circles in Spain, and abroad. It is not without irony that the anti-revolutionaries and so-called defenders of order became the supporters of rebellion. Franco had to stomach a great deal of unwelcome criticism from his Italian and German advisers, but their assistance was important, and at

[3] Quoted in Giuseppe Bottai, *Vent'anni e un giorno (24 Iuglio 1943)* (Milan, 1949), 113.

key moments critical. The more they committed men and equipment to prevent his defeat, the more confident he was of their continuing support. And nothing that the Axis representatives said deflected the *Caudillo* from fighting the kind of war he wanted or establishing his own kind of state, with himself as unchallenged leader. Franco's brutality, repression, and killing of his enemies and own supporters, shocked even his Fascist and Nazi advisers. For Franco, the war was a 'crusade', not only against Bolshevism but against all threats to his absolute rule.

The Spanish Civil War was not the first phase of the Second World War, but it was more than a sideshow. The diplomatic and strategic scene was changed by the murderous struggle in a country peripheral to the European balance of power. The very duration of the struggle acted as a catalyst in defining the alignments of states which, in one way or another, were drawn into the Spanish imbroglio. For some, the line-up in Spain reduced the possibility for diplomatic manoeuvre. The war tightened the bonds between Italy and Germany, limiting the former's choice of options and strengthening the anti-French and anti-British direction of Mussolini's planning. The reactions of the other powers to the civil war confirmed Hitler's perceptions of his would-be adversaries. It convinced him that Britain might still be wooed for a policy of non-involvement in central European affairs, and that France would follow in the British wake. In Britain, the seeming success of the policy of non-intervention encouraged Chamberlain's hopes for peace in Europe and his misplaced efforts to detach Mussolini from Hitler. Franco's victory increased France's sense of strategic vulnerability, and made the alignment with Britain central to its policies, whatever the differences between the two governments on handling Mussolini. It strengthened the ideological dimension of French military planning. Soviet attempts to convince Britain and France to join an anti-Fascist front heightened the hostility of those in London and Paris who distrusted the Russians and sought compromises with the Axis powers to preserve the peace. Their hostile reading of Soviet intentions coloured, though hardly determined, official responses to Hitler's *coups* during 1938. The Soviets sought, in vain, to use the Spanish Civil War as a way of persuading Britain and France to abandon their pursuit of agreements with Hitler. Their failure strengthened Bolshevik beliefs in the inevitable capitalist war, and intensified Stalin's obsessive fear of internal enemies, real and imaginary, who were to be stamped out at any cost. Under *Narodnyy Komissariat Vnutrennikh Del* (NKVD) direction, anarchists, the *Partido Obrero Unificación Marxista* (POUM) (anti-Stalinist Communists), and other 'Trotskyite subversives' were 'exposed' and liquidated. Many Soviet advisers sent to Spain from Moscow were recalled, imprisoned, and/or disappeared. The purges in Russia and Spain fed on each other.

Despite the horrors that the civil war spawned, for the foreign countries involved in the Spanish struggle, Spain was hardly more than a pawn in a much larger strategic game.

II

The Spanish Civil War had its roots in Spanish history. Its origins had little to do with other nations. Following the creation of the second Republic in April 1931, the next five years saw governments change from left-wing to right-wing and back again. The left wanted to weaken the influence of the Catholic Church, reform education, and cut down the size and importance of the swollen army. It was recognized that something had to be done to change the ownership and management of land, and to increase the rights of industrial workers. Separate cultures should be recognized, as in Catalonia and the Basque provinces, and granted greater political autonomy. Most army officers, clergy (except in the Basque region), landowners, and businessmen feared and opposed these reforms. The right stood for the Church, the army, and for 'tradition', order, and a unified Spain. On 16 February 1936, the right lost the national elections to a great coalition of the left known as the Popular Front, composed of liberals, Socialists, anarchists (the only politically significant movement of its kind in Europe) and Communists (a numerically small group with no representatives in the government). Alarmed by this, and by demonstrators seeking accelerated change, sections of the army conspired to overthrow the government as other soldiers had done so often before them. Open rebellion came with the shooting of Calvo Sotelo, a prominent right-wing deputy. General Emilio Mola sent out orders for revolt; the rising began in Morocco on 17 July. In the following two days further risings broke out on the Spanish mainland. After four days the rebels held about one-third of Spain, including the rich agricultural lands of the north and the ports of Galicia. Madrid, Barcelona, Valencia, and Bilbao remained in the hands of the republican forces.

If the *coup* had succeeded, there would have been no civil war. Instead, it unleashed the social revolution it was supposed to suppress. In Madrid, Santiago Casares Quiroga, the Republican prime minister, refused to arm the workers and resigned on 18 July. His successor tried to open negotiations with the rebels but it was too late. José Giral, a Socialist, assumed power the next day and the workers were armed. The defence of the Republic would be left to the left-wing militias and *ad hoc* revolutionary bodies. The civil war had begun. The generals had not anticipated this result; even Franco, the least optimistic of the participating generals, did not expect the struggle to last beyond

September. He had flown by private plane from the Canary Islands to Morocco where, by the time he arrived at Tetuan on 19 July, the rebels were in the ascendant. Their leaders quickly decided that foreign assistance would be needed if they were to succeed. The campaign in Spain was centred on taking Madrid, but General Mola's northern armies were stalemated by the workers' militias, while Franco's African troops were cut off in Spanish Morocco and in danger of being blockaded by the generally loyal Republican Navy. General José Sanjurjo, who was to have led the triumphal rebel entry into Madrid, was killed on his way from Portugal to Spain. This was an important turning point for Franco's future. In independent moves during the latter part of July, both Franco and Mola sent emissaries to Rome and Berlin to solicit assistance. These were the first steps towards the internationalization of the Spanish crisis.

Franco, though little known outside Spain, was the first to approach the Italians, on 22 July. While Ciano, the arrogant, ambitious, and newly-appointed foreign minister, was enthusiastic, Mussolini reacted cautiously to the Spanish requests. He began to consider limited intervention only after news from Paris and London that the French would not intervene in Spain, and that the British government was divided in its views and would not oppose Italian action. He appears to have definitely made up his mind after receiving, on 27 July, a detailed despatch from the Italian embassy in Moscow reporting the Kremlin's 'great embarrassment' regarding the civil war and suggesting that the Soviets might follow a policy of 'prudent neutrality'. Limited Italian aid might be decisive in the Spanish struggle. A squadron of twelve Savoia Marchetti S. 81 bombers was sent from Sardinia to Morocco (only nine arrived safely on 30 July), and went into operation as soon as the necessary fuel and additional Italian pilots arrived. Mussolini's decisions were not based on any careful calculation of Franco's possible success, but in the belief that a small amount of assistance could pay major dividends for Italy's position in the western Mediterranean, while destroying the threat of a 'red' Republic in Spain, and protecting the Fascist revolution in Italy. In Germany, too, Franco's emissaries proved successful. There had been extensive contacts between the German and Spanish armies and intelligence services in the years before the *coup*, but they had nothing to do with the initial revolt or with Hitler's decision to assist Franco. The first attempts, through Johannes Bernhardt, a German businessman and member of the Nazi *Auslandsorganisation*, and Adolf Langenheim, the Nazi chief in Spanish Morocco, were rebuffed. Assisted first by Alfred Hess, and then by his brother Rudolf, the deputy Führer favoured by Hitler, they were able to bypass the unsympathetic Wilhelmstrasse and War Ministry and reach Hitler himself, who was attending the Wagner festival in Bayreuth. Though he was at first contemptuous, by the end of the evening of 25 July, there were calls to Blomberg and Göring telling of his intention to launch *Unternehmen Feuerzauber* (redolent with overtones of Siegfried's passage through the flames to liberate Brünhilde) and to send even more planes than Franco requested. Göring, at first doubtful, rapidly became an enthusiast when he saw that Hitler was sympathetic. He organized a special staff to administer the military aid going to Franco. On 29 July, German planes sent to Morocco began transporting the élite troops of the Spanish North African Army to mainland Spain.

The arrival of the German and Italian planes was critical for the rebel forces in the first stage of the war, when the *coup* might have collapsed. Hitler's assistance, in particular, enabled Franco to move nearly 14,000 Spanish and Moroccan troops between 29 July and 11 October 1936, across the Straits of Gibraltar to Seville where they were most needed, leap-frogging the Republican navy. It was 'the first successful large-scale airlift in history'.[4] Hitler's much quoted 1941 boast—'Franco ought to erect a monument to the glory of the Junkers Ju-52. It is this aircraft that the Spanish revolution has to thank for its victory'[5]—contained more than a kernel of truth. It is possible that Franco would have transported his troops to the mainland even without foreign support, but not in such numbers or in so short a time. During September, Hitler expanded his intervention (dubbed 'Operation Otto') sending men, tanks, and radio equipment to Spain. The transport planes were converted into bombers and additional fighters were despatched from Germany. By mid-October, the Germans probably had some 600 men in Spain. Though the Germans appear to have been the main suppliers to the rebels in August and September, the Italians, not to be outdone, and without fear of international repercussions, increased their own shipments. Prompted by Franco, they took independent action in the Balearics, the islands (Majorca and Menorca) that lay across the main sea route between France's North African colonies and its Mediterranean ports. The rebels seized Majorca and, with Italian assistance, contained the Republican counter-attack. By mid-September, the island was in Falangist hands. Rome, however, did not want to go too far in provoking the already alarmed French or antagonizing the British: Ciano refused to sanction a Falangist *coup* on the island or to back a proposed invasion of Menorca. With the victory at Majorca, the rebels won control of the sea coasts and later the Straits of Gibraltar. The island served as a useful base for air

[4] Robert H. Whealey, *Hitler and Spain: The Nazi Role in the Spanish Civil War, 1936–1939* (Lexington, KY, 1989), 101.

[5] H. Trevor-Roper (ed.), *Hitler's Table Talk, 1941–1944* (London, 1953), 687.

attacks on private merchant vessels supplying the Republic. Majorca remained an Italian show; the Germans were not consulted.[6] In October, under pressure from Franco, the Germans and Italians sent submarines to Spanish waters to harass the Republic's fleet.

The success of the 'victory convoy' above the Straits of Gibraltar confirmed Franco's international credentials at Mola's expense, and made him a hero in the Nationalist armies. By mid-August, the Francoists were receiving regular shipments of armaments and ammunition, and controlling the flow of Axis supplies to Mola. The latter, hardly a match for his far more politically astute rival, agreed on 11 August to yield all authority over foreign assistance to Franco. Most of the early successes of the Nationalists in August were due to Franco's Army of Africa. He used fear and killings to paralyse his enemies, terrify the untrained citizen militias, and prevent future opposition to his rule. Even in the initial stage of his campaign, Franco's thoughts and strategy were directed to the fulfilment of his political ambitions. On 21 September, he was made *Generalísimo* of all the rebel armies, though with some degree of hesitation on the part of his military peers. His decision to move against Toledo rather than to march towards Madrid to join Mola's army, arose from calculations that the relief of the Alcazar in Toledo would silence all doubters and open the way to his becoming head of state. With the 'epic of Alcazar', re-staged two days later for cinema audiences across the world, Franco became an international name. On 1 October, he became the chief of state with 'absolute powers'. There was no one, either in the rebel military or civilian ranks, to challenge the authority of the new *Caudillo*. The forced unification of the rightist parties, a union of the Fascist *Falange* with the entirely separate Carlists, allowed Franco to create a new political movement totally under his own control, the *Falange Española Tradicionalista y de las JONS*. It ended the possibility of an independent Spanish Fascist movement. This physically unimpressive man, short, balding, and with a fluting voice, was transformed, through a massive propaganda campaign, into a modern *El Cid*.

Franco was slow to give his attention to the Madrid campaign. His armies were tired and their advance slowed by fierce Republican resistance. It was not until 20 October that he concentrated on the capital, though he took no direct part in the subsequent operations. The delay had given the Republicans time to see to the capital's defences. The Giral government in Madrid had fallen on 4 September and a

[6] Menorca, strategically the most important island of the group, stayed in Republican hands until early 1939 when, with British help, it was occupied by Franco's Spanish troops.

cabinet under Francisco Largo Caballero, with Communist representation, was installed in its place (though it had already fled the city for Valencia). When the attack on Madrid at last came, on 8 November, it was unexpectedly repulsed. It was a major defeat for the rebels and saw the employment, by the defenders, of Russian tanks and fighter aircraft and the first appearance of the international brigades. If the Republican forces had not been too depleted to mount a counter-offensive, this might have been the turning point in the civil war. Franco acknowledged defeat and abandoned the attack. He was fortunate not only in the loyalists' exhaustion, but in the joint German and Italian decision to grant formal recognition of his government on 18 November, without the capture of Madrid, as they had demanded. Franco told cheering crowds in Salamanca a day earlier that Germany and Italy were 'the bulwarks of culture, civilization, and Christianity in Europe'.[7] It was accepted in Berlin and Rome that only massive reinforcements could save the Nationalist cause.

The basis for possible Italo-German military co-operation in Spain had been laid at a series of meetings in August 1936 between Admiral Wilhelm Canaris, head of German military intelligence and a fluent Spanish speaker, and General Mario Roatta, his flamboyant Italian counterpart. It is highly probable that the Italians already knew that Hitler was helping Franco, though Canaris minimized the German contribution in the hope of securing greater Italian involvement. In Rome on 28 August, Canaris insisted that supplies be provided only to Franco, setting the seal on the latter's position. During September, a joint Italo-German mission to Franco drew up plans to meet the general's material requirements. Military co-operation was paralleled by steps towards a general political agreement. Mussolini, in particular, wished to cement the partnership with the Führer, hoping to find support for his imperial dreams. During August and September, Hitler sent strong signals to Mussolini assuring the Duce that he had no ambitions in the Mediterranean (the 'Baltic was Germany's Mediterranean') and was anxious for closer ties. At meetings between Ciano and Göring in Rome, both men denied that their countries had any territorial ambitions in Spain (apart from the Italian interest in the Balearic islands and Ceuta). Both stressed the threat to their plans from Britain, mainly to block any unilateral negotiations with London. At a subsequent meeting between Ciano and Hitler at Berchtesgaden on 24 October, the two men agreed on joint military efforts in Spain, the recognition of Franco as head of government as soon as Madrid was taken (expected within the next few days), and co-operation to prevent the creation of a separate Catalan state by France. Responding to Ciano's

7 Quoted in Paul Preston, *Franco: A Biography* (London, 1993), 106.

revelations from purloined sources that Britain's policies were directed against Germany as much as Italy, Hitler called for the formation of a bloc against the democratic powers, and promised that Germany would be ready for war within three years. Pleased with the promise of a future Mussolini–Hitler meeting, Ciano paid little attention to Hitler's boast.

In Spain, Franco's German and Italian advisers were deeply disturbed by his failure to pursue the Madrid campaign more energetically. At the end of October, clearly mystified by his tactics, Blomberg warned the Nationalist leader, through emissaries, that he would receive further reinforcements only under stringent conditions, in particular, the more systematic and active conduct of the war. Hardly pleased by such conditions, Franco had no alternative but to accept the German rebuke. After the defeat in Madrid the German intervention was again expanded. The German Condor Legion, consisting of specialized units with the most modern equipment, including aircraft of all types, tanks, and anti-tank artillery, was quickly assembled (the name came from the civilian transport planes of the German Lufthansa A.G., the Condor Lufthansa, which flew from Spain to the Canary Islands and then to South America). Five thousand Germans landed in Cádiz on 16 November and a further seven thousand on 26 November with artillery, aircraft, and armoured transport. This proved to be the last major escalation in the number of Germans fighting in Spain. Hitler had no wish to provoke French, and possibly British, intervention with a greater and more public build-up of German forces. It was at this point that Hitler probably decided Germany was only to play a secondary part in the Spanish drama, and that Mussolini was to be given the primacy he sought. At a meeting called by Mussolini in Rome on 6 December, attended by Ciano, Roatta, and Canaris, it was agreed to co-ordinate the delivery of military aircraft to Franco, and to give Italy the sole responsibility for patrolling Spain's Mediterranean coasts and for operations in Spanish harbours. The Germans limited themselves to Atlantic operations. Canaris warned Mussolini that Germany could not be seen to send large numbers of troops to Spain without international repercussions. On 21 December, Hitler, with his military advisers in full agreement, decided that only replacements for the Condor Legion and a small SS unit to train Spanish police officers would be sent to Spain. Enough material assistance would be offered in the form of aircraft, cannon, anti-aircraft guns, and ammunition to make sure that Franco was not defeated. Though the rebels' military situation took a turn for the worse in early 1937, the German leadership proved unwilling to expand its involvement. Hitler was content to leave to the Italians the main task of underwriting Franco's victory.

With Franco facing defeat in November 1936 and in need of massive assistance, Mussolini's commitment, though conditions were attached, became deeper and irrevocable. An economic and military agreement with Franco was concluded on 28 November which prohibited the free passage of troops of any third power, and provided for benevolent neutrality in case of conflict with a third party or the imposition of sanctions. The anti-French intent of the secret agreement was obvious. There was no specific Spanish commitment but Mussolini felt that he had tied Franco to Rome. In return, he was prepared to send the combat forces that the Nationalists so desperately needed. In mid-December, arrangements were made for two mixed brigades fully armed and equipped for combat to be despatched. In addition, Mussolini sent two contingents of 3,000 Black Shirts with their own officers and equipment, who were to be under Italian command. Irritated by this slight to his authority, Franco nonetheless used the Black Shirts as soon as they arrived, and then requested another 9,000 troops. Canaris's warning to Mussolini with regard to Germany failed to deter him; the strong doubts of two of his military leaders, Balbo and Badoglio, were disregarded. In Rome, in mid-January 1937, the new division of assistance to Franco was confirmed with Göring: there would be no large German contribution of men. The future agenda included a joint blockade, joint propaganda and intelligence activities, and a renewed invitation for the Duce to visit Berlin. Mussolini would have liked the Germans to shoulder more of the military burden but, hardly anxious to see Hitler establish any claim to the Mediterranean spoils, he did not ask for more. His impatience and dissatisfaction was directed at the *Caudillo* to whom, nevertheless, he continued to send more troops and material. To ensure the successful co-ordination of the now extensive Italian war effort, a new department, the *Ufficio Spagna*, was created in the Foreign Ministry under Ciano's direction, and Roatta, again due to Ciano's intervention, was put in charge of all the Italian military actions in Spain. While Mussolini refused Nationalist appeals for submarines, between December 1936 and February 1937 the Italians engaged in a major clandestine underwater campaign against Republican shipping, despite the risk of clashes with Britain. But the results were minimal. By mid-February, almost 49,000 ground troops had been shipped to Spain. In total, the Italians sent 80,000 men to the Spanish war, as compared with fewer than 19,000 Germans.[8] The decision made at the end of July 1936 in favour of limited assistance to Franco had become

[8] For comparative figures see Whealey, *Hitler and Spain*, 102–103; Brian R. Sullivan, 'Fascist Italy's Military Involvement in the Spanish Civil War', *Journal of Military History*, 59: 4 (1995), 718.

'an open-ended commitment that, within five months, would see Italy effectively at war with the Spanish Republic'.[9]

Why did Hitler and Mussolini intervene in the Spanish Civil War? Their governments had viewed the installation of the Popular Front in Madrid with distaste, but hardly with any great sense of alarm. The two dictators had different goals in mind, though for both the war was a way to prepare for the fulfilment of future expansionist ambitions. Mussolini's intervention was an attempt, like the Ethiopian campaign, to stimulate nationalist fervour and to further his imperial ambitions. Italy's strategic interest in the western Mediterranean was of key importance. According to the Duce, Italy was well placed to exercise its power, to strengthen its position at France's expense, and to turn the Mediterranean into an Italian lake. By intervening in Spain, Italy could solve, to its own advantage, the power relations in the Mediterranean. An alliance with Nationalist Spain, under Italian influence, offered the possibility of closing the Mediterranean to the French merchant and military fleets, and obstructing the movement of French troops from North Africa. 'If we use the base in Majorca, that in Pantelleria and others already in existence and equipped', Mussolini told Ribbentrop, 'not one negro will be able to cross from Africa to France by the Mediterranean route'.[10] Italian naval and air bases in the Balearic Islands would weaken both the British and French strategic positions. Combined with a Berlin–Rome partnership, a Fascist victory in Spain meant that France would be threatened on the Rhine, in the Alps, and in the Pyrenees. The Duce anticipated that a grateful Franco would follow Italy's lead, and imagined that Spain could be wedded to the Roman Empire. In ideological terms, Italian action in Spain allowed Mussolini to reclaim his role as the leader of the Fascist movement in Europe. Intervention in Spain would safeguard Fascism in Italy. As Mussolini wrote to his wife, 'Bolshevism in Spain would mean Bolshevism in France, Bolshevism at Italy's back, and danger of [the] Bolshevisation of Europe.'[11] Anti-Bolshevism also provided a common banner under which Italy and Germany could march together. As in 1922, it served Mussolini's domestic purposes and could be exploited to pave the way for public acceptance of an alliance with Germany that might otherwise prove generally unpopular. Arrogance blinded the Duce; he came to believe that 'his own superior intelligence would make him the senior partner in

[9] Paul Preston, 'Mussolini's Spanish Adventure: From Limited Risk to War', in Paul Preston and Anne L. MacKenzie (eds.), *The Republic Besieged: Civil War in Spain, 1936–1939* (Edinburgh, 1996), 49.

[10] Galeazzo Ciano, *Diplomatic Papers* (London, 1948), 145 (6 November 1937).

[11] Quoted in Glyn A. Stone, *Spain, Portugal and the Great Powers, 1931–1941* (Basingstoke, 2005), 29.

an Italo-German partnership'.[12] The partnership prospered. On 1 November 1936, Mussolini delivered his famous 'Axis' speech in Milan, denouncing the British and French, hailing the Germans, and publicly proclaiming that 'this Berlin–Rome Line is not a Diaphragm but rather an Axis' for all those states 'animated by a will to cooperation and peace'.[13] The Duce took no real interest in the internal politics of Nationalist Spain, beyond the far-fetched idea of persuading Franco to accept an Italian king. Fascism itself was to be vindicated through military action against the Popular Front government. As the war lengthened and increasing numbers of Italian troops were engaged in fighting, the prestige of Italy, the Fascist party, and of Mussolini, himself, became identified with victory in Spain. Mussolini became the prisoner of his megalomania.

The Italian military was already struggling with inadequate funds to re-equip and modernize an army which had squandered so much of its material resources in its African campaigns; it had no reason to welcome an engagement that might lead to a confrontation with France and Britain. Most senior officers, like most politicians, however, supported the intervention or failed to oppose it openly. Marshal Badoglio, the chief of the general staff, was one of the exceptions, disliking both the intervention and the pro-German orientation of Italian foreign policy. He had almost nothing to do with the planning or the execution of the Spanish campaign. In October 1936, at Ciano's urging, the unsympathetic chief of the army staff and under-secretary of war was dismissed, and was replaced by General Alberto Pariani, a Germanophile who redirected Italian war planning towards a future conflict with France and Britain, and who came to view Spain as a major asset in the forthcoming struggle in the Mediterranean. On two occasions, 5 November and 15 December, the chiefs of staff, notwithstanding Badoglio's reservations, considered a lightning land war against the Suez Canal, Egypt, and the Sudan, in the hope of linking Libya with the Italian possessions in East Africa. While indulging in imperial dreams at British expense, Mussolini held out the hand of friendship to London, intending to disguise his ambitions and to cut across Ribbentrop's efforts to conclude a bilateral Anglo-German agreement. Knowing that the European pot was boiling and assuming that France was too internally divided to act, Mussolini thought that the international currents were moving in Italy's direction. 'The next war will be a seven weeks war. We can do it. We don't need to consult anyone,' Mussolini boasted to

[12] Denis Mack Smith, *Italy and its Monarchy* (New Haven, CT, and London, 1989), 272.

[13] Benito Mussolini, *Opera Omnia*, vol. xxviii (Firenze, 1959), 69–70.

Giuseppe Bottai, an old comrade and long-serving minister, on 31 October 1936. 'Imagine the surprise of the Italians when, one day, they wake up, open the newspapers and read the news; an Italian air squadron has bombarded the English naval squadron in Malta. All the ships were sunk.'[14]

Franco's cunning defeated Mussolini's hopes for a quick victory in Spain; Hitler's own ambitions were to deprive him of some of the Spanish fruits. The Italians got relatively little in return for their military assistance. The economies of Italy and Spain were too similar, and the Germans exploited their economic advantage at Italian expense. Most of the Italian economic transactions with the Nationalists were conducted by Mussolini's brother working through the German agent, Johannes Bernhardt. The Spaniards considerably expanded their exports to Italy, including Moroccan iron ore, but this covered only a very small part of Italy's arms deliveries to the Nationalists. Franco agreed to pay back his war debts to Italy once in full control of Spain, but this would take three years to establish, and even then Spain could not afford to pay its debts in full. The Italian balance sheet remained in deficit. By April 1939, the three Italian armed forces had spent 6.1 billion lire in support of Franco and had lost 16,650 men, dead, wounded, or prisoners of war.[15]

As for Hitler, there is little evidence that in 1936 he had any fear of a social revolution in Spain or of a 'red wave' rolling over Europe. His initial reaction was, nevertheless, ideologically motivated, for he did not want to see a red triumph in Spain, particularly in view of the Popular Front victory in France. He rapidly perceived the strategic advantages of pursuing an anti-Bolshevik campaign. Anti-Bolshevism ('Judeo-Bolshevism') was a highly popular slogan in Germany, and was successfully employed in association with the decision to extend military conscription from one to two years, and to introduce the Four Year Plan in August and September 1936. The Spanish adventure, in which German investment was limited, was a useful device to further short-term aims. A Fascist victory in Spain would weaken France and draw Italy deeper into the German orbit. It might assist Hitler's efforts to build bridges to Britain, whose attention would be diverted from central Europe. He noted that 'Spain was a convenient sideshow which absorbed the energies of the other Great Powers thus leaving Germany a freer hand to pursue its ambitions.'[16] The unexpected length of the civil war played into Hitler's hands; in this respect, he had more luck

[14] Giuseppe Bottai, *Diario, 1935–1944*, ed. Giordano Guerri (Milan, 1982), 113–114.

[15] Robert Mallett, *Mussolini and the Origins of the Second World War* (Basingstoke, 2003), 92.

[16] Statement attributed to Hitler in Christian Leitz, *Economic Relations between Nazi Germany and Franco's Spain 1936–1945* (Oxford, 1996), 17, note 47.

than foresight. The prolonged struggle acted as a catalyst in polarizing European attitudes and in increasing fears of the Soviet Union. 'Germany's interests, which alone should be considered, were therefore not so deeply involved in an early conclusion of the Spanish Civil War as to risk a limitation of its own rearmament', Hitler explained. 'On the contrary, German policy would be advanced if the Spanish question continued for a time to occupy Europe's attention.'[17]

Military and economic considerations had not entered into Hitler's original decision. Yet during the course of the Spanish war, the Germans could test their new weapons and accustom officers to their use. There were also valuable tactical lessons learned, above all, the employment of tactical air strikes to support ground troops, a practice already part of the *Luftwaffe*'s programme but subsequently given greater prominence. It was in Spain, where the Soviet tanks proved far more effective than the German models, that the Germans learned that they had to increase the size and power of their tanks. Economic considerations rapidly became a major factor in German calculations. After the meeting at Bayreuth, Hitler and Göring, the key figure in managing the German commercial involvement in Spain, wanted to obtain the maximum economic benefits for the assistance given to Franco. Raw material shortages were already adversely affecting the German rearmament programme. Spain was rich in pyrites, used in making ammunition, iron ore, copper, lead, mercury, and zinc, all materials essential for rearmament, and in short supply. The country also had large reserves of untapped minerals that the Germans hoped to exploit. Hitler decided that the whole operation of supplying Franco should be kept secret. A private Spanish company, *Compañía Hispano-Marroquí de Transportes Limitada* (HISMA), was registered in Spanish Morocco at the end of July 1936 to organize aid to the Nationalists and to secure payment. It was headed by Johannes Bernhardt and a retired Spanish naval officer, Fernando Carranza. Under Göring's patronage, HISMA handled all the German deliveries of arms and ammunition to the Nationalists. In early October, Göring created a separate government corporation in Berlin, ROWAK (*Rohstoffe- und Waren-Einkaufsgesellschaft*) under the general authority of his Four Year Plan Commission, which was the sole distribution agent in Germany for all the Spanish raw materials supplied through HISMA. In the spring of 1938, it was integrated into the Nazified Economics Ministry under Göring's control. At first, because Franco was desperate for arms, he acquiesced in HISMA's monopolistic position. As the war dragged on, his forces became increasingly dependent on the war materials sent from

[17] Quoted in Robert Whealey, 'Foreign Intervention in the Spanish Civil War', in R. Carr (ed.), *The Republic and the Civil War in Spain* (London and Basingstoke, 1971), 219.

Table 5.1 German Trade with Spain, 1932–1939 (Million RM)

	1932	1933	1934	1935	1936	1937	1938	1939
Imports	98.9	86.5	99.7	118.3	97.7	123.4	110.1	118.9
Exports	90.6	85.5	87.5	87.5	69.3	58.7	94.1	67.7
Balance of Payments	−8.3	−1	−12.2	−30.8	−28.4	−64.7	−16	−51.2

Sources: Militärgeschichtliches Forschungsamt (ed.), *Germany and the Second World War*, Vol. I, ed. Wilhelm Deist (Oxford, 1990), 318. W. Schneider and C. Dipper, *Der Spanische Bürgerkrieg in der internationalen Politik 1936–1939* (Munich, 1976), 178.

Germany. As a result, the Germans were able to expand their purchases of Spanish raw material and to demand payment in scarce foreign exchange for materials sent. Although Spanish exports to the industrial powers declined, the Germans gained a larger share of the total than either the British or French. Whereas in 1935 Germany took 35% of Spanish exports of iron ore, pyrites, wood, and skins, at the end of 1939 80% of these products went to the Reich.[18] Pyrites from Spain constituted over half of Germany's total pyrite imports. With the balance of trade so heavily weighted in the German favour, the Nationalist debt soared.[19] In all, Germany claimed a total of $215 million from the Spanish Nationalists for war debts. After the *de jure* recognition of the Nationalist regime on 18 November 1936, the Germans intensified their efforts to secure control over mines and sources of other raw materials, intending to establish a permanent post-civil war stake in Spain in order to replace Britain's pre-eminent economic position. A series of agreements in 1937 allowed the Germans to create a network of enterprises that would control and extract the raw materials needed by the Reich. The project, code-named 'Montana', aroused considerable resentment in Spanish Nationalist circles. Forced to give way to the Germans in late 1938 when war material was needed to break the stalemate on the Ebro front, Franco reluctantly agreed to further concessions, and to partial payments of the accumulating debts to HISMA in foreign currency. But his attitude hardened and using new commercial arrangements with Britain and France, he was able to check the German economic offensive during the last stages of the civil war. The *Caudillo*, an ardent nationalist, had no wish to yield his future control over Spain's mineral wealth to foreigners, least of all to the domineering Germans.

[18] Whealey, *Hitler and Spain*, 85.
[19] See the discussion in Mogens Pelt, *Tobacco, Arms and Politics: Greece and Germany from World Crisis to World War 1929–1941* (Copenhagen, 1998), 167–168, 170–171, 176–177.

Table 5.2 Spain's Market Share of German Pyrites Imports, 1932–1940

	Germany total imports of pyrites ('000) t	Imports from Spain	%
1932	650	305	46.9
1933	849	393	46.2
1934	987	532	53.9
1935	1018	562	55.2
1936	1042	464	44.5
1937	1464	835	57
1938	1430	895	62.5
1939	1120	582	51.9
1940	482	27	5.6

Source: W. Schneider and C. Dipper, *Der Spanische Bürgerkrieg in der internationalen Politik 1936–1939* (Munich, 1976), 178.

In addition to handling trade with the Francoists, Göring was also secretly selling weapons to the Republic, using well-known arms traffickers, in particular, Prodromos Bodosakis-Athanasiadis, a Greek with close ties to Metaxas, the Greek dictator. German arms sales to the Republic reached their peak in 1937 and 1938. The Greek agent made a personal financial killing but he shared some of these earnings with Göring as well as making payments to Metaxas and other Greek officials. The practice continued, despite protests from the Francoists, until the very end of the civil war. Republican hard currency was as welcome as any Nationalist offerings to the high-spending Göring.

III

Franco had another key supporter, António de Oliveira Salazar, the dictator of Portugal. Finance minister and then prime minister (1932–1968) of the country, he created in 1933 a New State ('Estado Novo')—an authoritarian, anti-parliamentarian, one party, police state which enlisted the support of the Catholic Church, the army, and the rural and industrial élites. His regime was very much like that of Engelbert Dollfuss in Austria. Respectful of Mussolini, he was fiercely anti-Bolshevik and had already taken fright from the establishment of the Popular Front in Spain in February 1936. The outbreak of the Civil War and the failure of the Nationalist *coup d'état* only heightened Salazar's fears that a victory for the Republicans would lead to an invasion of Portugal and the establishment of an Iberian Bolshevik state. The British and French were careful not to encourage the Portuguese to expect any support should Spain invade Portugal as a result of the war. Salazar was clearly told that the best guarantee of Portugal's independence lay in the successful implementation of the Non-Intervention Agreement. Though aware of the danger that a victorious Franco might try to re-absorb Portugal, the dictator decided to actively support the Nationalists, supplying some 10,000 men and supplies, and providing facilities for the transport of German and Italian arms for Spain. The Soviets insisted that the Portuguese should join the NIC, the multinational Non-Intervention Committee meeting in London. Their representatives naturally cooperated with those from Germany and Italy and found themselves in repeated opposition to the Anglo-French attempts to implement the Non-Intervention Agreement. During 1937, these clashes, particularly with regard to the stationing of international observers on the Portuguese frontier, not only raised the diplomatic temperature in Paris, making communication difficult, but also led to tensions between Britain and Portugal. The latter was Britain's oldest ally; the alliance of 1386 was renewed in 1899, and though Lisbon may have suffered from Britain's benign neglect, it was always assumed in London that Portugal would remain a solid friend in war-time.

The Axis powers were quick to seize the opportunity of these conflicts in the NIC to court the Portuguese and to hasten the break-up of the Anglo–Portuguese alliance. Apart from ideological sympathies, their common anti-Bolshevism nourished Axis hopes of creating a Madrid–Lisbon–Rome–Berlin Axis that would bring important strategic advantages in its wake. Both Italy and Germany, particularly the latter, launched major propaganda campaigns to underline the ties between the dictatorships. The Germans established active cultural centres in Portugal and sponsored exchange visits between youth groups and organizations with similar interests. By using export subsidies, the Germans were able to acquire a larger share of the Portuguese home market, weakening Britain's dominant position as Portugal's chief foreign trader. The Berlin authorities also encouraged contacts with the Portuguese police and military authorities.[20] Directly threatening the position of Britain's main armament firms, from mid-1936 onwards, a concerted effort was made to win contracts to supply the Portuguese armed services. Arms contracts amounting to 28 million Reichsmarks were exchanged during 1937 and 1938. At the end of the Spanish Civil War, talks were underway for German arms to be exchanged for Portuguese products.[21]

The British had to respond to this challenge; the Anglo-Portuguese alliance was of considerable importance for Britain's naval and aerial

[20] Stone, *Spain, Portugal and the Great Powers*, 116–117. [21] Ibid., 118.

Atlantic strategy and the loss of the arms trade would bring a diminution of its already threatened political influence. London joined the propaganda war. Inspired articles, generally favourable to Salazar and his regime, appeared in *The Times* and in other journals. The British Council became active in promoting good relations during 1937 and 1938. The BBC broadcast its news programme in Portuguese and a series of short lectures from British establishment figures was organized in conjunction with the Portuguese broadcasting corporation. To counter German moves, the British established their own news agency in the summer of 1939 and appointed a press attaché to the embassy in Lisbon. The cultural offensive was only partly successful but, at the least, steps had been taken to re-establish the British presence in the country. With the balance of payments between the two countries roughly in balance and the London government unwilling to use German methods to expand trade, little could be done on the commercial front. Despite endless discussions in Lisbon and London, and considerable pressure from the British embassy and Foreign Office, the two governments agreed that matters were better left to private enterprises to arrange. At Foreign Office insistence, however, steps were taken to stop the erosion of Britain's traditional role of supplying the Portuguese armed services. Preceded by the visit of part of the British home fleet, which visibly dwarfed an earlier demonstration of German naval power, a military mission was sent to Lisbon in late February 1939. The mission stayed six months, advising the government and armed forces on military matters and gave considerable substance to London's efforts to convince Salazar to place defence orders in Britain. Export credits amounting to £1million were given to encourage the purchase of fighter aircraft, anti-aircraft guns, submarines, torpedo boats, and a coastal defence system for the port of Lisbon. Unfortunately, the orders could not be fulfilled because of prior military obligations. It was hoped, however, that by attaching permanent military, naval, and air attachés to the British embassy in Lisbon, Salazar would be convinced that Britain would take a continuing interest in Portugal's defensive capabilities. Apart from an order for mountain artillery from Italy, he did not sign any substantial contracts with the Axis powers during 1939.[22]

Events outside of Spain during 1938 underlined the dangers of too close an identification with the Axis powers. The German annexation of Austria, also a corporatist, dictatorial Catholic state, was a worry for Salazar. Franco's victories, moreover, could only have revived fears of a possible Spanish move into Portugal. It was not surprising that Salazar

[22] Ibid., 119. The information in this discussion comes from Professor Stone's study of Portuguese relations with Britain, France, Italy, and Germany.

welcomed the Anglo-Italian agreement of April 1938 and Chamberlain's attempt to seek a peaceful conclusion of the Czechoslovak crisis. Both the Portuguese and the British had an interest in preserving Iberian neutrality in any future conflict. In September 1938, the British thanked the Portuguese for encouraging Franco to remain neutral in case war broke out. That mediating role would become even more important with the signing of the Treaty of Friendship and Non-Aggression between Portugal and Spain on 17 March 1939 solidifying ties between the two countries. The Portuguese, courted by both the Axis and western countries, could use their improved diplomatic position to redefine the terms of the Anglo-Portuguese alliance in their favour without losing the benefits of British friendship.

IV

There had been little sympathy in London, Paris, or Washington for the Popular Front government in Spain during early 1936. The three ambassadors of the countries with the largest economic stake in Spain, with different degrees of emphasis, warned of the dangerous instability of the government and the possibilities of a Communist or anarchist triumph. There were sound strategic and economic reasons why the British wanted an orderly government in Madrid. The naval base at Gibraltar was essential for imperial communications and the territorial integrity of Spanish Morocco of considerable strategic importance. An estimated £40,000,000 was invested in Spain, a relatively small sum in terms of overall British investment, but constituting 40% of the total foreign investment in Spain. Most important was the British involvement in the mining industry: above all, in the pyrite mining and iron ore quarrying companies. Britain took 45% of its imported iron ore and 66% of all its imported pyrites from Spain in 1935. The British owned the Rio Tinto mining conglomerate, which was one of the largest industrial giants among Spain's primary producers. Since 1931, tension had risen between the new Republican government and British business interests. Neither the British in Spain nor the government in London were displeased by the rightward swing of the Spanish political pendulum in the November 1933 elections. Their confidence was rewarded by new labour laws and the blocking of further agrarian reform. All the multinationals benefited from the apparently more settled conditions of 1935. The election results of February 1936 and the widespread popular disturbances that followed convinced many foreign residents that the weak, vacillating, and vindictive Popular Front government would ultimately be forced to abandon its powers to the radicalized proletariat. The new government's efforts to counter domestic economic distress produced widespread dissatisfaction among British employers, and complaints to the Madrid embassy in London with reference to the 'communistic' regime. Diplomats echoed such sentiments. The British ambassador, Sir Henry Chilton, warned 'there will be hell to pay' should the extreme left not be checked. 'If the military *coup d'état,* which it is generally believed is being planned, does not succeed, things will be pretty awful.'[23]

Rumours of military *coups d'état* in Spain were so frequent and vague that they were not taken seriously at the Foreign Office, which remained surprisingly phlegmatic given the reports it was receiving. It was generally felt there was little to do except to wait for the expected *coup* or revolution. Spain was not high on that summer's diplomatic agenda. Parliament was in recess, the holidays were approaching and both Eden and Vansittart were away in August, the latter visiting Berlin. Attention at the Foreign Office was focused elsewhere—on the discussions for a new Locarno Pact and on the Anglo-Egyptian treaty, finally signed on 26 August. Ministers and their officials were still debating whether to coerce or conciliate the Italians in the eastern Mediterranean, now that the Ethiopian sanctions had been lifted. There were divisions, too, about the new Popular Front government in Paris and the possibility of chaos in France. The events in Spain of 17–18 July came as a surprise. The first reaction, apart from sending ships to rescue British nationals, was to avoid involvement. The cabinet, approached by the Spanish ambassador, refused to sell fuel to Republican naval vessels. While admitting the right of the Spanish government to buy arms in Britain, sales were discouraged.

Not much attention was given to the Spanish conflict during the summer months. Misgivings about the durability of any democratic government in Spain, and an exaggerated view of Soviet influence in the country, undoubtedly coloured the response to the generals' *coup.* There were those in the government, like Baldwin, Hoare, and Hankey, who were concerned by the 'communist' complexion of the Popular Front government in Spain and thought that to assist the Republicans would facilitate Bolshevik subversion in Western Europe. As early as 20 July, Lord Hankey, one of the most outspoken anti-Communists in Whitehall, warned ministers that '[i]n the present state of Europe, with France and Spain menaced by Bolshevism, it is not inconceivable that before long it might pay us to throw in our lot with Germany and Italy'.[24] Popular resistance to the rebels and the revolutionary reign of

[23] Douglas Little, *Malevolent Neutrality: The United States, Great Britain and the Origins of the Spanish Civil War* (Ithaca, NY, 1985), 196.

[24] TNA: PRO, CAB 63/51, Memorandum by Hankey, 20 July 1936.

terror instituted by armed workers and peasants in the Republican zone, convinced such men that the Giral regime was tarred with the Soviet brush. The French decision of 21 July to assist the Republic added to the fears, in Churchill's words, of 'a communist Spain spreading its snaky tentacles through Portugal and France'.[25] The British ambassador, roughly escorted from San Sebastian where the diplomatic corps summered, established himself at Hendaye, just inside the French border, from where he wrote a series of strong denunciations of the 'Reds' in Madrid. The Foreign Office preferred to rely on the less alarmist reports from Ogilvie Forbes, sent to Madrid on 16 August when the British ambassador declined to return to the capital. Despite the lack of sympathy for the Republican government, the commitment to non-intervention, whatever its pro-rebel implications, was motivated less by concern for what was happening in Spain, than by the wish to contain the conflict within Spanish borders. Spain was hardly discussed in Whitehall until the beginning of September. Most Labour and Liberal supporters approved of non-intervention, though they wanted it applied equally against both sides. Warnings that the civil war in Spain could hasten the division of Europe into opposing ideological blocs also predisposed the cabinet to non-intervention. Such a division would shatter British hopes of a five-power agreement and ruin any chance of a successful appeasement policy. Anticipating the rapid collapse of the Republic, there was in any case not much concern in London over future policy.

The French position was bound to be different. Since 1931, successive Paris governments had been cultivating good relations with Madrid, motivated by geography and uneasy relations with Rome. Insofar as the French expanded their influence in Spain, they could keep the Italians out. Like the Americans and British, the French welcomed the rightward shift of the Republic and in December 1935 France concluded a commercial agreement permitting the Spaniards to buy arms to the value of 20 million francs. The February 1936 victory of the Popular Front in Spain was much discussed in the run-up to that year's French elections. The victory of the Popular Front in France created new bonds of amity between the two governments, even as it unsettled the right in both countries. Distrust of the Republican government was shared by the upper echelons of the *Quai d'Orsay* as well as by much of the army's officer class. As General Gamelin was to admit later, 'in their hearts and their heads the sympathies of our soldiers favoured Franco'.[26]

[25] W. S. Churchill, *Step by Step, 1936–1939*, 3rd impression (London, 1939), 52.

[26] Quoted in Martin S. Alexander, *The Republic in Danger: General Maurice Gamelin and the Politics of French Defence, 1933–1940*, 101.

The military *coup* in Spain occurred only three days after the enthusiastic Popular Front celebrations of 14 July in Paris. The authorities were kept informed of the events in Spain from sources in French Morocco and French North Africa, as well as in Spain. The French ambassador to Spain, like his British counterpart, had little liking for the *Frente Popular*. It was natural, nonetheless, that the Spanish ambassador should have brought an appeal to Léon Blum from Prime Minister José Giral on 20 July, for arms and aircraft, just before the French premier set off for London. With the backing of Daladier, Delbos, and Cot, Blum agreed to supply arms up to the twenty million francs of the December 1935 commercial agreement. Preoccupied by his domestic programme and fully aware of the discord his actions might provoke, Blum acted discreetly, hoping that the revolt might be suppressed quickly before the political storm broke in France. The news, however, was leaked by pro-Franco members of the Spanish embassy; right-wing papers in Paris denounced the government's decision. In London, the subject of Spain was raised informally; Blum was warned by Eden (on the steps of Claridge's Hotel) to 'be careful'.[27] By the time of his return to Paris, on 24 July, the political winds were blowing in the non-interventionist direction. The powerful Senate Foreign Affairs committee opposed military assistance to Spain, as did the Radical party. Just before the cabinet meeting called on 25 July to discuss Spain, a visibly distraught Blum told the Spanish representative that he would stick to the decision 'at all costs'. But at this meeting, the stark divisions in the cabinet became clear. It was finally agreed that France would not 'intervene in the internal conflict of Spain'. This rather ambiguous statement was amplified by a *Quai* circular suspending all arms shipments to Spain, apart from private civil aircraft. Covert deliveries continued. The Senate Foreign Affairs committee and the Chamber were informed that no war material would be sent to Spain.

At a further cabinet meeting on 1 August, called after news that two Italian aircraft on their way to Morocco had landed in French Morocco, the premier's appeal for assistance to Spain was again rejected. Instead, a Non-Intervention Agreement proposal, drafted by the highly influential secretary general of the *Quai d'Orsay*, Alexis Léger, was produced and ministers agreed to submit it to Britain and Italy. As a gesture to the interventionists, until the agreement was accepted by the other powers, France would resume shipments to Spain. Between 5 and 8 August, sixteen planes were delivered, really intended as a warning to the Italians and Germans to desist from further military assistance to the rebels. Admirals

[27] Quoted in J. Edwards, *The British Government and the Spanish Civil War* (London and Basingstoke, 1979), 17.

Darlan and Decoux, hoping to use the crisis to promote joint Anglo–French naval staff talks, were sent to the Admiralty in London on a private visit, only to find the British naval chiefs strongly opposed to any action in the Mediterranean, and anxious to return the fleet to its normal state after the alarms of the Ethiopian crisis. They insisted on a policy of strict neutrality. Designated as the next chief of the naval staff, Darlan's concern with the Italian threat, and his distrust of the British, would have important consequences for future French naval planning. The Foreign Office, as anxious as the Admiralty to avoid involvement, responded positively and quickly to the French initiative, and on 6 August the *Quai d'Orsay* drew up the Non-Intervention Agreement to be circulated abroad. On the next day, just before a third French cabinet meeting, called to discuss the Spanish question, the British ambassador, Sir George Clerk, speaking privately but encouraged by officials in the *Quai d'Orsay*, expressed his fear that the Spanish government was 'a screen for anarchists', and that pending an agreement, the French should 'limit and retard' deliveries to Spain. Clerk warned Delbos, the foreign minister, that French involvement in the civil war might make co-operation between the two countries, with regard to Germany, more difficult. The warning was used at the cabinet to buttress the decision that all aid to Spain, whether public or private, should be suspended. After a stormy session, Delbos's proposal was accepted with the proviso that if the Non-Intervention Agreement was not rapidly signed, the position would be reviewed. The French decision for non-involvement was never reversed. It was one that caused Blum considerable personal anguish.

Although it was the Popular Front government in Paris that initiated the policy of non-intervention and called for a non-intervention committee to sit in London, Blum never denied the rumours that the French were forced into the policy of non-intervention by the British. It was a politically convenient way of parrying left-wing criticism. Blum was later to claim that a decision for intervention would have unleashed civil war in France. Spain was a highly emotive issue in a country already marked by fierce political debate. The parties of the right demanded total neutrality even where they favoured a rebel victory. The radical and socialist press wavered between support for Blum's non-intervention formula and demands for a stricter neutrality, when news of the delivery of French planes became known. By September, the Spanish Civil War was yet another issue dividing the French left. The leaders of the Radical party—including Herriot, Chautemps, and Delbos—all opposed involvement in Spain. Daladier, characteristically, shifted his position, but subsequently became adamant that no French military equipment should be squandered on Spain. If many Socialists favoured the Republican cause, there were fears, even in those circles, that active support for the Republic might lead to war. While Blum was aware of the danger of losing support to the Communists by adopting non-intervention, he was even more sensitive to the weakness of his government. He may have exaggerated the dangers of internal divisions, but any other policy except that of 'relaxed non-intervention' might well have led to the weakening or even collapse of his coalition. At Luna Park on 6 September 1936, he argued before a crowd that favoured assistance to the Republic, that non-intervention would prevent the escalation of the Spanish Civil War into an international struggle, and would avoid a 'necessarily unequal arms race' that would be won by the strongest industrial power, i.e. Germany. As at the British Foreign Office, the officials of the *Quai d'Orsay* believed that intervention in the Spanish Civil War would hasten the division of Europe along ideological lines with fatal consequences for France. It was in the hope of avoiding a European war that Blum would seek an agreement with Germany. The run-on effects of Berlin's exploitation of the Bolshevik theme were felt in Poland, Romania, and Yugoslavia, to the great disadvantage of the French efforts to strengthen their position in these countries. In Yugoslavia, Prince Paul was obsessed by the fear of Communism and the dangers of being dragged into a war because of the Franco-Soviet pact. Blum's government was particularly vulnerable to the ideological currents set off by Spain both at home and abroad. Even when threatened with the admittedly distant prospect of a war on three fronts, the leaders of France continued to believe that their policy of non-intervention in Spain was the best way to prevent a continental war and keep the prospect of European conciliation alive.

This did not mean that all assistance to the Republic ceased after the cabinet opted for non-intervention on 7–8 August. Early in August, Blum countenanced the sending of volunteers to Spain, French and foreign, as long as they had passports and travelled without arms. One quarter of the 40,000 members of the 'international brigades' were French, the largest national contingent. The air minister, Pierre Cot, assisted by Jules Moch, the head of Blum's secretariat, and Vincent Auriol, the finance minister, found ways to secure and deliver aeroplanes right through Blum's second ministry and, during 1937 and 1938, continued to organize clandestine shipments of arms to Spain with the tacit approval of Blum. At various times, the Pyrenean frontier was opened for the transport of arms and equipment.[28] Nonetheless, the military aid that came from France in no way compared either to the

[28] The French Pyrenean frontier was opened during July–August 1936, October 1937 – January 1938, March–June 1938 and then in January–February 1939.

quantity or quality of the war material sent by the Fascist powers, or that sent to the Republic by the Soviet Union. The Air Ministry's meagre efforts, for example, saw only a total of 282 aeroplanes, mostly obsolete models, delivered to the Republic. And it was to France that the 460,000 Spanish refugees fled, most in the mass exodus from Catalonia in the winter of 1939. Their immediate fate would be decided by a far from sympathetic French regime.[29]

The Americans remained aloof from the Anglo–French sponsorship of non-intervention, yet their policies, too, cut the Republic off from securing vital supplies. Washington was well prepared for the possibility of a right-wing *coup* and the State Department was not unhappy about the prospects of a more stable and orderly Spain. Officials did not anticipate the ability of the Republic to organize its own defence. Instead, the intelligence arriving in Washington seemed to confirm Hull's fears that the long expected Bolshevik reign of terror had begun. As most of the American firms were in the Republican zone, they felt the full blast of the local seizures of property and plants. Public opinion in the United States was as divided as in Europe, and supporters on both sides were quick to mount massive propaganda campaigns. But Congress was not in session and the president was cruising off the coast of New England, so the first steps towards non-involvement were taken by the State Department. It was already known that Germany and Italy were shipping arms to the 'so-called rebels', and it was assumed that Moscow would assist the Madrid government; Hull was also informed of the non-intervention plan submitted to London and Rome. On 5 August, he confidentially told the press corps of the State Department's informal decision for non-involvement. The American neutrality legislation of 1935 did not apply to civil wars, so no formal declaration could be made before Congress passed new legislation. There were some objections to Hull's announcement, but President Roosevelt, though sympathetically inclined towards the Republic, threw his weight behind the secretary of state. On 11 August, the moral embargo on arms sales became public policy. The replacement of Giral by Largo Caballero on 4 September, and the inclusion of two Communists in his cabinet confirmed Hull's apprehensions of a possible Communist takeover in Spain. Reports from the American ambassador, Claude Bowers, one of the few diplomats who defended the Madrid government and blamed the Germans and Italians for preventing the crushing of the rebels, were dismissed. He was considered out of touch in his 'embassy in exile'. The moral embargo won the support of both isolationists and internationalists

[29] For details of their subsequent fate and breakdown of figures, see David Wingeate Pike, *In the Service of Stalin* (Oxford, 1993), esp. Introduction, and David Wingeate Pike, *Les Français et la Guerre d'Espagne* (Paris, 1975), 381–392.

and was generally maintained until the end of 1936 with the exception of the despatch of nineteen aircraft to Le Havre for trans-shipment to Spain. In December, a company receiving money from the Soviet trade organization, Amtag, applied for a license to export planes and engines valued at almost three million dollars to the Republicans. The State Department was forced to comply and was soon asked by another company for a license to export an even larger shipment to the Republicans. Encouraged by the president, Senator Key Pitmann, the chairman of the Senate Foreign Relations Committee, introduced a joint resolution into Congress proposing a boycott on the shipment of arms, munitions, and implements of war to either side in Spain. Sales to neutrals for reshipment to Spain were also banned. The resolution was passed on 8 January 1937 by a unanimous vote in the Senate and with only one dissenting vote in the House of Representatives. To enforce its noninvolvement policy, the State Department refused to participate in any of the Latin American sponsored mediation plans. It was left to Mexico, alone among all the states, to openly supply the Republic with rifles and bullets. There were protests, mainly from the political left, against the embargo and demands that the president declare that a state of war existed in Spain. Hull, even at this time, continued to deny that German and Italian troops were engaged. Roosevelt, mindful of public divisions and future elections and fearing that such a declaration would increase the likelihood of expanding the war, decided that the embargo should stay in place. Senator Nye, a leading isolationist but anti-Franco, proposed in March 1937 that the embargo be extended to include all the countries involved in the Civil War but his initiative was blocked by Hull on the grounds that, by revealing the activities of all the other powers in Spain, it would undermine the Anglo-French non-intervention campaign. Nye's second proposal, to lift the embargo only on Republican Spain on a 'cash-and-carry' basis, was again buried due to Hull's intervention. It was not until 1938 that the president became alarmed at the prospect of a Francoist victory and sought ways to assist the Republicans. His remark in January 1939 that it had been a 'big mistake' not to have assisted the Loyalists underlines his greater awareness of the looming contest between the democratic powers and the Fascists.

V

With the continuing flow of arms from Germany and Italy to the rebels during August and September and its own supplies rapidly diminishing, the Republican government in Madrid had to look to Moscow. It was one of the more ironic aspects of the Spanish Civil War that the action of the western democracies left the Republic dependent on the Soviet

Union. Just as the supply of German and Italian transport aircraft was critical for the opening stage of the war, Russian assistance turned the tide in the battle for Madrid. Stalin had never shown any interest in Spain and the government was badly informed about what was happening there. It had neither diplomatic representation nor a press office in Madrid. The Spanish Communist party (*Partido Comunista de España* or PCE) was not only small but also out-flanked on the left by the stronger anarcho–syndicalist movement. Though in September 1934 it had agreed to participate in the socialist organized Worker's Alliance, the PCE had no representation in the pre-*coup* governments. Its early reports on the rebellion were absurdly optimistic; the party secretary predicted a rapid defeat of the rebels and expected to be asked to join the Madrid government. Misled as to the real situation in Spain, Moscow remained calm and reined in the over-enthusiastic PCE secretary, who was warned to stick only to the defence of the Republic and not to raise a popular militia. On 24 July, Dimitrov, the head of the Comintern, after consulting Stalin, instructed the Spanish Communist leaders to concentrate on defeating the mutiny and backing the Popular Front.

The first noted public reaction in Moscow to the Spanish crisis was a joint meeting of the Comintern and Profintern on 21 July. Plans were laid for a new meeting in Prague on 26 July, the same day that Hitler agreed to assist Franco. It was decided to raise a billion francs, nine-tenths from the trade unions of the Soviet Union. Popular Front organizations, both old and new, were instructed to collect funds and non-military supplies for Spain. Appeals came from Spanish Communists to party members and from sympathizers in Europe and in America. Individual Communists like André Malraux of France, and Nino Nanetti of Italy, travelled to Spain, the former returning to Paris to secure planes and pilots for the Republic. On 3 August, there was a massive demonstration in Red Square in support of the Republic though none of the leading figures of either the Soviet Communist party or the Comintern was present. Litvinov was away when the French presented their proposals for non-intervention. It was his deputy, Krestinskii, who replied on 5 August that the Soviet Union would return a positive answer provided Portugal was involved, and that 'certain states' would immediately cease aid to the rebels. Initially, most German aid was going via Portugal where Salazar, its dictator-president, was providing the rebels with a way of communicating between their two zones. By this date, over twelve million roubles had been deducted from the wages of Soviet workers and put at the disposal of the Republic. Unexpectedly, as the Russians knew of German and Italian assistance to the Nationalists, both those governments accepted the substance of the French proposals. The Russians had only the choice of acceptance or isolation in London without any chance of influencing the proceedings. On 23 August, the Soviet Union formally adhered to the French non-intervention proposal. Five days later the *Politburo* issued a decree forbidding the shipment of war material to Spain. The Russians, nonetheless, were moving beyond just the despatch of money. A naval and air attaché and a team of military advisers were sent to Spain. The veteran revolutionary Antonov-Ovseenko appeared in Barcelona on 25 August instructed to bridge the gap between the Madrid government and the Catalans and to make the anarchists in the city 'see reason'. He was convinced that it was imperative to organize a regular army if the Republic was to be saved. On 28 August, a hastily appointed new Soviet ambassador (the post had been empty since 1933), Marcel Rozenberg, flew into Madrid accompanied by a military attaché and a large military delegation. Nevertheless, it was still hoped in Moscow that the Republic would triumph without the supply of Soviet arms.

It was only slowly and in a step-by-step manner that the USSR entered the conflict. Stalin left Moscow for his usual summer holidays at the end of August and returned only in mid-September. Spain was one of the few cases where Moscow may have responded to pressures from the Comintern parties and foreign sympathizers.[30] Stalin appears to have concluded that he could not afford to have the Republic defeated, but preferred to follow a low-risk policy, working with the western democracies in order to prevent Germany and Italy from supplying Franco. He may too have been convinced by Litvinov's arguments that Spain could be used to build up an anti-Fascist front. Throughout this time, the commissar's attention was focused on Germany. On 7 September 1936, he wrote to Stalin advocating a renewed effort to consolidate the Soviet pacts with France and Czechoslovakia. He argued that a bloc of France, Czechoslovakia, Romania, Yugoslavia, and Turkey might encourage Germany 'to come to its senses and change its policies' and would attract the smaller nations: 'The chances of realizing such a bloc have significantly increased of late.'[31] The *Politburo* approved the formula though without enthusiasm.

Stalin's attention was centred on Moscow, where the first of the show trials of the 'old Bolsheviks' began on 19 August 1936 when Lev Kamenev and Gregorii Zinoviev were put on public trial while the other former members of the 'left opposition' (those who had opposed Stalin and Bukharin in 1927–1928) came under suspicion. Presented as a

[30] DGFP, series D, iii, 108–110.

[31] Michael J. Carley, 'Caught in a Cleft Stick: Soviet Diplomacy and the Spanish Civil War', in Gaynor Johnson (ed.), *The International Context of the Spanish Civil War* (Newcastle, 2009), 161. I owe the quotation and this interpretation of the Litvinov line to Professor Carley's article.

rightist, anti-liberal, pro-Fascist, and pro-Nazi plot masterminded by the exiled Trotsky, many contemporaries, including Winston Churchill, not only believed the story but also welcomed Stalin's moves against his Trotskyist enemies. Alas, this was just the beginning of a far more embracing attack on all men and institutions who might block Stalin's drive for absolute power.[32] All sixteen of the 'anti-Soviet joint Trotskyist–Zinoviev centre' were shot. Kamenev's confession implicated Bukharin and Rykov. The charges against Bukharin were dropped for a lack of evidence but Stalin was not to be denied. New trials (including that of Bukharin) followed and the 'Great Terror' spread. Events in Spain began to interact with the internal tensions in the USSR, intensifying Stalin's ruthless and personally directed campaigns of repression and executions.

It was in the aftermath of the Zinoviev–Kamenev trial that the decision to intervene in Spain was taken. Litvinov, but not Stalin, was reluctant to act. The situation did not really change with the resignation of Giral on 4 September and the entrance of the reluctant Spanish Communists into Largo Caballero's new ministry. With the Republican loss of San Sebastian on 13 September, the pressure on Litvinov, still trying to keep in step with the French, began to mount, particularly from foreign Communists in Moscow. Early in September, the decision was taken to ship arms to Spain. The Comintern executive committee advised a maximum increase in aid to the Republic, and on 18 September supplies of arms, labelled 'pressed meat', left the Black Sea coast. Later in the month, non-Russian military assistance was hastily organized in The Hague by Walter Krivitsky, the GRU's (military intelligence) resident in the Netherlands. A chain of import-export firms, usually with a silent NKVD agent in the background, was soon operating in Czechoslovakia, France, Poland, Holland and even Germany. The new system began to operate more efficiently during October.

The first shipment of arms, guns, tanks, planes, and other equipment, along with pilots and military advisers, reached Spain on 4 October. Three days later, the Soviet *chargé d'affaires* in London informed the NIC that the Soviet Union would not fulfil its obligations under the Non-Intervention agreement unless the German, Italian, and Portuguese violations ended. Like the other offenders, the Soviets remained active members of the NIC, knowing that the proceedings were a sham. Soviet shipments of heavy armaments left Odessa on the *Komsomol* and arrived at Cartagena on 15 October. On the same day, an exchange of telegrams took place between the Soviet and Spanish Communist

[32] For an extended discussion of the purges see pp. 460–67.

leaders that was subsequently published in *Izvestia*. In this manner, Stalin made known his declaration of support for the Republic. Stalin, himself, appears to have initiated the shift away from non-intervention, and would carefully monitor Spanish affairs in the months that followed. Eden's statement to the Commons on 19 November that 'there are other Governments more to blame than those of Germany or Italy', did not go unnoticed in Moscow. Right down to the end of the year, Ivan Maisky, the ambassador in London, tried to reassure Eden about Soviet intentions in Spain, but without relenting on the campaign to bring collective pressure on Germany and Italy. Even Litvinov, who had reservations about the Spanish intervention because of the possible consequences for relations with Britain and France, strongly criticized the 'bankrupt' policies of states that gave lip service to the concept of collective security, but did nothing. In early November, Litvinov had advised Maisky that after the arrival of new Soviet arms shipments, Soviet assistance might end. 'The Spanish question has undoubtedly significantly worsened our international position. It has spoiled our relations with England and France and sown doubt in Bucharest and even in Prague.'[33] Despite expectations that the Soviets would leave the Non-Intervention Committee, they continued as active participants. While wanting a Republican victory, they sought to avoid both a break with the western powers and an open conflict with Nazi Germany. There were divisions in Moscow about the events in Spain; attitudes changed as the optimistic forecasts of a rapid Republican victory gave way to predictions of a longer struggle. With the international climate darkening the paramount issue in Moscow was the security of the Soviet Union.

Direct aid sent by ship between October 1936 and March 1937, the period of greatest Soviet assistance, included planes, tanks, armoured cars, artillery pieces, machine guns, rifles, mortars, bullets, and shells in considerable numbers. Additional supplies were purchased from France, Czechoslovakia, Switzerland, and elsewhere. Most of the Republic's oil came from Russia.[34] The flow of material continued; a large consignment of arms was sent in December 1938 though by that date Spain was no longer of paramount interest to Moscow. As in the case of Germany,

[33] Quoted in Michael Jabara Carley, 'The Russian Connection: Soviet Perceptions of the Spanish Civil War', in Gaynor Johnson (ed.), *The International Context of the Spanish Civil War*.

[34] The figures vary according to the source. See Jonathan Haslam, *The Soviet Union and the Struggle for Collective Security in Europe, 1933–1939* (London, 1984), 145–146; G. Howson, *Arms for Spain: The Untold Story of the Spanish Civil War* (London, 1998), appendices.

Soviet assistance to the Republic came at a price. Deliberately inflated charges were levied for the arms supplied and, it is claimed, much of the equipment was obsolete. Between July 1936 and March 1937, the French provided facilities to the Bank of Madrid which was under Republican control, for the export of gold, while the Soviet *Banque Commerciale pour l'Europe du Nord* (BCEN), to which most of the gold sent to the Soviet Union was transferred, was allowed to operate legally in Paris. It appears that the Spanish Republic exported a total of $800 million worth of gold and silver to the USSR and France to pay for its war.[35] The Bank of Spain shipped to Moscow some 510 tons of gold worth $518 million, 72.6% of its total holdings; in the autumn of 1936 (the first shipments arrived on 6 November), $340 million was re-exported to the BCEN to pay for the services of the international brigades and to cover the $85 million Soviet loan spent by the Republic in 1938.[36] In addition to the gold, Spanish raw materials were also despatched in bulk to pay the debts to Moscow. The Soviets charged a great deal for their services.

The idea of the 'international brigades' was developed by Maurice Thorez, leader of the French Communists, when he arrived in Moscow on 22 September 1936. He suggested that brigades be raised by national Communist parties (though non-Communists were welcome), organized by the Comintern and led by Communist exiles mainly living in Russia. These would form the nucleus of an international Red Army, which, alongside the Spanish Communist Fifth Regiment, a tightly organized Communist militia, could be used to strengthen the other poorly armed and undisciplined working-class militias that were tied to other political or syndicalist groups and constituted the bulk of the Republican army. Stalin had some misgivings about the enterprise, but the brigade idea had the merit of providing a way of ridding the Soviet Union of Communist émigrés at a time when his campaign of terror was gaining momentum. It also meant that the Russians, apart from a relatively small group of technicians and advisers, would not have to

[35] Robert Whealey, 'How Franco Financed his War: Reconsidered', *Journal of Contemporary History*, 12 (1977), 139. See Whealey's balance sheet for the funding of Republicans and Nationalists, 135. Angel Viñas, 'Financing the Spanish Civil War', in Paul Preston (ed.), *Revolution and War in Spain, 1931–1939* (London, 1984), 268–273, and the far more detailed Angel Viñas, *El oro de Moscu. Alfa e omega de un mito franquista* (Barcelona, 1979). The exchange rate used here is 50 pesetas to £1 or 1 peseta to 10 cents.

[36] Whealey, *Hitler and Spain*, 22–3. For the difficulties in determining these figures see Viñas, *El oro de Moscú*, and his article 'Gold, the Soviet Union, and the Spanish Civil War', *European Studies Review*, 9 (1979), 105–128. Figures also given in Haslam, *Soviet Union and the Struggle for Collective Security*, 120. Howson, *Arms for Spain*. See also the more impressionistic account by Louis Fischer, *Men and Politics: An Autobiography*, 5th printing (New York, 1941, 1946), 365.

send their own soldiers to fight in Spain. There were probably between 2,000 and 3,000 Russians in Spain during the civil war, with 700 the maximum at any one time.[37] The formation of the international brigades became the major work of the Comintern. With main recruiting offices in Paris, other branches were opened in *Maisons des Syndicatís* around France and Belgium. Volunteers went from Paris to Spain either by boat or train, and were organized at Albacete, a base located between Madrid and Valencia. The volunteers were organized in battalions along linguistic lines and given appropriate national names. Most of the famous or infamous figures associated with the post-1945 Communist regimes were involved, including Klement Gottwald and Walter Ulbricht. Josip Broz, the future Marshal Tito, was in charge of volunteers from the Balkans and central Europe. Workers constituted the overwhelming majority of recruits; some 60% were Communists before volunteering and about another 20% joined the party while serving in Spain. As many as 59,400 men from over fifty countries including the United States served in the international brigades. This equalled about two-thirds of the combined forces of Germany and Italy.[38] The first group of volunteers arrived at Albacete on 14 October at the same time that the cargo ships carrying arms and ammunition started to dock at Cartagena and Alicante.

Spain's left-wing movements were divided and competitive, and even the anarchists were riven by faction. Already by late summer, the problems of Catalan nationalism and the anarchist dislike of rule from Madrid were leading to differences over how the war was to be fought. In Catalonia and Andalusia the anarchists were the dominant political force. They provided the inspiration for the militias, the movements towards local autonomy, and the seizures of land and factories that marked the social revolution unleashed by the military *coup*. Caballero was also under considerable pressure from the Communists, both the PCE and the *Partido Socialista Unificado de Cataluña* (PSUC), a united left-wing party formed in Barcelona under the domination of the Communists. Encouraged by Moscow, where the hunt against the so-called Trotskyites was in full progress, they favoured a regular army under central control and wanted both the movements towards local autonomy and social revolutionary action to be checked in the interests of political unity and a united front against the Nationalist forces of Franco. Until September, the anarchists held the upper hand but with defeats in the field and the growth of the more tightly organized and

[37] Stone, *Spain, Portugal and the Great Powers*, 43.

[38] Whealey, *Hitler and Spain*, 24. Whealey estimates there were 59,400 international brigadeers and 2,000 Russians on the Republic side compared to 16,800 Germans and 80,000 Italians fighting for the Nationalists.

better-disciplined Communist forces, the political balance both in Madrid and in Catalonia began to change in the Communist favour. The arrival of Soviet assistance and the international brigades naturally strengthened the position of the PCE at the moment when the Nationalists were moving on Madrid and the militias were fighting a stubborn but losing battle. Stalin believed that the Republic's difficulties were not just due to Fascist infiltration but to the divisions in the Republican camp. As in the Soviet Union, he was determined to impose tight Communist discipline. Along with Soviet assistance came the NKVD agents with instructions to destroy the 'Trotskyists' in Spain. The main target was POUM, a group of mainly ex-Trotskyist Catalans who had broken their formal ties to the 'Trotskyists', but who were critical of the Moscow trials and the Soviet desertion of its world revolutionary goal. The old historical feud between anarchists and Communists that had begun in the divisions between Bakunin and Marx, was renewed with a special vengeance in Barcelona, the one city in the world, albeit briefly, under anarchist rule. The final and terrible confrontation, local in origin, came in May 1937.

VI

In the autumn of 1936, there was a deep gulf between what was being said by the European governments and what was actually happening in Spain. It was characteristic of the diplomacy surrounding the civil war that would continue as long as that conflict lasted. A total of 28 nations signed the Non-Intervention Agreement. The Non-Intervention Committee, made up of the foreign ambassadors in London, held its first meeting in London on 9 September; within two weeks, the proceedings were deadlocked. Dino Grandi, the Italian representative, had received orders from Ciano 'to do his best to give the Committee's entire activity a purely platonic character'.[39] Maisky, the Soviet delegate, announced at an early meeting that the Soviet government would not consider themselves bound by the Non-Intervention Agreement to any greater extent than the other participants in the committee. The meetings were grand theatre. Dino Grandi, Prince Bismarck, the German embassy counsellor, and Ivan Maisky traded insults across the table. A brilliant portrait of the proceedings of the NIC's key sub-committee by Girard de Charbonnières, the ambassador's secretary at the French embassy in London, likened the atmosphere to an American Western saloon where all the poker players sat with their revolvers under the table. Lord Plymouth, the British parliamentary under-secretary

[39] *DGFP*, Ser. D, Vol. III, No. 73.

for foreign affairs, presided, detached from the often violent verbal battles and confining his interventions to calming the participants. Grandi, charming in private, theatrical in public, denounced Soviet violations of the agreement while proclaiming, with his hand on his heart, the goodwill of his own government. Ribbentrop, more often than not absent, exhibited an icy arrogance towards all, and lost his *sang-froid* only when engaged in combat with Maisky, a man who could speak for hours without raising his voice or changing his tone, whether reading from texts sent from Moscow or responding to accusations. The French ambassador and delegate, Charles Corbin, a man of the greatest delicacy, courteous, formal, and timid, was horrified by the polemics. Instructed not to form a common front with Maisky, the French ambassador was isolated, fighting the case for non-intervention almost single-handedly, as Plymouth refused to enter the fray.[40] The exchanges of invectives were replacements for the war that none of the powers wanted to fight.

The labours of the NIC and its sub-committees drifted on in an atmosphere of unreality for months. The Portuguese, whom the Soviet government demanded should be present, joined the proceedings at the end of September. It was not until 24 October, after Italy and Soviet Russia were accused of violating the Non-Intervention Agreement, that the British proposed a system of supervision in Spain to monitor breaches of the Non-Intervention Agreement. The contending parties in Spain refused to accept the recommendations. At the same time, an Anglo-French proposal for mediation in the war was allowed to lapse, in view of German, Italian, Portuguese, and Soviet reservations. While the battle for Madrid was still raging (October–November 1936), the Germans and Italians formally recognized the Franco government. For their part, the British decided not to accord belligerent rights to either of the warring sides, and to prohibit the export of arms. The Blum government ordered that their fleet should not assist merchant ships if attacked, but imposed no legal embargo. Nothing came of an Anglo-French offer of mediation nor, against Litvinov's advice, a Republican appeal to a specially summoned Council of the League of Nations in December. None of the powers involved, not even Republican Spain, wanted matters taken out of the hands of the NIC.

At the end of the year, the British and French governments, despite their earlier failures, asked that 'closely interested powers' outside the NIC prohibit the participation of foreign volunteers in the fighting in Spain. As might have been expected, there was no response to this appeal. The *entente* powers also proposed a revised scheme for the

[40] Girard de Charbonnières, *La plus evitable de toutes les guerres* (Paris, 1983), 114–122.

supervision of the sea and land frontiers of Spain and its dependencies, to control the entry of arms and munitions of war. In late December, a more detailed version of the proposals was sent to the contending parties in Spain, This revised control scheme was the main focus of discussion in the NIC during the early months of 1937.

After weeks of discussion and delay (Portugal was a major stumbling block unwilling to have patrols on the Portuguese–Spanish border), a 'scheme of observation' of the Spanish frontiers by land and sea was unanimously adopted on 8 March 1937. The Salazar government, deeply sympathetic to Franco, was still opposed to any international monitoring of its border, but the Portuguese knew that they were in no position to antagonize Britain, with whom they hoped to conclude an arms and military training programme. They finally allowed the British to take on the job of 'observation'; along the Spanish frontier, the word 'supervision' was rejected as too strong. The British, French, German, and Italian governments (the Soviets were persuaded not to participate) implemented a skeletal version of the NIC naval scheme, and began patrolling the Spanish waters on the night of 19–20 April 1937.

The other issue taken up by the NIC, initially as the result of British anxieties, was the flood of 'volunteers' into Spain. Plymouth raised the question on 7 December 1936, and started off a new round of discussions about the possible extension of the arms control scheme to cover volunteers. Efforts to get a declaration from all powers, to stop their nationals leaving to take part in the Spanish war, ran into immediate difficulties. The British and French pressed the governments of Germany, Italy, Portugal, and the Soviet Union to put a prohibition law in place on an agreed date in January. The Germans and Italians returned generally favourable replies to the Anglo-French request, as did the Soviet Union, yet this did not prevent the Italians from arranging to embark 9,000 troops between 11 and 17 January 1937. There could hardly have been a clearer demonstration of the fictional story being written in London. As one senior Foreign Office official wrote, when mocking a colleague for taking the NIC seriously: 'I thought it was generally admitted to be largely a piece of humbug. Where humbug is the alternative to war it is impossible to place too high a value upon it.'[41] The committee's prohibition on recruitment became 'effective' from midnight on 20 February. Even in Britain, the ban was not enforced; there was not a single prosecution brought under the Foreign Enlistment Act, and volunteers continued to be recruited, sent abroad and returned to Britain, admittedly in small numbers. The open Italian participation in

[41] Quoted in Jill Edwards, *The British Government and the Spanish Civil War, 1936–1939* (London, 1979), 137.

the battle of Guadalajara in March made a mockery of non-intervention, with charges and counter-charges echoing throughout the summer.

In contrast to the make-believe in the deliberations of the NIC, there was only grim reality in Spain. It was not only the Nationalists who had expected Madrid to fall quickly in early November. As the rebel armies advanced, panic spread through the capital, the Caballero government was hastily reformed to include the anarchists, though this had no effect on its sagging morale. Only the PCE and its highly disciplined Fifth Regiment appeared purposefully active. On 6 November, convinced that the capital would soon be taken, Largo Caballero and his government left Madrid for Valencia. So did the leading politicians of all the parties except the Communists. The defence of the city was put in the hands of a Defence Junta headed by the portly, balding, 58-year-old General José Miaja. His chief of staff had the good fortune to find the enemy's battle plan on the eve of the attack, but had little idea of what forces were at his command or their state of readiness. Apart from the city's inadequately armed citizens, there were the 1,900 men of the international brigades, who had arrived in mid-October, and the Fifth Regiment. The Communists and their Soviet advisers stepped into the vacuum left by the departing politicians and civil servants. The Communist–Socialist youth searched out the 'Fifth Column' of Nationalist supporters who General Mola had proclaimed, would assist his four columns of soldiers. Nearly all the political prisoners in Madrid were executed. The masses were mobilized to fight, both men and women—*La Pasionaria* (Dolores Ibárruri Gómez, a PCE leader) urged that boiling oil should be poured on those who attacked their homes—while children helped to build barricades. The Communists, both Spanish and Russian, instigated a campaign to maintain morale, shaken by the shelling and bombing of Madrid by the Condor Legion, which was purposely using incendiaries to produce maximum terror.

In the street-by-street fighting, the working class militias contained the Nationalist frontal assault. The XI and XII international brigades entered the battle. Three thousand anarchists arrived from Aragon; their attack (they had demanded their own front) was a failure, and was followed by three massive advances by the Nationalists, each repulsed at enormous cost. The Nationalists were finally able to cross the river; the anarchists fled and the way was open to the University City. It was in this sector that the battle for Madrid was really fought. After securing three-quarters of the area, Mola's troops found they could not advance. By 22 November, it was clear that the Nationalist assault on the capital had failed. The militias and citizens had defeated the smaller but infinitely more professional Nationalist armies. Much was owed to the energy of the Communists and the participation of the brigades. Their presence gave confidence and strength to the inexperienced militiamen. On 23 November, Franco, who had left the assault to Mola, called off the attack while insisting that the positions already won in the University City area had to be held. The Republican forces were too depleted to mount a counter-offensive. By mid-December, the two sides were exhausted, and dug in. For three weeks, the Madrid front was quiet, punctuated only by costly and bitterly contested small actions. Franco, after using the intervening weeks to consolidate his political authority, renewed the siege, but with only limited success and at a terrible cost. By mid-January, the fronts were again stabilized at the expense of some 15,000 men on each side.

The siege of Madrid was not just a Spanish battle. The Condor Legion, recently arrived in the country, showed what sustained aerial bombing could do in battle. It created panic but did not break the morale of the population, a lesson which the future belligerents failed to learn. Franco was fortunate; despite his failure, both Germany and Italy recognized his government and Mussolini decided to send massive help. External assistance enabled Franco to go forward from the deadlock in Madrid. While fuming over Franco's dilatory tactics and warning him of the consequences of further delays, his foreign supporters were willing to supply him in order to achieve victory. The Germans sent no further troops but quantities of aircraft, including state of the art bombers and fighters. The *Luftwaffe* tried out a variety of their aircraft in Spain. Except for the Soviet heavy tanks, the German equipment was generally superior to that of the other powers, and was further improved by its testing in battle. The Italians, hoping to end shipments by the end of January or February, sent over 10,000 Black Shirts and 10,000 army 'volunteers', a high proportion of the latter from southern Italy and the islands, and masses of war equipment.

The siege of Madrid set the seal of success on the Communist party in Spain. The Spanish Communists consolidated their position by supporting socialist unity and courting the Republicans. The PCE, acting as the party of order and unity, established its authority throughout the Republican territories in the south. More efficient and coherent in their aims and organization than their rivals, and backed by the only real source of assistance from abroad, they steadily gained in influence. The growing prestige of the PCE and the arrival of yet more Soviet advisers proved a mixed blessing for the Largo Caballero government. The battle against the 'Trotskyites', moving into high gear in Moscow, was also fought in Spain. The purges and repressions in Spain and in the USSR followed a parallel course. Over Madrid, Soviet fighter aircraft contested the previously unchallenged Nationalist air superiority. On 1 January 1937, seventeen Russian pilots were named 'heroes of the

TABLE 5.3 Italian War Material and Forces Sent to Spain, July 1936 – March 1939

Army and Militia

	Army	Militia	Total ground forces
Officers	3,301	1,736	5,037
NCOs	2,895	0	2,895
Troops	36,933	27,910	67,738
Total	43,129	29,646	72,775

Cannons	1,801
Mortars	1,426
Machine guns	3,436
Tanks	157
Motor Vehicles	6,791

Air Force

	Pilots	Other	Total air forces
Officers	862	203	1,035
NCOs	573	1,196	1,769
Enlisted	0	2,865	2,865
Total	1,435	4,264	5,699

	Bombers		Fighters
S81	84	Cr32	376
S79	100	Ro42	28
Br20	13	Other	10
CAS310	16		
Total	213	Total	414

Assault planes	44
Sea planes	20
Reconnaissance	68

Sources: John Coverdale, *Italian Intervention in the Spanish Civil War* (Princeton, NJ, 1975), 393. Robert H. Whealey, 'Foreign Intervention in the Spanish Civil War', in Raymond Carr (ed.), *The Republic and the Civil War in Spain* (London, 1971), 213–238.

Soviet Union' for 'difficult Government tasks'. The XI and XII Brigades, including Germans, French, Italians, Belgians, Poles, and Britons (among them Esmond Romilly, Winston Churchill's wayward cousin), made their reputations in the siege. New supplies, including planes, cannons, tanks, machine guns, trucks, artillery units, munitions, vehicles, and fuel, came from Russia by sea and via the Comintern across the French border. On the eve of the battle for Madrid, Stalin sent Caballero a letter asking, as a 'friend', for reports on the 'military comrades' sent as advisers and inquiring whether Rozenberg was 'satisfactory'. Stalin also offered advice; peasants' and foreigners' property should be respected, the small bourgeoisie not attacked, and the Republicans not cold-shouldered. Nothing should be done to give ammunition to the 'enemies of Spain'. Stalin did not want to scare off the bourgeois governments of Britain and France. Though Caballero was warned that the Soviets would not make a major contribution to the war effort, Stalin emphasized the need to aid 'Spanish democracy' in its battle against the rebels backed by 'international fascist forces'.[42] While possibly moving away from the seemingly bankrupt policies of collective action, Stalin was not prepared to take undue risks. Despite his caution, the Soviet Union was seen as irrevocably committed to the Republic and, in conservative and right-wing circles in France and Britain, the Republic was tarred with the Communist brush. Litvinov's efforts to build an anti-German front did not prosper. The Franco-Soviet military staff talks stalled. Maisky in London failed to convince Anthony Eden that the battle in Spain was part of the larger conflict between the aggressive fascist powers and the western democracies. It is true that Blum had initiated the first real rearmament programme in France despite the adverse financial and economic situation. At the end of 1937, too, a formerly divided Labour Party in Britain agreed to support rearmament and condemned non-intervention as a policy of 'one-sided intervention' that made the British government 'an accessory to the attempt to murder democracy in Spain'.[43] The outcome of the battle in Spain, nonetheless, remained of less interest to the Chamberlain government than the need to keep the door open to conversations with Mussolini and Hitler.

VII

What was going on in Spain made a mockery of the talks in London. Yet all the powers engaged in the battle for Madrid had finally sent back positive replies to the Anglo-French proposals on volunteers. The war went on, but the NIC succeeded in fulfilling the Franco-British aim of preventing the Spanish conflict from spreading. It may have been the French who initiated the policy of non-intervention, but it was the British who took the lead in making it a reality, and who insisted that the Spanish war should not disturb their efforts to promote peace in Europe. During January 1937, there was a war scare in Paris over German activity in Spanish Morocco. Apart from Eden, no one in London took the French alarm seriously. British ministers wanted nothing to do with any actions arising out of the Spanish conflict that might impede their quest

[42] See Silvio Pons, *Stalin and the Inevitable War, 1936–1941* (London, 2002), 71.

[43] Quotation from Clement Attlee in Kenneth Harris, *Attlee* (London, 1982), 139.

for agreements with Germany and Italy. The general reassessment of British strategy during 1936 had exposed the extent of the country's commitments and the paucity of its military resources. The chiefs of staff demanded that Britain avoid any form of threatening behaviour until it could fight a successful war, in their view not before 1939 at the earliest (some spoke of 1942). Even at a time when German and Italian contraventions of the Non-Intervention Agreements were too public to be ignored, the cabinet continued its pressure on the Foreign Office to restrict Britain's commitments and win time by conciliating and reducing the number of potential adversaries. It was not always clear that Britain could pursue both non-intervention and appeasement. If following the former policy seemed the best, safest, and most acceptable, if not the most morally correct, the continued involvement of other countries in Spain made it difficult to give teeth to the Non-Intervention Committee without running into conflict. Ultimately, the appeasement of the Fascist dictators overshadowed the requirements of Spain. As the British sought workable compromises, the balance was increasingly tipped in the direction of Franco in Spain and Mussolini and Hitler in Europe.

Nothing more clearly illustrates the British order of priorities than the negotiation of the 'Gentlemen's Agreement' with Italy late in 1936. This arrangement to maintain the Mediterranean status quo was intended to relieve the pressure on the Royal Navy and improve bilateral relations. Samuel Hoare, back in the cabinet as the first lord of the Admiralty after the Hoare–Laval fiasco, and one of its few open supporters of Franco, believed that such an agreement could lead to a permanent reduction of British naval forces in the Mediterranean. With the outbreak of civil disobedience in Palestine (the Italians provided the Arabs with clandestine support) in the summer of 1936, the anti-British Italian radio broadcasts from stations in Bari and in Libya were particularly troublesome. The Committee of Imperial Defence considered the unwelcome prospect of a possible Italian strike against Egypt or the Sudan from Libya or Ethiopia. It was thought imperative 'to get Italy out of the lists of countries with whom we had to reckon'.[44] The Foreign Office was split; Eden distrusted Mussolini but senior officials wanted to seize the opportunity to reduce tensions while the Duce was in a favourable mood. The reluctant Eden, who felt that pressure could be brought on Italy, nevertheless, entered the negotiations despite strong French objections. *Quai d'Orsay* warnings about the growing intimacy of the Germans and Italians were dismissed. Chamberlain, already seen as the next prime minister, was convinced that both countries were anxious for an agree-

[44] Quoted in Gaines Post, Jr., *Dilemmas of Appeasement: British Deterrence and Defense, 1934–1937* (Ithaca, NY, and London, 1993), 262.

ment with Britain and that their partnership was proof of Hitler's genuine interest in improving Germany's diplomatic position. He could hardly have been more mistaken.

The French objections to their exclusion from the talks were somewhat low-key. The fact was that neither Mussolini nor Blum was interested in an improvement in Franco–Italian relations. In November, the French ambassador was withdrawn from Rome, leaving only the *chargé d'affaires* to represent French interests. No change was made until October 1938. As in the case of non-intervention, it was politically prudent to let the British take the lead in negotiating with Mussolini. Even Delbos's rather mild reproofs were enough to provoke British complaints about French obstructionism. The Mediterranean Declaration, signed in Rome on 2 January 1937, pledged Britain and Italy to maintain stability in the Mediterranean. Separate notes were exchanged recognizing 'the integrity of the present territories of Spain'. Nothing was said of possible French involvement in future talks. Some British officials believed that Britain had achieved a major success and mistakenly predicted that this supposedly self-denying agreement would loosen Italy's ties with Germany.[45]

Eden rightly questioned Mussolini's trustworthiness and the value of the 'Gentlemen's Agreement', the title suggested by the Duce which the British foreign secretary particularly disliked. Mussolini entered the talks in bad faith and, three days after its signature, some 5,000 Italian 'volunteers' disembarked at Cádiz. This open disregard of the non-intervention policy provoked Eden's statement on 8 January 1937 that the Spanish Civil War 'has become an international battleground. The character of the future Government of Spain has now become less important to the peace of Europe than that the dictators should not be victorious in that country.'[46] The indignant foreign secretary pressed for the extension of non-intervention, and suggested that the British navy should patrol the approaches to ports both in Spain and in Spanish overseas possessions to prevent the entry of either 'volunteers' or war materials. This proved far too radical for his colleagues. Hoare, as might have been expected, led the opposition. Quite apart from the personal antipathy between Hoare and Eden, there were real political differences at issue. Eden believed that if Germany and Italy were not checked, they would, 'in effect, conquer Spain'. Hoare, on the other hand, warned his colleagues that they 'appeared to be getting near a situation where as a

[45] Glyn Stone, 'Sir Robert Vansittart and Spain, 1931–1941', in Thomas Otte and Constantine Pagedas (eds.), *Personalities, War and Diplomacy: Essays in International History* (London, 1997), 139–140.

[46] *DBFP*, 2nd ser., Vol. XVIII, No. 32.

nation we were trying to stop General Franco from winning. That was the desire of the left, but there were others, including perhaps some members of the cabinet who were very anxious that the Soviet Union should not win in Spain.'[47] The cabinet supported Hoare; Eden was forced to retreat. The proposals which ultimately went before the NIC were watered down to a mere extension of the committee's supervision plan to cover volunteers, with each state asked to take individual action to prohibit their enlistment.

Mussolini sank further into Spanish quicksand. There was little alternative since his prestige, that essential basis of his power, was now fully engaged. Once committed, he had to see the Spanish war through. An infuriated Duce chaffed at the deadlock in the siege of Madrid and Franco's apparent preference for a slow war of attrition. He feared that aid served only to make the *Caudillo* more confident of victory without encouraging him to move faster. Some in Rome opposed further involvement, but the Duce had become so fixated on success that he was prepared to send more troops and a vast amount of war material to hasten the rebels' triumph, before any control scheme became a reality. Convinced that a few decisive victories would end Republican resistance, he demanded a major attack on Málaga which would open the way to Valencia, the seat of the Republican government since November 1936. Assisted by separately led Spanish troops, the Italian forces took the poorly-defended city on 8 February. Its fall was followed by a terrible aftermath: Nationalist troops killed or imprisoned Republicans who were left in the city, and Italian aircraft strafed retreating militiamen and civilians on the single escape route purposely left open.

Mussolini and Ciano wanted to follow up Málaga with another Italian triumph that would bring the end of the war in sight. The unenthusiastic Franco preferred a slow and systematic advance into Republican territory, followed by purges to end all possibility of opposition. He disliked the whole idea of separate Italian forces and resented Málaga being trumpeted to the world as Mussolini's victory. Grudgingly, he agreed to an Italian attack on Guadalajara in early March, a distaste that explains, in part, its subsequent failure. The successful Republican counterattack, launched on 18 March, was a humiliating defeat for the Italians. Though the Italian offensive failed, so did the Republican counter-thrust, both at a high cost in men dead, wounded, or captured. Franco's unwillingness to send troops from his own front to assist the attack or to relieve General Roatta's demoralized forces, accounts for the rout that followed. Franco had not anticipated a defeat, but he wanted the Italians to bear the brunt of a struggle to exhaust the

[47] TNA: PRO, CAB 23/87, 8 January 1937.

Republican troops and provide time for his own soldiers to recover. He was not averse, moreover, to seeing the Italian forces humbled and his own position correspondingly strengthened, as he needed the Italians for the assault planned against Bilbao and wanted their army under his command. The Guadalajara defeat gave the wily leader just the weapon he needed; it was the last time Franco permitted the Italians to play an independent role. The psychological consequences of the Italian defeat were considerable, for it shattered the myths of Mussolini's omniscience and Italian invincibility. If Franco had gone on to capture Madrid in March as Mussolini had intended, the Duce would have fulfilled his Spanish goals. Instead, he became committed to Franco's 'creeping war of attrition'. Fully aware of his ally's duplicity, there could be no question of withdrawing. The Nationalists had to triumph if Mussolini's prestige was to be restored and opposition in Italy to the war silenced. The material and financial costs of Italian intervention spiralled while, thanks to Franco's way of waging war, Spain would be in no condition to give Italy any assistance in the foreseeable future.

In March 1937, still unable to break through in Madrid, Franco began an attack on the north, to deny the Republicans access to the sea and to gain control over the important industrial resources in the Basque region. The failure of the Guadalajara campaign convinced Franco that Madrid could not be taken except at unacceptable costs. During the summer of 1937 in a lengthy, methodical campaign, much of the north was taken. In the battles for the Basque territories, the German Condor Legion took the lead. The Germans were only too pleased to exhibit their superiority to the Italians and to show what close air support could accomplish. The Nationalist advance, nonetheless, proved unexpectedly slow as the Basques put up a dogged defence. The German and Spanish military leaders, angry at the sluggish pace of advance, talked of pulverizing Bilbao. Instead, the morale-shattering blow was struck at the small market town of Guernica in the late afternoon of 26 April 1937. High explosive bombs were dropped first, and then incendiaries created fires that destroyed the town. The presence of one Belgian and three British reporters, and the arrival of an articulate Basque priest during the bombing, turned the Nationalists' attempt to deny the destruction of the town into a world scandal. The ruin of an 'open city' was a chilling reminder of the devastating effects of bombing. The condemnation of Germany was worldwide; even Ribbentrop was embarrassed. Though the myth was revived again in the 1990s, few believed the Nationalist claims that Guernica had been destroyed by 'red separatist incendiaries'. The retreating Basque army had not yet reached Guernica; there was no question of cutting off their escape route by 'dynamiting the town'. It seems highly probable, however, that the attack was carried out at the request of the Spanish high command, and not on German initiative. Franco's main concern in the aftermath was that under international pressure, Hitler did not recall the Condor Legion from Spain. The purpose of the bombing was to terrorize the Basques and in this sense the Nationalists were successful. The Basque leaders were prepared to negotiate, though for the moment nothing came of it. The Italians, too, wanted Franco to accept a compromise peace in return for rapid surrender. In the meantime, the Nationalists renewed their march on Bilbao, under a new commander entirely faithful to Franco following the death on 3 June of General Mola in an unexplained plane crash. They entered the city unopposed on 19 June. The Basque authorities did not want to suffer the fate of Guernica. Everything was left intact. Franco allowed only small bodies of troops to enter the city so there was no pillage or reprisals. Mussolini interceded, with some degree of success, to urge moderation on Franco in his treatment of the Basques.

Once again, to mutual German and Italian disgust, Franco paused before finishing off the northern campaign. This gave the Republican armies what proved to be a fatal opportunity to launch their well-planned offensive at Brunete, a village just fifteen miles west of Madrid, on 6 July. The Communists chose the target and the international brigades played a prominent role. The thinly held Nationalist line broke. To contain the attack, Franco suspended the campaign in the north and sent divisions from Guadalajara, accompanied by the Condor Legion and the Italian air force. Neither side won a clear victory in this punishing campaign; there were casualties of an estimated 25,000 on the Republican side and 17,000 Nationalists. The Republicans were unable to sustain their offensive and gained little for their efforts. They lost so many experienced soldiers and so much valuable equipment that the battle was judged a major setback for the Communists, who had planned it. The Republican Madrid salient projecting into the Nationalist-held territory was now highly vulnerable to attack from three sides.

Franco was again in a position to attack Madrid and put an end to the war. Instead he deliberately held the army back and turned again to the northern campaign in mid-August. By the time of the Nationalist move against Santander, a port on the Bay of Biscay, they had an army of 60,000 men (facing 50,000 Republicans), well-equipped with modern tanks and artillery and supported by both the Condor Legion and the Italian *Corpo Truppe Volontarie* (CTV). It was an easy triumph. On 26 August 1937, after only a week's campaign, the Nationalists, led by the Italians, entered the city unopposed. The Italian 'volunteers' had secured their revenge for Guadalajara. The Rome propaganda machine went into high gear, undoubtedly assisted by the Republicans, who wildly exaggerated the number and importance of the Italian contribution to the victory, in the hope of securing additional assistance from France and the Soviet Union. The Basque leaders, who had withdrawn to the port of Santona, near Santander, surrendered their battalions to the Italians expecting the earlier guarantees of lenient treatment to be kept. With promises that there would be no reprisals, they were handed over to Franco. The *Caudillo* had no scruples about so-called moral obligations. There were summary trials, imprisonments, assignments to labour battalions, death sentences, and executions. At very little cost, Franco had humbled the troublesome Basques and inherited intact the industrial plant of the region. During September and October, the insurgents completed the subjection of Asturias. The conquest of the Basque country, Santander, and Asturias gave Franco a decisive military and industrial advantage over his enemies. With the whole north coast in their hands, the Nationalists could concentrate their naval forces in the Mediterranean and enforce the blockade of the Republican coast. The Army of the North was free to fight in the south. Franco paused, regrouped his forces, and considered his next offensive.

VIII

The Soviet Union continued to give no formal acknowledgement of its role in Spain, but its presence was unmistakeable. The Communist drive against 'spies and subversives' in Spain gathered pace as the Communists, especially those from Moscow, focused more on rooting out political enemies than on sustaining Largo Caballero's government. In December 1936, the first signs of new tensions were felt in Barcelona where the Communists, supported by the anarchists, expelled POUM from the *Generalitat*, the regional government of Catalonia, in December 1936. Clearly associated with the trials of the 'Trotskyists' in Moscow, the ruthless persecution of POUM now began. The roots of this repression were, in part, ideological; 'Trotskyism' in Spain, it was claimed, was part of an international Fascist conspiracy that had to be eliminated. It was mainly a local struggle for power aimed at the so-called threatening left. The Communists moved brutally against the Barcelona anarchists in early 1937; their leaders were arrested or assassinated either by the Spanish Communists or the Soviet-controlled security forces. The fiercest battles were fought over the militia system. The victory went to the better organized party. It was due to the Communist party and its advisers that a decree ending the militias and reorganizing the army in mixed brigades was introduced at the end of December 1936. While the militias continued to exist until mid-1937, the absence of a military hierarchy, poor training, and lack of equipment (they were purposely starved of weapons by the Communists) undermined their effectiveness. In Valencia itself, the seat of the Republican government, the Communists assumed a dominant role. Caballero, jealous of those who stayed in Madrid and resentful of the presence of the Soviet ambassador, Rozenberg, was, nevertheless, dependent on Soviet assistance. Rather than make use of the PCE, which was too independent for their purposes, the Soviets placed their own advisers in key positions and worked through the NKVD.

The Republican loss of the Basque territory in the summer of 1937 brought the political crisis in Valencia to a head. Since the start of the year, the conflict between Largo Caballero and the Communists and their Soviet mentors over control of the army had grown increasingly bitter. A conference of military commissars from all fronts was held on 2 April; its purpose was to increase the power and influence of the military commissars and the commissariat, at the expense of the Ministry of Defence. Caballero, as minister of defence, countered the challenge by trying to abolish the whole commissar organization. His efforts came to nought, mainly because of a bloody confrontation in Barcelona on 3 May between the anarchist *Confederación Nacional de Trabajo* (CNT) and POUM, on one side, and the forces of the Moscow-backed *Generalitat* and the Communist-dominated PSUC, on the other. The PSUC blamed the leaders of POUM and the 'uncontrollables' for their 'uprising' against the government. Though Largo Caballero was not responsible for the decisions taken in the Catalan capital, the suppression of the insurrection was done in his name, and was followed by arrests and executions and by a tightening of Communist control. There were demands from the PCE in Valencia for the unification of all the parties of the left and the creation of a united trade union movement, both moves intended to enhance Communist dominance. In mid-May, Caballero resisted a Communist proposal to outlaw POUM, and to reduce anarchist representation in the government. The Communists left the meeting, and on the following day Caballero resigned.

On 17 May 1937, Juan Negrín, who belonged to the right wing of the Spanish Socialist Workers' Party (PSOE), became prime minister. Negrín was not a Communist puppet; he was a moderate in politics and a competent administrator. His anti-revolutionary views, however, suited the Soviet government. It was intended that the PCE should only play a subordinate role in the Popular Front government, to reassure those who feared a Communist take-over of the country. Such a policy supposedly gave substance to ambassador Maisky's assurances to Anthony Eden that the Soviets did not want a Bolshevik government in Spain, but rather a liberal democratic anti-Fascist republic. José Giral, a moderate republican and former prime minister, was made foreign minister. There were only two Communist ministers in the cabinet; the Communists would work from behind the scenes. The anarchists were excluded altogether. POUM was quickly outlawed and its militias either broken up or merged with other units. Its leaders, including Andreas Nin, the former minister for justice, 'disappeared' for good. In the summer, a new counter-espionage agency was created; its activities extended to the extinction of all forms of opposition by the usual ghastly methods employed by such bodies. The Soviet actions in Spain and the purges of its own agents—Rozenberg was summoned home in February 1937 and, like so many others, eventually 'disappeared'—paralleled the ruthless purges at home. On 2 June 1937, the eve of the summary trial against the leaders of the Red Army, Stalin warned that the 'conspirators' wanted to 'make the USSR into a second Spain'.[48] The Soviet leader saw enemies and spies everywhere; the phantoms in Spain were as real as those in Moscow. Some pro-Republicans preferred to say nothing about events in Spain, given that only the Soviet Union provided any outside hope of saving the Republic. 'I was losing Russia', Louis Fischer, an American journalist and Communist with a home in Moscow, concludes his critical account of the trials. 'I did not want at the same time to lose Spain.'[49]

Accounts vary as to the mood in Republican Spain during the summer and autumn of 1937. Those appalled by the persecutions of the POUM and the treason trials in Moscow, claimed that the spontaneous revolutionary ardour motivating those who defended Madrid and volunteered for the international brigades had begun to wane. Apart from the divisions on the left, the inability of the Republicans to mount a successful offensive hardly encouraged an optimistic view of the future. Catalonia and Valencia held firm, as did Madrid and its environs, but two-thirds of Spain was now in Franco's hands. It was not just the Basques who were prepared to negotiate. Franco told the German ambassador in Salamanca on 23 May 1937 that Horacio Prieto, the minister of defence in Negrín's cabinet, had visited Blum to discuss a truce and hoped for either French or American mediation. Talk of peace went the rounds of Paris and Geneva. Valencia itself was considered unsafe and the government was transferred to Barcelona at the very end of October 1937. Though this strengthened Communist control, the strong pull of Catalan nationalism could not be subdued, nor the talk of a separate peace suppressed. Defection was openly preached in Barcelona and Soviet observers were well aware of the general longing for peace.

[48] Quoted in Pons, *Stalin and the Inevitable War*, 84

[49] Louis Fischer, *Men and Politics* (London, 1941), 443.

More important than the mood of defeatism or reports from western Communist parties of diminished interest in Spain, was the changing attitude of the Soviet Union. Material assistance continued to arrive in the Republic all through the summer of 1937 but Soviet advisers were recalled, more often than not to become themselves victims of the purges, and uncertainty and suspicion weakened the authority of those who remained. Both for domestic and foreign policy reasons, Stalin appears to have relegated Spain to a secondary position in his thinking. In the Soviet Union, the terror spread, affecting all the institutions of the state. Communist exiles and foreigners working or living in Russia were victims of the on-going repression. Measures supposedly taken to promote the internal consolidation of the regime in anticipation of a future war were, in fact, seen abroad as weakening its defensive structure.[50] Great efforts were made in Moscow to extol the power of the Soviet state and to warn off capitalist enemies. With the drive to establish a 'total security state', Spain ceased to be of major concern. There were rumours, too, that Stalin was moving away from the concept of anti-Fascist popular fronts, whether in Spain or in France but he was not yet ready to reverse gear.

If the turmoil in Russia, along with the series of Republican defeats in Spain raised doubts about the continued Soviet aid to the Republic, nevertheless supplies continued to be sent. Negrín, who, unlike some of his political colleagues, refused to consider a negotiated peace, knew that the prolongation of the war depended on Soviet assistance. A cultured and sophisticated man, he repressed his doubts about the actions of the Communists in Spain and his anxieties about the trials in the Soviet Union. The offensive in Brunete in July 1937 left the Republicans stripped of equipment; Negrín instructed his ambassador in Moscow to ask Voroshilov for more arms and supplies, particularly aircraft. The ambassador was at first unsuccessful, but once able to appeal to Stalin personally his request was subsequently fulfilled. Italian naval activity, however, made it almost impossible to send supplies via the Black Sea. Between October 1936 and July 1937, ninty-six Soviet merchant ships were captured and three sunk.[51] The Russians, whose naval power was weak, were unwilling to suffer further losses and began to cut their Black Sea shipments to the Republicans, leaving them more dependent on France's border policies, official or not. The outbreak of the Sino-Japanese war in July 1937 and, even more important, the decision to provide aid to the Chinese Kuomintang government, taken at the end of the month, contributed to the eventual downgrading of the Republican cause. Soviet planes and tanks, though fewer than

[50] For a discussion of the purges, see pp. 460–466.

[51] Figures in Haslam, *Soviet Union and the Struggle for Collective Security*, 146.

Chiang Kai-shek wanted, began to arrive in September and some 450 Russian pilots were in China by the end of 1937. One of the indirect results of the Soviet intervention in China, intended to strengthen the Chinese military effort so as to keep the Japanese tied up in China, was ultimately to strengthen the influence of the 'isolationists' like Molotov, Zhdanov, the Leningrad party secretary, and Potemkin, the first deputy commissar at the Narkomindel, who favoured a retreat into 'fortress Russia'. By the start of 1938, Litvinov, increasingly isolated, was contemplating resignation.

Table 5.4 Soviet War Material Sent to Spain by mid-May 1937

Airplanes	333	
Tanks	256	
Projectiles for tanks	970,700	until mid-March
Armoured vehicles	60	
Medium-calibre canons	236	plus 673,060 projectiles
Small-calibre canons	145	plus 1.52 million projectiles
Depth charges	200	
Torpedo longboats	2	
Torpedoes	8	
Marine radios	15	
Grenade launches	340	plus 165,000 projectiles
Heavy machine guns	4188	
Light machine guns	4150	
Machine rifles	3150	
Rifles	210,183	
Hand grenades	120,000	

Spare parts for aeroplanes, tanks, artillery, infantry; material for aerodromes, lubricant, and other materials for repairs

Source: Angel Viñas, *El escudo de la república: el oro de Espña, la apuesta soviética y los hechos de mayo 1937* (Barcelona, 2007), 420.

Table 5.5 Soviet Planes Sent to Spain by June 1937

Type	Sent	Lost	Active
I-15	148	35	113
I-16	76	8	68
SB	61	12	49
SSS	31	11	20
R-Z	93	0	93
Total	409	66	343

Source: Angel Viñas, *El escudo de la república: el oro de España, la apuesta soviética y los hechos de mayo 1937* (Barcelona, 2007), 423.

IX

The Italian roles at Málaga and Guadalajara, and the German bombing of Guernica, left no doubts in the spring and summer of 1937 that the non-intervention policy was a farce. Republican demands that either the NIC or the League of Nations raise the question of Italian violations, and Italian and German counter-demands for an investigation of the Soviet use of Spanish gold, simply confused the diplomatic picture and diverted attention from the main issue. In May, when representatives of many states, including Spain, gathered in London for the coronation of George VI, Eden took up the Republican suggestion for a mediated peace, only to find Franco, poised to attack Bilbao, monumentally uninterested. At the League Council meeting later that month, the foreign secretary admitted that his armistice proposal had failed. At the same time, when the Spanish representative complained of German and Italian intervention and questioned whether the NIC could achieve anything, both Delbos and Eden insisted that the committee had made real progress since the previous December. The non-intervention schemes, however flouted, contained the conflict in Spain, which was the main Anglo-French purpose.

The verbal battles in the NIC were never pursued to the point of disruption. More difficult was the task of defusing the quarrels that arose from a series of naval confrontations. In April 1937, Franco's forces began their campaign against the Basques in north-eastern Spain. The Nationalist naval commanders declared a blockade of Bilbao in an effort to stop provisions from reaching government forces. Franco, assuming that the British fleet would not intervene, informed the British ambassador, established at Hendaye, that if the four British merchant ships temporarily berthed at St. Jean de Luz attempted to enter Bilbao with their cargoes, his warships would attack. The four captains—three of them named Jones and dubbed 'Potato' Jones, 'Ham and Eggs' Jones and 'Corn-Cob' Jones, after their respective cargoes—became front-page news. The British were anxious that there should be no incidents, but such a direct challenge to Britain's neutral rights required a response. Franco was told that Britain would not accept any interference with its ships. At the same time, the Admiralty advised British ships not to go to ports on Spain's north coast and warned that, if they did so, they would be given no naval protection. Hoare, who opposed Britain's participation in the control schemes, argued that such warnings were essential if the British navy was not to be engaged against the Nationalist fleet. It seemed clear to irate Labour and Liberal Members that the government was following a pro-Franco policy, sentiments given expression during an unusually bitter Commons debate on 14 April. Even before the blockade was tested, it was clear that Franco's warning was deceptive. The Nationalist blockade was ineffective and the Admiralty warnings to British ships excessive. Subsequent insurgent efforts to interfere with British shipping were easily checked. The cabinet nevertheless remained concerned to avoid clashes with Nationalist ships, as was Franco, and a *modus vivendi* was negotiated to avoid incidents. As a result, the Admiralty in effect refused to protect ships that sailed into Spain's territorial waters or to rescue refugees stranded on the shore. Its policies provoked more denunciations from the Opposition benches. If the Conservatives, barring a dozen or so MPs who were strongly pro-Franco, were largely indifferent about events in Spain, the rank and file of the Labour party had taken up the Republic's cause. In October 1937, the Labour leadership was forced, somewhat reluctantly, to approve a nation-wide campaign for ending the Non-Intervention Agreement. The highly emotive issue of Spain helped to break the bipartisan approach to foreign policy established at the time of the Rhineland crisis.

Republican efforts to prevent German and Italian supply ships from reaching the Nationalists came close to scuppering the NIC. On 24 May 1937, the Italian ship *Barletta*, lying in the harbour of Palma de Majorca, was hit by a bomb. On 29 May, two Republican aircraft bombed the German battleship *Deutschland*. Neurath warned Hitler against declaring war on the Spanish Republic. The Germans retaliated by shelling the undefended city of Almeira on 29–30 May; Ribbentrop announced Hitler's decision to withdraw both from the control scheme and from the discussions of the NIC. Mussolini followed suit, anxious to use Spain as a means of reinforcing his ties with Hitler. The *Deutschland* incident created considerable alarm in London and Paris. Eden suspected that the incident had been provoked by the Republicans at the urging of Moscow, which he claimed would have liked to see a war between Germany and Britain and France. There were hasty Anglo-French efforts at damage limitation. It was agreed that in case of future attacks, the four patrol states would take joint action and if the country whose ships were attacked was not satisfied, it should have the right to take its own action. With this guarantee, Germany and Italy returned to the NIC. On 18 June, the Germans claimed that their cruiser, *Leipzig*, had been torpedoed by a Republican submarine, and demanded a four-power naval demonstration and the surrender of Republican submarines to a neutral body under four-power direction. The Admiralty doubted that the *Leipzig* had been fired upon, but bridled at French objections to concessions to the Nationalists, including the grant of belligerent rights to both sides in Spain, for it feared that the Royal Navy would have to make up the gap left by the departure of the Italian and German ships.

Neville Chamberlain became prime minister on 28 May 1937. Irritated by the slowness of the diplomatic machine, he personally intervened to get talks started with the dictators. But Chamberlain found his plans for the appeasement of the Axis powers blocked by the non-intervention accords and French stiffness over belligerent rights. His irritation with the Foreign Office, and with the French, was palpable, and fears at the French embassy, prompted by British officials, about the future direction of Chamberlain's diplomacy began to mount. As the Germans refused to allow any investigation of the *Leipzig* incident and the French were adamant in their refusal to give way to Hitler's demands, it was a frustrating time for the new prime minister. The Foreign Policy Committee, with Hoare dragging his feet, agreed that the German demands were excessive and backed the French in their rejection of the German note. They also agreed to Delbos's suggestion that British and French ships should fill the gap left in the naval control system. In the aftermath of the *Deutschland* affair, Eden had invited Neurath to London for a visit, to improve Anglo-German relations and to initiate wide ranging talks with the foreign minister. It was an attempt to establish direct contact with the German government through 'normal channels' rather than through Dr Schacht. Hitler did not want the visit to take place (nor did Mussolini) and the *Leipzig* incident, much played up by the Italians, simply provided the occasion for its cancellation. On 20 June, four days before Neurath was expected in London, Hitler called off the visit. At 10 Downing Street, the Foreign Office was blamed for yet another bungled effort at opening a dialogue with Berlin.

The first Blum government fell on the night of 21–22 June. Delbos remained as foreign minister in the new government of Camille Chautemps (whose main interests were domestic rather than foreign) and pursued a tougher line with regard to Spain and Italy. He had already begun to take a stronger stand against Axis violations of the NIC recommendations before the change of government, and now refused any concessions over the *Leipzig* incident until an investigation was held. If France was to abide by the non-intervention policy, there should be no grant of belligerent rights that would favour the Nationalists. Blum, for his part, appears to have made stronger support for the Valencia government part of his price for Socialist participation in the Chautemps coalition. The French demanded the withdrawal of the international observers on the closed French–Spanish frontier to register their displeasure, a threat renewed in July unless 'volunteers' were withdrawn.

The French, however, found themselves with relatively little influence on London where Chamberlain, having been checked by Hitler, turned his attention to the Italians. It was not the policy of non-intervention that was at issue between London and Paris, but differing attitudes towards the Italian role in the Mediterranean. The British prime minister was convinced that his personal intervention would cement relations with Mussolini. During the months following the 'Gentlemen's Agreement', the Italian anti-British propaganda campaign continued unabated. The Duce visited Tripoli in mid-March 1937 to open a new highway, a strategic road, hugging the North African coast from the Tunisian border all the way to Egypt. Mounted on a white stallion, he received 'the sword of Islam', laying claim to a protective role for all Muslims. In April, a High Command for North Africa was established and plans were laid for a white metropolitan army corps in Libya. The British press had a field day over the Italian defeat at Guadalajara and, in response, on 17 June, Mussolini published a violent, unsigned rejoinder in *Il popolo d'Italia,* denouncing Britain and warning that the dead at Guadalajara would be avenged. Even after the Neurath visit was cancelled, the Italian press continued its attacks in what was clearly a government-orchestrated campaign. Given the clear evidence of the Italian violations of the Non-Intervention Agreement and the lack of progress over the withdrawal of volunteers, the Foreign Office had no wish to resume talks with Rome. Misgivings (of which the Italians were fully appraised through their reading of intercepted British communications) about the Italian courtship of Yugoslavia and Turkey added to Eden's distrust of Mussolini's future intentions. In mid-June, Eden had presented a paper recommending that in future defence planning, Italy could no longer be considered a 'reliable friend' but should be regarded as a 'possible enemy'. Chamberlain rejected the Foreign Office formula, refusing to consider the Italian danger as comparable to that from Germany or Japan and proposed instead that Italy be counted an 'unreliable friend'. Backed by the Admiralty and War Office, Chamberlain thought an agreement with Italy in the Mediterranean possible and necessary if Britain was to reduce her over-extended defence burden. He was infuriated, as was the Admiralty, by French opposition to the grant of belligerent rights to both parties in Spain as a way of getting the Italians and Germans back into the naval patrols. There was considerable alarm in Paris at Chamberlain's turn towards Rome. The *Quai d'Orsay* wanted to use Spain to thwart Mussolini's ambitions in the Mediterranean, while Chamberlain, if not Eden, was prepared to ignore the Spanish question in the hope of coming to an understanding with Mussolini.

On 29 July, Chamberlain met with Grandi, the ambitious, self-confident, and unreliable Italian ambassador, who went well beyond his instructions from Ciano to win the prime minister's support. The ambassador, who had numerous contacts in Conservative circles, believed he could successfully play on the differences between the prime minister and the foreign secretary. Claiming that he had a personal message of friendship from Mussolini (probably untrue), he provided a summary of what he intended to say so that Eden would not ask to be present. According to Chamberlain's relatively short account of the meeting, Grandi quoted Mussolini as having no political or territorial ambitions in Spain, though he placed great importance on Franco's victory in order to avoid a 'red' government in Barcelona. Grandi claimed that the Duce regretted the bad relations between their two countries and would now like to fill in the framework of the January 1937 agreement. Finally, he concluded, Mussolini attached great importance to Britain's *de jure* recognition of Italy's conquest of Ethiopia. This was just the opportunity Chamberlain had been seeking. The prime minister insisted that *de jure* recognition could only be given as part of a general settlement. Even if Grandi's far more extensive account exaggerated his own cleverness and diplomatic skill, he obviously played on the prime minister's vanity and reminded him, too, of his father's and half brother's Italophile sympathies. The ambassador was rewarded with the offer of a personal letter to the Duce expressing Chamberlain's willingness to start conversations.

The two men met again alone (Eden was away on holiday) in London on 2 August. According to Grandi, Chamberlain told him he intended 'to continue to intervene directly in dealing with international problems' where his intervention was 'useful and necessary', but that he wanted Eden to maintain his authority and responsibility.[52] The foreign secretary, informed only some days later of Chamberlain's proceedings, expressed his strong disapproval and returned to London to protest. French complaints at their exclusion from talks over Ethiopia and the Mediterranean further annoyed the prime minister, who would not allow Chautemps and Delbos to block his new initiative. The prime minister and his foreign secretary clashed over the handling of Mussolini. 'Eden favoured intimidation', the British historian, R. A. C. Parker, concludes, 'Chamberlain conciliation'.[53] The prime minister thought it worthwhile to make sacrifices to gain Mussolini's friendship, including the recognition of Italian sovereignty over Ethiopia. Eden doubted whether the Duce's friendship was worth having if based only on hopes for future good behaviour. He wanted concessions before rewards were offered. Later events proved that Eden's doubts were well founded.

Early in August, the Nationalists sought Italian assistance to block Soviet shipments to the Republicans. If Mussolini needed any persuasion, Franco's warnings that if no action were taken the war would go on indefinitely, were sufficient to convince him to act. He agreed to

[52] ASMAE, SRD 963/3, Grandi to Ciano, 2 August 1937.
[53] R. A. C. Parker, *Chamberlain and Appeasement*, 108.

establish a blockade against all westbound shipping south of Sicily, tracking, intercepting, and sinking Spanish and Soviet ships as well as any 'enemy or suspicious merchant ships' carrying arms to Spain. Emboldened by the Italian victory at Santander, Mussolini would sanction any measures that would push Franco to finish the war. Between 6 August and 13 September, half the Italian fleet, unmarked and operating mainly at night, patrolled the Mediterranean and the Aegean. Italian submarines fired torpedoes at 24 vessels but only 4 merchant ships were sunk and one Republican destroyer damaged.

The Italian decision was made just as the exchanges between Chamberlain and Mussolini had begun. Given his opposition to the talks, Eden made much of the sinkings. The Admiralty had no wish to retaliate against the Italians, with whom they wanted an agreement. They continued to press for the granting of belligerent rights to the insurgents, as Franco was demanding. The replacement of Hoare by Duff Cooper as first lord of the Admiralty did nothing to alter the views of the naval chiefs. Nonetheless, on 17 August, Eden won ministerial support for a statement that if any British merchant ship was attacked without warning by 'anonymous submarines', the Royal Navy was authorized to counter-attack. The submarine campaign temporarily halted the Anglo-Italian talks, though no official protest to Rome was delivered. An announcement that Britain intended to maintain its current naval strength in the Mediterranean had no effect on the Italians. On 1 September, a torpedo from the Italian submarine *Iride* narrowly missed the British destroyer *HMS Havock*; two days later, a British merchant ship, the *Woodford*, was sunk near Valencia. There was a strong public reaction. Many newspapers, though not *The Times*, openly blamed Italy for these acts of 'piracy' and there were public demands for a British response.

The Chautemps government, too, pressed for action and threatened to reopen the Franco-Spanish frontier unless a conference was called to stop 'piracy' in the Mediterranean. Delbos first suggested a tripartite meeting but then proposed a conference of Mediterranean and Black Sea states with Italy excluded. After a 'somewhat acrimonious controversy' between Paris and London, the 'Valencia government' was omitted from the list and Russia, Germany, and Italy included. As the French insisted that Russia be present, the British won their demand that the Germans be invited as well. Invitations were issued on 6 September for a conference to be held at Nyon, a village near Geneva. The Russians, anxious to make their position clear, despatched a note to the Italian government on 5 September protesting at the aggressive activities of Italian naval vessels against Soviet merchant ships. After consultation with Mussolini, and knowing that the Germans would not attend,

Ciano refused the Nyon invitation, expecting that the meeting could not take place without Italy. He accused the Soviets of 'torpedoing' the conference.

But the Nyon conference took place, from 10–14 September 1937, and was judged a major success and a personal triumph for Eden. Though he had difficult times in the cabinet when he proposed joint action with France, he was backed by expressions of strong anti-Italian feeling in the country. Eden knew, through decrypted intercepts, that Ciano had called off the Italian submarine campaign on 4 September. In this sense, the conference was a success before the participants assembled. Eden and Delbos worked well together as did the British and French naval staffs, whom the other powers agreed should assume the major share of the patrolling responsibilities. Significantly, their co-operation stood in marked contrast to what had happened during the Ethiopian crisis. The partnership, however, depended on the two foreign ministers. In deference to Chamberlain's views, Eden made every effort to avoid offending the absent Italians. Bowing to majority opinion that the Russians should not patrol the Mediterranean, the Soviet Union waived its rights to participate in the patrols and confined its activities to the Black Sea. Since the British Admiralty claimed it was impossible to participate in both the Nyon Conference and NIC patrol schemes, the latter were abandoned. Once again, however, the British determination to appease Mussolini proved stronger than any concern for Spain or international justice. The preliminary agreement signed on 14 September was amended on 29 September to include Italy and permit Italian ships to patrol the Mediterranean. Litvinov was so indignant at this further example of hypocrisy that the proposal simply became an Anglo-French offer which the Italians accepted. At a meeting on 30 October, aboard *HMS Barham* at Bizerta, final arrangements were concluded so that Italian participation in patrolling could begin on 11 November. The poacher had become gamekeeper.

The Nyon conference marked the end of serious international tensions generated by the Spanish Civil War. There were no further submarine attacks reported until January 1938, when the patrols were reduced in strength because of their success. This was not due, as claimed by Winston Churchill in *The Gathering Storm*, to Anglo-French firmness at Nyon.[54] The Italians had called off the campaign before the conference, because their aims in Spain were being met by late August,

[54] Winston Churchill, *The Second World War*, Vol 1: *The Gathering Storm* (London, 1948), 192.

but also because they never intended to challenge the British directly.[55] In the weeks after the Nyon Conference, the Italians actually increased their aerial and naval assistance to the insurgents but took care not to flout the new naval regime. On 15 September, Ciano promised Franco two Italian submarines with a further two to follow shortly. Two destroyers, already sold to the Spanish Nationalists in August in clear contravention of the Non-Intervention Agreement, were only transferred in November, as Ciano insisted that the ships' silhouettes should be modified. And a month after Nyon, Mussolini was prepared to send another division to help Franco finish off the campaign in the north. The new troops were not despatched but only because they were not needed.

The French tried to follow up on Nyon with further joint action against the Italians. An Anglo-French invitation to open three-power talks on Spain, issued on 2 October, contained a threat to abandon non-intervention unless the policy was made effective, but also a plan that if progress was made on withdrawing 'volunteers', Franco might be granted belligerent rights. The Italians rejected the invitation a week later, refusing to discuss Spain outside the NIC or without German participation. The Italian press was unleashed against France; the latter proposed to respond to the Italian rejection by formally opening the border with Spain. The British blocked this 'provocative' action. For the moment, the French policy of 'relaxed intervention' remained in place. The tougher French mood was reflected by a demand, some weeks after Nyon, for a pre-emptive occupation of Menorca, still in Republican hands. The government and high command were united in their determination to keep Italy from establishing a permanent position in the Balearics. The Mediterranean, in the view of the influential Admiral Darlan, the new chief of the naval staff, was the key to French security. Its domination would secure Britain's and France's colonial possessions and free their hands for an assault against Germany. General Gamelin would not accept such a revolutionary change in French strategy: it would signal to the Germans a tacit loss of French interest in central Europe and increase the possibility of a German attack in the west. The focus of defence planning remained centred on a German attack against France, though a somewhat equivocal resolution emerged from the deliberations of the *Comité Permanent de la Défense Nationale*

[55] This caution did not prevent Mussolini from sending two new Italian corps to Libya in September 1937, nor Italian planning for moves against Egypt and the Sudan though there was no intention to mount an invasion of Egypt until much later. See Steven Morewood, *The British Defence of Egypt 1935–1940: Conflict and Crisis in the Eastern Mediterranean* (London and New York, 2005), 103–104.

(CPDN) at the end of December 1937: 'There are grounds for our eventually being able to pursue as a matter of first urgency, the defeat of Italy, while remaining in a position to face an attack from Germany at any moment, and to pin down its forces to the extent necessary in order to allow action by us or our allies in other theatres.'[56]

Mussolini's most pressing demand, as Grandi made clear in London, was for *de jure* recognition of Italian sovereignty over Ethiopia. The Duce had a curious predilection for having his conquests 'legalized'. The *Quai d'Orsay* was determined that this concession should be linked with the withdrawal of Italian 'volunteers' from Spain. The French encouraged an uprising in the Gojam, frustrating Mussolini's hopes of completing the pacification of Ethiopia and forcing him to increase the number of troops sent to East Africa. At the end of 1937, he resorted to a mustard gas campaign to defeat the Ethiopian rebels. Delbos insisted that France should participate in any British exchanges with Italy. The French foreign minister, it must be said, did not speak for the whole cabinet. Neither Chautemps nor Bonnet wanted to challenge Britain's primacy in charting policy over Spain or in the Mediterranean. Massigli and Léger argued that opening the French frontier as a counter-move would antagonize the British without saving the Spanish Republic. In London, possibly piqued by Eden's success at Nyon, but above all unwilling to have his efforts at conciliating Italy ruined by the Spanish question or by French obstinacy, Chamberlain was determined to deal with Rome on a bilateral basis. The prime minister could not ignore Delbos's demand for a part in the negotiations with Rome over Spain, but he was able to reassure Ciano that such tripartite talks would simply improve the diplomatic atmosphere before bilateral talks could start. In any case, the British could not meet the demand for recognition of Italian sovereignty over Ethiopia without League of Nations approval. Such a move would have been highly unpopular even in Conservative circles. The Italians were warned that their flagrant intervention in Spain made it difficult to secure League permission, particularly as the French would find it highly embarrassing to use their influence at Geneva in such circumstances. This shift of responsibility hardly did credit to either Chamberlain or Eden.

Notwithstanding Italy's adhesion on 6 November 1937, to the Anti-Comintern Pact, Chamberlain was anxious to begin the talks with Rome. Chamberlain grew impatient, particularly annoyed at the failure of the Foreign Office to get matters moving. A visit by Lady Chamberlain, Austen Chamberlain's widow, to Rome in December and her

[56] Meeting of CPDN, 8 December 1937, quoted in Nicole Jordan, *The Popular Front and Central Europe: The Dilemmas of French Impotence, 1918–1940* (Cambridge, 1992), 283.

friendly conversation with the Duce encouraged the prime minister's hopes. On New Year's Day 1938, after speaking with Chamberlain, Eden suggested ways for using the *de jure* recognition of Italian rule in Ethiopia as the base for future negotiations. As Eden went off for a holiday in southern France, Chamberlain took charge of the Foreign Office. It meant that he was in a position to thwart any French attempts to check Mussolini in the Mediterranean, while pressing on with his policy of appeasement.

X

After the Nyon Conference, Spain became little more than a pawn on the European chess-board. The bloody civil war continued because of Franco's tactics and the Republic's desperate determination to hold on to the territories under its control. None of the foreign powers engaged in Spain was prepared to withdraw their support, despite Axis impatience with Franco's tactics, and Soviet and French assumptions that the Republic's cause was lost. The ideological struggle between the two factions never broke out into open war. Instead, it was most openly and starkly displayed at the mammoth International Exhibition of 1937 in Paris, with the symbolic face-to-face confrontation of the massive, neo-classical pavilions of Hitler's Germany (designed by Albert Speer) and Stalin's Russian pavilion. Nearby was the Spanish pavilion containing Pablo Picasso's *Guernica*.

In Rome, Mussolini wanted a decisive demonstration of Italian prowess in the field, but was also anxious to attach Franco solidly to the Axis cause, to foster Italian ambitions in the Mediterranean. A subservient and grateful Franco, though the *Caudillo* showed no signs of being either, would confirm Italian domination of the Mediterranean and threaten France. Possession of the Balearics would interrupt British operations between its bases in Gibraltar and Malta; control over the Canary Islands would bring the Italian navy into the Atlantic. Neither the troubles in Libya nor in Ethiopia shook Mussolini's determination to see Franco victorious and linked to the Anti-Comintern Pact. Until Franco achieved victory, Mussolini would not withdraw his troops from Spain. The price was high. The arms and equipment used or left in Spain were to prove highly detrimental to Italy's performance in the Second World War. It has been estimated that with the material lost in Spain, the Italian army could have entered the field in June 1940 with fifty full-strength divisions instead of nineteen fully equipped and thirty-four incomplete divisions. Instead of two motorized divisions suitable for mobile operations in North Africa, the Italians could have fielded four or five against the British. Only some of the equipment left in Spain by the CTV was modern. Much was or would have been obsolete by 1940, but it was with this obsolete material that the Italians fought until 1943.[57]

Germany, though Hitler might tell Mussolini that it was vital to bring the Spanish conflict to an end as soon as possible, had every interest in allowing the war to continue. With Italy carrying most of the military burden, the conflict served to exacerbate Italian relations with Britain and France. At the high-level meeting of 5 November 1937, with his civilian and military advisers, Hitler was reported as saying: 'if one takes into account the length of time Franco has used in his offensives up to now, the war could possibly last about another three years. On the other hand, from Germany's point of view a 100% victory of Franco is really not desirable; we are more interested in a continuation of the war and the maintenance of tensions in the Mediterranean.'[58] Hitler was even prepared to see a 'red' Catalonia. The French would have to protect its threatened neighbour; Franco and France would become rivals and Britain would be blamed for the situation. As for Mussolini, 'a red Catalonia would be like a thick, fat bone before the Italian dog kennel and Mussolini could stand around gnawing at it, while he does not trouble himself worrying about other things in Europe, which he couldn't do anything about anyway'.[59] The Condor Legion was kept at approximately the same size from its arrival in Spain in the autumn of 1936 until Franco's final victory in the spring of 1939. Apart from a considerable rise in the spring of 1937 following the promises of support at the start of the year, the costs of assisting Franco were similarly constant. With a much smaller investment in men and materials, Germany gained the lion's share of the economic and diplomatic benefits.

In the case of France, Blum and his successor, Chautemps, initiated and followed the policy of non-intervention to keep the Popular Front together and to draw closer to Britain. It was a policy that they knew assisted Franco and hurt the Republic but if Blum agonized about this, he continued to endorse it. Non-intervention undoubtedly satisfied the great majority of Frenchmen. Nonetheless, the emotions generated by the issue continued to divide public opinion and to factionalize both left and right. Blum's fall in June 1937 left the Radicals in a dominant position in the new Chautemps government; they focused on France's perilous financial position. At the *Quai d'Orsay*, Delbos carried on Blum's policies, moving to a more pro-loyalist and anti-Italian position during the autumn months. This did not mean, however, any real

57 Sullivan, 'Fascist Italy's Military Involvement in the Spanish Civil War', 703.

58 *DGFP*, Ser. D, Vol. I, No. 31.

59 Quotation from Jaenecke, in Whealey, *Hitler and Spain*, 60.

departure from the policies of non-intervention. The *Quai d'Orsay* no longer hoped that there could be a compromise peace in Spain brokered by the Great Powers, or that the Italo-German *entente* might prove temporary. Whatever their fears about the implications of a Franco victory, neither the diplomats nor the French High Command were prepared to desert the NIC or move too far from London. Co-operation in Spain gave substance to an Anglo-French *entente* that was increasingly critical for France's future security.

It is true that the French continued to supply planes (probably less than three hundred), arms, and ammunition to the Republic, and refused to compromise on the issue of Spanish gold. The measures taken to assist the Republic were the minimum required to maintain a strained political coalition and to keep the allegiance of important sectors of the electorate. While the NIC debated the grant of belligerent rights subject to the withdrawal of a 'substantial proportion' of volunteers in October 1937, Delbos again threatened to open the frontier to force Italian acceptance. With Eden's somewhat cryptic approval, the frontier was opened, but only at night. It was closed again in January 1938 when the Socialists abandoned the Chautemps government, temporarily strengthening the hand of the Radicals. The divisions over non-intervention between the dominant Radicals on the one hand, and the Socialists, a few dissident Radicals, the CGT, and the Communists, on the other, deepened as the latter group demanded more assistance to the beleaguered Republic. Nonetheless, it was a gesture of despair (as well as an acknowledgment of guilt) that led Blum, who took office again in March 1938 just after Hitler's march into Vienna, to suggest an ultimatum to Franco and the despatch of French divisions to the Catalan front. His suggestions were rejected but the cabinet agreed to re-open the frontier in response to Negrín's personally delivered appeal. The flow of war material was of considerable short-term assistance to the Republicans. The Blum cabinet lasted just over six weeks and Daladier, who took over in late April, again had the border closed on 13 June. Emotions ran high but by the start of 1938 the problems in central Europe were already over-shadowing the issue of Spain.

From the British point of view, the policy of non-intervention was a success. However farcical the discussions in the NIC committee, there was no European war over Spain and the Great Powers had not divided into two opposing ideological blocs. France had not joined the Soviet Union in defence of the Republic, as some in the cabinet had feared, and despite all the evidence to the contrary, it was still believed, and not just by Chamberlain, that Italy could be separated from Germany. The cabinet ignored the shifts taking place on the continent as a consequence of the Spanish Civil War. Underestimating its impact on Mussolini, the

Spanish question, nonetheless, proved an additional barrier to a settlement with Rome. British policy-makers also failed to appreciate how the civil war contributed to the weakening of France's continental position. The British were content with the signs that the stricken Popular Front would follow their lead. Most satisfactory of all, the fictions of non-intervention and continuing NIC talks over 'volunteers' left open the possibilities of negotiations with Hitler and Mussolini, which were of paramount interest to the Chamberlain government, and to the prime minister in particular.

There were few worries in the cabinet about a Franco victory. Chamberlain stated the long-term basis for Britain's policies towards Franco when he told the cabinet: 'If and when General Franco won the Civil War . . . the situation would be very different and no doubt he would be looking round for help from other countries besides Germany and Italy. That would be the moment at which to put strong pressure upon him . . . that would be the time for action.'[60] During 1937, steps were taken to lay the basis for a renewal of Britain's ties with Spain. Convinced that Franco would win, the chiefs of staff were anxious about ensuring future Spanish neutrality in the event of a European war. Believing that post-war Spain would need British capital for its future reconstruction, ministers were convinced that Franco would not yield inalienable rights or territories to the Axis powers. Unlike the Germans, who tried to bully the Nationalists in order to secure their future economic position in Spain, the London cabinet preferred to speak softly, using Britain's considerable economic and naval clout to negotiate solutions to present difficulties in the hope of future rewards. Deals were struck to provide the Rio Tinto Company, the largest British mining interest in Spain, with monthly compensation for pyrites and other minerals sent to Germany and Italy. Negotiations also began to safeguard future British supplies of pyrites and iron ores. After many delays, the appointment on 16 November 1937 of Sir Robert Hodgson as commercial agent to the Nationalist authorities, despite the diplomatic niceties, amounted to a *de facto* recognition of the Nationalist government. In return, on 24 November Franco appointed the duke of Alba as agent in London, though the Spanish leader really wanted the formal recognition of belligerent rights. The hesitations of the Chamberlain government to go any further in the *Caudillo*'s direction had much to do with Britain's public identification with the policy of

[60] TNA: PRO, CAB 23/87, Cabinet 10(37)2, 4 March 1937, quoted in Smyth, 'Moor and the Money-lender', in Marie-Luise Recker (ed.), *Von der Konkurrenz zur Rivalität: das britisch-deutsche Verhältnis in den Ländern der europäischen Peripherie, 1919–1939* (Stuttgart, 1986), 167.

non-intervention. Its abandonment while the civil war continued would have represented a considerable blow to Britain's international prestige. Until the situation in Spain changed, it was simpler to maintain the balance between the two acknowledged governments in Spain while preparing the grounds for action after Franco's victory. During 1938 British opinion became increasingly and overwhelmingly pro-Republic but this did not create any effective opposition to the government's policies.

The Soviets were not prepared to write off their Spanish intervention. As part of the anti-Italian front at the Nyon Conference, the Russians made good propaganda use of their support for non-intervention however disappointed they might have been by its results. It may also be that, given the failure of both the Soviet Union's collective security policies and its efforts to settle directly with Germany, there was much to be said for keeping the struggle in Spain alive so as to prevent the complete victory of the Nationalists. In December 1937, urged on by their representatives at Valencia, the Soviets renewed their shipments to the Republic, sent from the Baltic and northern ports to France and across the Pyrenean frontier into Spain, the way opened by Blum's short-lived second ministry. Soviet assistance, dependent on French policy, was further diminished as the French political scene moved gradually to the right. There were no illusions in Moscow about the future of the Republic; the war-weariness of the people, the divisions in the Republican government, and the mistakes made by their own representatives pointed in only one direction. Stalin's thoughts lay elsewhere. Only a strengthened, purged, and united Soviet Union under his dictatorship could pursue a policy of isolation. As long as the war continued at minimal Soviet cost, it was not yet time to abandon the Negrín government. As the military situation deteriorated in the spring of 1938, Negrín's appeals for assistance were simply ignored. Some arms shipments continued but Stalin had other priorities. Most of the arms sent after August 1938 never reached the Republic. Some of it was later handed over by the French to the Nationalists. While the Soviet Union remained the chief source of supplies for the Republicans, it is impossible to know how far the pursuit of its own interests in Spain weakened the military efforts in the field.

The greatest and the only winner from all the conflict, confusion, and horror was Franco himself. It was not until December 1937 that he decided to launch a new attack on Guadalajara and then on Madrid. Against the advice of his own generals as well as from the highly impatient Italian and German military advisers, Franco called off the Guadalajara campaign to repel another Republican attack, this time an assault on the Nationalist-held city of Teruel, the bleak provincial capital of Aragón, 200 miles east of Madrid. The Republicans launched their offensive on 15 December and by Christmas were in the city. In a prolonged and savage battle in freezing temperatures, Franco's troops emerged triumphant and Teruel was re-occupied on 22 February 1938. The Republican army was shattered and Aragón opened to the Nationalists. With the loss of the best Republican units, it was the military turning point of the war. A series of victories for the Francoists followed. Still, the *Caudillo* would not end the death agony of Republican Spain. In ways which neither the Italians nor the Germans could fathom, Franco's military objectives served his political ambitions. He wished to annihilate the Republican army and to destroy or demoralize any opponents who might survive and challenge his rule. What was extraordinary was his continuing ability to secure the support from Mussolini and Hitler that enabled him to fight this kind of war.

A massive nationalist offensive in Aragón saw Franco's forces break through all Republican defences and reach the Mediterranean on 15 April 1938. Republican Spain was now split in two, with Catalonia severed from the rest of the Republic. Though civilian morale was low, Negrín was determined to fight on, counting on the new arms continuing to arrive over the French frontier. He reorganized his cabinet, a shift that increased Communist influence even further. A surprise attack against Franco's troops on the Ebro at the end of July 1938 produced temporary gains. But the Republican advance was halted by a series of counter-attacks and the fight degenerated into a costly battle of attrition, dragging on until November. With his superior resources, it was a fight that Franco was bound to win. On the wider scene, the Munich Agreement at the end of September 1938 ended hopes of further help for the Republicans for good. The formal withdrawal of the International Brigades, marked by a farewell parade in Barcelona, followed on 15 November. The final campaign of the war was a rout, as Franco began his advance into Catalonia towards Barcelona in late December. He had new German equipment and sufficient Spanish and Italian reserves to be able to relieve his troops every two days. As the Republican army disintegrated, Barcelona fell with barely a shot being fired. The war was grinding to an end, but the Negrín government refused to accept defeat. On 27 February 1939, France and Britain recognized the Nationalist government; a few hours later Azaña resigned his presidency. Bloody internecine fighting broke out in Madrid between survivors of the Republican government. Franco, on the verge of final victory, ignored all offers for a negotiated surrender. The final Nationalist advance, the *Caudillo*'s 'Victory Offensive', came against Madrid at the end of March; it met no resistance. On 1 April 1939, the civil war at last came to an end with the complete victory of Franco.

By this time, despite the ordeal and costs of three years of war, Spain was on the periphery of European international relations. Franco was free to begin the unopposed and bloody refashioning of his country. He would re-claim the European spotlight again in October 1940 when Hitler made his unsuccessful bid for the Spanish alliance.

In the deepest sense of all, the Spanish war was a prologue to the European war that followed. The devastation of the country and the bombings were a foretaste of what was to come. The divisions between right and left, deepened by the Great War and the new ideologies, Marxism and Fascism, though neither had roots in Spain, erupted into a savage struggle with atrocities committed on both sides. The term 'Fifth Column' was to take on a new resonance after 1939. When the refugees thronged towards Barcelona, they were subjected to the heaviest air raids of the war. Mussolini was 'delighted that the Italians should be horrifying the world by their aggressiveness for a change, instead of charming it by their skill at playing the guitar'.[61] Most of all, the fate of the defeated was a foretaste of the barbarism that was to come. In the civil war, the killings, over half a million, were not the end. Those on the losing side, regardless of political or class affiliation were arrested, thrown in jail, or executed in the long aftermath of the three year war. About 6,000 Spaniards came to the Soviet Union, including 3,000–4,000 children, mostly before 1939. The non-Communist Republicans, mainly airmen and merchant sea-man, were either sent to camps or killed. The children were put to work in factories and collective farms and were harshly treated; the requests of parents for their return were ignored. Many, abandoned in the Soviet retreat in the first phase of the German–Soviet war, joined the ranks of the vagabonds and delinquents, or formed highway gangs and ended in punishment camps and prison. The nearly half a million Spanish refugees who escaped to France over the Pyrenean passes were treated as criminals and not as exiles. They were confined behind barbed wire on open beaches, or, if politically suspect, sent to 'punishment camps' lest they foster revolution. Women and children, separated from the men, were herded into camps whose conditions became a minor international scandal. Daladier, under considerable domestic pressure to rid France of these unwanted exiles, bargained with Franco for their repatriation, refusing to return the Spanish gold unless they could be returned. Some 70,000 chose repatriation. Some were allowed to enlist in the Foreign Legion, the *Bataillons de Marche* or the *Compagnies de Travailleurs*, where they were put to work on roads, airfields, and fortifications. On the eve of the war, the camps still contained some 77,000 workers and 48,000 peasants. It was only in 1940 that steps were taken to empty the

[61] Quoted in Piers Brendon, *Dark Valley: A Panorama of the 1930s* (London, 2000), 146.

camps, leaving only the unfit (about 5,000) behind. The Spanish refugees were among the first to suffer the consequences of the capitulation. The Vichy authorities gave no protection and urged the Germans to deal more harshly with the Communists. Denied the status of prisoners of war, at least 10,000 found themselves back in the concentration camps where they had started, in the south-west of France. Some 30,000 were deported from France to Germany, of these 15,000 were sent to Nazi camps. More than 5,000 died at Mauthausen, the German concentration camp in Austria to which most of the Spanish Republicans were sent.[62] The aftermath of the civil war was not humanity's finest hour.

Books

ABENDROTH, H.-H., *Hitler in der spanischen Arena: die deutsch-spanischen Beziehungen im Spannungsfeld der europäischen Interessenspolitik vom Ausbruch des Bürgerkrieges bis zum Ausbruch des Weltkrieges, 1936–1939* (Paderborn, 1973).

ALEXANDER, M. S. and GRAHAM, H. (eds.), *The French and Spanish Popular Fronts: Comparative Perspectives* (Cambridge, 1988).

ALPERT, M., *A New International History of the Spanish Civil War* (Basingstoke, 1994).

AZCARATE, P. de, *Mi embajada en Londres durante la guerra civil española* (Barcelona, 1976).

BARGONI, F., *L'impegno navale italiano durante la guerra civile spagnola, 1936–1939* (Rome, 1992).

BEEVOR, A., *The Battle for Spain: The Spanish Civil War 1936–1939* (London, 1991).

BOLLOTON, B., *The Spanish Civil War: Revolution and Counterrevolution* (New York and London, 1991).

BUCHANAN, T., *Britain and the Spanish Civil War* (Cambridge, 1997).

CARR, E. H., *The Comintern and the Spanish Civil War*, ed. Tamara Deutscher (London, 1984).

COVERDALE, J. F., *Italian Intervention in the Spanish Civil War*, Foreword by Hugh Thomas (Princeton, NJ, 1975).

DUNTHORN, D.J., *Britain and the Anti-Franco Opposition* (London, 2000).

EDWARDS, J., *The British Government and the Spanish Civil War, 1936–1939* (London, 1979).

GOOCH, J., *Mussolini and his Generals: The Armed Forces and Fascist Foreign Policy, 1922–1940* (Cambridge, 2007).

GRAHAM, H., *The Spanish Republic at War, 1936–1939* (Cambridge, 2002).

HASLAM, J., *The Soviet Union and the Struggle for Collective Security in Europe, 1933–1939* (London, 1984).

HOPKINS, J. K., *Into the Heart of the Fire: The British in the Spanish Civil War* (Stanford, CA, 1998).

[62] Information and figures from David Wingeate Pike, *In the Service of Stalin: The Spanish Communists in Exile, 1939–1945* (Oxford, 1993), 3, 4, 36, 60, 161, 162.

Howson, G., *Arms for Spain: The Untold Story of the Spanish Civil War* (London, 1998).

Jackson, J., *The Popular Front in France: Defending Democracy, 1934–1938* (Cambridge, 1988).

Johnson, G. (ed.), *The International Context of the Spanish Civil War* (Newcastle, 2009).

Leitz, C., *Economic Relations between Nazi Germany and Franco's Spain, 1936–1945* (Oxford, 1996).

Little, D., *Malevolent Neutrality: The United States, Great Britain and the Origins of the Spanish Civil War* (Ithaca, NY, 1985).

Maier, K. A., *Guernica 26.4.1937: die deutsche Intervention in Spanien und der 'Fall Guernica'* (Freiburg, 1975).

Martínez, P. J., *Las fuerzas armadas francesas ante la Guerra Civil Española, 1936–1939* (Madrid, 1988).

Moradiellos, E., *Neutralidad benévola: el gobierno británico y la insurrección militar española de 1936* (Oviedo, 1990).

Morewood, S., *The British Defence of Egypt, 1935–1940* (Abingdon and New York, 2005).

Orwell, G. (Eric Blair), *Homage to Catalonia* (London, 2000).

Pike, D. W., *Conjecture, Propaganda, and Deceit and the Spanish Civil War: The International Crisis over Spain, 1936–1939, as Seen in the French Press* (Stanford, CA, 1968).

—— *Les Français et la guerre d'Espagne, 1936–1939* (Paris, 1975).

—— *In the Service of Stalin: The Spanish Communist in Exile 1939–1945* (Oxford, 1993).

—— *Franco and the Axis Stigma* (Basingstoke, 2008).

Pons, S., *Stalin e la guerra inevitabile, 1936–1941* (Turin, 1995). English trans. (slightly different) *Stalin and the Inevitable War 1936–1941* (London, 2002).

Preston, P. (ed.), *Revolution and War in Spain, 1931–1939* (London, 1984).

—— *The Spanish Civil War, 1936–1939* (London, 1986).

—— *Franco: A Biography* (London, 1993).

Radosh, R., Habeck M. R., and Sevostianov G. (eds.), *Spain Betrayed: The Soviet Union and the Spanish Civil War* (New Haven, CT, 2001).

Richardson, R. D., *Comintern Army: The International Brigades and the Spanish Civil War* (Lexington, KY, 1982).

Rovighi, A. and Stefani, F., *La partecipazione italiana alla guerra civile spagnola, 1936–1939: ufficio storico dello Stato maggiore dell'Esercito*, 2 vols. (Rome, 1992).

Salerno, R. M., *Vital Crossroads: Mediterranean Origins of the Second World War, 1935–1940* (Ithaca, NY, 2002).

Schieder, W. and Dipper, C. (eds.), *Der spanische Bürgerkrieg in der internationalen Politik, 1936–1939* (Munich, 1976).

Southworth, H. R., *Guernica! Guernica! A Study of Journalism, Diplomacy, Propaganda and History* (Los Angeles, CA, 1977).

Stone, G. A., *The Oldest Ally: Britain and the Portuguese Connection, 1936–1941* (Woodbridge, 1994).

—— *Spain, Portugal and the Great Powers, 1931–1941* (Basingstoke and New York, 2005).

Thomas, H., *The Spanish Civil War* (London, 1961).

Tierney, D., *FDR and the Spanish Civil War* (Durham, NC, 2007).

TRAINA, R. D., *American Diplomacy and the Spanish Civil War* (Bloomington, IN, 1968).

TUSELL, J., *Franco, España y la Segunda Guerra Mundial: Entre el Eje y la neutralidad* (Madrid, 1995).

VIÑAS, Á., *El oro español en la guerra civil* (Madrid, 1976).

—— *El oro de Moscú: alfa e omega de un mito franquista* (Barcelona, 1979).

—— *Franco, Hitler y el Estallido de la Guerra Civil: antecedente y consecuencia* (Madrid, 2000).

—— *El escudo de la república: el oro de España, la apuesta soviética y los hechos de mayo de 1937* (Barcelona, 2007).

—— *El honor de la República. entre el acoso fascista, la hastitidad britanica y la political de Stalin* (Barcelona, 2009).

—— and HERNÁNDEZ SÁNCHEZ, F., *El desplome de la República* (Barcelona, 2009).

WHEALEY, R. H., *Hitler and Spain: The Nazi Role in the Spanish Civil War, 1936–1939* (Lexington, KY, 1989).

Articles and Chapters

BLINKHORN, M., 'Conservatism, Traditionalism and Fascism in Spain, 1898–1937', in id. (ed.), *Fascists and Conservatives: The Radical Right and the Establishment in Twentieth Century Europe* (London, 1990).

CARLEY, M. J., 'Caught in a Cleft Stick: Soviet Diplomacy and the Spanish Civil War', in Johnson, G. (ed.), *The International Context of the Spanish Civil War* (Newcastle, 2009).

CEVA, L., 'Influence de la guerre d'Espagne sur l'armement et les conceptions d'emploi de l'aviation de l'Italie fasciste', in *Adaption de l'arme aérienne aux conflits, contemporains et processus d'indépendence des arm̃ees de ('Air des origines à la finde la seconde Guerre Mondiale.* Colloque internationale, Paris, École militaire, du 4 au 7 September, 1984, organisé par ('Institut d'historie des conflits contemporains et le service his torique de l'armée de l'air (Paris, 1985).

—— 'L'ultima vittoria del fascismo, Spagna, 1938–1939', *Italia Contemporanea*, 196 (1994).

FRANK, W. C. Jr., 'The Spanish Civil War and the Coming of the Second World War', *International History Review*, 9: 3 (1987).

GRETTON, P., 'The Nyon Conference: The Naval Aspect', *English Historical Review*, 60 (1975).

HABECK, M., 'The Spanish Civil War and the Origins of the Second World War', in Martel, G. (ed.), *The Origins of the Second World War Reconsidered: A. J. P. Taylor and the Historians*, 2nd edn. (London, 1999).

HARVEY, C. E., 'Politics and Pyrites during the Spanish Civil War', *Economic History Review*, 31 (1978).

JACKSON, P., 'French Strategy and the Spanish Civil War', in Leitz, C. and Dunthorne, D. J. (eds.), *Spain in an International Context, 1936–1959* (Oxford, 1999).

LEITZ, C., 'Nazi Germany's Interventions in the Spanish Civil War and the Foundation of HISMA/ROWAK', in Preston, P. and MacKenzie, A. L. (eds.), *The Republic Besieged: Civil War in Spain, 1936–1939* (Edinburgh, 1996).

LITTLE, D., 'Red Scare, 1936: Anti-Bolshevism and the Origins of British Non-Intervention in the Spanish Civil War', *Journal of Contemporary History*, 23 (1988).

MILLS, W. C., 'The Nyon Conference: Neville Chamberlain, Anthony Eden and the Appeasement of Italy in 1937', *International History Review*, 15: 1 (1993).

MONTEATH, P., 'Guernica Reconsidered: Fifty Years of Evidence', *War and Society*, 5: 1 (1987).

MORADIELLOS, E., 'Appeasement and Non-intervention: British Policy during the Spanish Civil War', in Catterall, P. and Morris, C. J. (eds.), *Britain and the Threat to Stability in Europe, 1918–1945* (London and New York, 1993).

PRESTON, P., 'Franco as Military Leader', *Transactions of the Royal Historical Society,* 6th Series, 4 (1994).

—— 'Mussolini's Spanish Adventure: From Limited Risk to War', in Preston, P. and MacKenzie, A. L. (eds.), *The Republic Besieged: Civil War in Spain, 1936–1939* (London, 1996).

SALERNO, R., 'Italy's Pirate Submarine Campaign of 1937', in Kennedy, G. C. and Neilson, K. (eds.), *Incidents and International Relations: People, Power and Personalities* (Westport, CT, and London, 2002).

SMYTH, D., 'The Moor and the Money-lender: Politics and Profits in Anglo-German Relations with Francoist Spain, 1936–1940', in Recker, M.-L. (ed.), *Von der Konkurrenz zur Rivalität: das britisch-deutsche Verhältnis in den Ländern der europäischen Peripherie, 1919–1939* (Stuttgart, 1986).

STONE, G. A., 'The Official British Attitude to the Anglo-Portuguese Alliance, 1910–1945', *Journal of Contemporary History*, 10 (1975).

—— 'The European Great Powers and the Spanish Civil War, 1936–1939', in Boyce, R. W. D. and Robertson, E. M. (eds.), *Paths to War: New Essays on the Origins of the Second World War* (London, 1989).

—— 'Britain, France and the Spanish Problem, 1936–1939', in Richardson, D. and Stone, G. (eds.), *Decisions and Diplomacy: Essays in Twentieth Century International History in Memory of George Grun and Esmonde Robertson* (London, 1995).

—— 'Britain, France and Franco's Spain in the Aftermath of the Spanish Civil War', *Diplomacy and Statecraft*, 6: 2 (1995).

SULLIVAN, B. R., 'Fascist Italy's Military Involvement in the Spanish Civil War', *Journal of Military History*, 59 (1995).

TIERNEY D., 'Franklin D. Roosevelt and Covert Aid to the Loyalists in the Spanish Civil War, 1936–1939', *Journal of Contemporary History*, 39 (2003).

VIÑAS, A., 'Gold, the Soviet Union and the Spanish Civil War', *European Studies Review*, 9 (1979).

WALTON, J. K., 'British Perceptions of Spain and their Impact on Attitudes to the Spanish Civil War: Some Additional Evidence', *Twentieth Century British History*, 5: 3 (1994).

WHEALEY, R. H., 'How Franco Financed his War: Reconsidered', *Journal of Contemporary History*, 12 (1977).

—— 'Economic Influence of the Great Powers in the Spanish Civil War: From the Popular Front to the Second World War', *International History Review*, 5 (1983).

6

'Loaded Pause': Rearmament and Appeasement, 1936–1937

I

During the first stages of the Spanish Civil War, Hitler pursued his preparation for a European conflict, while the British and French did everything possible to induce him to accept a peaceful resolution of his demands for changes in the status quo. In the summer of 1936 Hitler set 1939 as the year in which Germany should be prepared to go to war. His short-term aims were still imperfectly defined; his ultimate ambition, the conquest of living space in the East, remained unaltered. Though Germany was still in a weak military position, and faced economic and financial problems that might have discouraged a more cautious leader, Hitler was prepared to capitalize on the fluidity of the international situation. The other European states could hardly ignore what was happening in Berlin. While it was common knowledge that Hitler harboured expansionist goals, the signals emanating from Berlin were difficult to read. Hitler had the good fortune of the lucky gambler. With the creation of the Popular Front in France, and the latter's absorption in its domestic problems, Hitler could afford to wait on events. The political purges in the Soviet Union and its difficulties in the Far East confirmed his belief in Soviet weakness; anti-Bolshevik propaganda could be used with impunity, and Moscow's bids for friendship treated with disdain. The Spanish Civil War intensified the role of ideology in continental politics, making the creation of an anti-German coalition less likely than earlier. Only the perennial problem of Britain continued to disturb Hitler's equanimity. British support, or at worst its neutrality, remained a pre-condition for the Führer's long-term strategy.

The most important immediate consequence of Hitler's victory in the Rhineland was the spur it gave to rearmament planning. Flushed with success, the *Wehrmacht* prepared to speed up its military schedules. Hitler might speak of a thirty-six division army, but in March 1935 the

Reichswehr had only twenty-one divisions at its disposal, and these had not reached their full personnel and material strength. With Hitler's support, Heinz Guderian, one of a small group of officers working on the problem of developing mechanized units, won important backing for the idea of using armoured divisions as the key operational units in any future army. Both General Fritsch, the commander-in-chief, and General Beck, the army chief of staff, were converted to the possibilities of mobile warfare in the autumn of 1935; this represented an important turning point in the prolonged general staff debate over the restructuring of the army.[1] In Beck's view, the use of tanks would allow Germany to conduct a successful war on several fronts. 'Strategic defence', Beck wrote in a December memorandum to General Fritsch would 'only be successful if it is also conducted in the form of attack'. Beck's conversion to tanks opened the way for the creation of 48 armoured units. His detailed proposals for the mechanization and motorization of the army would allow the *Wehrmacht* to increase its mobility and capitalize on an already existing advantage with regard to its neighbours.

In early June, 1936, the general staff and the officers of the army high command began detailed planning and costing for the future development of both the peacetime and the wartime armies. With the exception of a large number of heavy motorized artillery and armoured units, the formations were to be virtually completed by the autumn of 1939. The wartime army projected for October 1940, when its build-up would be complete, would total 3,612,673 men; in 1914, the German army had gone to war with 2,147,000 men. Beck noted that such a massive build-up would be dependent on the availability of resources. He was willing to compromise on the calibre of the new armies; the ratio of officers to enlisted men would fall from 7% to less than 2%. More problematic was equipping the army in such a short time. The new summer programme, creating a wartime army of 102 divisions in a four-year period, was adopted in December 1936. It was the last comprehensive armaments plan before the outbreak of war, and built on the restoration of full German military sovereignty in March 1936. If implemented, Germany would be ready for war in 1939 with a vastly expanded army capable of taking the offensive.

The financial implications of the new programme were staggering. It was assumed that Hitler would deal with the question of the economy and that Blomberg would find ways to solve the raw materials and foreign currency shortages. Neither Blomberg nor the generals were

[1] Beck's memorandum in Militärgeschichtliches Forschungsamt (ed.), *Germany and the Second World War*, Vol. I, ed. Wilhelm Deist (Oxford and New York, 1990), 434.

prepared to consider the foreign policy consequences of their build-up. They saw the creation of an army capable of 'strategic defence' as the necessary instrument of an 'active great power policy' in Europe. General Beck cited the 'isolation' of Germany as the reason for expanding and accelerating the *Wehrmacht*'s rearmament. There was no discussion of how Germany's neighbours would view the new programme. Friedrich Fromm, head of the Central Administrative Office of the German army, warned Fritsch that 'following the rearmament period the *Wehrmacht* must either be used in combat very soon, or the situation must be alleviated by reducing the required level of war readiness'. Fromm raised the critical question: was it 'definitely intended to commit the *Wehrmacht* to action at some already determined time?'[2] He was given no answer. The process of mobilizing the whole economy to produce this war machine could not be prolonged indefinitely. The apparent blindness of the German high command to the foreign policy consequences of its planning may have been a reflection of its narrow professional perspective. Could it really be true that the generals ignored the aggressive implications of their planning and what it might portend for Germany's future?

It was not only the army that was embarked on expansion. The *Luftwaffe* began to produce a second generation of all metal aircraft and high performance aero-engines in 1935–1936. Factories had to be re-equipped as the production of older models was discontinued and new ones introduced. Moreover, though three different designs for medium-range bombers were adopted and produced, Germany was still without an effective strategic bomber. The search continued and yet another round of changes was anticipated. The navy, too, engaged in a major expansion, though Hitler hoped that Ribbentrop, sent to London as ambassador in August 1936, would come back with an agreement with Britain. New opportunities were opened, both by the Anglo-German naval agreement of 1935 and, after the failure of the London Naval Conference (December 1935 – March 1936), by the British decision to begin the construction of new battleships. Planning for the new ships and for faster construction times far outpaced implementation, as the shipyards were already operating at full capacity and available skilled workers were fully employed. Demands for raw materials and labour for rearmament soared.

It was clear in the autumn of 1935 that Hjalmar Schacht's New Plan could not keep pace with the regime's expanded rearmament programmes. In December, Schacht warned Blomberg, whose demands he had formerly backed, that he could not find the foreign exchange

[2] Militärgeschichtliches Forschungsamt, *Germany and the Second World War*, Vol.I, 443.

needed for the rearmament schedules. To add to the pressure, a bad autumn harvest in the autumn of 1935 forced Walther Darré, the agricultural minister, to demand foreign exchange to purchase food and feed stocks. Schacht struggled with the deteriorating balance of payments situation. By the spring of 1936, he had crossed swords both with Darré and with Wilhelm Keppler, Hitler's chief economic adviser, who favoured the exploitation of domestic sources, such as iron ore, rather than rearmament cuts, to relieve the pressure on imports and foreign exchange. In an effort to find a way out of the administrative impasse, Schacht and Blomberg supported Göring's wish to become the head of a new Raw Material and Foreign Exchange Office (April 1936), with instructions to 'ensure continued military preparations'.[3] Hitler had already used Göring as arbiter between Darré and Schacht. It did not take Schacht long to realize that Göring was a serious and dangerous rival. By the summer of 1936, shortages of raw materials were playing havoc with *Wehrmacht* orders. Industrial stockpiles were only sufficient for two months' work. Ammunition factories were working well below capacity and the motor vehicle industry was switched to a short-time schedule. There was, too, a shortage of skilled workmen, which led to competitive bidding for their services. The balance of payments situation was becoming disastrous. Though Schacht continued his programme of export subsidies and the daily rationing of foreign exchange, he pressed for a cut back on rearmament and an expansion of exports to ease the situation. He may even have considered devaluation, and German participation in the tripartite financial agreements being negotiated between France, Britain, and the United States. But Göring consolidated his own position and had Hitler's backing. He first collected all existing foreign currency assets, yielding enough to cover Germany's needs through the following year. A new organization, under his control, was created to launch an all-out drive to make Germany ready for war by expanding its domestic sources of food and raw materials. Schacht was on the defensive; his former military supporters deserted him. He tried to ally with Blomberg to check Göring, but found the defence minister unwilling to intervene. The minister was convinced that the Führer would find a way out of present difficulties.

In August 1936, at Obersalzberg, where he was considering the new *Wehrmacht* proposals as well as the situation in Spain, Hitler decided to resolve the clash between Göring and Schacht. In a long and wide-ranging memorandum prepared for Blomberg and Göring, the German

[3] Quoted in Adam Tooze, *The Wages of Destruction: The Making and Breaking of the Nazi Economy* (London, 2006), 210.

leader declared his intention of having 'the premier army' in Europe 'as rapidly as possible'.[4] Given the nature of the international threat, rearmament could not be 'too large, nor its pace too swift'. Economic considerations would have to give way to military requirements. The Führer warned that Germany had to prepare for the war against Bolshevism. Either it would have the best army in Europe or it would be lost. There was no point, he argued, in the 'endless repetition of the fact that we lack foodstuffs and raw materials; what matters is the taking of those measures which can bring about a final solution for the future and a temporary easing of conditions during the "transitional period"'. The 'final solution' lay in extending Germany's living space; the temporary measures would depend on creating an autarchic economy, and not on 'the throttling of armaments industries in peacetime in order to save and stockpile raw materials for war'. While accepting the need to use foreign exchange for imported foodstuffs to obtain the prerequisites for 'normal consumption', Hitler pointed to those areas—fuel, synthetic rubber, iron ore, industrial fats—where increased domestic production would permit rapid rearmament without depending on foreign imports. In his customary manner, Hitler accompanied exhortations to action with warnings to those who would question his goals. 'Either German industry will grasp the new economic tasks or else it will show itself incapable of surviving any longer in this modern age in which a Soviet State is setting up a gigantic plan. *But in that case it will not be Germany that will go under but at most a few industrialists.*' There remained, he reminded his readers, 'no such thing as a commercial balance of expenditure and profit. There is only a national balance of being and not being.'[5] The German people might well be called upon to make sacrifices; they would accept such a burden only if the party provided firm leadership. Hitler's memorandum concluded with two directives:

1. The German Army must be operational within four years.
2. The German economy must be fit for war within four years.

The timetable demanded by Fromm was now provided. As Hitler had always insisted, the solution to Germany's economic problems would come through conquest and not trade. Only Göring and Blomberg were given the complete text in September 1936. It was later given to Fritz Todt, the builder of the *Westwall* (Albert Speer inherited his copy in 1942). The memorandum meant that the army could go ahead

[4] J. Noakes and G. Pridham (eds.), *Documents on Nazism, 1919–1945* (London, 1974), 401–408, for whole document. See the German text in Wilhelm Treue, 'Hitlers Denkschrift zum Vierjahresplan, 1936', *Vierteljahrshefte für Zeitgeschichte*, 1 (1955).

[5] Noakes and Pridham, *Documents on Nazism*, 401–408.

Table 6.1 German Production Increases in the Four-Year Plan (output in '000 tons)

Commodity	1936	1938
Mineral oil	1790	6260
Aluminium	98	260
Buna synthetic rubber	0.7	96
Nitrogen	770	930
Explosive	18	300
Powder	20	150
Steel	19216	20480
Iron ore	2255	4137
Brown coal	161382	245918
Hard coal	158400	166059

Source: Dieter Petzina, *Autarkiepolitik im Dritten Reich* (Stuttgart, 1968), 182.

regardless of the economic costs. Hitler's memorandum made sense only on the assumption of an early war. Rearmament was given priority, over all other needs. Göring sounded an apocalyptic note when, on 17 December 1936, he exhorted German industrialists to expand their factories without worrying about surplus capacity. 'All selfish interests must be put aside. Our whole nation is at stake. We live in a time when the final battles are in sight. We are already on the threshold of mobilization and are at war, only the guns are not firing.'[6]

The Four-Year Plan was announced at the annual party rally at Nuremberg in September. There was no mention of war. Its only purpose was 'to secure the German standard of living and to provide employment for German workers beyond the end of the rearmament boom.'[7] Apart from general references to the battle against Bolshevism, there was no indication of the kind of war Hitler intended to fight. Who were the enemies and who were to be his allies? Was anything decided beyond the forthcoming struggle in the East? These were questions to which neither the military nor the Wilhelmstrasse were able to respond. On 18 October Göring was made the official head of the Four-Year Plan. Heads of the armed forces were told that financial constraints would no longer limit Germany's military expansion. Though Schacht still remained as Reich minister for economic affairs and president of the *Reichsbank*, Göring rapidly built up the new Four-Year Plan organization, securing the personnel and sufficient financing to increase the German capacity for the domestic production of food and raw materials.

[6] Quoted in Tooze, *The Wages of Destruction*, 21.
[7] Ibid., 223.

He hoped to cut Germany's import bill by half. The radical phase of Hitler's foreign policy had begun.

II

Foreign observers were aware of the speed-up of German rearmament but they could only guess at its extent and pacing. The introduction of two-year military service in August 1936, and the public announcement of the Four-Year Plan in September confirmed the suspicions of some, including the *Deuxième Bureau* in Paris, about Hitler's aggressive intentions and determination to engage in war. At the same time, Hitler's post-Rhineland peace campaign and his efforts to soothe the French and woo the British encouraged hopes that he might yet be deterred from an arms race and brought into a security system. Did the weakness of France, as proved by her passivity over the Rhineland, convince Hitler that Paris could be reached through London and so could be relegated to a secondary position in his thinking? In the post-Rhineland period, assurances were given to the *Quai d'Orsay* that Germany was prepared to conclude an agreement but that this would require the French abandonment of its eastern guarantees, including the Franco-Soviet treaty, which had been the excuse for Hitler's action in the first place. The Wilhelmstrasse was accurately informed of the domestic weakness of the Popular Front government. There was, in fact, only one positive German approach to the French and this came not from Hitler but from Hjalmar Schacht, his beleaguered economics minister. Though informed of Schacht's waning influence, *Quai d'Orsay* officials were impressed by his successful tour of the Balkan capitals in June 1936, which they thought might refurbish his reputation. Ambassador François-Poncet in Berlin and officials in Paris stressed the importance of Schacht's Paris visit and the opportunities it might present for *rapprochement*. Blum and Schacht met on 28 August; the latter, at a time when he was losing influence in Berlin, assured the French premier that he spoke with Hitler's general approval and would report back to the Führer. He claimed that Hitler was deeply concerned about Germany's financial and raw material difficulties and would respond favourably to a European settlement and arms limitation agreement, if offered commercial and colonial concessions. Blum welcomed this approach with good reason. The meeting took place only two weeks after the British, French, and Belgians had failed to find a way to bring Germany and Italy into a new Locarno arrangement. The *Quai d'Orsay* thought the financial and economic crisis in Germany presented an opportune moment to persuade Germany to scale back its rearmament. Blum accepted the prevailing view that German economic and financial difficulties might force the Nazi government to abandon the system of bilateral economic arrangements. The French devaluation and the tripartite currency agreement of 1936, with the United States and Britain, initiated by France, might compel the Germans to devalue the mark and seek foreign credits. Germany's financial embarrassment could be used to secure the European settlement that had so far proved unattainable. Blum intended that such an agreement would include a disarmament convention covering Germany, the Soviet Union, and France's eastern allies. Though he preferred a multilateral agreement, he held out the hope of a bilateral financial and colonial bargain and spoke of the surrender of the French 'portions of the Cameroons and Togoland provided that Britain would also part with its West African mandates'.[8] In line with these discussions, Blum proposed in early September that the Geneva disarmament talks be reconvened.

The French were slow to reveal the details of this exchange to the Foreign Office though Schacht was told that Blum would ask Britain to join in any colonial agreement. The British feared that Blum had suggested a colonial bargain at their expense, but these suspicions were unfounded. The premier never wavered in his belief that no agreement with Germany would give France the security she required unless Britain was involved. As Eric Phipps, now ambassador in Paris, pointed out, Hitler's 'sole and ultimate objective' was the isolation of France and the conclusion of a German agreement with Britain. Insofar as France was concerned, there was no immediate follow-up from Berlin. François-Poncet reported on 14 October that Schacht was 'disappointed and anxious' and that his personal credit was at a low point. Hitler reproached the French financial attaché with 'the vanity of these Franco-German conversations'.[9] He was not interested in an economic accord or a colonial bargain, and later efforts along these lines, pursued more energetically by the British (at French expense) than the French, ended in almost total failure. By the time of Schacht's second voyage to Paris in May 1937, Blum had given up any serious hope of securing concessions from Germany.

It may well be that Hitler continued to believe, as was stated in *Mein Kampf*, that a war against France had to precede a move in the East. In this case, too, his best hope of isolating France was to secure an agreement with Britain. He counted on the latter's disinterest in Eastern Europe, and the anti-Communist sentiments of the Baldwin cabinet to

[8] TNA: PRO, T 160/856/F 14545/3, S. D. Waley to Sir Richard Hopkins, report on the Blum–Schacht conversations, 16 September 1936.

[9] Jean-Baptiste Duroselle, *La décadence, 1932–1939* (Paris, 1979), 300; *DDF*, 2nd ser., Vol. III, Nos. 417, 462.

weaken, if not destroy, the French eastern alliance system. Britain's weakness during the Ethiopian crisis may have diminished Hitler's respect for its power but he continued his courtship. His efforts reached a crescendo during the early summer months when the 'Olympic pause' was used to impress and court his English guests. There was a stream of visitors to Germany, including Lloyd George and Robert Vansittart, the latter already branded in Berlin as a notorious anti-German. The numerous conversations held with Hitler and his most senior ministers, however, in no way affected the British cabinet's unwillingness to enter into bilateral talks and, in Vansittart's case, intensified his uneasiness and fears about this unfathomable leader, though without leading to a positive recommendation for action. Throughout 1936–1937 the cabinet remained focused on a 'Western Pact', or a revised Locarno, that would include Germany and Italy, and provide some form of security for the western powers, rather than relying on a bilateral arrangement with Hitler. Already a group of Hitler's advisers, including Göring, felt there was no need to woo the British, but the Führer was not prepared to drop his suit. He continued to procrastinate about the revised Locarno agreement, possibly hoping for British offers of specific concessions in eastern and central Europe. While assuring Eden that Germany would attend a five-power conference sometime in the distant future, he raised a multitude of reservations about German participation.

In the 'peace speech' of 7 March 1936, Hitler had publicly referred to the question of colonial revision though there were earlier hints of interest. The recognition of Germany's right to colonies was a favourite theme of conservative nationalists and business representatives during the Weimar period. Ribbentrop, seeking to strengthen and extend his power base in the highly competitive Berlin scene, was anxious to 'Nazify' and revive the existing colonial associations in the hope of launching a massive propaganda campaign in support of Germany's colonial claims. He appears to have convinced Hitler to back his cause as early as the summer of 1935. The older Colonial Society was wound up and a new, militant, and Nazi *Reichskolonialbund* was created under Ribbentrop's patronage and led by Ritter von Epp, a former colonial soldier and *Freikorps* leader, who was one of Hitler's earliest supporters. During 1936, the colonial propaganda campaign was launched. The colonial cause appealed to the older school of revisionists, some of whom were offended by the crudities of the Nazi movement, and to Schacht and some of his industrial backers. Neither these groups, nor the French and British understood that Hitler's colonial demands were tactical weapons that would not deter him from continental expansion. Nothing would be lost, however, by using the colonial card to sow difficulties between France and Britain and exploit its carrot and stick potential.

Other diplomatic moves were intended, at least in part, to push the recalcitrant British in Berlin's direction. Many were initiated from outside the Wilhelmstrasse, where Neurath found himself increasingly by-passed. This was true of the moves towards Italy and Japan. In the months before the outbreak of the Spanish Civil War, relations between Italy and Germany had remained uneasy. On the Italian side, this was due to continued contacts with the French, directed at the abandonment of the now useless sanctions, and the hopes for recognition of the annexation of Abyssinia. On the German side, there were fears that recognition might compromise the talks with London. There was no question in Hitler's mind that Britain was the preferred partner. Given Mussolini's backing for the Austro-German agreement, and the obvious advantage of permanently detaching Italy from its Locarno partners, the move towards Rome gathered pace. In late July 1936, Hitler instructed Hassell, his ambassador in Rome, to offer recognition of the Ethiopian annexation at a time of Mussolini's choosing, and to consider arrangements for a joint policy with regard to the abortive negotiations for a new Locarno. A series of unofficial visits during the summer were intended to reassure Mussolini about Hitler's peaceful intentions towards Austria, and German disinterest in the Mediterranean. Undoubtedly accelerated by their co-operation in Spain, the ground was prepared for the successful Ciano trip to Berlin in October 1936, and the protocol which was signed between Ciano and Neurath on 24 October 1936. These meetings in Berlin and Berchtesgaden revealed the common, but also the divergent interests of the two governments. Both proclaimed their anti-Bolshevist allegiance; in the Italian case, this meant the rejection of the pro-Soviet line that Italy had followed before 1935. The two governments agreed that any new Locarno-type arrangement in the West should not go beyond a promise of a non-aggression treaty between Germany and France.

If the assumption behind the October protocol was a free hand for the Germans in the Baltic and North seas in return for Italian predominance in the Mediterranean, there were still areas where the interests of the two countries clashed. The Italians accepted the German–Austrian agreement, but hoped that Austria might retain its independence. While both governments welcomed co-operation in the Balkans, each intended to press their claims to economic and political pre-eminence. Italy signed a commercial accord with Belgrade on 26 September 1936, and in November formally offered Yugoslavia a treaty of friendship or an alliance, while warning of the dire consequences of a refusal. There were Italian interests, too, in Romania and Bulgaria where Germany was an economic rival rather than a partner. Nor was Mussolini willing to turn his back on Poland, a country whose support the Italians had found particularly useful in the Balkans. Neurath, reflecting the traditional anti-Polish bias at the Foreign Ministry, warned Ciano that the Germans intended to settle the problems of Danzig and the 'Polish Corridor', but at some more appropriate time and in as peaceful a manner as possible. The more immediate danger lay elsewhere. At his eagle's nest at Berchtesgaden, Hitler called his guests' attention to nearby Austria, clearly visible through the massive glass window, but said nothing more. By the end of the year, Hitler had succeeded in bringing Mussolini to his side. The Duce had opted for the German partnership. It was a decision that was never reversed, whatever the differences and difficulties, and was to ease Hitler's way in central Europe, ultimately bringing disaster both to Mussolini and to Italy.

Across the street from the building where Neurath and Ciano signed their protocol on 24 October 1936, Ribbentrop and the Japanese ambassador, Mushakoji Kintomo, initialled the Anti-Comintern Pact. Earlier talks between Ribbentrop and the Japanese military attaché, Lt. Colonel Oshima Hiroshi, a Nazi enthusiast who saw the two countries as natural allies, began in 1935. They were suspended in December of that year, mainly due to the strong objections of Neurath who, like the *Wehrmacht* leaders, believed that Germany's best interests were served by its presence in China and its position of influence with Chiang Kai-shek. The German–Japanese talks, moreover, were publicized by the Soviet government, well informed of their contents by its agents in Japan, including Richard Sorge, an invaluable informant of what was transpiring in the German embassy in Tokyo. Despite denials from official sources in both capitals, the leaked news produced unwelcome international publicity and both sides beat a hasty retreat. Neither Foreign Ministry wanted to see the talks renewed though, as Dirksen, the newly appointed German ambassador in Tokyo and a strong supporter of the new understanding, pointed out, they would be difficult to stop. For the moment, the *Auswärtiges Amt* regained the initiative and Neurath was prepared to continue his country's traditionally pro-Chinese policies. German military advisers were assisting Chiang Kai-shek in the modernization of his army while military equipment, admittedly of inferior quality, was being sent from Germany. The main German interest in China was its raw material resources, especially tungsten, needed for rearmament. In April 1936, the German government concluded a major commercial treaty with the Chinese government, giving a credit of 100,000,000 marks for the purchase of German industrial and other products.

Unknown to the Wilhelmstrasse, Hitler was reconsidering the problem of relations with Japan in the summer of 1936. In conversations with Ribbentrop and Oshima at Bayreuth in late July, when the decisions to aid Franco and to send Ribbentrop to London were taken, the Führer agreed to sanction new negotiations with the Japanese. It was the Ribbentrop *Dienststelle* that produced the draft for the so-called Anti-Comintern Pact, initialled in October and formally signed on 25 November 1936. The treaty provided for co-operation in opposing the Communist International, and was open to any other country that wished to join. It was to have a five-year term. There were, as was generally suspected, secret commitments and reservations to the treaty reflecting the highly ambiguous nature of the new arrangements. The two states were committed to an anti-Soviet alliance: 'should one of the parties be unprovokedly attacked or threatened by the Soviet Union, the other party agrees not to carry out any measures which would relieve the position of the Soviet Union but will immediately consult on measures to preserve their common interests'.[10] Other reservations suggested that neither government was prepared to abandon alternative possibilities. The Germans, for instance, refused to recognise Manchukuo, which would have antagonized Chiang Kai-shek.

The announcement of the treaty raised a diplomatic storm. Though the Japanese ambassador had signed it, Oshima and the Japanese general staff were its real architects, and their role reflected the rising diplomatic power of the military in Tokyo. The Japanese Foreign Ministry accepted the pact with many misgivings, feeling that it was unnecessary and too one-sided. The Chinese took alarm and there was talk of Chiang replacing his German military and Italian air advisers with British officers. Neurath particularly feared the anti-British overtones of the new treaty. It hardly helped his cause that Ribbentrop, now ambassador in London, regarded the Anti-Comintern Pact as his special creation. It could be that Hitler hoped that this rather artificial agreement, given its anti-Soviet focus, might actually bring Britain to his negotiating table. In late October a very reluctant Ribbentrop finally arrived in London, supposedly to fulfil the Führer's instructions to 'Bring England into the Anti-Comintern Pact. That is my greatest wish.'[11] Hitler could not have made a worse choice if he harboured hopes of the British alliance. Neurath, finding it increasingly difficult to maintain either his own position or that of his office, had urged Ribbentrop's nomination only to get him out of Berlin and thus avoid his appointment as state secretary when Bülow died suddenly at the end of June. 'Ambassador Brickendrop', from the time of his arrival until his departure in August 1937, was nothing but a diplomatic disaster. Despite the lavish hospitality in the totally reconstructed German embassy,

[10] Frank William Iklé, *German–Japanese Relations 1936–1940* (New York, 1956), 38.
[11] John Weitz, *Joachim von Ribbentrop: Hitler's Diplomat* (London, 1992), 111.

his sheer incompetence, arrogance, and tactlessness, culminating in the 'Hitler salute' given to the new king, alienated even those sympathetic to the cause of Anglo-German friendship. During a very short posting (he seems to have spent only forty-six complete days at the embassy) Hitler's sycophantic envoy made more enemies than friends. He returned to Germany a convinced Anglophobe.

III

While courting the British, Hitler intended to isolate France, bring renewed pressure on Czechoslovakia, and extend German influence in south-east Europe. He applied a combination of persuasion and threat to achieve his purposes. The Führer had two major weapons that he used with skill: the German minorities living abroad and Germany's need for the foodstuffs and other raw materials that the south-eastern countries of Europe were desperate to sell. Self-determination and the return of the scattered German people to the Reich was a popular rallying cry, and a way of satisfying those, including Hitler, for whom racism was the essential dynamic in the New Order. The mobilization of the German minorities, to support the interests of the fatherland, was hardly a new tactic. Throughout the 1920s there had been strong support for the cause of the *Auslandsdeutsche* and for the government-sponsored 'private organizations' that were dispensing money to strengthen local minority groups. The Weimar governments had been cautious in their sponsorships and, in the Baltic, more concerned with promoting German economic interests than with territorial revisionism. Once the Nazis took power, the German minorities were enlisted in the Reich's cause because of their potential contribution to the expansion of Germany's racial base. Although at first playing minor roles, Alfred Rosenberg's *Außenpolitisches Amt* (APA) and the Nazi Party's *Auslandsorganisation* (AO) dwelt on the racial issue as one of the differentiating aspects of Nazi and Weimar policy. Relations with local 'agents of Nazism' were uneasy during the early years of the Nazi regime; in Austria and Czechoslovakia, in particular, there were divisions among local Nazi groups which were abetted and magnified by the bureaucratic rivalries in Berlin. Though the Nazification of large sections of the German minorities in these states provided the Nazis with a potentially destabilizing force, in 1936 there were major unsolved problems of control and utilization.

In Austria, with an eye on relations with Rome, Hitler followed a cautious line, unwilling to intervene in the competition between Göring, Hess, Himmler, and Goebbels, each of whom had his fingers in the Austrian pie. Hitler continued to waver between support for the respectable, legal, middle-class lawyer, Seyss-Inquart, and Josef Leopold, the plebeian, radical, volatile leader of the outlawed Austrian Nazi party. Eventually, the Austrian balance was tipped in favour of Seyss-Inquart and the SS, particularly after Hitler's appointment of Wilhelm Keppler in 1937. Hitler, alone, would decide when he was ready to move in Vienna. The Reich chancellor showed the same combination of cool calculation and patience with regard to the Nazis in the Memel territory of Lithuania, and in Danzig. An uneasy settlement was achieved over Memel, where Lithuanian measures against the Memel Germans designed to counter the growth of National Socialism had resulted in German economic reprisals. Since the Lithuanians had found other trading partners, and reprisals further depressed the economic conditions of the Memel Germans, Berlin was ready for a compromise. The Lithuanians, for their part, impressed by the Rhineland re-occupation and encouraged by Hitler's 6 March suggestion of a German–Lithuanian non-aggression pact, agreed somewhat reluctantly that a new economic treaty should be negotiated. The result, the commercial agreement of 5 August 1936, represented an uneasy truce. The question of the Memel Germans would be kept in reserve until the appropriate moment.

Similar caution was displayed over Danzig. In this instance, it was Hitler himself who re-opened the local conflict by allowing Albert Forster's National Socialists to step up their campaign against the remaining non-Nazi parties in the Free City. A combination of Reich German insults and local National Socialist attacks on the independent high commissioner, the Irishman Sean Lester, threatened to lead to a possible confrontation between the German and Polish governments. Beck, a slippery figure at best, summoned all his considerable reserves of diplomatic cunning to emerge from the Danzig imbroglio without either losing his reputation at home or alienating Germany. Charged to deal with the Danzigers by the Council of the League of Nations, whose members tried to avoid involvement despite their League-appointed role, Beck was able to broker a settlement that left Polish self-respect intact and the line to Berlin undamaged. This was at the expense of the Jews and non-Nazi parties in Danzig whom the National Socialists were free to treat as they wished. Beck insisted that all existing Polish rights should be respected. While he wanted to maintain the existing relationship between the Free City and the League and the office of high commissioner, he was prepared to see Lester go. The latter was forced to resign and was replaced by Carl J. Burckhardt in January 1937. Burckhardt, a still controversial figure, was a conservative Swiss, well suited by nationality if not by temperament to carry out the secretary general's instructions that he should keep a low profile and avoid taking any part in Danzig's internal politics. He mainly concerned himself with the maintenance of correct relations between Danzig and Poland. There was no interference with the measures taken by the local National Socialists.

Success went to Forster's head. Despite cautionary warnings from both Hitler and Neurath, he was soon denouncing the League and Poland and promising his followers that Hitler would enter Danzig within a few months. The Poles were furious and the Führer found it prudent to rein in his overzealous protégé. Assurances were given that Poland's existing rights would be respected, and the high commissioner's office (useful to both Germans and Poles as a buffer between them) would be kept in place. At the same time, Göring warned the Polish ambassador in Berlin, Józef Lipski, that Hitler would at some future date demand an extraterritorial passage across the Polish Corridor in return for unspecified compensations elsewhere. The status quo suited Hitler's purposes. There was no advantage to be gained from alienating Warsaw while Poland could be counted upon to provide a brake on any French movement towards the Soviet Union. And it was Hitler, or Hitler and Göring, and not Neurath who handled Danzig affairs.

Czechoslovakia became the object of a fierce German propaganda campaign in the months following the Rhineland crisis. Anticipating that, should the Germans occupy Austria, they would turn next on Czechoslovakia, Beneš had to consider the prospect of a hostile combination that would include Germany, Austria, Hungary, Poland, and Italy. The Little Entente, while united against Hungary, hardly a major threat in 1936, was difficult to mobilize against Germany. Doubts were raised about France's capacity to provide protection after the German occupation of the Rhineland. Relations with Paris remained uneasy. Past experience showed that little could be expected from Britain. The Foreign Office had scant patience with Beneš' position, and Joseph Addison, the long-serving British minister in Prague (1930–1936) was highly critical of Czech foreign policy in general, and the government's treatment of the Sudeten Germans in particular. Under such circumstances, it was hardly surprising that Premier Milan Hodža, the Slovak agrarian politician and Beneš' rival, was prepared to follow up Hitler's March offer of a bilateral non-aggression pact with Czechoslovakia. Hodža's efforts in this direction during the summer months of 1936 produced nothing concrete from Berlin. More worrying still for the Czechs was German support for the Sudeten Germans, an issue which, contrary to Beneš' hopes, now became a subject of international interest. The Prague government had outlawed the German National Socialist party in 1933, but a new organization, the Sudeten German Home Front, created by the Sudeten German gymnastics instructor

Konrad Henlein, had appeared on the scene. Henlein, who publicly disassociated himself from the Nazis and declared his loyalty to the Czechoslovak state, was already being subsidized by the Germans in the summer of 1934. His movement received regular monthly payments and backing against the 'old Nazi' leaders in Prague, who tried to discredit him. In the May 1935 election, Henlein's Front, re-christened the Sudeten German Party (SdP), and their Slovakian offshoot, the Carpathian–German Party (KdP), made their successful political debut, winning the votes of three-fifths of the entire German electorate in the country and emerging as the second largest party in the national parliament. Hitler now had in Czechoslovakia a legal party with a strong popular base, and a leader of considerable political skill.

Henlein made three visits to Britain in 1935–1936. During his first visit in December 1935, he delivered a lecture at Chatham House and met with several officials at the Foreign Office, one of whom assured the new British minister in Prague that Henlein was 'on a definitely anti-Nazi platform'.[12] In the summer of 1936, the way smoothed by the positive reports from the British minister in Prague, Henlein was received by Vansittart. He convinced the permanent under-secretary of his personal integrity and the loyalty of the Sudeten Germans to the Czechoslovak state. For his part, Hitler was content to let Henlein work out his own programme of action, both with regard to the 'old guard' of the Nazi party and in his dealings with the Hodža government. The Führer spoke to Henlein only briefly during the latter's visit to Berlin for the Olympic Games. Neurath, with whom Henlein had a more extended interview, warned him that there was no question that 'we should in the foreseeable future be embroiled in warlike enterprises for the sake of the Sudeten Germans' and insisted the latter 'would have to look after themselves'.[13] By the summer of 1936, it was clear to President Beneš and Hodža that additional steps would have to be taken to meet the Sudeten German demands, and that they would have to deal with Henlein, their popular spokesman.

In the summer of 1936, Hitler again pursued the offer of a non-aggression pact with Czechoslovakia. Following the Austro–German agreement, and in the face of French coolness towards the idea of an alliance with the Little Entente, he found willing listeners in Prague. Informal negotiations began in August and continued until January 1937. The German representatives in this exchange were Albrecht

[12] *DGFP*, Ser. C, Vol. V, No. 508 (14 August 1936).

[13] J. W. Bruegel, *Czechoslovakia Before Munich: The German Minority Problem and British Appeasement Policy* (Cambridge, 1973), 140, quoting from German Foreign Ministry Files, serial 2381, frames 499835–499842, Minute by Neurath, 14 August.

Haushofer from Ribbentrop's *Dienststelle* and Count zu Trauttmansdorff from the Ministry of Labour. As was the pattern in such matters, the German Foreign Ministry was told nothing, but the SS was informed through its contacts with the Sudeten Germans. The German negotiators arrived in Prague in mid-November 1936 for discussions with Beneš and Kamil Krofta, the foreign minister, who favoured negotiations with Germany. Though Beneš insisted that Czechoslovakia's two defensive alliances had to be preserved, he agreed to a non-aggression pact with a reservation about Czechoslovakia's obligations under the League of Nations covenant. The suggested settlement included a new trade agreement, a common stand on the Habsburg question, a press truce, and restrictions on émigré politics. The agreement would have allowed the Germans to press for improvements in the status of the Sudeten Germans.

On his return to Berlin, Haushofer reported to Hitler and Himmler and submitted a list of aims that he thought could be achieved, including the possibility of Czechoslovak neutrality in the event of a Russian attack on Germany, or in the case of a conflict with Russia over Spain. He warned that Czechoslovakia would not agree to neutrality if Germany attacked Russia. Hitler crossed out the reference to a non-aggression pact, re-arranged the order of aims, and wrote nothing at all about the Sudeten Germans but agreed to the continuation of the talks. The Czechs must have known that the possibility of keeping their defensive alliances and entering a pact with the Germans was most unlikely. At the funeral of the Hungarian prime minister, Julius Gombos, Göring boasted to the Hungarians that the conquest of Czechoslovakia would be easy. Neurath, when informed of the Prague exchanges, insisted that any alliance should depend on the abandonment of the French and Soviet alliances. Most important of all, Hitler told the Austrians that any improvement in relations with Prague would require the dropping of the Soviet connection. Haushofer and Trauttmansdorff returned to Prague on 18 December. It was agreed that both sides should prepare drafts of the pact amidst considerable optimism about the outcome. It was not to be. Hitler was not interested and the talks were broken off in January 1937.

Hitler had a second weapon in expanding German influence and undermining the French security system. This lay in the Reich's growing economic domination of south-eastern Europe. The political utility of this position was already demonstrated during the Rhineland *coup* when the sanctions against Italy made these countries particularly vulnerable to German displeasure. In 1933, the strong pre-depression position enjoyed by the Germans in south-eastern Europe had been eroded. At the same time, the Germans lacked the foreign currency needed to buy the raw materials necessary for fuelling recovery and rearmament. The East European states, anxious to export their surplus agricultural produce, were prepared to accept the clearing arrangements as proposed by Schacht as part of his 'New Plan'. With subsidies used to encourage exports and quotas imposed on imports, trade was directed towards those states (apart from the United States) which produced what Germany needed and who would buy German goods in return.

The agreements negotiated with Hungary and Yugoslavia in 1934 indicated that Germany was vitally interested in their grain and raw materials and would offer far more generous terms than any other buyer. For the Hungarians, badly hit by the German import quotas, the new agreement meant sales of grain and, above all, meat, at high market prices. Yugoslavia, too, would be able to sell its grain and meat products; the latter increased five-fold between 1934 and 1936. With higher domestic demand and the accelerated rearmament schedules, Germany's imports outpaced its exports and large Reichsmark balances accumulated in the East European states' clearing accounts. The dangers of these balances which were, in fact, loans without interest, were recognized and the Hungarians, Yugoslavs, and Romanians, particularly the latter, sought better terms to reduce the clearing balances. The pressing need to export agricultural surpluses and the absence of alternative markets (French weakness in this respect was critical) made it almost impossible to resist the German offers of preferential treatment.

Hjalmar Schacht's tour of Austria, Yugoslavia, Bulgaria, and Hungary in mid-June 1936 was intended to address the questions of raw materials and shortages of foreign currency. Bucharest, because of its foreign minister's (Nicolae Titulescu) pro-French orientation, and past difficulties on the economic side, was omitted from Schacht's ten-day trip. Schacht stressed the German need for agricultural goods and raw materials and offered 'payments' in technicians and machinery if these sectors were expanded. He emphasized his government's respect for the political integrity of the countries with which it traded. Schacht was able to establish, or re-establish, Germany's position of primacy in almost all the Danubian countries. There was a marked increase in German trade with Eastern Europe between 1933 and 1936 in both percentage and value, though it still provided only a little more than 13% of Germany's total imports. Hungary supplied corn and wheat and imported chrome and manganese. Yugoslavia exported cereals, livestock and animal products, bauxite, and copper, and took machines, iron products, coal, coke, and chemical and pharmaceutical produce in return. In 1933, Germany's share of Yugoslavia's foreign trade was half that of Britain, France, and Italy combined. By 1936, it was twice their combined share. Germany replaced Italy as Yugoslavia's best customer.

Romania supplied much-needed oil as well as wheat, animal feed, metals, and soya products. After Göring was made head of the Four-Year Plan, in October 1936, he lifted many of the trade restrictions imposed under Schacht. Imports of food and raw materials were greatly increased. Taking advantage of improving world prices and the rising German demand, many of the Eastern European countries won far better trading terms. Both Yugoslavia and Romania secured higher prices and more advantageous exchange rates on their clearing balances. They insisted on receiving capital, rather than the consumer goods that the Germans wanted to export and they were able to secure foreign exchange, or goods with foreign exchange potential, so that they could buy the raw materials overseas that they needed for their own industrialization programmes. In the important agreement negotiated between Germany and Romania in December 1937, the Romanians limited German purchases of oil through the clearings to 25% of their total clearing purchases; the rest had to be paid for through long-term German investments and the delivery of arms, an increasingly common way for Germany to pay for its imports, despite protests from the Reich defence representatives. Other Eastern European states, including Latvia and Estonia, either sought foreign exchange or took steps to divert trade to hard-currency countries. Between the summer of 1936 and the end of 1937, as world trade revived, both German imports and exports rose markedly. Poland was one of the few countries in the region able to resist the accumulation of large Reichsmark balances in its clearings.

Schacht's motivation was primarily economic, but as the German stake in the East European economies increased, the German representatives sought a more active political role. This was particularly true in Yugoslavia and Romania, where the Germans mounted major propaganda campaigns and subsidized right-wing parties and newspapers. The political stakes were high; a major German presence in these countries could undermine the Little Entente, isolate Czechoslovakia and further weaken the influence of France. It remained open to question whether, given their growing economic dependence on Germany, states like Yugoslavia and Romania with ties to France could avoid being drawn into the German orbit.

Without as yet launching any further military action, Hitler was reaping the rewards of his successful *coup* in the Rhineland. He had publicly demonstrated that Germany would accept neither external nor internal restraints on its rearmament. He had opted for expanded rearmament regardless of the economic costs and secretly proposed a date for possible military action. He had revealed, in the most public way, the fissures in the diplomatic structures designed to contain Germany, and demonstrated his ability to undermine them. In retrospect, it is difficult to understand why the French and the British governments continued to believe that Hitler could be brought into a new security arrangement. As Neurath warned the American ambassador to France, William Bullitt, as early as 18 May 1936, once Germany fortified its western frontiers it would take Austria, and no state would try to stop it.[14] At the same time, apart from taking the decision for rapid rearmament, Hitler had not settled on a specific course of short-term action. France could not be discounted, given its army, the relationship with Britain, and its eastern alliances. Hitler deliberately left his doors open so that both the French and the British governments continued their efforts to reach a settlement with Berlin, despite the obvious lack of progress.

IV

The diplomatic prospects of the Popular Front government that took office in June 1936 were daunting at best; yet the political and economic situation which Léon Blum inherited guaranteed that the premier's immediate focus would be on domestic policy. The occupation of the factories by well-organized and highly disciplined workers inspired fear and anger among the embattled employers. This baptism by fire proved to be a foretaste of what was to become one of the most debated premierships in France's inter-war history. Blum was an unlikely figure to emerge at a time when political passions and social tensions were at a peak. Born in Paris of Alsatian Jewish parentage, a moralist in politics whose socialism owed as much to Kant as to Marx, Blum believed in the power of reason and rational debate at a time when neither was in favour. His moral scrupulousness proved both a source of political strength and weakness, as did his fastidiousness in thought and manner. Slim, carefully groomed, and immaculately dressed, this highly intelligent man had nothing of the demagogue in his personality, and so consequently lacked the conviviality and common touch of the successful politician. His much-noted 'urbanity'[15] was hardly a quality that endeared him to the masses. Blum's appeal was an intellectual one but was buttressed by a deep sincerity that attracted supporters. 'He lived politics as a "personal moral drama"; "loyalty" and "fidelity" were his favourite words.'[16] An admirer of Franklin Roosevelt, Blum lacked the political acuity and pragmatic skills so critical to the American president's successful career. Given the bleak balance sheet that he inherited,

[14] *FRUS,* 1936, Vol. I, 301.
[15] Girard de Charbonnières, *La plus evitable de toutes les guerres* (Paris, 1983), 108.
[16] Julian Jackson, *The Popular Front in France: Defending Democracy, 1934–1938* (Cambridge, 1988), 280.

it is perhaps extraordinary that under Blum's leadership the Republic survived the vicissitudes of the next years, and embarked on a rearmament programme.

It was very much in keeping with the highly polarized society of 1936 that the new premier quickly became the object of virulent attack. He was an easy target; passions buried since the Dreyfus Affair came to the surface in their most extreme and divisive forms. Blum was not the only object of right-wing hostility. Pierre Cot, the minister of aviation, accused of being in the service of Moscow (an accusation later confirmed by evidence from Soviet sources), and Jean Zay, the Radical minister for education, were picked out for similarly savage attacks. The minister of the interior, Roger Salengro was driven to suicide in November by a campaign conducted by *Gringoire*, a right-wing paper, that accused him of desertion during the war. Blum was insistent that, after his unexpected victory at the polls, the electoral bargains made with political allies should be honoured, and nothing done that would violate the country's constitutional legalities. His party was the largest in the new coalition (which the Communists refused to join) but was dependent on Radical and Communist support in the Chamber. The cautious and legalistic Blum argued that the Socialists were not given a mandate to transform the social system and therefore had to work within it. His constitutionalism not only placed severe limits on what the government could do domestically, but inevitably opened his policies to attacks from both the extreme left and right. The Matignon agreements, intended to end the factory occupations by raising the wages of the workers, and the laws improving the workers' conditions of employment, including the forty-hour week and two week vacation periods, were concluded soon after the Popular Front took office. Within months, however, financial and economic crises brought the Popular Front 'experiment' to an end. In February 1937, Blum announced the need for a 'pause' in the implementation of further reforms.

The internal crisis of France precluded an adventurous foreign policy; foreign issues were not at the forefront of political debate. Attention was focused on the battle against Fascism within France, and not on the threat of Fascism abroad. Though Blum's chief interest lay in domestic issues, he was determined from the first to play a major part in the management of foreign affairs. After all, he had been the Socialist party spokesman on foreign affairs and was instrumental in shaping its foreign policy agenda. Once Herriot refused the *Quai d'Orsay*, Blum chose Yvon Delbos, a rather colourless Radical deputy from the Dordogne, but a friend and neighbour. Delbos, who had been minister of justice in Sarraut's cabinet and was well-known to Radical deputies in the Chamber, had little experience in foreign affairs. Somewhat lacking in

Table 6.2 French Military Expenditure, 1932–1937 (million francs) (constant prices, 1938)

	Army	Navy	Air	Colonies	Military Element in Civilian Ministries	Total
1932	11410	4229	2552	952	382	19525
1933	12010	4194	2554	910	229	19897
1934	10212	4539	2231	955	189	18126
1935	11180	5075	4035	1030	187	21507
1936	11941	5358	4090	937	382	22708
1937	13423	5247	4648	812	393	24523

Source: Robert Frank[enstein], *Le prix du réarmement, 1935–1939* (Paris, 1982), 304.

imagination and energy, he was conscientious and, above all, loyal to Blum. His appointment was taken as a signal of Blum's future intentions. The highly efficient premier read a good deal of the diplomatic correspondence, keeping a particularly close eye on the despatches coming from France's veteran ambassador in Berlin, François-Poncet. From the very start of his administration, Blum saw the need to adapt to the changed situation in Europe following the Rhineland occupation. Though a man of principle, Blum was not a single-minded ideologue. While still favouring a collective security pact in which Germany would join, the former spokesman for disarmament was quickly converted to the military case for rearmament. His government immediately embarked on the preparation of an extended rearmament programme. Alerted by French intelligence to the extent of Germany's war preparations, the superiority of its industrial strength, and the Nazi government's determination to press ahead with its military programmes whatever the costs, Blum acknowledged that France had no other choice but to rearm.

Blum's backing for the rearmament programme was a critical element in the conversion of the Socialists to a rise in defence expenditure. Three Radicals were appointed to the service ministries, each intent on securing funds for their respective forces. General Gamelin, the commander-in-chief and chief of the general staff, assured the new premier at a meeting on 10 June that the army would stay out of politics if the army was similarly left alone. Despite Gamelin's hostility to the Popular Front and personal dislike of Blum (reciprocated by the premier), the commander-in-chief kept the bargain. Insofar as he could control his officers' activities, he insisted on the political neutrality of the army. There were individuals, especially in the colonial armies, who were particularly hostile to the Blum government; officer support for Franco prompted government fears of right-wing conspiracies in the officer class. As revealed by the authorities in 1937, there was an extensive officers' network with cells (*Corvignolles*) intended to combat Communist and pacifist propaganda, and prepared to take counter-action in case of a Communist *coup* in France. They did not engage, however, in political intrigues against the government nor try to undermine the authority of the Republic. The *Comité Secret d'Action Révolutionnaire*, on the contrary, was an actively subversive civilian organization, but it was supported only by a few ultra-conservative officers, and failed to infiltrate the *Corvignolles*. There was no real threat to the government from within the army and Blum's confidence in Gamelin's assurances was justified. Right-wing fears that pacifist, Communist, and anarchist propaganda would undermine the morale of the troops proved similarly unfounded, and there was little need for the counter-measures prepared by the *Corvignolles*, should the threat from the left emerge.

Édouard Daladier, one of the most powerful politicians in France, returned to the Ministry of Defence at the rue St. Dominique, committed to the restoration of French military power. The Radical leader was made head of the newly created Ministry of War and National Defence, with co-ordinating authority over all three services. He and Blum had no differences over military issues. Daladier's working partnership with General Gamelin at this time was also harmonious. Complaints about the instability of pre-war political life in France should not extend to its defence establishment. Daladier stayed at the rue St. Dominique through five successive governments, from 6 June 1936 until 18 May 1940. There was hardly an important change in his team of advisers during these years, though whether this was an advantage or disadvantage is open to debate. Warned by Gamelin that without a major financial commitment to improve the armed forces France would soon be unable to withstand a German *attaque brusque*, Daladier immediately prepared for a massive rise in military expenditure. In September 1936 he actually increased the estimates proposed by the army chiefs from nine billion to fourteen billion francs over a four-year period.[17] Daladier's aggressive approach stands in marked contrast to his behaviour during 1933 when, in the struggle with General Weygand over *effectives*, he reduced the size of the French army. He must bear much of the responsibility for the country's military backwardness that he now tried to correct. Daladier left Blum in no doubt that the military balance was running strongly in the German favour. Given the latter's demographic advantage (a constant preoccupation of

[17] Jean Doise and Maurice Vaïsse, *Diplomatie et Outil Militaire, 1871–1969* (Paris, 1987), 321.

the French army) and its powerful industrial base, time could only increase the gap between the two nations unless France acted promptly. The September 1936 programme was the first major step taken towards the rearmament of France and the largest peacetime programme in French history. The amount to be spent on the acquisition of new materials would rise from the initial projection of 14.3 billion to over sixty-three billion francs by September 1939.[18] The army, the chief recipient of the new funding, was to be modernized with priority given to the production of tanks and anti-tank armament and to the motorization and modernization of the artillery. At the same time, a new aerial rearmament plan (Plan II) aiming at 1,500 combat planes by 1939 was launched by Pierre Cot, as well as a three year naval programme initiated by the navy.

The war industries nationalization bill, instituting a mixed enterprise system for the armaments industries, became law in August 1936. Göring's appointment as head of the Four-Year Plan was rightly seen in Paris as a German decision for unlimited rearmament and reduced the remaining military opposition to the nationalization programme. The new French law did not specify which industries were to be taken over; the decision was left to each service. The Air Ministry, for example, took possession of twenty-eight plants, the War Ministry nine, and the navy only two. Though there were disruptions in production in order to achieve long-term improvements, 'the war ministry nationalizations were far too limited in number and scope to be capable either of creating or removing industrial bottlenecks affecting army equipment delivery dates'.[19] Recent commentators place less importance on the forty-hour week as the cause of the crippling delays in production, than on a whole series of other contributing factors. Given its traditional industrial structure, the French system of production would have to be thoroughly reorganized before weapons or planes could be produced in any number. There were still thousands of small contractors and suppliers of component parts operating under artisanal conditions that served the larger producers. These smaller factories continued to be plagued by strikes even when they became rarities in the nationalized industries. Employers, hostile to the government and resentful of the new Popular Front legislation, mounted counter-offensives against the trade unions and against employee demands for higher wages, engendering further conflict and interruptions in production. As in Britain, skilled labour was in short supply and the unemployed unsuited for jobs in the defence industries. Unfortunately, relations between the military and the factory

[18] R. Frank(enstein), *Le prix du réarmement français* (Paris, 1982), 75, 91.

[19] Martin S. Alexander, *The Republic in Danger: General Maurice Gamelin and the Politics of French Defence*, 114.

managers were exceedingly poor. An unrealistic and ivory-tower approach to weapon design and manufacture resulted in a multitude of blueprints and prototypes, but little in the way of actual weaponry. There was a glaring gap between funding and planning, on the one hand, and the actual production of weapons on the other. Many of these problems were not basically dissimilar from those encountered in Germany and Britain, but France started later than either, in the middle of a depression from which the other two nations had emerged and proceeded from a weaker industrial base.

The whole rearmament programme has to be seen against the background of the Popular Front's efforts to take the country out of depression. Blum was warned that unless he was willing to introduce a managed economy and impose exchange controls to halt the flight of capital, neither of which he wished to do, there was no alternative but to devalue the franc. Already in May, Blum authorized conversations in Washington and London on exchange stabilization in preparation for the devaluation, which was carried out in September. Even then, Blum moved with great caution fearing that a sharp depreciation could bring his ministry down. A temporary economic upturn followed, but the devaluation proved too small and too late to kick-start the economy into a period of sustained growth. There was no way, in the autumn and winter of 1936–1937, that the government could fund its programme of further social reform, and rearmament. The former was cut back in the period of the 'pause' but rearmament expenditure was retained. While 'the effort directed to national defence did not provoke the financial crisis, it was by far the principal cause of its aggravation'.[20] In maintaining its arms expenditure, the Blum government increased its budgetary problems. Whereas in 1934 and 1935, 18% and 22% respectively of the ordinary budget went to military expenditure, the figure rose to 33% in 1936 and the same percentage was maintained in 1937. In 1938, it was increased to 37% and only in 1939, under the impact of the Munich crisis, to 64%.[21]

The beginning of French rearmament did not bring about any revision of traditional strategic thinking. The warnings from the *Deuxième Bureau* that Hitler was preparing for a series of swift, decisive campaigns while arming in depth, only served to reinforce the defensive caste of French planning. 'Now more than ever, the premier mission of the French military is to ensure the integrity of the national territory', Gamelin wrote to Daladier in July 1936.[22] The solutions offered to

[20] Frank, *Le prix du réarmement français*, 96. [21] Ibid., see Appendix.

[22] AN, Archives Daladier, 496 AP 28, dr. 4, Gamelin to Daladier, 10 July 1936, cited in Peter Jackson, *France and the Nazi Menace: Intelligence and Policy Making, 1933–1939*, 188–189.

the German challenge were the strengthening of the border defences, the conservation of French manpower for as long as possible, and the presence of powerful allies. An awareness of the current German emphasis on armour and mobility further strengthened the defensive priorities of the French army. The anticipated '*guerre de longue durée*' would be fought in stages. The army's first function was to preserve the integrity of the French frontiers and to secure France's industrial base from a German invasion. Gamelin thought in terms of a rapid movement (for which France's proposed mechanized and motorized forces would be used) into Belgium to take up positions along the Albert Canal in order to contain the projected German invasion. This depended on close co-ordination with the Belgian high command. In the second stage, Germany would be engaged in a long struggle during which the combined resources of the British and French empires would give the allies the material upper hand. Only when Germany had been sufficiently weakened would an offensive operation be launched to defeat the enemy. The general staff rejected the proposals of General de Gaulle and Paul Reynaud, revived during the summer of 1936, for the creation of a heavily armoured mechanized force consisting of professional soldiers. Such a change of emphasis from the inviolability of the frontiers to a war of movement, fought by a professional army, was judged both politically unacceptable and militarily dangerous, for it would expose France to an *attaque brusque* that would disrupt the whole mobilization process.

Gamelin, it is true, had fashioned offensive plans during 1935–1936 involving co-operation with Italy in a coalition war in central Europe that would bring together Italy, Yugoslavia, Romania, Czechoslovakia, and, it was hoped, Poland. However unrealistic such hopes were after the signs of an Italian turn towards Germany, the general staff clung to the plan of using Italy as a 'bridge' between France and her eastern allies. Such planning, however, did not obviate the continued focus on fixed defensive positions, and the key importance of the north-eastern front. Gamelin was loath to relinquish the Italian alliance, but like the officials at the *Quai d'Orsay*, his main diplomatic aim was to secure the British alliance, thought essential for France in any Franco-German war.

French military intelligence painted a very black picture both of German intentions and capabilities, correctly assessing the former but considerably exaggerating the latter, particularly the ability of German industry to keep pace with the planned expansion of the German forces. As at the time of the Rhineland crisis, Gamelin and the *Haut Comité Militaire* exaggerated the degree of German military preparedness in order to impress political leaders of the necessity to rearm and so to be able to deal with Germany from a position of strength. Intelligence rightly interpreted the Four-Year Plan as a signal of Hitler's intention to marshal the German economy for a forthcoming war. While concluding that the *Wehrmacht* was an offensive force designed to serve Hitler's expansionist purposes, there was far less certainty about German strategy or Hitler's future timetable. The *Deuxième Bureau*'s assessment that German military power would soon outstrip that of France, and that the gap would grow in the immediate future, was one that shaped military policies until after Munich.

While building up its forces, the French leaders intensified their efforts to repair their diplomatic bridges. With regard to the British, Delbos enjoyed some degree of success. French acceptance of the British lead in negotiating the abortive western pact with Germany fitted in with the military's preoccupation with German rearmament. Blum's well-founded belief, shared with Gamelin, was that since the balance of power had shifted in the German direction France could not afford a provocative policy. Moreover, France's military backwardness made a temporary *rapprochement* with Germany a practical necessity. Success in this endeavour would depend on London. Blum believed that the Schacht overture in the summer of 1936 could be used to bring Hitler's Germany into some form of multilateral agreement that would bring about a change of policy in Berlin. The August talks had the approval of the *Quai d'Orsay*; even René Massigli, one of the leading advocates of a policy of firmness towards Germany, welcomed the idea of a dialogue with Berlin. Whatever the unwarranted fears in London, Blum's main purpose was to get the Germans to join in a general European settlement and thus re-enter the world economy through offering colonial and economic concessions. Throughout the tortuous negotiations with Germany over a new Locarno, the French generally followed the British lead, stopping short only of compromising the right to assist their eastern allies. As the fear of German military power increased, so did the importance of Britain to the future security of France. In the summer and autumn of 1936, the Blum government's financial difficulties further strengthened the links between Paris and London. The success of the devaluation programme depended on American and British co-operation. The Finance Ministry would have liked a treaty formalizing the exchange relationship between the three countries; instead it had to accept a bargain which provided for a predetermined range of fluctuation for the franc. The tripartite agreement of 26 September 1936 was the first tentative step towards re-establishing the international monetary co-operation shattered in 1931. It was welcomed, prematurely, as an American step away from isolation. The French acquired a vested interest in the stability of the pound sterling, for any depreciation in its value would adversely affect the franc.

On other foreign fronts, the Popular Front faced a number of key reverses. Of these, the most important was King Leopold's declaration of Belgian independence on 14 October 1936. The French had watched with considerable alarm the mounting political tension in Brussels before the critical Belgian May elections. They were as disappointed as the Belgians with the outcome of the April 1936 tripartite military talks; and the failure to secure concrete British military support for the Belgians. This could only encourage the latter's retreat into neutrality. Subsequent visits of French military staff to Belgium and a high degree of cordiality between the Belgian and French commanders did nothing to counter the prevailing anti-French winds. The second van Zeeland government took office in June; it was intentionally vague about its foreign policy to avoid fanning pre-election political flames. The young and inexperienced Socialist, Paul-Henri Spaak, a strong advocate of military reform, was given the foreign affairs portfolio. He had the advice of two extremely experienced officials at the Foreign Ministry, the secretary general, Fernand van Langenhove, and the political director, Baron Pierre van Zuylen, both of whom believed that only 'a policy of complete independence ensures the maximum effectiveness of our army and our defensive system'.[23] Well before the May elections, the secretary general had advised that if there were new treaties of mutual assistance, Belgium's frontier should be guaranteed but that she should not offer any formal reciprocity. Belgium should be guaranteed, but not act as a guarantor.

By mid-July the Belgian decision had been taken. If van Zeeland's sympathies lay with Eden and Blum, his policies were those of Spaak. In a speech in front of the ministerial council on 14 October 1936, Spaak addressed the need to abandon the 'beautiful dreams' of the statesmen of 1918 and to adopt a foreign policy 'which is exclusively and wholly Belgian'.[24] During the next weeks Spaak assured the German ambassador that Belgium wanted only to pursue a policy of independence, news that the Wilhelmstrasse received with 'quiet pleasure'. In mid-September, as the British tried to set the much delayed five-power conference in motion, the Belgians and the French met privately in Geneva. Though Britain would accept the Belgian request to be a non-guarantor, the French would not. Delbos claimed that Belgium's attitude would weaken the position of both countries *vis-à-vis* the Germans and was barely compatible with Article 16 of the Covenant.

[23] *DDB*, Vol. IV, No. 92 (memorandum by van Langenhove, 9 July 1936).

[24] *DDB*, Vol. IV, No. 128, cited in J. Van Welkenhuyzen, 'Belgien am Vorabend des Zweiten Weltkrieges', in Klaus Hildebrand et al. (eds.), *1939: an der Schwelle zum Weltkrieg: die Entfesselung des Zweiten Weltkrieges und das internationale System* (Berlin, 1990), 232.

These assertions fuelled Belgian suspicions that the French intended to use Belgian territory for a war against Germany on behalf of Poland and Czechoslovakia. The Belgians left Geneva not only acutely conscious of the dangers of their still encumbered position, but determined to free themselves from the French link.

It was against this background that King Leopold, long opposed to the French connection and converted to the 'policy of independence' at least two years before his ministers, decided it was time for a royal intervention. He proposed a statement of principle intended to create cabinet unanimity for the military project. In a memo written mainly by his military adjutant but approved by van Zeeland, the king made the case for keeping Belgium outside the quarrels of her neighbours, and for abandoning the vestiges of the repudiated 1920 Franco-Belgian military agreement. Strangely enough, it was the ministers who suggested that the King's speech date be made public. Preoccupied with domestic considerations, they appear not to have considered the foreign reaction to the royal message, and gave Belgian representatives abroad no warning. It was in Paris that the alarm was greatest. It was not really the essence of Leopold's arguments that so provoked the French, for the *Quai d'Orsay* knew which way the Belgian wind was blowing. It was that the royal announcement came without any preparation or explanation, which infuriated the French officials. Despite an 'avalanche of assurances' and protestations of fidelity to their existing obligations, the Belgians were elusive and evasive in answering any French queries. What did it mean that Belgium wished to be guaranteed by France but would not guarantee France? Would staff talks be discontinued? What was Belgium's interpretation of its obligations arising from Article 16 of the Covenant? These problems had been discussed earlier but the French had preferred silence to enlightenment. Now the positions were reversed, particularly as there was little agreement within the van Zeeland cabinet on what the policy of independence actually meant. Blum and van Zeeland met secretly in November but there was no movement on the Belgian side. The French premier had to accept the decision that while France and Britain would continue to guarantee Belgium, the Belgians would not act as guarantor to France. By breaking its ties to France, the van Zeeland government succeeded in winning the Chamber's support for a military defence bill on 2 December.

The British reaction was mixed. The Air Ministry was far from happy but the British chiefs of staff argued that Belgian neutrality would discourage Hitler from westward expansion and would reduce the danger of war for Britain. If Germany did invade Belgium, there could be no argument, and Britain would have a clear-cut justification for military intervention. There was the additional argument that the

French would be less inclined to hopeless interventions on behalf of their eastern allies. The Foreign Office totally disagreed. It was the beginning of a long conflict between the diplomats and the military over the status of Belgium. Eden and Vansittart were sympathetic to the French strategic predicament. Though they resented the king's blunt statement and the lack of diplomatic finesse, they realized that nothing could be done to alter the Belgian decision and that Franco-Belgian arguments would only further delay the non-existent negotiations for a new Locarno.

The French now had to think again about the defence of their northern frontier and its all-important industrial sector. Daladier wanted to extend the Maginot system south to the Jura and north to the Channel, thus completing the continuous defensive position established by the building of the Maginot Line. General Gamelin, in considering the problems of the terrain, and estimating that an extension along the Franco-Belgian frontier would cost an additional 10 to 15 billion francs, wanted any additional money wrested from the Chamber to go on the expansion of the mechanized forces. He agreed only to improving a few fixed positions, around Dunkerque and the Monts de Flandres. Convinced that France lacked the funds to both extend its defensive fortifications and build up its conventional forces, Gamelin opted for the latter and looked to his special relationship with General van den Bergen, the chief of the Belgian general staff, for the re-opening of the joint planning which had been undermined by the Belgian declaration of independence. There is little doubt that Gamelin, thanks to van den Bergen's co-operation, was kept informed of the defensive plans of the Belgian army and that the French, in turn, furnished valuable technical assistance to the Belgians. Such a relationship was necessarily covert. Planning and coordination were carried on between the French military attachés in Brussels and van den Bergen, with no other Belgian officers involved. The Belgian general risked much, for he knew he was acting against the policy of his government. There could be no certainty that he could convince his civilian superiors to admit French troops before a German invasion was under way. All this was clear to Gamelin. The French general took a calculated risk in 1936.

No priority was given to fortifying the hilly Ardennes. Like his predecessors, Gamelin never believed that the Germans would attack through this natural barrier. Nothing was done to site artillery, or to adequately garrison the region though just after the Belgian announcement of neutrality attention was drawn to the danger of an '*attaque brusque*' in the Ardennes-Meuse sector. It was hoped to have a substantial mechanized reserve force in place, trained in the methods of sealing-off and counter-attack, to defeat a breakthrough. This force was supposed to be capable of crushing any rupture of the front on the Meuse (itself a 'formidable obstacle' to the invader) or of deploying north, south, or both against a German outflanking manoeuvre. The development of such a unit, the *Division Cuirassée de Réserve* (DCR) was much delayed, first by the bottlenecks that existed in the production of mechanized vehicles and armour plate, and then because the *Conseil Supérieur de la Guerre*, with some exceptions including Gamelin, was reluctant about concentrating tanks and mechanized infantry in the DCR. There was a further blow to Gamelin's strategic planning when Mussolini was seen to move into the German camp. During the spring and summer of 1936, Gamelin had continued to hope that Italy and Poland could be recruited for the defence of Austria and Czechoslovakia. Blum, himself, was not averse to a diplomatic arrangement with Rome. The *Quai d'Orsay* took up the multilateral possibilities, discussed by Flandin in April and May, of launching a new approach to Mussolini. Proposed reforms to the League Covenant took into account the lessons of the Ethiopian affair and were framed with Italy in mind. But attempts to extract Italian promises of support for Austria and Czechoslovakia, in return for the lifting of sanctions, produced nothing concrete and other French efforts ran into British obstruction. By the time the British agreed to end sanctions in mid-June, the French had no choice but to follow without having secured any compensation from Rome for their efforts.

The *Quai d'Orsay*, nevertheless, remained curiously optimistic about Mussolini's intentions. The Italophile ambassador, Charles de Chambrun, repeatedly and mistakenly reported that the Duce favoured the French rather than the Germans. Even after the announcement of the Austro-German agreement of July 1936, which laid the basis for *Anschluss*, some officials argued that the Italian–German *rapprochement* would not last, and that bilateral commercial arrangements in the Balkans, in which Italy would join, could be used to keep Mussolini apart from Hitler. During the summer of 1936, all the services supported the ever-retreating possibility of *détente* with Italy. French assurances that its assistance to the British fleet in the Mediterranean, in case of Italian attack, would be lifted, proved useless as did the formal lifting of sanctions and the departure of the main body of the British fleet from Alexandria on 18 July. The Italians made it clear that they would follow a joint policy with Germany with regard to any future meeting of the Locarno partners. Mussolini's military support for Franco strengthened Blum's personal distaste for the Italian dictator and confirmed his belief that Italy would ally with Germany. By November 1936, the general staff was abandoning its hopes of bringing the Italians into a Danubian or Mediterranean pact. The Duce insisted that the Franco–Soviet alliance was incompatible with Locarno (privately he had repeatedly denounced Locarno to the Germans), and that France, with its Popular Front government, had lost all credibility as an ally. The stupid affair of French accreditation in Rome made communication even more difficult. The Italians refused to accept as ambassador René de Saint-Quentin, the *Quai d'Orsay* nominee to replace the retiring Charles de Chambrun, unless he was accredited to the 'Emperor of Ethiopia'. Paris saw this as an intentional hostile gesture. The fracas meant that there was no French ambassador in Rome between Chambrun's departure in November 1936 and François-Poncet's arrival in November 1938, an absence which proved a major disadvantage for the French.

The French diplomatic options were few; the need to keep the British line intact became ever more necessary. The Spanish Civil War that threatened to divide Europe along ideological lines, the Belgian retreat into semi-neutrality, and Mussolini's moves towards Germany weakened France's strategic position. It was becoming obvious too, that unless the French took positive action, they would find their allies in Eastern Europe slipping into the German net out of necessity and fear. Military attention was focused on Poland. Given France's demographic weakness, the extension of German conscription from one year to two in August gave new importance to the eastern alliance. The Poles had an army of 305,000 men (the Czech forces numbered only 165,000) and were strongly anti-Soviet. The French army's efforts to revive the Polish connection had much to do with the general staff's hope to construct an eastern front without the Soviet Union. Fearing that the new Popular Front government might look to Moscow, Gamelin took a leading role in the negotiations that led up to the Rambouillet loan and arms agreement, concluded with Poland in September 1936. The *Quai d'Orsay*, for its part, remained suspicious of the Poles and highly doubtful about Beck's intentions. The Polish foreign minister's attitude during and after the Rhineland reoccupation convinced some senior officials that he was an enemy of France, and that there could be no improvement in Polish–Czech relations while he remained in office. Léger rejected a Polish proposal to revive the 1921 mutual assistance arrangements with its anti-Soviet clauses, and insisted that any financial aid for Polish rearmament should depend on an improvement of Polish relations with Czechoslovakia. But if the French were to improve their standing in Warsaw, a military loan was the only way to do it. The Polish army was large but woefully equipped. The Poles were asking for a one billion franc credit to purchase arms in France, and a one billion franc loan for the development of a Polish national war industry.

The loan was strongly supported by Léon Noël, the highly independent French minister in Warsaw, who believed that, if properly courted, the Francophile General Rydz-Śmigły who was both president of Poland and army chief of staff, would work for the dismissal of Beck, which would alter the whole tenor of Franco-Polish relations. Though the *Quai d'Orsay* was less than enthusiastic about proceeding along Noël's lines, Gamelin and Noël joined forces and made their arrangements even before the Blum government took office. Noël was overly optimistic about Rydz-Śmigły's intention to oust the Polish foreign minister. For like Beck, he was a good disciple of Piłsudski and whatever their political rivalries, the two men shared a similar reading of Poland's national interests. Knowing that the French always backtracked when it came to finance, the Poles resorted to a bit of diplomatic blackmail. Schacht had been offering to pay in weaponry for the Reich's share of a joint railway venture in Pomerania, and the offer was used to good advantage in Paris. Polish warnings to Daladier of a possible Polish–German *rapprochement* should the French not meet the Polish requirements, seem to have convinced the Blum government to act. The *Quai d'Orsay* agreed to a visit by Gamelin to Warsaw, in August, to confer with Rydz-Śmigły, but deliberately excluding Beck, in anticipation of the president's scheduled visit to Paris in September. The two generals got along splendidly. Gamelin, who was instructed to discuss France's concerns about Polish policy and Warsaw's continuing disputes with Prague, apparently concentrated on military matters and failed to raise such contentious issues except in an oblique manner. Rydz-Śmigły, who naturally consulted Beck, offered little in terms of future Franco-Polish military co-operation beyond an agreement to share intelligence. He accepted Gamelin's proposals for parallel action starting from a period of political tension, and an exchange of liaison missions during an actual conflict. With regard to Czechoslovakia and the USSR, Rydz-Śmigły said only that Poland had no engagements against either state. Gamelin appeared satisfied and assured the general that the Blum government would agree to the requested arms aid package.

Rydz-Śmigły paid his much publicized visit to Paris in September. Noël was later to complain that Blum and Delbos had not pressed for Beck's dismissal as a condition for the French loan, nor insisted on limitations on the Polish use of the French funds. But the accuracy of Noël's much quoted memoirs has been authoritatively challenged.[25] The French diplomat clearly wished to put the blame for failure in both these respects on the shoulders of the Popular Front negotiators,

[25] Nicole Jordan, *The Popular Front and Central Europe: The Dilemmas of French Impotence, 1918–1940* (Cambridge, 1992), 146–87, especially 153–157. Léon Noël, *L'Aggression allemande contre la Pologne. Une ambassade à Varsovie, 1933–1939* (Paris, 1946), 138–150.

rather than on his own misplaced optimism about Rydz-Śmigły's position in Warsaw. The Polish president proved an aggressive bargainer who ruffled the French feathers. On Beneš' insistence, Gamelin raised the question of Polish–Czech relations and asked what Poland would do if Germany attacked Czechoslovakia. He was told only that Poland would remain faithful to its League commitments and the alliance with France. This could not have given either the French or the Czechs much satisfaction. The French won no promises about Poland's future behaviour beyond verbal assurances that the Czechs did not need to fortify their frontier with Poland. There was also tough bargaining about finance. There was no difficulty about the total two billion franc loan, but the French wanted one billion francs to be spent in France, while the Poles wanted a larger share of the total to be spent on developing their own war industries. Fears that German activities in encouraging commercial arms agreements and investment in war-related industries might be extended to Poland, meant that Rydz-Śmigły could not be allowed to return to Warsaw empty-handed. The French, however, had no intention of erring on the side of liberality. Though the Poles got their two billion franc loan over a period of four years, a good many conditions were attached which favoured France. At least half the total funds to be spent would 'end up in French pockets'. The Poles got a credit of 800 million francs for purchases in France and the remainder was to be given for the development of war industries in Poland. Debates continued until the very last moment over interest rates and the French demand for a military control clause with regard to the use of funds in Poland. Rydz-Śmigły resented French insistence on the latter. Blum pointed out that France wanted to be sure that the money would not be used against Czechoslovakia or the USSR but would be spent in Poland and not elsewhere, for instance, in Germany. Gamelin reported to Daladier that Rydz-Śmigły agreed to Blum's demands, but no control clause appeared in the agreement. Nor was there any attempt to encourage Beck's ouster from the Polish government, a futile gesture that would have discredited the Popular Front. There was, at best, a hope that better Franco-Polish relations would 'sweep Beck along'. The Blum government counted on the president's promises to exercise full control over Polish foreign policy which it assumed meant a more pro-French direction in Warsaw's diplomacy. Nothing was put on paper.

The negotiations of the Rambouillet agreements showed only how little trust there was on either side. Noël's hopes that Beck would fall and Rydz-Śmigły would institute a more Francophile policy were totally misdirected. There was no government reshuffle in Warsaw; Rydz-Śmigły lost ground among the Piłsudski-ites when he accepted a marshal's baton and, as a result of illness, was sidelined during the autumn of 1936. Without a control clause, the French had little influence over how the Poles spent their money in Poland. The Poles intended to invest the French money in a vast industrial building programme, instead of building up stocks of munitions and raw materials. The French civilian authorities tried to rein them in, but it was far too late. The Blum government had allowed the army to set the terms of the Franco-Polish arms deal and, in the end, placed its trust in Rydz-Śmigły instead of demanding essential guarantees. Due to its own domestic difficulties, the French honoured less than 20% of the Polish arms credit in France. The new factories in Poland, as Noël was to later complain, 'only opened their doors in time to be bombarded by the *Luftwaffe*'.[26] Beck paid a private visit to Paris and was received by Delbos and Blum, but refused to be drawn with regard to Czechoslovakia.

Rambouillet turned out to be a one-off affair. It is possible that a massive injection of munitions and funds, which in any case the French did not have, would have restored Polish confidence in its ally. In June 1937, the Poles complained that they had received nothing in the many months since Rambouillet. French mobilization plans did not depend upon concerted action with the forces of its eastern allies. The age-old problem of attitude and tone adversely affected Franco-Polish relations. Even Gamelin found it difficult to treat the Poles as representatives of an independent nation with interests of their own. One suspects that he did not expect much from the Polish military leaders, though he hoped to profit from good relations with the generals, as in the case of Italy and Belgium. If Gamelin was surprised at the extent of Polish unpreparedness in 1939, it was not just the fault of the Poles, who admittedly concealed their military weakness, but also of the French general staff who, in their anxiety to create an eastern front without the Soviet Union, were content with the illusion of Polish power.

Poland received the lion's share of attention in the summer of 1936, but Blum and Delbos knew that something more had to be done to restore the confidence of the Little Entente powers if France was not to lose her influence by default. There were plenty of warnings from the French minister in Prague, who reported on the new German overtures to the Czechs, and who strongly supported first the Romanian and then the Czech project for a French alliance with the Triple Entente. 'Will France, separated from Central Europe, remain a Great Power?', the French minister asked. 'Can she furthermore cease to be a Great Power without risking her very life?'[27] The *Deuxième Bureau* issued a whole

[26] Jordan, *The Popular Front and Central Europe*, 182.
[27] *DDF*, 2nd ser., Vol. II, No. 475.

series of warnings about German intentions in the Danubian basin. Colonel Gauché, the head of the *Bureau*, had prepared a general survey of the situation after the remilitarization of the Rhineland, stressing the continuity of Hitler's intentions since the writing of *Mein Kampf*. He warned that should Germany gain control of the agriculture and raw materials of the Balkans, the country would become powerful enough to break the Maginot Line and successfully complete the 'Germanization of Europe'.[28] Four months later, in a note to Delbos, written by René Massigli, a solicitous observer of the south-eastern scene, the *Quai*'s political director called attention to the consequences of the Schacht voyage and the recent German successes in south-east Europe. 'Using its economic power, it [Germany] is gradually making the Danubian economy complementary to and dependent on its own', Massigli warned, 'and where it sees points of least resistance, it is attempting to break up the cluster of alliances blocking its way'. The French, he argued, had to make a special effort 'to furnish our allies with tangible proof that we intend to put our economic relations in harmony with our political ones, and practise our alliances'.[29] Massigli even proposed adopting the strategy used so successfully by the Germans of granting credits for purchases of war materials. His highly cogent analysis of French weakness in Eastern Europe still placed considerable weight on Italian economic activity in the region, as a counter-move to the German offensive.

Massigli's advice was not without effect. He had singled out, in his 9 July note, Austria (this was before the Austro-German accord), Poland, and the Little Entente countries as the main targets for French action. The Rambouillet credit to Poland two months later, and an agreement with Yugoslavia in December to buy 200,000 tons of wheat during 1937, with a substantial tariff rebate to facilitate the purchase, was evidence that the Popular Front government understood the need to meet the German challenge. Yet these and other efforts were restricted both by the domestic departments in Paris, concerned with France's commercial position, and by private industrial firms unwilling to take financial risks. A complex trade agreement reached in February 1936, intended to finance Romanian rearmament through orders to French industry, foundered in the face of a strong German counter-campaign, and France's unwillingness to absorb large enough quantities of Romanian products. While recognizing the need to subordinate economic

[28] SHD-DAT, 7N, 2522–2526, 'Note sur les conséquences à tirer de la renonciation par l'Allemagne du traité de Locarno', 8 April 1936, cited in Jackson, *France and the Nazi Menace*, 181–182.

[29] *DDF*, 2nd ser., Vol. II, No. 418.

interests to political necessities, the limited efforts made by the French were hardly likely to stem the loss of confidence in the French at a time when Germany was offering large-sized economic carrots.

The *Quai d'Orsay* showed little enthusiasm for an alliance with the Little Entente powers. In June 1936, the Romanian foreign minister, Nicolae Titulescu, seized the initiative. When the heads of the three Little Entente states met in Bucharest, Titulescu and Beneš warned the *Quai d'Orsay* that unless France acted, their countries would seek accommodations with the Germans. The same conclusion was reached by their chiefs of staff who, in mid-June, argued that any contingency planning against German expansion would depend on prior French military support. The military chiefs explored the possibility of Romanian and Yugoslav assistance to Czechoslovakia, provided that the French simultaneously opened a western front, and the Italian threat to Yugoslavia, the uppermost fear in Belgrade, was removed. Faced with these difficult prospects, Titulescu pursued two lines of diplomacy that were fundamentally inter-connected, one with regard to France and the other towards the Soviet Union. He wanted to create a broad anti-German coalition between France, the Little Entente, and the Soviet Union. At the June meeting in Bucharest, he urged his Little Entente partners to unify their policies and recommended that France be asked to conclude an alliance with the three powers. At the same time, with King Carol's support, he hoped to conclude a pact of mutual assistance with the Russians. Earlier talks with Litvinov in 1935 had been interrupted by the delay in the ratification of the Franco-Soviet pact but during the Abyssinian and Rhineland crises, both countries followed parallel lines of diplomacy. Taking advantage of Litvinov's presence at the Montreux Conference in June–July 1936, which had been called to consider Turkish demands for sovereignty over the Straits, Titulescu pressed for a bilateral agreement. It was a policy that aroused considerable opposition within his own country, abetted by the German, Polish, and Yugoslav representatives in Bucharest.

During a break in the Montreux Conference, Titulescu went to Geneva for the June session of the League Council and energetically lobbied Massigli for the Little Entente alliance. The French were suspicious, and disliked the anti-Italian tone of Titulescu's approach, deemed necessary in order to reassure the Yugoslavs. They were doubtful about assuming responsibilities that would necessarily fall on France should such an alliance be concluded. Officials were concerned, too, with the drift of Romanian politics and believed that Titulescu's bid was part of a political game to buttress his position. Romania, in the summer of 1936, was torn between its right- and left-wing parties, and both the government and the monarchy hoped to manipulate the right in order to stimulate nationalist feeling among the electorate, for their own purposes. As a result of the anti-Communist actions of the Bucharest government, Titulescu found Litvinov far less interested in a bilateral agreement. The commissar, suspecting that the Romanians might well join the Fascist camp, refused to commit the Soviet Union to Bucharest until the Franco–Soviet treaty was backed by a military accord. There was no desire in Moscow to replace France as the guarantor of the Little Entente.

Correctly gauging that Litvinov doubted whether he spoke for his government, Titulescu reverted to his usual tactic of offering his resignation in the hope of getting a fresh mandate. The gesture seemed to have again succeeded in its purpose. In fact, King Carol and his prime minister were manoeuvring to arrange Titulescu's political demise under circumstances that would not aggravate the political tension in Bucharest where the foreign minister had powerful supporters as well as detractors. Titulescu was given a new mandate for a mutual assistance pact with Moscow. Returning to Montreux, Titulescu secured Litvinov's consent to a pact to be signed at the September Geneva meeting. A protocol was initialled on 21 July 1936 providing for mutual assistance against any aggressor. This meant, for Romania, assistance against Hungary and Bulgaria as well as Germany and, for the Soviet Union, aid against Poland in spite of the Polish–Romanian treaty. The chief contentious point was Titulescu's insistence that the implementation of the pact should be dependent upon the intervention of the French army. The question was left unsettled until the autumn. The whole project came to nothing. At the end of August Titulescu was dismissed from the government. King Carol wanted to take control of Romanian foreign policy and was prepared to steer Romania along a non-aligned course using Poland as his model. The king wanted to keep the old alliances intact without strengthening them, and to maintain Romania's distance from both Germany and Russia. How far his vulnerable country could pursue a policy of non-alignment was open to doubt. The Romanians dropped Titulescu's Soviet policies and turned their backs on any schemes of security directed against Germany. While not unaware of the dangers involved, they continued to exploit their economic connections with the Reich.

French difficulties with Yugoslavia multiplied during the summer and autumn of 1936. The Yugoslavs had been moving away both from France and the Little Entente for a considerable time. When the aged and infirm Marshal Franchet d'Esperey returned from Belgrade in May 1936, having been sent by Daladier to reawaken memories of the French liberation of the Balkans in 1918, he reported signs that the Yugoslavs were intimidated by German tactics and urged that the

French mount an energetic military and diplomatic campaign. The more immediate problem in Belgrade was Yugoslav relations with Rome. Yugoslavia had suffered badly from its participation in sanctions against Italy and expected that once freed from military action in Ethiopia, the Italians would take their revenge. Milan Stojadinović, the Yugoslav prime minister and foreign minister, felt that he could not afford to affront his larger and stronger neighbour and when the Duce opened his campaign of conciliation, he found the door at least half-way open. In September, a bilateral trade agreement was signed, and in November Mussolini offered the Yugoslavs a treaty of friendship. By this time, of course, the Ciano–Neurath protocols were signed, and Mussolini was rethinking the Italian position in the Balkans not just with regard to France but to Germany as well.

Political as well as economic factors were pulling the Yugoslavs away from France. The Spanish Civil War and difficulties with Communists at home intensified the government's anti-Bolshevism and Prince Paul, in particular, became preoccupied with the Soviet menace. Closely related to the former Russian imperial family and surrounded by White Russian émigrés, he feared the spread of Soviet influence, and possible Yugoslav involvement in a war against Germany because of the Franco-Soviet alliance. He had little sympathy with either Beneš' or Titulescu's pro-Soviet orientation and found more in common with the Balkan League members, especially Turkey, than with Yugoslavia's Little Entente partners, Czechoslovakia and Romania. This became clear when Beneš, worried by Czechoslovakia's isolation, revived Titulescu's French alliance project in September 1936. The French warned that they would consider such a pact only if the Little Entente was transformed into an alliance against any aggressor. Beneš was rich in suggestions on how this might be done, but neither the Yugoslavs nor the Romanians were interested in turning the Little Entente into a tight alliance, least of all into an anti-German alliance. The Yugoslav *rapprochement* with Italy and Paul's anti-Bolshevism made them less than sympathetic to Beneš' proposals. The latters' warnings to the French and Mussolini's November 'Axis' speech, as well as the knowledge that the Czechs were considering a bilateral agreement with Germany, prompted Delbos to respond to Beneš' demand for an alliance with the Little Entente. It was a reluctant decision and linked to the prior creation of an alliance between the three Little Entente members. It was for negative rather than positive reasons that in December 1936 the *Quai d'Orsay* began to press actively for a French–Little Entente pact, intended to provide some measure of protection for Czechoslovakia against German attack.

The Soviet Union played an important part in the calculations of both the French and Little Entente powers. The outbreak of the Spanish

Civil War led to increased Soviet pressure in Paris for military staff talks while making the French ministers, with few exceptions, ever more reluctant to entertain them. Hitler singled out France as providing an advanced base for Soviet intervention in Spain and played on the possibility of a Bolshevik victory in France. His references to French domestic politics gave added point to Blum's conversations with Schacht, and increased the premier's anxiety to negotiate a general disarmament agreement with the Germans. 'But if Chancellor Hitler really wants to deliver France from the Soviet danger, I am going to tell you what would be the most sure method', Blum told Schacht. 'It would be to deliver France from the fear of German danger.'[30] Although the Blum–Schacht discussions produced no follow-up, they did succeed in alarming the Russians, who tried to force the French to open military conversations by warning of a possible German attack on France. When Litvinov met Blum in Geneva in early October 1936, he was able, because of the stalemate in the Locarno talks, to extract a promise of future negotiations. Blum agreed that after these negotiations were concluded, or when it became clear that they would not be held (which was increasingly likely), France would consider a pact involving the USSR, Poland, and the Little Entente, and would begin unofficial military conversations with Russia. In Paris, there was a raging battle between Pierre Cot, the air minister, and the French general staff regarding the negotiation of a military pact with Moscow. Cot wanted to associate the revival of the Little Entente accords with an *entente* with the Soviet Union and was, in fact, preparing for a trip to Bucharest to negotiate for Soviet air passage to Czechoslovakia. Quite apart from the high command's distrust of the Comintern and French Communist party, Delbos and his chief advisers remained distinctly cool about the Soviet connection. They pointed to warnings from London that closer relations with Britain would be jeopardized if a new strategic convention was concluded beyond the 1935 Franco-Soviet pact. They believed, along with the military, that the revival in any form of the Titulescu proposals would alienate the Yugoslavs, not to mention the Italians, and make negotiations with the Little Entente more difficult. Most important of all, there was still hope for an arrangement with Germany, which a military convention with Moscow would make impossible.

The result of the showdown between the Cot and Daladier factions at an inter-ministerial meeting on 6 November was a compromise. It was agreed to negotiate a pact with the Little Entente simultaneously with a mutual aid pact between the three countries. Despite the

[30] *DDF*, 2nd ser., Vol. III, No. 213.

accumulating evidence to the contrary, the general staff clung to its hope that Italy and Poland could be convinced to buttress this refurbishment of France's eastern ties. At the same time, Blum's promises to Litvinov were not without issue. While unwilling to sanction Cot's overtures on the air front or to allow the air minister to move on his own, the meeting agreed that the Soviets should be asked, through the military attachés, to define their concept of mutual aid. The conversations between General Schweisguth and the new Soviet military attaché in Paris, General Semenov, for a military agreement, began in January 1937 and were difficult from the start. Neither the approaches to the Little Entente countries nor to the Soviet Union met with success during the first half of the year. The simultaneous Anglo-French attempt to open talks with Hitler proved even more discouraging. Discussing France's position with William Bullitt a month after Blum's resignation in June, 1937, foreign minister Delbos told the American ambassador:

> Insofar as he [Delbos] could foresee the future, the position that France would take would depend entirely on the position of England. France would not undertake to fight Germany and Italy. The position of France would be the same as her position in the Spanish affair. If England should wish to stand firmly by the side of France against Germany and Italy, France would act. If England should continue to hold aloof, France could not act. France would never be caught in the position of having the Soviet Union as her only ally.[31]

This was the principle that would guide French policy right through to the outbreak of war in 1939.

V

In London, after March 1936, there was considerable confusion about Britain's future policy. For the most part, pre-crisis politics were simply recycled. Added to the difficulties with Germany were those with Japan, which had refused naval parity with Britain and the US and left the London Naval Conference and, more recently, the difficulties with Italy. Security in the Mediterranean was critical for Britain's lines of communication and supply routes to its east-of-Suez possessions. In response to the German challenge, it was decided to implement the already debated rearmament programme, but also to encourage Hitler to follow up his March peace plan. It was agreed that Britain would have to win time until it could negotiate with Germany from a position of strength. Some policymakers looked to a *modus vivendi* only until Britain

[31] O. H. Bullitt (ed.), *For the President, Personal and Secret* (Boston, MA, 1972), 222.

reached a point of comparative safety; more optimistic politicians believed there could be an acceptable settlement of German claims. United in their belief that war must be avoided, neither ministers nor their advisers could decide how this was best done. No one knew what Hitler's ultimate objectives were, or even what he wanted in the short-term. When would Germany be ready for war? When would Britain reach that point of comparative safety when negotiations could be carried out on equal terms? The Foreign Office feared German action before 1939; Vansittart, admittedly a pessimist, spoke of 1937. The defence chiefs thought there would be no danger until 1942. In the committees created to consider defence policy, such fundamental differences of opinion were either not addressed or were postponed in favour of short-term solutions that left open future options. Matters were not improved by an ailing and fatigued prime minister, Stanley Baldwin, and the lack of a clear lead from the foreign secretary, Anthony Eden.

No one questioned that Britain had to rearm, but how quickly and to what extent was a matter for debate. The new rearmament programme, prepared before the Rhineland reoccupation, was presented to the Commons on 10 March. Three days later, the former attorney general, Sir Thomas Inskip, valued by some for his legal training and administrative experience, was appointed to the new position of minister for the co-ordination of defence. He was thought a 'sound' appointment who, unlike Churchill, who wanted the job, would neither clash with the heads of the services nor upset the continentals. The appointment was described 'justifiably, though without originality, as the most extraordinary since Caligula made his horse a consul'.[32] On 21 April, a new budget was introduced raising taxes to cover the higher defence expenditure. It was well within the limits of what was thought to be politically acceptable The Defence Requirements Committee (DRC) report, on which it was based, had underlined the dangers of fighting a war on three fronts; the Foreign Office was called on to prevent such a catastrophe. The DRC pointed out that Britain had only one ally: 'our long-range policy should be so aligned that we can never get into a position where we would not have a certainty of French military support'.[33] Britain needed the French army to contain Germany. The Third Deficiency Programme of 1936 (the February and March 1934 programmes were intended only to bring the services up to standards previously set), despite its name, represented Britain's first major step towards the modernization and expansion of its forces. It

[32] A. J. P. Taylor, *English History, 1914–1945* (Oxford, 1965), 391.
[33] Defence Requirement Committee Report, 37, para. 18.

was a modest start. Though the costs went beyond the very cautious limits recommended in 1934, when the total estimates for 1935–1936 were set for £124 million, they were carefully calculated to appear reasonable.[34] Chamberlain was considering a loan to help cover costs but Treasury officials feared taking any inflationary risks. The same caution characterized the treatment of the 'shadow factory' scheme, created in 1934. This involved placing a small number of orders with firms not usually dealing with military production, in return for their preparations for rapid conversion and expansion, if needed for war mobilization. It was now agreed, despite the decision to do nothing to interfere with normal production, that some of this 'shadow' capacity would have to be put into operation in the near future.

The DRC proposals offered a balanced expansion programme for all three services. Britain's global supremacy rested on her naval power. But the Japanese challenge in the Pacific, and the possibility of a simultaneous war with Germany and Japan, required not the present one-power naval standard but a two-power standard. As this was thought impractical in terms of finance, shipyard space, material, and men, nothing was said of this new requirement in the parliamentary 'White Paper'. The new three-year programme proposed building five capital ships, five cruisers, and four aircraft carriers between 1936 and 1939, a flotilla of destroyers in 1936–1937 and a further flotilla of destroyers in alternate years up to 1942. In fact, only two capital ships would be laid down in 1936. In May, the existing building programme was accelerated. The Admiralty warned that more would have to be done to bring the navy up to standards that all agreed were already outdated and inadequate. The Admiralty favoured keeping up the DRC tempo unless Japan slowed her building programme or the Foreign Office could put Britain on better terms with Germany—in short foreign policy had to make up for naval weakness. The air force remained the favoured service. Provision had already been made for its expansion in May 1935; there was strong backing for the completion of the Scheme C programme which provided for a first line strength of 123 squadrons (1,512 aircraft) by April 1937. Intelligence sources indicated that Germany would have at least 2,000 front-line aircraft by that date and so it was necessary, for deterrence purposes, to increase the offensive power of the RAF.

[34] N. H. Gibbs, *Grand Strategy, Vol. I* (London 1976), 65. The estimates for 1936 through 1940 were as follows:
1936: £50,700,000
1937: £80,800,000
1938: £101,500,000
1939: £80,500,000
1940: £73,000,000

The planning period in the new 1936 programme was extended from 1937 to 1939, which was an arbitrary date as there was no agreement as to when Germany would be ready for war, or when Britain would attain the required position to negotiate from strength. Light bombers already on order were to be replaced with medium bombers, and the aircraft establishment of some squadrons increased in order to expand the overall size of the bomber element in the Metropolitan Air Force. In addition, the overall first line strength of the RAF would be increased by 182 aeroplanes, and money appropriated for war reserves of material and personnel omitted in the earlier expansion programmes.

There was little further ministerial debate about either the naval or air force recommendations, but the army estimates proved more contentious. In addition to maintaining garrisons overseas and providing for the military share in home defence, the DRC report recommended the creation of a Field Force, the term used in preference to Expeditionary Force with its unfortunate Great War connotations, consisting of 155,000 men provided with modern armaments and material. Part of this force would be available for continental service within a week of its mobilization and the remainder a week later. The Field Force would be reinforced by twelve Territorial Divisions and £26 million was allotted for the modernization that this would require. It was accepted that three years was not enough time to carry out the entire programme. As a result, the whole question of raising, equipping, and, most important, deploying the Territorial Army, was postponed, and nothing was said in the White Paper presented to Parliament. This postponement left unresolved the continuing disagreement over the future shape of Britain's defence posture. The army had long been the least favoured of the services and the easiest target for Treasury economies. With the turn to rearmament, Chamberlain, as chancellor of the exchequer, emerged as the most influential voice in ministerial debates over strategy. He argued that Britain could not simultaneously fight in Europe and in the Far East. As previously, Chamberlain focused on Nazi Germany as the main threat to British security. He believed that the air force, rather than the army, was the more effective deterrent to German attack. No power would dare to challenge Britain if it had an air force which could be converted from a 'defensive organ into a weapon of aggression with unprecedented powers of destruction'.[35] It would be easier to check Germany by building up Britain's defensive and striking air strength,

[35] Quoted in Gaines Post, Jr., *Dilemmas of Appeasement: British Deterrence and Defense, 1934–1937* (Ithaca, NY, 1993), 169.

rather than by equipping the Territorial Army for war on the continent. This would involve no deaths on the scale of 1914–1918, always a key consideration for Chamberlain. 'It was for consideration whether, from the point of view of a deterrent', Chamberlain argued, 'a strong offensive air force was not more effective than a Field Force which could not be put in the field for two weeks'.[36] If there were a war, he claimed, Germany would be able to occupy the Low Countries with terrifying speed and could establish air bases before the British army arrived.

If Chamberlain had succeeded, though he was blocked by Anthony Eden and the Foreign Office, he would have liked to warn the French that they should not count on reinforcements of the Field Force. In any case, there would be no repetition of the continental commitment of the Great War. Chamberlain was supported by Lord Swinton, the secretary of state for air, and by Lord Weir, a prominent Scottish industrialist and one of the founding fathers of the RAF, who, at Chamberlain's urging, had been added to the committee of ministers considering the DRC's recommendations. Chamberlain expected, too, that the newly appointed minister for defence co-ordination, Sir Thomas Inskip, would back his preference for an air, over a land deterrent. His strategic argument found some support in the War Office where there was less than unanimity about a future continental role for the army. Basil Liddell Hart, a highly influential journalist and commentator on defence issues, argued that the French army alone could make France and Belgium safe from a German invasion, on the grounds that a successful attacker would need three times the manpower of the defender, and so there was no need for a large British continental army. Air power could be used at the start of the war and the army held in reserve for imperial defence.

Chamberlain's arguments had a strong political *raison d'être* that also attracted fellow ministers. Rearmament was unpopular with the electorate and few voters were prepared to contemplate a new continental commitment of 1914–1918 proportions. Given the Opposition's slogan, 'Not a single penny for this government's rearmament programme', it was thought that there was little use in trying to build a coalition for rearmament, or even trying to explain the difficulties of the international situation to political enemies. On the contrary, the government would use its efforts to seek peace with Germany as a way of circumventing popular opposition to rearmament. Chamberlain, already acknowledged as Baldwin's successor, thought that if the Foreign Office, which he found wanting in energy, did its job properly, an

[36] Quoted in R. A. C. Parker, *Chamberlain and Appeasement*, 277.

agreement with Germany could be reached and a limited rearmament effort would be sufficient. In his view, Britain could rearm without interfering with the domestic economy and endangering the rise in the standard of living which the Conservative party had achieved and upon which Chamberlain's own considerable reputation rested. Chamberlain wanted 'business as usual'. There was to be no reduction in normal civilian activity or in the export trades and no interference with either management or labour. 'The maintenance of our economic stability is an essential element in our "defensive strength"', Edward Bridges, a senior official at the Treasury, wrote in December 1937, 'a fourth arm of defence'.[37] If Britain rearmed too rapidly, abandoned balanced budgets and accepted a condition of permanent deficits in its balance of payments, it would sacrifice its future safety.

The extent and pacing of rearmament was consequently determined by the domestic preoccupations of the government rather than by appraisal of the foreign threat. As there was little consensus between the services and the Foreign Office on the nature, urgency, and timing of this threat, Chamberlain's preoccupations shaped the ministerial agenda. His arguments were persuasive, clear, concise, and logically consistent. Fellow ministers were impressed by Chamberlain's energy and his unusual degree of certainty about the correctness of his views. The question of whether these views were strategically sound was not really debated.

The counter-case was put by Duff Cooper, the secretary of state for the army, and by the chiefs of staff and the Foreign Office. It had the support of Lord Hankey, the experienced secretary to the Committee of Imperial Defence, and Vansittart at the Foreign Office, a far more forthright critic of Chamberlain than Eden. Duff Cooper, whom Chamberlain dismissed as lazy, lightweight, and frivolous, demanded more money for the regular army and for equipping at least four Territorial Army divisions. Once again, the critical decisions were postponed, and the fundamental issues raised by the air vs. army debate, with all its ramifications, including Britain's policy towards France, were left undecided. Following Chamberlain's suggestion, the whole question of the army's role was referred to a future committee. By the time the subject was reconsidered, Chamberlain had succeeded Baldwin as prime minister.

Rearmament, so differently handled in Berlin and in London, was only one side of the coin; the Foreign Office was charged simultaneously with

[37] Cited in Robert Self, *Neville Chamberlain: A Biography* (Aldershot, 2007), 268. I am grateful to Professor George Peden for providing further clarification on the provenance of this quotation.

the task of securing a general settlement with Germany that might make the whole arms race unnecessary. Some Foreign Office officials saw no reason to offer further concessions to Germany in order to secure an agreement that would bring few positive advantages to Britain. Vansittart advised waiting until Britain rearmed and could argue from a position of strength and not be bullied by Germany. Cabinet ministers, however, were anxious to make a start on talks while Hitler was still favourably disposed towards Britain. Throughout the summer and autumn of 1936, the 'great German debate' continued in London.

British policy remained unclear, confused and, above all, unsuccessful. This was not due to any lack of advice. British visitors of all political complexions travelled to Berlin and conversed with Hitler, Göring, Schacht, or other senior Nazis. Vansittart himself visited the German capital for the Olympics, much to the surprise of the Nazi leaders who were well informed of his hostile views. He was received by Hitler. Once back in London, he wrote one of his familiar verbose and rambling discourses, studded with fine phrases but ultimately inconclusive. The 'Great Man', i.e. Hitler, remained a mystery whose ultimate intentions and desires were impossible to predict. Yet Vansittart took hope from Hitler's chameleon-like personality; he might yet 'opt for peace'. The permanent under-secretary claimed that he had tried to convince all his German interlocutors, including Hitler, that there had to be a return to normality, with a political settlement before an economic one, and that the 'area of appeasement', still a word with only positive connotations, should be as wide as possible.

While the British debated what steps should be taken to get Hitler to follow-up the March 1936 peace offer, there was the question of Anglo-French relations to be addressed, and the implications of the Popular Front victory in May. The British ambassador in Paris, Sir George Clerk, an experienced diplomat, but whose talents hardly equipped him for the choicest post in the service, warned that with a Popular Front government in power, France would sink into the mire of domestic upheaval and Socialist ruin. Far less anxious Foreign Office officials thought that Léon Blum and Yvon Delbos might prove more malleable than their predecessors, and that they would acquiesce in Britain's leadership. It was recognized in London, moreover, that Hitler would try to exploit any political differences between Britain and France in the interests of an Anglo-German agreement. 'If Hitler's policy appears obscure I think it is only because we are inclined to lose sight of his sole and ultimate objective', Orme Sargent, a key senior official at the Foreign Office wrote, 'as soon as we recognize that the isolation of France is the one and only thing he is working for, all his manoeuvres become clear'.[38] Throughout the summer, the British waited for a sign from Berlin that Hitler was interested in a comprehensive agreement, or was ready to take up his March 'peace offers'. There was considerable reluctance about a three-power meeting with France and Belgium to work out terms to be offered to Hitler as a replacement for the Locarno guarantees. If the Führer refused to negotiate, the British would be forced to expand the range of the military consultations with the French and the Belgians. When a pessimistic Eden returned from the July 1936 League Council meeting which acknowledged the failure of sanctions, he found his colleagues cool about proposed meetings with its two partners unless the Germans were informed. Ministers insisted that the talks be held in London and that their frame of reference be narrowly drawn. The cabinet would accept a replacement Locarno treaty guaranteeing the security of the western powers, but would not consider an alliance with France or any formal commitment in Eastern Europe. It also demanded further restrictions on the League's coercive powers in order to avoid a repetition of the Ethiopian fiasco. There was more enthusiasm for further consideration of colonial concessions to Germany.

The three-power London meeting lasted for one day; its short concluding communiqué called for a five-power conference which would negotiate a new Locarno treaty that would pave the way for a 'general settlement'. The British succeeded in keeping the negotiating ball in play and on their own terms, that is, concentrating on a western pact. As always, the British felt that the French guarantees to the successor states were a barrier to an agreement with Germany, but they could not question their legality, or modify their own guarantee to France. The chiefs of staff were more insistent than the Foreign Office that it was essential to protect Britain from being involved in an Eastern European war, even if France was attacked by Germany. On 29 July, addressing a group of Tory back-benchers concerned with the question of rearmament, including Winston Churchill and Austen Chamberlain, Baldwin admitted that 'none of us know what goes on in that strange man's [Hitler] mind', but added that 'We all know the German desire, and he has come out with it in his book, to move East, and if he should move East I should not break my heart.'[39] The cabinet agreed that 'our policy ought to be framed on the basis that we could not help Eastern Europe. We ought, however, to resist by force any attempt against our own Empire or Flanders.'[40] Unwilling to give Hitler a public green light, the

38 TNA: PRO, FO 371/19906, C3879/4/18, minute by Sargent, 28 May 1936.
39 *DBFP*, 2nd ser., Vol. XVII, No. 36, editors' note 7.
40 Quoted in Parker, *Chamberlain and Appeasement*, 69.

government's abandonment of Eastern Europe was stated in ambivalent terms. In a memorandum prepared under Lord Halifax's instruction while deputizing for the vacationing Anthony Eden, the Foreign Office advised, 'We should decline to disinterest ourselves from the East and Centre of Europe and continue to insist on the need for a general settlement, while urging France not to wreck a Western settlement by maintaining impossible demands in the East and Centre.'[41] British officials sought ways to revise the Franco-Soviet pact to make it acceptable to the Germans.

The cabinet's views were summed up in a note of 19 November, which the editors of *Documents on British Foreign Policy* pick out as 'perhaps the most important document in this volume, for it provided the basic definition of Great Britain's attitude towards German policy and aspirations and a point of reference in negotiations for the next year or more'.[42] The note reaffirmed Britain's desire for guarantees from France and Germany, but insisted that Britain and France had to carry out their obligations under the Covenant. It was again proposed that the Council of the League was the best body to pass judgement on the fact of aggression, but the British agreed to consider alternatives as the Germans demanded. Other questions affecting the peace could be discussed if progress was made with the Five-Power Conference. There were differences between the chiefs of staff and the Foreign Office, with regard to central and Eastern Europe and over the 'neutrality' of Belgium. In both instances, Eden was more solicitous of the French position than others. The chiefs of staff discounted French views that Belgian neutrality would have 'grave consequences' for Britain, arguing that the new Belgian position would be to Britain's advantage. Similarly, they argued that appeasement in Western Europe, 'a necessity for British security', would not be achieved if too much consideration was given to 'Russian interests'. Eden was able to keep the connection between a western pact and a general settlement, the latter also involving central and Eastern Europe, though the Foreign Office was forced to redraft this and other sections to make it less categorical.

This hardly pleased the more strident critics of current policy. Vansittart registered his disapproval; he claimed that the essential object of the draft was 'to get into conversations with the Germans'. 'That is a perversion. The essential object is to get a good, durable, defensible treaty with the Germans. And we shall only get that by firmness. There is nothing of that in all the watery amendments suggested.'[43] In a mood of rising frustration, different scenarios were discussed as the hopeless

[41] TNA: PRO, CAB 23/83, 6 July 1936. [42] *DBFP*, 2nd ser., Vol. XVII, ix.
[43] *DBFP*, 2nd ser., Vol. XVII, No. 389, footnote 1.

negotiations over the western pact continued. Senior Foreign Office officials thought it better to let the negotiations lapse rather than accept an emasculated compromise. While the diplomats pressed, without success, for faster rearmament, the chiefs of staff, doubtful of the value of France as an ally, continued to insist that the Foreign Office reduce Britain's overseas commitments. The search for a formula acceptable to the Germans proved to be purely academic. Hitler was not interested. On 8 December, Ribbentrop told the foreign secretary that the November memorandum was 'a grievous disappointment to the Chancellor'.[44] Six months of negotiation had produced nothing.

VI

Throughout these months, the debate over how to get the Germans into a 'general settlement' continued. Against a deteriorating security backdrop, complicated by the Spanish Civil War and the problem of Italy in the eastern Mediterranean, those arguing the case for financial or commercial concessions to Germany began to be heard. The so-called 'economic appeasers' were not a single or united group, and were found both within and outside official circles. Despite their many differences, they shared a belief that Germany's financial and economic difficulties, which were widely known, could be used as a means to promote a general political settlement. At the least, it was thought that offers of economic and financial assistance might strengthen the hands of the so-called 'moderates', who supposedly were trying to deflect Hitler from embarking on a massive armaments programme. If Germany became a partner in a much broader economic unit in which its 'legitimate' economic grievances would be met, there would be less reason for an aggressive foreign policy and positive incentives for 'normal behaviour'. Eden and Vansittart were both insistent that there should be no economic assistance 'without political return', a position at first shared by Neville Chamberlain. The arguments of the economic appeasers, pressed on Eden in the summer of 1936, became the subject of active debate in December. The lack of any progress in the five-power talks, and intelligence that the further and more rapid expansion of the German army was inevitable, gave point to the search for alternative means to institute a dialogue with Hitler. Various sources, including the air staff's intelligence directorate, predicted that the *Luftwaffe* would number 2,500 first-line machines by April 1939, while Britain's 'Scheme F' aimed at a first-line strength of about 1,700 aircraft by the same date.[45] The economic argument particularly appealed to Neville

[44] *DBFP*, 2nd ser., Vol. XVII, No. 455. [45] Post, *Dilemmas of Appeasement*, 255.

Chamberlain, frustrated by Baldwin's continuing hold on the premiership (in December, the prime minister was almost totally immersed in the abdication crisis)[46] and by what he believed to be the dilatory and obstructive ways of the Foreign Office. Inskip spoke for Chamberlain and others in the cabinet when he argued that the policy of addressing Germany's economic conditions at least held out 'some hope' of progress.

Within the Foreign Office, the case for economic appeasement was championed by Frank Ashton-Gwatkin and Gladwyn Jebb, members of the small economic relations section instituted in 1932 to strengthen the economic and financial competence of the Foreign Office. Ashton-Gwatkin argued that 'A weak, hysterical individual, heavily armed, is a danger to himself and others' while from 'a purely commercial point of view, a strong Germany would be one of our best customers'.[47] Ashton-Gwatkin joined with the young Jebb in setting out the arguments for encouraging German economic dominance in central and south-east Europe, and for the return of the ex-German colonies as a way of promoting peace. Jebb, significantly, was particularly fearful of the chaos that would result if the Nazis were overthrown or militarily defeated and a semi-Communist Germany emerged, prepared to join ranks with Soviet Russia. This paper sparked a considerable debate in diplomatic circles about whether it was better to have a 'lean' or 'fat' Germany. The debate rumbled on not just for months but for years and spread well beyond the walls of the Foreign Office.

Powerful backing for an economic offer came from Sir Frederick Leith-Ross, the chief economic advisor to the government, who reported to Chamberlain at the Treasury. Leith-Ross returned to London in July 1936 after almost a year's absence on an economic mission in the Far East and rapidly became a key figure in the governmental debate. He was convinced that British prosperity was ultimately tied to the international and not the domestic market, and that a turn from the existing protectionist and imperial preference system was becoming imperative. He feared, moreover, that an armaments race would create an inflationary situation making change and growth impossible and locking Britain into a tight protectionist structure. Germany was already Britain's best customer outside of the empire. Leith-Ross's backing for

[46] On 10 December 1936, Edward VIII abdicated the throne in preference to giving up Mrs Wallis Simpson, an American divorcée. The marriage question took up the attention of Baldwin as well as other political and Church leaders. Winston Churchill defended the king, adding to his reputation, already shaken by his opposition to the India Act, as an unreliable politician who lacked common sense.

[47] TNA: PRO, FO 371/18851, C7752/55/18, note by Ashton-Gwatkin on Germany's economic position.

some forms of financial and commercial concessions to Germany to assist that country's return to the international economy, along with his contacts with Schacht, were of considerable importance in the search for a new arrangement with the Germans in the winter of 1936–1937. Many, particularly in Liberal and Labour but also in Conservative circles, were urging that revisions should be made in British policy to encourage an expansion in world trade. Lord Lothian, the future ambassador to the United States, was a tireless critic of the protection and imperial preference system, and a leading proponent of concessions to Germany. Articles appeared in *The Times, The Economist*, the *Quarterly Review* and other journals sympathetic to the older liberal trading tradition. Economic appeasers and League enthusiasts, and they were often the same individuals, wanted the League to take up the question of raw material shortages and standard of living problems as a way of refocusing the League's activities and, with American participation, revitalize the much battered Geneva system.[48] It was proposed that Britain take the lead in establishing workable international agreements and encouraging international cartels that would de-politicize and de-nationalize the world economy. German participation was not only essential to their success but would prove a corrective to its current autarchic and rearmament policies. If left outside the western trading system, Germany might well return to its Rapallo orientation, creating a closed economic structure of its own.

The summer of 1936 was a particularly auspicious time to press for a reconsideration of Britain's financial and economic future. First, though the country's general economic situation was encouraging, the balance of payments surplus achieved in 1935 was being rapidly eroded (the surplus balance of £32 million in December 1935 became a deficit of £18 million in December 1936). Chamberlain hoped to reduce this accumulating deficit by encouraging foreign export customers to buy more British manufactures. One way would be to make a British loan to Germany to buy raw materials from the mainly agricultural and primary product producing countries, aiding both their economic recovery and ability to buy British (but not, presumably, German) goods. Second, what was known about Germany's mounting financial and economic problems encouraged hopes that concessions would be welcome to Berlin and might produce the elusive political breakthrough. Eden and Blum shared the illusion that Germany's difficulties could be used to create an arms limitation agreement within the framework of an

[48] This, too, was the advice of the League of Nations' Economic and Financial Organization. See Patricia Clavin, 'Europe and the League of Nations', in Robert Gerwarth (ed.), *Twisted Paths: Europe 1914–1945* (Oxford, 2007), 342–343.

economic settlement. Eden conceded that it was better to have a reasonably fat Germany with a political settlement than a desperately lean one left outside. He was cautious, however, and more concerned than his economic advisers that commercial concessions might encourage the German political penetration of south-eastern Europe, and a strengthening of its military position at British expense. The question was whether it was better to aid the Nazi regime so as not to drive it to extremes or leave it with its unsolved economic problems that might deter rearmament. The answer was not obvious at the time.

There were strong ties between British and German banking and commercial circles which resulted in important voices both in the City of London and among British exporters favouring an agreement. It was mainly for political purposes that the Anglo-French schemes were launched for reviving the ailing German economy. The appeal of long-term loans or preferential trading arrangements was tied to German willingness to enter a general European settlement. Some of the proposals were based on suggestions made in conversations with Schacht. As long as he remained a central figure in the Nazi establishment, it was thought in London that co-operation might encourage Germany to return to more orthodox economic practices and to participate in the world economy. These hopes persisted well after the announcement of the Four-Year Plan in 1936 and the signs that Schacht was losing out in the competition for Hitler's favour.

During the latter part of 1936, the cabinet proved reluctant to offer economic and financial assistance to Germany in anticipation of a future political settlement. There was no disagreement on this point between the economic departments and the Foreign Office. Officials in the Treasury, Board of Trade, and the Ministry of Agriculture were, moreover, strongly opposed to any modification of the Ottawa preferential structure, and reluctant to enter into raw material sharing schemes. They showed little interest in the programmes of the 'keep Germany fat' school. When discussing Schacht's commercial and colonial proposals, there was little enthusiasm at the Dominions or Colonial Offices for following up his initiatives. In general, the Treasury and Board of Trade refrained from using economic means to achieve political ends and jealously guarded their own jurisdictions. The Treasury, for instance, vetoed the Foreign Office Economic Section's recommendations that the British government renounce its 'most favoured nation' rights in central and south-eastern Europe to smooth the way for a German-led preferential area in the region. The Treasury and Board of Trade combined to block Yugoslav attempts to secure credits to purchase arms and military clothing, or to secure tariff concessions. In the Baltic, where Britain still enjoyed a lead over the Germans in imports, the

Board of Trade refused to impose clearings that would improve Britain's negative trade balance and strengthen its trading links at German expense. In this instance, the opposition of home producers to imports from the Baltic and Scandinavia were judged more important than foreign policy considerations.

Why, in the light of these observations, did the cabinet then repeatedly come back to the possibilities of economic concessions to Germany as a way of encouraging political dialogue? The government's high sensitivity to its own domestic financial and commercial concerns led to the belief that Hitler would also be influenced by the difficulties he faced in these domains. Neville Chamberlain took seriously the reports from the Department of Overseas Trade's industrial intelligence centre during 1937, which stated that Germany's foreign exchange difficulties, lack of gold reserves, and foodstuffs shortages would bring the economy to crisis point in the near future. As is now known, these observations were based on well authenticated reports, but Hitler's response was to speed up rearmament rather than curtail expenditure. Even after his demotion, Schacht kept the hopes of economic and colonial appeasement alive. In the autumn of 1936, in response to Schacht's suggestions, made in Paris, that Germany might join the Tripartite agreement talks between France, Britain, and the United States, Chamberlain proposed a joint Treasury and Foreign Office investigation into possible economic concessions to Germany, with the intention of increasing Germany's export potential. Unwilling to allow the French to take the initiative in these matters, Chamberlain and Leith-Ross decided that they should raise these questions directly with the German ministers. They believed that Schacht's emphasis on the return of colonies was only a way of securing more significant financial concessions. When in December the British took up the Schacht initiative, it was thought that trading concessions would prove more productive and acceptable to Hitler than any colonial concessions that might be offered. At the same time, the government gave its support to a League of Nations enquiry into the world trade in raw materials, as means of facilitating greater access for the 'have-not' nations without abandoning the Ottawa preferential schemes.

There was certainly less enthusiasm for colonial, as distinct from economic, concessions. On 9 March 1936, only two days after Hitler publicly referred to his interest in Germany's former imperial territories, the cabinet created a committee chaired by Lord Plymouth, the parliamentary under-secretary for the colonies, to report on the feasibility of colonial concessions. The Plymouth committee spent two months considering the subject. It had long been anticipated that the Germans would raise the colonial question and various efforts were made to decide what British policy should be. The answers were always ambivalent; departments were divided on the necessity of concessions that were known to be highly unpopular in all sections of the political spectrum at home, not to speak of opposition in the dominions and colonies. Attention centred on the mandates because no transfer of British colonial possessions could be considered.

The Plymouth committee's massive report, reviewing the history of the colonial question and presenting the moral, legal, practical, and strategic objections to satisfying Germany's claims, concluded on an uncertain note. The committee members agreed that however generously Germany might be treated, she would not necessarily be diverted from her European aspirations by the return of her ex-colonies. If circumstances demanded it, Britain and France should transfer the Cameroons and Togoland. Tanganyika, the territory that interested Hitler most, was ruled out on strategic grounds (its loss would spoil the British air route from Cairo to the Cape) and would raise fierce objections from white South Africa and Southern Rhodesia. France, which opposed *Luftwaffe* bases in West Africa, would have to carry the main burden of satisfying the German claims, if they had to be met. The announcement made by Eden in the Commons on 27 July, that the question of the transfer of mandated territories raised 'insuperable problems' for which the government could find no solution, was in keeping with the report's conclusions but did not reflect the unanimous view of the cabinet. Chamberlain, Hoare, who had returned to the cabinet in June, and Halifax each favoured some form of territorial concession and insisted that the parliamentary statement be modified to convince Hitler that the door was open to future negotiations. Because it seemed to indicate that the subject of transfers was under discussion, the statement did little to reassure British opponents of colonial appeasement, particularly among Conservative party backbenchers, including Churchill and Austen Chamberlain. A parliamentary protest against any cession of mandates and a negative vote at the Conservative party conference in October, suggested that cession was not a practical proposition.

The main thrust of British diplomacy in the summer and autumn of 1936 was concentrated on securing a new western pact, but Schacht's conversation with Blum on 27 August put Germany's economic problems and the colonial question on the front burner again. The Foreign Office was well aware of Schacht's preoccupation with the question of foodstuffs and raw materials, and his long-held hopes for the reacquisition of colonies. From Berlin, Ambassador Phipps dismissed Schacht's hysterical warnings that unless Germany received satisfaction in this respect, there could be an explosion that would take the form of war.

The Foreign Office viewed Schacht's colonial campaign as part of a larger effort to 'divert the pent-up forces which are at present threatening the economic structure which he has so laboriously built-up and defended during the last three years'.[49] In France, where imperial interests were less vital than continental security, the Blum government was more willing to consider the question of colonial appeasement. Blum raised the issue with Eden when the latter passed through Paris on 20 September 1936. Eden was surprised and cautious about what Blum believed to be an official German initiative. Eden's response was distinctly cool. The Germans, he insisted, should be aware that Britain adhered to its parliamentary statement of 27 July precluding the transfer of territory. He suggested, however, that any formal German colonial demands could be included within proposals for the agenda of the next Locarno conference.

At the same time, the prospect of using commercial and financial inducements to persuade Germany to participate in a general settlement was very much alive in London. By the end of the year, both Leith-Ross and Chamberlain were prepared to follow up Schacht's hints that Germany's financial and raw material needs might provide the key to the elusive general settlement. They thought it important, as well, to correct Schacht's impression, due mainly to his conversation with Blum on 26–7 August, that Britain was reluctant to discuss colonial or economic concessions. Eden and his senior officials were less optimistic than the Treasury about the outcome of such exchanges. It was agreed that Leith-Ross should meet with Schacht on 2 February 1937 in order to clear the air. The Blum government, which had made various suggestions for trade concessions to Germany in the autumn of 1936, each of which had been rejected by Chamberlain, acquiesced in the British decision to take up the talks with Schacht. The Popular Front government was faced with a major financial crisis at the end of the year. The devaluation of the franc had not restored confidence in the economy. There was no sign of reinvestment in industry and, after a brief influx of capital in October, the outflow of funds resumed. The budget deficit for 1937 was projected at 4.8 million francs and the extra-budgetary deficit (arms and public works) at sixteen million francs.[50] The financial crisis was postponed only because of advances from the Bank of France. With only Britain in a position to address Germany's economic needs, Chamberlain knew that France could be relegated to a secondary negotiating position.

[49] Minute by Sargent, 3 June 1936, on a despatch from Phipps to Foreign Office commenting on the Kennedy–Schacht interview, quoted in A. J. Crozier, *Appeasement and Germany's Last Bid for Colonies* (Basingstoke, 1988), 177.

[50] Jackson, *The Popular Front in France*, 178.

Anxious to keep the goodwill of Britain, Blum was content to follow where the British led. On 23 December, Delbos told the German ambassador, Count Welczeck, of France's hopes for a *rapprochement* with Germany, and assured him of the warm support of the British and Americans. He told the sympathetic ambassador that Germany should have 'raw materials, colonies and loans, in return for which the only compensation required . . . was peace'.[51] At the same time, the highly experienced French ambassador in Berlin convinced the *Quai d'Orsay*, rightly, that Schacht was fighting for his political life. Even if he should succeed, Hitler was unlikely to see in African colonies anything more than a temporary diversion from his plans for expansion in Eastern Europe:

> It is only a pity that, while the president of the Reichsbank is prolix in the exposition of German demands . . . he is vague and brief regarding the contributions that the Reich could make. What concessions would Germany be disposed to make for the realization of a general, European settlement? Would she agree to sign a new Locarno, taking account of French undertakings towards Czechoslovakia and Russia? Would she envisage resuming one day the way of the League of Nations? Neither M. Schacht nor M. Hitler have ever spoken on this precisely and explicitly.[52]

While Blum had his doubts about Britain's economic appeasement strategy, neither he nor Delbos would allow such questions to disturb the recent improvement in Anglo-French relations.

As in London, there were divided views in Paris about the wisdom of economic and colonial concessions. The French government, however, was quick to disassociate itself from any proposal or statement that might alarm the British. Blum immediately repudiated the suggestion of the French financial attaché in London that the signatories of the Tripartite agreement should offer sufficient loan capital to the Reichsbank to create a long-term foreign exchange reserve, so that it could compete in the open market. The *Quai d'Orsay* assured the British that the minister of colonies, who, in a series of press interviews in January and February 1937, had ruled out any territorial adjustments to the French empire, spoke only for himself. These mixed signals from Paris convinced the British of the wisdom of acting unilaterally.

VII

It was agreed in London that Leith-Ross's meeting with Schacht was to be an informal and exploratory one. Eden, anxious that the Foreign

[51] *DGFP*, Ser. D, Vol. III, No.164 (Welczeck to von Neurath, 24 December 1936).
[52] *DDF*, 2nd ser., Vol. IV, No. 187 (François-Poncet to Delbos, 21 December 1936).

Office should not be by-passed, insisted on a prior meeting with Chamberlain and Leith-Ross to straighten out the lines of command. There was a clash in expectations between the principals. Eden and Sargent did not want any new discussion of colonial issues. Nor were they ready to entertain any financial proposals unless Germany was prepared to enter into political negotiations. Chamberlain, conversely, had broader and more ambitious goals in mind. He was prepared to accept Schacht's claim that he spoke in Hitler's name, and welcomed the financial talks as a way to move towards a general settlement. Chamberlain wanted to seize the moment and be in a position to control any subsequent negotiations. Leith-Ross met Schacht at Badenweiler on 2 February 1937. Schacht pressed for colonies, especially the Cameroons and Togoland, and claimed that Hitler had little interest in financial matters and would take advice. He spoke of preliminary steps for a relaxation of exchange controls, and even suggested that the position of the Jews might be alleviated in order to improve the economic position in Germany. He did not ask for a loan or for a new credit for stabilization purposes, but concentrated on the return of German colonies. In return, Schacht claimed that Hitler would co-operate in assuring peace for all of Europe. He would give assurances about non-aggression as regards Russia, if only indirectly, and he would accept not only a non-aggression pact, but a non-interference pact, with regard to Czechoslovakia. Even an arms limitation agreement was not ruled out. Schacht suggested that Britain, France, and Germany should continue these discussions and, if a basis for agreement was found, approach the United States and invite Roosevelt to summon a conference, where the Americans might contribute to world peace by cancelling war debts. It was clear from this exchange that Schacht was more interested in colonies than in any financial arrangements. This hardly accorded with the Foreign Office view. Eden's response to this, and subsequent public pronouncements about the Reich's need for colonies, was to express regret at the slow progress of negotiations for a new western pact, and to refer to the official statement on 15 February that the government had not, and was not considering any transfer of territory under British control to Germany. The Standstill agreement between the two countries was renewed on the old terms; British efforts to secure some relief from German cancellations of credit lines met with no success. The Germans threatened that, should the agreement not be renewed, they would cancel the payment of interest on the debt. From Britain's point of view, the talks were a fiasco. The long awaited German reply to the British memoranda of 4 and 19 November, with regard to the Five-Power Pact, was received in London on 13 March. The Germans insisted that they required assurances with regard to the Franco–Soviet pact, and the French pacts with Poland and Czechoslovakia as well. Eden concluded that the chances of reaching agreement on a basis for a Five-Power Pact 'were very small indeed'.

It was in this context that the members of the cabinet committee on foreign policy, together with Leith-Ross and Hankey, met to discuss the forthcoming Schacht–Leith-Ross conversations. Despite Eden's doubts that Schacht's views represented Hitler's policy, as well as his own aversion to colonial discussions, Chamberlain gained the consent of the cabinet committee to raise the possibility in Paris of ceding the predominately French mandates of Togoland and the Cameroons to Germany. Ministers insisted on some kind of compensation for France. Chamberlain had put the colonial question back on the diplomatic agenda and he kept it there for many months to come. He was following a blind alley.

The events of 1935–1936 left the British convinced of the need to reassess their policies in the light of the diplomatic and military implications of the Ethiopian and Rhineland crises. Their goals remained the same, to negotiate a general settlement with Germany, and prevent France from taking any action that would make this more difficult. It would be necessary to rearm until Britain could bargain from a position of strength. This consensus on long-range policy hardly disguised the indecision and confusion that characterized British thinking about how to proceed. The Mediterranean crisis had already upset long-term planning; the Rhineland magnified British disarray. 'In fact we haven't got a policy', Alexander Cadogan wrote in his diary, 'we merely wait and see what will happen to us next'.[53] Matters were not helped by Baldwin's near nervous breakdown at the start of the year, and Neville Chamberlain's increasing impatience to enter into his rightful inheritance. While cabinet committees met and debated, the initiative remained with an ever-more confident Hitler, who had decided on a policy of all-out rearmament whatever the economic costs. The many foreigners who came to the Olympic Games held in Berlin in August 1936 were given a brilliant demonstration of the unity and self-confidence of the new Reich. They knew, or suspected, that Hitler was preparing further action, but believed that it was all the more necessary to come to an agreement before he took such a move. Both in London and in Paris, rearmament gathered pace, but so did the effort to find a way to avoid an accelerating arms race and the hateful prospect of threatening war. Hitler and the western powers were moving in opposite directions.

[53] Sir Alexander Cadogan, *The Diaries of Sir Alexander Cadogan, O.M.*, ed. David Dilks (London, 1971), 25 September 1936.

B. 1937–1938: FATAL DECISIONS

I

In 1937, Hitler decided to launch the Reich on his policy of territorial aggrandizement. François-Poncet observed in a dispatch of 22 July 1937 that:

> Hitler devotes less and less time to public affairs. He spends more of his time at his house at Obersalzberg and much less in the capital city. He leaves his collaborators free to carry on in their own manner in those areas which they have seized for themselves. He concerns himself, insofar as he does, with foreign policy. Primarily, he occupies himself in new and grandiose construction projects, especially for the beautification of Berlin, which haunts his imagination.[54]

The Führer, if impulsive and temperamental, could also be extraordinarily patient. On the few occasions when he indulged in lengthy expositions of his ideas for the benefit of his followers, his arguments were rational and well developed. Hitler had the ability to respond flexibly to changes in the European situation without losing sight of his ultimate goals. This made him a formidable opponent. He was aware, moreover, of the conflicting currents in his entourage; ministers were constantly appealing to him for support, and he framed explanations of policy to convince and soothe his audience. Though not available for consultation on any regular basis, he had a shrewd idea of what was being done in the Reich in his name. A purposely remote figure in one sense, he was an omnipresent leader in another. This sense of omnipotence was reflected both in the reactions of German officials to his orders, and in the testimony of the foreign visitors whom he agreed to receive. He could charm, confuse, or even threaten, but none left his presence doubting his power. The outside world identified Hitler with the Reich, and the combination of leader and country appeared a formidable one.

As in the case of the absolute kings of old, foreign statesmen tried to influence Hitler through his advisers, knowing that what ultimately mattered was what Hitler thought. Both British and French intelligence identified at least two groups competing for his attention, although they attributed less importance to these divisions than their political masters. There were the radical extremists, such as Goebbels, Himmler, and Ribbentrop on the one side, and on the other, the

[54] *DDF*, 2nd ser., Vol. VI, No. 444 (François-Poncet to Delbos, 22 July 1937).

'moderates', Blomberg, Fritsch, and, above all, Göring. Most British politicians, more optimistic in this respect than their French counterparts, thought that Hitler could be persuaded by the 'moderates' to follow the path of conciliation and compromise. British policy in 1937 was shaped by this illusory hope. The reverberations of German power, present and future, were felt throughout Europe. Statesmen tried to enhance their countries' security through a combination of diplomacy and rearmament. While Hitler's interests remained mainly continental, his ministers, competing with one another, looked beyond Europe, in part to enhance their own reputations. Hitler was already focused on *Mitteleuropa* as the necessary first step towards territorial expansion in the East.

II

French intelligence sources gave inflated estimates of the Reich's existing and potential strength, above all in the air, and provided exaggerated impressions of the pace of German rearmament. Too little attention was paid to the difficulties involved in fulfilling projected schedules, though German problems, above all the lack of raw materials, were accurately reported. Each of the French services adopted 'worst case scenarios'; the overestimation of German capability owed as much to a sense of France's demographic and industrial inferiority, as to a misreading of the existing German situation. The fact that neither the French armaments nor the aviation industries could meet the demands of the 1936 programmes hardly encouraged optimism about the future. It was easy to blame delays on lack of funding. But the problems of converting industries to war production, even on a limited scale, were due primarily to the backwardness of France's industrial plant and to the tense relationship between the state, military authorities, and employers under the Popular Front governments.

In London, a better balanced but equally gloomy appraisal of Germany's military and air strength emerged towards the end of 1936. The intelligence services warned that the German army was being developed for total war, and that Germany was well ahead in the race for bomber superiority. Only the Admiralty, convinced that Berlin would stick to the Anglo-German naval agreement of 1935, felt confident that, as long as Britain did not have to face three naval enemies at once, and could continue building ships, the sea lanes were secure. In London, as in Paris, there was an exaggerated respect for totalitarian efficiency which neither democratic state could match under peacetime conditions. The *Deuxième Bureau*, for instance, rightly predicted that whatever the domestic hardship involved, the German rearmament programme would continue and there would be no internal upheavals. There was, moreover, a fundamental difference between a state determined to prepare for war and those arming in the hope of preserving peace. 'The Germans have a formula which is the preparation of the state for war. It is not necessary for us to go so far but it is essential that we are aware of what they are doing and take the necessary precautions', Daladier told the Chamber Army Commission in February 1937. 'We have not adopted a programme similar to M. Göring's Four-Year Plan and our economy is not a war economy. If we choose to adopt the war economy principle we must renounce an international currency, create an internal market and envisage an extremely harsh policy of restrictions. We cannot take this step.'[55] French rearmament was constrained by the country's continuing financial and economic difficulties. The British, though in a much stronger position, were rearming at a pace that allowed the economy to function normally without 'any interference with or reduction of production for civil and export trade'. Neville Chamberlain, as chancellor of the exchequer and then as prime minister, was convinced that British safety could be secured without any setback to the rising standard of living, which guaranteed the popularity of his party, and without any compulsory redirection of industry or labour.

There was no agreement over the question of when Germany would embark on a policy of expansion. The *Deuxième Bureau* believed that war might come as early as 1938, but neither Blum, Chautemps, nor their military advisers accepted this pessimistic appraisal. They believed there would be sufficient time to improve the state of French armaments and to work for a political and economic settlement with Germany that could postpone war or even prevent it. Nor was there agreement on timing in London. Chamberlain, backed by the service ministers and chiefs of staff, assumed there would be a considerable breathing space, even up to five years, during which it would be possible to negotiate a *rapprochement* with Germany from a position of increasing strength. A few alarmists thought Hitler might act as early as 1938. While all agreed about the rapid progress of German rearmament, nobody knew if and when Hitler intended to embark on offensive operations in Europe. Anglo-French uncertainty was hardly surprising, given that none of Hitler's own defence chiefs were sure of his future timetable. Just as Hitler was deciding that the problem of 'living space' would have to be solved in the near future, Britain and France were preparing to launch yet another effort to achieve the elusive general settlement. In an

[55] AAN, Commission de l'Armée, 16ème Legislature, Carton #15, Daladier testimony, 24 February 1937, quoted in Peter Jackson, *France and the Nazi Menace*, 2000, 109.

astonishingly short time, Germany had become, as so many French leaders had feared since 1919, the major threat to the peace of Europe. Yet few believed that war was inevitable.

Professor Klaus Hildebrand cites 1937 as Hitler's '*Entscheidungsjahr*', the year in which Hitler chose to embark on a policy of 'foreign adventure'. In anticipation, the Führer rejected all the western attempts at co-operation that might compromise his free hand in central and Eastern Europe. It was only in November 1937 that he revealed to his military chiefs his intentions of moving into Austria and Czechoslovakia, even without the British alliance, and before Germany's military preparations were complete. Hitler's domestic position was unassailable and his popularity in Germany high. External events favoured his expansionist aspirations. Mussolini had been successfully wooed. The army purges in the Soviet Union confirmed Hitler's low opinion of Russia's military power and his disdain for Moscow's attempts at *rapprochement*. Hitler was conscious of one pressing problem. His possible opponents had embarked on rearmament programmes and Germany's window of opportunity would be relatively short. Increasingly obsessed with his own mortality, time took on a new importance in Hitler's thinking.

Diplomatic planning for *Anschluss* continued. Arriving in Rome in January 1937 to discuss Spanish affairs, Göring made clear Hitler's hopes for Italian assistance in assuring Austrian adhesion to the Austro-German accord of 1936, with its implied acquiescence in German domination. In return, Germany would support Italian ambitions in the Mediterranean. Mussolini was hesitant; he was not ready to abandon Austria until his own diplomatic preparations in the Balkans were complete. A compromise was reached; Italy would urge the Austrians to base their policies on the July agreement, but Germany would not actually change the status of Austria without further consultation. Nothing was set down in writing and Göring did not secure the green light he sought. The Duce, however, agreed to visit Germany to meet Hitler.

On 22 and 23 April 1937, the Duce and Ciano, at a meeting in Venice, warned Schuschnigg that he should work with the Germans and avoid any co-operation with Czechoslovakia. He was also cautioned against any flirtation with the idea of a Habsburg restoration. Any doubts about the direction of Mussolini's thinking vanished when Schuschnigg was sent to the railway station alone, while the Duce visited a German cruise ship. During the spring and early summer, Mussolini's attention was centred on Spain and the need to recoup Italian prestige in the Mediterranean. When Neurath, who unusually made a number of foreign visits in 1937, perhaps as a sign of his growing frustration at his loss of influence in Berlin, came to Rome in early May, he and Mussolini complained about Franco's slow progress. Neurath repeated Göring's advice that Italy should leave the League of Nations; Mussolini, responding to the controversy over the papal encyclical *Mit brennender Sorge* (*With Burning Anxiety*) published in March, urged the German government to make peace with the churches. It was agreed to bring Romania closer to the Axis if this could be done without alienating Hungary. As to Austria, the earlier assurances were renewed. The Austrian government would be told to make concessions to the National Socialists within Austria, but the status of the country should remain unchanged. As Neurath, unlike Göring, expected Austria to fall into the German orbit like 'ripe fruit', without any resort to force, he felt no need to belabour this sensitive question. There were renewed assurances about their respective hostility towards Britain, as each prepared to open its own dialogue with their joint 'enemy'. It was agreed that Mussolini would come to Germany during the period of army manoeuvres scheduled for September 1937. Neurath showed little interest in an expansion of the Axis or in a four-power consultation pact (Italy, Germany, Austria, and Hungary), which he saw as a back-handed guarantee of Austrian independence.

During his September visit to Germany, the Duce was wooed, flattered, and fêted. Hitler took great pains over the meeting. His new appointee in Vienna, Wilhelm Keppler, was specifically instructed to keep the Austrian National Socialists under control so as not to make trouble. In Mussolini's honour there were parades, demonstrations, manoeuvres, inspections and dinners. The vain Italian dictator was impressed, understandably given the dimensions of the army manoeuvres and the vast military parades in Berlin, and he was thoroughly moved by his reception. In a wonderfully transparent effort at emulation, the German goose-step was introduced into Italy as the *passo Romano*. The two dictators, who spent little time together in serious talk, discussed Austria as well as Spain, but few details of the conversations emerged. For the first time, however, the Italian navy began planning for an Axis naval policy, the essence of which was that the two navies should aim to build fleets equivalent to 50% of the Anglo-French fleets, and forge an alliance with the Japanese navy. The Duce was not asked for a free hand in Austria, as was widely rumoured, nor did Mussolini press the Führer as to his future intentions. The Duce was not blind to the dangers which a post-*Anschluss* Germany could pose to Italian interests in the Balkans. Ciano intended to use the Italo-Yugoslav friendship treaty of March 1937, itself both an aggressive and a defensive move, to create a 'horizontal axis' linking Rome, Belgrade, and Budapest as a way of safeguarding Italian interests in the region against an over-greedy Germany. Despite the vehemence of his anti-British propaganda campaign, Mussolini was not averse to a *détente* with Britain as a counter-weight to any Anglo-German agreement, and as a way to protect his interests in the Mediterranean. While Mussolini may have preferred to keep a foot in each camp, he knew that only the German option provided the chance for the implementation of the ambitious policies that he had in mind.

Public demonstrations of Italo-German friendship continued throughout the rest of the year. When Ribbentrop arrived for discussions in Rome on 6 November, he was told by Mussolini that 'the Austrian question should not be considered as a problem between Italy and Germany... Austria is a German country.'[56] The Duce went on to explain that the chief goal of Italian foreign policy was the creation of a Mediterranean empire with Sicily as its geographic centre, a proposition to which Ribbentrop rapidly assented. Following earlier Italo-German discussions, the Italians were prepared to join the Anti-Comintern Pact, thereby crowning Ribbentrop's long campaign to bring the Japanese and Italians into an anti-British tripartite agreement. It was hardly surprising that his reception in London was cool when he returned to his embassy for the coronation of George VI. Hassell, the German ambassador in Rome, never an enthusiast for an alliance, warned Neurath that 'we are dealing with a new orientation of German foreign policy, which, upon the promptings of no less a person than the ambassador to London, consciously pits Germany against Great Britain, and openly reckons with a world war'.[57] The Italians knew something of the pact's anti-Soviet secret protocols but did not become party to them. Though at best this was a weak ideological combination, Ciano was exultant. He wrote in his diary, on the same day the Italians joined the pact, that the three peoples 'were setting out on the same road—which perhaps will lead them to battle. A necessary battle, if we want to break the crust that suffocates the energies and aspirations of the young people.' According to Ciano, Mussolini claimed 'Italy is at the centre of the most formidable politico-military combination that has ever existed.'[58]

Italy's adherence to the Anti-Comintern Pact on 6 November was celebrated with as much fanfare as its departure from the League of Nations. The Italians recognized the Japanese puppet state of Manchukuo. At the same time, the ambitious Ciano, preparing for the visit of

[56] ASD, Archivio di Gabinetto, busta 3, fasciolo 2, minutes of meeting held at Palazzo Venezia, 6 November 1937.

[57] John L. Heineman, *Hitler's First Foreign Minister: Constantin Freiherr von Neurath* (London and Los Angeles, 1979), 168.

[58] Galeazzo Ciano, *Diario, 1937–1943* (Rome, 1990), 54.

the Yugoslav prime minister to Rome, reassured himself: 'The alliance with the Slavs allows us to view with calmness the possibility of the *Anschluss*.'[59] The break-up of the Little Entente would provide Rome with an insurance policy in the Balkans and pave the way for an extension of its influence. In January 1938, a new general directive for the Italian army was based, for the first time, on a coalition war aligning Germany and Italy against Britain and France. There was no formal alliance with Berlin. Even if Mussolini and Ciano might have welcomed it, its unpopularity with the king and with some of the military advisers acted as a powerful restraint. Nor would the public have welcomed the alliance even had the South Tyrol question been solved through the removal of German speakers to Germany, as was being considered in Berlin. Military objections on the German side were equally strong. Due to Italian actions in Spain, the *Wehrmacht* chiefs had decided that Italy would be more of a burden than an asset as a continental ally. The Duce's commitment to Germany was, nonetheless, irreversible. British beliefs and remaining French hopes that Mussolini could somehow be wooed away from Hitler were seriously misplaced.

Despite the extension of the Anti-Comintern Pact, Hitler continued to pursue the British alliance. This can be seen in his dealings with London during 1937. Ribbentrop repeatedly tried to enlighten Hitler as to the futility of his pursuit. The by now rabidly Anglophobic ambassador warned Hitler that Chamberlain's willingness to negotiate was only a way of gaining time for rearmament. It is difficult to know what Hitler actually thought of this vain, aggressive, and self-important figure. It was probably the ambassador's unquestioning loyalty and obedience that was his most commendable asset. Hitler expected little from Neurath, whom he considered a member of the old-fashioned, narrow-minded, and highly suspect upper class that he despised and scorned. Whatever his incompetence, Ribbentrop's negative view of British intentions was not entirely without importance. Much of his reporting bordered on the ludicrous. He was convinced, for instance, that the abdication of Edward VIII was due to an anti-German plot in which Churchill took an active part, and that the success of the plotters had effectively ended hopes of an Anglo-German *rapprochement*. Hitler seems to have swallowed this, and other equally extraordinary misrepresentations of the London scene. The British Foreign Office tried to bypass the German ambassador, a task made easier by his frequent and long absences from London, but its actions only fuelled the ambassador's Anglophobia without checking his influence. In his end-of-mission report of 28 December 1937, he argued that Britain would adhere to

[59] Ibid., 65 (5 December 1937).

its balance of power traditions, would always support France's policies in Eastern Europe, and could not accept German ascendancy on the continent. Britain would join France in fighting Germany, should a Soviet–German war occur. The ambassador recommended that in dealing with 'our most dangerous enemy', Germany should secretly construct a system of alliances, by consolidating German friendship with Italy and Japan and include other states with similar interests. 'Only in this manner can we meet England', Ribbentrop wrote, 'whether it be for a settlement someday or in conflict'.[60] It was a policy that he was to defend until the conclusion of the Nazi–Soviet pact.

As talks failed to produce the London offer that he sought, Hitler grew increasingly frustrated by British obstinacy and interference in 'German' matters. The Führer came to agree with Ribbentrop that no satisfactory agreement could be reached with London. Whereas Ribbentrop himself, however, believed that Britain would have to be prevented from defending its empire and the European balance of power, through the creation of an anti-British alliance system, Hitler was inclined to temporarily ignore Britain, which he thought would not intervene in Czechoslovakia. He planned to move before the British began to rearm seriously. Even when branding Britain as Germany's 'hate inspired adversary' and 'No. 1 enemy', in November 1937, he remained convinced that it would accept German expansion in central Europe. Hitler hoped to realize his programme, 'if no longer with England, but simply without her, but at the least, in so far as is possible, not against her'.[61]

III

Hitler's illusions owed much to the British reluctance to define their position in central Europe. The hope in London was to restrain Hitler through rearmament, while seeking accommodation. The French adopted a similar line despite their more exposed position in Eastern Europe. The leaders of both countries believed an agreement with Germany was possible. In France, Blum was determined that the new rearmament schedules should be maintained despite the cuts made in government expenditure. Nevertheless, he and Delbos simultaneously sought economic and colonial bargains with Germany that would lead to a political understanding. Rearmament and conciliation went hand in hand and, as in Britain, an improved military position was seen as a

60 *DGFP*, Ser. D, Vol. I, No. 93.

61 J. Henke, *England in Hitlers politischem Kalkül 1935–1939* (Boppard am Rhein, 1973), 101.

necessary part of successful negotiations with Hitler. Blum and Delbos were willing to associate France with the Leith-Ross-Schacht talks. Blum had his own agenda, a containment policy based on German participation in a general financial, economic, and arms limitation scheme, which would bring in most of the countries in Europe. At the same time, he wanted stronger ties with the Little Entente countries which should be encouraged to co-operate against Germany. He proved unable to fulfil either of these goals prior to his fall from power in June 1937.

At the start of the year, both Britain and France were still looking for a general settlement based on a Locarno-like agreement. Whitehall was considering what concessions would produce a positive German reply to its Western pact conference proposals. In an effort to move matters forward, the French took up a proposal from their ambassador in Berlin for a five-power agreement on maximum force levels, for which Germany would be offered preferential currency arrangements, new trading outlets, and possibly a colony. René Massigli, the political director at the *Quai d'Orsay*, was highly alarmed at the lengths his political chiefs were prepared to go in meeting German wishes. Neurath expressed interest but was non-committal; the Spanish war would have to be 'settled' before any progress could be made. The project died, as much the victim of French and British objections as to German temporization.

Meanwhile the Western pact negotiations stagnated. The French continued to demand an exceptions clause allowing aid to their eastern allies, and would not accept independent arbitration over the operation of mutual assistance. In the hope of compensating for the declaration of Belgian neutrality, Massigli sought British assent to the inclusion of a guarantee to Luxembourg under any new Western pact, but made little headway. The poor prospects for a five-power conference were hardly improved when Ciano claimed that the real obstacle to a resumption of the Locarno power talks was not the Franco-Soviet pact, but the Spanish Civil War. Early in February, Hitler observed that the Western pact talks were at an impasse because of French insistence on drawing Russia into Europe. There was no sign that either Rome or Berlin was interested in a revised Locarno. The full British cabinet did not even discuss the possibility between February and late April 1937.

Hitler did make a move, however, that set the diplomatic wheels moving. In his speech to the Reichstag on 30 January, he offered a non-aggression guarantee to the Low Countries. It reopened the Anglo-French debate about how to guarantee Belgian independence. The British and French, the latter with the greatest reluctance, had accepted the Belgian prime minister's statement that Belgium alone should interpret its obligations under Article 16 of the Covenant. They accepted, too, his assurances that Belgium did not intend to return to its pre-1914 position of neutrality. Contrary to all their previous thinking on the subject, Belgium now would be able to keep out of a war involving Britain and France against Germany. There matters stood until Hitler's speech. The Belgians saw in the German offer a chance to be freed of their Locarno obligations without losing the guarantee of their 'neutrality'. Though Brussels would have preferred a German guarantee of 'independence' rather than 'neutrality', the British were warned that the offer of a non-aggression pact would be accepted if the western settlement negotiations collapsed. On 11 February, Ribbentrop suggested to Halifax that as France refused to give way over exceptions, Germany would accept a Locarno guarantee of the Low Countries as a substitute for the Western pact. The Belgians made it clear that they wanted guarantees from the Locarno powers, without assuming any parallel obligations. The van Zeeland government demonstrated its commitment to defend its borders by securing a 24% increase in defence appropriations. On 2 March, foreign minister Spaak confirmed that any violation of Belgian air space would be treated as a *casus belli*.

Neither the Foreign Office nor the *Quai d'Orsay* wanted a four-power agreement limited only to Belgium. The Foreign Office, acutely aware of the connection between the security of France and that of Belgium, stood its ground in opposing the German proposal. Chamberlain, too, rejected the idea of a tripartite (Britain, France, and Germany) guarantee of Belgian independence, but for different reasons. He feared such a guarantee might be equated with an indirect alliance with France and open the way to staff talks. On 8 March, Eden proposed a network of declarations from Belgium's neighbours, promising abstention from aggression, and non-interference in its affairs, followed by unilateral British and French declarations that Belgian inviolability was a vital interest. This would avoid the creation of any new British treaty obligations, but would prevent a Belgian denunciation of the March 1936 agreement committing Belgium to the support of the League Covenant. Meanwhile, King Leopold was invited to London at the end of March to calm his anxieties about Belgium's Locarno obligations.

The German and Italian replies arrived together on 12 March and marched to the same tune. They effectively buried the possibility of a five-power settlement based on a revised Locarno pact. The only provision kept from the original treaty was the co-guarantor scheme, which meant that neither Britain nor Italy would be given non-aggression guarantees themselves. All non-aggression guarantees would be absolute, without exceptions, and the League would be excluded from any consultative role with regard to the workings of the treaty. As a consequence, France could not go to the aid of Poland or the Little Entente unless some other 'impartial body' (the Germans suggested that Britain and Italy could fulfil this function) adjudicated the dispute. All distinctions between 'flagrant' and 'non-flagrant' aggression were abolished, preventing any form of immediate action until after arbitration by Britain and Italy. Belgium would be guaranteed by the four Locarno powers in return for a promise of neutrality in any conflict.

Boiled down to its essentials, the Germans demanded the ending of the French alliance system, and a free hand in the East. Their memorandum restricted France's right not only to assist its allies, but the western powers' right to aid each other. The German rejection, as always with Hitler, was phrased so as not to cause a rupture with London, and the door was left open for future exchanges. François-Poncet rightly speculated that Hitler wanted to avoid diplomatic action until Chamberlain's imminent and welcome ascent to the prime ministership. It was expected in Berlin that he would prove to be reasonably sympathetic to the German cause.

For their part, neither the French nor the British seemed unduly depressed by the German 12 March reply. It was not unexpected and merely left the post-Rhineland status quo in place. The *Quai d'Orsay* took heart from Eden's public commitment to France and Belgium at Leamington on 20 November 1936, a speech not much liked by Chamberlain. French diplomats hoped that if Germany persisted in its opposition to any form of Western pact, comprehensive Anglo-French staff talks might actually start. In explaining why France had had no interest in a limited four-power pact, a Foreign Office official told the Belgians: 'We cannot lose sight of the fact that the present situation, proceeding for us from the unconditional defensive alliance of England and France, is far and away the most favourable diplomatic combination which we have known in the West since 1918 and that, therefore, France is by no means disposed to exchange so precious an advantage for a contingent and hypothetical advantage.'[62] No progress had been made in establishing any form of Anglo-French co-ordination, either with regard to rearmament or military–naval exchanges, beyond those associated with Spain. Nevertheless, the British 1936 guarantee remained as a concrete assurance of future British assistance. It was all the more important because of the Belgian decampment and the failure of the French–Little Entente negotiations, to be discussed in the next chapter. In June, faced with the increasing isolation of Czechoslovakia, the French tried a new initiative to reopen talks for a Western pact along Locarno lines, but the effort died.

[62] Pierre van Zuylen, *Les Mains libres: politique extérieure de la Belgique 1916–1940* (Brussels, 1950), 398–399.

Since the post-Rhineland 'effort of conciliation', however farcical, was still in place, the British did not have to fulfil their 1936 promises of Anglo-French staff talks. The main disadvantage to the continuation of the status quo was the Belgian situation, and it was to this problem that Eden turned his attention. A joint declaration issued by Britain and France was published on 24 April 1937 which released Belgium from all obligations resulting from Locarno or the 19 March 1936 arrangements, while reaffirming their own mutual obligations and guarantees under these agreements. The Belgians were expected to defend their frontiers against aggression or invasion, and so prevent their territory from being used by another state as a passage or base of operations for the purposes of aggression. Nothing concrete was said about Article 16 of the League Covenant or about staff talks. In a very real sense, France's acceptance of Belgium's guaranteed neutral state was a blow to French security. Acquiescence in the new situation was inevitable. The Belgian decision could not be reversed by any French action. In early 1938, as a symbolic gesture, the Belgian government started the construction of fortifications along the French frontier; summer manoeuvres were scheduled to take place near the border.

General Gamelin's whole forward defence strategy was in danger. He sought to balance the loss of staff talks by informal conversations with van den Bergen, the Belgian army's chief of staff. Colonel Edmond Laurent, Gamelin's personal appointment, was assigned to Belgium in July 1937, and from the time of his arrival until the outbreak of war in 1939, he became the sole intermediary between Gamelin and van den Bergen. Belgium was a security and not a diplomatic problem. Hoping to fight in Belgium and not in France, Gamelin was not interested in the defensive parameter recommended by Daladier. He proposed instead that select fixed positions along the Franco-Belgian border should be strengthened. This proved to be an ill-supervised and under-funded project, intended only to provide a 'backstop' for a French advance into Belgium. None of the directors of the French military between the wars thought of fortifying the Ardennes, which were considered a natural barrier against invasion.

On the British side, the Foreign Office, more pessimistic than the cabinet about the possibility of general agreement with Germany, wanted to take up the question of staff talks with the Belgians and French, but was blocked by ministerial as well as military opposition. No move was made until May 1938, and then only on the most limited basis with France, and solely with regard to the air in respect of Belgium. At the start of 1938, van den Bergen made contact with the British ambassador and the military and air attachés in Brussels. Even then, the British cabinet and CID took their time about approving such secret exchanges, which they argued left Britain open to the accusation of conspiring against the Belgian king and his government. The situation changed in 1939 when the danger of a German occupation of the Netherlands was thought acute. By that date, the Belgian government had become even more adamant about maintaining its 'independence' and van den Bergen had very little room for action.

The Germans, for their part, were anxious to capitalize on the new Belgian dispositions to counter the possible effects of the unwelcome Anglo-French guarantee to Belgium. At first they tried to move the Belgians towards a position of 'strict neutrality', but by June 1937 they were prepared to make concessions in order to minimize the anti-German bias in the Belgian promises to observe its League obligations. The Belgians were convinced that neither a Western pact nor a multilateral guarantee of Belgium and Holland would materialize, and that furthermore the Anglo-French guarantees were the best that could be won. Instead they preferred a parallel unilateral declaration from the Germans. A German declaration of 13 October 1937 took official notice of the Belgian position, the latter defined in almost identical terms as those found in the Anglo-French declaration. Germany confirmed its decision to respect the inviolability and integrity of Belgium, and to respect Belgian territory unless Belgium took any direct military action against Germany in any future conflict. Eden was furious that the Belgians had presented him with a *fait accompli*. He took umbrage at the statement that the German government, like the British and French, was prepared to give support to Belgium in the event of her being subjected to an attack or an invasion. No specific reference was made to Belgium's League obligations, but Germany 'took note' of Belgium's public declarations. The German declaration was well received in Brussels where it was hoped that it would provide some measure of safety against the threat of aggression. In his report of 21 May 1937, Davignon, the Belgian ambassador in Berlin, wrote that 'if unfortunately Germany must again break its promises vis-à-vis ourselves, it will result in a moral advantage of inestimable value for the cause of the allies during the war'.[63] Belgian 'independence' was defended in the Chamber as a policy of adaptation to the new European realities. The action was dictated as much by internal politics as by fear of Germany.

Unable to revive Locarno, the British and French turned again to the possibilities of financial, economic, and colonial appeasement. This gave Hitler another chance to spin out negotiations. Continuing reports of Germany's economic difficulties encouraged the illusory belief that

[63] Quoted in Fernand Vanlangenhove, *L'élaboration de la politique étrangère de la Belgique entre les deux guerres mondiales* (Brussels, 1980), 255.

international action to help Germany might yield positive results. Chamberlain and Leith-Ross insisted that the opportunity should not be missed. The chancellor of the exchequer, as so often in these years, was able to convince the foreign policy committee that the German government was deeply divided and that colonial concessions might ensure the triumph of the 'moderates'. The Foreign Office denied the existence of such a group. In its view, the German establishment was united in its belief that *Anschluss* was inevitable and that an attack on Czechoslovakia was probable unless the Sudetenland was transferred to Germany. Vansittart's secret informants in Germany reported that even Neurath subscribed to these views. In their opinion, Hitler would not be diverted from his goals. Chamberlain, nevertheless, carried his colleagues with him. The prime minister-in-waiting was looking for an opportunity to act.

On 1 March, Ribbentrop demanded the restitution of the German colonies as a gesture of international goodwill. On the very next day, Eden reaffirmed that the British government was not considering any transfer of territory. A week later, Germany was formally invited, but refused to join the League committee (the van Zeeland committee) to study the question of international access to raw materials, making a mockery of Schacht's economic arguments for colonies. On 15 March, Eden warned the cabinet that Schacht's proposed concessions were a sham, and threw cold water on his promise of Hitler agreeing to join some form of European pact. Chamberlain, however, pushed the colonial option forward. At a meeting of the foreign policy committee on 6 April, Chamberlain dealt with Eden's objections, the latter demanding that political guarantees must precede the transfer of colonies. Only Ormsby-Gore, the colonial secretary, continued to oppose using the African colonies to bribe Hitler. The French were asked whether they would agree to return Togoland and the Cameroons to Germany. If they agreed, Britain would offer Germany financial assistance of an equivalent value.

There was little here to interest Blum and Delbos. Few in Paris any longer believed that Hitler could be influenced by a so-called moderate party if offered colonial concessions. The French and Germans were already engaged in commercial negotiations arising out of the breakdown of the Franco-German clearing arrangements. There was a temporary agreement on iron ore and coke, concluded with Schacht in March, which was intended to promote a broader economic and political *détente* in the future. While Blum favoured these exchanges, he had become far less enthusiastic about a colonial bargain, particularly one at French expense. The pro-colonial current ran strong in Paris, and both the colonial ministry and the service departments took exception to the cession of the West African mandates. The French navy, in particular, took a special interest in the defence of the French empire, and examined in some detail the German (as well as the Italian) threats to the African centres of French colonialism. The British Admiralty was not unduly concerned with a German presence in Africa. The French naval chiefs concluded that the German demand for colonies was part of an overall strategic plan aimed at undermining Anglo-French imperial security. Darlan feared that once Germany was established in Africa, its fleet would harass French ships ferrying troops to France. One third of the French army was stationed in North Africa. The fact that neither the Cameroons nor Togoland could possibly be of any economic interest to Germany only confirmed this reading of German intentions. Combined with the powerful opposition of the colonial ministry, the naval protests were sufficient to block French acceptance of the British proposals.

Both the British and French ambassadors in Berlin denied that Schacht had any influence with Hitler or that a 'moderate party' existed. Both argued that Hitler's concept of *Lebensraum* already overshadowed traditional ideas of *Weltpolitik*. Phipps, in his final report from the German capital before moving to the Paris embassy, suggested that Hitler had let Schacht take up the colonial question only to secure British acquiescence in his plans for Eastern Europe. The ambassador rightly judged that Hitler had no interest in economic or colonial concessions. The question for Hitler was whether continental expansion should start without the co-operation of the British. On 2 May, shortly after taking charge of the British embassy in Paris, Phipps met Blum and Delbos. The two Frenchmen ruled out colonial concessions, arguing that the proposed cessions would be inoperable within a League of Nations framework and would not satisfy Hitler. The French refusal was taken calmly at the Foreign Office, and while blaming the French (and Phipps) for the rejection of their scheme, the foreign policy committee agreed on 10 May to put the colonial question on hold.

No progress was made during the meetings between Blum and Schacht in late May 1937. François-Poncet had advised the French premier that Schacht was out of favour and the conversation remained at the level of generalities. Blum was, in any case, soon absorbed in the political battle resulting from a new financial crisis. For a government still paying for 'the charges of the past' (debt charges and war pensions comprised half the total public expenditure) and spending a quarter of its budget on rearmament, there could be no respite from financial troubles. The June panic was, however, only partly the result of unexpected new armament expenditure. Political reasons, particularly the banking community's distrust of the Popular Front, undoubtedly were a major factor. Whether out of financial prudence or political calculation, bankers and bond holders anticipated a fall in the value of the franc. Blum was shaken by the intensity of the opposition that he faced and the fierce reactions it provoked among those on the left who believed their policies were being blocked by the '*mur d'argent*'. The crisis increased dissension within the Popular Front, and Blum's political position was further weakened. The Senate rejected the government's demand for financial decree powers and Blum resigned on 21 June 1937.

While it is highly probable that Blum resigned to prevent the collapse of the Popular Front coalition, it may well be that he was tired of the struggle and facing defeat on too many fronts, foreign as well as domestic. Before he left office, it was decided to go ahead with the much-debated staff conversations with the Soviet Union. Disappointment with the Schacht visit and the failure to revive the Little Entente could well account for Blum's turn towards Russia. Blum's concerns with the German threats to Austria and Czechoslovakia were shared by his successors, but whereas he had sought to reinforce the Czechoslovak position, the new prime minister, Camille Chautemps, and Georges Bonnet, his finance minister, envisaged a different direction for French foreign policy. Both assured Franz von Papen in mid-November, when the diplomat visited the Paris exhibition, that not only would they continue to search for an accommodation along Blum's earlier lines, but would accept the peaceful extension of German influence in Austria and Czechoslovakia, as long as German aims were limited and there were no surprises. 'I . . . was amazed to note that, like M. Bonnet, the Premier considered a reorientation of French policy in Central Europe as entirely open to discussion', von Papen reported to the Führer on 10 November 1937, ' . . . always under the condition, naturally, that Germany's ultimate aims in Central Europe were known'.[64]

With the French caught up in their domestic travails, Chamberlain was free to go ahead without much concern for the *Quai d'Orsay*. The new prime minister, who took office on 28 May 1937, sought for a new way to encourage Hitler to negotiate. The cabinet returned to the idea of using the League raw materials enquiry as a step towards satisfying German economic requirements. On 4 June, the prime minister told the imperial conference meeting in London that the German government was willing to let the colonial question stand, but might be willing to co-operate if given some assistance of a financial and economic character. 'Probably also they desired some political appeasement', the prime minister admitted, 'which would enable them to make some progress—not, of course, by force—with

[64] *DGFP*, Ser. D, Vol. I, No. 22.

neighbouring countries containing considerable numbers of persons of German race'. There was, Chamberlain claimed, 'a prospect of obtaining more definite information of the German willingness to co-operate in other directions'.[65] This was just the opposite of Hitler's true intentions.

Eden's invitation to the German foreign minister in early June to discuss Spain but also, as he made clear, a large number of other questions as well, was not particularly welcome in Berlin. It proved difficult to pin Neurath down as to dates. He demanded that the Western pact be excluded from the London agenda and tried to avoid any discussion of the *Deutschland* or the Spanish problem in general. The *Leipzig* incident was nothing more than an excuse to cancel the visit. The main historical interest in this meeting that never was, lies in the preparations made for it. The German discussions were relatively brief, with only the Spanish question covered in any detail. Ernst von Weizsäcker, the head of the political department, summed up the German view: 'If England would leave us alone where German interests are predominant and British interests are not affected, and if she would take our raw-materials situation seriously, and help us to improve it, Anglo-German co-operation in the interest of preserving peace would be assured.'[66] British preparations were far more detailed. Apart from Spain, thought to be a possible field for future Anglo-German collaboration, the Foreign Office tried to clarify its view of British policy in Eastern Europe. Neurath was to be warned that, as in 1914, 'any violent disturbance' in central and south-east Europe could lead to another European war. Britain could not disinterest herself in the independence of the countries of this area but might, as part of a general settlement, agree to accept commercial concessions in Germany's favour. At the same time, the German foreign minister would be contradicted if he raised phantom stories of Russian influence. Britain could not join or countenance any 'Anti-Communist Front'.

Behind the scenes, officials debated the ambiguities in Britain's central European policies. Anticipating that Germany would want a statement of British disinterest in the region, the British should refuse to give this. The government was prepared to accept the possibility of peaceful change, but had reached no decision as to what changes would be regarded as tolerable. William Strang, the head of the Central department, fearing that Neurath would recognize the weakness of the British case, warned the foreign secretary: 'The Secretary of State had clearly stated that we cannot confine our interests to the West and disinterest ourselves in German action in other parts of Europe . . . It is equally true

[65] *DBFP*, 2nd ser., Vol. XVIII, No. 575. [66] *DGFP*, Ser. D, Vol. III, No. 317.

that we cannot make any promise that we shall intervene by force of arms in any part of Europe other than Western Europe. As regards this, we do not say "Yes", and we do not say "No".' Negotiations over the present territorial status quo were only possible if Britain was 'prepared to acknowledge that Central Europe is the natural sphere for the operation of Germany's political and economic influence' if promoted 'by peaceful means'. That possibility, according to Strang, had been discussed 'ad nauseum [sic], and it has been settled, I think, that this is not our policy'. With regard to Austria, as Strang acknowledged, no final decision had been reached.[67] Orme Sargent, the assistant under-secretary wanted Neurath warned that the fate of Austria 'is of vital importance, not merely to peace but to *British* interests'.[68]

Such a statement was never made to the Germans. Neither of these officials' opinions accorded with the main thrust of opinion in the cabinet. Only some Foreign Office officials were prepared to draw clear lines in Eastern Europe. It seems highly dubious, even had Neurath come, that the conversations between foreign ministers would have cleared the air. Eden was wobbly and unclear in his own mind. Neurath's role in Berlin was extremely circumscribed; he rarely saw the Führer, he complained to personal intimates, and threatened resignation. Hitler had no wish to negotiate. The new British ambassador in Berlin, Nevile Henderson, though convinced that he had been picked by Providence to conclude an agreement with Germany, was forced to report that Hitler intended to settle the Austrian question and then move on to Czechoslovakia. What the Führer wanted, Göring informed him, was British (and French) agreement to German expansion in central and Eastern Europe. He would offer in return restraint in Germany's colonial demands. Warned about Hitler's intentions, there was still no consensus in London about what should be done. The chiefs of staff and the Foreign Office pulled in different directions; many in Whitehall thought the Foreign Office too biased against the dictators to negotiate successfully with either Germany, Italy or, for that matter, with Japan. Eden gave no consistent lead, sometimes opposing discussions with Germany until Britain rearmed while at other times ready to explore a settlement before this goal was reached. By the end of the year, the prime minister was thoroughly annoyed by his foreign secretary who needed constant prodding to take any positive action.

A further change at the Foreign Office assisted Chamberlain's plans. During December, Eden decided that Vansittart, whom he regarded as imperious and patronizing, should be shifted from his post. Though

[67] *DBFP*, 2nd ser., Vol. XVIII, No. 623.
[68] *DBFP*, 2nd ser., Vol. XVIII, No. 639.

'Van' had successfully fought off earlier attempts to send him either to Washington or Paris, he was now forced, mainly through Chamberlain's intervention, to accept the new but intentionally less influential position as 'Chief Diplomatic Advisor' without defined responsibilities.[69] Eden won the debate over his successor and named Alexander Cadogan, an experienced, sensible, and balanced diplomat (William Strang, who knew him well, was shocked when the post-war publication of the Cadogan diaries revealed the diarist as a man of the strongest feelings) who was, nonetheless, critical of the Foreign Office's policy of drift, and sympathetic to negotiations with the Axis powers. The change was announced on 1 January 1938. French diplomats in London felt they had lost a friend; Corbin interpreted Vansittart's transfer as a sign of the diminution of the power of both Eden and the Foreign Office. It should be said that it was not just the prickly and sensitive foreign secretary who found Vansittart's over-bearing and assertive personality difficult to take. With the exception of 'Van's boys', a small group of personally picked supporters, Vansittart was not a popular figure in the Foreign Office. His wealth, political connections, and an unconcealed intellectual arrogance set him apart from his subordinates, some of whom attributed the weakening of their influence to Vansittart's inflated sense of his own importance. As chief diplomatic adviser, he would still play a part in the making of policy mainly because of his intelligence sources in Germany. But during the next critical months his Francophile sentiments and opposition to the government's policies made little impact on either Neville Chamberlain, as the prime minister assumed control of British negotiations with Berlin and Rome, or on Lord Halifax, Eden's successor at the Foreign Office.

Chamberlain was convinced that he had to take matters into his own 'capable' hands. Energetic, efficient, and highly persuasive, he believed that he could personally bring about the accommodations with the dictators that he sought. He set about reorganizing and rationalizing the policy-making structure to develop a coherent and effective grand strategy, and put Britain's diplomacy into high gear. When Chamberlain asked about a renewed invitation to Neurath, the Germans told him that the moment was not appropriate. Still, Chamberlain refused to believe that Hitler was not interested in a comprehensive settlement. Reports that most of Hitler's entourage had given up the possibility of a settlement with Britain, and believed Chamberlain's peace efforts were a delaying tactic while his country rearmed, failed to dissuade the prime minister, or his enthusiastic ambassador in Berlin, from breathing new life into the peace process in the autumn of 1937.

[69] See John Ferris, *Intelligence and Strategy. Selected Essays* (Abingdon and New York, 2005), 93, for Vansittart's recovery of influence in the post-Munich period.

IV

The western powers were correct in their belief that Germany was suffering from an acute shortage of raw materials and foreign exchange. But they were seriously mistaken when they thought that this would lead Hitler to seek an accommodation that would bring Germany back into the world economy. Whereas in the pre-Hitler decade, the men who led Britain, France, and Germany, whatever their differences, shared common assumptions and hopes, this was no longer true. It was not difficult to understand that Stalin and Soviet Russia were driven by an alien ideology and played by different and objectionable rules; it was more difficult to accept that Hitler was intent on war and that only submission to his expansionist plans would postpone conflict. As a consequence, the British and French assumed that they could convince the Führer that he could make Germany strong and prosperous through peaceful means. There were many in Germany who would have been content to enjoy the benefits that Hitler had brought, not least, the restoration of pride as well as employment. For Hitler, the gains made were just the start of a process which would solve the age-old problem of an inadequate territorial base for an expanding population (who wanted to eat more and live better) and to rid the country of its 'parasitic' Jews.

The decision taken in the summer of 1936 to raise a wartime army of 102 divisions of some 3.6 million men put an enormous burden on the economy. A large percentage of the increase in Germany's national product was the result of defence spending either by the government or by private firms contributing to the autarkic and defence efforts of the regime. Steel and iron ore, essential for the export trade as well as for rearmament, were critical to the defence effort. In early 1937, rationing was introduced both for steel and for non-ferrous metals. In a sense, the rationing of steel was as important for the functioning of the German economy as the announcement of the Four-Year Plan.[70] The services found that they were faced with severe raw material shortages. The *Wehrmacht* was hardest hit though both the *Luftwaffe* and the Four-Year Plan had to cut back production as well. In the summer, the *Wehrmacht* leaders warned that they would not be able to equip the armies that they were raising and that the army would not be ready for offensive action in 1940, Hitler's target date. Technical and administrative difficulties added to the problems of the *Luftwaffe* but the shortage of steel was a major

[70] Adam Tooze, *The Wages of Destruction*, 231.

Table 6.3 German Military Expenditure, 1933–1938 (million RM)

	Reichswehrministerium (Army and Navy)	Luftwaffe	Total	Luftwaffe (%)
1933/4	670	76	746	10.2
1934/5	1311	642	1953	32.9
1935/6	1736	1036	2771	37.4
1936/7	3596	2225	5821	38.2
1937/8	5015	3258	8273	39.4
1938/9	11221	6026	17247	34.9

Source: Lutz Budrass, *Flugzeugindustrie und Luftrüstung in Deutschland* (Düsseldorf, 1988), 364.

factor. Aircraft output declined steadily from April 1937 until the second half of 1938. The navy was unable to carry out the increases planned within the framework of the London naval agreement. The competition for resources grew worse when exporters wanted to take advantage of improving world trade. To avoid a repetition of the crisis of 1934, it was essential to restrict imports and increase exports to secure hard currency. Despite his loss of influence, in early 1937 Schacht was able to secure a priority in the steel allocation process for the export industries. During 1937, this allotment equalled that of the *Wehrmacht* and Four-Year Plan combined. Göring's success in extending the power of the *Reichswerke Hermann Göring*, a giant conglomerate created in 1937, over the Ruhr firms which owned the German iron ore fields, and in assuming control over the manufacture of all steel capacity in private hands, did nothing to alleviate the immediate shortage of steel. During the whole pre-war history of Nazi Germany, 1937 was the only year in which military spending did not significantly increase.[71] Hitler's Four-Year timetable was in serious danger.

On 5 November 1937 Hitler met with his minister of war, the foreign minister, and the chiefs of the army, air force, and navy. His military adjutant, Friedrich Hossbach, took notes.[72] The reason for the meeting was the fights between the service ministries over the allocation of raw materials and, in particular, the navy's demand for more steel if it was to complete its construction programme. Hitler's purpose, while settling the problems of allocation, was to alert his listeners to the imminence of war and the need to accelerate German rearmament. As he told Göring before the meeting, he intended to 'light a fire' under Blomberg and Fritsch, for he was dissatisfied with the progress made in rearming the *Wehrmacht*. Claiming that his words should be taken as a

[71] Ibid., 241. [72] *DGFP*, Ser. D, Vol. I, No.19.

'last testament' (Hitler celebrated his 48th birthday on 20 April and with polyps recently discovered in his throat was obsessed with the fear that he might die before realizing his ambitions), the Führer argued that Germany's need for living space had to be satisfied by the seizure of agriculturally useful land, and that this involved war. He insisted that the 'German space question' would have to be solved by 1943–45 at the latest, as Germany's relative strength compared to its opponents would decline after that point. The Führer was fully aware that the time-scale set in the Four-Year Plan could not be met. Much would depend on international developments. Almost all of what followed dealt with an attack on Czechoslovakia, not mentioned in *Mein Kampf*, or on Austria and Czechoslovakia. The action against Czechoslovakia would have to take place in 1943–1945, the last possible date. Earlier action would be taken in case either the internal problems of France degenerated into civil war, or a war between France, or Britain and France against Italy, arising out of the Mediterranean struggle or the Spanish Civil War (as early as 1938). The conquest of Austria and Czechoslovakia, if the compulsory emigration of three million people was practicable, would provide foodstuffs for five or six million Germans. It would mean shorter and better frontiers, the freeing of forces for other purposes and the raising of twelve new divisions for the army, one new division per million inhabitants. Hitler's longer-range aim of 'solving the German space problem', the war for *Lebensraum*, was only implied. There was no mention of the conflict with the Soviet Union, only a reference to the unlikelihood of Russian intervention given the anticipated speed of the German operation against Czechoslovakia and the attitude of Japan. There was every reason for not stressing the difference between Hitler's short- and long-term views. He was, after all, trying to convince his subordinates that they could act against the Czechs without British or French intervention and that this could be done only if Germany moved swiftly before her enemies were ready.

Despite the reference to Germany's 'two hate-inspired antagonists, Britain and France, to whom a German colossus in the centre of Europe was a thorn in the flesh', Hitler took every opportunity to reassure his listeners about these would-be enemies. 'Actually, the Führer believed that almost certainly Britain and probably France as well', Hossbach reported, 'had already tacitly written off the Czechs and were reconciled to the fact that this question would be cleared up in due course by Germany'.[73] Hitler's reading of the situation was to be confirmed by Anglo-French actions during the first half of 1938. His belief that the

[73] *DGFP*, Ser. D, Vol. I, No.19.

British Empire 'despite its theoretical soundness, could not in the long run be maintained by power politics', suggests a more nuanced reading of Britain's position than found in *Mein Kampf*.

If Hitler exaggerated the weakness of the French republic and misread, as Neurath argued at the time, the situation in the Mediterranean, his assumption that France would follow Britain's lead in central Europe to Germany's advantage was not misplaced. His speech fully alerted its listeners to his intention of exploiting any situation thought suitable for the expansion of Germany's territorial base. It showed, too, that whatever Hitler's view of Britain's role in his future plans, he tried to reassure his subordinates by dismissing their fears of British intervention in central Europe. Neither Neurath nor the service chiefs doubted that Hitler was intent on war and earlier than any of them had anticipated. No one at the meeting or after objected to the proposed annexation of Austria or the destruction of Czechoslovakia. Hitler made no mention of the Sudeten Germans as such and referred only to the overthrow of Czechoslovakia as a state and 'the crushing of the Czechs'. His audience, however, was not convinced by these arguments. Neurath, Blomberg, and Fritsch questioned Hitler's reading of the western response to German action in Austria and Czechoslovakia and the army chiefs underlined the dangers of engaging in a general war before Germany was prepared to fight. Raeder said nothing; his turn came during the second part of the meeting when he got the allocation of steel he wanted. The importance of the occasion can be judged by the fact that Fritsch, four days later, before going off on an extended holiday in Egypt, requested a second meeting with Hitler and renewed his objections. Neurath, in a secret memorandum of late December 1937, noted that Britain and France were distinctly more friendly towards Germany and that the time had come to begin serious negotiations. In a covering letter, von Weizsäcker wrote, 'We ourselves are not yet strong enough to engage in European conflicts and shall therefore not seek any.'[74] Neurath made a number of attempts to speak with Hitler in December but always without success. Hitler, thoroughly irritated by this chorus of unexpected opposition, went off to brood at Berchtesgaden. When the opportunity arose, he would impose his authority and his own views with his purge of the military leadership and diplomatic élites in February 1938. Hitler would assume a direct role in the shaping of Germany's future policy, diplomatic, military, and economic.

No immediate action followed the 5 November meeting but subsequent changes made in German strategic planning suggest that the

[74] *DGFP*, Ser. D, Vol. I, No. 86 (memorandum by Weizsäcker, enclosing memorandum by von Rintelen).

Wehrmacht was shifting into a more aggressive mode. In late 1935, the army's first major deployment plan, 'Operation Red', dealt with the threat of a French invasion. At the start of 1937, 'Operation Green' postulated a pre-emptive strike against Czechoslovakia to prevent her intervention in case of a war with France. On 14 June 1937, a plan was drawn up that incorporated both 'Operation Red' and 'Operation Green' in which the former still took precedence over the latter. On 7 December, however, General Jodl, the chief of operations staff at *Oberkommando der Wehrmacht* (OKW), amended the plan giving precedence to 'Operation Green' with the invasion of Czechoslovakia no longer intended as a pre-emptive strike for defensive purposes but as an 'offensive war against Czechoslovakia' for the purpose of solving the 'German problem of living space'. There was a cautious approach to the question of timing but a warning that if Germany faced no other opponent but Russia on Czechoslovakia's side, 'Operation Green' 'will start' before the completion of Germany's preparedness for war. While it was not thought necessary to work out further military plans for the occupation of Austria, those regarding Czechoslovakia were prepared in considerable detail.

Hitler solidified his grip on the military and diplomatic bureaucracy. On 4 February 1938, he announced the replacement of dozens of the Reich's leading soldiers and diplomatic officials. These changes had been prompted by the 'scandal of the generals', namely the discovery that General von Blomberg's new wife (Göring and Hitler had attended the marriage on 12 January) had been a prostitute and some trumped-up charges of homosexuality against Werner Fritsch, the army's respected commander-in-chief, who had questioned Hitler's November 1937 proposals. Hitler quickly dealt with the crisis in army morale and then exploited the situation for his own purposes, aiming to astound Europe with a reorganization that would give an impression not of weakness but of 'concentrated strength'. He centred power in his own hands, taking personal command of the *Wehrmacht*, now a separate organizational entity, abolishing the office of minister of defence and changing the *Wehrmacht* office in the Defence Ministry into the High Command (OKW) of the armed forces, which derived its importance from its direct responsibility to himself. General Keitel, hardly a man to stand up to Hitler, became head of the OKW and acted as Hitler's chief of staff. The new commander-in-chief of the army, General von Brauchitsch, as his pre-appointment activities fully demonstrated, was prepared to court Hitler's favour whatever the cost to his professional standing and judgment. Simultaneously, Hitler retired seven army and six *Luftwaffe* generals, opening the way for younger and more avowedly pro-Nazi officers, while others were transferred to different commands.

With the enhancement of his personal authority over the armed services came their total subordination to the National Socialist state, as General Beck, the chief of the general staff, came to realize in the summer of 1938. Hitler's attack on the entrenched élites also extended to the diplomatic service. Neurath was dismissed in a humiliating fashion, but was kept on a short lead and, indeed, was present at the Munich conference. His replacement as foreign minister, the martinet Joachim von Ribbentrop, assembled the whole foreign ministry staff for review; each was expected to pledge his 'undying loyalty to the Führer's cause'. Since Hitler was content to let his subordinates go their own way, the incompetent and puffed-up Ribbentrop was able to interfere in many questions during the next 18 months, playing a part that neither his talents nor even his loyalty to Hitler justified. In the same decree nominating Ribbentrop, Hitler announced the recall of Hassell from Rome, Papen from Vienna, and Dirksen from Tokyo. Hassell was retired. The ever-resourceful Papen survived yet again, sent back to Vienna the day after his dismissal to handle the pre-*Anschluss* negotiations and then was saved by the disappearance of Austria. He was finally dispatched as ambassador to Turkey mainly because Ribbentrop wanted the untrustworthy aristocrat out of Berlin. Dirksen, a loyal Nazi who had served Hitler well in Tokyo, received the prized London embassy, due in part to the intervention of his mother who had tried years earlier to ease Hitler's entrance into Berlin society.

Hitler, too, would take on a new role in the direction of the economy. While not interested in the technical details of industrial policy, he carefully monitored the armament programme and the problems of rationing scarce raw materials. Walther Funk, Goebbels's close collaborator, replaced Schacht at the Ministry of Economic Affairs. Though Göring was disappointed not to get the position himself, he was able to merge the administration of the Four-Year Plan with the ministerial apparatus. All the key appointments were in the hands of politically reliable men who would carry out the new agenda of autarchy and rationing. Contrary to what has been assumed, Hitler kept a watching brief over the allocation of steel, the essential raw material for the German industrial economy.[75]

V

As Hitler was considering new 'surprises', Chamberlain searched for ways to establish 'good relations' in order to persuade the Führer to be a 'good European'. In other words, Chamberlain hoped to convince

[75] This information comes from Tooze, *The Wages of Destruction*, 243.

Hitler to use peaceful means to achieve his ambitions in central Europe. This was the background to the visit of Lord Halifax, a former viceroy of India, a much-respected Conservative and cabinet minister, on 19 November. Though not personally as close to Chamberlain as he had been to Baldwin, Halifax shared the new prime minister's views both with regard to Hitler and Mussolini. The invitation to the master of the Middleton foxhounds to attend a hunting exhibition came from Göring via the editor of the British sporting magazine, *The Field*. Chamberlain seized on this new opportunity to reach Hitler and enlisted Nevile Henderson's assistance in making the visit politically significant by arranging a Hitler–Halifax meeting in Berlin. Eden was less than enthusiastic and hoped to keep Hitler guessing until Britain had rearmed sufficiently to negotiate from strength. At an informal meeting with senior officials at Eden's home, when both Italian and German policy was discussed, 'we all favoured approach to Hitler and offer of a bilateral declaration of our policy, although none of us like the idea of the Halifax visit'.[76] Whereas the members of Eden's circle disagreed over the policy to be followed towards Mussolini, no one questioned the need for a fresh start with Germany.

It was arranged that Halifax would be received by Hitler at Berchtesgaden, giving his visit a special importance. Eden, who was absent at the Brussels conference dealing with the China situation when this was decided, and the Foreign Office, fought a fierce but losing battle to delay or even to cancel the visit to Hitler. They feared Halifax's trip to the Berghof would look 'almost like a Canossa'. Exaggerated expectations both in London and abroad intensified their discomfort. Rumours circulated and were reported from Prague, Warsaw, and Moscow that a deal would be struck in Berlin giving the Germans a free hand in the East in return for a renewed commitment to respect existing borders in the West. Earning a well-deserved rebuke from London, Henderson even told the Czechoslovak minister in Berlin, just before announcing Halifax's forthcoming visit, that as long as Prague continued to provide the link between Paris and Moscow, German agitation in Czechoslovakia would continue. He warned Mastny, the Czech minister in Berlin, that the Franco–Czechoslovak–Soviet pact was the main obstacle to European peace and that Prague would have to abandon it. From Paul Thummel, Czechoslovak agent no. A-54 working in the German *Abwehr*, came news that the Germans would offer to respect British colonial possessions in return for a free hand against Czechoslovakia. It was hardly surprising that Foreign

[76] John Harvey (ed.), *The Diplomatic Diaries of Oliver Harvey, 1937–1940* (London, 1970), 57.

Minister Kamil Krofta in Prague tried to pre-empt such a bargain by issuing, without any proof, a categorical denial asserting that 'all rumours to the effect that Great Britain was prepared to abandon Central Europe to Germany were absolutely untrue'.[77]

Judging from Halifax's preparatory notes for the meeting, Foreign Office forebodings were well founded. Their cautionary admonitions, as well as Eden's efforts to chivvy the prime minister over rearmament, had no effect. Chamberlain was enthusiastic about the meeting; as to Eden's concerns about rearmament, he advised his foreign secretary, who had been ill with flu, 'to go back to bed and take an aspirin'.[78] Halifax, in preparing for the visit, called for and read with approval Henderson's 10 May 1937 memorandum, which had caused much dismay at the Foreign Office on arrival. The ambassador had argued that the German absorption of Austria, the recovery of its African colonies and the drive for living space in Eastern Europe did not 'injure purely British national interests' and would restrain both Russian intrigues and Italian aspirations. For Henderson, the German was 'more civilized' than the Slav and Britain had no right to check the German effort to complete its unity or to prepare for war against Russia. The alternatives to an accommodation in central Europe, either to protest and do nothing or to revert to the bloc system and prepare for war, were, according to the ambassador, 'counsels of despair'. During the run-up to Halifax's visit, Henderson sent warm words of encouragement. The ambassador was anxious for Britain to be 'generous' in the concessions it would make. '[I]f we are not too niggardly, Germany will keep her word, at any rate for a foreseeable period', he wrote. 'We should not oppose peaceful evolution any more than we could condone forcible expansion.'[79] Halifax, who sent his preparatory notes to Chamberlain on 8 November without showing them to the unsympathetic Eden and Foreign Office, commented, 'I hope that we should not feel bound to (in Henderson's words) oppose "peaceful Evolution"—rather liberally interpreted perhaps.'[80] This would be the subsequent agenda for appeasement.

Halifax's account of his days in Germany, from 17 to 21 November, makes fascinating reading. The exhibition itself was a 'wonderful effort, down to a gramophone reproducing the roar of a stag in the imitation

[77] I. Lukes, *Czechoslovakia Between Stalin and Hitler: The Diplomacy of Edvard Beneš in the 1930s* (New York, 1996), 82.
[78] D. R. Thorpe, *Eden: The Life and Times of Anthony Eden, First Earl of Avon, 1897–1977* (London, 2003), 197.
[79] Quoted in R.A.C. Parker, *Chamberlain and Appeasement*, 97.
[80] TNA: PRO, PREM 1/330, Halifax to Chamberlain, 8 November 1937.

Forest and wild animal section'.[81] The conversation with Hitler showed how limited the grounds were for discussions. This was not, however, the conclusion drawn by either Halifax or Chamberlain, both of whom remained convinced that it was possible to discuss with Germany the 'practical questions' involved in a general European settlement. At their private meeting (Halifax was alone and Hitler accompanied only by Neurath and Paul Schmidt, his interpreter) the Führer made it perfectly obvious that he was not interested in Germany's return to the League or in disarmament. He thought the British government was living in 'a make-believe land of strange, if respectable, illusions'. It had 'lost touch with reality' and clung to shibboleths—'collective security', 'general settlement', 'disarmament', 'non-aggression pacts'. Though the Führer became excited only when speaking of Russia, there was less discussion of Communism than Halifax had anticipated. There was a strong attack on democracies and democratic methods but assurances that, though the status quo could not be preserved, there was a choice between war and settlement by reason and, of course, only the Russians wanted war. Halifax concluded, quite rightly, that 'All this is naturally disturbing to us and makes approach difficult. We are not talking the same language.'[82] Halifax, though patronizing about Hitler and his advisers, was clearly out of his depth in dealing with them.

It was Halifax and not Hitler who raised the possibility that England would accept alterations in Danzig, Austria, and Czechoslovakia if they came through 'the course of peaceful evolution' and without using methods that would cause 'far-reaching disturbances'. On at least two occasions, Halifax assured the German dictator that Britain was not wedded to the existing status quo. Hitler, who was reserved though courteous throughout the meeting (subordinates reported he was moody and out of sorts), showed no inclination to take up suggestions for further talks. His reluctance to engage in any dialogue was confirmed by his subordinates. On the next day, 20 November, Halifax travelled to Göring's vast estate at Karinhall. He found Göring 'frankly attractive'. He was, as Halifax wrote in a much quoted passage, 'Like a great schoolboy, full of life and pride in all he was doing, showing off his forests and animals, and then talking high politics out of the setting of green jerkin and red dagger . . . and producing on me an impression of a composite personality—film star, great landowner interested in his estate, prime minister, party manager, head gamekeeper at Chatsworth [the Duke of Devonshire's estate]'.[83] Göring looked forward to re-adjustments in central Europe brought about so as not to give 'an excuse

[81] *DBFP*, 2nd ser., Vol. XIX, No. 336.
[82] *DBFP*, 2nd ser., Vol. XIX, No.336.
[83] *DBFP*, 2nd ser., Vol. XIX, No.336.

or opportunity' for any outside power to intervene. Colonies were the only issue dividing Britain and Germany; this could be solved without 'too much difficulty'. At an evening dinner party, Halifax had a long conversation with Blomberg. The war minister warned Halifax that colonies were of secondary importance and that Germany's vital interests concerned her central and Eastern European position. Just as France had her position of power and influence in Western Europe and the Mediterranean, she had to recognize Germany's right to a similar position in central Europe. Czechoslovakia, whom nobody liked, was only an outpost of Russia. Blomberg returned to the same theme in a later note to the lord president intended to clarify his views. The war minister assured Halifax that Germany had no aggressive designs in the West and could not understand why France 'so bitterly opposed the satisfaction of Germany's vital needs'. Halifax also met Schacht, who was to 'resign' the post of German economic minister the following week, and Goebbels, whom he 'unexpectedly failed to dislike' ('some moral defect in me') and who complained about the attitude of the British press, eliciting a sympathetic reply from Halifax who, subsequently tried to amend the situation.

Halifax appears to have speedily recovered from the mixture of 'astonishment, repugnance and compassion' with which he heard Hitler explain how to solve the problem of India: 'Shoot Gandhi and if that does not suffice to reduce them to submission, shoot a dozen leading members of Congress; and if that does not suffice, shoot 200 and so on until order is established.'[84] On his return to London, Halifax thought it possible to do business with the Germans. He assured fellow cabinet ministers that there would be no German policy of 'immediate adventure' though they should expect 'a beaver-like persistence' in pressing German claims in central Europe. Halifax recommended that the British take up the possibility of a colonial settlement and use this to 'pursue a policy of real reassurance in Europe'.

If Halifax's qualified optimism is difficult to understand, Chamberlain's belief that the visit was 'a great success' serves only to illustrate the degree to which wishful thinking had distorted ministerial judgement. It was not that Chamberlain had misread Hitler's message. As he explained in a letter to his sister, 'the Germans want to dominate Eastern Europe'. He went on to say, 'I don't see why we shouldn't say to Germany, give us satisfactory assurances that you won't use force to deal with the Austrians and Czecho-Slovakians and we will give you similar assurances that we won't use force to prevent the changes you want if we can

[84] Quoted in I. Kirkpatrick, *The Inner Circle* (Macmillan, 1959), 97.

get them by peaceful means.'[85] The prime minister hoped to extract, in return, German co-operation and participation in reforming the League and negotiating a general disarmament agreement through limiting the size of tanks, aircraft, and guns.

It was Laurence Collier, the head of the Northern department and the most consistent Foreign Office opponent to an agreement with Germany, who made the strongest case against a new initiative in Berlin. He preferred the continuation of the 'present state of armed truce' and the 'unheroic policy of so-called "cunctation"'.[86] Europe had lived in the past, Collier wrote, without a general settlement but also without war. This was far better than opening the floodgates of territorial expansion by public acquiescence in German, Italian, or Japanese expansion, before it actually occurred. Eden repeated these same arguments in a memorandum of 26 November circulated to the Committee of Imperial Defence.

This was not the policy Chamberlain intended to follow. He thought it had brought no positive results in the past and was not the way to avoid a conflict over changes in the European status quo that were in any case inevitable. The prime minister knew what a difficult task he faced. Henderson reported that Hitler was 'deeply disappointed' with the British attitude and their failure to understand him. This would hardly stop him. Eden was pessimistic about the possibility of success but he was unwell and visibly tired. On 3 January 1938, Eden went off to the south of France for an overdue break, having decided against a more extended holiday in Madeira. Chamberlain was left in control of foreign affairs. The foreign secretary knew it was not a good time to be away. Quite apart from his differences with Chamberlain over both German and Italian affairs, President Roosevelt had decided to explore joint naval action in the Far East as the result of the Japanese bombing of the American S.S. *Panay*. Eden was able to receive the American naval representative just before leaving for France but had to leave any further exchanges in the prime minister's less than sympathetic hands. According to Thomas Lamont, the American banker, 'if it could be said that any Englishman was anti-American, Chamberlain was that anti-American Englishman'.

The Chautemps cabinet was content to let the British take the initiative in continental affairs. Though the French cabinet was more sanguine about a Franco victory in Spain than its predecessor, it could hardly ignore the military implications of a German–Italian–Spanish alignment. The fear of future encirclement not only fuelled the

[85] *DBFP*, 2nd ser., Vol. XIX, No. 349 (N. Chamberlain to Ida Chamberlain, 26 November 1937).

[86] *DBFP*, 2nd ser., Vol. XIX, No.348.

continuing search for an accommodation with Germany but drove the French closer to Britain. This acquiescence in British leadership was the notable feature of the meeting between Chautemps and Delbos with Chamberlain and Eden and their respective staffs in London on 29–30 November. The French had come to hear a report on the Halifax–Hitler conversation and to review all the other issues (Spain, Italy, Danzig, the Far East), of mutual concern. The *Quai d'Orsay* had been badly informed about the background to the Halifax trip. François-Poncet had tried to persuade Henderson that the Germans aimed at disrupting the Anglo-French *entente* as well as France's eastern treaty system but was unable to check the ambassador's open assurances of Britain's disinterest in Eastern Europe. Though the *Quai* officials discounted the rumours of a possible bargain over central Europe, there was considerable unease in Paris. Trying to calm his colleagues, Corbin compared the visit to Lord Haldane's trip to Germany in 1912 with its ultimately beneficial results for France.[87]

At the November meeting, Lord Halifax provided the French ministers with a summary of what had transpired in Germany and his own personal impressions of the visit. The two records of the meeting, apart from a somewhat more positive French reading of Britain's future role in central Europe, indicate there was no major difference between the two governments.[88] After Halifax's presentation, it was agreed that the colonial question should be considered but only in the context of a general agreement—i.e. the Western pact, disarmament, the League, central and Eastern Europe. The French emphasized the unwillingness of the French public to accept any colonial sacrifice without a substantial *quid pro quo*. The two governments would also confer on the list of demands to be made in Berlin. Their joint reply to the Hitler–Halifax exchanges would be delivered through Nevile Henderson.

The key question for France was that of central and Eastern Europe. Delbos was about to start on a tour of East European capitals that would include Poland, Romania, Yugoslavia, and Czechoslovakia but not the Soviet Union, an omission welcomed in London. It was assumed in London that the Chautemps government would not line up with a Left bloc in Europe nor strengthen its ties with Moscow. Delbos's visits were intended to convince London of the continuing viability of France's eastern alliances. Nonetheless, it was already clear at this meeting that the French leaders were prepared to trim their sails to British winds in central Europe. Czechoslovakia posed the greatest difficulties for the two countries; the French had an alliance and the British did not.

87 *DDF*, 2nd ser., Vol. VII, No. 238.
88 *DDF*, 2nd ser., Vol. VII, No. 287; *DBFP*, 2nd ser., Vol. XIX, No. 354.

Chamberlain agreed that the conversations with Germany could only proceed on the basis of an understanding about central Europe. It had to be assumed, he observed, that Germany's ultimate aim was to gain territory: 'our policy ought to be to make this more difficult, or even to postpone it until it might become unrealisable'.[89]

This was as far as the prime minister was willing to go. Eden joined Chamberlain in urging Delbos to press Beneš to satisfy the grievances of the *Sudetendeutsche*. Delbos insisted, rightly as the Hossbach account suggests, that the minorities question was only a pretext for territorial expansion and argued that Germany should not be given a blank cheque for an operation of conquest. It was essential, he said, according to the French account of the meeting, that any pressure on the Czechs should be accompanied by a promise that if the legitimate grievances of the Sudetens were satisfied, Czechoslovakia should have the right to count on the sympathy of Britain and France if it became the victim of aggression. Chamberlain demurred; he 'thought that the British government could not go so far, nor give an assurance in the case of aggression'.[90] He told his French visitors that his government could not state 'what their action would be in the event of an attack'. There was strong public feeling, he warned, against being entangled in a war over Czechoslovakia, 'which was a long way off and with which we had not a great deal in common'.[91] The French insisted that the Germans should show their good will by accepting a new Locarno in which they 'must mark their desire for security not only in the West, but also in the East'. Eden countered by suggesting that Germany be asked whether it was 'disposed' to renew the undertaking not to go to war against Czechoslovakia. Neither side anticipated a German attack on Czechoslovakia but feared an indirect assault on Czech independence. The French reserved the right to wait on events before deciding whether and when their treaty should come into operation and rejected Chamberlain's efforts to get them to reassure the Germans in this direction.

Chautemps and Delbos could hardly have been surprised by the British refusal to make any commitment to support France in the case of a war over Czechoslovakia. Eden had warned Delbos as early as 8 October of his colleagues' unwillingness to consider engagements with regard to events which were 'so complex and so badly defined'.[92] The French leaders did not press their hosts unduly. Apart from stressing the difficulties of the situation in Prague, they agreed that the Czechs should be asked to make greater concessions to the Sudeten Germans and that the British should launch the new attempt

[89] *DBFP*, 2nd ser., Vol.XIX, No.354.
[90] *DDF*, 2nd ser., Vol. VII, No.346.
[91] *DBFP*, 2nd ser., Vol. XIX, No.354.
[92] *DDF*, 2nd ser., Vol. II, No. 41.

at a general settlement with Germany. In Delbos's explanatory dispatch circulated to the key French diplomatic posts on 2 December, the foreign minister claimed that, if the necessary concessions were made to the Sudeten Germans, Britain would associate itself with French efforts to secure new German guarantees of Czechoslovakia's territorial integrity. This was an over-optimistic interpretation of what Chamberlain and Eden had said. At most, the French were assured that Britain would not abandon its interest in Austria and Czechoslovakia. It was little enough but acceptable to those in Paris who believed that the extension of German influence in central Europe was inevitable. William Bullitt, the well-informed American ambassador in Paris, wrote to Roosevelt on 23 November. 'Chautemps will wish personally to enter into direct negotiations with Germany and perhaps make the necessary concessions', he cabled Washington, 'in other words to abandon Austria and the Germans of Czechoslovakia to Hitler. But he will know that his government will fall if he tries to put this policy into practice.'[93] Chautemps, Delbos, and Bonnet were prepared for a retreat from central Europe even before the meetings with Chamberlain and Eden took place. It was politically convenient to walk in the British shadow; it would help insure London's future support in any *guerre de longue durée* and provide an acceptable excuse at home to cover a further withdrawal from Eastern Europe. In so far as the French were reluctant to face the full strategic consequences of a German advance into Austria and Czechoslovakia, co-partnership with Britain in the region, however limited, was almost a necessity.

Chautemps and Delbos also were prepared to allow the British to open bilateral talks with the Italians despite *Quai d'Orsay* agitation about Mussolini's anti-French press and radio campaign and officials' strong doubts about the possibility of detaching the Duce from Hitler. The attempt at an independent policy towards Italy had failed and had irritated Chamberlain. For the moment, too, the French and British had moved closer regarding Spain. Both governments congratulated themselves on the success of the policy of non-intervention. Since the middle of October 1937, relatively little outside help had arrived for either side. The British were preparing for the inevitable, if delayed, Francoist victory. Differences between the two governments over Spain would emerge again somewhat later but for the moment, Delbos and Chautemps assured Eden that a Franco victory would not necessarily menace French interests unless Franco ceded territory to Italy or Germany for air or naval bases. Still concerned about Italian actions in the

93 Bullitt, *For the President*, 237.

Mediterranean, the French acquiesced in the opening of direct talks between London and Rome asking only, as they had in 1936–1937 and with as little success, that they be kept informed of the exchanges.

VI

The Chautemps–Delbos visit in November was judged a success in London. The Radical premier was considered more acceptable than Blum and preferable to more right-wing politicians who might prove less amenable to British direction. Except with regard to the air force, there was a surprising lack of concern in London about the military weakness of France. It was assumed in both capitals that the French army could contain a German attack on France. Gamelin walked a very narrow path between wanting a new continental commitment from Britain and not wishing to reveal the true extent of France's military deficiencies in case the British would concentrate on their own defensive requirements. He asked only that a small but powerful British mechanized force be prepared for intervention in Belgium. The chief of the imperial general staff attended the French army manoeuvres in September 1937, along with the Czechs and Poles. He reported on the weaknesses of the French army, the slow speed and poor performance of its tanks and, most strikingly of all, on the possible vulnerabilities of the Maginot Line. None of these worries made any impression on Hore-Belisha, the British war minister, who was also present at the French exercises. He remained convinced that the French fortifications were 'virtually impregnable' and so backed Chamberlain's refusal to consider further commitments to France or to take any steps towards closer collaboration. The supposed strength of the French army provided powerful ammunition for those like Chamberlain who argued in the winter of 1937–1938 that Britain should prepare only a small token expeditionary force. It was one of those 'unspoken assumptions' that do not appear in the cabinet papers.

On 22 December 1937, the British cabinet considered the general review of future spending prepared by Sir Thomas Inskip, minister for the co-ordination of defence. Faced with an unacceptable rise in arms expenditure and fearful of its consequences on the stability of the economy, savings had to be made. Inskip, while warning his colleagues of the risks involved should France be in danger of being overrun, saw no alternative but to reduce the already circumscribed role of the army. 'On the basis of the policy now proposed the Continental hypothesis ranks fourth in order of priority and the primary role of the Regular Army becomes the defence of Imperial commitments, including anti-aircraft

Table 6.4 Comparison of Annual Expenditure on the Three Services in Britain, 1933–1939

	Army	Navy	Air Force	
1933	37,592,000	53,500,000	16,780,000	
1934	39,660,000	56,580,000	17,630,000	
1935	44,647,000	64,806,000	27,496,000	
1936	54,846,000	81,092,000	50,134,000	
1937	63,010,000	77,950,000	56,290,000	
	14,867,000	24,000,000	26,000,000	Issues under the Defence Loans Act, 1937
1938	86,661,000	95,945,000	72,800,000	
	35,700,000	31,350,000	61,000,000	Issues under the Defence Loans Act, 1937
1939	88,296,928	97,960,312	105,702,490	

Source: N. H. Gibbs, *Grand Strategy*, Vol.I: *Rearmament Policy* (London, 1976), 532.

defence at home'.[94] Instead of a Field Force of five divisions capable of disembarking on the continent within fifteen days of mobilization, the new Field Force was destined to operate in an eastern campaign, possibly in Egypt. As it was, arms production had failed to reach its 1937 goals.

Given the new lowered priorities, preparations for a land war with Germany practically reached vanishing point. Hore-Belisha argued that the French, in the event of war, did not expect Britain to supply an expeditionary force on the scale hitherto proposed and counted on a contribution in naval and air power and finance. He admitted that to provide even the two mechanized divisions wanted by Gamelin he would have to divide the existing division into two parts. The cabinet unanimously accepted Inskip's recommendations, with Eden expressing some doubts and suggesting only that Britain and France should confer on measures for their joint defence. Gamelin would have liked a far more substantial commitment from London but accepted, as did his colleagues, that there would be no large-scale British military intervention as in 1914–1918. The French had to acquiesce in Britain's pre-occupation with its home and imperial defence. Whatever the warnings of the intelligence services about the *Wehrmacht*'s superiority over the French, both numerical and technical, Gamelin still thought his army could contain a German attack.

There was less British complacency about the weakness of the French air force. This had a good deal to do with their distrust of Pierre Cot, the air minister, in sharp contrast to their faith in Gamelin. In February

[94] Quoted in N. H. Gibbs, *Grand Strategy*, Vol. 1 (London, 1976), p. 468.

1937, the two countries agreed to share air intelligence; exchanges of information began in the spring of that year. Cot, an exponent of strategic bombing and a voluble advocate of a military alliance with the Soviet Union, was engaged throughout his tenure at the ministry in fierce political battles with fellow defence ministers and with the Senate's Air Commission, which strongly opposed the nationalization programme and the forty-hour week. In response to the latter's repeated critiques, Cot deliberately disguised the long-standing production difficulties that had led to a drastic drop in industrial output (the number of planes received by the air force fell by nearly 30% during the first 12 months of Cot's tenure) which made a mockery of his estimates for the future production of aircraft.[95] It would take far more time than Cot suggested for the Popular Front reorganization of the aviation industry to take effect. Pessimistic reports from the British air attaché in Paris and the Department of Overseas Trade Industrial Intelligence Centre prompted Eden to query Delbos in Geneva in November 1937 about the drop in French production. Delbos denied that the situation was critical but there was considerable alarm at the *Quai d'Orsay* when alerted to Cot's false claims. At the December Anglo-French meeting, Chamberlain and Inskip confronted their French visitors. 'You have no modern aircraft', Chamberlain told the French premier, 'and no prospects of producing any in the near future'.[96] Chautemps admitted only that production had 'fallen a little behind' but that France was going to 'spend a great deal of money' and 'make purchases in the United States'.[97] It was only before the CPDN (*Comité Permanent de la Défense Nationale*) on 8 December that Cot revealed the full extent of the air crisis and for the first time since the autumn of 1936 demanded a large increase in funding. By this date, he was considered a political liability and out of step with the policies of the Chautemps government. In January, when the cabinet was reconstituted, he was replaced by Guy Le Chambre, a young Radical close to Daladier. Cot's many battles and his repeated distortions of the true situation in the air proved costly for an air force already two years behind the Germans in starting to rearm. Whatever their concerns, however, about the French air situation, there was no move in London to co-ordinate planning or production schedules with the French.

Despite the alarmist reports of the *Deuxième Bureau* on the shifting balance of power in Europe, Daladier joined fellow ministers in assuming

95 R. Frank[enstein], *Le prix du réarmament français, 1936–1939*, 316.

96 John McVickar-Haight, Jr., *American Aid to France, 1938–1940* (New York, 1970), 5.

97 TNA: PRO, FO 371/20694, C8237/122/17, 29 December 1937 quoted in Jackson, *France and the Nazi Menace*, 240.

that there was no imminent crisis. The successful containment of the Spanish Civil War appeared to quieten fears of an immediate threat to France. Until December 1937, at least, Chautemps, Daladier, and Bonnet still thought it possible to either postpone or avoid war altogether. The French government's willingness to seek an accommodation with Germany in the winter of 1937–1938 cannot be explained solely in terms of submission to the 'English governess'.[98] France's political weakness and financial and economic difficulties, dictated a policy of caution and passivity in a deteriorating international environment. With but few exceptions, those engaged in foreign and defence policies felt constrained by the disunity of the country, its unhealthy currency and its unbalanced budget. This meant, in terms of foreign affairs in 1937–1938, the elusive settlement with Germany and a good relationship with the British. Those urging alternative policies had a difficult time, either for political reasons, as in the case of Cot, or, in Admiral Darlan's case, because of the army's traditional domination of the country's defence strategy.

Weak executives, aware of their impermanence and unsure of parliamentary support, do not embark on active foreign policies. The substitution of Chautemps for Blum meant that the Radicals were the dominant voice in the ministry, and that the government moved to the centre-right. The appointment of Georges Bonnet as finance minister in the cabinet was an indication of this conservative turn. Bonnet was an able, ambitious, but highly conservative anti-Popular Front Radical, who had been 'exiled' as ambassador in Washington in 1936. Even so, Chautemps had the greatest difficulty in maintaining his sagging coalition of Radicals and Socialists, dependent as it was on Communist support in the Chamber. The Radical party had become fiercely anti-Communist, and impatient to disassociate itself from the Socialists, the forty-hour week, and the remnants of Blum's economic and social programmes. The possibility of a centre-right coalition was already being mooted. The Socialists, never a united party, were losing votes to the Communists. They wanted to distance themselves both from the Radicals and the Communists. Divisions in the Socialist party were accentuated by growing differences over foreign policy. The debates over non-intervention in Spain were subsumed by splits between those supporting or opposing the appeasement of Germany. There were differences, too, over the USSR. The party contained an important group of pacifists who were convinced that the Soviet Union

[98] The evocative phrase of J. Bédarida, 'La gouvernement anglaise', in René Rémond and Janine Bourdin (eds.), *Édouard Daladier, chef de gouvernement, avril 1938 – septembre 1939* (Paris, 1977).

posed a far greater threat to internal order and the European peace than Nazi Germany. The Russians were suspected of trying to engage France in a war against Germany which would leave them supreme in Europe. These views found an echo in the equally fragmented ranks of the political right, where many, though not all, were prepared to abandon traditional preferences for military alliances against Germany, in favour of *rapprochement* with Berlin. The combination of pacifist left and anti-Communist right was to coalesce in the summer and autumn of 1938 to provide support for the Munich agreement. The Communist party, consistent in its ultimate aims, followed a tortuous political route during the winter of 1937–1938 as its leaders tried to balance the need to secure the party's popular base in a highly volatile anti-government atmosphere, and the need to keep the Chautemps ministry in office in order to keep its political influence. On foreign policy issues, the Communists and the government moved in opposite directions, the former demanding the strengthening of the Franco-Soviet alliance, and the latter seeking to cut its links with Moscow in the interests of domestic and foreign stability. Anti-Fascism, so important in the creation of the Popular Front, was no longer a source of unity for the parties of the left.

Unsettled financial and political conditions put further pressure on the government to look for an accommodation with Germany. Accepting the advice of his financial experts, who enjoyed close links with the British Treasury, Bonnet not only proposed tax increases and further cuts in civil expenditure but also the freezing of armament expenditure for the next three years. The final budget accounts for 1937 showed that civil expenditure was two million francs below the original estimates but military expenditure 800 million francs higher.[99] Bonnet also decided it was far too costly to maintain the franc within the limits decided in October 1936. After consulting with the Americans and British who agreed to temporarily close their exchange markets, the franc was allowed to 'float' in June without regard to any upper or lower limits. This meant, in effect, another devaluation. There was a temporary repatriation of funds, encouraged by the government's announcement that there would be no export controls and tougher measures against strikers. The respite was short. Bonnet's budget cutting did not affect expenditure in 1937 and the effects of the American depression that began in June 1937 added to the country's problems. The Treasury again had to rely on advances from the Bank of France. In December 1937, there was a huge strike at the Goodrich tyre factory near Paris and at Christmas, a strike of the public services, supported by the Communist

[99] Julian Jackson, *The Popular Front in France: Defending Democracy, 1934–1938* (Cambridge, 1988), 180.

party, that left the capital without transport, gas, or electricity. The signs of worker discontent further undermined financial confidence in the government. Afraid of alienating the investing classes and of offending the British and Americans, the government would not consider exchange controls. By the start of 1938, funds were again being exported; the massive flight of capital drained the gold reserves of the Bank of France. Industrial production levelled off and plunged in March 1938 to its lowest level since 1935. Apart from the Communists and some Socialists, politicians blamed French economic weakness on the anticipation of confrontations with labour and further political instability.

Bonnet's decision to impose a three-year ceiling on defence spending with an annual maximum to be spent each year meant the extension of the 'pause' to the effort of rearmament. On 19 July 1937, at an interministerial conference attended by the heads of the three services and the director of the budget, Bonnet demanded and won a limit of 11 million francs for 1938, more than two and a half million francs lower than requested by the three services. The move was welcomed in Washington where Henry Morgenthau, the secretary of the Treasury, believed that no financial assistance could save the French while a 'constantly increasing' proportion of their budget was going for 'war purposes'. In London, Chamberlain was delighted that the Rue de Rivoli had finally understood that financial strength was the 'fourth arm of defence'. 'France must have a strong army, a powerful navy and a modern air force', Bonnet told the Chamber of Deputies, 'but it is equally vital that she safeguards her wartime finances, that is to say, her gold'.[100]

Neither Daladier nor Cot, kept in the Chautemps cabinet at Blum's insistence, protested against Bonnet's 'pause' though they were the ministers most worried by the resurgence of German strength. War was not thought to be imminent; there was still time for France to recover and marshal its forces. In the battle over the allocation of available funds, Daladier was able to increase the army's share of the budget from 45% to 49%, securing sufficient additional funds to ensure continuity in the War Ministry's programme. Cot protested against the proposed cuts in the air estimates (from 4,620 to 2,439 million francs) to be spent over four years instead of three and due to Blum's support, won a compromise figure of 3,250 million francs. These cuts had the unfortunate effect of discouraging aircraft manufacturers from further investment in their plants and delayed the acceleration in production schedules, which were already far behind their 1937 targets. It was, however, the navy that suffered most; it was the only service that

[100] Quoted in Frank, *Le prix du reármament français*, 165.

obtained less money for 1938 than for 1937 without taking into account the losses due to subsequent devaluations. Admiral Darlan complained bitterly, pointing out the strategic folly and long-term consequences of interruptions in ship-building programmes. He warned that by 1942 France would rank fourth among the European naval powers and would depend on Britain in any war against Germany and Italy. Recalling that Britain and France could have different national interests, Darlan repeated his warnings of the previous spring that the 'French government would be forced "to model exactly" its foreign policy on that of the English'.[101] The admiral won a supplementary credit in November though the sharp depreciation of the franc wiped out most of this additional gain.

After July 1937, the decision to slow down France's rearmament programme increased the country's vulnerability to German attack and made it more important to secure British underwriting. As France imported many of the raw materials needed for the defence industries, such as coal (some 30% came from England), copper, oil, and rubber, bought from either Britain or its empire and much of this trade was carried in British ships, the French were at a disadvantage in any trade negotiations. With the Chamberlain government determined to maintain and expand its export trade, the French had to make unwelcome commercial concessions to preserve the financial backing from London that made rearmament possible. It is easy, however, to exaggerate the extent to which the need for British support and protection shaped French diplomacy at this time. The Chautemps government still hoped for an arrangement with Germany and was prepared to pay a price to achieve it. Though British disapproval of French commitments in Eastern Europe was a contributing factor to the French retreat, there were equal or more compelling reasons for the failure to resuscitate the Little Entente or to negotiate a military alliance with the Soviet Union. The battle to stay in office appears to have absorbed the energies of those in power. A mood of fatalistic pessimism spread among the diplomats at the *Quai d'Orsay* during the winter of 1937–1938. Léger, 'an institution within an institution', who as secretary general of the *Quai d'Orsay* since 1933 had outlasted six ministers and twelve governments by 1938, threw his weight in the direction of Britain and away from negotiations with Italy or Russia. Highly intelligent and a poet of note, Léger was reserved, formal, and ultimately enigmatic. He seems to have been unwilling to push his views too hard and was almost fearful of debate and open confrontation. Even the ablest and most outspoken of officials, such as René Massigli, were conscious of their inability to devise a policy

[101] Frank, *Le prix du reármament français*, 170.

that would stop the erosion of French influence. A majority hoped, though with mounting pessimism, that Germany could be contained through multilateral pacts in which both Britain and France would participate. The excessive legalism of the *Quai d'Orsay*, its preoccupation with the forms of diplomatic intercourse, and its hothouse atmosphere hardly prepared functionaries for dealing with the gangster tactics of its chief opponents.[102] The ardently Anglophile French diplomats in London, though full of forebodings about Chamberlain's direction of foreign affairs, offered no suggestions as to how he could be convinced of the two countries' mutual dependence.

December 1937 was a particularly bleak month for French foreign policy. On 8 December 1937, the CPDN considered the possibility of a war against Germany and Italy. The Delbos tour of the eastern capitals proved only that the Little Entente was a hollow grouping and confirmed the loss of Yugoslavia to the Axis powers. The isolation of Czechoslovakia and the threat of German action in central Europe posed more immediate dangers to France than any previous Popular Front government had faced. The meetings with Chamberlain and Eden on 29–30 November had shown how limited were British interests in the region and their unwillingness to offer any commitment to Czechoslovakia. Serious rearmament had begun in both countries but with little co-ordination of effort or joint planning. If the Anglo-French *entente* appeared firmer than before, the improvement was at the price of the French accepting an unequal partnership. The Chamberlain government insisted on 'business as usual' and tried to avoid being drawn into a more active economic role even as pressures mounted on the cabinet to expand the rearmament effort and to address the bottlenecks in production, particularly the shortage of skilled labour. Chamberlain was hardly a warm friend of France. His continuing exasperation with the political instability of the French Republic and what he thought to be its financial and economic incompetence lay very close to the surface. His direction of Britain's diplomacy was based on a narrow conception of Britain's national interests. In Paris, even in these dismal months, it was still assumed that once political unity was restored, finances put in order and its military strength increased, France could sustain its position as one of the great powers of Europe. In London, this vision, seemingly so far removed from the realities of its political and economic situation, had little place in Chamberlain's thinking. In the 1920s and the early 1930s, Britain's declared aim had been to recreate the balance of power in Europe, sometimes by weakening France and strengthening Germany. By 1937 this goal had been abandoned.

[102] Jean-Baptiste Duroselle, *La décadence, 1932–1939*, 269–275.

Breaking with traditional policies, under Neville Chamberlain's leadership, Britain would enter into direct bilateral relations with Germany to keep the peace of Europe. It was over central Europe that this policy had its first and also its final test.

Books

ADAMTHWAITE, A., *France and the Coming of the Second World War, 1936–1939* (London, 1977).

—— *Grandeur and Misery: France's Bid for Power in Europe, 1914–1940* (London, 1995).

ALEXANDER, M. S., *The Republic in Danger: General Maurice Gamelin and the Politics of French Defence, 1933–1940* (Cambridge, 1992).

BELL, P. M. H., *Britain and France 1900–1940: Entente and Estrangement* (London and New York, 1996).

BIALER, U., *The Shadow of the Bomber: The Fear of Air Attack and British Politics, 1932–1939* (London, 1980).

BOND, B., *British Military Policy between the Two World Wars* (Oxford, 1980).

BOYCE, R., *The Great Interwar Crisis and the Collapse of Globalization* (Basingstoke, 2009).

—— and ROBERTSON, E. M. (eds.), *Paths to War: New Essays on the Origins of the Second World War* (London, 1989).

BUDRASS, L., *Flugzeugindustrie und Luftrüstung in Deutschland* (Düsseldorf, 1988).

BURLEIGH, M., *Germany Turns Eastwards* (Cambridge, 1988).

—— *The Third Reich: A New History* (London, 2000).

CAPUTI, R. J., *Neville Chamberlain and Appeasement* (Selinsgrove, PA, 2000).

CARR, W., *Arms, Autarky and Aggression* (London, 1972).

CHAPMAN, H., *State Capitalism and Working-Class Radicalism in the French Aircraft Industry* (Oxford, 1991).

CHILDERS, T. and CAPLAN, J. (eds.), *Re-evaluating the Third Reich* (New York, 1993). See H. Mommsen.

COLLOTTI, E., *Fascismo e politica di potenza: politica estera, 1922–1939* (Milan, 2000).

COWLING, M., *The Impact of Hitler: British Politics and British Policy, 1933–1940* (Chicago, IL, and London, 1977).

CROWSON, N. J., *Facing Fascism: The Conservative Party and the European Dictators, 1935–1940* (London, 1997).

CROZIER, A. J., *Appeasement and Germany's Last Bid for Colonies* (Basingstoke, 1988).

—— *The Causes of the Second World War* (Oxford, 1997).

DENNIS, P., *Decision by Default: Peacetime Conscription and British Defence, 1919–1939* (London, 1972).

DOCKRILL, M., *British Establishment Perspectives on France* (London, 1999).

DOISE, J. and VAÏSSE, M., *Diplomatie et outil militaire, 1871–1991*, new and rev. edn. (Paris, 1991).

DREIFORT, J. E., *Yvon Delbos at the Quai d'Orsay* (Lawrence, KA, 1973).

DÜLFFER, J., *Weimar, Hitler und die Marine* (Düsseldorf, 1973).

Evans, R. J., *The Coming of the Third Reich* (London, 2003).
—— *The Third Reich in Power, 1933–1939* (London, 2005).
Ferris, J., *Intelligence and Strategy: Selected Essays* (Abingdon and New York, 2005).
Forbes, N., *Doing Business with the Nazis: Britain's Economic and Financial Relations with Germany, 1931–1939* (London, 2000).
Förster, J., *Die Wehrmacht im NS-Staat: Eine strukturgeschichtliche Analyse* (Munich, 2007).
Frank(enstein), R., *Le prix du réarmement français, 1935–1939* (Paris, 1982).
Fridenson, P., *La France et la Grande-Bretagne face aux problèmes aériens: 1935 – mai 1940* (Vincennes, 1976).
Funke, M. (ed.), *Hitler, Deutschland und die Mächte* (Düsseldorf, 1976). See J. Dülffer.
Gibbs, N. H., *Grand Strategy*, Vol. I: *Rearmament Policy* (London, 1976).
Hayes, P., *Industry and Ideology: IG Farben in the Nazi Era*, new edn. (Cambridge, 2001).
Hehn, P. N., *A Low, Dishonest Decade: The Great Powers, Eastern Europe and the Economic Origins of World War II, 1930–1941* (New York and London, 2002).
Heineman, J. L., *Hitler's First Foreign Minister: Constantin Freiherr von Neurath, Diplomat and Statesman* (Berkeley, CA, 1979).
Henke, J., *England in Hitlers politischem Kalkül* (Boppard am Rhein, 1973).
Higham, R., *Armed Forces in Peacetime: Britain, 1918–1940: A Case Study* (London, 1962).
—— *The Military Intellectuals in Britain, 1918–1939* (New Brunswick, NJ, 1966).
Hildebrand, K., *Vom Reich zum Weltreich: Hitler, NSDAP und koloniale Frage, 1919–1945* (Munich, 1969).
—— *Das vergangene Reich: Deutsche Außenpolitik von Bismarck bis Hitler* (Stuttgart, 1995).
—— and Werner, K. F. (eds.), *Deutschland und Frankreich 1936–1939* (Munich, 1981).
—— Schmädeke, J., and Zernack, K. (eds.), *1939: An der Schwelle zum Weltkrieg: die Entfesselung des Zweiten Weltkrieges und das internationale System* (Berlin, 1990).
Homze, E. L., *Arming the Luftwaffe: The Reich Air Ministry and the German Aircraft Industry, 1919–1939* (Lincoln, NE, 1976).
Howard, M., *The Continental Commitment: The Dilemma of British Defence Policy in the Era of Two World Wars*, new edn. (London, 1989).
Hudemann, R. and Soutou, G.-H. (eds.), *Eliten in Deutschland und Frankreich im 19. und 20. Jahrhundert*, Vol. 1 (Munich, 1994). See W. Serman, M. Messerschmidt, J.-C. Allain, P. Krüger, and G.-H. Soutou.
Jackson, J., *The Politics of Depression in France, 1932–1936* (Cambridge, 1985).
—— *The Popular Front in France: Defending Democracy, 1934–1938* (Cambridge, 1988).
Jackson, P., *France and the Nazi Menace: Intelligence and Policy Making, 1933–1939* (Oxford, 2000).

Jacobsen, H.-A., *Nationalsozialistische Außenpolitik 1933–1938* (Frankfurt am Main, 1968).

Kershaw, I., *The Nazi Dictatorship: Problems and Perspectives of Interpretation* (London, 1989).

Kieft, D. O., *Belgium's Return to Neutrality* (Oxford, 1972).

Kiesling, E., *Arming against Hitler: France and the Limits of Military Planning* (Lawrence, KA, 1996).

Kopper, C., *Hjalmar Schacht: Aufstieg und Fall von Hitlers mächtigstem Bankier* (Munich, 2006).

Lamb, R., *The Drift to War, 1922–1939* (London, 1989).

Langhorne, R. (ed.), *Diplomacy and Intelligence during the Second World War* (Cambridge, 1983). See B. Lee.

Leitz, C. (ed.), *The Third Reich: The Essential Readings* (Oxford, 1999).

—— *Nazi Foreign Policy, 1933–1941* (London, 2004).

Lukes, I., *Czechoslovakia between Stalin and Hitler: The Diplomacy of Edvard Beneš in the 1930s* (New York, 1996).

Macdonald, C. A., *The United States, Britain and Appeasement, 1936–1939* (London, 1981).

Maiolo, J., *The Royal Navy and Nazi Germany, 1933–1939: A Study in Appeasement and the Origins of the Second World War* (London, 1998).

—— *Cry Havoc: The Arms Race and the Second World War 1931–1941* (London, 2010).

Mallett, R., *The Italian Navy and Fascist Expansionism, 1935–1940* (London, 1998).

—— *Mussolini and the Origins of the Second World War, 1933–40* (Basingstoke and New York, 2003).

McKibbin, R., *Classes and Culture: England, 1918–1951* (Oxford, 1998).

Messerschmidt, M., *Die Wehrmacht im NS-Staat* (Hamburg, 1969).

Meyers, R., *Britische Sicherheitspolitik, 1934–1938: Studien zum außen- und sicherheitspolitischen Entscheidungsprozess* (Düsseldorf, 1976).

Michalka, W., *Ribbentrop und die deutsche Weltpolitik, 1933–1940: außenpolitische Konzeptionen und Entscheidungsprozesse im Dritten Reich* (Munich, 1980).

Minniti, F., *Fino alla guerra: strategie e conflitto nella politica di potenza di Mussolini, 1923–1940* (Naples, 2000).

Mommsen, W. and Kettenacker, L. (eds.), *The Fascist Challenge and the Policy of Appeasement* (London, 1983). See R. M. Smelser, W. Michalka, R. F. Cruault, R. Frankenstein and J. Dunbabin.

Müller, K.-J., *Das Heer und Hitler* (Stuttgart, 1969).

—— *The Army, Politics and Society in Germany, 1933–1945* (Manchester, 1987).

Neville, P., *Appeasing Hitler: The Diplomacy of Sir Nevile Henderson, 1937–1939* (London, 2000).

Overy, R. J., *War and Economy in the Third Reich* (Oxford, 1994).

Parker, R. A. C., *Chamberlain and Appeasement: British Policy and the Coming of the Second World War* (Basingstoke, 1993).

—— *Churchill and Appeasement* (London, 2000).

Peden, G. C., *British Rearmament and the Treasury, 1932–1939* (Edinburgh, 1979).

—— *The Treasury and British Public Policy 1906–1959* (Oxford, 2000).

—— *Arms, Economics and British Strategy from Dreadnoughts to Hydrogen Bombs* (Cambridge, 2007).

PETERS, A. R., *Anthony Eden at the Foreign Office, 1931–1938* (Aldershot, 1986).

POSEN, B. R., *The Sources of Military Doctrine: France, Britain and Germany between the World Wars* (Ithaca, NY, 1984).

POST, G. Jr., *The Dilemmas of Appeasement: British Deterrence and Defense, 1934–1937* (Ithaca, NY, and London, 1993).

RENOUVIN, P. and RÉMOND, R. (eds.), *Léon Blum, chef de gouvernement 1936–1937* (Paris, 1967).

ROBERTSON, E. M., *Hitler's Pre-war Policies and Military Plans, 1933–1939* (London, 1963).

ROCK, W. R., *British Appeasement in the 1930s* (New York, 1977).

ROI, M. L., *Alternative to Appeasement: Sir Robert Vansittart and Alliance Diplomacy, 1934–1937* (Westport, CT, 1997).

ROSKILL, S. W., *Naval Policy between the Wars*, Vol. 2 (London, 1976).

ROSTOW, N., *Anglo-French Relations, 1934–1936* (London, 1984).

RUGGIERO, J., *Neville Chamberlain and British Rearmament: Pride, Prejudice, and Politics* (Westport, CT, 1999).

SALERNO, R. M., *Vital Crossroads: Mediterranean Origins of the Second World War, 1935–1940* (Ithaca, NY, 2002).

SCHMIDT, R. F., *Die Außenpolitik des Dritten Reiches 1933–1939* (Stuttgart, 2002).

SHAY, R., *British Rearmament in the Thirties: Politics and Profits* (Princeton, NJ, 1977).

SHORROCK, W. I., *From Ally to Enemy: The Enigma of Fascist Italy in French Diplomacy, 1920–1940* (Kent, OH, 1988).

SMELSER, R. M., *The Sudeten Problem, 1933–1938: Volkstumspolitik and the Formulation of Nazi Foreign Policy* (Dawson, 1975).

STERNHELL, Z., *Ni droite, ni gauche: l'idéologie fasciste en France* (Paris, 1983).

THOMAS, M., *Britain, France and Appeasement: Anglo-French Relations in the Popular Front Era* (Oxford, 1996).

TOOZE, A., *The Wages of Destruction: The Making and Breaking of the Nazi Economy* (London, 2006).

TURNER, J. (ed.), *Businessmen and Politics: Studies of Business Activity in British Politics, 1900–1945* (London, 1984). See G. Peden.

VANLANGENHOVE, F., *L'élaboration de la politique étrangère de la Belgique entre les deux guerres mondiales* (Brussels, 1980).

WEINBERG, G. L., *The Foreign Policy of Hitler's Germany*, Vol. I.: *Diplomatic Revolution in Europe, 1933–1936* (Chicago, IL, and London, 1970).

—— *The Foreign Policy of Hitler's Germany*, Vol. II.: *Starting World War II, 1937–1939* (Chicago, IL, and London, 1980).

WENDT, B.-J., *Economic Appeasement: Handel und Finanz in der britischen Deutschland-Politik, 1933–1939* (Düsseldorf, 1971).

WRIGHT, J., *Germany and the Origins of the Second World War* (Basingstoke, 2007).
YOUNG, R. J., *In Command of France: French Foreign Policy and Military Planning, 1933–1940* (Cambridge, MA, 1978).
—— *France and the Origins of the Second World War* (Basingstoke, 1996).

Articles and Chapters

ALEXANDER, M. S., 'In Lieu of Alliance: The French General Staff's Secret Co-operation with Neutral Belgium, 1936–1940', *Journal of Strategic Studies*, 14: 4 (1991).
—— and PHILPOTT, W. J., 'The Entente Cordiale and the Next War: Anglo-French Views on Future Military Co-operation, 1938–1939', *Intelligence and National Security*, 13 (1998).
BECK, P., 'Britain and Appeasement in the Late 1930s: Was there a League of Nations Alternative?', in Richardson, D. and Stone, G. (eds.), *Decisions and Diplomacy: Essays in Twentieth Century International History in Memory of George Grün and Esmonde Robertson* (London, 1995).
BÉDARIDA, F. 'La "Gouvernante anglaise" ', in R. Rémond and J. Bourdin (eds.), *Édouard Daladier, chef de gouvernement* (Paris, 1977).
BIALER, U., 'Elite Opinion and Defence Policy: Air Power Advocacy and British Rearmament during the 1930s', *British Journal of International Studies*, 6 (1980).
BLATT, J., 'The Cagoule Plot, 1936–1937', in Mouré, K. and Alexander, M. S. (eds.), *Crisis and Renewal in France, 1918–1962* (New York and Oxford, 2002).
BOADLE, D., 'The Formation of the Foreign Office Economic Relations Section, 1930–1937', *Historical Journal*, 20: 4 (1977).
BUFFOTOT, P., 'The French High Command and the Franco-Soviet Alliance, 1933–1939', *Journal of Strategic Studies*, 5 (1982).
CASSELS, A., 'Deux Empires Façe à Façe: La Chimère d'un Rapprochement Anglo-Italien (1936–1940)', *Guerres mondiales*, 161 (1991).
CEADEL, M., 'Interpreting East Fulham', in Cook, C. and Ramsden, J. (eds.), *By-Elections in British Politics* (London, 1973).
—— 'The First British Referendum: The Peace Ballot, 1934–1935', *English Historical Review*, 95 (1986).
CROZIER, A. J., 'Prelude to Munich: British Foreign Policy and Germany, 1935–1938', *European Studies Review*, 6 (1976).
—— 'Imperial Decline and the Colonial Question in Anglo-German Relations, 1919–1939', *European Studies Review*, 11 (1981).
DAUNTON, M., 'Payment and Participation: Welfare and State-Formation, 1900–1951', *Past and Present*, 150 (1996).
DILKS, D., ' "We Must Hope for the Best and Prepare for the Worst": The Prime Minister, the Cabinet and Hitler's Germany, 1937–1939', *Proceedings of the British Academy*, 73 (1987).

FRANK(ENSTEIN), R., 'The Decline of France and French Appeasement Policies, 1936–1939', in Kettenacker, L. and Mommsen, W. J. (eds.), *The Fascist Challenge and the Policy of Appeasement* (London, 1983).

GIRAULT, R., 'Léon Blum, la dévaluation de 1936 et la conduite de la politique extérieure de la France', *Relations internationales*, 13 (1978).

—— 'The Impact of the Economic Situation on the Foreign Policy of France, 1936–1939', in Kettenacker, L. and Mommsen, W. J. (eds.), *The Fascist Challenge and the Policy of Appeasement* (London, 1983).

GOLDMAN, A. L., 'Sir Robert Vansittart's Search for Italian Co-operation against Hitler', *Journal of Contemporary History*, 9: 3 (1974).

GREENWOOD, S., 'Caligula's Horse Revisited: Sir Thomas Inskip as Minister for the Co-ordination of Defence, 1936–1939', *Journal of Strategic Studies*, 17 (1994).

HILLGRUBER, A., 'England's Place in Hitler's Plans for World Dominion', *Journal of Contemporary History*, 9: 1 (1974).

—— 'England in Hitlers außenpolitischer Konzeption', in Hillgruber, A. (ed.), *Deutsche Grossmacht- und Weltpolitik im 19. und 20. Jahrhundert* (Düsseldorf, 1977).

JOHNSON, G., 'Sir Eric Phipps, the British Government and the Appeasement of Germany, 1933–1937', *Diplomacy & Strategy*, 16: 4 (2005).

JORDAN, N., 'Maurice Gamelin, Italy and the Eastern Alliances', *Journal of Strategic Studies*, 15: 4 (1991).

KENNEDY, P. M., 'British "Net Assessment" and the Coming of the Second World War', in Murray, W. and Millet, A. R. (eds.), *Calculations: Net Assessment and the Coming of World War II* (New York, 1992).

KNIPPING, F., 'Frankreich in Hitlers Außenpolitik, 1933–1939', in Funke, M. (ed.), *Hitler, Deutschland und die Mächte* (Düsseldorf, 1976).

KNOX, M., 'Il fascismo e la politica estera italiana', in Bosworth, R. J. and Romano, S. (eds.), *La politica estera italiana, 1860–1985* (Bologna, 1991).

MCKERCHER, B. J. C., 'National Security and Imperial Defence: British Grand Strategy and Appeasement 1930–1939', *Diplomacy and Statecraft*, 19 (2008).

—— 'The Foreign Office, 1930–1939: Strategy, Permanent Interests and National Security', *Contemporary British History,* 18: 3 (2004).

NEVILLE, P., 'The Appointment of Sir Nevile Henderson, 1937—Design or Blunder?', *Journal of Contemporary History,* 33: 4 (1998).

OVERY, R., 'The German Pre-war Aircraft Production Plans, November 1936 – April 1939', *English Historical Review*, 90 (1975).

PARKER, R. A. C., 'British Rearmament, 1936–1939: Treasury, Trade Unions and Skilled Labour', *English Historical Review*, 96 (1981).

PEDEN, G. C., 'A Matter of Timing: The Economic Background to British Foreign Policy, 1937–1939', *History*, 69 (1984).

ROLLINGS, N., 'Whitehall and the Control of Prices and Profits, 1919–1939', *Historical Journal*, 44: 2 (2001).

SCHWARZ, L. D., 'Searching for Recovery: Unbalanced Budgets, Deflation and Rearmament in France during the 1930s', in Garside, W. R. (ed.), *Capitalism in Crisis: International Responses to the Great Depression* (London, 1993).

STANNAGE, T., 'The East Fulham By-Election, 25 October 1935', *Historical Journal*, 14: 1 (1971).

STEDMAN, A. ' "Then what could Chamberlain do other than what Chamberlain did?": The Enduring Need for a More Nuanced Understanding of British Foreign Policy and Alternatives to Appeasement', in G. Johnson (ed.), *The International Context of the Spanish Civil War* (Newcastle, 2009).

STONE, G. A., 'Britain, France and the Spanish Problem, 1936–1939', in Richardson, D. and Stone, G. (eds.), *Decisions and Diplomacy: Essays in Twentieth Century International History in Memory of George Grün and Esmonde Robertson* (London, 1995).

SULLIVAN, B., 'The Italian–Ethiopian War, October 1935 – November 1941: Causes, Conduct and Consequences', in Ion, A. H. and Errington, E. J. (eds.), *Great Powers and Little Wars: The Limits of Power* (Westport, CT, 1993).

—— 'From Little Brother to Senior Partner: Fascist Italian Perceptions of the Nazis and of Hitler's regime, 1930–1936', in Alexander, M. S. (ed.), *Knowing Your Friends: Intelligence Inside Alliances and Coalitions from 1914 to the Cold War* (London, 1998).

THOMAS, M., 'French Economic Affairs and Rearmament: The First Crucial Months, June–September 1936', *Journal of Contemporary History*, 27 (1992).

—— 'Appeasement in the Late Third Republic', *Diplomacy and Statecraft*, Vol. 19, no. 3 (September 2008).

VOLKMANN, H.-E., 'The National Socialist Economy in Preparation for War', in Militärgeschichtliches Forschungsamt (ed.), *Germany and the Second World War*, Vol. 1., ed. Wilhelm Deist et al. (Oxford, 1990).

WADDINGTON, G. T., ' "An Idyllic and Unruffled Atmosphere of Complete Anglo-German Misunderstanding": Aspects of the Operations of the Dienststelle Ribbentrop in Great Britain, 1934–1938', *History*, 82: 265 (1997).

WEINBERG, G. L., 'Hitler and England, 1933–1945: Pretence and Reality', *German Studies Review*, 8 (1985).

WHEALEY, R. H., 'Mussolini's Ideological Diplomacy: An Unpublished Document', *Journal of Modern History*, 39: 4 (1967).

WRIGHT, J. and STAFFORD, P., 'Hitler, Britain and the Hossbach Memorandum', *Militärgeschichtliche Mitteilungen*, 42 (1987).

YOUNG, R. J., 'The Strategic Dream: French Air Doctrine in the Interwar Period, 1919–1939', *Journal of Contemporary History*, 9: 4 (1974).

—— 'Soldiers and Diplomats: The French Embassy and Franco-Italian Relations, 1935–6', *Journal of Strategic Studies*, 7 (1984).

—— 'French Military Intelligence and the Franco-Italian Alliance, 1933–1939', *Historical Journal*, 28: 1 (1985).

7

Illusions of Neutrality: Eastern Europe, 1936–1938

I

Hitler's preparations for war, and the Anglo-French attempts to avoid that catastrophe through rearmament and negotiation, set the parameters for European politics between 1936 and 1938. As a consequence, the smaller powers, although diplomatically active, found their room for manoeuvre limited. All had to adjust to the conditions created by the Ethiopian and Rhineland crises, and by the outbreak of the Spanish Civil War and the deepening ideological divisions in Europe. The Eastern European states (Albania, Austria, Czechoslovakia, Poland, Hungary, Yugoslavia, Romania, Bulgaria, Greece, Lithuania, Latvia, Estonia, Finland) and Turkey, were soon to find that the differences between Western and Eastern Europe, already present in post-Locarno Europe, became more marked and dangerous to their national independence and security. As in the past, moreover, the differences between individual countries, even when they were neighbours, precluded any common regional response. One of the fundamental problems blocking such actions was often the absence of a common enemy. Depending on geography, any one or combination of states—Germany, Italy, and the Soviet Union—could seriously threaten any individual state. Particularly important in south-eastern Europe was the *rapprochement* between Italy and Germany; one or the other might be considered the primary threat. At the same time, almost all the smaller states were faced not only with the undermining of the League security system but also by the absence of any strong defender of the status quo. The former 'neutrals' from the First World War—Denmark, Finland, the Netherlands, Norway, Spain, Sweden, and Switzerland—responded to the failure of the League sanctions policy with a joint declaration on 1 July 1936 castigating the League for its inconsistent application of the Covenant and announcing that until the international community agreed to abide by the rule of law, they would not consider themselves bound by Article 16. Whether with regard to the major and even the minor diplomatic issues of the day, Geneva was relegated to a minor role and the real diplomatic action took place elsewhere. Just as there was no commonly recognized foe, there was no single Great Power patron. For the status quo nations, France still remained the most important source of potential protection. Yet its alliances had lost much of their potency and the agreements with Romania and Yugoslavia were in dire need of radical refurbishment. France, itself, was seriously weakened by the setbacks of the previous years and the Popular Front governments faced the same financial problems that had beset their predecessors. France was hardly in a position to offer the kinds of assistance that might have reassured its allies and friends. Nor could the French leaders afford to compromise their relations with the British, who repeatedly made clear their relative disinterest in Eastern Europe and strong dislike of France's eastern alliance system. Though Britain was a major investor in the region, this had not brought political influence or, in central or south-eastern Europe, expanded trade. For this reason, in the absence of any clear security concerns, Britain could take a more detached view of German involvement in Eastern Europe than France. The weakening of France and British disinterest left a power vacuum in Eastern Europe just as the aggressor nations were seizing the initiative. Few of the smaller states, even if they did not feel directly threatened by an arming Soviet Union, placed much trust in Moscow's conversion from a revisionist to a status quo power. Despite excellent intelligence and the clear signs of impending danger, regional quarrels continued to prevent or delay the adoption of measures of common defence. As almost every state feared an immediate as well as a far-off neighbour, nationalist and revisionist sentiments made it difficult to form any regional defence systems regardless of their initiator or the dangers they faced.

II

Everyone knew that Hitler intended to move and that Austria would be one of his first victims. No one could predict when or how. In fact, the Führer continued to play a waiting game while clearing the diplomatic decks for action. The Italians had been squared. The Duce's fateful journey to Berlin (25–29 September 1937) sealed the Austrian fate. Hitler could be confident that Mussolini would not object to *Anschluss*. Italy's heavy involvement in Spain could have only encouraged his optimism. France and Britain were already adjusting to the prospect of a German move into Austria. As early as February 1937, the French foreign minister told the American ambassador that France would not fight for Austrian independence and in late April, with the British ambassador present, admitted to Bullitt that Germany could take Austria

Map 5. Eastern Europe, 1933–1938

at any time.[1] In November, Papen held private conversations with Chautemps and Bonnet who told him that France would raise no objection 'to an evolutionary extension of German influence in Austria . . . or in Czechoslovakia'.[2] By early 1937, the British too had accepted the idea of German expansion in central and south-eastern Europe though they hoped that Hitler would refrain from armed aggression and any resort to force. Once Chamberlain became prime minister, he reinforced the Foreign Office view that Germany had become far too powerful for Britain to prevent some form of German predominance in the East. According to Papen's report to Hitler on 26 May, when Guido Schmidt, the Austrian foreign minister, visited London to represent Austria at the coronation ceremonies, Eden assured him that the Austrian question was arousing England's 'keenest interest' but that he was particularly pleased that Austria did not ask for commitments of any kind from third nations.[3] During Lord Halifax's conversation with Hitler at the time of his visit to Germany in November, he made clear that Britain's main interest in central Europe was the peaceful solution of the problems of Danzig, Austria, and Czechoslovakia. He assured the Führer that the British people would never approve of going to war over the issue of union between two German states. In essence, this was the British line when Chautemps and Delbos visited London in late November 1937 and agreed to let the British take the initiative in securing an agreement with Hitler.

By the early summer of 1937, Hitler was already considering a number of possibilities that could lead to German intervention and annexation, but he was prepared to wait on events until the circumstances were right for action. In Vienna, Papen was left in place to bring increasing pressure on the Austrian chancellor in the German direction. The feuding between the Austrian National Socialists, led by the 'radical' Joseph Leopold and the Seyss-Inquart gradualist faction, continued with both sides demanding that Schuschnigg implement the terms of the July 1936 accord by bringing the 'National Opposition' (National Socialists) into the government. Schuschnigg, repeatedly warned of future German action, revived the idea of a Habsburg restoration mainly as a negotiating gambit. It served only to weaken his domestic position and alarm the Italians and Hungarians. In May, the Germans made contingency plans for a military riposte to occupy Austria, ('Operation Otto'), claiming that they intended to defend the Republic. Göring strongly favoured *Anschluss* as soon as possible but Hitler held back, not

[1] *FRUS*, 1937, I, 52 and 85. [2] *DGFP*, Ser. D, Vol. I, No. 63.
[3] *DGFP*, Ser. D, Vol. I, No. 225.

yet willing to intervene either in Vienna or in Berlin where the authorities were backing different Austrian Nazi factions.

As pressures on Schuschnigg mounted, the Austrian chancellor made desperate but unsuccessful efforts to link Austria with Czechoslovakia or Hungary. Nor would the other two members of the Little Entente, despite their apprehensions about a German move into Austria, take any steps to assist him. The Hungarians, who feared the annexation of Austria and the creation of a common German–Hungarian border, were too intent on the fulfilment of their revisionist hopes and too dependent on Germany economically to take up the Austrian cause. The Romanians were less immediately threatened by *Anschluss* though an independent Austria kept Germany further away from Bucharest and gave them greater breathing room. They, too, however, were not going to challenge Hitler over Austria. Schuschnigg's attempts to seek a *détente* with Berlin during the summer months of 1937 were similarly futile; Papen only intensified his campaign of intimidation and bullying while the Austrian Nazis, with the knowledge of the Reich authorities, stepped up their activities in the country. Schuschnigg even considered an agreement with Leopold and his Austrian Nazis if their leader would give an assurance of maintaining Austrian independence, but Leopold's position was weakened when he was rejected by Papen, who feared a premature move by the uncontrollable radical leader. Schuschnigg's plans for a direct settlement came to nought. The chancellor turned to the relatively more moderate Artur Seyss-Inquart, the Vienna lawyer favoured by Papen, who proposed a form of enlarged Reich in which Austria would still play an important part. He entered the cabinet in June 1937 and easily out-manoeuvred Leopold to become the main link with the Austrian Nazi faction. Successfully disguising his extreme nationalist and Nazi convictions, he deceived Schuschnigg into thinking that he was a loyal supporter of the Republic.

Hitler still had not decided on a specific course of action. In July, Schuschnigg called a meeting of the commission set up in the July 1936 agreement to implement its programme for the *rapprochement* of the two German countries. Wilhelm Keppler, Hitler's 'eyes and ears' in Vienna and the head of the German delegation, met with Schuschnigg and other members of his cabinet but no progress was made. Papen and Keppler reported personally to Hitler on the proceedings. In response to Papen's complaints that too many German officials were fishing in the muddy Austrian waters, Keppler was made the sole Reich representative in Austria responsible for conducting relations with NSDAP. Göring and Keppler were each convinced that Hitler would settle the Austrian problem by the spring or summer of 1938. No dates were mentioned at Hitler's 5 November conference but no one present had any doubts that

Hitler intended to start on his expansionist programme in the very near future. Hitler's listeners had few concerns about Austria. No outside power was expected to intervene and there would be no military difficulties involved if German troops had to move into Austria. In Vienna, Schuschnigg refused to consider German Foreign Ministry proposals for a customs and currency union and continued to resist the German and Austrian Nazi demands that he should meet with Hitler. As Nazi activity in Austria mounted, however, he finally agreed and the meeting, postponed because of the Blomberg–Fritsch affair, took place on 15 February 1938.

III

The prospects for a German move into Czechoslovakia required more preparation than any action in Vienna given Prague's alliances with France and the Soviet Union. Once Hitler broke off the talks with Prague in early 1937, the Germans adopted a stiffer line towards Czechoslovakia. Beneš' attempts to revive the negotiations were rejected. A violent German press campaign against the Republic was paralleled by a slow tightening of controls over the Sudeten German party where Henlein had enjoyed a semi-independent position. The campaign increasingly centred on the oppression of the German minority in Czechoslovakia. The German charges were given a new boost at the start of the year when the Prague government failed to secure support for its offers of cultural and economic concessions to all the national minorities. Henlein brought in his own proposals which, in substance, would have created separate 'national groups', a solution totally unacceptable to the Hodža government as it would largely destroy the central government. The nationalities issue was a valuable propaganda tool, particularly in London where Henlein was a welcome guest during the summer of 1937 and was again received by Vansittart and by Churchill. The Foreign Office knew of the financial links between the Reich and the Sudeten German party but diplomats, including Basil Newton, the British minister in Prague, and politicians showed considerable sympathy for the Sudeten complaints. From the time that George Clerk left the legation in 1926, his successors had showed a strong distaste for the voluble Beneš, the 'Little Jack Horner' of European politics, and for the 'lumpy' and 'bourgeois' Czechs. There was something more behind their complaints about Czech xenophobia and lapses from democratic practice than mere prejudice and social snobbery, although both were demonstrably present. There were incidents in which the Prague government had behaved oppressively and had refused to acknowledge any fault. Even Jan Masaryk, the Czech minister in London, was sometimes critical of his own government. To be sure, the Czechs were far better than most of the multi-ethnic Eastern European states in their handling of minority grievances but, as a functioning democracy, their government tended to be singled out for sharp criticism in London.

Hitler's thinking about the future of Czechoslovakia had not yet crystallized into any concrete plan. At the 5 November 1937 meeting Hitler only told his officers that the question of Czechoslovakia would be solved by force and authorized 'Operation Green', the planned attack against Czechoslovakia. The timing of the immediate action had not been settled. Beneš, concerned about the loyalty of the Sudeten Germans, was increasingly disinclined to go any further in the direction of offering autonomy. Once the Germans internationalized the issue, Sudeten German grievances became diplomatic dynamite. The *Quai d'Orsay* took a sympathetic view of Beneš' nationality problems and repeatedly rejected Foreign Office demands that they press him to make greater and more rapid concessions to the Sudeten Germans. Naturally, Hitler played on the differences between London and Paris. While stoking the embers of domestic dissatisfaction, Hitler considered the possibilities of launching his military action. The wooing of Poland and of Yugoslavia and Romania was intended to isolate Czechoslovakia and make it difficult, if not impossible, for the French to turn the Little Entente into an anti-German bloc.

IV

Hitler kept a close watch over Polish affairs where Göring maintained his own special interest. German–Polish relations could not be left to the traditionally anti-Polish Wilhelmstrasse. The major problem remained Danzig where Hitler took special pains not to allow disputes there to disrupt his Polish treaty. He intervened when Albert Forster, the head of the National Socialists in the Free City, grew too assertive or when Forster's rivalry with the nominal head of the Danzig government, the more cautious Arthur Greiser, grew too intense. Unlike Neurath, Hitler was prepared to compromise with the Poles when it appeared useful. This was clear when the two sides clashed over the Convention of 1922 which assured minority rights to those living on both sides of divided Upper Silesia. The convention ran out in July 1937 after which the Germans would be free to apply their anti-Semitic laws to the few hundred Jews living in their sector.[4] The Nazis pressed the case of the

[4] Jewish representatives brought the case of Bernheim, a Jew who had lived in Upper Silesia, to the League minorities committee and scored a major success.

many thousands of German-speaking people living under Polish rule in what they called East Upper Silesia. The Poles, having repudiated the League's role in protecting minorities in 1934, refused to renegotiate the treaty but were prepared for simultaneous Polish–German declarations. Due mainly to Polish obstruction, little progress had been made when the convention expired in July.

Because of repeated anti-Polish incidents provoked by Forster and the possibility, admitted by Carl Burkhardt, the high commissioner, that the League of Nations might soon withdraw from the Free City, Józef Beck, the all-powerful Polish foreign minister, moved to secure his country's rights. Both sides continued to complain about the treatment of their nationals but neither were willing to take up the issue in the months that followed. Beck visited Berlin in January 1938; Göring made one of his frequent trips to Warsaw in February. On both occasions, Beck was told that there would be German action against Austria and Czechoslovakia but was assured that Polish economic interests in Austria would be respected and that Poland itself would be treated as a friend. In his speech on 20 February 1938, with his attention already focused on Vienna, Hitler spoke of his deep concern for the fate of Germans living in Austria and Czechoslovakia while praising Poland's leaders and dwelling on the happy situation in Danzig as an example to all. How far Beck trusted the Germans is open to debate. Beck, though vain, was no fool; when he made the 1934 treaty with Germany, he had spoken of a ten-year respite. Quite apart from the strong Francophile sentiments in the army and in the upper classes, there was no disposition in Warsaw to abandon the French alliance or to substitute German for French armaments. German–Polish trade was kept within strictly defined limits and no massive clearing balances were allowed to accumulate. Though the Germans, and in particular Göring, would have liked to include Poland in the Anti-Comintern alliance and dangled the Ukraine as bait, Beck was not tempted. Like Piłsudski, he considered the Soviet Union more dangerous than Nazi Germany and would have nothing to do with any 'Paris–Prague–Moscow Axis' but this did not mean dropping France. Overtures were made to the British but Beck was as much disliked and distrusted in London as in Paris, and the Foreign Office had no wish to meddle in Polish affairs. Eden reflected Foreign Office thinking when he commented on a survey sent by the British minister in Warsaw, '[Beck] is an unsatisfactory individual to work with and shifty even to the extent of injuring his own country.'[5]

[5] Quoted in Gerhard L.Weinberg, *The Foreign Policy of Hitler's Germany: Diplomatic Revolution in Europe, 1933–1936* (Chicago, IL, 1970), 208 (fn. 63).

Poland was almost as exposed as Czechoslovakia to domestic difficulties and to shifts in Hitler's policies. Political life after Piłsudski's death in 1935 was tumultuous. The effects of the depression were long-lasting and peasants and urban workers moved to the extremes of the political spectrum. Minority discontents were intensified and without the protection that Piłsudski had offered the Jews, anti-Semitism again blazed in the country. Poised between two dangerous enemies and protected only by its weakened alliance with France, Beck's dreams of a Polish sphere of influence extending from the Baltic to the Black Sea lacked all substance. More realistically, the Polish foreign minister believed he could buy time by keeping Hitler's attention centred on Austria and Czechoslovakia. Not only did he refuse to take any step towards Prague as urged by the French, but he worked closely with the Hungarians and Romanians in preparation for Czechoslovakia's possible dismemberment. He sought to promote agreements between Hungary and Yugoslavia and between Hungary and Romania. Both *rapprochements* would facilitate the division of Czechoslovakia between these would-be heirs. This proved far too ambitious a programme, particularly as the understanding between Italy and Poland, which might have given substance to this edifice, never actually materialized. For the moment, the existing state of German–Polish affairs suited both parties.

V

Hitler was not slow in capitalizing on his anti-Bolshevik crusade, as well as his new partnership with Mussolini, in courting Yugoslavia and Romania. The French loss of prestige after the Rhineland occupation and the ideological overtones of the Spanish Civil War paved the way for a sea-change in south-eastern Europe. Yugoslavia, Hitler knew, was the weakest link in the 'rusted chain' that bound the Little Entente together and Belgrade became the centre of considerable activity during 1937. On 24 January, Yugoslavia and Bulgaria signed a treaty promising 'inviolable peace and sincere and perpetual friendship' between the two nations. This settlement with the 'outcast' of the Balkans alarmed the other Balkan states and caused the Romanians and the French particular anguish. Each tried to block the new arrangement fearing that Yugoslavia would detach herself from the Little Entente and move out of its former regional orbit. Their efforts proved unavailing, particularly as Beneš gave his unconditional approval to the new pact, possibly because he felt liberality might keep Yugoslavia loyal to the Little Entente.

The Italians, too, were active in Belgrade. On 25 March 1937, Ciano and Stojadinović, the Yugoslav foreign minister (January 1935 – February 1939), signed new political and economic accords on terms highly favourable to Yugoslavia. The Germans had been urging such a treaty since the autumn of 1936 hoping that Prince Paul's policy of neutrality would lead him away from France. Ignoring the possible anti-German aspect of the treaty and rightly believing that the Italians could not challenge the German mastery of the Yugoslav economy, Germany would benefit from the disruption of the Little Entente and the straining of Belgrade's ties with Paris. The political agreements were negotiated between the Italian officials and Dr Ivan Subotić, a highly experienced and much respected diplomat sent from Geneva to Rome. The final talks between Ciano and Subotić in early March were conducted in the greatest secrecy. The Germans were kept informed of their progress but nothing was said to the French. After much argument, both parties agreed not to seek any special or exclusive political and economic advantages that would compromise the independence of Albania. No mention was made of the existing Italian position in Albania, confirmed in March 1936 by new financial, trade, and economic agreements with Tirana. The Italians promised to respect the territorial integrity of Yugoslavia and not to tolerate the activities of the terrorists in Italy, the Croatian Ustaši, who were still receiving Italian subsidies. Each power gave a pledge of neutrality in case of unprovoked aggression. Subotić withstood Italian pressure for an alliance and forced the Italians to recognize existing Yugoslav obligations as a member of the Little Entente, the Balkan Entente, and the League of Nations. Stojadinović was able to claim in Paris that his country was only following a policy of equilibrium and would maintain her friendship with France. The economic accords with Italy were also favourable to Belgrade. Italy agreed to increase its imports and to extend 'most favoured nation' treaty rights to its neighbour. The increase in trade was mainly at Czech expense.

When Ciano came to Belgrade to sign the treaty in March, he and the cynical, tough-minded, and supremely self-confident Stojadinović found much in common. Stojadinović assured Ciano that an eventual Italian–Yugoslav alliance was 'natural and inevitable' and that there would be no alliance with France. He anathematized the Blum government for its niggardly ways and deplored the 'truly deleterious and disruptive influence of the Jewish, Masonic and Communistic mentality' of Blum's France.[6] 'The French always accuse anyone of selfishness', he told Ciano, 'who is not prepared to let himself be killed for them'.[7] The question of Germany was delicately handled. The two men extolled their good relations with Berlin yet each hoped to deter a German movement towards the Adriatic after the inevitable *Anschluss* took

[6] Quoted in Nicole Jordan, *The Popular Front and Central Europe*, 255.

[7] J. B. Hoptner, *Yugoslavia in Crisis, 1934–1941* (New York and London, 1962), 81.

place. While not anticipating immediate German action, Stojadinović tried to enlist Italian support for making Yugoslavia the principal power in the region. In a later conversation with Prince Paul, Ciano returned to earlier themes: 'Germany is a dangerous enemy but a disagreeable friend. *Anschluss* is inevitable, the Italo-Yugoslav union a necessity in our future relations with Germany. As for the rest, our pact should attract other countries into our orbit. An understanding with Hungary is desirable. When Vienna becomes the second German capital, Budapest should be ours.'[8] The Italian courting of Yugoslavia was intended to offset the extension of German influence in the Balkans.

Though the French put a good public face on the agreement, there was consternation in Paris. The *Quai d'Orsay* was not officially informed until February 1938. Delbos thought that the new Rome–Belgrade treaty, which the French had so eagerly sought in the past, would protect Mussolini's position in the Balkans and allow him to concentrate on Spain. Coming after the Italian defeat at Guadalajara, Delbos interpreted the Italian action as the preliminary to a large-scale military intervention in Spain. The *Quai d'Orsay* was not taken in by Stojadinović's assurances during his Paris visit in November 1937 about the fragility of the Axis. The French had to accept that the new treaty dealt a major blow to their Balkan strategy.

A worried Beneš followed Ciano to Belgrade. Whether because Prague was running out of alternatives or because of some lingering hopes of a settlement with Germany, Beneš told Prince Paul that he did 'not believe in the German danger, German strength or German designs on Czechoslovakia' and argued that Hitler was a 'puppet' in the hands of his army.[9] On his return to Prague, Beneš not only minimized the dangers of the new agreement but put out unrequited overtures to Rome vainly hoping to resurrect the idea of an Italian–Little Entente agreement to block *Anschluss*. During the latter half of 1937, Mussolini turned a deaf ear to Beneš' importunings. Whatever his attempts to downplay the German danger to Prague, Beneš could not have under-estimated the importance of the Yugoslav defection. The Foreign Office, like the *Quai d'Orsay*, made equally vain efforts to keep Yugoslavia out of the Italian orbit. Its warnings to Stojadinović had little effect in the face of its own efforts to come to an agreement with Italy. As the British opposed a French treaty with the Little Entente powers, they urged Delbos to accept the new treaty as a *fait accompli*.

In Bucharest, too, where King Carol was keeping the Iron Guard at bay, support for a policy of 'neutralism' provided an opening for the Germans notwithstanding the widespread Francophile sentiments in

[8] Ibid., 83. [9] Ibid., 84.

the capital based on the traditional cultural links between the upper classes of the two countries and a special relationship between the general staffs. The French, and more importantly, the Czechs, were supplying the bulk of the desperately needed arms to the Romanians on generous terms. The Germans also faced the problem of the insoluble Romanian–Hungarian conflict. Transylvania with its large Magyar population made it highly unlikely, whatever the Germans proposed, that the Romanians and Hungarians would bury their differences. As long as Nazi Germany appeared as Hungary's protector, there were limits on any *rapprochement* between Berlin and Bucharest. Nonetheless, once King Carol and Antonescu, his foreign minister, abandoned Titulescu's earlier Russophile and Francophile policies and moved to establish a more neutral position in European politics, they were prepared to follow Poland's example and conclude bilateral treaties wherever they could. In the winter and spring of 1937 they even offered the Soviet Union a non-aggression treaty in return for an acknowledgment of Romanian sovereignty over Bessarabia. Litvinov was rightly suspicious, for neither the king nor Antonescu would consider a treaty of mutual guarantee nor enter into any arrangement permitting Russian troops to move through their country as Titulescu had been prepared to consider. In March 1937, in Geneva, Litvinov denounced the earlier Gentlemen's Agreement made over Bessarabia and warned that the Soviet Union would press its claims should Bucharest draw closer to Berlin. While sounding out the Russians, the Romanians were actively discussing new political as well as commercial links with Germany. To counter the Romanian talks with Russia and France, Göring offered the possibility of a bilateral agreement, a 'precise state guarantee' of Romania's territorial integrity. The Romanians were not totally immune to Göring's diplomatic carrot. The German alliance would provide protection against Hungary and Bulgaria and the German demands, a long-term commercial pact, rejection of talks with the Soviet Union over the passage of troops through Romania, and the refusal of the French–Little Entente pact, was very much in line with the king's own priorities. An actual alliance with Germany, however, was not. Once the possibility of the French pact was buried, nothing more was heard of Göring's alliance offer. The Germans 'did not yet possess the leverage necessary to bring about a reversal of Romania's orientation'.[10]

The German and Italian wooing of Yugoslavia and Romania was bound to complicate relations with the Hungarians. The Italians lost considerable influence in Budapest once their interest in Vienna and in

[10] Dov Lungu, *Romania and the Great Powers, 1933–1940* (Durham and London, 1989), 103.

the three-power agreement faded. At the same time, though Ciano might have been willing to sacrifice Hungary in favour of Romania, Mussolini was unwilling to drop the Hungarians. Ciano had to tell Stojadinović that 'Italy's friendship with Hungary prevented her from going too far in her relations with the Romanians, although, apart from Hungarian revisionism, there was no difference between Italy and Romania.'[11] Neurath took the same line with the Hungarian foreign minister, Kálmán Kánya. It was not just Romania that stood between Germany and Hungary. German relations with Budapest, particularly after the death of Prime Minister Gömbös in October 1936, were distinctly uneasy. Some of these difficulties predated Gömbös' death, for the prime minister, while welcoming Hitler's advice to direct his forces against Czechoslovakia, would not renounce the Hungarian territories annexed by Yugoslavia and Romania. In this respect, his successors were only continuing Gömbös' policies. There were other sources of tension. The German element in Hungary resisted Magyarization and was attracted by the Reich's siren calls. The German sympathizers found fertile grounds for political intrigues in extreme right-wing circles. This hardly endeared them to the Budapest government, already worried by the increasing popularity of the native Nazi admirers who had the support of highly placed officers on the general staff and permanent officials in several ministries.

For their part, neither Admiral Horthy nor Kánya, though both strong revisionists, were overly sympathetic to Hitler or to his Nazi regime. Both men had served the Habsburgs; Horthy, moreover, as an ex-admiral in the Habsburg navy, had little time for a one-time army corporal. More important, neither man believed that Germany would prevail in a new European war and their views were shared by the older generation of Hungarian politicians. These men instinctively assumed that British naval power would prove decisive in any future European struggle and were determined that Hungary should not again join the losing side. The officer corps, on the contrary, which had considerable political clout, believed that Hungary would inevitably be drawn into the next war, if only because the Little Entente powers would invade Hungary at the outset of any conflict. They wanted Hungary to be prepared to fight alongside the Germans. Admirers of the Nazi system, the Hungarian officers, many of German ethnic background, sought a firm military and political alliance with Berlin. In the spring and summer of 1937, the general staff demanded that the Budapest government adopt a massive programme of military modernization but their

[11] Ciano Papers, p. 102, quoted in C. A. Macartney and A. W. Palmer, *Independent Eastern Europe* (London and New York, 1966), 361.

proposals were rejected on both political and economic grounds. Kánya thought their adoption would dangerously increase Hungary's reliance on Germany and strengthen the hand of the Arrow Cross movements already capitalizing on the economic discontent in the country and the intensifying anti-Semitic mood. Horthy's advisers thought the plans financially ruinous and the downturn in world prices for agricultural produce in the spring of 1937 increased their hesitancy. The Hungarians were militarily exposed and serious rearmament had just begun. Kánya had no wish to be involved in a war against Czechoslovakia. The foreign minister preferred to keep a low profile and to rearm slowly so as not to alarm Hungary's neighbours. Due to Italian and German urgings, talks were opened with Yugoslavia in March 1937 but they dragged on without successful issue. Stojadinović, whose new diplomatic initiatives had so upset his Little Entente partners, could not afford to affront them further by making a separate treaty with the Hungarians. Very much to Hitler's displeasure, in the light of his forthcoming plans, the Hungarians decided to negotiate with each of the three Little Entente states simultaneously and did so successfully in the summer of 1938 just when Hitler wanted to see Czechoslovakia totally isolated.

Furious at Kánya's resistance to their programme and the delays in rearmament that were blamed on the Jews and Socialists, the army officers grew restive. Using the Hungarian ambassador in Berlin, Döme Sztójay, a former general staff officer, they pressed the Germans for joint staff talks. They also approached the regent and lobbied for a more active rearmament programme and the replacement of his 'ineffective' civilian government by an authoritarian right-wing government based on military support. Horthy refused to co-operate. He accepted the advice of his civilian advisers that an army engaged in politics was 'not only worthless but harmful too'.[12] This check to military ambitions was compromised, however, when in late November 1937 the Hungarian government was informed of Hitler's plans for the future destruction of Czechoslovakia. Kálmán Darányi, Gömbös' successor as prime minister, and his foreign minister, Kálmán Kánya went to Berlin on 21 November 1937 to confer with Hitler and Göring. The Führer made it clear that with the dismemberment of Czechoslovakia, the Hungarians could have all of Slovakia including Pressburg and sub-Carpathian Ukraine. Darányi was told that if Hungary concentrated all its efforts on Czechoslovakia, Hitler would support its demand for Yugoslav non-involvement in any conflict with Czechoslovakia and

[12] Quoted from a speech of Horthy's on 3 April 1938, in Thomas L. Sakmyster, 'Army Officers and Foreign Policy in Interwar Hungary, 1938–1941', *Journal of Contemporary History*, 10 (1975), 28.

would, at some later date, consider a revision of the Hungarian/Romanian border in Budapest's favour. Hitler and Darányi agreed to joint political and military action against Prague and to joint consultations between the two general staffs. Hungarian soundings in Warsaw were favourable; the Poles had no interest in the German promised territories and would not contest the Hungarian claims. The situation would change at the beginning of 1938.

It was a bargain that the Hungarian leaders could not resist. Public opinion in Hungary had been indoctrinated for nearly twenty years to support the return of the seized territories. The internal pressures exerted by the Fascist 'Arrow Cross' movements were intensifying. Believing that war would break out in 1940 or 1941, government plans were laid (Kánya was excluded from the relevant meetings) for a massive rearmament programme. Early in 1938, a Five-Year Plan for public works and rearmament was adopted. The Darányi government, hoping to lessen the growing appeal of the 'Arrow Cross', introduced in May 1938 a long-heralded but much delayed anti-Semitic bill providing for the gradual elimination of Jews from business, the professions, and public service within five years. It was a measure bound to radically shake the national economy, for the Magyars, since the creation of the Dual Monarchy in 1867, had considered trade, commerce, industry, and banking as unfit occupations for landowners and had left such matters to the relatively well-placed Jews.

VI

While Hitler took an active part in both the diplomatic and military preparations for his first moves towards territorial expansion, the German economic offensive in south-eastern Europe gathered new momentum. This owed little to Hitler. Reference has been made to Schacht's strategies to meet the balance of payments crisis of 1934. The repudiation of the American debts and the conclusion of the Anglo–German Payments Agreement of 1934 was followed by a dramatic drop in trade with the United States and serious cuts in trading with Britain and France. It has been convincingly argued that the German policy of autarchy consisted mainly of selective disengagement from trade with the United States, Great Britain, and France.[13] Imports from the rest of the world remained basically unchanged from the pre-depression peak

[13] A. O. Ritschl, 'Nazi Economic Imperialism and the Exploitation of the Small: Evidence from Germany's Secret Foreign Exchange Balances, 1938–1940', *Economic History Review*, 54 (2001), 344.

Table 7.1 Germany's Share of East European Trade (%) (Figures for 1938 include Austria. The1929 figures for Czechoslovakia and Poland refer to 1928.)

	Exports to Germany				Imports from Germany			
	1929	1932	1937	1938	1929	1932	1937	1938
Bulgaria	22.9	26	43.1	59	22.2	25.9	54.8	52
Czechoslovakia	22.1	19.6	13.7	20.1	24.9	22.9	15.5	19.1
Hungary	11.7	15.2	24	40	20	22.5	25.9	40.9
Poland	34.2	16.2	14.5	24.1	26.9	29.1	14.5	23
Romania	27.4	12.5	22.3	26.5	24.1	23.6	28.9	40
Yugoslavia	8.5	11.3	21.7	42	15.6	17.7	32.4	39.4

Source: Derek H. Aldcroft and Steven Morewood, *Economic Change in Eastern Europe since 1918* (Aldershot, 1995), 67.

Table 7.2 Changes in the Direction of German Trade, 1929 and 1938 (%)

	German Imports		German Exports	
	1929	1938	1929	1938
Europe				
Southern and Eastern Europe	9.8	18.7	11.2	20.8
Scandinavian countries	7.4	11.3	10.2	12.9
Austria	1.5	n/a	3.3	n/a
Gold bloc and Czechoslovakia	23.6	16.1	35.2	26
United Kingdom	6.4	5.2	9.7	6.7
Total Europe	48.7	51.3	69.6	66.4
Rest of the World				
British dominions and colonies	12.5	10.3	4.3	6.1
United States	13.3	7.4	7.4	2.8
Latin America	12.1	16.8	7.8	12.1
Other countries	13.4	14.2	10.9	12.6
Total rest of the world	51.3	48.7	30.4	33.6

Source: Charles H. Feinstein, Peter Temin, and Gianni Toniolo, *The European Economy between the Wars* (Oxford, 1997), 164.

though the ratio of imports to national product was lower in 1938 than in 1928.

Schacht hoped to compensate for this contraction in trade by cultivating links with producers in south-east Europe and in Latin America, where Brazil (cotton and coffee) and Chile (copper and saltpetre) became important suppliers. The German share of trade with Latin America grew significantly between 1933 and 1936, sometimes at American expense. In 1934, Germany supplied 14% of all Brazilian

TABLE 7.3 Disengagement of Germany from Trade with Western Powers, 1928–1938 (million RM/million RM of 1928)

(a) By Country Imports

	From US		From Britain		From France	
	Nominal	Deflated	Nominal	Deflated	Nominal	Deflated
1928	2062.2	2062.2	893.8	893.8	740.8	740.8
1938	404.6	965.8	282.8	619.5	143.7	346.1
% change	−80.4	−53.2	−68.4	−30.7	−80.6	−53.3

(b) Effect of Trade Total

	Total		Minus US, Britain, and France	
	Nominal	Deflated	Nominal	Deflated
1928	14001.3	14001.3	10304.5	10304.5
1938	6051.7	11973.3	5220.6	10041.9
% change	−56.8	−14.5	−49.3	−2.5

Source: A. O. Ritschl, 'Nazi Economic Imperialism and the Exploitation of the Small: Evidence from Germany's Secret Foreign Exchange Balances, 1938–1940', *Economic History Review*, New Series, 54: 2 (2001), 343.

imports compared with America's 23.6%. By 1936, the figures were 23.5% and 22.1% respectively, despite a trade agreement between Brazil and the United States. In Chile, too, Germany supplied 28% of all imports compared with 25.4% for the United States. In 1938, 15% of total German imports came from Latin America compared with 10% from south-eastern Europe.[14] Between 1934 and 1936, when there was a sharp reduction in imports from the United States and the Western European countries, imports from these other regions rose and German exports almost doubled. Because of improved world trading conditions, Schacht's export subsidies, and other controls, Germany actually showed a positive trade balance of 440 million marks at the end of 1936, almost four times that of 1935 despite the marked rise in imports. By the end of 1935, over half of Germany's total foreign trade was conducted within the clearing system; nine of the twenty-three countries involved were in central and south-east Europe with Romania, Hungary, Bulgaria, and Yugoslavia, holding the largest credit balances in the German Clearing Accounting Office in Berlin. The clearings did not actually lead to the flows of real resources or convertable currency

[14] William Carr, *Poland to Pearl Harbor: The Making of the Second World War* (London, 1985), 14.

that would have allowed Germany to exploit its smaller trading partners though the Germans established a dominant place in south-eastern Europe comparable to that enjoyed by Imperial Germany and Austria-Hungary before the First World War.[15] Germany's improved performance could not solve either its import needs or its chronic foreign exchange problems. These increased during the autumn and winter of 1936–1937 because of rising world food prices and new demands for basic foodstuffs resulting from increased employment. The disproportionate development of the capital investment sector, stimulated further by rearmament orders, further increased the demand for raw materials that required the use of foreign exchange. Even with its temporary positive trade balance, Germany had only about half the foreign exchange needed for essential imports. Neither the requisition of foreign currency in private hands nor the development of the synthetic industries provided a satisfactory solution.

In the winter of 1936–1937, Göring, who as a result of Hitler's decision to accelerate the preparations for war had replaced Schacht as the real power in the armament recovery, faced a major food crisis that required a rapid and large increase in agricultural imports. He had to use Schacht's tactics in the Balkans and Baltic even as the latter's influence waned. Schacht had already agreed, in his difficult negotiations with Yugoslavia and Romania during 1936, to pay higher than world market prices and to accept import quotas. He also gave way to demands for certain kinds of German exports and was driven to accept partial payment in foreign exchange or in foreign exchange-worthy goods. Both Belgrade and Bucharest won concessions with regard to the clearing balances, either through the pegging of exchange rates or guarantees of existing exchange rates. In other words, Göring inherited a situation in which the Yugoslavs and Romanians were in an excellent position to extract good terms from the Reich if bargains were to be concluded. In practice, neither side favoured the accumulation of large balances in Reichsmarks. Though Schacht had exploited the clearing system to meet the German need for imports, he was concerned, as were German industrialists at the time, to stimulate exports and even to create a permanent export surplus that would allow Germany to re-enter the world trading system. He had demanded that the Yugoslavs and the Romanians increase their imports from Germany and provide entry for German industrial firms into their country. In 1936, for instance, Krupp won a contract for the construction of a rolling mill at Zenica in Yugoslavia. Protracted negotiations, continued throughout 1937, were begun between the Romanian state-owned mining company,

[15] Ritschl, 'Germany's Foreign Exchange Balances, 1938–1940', 336–337.

Rimma, and Ferrostaal, a German subsidiary of the Ruhr steel-coal combine GHH (*Gutehoffnungshütte*). Since lack of investment capital made it almost impossible for Germany to compete with the dominant British and French, the entry of German firms into these countries was one of the most promising ways of establishing an industrial presence and securing an independent raw materials base.

The bilateral negotiations involved tough and prolonged bargaining by state bureaucrats and representatives of industry. The food-producing nations drove hard bargains though no other importing country could purchase the large amounts of foodstuffs required by Germany nor at the higher than world market prices the Germans paid. Göring's own administrative incompetence and interdepartmental competition as well as difficulties with private industrial concerns anxious to exploit the opportunities for exports, added to the Reich's difficulties. There was, however, more co-operation among the bureaucrats and even between the Four-Year Plan and the older government departments than actually appeared. An important co-ordinating body, the *Handelspolitischer Ausschuss,* chaired by the head of the Wilhelmstrasse's trade policy department (Karl Ritter for most of the period), was still working quite effectively in the late 1930s. Whatever the difficulties, the Reich was achieving many of its major import objectives in south-east Europe. The figures show how successful the Germans were in Bulgaria, Hungary, Romania, and Yugoslavia but also, though to a lesser degree because of the British presence, in Turkey and Greece.

The Germans increased their share of both Turkish imports and exports and participated in the country's various development plans launched in 1937. It was, however, British capital that took the lion's share both in these projects and in Turkey's rearmament programmes. In Greece, King George, who had returned from exile in 1932, ended four years of political struggle by appointing General Ioannis Metaxas as minister for army affairs in March 1936. Metaxas assumed dictatorial powers in August. A traditionalist, paternal authoritarian rather than a Fascist, Metaxas instituted, along with the usual political trappings of an authoritarian state including the abolition of all parties and suspending civil rights, major investment and public work schemes. The Germans traded on their already existing position in Greece; they bought large quantities of tobacco and provided foreign exchange with which Greece could buy arms and fortify her frontier with Bulgaria. Once again, however, like the Turks with whom Greek diplomatic ties were tightened, Metaxas wanted to keep out of bloc politics. While strongly favouring Germany in matters of trade, he had no wish to quarrel with Britain and repeatedly assured London that Greece was 'irrevocably and unreservedly devoted to the British connection'.[16] King George was a known Anglophile and Metaxas, at first, needed royal support for his regime. The British were somewhat critical of Metaxas' dictatorial methods and had watched with some apprehension the increase in Greek–German trade, including extensive arms purchases particularly in 1936 and 1937.[17] Between 1935 and 1937, the value of Greek exports to Germany, especially of tobacco, more than doubled.[18] With imports far exceeding exports, large Greek credits were built up in Berlin. The Greeks tried without success to have these assets liquidated into hard and convertible currency but the Germans demanded increased imports of German goods. It was not until the conclusion of a German–Greek arms deal in late 1936 and huge purchases of German war material that the Greek clearing credits were finally reduced. Though the French conglomerate, Schneider-Creusot, through its Škoda plant, still had a major position in Greece, Romania, and Yugoslavia, in Greece, a German firm in which *Reichswerke Hermann Göring* had a major share, *Rheinmetall-Borsig*, took over its contracts with the Greek Powder and Cartridge Company, a private company controlled and managed by Prodromos Bodosakis-Athanasiadis. Not only did the company supply the Greek army with arms and ammunition but, with Bodosakis as the main intermediary, it was an important arms exporter to Republican Spain, Turkey, Romania, and China. The Germans supplied much of the machinery, steel, tools, and technical know-how needed by the company and were paid in hard currency and gold. It is hardly surprising that Göring allowed, or even encouraged the Greek arms sales abroad, including to Republican Spain.[19]

There was some resistance to the German demands. When the Germans, at Göring's insistence (in a decree issued in July 1937), demanded 100% payment in hard currency for the new Dornier Do 17 bomber, the Greeks refused, rejecting even a later compromise offer and ordered their bombers from France. There were, moreover, important British concessions in Greece and while Metaxas was anxious to nationalize the telecommunications and electrical supply companies, in both cases

[16] Quoted in John S. Koliopoulos, *Greece and the British Connection, 1935–1941* (Oxford, 1977), 60.

[17] Ibid., 125. Value of arms sold to Greece by Germany in million RM according to *Ausfuhrgemeinschaft für Kriegsgerät*: 1936—23.5, 1937—16.5, 1938—9.8, 1939—7.0.

[18] Half of Greece's export trade was in tobacco and Germany bought about 50%. See the details in Mogens Pelt, *Tobacco, Arms and Politics: Greece and Germany from World Crisis to World War, 1929–1941* (Copenhagen, 1998), 110–132.

[19] In May 1938, the Germans officially banned arms exports to Greece and Turkey because of resales to countries on the German blacklist and to China. This did not prevent Greek purchases of war material or further delivery of arms to China. Mogens Pelt, *Tobacco, Arms and Politics*, 145–171. Patrick Finney, University of Wales at Aberystwyth brought this book to my attention.

the British concessions were renewed. Whatever the strength of the German economic position in Greece, as a maritime nation dependent on its sea imports for foodstuffs and other essential commodities, the Greeks could ill afford to alienate the British. Their highly profitable merchant fleet earned most of its income through the carrying trade for Britain and was, of course, insured in London. Whatever the doubts of the British government about the Metaxas dictatorship, the British Foreign Office opted to pursue a hands-off policy as far as Greek domestic politics were concerned. There seemed no reason to take any active steps to strengthen its ties with Greece. King George's visit to London in November 1937 resulted in little more than a reiteration of Britain's traditional friendship and sympathy for the Greek people and their government.

By the end of 1937, despite the slight decrease in trade with Czechoslovakia, the German penetration of the Danubian and Balkan states was sufficient to provide it with important, if still woefully inadequate, supplies of foodstuffs and raw materials. Imports from the agricultural states of Eastern Europe increased from 364.5 million RM in 1936 to 555.8 million RM in 1937. Enough grain was purchased to avoid a repetition of the winter crisis of 1936–1937.[20] Raw materials were available for consumer goods and limited quantities of metals and ores were imported for rearmament purposes. Admittedly, German successes varied from state to state and what was won, as in Bulgaria where Germany took almost the whole of the country's tobacco output, was not necessarily critical for the country's economy.[21] Some governments were more co-operative than others; most put up a stiff fight to get the best terms possible. The Poles refused to run up Reichsmark balances in the clearings and German imports of cereal grains remained at a relatively low level. The Hungarians, having accumulated a large Reichsmark balance during 1936, refused to sell wheat through the clearings in the next year. According to the German negotiators, during the first half of 1937, the Hungarians offered less than what had been promised under the terms of the 1934 treaty. New talks began in June and resulted in Hungarian promises to provide 100,000 tons of corn and 50,000 tons of wheat during the next year. This was, however, less than 10% of the Hungarian annual surplus and only half of what the Germans

[20] D. Kaiser, *Economic Diplomacy and the Origins of the Second World War* (Princeton, NJ, 1980), 160.

[21] Macartney and Palmer, *Independent Eastern Europe*, 338–339. In 1937, Germany was taking 67.6% of Bulgaria's exports and providing 59% of her imports and was Bulgaria's only source of arms.

wanted. In return, Germany had to supply Hungary with cellulose, artificial silk, and various mineral products that the Hungarians needed for rearmament but could not afford to buy on the world market.

Germany's greatest success in 1937 was in Yugoslavia. Germany already held almost one-third of the Yugoslav market in 1936 and had replaced Italy as Belgrade's chief trading partner. In the following year, Yugoslavia sent 35% of her total exports to Germany and took 43% of her total imports from Germany. She sent only 9% of her exports and took only 8% of her imports from Italy. In the tortuous negotiations which followed Schacht's visit to Belgrade in 1936 and finally concluded at Dubrovnik in October 1937, the Germans won much of what they wanted though at a considerable price. They conceded the principle of prior German payments through exports before the Yugoslavs would deliver the raw materials ordered. The promise of prior exports, however, was restricted only to the new additional grain quotas of cereals for 1938, without any reference to the large clearing debts resulting from earlier grain purchases. The Germans succeeded in nullifying the punitive Yugoslav quota system introduced the previous spring and were able, as their grain shortage became less acute, to adjust the quota structure to favour industrial raw materials, particularly iron ore, over imports of agricultural goods. It was at this time, too, that Stojadinović expressed an active interest in buying aircraft, submarines, and a destroyer from Berlin. The rolling mill at Zenica built by Krupp, was officially opened. Stojadinović made it perfectly clear that the project was part of Yugoslavia's disengagement from France. He assured the Germans that Belgrade would not grant preference to Czech industrial goods and would have nothing to do with suggestions for closer Little Entente economic co-operation.

The Germans did well in Romania, too, though success did not come easily and again they had to pay higher than world prices for the Romanian goods. Oil was one of the major stumbling blocks in the negotiations between the two states. Romania was the fourth largest oil exporter in the world and was rapidly increasing its production with fields that could be further exploited. Domestic production in Germany, whether of regular or synthetic fuels, could hardly match the needs of a hoped-for mechanized and motorized army and an expanding air force. Though supplies came from Venezuela and the United States, Romania was a far more attractive and safer source that would not require hard currency for payment. The Romanians had a first-class negotiating tool and exploited it as far as possible. The Bucharest negotiators who met the Germans in the autumn of 1936 insisted that the latter's imports of oil and oil products should be restricted to one quarter of all German imports from Romania. It was finally agreed with Helmuth Wohlthat, the representative from the *Reichsstelle für Devisenbewirtschaftung* and chairman of the government committee for trade with Romania, that Germany would be allowed to purchase extra oil through supplementary compensation agreements highly favourable to Romania and the shipment of armaments to Bucharest. These autumn arrangements created large clearing balances in the Romanian National Bank accounts in Berlin, a problem that hampered further talks when the Germans again sought to increase their grain and oil imports in 1937. The Romanian National Bank, whose directors were strongly Francophile in their sympathies, was unwilling or unable to support the exchange rate of the mark. Its value fell and wild fluctuations occurred in the exchange rates. As a consequence, there was growing resistance to any further bargaining until the problem of the clearings was addressed. Göring, like Schacht, tried to promote state contracts for German firms as a possible way out of the German difficulties but German efforts in 1936 raised opposition both in Romania and in Germany from other industrialists. Talks stalled in the summer of 1936 because the German firm demanded a Reich guarantee of the credit to be extended to the Romanian firm. The German Finance Ministry thought the whole bargain highly risky and only reluctantly agreed to back the transaction in September 1936. A Finance Ministry official wrote that

> decisive for my decision were the trade policy considerations cited by you, that because of the significance of the Romanian markets for the total German raw materials and food economy it appears suitable to remain in many-sided transactions, even in the case of possible sacrifices. In this connection there comes into play the significance of the treaty in terms of foreign policy and its impact upon later armament transactions at a point when it appears that a shift of the Romanian conception of politics to one near our own point of view seems to be in preparation.[22]

The protracted negotiations between Rimma and Ferrostaal were not finally concluded until the end of 1937, despite pressing German demands for ore and petroleum. In the summer of 1937, too, a German–Dutch firm concluded a small U-boat deal that proved to be a breakthrough into the Romanian armaments market which still remained mainly in French and Czech hands.

It was only after eight months of Romanian procrastination that in the summer of 1937 the Germans were assured of the bread and fodder grains they demanded as part of a trade deal with Bucharest. There were

[22] Quoted in William S. Grenzebach, *Germany's Informal Empire in East-Central Europe: German Economic Policy toward Yugoslavia and Rumania, 1933–1939* (Stuttgart, 1988), 93.

still problems with regard to the clearings and to the question of oil, particularly aircraft fuel, which could only be bought on the world market for cash. The blocked marks in Berlin were of little use to Romania's oil producers who, because of the fluctuations in the value of the mark, could not obtain their cash equivalent in lei. Exporters refused to deliver oil in the summer of 1937 and in September the *Luftwaffe* faced a supply crisis. Except for grain, which the Germans had to buy, Romanian imports had become so expensive that only small purchases could be made. While the Germans wanted increased wheat and feed imports, it was the oil problem which pressed most heavily on Helmuth Wohlthat when he came to Bucharest to negotiate in November 1937. The Romanians had every intention of reducing their bilateral trade to its 1936 level and hoped, in particular, to limit German imports to the value of German exports in the previous quarter. They also wanted to change the composition of agricultural exports from grains to pigs, pig products, and eggs, all of which were difficult to sell on the world market. There were weeks of talks and the final arrangements were the usual 'patchwork of compromises'.[23] Germany was guaranteed purchases of 250,000 tons of wheat and 500,000 tons of feed grains during 1938 and was assured of import permits for shipments to Romania. The Romanians, for their part, were guaranteed high prices on a series of agricultural commodities hard to sell elsewhere. A compromise was reached on the clearing debt. As in Yugoslavia and Turkey, the Germans refused to establish a fund to guarantee the mark but promised that the balance of payments would be assured by the regulation of German imports of goods. If against expectations the balance did not decrease or should again increase, German imports would be correspondingly curtailed. A formula was reached on the Reichsmark/lei exchange.

For the first time, too, quotas were set for armament deliveries. There was a general quota of ten million marks to be paid in wheat for transactions up to 100,000 marks. Above this level, there would be individual negotiations; in the protocol, the Germans made special reference to their preference for payment in petroleum and wheat. The signing of the agreement at the end of 1937 was followed by a meeting between King Carol and Wohlthat. The king spoke of his interest in further economic co-operation between the two countries and sought Wohlthat's advice with regard to 'the state direction of foreign trade and the domestic economy'. Prime Minister Gheorghe Tătărescu, prepared to bow to the prevailing winds, sought future German co-operation as he outlined for Wohlthat's benefit his far-reaching economic plans designed to modernize agriculture,

[23] The details will be found in Grenzebach, *Germany's Informal Empire*, 184–185.

improve the transportation system, exploit the country's raw material resources, and open new oil fields. Many of these projects were to reappear in the Wohlthat treaty of March 1939.

All these bilateral agreements, of which the Yugoslav and Romanian were the most important, had their basis in the Reich's economic needs, but future political considerations were not excluded. Quite apart from the official negotiations, individual German firms were also involved, often following their own economic strategies that did not necessarily coincide with the more restricted Reich aim of creating a self-sufficient *Großraumwirtschaft*. Some of these agreements eased the bottlenecks in the German domestic market but trade never grew fast enough to meet Germany's steeply rising raw material requirements resulting from its rearmament needs. Only three Danubian countries, Bulgaria, Yugoslavia, and to a lesser extent Romania, were truly complementary to industrial Germany. As world terms of trade improved, the exporting countries, particularly Romania, were able to resist German pressure for larger deliveries and, contrary to the German intention of discouraging their further industrialization, were able to demand investment goods and armaments in return for any new agreements. How far the new agreements benefited Germany's trading partners is still a matter of debate. There were short-term benefits; Yugoslavia enjoyed boom conditions during the second half of 1937 and the pick-up in trade for the smaller Balkan states has been attributed to German action. A number of economic historians, including Professor Alan Milward, have argued that the south-eastern economies benefited from the German purchases of their agricultural products and that the bilateral treaties encouraged industrialization.[24] These arguments have been given strong statistical support by A. O. Ritschl who has shown that the countries of the Danube basin received outflows of German foreign exchange reserves. An examination of the cash and clearing accounts show that though a country like Hungary (and Italy) was a 'weak' country, that is a country with low cash revenues and large credit extensions to Germany, Yugoslavia, Romania (until the 23 March 1939 agreement), and Turkey were relatively 'strong' countries that

[24] Alan S. Milward, 'The Reichsmark Bloc and the International Economy', in Gerhard Hirschfeld and Lother Kettenacker (eds.), *Der "Führerstaat": Mythos und Realität* (Stuttgart, 1981), 377–413. Strong counter arguments have been made by Bernd-Jürgen Wendt, 'Südosteuropa in der nationalsozialistischen Grossraumwirtschaft. Eine Antwort auf Alan S. Milward', 414–428 in Hirschfeld and Kettenacker and by Alice Teichova, 'Bi-lateral Trade Revisited: Did the South-east European States exploit National Socialist Germany on the Eve of the Second World War?', in Ferenc Glatz (ed.), *Modern Age—Modern Historian: In Memoriam György Ránki (1930–1988)* (Budapest, 1990), 200–201.

benefited from German payments of foreign exchange cash. It was only when German troops actually occupied the Balkan countries that the Reich was able to exploit their economies. It may be true, nonetheless, as Professor Alice Teichova has argued, that German domination of the region ultimately reinforced dependence on the production of agricultural and other raw material products to the detriment of the development of the industrial sector.[25]

How far did the concepts of *Lebensraum* and *Wehrwirtschaft* shape the actions of the German negotiators in these early years? They were particularly careful in 1937 in their handling of the political aspects of their commercial transactions, disassociating agreements from any border or nationality disputes and from either Hungarian or Bulgarian revisionist goals. Even the armaments agreements appeared to be aimed at achieving economic goals. It was not without significance that responsibility for overseas sales of arms was switched from the Political to the Economic Department of the Wilhelmstrasse in May 1937. Due to pressure from individual armaments firms still seeking export orders, arms sales were used mainly to reduce the clearing balances. In the summer of 1937, however, German negotiators again demanded payment in either foreign exchange or goods that could only be purchased for foreign exchange (the latter almost always materials that the East Europeans refused to sell through the clearings as they could be sold on the world market). In the agreements concluded in early 1938, Hungary, Romania, Yugoslavia, and the Baltic countries were each required to follow this trading pattern. The American downturn in 1937 caused a sharp decline in the volume and value of world trade. This recession, lasting from the last quarter of 1937 until mid-1938, reduced German exports. As the world economy slumped in the first half of 1938, global trade fell by 20%.[26] With raw material demands exceeding all expectations, the Reich again faced a severe balance of trade deficit and an acute shortage of foreign exchange. *Anschluss* would bring only temporary relief.

Already in 1935, the official German trade statistics included Austria and Czechoslovakia trade figures along with those of the German Reich as if they were already part of 'Greater Germany'. Even these countries would only supply middle-term solutions in the movement towards *Lebensraum*. Hitler had never believed that an East European economic bloc or an informal empire would provide the economic base needed to

[25] Teichova, 'Bilateral Trade Revisited: Did the Southeast European States Exploit National Socialist Germany on the Eve of the Second World War?'

[26] Adam Tooze, *The Wages of Destruction*, 246.

assure the Reich's future. He knew, as he told his listeners in 1937, that the boom caused by rearmament 'could never form the basis of a sound economy over a long period and the latter was obstructed above all also by the economic disturbances resulting from Bolshevism'. Nor could Germany depend on foreign food supplies in war-time given Britain's command of the seas. 'The only remedy, and one which might appear to us as visionary', Hitler concluded, 'lay in the acquisition of greater living space—a quest which has at all times been the origin of the formation of states and the migration of peoples'.[27] The expansion of East European trade was impressive. With regard to foodstuffs and certain minerals, i.e. lead, copper, zinc and, of course, oil, such imports were critical but they fell far, far short of what was needed to sustain the rearmament programme outlined in 1936 and, in many cases, resulted in an outflow of foreign exchange reserves. As Schacht's unofficial and unsuccessful negotiations with the French and the British suggested, he continued to seek a solution through devaluation and expanded international trade. Such ideas were totally foreign to Hitler's way of thinking. The Führer needed to act soon if Germany was to launch the wars of conquest that he had in mind while it enjoyed the advantages of its head-start in rearmament.

The economic emphasis of these early bilateral settlements did not mean that either the Germans or their trading partners were unaware of their political implications. Already in 1936, Schacht's Balkan tour alerted foreign observers to the threat implicit in the German offensive. 'It is my opinion that he [Schacht] is conducting an astute economic political policy designed to bury the states of Eastern and South-Eastern Europe economically under German dominance', the American minister in Belgrade wrote to Cordell Hull, 'and which will possibly eventuate in their political dependency'.[28] Not only did the Germans resort to political means to achieve their bargains but they used their financial gains to build up pro-Nazi parties and public sentiment. As parallel political negotiations indicated, Göring engaged in both, either personally or through his agents. Economic arrangements were not divorced from an interest in drawing the Balkan and Danubian states out of the French political orbit. The smaller states knew that there were risks involved; there were few politicians in eastern Europe who did not realize that German economic policy posed a threat of a different order than that of its Weimar predecessor. Few, nevertheless, thought that Germany's commercial '*Drang nach Osten*' would reduce them to a state of economic servitude from which they could not escape. To avoid

[27] *DGFP*, Ser. D, Vol. I, No. 19.

[28] Wilson to Hull, TNA: PRO, RG59 600, RG 59 600 H 6231/66, 25 June 1936.

German domination, all tried to increase their trade with Britain, France, and the United States. Most of their credits from these exports were used to pay off old debts, however, rather than to buy the raw materials and machinery needed for industrialization. In the end, most of the Balkan states proved more resistant than Hitler anticipated, though some, like Romania and Hungary, were pulled deeper into the German net.

VII

The German drive for *Wirtschaftsraum* was not confined to the Danubian and Balkan states. Already at the start of Hitler's reign, when new ideas for getting out of the depression were canvassed, there was pressure to include the states on Germany's northern borders in a German-dominated protected zone based on preferential trading agreements. Hans Ernst Posse, the head of the trade division and later state secretary at the Ministry of Economics, was a strong proponent of the *Wirtschaftsraum* idea citing the Ottawa agreements as a precedent. A memorandum embodying his ideas was submitted to Hitler in May 1933. The Germans would play a leading role in a European trading block that would take in 'Scandinavia, Belgium and Holland on the one hand, and Austria, Hungary, Yugoslavia, Bulgaria and Romania on the other'.[29] It was agreed to implement the new policy in October 1933, first in the markets 'dominated by German businessmen . . . especially south-east Europe and the countries of north and northwest Europe'. The first trade agreement was made with the Dutch in December 1933; in the spring of 1934, new bilateral agreements were concluded with Denmark and Finland as well as with Hungary and Yugoslavia. The arrangements with the Nordic states reversed Germany's high protection policies of the post-1929 period originally devised to assist its hard-pressed and inefficient agricultural sector. The new tariffs resulted in a disastrous reduction in German trade with both the Baltic and Nordic states which reached its nadir point during the early months of 1933 when Hugenberg was at the Ministry of Agriculture. It was during these same years that the British, after the adoption of the Ottawa preference system, began to negotiate bilateral treaties with the northern states. The British government was being urged to assist the ailing export industries and to meet the chorus of criticism from those Liberal free traders or ex-free traders, like Walter Runciman, the Liberal head of the

[29] Patrick Salmon, *Scandinavia and the Great Powers 1890–1940* (Cambridge, 1997), 378. See Tim Rooth, *British Protectionism and the International Economy* (Cambridge, 1992).

Board of Trade who feared the international consequences of the abandonment of free trade. The Foreign Office warned that the Ottawa regime would be seen abroad as a retreat from Europe and would result in a serious loss of influence in continental affairs.

The Board of Trade turned first to those countries most dependent on the British market and therefore most anxious to negotiate. A series of bilateral trade agreements were concluded, with the Scandinavian countries in 1933 and with Estonia, Latvia, and Lithuania in July 1934.[30] London offered guarantees of existing market shares and security against further tariff increases in return for assured markets for British exports, coal being one of the most important. In Scandinavia, British exports rose from £26.6 million in 1932 to £47.3 million in the boom year 1937. In contrast, British imports at first fell and only exceeded the 1931 figures in 1937.[31] The treaties with the Baltic states were somewhat less effective in part because the Germans abandoned their protectionist policies and were willing to pay more than world prices for Baltic agricultural goods. Nonetheless, both the volume and value of British exports to the Baltic increased each year until 1938. The difficulty was that Britain suffered from an adverse balance of trade and lagged behind Germany in its exports to both Latvia and Estonia. Lithuania was the exception. Britain's success in capturing and keeping the major share of both its import and export trade was due less to any special government or private initiative than to the quarrels between the Germans and the Lithuanians over the latter's treatment of the Germans living in the Memelland.

The renewed interest of both the British and the Germans in finding export markets in these countries obviously created more competitive conditions for their traders. Though the structure of their economy gave the Germans a decided advantage, Britain's presence in the Nordic and Baltic states meant that Germany could not establish the same degree of domination that they enjoyed in south-east Europe. The Germans used the same techniques in the Baltic as in the Balkans. The large increases in Latvian and Estonian exports of butter, eggs, timber, and meat created Reichsmark balances that had to be spent on German products. By 1938, moreover, each of the three Baltic countries was paying for German arms through sales of raw materials and the payment of foreign exchange. In Scandinavia, too, clearings and payment agreements were the principal instrument of German commercial policy. A real effort was made, however, to maintain the flow of German exports to pay for

[30] For a detailed study of these agreements, see Rooth, *British Protectionism and the International Economy*, 134–143 (for Scandinavia) and 192–202 (for the Baltic).

[31] Salmon, *Scandinavia and the Great Powers*, 375.

Table 7.4 British and German Exports as a Percentage of the Total Imports of the Nordic Countries, 1929–1939

	Denmark		Finland		Norway		Sweden		Total	
	Germany	UK	Germany	UK	Germany	UK	Germany	UK	Germany	UK
1929	32.9	14.7	38.3	13	24.3	20.7	30.7	17.3	31.6	16.4
1930	34.2	14.5	37.1	13.7	21.5	25.7	32.1	15.8	31.2	17.4
1931	33.5	14.9	35	12.6	23	20.2	33.1	14.1	31.2	15.5
1932	25.9	22.3	28.6	18.3	21.3	21.6	29.4	16.8	26.3	19.8
1933	22.7	28.1	27.5	20.6	20.9	22.9	29.2	18	25.1	22.4
1934	21.3	30.1	20.7	22.8	19.1	22.9	26.8	19.5	22	23.8
1935	22	36	20.4	24.2	17	17.8	24.3	19.3	20.9	24.3
1936	25.3	36.5	19.3	24.2	17.6	17.8	24.4	19.2	21.7	24.4
1937	23.9	37.7	19.7	22.5	16.9	18.3	22.8	19	20.8	24.4
1938	24	33.8	20.3	21.9	18.4	16.2	24	18.3	21.7	22.6
1939	26.4	32.2	22	19.1	19	16.8	26.1	18.1	23.4	21.6

Source: Patrick Salmon, *Scandinavia and the Great Powers, 1890–1940* (Cambridge, 1997), 275.

Table 7.5 British and German Shares of the Export Trade of the Baltic States, 1920–1938 (% of total value)

	Estonia		Latvia		Lithuania	
	Britain	Germany	Britain	Germany	Britain	Germany
1920			67.5	1.2		44.4 / 80
1921			35.6	17.9	27.1	51.3
1922	22.2	12.7	40.3	13	39	36.2
1923	34.1	10.8	46.3	7.6	26.9	43.3
1924	33.5	22.6	41.5	16.4	27.9	43
1925	25	31.2	34.6	22.6	24.2	50.7
1926	28.8	23.1	34	24.3	24.9	46.8
1927	31.4	29.8	34	26.4	24.8	51.5
1928	34.8	25.9	27	26.4	20.4	57.7
1929	38.1	26.6	27.4	26.5	17.4	59.4
1930	32.3	30.1	28.4	26.6	19.5	59.9
1931	36.6	24.3	25.4	27	33.1	45.9
1932	36.7	26.2	30.8	26.2	41.4	39.1
1933	37.1	21.2	42.5	25.9	44.7	32.8
1934	40.5	22.5	35.8	29.5	42.6	21.6
1935	37.5	24.4	30.2	33.5	45.7	33.6
1936	36.6	22.5	35	30.8	48.4	10.8
1937	33.9	30.5	38.4	35.1	46.4	16.6
1938	34	31.4	41.9	33.5	39.4	26.8

Source: Merja-Liisa Hinkkanen-Lievonen, 'Britain as Germany's Commercial Rival in the Baltic States, 1919–1939', in Marie-Luise Recker (ed.), *Von der Konkurrenz zur Rivalität: From Competition to Rivalry* (Stuttgart, 1986), 46.

Table 7.6 British and German Shares of the Import Trade of the Baltic States, 1920–1938 (% of total value)

	Estonia		Latvia		Lithuania	
	Britain	Germany	Britain	Germany	Britain	Germany
1920			20.7	18.6		72
1921			14.3	48.1	0.9	70.7
1922	14.9	54.7	18.7	42.6	1.8	78
1923	19.7	51	17	45.2	5.3	80.9
1924	14	36.6	16.2	39	8.1	62.6
1925	12.3	29.4	13.8	41.5	8.3	56.6
1926	12.1	29.1	9.9	39.9	7.9	53.8
1927	14.3	26.4	10.6	40.6	6.8	53.2
1928	11	30.3	9.5	41.2	6.6	50.4
1929	10.1	30.1	8.4	41.2	8.5	49
1930	8.6	28.3	8.5	37.1	7.7	48.5
1931	7.7	30	8.6	37.1	7.1	47
1932	13.8	32	13.9	35.8	10.8	40.3
1933	18	22.5	21.9	24.5	17.1	36.1
1934	16.4	21.2	22.6	24.5	25.3	28
1935	19	26.3	20.4	36.8	37.3	11.4
1936	17.9	29.8	21.5	38.4	36.5	9.2
1937	16.7	26.1	20.7	27.1	27.9	21.8
1938	17.9	31.1	19.3	39	30.9	24.5

Source: Merja-Liisa Hinkkanen-Lievonen, 'Britain as Germany's Commercial Rival in the Balti States, 1919–1939', in Marie-Luise Recker (ed.), *Von der Konkurrenz zur Rivalität: From Competition to Rivalry* (Stuttgart, 1986), 47.

imports and to tap into the proceeds of Scandinavian trade with Britain which supplied the Germans with much needed foreign exchange. Particularly in Denmark, the most Germanophile of the Scandinavian states, political as well as economic reasons favoured the maintenance of bilateral trade. From 1937 onwards, the Germans launched an 'export offensive', mainly aimed at Sweden, the key source of German iron ore, but also directed to Norway and Finland, countries that were supplying increasing amounts of raw materials to Germany. At the same time, Denmark was given preferential treatment both in the supply of raw materials and semi-finished goods. There was a combined effort on the part of the German legations and chambers of commerce, the *Reichsgruppe Industrie* and its associates, and interested departments in Berlin that produced a major increase in German exports in 1938. Their value far exceeded those of Britain. While the British continued to buy more from Scandinavia than the Germans, the Scandinavian share of the German import market increased from 7.4% in 1929 to 11.4% in 1938 while the share of the British market remained relatively static.

The German economic drive did not go unnoticed in London. There were those at the Foreign Office, Laurence Collier of the Northern department and Ashton-Gwatkin and Gladwyn Jebb of the economic relations section, who, for quite different reasons, demanded a positive response to Germany's effort to regain its economic position in the north. Ashton-Gwatkin was prepared to recognize a German sphere of economic interest in the Danubian and Balkan countries by renouncing Britain's most-favoured-nation rights in the region, if Germany would do the same in Scandinavia and the Baltic which was a larger and more profitable market for Britain. Collier, who was no friend of economic appeasement, campaigned vigorously for the extension of clearings to the Baltic and Scandinavian trade to tie these states more tightly to Britain and increase its political influence there. His efforts to 'take a leaf out of the German book' found only qualified support from Ashton-Gwatkin and none from the Treasury, which opposed the use of clearings for anything but the collection of debts. Collier was particularly concerned with Germany's ultimate aims in the north-east which he predicted in 1936 would include the recovery of Memel and the creation of '"a protectorate, probably political & certainly commercial" over all three Baltic republics'.[32] The question of German competition in north-eastern Europe was part of a much broader problem and during 1936, the government found itself faced with demands from exporters for assistance against German competition. In October 1936, having ruled out export subsidies or clearings, an interdepartmental committee decided that the best solution lay in encouraging British and German industrialists to divide export markets between themselves. Leith-Ross, an important economic appeaser in Whitehall, was a strong proponent of cartel arrangements and raised the question with a group of German industrialists. In mid-November, 1936, Runciman authorized the Federation of British Industries to contact German producers. The Foreign Office economic section also responded favourably to the idea of cartels; Collier strongly objected but he was in a minority of one. No economic department in London favoured unnecessary government intervention in trade and the Foreign Office economic section, the only one actively involved in trade questions, wanted accommodation with Germany and not confrontation. In fact, though cartel agreements, both open and concealed, played their part in north-east trade, they neither promoted exports (ICI and

[32] Quoted in Merja-Liisa Hinkkanen-Lievonen, 'Britain as Germany's Commercial Rival in the Baltic States, 1919–1939', in Marie-Luise Recker (ed.), *Von der Konkurrenz zur Rivalität: From Competition to Rivalry* (Stuttgart, 1986), 43.

I.G. Farben only confirmed their respective monopolistic positions in the chemical field) nor served Anglo-German understanding.

For the British, the northern markets represented only a small fraction of their overseas trade. Until the recession of late 1937 and the German push in the region, exporters were not prepared to fight for a larger share of trade. Britain's trading position in the region, though weaker in comparative terms, was considerably stronger and more profitable than in 1929. Despite Collier's repeated insistence on the need to strengthen Britain's political presence in the region, the British government remained ambivalent about contesting the German offensive in northern Europe. This was partly because of its concern with domestic and imperial markets and the still lingering dislike of government intervention in trade matters. It was also because few in Whitehall believed that Hitler intended to absorb the northern states into his Greater Germany.

The Baltic did not loom large in British strategic thinking. The Anglo-German naval agreement of June 1935 was concluded without considering its effects on the Baltic and Scandinavian states. The latter saw the treaty as confirmation of their view that nothing was to be expected from the British in terms of security arrangements. There was little in the subsequent behaviour of Britain or France in 1936 to halt their already shaken confidence in collective security. In 1937, at Vansittart's suggestion, Lord Plymouth, the under-secretary of state for foreign affairs, visited Finland and the Baltic states, a gesture intended to show the flag. Neither the visit nor Britain's post-Munich commercial campaign refurbished its image or restored its political influence. The description of Anglo-Scandinavian political relations as 'amicable, but non-committal and relatively distant' applies to the Baltic states as well.[33]

The case of Finland was exceptional. Here, too, the growth of German influence had been watched by the Northern department of the Foreign Office with some alarm. The Germans could capitalize on Finnish fears of the Soviet Union and their need for all types of military equipment, especially modern aircraft. The majority of Finns, however, had little liking for Nazi doctrines. Their arms purchases were dictated by political as much as technical considerations. In 1936, for instance, they bought aircraft from the Dutch and artillery from Sweden rather than from Germany, in the first instance, and Vickers in the second. In sharp contrast to its behaviour in south-eastern Europe, in Finland, the British government made a concerted effort to court the Finnish

[33] Patrick Salmon, 'Anglo-German Commercial Rivalry in the Depression Era', in Recker (ed.), *Von der Konkurrenz zur Rivalität*, 134.

military establishment in order to keep Finland out of the German orbit. The military wooed Finnish officers, including Field Marshal Mannerheim who visited London twice in 1936. At the same time, an air attaché was appointed for Finland and the Baltic states. Britain was rewarded with a major success when the Finns bought Bristol Blenheims for their bomber fleet. Economic and political reasons lay behind the British effort. Britain had a huge balance of trade deficit with Finland and this was one way to maintain a political presence in the eastern Baltic.

What were Hitler's intentions in northern Europe at this time? As early as 1928, he had written, 'What the Mediterranean Sea is to Italy, the Eastern Coast of the Baltic Sea is to Germany', a statement he would repeat to Ciano on 12 August 1939.[34] In his long-term plans, the Baltic and Nordic states may have been part of 'the wider schemes to establish a German *Großwirtschaftsraum* and gain living space in the East'.[35] The incorporation of the northern states into the German empire was both natural on economic and racial grounds and necessary given British and Soviet interests in these countries. Yet apart from scattered remarks to visitors and officials, there is no indication of any clear view or unifying idea in Hitler's approach towards these countries. In 1937, it seems to have been economic rather than strategic or racial considerations that were in the forefront of Nazi policy. The Baltic was still seen within the context of Hitler's policies towards Poland and the Soviet Union which meant the rejection of any Eastern Locarno pact and an aversion to the conclusion of non-aggression treaties with individual states. There were local German colonies in the Baltic and in Scandinavia, Nazi ideologues, like Alfred Rosenberg and Walther Darré, made much of the 'Nordic community of fate' and common racial ties. Yet their efforts in the early years of the Hitler regime to launch racial propaganda campaigns in the region were unproductive and only annoyed German industrialists intent on expanding their export trade. A much lower-keyed approach was subsequently followed but even this failed to attract any mass support for Nazi ideas in Scandinavia. The National Socialist-type parties in the region lost electoral support. There were, however, in the late 1930s, as Vidkun Quisling's 'Northern Coalition' would later suggest, enough Nazi sympathizers, some with influence in élite circles, for the Germans to find willing assistance when their attention became

[34] G. Weinberg (ed.), *Hitlers Zweites Buch* (Stuttgart, 1961), 206; *DGFP*, Ser. D, Vol. VII, No. 43.

[35] Rolf Ahmann, 'Nazi German Policy towards the Baltic States on the Eve of the Second World War', in J. Hiden and T. Lane (eds.), *The Baltic and the Outbreak of the Second World War* (Cambridge, 1992), 51.

focused on the north. In the hope of maintaining good relations with Denmark, the questions of North Schleswig and border revision were not officially raised.

There were some moves during 1937 to expand established naval and intelligence contacts with Latvia and Estonia, which was already supplying the German navy with shale oil. A German armoured cruiser visited Tallinn and German officers observed the Latvian military manoeuvres. Soviet interest centred on Latvia, thought to be useful as protection against a German blockade. A Soviet armoured cruiser went to Riga in 1937 and Latvian officers were invited to the Red Army's manoeuvres. With his attention focused on central Europe in 1937, Hitler probably gave very little attention to the position of the northern states. For their part, the Baltic and Scandinavian states preferred to continue trading with both Germany and Britain. Sweden, Norway, and Denmark enjoyed a high standard of living and the Anglo–German competition for their favours was not without its use. At the same time, they did not wish to be drawn into any bloc or to give offence to their neighbours, Poland and the Soviet Union as well as Germany. Fears of a two-front war mounted after 1937. Neither the Baltic Entente (which Finland refused to join) nor the even looser Oslo group provided any real protection. The general retreat from the League of Nations was symbolized by a withdrawal from any obligations incurred through Article 16. 'Realism' dictated a policy of neutrality. After all, the Scandinavian states had managed to stay out of the 1914–1918 war. It was hardly surprising that their leaders hoped that policies of strict neutrality would protect them once again.

VIII

Germany's economic offensive provoked a French reaction. If anything was to be saved of France's eastern defensive system, a more positive approach had become essential. As discussed earlier, the most concrete step taken was the Rambouillet offer to Poland with its two billion franc credit for military purposes. This was not followed up, however, in any way that promoted joint Franco-Polish military co-operation against Germany or the ever elusive Polish–Czech agreement that France so much wanted. Gamelin clearly preferred the Polish alliance to any form of Soviet military assistance in Eastern Europe. He continued to exaggerate the power of the Polish army and assumed, even with the Italian alliance slipping out of sight, that Poland would act as France's surrogate to contain the German threat to Czechoslovakia. Not only did the French army chiefs fail to monitor the Polish use of the Rambouillet loans and credits but they failed to monitor Polish war planning which was increasingly directed against the Soviet Union rather than against Germany. Pierre Cot, at the Air Ministry, created a special office intended to advance sales of French aircraft abroad, especially to Poland. The head of the French air staff intelligence section and his Polish counterpart exchanged visits and discussed provision for French bombers to operate from Polish airfields. Cot, backed in this instance by Léon Nöel, the French minister in Warsaw, argued for a mutual air assistance agreement leading to a regional air pact that would include the Soviet Union, hoping that this might prove acceptable to the Poles. But these exchanges produced nothing in the way of joint operational planning and very little in the way of technical co-operation. Polish interest was centred less on co-operation than on acquiring French equipment for their own aircraft and securing training opportunities for their bomber pilots for an independent air force. None of the French army's maturing mobilization plans were based on co-operation with Poland. The French, moreover, were slow in fulfilling their Rambouillet promises and the Poles complained bitterly in 1937 that they had received almost nothing in the way of promised military equipment. The difficulties, as in the case of Yugoslavia and Romania, lay in the inability of France's defence industries to fill the new orders for their own armed services. There were also bureaucratic tangles and a lack of clear command in Paris that blocked the flow of what equipment might have been sent to Poland. A greater effort could have been made if the Polish orders had been followed up.

For their part, the Polish military authorities, though strongly Francophile, were less than candid with their French counterparts about the state of Polish preparedness or their future military planning. Beck remained in power, distrusted and disliked by the *Quai d'Orsay* but seemingly immovable. The foreign minister was playing a dangerous game. Having abandoned Piłsudski's balancing act between Germany and the Soviet Union, he still thought he could move between France and Germany keeping Poland's future options open. In April 1937, he travelled to Bucharest hoping to strengthen Polish–Romanian co-operation against the Soviet Union by reviving their 1922 treaty. Beck strongly opposed the Franco-Little Entente pact and backed the Italian overtures to Yugoslavia to weaken the Little Entente. He nursed Poland's ties with Romania and Hungary despite their mutual antipathy. All these moves were intended to increase Prague's isolation; Beck believed that Poland had everything to gain from focusing Hitler's attention on Austria and Czechoslovakia. Far too shrewd to go too far in the German direction, he was content, like Hitler, with the existing state of Polish–German relations. While Beck's diplomacy, however tortuous, had a logic of its own, the passivity of the French high command, given Gamelin's assumption that Poland would take a leading part in any campaign in the East, is more difficult to defend.

René Massigli of the *Quai d'Orsay* had not been the only voice at the *Quai* insisting on the necessity of a more positive French policy in south-eastern Europe in 1936–1937 but little was actually done. An unofficial visit by Robert Blum, the premier's son who had spent a year working in Belgrade in 1931, to the Yugoslav capital in December 1936 revealed how much ground France had lost in terms of position and influence. On his return, the young Blum urged that the British be pressed to intervene in the region and that the French economic presence should be expanded. He pushed for a major propaganda and cultural campaign intended to restore France's former reputation. On the cultural side, the response from Paris was decidedly lukewarm. Much had been hoped for, by those few believing in the importance of cultural diplomacy, from the 1937 Paris exhibition. The slowness with which the buildings had been constructed and the difficulties incurred by the exhibitors stood in marked contrast to the brilliance of the 1936 Berlin Olympics, discouraging those willing to put government money into such efforts. A general distaste for the crudities of a propaganda campaign and an ingrained sense of French cultural superiority that hardly needed demonstration left France well behind both Germany and Italy in the paper and film wars of the 1930s. The Blum warnings, nonetheless, added to the alarms raised by the reports from French ministers in Belgrade and Bucharest, had some effect on the Popular Front government.

The *Quai d'Orsay* had been slow to consider the revitalization of the Little Entente as a way of securing protection for Czechoslovakia. It showed little enthusiasm for Krofta's revival of the Titulescu idea of a French alliance with the Little Entente which would have increased French obligations without any compensating advantages. Delbos insisted that a mutual aid pact should be concluded first between the three Little Entente partners before France would enter the scene. The fear of a forthcoming German move in central Europe and the Italian moves towards Germany contributed to the change in French policy. It was, however, only on 6 December 1936 at the inter-ministerial meeting called to discuss Pierre Cot's ideas for inter-allied air co-operation that it was agreed to go forward with the idea of a pact with the Little Entente countries and military talks with the Soviet Union. Though linked at the time, both the *Quai d'Orsay* and the defence chiefs were determined that the talks should be conducted separately. Delbos's doubts about any connection between the two initiatives were further strengthened when Antonescu, the Romanian prime minister, angered by Cot's attempt to arrange an agreement with his counterpart for

Soviet use of Romanian air bases, warned that the friendship between France and the Soviet Union lay behind his reluctance to back the Franco-Little Entente pact negotiations. It must be remembered, too, that Cot was regarded with distaste, particularly in military and naval circles, and that apart from Blum and one or two other ministers, his advocacy of any move towards the Soviet Union was viewed with hostility.

The French circulated their draft proposals on 18 January 1937. Neither the Yugoslavs nor the Romanians showed much interest. The draft was carefully drawn so that France would only contract new obligations to assist the two states when they had committed themselves to the defence of Czechoslovakia against German attack. The project was partly based on the application of paragraph 3 of Article 16 of the Covenant which stipulated that each League member should allow the passage of troops through its territory sent to assist the victim of aggression. Even the Czechs were lukewarm to the French proposal for it was far less ambitious than Krofta's November scheme which, to his intense irritation, was now made public. The Czechs were still hoping that something might come out of the German talks. In any case, Beneš, who could not afford to alienate Yugoslavia, rejected French suggestions that arms sales to Belgrade might be cancelled or that Yugoslavia should be threatened with expulsion from the Little Entente if she did not initial the French draft. Milan Stojadinović, the Yugoslav prime minister, with his Bulgarian and Italian treaties in mind, argued that the French proposals would provoke Germany and Italy, both of whom would take economic reprisals. 'If one remembers the general indecisiveness of French policy along with its lack of firmness in dealing with Germany on the question of the Rhineland as well as towards Italy in recent days and in connection with the events in Spain', Stojadinović wrote to the Yugoslav minister in Paris on 15 March 1937, 'then one can understand why we want to achieve a policy of equilibrium in relations with all the great powers. A relationship which will not blindly bind us to any one of them.'[36] The Yugoslavs were not interested in the French proposal and the Romanians hid behind Belgrade's opposition to disguise their own doubts. With Göring dangling the prospect of a German guarantee if Romania turned down the French offer, General Ion Antonescu suggested as a substitute for the French pact, three separate French treaties with each of the Little Entente states along the lines of the 1921 Franco-Polish treaty. This hardly suited Delbos' purpose which was, above all, to secure Yugoslav and Romanian assistance to Czechoslovakia in case of German attack.

[36] Hoptner, *Yugoslavia in Crisis*, 91.

The Yugoslav treaty with Italy and intimations of the Romanian 'policy of independence' predetermined the fate of the French initiative. At their conference in April 1937, the three Little Entente powers decided to postpone indefinitely the entire question of an alliance between the Little Entente and France. The Germans had succeeded, by encouraging the Italian–Yugoslav *rapprochement*, in detaching Belgrade from the Little Entente to the detriment of Prague. The French correctly gauged the more general importance of the changing direction of Italian diplomacy. Delbos warned Corbin, the French ambassador in London, on 1 May, that because of Mussolini's involvement in Spain, he 'will find himself almost inevitably led to abandon Italy's own interest in Danubia, once the weakening of the Petite Entente is assured, in order to bring his effort to bear on the Mediterranean, presenting this evolution, imposed by Germanic pressures, as a normal consequence of the creation of the Empire'.[37] This was hardly an encouraging outlook for France's efforts to protect Czechoslovakia.

Blum and Delbos tried to involve Britain in their Little Entente talks. As the French proposal was partly based on the hope that a pact between France and the Little Entente powers would obviate the need for Soviet participation in any second front, British support was essential to give the initiative any real credibility. Given the Foreign Office dislike of Beneš and its belief that the *Sudetendeutsche* were being oppressed by the Czechs, there was little sympathy for the French efforts to underwrite Prague. British officials preferred a German–Czech settlement that would reduce tensions in central Europe and make Hitler more amenable to a general European settlement. In early 1937, even before the French draft of the Little Entente pact was officially presented to the Foreign Office, interested officials expressed their disapproval of the French proposal. Officials feared that the pact would draw Italy closer to Germany and ruin the chances of improved relations between London and Rome. Orme Sargent, the assistant under-secretary, recommended that nothing should be done in the Balkans until Prague solved its minority problems and the Western pact negotiations with Germany had definitely failed. Sargent claimed that Britain's explicit guarantees to France in 1936 entitled her 'to exercise a definite control over policy in the East of Europe'.[38] It was argued that if any country was to save Czechoslovakia, it had to be France. If it would not or could

[37] Quoted in Jordan, *The Popular Front and Central Europe*, 258.

[38] TNA: PRO, FO 371/21136, R501/26/67, FO minutes, 29 January – 1 February 1937.

not act, neither Yugoslavia nor Romania would be in a position to do so. In their dislike for the French initiative, the foreign secretary and his advisers were at one. In early February, Eden told Delbos that Britain lacked the necessary means of persuasion. He tried to reassure him by claiming that he was not unduly alarmed by the weakening of the Little Entente or by the failure of the French proposal. He pointed out that nothing prevented France from reaffirming its obligations to Czechoslovakia. The Admiralty, too, rejected any association with France's Little Entente pact, claiming that such an attachment would mean support of an encirclement strategy, the collapse of appeasement, and the perpetuation of the three-power threat. The Admiralty recommended that the cabinet should 'admit openly to Britain's withdrawal from Eastern Europe'. The CID amplified this argument when discussing the Singapore strategy on 25 February, claiming that involvement in Eastern Europe would leave 'the Empire needlessly exposed, not just to German but to Japanese or Italian attack'.[39]

In one of those persuasively logical analyses of French policy for which the *Quai d'Orsay* was famous, officials examined the reasons for their failure with the Little Entente. The recommendations for action were far less impressive than the analysis of the failure. It was suggested that a new balance sheet be drawn up to see what really could be expected, in political and military terms, from 'our friends' and a decision reached as to how much should be done to avoid a further erosion of the French position. The Political Directorate argued 'that a Danubian policy could only be validated by substantive British support' and recommended that the French threaten to pull out of the region as a way of forcing the British hand.[40] In other words, Massigli's directorate was preparing to follow the British lead in a region where the latter's lack of sympathy was well-known.

British backing was not forthcoming, their unwillingness to engage buttressed by the knowledge that both the Romanian and Yugoslav governments opposed the French–Little Entente pact. The British were not totally uninterested in the region; there were British financial interests in Romania, where the greater part of its industries and banks was in British, French, and American hands, and in Yugoslavia. British trade with the Danubian states, however, was negligible. Throughout the 1930s, imports from the region never exceeded 2.3% of total British

[39] Martin Thomas, *Britain, France and Appeasement: Anglo–French Relations in the Popular Front Era* (Oxford and New York, 1996), 189.

[40] See Jordan, *The Popular Front and Central Europe,* 251, for an extensive discussion of an unsigned memorandum, 12 Feburary 1937, taken from the Massigli papers.

imports and exports to the region never amounted to more than 1.4%.[41] The imperial preference system meant that Britain, although the world's largest importer of cereals, did not have to buy in south-east Europe. As trade was limited, sterling was in short supply yet both Hungary and Romania had to service long-term and commercial debts in London contracted during the earlier depression years. The Yugoslavs were in a slightly better position. They had won larger import quotas and lower duties on agricultural exports in November 1935 as compensation for losses resulting from the imposition of sanctions against Italy. But when the Yugoslav foreign trade expert, who was also handling the German negotiations, tried to counter Yugoslavia's increasing dependence on German trade by seeking preferential tariff concessions in London, he met with no encouragement. The most he could secure after his visit to London in mid-November was an agreement tying the granting of import licences to the level of Yugoslav exports to Britain. Nor was Belgrade successful when an attempt was made at the end of 1936 to secure a large long-term credit to purchase arms and military equipment. The British legislation of 1933 prohibiting credits for the purchase of 'munitions of war', an all-embracing term which included clothing, was still in place in 1937. Though Vansittart and Sargent favoured a positive response to Belgrade's request if only to prevent the reorientation of Yugoslav policy, Neville Chamberlain, the chancellor of the exchequer, vetoed any changes in the law and blocked the credit guarantee. He did not want to increase arms production beyond the minimum needed to meet Britain's deficiencies. Even in private negotiations, the Yugoslav efforts were thwarted by government intervention. The Yugoslavs made an attempt to buy twelve Bristol Blenheim bombers but the Air Ministry sanctioned the purchase of only one, agreeing to two only after intense lobbying by the British minister in Belgrade and the Foreign Office. The Romanians, too, tried to enlist British assistance in resisting pressure from both Paris and Berlin. King Carol, who had an 'obsessive admiration' for Britain, believed that only the latter could replace the weakened French as Romania's Great Power protector. In July 1937, the king paid an unofficial visit to London. Despite friendly conversations with Chamberlain and Eden, he received nothing concrete in the way of assistance. 'More and more people in Romania', he told Chamberlain, 'were turning away from France and crying for Britain, Britain'.[42] Apart from a willingness to keep in direct

[41] Alice Teichova, *An Economic Background to Munich* (Cambridge, 1974), 21; Kaiser, *Economic Diplomacy and the Origins of the Second World War*, 175.

[42] Lungu, *Romania and the Great Powers*, 112.

touch, the British offered no increase in trade, no new investments and, above all, no deliveries of arms.

In February 1937, the chiefs of staff prepared a memorandum for the cabinet outlining British defence priorities. Home defence, France, and the Low Countries came first. This was followed in order of importance by defence of British possessions in the Far East, defence of the eastern Mediterranean, and defence of India against any potential Soviet threat.[43] In May, an arms priority list was drawn up in the Foreign Office to provide guidance for export sales. In order of importance, the first twenty countries were Egypt, Afghanistan, Belgium, Portugal, Turkey, Saudi Arabia, Yugoslavia, Greece, Argentina, the Netherlands, Finland, Estonia, Latvia, Lithuania, Poland, Romania, Iran, Yemen, Brazil, and China. Those omitted were either unfriendly (Germany, Italy, and Japan), self-sufficient in armaments (the United States and Czechoslovakia) or of little strategic interest to Britain. It was hardly likely given home requirements in 1937 that there would be sufficient arms for export even to the first five countries on the list.

The French embassy in London warned Paris of the consequences of Chamberlain's accession to the prime ministership. The French could not count on British underwriting of their eastern alliances. If anything was to be done in Eastern Europe, they would have to do it themselves. The Neurath visit to the region in June 1937 and the highly alarmist reports from the *Deuxième Bureau* about German action in Yugoslavia stirred Gamelin into action. There had been a continuous litany of complaints from the energetic and well-informed French military attaché in Belgrade, Marie-Emile Béthouart, during 1936 and the first half of 1937, about the poor condition of the Yugoslav army and the political leadership's loss of confidence in France. He warned that Prince Paul's 'inordinate preoccupation' with the Bolshevik menace was pulling Yugoslavia into the German orbit despite the Francophile sympathies of the military high command. Gamelin was urged to make a major effort to encourage co-operation between the two armies in order to repair the military line to Belgrade. The French pulled out all the stops when the Yugoslav and Romanian chiefs of staff attended the French manoeuvres in July 1937. Everything was done to impress them with France's military preparedness. Gamelin visited both countries to attend their respective military manoeuvres in September. He saw for himself how poorly equipped the Yugoslav army was and noted the absence of armour and anti-tank guns and the poor prospects for creating an armaments industry. He observed, too, the 'troubled atmosphere' in Belgrade and the abundant evidence of Stojadinović's political

[43] Kaiser, *Economic Diplomacy and the Origins of the Second World War*, 182.

opportunism. There was a better reception in Bucharest and Gamelin judged that the position was redeemable if a major effort was made. What could be done to help these states modernize their military forces and to make certain that their use would assist the French? France did not want the foodstuffs and raw materials the Yugoslavs had to sell and refused to offer the kind of advantageous clearing terms that marked the Yugoslav–German arrangements. French farmers resisted any lowering of tariffs. The French colonies, particularly those in North Africa and Indochina, excluded from the French import quota system, had become major exporters of cereals to France. Neither Yugoslavia nor Romania had the funds needed to pay for French military equipment. Yugoslavia won a moratorium on repayments for equipment supplied under a French agreement of 1924. In 1935, despite Belgrade's impoverished condition, Paris agreed to further loans of war material with a book value of some ten million francs. At the same time, a twenty-five million franc contract for mortars and ammunition was concluded in return for Yugoslav tobacco exports.[44] Subsequent negotiations stalled. The Yugoslavs lacked the foreign exchange to pay for war materials and the French Finance Ministry, faced with its own financial problems and pressure on the franc, refused to underwrite purchases that the Yugoslav army chiefs wanted to make. Despite their Francophile sympathies, the German arms deals would be difficult to reject.

Romania's geographic position, a border with the Soviet Union but over 600 kilometres from Germany's pre-*Anschluss* frontier, made it less important strategically for France than Yugoslavia, with the exception of Cot's plans for an eastern air assistance pact in 1936–1937. Cot hoped to use the Romanian air fields should the French be forced to retreat from Czechoslovakia. The Romanians, under King Carol, had been making substantial efforts to strengthen their air force and modernize their ill-equipped and ineffective army. Even as King Carol and Victor Antonescu, his foreign minister, entered into closer economic relations with Germany, they concluded new armaments agreements with Prague. The Czechs hoped that a rearmed Romania would free Czechoslovakia from the fear of Hungarian attack while they were fighting the Germans. The Romanian leaders were amenable to new arrangements with France. In 1936, the Romanians embarked on a twelve year military modernization programme which depended on French material supplies and technical support. Though warned that Romania's attachment to France would waver if French industry

[44] Martin S. Alexander, *The Republic in Danger: General Maurice Gamelin and the Politics of French Defence, 1933–1940*, 231.

was unable to support Romanian rearmament, neither the French government nor the arms producers proved sympathetic to Bucharest's requirements. There were multiple problems as the French arms suppliers, particularly Hotchkiss and Schneider, refused to sign contracts with Bucharest unless given special repayment guarantees which the Romanian government refused to sanction. The French government similarly refused to underwrite their agreements should the Romanians default on their payments. Neither the French Treasury nor the ministries of commerce and agriculture were willing to accept Romanian payments in kind which could involve the flooding of the French market with cheap food stuffs. Despite the joint planning for air co-operation, the French failed to supply the aircraft the Romanians wanted. The Romanian demands were far greater than their means of payment. In any case, by 1937, the French were faced with a massive deficiency in their own aircraft production figures.

By the time of *Anschluss,* the Romanian general staff was looking to Germany to meet the major share of its munitions requirements. Romanian oil should have given Bucharest an excellent negotiating card with the French as well as with Germany. Yet even here there were endless difficulties. The Romanians wanted to export refined oil that generated higher profits than unrefined crude but the French, with refining facilities of their own, preferred to import the cheaper unrefined crude that could be purchased from the Soviet Union, Venezuela, and the United States. A compromise was reached combining both crude oil and refined aviation spirit and the Bucharest government was provided with some 725 million francs to purchase French war materials. The supply deal was ratified in May 1936 but the contracts were never completed. The arrangements proved unsatisfactory, as was the highly complex trading system put into place in 1937. The Germans were far more successful with the Romanians than the French.

Why did the French not make a greater effort, given Gamelin's alarm about German incursions into Yugoslavia and Romania? There was, of course, the problem of a late awakening after years of relative neglect. France's friends had complained repeatedly of its niggardly ways and condescending attitudes. A Popular Front government was in a particularly difficult position. On the one hand, there were doubts in both Belgrade and Bucharest about dealing with a left and Communist-backed government in the more highly charged ideological atmosphere of 1936 and 1937. On the other hand, the orthodox financial policies of the Popular Front discouraged the kinds of offers that could be made by the Germans. Most important of all, France suffered in the competition with the Reich from its own military and industrial inadequacies. With serious rearmament just begun, the French were reluctant to sanction arms sales abroad. Having already discovered in 1937 that rearmament problems arose more from industrial bottlenecks than from any shortage of funds, the army heads recognized that the armaments industries would have to be reorganized before French needs could be met. While acknowledging the justice of the complaints coming from his military attachés in Eastern Europe, Gamelin could not take the risk of sending equipment to Yugoslavia or Romania that was needed in France. What was sent abroad tended to be obsolete equipment that was not wanted. The intelligence services warned of the importance of raw materials and oil for Germany's military mobilization. Berlin's economic weaknesses in these respects was one of the few grounds for optimism when the bleak future of a German–French arms race was assessed. Any steps blocking German access to the markets of south-eastern Europe would have been highly welcome but while France's own defensive capacity was at risk, its needs, far greater than Gamelin would publicly admit, had to take precedence over those of its allies. Only a minimum could be done to assist states whose own military weaknesses precluded a major contribution to any joint defence against German attack. Sending scarce arms and aircraft to countries whose military establishments were weak and backward made little strategic sense.

Unwilling or unable to compete with the Germans commercially, the French resorted, with diminishing confidence, to old ideas for creating greater solidarity among the Danubian countries. In May 1937, Premier Hodža of Czechoslovakia proposed a system of tariff preferences that would link Austria and Hungary with the Little Entente. The Germans took no interest in the scheme which was quietly buried. In the autumn of 1937, the French backed a plan for the financial reconstruction of central Europe based on central bank support for new exchange rates for the Danubian countries that would end the existing system of exchange controls. Suggested by Richard Schuller, the foreign trade specialist of the Austrian Foreign Ministry, it was aimed at reducing German influence in the region. Delbos raised the question with Eden, whose response was not unfavourable. On the eve of the Halifax visit to Germany, however, neither Neville Chamberlain nor Sir John Simon, the chancellor of the exchequer, would endorse any proposal that could be interpreted as part of the 'encirclement' of Germany. As late as January 1938, just prior to the publication of the van Zeeland plan, the League of Nations' attempt to tackle the raw materials problem supposedly aggravating the tensions between the 'have' and 'have-not' nations, the French suggested that France, Britain, and other hard currency countries issue credits to the amounts held by the Danubian states in their clearing balances. This would provide a way of diverting trade from Germany to the free exchange countries. The idea was dismissed; the whole intention of the van Zeeland report was to ease Germany's economic situation and not to aggravate it. New French suggestions in February and March 1938 were rejected by the British. *Anschluss* buried the Schuller plan and all its possible variations.

None of these French gestures, which depended on British co-operation, could turn back the clock. During the last months of 1937, Stojadinović made his own tour of the European capitals. In Paris, in October, he insisted that his policies were essential for the internal consolidation and strengthening of his country. Reaffirming the Franco-Yugoslav pact of 1927, he assured his hosts that if war came Yugoslavia would be on the side of France. The Yugoslav premier arrived in Rome on 5 December where he was fêted by Ciano and received by Mussolini. The Duce was assured that there would be no agreement with France nor any Yugoslav move towards the Soviet Union. Stojadinović promised, too, that he would seek an agreement with the Hungarians. The Hungarian prime minister and the Yugoslav foreign minister had already met in Berlin in November but neither German nor Italian promptings produced the desired result. Possibly to ingratiate himself with the Italians, Stojadinović claimed that he was not at all sympathetic to *Anschluss* though when the time came, the Yugoslavs like the Italians gave no sign of disapproval. After a highly enjoyable stay, Stojadinović left Rome to return to Belgrade just in time to receive Delbos who had embarked on his own three-week voyage in a replay of Barthou's successful tour of 1934. If there were any doubts in the *Quai d'Orsay* about Stojadinović's position after the inconclusive talks in the capital, they were resolved when Stojadinović journeyed to Berlin and was received by Hitler on 17 January 1938. Hitler assured him that he favoured a strong Yugoslavia and that German ambitions were centred on the Baltic and not on the Balkans where they wanted 'nothing more than an open door for our economy'.[45] Stojadinović claimed he had removed his 'French eyeglasses' and was ready to march with Germany against a Habsburg restoration, a reference to Schuschnigg's gesture in this direction. Even allowing for Stojadinović's willingness to tell each of his interlocutors what they wished to hear, there was no disguising Yugoslavia's departure from the French diplomatic circle.

'We will not abandon Czechoslovakia', Yvon Delbos, the French foreign minister, told Anthony Eden on May 1937. 'We could not do so without disappearing from the European map as a great power.'[46] While

[45] Quoted in Hoptner, *Yugoslavia in Crisis*, 88.

[46] Quoted in Martin Thomas, 'France in British Foreign Policy: The Search for European Settlement, March 1936 – June 1937', D.Phil. thesis (Oxford, 1990), 352.

the French were not prepared to drop Czechoslovakia in the summer of 1937, none of their efforts during the next months to secure assistance for Prague succeeded. They had accepted the collapse of the Little Entente negotiations. With regard to Germany, the *Quai d'Orsay* was trimming its sails to British winds that did not blow fair for Czechoslovakia. By October, if not earlier, Prime Minister Chautemps and Delbos were considering a retreat from central Europe. Delbos's end of year tour, intended as a morale boosting exercise, came to represent the 'dying song of the swan'. On the way to Warsaw, there was a brief railway stop-over in Berlin where the French foreign minister, fresh from his meeting with Chamberlain and Eden, assured Neurath that France was anxious for a settlement with Germany. In Warsaw, little was accomplished. Delbos was not allowed to see Rydz-Śmigły alone for military discussions and was accompanied everywhere by Beck. It was reported that Beck told Delbos that its Soviet orientation provided the real grounds for Polish enmity towards Czechoslovakia. Prague, he claimed, had become the centre of the Comintern.

Delbos's arrival in Bucharest occurred during what turned out to be the last and most controversial election in Romania's inter-war history. The Iron Guard, under its new electoral name, attracted large and enthusiastic crowds much to King Carol's distress. Delbos' conversations with his hosts were restricted to banalities. At this very moment, the Germans were in Romania, negotiating the economic agreements that would open the way for a major increase in German imports and arms exports. 'The French visit', Dov Lungu concludes, 'had all the appearances of *politesse* rather than *politique*'.[47] The next few months in Bucharest were dominated by domestic politics. The ruling Liberal party failed to secure the vote it needed to rule and the Iron Guard did surprisingly well in the November elections. Faced with this situation, King Carol called to power the extreme-right, anti-Semitic but pro-monarchy, National Christian party, whose leaders Octavian Goga and Alexander Cuza were known for their Nazi sympathies and German connections. A series of anti-Semitic laws was introduced sparking a Jewish boycott that threatened to destabilize the whole economy. Romanian threats to denounce the Minorities Treaty brought rebuffs from both Paris and London. The Soviet Union, convinced that King Carol would now openly identify with Germany, withdrew its minister from the country. On 10 February, the king dismissed the government (which, unknown to Carol, had been negotiating with the Iron Guard) and established a personal dictatorship appointing to ministerial office a number of pro-western advisers. For a brief moment before *Anschluss*,

[47] Lungu, *Romania and the Great Powers*, 112.

there was a window of opportunity for the western powers. Delbos's meeting with Stojadinović could not have been a happy one as the Yugoslav premier had just returned from his much publicized visit with Mussolini and Ciano.

Delbos must have reached Prague, the last stop on his journey, with a deep sense of relief. The ever-optimistic Beneš clung to his belief that the 'dynamic regimes' would 'eventually either sink in competition with the democratic world, or like Stalin's Soviet Russia, gradually abandon their aggression'.[48] Sheila Grant-Duff, a well-connected British journalist with excellent contacts in Prague, wrote to Winston Churchill that:

> Beneš thinks that in 1938, a detente if not an entente is possible between Germany and her neighbours. While Beneš is in power, it is certain that the Czechs will not go any further than the French nor do anything which the French would disapprove or anything which would weaken the chance of a general settlement... I think Beneš' view that a detente is possible is as much a wish as a thought and that he does not believe in the possibility of a permanent understanding with Hitler Germany. Behind the wish is the urgency of calling a halt to the armaments race.[49]

Beneš retained his confidence in France. Jan Masaryk in London kept his countrymen informed about the Chamberlain government's views and warned that France was prepared to follow Britain's lead. Nonetheless, Beneš thought it possible to negotiate with the minorities and to deal diplomatically with Germany's complaints. Delbos's visit to Prague was the occasion for a strong avowal of France's loyalty to its existing treaties. The French foreign minister did raise the question of the *Sudetendeutsche* as the British had requested. Beneš dismissed the possibility of giving autonomy to the German minority but expressed his willingness to listen to what others thought he should do. He assumed that the relatively minor but immediate improvements he was suggesting would satisfy the British as well as the French. The two men each claimed that their meeting was a great success. Arriving in Paris, a smiling Delbos told the press, 'J'ai fait un excellent voyage.' The real truth emerged when Delbos appeared before the Foreign Affairs Committee of the Chamber of Deputies a few days later. He admitted that though France remained popular among the peoples of Poland, Yugoslavia, and Romania, official circles in these countries did not share the pro-French sentiments of the subjects. When Delbos entered

[48] Quoted in Igor Lukes, *Czechoslovakia between Stalin and Hitler: The Diplomacy of Edvard Beneš in the 1930s* (Oxford, 1996), 84.

[49] Chartwell Trust Papers, 2/328, Sheila Grant-Duff to Winston Churchill, 5 January 1938.

Prague, Alexander Werth, the well-informed *Manchester Guardian* correspondent in Paris reported, he exclaimed 'at last we are going to see some real friends'.[50]

The smaller states, drawing their lessons from the events of 1936, were prepared to follow the paths of Poland and Belgium. Those leaders who had looked to Paris for protection in the past were highly conscious of 'the shorn locks of the French Samson'. During 1937, apart from Austria and Czechoslovakia, neither of which had much choice, they would try to reaffirm their neutrality and pursue 'policies of independence'. Governments tried to avoid too clear an identification with any bloc. Only Yugoslavia moved towards the Axis powers in what was intended as a first step towards the adoption of a policy of neutrality. Unwilling to be drawn into Great Power quarrels, member states stressed the regional limitations of the Little Entente and Balkan Alliance, the former restricted to co-operation against Hungary and the latter, due to Turkish and Greek insistence, confined to purely Balkan affairs. While all governments engaged in rearmament, no decisive move was made towards military co-operation. Each of the Little Entente states had bilateral military arrangements covering security concerns that diverged from those of its partners. Few governments in the region were prepared to associate themselves too closely with the 'Paris–Prague–Moscow' axis, whatever their fears of Germany or Italy.

It was clear by 1937 that the European balance of power was shifting away from France towards Germany. With no alternative protector in sight and with politically influential groups often divided in their sympathies, the leaders of the status quo countries increasingly believed that safety lay in conducting independent foreign policies without fully committing themselves to any one Great Power, particularly as Britain, the most preferred substitute for France, showed no interest in their economic or security problems. Neither the leaders of Hungary or Bulgaria had much respect for Hitler, the 'upstart corporal'; King Boris regarded him as 'a showcase in hysteria'.[51] Yet they lacked the power to challenge his influence and retained revisionist ambitions which only Germany could fulfil. It was the latter which brought the Hungarians closer to Berlin towards the end of 1937. Rulers, nevertheless, tried to preserve some measure of independence while balancing between their conflicting goals. There appeared no immediate threat to any of these states. Both the Baltic and Balkans were only of secondary

[50] Alexander Werth, *The Twilight of France, 1933–1940* (London, 1940), 148.

[51] Vesselin Dimitrov, 'Bulgarian Neutrality: Domestic and International Perspectives', in Neville Wylie (ed.), *European Neutrals and Non-Belligerents during the Second World War* (Cambridge, 2002), 192.

interest to Hitler. His more immediate goals lay in central Europe. Mussolini, still heavily engaged in Spain and in East Africa, concentrated on strengthening the ties with Germany. Ambitions in the Red Sea and Mediterranean took precedence over the Balkans where Italian suspicions of German intentions remained in place. Despite the central preoccupation of the Romanians with the Soviet Union, the Russians were still pursuing a defensive policy. Regardless of the increasing German economic hold over these countries, statesmen still believed they had room for manoeuvre.

The Popular Front effort during 1937 to strengthen its ties with the Little Entente nations in order to protect Czechoslovakia ended in failure. The prestige lost over the Rhineland and Ethiopia could not be restored and the ideological reverberations of the Spanish Civil War further weakened the *Quai d'Orsay*'s negotiating hand. Quite apart from the political pressures within which the Popular Front operated, the government lacked the necessary resources, financial and economic, to challenge the German economic offensive in Eastern Europe. The contrast between German strength in 1937 and French weakness made the revival of France's influence unlikely. Viewed from Paris, the Belgian retreat into neutrality and the Italian–Yugoslav pact meant that France could not assist Czechoslovakia without facing the danger of fighting on her own soil. The failures in south-east Europe could only serve to reinforce the defensive caste of French military planning. It was doubly unfortunate for Czechoslovakia that their most important ally was becoming more dependent on co-operation with Britain just at the moment when Chamberlain was prepared to bargain with Hitler over central Europe. Whereas the Foreign Office had tried to disguise Britain's unwillingness to check German expansion into Austria and Czechoslovakia, hoping that warnings even without commitments might deter Hitler, Chamberlain wished to abandon such unsatisfactory games in an effort to convince the Führer to act in accordance with the normal diplomatic rules. If Germany moved in an orderly and peaceful manner, the injustices of the Treaty of Versailles could be corrected. The prime minister set the pace and expected France to follow. The only other way for France was through Moscow. As will be discussed in the next chapter, strong doubts both about the reliability of the Bolsheviks and the offensive capacities of the Red Army, reinforced by British disapproval of Franco-Soviet military links, closed this road off as well. Yet only the Soviet Union could provide the two-front war needed to assure French security. The safety of France appeared to depend on a settlement with Hitler which Britain could deliver. If appeasement failed and war came, France would need British backing to win the anticipated long war of attrition. In the winter of 1937–1938, with serious rearmament just beginning, France's ability to pursue an independent policy towards Germany reached one of the low points in its inter-war history. Within six months, its continued existence as a European Great Power would be put in question.

Books

AHMANN, R., *Nichtangriffspakte: Entwicklung und operative Nutzung in Europa, 1922–1939, mit einem Ausblick auf die Renaissance des Nichtangriffsvertrages nach dem Zweiten Weltkrieg* (Baden-Baden, 1988).

ALDCROFT, D. H., and MOREWOOD, S., *Economic Change in Eastern Europe since 1918* (Aldershot, 1995).

BEREND, I., *The Crisis Zone of Europe: An Interpretation of East-Central European History in the First Half of the Twentieth Century* (Cambridge, 1986).

—— *Decades of Crisis: Central and Eastern Europe before World War II* (Berkeley, CA, 1998).

BOELCKE, W. A., *Deutschland als Welthandelsmacht, 1930–1945* (Stuttgart, 1994).

BRUEGEL, J. W., *Czechoslovakia before Munich: The German Minority Problem and British Appeasement Policy* (Cambridge, 1973).

BURLEIGH, M., *Germany turns Eastwards: A Study of Ostforschung in the Third Reich* (Cambridge, 1988).

CIENCIALA, A., *Poland and the Western Powers, 1938–1939: A Study in the Interdependence of Eastern and Western Europe* (London, 1968).

EVANS, R. J. W. and CORNWALL, M. (eds.), *Czechoslovakia in a Nationalist and Fascist Europe, 1918–1948* (Oxford, 2007).

FEINSTEIN, C. H., TEMIN, P., and TONIOLO, G., *The European Economy between the Wars* (Oxford, 1997).

FORSTMEIER, F. and VOLKMANN, H.-E. (eds.), *Wirtschaft und Rüstung am Vorabend des Zweiten Weltkrieges* (Düsseldorf, 1977). See M. Funke, H.-E. Volkmann.

FUNKE, M. (ed.), *Deutschland und die Mächte: Materialen zur Außenpolitik des Dritten Reiches* (Düsseldorf, 1976). See M. Broszat, M. Geyer.

GRENZEBACH, W. S. JR., *Germany's Informal Empire in East-Central Europe: German Economic Policy toward Yugoslavia and Rumania, 1933–1939* (Stuttgart, 1988).

GROMADA, T. V. (ed.), *Essays on Poland's Foreign Policy, 1918–1939* (New York, 1970).

GUILLEBAUD, C. W., *The Economic Recovery of Germany: From 1933 to the Incorporation of Austria in March 1938* (London, 1939).

HIDEN, J., *The Baltic States and Weimar Ostpolitik* (Cambridge, 1987).

—— and LOIT, A. (eds.), *The Baltic in International Relations between the Two World Wars* (Stockholm, 1988). See P. Salmon and R. Misiunas.

HILLGRUBER, A., *Hitler, König Carol und Marschall Antonescu: die deutsch-rumänischen Beziehungen, 1938–1944*, 2nd edn. (Wiesbaden, 1965).

HIRSCHFELD, G. and KETTENACKER, L., *Der Führerstaat: Mythos und Realität: Studien zur Struktur und Politik des Dritten Reiches* (Stuttgart, 1981). See A. S. Milward, B.-J. Wendt.

HITCHENS, M. G., *Germany, Russia and the Balkans: Prelude to the Nazi–Soviet Non-Aggression Pact* (New York and Boulder, CO, 1983).
HOPTNER, J. B., *Yugoslavia in Crisis, 1934–1941* (New York, 1962).
JORDAN, N., *The Popular Front and Central Europe: The Dilemmas of French Impotence, 1918–1940* (Cambridge, 1992).
KAISER, D. E., *Economic Diplomacy and the Origins of the Second World War: Germany, Britain, France and Eastern Europe, 1930–1939* (Princeton, NJ, and Guildford, 1980).
KIMMICH, C. M., *The Free City: Danzig and German Foreign Policy, 1919–1934* (New Haven, CT, 1968).
KLIMEK, A., *Diplomacy at the Crossroads of Europe: Czechoslovak Foreign Policy, 1918–1938*, trans. Libor Trejdl (Prague, 1989).
KOLIOPOULOS, J. S., *Greece and the British Connection, 1935–1941* (Oxford, 1977).
LE GOYET, P., *France–Pologne 1919–1939: De l'amitié romantique à la méfiance réciproque* (Paris, 1991).
LITTLEFIELD, F. C., *Germany and Yugoslavia, 1933–1941: The German Conquest of Yugoslavia* (New York and Boulder, CO, 1988).
LUKES, I., *Czechoslovakia between Stalin and Hitler: The Diplomacy of Edvard Beneš in the 1930s* (Oxford and New York, 1996).
LUNGU, D. B., *Romania and the Great Powers, 1933–1940* (Durham, 1989).
MARGUERAT, P., *Le IIIe Reich et le pétrole roumain, 1938–1940* (Geneva, 1977).
MAZOWER, M., *Greece and the Inter-War Economic Crisis* (Oxford, 1991).
Militärgeschichtliches Forschungsamt (ed.), *Germany and the Second World War*, Vol. 1: *The Build-up of German Aggression*, ed. Deist, W. (Oxford, 1990). See Part II by H.-E. Volkmann.
—— (ed.), *Germany and the Second World War*, Vol. III: *The Mediterranean, South-east Europe and North Africa, 1939–1942*, ed. Schreiber, G., Stegemann, B., and Vogel, D. (Oxford, 1995). See G. Schreiber, 'Germany, Italy and South-east Europe: From Political and Economic Hegemony to Military Aggression', Parts 1 and 2.
MILLMAN, B., *The Ill-made Alliance: Anglo–Turkish Relations 1934–1940* (London, 1998).
OPREA, I. M., *Nicolae Titulescu's Diplomatic Activity* (Bucharest, 1968).
PELT, M., *Tobacco, Arms and Politics: Greece and Germany from World Crisis to World War, 1929–1941* (Copenhagen, 1998).
PETZINA, D., *Autarkiepolitik im Dritten Reich: der nationalsozialistische Vierjahresplan* (Stuttgart, 1968).
POLANSKY, A., *The Little Dictators: The History of Eastern Europe since 1918* (London, 1975).
RÁNKI, G., *Economy and Foreign Policy: The Struggle of the Great Powers for Hegemony in the Danube Valley, 1919–1939* (Boulder, CO, and New York, 1983).
RECKER, M.-L. (ed.), *Von der Konkurrenz zur Rivalität: das britisch-deutsche Verhältnis in den Ländern der europäischen Peripherie, 1919–1939* (Stuttgart, 1986).
ROOS, H., *Polen und Europa: Studien zur polnischen Aussenpolitik 1931–1939* (Tübingen, 1957).
RUSINOW, D. I., *Italy's Austrian Heritage, 1919–1946* (Oxford, 1969).

SADKOVICH, J. J., *Italian Support for Croatian Separatism, 1927–1937* (New York, 1987).

SAKMYSTER, T. L., *Hungary, the Great Powers and the Danubian Crisis, 1936–1939* (Athens, 1980).

SALMON, P., *Scandinavia and the Great Powers, 1890–1940* (Cambridge, 1997).

SCHRÖDER, H. R., *Deutschland und die Vereinigten Staaten 1933–1939* (Wiesbaden, 1970).

SCOTT, W. E., *Alliance against Hitler: The Origins of the Franco-Soviet Pact* (Durham, 1966).

SMELSER, R. M., *The Sudeten Problem, 1933–1938: Volkstumspolitik and the Formulation of Nazi Foreign Policy* (Folkestone, 1975).

TEICHOVA, A., *An Economic Background to Munich: International Business and Czechoslovakia, 1918–1938* (Cambridge, 1974).

—— and COTTRELL, P. L. (eds.), *International Business and Central Europe, 1918–1939* (Leicester, 1983).

VAN ROON, G., *Small States in Years of Depression: The Oslo Alliance, 1930–1940* (Assen, 1989).

WENDT, B.-J., *Economic Appeasement: Handel und Finanz in der britischen Deutschland-Politik, 1933–1939* (Düsseldorf, 1971).

Articles and Chapters

AHMANN, R., 'Nazi German Policy towards the Baltic States on the Eve of the Second World War', in Hiden, J. and Lane, T. (eds.), *The Baltic and the Outbreak of the Second World War* (Cambridge, 1992).

CAMPBELL, F. G., 'Central Europe's Bastion of Democracy', *East European Quarterly*, 11: 2 (1977).

CAMPUS, E., 'La diplomatie roumaine et les relations franco-allemandes pendant les années 1933–1939', in Colloque international sur les relations franco-allemandes de 1933 à 1939 (ed.), *Les relations franco-allemandes, 1933–1939* (Paris, 1976).

CLIADAKIS, H., 'The Political and Diplomatic Background to the Metaxas Dictatorship, 1935–6', *Journal of Contemporary History*, 14: 1 (1979).

CORNWALL, M., 'A Fluctuating Barometer: British Diplomatic Views of the Czech–German Relationship in Czechoslovakia, 1918–1938', in Schmidt-Hartmann, E. and Winters, S. (eds.), *Great Britain, the United States and the Bohemian Lands* (Munich, 1991).

—— 'The Rise and Fall of a "Special Relationship"? Britain and Czechoslovakia, 1930–1948', in Brivati, B. and Jones, H. (eds.), *What Difference did the War Make?* (Leicester, 1993).

DAVENPORT-HINES, R. P. T., 'Vickers' Balkan Conscience: Aspects of Anglo-Romanian Armaments, 1918–1939', *Business History*, 25 (1983).

D'HOOP, J.-M., 'La France, la Grande Bretagne et les pays balkaniques de 1936 à 1939', in Imperial War Museum and Comité d'histoire de la Deuxième Guerre Mondiale (eds.), *Les relations franco-britanniques de 1935 à 1939* (Paris, 1975).

DIMITROV, V., 'Bulgarian Neutrality: Domestic and International Perspectives', in Wylie, N. (ed.), *European Neutrals and Non-Belligerents during the Second World War* (Cambridge, 2002).

HINKKANEN-LIEVONEN, M.-L., 'Britain as Germany's Commercial Rival in the Baltic States, 1919–1939', in Recker, M.-L. (ed.), *Von der Konkurrenz zur Rivalität: From Competition to Rivalry* (Stuttgart, 1986).

HOPTNER, J. B., 'Yugoslavia as Neutralist, 1937', *Journal of Central European Affairs*, 16 (1956).

JACKSON, P., 'La faillite de la dissuasion française en Europe Centrale', in Vaïsse, M. (ed.), *Bâtir une nouvelle sécurité: la coopération entre la France et les États d'Europe centrale et orientale dans l'entre-deux-guerres* (Paris, 2001).

JORDAN, N., 'Maurice Gamelin, Italy and the Eastern Alliances', *Journal of Strategic Studies*, 14 (1991).

MAŁECKA, T., 'Amerikanisches Kapital in Polen in der Zwischenkriegszeit', in Schroeter, H. G. and Wurm, C. A. (eds.), *Politik, Wirtschaft und internationale Beziehungen: Studien zu ihrem Verhältnis in der Zeit zwischen den Weltkriegen* (Mainz, 1991).

MAZOWER, M., 'Economic Diplomacy between Great Britain and Greece in the 1930s', *Journal of European Economic History* 17: 3 (1988).

MILLMAN, B., 'Turkish Foreign and Strategic Policy, 1934–42', *Middle Eastern Studies*, 31: 3 (1995).

MILWARD, A., 'The Reichsmark Bloc and the International Economy', in Hirschfeld, G. and Kettenacker, L. (eds.), *Der "Führerstaat": Mythos und Realität: Studien zur Struktur und Politik des Dritten Reiches* (Stuttgart, 1981).

ORVIK, N., 'From Collective Security to Neutrality: The Nordic Powers, the League of Nations, Britain and the Approach of War, 1935–1939', in Bourne, K. and Watt, D. C. (eds.), *Studies in International Relations: Essays Presented to W. Norton Medlicott* (London, 1967).

RITSCHL, A. O., 'Nazi Economic Imperialism and the Exploitation of the Small: Evidence from Germany's Secret Foreign Exchange Balances, 1938–40', *Economic History Review*, 54 (2001).

SAKWA, G., 'The "Renewal" of the Franco-Polish Alliance in 1936 and the Rambouillet Agreement', *Polish Review*, 16: 2 (1971).

SALMON, P., 'Anglo-German Commercial Rivalry in the Depression Era: The Political and Economic Impact on Scandinavia, 1931–1939', in Recker, M.-L. (ed.), *Von der Konkurrenz zur Rivalität, 1919–1939* (Stuttgart, 1986).

SCHRÖDER, H.-J., 'Südosteuropa als "Informal Empire" Deutschlands, 1933–1939: das Beispiel Jugoslawien', *Jahrbücher für Geschichte Osteuropas*, 23 (1975).

SCHRÖDER, H.-J., 'Eastern Europe in Transition: Economic Development during the Interwar and Postwar Period', in Teichova, A. (ed.), *Central Europe in the Twentieth Century: An Economic History Perspective* (Aldershot, 1997).

TEICHOVA, A., 'East-Central and South-East Europe', in Mathias, P. and Pollard, S. (eds.), *The Cambridge Economic History of Europe*, Vol. VIII, 2nd ed. (Cambridge, 1989).

—— 'Bilateral Trade Revisited: Did the Southeast European States Exploit National Socialist Germany on the Eve of the Second World War?', in Glatz, F. (ed.), *Modern Age—Modern Historian: In Memoriam György Ránki, 1930–1988* (Budapest, 1990).

Ten Cate, J. H., 'Deutschland und die neutralen Kleinstaaten in Nord- und Nordwesteuropa in der Zwischenkriegszeit. Ein Abriß', in Schroeter, H. G. and Wurm, C. A. (eds.), *Politik, Wirtschaft und internationale Beziehungen: Studien zu ihrem Verhältnis in der Zeit zwischen den Weltkriegen* (Mainz, 1991).

Thomas, M., 'To Arm an Ally: French Arms Sales to Romania, 1926–1940', *Journal of Strategic Studies*, 19 (1996).

Wendt, B.-J., 'England und der deutsche "Drang nach Südosten": Kapitalbeziehungen und Warenverkehr in Südeuropa zwischen den Weltkriegen', in Wendt, B.-J. and Geiss, I. (eds.), *Deutschland in der Weltpolitik des 19. und 20. Jahrhunderts* (Düsseldorf, 1973).

Zorach, Jonathan, 'The Nationality Problem in the Czechoslovak Army between the Two World Wars', *East Central Europe*, 5: 2 (1978).

—— 'The British View of the Czechs in the Era before the Munich Crisis', *Slavonic and East European Review*, 57 (1979).

8

Whither the Soviet Union? Moscow and the West, 1936–1938

There was another card that could be played in Eastern Europe, but in 1937 neither the French nor the British were willing to play it. In the world of the theoreticians, where states strive either to expand or maintain their power positions and act as unitary rational agents on the international stage, Britain and France should have responded favourably to Litvinov's efforts to create a 'collective security' front. Few doubted in 1937 that Germany represented the major threat to the European peace, and that Hitler, in his writings and his speeches, had made clear German enmity towards the Soviet Union. The drive for *Lebensraum* had defined territorial goals; they centred on the agriculturally rich lands of the Ukraine. In Hitler's speeches, Bolshevism was identified with the Jews, and the international ideological battle was most frequently presented in terms of a struggle with Judeo-Bolshevism. The Spanish Civil War gave Hitler's ideological campaign a new edge and resonance. Given the problems faced by the British and French in negotiating a general settlement with Germany, there were compelling reasons for including the Soviet Union in any anti-revisionist bloc, if only to encourage the Germans to come to the bargaining table or to deter Japan and Germany from joining together. Yet neither the French nor the British picked up the Soviet card, and during 1937 the door to *rapprochement* was almost shut.

The continuing deterioration in relations can be linked both to the ongoing conflict in Spain, and to the purges that convulsed the Soviet Union. The Spanish Civil War, with its heavy impact on French domestic politics, restricted Léon Blum's freedom of diplomatic manoeuvre. With the fall of his ministry in June 1937, power in the Popular Front government shifted to those sections of the coalition most hostile to the French Communist party, and to the Soviet Union. In Britain, too, though the Communist party was small and politically irrelevant, the Spanish imbroglio affected political attitudes, and, in certain parts of the Conservative party heightened the traditional hostility towards the USSR, which had so marked the policies of the 1920s. Of crucial importance in confirming these suspicions and doubts was not the arrests, trials, and executions of the 'old Bolsheviks', but the increasing pace of the purges engulfing the upper echelons of the Soviet military establishment. The behaviour of the Stalinist government was judged, both at the *Quai d'Orsay* and at the Foreign Office as far worse than that of the Fascist states. The purges of the army, which was beginning to gain international respect, devalued the importance of the Soviet Union as a potential friend or enemy, as a deterrent or wartime ally, whether in Europe or in the Far East. It confirmed long-held doubts in the French and British military establishments that the Soviet Union could, or would be able to, influence the future balance of power. It convinced Hitler, who had needed no further confirmation that the USSR was weak, morally corrupt (!), and incapable of mounting a threat to the fulfilment of his short-term goals.

I

Given its exposed position with regard to Germany and its alliances in the East, France was the more likely candidate for an agreement with Moscow than Britain. It was a reluctant Laval who concluded the mutual assistance pact with the Soviet Union in May 1935 and who enjoyed a highly successful trip to Moscow where he promised speedy ratification, and the possibility of military staff talks. Though welcoming the new agreements with France and Czechoslovakia, Soviet expectations were not high. Laval was distrusted, and Soviet suspicions were soon confirmed by his publicly declared preference for a settlement with Germany, which the pact with Russia only made more difficult. The new Franco-Soviet pact was only ratified in February and March 1936; the large majority in the French Senate a reaction to the German remilitarization of the Rhineland. The Russians closely monitored the highly volatile political situation in Paris; the times were hardly propitious for the start of the military talks which alone, in the Soviet view, would give substance to the new alignment. At the start of 1936, Litvinov increased earlier Russian spending on the French press, particularly on the semi-official *Le Temps*, on the grounds that without subsidies, the already vitriolic newspaper attacks on the Soviet Union would become even worse, making public relations more difficult. The fall of Laval in January brought little change, as the political unrest in France continued during the run-up to the May elections. Even the advent of the Popular Front government, with Communist party support, did not promise an easy passage for the Franco-Soviet military talks. The Popular Front success reactivated anti-Communism and denunciations of Moscow-inspired subversion, in the ranks of the centre and right-wing parties. Litvinov warned that 'Even though, at first sight, these results are good, especially the victory won by the Communist party, I foresee as the effect of the elections a reinforcement of the activity of the right-wing parties and a subsequent drift towards the fascistation of France'.[1] The British, too, made clear their strong opposition to the Franco-Soviet staff talks at a time when the Popular Front government was anxious to draw closer to London. Nonetheless, in October 1936, Blum promised Litvinov that he would open negotiations if the new Locarno exchanges with Germany failed. The *Deuxième Bureau* was warning that the Reich had already established a decisive superiority over France on the ground and in the air. Belgium was moving towards neutrality. The prospect for a French–Little Entente pact was poor; France's relations with Yugoslavia and Romania were deteriorating and Yugoslavia was moving in the Italian direction. The public signs of the growing Italo-German friendship, and Mussolini's increasing activity in the Balkans, cast doubts on any settlement with Rome. Though Anglo-French relations began to improve, the British efforts, like those of Blum, to negotiate a general settlement with Germany had stalled. There was, moreover, little hope in Paris that Britain would provide an insurance policy against the anticipated German move against Czechoslovakia. On 6 November 1936, the Popular Front government decided to open military exchanges with the Soviet Union, despite the opposition of the military high command and the upper echelons of the *Quai d'Orsay*. Officers did not believe that the Soviet Union possessed either the will or the capability to defend Czechoslovakia against German attack. At the *Quai d'Orsay*, secretary-general Alexis Léger, already highly apprehensive about the activities of the Comintern in France and in Spain, feared that any military conversations with the USSR would provoke the Poles and, more dangerously, provide a pretext for German aggression. Léger had never believed that the Franco-Soviet pact of 1935 had any military value beyond preventing a Soviet–German accommodation. His views were shared by many of the senior officials at the ministry.

The French military dragged their feet. With but few exceptions, the army chiefs continued to argue that little would be gained and much harm would result from any exchange of information between the French and Soviet military forces. Even the highly pragmatic Gamelin, who was less ideologically engaged than some of his fellow officers, shared their anxieties about the risks involved in opening

[1] Quoted in Sabine Dullin, 'Litvinov and the People's Commissariat of Foreign Affairs: The Fate of an Administration under Stalin, 1930–1939', in Silvo Pons and Andrea Romano (eds.), *Russia in the Age of Wars, 1914–1945* (Milan, 2000), 129.

military conversations with Moscow. He indirectly informed London that he 'was going to resist military exchanges with the Red Army, so long as he was chief of the general staff and in a position to do so'.[2] For officers such as generals Schweisguth, Colson, and Vuillemin, a combination of distrust and scepticism coloured perceptions of Soviet military capabilities. Schweisguth's highly negative report on the September 1936 manoeuvres buried an earlier and far more positive assessment of the Red Army. The report's highly alarmist final section, drafted by Vuillemin of the air staff, who was also the general staff's liaison officer with the *Quai d'Orsay*, suggested that the Russians were seeking a military alliance with France to encourage German fears of encirclement. It was intended to provoke a German–French war from which 'the Soviet Union would emerge as the unopposed arbiter of Europe's destiny as had the United States in 1918'.[3] Schweisguth warned that France should not be deceived by Red Army propaganda concerning its ability to provide assistance against Germany. The report played on the anxieties of senior officers, already alarmed by the political situation in France, and their fears that the French Communists were working to undermine the morale of the army.

Neither Daladier, the minister for war and national defence, nor Gamelin, the chief of staff, wanted the preliminary talks to succeed. Daladier was widely known to oppose the exchanges, and was the subject of constant attacks by the Communist party and paper, *l'Humanité*. The very fact that Schweisguth and Vuillemin were appointed to negotiate with General Semenov, the new Soviet military attaché who arrived in Paris at the start of 1937, suggested that the French high command was unwilling to implement the November decision. Gamelin told Schweisguth, 'We need to drag things out', and later advised him that 'we should not hurry, but avoid giving to the Russians the impression that we were playing them along, which could lead them into a political *volte-face* [i.e. *rapprochement* with Germany]'.[4] On 17 February, the Soviet ambassador in Paris called on Blum, while Semenov met with Colson and Schweisguth. The ambassador told the premier, who had been alerted to British displeasure about the talks, that the Red Army would assist France or Czechoslovakia with all of its forces against a German attack. This assistance would have to be sent through either Poland or Romania. If this proved impossible,

[2] Martin S. Alexander, *The Republic in Danger: General Maurice Gamelin and the Politics of French Defence, 1933–1940*, 299.

[3] Report Schweisguth, 5 October 1936, *DDF*, 2nd ser., Vol. III, No. 343 (annexe).

[4] Both quotations from Michael Carley, 'The End of the "Low, Dishonest Decade": Failure of the Anglo-Franco-Soviet Alliance in 1939', *Europe–Asia Studies*, 45: 2 (1993), 308.

Soviet troops would be sent by sea, and the air force would be dispatched to France and Czechoslovakia. The USSR would also provide material aid to both countries. In return, the Soviet high command demanded formal military accords. It wanted to know what assistance France would offer in the case of German aggression against the USSR, and what materials would be supplied to the Soviet Union. Blum explained that the French general staff needed to know how the Red Army commanders thought they could bring their military force to bear on Germany, and warned of his own concerns that the Poles, Romanians, and Baltic republics would never allow the passage of Soviet troops across their territories.

While Semenov was in Moscow, the French generals drafted a response for Daladier to present to Blum. The Soviet *démarche* was judged technically unsatisfactory, and more details about the nature of possible Soviet assistance were required. The generals recommended continuing the conversations but postponing any decision about more substantive talks until their conclusion. Daladier was, if anything, more reluctant to act than his generals, and postponed a meeting with them until 19 March, weeks after receiving their recommendations, and on the eve of Semenov's second return to Moscow. The minister of defence hoped that the proceedings might be delayed by asking for additional information, particularly with regard to the question of Soviet air assistance. At the meeting between Schweisguth and Semenov, the French general pointed out that co-operation on the ground would depend on 'political factors' with respect to Poland, the Baltic and elsewhere. Semenov, in turn, warned Schweisguth that the Soviet military chiefs would probably refuse to answer the latest French questions, which could only be discussed in authorized official conversations. Even the purely technical matters proposed for examination would depend on French mediation in Poland and Romania, to bring about a change in their respective diplomatic attitudes towards Moscow. A few days later, when Delbos met with Potemkin, the Soviet ambassador, the foreign minister was more encouraging. Potemkin, already reassigned to take up the important post of deputy commissar for foreign affairs (his predecessor was to die in Stalin's purges), refused to speculate on the reaction of the Soviet general staff, but was already pessimistic about the outcome.

Though Blum and Delbos may have hoped for some progress, it was Pierre Cot, the minister for air, who was the real enthusiast for a military alliance. Cot had made various attempts during 1936 to develop an offensive air strategy that would at the same time free the air force from army control. He had instituted equally unsuccessful talks with the Romanians in the hope of securing their assent to Soviet air passage. Neither this failure, nor Daladier's veto of his proposals in late January for opening joint army–air force talks in Moscow, dampened Cot's enthusiasm for an independent approach to the Russians. In mid-February, with Blum's approval, he sought to hasten the stalled negotiations via Prague, to gain Franco-Czech-Soviet air collaboration. Cot and the Czech representative sent by Beneš for joint conversations discussed how the existing mutual security treaties could be used as the basis for such co-operation. The French military authorities took alarm, though there was no Soviet participation in the exchanges and Cot knew of Moscow's objections to any piecemeal arrangements. At the 19 March meeting between Daladier and his generals, the defence minister voiced his doubts about the value of Soviet air assistance, citing the need for intermediate bases, and Romanian opposition to the granting of air passage. When Gamelin raised the possibility of formal Soviet guarantees to Poland and Romania, Daladier blocked further discussion. He stressed Britain's hostility to any form of Franco-Soviet military collaboration, and insisted that France could do without Soviet, but not without British, assistance. He announced his intention of visiting London in April, supposedly to 'rouse the British to the dangers of allowing Germany to reconstruct a *Mitteleuropa* on the Baghdad Axis', but mainly in the hope of marshalling British support against the talks.[5] In early April, in response to the Belgian defection, and again in the hope of breaking the continuing stalemate, Cot, with Blum's approval, sent an air mission to Russia. Though favourably impressed, particularly by the Russian industrial mobilization for creating an offensive air force, General Pierre Keller, the head of the mission, found the Soviets unwilling to discuss the question of air collaboration in isolation. Voroshilov, the commissar for war, warned that he was not prepared to continue the Paris talks as long as the French refused to say what they would do should the USSR be attacked by Germany. Keller returned to Paris with warnings about the need to make progress at the official level.

While waiting for Semenov's expected return, Blum and Delbos, disturbed by rumours of a German–Russian *rapprochement*, and apprehensive, too, about the domestic consequences of a breakdown in the talks, tried to get Daladier to break the deadlock in the military conversations. The defence minister, still unconvinced, approached Gamelin and suggested a secret meeting with a Soviet military representative, possibly in London, during George VI's coronation ceremonies in May.

[5] Nicole Jordan, *The Popular Front and Central Europe*, 264.

Gamelin refused to act without informing the British and Poles, and would do nothing if military negotiations would alienate either. In a written deposition, he restated his doubts about whether the problems of passage through Poland or Romania could be solved. When Daladier visited London in late April, to promote the cause of Franco-British co-operation in the Mediterranean, he was told that France was naturally at liberty to proceed with the Soviet talks, but that Germany was issuing warnings and that France should not be surprised at the consequences. Vansittart repeated the same message, in conversations with Ambassador Corbin in April and May, claiming that the Germans would use any military conversation as a pretext to wreck the Western pact negotiations and throw all the blame on France.

British opposition sealed the fate of the talks as far as Daladier and Gamelin were concerned. While waiting for Semenov, Gamelin decided to freeze the talks by informing the Soviet military representative, in London for the coronation festivities, 'that the French soldiers were in favour of an agreement, but were unable to admit of Russian interference within the French army, intended to weaken it'.[6] There was no need for subterfuge. Semenov, who had been expected back in April, never reappeared. He was a victim of the purges that spread to the Red Army high command during the spring and summer of 1937. Nonetheless, the Soviets pressed the French for a decision. Neither Blum nor Delbos wanted to close the door on future contacts. Ministers discussed the terms of a *démarche* to be made by Ambassador Coulondre (who arrived in Moscow in November 1936), to the Russians. In consultation with Gamelin, the *Quai d'Orsay* worked out an ingenious legalistic solution, placing the proposed staff talks under the aegis of the 1935 Franco-Soviet pact, which would avoid any formal discussions of a political character. The Soviets might be asked, in their own interest, to give air support to Czechoslovakia and provide local aid for the Little Entente powers. Nothing was said of any French contribution to the defence of the USSR. Even the so-called technical covenants were subject to conditions, i.e. no publicity, and Soviet acceptance of France's obligations to inform allied governments. It was a one-sided formula resulting from the French distrust of Soviet intentions, and military fears that having provoked a Franco-German war, the USSR would stand aside when the conflict began.

Why did Blum and Delbos press for the continuation of staff talks, even in an attenuated form? The ostensible reason was the fear of a Russo-German *rapprochement*, rumours of which were intentionally spread by Stalin's agents in anticipation of the denunciations of

[6] Quoted in Alexander, *The Republic in Danger*, 301.

Tukhachevsky and other senior officers, as German spies. But in Paris there was also rising apprehension over the exposure of Czechoslovakia to German attack. When approached by Beneš on 8 April 1937 to sanction Czech attempts to seek an arrangement with Berlin, Delbos responded positively, judging that Britain's attitude towards Czechoslovakia, so important in French calculations, would depend on Czech efforts to conciliate Germany. The foreign minister may have viewed the promise of Soviet assistance as the only available short-term option. The Soviets marked the anniversary of the signing of the Franco-Soviet pact with warnings in *Pravda* and *Izvestia* that France needed the pact more than the Soviet Union, which could defend its own borders without foreign assistance. Delbos assured Moscow that he was determined 'to respect the Franco-Soviet Pact and to preserve its significance', but exchanges with Eden during the May coronation ceremonies in London confirmed his decision to avoid a military agreement with Russia. He defended the proposed staff conversations, which he characterized as 'entirely harmless', and necessary to avoid affronting the Soviet Union and a Soviet approach to Germany. Warned by Eden of the 'psychological effects' of such collaboration, both in England and 'in the lesser countries of Central Europe', Delbos held his ground, arguing that any postponement in agreeing to limited collaboration would intensify Soviet suspicions of western intentions. He argued, too, that technical aeronautical talks were urgently needed. Soviet air assistance was indispensable if Czechoslovakia, whose defence was vital to France, was attacked by Germany.

On a tour through Europe, Litvinov stopped off in Paris on 18 May, and saw Blum and Delbos. Though he made a strong case for joint action in the defence of Czechoslovakia, there was no mention of military conversations in the final joint communiqué. A few days after the Litvinov visit, Blum unburdened himself to the American ambassador, William Bullitt. Speaking of the tragic similarity of the 1937 international situation to that of 1914, he told Bullitt that there appeared to be no alternative to the re-creation of the pre-war Anglo-Franco-Russian alliance. Bullitt was closer to the mark when he wrote to Roosevelt, 'The general situation is this; Delbos and Blum are more or less in despair with regard to the possibility of keeping Austria and Czechoslovakia out of the hands of Germany. Hitler has the ball and can run with it in any direction he chooses.'[7] At Litvinov's meeting with Blum and Delbos, he was told that

[7] Orville Bullitt (ed.), *For the President, Personal and Secret: Correspondence between Franklin D. Roosevelt and William C. Bullitt* (Boston, MA, 1972), 213. The president

though the air minister and minister of marine had agreed to pursue limited staff talks, Daladier had not yet given his response. A few days later, the French agreed on the terms of the *démarche* to be sent to Coulondre in Moscow. On 15 April, the three service chiefs were authorized to renew technical conversations with their Soviet counterparts. The military men remained convinced that even 'technical conversations' between military attachés would alarm Poland and Romania, and lead both states into the German camp, freeing Hitler for war against France. General staff officers warned the politicians that 'a Franco-Soviet military agreement risks putting in jeopardy the warmth and candour of Franco-English relations'.[8] It seems unlikely, had the *démarche* been presented, that there would have been any real follow-up on the French side.

The purge of the Soviet high command gave the *coup de grâce* to the prospects of technical conversations, and brought to an end the half-hearted efforts to conclude a new trade deal. It was first thought that Stalin was acting mainly to rid himself of domestic rivals, but the spreading campaign against the higher echelons of the Red Army raised more far-reaching questions. As thousands of senior officers were purged, the French high command dismissed the advice of their military attaché in Moscow that the Red Army remained a formidable fighting force, and would recover. Long-held doubts about the Red Army's ability to pursue an offensive war, quite apart from the problems of transit, were now thoroughly vindicated. It was widely believed that the stability of the Soviet state itself might be shaken. The threat of a Soviet–German *rapprochement* receded though it did not disappear. With the Soviet Union 'annihilating itself', Gamelin recommended renewed appeals to the Poles and Romanians to stand up against the German threat. 'This [the purges] should make us more prudent than ever, do not break off in order not to risk throwing Stalin into Hitler's arms', Gamelin advised, 'but do not commit ourselves and do not show the Russians anything of interest. The USSR is increasingly outside the European game.'[9] Beneš warned the French minister in Prague: 'Russia is a good card, it is perhaps not necessary to play it, but we must not abandon it for fear that Germany pick it up.'[10]

had just signed the new Neutrality Act (1 May 1937) providing that goods from the United States sold to belligerents had to be on a 'cash-and-carry' basis.

[8] *DDF*, 2nd ser., Vol. V, No. 480.

[9] Pierre Le Goyet, *Le mystère Gamelin* (Paris, 1976), 205–206, cited in Jordan, *The Popular Front and Central Europe*, 276–277.

[10] *DDF*, 2nd ser., Vol. V, No. 315.

For the French, the exchanges with the Soviet Union were always subordinate to the need to improve relations with London. Both Blum and Chautemps were careful to keep the British informed of their dealings with the Russians, and it was because the Foreign Office was convinced of the narrow scope of the Franco-Soviet pact that they came to accept its utility in preventing an agreement between the Soviet Union and Germany. The French, moreover, were more concerned with the preservation of the alliance with Poland and their lingering hopes for an alliance with the Little Entente, than with the ties with Russia. There seemed little possibility that either Poland or Romania would allow Soviet troops access to Czechoslovakia through their countries. Though the results were very disappointing, air and military collaboration with Poland went much further than with the Soviet Union. In these years, the Soviet forces were not factored into French war planning. There was always the fear that French reliance on Czechoslovak and Soviet military support would drive the Poles further into the arms of Germany. The French were well aware that the Russians would remain faithful to France only as long as there were substantial gains to be won in terms of security against Germany. In both countries, attention was focused on the Reich. Each wanted to dissuade Hitler from an attack in the East but neither wished to provoke him. The French knew that Moscow would keep the door open to Germany, just as the British and French intended to do. The purpose of the Franco-Soviet collaboration was 'essentially dissuasive or negative.'[11]

The abortive negotiations left behind a bitter aftertaste. French reluctance to play the Soviet card made it likely that Stalin would approach the renewed efforts at negotiation in the spring and summer of 1939, with suspicion and cynicism.[12] In France, the assumption, not necessarily true, that worker discontent and the PCF attacks on the government were Moscow-inspired, led to numerous complaints about 'Comintern meddling', and warnings that if Soviet interference did not cease, the mutual assistance pact would become a 'dead letter'. Litvinov turned on Coulondre during their 17 June meeting, insisting that he could do nothing 'to suppress the French Communist Party . . . [but he] did not care in the least what the French Government did to them. All that interested Russia was a military alliance with France.'[13] To be sure, it became increasingly difficult for foreigners to do any serious business

[11] Sabine Dullin, 'Le rôle de l'Allemagne dans le *rapprochement* franco–soviétique 1932–1935', in Pierre Guillen and Ilja Mieck (eds.), *Deutschland–Frankreich–Russland: Begegnungen und Konfrontationen* (Munich, 2000).

[12] Alexander, *The Republic in Danger*, 302.

[13] Quoted in M. J. Carley, 'Five Kopecks for Five Kopecks: Franco-Soviet Trade Negotiations, 1928–1939', *Cahiers du Monde russe et soviétique*, 33: 1 (1992), 49.

in Moscow. Buffeted by a new wave of arrests at the Foreign Affairs Commissariat in the autumn, and the cold winds from Paris and London, Litvinov was struggling to maintain an increasingly battered position. In Paris, the Blum government fell on 21 June 1937 and in the new Radical-dominated Chautemps cabinet, Pierre Cot was left isolated and powerless. The Radical party conference at Biarritz in October was marked by intense anti-Communist feeling, mainly directed against the PCF. The collapse of the military talks left few opportunities for further negotiations. Though the provisional trade agreement of 1935 was renewed annually up to 1939, trade between the two countries was relatively unimportant, and when pursued by the USSR was intended mainly to create a better atmosphere for political negotiations. The French chipped away at the USSR's positive trade balance, but discussions between the government departments over quotas, tariffs, and such matters, were 'reduced to quibbling over trifles'.[14] There was no economic bridge to a Franco-Soviet *rapprochement*.

Yakov Surits, an ex-Menshevik, and like his chief, Litvinov, a Jew, left the Soviet embassy in Berlin to succeed Potemkin as ambassador in Paris in June 1937. He shared Litvinov's hopes for an anti-German front, but at the end of the year he sent to Moscow a gloomy, if accurate, account of the situation in Paris. The French government, he claimed, was not interested in strengthening the mutual assistance pact; its sole value for France was as a hindrance to Soviet–German relations. French policy, Surits warned, was totally subservient to Britain, and deeply rooted in 'fear of the Red danger' and 'hatred of social revolution'. The ambassador noted the fundamental divergence between Soviet and French policy; the French would not move, unless there was 'pressure from below'.[15] Potemkin's reading of the situation was even more pessimistic. 'The western powers join the other side [i.e. the Germans],' he wrote to Surits at the end of the year, 'and this is the end of collective security; the Soviet Union has to take the consequences'.[16] By early 1938, it was clear that the Soviets had lost patience. 'We are very dissatisfied with the present line of French foreign policy and the personal conduct of Delbos', Potemkin wrote to Surits. 'It has been decided to hold the French rather far off, not seeking any closeness with them, and even more, not making to them any advances. They must

[14] Carley, 'Five Kopecks for Five Kopecks', 50.

[15] *DVP*, Vol. XX, No. 423 (Surits to Litvinov, 27 November 1937). See the extracts given in M. J. Carley, 'A Soviet Eye on France from the Rue de Grenelle in Paris, 1924–1940', *Diplomacy and Statecraft*, 17 (2006), 328.

[16] Quoted in René Girault, 'En guise de conclusion: Quelques réalites à propos de quelques mythes', in 'Munich 1938, Mythes et réalités', *Revue des études slaves*, 52: 1–2, (1979), 212.

understand that their tactics are clear to us, and that we do not entertain any illusions concerning the present government's attitude toward Franco-Soviet co-operation. France needs the USSR, but we after all can without difficulty get along without the French.'[17] Litvinov was less abrupt, the Soviets would keep quiet and wait 'but we will support proposals by others which go in the direction of our policies. As for Delbos, don't reproach him and don't push him.'[18] Litvinov was still hoping for a coalition of powers, however loose, that would balance the German–Italian–Japanese combination. For the moment, under the shadow of the purges, there was little that he could do.

II

British opposition to the Russo-French staff talks contributed to their failure. There had been a long history of hostility and distrust of the Soviet Union.[19] Successive governments in London had been slower than the French to respond to the re-orientation of Soviet policy in 1934 and viewed both Barthou's policies and Litvinov's efforts to begin a dialogue with London, with suspicion. Even commercial relations were dogged by disputes. The Soviets did not use the proffered credits resulting from the 1930 trade agreement to buy British products; it was widely believed that they maintained their high trade surplus by dumping goods on the British market. In March 1933, six British engineers employed by Metro-Vickers in Moscow, were arrested; an embargo on Soviet goods and heavy diplomatic pressure were necessary to secure their release and repatriation. The affair reminded the Foreign Office that Soviet 'justice' was a farce, and that the conduct of relations with Moscow was not like that with any other country. The strong public reaction meant that the politicians would be doubly cautious about dealing with the Soviet government, even as it moved from the 'revisionist' to the 'anti-revisionist' camp. Although Sir Percy Loraine, the British ambassador to Turkey, thought it 'better to give the Russians a seat at the dining table, rather than have them poisoning the soup in the kitchen', Simon, then foreign secretary replied, 'the fact that the Government leaders sit at the dining table will not deter the Comintern cooks from brewing potions in the kitchen which they will not hesitate to serve up to us at any suitable opportunity'.[20]

[17] Quoted in Carley, 'A Soviet Eye on France', 329. [18] Ibid.

[19] For the most part, I have followed the arguments found in Keith Neilson, *Britain, Soviet Russia and the Collapse of the Versailles Order, 1919–1939*, 166–253, in sketching in the background to British policy towards the Soviet Union.

[20] *DBFP*, 2nd ser., Vol. VII, Nos. 576 and 582 (22 February 1934 and 29 March 1934).

Still, global circumstances should have worked in the direction of *détente*. The study of imperial defence undertaken in October 1933, focused attention on the implications of the Soviet–Japanese conflict for British interests in the Far East. The subject was again indirectly canvassed in the discussions of the newly created DRC (Defence Requirements Committee) in 1934. The final DRC report concluded that the Far East should be considered Britain's most immediate threat and Germany its most important long-range threat, and recommended a large increase in defence expenditure, with the increase to be divided among the three services. The Russian danger to India, a subject of perennial British concern, was reduced to a tertiary threat. Thus, one of the long-standing issues in imperial defence almost vanished, though the subject rose periodically, until the end of the 1930s. If Britain could make good its deficiencies elsewhere, the Defence Requirements Committee concluded that the requirements for the defence of India could be met. The DRC perspective meant that the Soviet Union would no longer be viewed in isolation, but within the context of Far Eastern and German affairs. The DRC report was not the final word. Neville Chamberlain as chancellor of the exchequer, convinced his fellow ministers that Germany and not Japan should be the main object of British rearmament. He argued for a settlement with Japan, despite any American objections. The ensuing debate raised the issue of Russia's role in the Far East where it could restrain Tokyo from war-like adventures against other powers but might lose in a direct conflict with Japan. Though most officials agreed that the best result for Britain would be continued tension between the two powers, there were divided opinions over the likely result of a Japanese victory over the USSR. Some believed that as long as Japan could not conquer China, a Japanese victory posed no real danger for Britain. Lawrence Collier of the Northern department, which handled the Soviet Union, and Ralph Wigram of the Central department, stressed instead the restraining Soviet role in the Far East, and the importance of its ability to deter Germany in Europe. Vansittart, as permanent under-secretary, refused to commit himself, declaring that victory by either country would be equally bad. As one of the fiercest critics of the Soviet Union in the Foreign Office, whose suspicions were constantly re-enforced by his reading of intelligence reports on Comintern activities, Vansittart remained highly sceptical about the 'new course' in Soviet foreign policy and thought that Russia was 'no more pacific in heart than either Germany or Japan'.[21] He showed scant

[21] Simon Bourette-Knowles, 'The Global Micawber: Sir Robert Vansittart and the Global Balance of Power, 1933–1935', *Diplomacy & Statecraft*, 6: 1 (1995), 104.

sympathy with the French efforts to draw the Russians into protective schemes against Germany.

In the summer of 1934, the breakdown of the Disarmament Conference and the perceived changes in Soviet diplomacy modified British opposition to the conclusion of an Eastern Locarno. It was thought that a pact in Eastern Europe, if it included Germany, would encourage a French compromise over disarmament. At the same time, Vansittart's misreading of the Röhm purge (30 June), and his fear that a return of the *Reichswehr* and Junkers to power would lead to a revival of the Rapallo connection, contributed to his altered view of the Soviet Union. Convinced that events in Germany were 'ominous for the general peace of Europe', he argued that Britain could not afford to discourage the emerging Franco-Soviet alignment, and was prepared to take the initiative in supporting the Soviet application for League membership. Opposition to Chamberlain's renewed campaign for an Anglo-Japanese settlement prompted Vansittart to link the Far Eastern and the European situations. A defeat in the Far East would weaken Russian opposition to Germany in Europe. Anthony Eden, the minister with special responsibility for League affairs, in one of his rare interventions in Far Eastern affairs, queried the concept of a Soviet 'makeweight' to Germany in Europe. 'I do not believe that Russia is a weight, only a mass, in Europe', he minuted.[22] The debate was suspended when the Japanese showed little interest in an agreement with Britain.

Vansittart's changing attitude towards the Soviet Union owed something to the efforts made by Ivan Maisky, the Soviet ambassador in London. Most unexpectedly, Vansittart and Maisky became personal friends. There were dinners *à quatre* (Vansittart's American wife had taken the initiative and the two wives got on splendidly) at Vansittart's lavish Park Street home, and larger dinner parties, at one of which Winston Churchill was present. The latter, though out of office and somewhat isolated in the Conservative party, became, with mixed results, one of Maisky's most important contacts in London. The friendship between the wealthy and rather lordly Vansittart, and the peppery Soviet ambassador was unusual but productive. The former was given information not available to Lord Chilston, the British ambassador in Moscow, who like so many foreign representatives in the Soviet Union, enjoyed only the most limited contacts with his host government, and suffered from the frustrations of his isolation. Reporting to Litvinov on one of a series of meetings in the summer, Maisky quoted the permanent under-secretary as saying:

[22] Ibid., 108.

'High political' issues should override all other interests; those of domestic politics and of various ideologies. It is because of the interests of 'high politics' that I consider the Anglo-Soviet *rapprochement* to be an extremely important peace factor... The very course of events (here Vansittart used the French expression, 'La marche des événements') and the logic of things incite our two countries to get closer both in Europe and in the Far East.[23]

Priding himself on being a realist in international affairs, Vansittart concluded that 'the real world situation' necessitated a more open mind with regard to the Soviet Union.

Those sympathetic towards an improvement in Anglo-Soviet relations feared that, should the 'Litvinov line' fail to produce results, the Soviet Union would turn to Germany. Vansittart stressed the importance of avoiding any action that would make Russia feel that Britain and France would 'leave her in the lurch' and persuade Moscow to come to terms with Germany before it was too late. As realists, it was important to take advantage of Russia's year-long fear of Germany without overrating its recent change of heart. To influence the situation in Moscow, Vansittart suggested that the cabinet take up Maisky's suggestion of a ministerial visit to Moscow in order to bolster Litvinov's position.

Asian factors, along with events in Germany convinced Vansittart and other Foreign Office officials, including Collier, that Britain should assist the French efforts to prevent the Soviets from returning to its revisionist past: 'We must not for a moment imagine that it is only a French interest to ménager Russia', Vansittart minuted. 'On the contrary, it is very much a British interest also; and we must have this fact constantly present to our minds, if we are to be the political realists, which the gravity of the times demands.'[24] Another faction, led by Orme Sargent, the tall, lean, reserved but highly influential assistant under-secretary responsible for German affairs, strongly opposed any gesture towards Moscow. Sargent distrusted the Soviet Union and feared that any French agreement with the Soviet Union would be dangerous for Britain. Sargent and Collier clashed openly, and in print. The former thought the possibility of a Russo-German settlement much exaggerated, while the dangers of the Franco-Soviet alliance were insufficiently understood. Convinced that Litvinov wanted a Franco-Soviet pact and not a regional agreement, he warned in January 1935 that such an alliance would be the first step towards the return to the pre-war grouping of powers, a prospect 'so horrible' that the British should use all their influence to prevent it. He wanted, above all, to

[23] *DVP*, Vol. XVII, 552–557.

[24] Bourette-Knowles, 'The Global Micawber', 115.

avoid a return to the 'balance of power' system of pre-1914. The debate continued throughout 1935, especially after Hitler blamed the Franco-Soviet pact of May 1935 for the failure to reach a general agreement.

While Vansittart shared Sargent's apprehension about a revival of the pre-1914 constellation and feared German complaints about encirclement, he nonetheless convinced the cabinet to agree to a ministerial visit to Moscow, to give Litvinov a much needed success 'at little or no cost to ourselves'. As the British prepared for the Simon–Eden visit to Berlin in the spring of 1935, it was decided that Eden should go on to Moscow to ease Soviet fears of a western bloc against the USSR. The events of March, including Hitler's announcement of conscription, were hardly a reassuring prologue to the Moscow talks. Yet there was some optimism about what could be accomplished. Maisky later cited Eden's visit as the high point of the thaw in Anglo-Soviet relations. Stalin agreed to meet Eden, the first major western statesman to be so honoured. Maisky's high expectations were not matched by the results of the meetings, notwithstanding a final communiqué extolling co-operation for the 'collective organization of peace and security'. The conversations took place in Moscow on 28 and 29 March and centred on the Eastern Pact. Eden had second thoughts about the possibility of a general settlement after meeting Hitler, who rejected any form of Eastern Pact involving mutual assistance. Eden therefore asked the cabinet to agree to the offer of a modified Eastern Pact that would include the Soviet Union, the Baltic States, Czechoslovakia, and France, with the proviso that Germany and Poland could join later, and that it would operate under the auspices of the League. In agreeing, Simon warned Eden that any such agreement had to be delayed until after the Stresa meeting. In conversation with Eden, Litvinov reviewed his concerns about Eastern Europe and the direction of future Soviet diplomacy. He argued that the Great Powers must adhere to the collective system in order to thwart Hitler, who was building his policy on the assumption of Anglo-Soviet antagonism. He insisted that he did not regard mutual assistance pacts as a real guarantee of defence, but rather as a deterrent and warned of a possible Soviet retreat into isolation if no arrangements were concluded. Stalin, who had received a distorted report of the Berlin talks, edited to confirm his own prejudices, also stressed the importance of mutual security pacts with several nations in order to thwart Hitler.[25] Illustrating his theory of collective

[25] The report of the talks in Berlin had been amended by Stalin's security people to make it seem that an Anglo-German *rapprochement* was occurring. Christopher Andrew and V. Mitrokhin, *The Mitrokhin Archive: The KGB in Europe and the West* (London, 1999), 71–72.

security, he said: 'We are six of us in this room; if Maisky chooses to go for anyone of us then we must all fall on Maisky.'[26] Relaxing at tea, Eden noticed a very large wall map of the Soviet Union and commented upon the size of the USSR. According to the Soviet account, Stalin jokingly replied, 'Yes, a large country with many problems.' Eden then remarked on the small size of the British Isles in comparison. 'A small island', replied Stalin, 'but one on which much depends. What if this small island said to Germany, 'We will give you neither money, nor raw materials, nor steel, peace in Europe would be assured.'[27] Eden left with a very clear impression of the dictator, 'a man of strong oriental traits of character with unshakeable assurance and control whose courtesy in no way hid from us an implacable ruthlessness'.[28]

There was no movement in Anglo-Soviet affairs in the months that followed the Eden visit. Attention was focused on the forthcoming Stresa meetings. The French were pressed to delay the conclusion of the Franco-Soviet pact whose terms should be made compatible with both Locarno and the League Covenant. They were warned, hardly for the first time, that Britain would not assume any responsibilities beyond Locarno. Laval was not forthcoming about the Franco-Soviet talks, and though the terms of the treaty signed on 2 May 1935 met the British demands, it received a mixed reception in London. Some hoped it might have a 'salutary' effect on Germany. Others argued that the Soviets were interested only in protecting themselves, and would support the status quo in Europe and in Asia only as long as their fear of Germany and Japan persisted. Commenting on Laval's warm reception in Moscow in mid-May, Collier noted the parallels between Soviet, German, and Italian policy, 'each of them refrains from aggression and preaches peace so long as it pays her, and no longer, and, for the next few years at least, this is likely to pay Russia more than unfortunately it pays either of the other two'.[29]

Exclusion from the Stresa meetings revived the *Politburo*'s fears of a bloc of capitalist powers against the USSR. The Anglo-German naval agreement of 18 June 1935, though the Russians were told they would be invited to the general naval conference that would follow, confirmed Moscow's suspicions that Britain would give way to Hitler in any

[26] *DBFP*, 2nd ser., Vol. XII, No 669.

[27] M. J. Carley, '"A Fearful Concatenation of Circumstances": The Anglo-Soviet *Rapprochement*, 1934–6', *Contemporary European History*, 5 (1996), 46. Compare also *DBFP*, 2nd ser., Vol. XII, Nos. 669 and 670, and *DVP*, Vol. XVIII, 246–251.

[28] Quoted in Neilson, *Britain, Soviet Russia and the Collapse of the Versailles Order*, 135.

[29] Quoted in ibid. 140.

region, whether in Eastern Europe or in the Baltic, where British interests were not directly engaged. Nor did the Russians welcome, despite Vansittart's attempts to remove Maisky's apprehensions, the June changes in the British government that brought Sir Samuel Hoare, who had been the British military agent at the Tsar's headquarters during the war, to the Foreign Office in place of Simon. Hoare despised the Russians, and feared that Moscow would lead the French into arrangements that would compromise Britain's freedom of action. The chief encouragement for the Soviets during the summer of 1935 was Maisky's conversations with Winston Churchill and Lord Beaverbrook. Both men, staunch anti-Communists, had now converted to hopes of a defensive alliance because of the German threat to Britain. According to Maisky, Churchill wanted an alliance 'but from a tactical–political point of view this alliance had to go by the pseudonym of "collective security" and exist under the aegis of the League of Nations'. Churchill assured Maisky that though there was now a strong tendency towards organizing western security on the basis of an agreement with Germany granting it freedom of action in the East, 'in the end the partisans of "indivisible peace" and *rapprochement* with France and the USSR will win out'.[30]

There was a real gulf between the two countries that made *rapprochement* difficult. The British still hoped that it was possible to bring Germany into a general European arms agreement that would recognize its legitimate interests, but limit its rearmament. The Soviets believed that such a policy was weak and naïve and that aggressors could only be checked by force. They wanted to put into place the mechanisms that could be used to safeguard their position against a German threat. These fundamental differences, as well as mutual suspicions, blocked even modest steps towards improving relations. Litvinov's approaches to France and Britain were not always welcome in Moscow. He was forced to take a very cautious line in Geneva during the Ethiopian crisis though he finally won *Politburo* backing for sanctions against Italy.[31] For the British, the Abyssinian affair changed the atmosphere in which Anglo-Soviet diplomacy was conducted. The difficulties in the Mediterranean again focused attention not only on Italy and France, but also on the country's naval weakness in the Far East at a time when Anglo-Japanese relations were steadily deteriorating. This again raised the possibility of including the Soviet

[30] *DVP*, Vol. XVIII, 397–398 (15 June 1935).

[31] For the Soviet Union's uneven application of sanctions see, Lowell R. Tillett, 'The Soviet Role in League Sanctions Against Italy, 1935–36', *The American Slavic and East European Review*, 15: 1 (1956), 11–16.

Union, as well as the United States in an anti-Japanese front, yet no step towards Moscow followed. Intelligence reports in the autumn of 1935, that Germany and Russia might try to compromise their differences and conclude an agreement that would include Japan, spurred on the Foreign Office advocates of an Anglo-Soviet *détente* to press for a guaranteed loan to Moscow. The proposal had been canvassed in early 1935, but the Treasury had been cool and the subject was still under discussion in the months before the Hoare–Laval affair brought Anthony Eden to the foreign secretaryship. After many delays and fierce arguments within the Foreign Office, Eden vetoed the idea in February 1936, despite the fact that the Germans agreed to extend new credits to Russia in late January. He feared that the guaranteed loan, coming at the same time as the ratification of the Franco-Soviet pact, would give substance to Hitler's fear of encirclement, and put in jeopardy the British plan to restart talks with Berlin. Eden's antipathy towards, and distrust of the Soviets, was deep-seated. This was due, in part, to Communist intervention in his constituency during the recent British elections, but also to Moscow's propaganda offensives, and its carefully monitored covert activities in Britain and in the empire. Commenting on Vansittart's support for the loan, Eden minuted that he had 'no sympathy to spare for M. Maisky. I hope the next time M. Maisky comes with complaints he will be told that our goodwill depends on his Govt's good behaviour, i.e. keep their noses & fingers out of our domestic politics.'[32] While still considering the alternatives, he noted: 'I want good relations with the bear, I don't want to hug him too close. I don't trust him, and am sure there is hatred in his heart for all we stand for.'[33] Reports from Ambassador Phipps in Paris, that Hitler might use the loan, along with the ratification of the Franco-Soviet pact, as an excuse for occupying the Rhineland, confirmed Eden's decision. Eden's preference for a credit was partly political; a guaranteed loan required legislation that would bring the anti-Soviet lobbies in the House of Commons into action. He also had doubts about the real intentions of the Soviet government in seeking a loan. The cabinet agreed to the less contentious offer of a million pound credit. This proposal proved to be the last serious effort made to improve Anglo-Soviet relations until the spring of 1939.

Foreign Office debates over Russian policy continued, especially because they entailed two different approaches to the German threat.

[32] Quoted in Carley, 'A Fearful Concatenation of Circumstances', 56.

[33] Quoted in Robert Manne, 'The Foreign Office and the Failure of Anglo-Soviet *Rapprochement*', *Journal of Contemporary History*, 16: 4 (1981), 749.

If Collier was the leading advocate of a *rapprochement* with the Soviet Union on the grounds of 'grim reality', Sargent remained its most vehement opponent. Vansittart's advice, both with regard to the negotiations with Germany and the question of a loan or credits, became somewhat more equivocal during 1936. Conscious perhaps of his loss of influence after his leading role in the Hoare–Laval fiasco, and of his reputation as a Germanophobe, he moved closer to the Eden line, advocating the exploration of coming to terms with Germany, if that course 'proves possible, honourable and safe' (such as the restitution of German colonies). The choice of credits or loan should depend on the decision to approach Germany.[34] Increasingly, Eden opted for Sargent's arguments in favour of an accommodation with Germany, and against the *rapprochement* with Russia. The foreign secretary did not believe that 'peace was indivisible'. He wanted 'correct relations' with the Soviet Union, but nothing more. As a result, while Hitler dallied with the British, Anglo-Soviet relations remained correct, but did not prosper. In the Far East, where the British carefully monitored the Russo-Japanese relationship when assessing Japanese offers of co-operation in China, the Foreign Office recommended a neutral course, moving neither towards nor away from Tokyo. Well informed about the negotiation of the Anti-Comintern Pact between Germany and Japan, officials acknowledged its anti-British intent, but took comfort from the increased tension between Japan and the Soviet Union that would inevitably result. For the moment, Britain could benefit from the existing situation without taking any positive action.

In Europe, the Spanish Civil War heightened British distrust of Moscow. While adopting and implementing the French proposed policy of non-intervention, Baldwin and Eden continued to fear that the conflict would result in the division of Europe into two hostile ideological blocs. Vansittart cautioned Blum and Léger in September 1936: that 'the British government was upheld by a very large Conservative majority, who were never prepared and now probably less than ever, to make much sacrifice for red eyes'.[35] He warned the French that many in Britain blamed Russian Communist propaganda and intrigues for the trouble in Spain, and any French move toward Communism would revive a strong wave of pro-German feeling in Britain. Even Churchill was not immune from old fears of the 'Red danger', turning a

[34] Quoted in Neilson, *Britain, Soviet Russia and the Versailles Order*, 162. See the important article John Ferris, ' "Indulged in all too little?" Vansittart, Intelligence and Appeasement', *Diplomacy and Strategy*, 6: 1 (1995).

[35] Quoted in Neilson, *Britain, Soviet Russia and the Versailles Order*, 183.

deaf ear to Maisky's protestations that the Spanish war was 'part of the struggle against Nazi Germany.'[36] In the Commons, on 5 November 1936, in a long speech criticizing the government's defence policies, Churchill spoke of Russia's intervention in Spain as 'insensate folly', making it quite impossible for the free nations of the world to interest themselves in the Soviet fate.[37] Eden's attitude hardened as the proceedings of the Non-Intervention Committee dragged on. The foreign secretary hardly disguised his delight that he and Delbos had managed the Mediterranean crisis in the autumn of 1937 without the direct involvement of the Soviet Union.

The War Office, too, had an interest in the Soviet Union. There was basically little difference between the evaluations of the British and French military staffs, either about the military contribution that the Soviet Union could make in a war against Germany, or about the opposition of the Poles to any form of co-operation with the Soviet Union. The British attachés had returned from the Soviet manoeuvres in the autumn of 1935 with mixed impressions. Though less impressed than the French and American observers, they noted the improvement in the quality of staff officers, and the discipline and energy of the officers and men in the air force. Neither the Red Army nor the Red Air Force was as yet an 'efficient instrument of war', but both were improving rapidly. International observers took note of the vast airlifts and parachute drops of large formations of Soviet troops. According to the War Office appraisal of January 1936, the Red Army was in 'an infinitely better state, from a material point of view, than the Imperial army was in 1914', and was backed by an armaments industry that would make the Russians less dependent on outside sources of supply than in 1914.[38] Nonetheless, Russia's army still suffered from being 'horsed', and was without proper railway transportation. It could not mount a large-scale offensive campaign against a first-class power, but it would be risky for any power to attempt a war of aggression against it.

In the autumn of 1936, General Archibald Wavell, who had observed the pre-war Tsarist army, attended the Red Army manoeuvres in Minsk, along with the French and other military missions. Unencumbered by some of the ideological hang-ups of General Schweisguth, Wavell was impressed by the great improvements made in materials and

[36] *DVP*, Vol. XIX, 531–532. See Carley, 'A Fearful Concatenation of Circumstances', 67.

[37] *Hansard*, HC Deb, 5 November 1936, Vol. 317, Col. 318.

[38] Keith.Neilson, '"Pursued by a Bear": British Estimates of Soviet Military Strength and Anglo-Soviet Relations, 1922–1939', *Canadian Journal of History*, 28 (1993), 210.

armaments, especially in the design and performance of the army's armoured machines (the Soviet BT tank, derived from the American Christie prototype, was the forerunner of the later T-34 tank), but stressed the poor tactical use made of Soviet armaments.[39] The air force attaché reported that Soviet fighters and medium bombers were 'well-armed, fast and manoeuvrable', but that its light bomber and reconnaissance aircraft were slow and cumbersome, and air tactics were clumsy and unimaginative. In his balanced assessment of the Red Army, Wavell concluded that it was still a 'bludgeon', incapable of rapier work but better led than its predecessor, and undoubtedly a formidable opponent in defence of its own territory. While at present 'clumsy and less formidable in attack', he observed that, 'its size and the extent of its mechanical equipment would make it dangerous'.[40]

By early 1937, the chiefs of staff agreed that the Soviet Union was rapidly becoming a powerful military force. It had the largest army and air force in the world, and the entire country was already placed on a war footing. Nevertheless, they remained equivocal about the value of the Soviet Union as an ally, either in Europe or in the Far East. Against Germany, Soviet intervention would not be particularly helpful without the active co-operation of Poland. In the Far East, Russian neutrality was 'infinitely preferable' to intervention, should Japan enter a European war. Such appraisals, as well as serious doubts about the wisdom of sharing any military intelligence with the USSR, strengthened opposition to the Franco-Soviet staff talks in the winter months. The chiefs of staff agreed, however, that Germany's fear of Soviet intervention was a 'powerful moral deterrent against Germany going to war', and that there were still practical reasons for maintaining the Franco-Soviet pact.[41]

This argument lost its force in the wake of the purges of the Soviet high command. As Collier noted, it was not 'Trotskyism' in the army that Stalin feared, but 'independence of any sort'. Chilston, reporting on the trial and execution of Tukhachevsky and his colleagues, insisted that the charges were totally fabricated, a judgment generally accepted in London. By the summer of 1937, the horror of what was going on in the Soviet Union united both the Foreign Office and the War Office in a sense of outrage. Nevertheless, it took time to evaluate the cost to the Soviet Union of the on-going dismissals, arrests, and the liquidation of even senior officers. Major E. C. Hayes, a military intelligence officer

[39] The British immediately ordered a Christie prototype. On 19 November 1936, Lord Lloyd informed the Lords that Britain had no modern medium tanks at all and only 100 tanks of the 1923 model, barely fit for use in practice. The Soviet Union, he reminded the peers, was estimated to have between five and six thousand tanks.

[40] Neilson, 'Pursued by a Bear', 213. [41] Ibid., 215.

at the War Office in close contact with Collier, argued that the losses would retard, if not stop, further progress in modernizing the army. 'If the value for war of the Red Army has declined as a result of recent events then the value of the Soviet Union as an ally to France has decreased to a corresponding extent', he wrote, 'and, conversely, her danger to Germany as an enemy has also declined. In these circumstances it is not surprising that Germany, Japan and Italy are jubilant over this affair.'[42]

In London, as in Paris, fears of a Soviet–German *rapprochement* receded. The Moscow embassy believed, correctly in the light of present evidence, that the possibility of a Red Army–*Reichswehr* connection had been purposely exaggerated in order to entrap the Soviet commanders. Public revulsion at the Soviet proceedings spread. Most of the Labour party was as repelled as the fiercely anti-Bolshevik sections of the Conservative party. The purges convinced the Chamberlain government that little attention need be paid to the Soviet Union. Beset by internal convulsions, it was far too weak to play any part in European politics. It was predicted that Soviet diplomacy would become increasingly passive, and that Moscow might retreat into a position of isolation. Though Anthony Eden showed some signs of concern, the possibility hardly disturbed Neville Chamberlain. It was, of course, thought inappropriate to interfere in any way with what was happening within that 'suicidal country.'

The period of the 'thaw' in Anglo-Soviet relations was a short one. The friendly exchanges between the two governments during 1934 and 1935 never actually pointed in the direction of a *rapprochement*. The arguments from *Realpolitik* were never strong enough to overcome suspicion of Stalin's intentions. The real key, however, to the ministerial and official opposition to the Eastern Pact, and to the Franco-Soviet treaty was the fear of alienating Germany and foreclosing the possibility of a multilateral understanding. It was felt that any British gesture of friendship towards the Soviet Union would compromise the government's efforts to get Hitler to accept a new arms settlement. While Britain benefited from the strains in Soviet relations with Germany and Japan, there seemed little purpose in settling with Russia. In Europe, London did not want any new engagement in Eastern Europe, and continued to fear that France's links with Moscow would drag Britain into quarrels in which it had no interest.

[42] Quoted in James S. Herndon, 'British Perceptions of Soviet Military Capability, 1935–39', in Wolfgang J. Mommsen and Lothar Kettenacker (eds.), *The Fascist Challenge and the Policy of Appeasement* (London, 1983), 306.

Just as 'grim reality' was exposing the difficulties of the British policy of 'deterrence' in 1937, a debate began, encouraged by Lawrence Collier, over the relative dangers of the Fascist and Communist threats to the western democracies.[43] Such discussions are rare in foreign ministries at any time, but were particularly uncommon in the Foreign Office where officials took positive pride in their pragmatism. On one side of this debate, D'Arcy Godolphin Osborne, the British minister to the Vatican, provided the most comprehensive case for the argument that the 'Communist danger' posed the greater threat to the western democracies. It was the most aggressive force in the contemporary world. There was no possible compromise or adjustment with Communism, which was a form of ideological imperialism. The Fascist states (the term used to include both Italian Fascism and National Socialism), on the contrary, could be brought back to peaceful ways if their economic distress was alleviated and the 'idiosyncrasies' of the dictators accepted. On the other side of the debate, Collier argued that in foreign policy one had to deal with the immediate future, and that while Russia might pose the ultimate challenge to the democracies, the German and Italian dangers were more immediate and pressing. He believed that British public opinion was 'unalterably opposed' to the idea of an anti-Communist crusade, and that if forced to choose would support anti-Fascism instead of anti-Communism. Apart from the fact that both men were born in the late Victorian period, it is hard to think of a greater contrast than that between Osborne, a representative of the old school of diplomats and already a somewhat archaic figure in the diplomatic service, and the academic Collier, an official in the 'Eyre Crowe mould', who had no interest at all in the *haute monde*. Most of those who had served in the Rome embassy, including Gladwyn Jebb, now in the economic section of the Foreign Office, supported Osborne. Jebb believed that 'the Soviet regime is far more horrible than the Nazi one, & that I am not in favour of fighting everybody at once'.[44] The 'realists' (the term, itself, ambiguous, and used in a variety of ways), backed the Collier line that it was Germany and not the Soviet Union which was bringing Europe to the brink of war, and that Britain should resist whichever was the more aggressive and powerful. Their exchanges, and the commentary of officials and diplomats on their letters, are exceptionally revealing of the Foreign Office 'mind' in the

[43] See Donald N. Lammers, 'Fascism, Communism and Foreign Office, 1937–1939' *Journal of Contemporary History*, 6: 3 (1971) which includes numerous extracts from the Foreign Office documents.

[44] Minute by Jebb, 29 October 1937, TNA: PRO, FO 371/21103, N4924/272/38.

late 1930s. No consensus emerged, making it difficult to arrive at a settled policy.

The issues raised by this debate took on new importance during the first half of 1938, when officials were asked to prepare a formal memorandum comparing the two systems as they affected British foreign policy. Collier responded with an extended lesson on the theoretical differences between Communism, on the one hand, and Nazism and Fascism on the other, and then examined the reasons for their similarities in practice. He attributed Soviet behaviour to the inherent impracticability of a major part of pure Communism, and to the historical circumstances that forced the Soviet rulers to adopt measures to make the Soviet state strong enough to face its external enemies. He was under no illusions:

> the Soviet system at present surpasses both the Nazi and Fascist systems in wholesale ruthlessness and cruelty, being controlled, as stated above, by 'semi-Asiatic savages'; whereas the regimes in Germany and Italy are conducted by men who, whatever they may preach, have not yet been able to free themselves entirely from the comparatively liberal atmosphere in which they were brought up, and still less from that of the whole west European civilisation which they are attempting to repudiate or to remodel.[45]

While no other country had adopted measures of political repression comparable to the 'purges', both systems were, in practice, expansionist and aggressive in ways that would inevitably lead to a conflict with British interests. Collier concluded that, for the moment, Communism was the weaker of the two forces, and Britain's major preoccupation had to be with the stronger and more aggressive Fascist states.

The most important official voice was that of Alexander Cadogan. Although the permanent under-secretary who replaced Vansittart in 1938 warned that the Foreign Service should not be turned into a 'debating society', he added that: 'I personally—with all humility—think it otiose to discuss whether Fascism or Communism is the more dangerous to us. It is quite plain that, *at the moment*, the former is more dangerous, because it is the more efficient, and makes more and better guns and aeroplanes.'[46] There was little profit to debating the issue further; it was like determining the relative disagreeableness of mumps and measles. Practical politics, and not ideological considerations, should determine British foreign policy. Were such clear distinctions possible in the summer of 1939?

[45] Draft memorandum by Collier, 16 August 1938, TNA: PRO, FO 371/22289, N4071/97/38.

[46] Minute by Cadogan, 12 February 1939, TNA:PRO, FO 371/22289, N6227/97/38.

III

How did Moscow view the situation? The erratic opening of the Soviet archives still leaves many questions unanswered. Some fundamental questions with regard to Stalin's views, the only important figure in Moscow, may never be answered, although this is equally true for Hitler, or even for Franklin Roosevelt, who was not a dictator, and whose voluminous personal files have long been open to researchers. Historians know enough today to dismiss the simplistic views of those official Soviet historians who pictured the USSR as the determined and consistent champion of collective security against the menace of Fascist aggression. Equally doubtful are the interpretations of those western historians who dismissed Soviet policies of collective security as smokescreens for Stalin's real aims that were finally realized in the Nazi–Soviet pact. Neither a picture of contrasting public and private diplomatic moves, nor an emphasis on the differences in the policies pursued by Stalin's subordinates, gets to the heart of the matter. As Soviet diplomacy, apart from deeply held ideological assumptions, was often shaped by reactions to current domestic and foreign situations, no simple explanation of Stalin's behaviour is possible. The Soviet specialist Teddy J. Uldricks has concluded, in a highly influential essay, that 'throughout the decade, suspicion of all imperialist powers and a desperate search for security remained constant'.[47] It is possible, however, to look at the roots of these suspicions, and the consequences of Stalin's perceptions of the capitalist world for the country that he so brutally ruled. It may well be that had the Soviet Union been more powerful and fully armed, Stalin would have followed the isolationist policy he favoured, knowing that the Soviet Union could avoid being drawn into the European civil war which he believed was inevitable. The Soviet Union could then have waited for its opportunity to overcome its capitalist opponents when they fell out against each other. Given the prevailing conditions, and Stalin was a realist, isolation was difficult. Soviet policies were, for the most part, defensive as the Kremlin sought to avoid or, at least, postpone armed conflict.

Fear of 'capitalist encirclement', and the belief in an 'inevitable war' with the capitalist powers, was an integral part of Bolshevik ideology. Its origins date back to Lenin's theory of imperialism, and his prediction of a showdown between a capitalist coalition and the Soviet Union. The

[47] Teddy J. Uldricks, 'Soviet Security Policy in the 1930s', in Gabriel Gorodetsky (ed.), *Soviet Foreign Policy, 1917–1991: A Retrospective* (London and Portland, OR, 1994), 73.

sense of living in a dangerous and hostile world dominated both Lenin's and Stalin's thinking even when imagined 'war scares' failed to materialize. The Allied interventions of 1918–1921 set the pattern for future interpretations of foreign behaviour. The war scare of 1927, however politically motivated, was fuelled by fears of a 'united imperialist front' led by Britain and France and spearheaded by Poland.[48] In 1931–1932, and again in 1934–1935, events in Europe and in the Far East raised the chilling spectre in Moscow of a two-front war.[49] In the first instance, intelligence sources reported that Japan would join France, Poland, and even Britain in an assault on the Soviet Union. In the second case, the sense of security induced by the success of the Five-Year Plan, and the huge increase in defence spending gave way to predictions of war as Stalin came to terms with Hitler's hostility and the supposed defection of Poland to the German side in 1934. In the summer and autumn of 1935, Soviet intelligence sources reported to Stalin, erroneously, that the Poles, Germans, and Japanese were planning for an invasion of the Soviet Union. Though Soviet intelligence was as good, if not better, than that of their European counterparts, agents, instructed to report on foreign threats to the USSR, inevitably found confirming evidence. While Stalin may have believed that the Franco-Soviet pact had helped to avert a German, Polish, and Japanese attack on Russia in 1935, he never accepted that the Soviet Union had won anything more than a temporary respite. It was hardly surprising, against this background, that the Spanish Civil War came to be seen as the prologue of the new war that he had so long anticipated, rather than a last effort to preserve the European peace by checking the aggressors. Not only had Litvinov failed to create an anti-Fascist front, but it was believed that Britain and France were seeking to avoid confrontation with Germany and Italy by encouraging Hitler to look eastwards. The announcement of the Rome–Berlin axis on 1 November 1936, and the German–Japanese Anti-Comintern Pact on the 24 November, though the details and the debates in Tokyo revealing its limitations were reported by Soviet intelligence, were seen by some in Moscow as portents for the future formation of a coalition against the USSR, and the onset of the war between 'the world of Communism and the world of Capitalism'.[50]

[48] See the discussion in Zara Steiner, *The Lights that Failed: European International History, 1919–1933*, 533–546 for a summary of the debates about the 1927 war scare.

[49] For an extended discussion of these war scares, based on material from intelligence sources in Stalin's private papers as well as diplomatic and military papers see James Harris, 'Encircled by Enemies: Stalin's Perceptions of the Capitalist World, 1918–1941', *Journal of Strategic Studies*, 30: 3 (2007), 515–537.

[50] Quotation from Zhdanov's speech on 28 October 1936 in S. Pons, *Stalin and the Inevitable War* (London, 2002), 68.

Table 8.1 Soviet Budget Outlays, Total and on Defence, 1928/29–1940 (million roubles and %)

	Budget total million roubles	Defence outlays million roubles	% of budget
1928/29	8784	880	10
1929/30	13322	1046	7.9
1930	5038	434	8.6
1931	25097	1790	7.1
1932	37995	4034	10.6
1933	42081	4299	10.2
1934	55445	5393	9.7
1935	73572	8174	11.1
1936	92480	14858	16.1
1937	106238	17481	16.5
1938	124039	23200	18.7
1939	153299	39200	25.6
1940	174350	56752	32.6

Source: M. Harrison and R. W. Davies, 'The Soviet Military–Economic Effort during the Second Five-Year Plan, 1933–1937', *Europe–Asia Studies*, 49: 3 (1997), 372.

Fears of a capitalist attack were shared by the military and civilian leadership. Believing that war with the capitalist powers was inevitable, both insisted that the Soviet Union had to industrialize and prepare the armed forces for the expected onslaught. Soviet war production rose rapidly after 1935 when the drop in production was principally due to a change-over to mass production methods. During 1936, the budget share devoted to defence rose from 11% to 16% and continued to rise in subsequent years. There were some difficulties during 1937, due in part to the effects of the Terror. By 1940, almost one-third of the budget was allotted to defence, which was consuming more roubles than the entire state budget of 1934.[51]

As the Soviet authorities repeatedly exaggerated the immediate military threat and over-estimated the strength of their enemies, current production of some weapons, such as tanks, was greater than what was required for immediate purposes. As a result, by 1941, much of the large stock of Soviet armament was out of date.[52] The share of defence in investment and production increased substantially in 1931–1932, because of the Japanese threat, and still further from 1936 onwards.

[51] M. Harrison and R.W. Davies, 'The Soviet Military–Economic Effort during the Second Five-Year Plan, 1933–1937', *Europe–Asia Studies*, 49: 3 (1997), 371.

[52] R. W. Davies 'Preparations for Mobilisation of the Soviet Economy in the 1930s', in Mark Harrison (ed.) *Guns and Rubles: The Defense Industry in the Stalinist State* (New Haven, CT, 2008).

Table 8.2 Gross Production of Soviet Armaments Industries, 1932–1937 (million roubles at 'unchanged' 1926/1927 prices)

	Series A		Series B		Series C	
	armament	total	armament	total	armament	total
1932	1500	2900				
1932			1094	2084		2795
1933			1265	2083		2387
1934			1414	2742		3015
1935						4319
1936					3846	6620
1937 plan	6550	9140			6558	9054

Series A: RGAE, 4372/911/3217, 114–113 (report from the defence sector of Gosplan to the head of Gosplan, dated 20 May 1937).
Series B: GARF, 8418/10/148, 13 (report to Molotov, dated 11 January 1935); 1934 is preliminary.
Series C: RGAE, 4372/91/3217, 118–116 (20 May 1937).

Source: M. Harrison and R. W. Davies, 'The Soviet Military–Economic Effort during the Second Five-Year Plan, 1933–1937', *Europe–Asia Studies*, 49: 3 (1997), 383.

Table 8.3 Soviet Weapons Procurement, 1933–1936 (million roubles, current prices)

	1933	1934	1935	1936
Aviation	411.8	510.3	596	1614
Auto-tank	334.2	344.8	535	1093
Artillery	478	585.8	947	1416
Chemical weapons	45	45.7	60.5	91
Radio and telecoms	90	92	74.6	121
Special technology	0	0	32.8	45
Engineer	52	52.7	53.7	100
Naval construction and aviation	335	645.5	881.5	1370
Railroads	7	15	13	48
Fuels	0	0	0	14
Total	1753	2291.8	3194.1	5912

Source: Lennart Samuelson, *Plans for Stalin's War Machine: Tukhachevskii and Military–Economic Planning, 1925–1941* (Basingstoke, 2000), 180.

Though ideology remained one of the keys to Soviet diplomacy, practical and pragmatic considerations led to repeated retreats from orthodoxy. The adoption of 'socialism in one country' and the abandonment of the hope of 'permanent revolution' was one such major change. Another occurred when the *Politburo* passed its resolution in favour of collective security on 12 December 1933. The Comintern's approval of the Popular Front strategy, given Stalin's personal imprimatur on 1 May 1935, was yet another. None of these deviations were meant to be more than temporary revisions of the Bolshevik inheritance. In Leninist theory, there was no difference between the capitalist states, and all were to be regarded as enemies. The new policies adopted in 1934 postulated a distinction, in Litvinov's terminology, between those identified as 'deeply pacifist' and the 'more militaristic' imperialist powers, a view contested by others in the *Politburo*, and in certain sections of the Comintern. The opposition to aligning with one set of capitalist states against another shadowed Litvinov's efforts at bloc building. The Spanish Civil War provided new ammunition for those arguing for the undifferentiated view of the outside world. Always suspicious of all foreign powers, Stalin remained cautious, prepared to give Litvinov's policies a chance, if doubtful of the prospects for success. While members of the Comintern in 1936 might debate whether war was inevitable or could be postponed or averted, the Soviet Union increased its efforts to build up its military establishment in the full knowledge that ultimately it might have to fight on its own.

Within this ideological framework, Stalin, like the leaders of the western powers, considered alternative responses to the threatening international situation. He ended the debates over foreign policy, and the Comintern, despite and because of its role in Spain, rapidly lost its influence in Moscow. The pragmatic Soviet leader was prepared to pursue different options, simultaneously and sometimes in contradiction to each other. One option, as proposed by Litvinov, centred on an anti-Fascist coalition of powers as a deterrent to aggression. Litvinov's defensive policies took various forms. The non-aggression treaties of 1933 and 1934, a treaty formula developed by the Soviet Union, with its neighbours were intended to safeguard the Soviet borders.[53] Joining the League of Nations and concluding the Franco-Soviet Pact, in part with the hope of reaching London through Paris, represented more decisive moves towards the creation of a common front against the aggressors. As shown above, Litvinov's efforts in Paris and London met with very limited success, the French–Soviet Pact failed to fulfil his hopes and the intervention in Spain, despite his efforts, further alienated the British and French governments. There was neither the trust nor the identity of aims that would have brought the USSR and the western powers together. Bolshevik ideology and the activities of the Comintern reinforced existing suspicions about the aims of the Soviet government. Past history and

[53] See the discussion of Soviet non-aggression pacts found in R. Ahmann, *Nichtangriffspakte: Entwicklung und operative Nutzung in Europa 1922–1939 : mit einem Ausblick auf die Renaissance des Nichtangriffsvertrages nach dem Zweiten Weltkrieg* (Baden-Baden, 1988).

geography worked against the Soviet concept of collective security; the unwillingness of Poland and Romania to give Soviet forces rights of passage through their territories, reduced the value of Soviet assistance to France and Czechoslovakia. The western efforts to reach an accommodation with Germany confirmed Soviet conspiracy fears, but also strengthened the reluctance of the smaller states to enter multilateral agreements that would include Moscow. There was, even in Prague, strong right-wing opposition to Czechoslovakia's increasing reliance on the Soviet Union. It was one of the reasons for the fall of the Hodža government in mid-July 1937. Litvinov persisted in pursuing the idea of a pan-European bloc; Munich was a heavy blow that almost destroyed his position.

The second alternative for the USSR, which dated back to Rapallo and the treaty of Berlin, was an arrangement with Germany. There were those of Stalin's advisers, such as Molotov and Zhdanov, the Leningrad party secretary, who believed that this was the better and safer option for the Soviet Union. They argued that Germany might direct its hostility against France and Britain before turning on the Soviet Union, and that an agreement with Berlin would postpone an attack on the USSR whatever Hitler's final intentions. If Litvinov's diplomats, Surits, the *polpred* in Paris, and Maisky in London shared his views on the need for some form of collective action, there were others, even in the Foreign Ministry, who favoured a settlement with Germany. It was not the Foreign Ministry, however, but the People's Commissariat of External Trade that took the lead in the ongoing commercial and financial negotiations with Berlin. These exchanges, like the British and French economic initiatives, were conducted with political goals in mind. David Kandelaki, the Commissariat's agent, was backed by Stalin in the hope of paving the way for the normalization of Soviet–German relations. Between 1935 and 1937 an open rivalry developed between the Narkomindel and the Foreign Trade Commissariat and the Soviet leadership appears to have favoured the latter. The key figure in all these matters was Stalin. There remains some disagreement over how closely Stalin monitored the conduct of foreign affairs (he undoubtedly kept a very sharp eye on matters relating to Spain) whether by the ministries, Comintern, or the security services. It appears that between 1933 and 1936, although Litvinov was not a member of the *Politburo* and rarely met Stalin alone, he often took the initiative in making proposals to Stalin and the small group of men in the *Politburo* who handled foreign affairs. These were discussed, amended or rejected, but generally won acceptance. Already, in 1936, the Narkomindel began to lose influence. The formal system of consultation changed in 1937 when the Soviet government became more centralized and even more focused on Stalin. *Politburo* meetings became irregular and less frequent; foreign policy was handled by a permanent commission (Stalin, Molotov, Voroshilov, Kaganovich, and Yezhov, the latter responsible for internal security), in which, of course, Stalin remained the dominant figure. As earlier, Litvinov was still summoned to the Kremlin on average about twice a month, sometimes more often and for longer interviews during moments of crisis, but Stalin and Molotov appear to have become more active in handling foreign affairs than earlier. But whereas previously, the commissar was sometimes accompanied by other members of the ministry, after 1937, senior officials, including Potemkin, Litvinov's deputy, were summoned to come alone to the Kremlin and given their orders.

Individual diplomats were also brought back to Moscow to report to Stalin and the commission. In 1938, the *polpred* in Berlin was summoned to the Kremlin five times, three times without Litvinov. In February 1939, a system was established by which diplomats would return home regularly each year, further reducing the power of the Commissariat as an intermediary between the diplomats and Stalin.[54] In any case, by this date, the NKVD had established itself at the Narkomindel and in the missions abroad and the first big waves of arrests had begun. Decisions to open talks with the Germans were taken by Stalin, as was true of most diplomatic initiatives in these years. Litvinov constantly asked for approval before acting even on questions of secondary importance. Possibly less sure of his grasp of foreign rather than domestic matters, Stalin favoured a more passive line abroad than Litvinov would have preferred to follow.

The real difficulty for Moscow in approaching Berlin, and this had been true since 1933, lay in Hitler's opposition to any political agreement. With regard to Britain, and to a far lesser extent France, Hitler repeatedly raised the possibility of peaceful change while preparing for war. When it came to relations with the Soviet Union, even where his subordinates took the initiative, the Führer never allowed their efforts to go too far. In 1935, he reportedly refused Stalin's secret offer of a non-aggression pact.[55] The new German–Polish pact increased Hitler's freedom of action vis-à-vis France; it was to his advantage that the Poles neglected military planning against Germany, and that Polish–Czechoslovak relations deteriorated. During 1936–1937, Hitler's anti-Bolshevik rhetoric reached a new pitch and was matched by his growing disdain for Russia's military power. For the moment, the road to Berlin was blocked.

[54] Sabine Dullin, *Des hommes d'influences: Les ambassadeurs de Staline en Europe 1930–1939* (Paris, 2001), 263.

[55] Ahmann, *Nichtangriffspakte*, 368.

Table 8.4 State Budget Appropriations to NKVM-NKO (the Defence Budget) in the First and Second Five-Year Plans (October 1928–1932 and 1933–1937) (million roubles at current prices)

	Military equipment	Construction	Maintenance	Total
First Five-Year Plan				
Plan	1,683	466	3,386	5,535
Actual	3,919	1,342	2,683	7,944
Second Five-Year Plan				
Plan	13,000	4,480	14,020	31,500
Revised	20,745	6,924	28,775	56,444
Actual	15,896	6,977	27,918	50,791

Source: M. Harrison and R. W. Davies, 'The Soviet Military–Economic Effort during the Second Five-Year Plan, 1933–1937', *Europe–Asia Studies*, 49: 3 (1997), 388.

There was a third option, which Stalin may have preferred, though it was not without risks. A policy of isolation depended on a strong military base that would discourage any future attack. New efforts were being made to achieve this military independence, even while the purges decimated the officer ranks. In 1936, there was an additional injection of funds for the modernization programme, followed by subsequent increases in 1937 and 1938. A 'third phase' in Soviet defence spending began in 1936, one in which growth in real terms accelerated sharply as did its relative burden on the Soviet economy. During the period of the second Five-Year Plan, 1933–1937, 'rapid rearmament gave way to intense mobilization'.[56]

Given the growing importance of foreign affairs and the increasing dangers of war, it was essential that Russia not only rearm, mechanize, and modernize, but that any possible source of domestic instability should be eliminated. Stalin believed that the unity of the country was an invaluable asset in case of war and judged, mistakenly, that Nazi Germany was weaker than the Soviet Union in this respect. The apprehension of war, given Stalin's pathology about opposition of any kind, strengthened his extreme suspicion about a potential 'fifth column'. However attractive a retreat into isolation might appear, Stalin still hoped to improve Russia's position diplomatically, or at the very least, avoid a premature war. As a result, he supported Litvinov's attempts at bloc building while considering new approaches to Germany that, at the least, would normalize Russo-German relations. With the failure to secure protection from Britain and France against Nazi

[56] Davies and Harrison 'The Soviet Military–Economic Effort', 397.

Germany and in the knowledge that both countries were trying to reach a settlement with Hitler, the hard-headed Stalin would naturally try to open the closed door to Berlin.

The talks with the Germans were, for the most part, handled by outside agents, a common practice in both Nazi Germany and Fascist Italy. At the very time that the Franco-Soviet pact was signed, Soviet representatives began to explore the possibilities of a move towards Germany, using Russia's economic assets as a way of opening the door to political arrangements. Already at the start of 1934, the German ambassador in Moscow, Nadolny, suggested that improved economic relations might promote a better political atmosphere. In the early Hitler years, Germany was still the Soviet Union's second best customer (after Britain), and the ending of military links between the two countries did not destroy their financial and commercial connections.

A trade and payments agreement was concluded in March 1934, and a German credit to the Soviet Union extended in April. In May, negotiations began for a new credit agreement that would finance further Soviet purchases from Germany. In December David Kandelaki was sent by the Commissariat of Foreign Trade to facilitate the talks that finally resulted in an important credit treaty signed in April 1935. The Russians were given a loan of 200 million marks, repayable over five years at 2% interest. It was tied, as was customary in such cases, to the purchase of designated German goods.

These negotiations were conducted on the Russian side by Kandelaki and Bessonov, the counsellor at the Soviet embassy and a GPU agent, and by Schacht for the Germans. The latter not only pressed for an increase in trade, but also suggested the possibility of a political agreement, claiming that his policies were being carried out with Hitler's approval. In late June 1935, the Germans offered the Russians a one billion RM credit, repayable over 10 years, in return for oil and raw materials from the USSR. Kandelaki recommended confirmation of the loan in writing, but Litvinov, dismissing the offer as a 'German manoeuvre' designed to sabotage the Franco-Soviet *rapprochement*, objected. The French were informed, and Kandelaki was told to avoid further discussions, and to complain about German obstruction in implementing the earlier 200 million mark loan. The Russian negotiator returned to Moscow for instructions. Stalin, contrary to Litvinov's advice, appears to have decided to explore the Schacht offer. There was a meeting between the Russian negotiators and Schacht on 15 July 1935. According to the latter's account, Kandelaki, who emphasized that he had spoken not only to the commissar for foreign trade, but also with Molotov and Stalin, raised the question, in a somewhat embarrassed way, of some form of assistance from Schacht,

Table 8.5 Soviet–German Trade, 1932–1940 ('000 roubles, current prices)

	Total	Machinery	Energy Gen./Elec.	Light industrial	Energy minerals	Iron/Steel	Chemicals	Building materials	Plan/animal raw mat.	Foodstuffs	Live animals	Meat, milk, etc.	Consumer products
1932	1,142,067	772,761	144,600		337,825	310,694	12,201	8,821	4,192	320	303	2,139	2,693
1933	515,903	325,467	31,993		40,075	165,350	6,110		1,898	31		3	1,590
1934	100,225	62,983	12,651		39,014	24,110	9,466		1,477	6	3	0.3	157
1935	75,634	45,107	8,638	474	17,130	15,463	7,423		2,040	101	94		3,021
1936	245,444	201,890	17,436	9,022	27,481	24,817	11,106		2,649	529	529	8	555
1937	151,322	120,824	6,289	12,956	23,282	22,257	5,355		1,055	60	60	1	108
1938	50,736	31,466	1,805	11,111	12,414	9,624	5,766	32	330				728
1939	42,325	34,507	1,336	5,439	6,020	5,540	1,238		218				15
1940	316,301	147,652	28,917	14,600	139,366	74,147	9,926		1,146	73	72	0.4	1,015

Source: Figures derived from *Vneshnaya torgovla SSSR za 1918–1940 gg: statistischeskii obzor* (Moscow, 1940)

mentioning the Eastern Pact. Schacht advised that such matters should be handled by the Russian ambassador and German Foreign Ministry. While it seems likely, from what is known from Schacht's dealings with the British and French, that the *Reichsminister* may have misrepresented the nature and tone of the exchanges, it could well be that Kandelaki did make some kind of indirect political approach.

There was no such hesitation in the autumn of 1935 when, worried by reports of Franco-German meetings in late October, the Soviets mounted a diplomatic offensive intended to sound out the Germans. In Moscow, Tukhachevsky, generally considered to be pro-French, arrived at a farewell reception for Fritz von Twardowsky, the councillor of the German embassy. This was his first visit to the German premises since 1933. According to Twardowsky's report, the marshal spoke warmly of his hopes 'that Germany and the Soviet Union would come together again'. Litvinov himself, sharing a table with Werner von der Schulenburg, the German ambassador, at a commemoration dinner for the October Revolution, 'suddenly raised his glass and said in a loud voice: "I drink to the rebirth of our friendship"'.[57] While such comments from known Francophiles can be dismissed as gestures of frustration with Laval, this was hardly true of Kandelaki's efforts on his return to Berlin. On 30 October, he and Schacht met to discuss the April 1935 credit agreement; the *Reichsminister* again raised the question of a large scale, long-term credit for the Soviet Union. Kandelaki returned to Moscow the same day for further instructions. Surits, the Soviet ambassador in Berlin, also returned home for a short, though important, consultation. It is clear from his letter to Litvinov on 28 November that the ambassador had been instructed to activate his contacts with the Germans (he was to visit or entertain, among others, Neurath, Goebbels, Göring, Rosenberg, Schacht, and Blomberg) and to explore the possibility of a future change in German policy towards the USSR. Stalin's (or the *Politburo*'s) directive might well have been connected with Laval's well-reported retreat from the Franco-Soviet pact, which still awaited ratification.

Surits was wary. 'All my contacts with the Germans merely reinforced the conviction I already held that the course against us taken by Hitler remains unchanged', Surits wrote to Litvinov, 'and that we cannot expect any serious alterations in the immediate future'.[58] He was told

[57] Quoted in Jiri Hochman, *The Soviet Union and the Failure of Collective Security, 1934–1938* (Ithaca, NY, and London, 1984), 107. *DGFP*, Ser. C, Vol. IV, Nos. 383 and 407 respectively.

[58] This and subsequent quotations in this paragraph are from Jonathan Haslam, *The Soviet Union and the Struggle for Collective Security in Europe*, 91–92.

by his German interlocutors that Hitler had three 'obsessions': hostility towards the USSR (towards Communism), the Jewish question, and *Anschluss*. His hostility towards the Soviet Union 'flows not only from his ideological attitude *vis-à-vis* Communism, but [also] constitutes the basis of his tactical line in the field of foreign policy'. For the short-term, Surits recommended waiting patiently, building up Soviet strength and expanding work on the economic front. He argued that both sides would benefit from strengthening economic ties along the lines suggested by Schacht. This was the only reason that Hitler had sanctioned the *Reichsminister*'s initiative in the first place. Surits' reports confirmed Litvinov's reading of the German situation; both men remained highly sceptical of any change in the 'primitive anti-Soviet positions' of Hitler and his entourage. In an attempt to block further political discussions, Litvinov wrote to Stalin attacking Schacht's credibility and calling the leader's attention to Surits's negative assessment of future German policy. While Litvinov agreed that the economic conversations should continue, he opposed directing more or all of the Soviet Union's future foreign orders to Germany which would strengthen the hard-pressed Germans and, with no counter-balancing political advantages for the Soviet Union, would weaken foreign economic interest in the USSR. Contrary to the recommendations of the People's Commissariat of Heavy Industry, Litvinov proposed that credit orders to Germany be limited to 100 or a maximum of 200 million marks. He called for a counter-propaganda campaign to match the Hitlerites' 'Homeric' efforts instead of the current 'passive Tolstoyian position' taken by the Soviet Union.

We do not have Stalin's reply, but what is interesting is that Litvinov was willing to contest a policy that had the support of the *Politburo*. His efforts were to no avail; Soviet soundings in Berlin continued. German and Soviet reports of these probings naturally attribute the initiative in each case to their opposite number. In separate actions, the Russian negotiators called on a wide range of German officials. In early December, Bessonov held a series of meetings with representatives from the War Ministry and Foreign Ministry, with Erhard Milch of the Ministry of Aviation and with Brinkman, Schacht's main adviser, and Herbert Göring, Hermann Göring's cousin and an official in Schacht's office. The Germans reported that Bessonov and Surits were eager for improved Soviet–German relations, and had linked this issue to success in the economic negotiations. The deputy director of the German Foreign Ministry's Eastern department claimed that Bessonov had suggested supplementing the Berlin treaty by a bilateral non-aggression pact. Bessonov, in two letters to Moscow, confirmed the 'presence in Germany of sections and groups which for a variety of reasons are interested in a normalization of relations with the USSR'.[59] He specifically cited military, industrial, and diplomatic circles but excluded the leaders of the Nazi party. Surits's report to Litvinov in December 1935 confirmed Bessonov's reports and went on to claim that even sections of the Nazi party were critical of the official anti-Soviet line. This was hardly welcome news for Litvinov, who minimized the importance of the embassy's findings. At the annual reception for the diplomatic corps in Berlin in January 1936, much to the surprise of the assembled diplomats, Hitler spoke more freely with ambassador Surits than with the others.

The question of who took the initiative is actually of secondary importance. Both sides had an interest in continuing the dialogue. The Soviet government decided to take up the old German credit offer of 500 million marks, and Kandelaki returned to Berlin in mid-December 1935 for new negotiations. It was at this time that Maisky was pushing for the guaranteed loan in London. There were financial and trade difficulties on both sides that delayed agreement; the Rhineland crisis led to their temporary suspension. Reports of Kandelaki's activities were noted by the British embassy in Moscow, which prepared an extensive account on the possibility of a Soviet–German *rapprochement*, partly based on secret information. After further consultation, the material was sent back to ambassador Chilston, who, during the course of 1936, prepared two reports, in February and in November, both highly sceptical about a Berlin–Moscow agreement, and suggesting that the initiatives were coming from Germany. It was not untypical of the isolated conditions in which the embassy operated, that neither Chilston nor his military attaché could report on the attitudes of either the Soviet government or the Soviet high command. There were, to be sure, warnings from Litvinov, and from the Soviet ambassadors in Paris and London, that 'many in Russia' were beginning to doubt the wisdom of the policy of collective security. Stopping off in Paris in February 1936, Litvinov warned that any delay in ratifying the Franco-Soviet pact would lead to a 'growth of isolationist tendencies' in the USSR. That note had already been sounded on 10 January, when Molotov told the central executive committee of the Supreme Soviet that 'we toilers of the Soviet Union must count on our own efforts in defending our affairs, and above all on our Red Army in the defence of our country'.[60] These and other pronouncements, backed by further extensions of the defence budget, were given new importance by the reports of the

[59] Geoffrey Roberts, *The Soviet Union and the Origins of the Second World War* (Basingstoke, 1995), 34.

[60] Haslam, *The Soviet Union and the Struggle for Collective Security in Europe*, 93.

growing friendship between the Germans and Japanese, based on their shared hostility towards the Soviet Union.

Whatever Stalin's doubts about the wisdom of the policies of collective security, they were still in the ascendant on the eve of the Rhineland crisis. On 1 March 1936, Stalin gave an interview to the proprietor of an American newspaper during which, for the first time in two years, he spoke publicly about foreign affairs. He told Roy Howard that the Italian–Ethiopian war was only an episode, and that it was still difficult to judge which of the two centres of war danger, Japan in the Far East and Germany in Europe, was the most dangerous. It was possible that the 'emphasis may shift to Europe'. Welcoming the ratification of the Franco–Soviet pact by the French Chamber of Deputies, Stalin, most unusually, attacked Hitler personally when the Führer, in a supposedly 'pacific' reply to the French vote, threatened both France and the USSR. There was, however, no allusion to collective security in Stalin's interview, an omission that suggests that the Soviet leader expected little from the League of Nations.

If the Ethiopian crisis could be downplayed, the Rhineland re-militarization and its aftermath was a major check to Litvinov's diplomacy, and provoked considerable debate in Moscow about the future direction of Soviet policy. The failure of the western powers to stand up to Hitler, or to include the Soviet Union in its deliberations, may have strengthened Stalin's instinctive preference for a policy of isolation. There were signs of disarray in high government circles, and in the Comintern executive which met in Moscow during the last week in March and first week in April. During the crisis itself, Litvinov and Molotov sent out different signals. After maintaining a week's silence until the French Senate hurriedly ratified the Franco–Soviet pact on 12 March 1936, Litvinov took an active part in the League Council meetings in London, trying to push France and Britain into a more resolute stand against Germany, but leaving the door open for a Soviet retreat. The commissar for foreign affairs argued that unless sanctions were imposed on Germany, the League's position would be dangerously compromised, and all the mechanisms for maintaining peace and security in Europe would be weakened. At the same time, Molotov's interview with the editor of *Le Temps* in late March, struck a different note. It served as a warning to the western powers, and a hint to the Germans, that the Soviet Union was still interested in *détente*. Molotov reminded Chastenet, the editor, of the importance of the Soviet alliance for France's future security. Answering the latter's question about Soviet opinion regarding a *rapprochement* with Germany, he replied: 'Among a certain section of the Soviet people there is a trend with an extremely hostile attitude towards those currently ruling Germany, particularly in connexion with constantly repeated hostile outbursts by German leaders against the Soviet Union. However, the chief trend determining the policy of the Soviet authorities considers it possible to improve relations between Germany and the USSR'.[61] Molotov would not have made such a statement if it had been unacceptable to Stalin.

The Comintern debates of March–April 1936 revealed a great diversity of opinion about the future path that Soviet policy should take. The main lines of division were between those who wanted peace maintained as long as possible, and those who thought that as war was coming anyway, the Soviet Union should hasten its arrival, and create the conditions for the Communist revolution in Europe. In a final unpublished resolution of 1 April 1936, delegates denounced the passivity of the League of Nations, and blamed Britain for its failures. If the USSR was threatened by war, the danger was even greater for the other European countries, as the first aggression would not be directed against the Soviet Union, but against France and Britain. The Comintern resolution also asserted that the Communists should not assume any political responsibility for the defensive measures adopted by bourgeois governments, though this did not exclude the possibility of support in special cases. Such conclusions echoed the Kremlin's suspicion of both Britain and France and its doubts about achieving peace through collective security. The wording of the final resolution bore Stalin's mark, for he and Molotov were determined to put off war as long as possible. The arguments made for an early war and revolution were buried. Nonetheless, the sharp divisions in the ranks of the Comintern could not be disguised. Given Stalin's preoccupation with any latent opposition that might raise its head again in wartime, those whose foreign policy views differed from the official (Stalin's) line were clearly in danger. Among the victims of the first show trial were those in the Comintern who were defending positions finally rejected by Stalin and Molotov.

The mood in Moscow in the spring of 1936 was increasingly pessimistic. There was not much satisfaction from either Paris or London. Ambassador Potemkin, an alert observer of the French scene who had pushed for Franco-Soviet staff talks, reported from Paris on 26 March that, 'Hopes of our support in the event of armed conflict with Germany are manifestly weak in France.' The *polpred* described the 'atmosphere of doubts, fears, mistrust and hesitations, in which the French government must act at the present critical moment'.[62] The fact that the PCF

[61] Ibid., 100.
[62] Quoted in Haslam, *The Soviet Union and the Struggle for Collective Security in Europe*, 101–102.

continued to block the French defence efforts reflected Soviet doubts about France's intentions. As the next months showed, the Franco-Soviet pact was a weak reed on which to build an anti-German combination, and was failing to create a bridge to Britain whose greater weight in the Anglo-French *entente* was clearly demonstrated during and after the Rhineland crisis. The Soviet Union again turned towards Germany. Commercial negotiations were resumed, and a new trade and payments agreement was signed in April 1936 that dealt exclusively with arrangements within the 200 million mark credit, much of which was still unused. At the same time, Schacht, according to Bessonov, again raised the question of the 500 million RM credit which the *Reichsminister* was anxious to disassociate from any political discussions. The Soviet negotiators, however, made it clear at a lunch given by Kandelaki on 4 May that 'the Soviet government—despite the increasing scepticism in Moscow—still saw the possibility of achieving a political *détente*'.[63] Prodded by his cousin Herbert, who worked in Schacht's office, Hermann Göring, now head of the newly created Raw Materials and Foreign Exchange Office, met with Kandelaki and his deputy on 13 May. Welcoming the new credit agreement, Göring assured the Soviet representatives that the 'time was ripe' for more friendly economic and political relations. However genuine his sentiments, the onerous restrictions on Soviet trade were not lifted, and there were no signs of an improvement in political relations. The Soviets did not want a large German credit if they could not earn the marks to pay back their debt. There were to be no accumulating clearing balances as in south–eastern Europe.

Krestinsky, the deputy commissar for foreign affairs, wrote to Surits in early August that German affairs had not been discussed for a long time in Moscow, but that it was unlikely that the loan would proceed. The offer was exclusively for German economic purposes, and 'We have no motives for supporting the Germans politically.' Krestinsky claimed 'this is mine (and Litvinov's) point of view and it seems in any case to a considerable degree to coincide with the views of leading comrades'.[64] A week later, Krestinsky informed the ambassador that the decision had been taken not to proceed, though the subject could be raised again if Germany agreed to Soviet demands for military equipment. Behind this rejection were the hopes raised by the victory of the Popular Front in France, and, in the early stages of the Spanish Civil War, the belief that support for non-intervention might assist the

[63] *DGFP*, Ser. C, Vol. V, No. 312, cited in Roberts, *The Soviet Union and the Origins of the Second World War*, 40.

[64] Roberts, *The Soviet Union and the Origins of the Second World War*, 41.

Republic and prevent Italo-German assistance to Franco. The charges made against Zinoviev, Kamenev, and the others in August 1936, involved accusations of a Gestapo–Trotskyite connection and were strongly anti-Nazi in tone. Yet the Soviet response to Hitler's fierce attack on the Bolshevik–Jewish conspiracy at the Nuremberg rally in September, was surprisingly low-keyed. Surits suggested a strong note of protest, a public statement, and the suspension of sales of raw materials to Germany, even if this meant payment of Russian bills of exchange in gold. His advice was rejected; instead the official response was restricted to press articles and instructions for the ambassador to raise the question sharply with the German leaders. The events of the next months suggest that Soviet caution was justified. As anticipated by Litvinov, Communist party backing for the new Popular Front government made it more difficult to deal with the Blum government as it had to fend off attacks from the anti-Bolshevik right. By October, too, the Soviet Union was threatening to quit the Non-Intervention Committee and was supplying arms to the Republicans. The Russians walked a thin diplomatic line in Spain, with Litvinov denouncing the policy of non-intervention and Anglo-French hypocrisy, but remaining in the NIC and avoiding any action that would cut the lines to London or Paris.

There was a similar disjunction in Soviet policy towards Germany. German–Soviet relations publicly deteriorated. Hitler's speeches grew more menacing, the 'axis' was consolidated, the Anti-Comintern Pact concluded, and the situation in the Far East appeared ever more ominous. While Maisky in London denounced German and Italian activities in Spain, Kandelaki, Schacht, and the two Görings continued their talks on German–Soviet trade. At a meeting on 14 December between Surits and Göring at the latter's invitation, the rising star in the Nazi firmament stressed Schacht's commitment to the further development of German–Soviet economic relations, and to the normalization of political relations. The latter would depend on the realization of the former. Surits reported; 'Referring to his [Göring's] genuine wish to develop economic relations with the USSR, he said that this also fits with his view of the desirability of normalizing political relations as well; and in that regard he recalled the precepts of Bismarck and even the mistake which Wilhelm II made in retreating from these precepts.'[65] Ten days later, Kandelaki met with Schacht, who in a retrospective report to Neurath claimed that he had told the Soviet trade negotiator that only a

[65] Doc. 250, Protocol 44, 9/12/36 in Politburo TsK RKP (b). Rossiya i Evropa. Reshenia 'Osoboi papki' 1923–1939 (Moscow, 2001). I owe this reference and the translation to Professor Jonathan Haslam.

statement from the Soviet ambassador, promising that the Russian government would refrain from Communist agitation outside the Soviet Union, would lead to a 'more active development of trade'. 'M. Kandelaki, apparently involuntarily', Schacht wrote, 'let it appear that he sympathized'. Without Kandelaki's account, it is hard to judge the veracity of Schacht's report. Surits claimed that it was Schacht who took the initiative, and that in his many talks with Kandelaki and his deputy, the economics minister expatiated on his favourite political themes: Soviet withdrawal from Spain, and from the Popular Front in France, and an end to the policy of the 'encirclement' of Germany. In any case, Kandelaki returned to Moscow at the end of the year, just when Soviet military talks were about to begin in Paris, and was instructed on 8 January 1937 by the *Politburo*, (the draft oral reply was prepared by Litvinov), to tell Schacht that the Soviet government had no objection to new negotiations with the German government, through official channels. The talks would be kept confidential if the German government insisted.[66]

This overture, the first by the Soviet Union to the Germans since the spring of 1935, was undoubtedly a response to its deteriorating diplomatic situation, and to fears that the British and French would strike a deal with Germany. Kandelaki, on 29 January, delivered the message to Schacht who, according to his own account, again repeated the demand that political conversations be conducted through the ambassador. In Litvinov's report to Stalin on 4 February, he queried Kandelaki's handling of the talks and made known his opposition to their continuation. It was unnecessary for either Surits or Kandelaki to return to Moscow, Litvinov insisted, as it had already been decided that the initiative should be left to the Germans. All that was necessary was to give Surits the authorization to open negotiations, but to leave time for the French and Czechs to be informed. With Stalin's agreement, Litvinov sent off the new instructions to Berlin. The Soviet leaders waited for developments. Nothing happened. Neurath saw Hitler on 8 February; the German leader rejected the idea of political conversations. On 21 March, Schacht told the Soviet ambassador that there was no prospect for any change in German–Soviet relations. This was the end of the 1937 negotiations.

It is easy to understand why Stalin and Molotov seized on the opportunities opened by Germany's economic requirements. The situation in Spain had increased Soviet suspicions of both Britain and France. In early 1937 the British concluded their 'gentleman's agreement' with Italy, and there were persistent rumours that the French and Germans

[66] Roberts, *The Soviet Union and the Origins of the Second World War*, 44.

were entering into new talks. The second show trial, involving the so-called 'Anti-Soviet Trotskyist Centre', opened on 23 January 1937. This attack on the 'right opposition' included those involved in negotiations with Britain and France. Much was made of the argument that as the Trotskyites could only take power if the USSR was defeated in war, 'the Trotskyist criminals have banked on forcing a war by the fascist states against the USSR'.[67] Both the German military, and the press attachés were implicated in the Radek treason trial. There were demands for their recall, but the Germans refused to be bullied, and the two men stayed in Moscow. The charged atmosphere and the accusations against the 'revolutionary internationalists' did not leave either the diplomats or the Comintern untouched. Already in February 1937, Coulondre cancelled his visit to Paris, reporting that Litvinov was in personal danger; his English wife had already been despatched to teach English in the Urals. With the execution of the former deputy commissar of foreign affairs, Sokolnikov, in late January, the NKVD moved into the precincts of the Foreign Ministry.

It is typical of Stalin's tactics that even as the Soviet security services were planting the material incriminating Tukhachevsky, the Soviet leader authorized the opening of political negotiations with Germany. He may have been convinced that there might be trouble with the army. As he told the Central Committee plenum, in his speech on 3 March 1937: 'To win a battle in time of war may require several corps of Red Army men. But to lose this prize at the front would take only several spies somewhere'.[68] History hung heavy on Stalin's shoulders, he needed to show these men were involved in treasonable activities, providing an acceptable reason for his irrational behaviour. An attack on the Soviet Union could bring, in the first instance, military defeat. Traitors in the party, in the army, or in the bureaucracy would try to effect a *coup*. Following First World War precedents, they would seek foreign support and pay a price in the non-Russian territories of the USSR. It was therefore necessary to root out all sources of opposition, real or potential, and to brand any form of criticism of the regime as treasonable. Undoubtedly, the arrests, trials, and 'confessions' of so many of the best known figures in the Soviet hierarchy convinced many in the Soviet Union that the charges were true. The Soviet leadership believed, or were convinced (fear was a great educator), that the party, the army, and even the secret services contained opponents to Stalin's rule.

[67] *Pravda*, 1 February 1937, quoted in Haslam, *The Soviet Union and the Struggle for Collective Security in Europe*, 125.

[68] Quoted in Haslam, *The Soviet Union and the Struggle for Collective Security in Europe*, 136.

In the summer of 1937 there was a temporary Soviet retreat from world affairs. Japan's invasion of China in July and the rising tension in international politics resulted in the increasing isolation of the USSR. The abstention from action in Spain and in China proved only temporary. In both conflicts, it was in the interests of Soviet security to prolong the confrontations, and avoid any rapid defeats that would shift the danger points to central and Eastern Europe. Nevertheless, Soviet aid to the Republicans in Spain, and to Chiang Kai-shek, serving Soviet national interests, was carefully gauged so as not to provoke major reactions from the Great Powers. Elsewhere, too, Soviet diplomacy was marked by extreme caution and self-absorption. The purges took their toll. Surits left Berlin for Paris and was replaced by Yurenev, a highly experienced diplomat, who was more optimistic about the possibilities of a normalization of relations with Germany. Kandelaki and his deputy Friedrikson returned to Moscow, and became deputy commissars of foreign trade, prior to their arrest and imprisonment. Hitler received Yurenev at Obersalzberg and warm words were exchanged; Neurath was an old acquaintance and both he and Weizsäcker, the head of the Wilhelmstrasse's political section, made encouraging noises about German–Soviet relations. Yurenev misread the signs for Hitler had no intention of engaging in political talks whatever Germany's economic problems. The ambassador's reception at the Führer's Alpine villa was probably nothing more than a wish to minimize the importance of the interview. When Yurenev returned to Moscow on leave later in the summer of 1937, he was arrested.

Contacts between Moscow and Berlin continued. Talks on credits were begun in January 1938 but were broken off in March due to Soviet unwillingness to accept the German terms. At their meeting on 11 July, when European attention was focused on Prague, Merekalov, the new Soviet representative in Berlin, and Weizsäcker, both expressed their willingness to continue the credit talks although Merekalov noted that 'since the German proposals on credits had turned out to be unacceptable to the Soviet government, it was Germany which should take the initiative'.[69] Though the documentary trail is difficult to trace in the published documents, it appears that no agreement was reached on credits. It is known that in March 1938, the two countries signed an agreement regulating their trade. This was renewed for a year on 19 December 1938, when the Germans suggested the resumption of the credit talks.[70] These latter talks,

[69] AVP RF. Astakov Diary, 11 July, f.05, p. 142, d.56. I. 196.
[70] *DVP*, Vol. XXI, No. 59.

which also broke down, belong to the post-Munich story and will be discussed in a later chapter.

It was due mainly to Hitler that there was so little success in Berlin, but the possibilities for an anti-revisionist front also diminished, almost to vanishing point. The military purges confirmed and strengthened the doubts in London and Paris about the utility of a *rapprochement* with the Soviet Union. There was every sign in the autumn of 1937 that the Soviet Union was not a real factor in Anglo-French calculations about Hitler's next moves. In his speech to the electors of Leningrad (irony of ironies, there was an election campaign for the Supreme Soviet just as the Terror was reaching its high point) on 27 November 1937, Litvinov again rehearsed the differences between the aggressor and pacific powers but cautioned that:

> there are states which do not believe their statements about their aggressive designs and devote all their diplomacy to obtaining confirmation and clarification of these completely unambiguous statements. We want to know, whether we have correctly understood you and whether you really believe what you saw. Would you be so kind as to confirm and clarify this . . . (Laughter). Replies to these enquires are sometimes received in an unambiguously insulting form. But even then they ask for confirmation and clarification. Thus we are left with a division of labour in the international arena, whereby some states attack, and others make enquiries and await confirmation and clarification (Laughter).[71]

Litvinov's satirical characterization of British and French policy following Halifax's November visit to Hitler, suggests the degree of his disillusionment with the western powers. Delbos's end of year trip, his meeting with Neurath on 3 December 1937, and the omission of the Soviet Union from his itinerary, fed Soviet fears, xenophobia, and sense of exclusion.

Litvinov was surprisingly open with the *Le Temps* correspondent in Moscow on 25 December. Asked whether it was correct to describe the Soviet position as isolation, a withdrawal into itself, Litvinov responded: 'Obviously, since at the moment no one wants anything to do with us. We will carry on waiting . . . and then we'll see.' The conversation went on. When pressed as to his meaning, the commissar replied, 'There are other possible combinations.' 'With Germany?' 'Why not?' Litvinov said. The commissar went on to explain that when Hitler came to power, he had renewed the Berlin treaty and had only changed his mind when convinced the Russians were opposed to German expansion in central Europe. If, however, the Soviets 'gave him to understand that we have no interest in maintaining the status quo', the situation would be different. The USSR would not be touched by territorial

[71] Extracts from quotation in Haslam, *The Soviet Union and the Struggle for Collective Security*, 151–152.

revision and could disinterest itself. It would not be a question of signing new treaties, Litvinov claimed, 'Things would happen differently!'[72] Few in Paris or London believed that Germany would seek an arrangement with Moscow, and given their assumptions of German strength and Soviet weakness, assumed that the danger that they most feared could be temporarily ignored. They could deal directly with Hitler without paying attention to the USSR, a state whose doctrines and behaviour were as threatening to their interests as Nazism but which lacked the strength to project them.

IV

The 'Great Terror' dominated Soviet life in these pre-war years. What began with the trials, arrests, and expulsions following the assassination of the Leningrad party boss, Sergei Kirov, on 1 December 1934, reached a climax of horror between the autumn of 1937 and the spring of 1938. The waves of mass repression engulfed the party, bureaucracy, Narkomindel, Comintern, foreign Communists who had sought refuge in Russia, and sympathizers and loyalists living abroad. It was only in the autumn of 1938 that at Stalin's command, the Central Committee began to rein in the perpetrators, most of whom in turn were liquidated. One will never know how many people perished in this bloodletting, possibly between one and one and a half million people. More were executed or died because of inhuman treatment in 1937–38.[73] There is no doubt that the purges were directed from the centre, and that Stalin was personally responsible. In many cases, he dispatched telegrams with his own instructions, naming the victims. Selection was arbitrary. Regional quota systems were set for the major territorial units, along with the number to be shot, or sent to labour camps or prison. The victims were tried by trios, typically consisting of the local NKVD chief, the party secretary, and the procurator.[74] Accusations and sentences had little to do with guilt or innocence; all were subject to arbitrary judgments. There were instances of spontaneous action at the local level, and it was not unusual for the quotas for arrests and shootings to be exceeded. It was, nevertheless, Stalin who set the Great Terror into motion, removing in the process all those strata of the population whom he judged hostile, or potentially hostile, to his personal regime. Again and again, he rejected arguments for attenuating the bloodbath.

72 From Haslam, *The Soviet Union and the Struggle for Collective Security*, 153–154.

73 According to official central Soviet archives record 681,692 persons were executed.

74 Robert Service, *A History of Twentieth-Century Russia* (London, 1998), 222.

As 'internal enemies' were everywhere, they had to be rooted out in the interests of unity, and in anticipation of an armed attack from abroad.

Beyond attributing the purges to Stalin's bloodlust, which surpassed that of Hitler's, and his pathological distrust of all possible opponents, some historians have postulated a link between the purges, past practices, and the long-held belief in an inevitable war. Though Stalin's purges went far beyond Lenin's imaginings, such ideas and practices date from the Leninist period. The Four-Year Plan was enforced through violent means, and the purges of 1933 and 1934 demonstrated Stalin's determination to drive home his programme, even at high human cost. There was a connection between the centralization and 'purification' of the regime, and the external environment. During 1937–1938, the Soviet Union not only faced heightened threats from Germany and Japan, but also suffered from diplomatic isolation in Europe and in the Far East. The situation in Spain hammered home the dangers of 'sabotage', 'fifth columns', and internal divisions (created, in part, by the Spanish Communists and the Soviet representatives) while increasing the danger of a combined European front against the Soviet Union.[75] Given Stalin's desire for absolute power and his ideologically based belief in the coming war, re-enforced by contemporary events, his violent repression was the most obvious response to the fault lines in Soviet society, and the most effective way to root out opposition, real, potential, or imaginary. Repeatedly in public forums, Stalin linked his spurious accusations with the threats from abroad. The accused in each of the three public trials were denounced as 'proponents' of a destructive war against the Soviet Union, and accused of serving as agents of Russia's external enemies. In order to mobilize the country for the impending struggle, Russia's 'internal enemies' and their relatives had to be liquidated. At a deeper level, the purges were rooted in Stalin's fierce determination to establish his absolute control over all men and institutions that might threaten his monopoly on power.

Though actions against individuals were often indiscriminate and without defined political aims, specific institutions such as the party, the Central Committee, Narkomindel, Comintern, Red Army, and intelligence services, were each targeted. Only one in thirty delegates to the Seventeenth Party Congress in 1934 returned to the Eighteenth Congress in 1939. Only sixteen out of seventy members of the Central Committee survived. At least 34% of the personnel of the Narkomindel disappeared during the purges; the figure being much

[75] See pp. 211, 213–15 for the discussion of the links between the purges and the Spanish Civil War.

higher, 62%, among the approximately one hundred holders of senior posts.[76] Thousands of Red Army officers were purged, including fifteen of the sixteen army commanders. Even the NKVD was purged; more than 20,000 men fell victim to Stalin's wrath. National and ethnic groups were suspect; Poles, Kurds, and Koreans were forcefully removed and settled elsewhere. Kazakhstan became a dumping ground for those who incurred Stalin's suspicions.[77] Agents and sympathizers abroad became 'enemies of the people'; they fled, or tried to disappear, or were assassinated, as Soviet agents infiltrated both loyalist and émigré groups. Stalin's bloody purges involved the elimination of all men and women, who for any reason, be it birth, background, occupation, area of residence, or foreign nationality might become an enemy of the regime. In institutional terms, this meant not just the destruction of any potential 'fifth column', but also the elimination of the members of the older élites who would be replaced with younger and more recently indoctrinated men, more amenable to Stalin's total control. The denunciations, arrests, and killings generated yet more atrocities. The perpetrators were themselves purged, and then their replacements too were purged. Local scores were settled; family feuds took ominous forms. Even in this atmosphere of hatred and suspicion Stalin appears to have escaped personal censure.

Already distrusted by party officials, and tainted by its cosmopolitanism and contacts with foreigners, the Foreign Ministry was a natural target. Two waves of arrests took place, in 1937, following the execution of Radek and Sokolnikov, the deputy commissar of foreign affairs, and again, with more devastating results, after Litvinov's dismissal in May 1939. The Central Committee plenum meeting in February–March 1937 specifically called for an investigation into the 'lessons of sabotage' by 'Japanese–German–Trotskyite' agents. After the Tukhachevsky trial and execution, a number of arrests were made. At the same time, a campaign was launched to reduce the number of foreign consulates and foreigners living in the USSR. By the end of the year, a new sweep of Narkomindel officials and diplomats who had served in Spain took place. The victims were sent to labour camps or were killed.[78]

[76] T. J. Uldricks, 'The Impact of the Great Purges on the People's Commissariat of Foreign Affairs', *Slavic Review*, 36: 2 (1977), 190.

[77] For references see Service, *A History of Twentieth-Century Russia*, 222–225.

[78] For the following details, see Uldricks, 'The Impact of the Great Purges on the People's Commissariat of Foreign Affairs', 187–204; Sabine Dullin, *Des Hommes d'Influences: les ambassadeurs de Staline en Europe, 1930–1939* (Paris, 2001), 240–277, and Pons, *Stalin and the Inevitable War*, 89–96; Alastair Kocho-Williams, 'The Soviet Diplomatic Corps and Stalin's Purges', *Slavonic and East European Review*, 86: 1, (2008), 102–105.

Missions abroad were stripped of so-called 'spies, saboteurs and terrorists'. Anyone dealing with foreigners even in an official capacity could be denounced as 'foreign agents' or 'Trotskyist'. There was little point, and much danger, in any diplomatic activity. The Central Committee and NKVD vetted serving and incoming officials. In the summer of 1938, for the first time Litvinov, under extreme pressure, failed to take his summer vacation in Karlsbad. Plots and intrigues against the commissar, possibly orchestrated by Potemkin, undermined his authority. In December, Litvinov was twice summoned to the Kremlin at unusual hours, between 1.30 and 2.00 in the morning; the meetings appear to have been connected with the purging of the Narkomindel. For the most part, the commissar acquiesced in the attacks on his personnel, occasionally acting to protect some of his close collaborators by refusing to allow them to return home. The assaults on the Narkomindel and the missions abroad left the service acutely short of diplomats and support staff. In a letter of complaint to Stalin in February 1939, Litvinov pointed out that there were eight embassies without ambassadors: Washington, Tokyo, Warsaw, Bucharest, Barcelona, Kaunas, Copenhagen, and Sofia. (Teheran would soon be added to the list.) The situation with regard to counsellors and secretaries of embassies was almost as bad. Litvinov complained, too, that because of the interventions of the NKVD and the Central Committee, diplomats on leave or recalled to Moscow (such as Boris Shtein from Rome) were not permitted to return to their posts. Trained replacements could not be sent abroad. Litvinov warned of the damage done to Soviet prestige and the difficulties of doing business given the number of diplomats who were purged or had defected. His protests were ignored; the arrests continued and posts remained unfilled. It was not until Molotov replaced Litvinov in 1939 that a programme for the replenishment of the cadres was introduced, and a new generation of diplomats, markedly different in background, education, and training entered the service.

Buffeted by the NKVD attacks and a series of diplomatic defeats, Litvinov was driven to consider resignation at the end of 1938. A letter written to Stalin was never sent, but fell into Molotov's hands who undoubtedly informed his leader of its contents.[79] In a mood of general despondency, Litvinov carried on trying to protect some of his more senior protégés (his private secretary was arrested in the commissar's own room) but outwardly at least, he toed the Stalinist line. The dictator's new

[79] The source of the story is found in the far from reliable memoirs of Z. Sheinis, the *polpred* in Rome, *Litvinov, revoliutsioner, diplomat, chelovek* (Moscow, 1989), cited in Sabine Dullin, 'Litvinov and the People's Commissariat of Foreign Affairs', in Pons and Andrea Romano (eds.), *Russia in the Age of Wars, 1914–1945* (Milan, 2000), 140–146.

favourite, and one of a handful of advisers on foreign policy, Andrei Zhdanov, the Leningrad party secretary, publicly established himself as Litvinov's opponent, and along with Molotov, a long-standing rival, emerged as the most forceful critic of collective security. With the Narkomindel engulfed in an atmosphere of suspicion and fear, Soviet diplomacy entered a phase of passivity and semi-paralysis.

The Comintern, too, came under siege. 'All of you in the Comintern are working for our enemy,' Stalin told Georgi Dimitrov, the Comintern secretary, on 11 February 1937.[80] Dimitrov remained in office, working under a dark cloud and receiving visitors 'privately' at home rather than in the office. There was talk in Moscow of uniting the Second and Third International and reducing the Comintern to a skeletal structure. In Spain, the campaign against 'Trotskyism' reached its terrifying heights with the Communist repression of May 1937 and the assassination of Andrés Nin. During the second half of the year, the national Communist parties became the victims of a 'general blitz'. The heads of the German Communist party were charged in September 1936 and the sentences carried out during the following spring and summer. The entire political office of the Polish Communist party, most of whom lived in Moscow, was arrested in September 1937. Hungarian Communists (including Béla Kun) as well as Austrian, German, Latvian, Estonian, Lithuanian, Finnish, Romanian, and Yugoslav exiles, who had sought sanctuary in Moscow, were either banished, imprisoned, or liquidated. The national Communist parties were commanded to rid their ranks of Trotskyist and Bukharinist 'traitors'. Though some of the internal battles were fierce and prolonged, all were brought to heel. While Stalin still wanted to preserve the policy of 'popular fronts' against Fascism, there was no room for comrades suspected of ideological deviation or party indiscipline. The Comintern was rendered impotent.

Most astonishing of all to observers of the Soviet scene, Stalin turned on the Red Army. Hitler's accession to power had resulted in a major expansion; appropriations were increased, special privileges granted to officers, and even some Tsarist ranks restored. As the purging of the party gathered momentum, there was a striking diminution of party members in the armed forces. When the NKVD supplied so-called information about sedition in high ranks, the ever-suspicious Stalin was quick to react. Primakov, a hero of the civil war, was arrested in November 1936; evidence about Tukhachevsky began to be gathered. During the winter months, reports were circulated, probably emanating from Soviet sources, but possibly involving the Gestapo as well as the NKVD, of links between the Red Army and the *Reichswehr*. In January

[80] Quoted in Pons, *Stalin and the Inevitable War*, 96.

and again in May 1937, Beneš, repeating the deliberately fabricated intelligence leaks, communicated to Moscow the details of a plot involving senior Soviet officers, and plans for a future *coup d'état*. Daladier, too, alerted Moscow to the connections between the Red Army chiefs and the German high command.[81] The reports given to the February–March 1937 Central Committee plenum did not directly refer to the army, but speeches by Stalin and Molotov made it plain that it would not be exempted from the search for 'Fifth Columnists'. Early in May, military councils were introduced and the civil war practice of appointing military commissars was restored. Stalin, himself, proposed the expulsion of Tukhachevsky and other commanders from the party and authorized the NKVD to handle the whole affair. The story was quickly spread that Tukhachevsky was implicated in a Soviet–German plot, and that the Germans believed that once the Red Army seized power, a Berlin–Moscow *rapprochement* would be possible. Though dismissed by the British and French military attachés in Moscow, as well as by the German embassy, it found acceptance among some foreign diplomats. The fictitious plot of the 'counter-revolutionary military Fascist organization', prepared by the NKVD, was elaborated by Voroshilov, Tukhachevsky's superior and a marshal always closer to Stalin than his abler and more independent deputy. In the fervid atmosphere of 1937, the lines between fact and fiction totally disappeared. Tukhachevsky and the other senior officers were denounced as German agents recruited during the Rapallo years. All were sentenced to death at a closed trial and shot on the night of 12 June 1937.

The army purges that started in 1937 continued through 1941. They left the Red Army leaderless, and the officer ranks decimated and in a state of confusion. They affected the army in the Far East and the Red Navy as well. The grisly toll of officers (the figures are debated and many who were purged were reinstated) had a catastrophic effect on planning and combat efficiency. The rostra of purged officers included '3 of 5 marshals of the Soviet Union, 2 of 4 army commanders 1st rank, 12 of 12 army commanders 2nd rank, 60 of 67 corps commanders, 136 of 199 division commanders, and 221 of 397 brigade commanders'.[82] There was a serious shortage of officers and men in a rapidly enlarged army; in 1938 it was

[81] Igor Lukes, *Czechoslovakia between Stalin and Hitler: The Diplomacy of Edvard Beneš in the 1930s* (New York and Oxford, 1996), 91–107; Pons, *Stalin and the Inevitable War*, 86. See M. J. Carley, 'Caught in a Cleft Stick: Soviet Diplomacy and the Spanish Civil War', in G. Johnson (ed.), *The International Context of the Spanish Civil War* (Newcastle, 2009).

[82] See David M. Glantz, *Stumbling Colossus: The Red Army on the Eve of World War II* (Lawrence, KA, 1998), 30–31. The total number of those penalized, 1937–1941, has been put at 54,714 men. But see Reger R. Reese, 'The Red Army and the Great Purges', in J. A. Getty and R. T. Manning (eds.), *Stalinist Terror: New Perspectives* (Cambridge, 1993), 213, for a much lower estimate.

estimated that the army lacked almost 100,000 men. The newly appointed officers were well rewarded and totally loyal to Stalin but loyalty was based largely on fear. Initiative and creativity were crushed, and the earlier revolutionary zeal of the military smothered. Morale was severely shaken, both in the officer corps and among serving soldiers. The price paid was seen in the war against Finland and the performance of the Red Army in western Russia in the summer of 1941. Military leaders were well aware of the army's deficiencies, but it was only in 1940 that Timoshenko, the newly appointed commissar of defence, initiated a sweeping reform programme to address the worst problems. The Terror hit the Soviet economy and the defence industries suffered. 'While economic difficulties did not lead to the purges,' R. W. Davies has written, 'the purges themselves caused major difficulties for the economy'.[83] The dismissals and arrests of administrators and technicians disrupted the work of the defence industries; younger and less experienced officials replaced the old. Some of these were purged in turn and even more inexperienced and untried men were appointed. The present consensus is that the decline in investment and the considerable slow-down in the rate of growth in 1937 was in large measure due to the effects of the purges.[84] The terror also had a disastrous effect on important Gulag operations.[85] The Soviet leaders, themselves, saw a direct connection between the purges, falling production rates, and labour discontent.[86] What is remarkable is the speed with which the defence industries recovered and their subsequent very rapid expansion. Not only did expenditure on defence increase but 'both production and investment in military preparations and in the armament industries, all grew rapidly, as did strategic stocks'.[87] This was apparently accomplished despite the blow administered by the repressions. It may have been due to the solid grounding of the industries in the early thirties and the training of sufficient numbers of technicians to supply the necessary

[83] R. W. Davies, 'The Soviet Economy and the Launching of the Great Terror', in M. Ilic (ed.), *Stalin's Terror Revisited* (London and New York, 2006), 31.

[84] Ibid., 31–32. See Barbara G. Katz. 'Purges and Production: Soviet Economic Growth, 1928–1940', *Journal of Economic History*, 35: 3 (1975); Paul R. Gregory and Mark Harrison, 'Allocation under Dictatorship: Research in Stalin's Archives', *Journal of Economic Literature*, 43: 3 (2005), 740–741.

[85] Simon Ertz, 'Building Norilsk' in Paul R. Gregory and Valary Lazarev (eds.), *The Economics of Forced Labour: The Soviet Gulag* (Stanford, CA, 2003).

[86] R. W. Davies, 'The Soviet Economy and the Launching of the Great Terror', in Ilic (ed.), *Stalin's Terror Revisited*, 30.

[87] Ibid., 32. In this article, Professor Davies argues that the drastic increase in defence expenditure was an important cause of the country's economic difficulties between 1937 and 1940.

replacements.[88] The figures, of course, give no indication of the inefficiencies of the system, and the poor quality of much that was produced. Nor do they give any indication of the conditions under which the war materials were manufactured.

Outside of the Soviet Union, the trials gave added weight to those prepared to minimize any Soviet contribution to an anti-Fascist front and strengthened hopes that some arrangement could be made with Hitler. The Führer, who had never attributed much importance to the Red Army, could take the initiative without undue concern about Moscow. According to a retrospective Soviet account, 'Hitler's military was ecstatic. The chief of the German general staff, General Beck, in assessing the military situation in the summer of 1938, said that the Russian Army could not be considered an armed force, for the bloody repressions had sapped its morale and turned it into an inert military machine'.[89] In Moscow, Stalin was prepared to watch and wait until the Soviet Union was in a position to call for new cards in the diplomatic game. While he would pay a heavy price for the ravages of terror, he believed that he had eliminated all those who might question his authority. There was to be no 'Fifth Column' in the Soviet Union. Just as Hitler began to implement his plans for expansion, the USSR became a seemingly marginalized power. There were no Soviet representatives at Munich and none of the participants regretted their absence.

It was not only events in Europe that account for the defensiveness of Soviet policy in the later 1930s. The Far Eastern situation provided an ever-present backdrop to Soviet attitudes towards Britain and Germany. The fear of a two-front war runs as a continuous thread in any analysis of Stalin's thinking. The outbreak of the undeclared war between China and Japan in 1937 affected the Soviet Union more directly than it did any other European power, including Britain. Military clashes took place between the Russians and Japanese in July 1937 and a series of incidents in July–August 1938 culminated in the battle of Lake Khasan on the Manchurian border. As will be argued in the next chapter, while the Far Eastern crises resulted in new connections between Britain and the United States, common interests in checking a Japanese advance in China did not bring the Russians and British closer together. Until 1939, moreover, although the German agreement with Tokyo might have distracted Britain, the United States, and the Soviet Union from the German threat in central Europe, it did

[88] Communication from Professor R. W. Davies to author (2008).

[89] O. F. Suvenirov, 'Vsearmeiskaia tragediia', *Voenno–istoricheskii zhurnal* (1989), 44, cited in Glantz, *Stumbling Colossus*, 31–2.

not fundamentally alter Germany's relations with any of the powers concerned. It is possible to treat the Far Eastern situation separately from the sequence of events that led to the origins of the European war in 1939, but because it affected the broader context in which European, American, and Soviet policy operated, it needs to be addressed in this global context.

Books

AHMANN, R., *Nichtangriffspakte: Entwicklung und operative Nutzung in Europe 1922–1939. Mit einen Ausblick auf die Renaissance des Nichtangriffsvertrages nach den Zweiten Weltkrieg* (Baden-Baden, 1988).

ANDREW, C., *Secret Service: The Making of the British Intelligence Community* (London, 1985).

—— and GORDIEVSKY, O., *KGB: The Inside Story of its Foreign Operations from Lenin to Gorbachov* (London, 1990).

—— and MITROKHIN, V., *The Mitrokhin Archive: The KGB in Europe and the West* (London, 1999).

—— and NOAKES, J. (ed.), *Intelligence and International Relations, 1900–1945* (Exeter, 1987). See C. Andrew.

BARBER, J. and HARRISON, M., *The Soviet Defence Industry Complex from Stalin to Krushchev* (Basingstoke, 2000).

CARLEY, M. J., *1939: The Alliance that Never Was and the Coming of World War II* (Chicago, 1999).

CARR, E. H., *The Twilight of the Comintern, 1930–35* (London, 1982).

COEURÉ, S., *La Grande Lueur à l'Est: Les Français et l'Union soviétique, 1917–1939* (Paris, 1999).

CONQUEST, R., *The Great Terror: A Reassessment* (London, 1990).

COURTOIS, S. et al., *Le livre noir du communisme: crimes, terreur et répression* (Paris, 1997).

D'AGASTINO, A., *Soviet Succession Struggles: Kreminology and the Russian Question from Lenin to Gorbachev* (Boston, MA, 1988).

DAVIES, R. W., HARRISON, M., and WHEATCROFT, S. G., *The Economic Transformation of the Soviet Union, 1913–1945* (Cambridge, 1994).

DULLIN, S., *Des Hommes d'Influences: Les ambassadeurs de Staline en Europe, 1930–1939* (Paris, 2001).

ERICKSON, J., *The Soviet High Command: A Military–Political History 1918–1941* (London, 1962).

GETTY, J. A. and NAUMOV, O.V., *The Road to Terror: Stalin and the Self-destruction of the Bolsheviks, 1932–1939* (New Haven, CT, 1999).

—— and MANNING, R. T. (eds.), *Stalinist Terror: New Perspectives* (Cambridge, 1993).

GLANTZ, D. M., *The Military Strategy of the Soviet Union: A History* (London and Portland, OR, 1992).

—— *Stumbling Colossus: The Red Army on the Eve of World War* (Lawrence, KA, 1998).

GUILLEN, P. and MIECK, I., *Deutschland–Frankreich–Russland: Begegnungen und Konfrontationen. La France et l'Allemagne face à la Russie* (Munich, 2000).

HABECK, M. R., *Storms of Steel: The Development of Armor Doctrine in Germany and the Soviet Union, 1919–1939* (Ithaca, NY, 2003).

HAIGH, R. H., MORRIS, D. S., and PETERS, A. R., *Soviet Foreign Policy, the League of Nations and Europe, 1917–1939* (Aldershot, 1986).

HARRISON, M. (ed.), *Guns and Roubles: The Defense Industry in the Stalinist State* (New Haven, CT, 2008). See articles cited below.

HASLAM, J., *The Soviet Union and the Struggle for Collective Security in Europe, 1933–1939* (London, 1984).

—— *The Soviet Union and the Threat from the East: Moscow, Tokyo and the Prelude to the Pacific War* (London, 1992).

HOCHMAN, J., *The Soviet Union and the Failure of Collective Security, 1934–1938* (Ithaca, NY, 1984).

HUGHES, M., *Inside the Enigma: British Officials in Russia, 1900–1939* (London and Rio Grande, 1997).

ILIC, M. (ed.), *Stalin's Terror Revisited* (London and New York, 2006). See articles cited below.

LARS, T. L., NAUMOV, O. N, and KHLEVNIUK O. V. (eds.), *Stalin's Letters to Molotov* (New Haven, CT, and London, 1995).

LUKES, I., *Czechoslovakia between Stalin and Hitler: The Diplomacy of Edvard Beneš in the 1930s* (New York and Oxford, 1996).

MORRELL, G. W., *Britain Confronts the Stalin Revolution: Anglo–Soviet Relations and the Metro-Vickers Crisis* (Waterloo, Ontario, 1995).

NARINSKY, M. and ROHWER, J. (eds.), *Centre and Periphery: The History of the Comintern in the Light of New Documents* (Amsterdam, 1996).

NEILSON, K., *Britain, Soviet Russsia and the Collapse of the Versailles Order, 1919–1939* (Cambridge, 2006).

NEKRICH, A., *Pariahs, Patriarchs, Predators: German–Soviet Relations, 1922–1941* (Chichester and New York, 1997).

OBERLANDER, E., *Hitler–Stalin-Pakt 1939: Das Ende Ostmitteleuropas?* (Frankfurt am Main, 1989). All the essays are interesting though some need updating.

PONS, S., *Stalin e la guerra inevitabile, 1936–1941* (Turin, 1995). English translation (slightly different) *Stalin and the Inevitable War, 1936–1941* (2002) (London and Portland, OR, 1995).

—— and ROMANO, A. (eds.), *Russia in the Age of Wars (1914–1945)* (Milan, 2000). See S. Main, L. Samuelson, and articles cited below.

RAACK, R. C., *Stalin's Drive to the West, 1938–1945* (Stanford, CA, 1995).

ROBERTS, G., *The Soviet Union and the Origins of the Second World War: Russo-German Relations and the Road to War, 1933–1941* (Basingstoke, 1995).

ROI, M., *Alternative to Appeasement: Sir Robert Vansittart and Alliance Diplomacy, 1934–1937* (Westport, CT, 1997).

SAMUELSON, L., *Plans for Stalin's War Machine, Tukhachevskii and Military–Economic Planning, 1925–1941* (London, 2000).

SHAW, L. G., *The British Political Élite and the Soviet Union, 1937–1939* (London and Portland, OR, 2003).

THURSTON, R., *Life and Terror in Stalin's Russia* (New Haven, CT, 1996).

ULAM, A. B., *Expansion and Coexistence: Soviet Foreign Policy, 1917–1973* second edn. (New York, 1976).

Articles and Chapters

AHMANN, R., 'Soviet Foreign Policy and the Molotov–Ribbentrop Pact of 1939: An Enigma Reassessed', *Storia delle Relazioni Internazionali*, 2 (1989).

—— ' "Localization of Conflicts" or "Indivisibility of Peace": The German and the Soviet Approaches towards Collective Security and East Central Europe 1925–1939', in Ahmann, R., Birke, A. M., and Howard, M. (eds.), *The Quest for Stability: Problems of West European Security, 1918–1957* (Oxford, 1993).

BOURETTE-KNOWLES, S., 'The Global Micawber: Sir Robert Vansittart, the Treasury and the Global Balance of Power, 1933–1935' *Diplomacy and Statecraft*, 6: 1 (1995).

CARLEY, M. J., 'Five Kopecks for Five Kopecks: Franco-Soviet Trade Negotiations, 1928–1939, *Cahiers du monde russe et soviétique*, 33: 1 (1992).

—— 'Down a Blind Alley: Anglo-Franco-Soviet Relations, 1920–1939', *Canadian Journal of History*, 39 (1994).

—— 'Prelude to Defeat: Franco-Soviet Relations, 1920–1939', *Historical Reflections/Reflexions Historiques*, 22: 1 (1996).

—— ' "A Fearful Concatenation of Circumstances": The Anglo-Soviet Rapprochement, 1935–1936', *Contemporary European History*, 5: 1 (1996).

—— 'A Soviet Eye on France from the Rue de Grenelle in Paris, 1924–1940', *Diplomacy and Statecraft*, 17 (2006).

—— 'Caught in a Cleft Stick: Soviet Diplomacy and the Spanish Civil War', in Johnson, G. (ed.), *The International Context of the Spanish Civil War* (Newcastle, 2009).

CHAPMAN, J. W., 'A Dance on Eggs: Intelligence and the "Anti-Comintern" *Journal of Contemporary History*, 22 (1987).

DAVIES, R. W., 'The Launching of the Great Terror', in Ilic, M. (ed.), *Stalin's Terror Revisited* (London and New York, 2006).

—— 'Preparations for Mobilisation of the Soviet Economy in the 1930s', in Harrison, M. (ed.), *Guns and Rubles: The Defense Industry in the Stalinist State* (New Haven, CT, 2008).

—— and HARRISON, M., 'The Soviet Military–Economic Effort during the Second Five-Year Plan (1933–1937)', *Europe–Asia Studies*, 49: 3 (1997).

DULLIN, S., 'Le rôle de Litvinov dans les années 1930', *Communisme*, 42–44 (1995).

—— 'Litvinov and the People's Commissariat of Foreign Affairs: The Fate of an Administration under Stalin, 1930–1939', in Pons, S. and Romano, A. (eds.), *Russia in the Age of Wars, 1914–1945* (Milan, 2000).

—— 'Le rôle de l'Allemagne dans le *rapprochement* Franco-soviétique, 1932–1935', in Mieck, I. and Guillen, P. (eds.), *Deutschland–Frankreich–Russland: Begegnungen und Konfrontationen. La France et l'Allemagne face à la Russie* (Munich, 2000).

—— 'Litvinov, les diplomates soviétiques et l'Europe au seuil des années 1930', in Narinski, M., de Réau, E., Soutou, G.-H., and Tchoubarian, A. (eds.), *L'URSS et l'Europe dans les années 1920* (Paris, 2000).

Dreifort, J. E., 'The French Popular Front and the Franco-Soviet Pact, 1936–7: A Dilemma in Foreign Policy', *Journal of Contemporary History*, 11 (1976).

Ellman, M., 'Soviet Repression Statistics: Some Comments', *Europe–Asia Studies*, 54 (2002).

Erickson, J., 'Threat Identification and Strategic Appraisal by the Soviet Union, 1930–1941', in May, E. R. (ed.), *Knowing One's Enemies: Intelligence Assessment before the Two World Wars* (Princeton, NJ, and Guildford, 1984).

Fleischauer, I., 'Soviet Foreign Policy and the Origins of the Hitler–Soviet Pact', in Wegner, B., *From Peace to War: Germany Soviet Russia and the World, 1939–1941* (Providence, RI, and Oxford, 1997).

Getty J. A., ' "Excesses are Not Permitted": Mass Terror and Stalinist Governance in the Late 1930s', *Russian Review,* 61 (2002).

Girault, R., 'Les relations Franco-Soviétiques à la veille de la Seconde Guerre mondiale: bilan des anneés, 1937–1940', *Revue des études slaves*, 50: 3 (1977).

Gregory, P. R. and Harrison, M., 'Allocation under Dictatorship: Research in Stalin's Archives', *Journal of Economic Literature*, 43: 3 (2005).

Harris, J., 'Encircled by Enemies: Stalin's Perceptions of the Capitalist World, 1918–1941', *Journal of Strategic Studies*, 30: 3 (2007).

Harrison, M., 'The Dictator and Defense' in Harrison, Mark (ed.), *Guns and Rubles: The Defense Industry in the Stalinist state* (New Haven, CT, 2009).

Haslam, J., 'The Comintern and the Origins of the Popular Front 1934–1935', *Historical Journal*, 22: 3 (1979).

—— 'Soviet–German Relations and the Origins of the Second World War: The Jury is Still out', *Journal of Modern History*, 79 (1997).

Hauner, M., 'The Soviet Threat to Afghanistan and India, 1938–1940', *Modern Asian Studies*, 15: 2 (1982).

Ingram, E., 'Great Britain and Russia', in Thomson, W. R. (ed.), *Great Power Rivalries* (Columbia, SC, 1999).

Jones, D. R., 'Motives and Consequences of the Red Army Purges, 1937–8', *Soviet Armed Forces Review Annual*, 3 (1979).

Katz, B. G., 'Purges and Production: Soviet Economic Growth, 1929–1940', *Journal of Economic History*, 35: 3 (1975).

Khlevniuk, O., 'The Objectives of the Great Terror, 1937–8', in Cooper, J., Perrie, M., and Rees, E. A. (eds.), *Soviet History, 1917–1953: Essays in Honour of R. W. Davies* (London and New York, 1995).

—— 'The Reasons for the Great Terror: The Foreign Political Aspect', in Pons, S. and Romano, A. (eds.), *Russia in the Age of Wars, 1914–1945* (Milan, 2000).

—— 'Economic Officials in the Great Terror, 1936–38', in Ilic, M. (ed.), *Stalin's Terror Revisited* (London and New York, 2006).

Kocho-Williams, A., 'The Soviet Diplomatic Corps and Stalin's Purges', *Slavic and East European Review,* 86: 1 (2008).

Kuromiya, H., 'Accounting for the Great Terror', *Jahrbücher für Geschichte Osteuropas*, 53 (2005).

—— 'Stalin and his Era', *Historical Journal*, 50: 3 (2007).

LAMMERS, D. N., 'Fascism, Communism and the Foreign Office, 1937–1939' *Journal of Contemporary History*, 6 (1971).

LARGE, J. A., 'The Origins of Soviet Collective Security Policy, 1930–1932', *Soviet Studies*, 30: 2 (1978).

MAIN, S. J., 'The Arrest and "Testimony" of Marshal of the Soviet Union, M. N. Tukhachevsky (May–June 1937)', *Journal of Slavic (formerly Soviet) Military Studies*, 10: 1 (1997).

MANN, R., 'The Foreign Office and the Failure of Anglo-Soviet *Rapprochement*', *Journal of Contemporary History*, 16 (1981).

MCDERMOTT, K., 'Stalinist Terror in the Comintern: New Perspectives', *Journal of Contemporary History*, 30 (1995).

NEILSON, K., ' "Pursued by a Bear": British Estimates of Soviet Military Strength and Anglo-Soviet Relations, 1922–1939', *Canadian Journal of History/Annales canadiennes d'histoire*, 28 (1993).

—— 'A Cautionary Tale: The Metro-Vickers Incident of 1933', in Kennedy, G. and Neilson, K. (eds.), *Incidents and International Relations: Personalities, Perceptions and Power* (Westport, CT, 2002).

—— 'The Defence Requirement Sub-Committee, British Strategic Foreign Policy, Neville Chamberlain and the Path to Appeasement', *English Historical Review*, 118: 477 (2003).

—— 'Arms Control and the Anglo-Soviet Naval Agreement of 1937', in Hamilton, K. and Johnson, E. (eds.), *Arms and Disarmament in Diplomacy* (London and Portland, OR, 2008).

NEVILLE, P., 'Rival Foreign Office Perceptions of Germany, 1936–1939', *Diplomacy and Statecraft*, 13: 3 (2002).

PONS, S., 'The Comintern and the Issue of War in the 1930s: The Debate in March–April 1936', in Narinsky, M. and Rojahn, J. (eds.), *Centre and Periphery: The History of the Comintern in the Light of New Documents* (Amsterdam, 1996).

POZNIAKOV, V., 'The Enemy at the Gates: Soviet Military Intelligence in the Inter-war Period and the Feasibility of Future War, 1921–1941', in Pons, S. and Romano, A. (eds.), *Russia in the Age of Wars, 1914–1945* (Milan, 2000).

RESIS, A., 'The Fall of Litvinov: Harbinger of the German–Soviet Non-Aggression Pact', *Europe–Asia Studies* 52: 1 (2000).

ROBERTS, G., 'The Fall of Litvinov: A Revisionist View', *Journal of Contemporary History*, 27 (1992).

—— 'A Soviet Bid for Coexistence with Nazi Germany, 1935–1937: The Kandelaki Affair', *International History Review*, 16: 3 (1994).

—— 'On Soviet–German Relations: The Debate Continues—A Review Article', *Europe–Asia Studies*, 50: 8 (1998).

—— 'The Fascist War Threat and Soviet Politics in the 1930s', in Pons, S. and Romano, A. (eds.), *Russia in the Age of Wars* (Milan, 2000).

SHAW, L. G., 'Attitudes of the British Political Elite towards the Soviet Union', *Diplomacy and Statecraft*, 13: 1 (2002).

SPAULDING, M. R., *Osthandel and Ostpolitik: German Foreign Trade Policies in Eastern Europe from Bismarck to Adenauer* (Providence, RI, and Oxford, 1997). Chapter 6, section on Soviet Union.

Tillett, L. R., 'The Soviet Role in League Sanctions against Italy, 1935–6', *The American Slavic and East European Review*, 15: 1 (1956).

Thurlow, R. C., 'Soviet Spies and British Counter-Intelligence in the 1930s', *Intelligence and National Security,* 19 (2004).

Uldricks, T., 'The Impact of the Great Purges on the People's Commissariat of Foreign Affairs', *Slavic Review*, 36: 2 (1977).

—— 'A. J. P. Taylor and the Russians', in Martel, G. (ed.), *The Origins of the Second World War Reconsidered: The A. J. P. Taylor Debate after 25 Years* (London and Boston, MA, 1986).

—— 'Soviet Security Policy in the 1930s', in Gorodetsky, G. (ed.), *Soviet Foreign Policy1917–1991: A Retrospective* (London, 1994).

Vaïsse, M., 'La perception de la puissance soviétique par les militaires françaises en 1938', *Revue historique des Armées*, 3 (1983).

—— 'Les militaires français et l'alliance franco-soviétique au cours des anneés 30', in *Forces armées et systeme d'alliances, actes du colloque international d'histoire militaire et d'études de défense nationale, Montpellier, 2–6 septembre 1981*, Vol. III (Paris, 1983).

Watson, D., 'Molotov's Apprenticeship in Foreign Policy: The Triple Alliance Negotiations in 1939', *Europe–Asia Studies*, 52: 4 (2000).

—— 'The *Politburo* and Foreign Policy in the 1930s', in Rees, E. A. (ed.), *The Nature of Stalin's Dictatorship: The Politburo, 1923–1953* (London, 2004).

Watt, D. C., 'Francis Herbert King: A Soviet Source in the Foreign Office', *Intelligence and National Security*, 3: 4 (1983).

—— 'Who Plotted Against Whom? Stalin's Purge of the Soviet High Command Revisited', *Journal of Soviet Military Studies*, 3: 1 (1990).

Wheatcroft, S. G., 'Towards Explaining the Changing Levels of Stalinist Repression in the 1930s Mass Killing', in Wheatcroft, S. G. (ed.), *Challenging Traditional Views* of *Russian History* (New York, 2002).

9

Thunder from the East: The Sino-Japanese Conflict and the European Powers, 1933–1938

The story of the Sino-Japanese conflict had a history of its own, touched but not shaped by European and American reactions to its tortuous course. Yet instability in Asia clearly had implications for Europe. A number of European countries (Britain, France, the Netherlands, Portugal, Germany, Italy, and the Soviet Union), as well as the United States, had interests in China or the South Pacific. For almost all these countries, European events took precedence over East Asian problems. Even for the USSR, an Asiatic as well as a European power, and for Britain, the centre of an empire with imperial interests, the situation in Europe necessarily influenced their perceptions of the Japanese threat. It can be argued that European relations were only marginally affected by the conflict in China, even when from July 1937 it became first a ferocious, and then an undeclared war of attrition. In this sense, the origins of the European war of 1939 and the world war of 1941 can be separately plotted. Paradoxically, it was the Nazi victories of 1940, and above all, the fall of France, that set in train the circumstances that led Japan to expand into South-East Asia, and the Americans to intercede in the Pacific, turning the European war into a global conflict. In another sense, however, because the Soviet Union and Britain had vital interests to defend in the region, their vulnerabilities and responses affected their relations with one another and with a host of other players, influencing not only the balance of power in the Pacific but in Europe as well. Viewed from this perspective, the Sino-Japanese conflict is very much part of the European story well before the outbreak of the war in 1939.

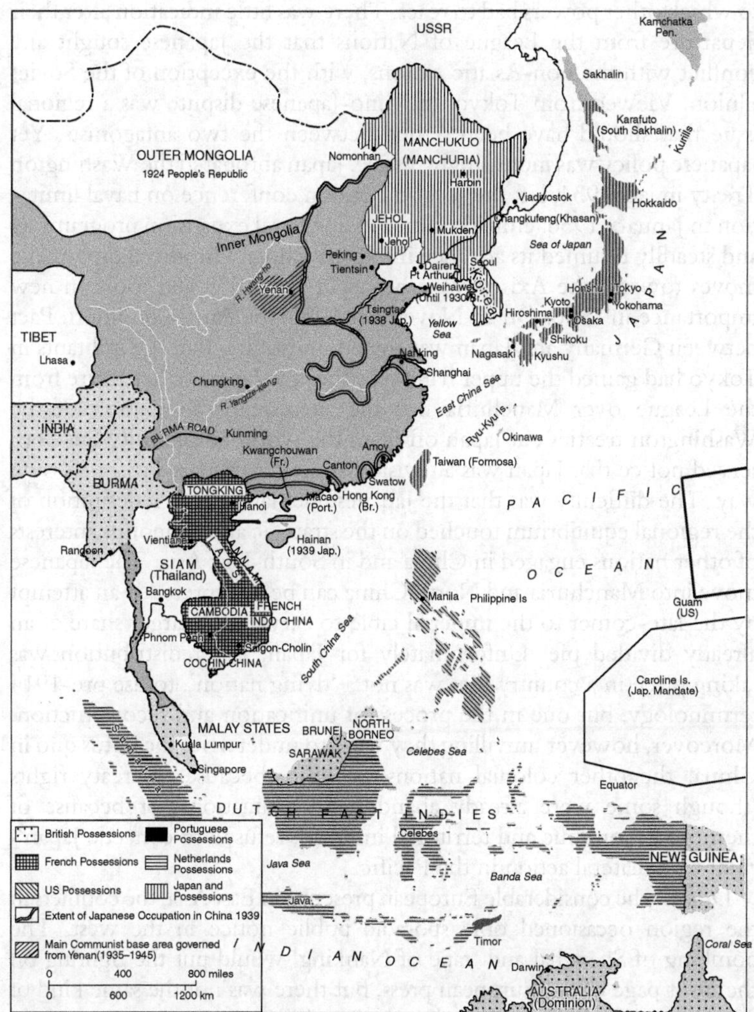

Map 6. East Asia 1931–1939

The European Powers and the Problem of Japanese Ambitions

I

As with the course of events in Europe, it was a revisionist power pursuing an expansionist and aggressive foreign policy that set the agenda to which other powers had to react. There was little indication after their departure from the League of Nations that the Japanese sought any conflict with the non-Asiatic nations, with the exception of the Soviet Union. Viewed from Tokyo, the Sino-Japanese dispute was a regional issue that should have been settled between the two antagonists. Yet Japanese policy was increasingly restive. Japan abrogated the Washington Treaty in late 1934, left the second London conference on naval limitation in January 1936, embarked on a major naval expansion programme, and steadily resumed its advance in North China. Unofficial diplomatic moves towards the Axis powers began in July 1935 and took on new importance in 1936. On 25 November 1936, the Anti-Comintern Pact between Germany and Japan was signed, indicating that the militants in Tokyo had gained the upper hand. Neither the Japanese departure from the League over Manchuria nor the subsequent abrogation of the Washington treaties cut Japan off from the world community but both served notice that Japan was a revisionist power prepared to go its own way. The difficulty was that the Japanese demands for a redefinition of the regional equilibrium touched on the strategic and economic interests of other nations engaged in China and in South-East Asia. The Japanese move into Manchuria and North China can be interpreted as an attempt by the late-comer to the imperial table to carve out a larger share of an already divided pie. Unfortunately for Japan, the redistribution was taking place in a country that was not a 'dying nation', to use pre-1914 terminology, but one in the process of unification and reconstruction. Moreover, however unwilling they were to underwrite the status quo in China, the other colonial nations, whether because of treaty rights (though some were already abandoned), obligations, or because of their own economic and territorial interests, refused to concede Japan's right to unilateral action in the Pacific.

Despite the considerable European presence in East Asia, the conflicts in the region occasioned only sporadic public notice in the west. The bombing of Shanghai and 'rape of Nanking' would put the fighting on the front page of the European press, but there was not the same kind of public reaction as was provoked by the Spanish Civil War. It was mainly in the United States that a major pro-China lobby developed after 1937. Few European statesmen took a sustained interest in Far Eastern affairs; most left much of the daily business of the region to their experts, often men with considerable knowledge of the area. Because of the distances involved, diplomats sometimes could conduct negotiations without the kinds of control exercised over ambassadors stationed closer to home. Even the Soviet ambassador in Nanking had to be reined in when it was felt he had conceded too much to the Chinese. Some ambassadors served for unusually long periods of time: Oskar Trautmann represented Germany in China from 1931 until 1938; Joseph Grew was the American ambassador in Tokyo for ten years from 1932 until 1941. Representatives could call on the expertise of men long resident in the East whose knowledge went far deeper than that which was available at home. Admittedly, such men often suffered from 'localitis'. It was not unusual for contradictory advice to be received from men stationed in China and Japan. There were differences, too, in many foreign ministries, between regional 'experts' cut off from the main streams of diplomatic business, and those serving in other departments for whom East Asian affairs were but a remote part of a far more complex diplomatic picture. In Britain and Germany, for instance, policy-making was marked by inter-ministerial disputes between men with differing financial, economic, or strategic priorities. When East Asian questions rose to the top of the diplomatic agendas, the politicians had to consider other parts of the world as well. The simultaneous assaults on the status quo in Europe and in China made it impossible for either the Soviets or the British to consider the Sino-Japanese conflict in isolation.

Geography and history dictated the Soviet concern with the new course of Japanese foreign policy. The USSR shared a three thousand mile, and much disputed, border with Japan. As Stalin argued in 1936, the danger posed by Japan to the peace was more immediate than that of Germany. The Soviet Far East provided a tempting target for the Japanese military. The army's drive for influence in North China was specifically aimed at the Soviet Union, and there was good reason for the Russians to fear a pre-emptive strike. Moscow was well informed about the debates among the Japanese leadership; among other agents, the well-placed Richard Sorge sent a stream of first-rate intelligence back to military intelligence (GRU), which reached Stalin as well as the Soviet Foreign Ministry. The Soviets could not ignore the powerful position of the military in Tokyo or the open Japanese denunciations of the Soviet Union. A Pacific war would not put the survival of the regime in danger, but the Soviet leadership was in constant fear of a two-front conflict which posed an even greater danger to the USSR than the Allied interventions of 1918–1919. Stalin wanted peace in the Far East until the Soviet Union was militarily strong enough to face its enemies on both fronts. The traditional Tsarist conflict with Japan, quite apart from any revolutionary goals, meant that the Far East was given a higher priority in Soviet foreign policy than was necessary in any other European capital.

The western countries involved in East Asia differed widely in the degree of their engagement in the Sino-Japanese conflict. Britain, the dominant imperial power in the region, was bound to feel its effects. It was a major investor and trader in China and its commercial involvement extended well beyond the concessions in Shanghai, Tientsin, and

Hankow, into the interior of the country. Over half of all foreign investment in Chinese manufacturing was British.[1] British enterprises in Shanghai and elsewhere were well placed to bring pressure at home and were vociferous in their complaints about government inactivity. Until the bombing of Shanghai in 1937, many British traders in the city favoured an agreement with the Japanese, whose discipline, orderly ways, and sensible attitudes contrasted favourably to Chinese indolence and corruption. As with the Americans, the hope of penetrating the vast China market in the future was a constant incentive to protect existing trade. Despite Britain's powerful economic position, its leaders felt unable to defend its multiple interests in either China or in other parts of East Asia, without weakening its position in Europe. The British could not check the Japanese military advance in China with troops or ships. The military intervention of 1927 for the defence of Shanghai would be hard to duplicate. Still the world's leading naval power, the existing fleet could not cover both oceans. Britain was committed through the Nine Power Treaty to uphold Chinese independence and territorial integrity, and while these principles had been compromised, they could not be abandoned without a loss of prestige in China and more generally in Asia. Given their limited military resources, prestige was a key element in maintaining influence in the region. Ultimately Japan's bid for a dominant position in the Pacific would threaten Britain's vast and resource-rich possessions in South-East Asia, and its lines of communication with Australia and New Zealand. The Pacific Dominions and Britain's dependencies expected the mother country to provide for their defence. It was a formidable burden, even without the fears of a two-ocean war that increasingly dominated Britain's strategic thinking. The very safety of India might be put at risk if British rule in South-East Asia was threatened. The country needed access to the raw materials of Burma, Malaya, and Borneo as well as to the Pacific Dominions, if it was to fight a long European war. In a very real sense, Britain's Great Power position in Europe depended on its imperial standing in the Pacific.

Having access to the Japanese diplomatic codes, the British were aware of Japan's political ambitions even after the fighting between China and Japan stopped in May 1933. The British defence chiefs believed that British possessions in Asia were 'dangerously' vulnerable. The Shanghai and Jehol conflicts of 1932–1933 had revealed the weaknesses of the Royal Navy in any attempt to deal with an aggressive

[1] The British share was 54.1% compared to its nearest rival, Japan, at 40.3%. Figures quoted from Chi-Ming Hou, *Foreign Investment and Economic Development in China, 1840–1937* (Cambridge, MA, 1965), 81.

Japan. Work on the Singapore base was restarted in 1933, and the Admiralty laid plans for the building of a two-ocean fleet, but these would take time to complete even if all the necessary funds were made available. The Ethiopian crisis of 1935 brought a new challenge to Britain's imperial sea-lanes. Now facing threats in the Mediterranean and the Atlantic, the viability of the Singapore strategies was put in question but not found wanting in the longer run. As long as Britain was strategically isolated in East Asia, the chiefs of staff wanted to avoid any conflict with Japan. Insofar as Tokyo's advance into the South-West Pacific was 'an inevitable and necessary course', Britain appeared to have a variety of diplomatic options, none really satisfactory. There was general agreement that, given Britain's responsibilities, its resources were over-stretched. Various possibilities were canvassed. There could be an agreement with Japan, the traditional British way of dealing with imperial competition. This was the course favoured by Neville Chamberlain and the Treasury. With no immediate danger of a clash between Britain and Japan, financial and economic arrangements in China could satisfy both powers. Building a two-ocean fleet was expensive. To Chamberlain's satisfaction, an agreement with Tokyo would make Britain far less dependent on American backing in East Asia. Others, officials in the Foreign Office dealing with Far Eastern affairs, and navalists were far more globally and imperially minded. The former underlined the connection between the balance of power in the Far East and in Europe. The latter believed that the navy and the empire were the real sources of British strength and were essential both to keep the peace and win the war. Repeatedly, as chancellor of the exchequer and then as prime minister, Chamberlain favoured a settlement with Japan, even at the expense of relations with Washington, but none of his efforts succeeded in the face of Japanese aggression and American objections to the appeasement of Japan.

The possibility of containment, or at least the maintenance of the existing situation in China, which was backed by many Foreign Office officials, was frustrated not only by events in China, but by uncertainties about American policy, and Washington's clear preference for parallel rather than joint action. Officials repeatedly argued that the safest way to safeguard British interests in the Pacific was to keep in step with the United States, and avoid any initiative that might alienate Washington. 'It may be that in no circumstances could we count on any assistance from the US. But by an alliance with Japan we should forfeit all chance of it,' wrote Alexander Cadogan, the former ambassador to China now serving as deputy under-secretary in the Foreign Office, in May 1937. 'It must be the USA every time I think,' Robert Vansittart, the permanent under-secretary at the Foreign Office, minuted on the same despatch.[2] As the more exposed country, Britain was the more dependent power in the relationship with Washington. After 1935 there was increasing co-operation on naval issues and relations between the two governments undoubtedly improved but there was no joint action and no assurance of American backing should Britain be forced to engage with Japan.

The British had found the Americans frustrating partners. In their estimation, Washington proclaimed the principles of the open door and the independence and territorial integrity of China, while refusing to back their words with concrete actions. The Simon–Stimson quarrel during the Manchurian crisis left bad memories in both capitals; the publication of Stimson's account of the affair in 1936 re-kindled the old animosities. State Department officials disliked Sir John Simon, and the quarrels of 1931 coloured their views of British policy. Vansittart deeply distrusted the Americans and hardly disguised his antipathy. Yet Britain's inability to maintain her position in the Pacific by the use of her own forces when faced by threats in Europe tied London to its 'unwilling and undependable partner'. Whereas during the Manchurian affair the Americans took the lead in suggesting some form of response to Japan's challenge, and the British proved reluctant partners, thereafter, the position was reversed. American non-participation was a critical issue, for some officials believed that the long-term status quo in South-East Asia could only be preserved with American naval support. Without a fleet based in the Pacific and still without a two-ocean navy, only the threat of American naval action would give substance to the British deterrent. Careful diplomacy was needed to balance between Japan and China, without provoking the former or deserting the latter whose resistance was critical in delaying the Japanese advance. It was equally, if not more, difficult to manage relations with the Americans, particularly as President Roosevelt's initiatives too often carried no promise of delivery and could result in Japanese retaliatory action against Britain. The American role in the Pacific restricted British diplomacy more than its abstention from European security affairs.

While the United States had fewer territorial and commercial interests to defend in the region than Britain, it had a moral obligation to defend China's independence and territorial integrity. Since the end of the nineteenth century, the Americans were pledged to the maintenance of the 'open door' in China and this principle, however compromised, maintained its place in American foreign policy priorities.

[2] Quoted in N. Tarling, *Britain, Southeast Asia and the Onset of the Pacific War* (Cambridge, 1996), 13.

This moral presumption in favour of Chinese independence helped to shape Washington's diplomacy in the Far East right up to Pearl Harbor. In addition to Alaska and the Philippines (which was promised independence in 1946), American possessions in the Pacific included Hawaii and numerous islands (Wake, Midway, Guam, and Western Samoa). American trade with Japan, though not at pre-Depression levels, was substantial and far larger than with China. American investment in China was small, well behind that of Japan and Britain. Apart from the Philippines, there were major American investments in Malaya, the Indies, and Thailand (Siam); American oil companies were active in Thailand and in the Dutch East Indies. Large quantities of rubber, tin, and other minerals were imported from Malaya, the Dutch East Indies, and Indochina. Whatever the influence of American commercial interest groups, the political leadership in Washington did not believe that either trade or investment was under immediate threat from the Japanese engagement in China. The American navy, it is true, thought in terms of a potential war with Japan, but only at some indeterminate future date. The fleet had not been built up to treaty limits and Congressional opinion made it difficult to initiate any major rearmament programme.

President Roosevelt was absorbed by domestic problems when he assumed office in 1933; he was prepared to honour the Stimson doctrine of non-recognition, but unwilling to go much further. He adopted the same *ad hoc* pragmatic approach to foreign affairs as he did to domestic questions. He was, above all, a consummate politician with an ear finely tuned to the Congressional sound waves that were, at this juncture, pacific and opposed to intervention in foreign quarrels. Roosevelt's secretary of state, Cordell Hull, cautious by temperament and inclination, placed considerable faith in the ability of mutual trade agreements to keep the peace. Both men were prepared to recognize Japan's post-Manchurian position; neither wanted to 'stir up matters with Japan' by taking up the Chinese cause. While reminding the Japanese of their treaty obligations when they were too flagrantly disregarded, neither the president nor the secretary of state was prepared for action in the Pacific, or was willing to consider the reconstruction of the battered security system in the region. There was, above all, no wish to involve the United States in Britain's quarrels with Japan. The State Department insisted that British and American interests in East Asia were distinct, and preferred, when action was required, to move independently. Frequently annoyed by British airs of condescension (the 'habit of treating us as their seventh dominion'), Roosevelt took special pains not to have his policies seen as the 'tail to the British kite'. This did not prevent the State Department from viewing British moves towards an agreement with Tokyo as destructive of the moral principles for which both governments stood. Nor were Anglo-American relations made easier by American suspicions, not entirely without foundation, that the British saw a partnership in the Far East as the prelude to involving the United States in Europe.

The British might have looked to Moscow for co-operation in containing Japanese expansion. As argued in the previous chapter, though officials took seriously the Soviet role in maintaining the balance of power in East Asia, common interests were not sufficient to bring about a *rapprochement*. British intelligence indicated that the Soviet Union could keep Japan engaged in the north, and defer any move southwards where British interests were engaged. For the most part, it was thought that Britain could benefit from the tensions between Tokyo and Moscow without aligning with either side and remaining detached from their quarrels. The British favoured continuing hostility between Moscow and Tokyo, but not war as Stalin sometimes believed. It was an insurance policy for which few premiums had to be paid. Admittedly, Soviet assistance to Chiang Kai-shek was viewed with mixed feelings, for while hoping that Chinese resistance would continue, neither Britain nor the United States wanted to see a Soviet-dominated Nationalist government.

Other European countries were also threatened by Japan's ambitions. Both France and the Netherlands had colonial possessions in the Pacific to which they attached considerable importance.[3] More was involved than investments and commerce; colonies gave each a special status. Yet neither of these powers could defend their possessions, which had no forces of their own and, in the case of France, were never given the funds needed for minimal self-defence. The French had trading and investment interests in China, well behind Britain, Japan, and the United States, but of sufficient importance to be cherished in a period of financial and export difficulties. There were investments in Shanghai, Tientsin, and Hankow, as well as in southern China where ownership of the only railway that ran from the seaboard to Yunnan put France in a particularly favoured market position. As long as Japan concentrated its attention on Manchuria and North China, the French could breathe easily. During the Manchurian affair, French sympathies lay with Japan rather than with China, whose newly strengthened position was seen as a threat to Indochina, the focus of French concern. One and a half times the size of France and, in myth at least, a 'matchless source of wealth', Indochina was an attractive investment area, despite the current low returns, and was a valuable, though small, protected market for French

[3] Portugal also had possessions in the region as well as in Africa.

goods. Should France be involved in a European war, Indochina would be a useful source of manpower, funds, timber, and minerals. As France began to lose influence in Europe, the empire was fêted as the symbol of great power status. Whatever the official neglect of Indochina, French *amour propre* was engaged in its possession. Yet with only 40,000 troops in Indochina and almost non-existent defences, it was vulnerable to attack. Any Japanese moves in the South China Sea, or rumours of its potential strategic co-operation with Thailand (Siam), rang alarm bells in Indochina and in Paris. The French wanted peace in the Far East but looked in vain to Britain and the United States to provide the defence forces they needed should war come.

As for the Dutch, the economic value and resources of the East Indies was more than sufficient to silence the voices of the few who, worried by the nationalist movements on the islands, argued for giving the colony its independence. It was a common Dutch saying at the time that 'the Indies are the cork which keeps the Netherlands afloat'.[4] With a large indigenous population, a considerable Dutch presence in its civil service (about 20,000 Dutchmen employed in the administration), and a growing post-depression investment estimated to amount to 15.7% of the Dutch national income, the colonial authorities kept a close watch on the Indonesian nationalists, and on any Japanese attempts at the economic penetration of the islands. It was, after all, possession of the East Indies that distinguished the Netherlands from the other small powers of Europe, and buttressed the illusion that it could continue with its traditional policies of neutrality on the continent. Any retreat in the face of an external threat could easily shake the imperial structure, already under pressure from native protest groups. It was anticipated that in any Pacific war Japan would turn its attention to the rich Borneo oil fields. When the European conflicts of 1935–1936 posed the possibility of an unopposed Japanese thrust southward, the Dutch sought a formal guarantee for the independence of the islands from Britain. While admitting that Dutch rule in the East Indies was critical for the safety of Singapore, the nervous British chiefs of staff rejected requests for a public statement of Britain's 'deep interest' in the security of the islands. Such a statement could lead to commitments 'we might not be in a position to fulfil.'[5] While the Dutch waited to see what the British (and Americans) would do, they assured the Japanese of their wish for good relations with Tokyo.

[4] Christopher Thorne, *The Issue of War: States, Societies, and the Far Eastern Conflict of 1941–1945* (London, 1985), 38.

[5] Tarling, *Britain, Southeast Asia and the Onset of the Pacific War*, 32.

Though without colonies in the region, both Germany and Italy were also engaged in Asian affairs. German policy-makers pursued a complicated and much debated policy after the Nazi take-over. Even at the time of the Manchurian affair, the Germans had tried to balance between the two protagonists, and opposed League intervention. After 1933, Germany's expanding investment and trade in China had to be defended, but there were also new business opportunities opening up in Japanese-held Manchuria. The *Reichswehr* and the Economics Ministry favoured the Chinese Nationalists, and concluded a number of agreements securing much-needed raw materials in return for arms. Chiang Kai-shek was encouraged to use retired German officers as his main military advisers. Hitler, some Nazi party leaders, and the new ambassador in Tokyo, Herbert von Dirksen, admired the Japanese challenge to the Anglo–Americans and their defiance of the League. Tokyo's anti-Soviet position, too, fitted well into Hitler's ideological and strategic considerations. But though the German leader was sympathetic to the idea of closer relations with Japan, he was uneasy over the racial dimension, and in any case was unwilling to interfere in matters not of primary interest to him. Neurath and the Wilhelmstrasse continued to follow a policy of 'balance' in the Far East, trying to preserve good relations with both China and Japan. They had a real stake in Chiang's survival and depended on ambassador Oskar Trautmann in Nanking to implement their delicate and complex policy. Dirksen, a Nazi party member anxious to make his name, and far more favourable to a German–Japanese alliance, was more difficult to control. In the background was Joachim von Ribbentrop, Neurath's rival, who, in the summer of 1935, began conversations with the fiery Japanese military attaché in Berlin, Lt. Col. Oshima Hiroshi, who was an admirer of the Nazi movement and deeply hostile towards the Soviet Union. It was Oshima who initiated the negotiations for the Anti-Comintern Pact (25 November 1936) against the opposition of both the Japanese ambassador in Berlin and most of the officials in the Japanese Foreign Ministry, who were unwilling to antagonize either the Russians or the British. The pact was accepted in Tokyo but resistance to any expansion of the ties with Germany was strong.

The Anti-Comintern Pact, as the Soviets knew from their intelligence agents, did not represent any fundamental change in either Japanese or German diplomacy. The pact itself was anodyne; both countries were committed to vigilance against the Communist International. The secret supplementary protocol was more forthright, but carefully framed to safeguard future freedom of action. If one of the parties was attacked without provocation or was threatened by the Soviet Union, the other would not take any measures to relieve its position but would consult together to promote their common interests.

There was also a guarantee, much debated in August 1939, that neither side was to enter into any political treaties with the Soviet Union contrary to the spirit of the pact, without their mutual consent. Both sides had reservations about the treaty. Those in the Japanese army who favoured the pact thought it would warn Chiang Kai-shek that little could be expected from the USSR. The Japanese naval chiefs were hesitant, however, and the Foreign Ministry divided, opponents feared that the treaty would alienate Britain and the United States. In Berlin, the Wilhelmstrasse and the military leadership strongly opposed Ribbentrop's negotiations. His success was a blow to Neurath's prestige, though the latter was able, at first, to prevent any extension of Germany's political obligations to Japan, while managing to assure the Chinese that the new agreement was irrelevant to the Sino-Japanese dispute. The German minister of defence, Blomberg, who neither considered Japan a viable military partner nor believed that a Russo-Japanese war would improve Germany's European position, vehemently opposed strengthening any links between the German and Japanese armies. As the *Wehrmacht* was able to keep the military conversations in its own hands, the Japanese were offered only an agreement on intelligence co-operation (July 1937). Steps were taken to safeguard and extend the army's economic and military ties with China, which received approximately 37% of Germany's total export of arms for 1937.[6] In April 1937, the retired German general, Alexander von Falkenhausen, was appointed Chiang's chief military adviser. By the autumn, there were over seventy German military and other advisers in China, who, to the fury of the Japanese, were engaged in the war against them.

The Anti-Comintern Pact served Hitler's immediate needs. He could use it in the future as a carrot or a stick to induce Britain to enter into an alliance. Though Ribbentrop wanted to extend the pact to include Italy, as well as Poland, Bulgaria, Latvia, and Romania, Hitler took no action, preferring to preserve Germany's current position in the Far East, and avoid making any real choice between Japan and China until it was necessary. In June 1937, H. H. Kung, the Chinese minister of finance, came to Berlin after attending George VI's coronation festivities. His hosts assured him that German policy towards Japan was based on general political considerations and not Far Eastern ones, and that it should be viewed from the standpoint of Germany's struggle against Bolshevism. Hitler remarked on the complementary nature of Sino-German economic interests, and told Kung that Germany had no political aims in the Far East. He informed the finance minister that he

[6] John P. Fox, *Germany and the Far Eastern Crisis, 1931–1938* (Oxford, 1982), 241.

favoured some form of détente between Nanking and Tokyo, and offered German mediation should it be required. All this was to change with the outbreak of the Sino-Japanese war in July 1937 and Hitler's preparations for a move in Europe.

The Italians, who had a concession in the International Settlement in Shanghai, and were represented in the League-appointed Lytton Commission, had opposed sanctions in 1932 and followed a circumspect policy in China where they tried to take advantage of the existing situation without alienating either side. Various military and financial missions were sent to Nanking, and a considerable number of aeroplanes were sold to Chiang Kai-shek. This profitable trade was supposedly stopped in the autumn of 1937, after the Germans had ended their own shipments to the Nationalists. The real turn in Italian policy towards Tokyo resulted from the changes in Mussolini's diplomacy, with the moves towards Berlin after 1935, and the adoption of an anti-British policy during and after the Ethiopian affair. In 1936, Ribbentrop had suggested that Italy join the Anti-Comintern Pact but Mussolini and Ciano turned him down. Mussolini's expanded imperial ambitions, directed against Britain and France, brought Japan back into the Italian picture. Serious exchanges began in the autumn of 1937 when Ciano proposed a bilateral agreement along the lines of the Berlin–Tokyo pact. The move was warmly supported by the Italian navy, which believed this would weaken the Royal Navy in the Mediterranean. The Japanese were cool, but proved more amenable to the idea of an expanded Anti-Comintern Pact that was less overtly anti-British. When Ribbentrop again raised the possibility the Italians were quick to respond. Italy signed the Anti-Comintern Pact on 6 November 1937, consolidating its ties with Germany and hopefully strengthening its position with regard to Britain.

However different their policies might have been, the Europeans and Americans shared certain unspoken, and sometimes spoken, assumptions about the Asiatics. Contemporaries talked of the differences between 'East' and 'West', and were highly sensitive to what is currently known as the 'clash of civilizations'. There were exceptions, but many western diplomats believed that Asian societies were inferior to those of the West and would progress only in so far as they adopted western ways. Such assumptions account for the patronizing attitudes taken towards the Chinese who were, according to perceptions at that time, at an early stage of modern nation-building and industrialization, and whose government was riven by internal conflicts. When asked by Chiang Kai-shek what was wrong with his country, an admittedly embarrassed Sir Alexander Cadogan replied that, 'What was wrong with China was that there was something wrong with the

Chinese—something at least that did not conform to western standards and made them unable properly to adjust [to] western standards.'[7] Admittedly, many, both in Britain and the United States, saw the Nationalist Government in Nanking as a progressive force for good, despite the reports of corruption, factionalism, and cruelty that filtered through to the West. Japan was acknowledged as the more modern and enterprising of the two nations, but ethnocentric and racial views led to an underestimation of Japan's capacity to mobilize its society to fight a modern war. This negative image was based on national stereotypes that were common currency in western circles. Thus, although Japan's armed services were admired for their high morale and exemplary discipline, there was, at the same time, criticism of their lack of tactical flexibility and technological backwardness. In 1935, the British naval attaché, Captain Guy Vivian, reported that 'I have to strain my imagination to the utmost to believe that these people are capable of springing a technical surprise of any importance on us in war.'[8] The Japanese army was judged as in no way comparable to either Soviet or western forces and the quality of its navy downgraded. In Japan, meanwhile, particularly in naval circles, anti-British as well as anti-American feeling intensified. Britain incurred a good deal of the blame for the Japanese failure to achieve naval parity at the London naval conferences and was seen as the main obstacle to Japanese ascendancy in China.

Similar attitudes coloured relations between the white colonial élites and the native populations in many of the European dependencies. In only a few of them was there any sense of partnership between Europeans and Asians; it was not at all clear that the Europeans would be able to enlist the support of the peoples of South-East Asia against an invasion by another Asiatic nation. The racial factor proved to be a two-edged sword. The Europeans were acutely conscious of the need to maintain their prestige in the 'East'. By acting as 'bystanders with crossed arms', the *Quai d'Orsay* warned in May 1933, the western powers were 'diminishing their prestige and facilitating the elimination of the white race from a domain where the latter has still made prodigious efforts and realized a great achievement'.[9] As might have been anticipated, the Nazis, whatever their admiration for Japan's actions over Manchuria, had considerable difficulty in dealing with the 'yellow races'. The

[7] Quoted in Wm. Roger Louis, *British Strategy in the Far East, 1919–1939* (Oxford, 1971), 234.

[8] Quoted in Antony Best, 'Constructing an Image: British Intelligence and Whitehall's Perception of Japan, 1931–1939', *Intelligence and National Security*, 11: 3 (1996), 413.

[9] Quoted in John Dreifort, *Myopic Grandeur: The Ambivalence of French Foreign Policy towards the Far East, 1919–1945* (Kent, OH, and London, 1991), 95.

Nuremberg racial laws of 1935 were carefully drawn so as to avoid inflaming Japanese sensibilities, but with a great deal of difficulty and hesitation. Hitler, who did not sever longstanding German ties to China until 1938, and whose attitude towards Japan remained ambivalent, continued to refer to the 'innate superiority' of the white man and gave little consideration to Japan's military capabilities. A few weeks after the Japanese attack on Pearl Harbor, he regretted 'the loss of a whole continent... with the white race the loser'.[10] The Japanese were to invoke the twin concepts of anti-western imperialism and racial solidarity in their subsequent calls for a 'new order in East Asia'. Given the record of the European imperial powers, it could well have been a potent Japanese propaganda weapon.

II

Whatever happened in the Far East would depend on what happened in China. At first the Pacific struggle was between Japan and China, both Asiatic powers though of a different order of economic and military development. For the most part, the course of events between 1933 and 1937 was driven not by the external situation but by the domestic politics of each country. The Tangku truce of 31 May 1933, which Chiang Kai-shek had no choice but to accept, had ended the earlier bout of Sino-Japanese fighting, but left the initiative in Japanese hands. It confirmed Japan's possession of Manchuria and, through the creation of a demilitarized zone south of the Great Wall, separated the 'four eastern provinces' from the rest of China. With Japanese attention primarily focused on the reorganization of Manchukuo into an economic powerhouse, there was a lull in military activity.

In Tokyo, the foreign minister, Hirota Koki (1933–1936, 1937–1938), a basically pragmatic but weak and vacillating figure, was probably neither militaristic nor dominated by the military. On taking office he was prepared to negotiate a permanent peace with the Chinese based on the recognition of Manchukuo, in return for the cessation of any further Japanese military action in China. As an ex-diplomat with considerable foreign experience, Hirota was aware of the dangers of isolation and anxious to settle with all the main powers, based on their acceptance of Japan's new position in the Pacific. On 17 April 1934, a Foreign Ministry spokesmen, Amau Eiji, issued a statement declaring that it was Japan's 'mission' to maintain the peace and order in East Asia, and that other nations were expected to accept the changed situation in Asian affairs. Foreigners were warned against any form of political or

[10] H. Trevor-Roper (ed.), *Hitler's Table Talk* (London, 1953), 181.

economic activity in China, even under the name of technical or financial assistance. The Amau declaration was a simultaneous warning to China, and to foreign nations, that Japan was now the major player in China. None of the western powers, in spite of Chinese representations, were prepared to take up the challenge implicit in what was seen as an 'Asian Monroe Doctrine'. Whatever their misgivings, they accepted Japanese assurances that there was no intention of infringing the rights of western nations in China. Hirota lacked the determination to carry out his programme. The Manchurian crisis had permanently eroded the position of the civilians in the government, and the influence of the Foreign Ministry. Though the formal structure of the state remained intact, there had been a transfer of power from its traditional base into the hands of the more radicalized sections of the army and navy, which were at odds with each other and each, in turn, divided into different factions. No single leader emerged to provide unity of direction. This was partly the consequence of the singular position of the emperor, but was also the result of an ethos which discouraged assertions of individual authority. The Foreign Ministry, itself, was a divided house. Diplomats tended to be executants rather than policy makers, often choosing between different lines posed by the military.

In looking at Sino-Japanese relations, it is possible to differentiate between the years 1933–1935 and 1936–1937. In the earlier period, a settlement seemed possible; in the latter period, attitudes hardened and the grounds for compromise almost disappeared. In 1933, Chiang Kai-shek, the *Kuomintang*'s (KMT) most powerful political and military leader, would have welcomed a permanent peace. Devious, subtle, resourceful, and above all tenacious, Chiang led a group of 'appeasers' or 'gradualists' who believed that China needed a period of calm to complete the process of political unification, and who favoured an accommodation with Japan. Chiang reasoned that China would eventually be saved by a war between Japan and one of the other Great Powers, and that the resulting changes in the enemy's country 'will give our nation a ray of hope in our desperate condition'.[11] The views of such 'appeasers' were contested by the 'internationalists', men such as T. V. Soong, Chiang's brother-in-law and finance minister, and the Chinese ambassadors in all the major powers, who wanted closer relations with the West to make possible a policy of economic resistance to Japan's expansionism. Despite Soong's efforts to raise western loans, in September 1933 the majority of the KMT leadership adopted Chiang's gradualist strategy—'compromise in order to preserve the whole'. Apart

[11] Quoted in Youli Sun, *China and the Origins of the Pacific War, 1931–1941* (New York, 1993), 43.

from the actual recognition of Manchukuo, or the cession of territories to Japan, the Nationalists were prepared to make further concessions to achieve peace. While imposing his will on the KMT, Chiang also tried to extend his control over the remaining dissident warlords and began, with the help of General Hans von Seeckt, the former commander-in-chief of the *Reichswehr*, to reorganize his army in preparation for a new campaign against the Chinese Communist Party (CCP). In the autumn of 1934, he decisively defeated the Red Army, and forced the routed CCP to leave Kiangsi on its 5,000 mile 'Long March' to Shensi, in the extreme north-west of China. Without a politically and economically viable nation, Chiang had every inducement to work out a *modus vivendi* with Japan.

The early exchanges between the two governments were cordial and hopeful. Despite many ups and downs, the talks continued right up to the summer of 1935. It was, perhaps, because the negotiations were so promising that the leaders of the Japanese field armies (the Kwantung and Tientsin armies) became impatient after two years of inaction, and began their campaign to promote autonomy movements in North China. They intended to create a number of autonomous regimes under Japanese tutelage, separated from the rest of China, which would act as a buffer zone against the Soviet Union. They sought, too, to establish a protectorate in Inner Mongolia that directly threatened Russian interests. By June 1935, a number of treaties were concluded that left the local North China warlords in place, but cut most of their links with Nanking. By the end of the year, proposals for an autonomous region were on the Tokyo–Nanking negotiating table. The resumption of military action was hardly welcome news to those in Tokyo who were hoping for improved relations with Nanking, but the cabinet approved the treaties and Hirota accepted a succession of military *fait accompli*, undermining Chiang's authority. Hirota nonetheless continued with his peace efforts. He was authorized to negotiate a friendship treaty with the Nanking government, based on the 'Three Principles': China was to end its reliance on Europe and America, prevent any conflict between Manchukuo and the neighbouring provinces, and join with Japan in a common defence against the spread of Communist influence in the areas bordering on Outer Mongolia. The army inroads into North China, and the peace talks, proceeded simultaneously.

Chiang, disregarding demands from some KMT politicians for a policy of resistance, was prepared to negotiate, but tied further talks to Japan's recognition of China's independence and territorial integrity. He offered the Japanese military co-operation against the Soviet Union and improved economic and cultural relations, but also sought British and

American diplomatic assistance in Tokyo. Neither government would go beyond separate verbal protests; the Americans were reluctant to act at all. Chiang needed the Japanese agreement before he could move against the CCP. He was faced, however, with rising anti-Japanese feeling in China, and increased opposition to his policies, particularly after the change in Comintern tactics when it appeared that the CCP might make a bid for the ending of the civil war and support the creation of a 'united front' against Japan. The continued harassment of the Chinese by the Kwantung field army around Peking and Tientsin sparked a huge demonstration in Peking in December 1935 that spread to all the main Chinese cities. In May 1936, a National Salvation Association was created, linking the various opposition groups and demanding that the KMT 'resist Japan first'. Some of the Salvationists considered the Soviet Union to be China's most reliable ally, not because of any ideological preference, but because of Russia's geographic position and its age-old conflict with the Japanese.

Though an uneasy peace was maintained, continuing Japanese army activity in North China meant that there could be no freezing of the status quo. In 1936 and 1937, the diplomatic situation deteriorated. In Tokyo, divisions within the army climaxed in an abortive putsch of young officers on 26 February 1936; the emperor had to intervene, and loyal military and naval forces were used to crush the revolt. Though unsuccessful in its attack on those who had taken a more global approach to Japanese concerns, the attempted *coup* revealed the strength of nationalist feeling in Japan and the power of the military. The revolt led to the fall of the government and opened the way for the 'total mobilization faction' or 'control faction' to take command. This faction was dedicated to the creation of a militarized Japan and the establishment of a self-sufficient economic bloc in East Asia, as opposed to the fiercely anti-Communist army group that favoured an immediate war against the Soviet Union. The 'control faction' put into operation the long-term planning thought necessary for the eventual war against Russia. The Japanese economy was transformed, with massive increases in military expenditure and heavy industry. Divisions both within the army, and between the army and navy, continued even as the militarization programme was put in place. Preparation for an extended war in the future would require a period of peace, but there was to be no abandonment of the position already won in China. When Hirota again returned to the Foreign Ministry in 1936, he adopted a sharper line towards the Nationalists.

At the same time, the Chinese, too, became less forthcoming about offering any further concessions in North China. In September 1936, an incident at Fengt'ai', a key railway junction just south of Peking, led to the defeat of the local warlord who, with considerable local support, had tried to resist the imposition of Japanese control. This left only one remaining rail link from North China to the south, at Lukouchiao, the scene of a far more explosive incident in July 1937. Trouble also broke out in Mongolia, where an unauthorized Japanese–Mongolian army moved into the neighbouring province of Suiyuan. The attack was successfully repulsed, giving an important psychological boost to the anti-Japanese movement. However much Chiang may have wanted an agreement with Tokyo, he had to deal with the powerful opposition from both within and outside the KMT. Chiang continued to temporize, preferring to defeat the Communists before facing Japan.

III

It is against this background of Japanese action and the toughening of the Chinese mood, that the changing Soviet role in China must be assessed. For the Soviet Union, there was always the danger of an unwanted war with Japan; the authorities in Tokyo had been vociferous in their anti-Soviet pronouncements, and Moscow was kept informed of Japanese army hopes for a pre-emptive strike against the USSR. In the background was the difficult European situation, and Litvinov's vain attempts to create a common front with France and Britain against Hitler. There were, as elsewhere, divided counsels on how to handle the Japanese. Litvinov was prepared to appease Japan in the interests of creating a bloc in Western Europe against Nazi Germany, which he regarded as the more dangerous enemy. He reduced the influence of those officials in the Ministry who advocated a strong line against Japan, and sought to court the moderates in the Japanese army command. His efforts at appeasement were opposed by the Comintern leaders, Karl Radek and Bukharin (soon to fall victim to Stalin's purges), who nourished illusory hopes of an internal Japanese revolution. He was also opposed by his well-placed rival, Vyacheslav Molotov, who was prepared to appease Germany but wanted to stand up to Japan. Stalin allowed Litvinov to negotiate the sale of the Chinese Eastern Railway (CER) to the Japanese, in order to win a breathing space. The negotiations, lasting almost two years, were punctuated by frequent frontier incidents and constant worries that the extremists in the Japanese army would gain the upper hand in Tokyo. Litvinov's hopes that the sale might smooth the way to further negotiations were not without substance. In January 1935, the Japanese suggested that the sale might be followed by the negotiation of a non-aggression pact if the USSR would withdraw their forces from their Far Eastern border. Litvinov was prepared to explore this offer, but no progress was made. The revived Japanese military campaign in North China and Outer Mongolia cancelled out the favourable atmosphere created by the completion of the sale of the CER on 23 March 1935, after a total of fifty-six meetings. Responding to the Kwantung field army's advances, Litvinov appealed for joint protests from Britain and the United States but with no success. Mongolian troops drove the Kwantung army back in the autumn of 1935, and again in the following year. The government of Outer Mongolia appealed to Moscow for support and a protocol of mutual assistance was concluded in March 1936. The Russians preferred to leave Outer Mongolia within China, but to utilize its forces for Soviet defence. In the interview with an American journalist described earlier, Stalin insisted that Japan rather than Germany was the primary danger to peace.

Given the situation in Europe, Stalin and Litvinov tried to avoid an open confrontation with Japan. While they believed that Hirota was pacifically inclined, they knew that he had to contend with warring factions in Tokyo, and anticipated a 'trail of zig-zags' in Japanese policy towards Moscow. Having shown their determination to check Japanese aggression in Mongolia, the Soviets hoped that Japan would be deterred from further action and might seek an agreement in order to have a freer hand in China. While the Soviet Union could hardly regard a Japanese victory over the Chinese with equanimity, the continuing Sino-Japanese tension was very much to Russia's advantage. Through excellent intelligence reports the Russians were fully aware of Chiang's efforts to secure a settlement with Hirota; Litvinov was prepared to encourage Chinese resistance. He moved cautiously, wary of being trapped by the Chinese into a Russo-Japanese conflict from which only Chiang Kai-shek would benefit. Chiang's determination to wipe out the Chinese Communists posed another set of problems for Moscow. While primarily concerned with Russian security, Stalin could not and would not allow the destruction of the CCP. Stalin's relations with Mao Tse-tung and the CCP had long been difficult, for he had previously discounted the possibility of an early successful Socialist revolution in China; Mao believed, on the contrary, that a revolution, based on co-operation between peasants and workers was possible and that Chiang could be effectively challenged. The physical distance and lack of contact between Moscow and Wayaobao in northern Shensi, where the CCP was first quartered, gave the party an unusual degree of independence. In essence, Stalin and Mao had different interests in mind: Stalin's primary concern was with the USSR, Mao's was with the preservation of his own power, and the CCP and its triumph in China. The Comintern's adoption of the 'united front tactics' in April 1935 brought these differences to the forefront of their relationship.

Recently released selected items from Chinese and Soviet sources have fuelled the on-going debate about the degree of Mao's independence from Moscow in the 1930s, which remains an historical minefield. The original 'united front' concept, adopted for the Far East, did not apply to Chiang Kai-shek, his armies, or the KMT. After many months of discussion following the end of the 7th Comintern Congress, the CCP delegation in Moscow finally agreed, possibly as late as December 1935, to include Chiang in an anti-Japanese front. But communication problems made it nearly impossible to transmit the new policy line to the CCP leadership in their remote headquarters at Wayaobao. It was not until late 1935 that Mao learned of the 'united front' line but possibly not the post-Congress decisions regarding the inclusion of Chiang Kai-shek. Though hardly welcome, the Comintern decision was accepted, and the CCP duly called for a united anti-Japanese national front, but excluded the Nationalists. Encouraged by splits within the KMT, the Chinese Communists had no intention of abandoning their anti-Chiang campaign. Moscow was by this time considering an agreement with the Nanking government, and in late May 1936 the Comintern dropped the idea of a struggle for Soviet power in China. With radio communication restored in June 1936, the Comintern learned that the CCP leadership, while accepting the united front line, was continuing its fight against Japan and Chiang Kai-shek. This was a complete misreading of Moscow's new strategy. In a letter personally approved by Stalin, and radioed to the CCP in August 1936, the Comintern secretariat specifically ordered their Chinese colleagues to stop fighting the Nationalists, and concentrate instead on the anti-Japanese offensive: 'We think that it is incorrect to place Chiang Kai-shek in the same category as the Japanese occupiers.'[12] The Comintern outlined the terms which the CCP must offer when negotiating with the KMT, taking care to assure the CCP that its instructions presupposed the strengthening of the party and the Red Army, in every possible way. After considerable discussion the CCP *Politburo* agreed to issue an open letter to the KMT calling for the formation of an 'all Chinese united government of national defence'. Secret talks were opened with the KMT, but no progress was made.

The differences between Moscow and the CCP came to the fore when there was a rebellion of the south-western warlords against Chiang Kai-shek. The CCP welcomed the revolt and offered to support

[12] Alexander Dallin and F. I. Firsov (eds.), *Dimitrov and Stalin, 1934–1943: Letters from the Soviet Archives* (New Haven, CT, and London, 2000), 104.

the rebellion only to be thwarted in their resolve by the warlords' decision to settle with Chiang. The Comintern strongly disapproved of the rebels who were dividing the Chinese anti-Japanese movement at a critical moment. Similarly, the CCP was warned to be careful of the 'Young Marshal', Chang Hsueh-liang, the head of the north-eastern army who had been recruited by Chiang Kai-shek to fight the Reds, but who was in contact with the CCP. In the autumn of 1935 the Chinese Communists had approached General Yang Hu-ch'eng, the head of the north-western army, to join an anti-Japanese front. In February and March 1936, they began to cultivate Chang, whose large army had been driven out of Manchuria by the Japanese, and who was more interested in fighting Japan than in confronting the Communists. Talks were held in Yenan in April 1936, and an agreement was reached, but Chang demanded that Chiang Kai-shek be included in the united front. Desperately needing Chang's assistance, the CCP leadership agreed to 'compel' Chiang to fight Japan, and again entered into endless but unsuccessful negotiations with the Nationalists in Shanghai. Further talks between the KMT and CCP representatives in the summer and autumn of 1936, demanded by the Comintern, proved equally fruitless. On 24 October, the (Chinese) Red Army launched its western campaign but the attack had to be abandoned almost immediately due to the successful resistance of the KMT armies. Even at this date, however, Moscow was apparently still considering plans to arm the CCP, and was encouraging the CCP's approaches to Yang and Chang. Chinese sources, if correctly reported, suggest that Stalin was following two contradictory policies throughout 1936, negotiating with Chiang and promoting the united front strategy in China, but prepared to arm the CCP and support its efforts to establish a Communist-led buffer state in China's north-west.[13] If Chiang reached a settlement with Tokyo, (the Sino-Japanese talks were continuing), an armed Chinese Red Army and a base in north-west China near to the USSR would provide a valuable defence against the KMT. The KMT armies were a better option, but if that tactic failed, Moscow would fall back on the CCP.

The complexities of the situation in China were due to suspicions on all sides, as well as Chiang Kai-shek's continuing determination to destroy the CCP. There was, moreover, little trust between Nanking and Moscow. It was only after the Japanese renewed their campaign in

[13] I have followed the account in John W. Garver, 'The Soviet Union and the Xian Incident', *Australian Journal of Chinese Affairs*, 26 (1991), 146. For the controversy on this point, see Michael M. Sheng and John W. Garver, 'New Light on the Second United Front: An Exchange', *Chinese Quarterly*, 129 (1992), 149–183. For a very different interpretation, see Chang Jung and Jon Halliday, *Mao: The Unknown Story* (London 2006), 184–189.

North China in mid-1935 that Chiang became seriously interested in a mutual assistance pact with the USSR, and intimated to the Soviet ambassador, Dmitrii Bogomolov, that he was prepared to open contacts with the CCP. Bogomolov was cautious and Litvinov cool about Chiang's approach, the latter because he did not want trouble with Japan at a time of difficulty in Europe. The talks continued throughout the winter of 1935–1936. As the Soviet Union's security position in Europe deteriorated, Moscow became more receptive to the idea of a deal with Chiang. The Russians were willing to supply arms to the KMT and were prepared to offer a non-aggression pact, but not the mutual security pact that the Nationalists wanted. While Chiang continued to negotiate with the Japanese, the Russians remained uneasy, fearing that the Sino-Russian talks might be used to secure better terms from Tokyo. Changing circumstances during 1936 drew the two countries together. On the Chinese side, the talks with Japan did not prosper and rising nationalist feeling in both countries made compromise impossible. By the autumn of 1936, relations between Nanking and Tokyo were extremely tense, and Chiang decided on a new bid for a secret military treaty with Moscow. On the Russian side, the signing of the Anti-Comintern Pact in November, and the fear that the Chinese would join the Soviet Union's two enemies (as the Japanese suggested to Chiang), made the Soviets more receptive to the KMT bid. Moscow was still cautious, wanting to know precisely what Chiang intended, but also anxious to proceed and willing to bring pressure on the CCP to come to terms with the Nanking government. In early December 1936, formal negotiations began. The Soviets offered a non-aggression pact and loans for the purchase of Soviet military equipment. The KMT representatives, fearing that Moscow might try to manoeuvre China into a conflict with Japan without its own involvement, continued to demand a mutual security pact. Both sides, however, were ready to co-operate against Japan. It proved impossible to disassociate the Nanking–Moscow talks from the conflict between the KMT and the CCP. As relations between the latter two became increasingly fraught, it was difficult for Stalin to pursue the Nanking agreement without bringing the CCP into line.

It was Chiang's attempt to crush the CCP that sparked the bizarre incident in Sian in December 1936 when he was arrested by warlord generals Chiang Hsueh-liang and Yang Huch'eng. In the previous month Chiang Kai-shek had flown to Sian to convince the two generals quartered there to move their troops against the Communists. Furious at their refusal, he sent his own men against the Communists only to be defeated. Without any choice, he returned to Sian and issued an ultimatum to the dissident generals. Chang and Yang placed him under arrest and appealed to the CCP to send a delegation to Sian. It is still not clear whether the arrest was done with the knowledge of Mao and the CCP. They certainly reacted positively to the news. Mao, in a moment of exaltation, appears to have hoped for Chiang's execution. The CCP radioed Moscow for instructions. Stalin, however, took extreme alarm when the news reached Moscow. The CCP was told that Chang's actions endangered the unity of the anti-Japanese front and could only promote Japan's invasion of China. The party was instructed to seek a peaceful ending to the incident providing that Chiang Kai-shek would fulfil four conditions. These were to reform his government to include all the anti-Japanese movements, to guarantee the rights of the Chinese people, to end the policy of suppressing the Red Army and co-operate with it to resist Japan and, finally, to co-operate with countries sympathetic to the Chinese resistance to Japanese imperialism, but not to advance the slogan 'unite with the Soviet Union'. Behind the Comintern order was Stalin's fear that Chiang Kai-shek would believe that Moscow had a hand in his arrest and was working in partnership with Chang. Chiang's kidnapping, if engineered by the USSR, would appear as particularly provocative at a time when the Sino-Soviet negotiations were bearing fruit. And if the negotiations with the Nanking government failed, the Soviet Union would be left isolated in the Far East. Further, if Chiang Kai-shek was eliminated, it was possible that he would be succeeded by a more pro-Japanese and anti-Communist leader.

The subsequent negotiations between CCP and KMT were conducted mainly on the basis of the Comintern instructions. It appears that the KMT negotiator agreed to CCP terms and that Chiang gave his oral consent to the Communist terms in a general fashion, but insisted that he would negotiate with Chou En-lai only if allowed to return to Nanking. Chang felt betrayed by the CCP, which had led him to believe that Moscow would support an anti-Japanese regime in north-west China. Whatever the reasons, Chiang was released and he and Chang returned to Nanking on Christmas Day 1936. On their arrival, Chang was promptly arrested, and while subsequently released, his army was later brought under Chiang Kai-shek's control.[14] The latter's reputation soared as a consequence of his imprisonment and release. Supposedly converted to the anti-Japanese cause, he was

[14] For an entirely different view of what happened at Sian and the events leading up to it, see Jung Chang and Jon Halliday, *Mao: The Unknown Story*, 181–196 for discussion. I adhere, at the time of writing, to the Garver view and Jonathan Haslam's admittedly earlier account in *The Soviet Union and the Threat from the East, 1933–41* (London, 1992), 70–87, but further evidence from either the Russian or Chinese sources may lend support to the Chang–Halliday thesis.

regarded as indispensable to the united front and victory. Mao accepted the Comintern directive, though he felt that the Soviets were misguided to trust Chiang Kai-shek.

The next steps pointed to a possible resolution of the civil war. A new government was created in Nanking, the anti-Communist campaign was halted, and talks with the CCP begun. Chiang, now in a stronger position, proved a reluctant and tough negotiator, demanding a reduction in the Communist forces and a change in Red Army tactics. The Chinese Communists fought hard to protect their position, hoping that their party would expand its popular base and push to the left. The Comintern leaders, anxious about Mao's ultimate intentions, repeatedly prompted the CCP along the path of conciliation. Only slow progress was made in the KMT–CCP talks during the first half of 1937. The KMT did not endorse the united front until September 1937—after the first skirmishes of what became the Sino-Japanese war. If there was much to be settled and little love lost between Chiang and Mao, the civil war appeared to be suspended.

Stalin sought to buy protection for the USSR at the lowest possible cost. In the last analysis, there was no question of abandoning the CCP, but the Nanking government offered a better defence against future Japanese aggression than the CCP army in China. The USSR was still in an exposed position in China. The danger from Japan to its eastern borders remained. The Russians were cautious about supplying the Chinese and were wary of any attempt by Chiang to set off a Soviet–Japanese war. The Soviet situation in the summer of 1937 allowed little room for belligerency. The Spanish Civil War had driven the USSR into diplomatic isolation in Europe, and its hopes for a collective front against either Nazi Germany or Japan had diminished almost to vanishing point. The illusion that the Americans would back the Soviet Union in the Far East, as Litvinov had hoped, had to be abandoned. At home, the purges of the Red Army left the USSR temporarily vulnerable, even though the Soviet Far Eastern Army was less badly affected than the military elsewhere. The disruption in the army's command structure reduced its efficiency at a time when Japan was increasing the size of their garrisons in Manchuria. Soviet weakness, Moscow believed, could well tempt the Japanese army radicals. Supporting China was the least dangerous and costly way to buy protection.

IV

British thinking about the Far East was plagued by uncertainty about the nature and extent of Japanese ambitions, about the stability of China, and about what could be expected from the United States. Decisions about the

Pacific were repeatedly overshadowed by the crises in Europe. Britain could not simultaneously fight three major enemies (Germany, Italy, and Japan) on its own. Could it even fight two without assistance? How to prevent such a situation from developing preoccupied its leaders right up to, and after, the outbreak of war. Policy-makers explored a number of options, all intended to maintain a status quo already upset by Japan's actions. Was it better to accept the existing situation in the Far East and trust that Japan would confine her ambitions to Manchuria and northern China, or was it necessary to prepare for a further Japanese advance in central and south China? Would an improvement in relations with Japan, or the strengthening of China, contribute more to the stabilization of the region? Should Britain's efforts be directed to conciliating Japan, or to deterring her by building up the Singapore base, enlarging the Pacific fleet, and seeking American (or even Soviet) co-operation in the interim? Finally, and far from the least important problem: how far could Britain pursue its own policies without the approval or participation of the United States? Encouragingly, in mid-1935, the Japanese showed every indication of wanting to conclude agreements with Britain and the United States but there was considerable unease about their ultimate intentions.

The British wanted a diplomatic solution to the Japanese problem, but no clear or consistent strategy emerged. Uncertainties about what was happening in China, political shifts in Tokyo, and the unwillingness of the United States to act in tandem, added to the difficulties of implementing even a do-nothing policy. There were continuing hopes that Russo-Japanese tensions would prevent Japan from moving southwards where Britain's interests were concentrated. The Foreign Office, only one of the interested departments, backed the least adventurous option, maintaining the status quo by keeping the lines open to both Japan and China, and discouraging any agreement between them which would be to Britain's disadvantage. Such a passive policy hardly suited either the Treasury or Board of Trade, each of which preferred a political arrangement with Japan that would make economic co-operation possible, and smooth the way for a rearmament programme that would allow Britain to concentrate on Europe. Chamberlain's antipathy towards Roosevelt and the Americans coloured his views. The chancellor of the exchequer believed that an agreement with Japan would make American assistance in the Far East unnecessary. The Foreign Office argued, on the contrary, that unless backed by the Americans, 'Britain must eventually be done for in the Far East' and was unwilling to risk American displeasure by settling with Japan.[15]

[15] *DBFP*, 2nd ser., Vol. IX, No. 238, footnote 2, note by Vansittart.

It was the American decision to placate the powerful silver lobby in Congress that provided Chamberlain and the Treasury with an opportunity for intervention. In June 1934, Roosevelt signed the Silver Purchase Act, requiring the government to buy silver until it reached one-fourth of the country's monetary reserve, or until its price reached $1.39 on the world market. Within three months, Chinese silver exports had increased sevenfold and Nanking was imploring the Americans for relief. Henry Morgenthau, the highly influential Treasury secretary, backed a substantial loan to China. The State Department, worried by Japanese hostility towards any unilateral American action, suggested international co-operation. Roosevelt reacted coolly to both proposals; he was unwilling to challenge the silver bloc and felt that China should learn to stand on its own feet rather than seek foreign assistance. The Chinese went hunting for financial assistance in London, but were given little satisfaction. In December 1934, the British banks in China responded positively to a Chinese request for a credit that would allow Nanking to control the exchanges. The banks turned to London for diplomatic underwriting. Despite doubts about the practicality of the Chinese proposals, the Treasury seized the opportunity to solicit Japanese co-operation in strengthening the Nationalist economy. T. V. Soong, the president of the Bank of China, took over the negotiations for a £20 million loan and found the Treasury and Board of Trade co-operative. The Foreign Office, convinced that Japan was ready to embark on a forward policy in China, felt that Britain should avoid any financial action.

As always in London, when faced with conflicting views, a cabinet subcommittee was established. It was to consider the Chinese loan and the financial rehabilitation of China. A majority preferred to leave it to the Chinese to make concrete suggestions before reaching any decision. Unknown to the Foreign Office, the Treasury and Board of Trade had already decided to send out financial experts to China in preparation for a big trade drive and a policy of co-operation with Japan in under-writing China's finances. On 4 June 1935, the cabinet approved the Treasury plan to send Sir Frederick Leith-Ross, the government's chief economic adviser, to the Far East. Leith-Ross's plan was to use British recognition of Manchukuo as bait for Japanese participation in a loan to China. China experts in London were hardly sanguine about the idea; one official claimed that to 'undertake the rehabilitation of China is like trying to pin apple jelly to the wall'.[16] Washington was cool, if not positively cold, and Leith-Ross travelled to Asia via Canada in the absence of an

[16] *DBFP*, 2nd ser., Vol. XX, No 329, footnote 5.

invitation to visit the American capital. In Tokyo, Leith-Ross found the Japanese uniformly discouraging. Having accomplished nothing, he went on to China where his activities generated a stream of complaints from the irate Japanese. In terms of Anglo-Japanese co-operation, the Leith-Ross mission badly misfired. A positive British policy in China was fundamentally incompatible with a *détente* in Anglo-Japanese relations, though Chamberlain was singularly slow in recognizing the fact. In November 1935, faced with financial catastrophe, the Nanking government acted on its own, without a British or international loan. The banknotes of the three major government banks were made the only legal tender in China. Britain supported the move by prohibiting British firms from using silver, and the Americans helped by buying silver during the next six months, with the proceeds used to buy American cotton and foodstuffs. The Chinese monetary action was a great success. The move strengthened the authority and prestige of the KMT, and allowed Nanking to cover its chronic deficits by printing money.

The presence of Leith-Ross in Nanking may have encouraged the Chinese to reform their currency but stoked Japanese impatience to create an economic bloc in North China. The Kwantung army leaders, furious at the British intervention, singled out Britain as the main obstacle to Japanese expansion. Increased army pressure was brought to bear on the Chinese regional leaders in North China, to make their provinces autonomous and free from Nanking's influence. This renewed outburst of Kwantung army activity confirmed the Foreign Office view that Japan was 'mistress of the Far East' and any British initiative in China would need her assent. The Japanese needed a 'licking', but Britain was in no position to administer it. The Foreign Office wanted Leith-Ross recalled; Chamberlain dragged his feet, and it was not until May 1936 that it was agreed that the 'gallant hero of this lost cause' should return home. Leith-Ross's many-paged report was read in both the Treasury and Foreign Office, and the latter's comments were forwarded to the appropriate cabinet sub-committee in preparation for a future meeting that was never held. The inter-departmental battles over East Asia were soon overshadowed by events in Europe.

Anthony Eden was determined to keep a low profile in East Asia. While agreeing that closer Anglo-Japanese relations were desirable, nothing emanating from Tokyo encouraged optimism. As Japanese military activity in China intensified and Chinese opposition to Chiang's policies of appeasement spread, Eden turned away from any recommendations that would stiffen Nanking's resistance to Japanese encroachments. Britain was neither willing nor able to protect China's territorial integrity, yet would not abandon its existing position in

China. The difficulty of maintaining this policy may explain why the very sceptical Eden listened with some interest when the new Japanese ambassador, Yoshida Shigeru, an experienced diplomat and known Anglophile, visited him in July 1936 and spoke of hopes for a future understanding between Japan and Britain. His proposals were vague and, as he admitted, purely personal. In September, Yoshida claimed that new instructions from Tokyo encouraged hopes for improved relations and co-operation in China. Alexander Cadogan, the deputy under-secretary, considered this highly dubious. In the long run, a member of the Far Eastern Department concluded, China was 'too big a nut for Japan to crack' and its doors had to be kept open for British trade.[17] Officials underlined the danger of antagonizing the Soviet Union and, above all, the consequences of antagonizing the Americans.

In October 1936, new Japanese talks with Nanking were started. They were intended to persuade Chiang to recognize Japan's dominant position in China. While uncertain of the meaning of the Sian incident of December 1936 and the events that followed, the Japanese were aware of the strengthening of Chinese nationalist and anti-Japanese sentiments, but were unable to agree on an appropriate policy. A financial crisis and attacks on the army in the Diet brought down the cabinet in January 1937. It was finally replaced by a moderate government led by General Hayashi Senjuro, a former war minister acceptable to the army. His foreign minister, Sato Naotake, a professional diplomat and former ambassador to France (1933–1937), sought to revise Japanese policy in China. He believed that Japan's future lay in an open international economic system in which it could secure both the raw materials and the markets it needed to promote industrialization and its export trade. The Japanese position in Manchukuo had to be recognized, but Sato proposed abandoning the existing policy of trying to create autonomous movements in the northern provinces around Peking. He argued, too, that relations with the Soviet Union should be improved. Sato's recommendations won the approval of both the army and the navy ministers. In April 1937, four Japanese cabinet ministers (foreign affairs, finance, war, and navy) agreed that Japanese policy in North China should be primarily economic and not aim at its political separation from the rest of China. The Kwantung army took alarm. The new turn in government policy ran contrary to its intention to contain

[17] Quoted in Ann Trotter, *Britain and East Asia, 1933–1937* (Cambridge, 1975), 193. It should be noted that this still useful book came out before *DBFP*, 2nd ser., Vol. XX, was published.

the Nationalist opposition and strengthen Japan's control over North China.

The British waited to see whether the 'moderate and eminently sane' Sato would succeed in checking expansion into China, rightly judging that he had only a limited period of grace. And so it transpired. General Hayashi resigned in June and was replaced by the respected and much-liked Prince Konoe Fumimaro. The patrician Konoe had been part of the Japanese peace delegation to Paris in 1919 and had written a pamphlet in the 1920s entitled 'Rejecting the Anglo-American Peace'. As prime minister, while believing that the time was not yet ripe for action, he insisted that in a divided world, Japan, as a 'have-not' country, must secure for itself 'the right of survival'.[18] It was hoped in Tokyo that he would bring together bureaucrats, military men, and party politicians, but in fact he was unable to re-establish civilian control over the military. Not only did the military exercise greater political influence in Tokyo and in the missions abroad, but their policies were far more popular than the cautious, anti-expansionist line of the traditional diplomats. The bespectacled Konoe, in his wing collar and frock coat, proved to be a vacillating leader, caught up in the long and bitter struggle in Tokyo over the policy to be followed in China.

The British government continued to follow its circumspect policy towards Tokyo. Not only were ministers divided as to how to handle the Japanese, but the American reaction was carefully monitored. While continuing discussions with Ambassador Yoshida, the Foreign Office intensified its efforts to create a common front with the Americans. The situation was complex. Roosevelt sent out contradictory signals and the Foreign Office was fully aware of the strong isolationist current in the United States that restricted his freedom of action. When the president raised the possibility of summoning a peace conference, an idea he had long favoured, in order to force the 'gangster powers' into the open, the Foreign Office feared the possible consequences, and asked Lindsay, the very able British ambassador in Washington, to discourage the president without actually quashing the president's idea. Lindsay handled the matter with consummate tact and when the proposal ran its course without producing concrete results, the president was still willing to speak of co-operative action with London. In early February 1937, the president of the Board of Trade, Walter Runciman, travelled to Washington, following a presidential invitation, to discuss the possibilities of an Anglo–American trade agreement. Roosevelt told Runciman that the Japanese situation was causing him great anxiety and

[18] Quoted in A. Iriye, *The Origins of the Second World War in Asia and the Pacific* (London and New York, 1987), 39.

that he would welcome a 'closer examination of the situation by our two governments so that if and when action is called for we could act in accordance with a consistent policy'.[19] British officials were sceptical but Eden was encouraged by Roosevelt's openness with regard to the Far East.

There were, at the same time, signals in the opposite direction. In March 1937, Chamberlain considered approaching Henry Morgenthau at the Treasury about a joint guarantee by Britain, China, Japan, the USSR, and the United States, of the 'territorial status quo' in the Far East. The idea was rapidly abandoned; Chamberlain had to be satisfied with the desirability of putting relations between the United States, Britain, and Japan on a 'footing of harmonious co-operation'. Washington was apprehensive about the Yoshida–Eden talks, and sought reassurance that there would be no change in Britain's policy towards China, in order to secure Japan's friendship. In April, the Americans put forward an old presidential idea for a multilateral 'neutralization of the Pacific', that would have solved their problem of defending the Philippines. There was no expectation in London that the Japanese would agree, or that the United States would offer any explicit guarantees to maintain the neutrality of the region. Britain had to accept the unpalatable fact that the Americans intended to preserve their full independence, without relinquishing their interest in British policy. The most that could be done was to build on the existing goodwill shown by the president and some members of his administration. In the Far East, the Foreign Office continued to favour a 'no bloc' policy, directed at keeping Britain's potential enemies 'in a state of mild friction' without directly aligning itself with any combination of states.

No major crisis was anticipated in the spring and summer of 1937. By this date, the combined services intelligence and cryptographic organization, the Far Eastern Combined Bureau, was fully in service and providing good diplomatic and naval, if not military, intelligence. It was known that Japan was laying the basis for a war economy but there were strong doubts about Japan's ability to finance an ambitious rearmament programme, or to acquire the technological skills needed to fight a modern war. British observers in this field had a more accurate appreciation of the Japanese situation but their intelligence did not always reach the higher levels of decision-making in London. Much was known, too, about Japanese ambitions and spying activities in Singapore and Hong Kong. The British believed, nonetheless, that with American co-operation they could maintain the status quo until an expanded

[19] Runciman to Eden, 8 February 1937, quoted in Greg Kennedy, *Anglo-American Strategic Relations and the Far East, 1933–39* (London, 2002), 225.

Royal Navy would provide the degree of force needed to neutralize the Japanese threat. The interim situation was an uneasy one, but few in London shared Chiang Kai-shek's view that a clash between the West and Japan was inevitable. It was assumed that there would be no Japanese move against Britain unless the latter was actually engaged in a European war. Faced with the hostility of both the Chinese and the Russians, Japan could hardly afford to pursue its ambitions in south China, and in the South Seas, at the expense of the British Empire. Efforts at conciliation were restricted to the actions of a few individuals in each country. None were successful.

The divisions in Tokyo, and the Japanese army's increasing domination of the decision-making process, explains, in part, why British overtures proved unproductive. In London, diplomatic and commercial considerations blocked any deal with Tokyo. Ministers were not only concerned with the American reaction but feared that any such move toward Japan might push Stalin in the direction of Berlin. Not even Chamberlain, the main ministerial advocate of appeasing Japan, was willing to sacrifice Britain's commercial interests in China in order to foster Anglo-Japanese friendship. The Leith-Ross mission of 1935 was intended to lay the basis for an Anglo-Japanese condominium in China, and not to prepare the ground for a British withdrawal. Proposals to reform the Chinese currency were devised, in the hope of linking it to the pound, a plan which ran contrary to American ambitions and to Japan's hopes of establishing a yen bloc in the region. Though there was some sympathy for Japan's need for raw materials and markets in London, Britain appeared unwilling to liberalize its own trading system in the Japanese direction. When government proposals for a cartel agreement between the Lancashire cotton producers and their Japanese competitors failed to materialize, the British abrogated the Anglo-Japanese commercial treaty for its West African colonies and introduced quotas to keep out the cheaper Japanese goods. The Foreign Office admitted that 'Britain's imperial preference policy has given a great impetus to economic nationalisms, great and small, and has had a direct effect on Japan's policy in China.'[20] The trade issue provoked hostility on both sides. There was little public sympathy for an agreement between the two countries and no outside pressure for a *rapprochement*. On the contrary, Japan's alignment with the Axis powers, however tenuous, pointed in the opposite direction. The level of threat

[20] Quotation from Ashton Gwatkin, head of the Foreign Office Economic Section, in Antony Best, 'Anglo–Japanese Relations in the 1930s: The Inevitable Road to War?', *Bulletin of Asia-Pacific Studies*, 8 (1998), 71.

to Britain's security was not high enough to either confront or appease Japan.

V

The British were preparing to summon an expected new naval conference early in 1935, as both the Washington and London naval treaties would end in 1936. The former, automatically renewed, could be terminated at the end of 1936 on two years' notice. The latter would end in December when signatories were required to hold a new conference to negotiate a successor treaty. The difficulties became apparent even before informal conversations began with the Americans and Japanese. Given the stormy aftermath in Tokyo of the 1930 London treaty, and the changes in the command structure of the Japanese navy, the British expected that Japan would insist upon parity with the two other fleets. The hard-liners in the Japanese navy demanded that Japan be freed from the 'fetters' of the naval treaties, and that the ratio restrictions should be abolished. The chief of the Japanese naval staff, like most of his colleagues, viewed the United States as Japan's greatest adversary in East Asia. Plans to ward off an American attack meant that Japan had to plan for a two-phase war in which its submarines would first reduce the fighting capacity of the Americans, and its fleet engage only when the United States navy had advanced into the western Pacific. The Japanese needed to build submarines, large battleships, and big guns well beyond the existing treaty limits. President Roosevelt's decision in 1934 to build the American fleet up to maximum treaty standards, and information about the American war plan 'Orange', for hostilities with Japan, confirmed the Japanese view that offensive planning was the best defence against an American attack. The navy's new programme was approved by the throne in September 1934. Japan would seek parity with the United States and, if the claim was denied, announce its decision to abrogate the Washington treaty at the end of the year, giving the required two-year notice.

The Americans were adamantly opposed to any change in the existing naval ratios. Roosevelt, who had been Woodrow Wilson's under-secretary of the navy and was more sympathetic to the navalists than Hoover, wanted a larger fleet. Aware of the strength of the anti-war and anti-big navy opposition, the president's programme was presented as part of the administration's plans to combat unemployment. Thirty-two warships were funded under the NIRA (National Industrial Recovery Act) and considerable sums appropriated for the improvement of existing bases and dockyards. The subsequent

Vinson–Trammell Naval Bill, passed by Congress in 1934, authorized the building of 1,902 vessels and 1,181 naval aircraft over a seven-year period. This would put the Americans well ahead of the Japanese in all the most critical categories, while still falling within treaty limits. Most of the new ships and submarines were needed to replace obsolete vessels laid down during the Great War. Roosevelt was suspicious of Japanese intentions in the Pacific, and during his early years in office took seriously even ludicrous reports of Japanese surveying of the United States and its possessions. But though he supported the naval building programme, the president also backed the Tydings–McDuffie Act of 1934 providing for future Philippine independence, and remained undecided whether to demand a naval base on the islands as his naval chiefs wanted, or accept the military verdict that the Philippines would fall to the Japanese before the fleet arrived. Aware of the strong public pressure for disarmament, Roosevelt wanted something positive to come out of the new London talks. If there could be no compromise on ratios, some quantitative reductions, and, more realistically, qualitative restrictions, on future ship-building should be sought. It was agreed with Norman Davis, again selected to be Roosevelt's chief disarmament negotiator, that American policy should be co-ordinated with the British, whom it was assumed were equally opposed to Japan's demand for parity and would favour further reductions in naval construction.

This assumption was only partly correct. As a result of the Manchurian crisis, Britain's 'Ten-Year Rule' governing defence planning was abolished, and in April 1933 it was decided to renew work on the still far from complete Singapore base. The Royal Navy, despite appropriation cuts, had managed to use the provisions of the London naval treaty of 1930 to secure a steady replacement programme of cruisers, destroyers, and submarines between 1930 and 1933. Apart from the United States, which was making up its cruiser deficiencies, Britain was outbuilding every other naval power, including the Japanese, in other categories. Nonetheless, Japan's earlier actions in Manchuria and Shanghai had revealed the weaknesses of Britain's position in East Asia, and the shortages restricting the world-wide mobility of the fleet. Efforts were in progress to address some of these problems, but the Admiralty was planning for the expiry of the naval agreements in 1936, and the creation of a much larger fleet than permitted under the existing tonnage allowances, a fleet that would allow Britain to protect the Empire against Japanese attack, and to provide security in home waters. The enlarged fleet was to be achieved through a ten-year building programme. There was a set-back when Chamberlain won ministerial backing for a revision of the Defence Requirements Sub-Committee

(DRC) report of 1934.[21] The chancellor of the exchequer had dismissed the threat of imminent war in the Far East, and insisted that Britain could not afford to fund the DRC recommendations for a balanced funding for all three services. He rejected the emphasis on imperial strategy in favour of concentrating on home defence and enlarging the RAF with cuts in the naval and army estimates to increase those of the RAF. The first sea lord, Sir Ernle Chatfield, convinced that Japanese intransigence would make the Admiralty case for funding, was prepared to reject Chamberlain's offer of 60% of the DRC recommendations, and to take only a small increase in the proposed 1935 estimates but demanded the eventual fulfilment of the Admiralty's full programme, including the target of seventy cruisers that had caused so much trouble with the Americans in the past. The policy battles in London coloured British diplomacy in the Far East for the next three years. Chamberlain and the Treasury preferred an accommodation with Japan, even if this meant recognizing Manchukuo and following a policy independent of Washington. The Admiralty, while rejecting Chamberlain's views on strategy and expenditure, was inclined to an agreement with Japan in the short-term, at least until the Singapore base was completed and the defence deficiencies addressed. The Admiralty was concerned, too, with the increases in the German naval budget of 1933, and the possibility of a new naval race in the Mediterranean. In response to new German naval construction, the French laid down another *Dunkerque*-class ship of 26,000 tons in 1933, and the Italians responded in late 1934 by announcing their intention to lay down two 35,000 ton ships. Faced with the possibility of an arms race in the Mediterranean, the British tried, but failed, to bring the two powers into the naval limitation schemes. The Italians, intent on achieving parity with France, began their new programme on 28 October 1934, the anniversary of the Fascist march on Rome. While giving little thought to war with Italy, the Admiralty argued that a two-ocean British fleet was a minimum requirement for naval security.

The British thought they could achieve their aims by prolonging the arms limitation system, particularly in the area of qualitative restrictions. This would allow them to capitalize on their existing advantages without facing the possibility of a rival developing a revolutionary type of warship, which would put whole classes of ships out of date. The problem was to salvage something from the naval treaties without alienating either Washington or Tokyo. Having just emerged from the Geneva disarmament fiasco, the Foreign Office wanted to avoid public defeat in the Pacific. It recommended, and the Admiralty agreed, that

[21] See pp. 50–2.

Britain should follow a middle course, avoiding alignment with either side and seeking to bridge the gap between Washington and Tokyo. The Admiralty reluctantly reduced its cruiser requirements from seventy to sixty (still an increase of ten over the 1930 London treaty limits) if subject to a six instead of a ten-year treaty restriction. As might have been expected, in the several months of uncomfortable preliminary exchanges during mid-1934 the Americans took umbrage at the British claim for cruisers. As their instructions called for a ten-year treaty renewal, with existing ratios and a 20% reduction in tonnage, the Anglo-American impasse lasted the whole summer. The atmosphere was further poisoned by rumours of an Anglo-Japanese deal. Both sides wanted to tie Japan to the existing ratios; each wanted the other to bear the brunt of Japanese anger. Each was suspected, in turn, of seeking a bilateral arrangement with Japan, with some cause as far as Britain was concerned. Neville Chamberlain repeatedly tried to promote an Anglo-Japanese *rapprochement* before the naval conference met. In the summer and autumn of 1934, despite Foreign Office opposition, he pushed for talks on a non-aggression pact, only to find that Japan would not accept any agreement that limited gains in China. There was also an effort, again supported by the Treasury and opposed by the Foreign Office, to come to an economic accommodation in Manchukuo in the hope that this would lead to a political understanding. Chamberlain encouraged plans to send a Federation of British Industries (FBI) mission to Manchukuo to lay the basis for a joint Anglo-Japanese investment agreement. The Foreign Office backed the idea until it became obvious that Japan would not countenance an 'open door' in the region. The mission's discussions in Tokyo set off a host of rumours, widely printed in the Japanese press, that Britain would recognize Manchukuo, renew the old alliance, break with the United States, and join Japan against the Soviet Union. The members of the FBI mission returned with glowing reports of the opportunities for future investment and development in Manchukuo, but there was no Japanese follow up to its visit to Tokyo. By the time the Anglo-American preliminary naval talks ended, the British had opted for an agreement with the Americans if the tripartite treaty could not be negotiated, and if the Americans abandoned their claim for a 20% reduction in treaty limits and agreed to keep the existing ratios.

Efforts to achieve a political agreement leading to co-operation at the forthcoming naval conference failed, because the Japanese were single-mindedly intent on freeing themselves from the ratio restrictions. The Japanese advocated a common upper limit on overall tonnage; they also recommended abolishing arms for attack, including both aircraft carriers and battleships. Already in September 1934, London and

Washington were informed of Japan's intention to pull out of the Washington naval treaty before the end of the year. The Japanese were concerned mainly with the American fleet since, (in the words of one Japanese negotiator), 'the British Empire is already an old man'.[22] Captain Shimomura was sent to Washington and London to underline Tokyo's objections to the existing ratios. He warned the Americans that no Japanese delegate signing such a treaty without the promise of equality 'could return to Japan to live and that no government which had so agreed would survive such an agreement'.[23] In mid-October 1934, the American and Japanese delegations arrived in London from the United States, on separate ships, for the preliminary conference. The British embarked on their 'middle course', approaching the Japanese with an offer of equality of status, and suggesting a secret three-power 'gentlemen's agreement' to regulate construction by establishing qualitative limits. There were to be procedures for communicating yearly outlines of building programmes. In reaction, Roosevelt warned in a letter to *The Times* that Britain should not sacrifice Anglo-American co-operation for the mirage of an agreement with Japan. Roosevelt wrote to Davis: '[I]f Great Britain is even suspected of preferring to play with Japan to playing with us, I shall be compelled, in the interest of American security, to approach public sentiment in Canada, Australia, New Zealand, South Africa in a definite effort to make these Dominions understand clearly that their future security is linked with us in the United States. You [Davis] will best know how to inject this thought into the minds of Simon, Chamberlain, Baldwin and MacDonald in the most diplomatic way.'[24] The president was in earnest, but he need not have worried, for the Japanese rejected the British proposal. They would not accept a fleet inferior to either of the other two naval powers, though they were willing to continue with other parts of the Washington treaty. Neither the Admiralty nor the American Navy Department were interested in the Japanese offer to refrain from building up to the 'upper limit', if all the powers agreed to such a limit. Neither was prepared to concede the right of parity to Japan. Still Chamberlain refused to give up hope. Without informing the Americans, he helped to devise a new formula allowing Japan to achieve parity with Britain, but only slowly until 1942, that is, during the dangerous years of British rearmament. Nothing was

[22] *FRUS,* 1934, I, 271.

[23] Quoted in Christopher Hall, *Britain, America and Arms Control, 1921–1937* (Basingstoke, 1987), 157.

[24] FDRMss. Roosevelt to Davis, 9 November 1934. I owe this reference to Dr. Phillips O'Brien.

said to the Americans but again there was no response from Tokyo. The pre-conference talks were at an end. Often acrimonious, the Anglo–American talks actually brought the two nations closer together. The need to limit Japanese naval expansion proved stronger than their continuing technical disagreements. On 19 December 1934, the three delegations had their first and only meeting together. Ten days later, Japan gave the two-year formal notification of its intention to withdraw from the treaties.

A year was to elapse before the second London Naval Conference was formally convened on 9 December 1935, the same day that the Hoare–Laval pact became public. The Washington treaties were practically dead. Their political basis had long been eroded, and with the impending withdrawal of Japan from the second London naval treaty, little remained of their security provisions. Though the British and Americans were to remind Tokyo of the existence of the Nine Power Treaty, neither showed any intention of enforcing it. The actual death of the naval treaties was a prolonged affair. Delegations came from Britain, the United States, Japan, France, and Italy. Germany and the Soviet Union were requested to accede to the treaty. The British asked that the participants disclose their future naval building programmes. The Japanese refused, demanding acceptance of their proposed 'common upper limit'. Compromise proved impossible and the Japanese withdrew from the conference on 15 January 1936, with its delegates thereafter attending only as observers. With the possibility of quantitative limits eliminated, delegates discussed an annual notification system, and qualitative limits on capital ships, aircraft carriers, cruisers and submarines. There was a five-year building 'holiday' for heavy cruisers, with exceptions for the Americans who had fallen below current treaty limits. Signatory states were forbidden from building capital ships which exceeded 35,000 tons and carried guns of more than 14-inch calibre. Although the 1930 London Naval Treaty prohibited 8-inch guns on cruisers, the United States and Japan began to lay down ships of up to 10,000 tons, with large numbers of 6-inch guns. In the new treaty, the signatories agreed to a new maximum displacement of 7,000 tons, with guns up to 6 inches. Escalator clauses allowed signatories to evade the treaty restrictions. At the final plenary session, the treaty was signed by Britain, most of the Commonwealth (the Irish Free State and South Africa had no naval vessels), France, and the United States. The Italians suddenly withdrew at the end of February, supposedly because of League sanctions, but in practice to avoid any blockage to their naval construction programme.

The Second London Naval Treaty was signed on 25 March 1936 and actually came into force on 29 July 1937. Despite an 'ultimatum' from Britain, the United States, and France in February 1938, the Japanese refused to disclose the details of their naval building programmes. Britain and the United States, with French consent, invoked the escalator clause of the new treaty, allowing them to agree on a qualitative escalation to counter the building of a non-signatory state. The Americans wanted no upper limit on displacement, only on gun size, but the British insisted, and a 45,000 ton/16-inch gun limit was set. For reasons of economy, dockyard limits, and design, the Admiralty preferred a 40,000 ton ship and tried to convince the other Europeans, with limited success, to accept the lower tonnage. Britain negotiated separate bilateral treaties with Germany (June 1938), the Soviet Union (July 1938), and Italy (December 1938); talks with Turkey continued into 1939 without result. After a prolonged correspondence, Finland and the Scandinavian countries joined at the end of 1938.[25] The Japanese, with whom bilateral talks were also begun, would not accept any qualitative limits and showed no interest in revealing the details of their building programmes. The Americans considered the qualitative restrictions (some of which they disregarded) and the notification clauses of scant importance, and dismissed Britain's bilateral treaties as mere window dressing. Nothing could prevent signatory nations from cheating on displacement limits, or from using the treaties to disguise qualitative improvements. An additional protocol signed in London in 1936 extended the 1930 prohibition of submarine warfare against unarmed merchant ships; Britain, USA, Japan, France, and Italy all signed and ratified it, while Germany and the USSR also acceded. By the time war broke out, over forty states, including all the chief maritime powers, had either ratified or acceded to the Protocol. The prohibition did not withstand the test of war.

The second London Naval Conference marked the end of the naval arms control experiment initiated in 1921. The naval arms race had already begun. Japan embarked on its 'second building programme' for the years 1934–1937 in March 1934. By December 1935, its navy had already exceeded the Washington and London quotas. It subsequently pursued an even larger 'third building programme' with the emphasis on large ships. There were plans for the construction of four monster 70,000 ton battleships armed with 18-inch guns. Japan's new naval strategy, the southern advance, was approved as part of the new Imperial

[25] See the articles by Joseph Maiolo, 'Anglo–Soviet Naval Armaments Diplomacy before the Second World War', *English Historical Review*, 123 (2008), 351–378, and 'Naval Armaments Diplomacy in Northern Waters: The Origins of the Anglo–Scandinavian Naval Agreement of 21 December 1938', in R. Hobson and T. Kristiansen (eds.), *Navies in Northern Waters, 1721–2000* (London, 2004). For further details on Stalin's decision to build a high sea fleet, see chapter bibliography for Chapter 16.

Defence Plan formulated in June 1936. The country was to maintain its position on the Asian continent, deal with the Soviet threat in the north, and expand into the South Seas, using peaceful means to avoid clashes with other powers. The army and navy's differing strategies were both sanctioned: the army's war against the Soviet Union and eventual primacy in Asia, and the navy's southward move to secure the riches of the colonial empires and ensure its command of the western Pacific against the Americans. There was no agreement on which war would be fought first; China, the United States, Britain, and the Soviet Union were all named as hypothetical enemies. This was the first time Britain was added to the list of budgetary targets. The new strategy was intended to satisfy the demands of both services without deciding on priorities or feasibility.

The British and Americans had also embarked on naval building programmes before the collapse of the conference. The total British estimates for 1936–1937 provided the funding needed to embark on the building of the expanded fleet. This building programme was by far the largest since 1918. In 1937, a peak year for the placing of rearmament contracts, more keels of capital ships were laid down than the combined totals for the United States, Japan and Germany. Some ships were replacements for obsolete vessels. The Admiralty continued to plan for its 'New Standard Navy', a greatly enlarged programme that would allow Britain to fight against its potential enemies in both European and Far Eastern waters. War was not anticipated before 1942, by which time the new programme would be completed. The British seem to have underestimated the Japanese navy's determination to achieve supremacy in the western Pacific through qualitative one-upmanship.

The Japanese withdrawal in December 1934 also had another ramification. Japan was determined to build over-sized cruisers. This would lead to both the United States and Soviet Russia's building similar ships, and Moscow's building would provoke a German response. The Royal Navy would find itself enmeshed in a naval building race that, given the Treasury's parsimony, it could not win. In these circumstances, the German offer to limit their fleet tonnage to 35% of the British total was particularly welcomed. If this could be achieved, and a qualitative naval race could be avoided, then the Admiralty would be able to fulfil its global responsibilities until the funds for a two-ocean fleet were available. The result was the signing of the Anglo-German Naval Agreement of 18 June 1935. While the Admiralty hailed this agreement, it had drawbacks. The unilateral British action undercut the solidarity that had been expressed at the Stresa conference in April.

Though warned of German violations of the naval agreements in 1937–1938, British naval opinion was divided over how important or extensive these violations were. It was only in the spring of 1938 that the Germans began to draft plans for a navy designed to defeat the Royal Navy. For the moment, except for trying unsuccessfully to get the sea powers to agree to raising the upper displacement for battleships to 45,000 tons, the British continued to hope that the naval treaties would provide some kind of protection against a qualitative arms race. The Admiralty proposals for the New Standard Navy were rejected in July 1938 on the grounds that they were far too expensive to implement. This made relatively little difference to the ongoing construction programme, as shipyards were already at maximum capacity building the sanctioned 'DRC Fleet'. Five ships of 35,000 tons with 14-inch guns (the *King George V* class) were laid down in 1937–1938. In addition, the Admiralty wanted to build 40,000 ton/16-inch gun *Lion* class ships; four were authorized for 1939–1940 (two each year). Although the ships were started, the outbreak of war led to their cancellation.

The demise of the Washington–London treaty system relieved the US navy of the impediments to its future expansion. It was now free to fight for the building programmes it wanted. For the moment, Roosevelt still hoped for a new plan to limit naval armaments and the US Navy was engaged only in bringing its forces up to the Washington–London limits. In February 1938, 'Plan Orange' was revised so that a blockade of Japan was combined with the old strategy of a frontal assault on the main Japanese fleet. In May, in response to the Japanese naval building, a new Vinson–Trammel Act was passed in Congress, authorizing the construction of sixty-nine more ships. One of the most important results of the naval discussions was the major improvement in Anglo-American relations. Joint planning, however, remained in an embryonic state and there was, of course, no American commitment to future action.

In retrospect, the Japanese departure from the naval limitation system represented a final blow to the dream of multinational disarmament. At the time, the importance of its demise was overshadowed by the German march into the Rhineland. The failure of the London conference made little impact on the continued public demands for disarmament in Britain, though there was less pressure for unilateral disarmament. As late as June 1937, an admittedly narrow majority of people interviewed for the Gallup pollsters considered the time ripe for the calling of another disarmament conference. In strategic terms, the Japanese abrogation of the Washington treaties meant that Britain's imperial position in the Pacific was under threat. The Admiralty may have exaggerated British weakness in its fight for increased appropriations, but questions were asked about the Singapore strategies. The

Defence Plans (Policy) Committee was told in 1937: 'Recent indications have shown clearly that there is doubt whether under existing political conditions in Europe and with the rise of the German navy, we should, in fact, be able to send an adequate fleet to the Far East if a menace were to arise in that area.'[26] At the Imperial Conference of May–June 1937, held at the time of George VI's coronation, the Australians and New Zealanders raised questions about the absence of a peace-time fleet in the Pacific, and the long period that would elapse before Singapore could be relieved. They were forced to accept evasive answers, although the Australians were assured that the safety of Singapore could almost certainly be guaranteed, and could be regarded as a 'first class insurance' for Australian security. In February 1938, the Singapore base was opened. Yet in the spring of that year, the Admiralty questioned whether it could send an 'adequate fleet' to the Pacific, since it was impossible to fight a war on three fronts. Defence of the Pacific Empire would depend on holding the balance in China, on implementing the Admiralty's construction programme, and seeking the co-operation of the Americans. At best, this was a formidable task for the overstretched home country.

The Undeclared War in China: International Implications, 1937–1938

I

The uneasy peace in China was shattered when on 7–8 July 1937 at Lukouchiao (Marco Polo Bridge), just south of Peking, there was a local clash of Chinese and Japanese troops. The isolated incident of Chinese soldiers firing on a Japanese army company during night manoeuvres, and a Japanese counter-attack, could have been settled by the local commanders. A local ceasefire was actually arranged, but despite many voices for containment on both sides, reinforcements and recurring incidents broadened the area of combat and made withdrawal difficult. Tokyo favoured localization mainly out of fear of Russian intervention, but also because neither the general staff nor the political leadership wanted a war in China. Nevertheless, troops were brought into the area from other garrisons in North China. Nationalist leaders also wanted a settlement, yet two days after the initial clash Chiang Kai-shek ordered four Nationalist divisions to reinforce the army in southern Hopei, thereby violating the summer agreements of 1935. The Japanese cabinet warned Chiang on 11 July not to interfere with the local agreement,

[26] TNA: PRO, CAB 16/182, Admiralty memorandum, 26 April 1937.

followed by a strongly worded *aide-mémoire* delivered on 17 July demanding that the Chinese authorities refrain from interfering in North China. In response, Chiang declared that any settlement with Japan must not compromise China's sovereignty, and warned that China was reaching the limits of her patience and would not allow 'one more inch' of territory to be lost. He also appealed to Britain, France, and the United States for mediation in the Sino-Japanese conflict. By the end of July, with Japanese troops crossing the Great Wall and local skirmishes becoming more frequent, hopes for localization began to fade. The Japanese marched into Peking on 29 July, routed the Chinese and took Tientsin the next day. The bombing of the university in Tientsin, a centre of anti-Japanese resistance, was the first taste of the destructive air war that was to come. By the end of the first week of August, all Chinese troops had been withdrawn from the Peking–Tientsin area. Still without any decision for a longer campaign, the government of Prince Konoe agreed to send an expeditionary force into China, supposedly to protect Japanese property and civilians. Enraged by this provocation and urged on by the CCP, the Nationalist government, assisted by its German advisers, reorganized its army in preparation for conflict. An undeclared war began that was to last for eight more years. It was the curtain-raiser for the global war.

Despite rising tension in the Peking area in the months prior to the Marco Polo Bridge incident, the initial military confrontation had been unexpected and accidental. Neither Prime Minister Konoe nor Foreign Minister Hirota sought a war, yet they proved incapable of halting the subsequent spiralling military involvement. For the next eighteen months, the Konoe cabinet sanctioned one military advance after another in China, seemingly unable to control or check the more radical army officers. The cabinet was carried along by the waves of nationalist feelings fed by the victories in China. Konoe's impulse to offer conciliatory terms to the Chinese was repeatedly checked by a divided cabinet unable to decide what its goals in the China war should be. Chiang Kai-shek, for his part, had no wish to fight the Japanese. His aim was to avoid or postpone a confrontation until other foreign powers became involved and provided sufficient assistance for the KMT to deal with both the Japanese and the Communists. After Sian, he could not offer further concessions to Tokyo. Once the 'incident' became a war in everything but name (neither side wanted a declaration of war for fear of complicating relations with other nations), any compromise would lead to renewed attacks on his leadership and a revival of the civil war. After six months of fighting and in the face of terrible Chinese casualties, there was no question of going back to the status quo *ante bellum*. Despite massive defeats, Chiang remained optimistic, convinced of the inevitable war between Japan and one or more of the other Great Powers, probably the United States. In reprisal for Japan's activities in the north, he decided to make a stand at Shanghai and 'wipe out the enemy army in one stroke'.[27] As Shanghai was an international city, Chiang thought that the conflict might lead to foreign mediation or intervention. His gamble failed disastrously. After seven weeks of intense fighting, including an air war observed by the horrified foreign population of Shanghai, the city fell in November. As the Japanese moved up the Yangtse towards Nanking, Japanese reinforcements and aircraft were sent, and a 'total war' of appalling ferocity on both sides developed. The longer the fighting continued, the more bitter it became. As the casualties mounted, peace became less and less likely.

The three-month Shanghai campaign was not only a military disaster consuming Chiang's best trained and best equipped troops; it also failed to elicit the western response anticipated by the Chinese leader. Representatives of the Great Powers in Shanghai had tried to prevent hostilities from breaking out, but their efforts at mediation, as well as those of the foreign ambassadors in Nanking, were equally futile. British attempts to elicit American support for joint action in both the combatants' capitals, in order to secure the suspension of troop movements and the acceptance of Anglo-American mediation, were abandoned when Hull insisted on 'parallel' as distinct from 'joint' representations. At the start of August, the American and British ambassadors saw Hirota separately to offer their good offices. The Japanese minister stalled. When the Japanese authorized the sending of an expeditionary force to central China, Eden again tried for joint representations without success. At one point, Britain offered to send a military force to Shanghai to protect Japanese nationals if other states would join in and both China and Japan would withdraw their forces. This initiative, too, was stillborn. Admiral Charles Little, the commander-in-chief of Britain's China squadron, spelled out his sense of frustration: 'It is humiliating for the white man not to have the power to prevent them from damaging and making use of the fine city which he, and most especially the British, have laboriously built up and which is such an asset to the Far East.'[28] When the British ambassador in China, Sir Hughe Knatchbull-Hugessen, was wounded on 26 August by Japanese aeroplanes while travelling from Nanking to Shanghai, Tokyo refused to apologize. They offered an expression of 'deep regret' only when threatened with the withdrawal of Sir Robert Craigie, the newly-appointed

[27] Sun, *China and the Origins of the Pacific War, 1931–1941*, 91.

[28] Bradford Lee, *Britain and the Sino-Japanese War, 1937–1939: A Study in the Dilemmas of British Decline* (Stanford, CA, 1973), 39.

British ambassador to Japan. The Japanese offer was accepted. Neither side wanted to make anything more of the incident.

The Japanese instituted a 'pacific blockade' covering most of the coast of China, warning that they reserved the right to ascertain the identity of foreign vessels, and might feel compelled to apply the blockade to third-party vessels carrying war supplies to China. The British accepted a circumscribed verification procedure if Japan refrained from more serious interference with their shipping. In this, London acted alone. The Americans announced on 14 September that no government-owned ships could carry munitions to either country, while other American-owned vessels would move at their own risk. The Neutrality Act of 1 May 1937 gave the president the right to proclaim a state of war that would make it unlawful to sell and transport arms and ammunition or grant loans to any of the belligerents. There was a 'cash and carry' provision, however, that allowed the purchase of certain goods to be transported in foreign ships; if put into effect, this provision could well have assisted Japan. With Senatorial and newspaper opinion divided, Roosevelt decided not to invoke the Neutrality Act, making it possible to ship arms to both combatants, and to wait on events. Cordell Hull took the moral high road, underlining the government's commitment to peace and peaceful change through co-operative efforts, but reiterating America's policy of no alliances or entangling commitments. In a later press statement, he expanded on the administration's support for these principles in the Pacific and in the rest of the world. Applauded in the United States as a clear statement of intent, Hull's statement hardly advanced matters in China. The British condemned American policy as excessively timid, but in fact were as unwilling as the Americans to risk any kind of intervention. Both governments assumed that a tougher policy might provoke the conflict they wanted to avoid.

II

It might have been anticipated that the Germans would support Tokyo and the Soviets back Chiang Kai-shek. Both governments, however, moved with great caution. Almost from the start of the new conflict, the Germans were pressed by both the Japanese and Chinese for assistance. The war was not welcomed in Berlin. Though Japanese envoys argued that the war was part of the fight against Communism and consequently covered by the Anti-Comintern Pact, the Wilhelmstrasse refused its backing and responded that the only beneficiary of the conflict would be the Soviet Union. Japanese queries about German shipments of arms to China, and the role of the German military advisers with the KMT,

Table 9.1 Arms and Munitions to China up until 1937 (in pounds sterling)

Germany	883000
France	378000
Switzerland	158000
Belgium	137000
United States	127000
Great Britain	122000
Aircraft and parts of aircraft (in pounds sterling)	
United States	683000
Great Britain	192000
Italy	85000
Germany	17000

Source: Aron Shai, *Origins of the War in the East* (London, 1976), 171. No date given, presumably until 1937.

were carefully side-stepped. A promise to Tokyo to cease arms shipments to China was violated; Germany's 'strict neutrality' was stressed. Hitler, at a meeting with Neurath and Blomberg on 17 August 1937, stated that 'he adhered, in principle, to the idea of co-operating with Japan, but that, in the present conflict between China and Japan, Germany must remain neutral'.[29] As the Japanese blockade took effect in late August, the continued German shipments of war materials, mostly through Hong Kong, resulted in further difficulties. Chiang's refusal to consider the Japanese terms in the summer of 1937 was strengthened by the encouragement of his German military adviser, General Falkenhausen, who believed that the Chinese army could drive the Japanese over the Great Wall if German advice was followed. German arms continued to arrive in China (during the first 16 months of the conflict, Germany supplied around 60% of China's total arms imports) and the Chinese asked for more. Yet in September, Hitler assured Emperor Hirohito's younger brother that Germany would adhere to the principles of German–Japanese co-operation in world affairs. The real question was how long Germany could resist the pressure to take a more partisan role. Dirksen, the pro-Japanese ambassador in Tokyo, urged Berlin to mediate between the two combatants, but also to continue its double role in the two capitals. The Germans decided to do nothing until both parties requested mediation. It was not until the last week of October that this opportunity would arise.

[29] *DGFP*, Ser. D, Vol. I, No. 478 (memorandum by Neurath, 17 August 1937).

Moscow was convinced that the best way to avoid a Japanese attack on the Soviet Union in the Far East was to offer arms to the KMT and encourage Chiang to fight Japan. The Soviets wanted to avoid direct confrontation with Tokyo. On 29 July, at the same time that the decision was taken to increase aid to Spain, the *Politburo* agreed to provide arms to the KMT after the conclusion of a non-aggression pact with China. Moscow insisted that the arrangement be kept secret, a proviso that the Chinese disregarded as their representatives from all over Europe converged on Moscow. The pact was signed on 21 August 1937. The Soviet intention, backed by shipments of planes, vehicles, machine guns, rifles, bombs, shells, and other equipment, was to underwrite the Chinese military effort in order to keep the Japanese tied up in China. At first, Chiang had been reluctant to solicit Soviet assistance for fear of a major Japanese attack, but once hostilities accelerated, he requested supplies and men (mainly officers, technical advisers, and pilots). In mid-August, he presented his list of needs; he was to receive about half of what was requested, and later than he had hoped. Some 200 planes and 100 tanks arrived within a month of signing the contract, and 450 Russian pilots were in China by the end of the year. Chiang was given a very large credit to spend on arms, in return for which the Russians received raw materials needed for rearmament, including tungsten. From the autumn of 1937 until mid-February 1938, some 3,665 Soviet military specialists had come and gone.[30] When, finally, the German military mission in China was withdrawn in the summer of 1938, Soviet advisers were appointed to take their place. The Russians carefully monitored the Japanese response and tried to avoid direct provocation. Bogomolov, the Russian ambassador to China, was actually reproved by Litvinov when he suggested to the Chinese that the Soviet Union might be prepared for a pact of mutual assistance. The ambassador was recalled to Moscow and, like Rosenberg, the Soviet representative in Spain, perished in the Terror.

III

On 11 September, within days of the battle at Shanghai, Dr Wellington Koo, China's delegate to the 1937 League Assembly, formally requested that the League take cognizance of the fact that his country had been invaded. Eden went straight from the Nyon Conference to Geneva.[31] Along with Delbos, the French foreign minister, and Avenol, the League's secretary general, he told the Chinese ambassador that there should be no

[30] Haslam, *The Soviet Union and the Threat from the East*, 93–94.
[31] See p. 238.

appeal under Article 17 that might bring the sanctions article (Article 16) into operation. The Chinese agreed that the Assembly should refer the matter to the Advisory Committee, created in 1933 (the old 'committee of nineteen' appointed at the time of the Manchurian affair) to monitor the Sino-Japanese situation. The committee held its first meeting on 22 September. Under Anglo-French leadership, the ground was prepared for a conference of the Washington treaty powers under terms that it was hoped the Americans would accept. There was a great deal of sympathy for China in Geneva but delegates were unwilling to discuss either Koo's demands for sanctions, or for a declaration citing Japan as an aggressor nation. The Ethiopian fiasco left unpleasant memories. The League Assembly criticized Japan for the violation of its treaty obligations and recommended that member states avoid actions that would weaken China. They were encouraged to extend aid on an individual basis. Their recommendations infuriated the Japanese, without rendering any effective assistance to China. Unwilling to go any further, delegates agreed to refer the question to a special conference in Brussels of the Nine Power Treaty signatories and other concerned powers. Attention was focused on Washington, for American participation in the international peace effort was considered vital for success.

Eden tested the American waters. On 30 September, he raised the possibility of an economic boycott, citing the strength of British public feeling. To Eden's fury, a sceptical Chamberlain altered the draft so as to suggest that his government did not believe any such action would be effective. The usual Admiralty reservations about sanctions gave added weight to the prime minister's opposition. The State Department settled the argument in Chamberlain's favour. The Americans referred only to Hull's earlier statements of principles, though they suggested that some action under the Nine Power Treaty might be possible. A qualified American agreement to participate in a conference was followed by President Roosevelt's 'quarantine speech', given in Chicago on 5 October 1937. Already in difficulties over his attempt to 'pack' the Supreme Court, the president was faced with a sharp contraction of the American economy in the autumn and widespread fears of a 'second depression'. Hardly in the mood to risk a major diplomatic move, Roosevelt, nonetheless, toyed with the idea of some kind of international gesture that might divert attention from domestic affairs. Hull and Norman Davis, one of the president's favoured freelance advisers, proposed a speech on international co-operation 'in a large city where isolation was entrenched'.[32] In discussions with his associates, Roosevelt

[32] Quoted in Robert Dallek, *Franklin D. Roosevelt and American Foreign Policy, 1932–1945* (New York, 1979), 147.

made it clear that he wanted to make a dramatic statement that would educate the American people about the dangerous state of the world, but would also serve as a warning to nations that were 'running amok' that they would be cut off from trade and access to raw materials if they continued their lawless ways. In Chicago, the president told his audience that the 'peace-loving nations' had to oppose those 'creating a state of international anarchy and instability from which there is no escape through mere isolation or neutrality'. He warned that: 'The epidemic of world lawlessness is spreading. When an epidemic of physical disease starts to spread, the community approves and joins in a quarantine of the patients in order to protect the health of the community against the spread of the disease.' The speech ended on an ambiguous note. 'There must be positive endeavours to preserve peace. America hates war. America hopes for peace. Therefore, America actively engages in the search for peace.'[33] It was a characteristically brilliant performance, yet there was no plan behind it. Contemporaries believed that Roosevelt had something concrete in mind, but it was unlikely that he was considering any specific action against Japan. He was merely looking for some *international* gesture to promote peace. Sanctions were inadmissible, 'a terrible word to use', he told reporters. 'They are out of the window.' His speech, as he explained when pressed, expressed an 'attitude'. 'We are looking for a programme', the president said.[34] When, on 6 October, the League Assembly met, delegates denounced the Japanese action and called for a Nine Power Conference. Roosevelt backed American attendance as 'one of the possible paths' to peace. There were high hopes that the United States was about to re-enter the international arena.

Eden asked for a more exact interpretation of Roosevelt's speech. His efforts to seek elucidation only irritated the president. Chamberlain, an emphatic opponent of sanctions, insisted rightly that the Americans, despite the 'ballyhoo', would not propose or join any sanctions against Japan. Economic sanctions, the prime minister asserted, were of no use unless backed by overwhelming force, which neither Britain nor the United States could consider. Unlike Eden, who was prepared to follow up any indication of American interest in co-operation, Chamberlain's main interest in approaching Washington was to prevent the Opposition parties in London from arguing that the British government was standing in the way of effective restraints on Japan. When questioned by Ambassador Lindsay, the American under-secretary of state, Sumner

[33] Franklin D. Roosevelt, *The Public Papers and Addresses of Franklin D. Roosevelt. 1937 Volume: The Constitution Prevails*, ed. Samuel I. Rosenman (London, 1941), 411.

[34] Quoted in Dallek, *Roosevelt and American Foreign Policy*, 149.

Welles, a presidential appointee and confidant, said that the emphasis should be on the last sentences of the president's speech and that 'quarantine' was a remote and vague objective. He warned that the United States would not be drawn into any armed conflict. The American ambassador in London also cautioned Eden that Roosevelt hoped Britain would not rush ahead at the Nine Power Conference in Brussels for he feared accusations of being 'dragged along as Britain's tail'. The ambassador explained that while the United States would not take the lead at Brussels, Roosevelt hoped that the American presence alone would promote something in the nature of a 'common front'. By working with the British, he intended to familiarize the American people with the idea of co-operation in international affairs. In other words, this was to be an educational experiment.

Despite these disclaimers, there were signs of a possible American move away from isolation. The defence of Shanghai made China front-page news. The war picture of a crying baby sitting on tracks in the middle of a blasted empty street had the same emotional impact on newspaper readers as that of the burned child in Vietnam so many years later. The Japanese bombings set off a wave of public sympathy for the Chinese, whose heroism and sufferings were reported by American journalists in Shanghai. Sympathy for the apparently steadfast Chiang and his attractive, Wellesley College-educated wife, produced editorial demands for economic and financial assistance for China. The couple was featured on the cover of *Time Magazine* as 'Man and Wife of the Year' for 1937. Its editor-in-chief, Henry Luce, born in China of missionary parents, was a natural backer of the growing 'China lobby,' spearheaded by the missionary societies. Such backing, however, did not mean support for threats of intervention or the use of force. At most, those who hailed the Chicago speech thought that Roosevelt was thinking of some form of economic pressure on offending nations. On 8 October, buoyed up by the initial acclaim for his speech, Roosevelt had told Hull, Welles, and Davis that if the Brussels conference mediation failed, the US should not 'pack up and come home', but rather consider further steps. It was only as the president reflected on the arguments of his critics that he decided that this was neither the time nor the place for the United States to take the lead in world affairs. Pacifist organizations were in the midst of a joint campaign for twenty-five million signatures to 'Keep America Out of War'. Congressional opinion ran strongly against joining the League of Nations in collective action in the Far East. The president acted in harmony with his perception of the prevailing mood; a combination of moral indignation and the avoidance of international action would suit both Congress and the electorate.

Twice the Japanese were formally invited to Brussels and twice they had refused to come. Given the unanticipated extent of Japan's military involvement in China and the prolonged battle for Shanghai, Hirota and the service ministers agreed in early October to discuss terms with Chiang. Fearing possible Soviet intervention, they wanted to conclude the 'incident' as rapidly as possible. The army suggested using Germany and Italy as the 'letter carriers' between the two warring countries, and its recommendation was formally adopted. While there was to be no question of mediation, arbitration, or conciliation, the Germans, who had refused to participate in the League advisory committee or to attend the Brussels Conference, were the natural intermediaries. In early October, moreover, the Japanese campaign to curtail German assistance to China began to make headway. Ribbentrop, flying back and forth between his London embassy and Berlin, convinced Hitler that unless Japan's grievances were addressed, the Anti-Comintern Pact would be in danger. He won the Führer's support, against all the efforts of the Wilhelmstrasse, for pressure on Mussolini to suspend the on-going Italian–Japanese talks, and to accept Italian participation in the Anti-Comintern Pact. Though instructed by Hitler to work with Neurath, the ambassador (with his eye on the foreign minister's job) despatched his own agent to Rome, and went himself on 22 October to take charge of the final negotiations with the Italians. Ribbentrop's success in Rome had immediate consequences for Germany's China policy. A startled and disapproving Foreign Ministry found that Göring had ordered, at Hitler's command, that all deliveries of arms to China should cease. Göring and Ribbentrop each informed the army heads that Hitler had decided on an 'unequivocal attitude' of support for Japan and that the *Wehrmacht* was to avoid obstructing Japan's goals. Hitler's decision, made on 18 October, set off a bureaucratic scramble in Berlin, as the army and Foreign Ministry fought a delaying action against the stoppage of shipments and the withdrawal of the German officers. Hitler's position was not entirely clear. It is probable that he wanted the best of both worlds. If peace could be restored, China might join the Anti-Comintern Pact, and Germany could keep both its doors open. At the end of October, Hitler agreed that Oskar Trautmann, the German ambassador in Nanking, should act as an intermediary to work out the conditions for a ceasefire. Though ordered not to go beyond the role of letter carrier, Trautmann departed from his instructions to save Chiang from what he thought would be defeat and deposition. On 2 November, Foreign Minister Hirota outlined his peace terms. They involved an autonomous Inner Mongolia, a demilitarized zone in North China administered by Nanking through a pro-Japanese official, the end of anti-Japanese activities, and co-operation in fighting Communism. If the conflict continued, Japan would aim at China's total defeat and exact far harsher terms. Not unexpectedly, Chiang refused to negotiate unless Japan was prepared to restore the pre-conflict status quo.

Chiang expected much from the Brussels Conference; he was possibly the only one who did. By the time the meetings opened on 3 November, whatever hopes there had been for success were already dissipated. American policy remained equivocal: the State Department's Far Eastern expert wanted forceful action against Japan, while the head of the European division was suspicious of the British and opposed any form of American involvement. At the conference, the American delegate, Norman Davis, impatient at the lack of progress, went beyond his instructions, and though warning that his suggestions were personal, detailed different ways by which Japan could be contained. Some members of the American delegation hinted at the unwillingness of the European states to follow America's 'positive' lead. Faced with these accusations, Eden, worried that some form of ineffective sanctions would lead to Japanese retaliation against the British Empire, tried to clarify his country's position. It could not go forward in the Far East unless assured both of American participation in sanctions and its naval backing in case of war. The British and French told Davis, in blunt terms, that neither of their countries was prepared to act alone, given their difficulties in Europe, but would consider joint actions with the Americans. Davis admitted that everything depended on Roosevelt's attitude and the American mood when the conference ended. Ambassador Lindsay, too, warned Eden that there was little public interest in the Brussels meetings, and that public opinion would not support positive action if the conference failed. He anticipated a new isolationist campaign when Congress re-assembled in mid-November.

In London, despite another negative special committee report on the question of sanctions and Chamberlain's strong opposition, Eden still wanted to examine the Davis proposals to ensure the promotion of good relations between the two governments. With the European situation very much in mind, Eden was prepared to approach the president to discuss some form of common action, even ineffectual sanctions might be useful. Lindsay thought the whole idea a non-starter, but agreed to see Sumner Welles rather than the president. As the ambassador had anticipated, Welles claimed that Davis's suggestions were strictly exploratory and there was no intention of introducing any legislation that might be needed for 'so-called sanctions'. Instructions would be sent to Davis to support the appointment of a standing committee to monitor future developments, a euphemism for doing nothing. The conference proved to be Davis's swan-song, for his performance was judged a disaster. Having been forewarned that the United States would not take a leading role at Brussels or back any action that might lead to isolationist accusations of American policy being a 'tail to the British kite', Eden could hardly have expected the conference to result in any action to check Japan. He had, nonetheless, been encouraged by the signs of increasing American involvement in the Far East and by a commonality of views that could open the door to future co-operation.

The Brussels conference was being held at a time when Chamberlain and Eden were already in disagreement over British policy in Europe. Eden was annoyed at Italian obstruction in the Non-Intervention Committee on Spain and Grandi's opposition to the withdrawal of foreign troops from Spain. Chamberlain had decided on a new approach to the Italians, and the Spanish question seemed an unnecessary impediment to his initiative. There were differences, too, over Halifax's visit to Germany in the autumn of 1937. Both these problems climaxed in mid-November when Eden was dealing with Davis's proposals. Chamberlain's failure to appreciate the full importance of the United States in Britain's foreign and defence policy would precipitate a break between the two men and Eden's subsequent resignation on 20 February 1938.

The French were equally unsuccessful in prodding the Americans to give a lead. Like the British and Americans, they had not wanted to become involved in the Sino-Japanese conflict. Preoccupied with the Spanish Civil War, Foreign Minister Delbos had tried to prevent the Chinese appeal to the League of Nations, fearing that 'the only result of a Chinese appeal would be [that] the cipher would become the shadow of a cipher. The League still had some utility in Europe and he did not wish to see it made ridiculous.'[35] Ineffective sanctions would only infuriate Japan and lead to action against western colonial interests in South-East Asia, including French Indochina. Efforts to secure special protection from the United States and Britain fell on deaf ears. Fears of French involvement had not prevented the sending of considerable material assistance to China by rail, through Indochina from Haiphong to Kunming in Yunnan province. As the Japanese moved southward, the French anticipated that their next move might be either against Yunnan province or Hainan in the Gulf of Tonkin, threatening the security of Indochina itself. In late September, the Japanese warned the French that they would bombard the Chinese part of the railway to stop the arms trade. The French governor general of Indochina took alarm and complained bitterly about the inadequacy of the arms at his disposal. He warned of a possible Japanese occupation of Hainan, or even of an attack on Indochina by the Japanese-backed and -equipped Siamese army. The *Quai d'Orsay* decided to take defensive action and formally

[35] Quoted in Dreifort, *Myopic Grandeur*, 105–106.

banned arms and munitions moving across their colony, except those ordered before 15 July 1937. Both the British, who feared that Japan would focus its attention on Hong Kong, the other main channel for shipping arms, and the Americans, who thought that the French move would prejudice the Chinese position before the Brussels Conference met, protested but without success. In fact, supply intermittently continued despite fierce opposition from the *Quai d'Orsay*, who were under strong pressure from Japan. As the French ambassador in Tokyo reminded his chief, 'our situation in the Far East is extremely vulnerable in relation to a country as militarily powerful and ferociously egoistic as Japan'.[36]

Delbos had welcomed the idea of the Brussels Conference and was encouraged by Roosevelt's quarantine speech, despite warnings that neither would result in positive American action. In the event, like his simultaneous effort to promote a united front with the United States in Europe, Delbos's hopes of American assistance proved ill-founded. The misreading of Roosevelt's intentions was not entirely his fault. In response to the French ambassador's defence of the decision to ban the transport of arms through Indochina, Roosevelt had asked 'do they not clearly realize in France that a Japanese attack against Hong Kong, or Indochina or the Dutch Indies would constitute equally an attack against the Philippines? In this eventuality, our common interests would be endangered and we would have to defend them together.'[37] It was not until 9 November that the French were told that there was no possibility of an American guarantee for Indochina or, indeed, for any kind of support in opposing aggression in East Asia. In Washington, Delbos launched the idea of joint Anglo-French representations to secure a clear statement of American policy, but Eden was not interested. The *Quai d'Orsay* signalled its own lack of interest in the final conference proceedings by failing to return its delegation to Brussels.

On 24 November, the Brussels Conference was adjourned after affirming that 'a prompt suspension of hostilities in the Far East would be in the best interests not only of China and Japan but of all nations'.[38] Beyond these pious words, no action was proposed. Nothing was done to reconsider the Far Eastern situation, given the collapse of the Nine Power Pact. The short-lived hopes for collective action vanished; it was not good news for a common front in Europe. In this sense, the Brussels

[36] Quoted in John F. Laffey, 'French Far Eastern Policy in the 1930s', *Modern Asian Studies*, 23: 1 (1989), 134.
[37] Quoted in Dreifort, *Myopic Grandeur*, 115–116.
[38] *DBFP*, 2nd ser. Vol. XXI, No. 391.

Conference was a frustrating fiasco. An affirmation of moral disapproval was hardly a warning signal, either to Japan or to Nazi Germany. Nor was the conference an educative experience for the Americans, as the president had intended. For the Soviets, the experience was an entirely negative one, serving only to confirm Moscow's diplomatic isolation. The Russians had been invited at Litvinov's insistence; both he and Potemkin, who took his place when the commissar went back to Moscow, would have liked joint intervention but were careful not to move ahead of the western powers, who showed no wish to co-operate with Moscow.

The failure of the Brussels Conference left Chiang Kai-shek with few options but to consider Japan's German-delivered terms. It is true that Soviet arms (more than were committed to Spain) and advisors were arriving in significant numbers, but there was no possibility that the USSR would mobilize its troops on the Japanese frontier as the Nationalists would have liked. Chiang declared on 2 December that he would negotiate on the basis of Japan's terms, but only if there was no 'ultimatum', North China's independence was assured, Germany would act as mediator, and that China's agreements with third parties (i.e. the Soviet Union) should not be affected. Unfortunately for the Nationalists, as the military situation changed in Tokyo's favour, the Japanese raised the price of peace. With the triumphs of late 1937, the extremists, who wanted to pursue the China campaign to eliminate Chiang entirely, gained the upper hand. This time it was Konoe, rather than the Japanese military chiefs, who insisted on terms that would bring China under Japan's virtual control. Trautmann, the German ambassador, fearful of a terrible struggle and a Chinese defeat, tried to get Chiang to consider the revised and even stiffer terms transmitted on 21 December, but the Nationalist leader could not accept them.

IV

On the night of 12–13 December, Nanking fell. Its defence had lasted only five days. The Chinese troops, their morale shattered, were in chaotic retreat. Determined to make an example of the city, in part to bring the war to an end, the Japanese army was given its head. The scenes of massacres of civilians, burnings, and rape, made future acceptance of any Japanese terms almost impossible, and shocked foreign witnesses and the outside world. Japanese pictures, developed in the camera shops of Shanghai, made their way to the foreign correspondents and appeared in the world press. Discipline was only very slowly restored, and Japanese diplomats were left with the impossible job of dealing with complaints and protests from Germany, as well as from other powers. From the 'rape of Nanking' came the widespread western image of the Japanese army as savage and barbaric. For the Japanese, the atrocities at Nanking became a non-event. Even today some Japanese find it difficult to admit what happened so many years ago, and efforts continue to be made to airbrush many of these incidents from the Japanese past.

Both in Tokyo and Hankow, where the Chinese government and diplomatic corps had withdrawn some 400 miles up the Yangtze River, the Germans tried to promote a compromise between the combatants. The Japanese hard-liners outmanoeuvred the more moderate general staff officers, and an even tougher list of conditions was prepared at an imperial conference called on 11 January 1938. Chiang for his part refused to negotiate on the basis of the earlier peace terms. 'The time must come,' he explained, 'when Japan's military strength will be exhausted thus giving China the ultimate victory'.[39] The situation in Hankow was chaotic and Chiang received contradictory advice. There was little detailed information on the state of the military situation or what the future might be. The pro-resistance group counted on an inevitable war between the Fascists and the democracies that would save China; opponents of resistance argued that the international situation had changed for the worse and there was no alternative to peace with Japan. The pro-peace group coalesced around Wang Ching-wei, who was emerging as Chiang's only possible rival. Chiang's refusal to accept the Japanese peace terms, all-important at this juncture, was based on hopes of outside intervention, and on well-based fears that Tokyo would demand his resignation as part of the price for settlement. He warned the new Soviet ambassador that 'the situation is such that should the USSR not intervene openly and militarily in support of China, then China's defeat is inevitable'.[40] Fearful that Chiang might make peace, the USSR increased its aid to the Nationalists. The Comintern, despite all the difficulties caused by the Terror, emerged from a period of non-interference and demanded that Mao cease his independent guerrilla war and co-operate fully with Chiang Kai-shek. Further promptings from Moscow, and a change in KMT policy, had the desired effect. At the start of 1938, Dimitrov reported to Stalin that the CCP had unanimously accepted the Comintern directives to co-operate with the KMT. Needing money, arms, and equipment from Moscow, the CCP fell into line but Mao refused to abandon his struggle against Chiang Kai-shek.

[39] Barbara Tuchman, *Sand Against the Wind: Stillwell and the American Experience in China, 1911–1945* (London, 1970), 178.

[40] Haslam, *The Soviet Union and the Threat from the East*, 102.

While debating whether China should be given any form of assistance, the most positive decision reached in London was to build an all-weather road from Burma to China, opening up a much-needed additional supply route. The British considered and rejected the possibility of sending a fleet to East Asia as a warning to Tokyo. At least eight or nine battleships would have to be sent and this would leave Britain vulnerable elsewhere. These were the same arguments in reverse as used during the Ethiopian crisis. Chamberlain rightly questioned whether the Americans would be interested. After a negative response from Washington at the end of November, the idea was put in cold storage. On 12 December 1937, just before Nanking fell, Japanese planes attacked and sank the USS *Panay,* which was preparing to evacuate American diplomats and residents. Three Standard Oil tankers were bombarded as well. HMS *Ladybird*, the *Bee*, and two other British gunboats on the Yangtze River were shelled from the shore. These attacks made by the Japanese pilots on their own initiative, and by local Japanese officers, created consternation in Tokyo. Acting with an unusual degree of promptitude, the Japanese immediately expressed regret. An infuriated Chamberlain demanded action. Eden at once proposed supporting any American protest and considered joining in more menacing actions. As always, caution prevailed. The next moves were left to the Americans who, while considering their own response, showed scant interest in a joint protest.

For a week after the *Panay* incident, Roosevelt, believing that the attacks were deliberate, considered naval and economic action against Japan, even a blockade (called a 'quarantine') of Japan, or an embargo on raw materials such as cotton and oil. The president proposed sending a naval expert to London to arrange the blockade, but also to establish a more permanent exchange of information as had taken place in 1915 and 1917. The horrified British ambassador in Washington pointed out that a blockade would mean war; Roosevelt insisted that his scheme might provoke hostilities but would prevent war. The president consulted his secretary of the Treasury to see what authority he had for using exchange controls against Japan, and was assured this was possible. On 17 December, the president told his cabinet he had the right to impose economic sanctions on Japan and to specifically embargo cotton, oil, and other items. He told his listeners that a joint blockade with the British would bring Japan to its knees in a year.

This time, London rejected both economic sanctions and exchange controls, as likely to lead to war. Warren Fisher at the Treasury was scathing: 'Over & above the imbecility of economic sanctions, we [should] find ourselves left in the lurch sooner or later by the USA (who incidentally have no very special stakes in Asia) & Japan [would] scoop Hong Kong. [Should] we then add the fatal folly of going to war with Japan & so committing suicide in Europe?'[41] Nonetheless, the British were anxious to make some move in the Far East to restore their prestige and to take advantage of Roosevelt's anger. Eden tried to tie the president down to the 'present movement of ships' rather than to a future and provocative blockade. Even Chamberlain was optimistic that the president's mood might be successfully exploited. He wrote to his sister on 17 December (in a much quoted, if often shortened letter): 'It is always best & safest to count on nothing from the Americans except words but at this moment they are nearer to "doing something" than I have ever known them and I can't altogether repress hopes.'[42] The Foreign Office experts were prepared to give up Manchukuo and North China, but believed that in Shanghai and the Yangtze Valley Britain should take a stronger stand on an international basis. Any Japanese landing on the coast south of Shanghai, particular in Canton, would threaten Hong Kong and could not be tolerated. The chiefs of staff opposed the experts' suggested warnings to the Japanese, arguing that if Japan occupied the mainland behind Hong Kong, there was nothing Britain could do. They added, 'it seems scarcely conceivable to us that [Japan] will deliberately do anything at Hong Kong which is bound to involve her in war with the British Empire'.[43] It was, in fact, because of its difficulties in Europe that Britain was unwilling to contemplate a demonstration of strength in the Far East, without being certain of American involvement.

It rapidly became clear that the Americans would not join in any simultaneous naval demonstration. By calling for a 'quarantine', instead of outright sanctions, the president thought Japan could be deterred from provoking hostilities. 'After all', he told his cabinet, 'if Italy and Japan have developed a technique of fighting without declaring war, why can't we develop a similar one. There is such a thing as using economic sanctions without declaring war. We don't call them economic sanctions, but call them quarantines. We want to develop a technique which will not lead to war. We want to be as smart as Japan and Italy.'[44] This idea of 'quarantining' Japan was one that Roosevelt was to revive repeatedly before Pearl Harbor. The belief that he could somehow initiate collective action against aggressor states without involving the United States in war, and without recourse to a hostile and isolationist Congress, was to provide new opportunities for presidential

[41] *DBFP*, 2nd ser., Vol. XXI, No. 437, footnote 4.
[42] *DBFP*, 2nd ser., Vol. XXI, No. 431, footnote 4.
[43] *DBFP*, 2nd ser., Vol. XXI, No. 438, footnote 3.
[44] Quoted in Dallek, *Franklin Roosevelt and American Foreign Policy*, 154.

diplomacy after Munich. Those in London who saw hope in these signs of presidential activity had grounds for optimism, but there was no possibility of open co-operation in the Pacific. Roosevelt's ardour for action cooled quickly. Less than twenty-four hours after telling the cabinet of possible economic and naval moves against Japan, he was already pulling back, due in part to the absence of any strong public support for action against Japan, and isolationist calls for the withdrawal of all Americans from China. The blockade idea was quickly abandoned, though the president considered more modest forms of Anglo-American co-operation. On 21 December, he accepted an Australian invitation for a visit of part of the fleet to Sydney, three of the four American cruisers were subsequently to stop in Singapore for the opening of the new British naval base there. On the same day, Captain Royal E. Ingersoll, the director of the navy's War Plan division, was instructed to go to London to discuss technical problems with the Admiralty, relating to new naval construction programmes and co-operation, should the two countries become involved in a war with Japan.

On Christmas Eve, Hirota apologized to the Americans, agreed to pay an indemnity for the *Panay* and promised to safeguard the rights and interests of Americans in China. Roosevelt accepted the apologies and the $2 million indemnity, without any prior consultation with the British. The *Panay* incident was closed. The Japanese answer to London was less conciliatory. The Foreign Office pressed the British case, despite warnings from their ambassador in Tokyo that complaints about Japanese disregard for Britain's interests in China were only antagonizing the Tokyo government, which had discounted any independent British action.

The Ingersoll talks in London cleared the air for future naval co-operation. Ingersoll made it clear that the Americans would not make any move in the Pacific. The British explained that if drawn into war with three powers, they could only send those vessels not needed for home protection. American naval assistance would be required against Japan, while the British navy would serve as a barrier against Germany in the Atlantic. The private visit resulted in an informal understanding that if the two fleets had to work together against Japan, Britain could use American waters and the Americans the waters of the British Commonwealth. If a distant blockade was established against Japan, the Royal Navy would patrol an arc from Singapore to east of New Zealand, while the American navy would patrol an arc from the east coast of New Zealand to the Pacific coast of the United States. Attempts would be made to arrange for the simultaneous arrivals of their respective fleets at Singapore and Honolulu, and for an exchange of information on codes, tactical formations, and other details. Despite unresolved differences, the

Admiralty found the talks encouraging, and welcomed the American willingness to participate in a future distant blockade of Japan, the key feature of British naval planning. As if to buttress the naval talks, on 10 January Roosevelt transferred the bulk of the American fleet from the Atlantic back to the Pacific. The talks were secret, non-committal, and hypothetical. Great care was taken so as not to reveal too much about their respective code-breaking activities (against each other and friendly nations, as well as against Japan) but exchanges of intelligence and informal consultations brought the two naval establishments closer together. While this did not mean any American commitment to joint action in the Far East, the British had some reason to believe that they could rely on American goodwill in the Pacific. American caution was justified; leaked reports of the talks caused a furore in Congress.

Administrative attention in Washington became focused on Europe. At the State Department, Hull argued that Japan was working closely with Germany and Italy, and recommended parallel Anglo-American naval measures in the Pacific, as well as commercial and monetary agreements intended to demonstrate their mutual friendship. He also proposed schemes for the limitation and reduction of armaments, in which Germany and Italy would be invited to participate. Their refusal would mean that Britain and the United States would have to depend on their combined strength. Sumner Welles found Hull's ideas impractical; he revived his old proposals for a meeting of government representatives at the White House, to give fresh impetus to the Anglo-French attempts to reach an understanding with Germany and Italy. With a *rapprochement* in Europe, the Axis powers would withdraw their support from Japan. The president believed that an American gesture would be useful at this time, though little was known of Chamberlain's intentions. The proposal for talks in Washington was secretly conveyed to the British embassy on 11 January, with a demand for assent not later than 17 January. The plan was intended to link arms limitation with the offer of equal access to raw materials; it was to be accompanied by hints of possible revision of the peace settlements to attract the revisionist nations. Eden was away on vacation in the south of France and Chamberlain was in charge of the Foreign Office. The prime minister had little liking for a proposal that cut across his own peace initiatives, and having just received a half-hearted presidential response to a request for parallel action with regard to the beatings of two British policemen in Shanghai, had no illusions about the possibilities for co-operation. He vetoed any independent demonstration against Japan, and, scrapping a positive reply to Roosevelt's conference idea, sent a truncated message asking for a delay until the British negotiations with Germany and Italy were concluded. The message indicated that as part of the negotiations with Italy, Britain was offering to recognize the conquest of Ethiopia, a move hardly calculated to win the approval of an administration that put its main (or even sole) emphasis on the moral foundation of international law. The British reply was meant to bury the presidential proposal. Eden was contacted but was delayed in his rush back to London, and the Chamberlain telegram went without his approval. On Eden's return, he was able to have the decision reversed, and a warmer and more conciliatory message was sent. The foreign secretary, his nerves very much on edge, found his victory short-lived; Roosevelt at first delayed and then dropped his scheme entirely. It may well have been that the president's move had only been intended to assist Chamberlain's efforts in Rome and Berlin. According to Welles, Roosevelt thought Chamberlain's diplomatic initiative in Europe to be 'entirely right', and had decided to hold his plan in abeyance.

Chamberlain considered Roosevelt's peace plan vague, inept, and dangerous. The moment was an important one for the prime minister: Italy had agreed to negotiate and his hopes were high that Hitler, too, might be willing to talk. British association with a Roosevelt 'bombshell' could torpedo both conversations. Supremely confident in his own ability to deal with the dictators, the prime minister did not want to become enmeshed in Roosevelt's impractical schemes. It was not that he underestimated the importance of American influence. During the spring and summer of 1937, the prime minister, in the face of opposition from his own backbenchers as well as from business supporters, had backed the difficult and protracted Anglo-American trade talks, initiated in the first instance by the Americans. Admittedly, the talks had considerable support from the Treasury and the Foreign Office despite the economic disadvantages of the bargain, and a wide range of non-governmental bodies. As Chamberlain explained:

> the reason why I have been prepared ... to go a long way to get this treaty is precisely because I reckoned it would help to educate American opinion to act more and more with us and because I felt it would frighten the totalitarians. Coming at this moment it looks just like an answer to the Berlin–Rome–Tokyo axis and will have a steadying effect.[45]

The American card was to be kept in play, but this did not mean having the erratic president throwing his weight around Europe. It was because Roosevelt took umbrage at the prime minister's reply that Eden was

[45] David Reynolds, *The Creation of the Anglo-American Alliance, 1937–1941: A Study in Competitive Co-operation* (London, 1981), 18.

able to persuade Chamberlain to reverse his stand. Other differences, quite apart from the 'Roosevelt offer', contributed to the underlying strains in the Chamberlain–Eden relationship that led to the foreign secretary's resignation in February. With the dropping of the presidential peace scheme and Eden's resignation, Chamberlain was free to implement his European policies. As a consequence, Chamberlain had relatively little time to devote to the complex situation in China, and left matters in the hands of the Foreign Office.

At the departmental level and in China itself, Anglo-American relations became closer after the Japanese attack on China. While neither Ambassadors Grew nor Craigie in Tokyo favoured a united front against Japan, which they thought would only antagonize the Japanese, in London, the Foreign Office welcomed the State Department's willingness to check Japan, even if only in an informal and parallel manner. The two navies were sharing information about their naval programmes as well as intelligence on Japanese ship-building and modernization plans. In the absence of any Japanese demonstration of goodwill, the British were determined to stick to their 'stalemate' policy, based on the belief that China and the Soviet Union would enmesh the Japanese in China until Tokyo would be forced to deal more amicably with its neighbours. The positive side of the story was the closer contact between London and Washington over Far Eastern questions which, at least on the British side, encouraged optimism about future prospects for co-operation.

V

Given its recent military successes and the domestic pressures for a quick end to the war, the Konoe government believed in early 1938 that it was time to settle the China conflict as quickly as possible. Though it accepted that neither Britain nor the United States would endorse the changes made through military action in China, no counter-action was anticipated. On 16 January 1938, Konoe announced that Japan would stop dealing with the *Kuomintang* government and wait for the establishment of a new Chinese administration, 'with which she would co-operate wholeheartedly in adjusting Sino-Japanese relations and building a new China'.[46] This proved to be a mistake. Two days later, both countries withdrew their respective ambassadors. The Japanese announced their intention to wage a war of annihilation against the Nationalists. In his speech to the Diet on 22 January, Hirota told the politicians that Japan would seek a 'new order' in Asia, one which would have no place for the western powers. Konoe and Hirota, tired

[46] Iriye, *The Origins of the Second World War*, 52.

of Chinese equivocation, felt that the Japanese moderates were exaggerating the danger of Soviet intervention, particularly with the Red Army in a state of self-destruction. Reinforcements were sent and a new campaign opened in central China. Plans were laid for the taking of Hankow and possibly Canton. Believing that the Chinese war would soon be over if Chiang Kai-shek was removed from power, contact was made with Wang Ching-wei, Chiang's second-in-command, who favoured a ceasefire. The 'China incident' became the 'Great Patriotic Endeavour'. The cabinet devised and, in February, won the unanimous support of the Diet and the *zaibatsu* (the large industrial firms) for sweeping reform measures that allowed the government to implement the ambitious 1936 imperial defence plan incorporating both army and navy objectives. To win backing for this vast extension of state power, Konoe committed Japan to the domination of China and the creation of an alternative puppet regime. The expansion of Japanese aims meant that the country was embarked on a programme that was well beyond its available resources.

The Japanese militants expected only verbal protests from Britain and the United States. If London continued to seek some form of settlement with Tokyo, neither Chamberlain nor the new foreign secretary, Lord Halifax, was prepared to move as far in the Japanese direction as the British representatives in Tokyo, Ambassador Craigie and his strongly pro-Japanese military attaché, Major General Piggott, thought necessary. Still, the Chamberlain government remained hesitant about assisting the Chinese war effort, especially since reports from China were contradictory. Those from Hankow stressed the 'supineness, incapacity, disunion, irresponsibility and ill-founded optimism of the Chinese government', and were pessimistic about Chiang's future, while those from Shanghai claimed that in the unlikely event that Chiang should fall, he would be replaced by an even stronger anti-Japanese government, and China would fight on.[47] In the spring and summer of 1938, the Foreign Office preferred to think that Chiang would survive, and that there would not be a Communist take-over of the *Kuomintang*. No move was made to approach the Soviet Union itself, the object of a frenzied anti-Soviet campaign in Tokyo. Though the British hoped that the Russians would continue to deter further Japanese aggression, they certainly did not want a Communist-dominated *Kuomintang*. The Soviets, particularly after Eden's resignation, suspected that Chamberlain would try to move closer to Japan. Given the on-going British approaches to Hitler in Europe, Moscow was convinced that the appeasement of Germany was to be paralleled by an Anglo-Japanese

[47] Lee, *Britain and the Sino-Japanese War*, 126–133.

agreement intended to deflect Japanese aggression away from south China and northwards against the USSR. British policy was less Machiavellian than Stalin thought. Halifax had no wish for a Russo–Japanese war. It was the fear of unnecessarily provoking Tokyo, combined with the need to keep in step with the Americans, that explained why Britain was careful about underwriting the Nationalists. As the European scene darkened, cabinet attention focused on Germany and Italy, almost to the exclusion of East Asian affairs. When Chiang, not for the first time, appealed for a British loan in late April 1938, he took his case again and again to the League of Nations in part to increase the pressure on London. A protracted debate in the Chamberlain cabinet began that extended well into the summer. The adverse European situation contributed to the decision to reject the Chinese request. The only concrete action was official support for the building of the Burma Road, the desperately needed supply route into unoccupied China. The British, like the Americans and the Russians, thought (and hoped) that the war in China would go on and result in stalemate when mediation would be welcomed by both sides.

Whatever the superiority of the Japanese military machine, the very size of China and the financial and economic strains of pursuing their full mobilization programme, were clearly weighing on the Konoe government. Members of the Japanese general staff were concerned that the continuing war in China would make it difficult to prepare for the war against the Soviet Union, which had always been their main preoccupation. Japan's increasing dependence on the United States for oil, and on the Americans and the British Empire for imports of raw materials, machine tools, and armaments, led to a brief reversal of policy in May 1938.

Table 9.2 Japanese Oil Imports

	1000 tons	%
US	3043	66
Dutch Indies	991	21
British Borneo	301	7
Manchukuo	73	2
North Sakhalin	26	1
Others	191	4
Total	4645	100

Source: Chihiro Hosoya, 'Miscalculations in Deterrent Policy: Japanese–US Relations, 1938–1941', *Journal of Peace Research*, 5: 2 (1968), 114.

In a reconstructed cabinet, the vacillating Konoe dropped Hirota and allowed his new foreign minister, General Ugaki Kazushige, to embark on a short-lived attempt in the summer of 1938 to negotiate with Chiang, and seek agreements with Britain and America. At the same time, however, a new war minister was appointed to deal with Germany, with the intention of strengthening the Anti-Comintern Pact. Ugaki hoped that Chiang would come to terms; the Japanese advance into central China was continuing, and no other country but the Soviet Union was sending major assistance to the Nationalists. The Chinese leader might have considered talks if he had had more confidence in Ugaki, and if there had not been a clash between Japan and the Soviet Union at Changkufeng on the Korean–Mongolian border. This had raised hopes of further conflicts in the north that might slow the Japanese advance elsewhere in China. Skirmishes between the Japanese army in Korea and the Soviet military became a little war in July–August 1938. Both sides were badly mauled, but mainly for political and logistic reasons the Korean army surrendered its tactical gains to an overwhelmingly superior Soviet force. Well-supplied with military intelligence, the Soviets knew that the incident would not lead to war between the two countries. A truce was rapidly concluded. The Soviets trumpeted their victory while knowing how poorly their troops had performed. In Tokyo, it was decided not to risk escalation while the situation in China remained unresolved. Blyukher, the commander of the Red Banner Far Eastern Army, though he had testified against Tukhachevsky, was summoned home. Thought to have been indecisive and ultra-cautious in his encounter with the Japanese, he was arrested in October 1938, just as the purges were slowing down. He died in prison in November. It was believed in Moscow that the Japanese would attack again, and that the Far Eastern army and navy required reinforcements.

The Japanese made no progress either in their talks with the KMT, or in those with the sympathetic British ambassador, Sir Robert Craigie, in Tokyo. Preoccupied with the crisis in Czechoslovakia, Chamberlain and Halifax wanted to avoid problems in China. While unprepared to formally recognize the separate existence of Manchukuo, they backed Craigie's efforts to negotiate a compromise in China. The talks begun in July were soon deadlocked. The British produced a formidable list of complaints about Japanese violations of Britain's commercial interests in China; Ugaki countered by demanding that Britain cease to support Chiang, and 'co-operate' with Japan in developing China. After only four months in office, Ugaki resigned in late September. He had embarked on an unpopular course, and had been fighting a rearguard action against those pressing for an all-out war in

China and stronger ties with the Axis. The way was now opened for the hardliners in Tokyo.

VI

An all-out offensive was planned to end Chinese resistance. In October 1938, the Japanese occupied Hankow, the last Chinese major industrial centre, and Canton, which with Hong Kong, handled much of China's arms supplies. With the fall of Hankow, the *Kuomintang* was forced to retreat some thousand miles and establish a new provisional capital in Chungking, a town in the remote province of Szechwan, bordering on Tibet. The taking of Canton and the area north of Hong Kong severed one of the main arteries sustaining the Chinese war effort. Hong Kong was threatened with encirclement, and a serious blow had been dealt to Britain's prestige in south China. The French and Portuguese took fright; each tried to appease the Japanese. The French cut the flow of arms through Haiphong in Indochina to a trickle; the Portuguese took similar action in Macao. The Japanese leaders thought the time appropriate to challenge the western powers. On 3 November 1938, Konoe published his proposals for a New Order in East Asia based on the union of Japan, Manchukuo, and China: 'The Asian people must turn their backs on the self-centred individualistic materialism of Europe, accept the common ideals of Asia and devote themselves to lives rooted in Asia.'[48] Arita Hachiro, Ugaki's successor as foreign minister, in an answer to American protests against Japanese violations of the Open Door and other infringement of their rights, made clear that there was no place for the western powers in the New Order, and that the old principles and treaties no longer applied to the situation in East Asia. The Japanese had publicly abandoned the Washington system and, after some hesitation, 'finally crossed the bridge of no return'.[49] The Konoe–Arita leadership turned to Germany, preparing to negotiate a military alliance against the Soviet Union.

The failure of the first German effort at peacemaking in the winter of 1937–1938 had been followed by a Japanese campaign to secure German recognition of Manchukuo and thus end the flow of arms to China, and military advisers to Chiang. The omens became more favourable when Ribbentrop replaced Neurath at the Foreign Ministry on 4 February 1938. The 'arch-apostle of the pro-Japanese course' was determined 'to establish an iron bridge and not merely a wooden

[48] Quoted in Ian Nish, *Japanese Foreign Policy, 1869–1942: Kasumigaseki to Miyakezaka* (London, 1977) 304.

[49] Iriye, *The Origins of the Second World War in Asia and the Pacific*, 68.

one between Berlin and Tokyo'.[50] On 20 February, Hitler told the *Reichstag* that he was ready to recognize Manchukuo. In a speech full of praise for Japan's political ideology, the Führer stressed its value as an anti-Bolshevik ally, while assuring his audience that 'Japan's greatest victory would not affect the civilization of the white races in the very least'.[51] It was not, however, until June 1938 that all deliveries of war material to China ceased (the Japanese refused to make good the resulting loss of foreign exchange) and the German military advisers and ambassador left China. Hitler abandoned his hopes of running with the hare and with the hounds. Having initially tried to remain neutral in the Sino-Japanese war, the real change in German policy resulted from Hitler's European ambitions. Both he and Ribbentrop believed that a military alliance in the Far East would make the British more amenable to German expansion in central Europe. Whether Japan could be weaned from her ambitions in North China and focus on Britain was an open question.

Relations between Tokyo and Berlin remained unsettled. Ribbentrop, the main German mover for the extension of the Anti-Comintern Pact, sought its transformation into a comprehensive military agreement against the western powers as well as the Soviet Union. Majority opinion in Tokyo, on the contrary, wanted to limit the alliance to operations against the Soviet Union. Japan was hardly in a position to antagonize the Soviet Union and the western powers simultaneously. Nonetheless, unable to force Chiang Kai-shek to accept a ceasefire, and vulnerable to a Soviet advance in the north-west, in August 1938 the Japanese agreed to consider a German draft extending the pact's terms. Opinion in Tokyo remained divided; the war minister supported its extension but Arita, the naval chiefs, and the finance minister opposed, fearing that the projected alliance could involve Japan in war with Britain, France, and the United States, as well as with the Soviet Union. No consensus was reached; disagreements on this and other issues brought the Konoe cabinet down in early 1939. The Germans became visibly annoyed by the caution and indecision in Tokyo as their timetable for action in Europe shortened.

By the end of 1938, there was stalemate in China. Large-scale fighting diminished in the years that followed. The Japanese did not resume offensive operations until 1944. They had already won all the important battles. Japan controlled the major cities and principal seaports, and held most of the key river systems. It had imposed a tight

[50] John P. Fox, *Germany and the Far Eastern Crisis: A Study in Diplomacy and Ideology* (Oxford, 1982), 297.

[51] Ibid., 304.

blockade along the entire Chinese coastline. Yet Chiang Kai-shek refused to capitulate. He could wait in Chungking, where he was safe, trading space for time, and sacrificing territory and manpower to avoid surrender. He still hoped that foreign aid and, in particular, possible American assistance, would sustain Chinese resistance until a general war broke out. The Japanese recognized Chiang's determination to resist when they opened negotiations with Wang Ching-wei, who had secretly left Chungking and flown to Hanoi in late December 1938, prepared to set up a pro-Japanese regime in China. Most Chinese politicians and generals, as well as much of the population, continued to back Chiang Kai-shek. Neither London, Washington, nor Moscow recognized the new regime. The interior of China was still in Nationalist hands and guerrilla warfare spread behind the Japanese lines. If the Chinese Communists showed as much interest in fighting the KMT as in the anti-Japanese campaign, they nevertheless remained implacable foes of any negotiated peace with Tokyo.

The Far Eastern situation at the end of 1938 witnessed the increasing inter-connection between the regional conflict and the global crisis. Most of the non-Asiatic players looked at the war through European-tinted glasses. European preoccupations crowded out regional concerns even when, as in the case of France and the Netherlands, these were of considerable importance. In the spring and summer of 1939, the French considered British plans for the defence of its East Asian empire a dangerous strategic distraction from the war against the Axis. For Germany and Italy, the Anti-Comintern Pact was more important as a weapon against Britain, rather than against the Soviet Union. This was why the Japanese moved so uneasily into the German orbit.

The case was somewhat different in Moscow and London, and, of course, in Washington. Faced with a deteriorating European situation and diplomatic isolation in both Asia and Europe, the Soviets wanted to see Japan tied down in Asia. They were not yet prepared for war with Japan and, above all, wanted to avoid having to fight in Europe and in Asia. Sustaining the Chinese struggle against the Japanese was seen as a way of deterring a Japanese attack on the Soviet Union. Moscow became the largest supplier of war material, especially planes, to China; in 1938 and 1939, new credit agreements were signed and steps were taken to improve the highly dangerous land and air routes through Sinkiang to Lanchow. The CCP was still a problem. The Chinese Communists wanted Soviet arms to go directly to their own Eight Route Red Army. They responded to Chiang's veto by intercepting arms shipments and disappearing into the hills with all they could carry. Stalin was well aware of Mao's intention to strengthen the CCP at Chiang's expense, and harboured his own doubts about

Chiang's steadfastness. If he kept a waiting brief in China, his support for the war against Japan was unequivocal. During the early months of 1939, not only was Moscow on the defensive in Europe, but there were more than thirty Japanese infringements of the Manchurian frontier, which suggested that the Japanese were testing the Soviet defences. There were good reasons for following a low-risk policy in East Asia.

The British, too, had to think globally as they faced threats in both Europe and East Asia. Believing that Japan was getting enmeshed in China, the cabinet concluded that Britain could outlast Japan without a war or making damaging concessions. While hopeful about the outcome of the Asian war, and even about the prospects of American assistance in maintaining the existing balance of power, the British tried to maintain its non-committal policy in East Asia, neither conciliating nor resisting Tokyo. The crisis over Czechoslovakia restricted what could be done in China. The Japanese moves around Hong Kong and Konoe's announcement of 'The New Order in East Asia' were seen as direct challenges to Britain's position. If British attitudes hardened, their policies remained circumspect. Intelligence sources reported on the perilous state of the Japanese economy, and the relative weakness of its army and air force, suggesting that the dangers of retaliation were less than assumed. There was again talk of economic sanctions against Japan. They were rejected as dangerous without joint American action. Instead the government introduced modest measures to assist the KMT. Whereas at the beginning of 1938, the cabinet had rejected Chinese requests for credits and loans, the decisions were reversed in December, in part because of the American $20 million credit to China announced in December. The British first offered a long overdue loan to buy lorries for use on the Burma Road, followed by a £2.5 million credit to buy products in Britain. Other measures taken to support the Chinese currency (serving British interests as well) were presented with great care to avert Japanese anger. A proposed rail line between northern Burma and China's Yunnan province was dropped because of objections from Burma, but work was expedited on the 350-mile Burma Road extending from Kunming, the provincial capital of Yunnan, to Lashio in northern Burma. Because only small shipments of supplies were reaching China through Hong Kong, and the Haiphong route was subject to French closures, an alternative route was essential if assistance was to reach the Chinese. The Burma Road was opened in December 1938 and became China's main supply line to the outside world. A total of about 1,000 tons per month were despatched during 1939; the totals reached 18,000 in 1942. The first consignment contained shipments of ammunition from Germany and Czechoslovakia. Great care was taken with regard to all these moves to underwrite China so as not to provoke Japan. No real effort was made, however, to conclude a general settlement of differences with Tokyo. The Craigie–Utaki conversations in the summer of 1938 had shown how deep the impasse between the two countries was. It was thought that any agreement with Tokyo, as urged by Ambassador Craigie, would discourage Chiang Kai-shek and alienate the Americans who were becoming more active in China. Contrary to Japanese expectations, Britain's European preoccupations and assumed hostility towards the Soviet Union did not result in the appeasement of Japan. There was no Munich in the Far East because there was no need for one. Britain's existing strategy in the Far East appeared to be containing Japan without provoking retaliation against the British Empire.

American attitudes towards Japan stiffened during the course of 1938 and though they and the British followed separate paths, they were leading in the same direction. While Congress refused to consider intervention either in Europe or East Asia, there was some dissatisfaction with the effects of the arms embargo on Spain and deep unease about Hitler's campaign against Czechoslovakia. There was, too, a public reaction against the export of arms to Japan and the Japanese bombing of the Chinese cities. A new pressure group, the American Committee for Non-Participation in Japanese Aggression, and organizations condemning Japanese military action called for punitive sanctions. Roosevelt took particular umbrage at the Konoe announcement of a 'New Order' in East Asia, which he and Hull regarded as a unilateral repudiation of Japan's international obligations. Arita's response to American complaints was unequivocal: 'the concepts and principles of the past did not apply to the present situation'. Japan appeared to have 'finally crossed the bridge of no return'. It was at this point that American officials began to think of specific ways to check Japan, either through the abrogation of the 1911 treaty of commerce which would allow the United States to regulate its trade with Japan or by granting a loan to China. In March–April 1938, Henry Morgenthau, the secretary of the Treasury, arranged for the purchase of fifty million ounces of Chinese silver so that China could buy military supplies. Hull thought this move, the first such offer to the Chinese, premature and an unnecessary affront to Japan. The Japanese moves in China and Hitler's success at Munich strengthened the hand of the pro-Chinese lobby in Washington. In December, the Americans agreed to the offer of the $20 million loan secured by future deliveries of tung oil. It was the start of a flow of loans made in 1940. The Americans still remained cautious about their relations with the British though Japanese policies were pushing the two countries together. The American ambassador in Tokyo insisted that Anglo-American interests were different and common action would only provoke the Japanese. Britain would have to be satisfied with separate representations in Tokyo without the promise of active support.

In retrospect, but even at the time, this tougher American attitude towards the Japanese in contrast to the more tentative policies pursued by the British, is a further indication of the shift in power. Faced with the enmity of Germany and Italy, Britain mounted a holding operation in the Far East until the completion of the two-ocean fleet programme. Success depended on the continuation of the war in China, Soviet pressure on Japan, and American support. The need to keep the Americans in play was a major factor in rejecting Chamberlain's plans to appease the Japanese. With so little hope that the Americans would intervene in Europe, such reservations did not apply to the appeasement of Germany. President Roosevelt felt he had a freer hand in East Asia than in Europe though there were limits to any action. Moral indignations over Japan's denunciations of all the Pacific treaties, the pro-Chinese sympathies of parts of the American press, and the activities of the pro-Chinese lobby weakened the prevailing isolationist winds. The economic arguments, in terms of trade, favoured Japan but these were balanced by American attachment to the Open Door and the hopes of a future market in China. Roosevelt assumed he could take a stronger line in Tokyo without provoking a hostile Congressional reaction. This left Britain in an awkward position. They could not appease the Japanese for fear of alienating the Americans but they could not provoke Tokyo for fear of unleashing a response which they would have to face alone. The two naval powers needed each other for a war in the Pacific but whereas the American navy could concentrate its fleet in one ocean, the British Admiralty had to plan in terms of a global war. This pressure would soon result in a re-thinking of the Mediterranean–Pacific dilemma. The Americans had a freedom of action to which the British could not aspire. Yet the burden on the British navy, given Britain's scattered empire and the home island's defence requirements, was far greater than that on the American fleet. The problem took a concrete form at Tientsin in the summer of 1939.

VII

The Sino-Japanese struggle was a regional conflict that had implications for the global crisis. Its roots were primarily domestic and the conflict restricted to China. The conflict began as a clash between Japanese imperial aspirations and revived Chinese nationalism. Yet from 1931 onwards, the Soviet Union had played a crucial part in shaping both the Japanese imperial drive and the Chinese Nationalist response. There was another dimension, too, which drew other powers into the China quagmire and connected the hemispheres. The Japanese decision to abandon the treaty systems raised difficulties with both Britain and the United States; in particular, the collapse of the Washington–London naval structure opened the way to a naval race in the Pacific which compounded the problems of peace-keeping. The core of the struggle in China was and remained a struggle between the two Asiatic powers. The undeclared war had its own history divorced from what was happening in Europe. There are good reasons why the belligerents in the Second World War adopt different starting dates for the conflict. The war remained confined to the two countries; the Japanese may have considered a campaign against the Russians but hardly a war against Britain and the United States. But because a stalemate developed and the Chinese would not accept their defeat, the powers with strategic and economic interests in the region became increasingly involved. Both combatants sought outside assistance; the Japanese became convinced that foreign assistance explained the Chinese resistance and had to be stopped. Both Asiatic powers responded to and exploited the crises in Europe. For those Great Powers who had interests both in East Asia and Europe there could be no divorce between the continental conflicts. Policies in East Asia were in part responses to events in that region but they also reflected the quarrels in Europe. For most, particularly after 1938, European considerations took precedence over any engagements in East Asia though for Britain, which relied on the global balance of power for its security, and for the Soviet Union, Far Eastern questions could hardly be ignored. The Sino-Japanese war, though it might raise security issues, did not alter the situation in Europe or change the relationships between the European powers. There were links between the Far Eastern war and the global strategic conflict but there were also two separate and distinct crises occurring simultaneously. It was Hitler's challenge in central Europe that would dominate the headlines and engage Europe's statesmen in 1938–1939.

Books

ALDRICH, R. J., *The Key to the South: Britain, the United States and Thailand during the Approach of the Pacific War, 1929–1941* (Oxford, 1993).

ASADA, S., *From Mahan to Pearl Harbour: The Imperial Japanese Navy and the United States* (Annapolis, MD, 2006).

BARNHART, M. A., *Japan Prepares for Total War: The Search for Economic Security, 1919–1941* (Ithaca, NY, 1987).

—— *Japan and the World since 1868* (London, 1995).

BELL, C. M., *The Royal Navy, Sea-power and Strategy between the Wars* (Basingstoke, 2000).

BELL, P., *Chamberlain, Germany and Japan, 1933–34* (Basingstoke, 1996).

Best, A., *Britain, Japan and Pearl Harbor: Avoiding War in East Asia, 1936–41* (London, 1995).

—— *British Intelligence and the Japanese Challenge in Asia, 1919–1941* (London, 2002).

Borg, D., *The United States and the Far Eastern Crisis of 1933–1938: From the Manchurian Incident through the Initial Stage of the Sino-Japanese War* (Cambridge, MA, 1964).

—— and Okamoto, S. (eds.), *Pearl Harbor as History: Japanese–American Relations, 1931–1941* (New York and London, 1973).

Boyce, R. and Maiolo, J. A., *The Origins of Word War Two: The Debate Continues* (London, 2003). See A. Best (Imperial Japan) and J. Garver (China).

Boyd, C., *Extraordinary Envoy: General Oshima Hiroshi and Diplomacy in the Third Reich, 1934–1839* (Washington, DC, 1980).

Brook, T. (ed.), *Documents on the Rape of Nanking* (London, 1999).

Burns, R. D. and Bennett, E. M. (eds.), *Diplomats in Crisis: United States–Chinese–Japanese Relations, 1919–1941* (Santa Barbara, CA, 1974).

Calvocoressi, P., Wint, G., and Pritchard, J., *Total War: The Causes and Courses of the Second World War*, revised 2nd edition (Harmondsworth and New York, 1989), Epilogue, Part I.

Carr, W., *Poland to Pearl Harbor: The Making of the Second World War* (London, 1985).

Chang, J. and Halliday, J., *Mao: The Unknown Story* (London, 2006).

Coble, P. M., *Facing Japan: Chinese Politics and Japanese Imperialism, 1931–1937* (Cambridge, MA, 1991).

Cole, W. C., *Roosevelt and the Isolationists* (Lincoln, NE, 1983).

Crowley, J. B., *Japan's Quest for Autonomy: National Security and Foreign Policy, 1930–1938* (Princeton, NJ, 1966).

Dallek, R., *Franklin D. Roosevelt and American Foreign Policy, 1932–1945* (New York, 1979).

Dallin, A. and Firsov, F. I. (eds.), *Dimitrov and Stalin, 1934–43: Letters from the Soviet Archives* (New Haven, CT, and London, 2000).

Divine, R. A., *The Illusion of Neutrality: Franklin D. Roosevelt and the Struggle over the Arms Embargo* (Chicago, IL, 1962).

Dower, J., *Empire and Aftermath: Yoshida Shigeru and the Japanese Experience, 1878–1954* (Cambridge, MA, 1979).

Dreifort, J. E., *Myopic Grandeur: The Ambivalence of French Foreign Policy toward the Far East, 1919–1945* (Kent, OH, 1991).

Eastman, L., *Seeds of Destruction: Nationalist China in War and Revolution, 1937–1949* (Stanford, CA, 1984).

Endicott, S. L., *Diplomacy and Enterprise: British China Policy, 1933–1937* (Vancouver, 1975).

Fogel, J. A., *The Nanking Massacre in History and Historiography* (London, 2000).

Fox, J. P., *Germany and the Far Eastern Crisis, 1931–1938: A Study in Diplomacy and Ideology* (Oxford, 1982).

Garver, J., *Chinese–Soviet Relations, 1937–1945: The Diplomacy of Chinese Nationalism* (New York, 1988).

GORDON, G. A. H., *British Sea-power and Procurement between the Wars* (Annapolis, MD, 1988).

GOW, I., HIRAMA Y., with CHAPMAN, J. (eds.), *The History of Anglo-Japanese Relations, 1600–2000, Vol. III: The Military Dimension* (Basingstoke and New York, 2003). See J. Ferris, I. Gow, T. Kuramatsu, Y. Aizawa, J. W. M. Chapman.

HAGGIE, P., *Britannia at Bay: The Defence of the British Empire against Japan, 1931–1941* (Oxford and New York, 1981).

HALL, C., *Britain, America and Arms Control, 1921–1937* (Basingstoke, 1987).

HASLAM, J., *The Soviet Union and the Threat from the East 1933–1941: Moscow, Tokyo and the Prelude to the Pacific War* (Basingstoke and London, 1992).

HATTENDORF, J. and JORDAN, R. (eds.), *Maritime Strategy and the Balance of Power* (London, 1989).

HEINRICHS, W. H., *American Ambassador: John Grew and the Development of the United States Diplomatic Tradition* (Boston, MA, 1966).

—— *Threshold of War: Franklin D. Roosevelt and American Entry into WWII* (New York, 1988).

HERZOG, J., *Closing the Open Door: Anglo-Japanese Diplomatic Negotiations, 1936–1941* (Annapolis, MD, 1973).

HOU, C.-M., *Foreign Investment and Economic Development in China, 1840–1937* (Cambridge, 1965).

HUNT, M. H., *The Genesis of Chinese Communist Foreign Policy* (New York, 1996).

IRIYE, A., *The Chinese and the Japanese: Essays on Political and Cultural Interaction* (Princeton, NJ, 1980).

—— *The Origins of the Second World War in Asia and the Pacific* (London and New York, 1987).

KENNEDY, G. C., *Imperial Crossroads: The Influence of the Far East on Anglo-American Relations, 1933–1939* (London, 2002).

KENNEDY, P., *The Rise and Fall of British Naval Mastery* (New York, 1976).

KREBS, G. and MARTIN, B. (eds.), *Formierung und Fall der Achse Berlin–Tokyo* (Munich, 1994).

KREINER, J. and MATHIAS, R. (eds.), *Deutschland—Japan in der Zwischenkriegszeit* (Bonn, 1990). See T. Leims, and D. Schauwecker.

KUTAKOV, L. N., *Japanese Foreign Policy on the Eve of the Pacific War: A Soviet View* (Tallahassee, FL, 1972).

LAMB, M. and TARLING N., *From Versailles to Pearl Harbor: The Origins of the Second World War in Europe and Asia* (Basingstoke, 2001).

LARGE, S., *Emperor Hirohito and Showa Japan* (London, 1997).

LEE, B., *Britain and the Sino-Japanese War, 1937–1939: A Study in the Dilemmas of British Decline* (London, 1973).

LEIGH, M., *Mobilizing Consent: Public Opinion and American Foreign Policy, 1937–1945* (Westport, CT, 1976).

LEUTZE, J. R., *Bargaining for Supremacy: Anglo-American Naval Relations, 1937–1941* (Chapel Hill, NC, 1977).

LOUIS, W. R., *British Strategy in the Far East, 1919–1939* (Oxford, 1971).

LOWE, P., *Great Britain and the Origins of the Pacific War* (Oxford, 1977).

—— *Britain in the Far East* (London, 1981).

MacDonald, C. A., *The United States, Britain and Appeasement* (London, 1981).

Marder, A. J., *Old Friends, New Enemies: The Royal Navy and the Imperial Japanese Navy. Vol. 1. Strategic Illusions, 1936–1941* (Oxford, 1981).

Marks III, F. W., *Wind over Sand: The Diplomacy of Franklin Roosevelt* (Athens, OH, 1987).

McIntyre, W. D., *The Rise and Fall of the Singapore Naval Base, 1919–1942* (London, 1979).

Morley, J. W. (ed.), *Deterrent Diplomacy: Japan, Germany and the USSR, 1935–1940* (New York, 1976).

—— (ed.), *The China Quagmire: Japan's Expansion on the Asian Continent, 1933–1941* (New York, 1983).

Murfett, M. H., *Fool-Proof Relations: The Search for Anglo-American Naval Cooperation during the Chamberlain Years 1937–1940* (Singapore, 1984).

Neidpath, J., *The Singapore Naval Base and the Defence of Britain's Eastern Empire, 1919–1941* (Oxford, 1981).

Nish, I., *Japanese Foreign Policy, 1869–1942: Kasumigaseki to Miyakezaka* (London and Boston, MA, 1977).

—— (ed.), *Anglo–Japanese Alienation, 1919–1952: Papers of the Anglo-Japanese Conference on the History of the Second World War* (Cambridge, 1982).

—— *Some Aspects of Soviet–Japanese Relations in the 1930s* (London, 1982).

—— *Britain and Japan: Biographical Portraits* (Folkestone, Kent, 1994). See I. Nish (Ashton–Gwatkin), A. Best (Craigie)

—— *Japanese Foreign Policy in the Interwar Period* (Westport, CT, and London, 2002).

—— and Kibata, Y. (eds.), *The History of Anglo-Japanese Relations, 1600–2000 Vol. II: The Political–Diplomatic Dimension, 1931–2000* (Basingstoke and New York, 2000). See K. Yoichi, A. Best, I. Osamu, and J. Sharkey.

O'Brien, P., *Technology and Naval Combat in the Twentieth Century and Beyond* (London, 2001). See M. R. Peattie, S. T. Sumuda, and P. O'Brien.

Oka, Y., *Konoe Fumimaro: A Political Biography*, trans. Shumpei Okamoto and Patricia Murray (Tokyo, 1983).

Ong, C., *Operation Matador: Britain's War Plans against the Japanese, 1918–1941* (Singapore, 1997).

Pelz, S. E., *Race to Pearl Harbor: The Failure of the Second London Naval Conference and the Onset of World War II* (Cambridge, MA, 1974).

Pritchard, R. J., *Far Eastern Influence upon British Strategy Towards the Great Powers, 1937–39* (New York, 1987).

Reynolds, D., *The Creation of the Anglo-American Alliance, 1937–1941* (London, 1981).

—— *From Munich to Pearl Harbor* (Chicago, IL, 2001).

Roskill, S., *Naval Policy between the Wars, Vol. II: The Period of Reluctant Rearmament, 1930–1939* (London, 1976).

Shai, A., *The Origins of the War in the East: Britain, China and Japan, 1937–1939* (London, 1976).

Sommer, T., *Deutschland und Japan zwischen den Mächten, 1935–1940: Vom Antikominternpakt zum Dreimächtepakt* (Tübingen, 1962).

SPENCE, J. D., *The Gate of Heavenly Peace: The Chinese and their Revolution, 1895–1980* (Middlesex, 1982).

STORRY, G. R., *Japan and the Decline of the West in Asia, 1894–1943* (London, 1979).

SUN, Y., *China and the Origins of the Pacific War, 1931–1941* (New York, 1993).

TARLING, N., *Britain, Southeast Asia and the Onset of the Pacific War* (Cambridge, 1996).

TILL, G., *Air Power and the Royal Navy* (London, 1979).

TROTTER, A., *Britain and East Asia, 1933–1937* (Cambridge, 1975).

UTLEY, J. G., *Going to War with Japan, 1937–1941* (Knoxville, TN, 1985).

WHYMANT, R., *Stalin's Spy: Richard Sorge and the Tokyo Espionage Ring* (London, 1996).

YOUNG, L. D., *Japan's Total Empire: Manchuria and the Culture of Wartime Imperialism* (Berkeley, CA, 1998).

Articles and Chapters

AGBI, S. O., 'The Foreign Office and Yoshida's Bid for *Rapprochement* with Britain in 1936–7', *Historical Journal*, 21 (1978).

—— 'The Pacific War Controversy in Britain: Sir Robert Craigie versus the Foreign Office', *Modern Asian Studies*, 17 (1983).

BARNHART, M. A., 'The Origins of World War II in Asia and the Pacific: Synthesis Impossible?', *Diplomatic History*, 20 (1996).

BENNETT, G., 'British Policy in the Far East, 1933–1936: Treasury and Foreign Office', *Modern Asian Studies*, 26: 3 (1992).

BEST, A., 'Constructing an Image: British Intelligence and Whitehall's Perception of Japan, 1931–1939', *Intelligence and National Security*, 11 (1996).

—— 'Anglo-Japanese Relations in the 1930s: The Inevitable Road to War?', *Bulletin of Asia-Pacific Studies*, 8 (1998).

—— 'Economic Appeasement' or Economic Nationalism? A Political Perspective on the British Empire, Japan and the Rise of Intra-Asian Trade, 1933–37', *Journal of Imperial and Commonwealth History*, 30 (2000).

BLOSS, H., 'Deutsche Chinapolitik im Dritten Reich', in Funke, M. (ed.), *Hitler, Deutschland und die Mächte* (Düsseldorf, 1976).

—— 'Die Zweigleisigkeit der deutschen Fernostpolitik und Hitlers Option für Japan 1938', *Militärgeschichtliche Mitteilungen*, 1 (1980).

BOURETTE-KNOWLES, S., 'The Global Micawber: Sir Robert Vansittart, the Treasury and the Global Balance of Power, 1933–35', *Diplomacy and Statecraft*, 6: 1 (1995).

CROWLEY, J. B., 'The Marco Polo Bridge Incident, 1937', in Morley, J. W. (ed.), *The China Quagmire: Japan's Expansion on the Asian Continent, 1933–1941* (New York, 1983).

DOERR, P. W., 'The Changkufeng/Lake Khasan Incident, 1938', *Intelligence and National Security*, 5 (1990).

DREA, E. J., 'Reading Each Other's Mail: Japanese Communication Intelligence, 1920–1941', *Journal of Military History*, 55 (1991).

Ferris, J., 'From Broadway House to Bletchley Park: The Diary of Captain Malcolm Kennedy, 1934–46', *Intelligence and National Security*, 4 (1989).

Ferris, J., 'Worthy of Some Better Enemy? The British Estimate of the Imperial Japanese Navy, 1919–1941, and the Fall of Singapore', *Canadian Journal of History*, 28: 2 (1993).

Garver, J. W., 'The Soviet Union and the Xi'an Incident', *Australian Journal of Chinese Affairs*, 26 (1991).

—— 'Comment: Mao, the Comintern and the Second United Front', in 'New Light on the Second United Front: An Exchange of Views', *China Quarterly*, 142 (1992).

Haslam, J., 'Soviet Aid to China and Japan's Place in Moscow's Foreign Policy, 1937–1939', in Nish, I. (ed.), *Some Aspects of Soviet–Japanese Relations in the 1930s* (London, 1982).

Hata, I., 'The Japanese–Soviet Confrontation, 1935–1939', in Morley, J. W. (ed.), *Deterrent Diplomacy: Japan, Germany and the USSR, 1935–1940* (New York, 1976).

Hatano, S., and Asada, S., 'The Japanese Decision to Move South', in Boyce, R. W. D. and Robertson, E. M. (eds.), *Paths to War: New Essays on the Origins of the Second World War* (London, 1989).

Hosoya, C., 'Miscalculation in Deterrent Policy: Japanese–U.S. Relations, 1938–1941', *Journal of Peace Research*, 11 (1968).

Iriye, A., 'Imperialism in East Asia', in Crowley, J. B. (ed.), *Modern East Asia: Essays in Interpretation* (New York, 1970).

Kennedy, G. C., '1935: A Snapshot of British Imperial Defence in the Far East', in Neilson, K. and Kennedy, G. C. (eds.), *Far-Flung Lines: Studies in Imperial Defence in Honour of Donald Mackenzie Schurman* (Portland, OR, and London, 1997).

—— 'The Keelung Incident and Britain's Far Eastern Strategic Foreign Policy, 1936–1937', in Kennedy, G. C. and Neilson, K. (eds.), *Incidents and International Relations: People, Power and Personalities* (Westport, CT, and London, 2002).

Kennedy, P., 'British "Net Assessment" and the Coming of the Second World War', in Millet, A. R. and Murray, W. (eds.), *Calculations: Net Assessments and the Coming of World War II* (New York, 1992).

Louis, W. R., 'The Road to Singapore: British Imperialism in the Far East, 1932–1942', in Mommsen, W. J. and Kettenacker, L. (eds.), *The Fascist Challenge and the Policy of Appeasement* (London, 1983).

Lowe, P., 'The Dilemmas of an Ambassador: Sir Robert Craigie in Tokyo, 1937–1941', *Proceedings of the British Association for Japanese Studies*, 2 (1977).

Martin, B., 'Die deutsch-japanischen Beziehungen während des Dritten Reiches' in Funke, M. (ed.), *Hitler, Deutschland und die Mächte* (Düsseldorf, 1976).

Murfett, M. H., 'Living in the Past: A Critical Re-examination of the Singapore Naval Strategy, 1918–1941', *War and Society*, 11 (1993).

Nish, I., 'Japan in Britain's View of the International System, 1919–1937', in Nish, I. (ed.), *Anglo-Japanese Alienation, 1919–1952: Papers of the Anglo-Japanese Conference on the History of the Second World War* (Cambridge, 1982).

—— 'An Overview of Relations between China and Japan, 1895–1945', *China Quarterly*, 124 (1990).

OHATA, T., 'The Anti-Comintern Pact, 1935–1939', in Morley, J. W. (ed.), *Deterrent Diplomacy: Japan, Germany and the USSR, 1935–1940* (New York, 1976).

O'NEILL, R., 'Churchill, Japan and British Security in the Pacific, 1904–1942', in Blake, R. N. W. and Louis, Wm. R. (eds.), *Churchill* (Oxford, 1993).

ROTHWELL, V. H., 'The Mission of Sir Frederick Leith-Ross to the Far East, 1935–1936', *Historical Journal*, 18 (1975).

SHENG, M. M., 'Response: Mao and Stalin: Adversaries or Comrades?', *China Quarterly*, 129 (1992).

—— 'Mao, Stalin and the Formation of the Anti-Japanese United Front, 1935–7', *China Quarterly*, 129 (1992).

SHIMADA, T., 'Designs on North China, 1933–1937', in Morley, J. W. (ed.), *The China Quagmire: Japan's Expansion on the Asian Continent, 1933–1941* (New York, 1983).

SUMIDA, J., '"The Best Laid Plans"': The Development of British Battle Fleet Tactics, 1919–1942', *International History Review*, XIV (1992).

TILL, G., 'Perceptions of Naval Power between the Wars: The British Case', in Towle, P. (ed.), *Estimating Foreign Military Power* (London, 1982).

TSOKHAS, K., 'Anglo-Australian Relations and the Origins of the Pacific War', *History*, 80 (1995).

WARK, W., 'In Search of a Suitable Japan: British Naval Intelligence in the Pacific before the Second World War', *Intelligence and National Security*, 1: 2 (1986).

WATT, D. C., 'Chamberlain's Ambassadors', in Dockrill, M. and McKercher, B. (eds.), *Diplomacy and World Power: Studies in British Foreign Policy, 1890–1950* (Cambridge, 1996).

WILSON, S., 'The "New Paradise": Japanese Emigration to Manchuria in the 1930s and 1940s', *International History Review*, 17: 2 (1995).

YANG, D., 'Convergence or Divergence?: Recent Historical Writings on the Rape of Nanking', *American Historical Review*, 104: 3 (1999).

YOUNG, L., 'Japan at War: History-Writing on the Crisis of the 1930s' in Martel, G. (ed.), *The Origins of the Second World War Reconsidered: A. J. P. Taylor and the Historians*, 2nd edn. (London, 1999).

10

Hitler Moves: Austria and Czechoslovakia, 1938

I

On 12 March 1938, German troops marched into Austria. The next day, to cheering crowds, Hitler proclaimed the union of Austria and Germany. It was a long expected move though the actual sequence of events took many by surprise. Already in mid-December 1937, Papen had suggested a meeting with Hitler to Schuschnigg, apparently in accordance with the Austrian chancellor's wish for a personal discussion with the Führer. The date was set for the end of January, but because of the Blomberg–Fritsch crisis it was postponed until 12 February. Schuschnigg arrived at Berchtesgaden thinking he would be offered a confirmation of the German guarantee of Austrian independence, in return for concessions that he had already outlined to Seyss-Inquart, who naturally informed Hitler. After a friendly greeting the Führer ranted about Austrian 'treason' against Germany. Elsewhere, Ribbentrop presented the terms of the ultimatum to be implemented by 15 February to the Austrian foreign minister. They included the lifting of all restrictions on the National Socialists, an amnesty for Nazis already arrested, the appointment of Seyss-Inquart as minister of the interior with control over the security forces, Edmund von Glaise-Horstenau to be made war minister, and steps taken to integrate the Austrian and German economies. Schuschnigg had already privately accepted most of these terms, but the appointment of Seyss-Inquart came as an unexpected shock. Hitler summoned three of his generals to be in attendance at lunch. When in the late afternoon, Schuschnigg was informed of the terms, he claimed that only the Austrian president could make cabinet appointments and grant amnesties; Hitler summoned General Keitel to act briefly as a silent witness. The implied threat of a military invasion proved successful. With some modest changes, Schuschnigg gave in and agreed to Hitler's demands. The shaken and depressed Austrian delegation, accompanied by Papen, returned to Salzburg that evening. They were far too demoralized to have accepted Hitler's invitation to dine.

Schuschnigg complied with the terms of the ultimatum on 15 February. Hitler believed that Austria would fall into his lap without any military action through a combination of internal subversion and external threat. His 20 February speech praised the Berchtesgaden agreement, but made no mention of the promised reference to non-interference in Austria's internal politics. Schuschnigg's chief concern now was to avoid a German invasion. Late in February, with a small group of associates he began to plan for a plebiscite intended to show that an overwhelming majority of the public supported Austrian independence. The vote was planned for Sunday, 13 March.

Schuschnigg's announcement on 9 March took Hitler completely by surprise. First incredulous, and then infuriated, he called for General Keitel and demanded to see the plans for a march into Austria. There were no such plans. 'Operation Otto', a proposed action in case of a Habsburg restoration, was resuscitated and revised. The pace of activity at Berchtesgaden became frantic as Hitler's advisers were summoned to give advice. Goebbels and Göring were each called to see Hitler. The Führer wanted action, but he wanted it given a cloak of legality. According to his own account, Göring assumed control of the operation during Saturday, 12 March. Seyss-Inquart and Glaise-Horstenau were to demand that the referendum be postponed for two weeks allowing for a plebiscite similar to that held in the Saarland in 1935, Schuschnigg should resign to make room for Seyss-Inquart, and all restrictions on the National Socialists should be lifted. The first ultimatum was sent to Schuschnigg around 10 a.m. The Austrian chancellor accepted the postponement but refused to resign. His appeals to London for support proved futile. At about 3.30 he resigned, but the Austrian president refused to appoint Seyss-Inquart to replace him. A new ultimatum was sent off to Vienna with an expiry time of 7.30. At 8 p.m. Schuschnigg went on the air, describing the ultimatum, and claiming that Austria had yielded to force. In order to avoid bloodshed, troops would offer no resistance.

By this time, with German encouragement, local Nazis were rampaging through the Austrian cities. Göring wanted Seyss-Inquart to send Berlin a pre-arranged telegram asking for German help to restore order. Seyss-Inquart refused, hoping to avoid German occupation, and thus preserve some remnants of Austrian independence. Göring replied that oral agreement would suffice. Eventually, the telegram was sent, but it was irrelevant because, prompted by Göring, Hitler had already given the *Wehrmacht* the order to march. It was only at midnight that the Austrian president gave in and appointed Seyss-Inquart as chancellor. All the German demands had been met, but no change in orders took place. A last attempt by Seyss-Inquart to stave off the inevitable was brusquely rejected by Hitler. At 5.30 a.m. on 12 March, German troops began their 'friendly visit' to Austria. Hitler later flew to Munich to prepare for his triumphal entry into the land of his birth.

Steps were taken to reassure Mussolini, who had been promised that he would be consulted before any action was taken over Austria. On the Saturday, Hitler had sent a handwritten letter with Prince Philipp of Hesse, explaining his decision and assuring the Duce of his undiminished sympathy. In fact, the decision to march was taken before Mussolini's reply was received. Nonetheless, Hitler was relieved and grateful to receive Mussolini's positive response. 'Please tell Mussolini I will never forget him for it, never, never, never, come what may', he told Hesse over the telephone. 'Should he ever need any help or be in any danger, he can be sure that, do or die, I shall stick by him, come what may, even if the whole world rises against him.'[1] Hitler actually remembered his promises to the Duce. Göring squared the Czech minister in Berlin. In return for a promise not to mobilize, the Czechs were assured that their country had 'nothing to fear' from the Reich. His assurances were welcomed in Prague where, in any case, there was no inclination to act. It was only after *Anschluss* that Beneš became nervous, but perhaps not nervous enough, about its consequences.

As the German army entered Austria, they were warmly welcomed; tanks were decked with blooms in this first of the 'flower wars'. Hitler made his way more slowly, stopping at Braunau-am-Inn, his birthplace, and at Linz where he had gone to school. He took there the decision to incorporate Austria directly into the Reich, instead of creating a satellite state. *Anschluss* was completed on 13 March, the day designated for the Austrian plebiscite. The Austrian army took an oath of allegiance to Hitler. A member of the 'old guard', Josef Bürckel, was brought in from the Saar to reorganize the Austrian Nazi party, for Hitler was not going to leave the party in the hands of the highly unreliable Austrian Nazi leadership. In Vienna, Hitler proclaimed the 'entry of my homeland into the Reich'. Before leaving, he signed decrees prohibiting the formation of any political party but the Nazi party, and excluding Jews from public service. Behind the German army came the police and SS Death's Head formations. Arrests began immediately, as did the persecution of Austria's 200,000 Jews helped by the long tradition of anti-Semitism in the country. During these first days, jeering crowds in Vienna watched the so-called 'rubbing parties', as Jews were forced to erase the pre-plebiscite slogans and Jewish shopkeepers were compelled to paint '*Jude*' on their storefronts. The horrors of these demonstrations of Austrian anti-Semitism created consternation elsewhere, particularly

[1] Quoted in Ian Kershaw, *Hitler,* vol 2. *Nemesis, 1936–1945, 78.* My account follows that of Kershaw.

among the already embattled Jewish community in Germany. By the autumn, thanks to the efficiency of Adolph Eichmann, 45,000 Jews had emigrated, having paid handsomely for the privilege. New Reich elections were announced for 10 April, and a plebiscite called for all of Germany, including Austria. The results were a triumph for Hitler. His popularity soared as he travelled from one end of Germany to the other, 'electioneering'. The last ten days were spent in Austria, and climaxed in Vienna with a final exhortation by the 'Man of Destiny' to a wildly cheering crowd of some 200,000 Austrians.

Anschluss, long predicted, was an improvised affair in execution. Hitler's anger and rages were brilliantly used to achieve his long-intended ends. An unusual combination of uncertainty and determination, spontaneity and calculation, characterized his policies during this short-lived crisis. He had taken only the most modest gamble when he sent his army into Austria, though the army was ill-prepared even for this limited action. Schuschnigg's last-minute attempt to appeal to the people was a reversal of the policies the Austrian chancellor had followed towards Berlin for the previous two years, and which he abandoned because no other country came to his support and Hitler had ceased to tolerate the status quo. Though Schuschnigg's later critics have argued that even a brief struggle might have cast doubts on the story of a 'festive entry', the welcome accorded Hitler suggests otherwise. The Austrian National Socialists had done their job well; those who opposed *Anschluss* were scattered and powerless. The '*Anschluss* from inside', a recent study has concluded, worked better in many cases than the invasion of the German *Wehrmacht*, which was by no means perfect.[2] Hitler was equally correct in his assumption that the other powers would accept a *fait accompli*. Britain, France (with only an interim government in place), the Soviet Union, and Poland had each written off Austria months before Hitler made his move. Apart from its very positive effect on German national pride, *Anschluss* was important mainly in the context of Hitler's future expansionist programme. Both before and after the Austrian annexation, Hitler's attention was focused on Czechoslovakia, the far more important, but also more dangerous, acquisition that he sought. *Anschluss* put Germany in an excellent position to threaten Prague. Bohemia was now encircled on three sides. Once in occupation, the Reich could revive Vienna's traditional financial and trade links with the countries of south-eastern Europe, and

[2] Oliver Rathkolb, 'The Anschluss in the Rearview Mirror, 1938–2008: Historical Memories Between Debate and Transformation', in Günter Bischof et al. (eds.), *New Perspectives on Austrians and World War II: Contemporary Austrian History, 17* (New Brunswick, NJ, and London, 2009).

make it the centre of Germany's informal empire in the region. The actual economic effects of *Anschluss* were mixed. Austrian industry was integrated into the German rearmament effort and the country, assisted by the initial German investment, enjoyed an economic boom. The key industrial prize was the 'Alpine', Austria's chief steel producer and exporter of high-grade iron ore, mainly to Czechoslovakia and Hungary. *Reichswerke Hermann Göring* seized the firm, which was used to establish a strong bargaining position in south-eastern Europe.[3] While *Anschluss* increased Germany's overall industrial capacity, the gains proved limited. The country was poor in heavy industrial resources and required considerable food imports to survive. More valuable to the Germans was the large number of unemployed workers but, above all, the considerable reserves of gold and foreign exchange held in the Austrian state bank. By forcing the Austrians to surrender privately held gold and foreign deposits as well, the Germans considerably increased their holdings at a time when the foreign exchange situation in Germany was again looking critical. Germany acquired 'at least 782 million Reichsmarks, more than the combined total of all the existing German foreign exchange holdings'.[4] On the negative side of the ledger, in the longer run, Austria's need for imported foodstuffs and industrial raw materials added to the problems of the Reich's balance of payments problems, the crucial constraint on its rearmament programme.

The Austrian crisis disrupted the British search for a settlement with Germany which had begun with the Halifax visit in November 1937. On 3 March, Sir Nevile Henderson had met Hitler who, 'glowering in his chair', was infuriated by Britain's new proposals for a settlement. Henderson's upper-class appearance and manner, representative of the social milieu that Hitler so resented, could hardly have made the ambassador's task any easier. Henderson spoke of limitations on Germany's armed strength, particularly its bombers, and suggested that future changes in Europe should take place only by agreement. Hitler dismissed the British feeler. He was not going to let anyone interfere in Germany's relationship with countries of the same nationality, which had large German populations, and if 'internal explosions' took place, he warned, Germany would not remain neutral, but 'would act with lightning speed'.[5] As for aerial disarmament, he insisted that German armaments were a response to Russia and that Britain should start its

[3] Details are from Adam Tooze, *The Wages of Destruction*, 245–249.

[4] Ibid., 246.

[5] *DBFP*, 2nd ser., Vol. XIX, No. 615: 'glowering in his chair'; *DGFP*, Ser. D, Vol. I, No. 138: 'lightning speed'.

disarmament efforts there. The vague promises of giving Germany limited rule over territories in tropical Africa, an offer conceived and elaborated by Chamberlain, was no temptation to agreement. In London, on 11 March, Chamberlain and Halifax gave a farewell lunch for Ribbentrop who was relinquishing the London embassy. With the Austrian crisis already under way, they lectured the new foreign minister on this 'exhibition of naked force', without making any impression. As Hitler anticipated, apart from verbal denunciations, no action was contemplated or taken. No warning was issued to Berlin about the outcome of any future German aggression, as Winston Churchill and some members of the Opposition demanded. The Austrian *coup* only proved to Chamberlain that the policy of seeking an agreement with Italy should have been adopted earlier. As with his view of Hitler, Chamberlain seriously misjudged Mussolini and his imperial aims. On 13 March, writing to his sister, the British prime minister explained that though talks with Germany would have to be abandoned and rearmament increased or accelerated to show that Britain would not be bullied, 'if we can avoid another violent *coup* in Czechoslovakia, which ought to be feasible, it may be possible for Europe to settle down again, and some day for us to start peace talks again with the Germans'.[6] Once again, however, as far as Chamberlain was concerned, it seemed to be the French who were making difficulties.

On the day the Germans entered Austria, France was between governments, with the Chautemps ministry acting as caretaker, and the politicians occupied with the cabinet crisis. A Blum government took office on 13 March. There was no *Union Sacrée* as Blum wished, and from the start his political situation was highly precarious. French protests over Austria, though stronger than those of the British, were more a matter of form than substance. Several months earlier, the small country had been written off as a lost cause both by the *Quai d'Orsay* and the service departments. Well-informed about the negotiations in Berchtesgaden (the French were reading the Austrian diplomatic traffic), Daladier and Gamelin had decided during the second week of February that Austrian independence was not worth a war with Germany. In keeping with its retreat from Eastern Europe, the Chautemps government accepted that France would do nothing. Once in office, Blum and Paul-Boncour, the new foreign minister, appeared more resolute. As with the British, the key question was Czechoslovakia. Rumours of a threat to Prague had circulated before the annexation of Austria; post-*Anschluss,* there was general agreement that Czechoslovakia would be Hitler's next victim. On 14 March, Paul-Boncour

[6] Robert Self (ed.), *The Neville Chamberlain Diary Letters,* Vol. 4 (Aldershot, 2005), 305.

assured the Czech minister in Paris that France would fulfil all its obligations to his country. The following day, Blum asked the Council of National Defence what direct assistance could be given to Czechoslovakia if Germany were to attack her. As defence minister, Daladier replied that France could offer no direct aid, as it still lacked the necessary mobile armoured force, and that the only possible action would be to mobilize and thereby to 'hold German troops on our frontier'. Gamelin and General Vuillemin, the newly appointed Air Force chief of staff, dismissed the possibility of Soviet assistance to Czechoslovakia, citing Polish and Romanian objections to the passage of Soviet land forces and the anticipated early German destruction of Czech airfields so that no Soviet aircraft could land. Spain was also discussed, including Blum's idea of an ultimatum to Franco. Daladier and Gamelin opposed any French military intervention. 'Such an intervention, not motivated by new developments, risks leaving us alone before Germany and Italy without any assurance of British assistance', Daladier argued, 'and with only the mediocre aid of a Russia that is far off and weakened'.[7] Though the official policy of 'non-intervention' remained in place, French and Soviet arms were allowed to cross the Pyrenean frontier in increasing quantities. The border was not sealed again until June, when Daladier finally acceded to British demands for closure.

On 4 April, the French representatives from central and Eastern Europe were summoned to the *Quai d'Orsay* where they reported that Czechoslovakia had little to hope for from either Poland or Romania. Paul-Boncour attempted to counter this mood of defeatism, but the Blum government fell on 8 April after the Senate rejected Blum's demand for plenary powers to institute a programme of financial reform and industrial expansion, based on a vastly increased rearmament programme. The model was to be Schacht's war economy programme, centred on exchange controls. In addition to British doubts about the Popular Front government, Sir Eric Phipps and the Foreign Office were particularly glad to see the back of Paul-Boncour. They judged him, on past performance, as a dangerous and unreliable 'light-weight', whose strong anti-Italian views would make agreement with Mussolini difficult. In an extraordinary intervention, Orme Sargent advised Phipps that 'anything we can do to weaken the present French government and precipitate its fall would be in the British interest'.[8] When the Blum ministry duly fell, Phipps actively and successfully opposed Paul-Boncour's return to the *Quai*

[7] *DDF*, 2nd ser., Vol. VIII, No. 446 (minutes of the Comité Permanent de la Défense Nationale, 15 March 1938).

[8] Sargent to Phipps, 17 March 1938 (from Phipps papers), quoted in Anthony Adamthwaite, *France and the Coming of the Second World War, 1936–1939* (London, 1977), 84.

d'Orsay. Édouard Daladier, the new premier, appointed Georges Bonnet, a leading anti-Popular Front Radical and a strong proponent of conciliating Germany. Bonnet would bring added political backing to a weak right-centre coalition ministry. According to Paul-Boncour's memoirs, Daladier, in rejecting his appeal to stay at the *Quai d'Orsay*, replied: 'The policy you propose is a good one, the honourable course for France to follow. I do not believe, unhappily, that we have the capability to follow such a policy. I will take Bonnet.'[9] The British would have preferred the more easily influenced Chautemps—for Bonnet was known to be clever, ambitious, and untrustworthy—but the new French ministers were invited to London to bolster the team and to make certain that France would follow Britain's lead. The two-day meetings on 28 and 29 April served to confirm Britain's leadership.

In Moscow, as elsewhere, *Anschluss* was anticipated well before it happened, but no preparations were made for any response. The march into Austria occurred on the eve of the sentencing of Bukharin, Krestinsky, and the other unfortunate Bolsheviks accused of being 'War Provocateurs', in the latest and what proved to be the last, of Stalin's 'show trials'. It was not until 14 March that the Moscow papers began to comment on the events in Austria, with Britain depicted as the chief villain, and German actions blamed on Chamberlain's policy of appeasing Hitler. Litvinov wanted a more active Soviet response to the German move; he thought it possible to mobilize the anti-appeasers in Britain and France, put the responsibility for further inaction clearly on Britain, and refute insinuations about Soviet weakness. Already on the defensive, and aware of the growing opposition to collective security, he assured the *Politburo* that none of his proposals would create new Soviet obligations in Europe. He appears to have secured Stalin's permission for a declaration to foreign journalists that condemned *Anschluss* and stated that the Soviet Union was ready to enter immediately into discussions with the western countries both in and outside the League of Nations, for the adoption of practical measures to handle the existing circumstances. He warned the journalists that 'Tomorrow may already be too late.'[10] Litvinov had long seen the problems of Austria and Czechoslovakia as one. As he wrote to the Soviet *polpred* in Prague, he feared that Beneš, like Schuschnigg, would go down 'the path of gradual concessions, and will end up falling in the same pit'. His declaration, he warned, 'is, perhaps, our last call for co-operation in Europe; after that we shall probably take a position of little interest in the future developments in Europe'.[11]

9 Joseph Paul-Boncour, Entre deux guerres, III, 101.

10 *DVP*, Vol. XXI, No. 82.

11 Quoted in Zara Steiner, 'The Soviet Commissariat of Foreign Affairs and the Czechoslovakian Crisis in 1938', *Historical Journal*, 42: 3 (1999), 755.

Everywhere, and most of all in Berlin, *Anschluss* returned the spotlight onto Czechoslovakia. Hitler's new appointees to the *Wehrmacht* were already working on 'Case Green', adapting the revised 1937 plan for the invasion of Czechoslovakia, to take account of the annexation of Austria and Hitler's preference for 'a lightning-like operation following an incident'.[12] Once the surprise attack began, it would be necessary to break through the Czech frontier defences and win a decisive victory within four days, in order to encourage Hungary and Poland to seize their share of the booty and keep other states from intervening. The army plan was submitted to Hitler on 20 May, the day of a partial Czechoslovakian mobilization in response to false rumours of an impending German attack. Hitler stepped up the preparations for military action and altered the general introductory statement with regard to its timing, without, however, setting any definite date. The annexation of Austria also had an almost immediate effect on German efforts to use the discontents of the Sudeten Germans to further Hitler's cause. Prior to *Anschluss*, relations with Czechoslovakia were correct, if tense. Hitler's reference in his Reichstag speech of 20 February, to the 'ten million Germans' whose 'right of racial self-determination' he intended to protect, did not pass unnoticed in Prague. Prime minister Hodža warned the Germans off any interference in domestic affairs, but also promised new concessions to the Sudetens and future consultations with Henlein. On 27 March there were enthusiastic demonstrations in the Sudetenland, and rumours that the *Wehrmacht* would enter Czechoslovakia after the coming plebiscite in Germany. The next day Henlein was received by Hitler, who directed him on the tactics the Sudeten German party should follow. Henlein repeated the formula back to Hitler: 'we must always demand so much that we cannot be satisfied'.[13] More detailed instructions came in a conference with Ribbentrop on 29 March, including cautions not to move faster than his mentors in Berlin wanted. Such instructions, unknown in London, Paris, or Prague, made a mockery out of subsequent Czech efforts to find an acceptable solution to the Sudeten problem, whatever the illusory hopes of the British and French. Hitler hoped to use the Sudeten demands either to stage or to take advantage of some incident without incurring the dangers of western intervention.

The German instructions provided the base for Henlein's famous Karlovy Vary (Carlsbad) speech of 24 April 1938, in which he outlined

[12] Quoted in Wilhelm Deist, 'The Rearmament of the Wehrmacht', in Militärgeschichtliches Forschungsamt (ed.), *Germany and the Second World War.* Volume I: *The Build-up of German Aggression,* ed. Wilhelm Deist (Oxford, 1990), 531.

[13] *DGFP*, Ser. D, Vol. II, No. 107 (Report of a meeting between Hitler and Henlein, 28 March 1938).

the conditions for political autonomy and the grant of rights that aimed at the subversion of the Czech state and constitution. Not surprisingly, the Prague government found Henlein's points unacceptable, particularly the demands that the Czechs change their foreign policy, recognize the Sudeten Germans as a distinct legal entity within the state, and allow them the freedom to profess and propagate the Nazi ideology. Meanwhile the Prague government transmitted its own proposals for settling the Sudeten problem to London and Paris; these were judged not extensive enough to convince either government that the Czechs really wanted a settlement. The Czech president continued to believe that time would solve the Sudeten problem if it could be removed from the international agenda. Given the background of British distrust of Beneš and the belief in London that Sudeten German claims were the key to the problem, the government argued that greater pressure on the Czechs could lead to a breakthrough. These impressions were confirmed when Henlein, instructed by Hitler to try to assure Britain's neutrality, came to London in mid-May. With the approval of Chamberlain and Halifax, he saw Vansittart and others, including Churchill. Henlein's arguments that he only wanted autonomy and a fair deal for the Sudeten Germans appeared convincing and, indeed, it may be true that the Sudeten German leader still hoped that he might play an independent role in a reconstituted Czechoslovakia. Henlein insisted that Beneš could conclude a satisfactory agreement with the Sudeten Germans if only he would act quickly. If no settlement was reached, Henlein proposed that a plebiscite be held under international supervision. The British were completely taken in; Churchill accepted the general view in London that if only Beneš behaved properly, there need be no crisis over Czechoslovakia. Henlein visited Hitler at Berchtesgaden shortly after his return from London. The Führer had every reason to believe that he might soon have a situation in Prague which could be exploited to launch his little war.

Hitler, meanwhile, was anxious to explore co-operation with Italy. The meetings between Ribbentrop, Mussolini, and Ciano in November 1937 had made it clear that the Italians were prepared to trade Austria for German recognition of Italy's ambitions in the Mediterranean. Arguably this process had begun in January 1936 with Mussolini's declaration to Hassell of the 'Germanness' of Austria. Though he had expressed his gratitude to Mussolini over Austria in the most fulsome terms, Hitler knew that Mussolini's willingness to accept *Anschluss* did not mean that the Duce and Ciano welcomed the last-minute announcement in Rome, or the disappearance of Austria. If Mussolini was impressed by Hitler's easy *coup*, and aware of his future intentions, there was a certain frustration about being left behind by his Axis partner. The Italians had still not managed to pacify Abyssinia, despite the increased number of Italian troops engaged and the extensive use of poison gas. Other Italian forces were still engaged in Spain. Yet the absence of resources produced no diminution of Mussolini's ambitions. In the Mediterranean, time was short as Mussolini wanted an agreement with Britain before Hitler took his next step in central Europe. At the same time, Ciano was active in the Balkans, seeking the mutual defence pact with Yugoslavia that had eluded his grasp in 1937, and trying to improve relations with both Hungary and Romania.

The Italian effort to seek an accord with Britain provoked the clash between Eden and Chamberlain that ultimately resulted in the British foreign secretary's resignation on 20 February, much to the delight of the Italians and to the dismay of the French. The differences between the two men were more marginal than Chamberlain made out. The prime minister believed that the German threat to Austria provided an excellent opportunity to stiffen Mussolini's back against Hitler; Eden, who never liked negotiating with the Italian 'gangster', quite rightly suspected that Mussolini had already sold Austria out for some kind of quid pro quo. The issue was brought to the cabinet where Chamberlain, anxious to have Eden out, spoke of 'a fundamental difference of outlook' with the foreign secretary with regard to both Italy and Germany. An overwhelming majority of the cabinet sided with the prime minister and Eden resigned. Chamberlain chose Lord Halifax, a former viceroy of India and a much-admired statesman who prayed 'regularly and repeatedly' without, alas, achieving any degree of certainty, as successor. Halifax's considerable reputation in Conservative circles, as well as his modesty and detachment from the rough and tumble of domestic politics, commanded the respect of his colleagues. The choice underlined the prime minister's intention to have a directing role in shaping foreign policy. Until Godesberg, Chamberlain could count on a reliable and politically popular partner at the Foreign Office.

Stopped from further approaches to Hitler because of *Anschluss*, Chamberlain lost little time in following up Ciano's initiative. By eliminating one of Britain's three potential enemies, he could pursue his 'general settlement' with an easier mind. Chamberlain believed, and continued to believe, that Mussolini could act as a calming and restraining influence on Hitler, a judgment which was not entirely wrong. The so-called 'Easter Accords' were quickly concluded. Signed in Rome on 16 April 1938, they were regarded by the Italians as a major diplomatic success, for they believed they had won a free hand in the western Mediterranean. The British agreed to recognize the Italian empire in Ethiopia, once the League gave its permission; the Italians promised to support the status quo in the Mediterranean, settle the Spanish question, and reduce the Libyan garrison by an unspecified amount. The two countries would exchange information about substantial military movements in their respective possessions in the Mediterranean, Red Sea, and north-east Africa. The accords were to come into operation when some 'volunteers' left Spain; full evacuation would take place only after the Spanish war ended. For the French, the agreement was a blow. It strengthened Italy's Mediterranean position and *Quai* officials had the strongest doubts about Mussolini's promise to negotiate a similar arrangement with France. The British, however, particularly the Admiralty, which could now concentrate on securing its two-ocean fleet, thought they had eliminated Italy from the list of potential enemies and had driven a wedge between the two dictators.

The British cabinet had already agreed on its policy towards Czechoslovakia. Chamberlain and Halifax were at one in not believing that Hitler wanted to absorb all of the country and in thinking that the only permanent settlement of the problem was division along national lines. Ministers, called to a Foreign Policy Committee meeting on 18 March, presented a multitude of reasons why Britain could not intervene to support Czechoslovakia. The Foreign Office did not speak with a single voice. The permanent under-secretary, Alexander Cadogan, was more optimistic about the future direction of German policy than the experienced Orme Sargent. Halifax rejected any provisional British promise to assist France against a German attack after she had gone to help Czechoslovakia, and preferred instead a no-commitment policy that would restrain France. Chamberlain, backing Halifax, claimed that the only solution to the Czech problem was one acceptable to Germany, and predicted that if she could get 'her *desiderata* by peaceful means', she would not opt for force. He did not see, as some did, that the Sudeten Germans were not the issue. Only the intervention of his 'weak-kneed colleagues', as the prime minister was to call them, and the prospect of defending the government's case in the Commons, resulted in the adoption of a friendlier version of the British refusal of any guarantee to France. To calm the public, measures to speed up rearmament were to be announced in the near future. On 24 March, the prime minister informed the Commons of the government's decision. He warned that, if war broke out, 'the inexorable pressure of facts might well prove more powerful than formal pronouncements, and in that event it would be well within the bounds of probability that other countries, besides those which were parties to the original dispute, would almost immediately be involved. This is especially true in the case of two countries like Great Britain and France. . . .'[14] The French were informed on the same

[14] *Hansard*, HC Deb, 24 March 1938, Vol. 333, Cols. 1405–1406.

day that there would be no guarantee should France come to Czechoslovakia's assistance. The British stance was hardly one to set off alarm bells in Berlin.

At the Anglo-French meetings in London on 28 and 29 April, Spain and Italy were the first items on the agenda. The very fact that such meetings were held in London gives an indication of the balance between the two governments. The French agreed to revert to the policy of non-intervention to get the Axis troops out of Spain, and to seek an agreement with Italy parallel to the Easter Accords. There remained, however, a considerable gap between the British and French positions on Italy. The British believed that Mussolini's discomfort over *Anschluss* had highlighted the differences between the two Axis powers, and that the Anglo-Italian agreement would separate Rome and Berlin even further. Daladier, pressed by Darlan and the officials at the *Quai d'Orsay*, was convinced, correctly as is now known, that the recent signals from Rome pointed to a hardening of the Italian–German partnership. In the French view, by retreating from the Red Sea the British were offering the Italians a strengthened strategic position that would allow them to threaten France's lines of communication to the Near and Far East. They proposed naval staff talks to address the situation. The British hardly welcomed the idea. It was only after considerable wrangling that Chamberlain agreed 'in principle' to naval talks, sometime after Hitler's visit to Italy. They were to be concerned only with Germany. With Daladier and Gamelin convinced that France could not fight a war without Britain, Darlan was forced to swallow these narrowly drawn limits to any future exchanges. The French continued to believe that Italy would back Germany in any future war. The British were no more forthcoming over French demands for staff contacts. Chamberlain suggested that low-level conversations be restricted to the air staff, and address only the co-ordination of the two air defence systems and plans for a British strike force based in France. He explained that there was no need for army staff talks since Britain, at the outset, could send only two incomplete divisions to France. Daladier's efforts on the first day to shake the British resolve to avoid joint military planning produced only Chamberlain's grudging admission that he 'would not be unwilling' for contacts to be established through the military attachés, as long as it was clearly understood that these involved no commitment to send troops to France in case of war.

It was on the morning of the second day of talks that the issue on everyone's mind was finally addressed: Czechoslovakia. Halifax outlined the British position as explained to the French and to the Commons on 24 March. Britain would give no guarantee to take military action in case of German aggression. Arguing that Czechoslovakia could not be protected against Germany, Halifax asked that the French join in urging Beneš to negotiate a settlement with Henlein. Daladier's response was blunt and passionately delivered. He fiercely attacked Halifax's arguments, and insisted that the only way to save the peace of Europe was for Britain and France to make it clear that they would not permit the destruction of Czechoslovakia. Having been carefully briefed by Charles Corbin, the distinguished French ambassador, and his two chief advisers, Roland de Margerie and Girard de Charbonnières, all critical of Chamberlain's appeasement diplomacy, Daladier insisted that Henlein was seeking the destruction of Czechoslovakia, and that Germany was intent on tearing up treaties and destroying the equilibrium of Europe. If the current military situation was poor, the destruction of the valuable Czech army would hardly improve it. He called attention, somewhat surprisingly given his previous attitude towards the USSR, to the power of the Soviet Union, which still had the largest air force in Europe, some 5,000 planes. Chamberlain, claiming to share Daladier's indignation at Hitler's actions, but forced to dismiss such dangerous 'sentimental considerations', carefully set out the arguments against a policy of firmness. Germany would destroy Czechoslovakia whatever other countries might do, and only a long war, whose outcome was uncertain, would allow the Allies even if they won, to reconstruct Czechoslovakia, if that was what they wanted to do. The prime minister believed the situation was not as black as Daladier painted it. He did not think Hitler intended to destroy Czechoslovakia or wished to bring about an *Anschluss* of the Sudeten areas with Germany. Daladier's concluding remarks appeared to leave the two sides irreconcilable. He 'feared that, if...there were no signs of a determined policy and a common agreement between His Majesty's Government and the French Government, we should then have decided the fate of Europe, and he could only regard the future with the greatest pessimism'.[15] The historian, with the advantage of hindsight, cannot resist quoting Cadogan's false verdict on Daladier's argument: 'Very beautiful, but awful rubbish.'[16] Despite the French premier's indignation, in the afternoon session he gave way to Chamberlain on all the essential points. The British and French would encourage the Czechs to offer the maximum concessions to the Sudeten Germans. The former would intervene in Berlin and find out what the Germans wanted in Czechoslovakia. If a peaceful solution was not found, and the Germans intended to resort to

[15] *DBFP*, 3rd ser., Vol. I, No. 164 (Record of Anglo-French conversations, 28–29 April 1938: Third meeting, 29 April 1938, 10.45 a.m.).

[16] David Dilks (ed.), *The Diaries of Sir Alexander Cadogan, O.M., 1938–1945* (London, 1971), 73.

force, they would do so knowing 'that France would be compelled to intervene by virtue of her obligations, and that His Majesty's Government could not guarantee that they would not do the same'.[17] Specific reference would be made in Berlin to Chamberlain's 24 March warning. Halifax emphasized the great importance of repeating this directly to Hitler; yet, when he saw the German chargé after the meeting broke up, he only asked, in a 'friendly manner', that Ribbentrop be told that 'Britain would undertake no new commitment'.[18]

Was Daladier's spirited defence of Czechoslovakia honestly meant or was he hoping, as Chamberlain assumed, that the British would force him into the policy he actually wanted to follow? It is highly probable that Daladier wanted it both ways, to maintain the alliance with Czechoslovakia but keep close to Britain, for he knew that France was in no position to meet its obligations except in partnership with the British. The premier's case was based on the assumption, shared with the French military leadership, that if Germany established its hegemony in east-central Europe, the independence of France would be threatened with destruction. Informed of the great disparity between French and German air power, and believing that the French army was incapable of striking a decisive blow at Germany, Daladier accepted that France could not go to the aid of Czechoslovakia alone. On all sides, he was warned (though he hardly needed such promptings) that it was vitally important to secure British support. Just before his departure for London, the *Secrétariat Général de la Défense Nationale* (SGDN) had prepared a long memorandum emphasizing France's air and demographic weakness, and underlining the danger that she would have to fight against both Germany and Italy. 'France cannot resist forces three times as numerous', the SGDN insisted. 'British support would be essential.'[19] The French financial situation, on the eve of a new devaluation that would link the franc to the pound sterling (the 'franc-sterling'), increased France's dependence on co-operation with the British and American treasuries. Furthermore, it was argued in Paris that the Anglo-French partnership, alone, could provide Prague with greater room to manoeuvre in its dealings with Germany. There were few to be found in Paris who did not believe that only an alliance with Britain would assure French safety in the future.

It may be that Daladier felt it necessary to assess how far Britain was prepared to go in central Europe, or that he was seeking to share the

[17] *DBFP*, 3rd ser., Vol. I, No. 164 (Record of Anglo-French conversations, 28–29 April 1938: Fourth meeting, 29 April 1938, 2.45 p.m.).

[18] *DBFP*, 3rd ser., Vol. I, No. 165 (Halifax to Henderson (Berlin), 29 April 1938).

[19] MAE, Papiers 1940, Fonds Daladier, volume 1, 24 April 1938.

burden of responsibility that he was unwilling to carry alone. There are no final answers as to why Daladier took so firm a stand in the morning, and capitulated so easily in the afternoon, though it was not unusual for the premier to retreat when decisive action was required. Further, while the goals of Daladier differed from those of Bonnet, they both produced the same result. Daladier's immediate aim was to redress the economic situation in order to accelerate rearmament so that France could stand the initial shock of war and become 'alliance worthy' in the eyes of the British. The time factor was all-important; neither arms nor the British alliance would be quickly acquired. Well aware, as the long-serving defence minister, of the magnitude of the task of rearmament, Daladier felt he had to play for safety. Bonnet, for his part, believed that only an agreement with Germany could ultimately save France. He assumed that France's financial and economic position precluded negotiating from a position of strength, whether with regard to Britain or Germany. As a 'realist', he felt that France had no choice but to abandon its commitments in central Europe and avoid, at any cost, a rupture in Anglo-French relations. Until Munich at least, Daladier did not follow any consistent policy. Bonnet was given a free hand in the conduct of France's foreign policy while the premier concentrated on the economy and rearmament. At the same time, Daladier kept in close touch with Paul Reynaud and Georges Mandel who, along with their chief British contact, Winston Churchill, were prepared to stand up to Hitler over Czechoslovakia, believing that this would force the Germans to retreat.

This meant in practice, as far as the Czech situation was concerned, that the British would take the lead in pressing Beneš to satisfy the Sudeten Germans, so that France would not face the choice between dishonour and war. Ambassador Bullitt reported to the American secretary of state, Cordell Hull, that Daladier gave him the impression 'that the French and British action with regard to Czechoslovakia will be based on the assumption that the ultimate dissolution of Czechoslovakia is inevitable . . . '.[20] Bonnet, too, wanted an agreement with Italy, hoping, unlike his senior officials, that Mussolini could be weaned away from Hitler. The French chargé d'affaires in Rome (there was still no ambassador) presented a twelve-point programme to Ciano that included a joint declaration of non-interference in Spain, the negotiation of a new Tunisian convention, the reduction of the Italian presence in Libya, recognition of French interests in the Red Sea, and other more minor controversial issues. The Italians took umbrage at this list, and refused any response at all until Ciano visited Albania and Hitler made his much-awaited visit to Italy in May. Mussolini broke off the

[20] *FRUS*, 1938, I, 493–495 (Bullitt to Hull, 9 May 1938).

conversations with the French, citing the arms traffic across the Pyrenean frontier as an excuse. It was not long before the full extent of Mussolini's hostility to France became clear.

Italy loomed large in German considerations as Hitler considered the future of Czechoslovakia. Though Mussolini had shown no particular interest in the country's fate, Hitler wanted more than mere indifference. There was as yet no German timetable; Hitler had told Henlein only that he intended to settle the Sudeten German question in 'the not too distant future'. The Führer had to make sure that the Anglo-Italian agreement would not adversely affect Italy's ties with Germany. He needed to sound out Mussolini on the Czech question, and gauge the Italian response to a possible war between Germany and Britain and France. He calculated that Italian support would further deter the western powers from intervening in his Czech war. Hitler assessed the relationship between Mussolini's future plans and his own timetable: 'Either Mussolini regards his work as finished, or not. a) If so, Czechoslovakia in distant future. Close the Western frontier, then wait and see. "Return with empty bag." b) If not, then African "Empire". Impossible without German aid. Precondition Czechoslovakia. "Return with Czechoslovakia in the bag".'[21] Surrounded by a huge and assorted entourage, Hitler set off for Rome on 2 May. His recent 49th birthday was very much on his mind, as were the polyps lately found in his throat, and he spent much of the journey from Berlin drawing up his will and putting his affairs in order. While annoyed at being the official guest of the unsympathetic king, as well as by the early coolness of the Italian crowds, he was impressed by the full programme of demonstrations, balcony appearances, and military reviews. At a state dinner held at the Palazzo Venezia on 7 May, Hitler proclaimed that the Brenner frontier was to be considered 'untouchable forever'. In Florence two days later, Mussolini told Hitler, 'henceforth no force will ever be able to separate us'.[22]

No alliance was concluded. During the German visit, Ribbentrop proposed what Ciano regarded as 'a pact of military assistance, public or secret, whichever we prefer' but, on the latter's advice, Mussolini postponed acceptance. He was, of course, fully aware of Hitler's intentions to move against Czechoslovakia. Almost immediately after his visitors' departure, he warned Ciano that 'a diplomatic crisis will be precipitated and France and England will inevitably be against us', making a pact with Germany essential.[23] Nevertheless, an alliance at

[21] The document probably dates from about 20 April 1938. Quoted in Telford Taylor, *Munich: The Price of Peace* (London, 1979), 382.

[22] Galeazzo Ciano, *Diario* (Milan, 1946, 1998), 134 (9 May 1938).

[23] Ciano, *Diario*, 134 (10 May 1938).

this juncture might weaken Chamberlain's political position just when the British were prepared to lobby for the recognition of the Ethiopian conquest at the League of Nations. In late June, Ribbentrop broached the idea of a military alliance, assuring the Italian ambassador in Germany that Germany could 'liquidate' Czechoslovakia alone and would not need Italian help should a general war break out. Although Mussolini and Ciano were favourable to the idea, they were not yet ready to go down this path, partly because of unfinished business in London. General Pariani suggested to Mussolini that the Italians conclude a convention with the Germans for technical military collaboration which the Hungarians might also join. The acceptance of his recommendation was 'another step on Italy's road from Axis partner to ally'.[24]

Mussolini remained cautious about concluding a full military alliance. Quite apart from the anticipated German attack on Czechoslovakia, Italian and German interests did not necessarily coincide. Italian intelligence reports suggested that the Germans were pursuing industrial and commercial goals in Spain, Hungary, and Yugoslavia that would adversely affect Mussolini's ambitions in those countries. The Germans were also reported to have been active in Albania. When Pariani was sent to Berlin on 10–11 July to prepare the ground for closer military collaboration, he was told by Hitler that other powers were trying to split Germany and Italy apart. He claimed that the two countries had no conflicting interests but if there were any, they should be cleared up. While Pariani reported that Germany was actively preparing for war, he did not think it would reach 'substantial efficiency' until 1940–1941.[25]

There were suspicions on both sides. Mussolini and Ciano were already thinking of annexing Albania but preferred not to fully reveal their intentions. Hitler had made no mention of his programme for Czechoslovakia though he had reviewed possible scenarios for action with General Keitel on 21 April. Despite Ribbentrop's offers, there was not a great deal of enthusiasm in German military and naval circles for an alliance. Neither General Beck nor Admiral Raeder had much time for the Italians and 'feared that German policy would be tied to Italian escapades'.[26] After the Führer's visit, the Duce mounted a massive anti-French press campaign. With British support for the League's recognition of the Italian empire in Ethiopia, he no longer required France's backing. On 14 May, at Genoa, in a highly bellicose speech, the Duce

[24] John Gooch, *Mussolini and his Generals: The Armed Forces and Fascist Foreign Policy, 1922–1940*, 393. Material in this paragraph comes from Gooch.

[25] Ibid.

[26] Manfred Messerschmidt, 'Foreign Policy and Preparation for War', in Militärgeschichtliches Forschungsamt (ed.), *Germany and the Second World War*, Vol. I, ed. Wilhelm Deist (Oxford, 1990), 655.

declared that Italy and France were 'on opposite sides of the barricades' in Spain, and that amicable relations were impossible. He praised *Anschluss*, reviled the democracies, and declared that the Stresa front was dead. By June, despite Bonnet's continuing efforts, hopes for renewed talks were diminishing and France faced the possibility of simultaneous crises in central Europe and in the Mediterranean. The British hardly fared better. Ratification of the Easter Accords was delayed as the bombings of British ships in Spanish ports continued unabated. The Foreign Office demanded that the Duce withdraw his forces from Spain, agree to an armistice, and begin talks with France along the lines of the agreement with Britain. Mussolini would hear none of this; in particular, he was not prepared to bring his 'volunteers' home from Spain. He had, of course, no genuine interest in a meaningful Anglo–Italian entente, except as a means to bring pressure on Germany. There was trouble, too, brewing in the Maghreb where the rapid Italian build-up of the Libyan garrison, in violation of the Easter Accords, caused considerable alarm at the Colonial Office. The Arab rebellion in Palestine forced the British to despatch troops from Egypt just at the time when Mussolini, wanting to prepare his position before the Sudeten crisis erupted, doubled the size of his army in Libya. He hoped to have two Italian army corps in place, one facing French Tunisia and the other threatening Egypt. As extraordinary as it seems, with Italian troops and aircraft engaged in simultaneous wars in Spain and Ethiopia, Mussolini continued to dream of a vast empire to be acquired at British and French expense when the inevitable European war broke out.[27] What was even worse, his three chiefs of staff, knowing that their services were woefully ill-equipped and that Italy had neither the essential natural resources nor the industrial structure to prepare the country for war, nevertheless encouraged Mussolini to believe that Italy could launch a successful campaign against Britain and France in North Africa. Though their long itinerary of negative statistics made some impression on the Duce, he seemed to accept their assurances that progress was being made towards the goals of autarky, essential given the entirely realistic fear of blockade and war.

The most unexpected demonstration of ideological solidarity with Nazi Germany came on 14 July when the 'Manifesto of the Race' was announced. Part of a campaign launched by the Fascist party to advance the cause of Fascist 'totalitarianism', its publication came as a shock to a country where anti-Semitism had few roots and no popular following.

[27] Brian R. Sullivan, 'The Italian–Ethiopian War, October 1935 – November 1941: Causes, Conduct and Consequences', in A. H. Ion and E. J. Errington (eds.), *Great Powers and Little Wars: The Limits of Power* (Westport, CT, and London, 1993), 190.

Italians, unlike Jews, Mussolini proclaimed, were Aryans. Marriage and sexual intercourse with Jews threatened the racial superiority of the Italian people. Racial consciousness was also invoked to mark the difference between the triumphant white Fascist warriors and the mentally deficient defeated Ethiopian masses. By proclaiming Italy's racial supremacy, the Duce hoped to arouse that militaristic and self-confident spirit in the 'new man' that would lead to conquest of empire and victory in war. Such a spiritual revolution would teach Italians to become hard and full of hate in order to be 'masters'. Party members, among whom there were Italian Jews, were surprised to learn in September 1938 that the Jewish world was 'an irreconcilable enemy of Fascism'. Mussolini acted on his own without any promptings from Hitler. His intention was to underline Italy's ideological unity with the Third Reich.

Hitler returned from Italy on 10 May, reassured that Mussolini's friendship had survived *Anschluss,* and that there was no danger of a revival of the Stresa front. He knew of the British and French efforts in Prague and the Foreign Office request for a 'confidential statement' of what Germany wanted, so that the Czechs could be pressured to accede to German wishes. He also had Henlein's report on his successful visit to London. While resting at Berchtesgaden, the Führer bombarded the OKW with a series of questions about the state of German forces near the Czech frontier, and the nature and strength of the Czech fortifications. The arrival of the revised 'Case Green' coincided with the May weekend diplomatic crisis.

II

On 20 May, separate reports reached the Foreign Office and *Quai d'Orsay* of German troop concentrations near the Czechoslovak border. There was a detailed warning to Czech intelligence that German agents were preparing a revolt in the Sudetenland to coincide with the municipal elections on 22 May, and that this would provide the pretext for German troops to cross the border. The identity of the informant remains unknown.[28] The incoming report was at first believed by Czech intelligence, though questions began to be asked just hours after the partial mobilization order was issued. On 23 May, the intelligence analysts in Prague realized that the operational section had mistaken routine German manoeuvres near the Czech border for the real thing. Meanwhile, on 21 May, the Prague government mobilized an extra

[28] See I. Lukes, *Czechoslovakia between Stalin and Hitler: The Diplomacy of Edvard Beneš in the 1930s* (New York and Oxford, 1996), 148.

199,000 men, bringing the Czech army up to a total of 383,000 men. The mobilization went smoothly; the men occupied the front-line fortifications in the Sudetenland and morale was high. The scheduled municipal elections were held the next day without any major incidents. Though none of the military attachés in Berlin could find any signs of unusual German military action, the *Deuxième Bureau* in Paris and the Secret Intelligence Service (SIS) in London each warned their governments of the dangers of a German attack. On 21 May, the British and French made strong protests to the Germans, to the considerable surprise and alarm of the Wilhelmstrasse. The Soviets, who were also taken by surprise, announced they would stand by their obligations to Czechoslovakia. There is no proof of Soviet involvement in the scare.[29] In Paris, Daladier invited the German ambassador to his home, in order to speak frankly 'as a French ex-serviceman to his German comrade'. He warned him that if Germany attacked Czechoslovakia, France would have to fight if she was not to be dishonoured. Bonnet also announced that France would act if German troops entered Czechoslovakia. In Britain, Halifax instructed Sir Nevile Henderson to tell Ribbentrop that if a conflict arose the British 'could not guarantee that they would not be forced by circumstances to become involved also'.[30]

The rumours were false. The Wilhelmstrasse issued a formal denial of any intention to invade Czechoslovakia, and by 24 May the weekend crisis was over. The incident had important consequences. Hitler was furious with the Czechs, and with the reports that he had bowed to Anglo-French pressure to retreat from a *coup* that he had never planned. Henlein, who had broken off the talks in Prague, was summoned and told to hold fast to the Carlsbad programme, but not to let matters get out of hand as Germany had to fill the gaps in its western fortifications. Keitel received a telegram from Hitler's adjutant, Schmundt. The general was told: 'The Führer is going into Green in detail. Basic ideas unchanged. Surprise factor to be more emphasized.' Hitler advised his generals that exercises should be held in taking fortifications by surprise (the planned exercises for September were too late) and that the fortification work in the west should be accelerated. The sending of this directive to Brauchitsch as well as Keitel indicates that Hitler believed that the *Oberkommando des Heeres* (OKH) should now be involved in this planning. At the 28 May meeting with his military and civilian officials, it was made clear that he would not be deterred by the threat of a

[29] See the hypothesis suggested by Lukes 'The Czechoslovak Partial Mobilisation in May 1938: A Mystery (Almost) Solved', *Journal of Contemporary History*, 31: 4 (1996), 714–715.

[30] *DBFP*, 3rd ser., Vol. I, No. 250 (Halifax to Henderson (Berlin), 21 May 1938).

conflict with the western powers. According to one participant, Fritz Wiedemann, Hitler's adjutant, the Führer declared: 'It is my unshakeable will that Czechoslovakia shall disappear from the map.'[31] Two days later Hitler signed the revised directive for 'Case Green'. Only the opening paragraph was decisively altered: 'It is my unalterable decision to smash Czechoslovakia by military action in the near future. It is the business of the political leadership to await or bring about the suitable moment from a political and military point of view.'[32] The *Wehrmacht* was instructed to begin preparations immediately. A covering letter from Keitel set 1 October as the latest date for the execution of the plan. During the next months, Hitler repeatedly intervened to question and criticize the preparations being made for a forcible solution to the Czech question, and monitored the construction of the defensive fortifications against Belgium and France. In so doing, in his position as both chancellor and commander-in-chief, he disrupted the previous command structure and reduced the influence of the *Wehrmacht* chiefs. General Keitel never issued a comprehensive directive for the *Wehrmacht* defining its future tasks; planning consisted of 'directives for particular current tasks'. These were determined by Hitler's immediate political objectives.[33]

At the same 28 May meeting, when speaking of the need to move against Czechoslovakia, Hitler told his listeners that its elimination would 'clear the rear for advancing against the West, England and France'.[34] He believed it would be years before Britain and France would be ready to fight. Britain would not be prepared until around 1941, France could be knocked out at once, Germany's coastal base would be enlarged by taking Holland and Belgium, and Britain would be expelled from the continent. The operational planning involved in 'Case Green', almost Hitler's sole concern during the summer months, was based on the assumption that the western powers would not intervene in Czechoslovakia and that there would be no European war at that time. On 27 May, he issued orders for a vast acceleration of work on the West Wall, demanding that the defence line along the French and Belgian borders be completed by 1 October. The rushed construction would frighten and deter the French and, he argued, protect the German forces should the western powers attack. Through the summer months, there came a steady stream of detailed questions from the Berghof, and a procession of officers and civilians arrived to report to Hitler.

[31] *DGFP*, Ser. D, Vol. VII, Appendix III, H, (v), p. 632.
[32] *DGFP*, Ser. D, Vol. II, No. 221 (Directive for Operation 'Green', 30 May 1938).
[33] Deist, 'The Rearmament of the Wehrmacht', 532.
[34] *DGFP*, Ser. D, Vol. VII, Appendix III, H, (v), p. 632.

The May crisis not only accelerated German rearmament but also affected Hitler's thinking about Britain. The full wartime army was to be completed by April 1939 instead of the original target date of April 1940. Large sums were earmarked for the construction of the West Wall. Following the Führer's line of reasoning, the naval chiefs began to include Britain in their operational planning. Admiral Raeder had already begun to move in this direction after the Hossbach conference, though not in any open way. On 28 May Hitler ordered the accelerated completion of battleships F and G (*Bismarck* and *Tirpitz*), as well the construction of U-boats, both aimed at Britain. Six 'super-battleships', originally planned for construction in sequence, were now to be constructed simultaneously. In June, Raeder asked Commander Heye of the operations department to prepare a memorandum on a naval war with Britain. Submitted in August 1938, it initiated an intense debate that culminated in a clash between Hitler and Raeder over whether Germany should build battleships or cruisers and pocket-battleships. The decision to adopt 'Plan Z', a wildly over-ambitious expansion plan intended to prepare Germany for a naval war against Britain, was only taken in early 1939. *Luftwaffe* planning also underwent a major change of direction, despite the many difficulties that had already led to stagnation in aircraft production. Due to a major campaign by Heinrich Koppenberg, the director general of Junkers, who promised to organize a Ford-like system of mass production, Göring and the air chiefs agreed to make the Ju-88 twin-engine bomber the sole standard bombing plane of the *Luftwaffe*. Immediately after the May crisis, Göring placed an order for a fleet of 7,000 Ju-88s. In so doing he committed over half the *Luftwaffe*'s workforce to the production of a medium range bomber, whose sole strategic rationale was offensive operations against France and Britain. In fact, the Ju-88 had limited capacities as a strategic bomber. Again, it was after Munich that the Germans began thinking of a long-range four-engine bomber (the He-177) that could present a real aerial threat to Britain.

This accelerated programme could not be accomplished without serious strains on Germany's already difficult raw material, foodstuff, and animal feed situation. The new demands for increased armaments forced Göring to revise the Four-Year Plan in the spring of 1938. The New War Economy Production Plan, administered by Carl Krauch, the managing director of IG-Farben, concentrated on the development of synthetic products and on vital war products such as gun powder, explosives, and chemical weapons, which would be needed in any future conflict. In August 1938, the plan was extended; the '*Schnellplan*' (Rapid Plan) shortened the scheduled rearmament programmes for 1942–1943 by a year. Even with massive cuts in the non-war sectors of the economy, the production figures laid down in the '*Schnellplan*' could not be met. There was severe pressure on the foreign exchange and currency accounts at a time when import demands were rising and exports falling. Germany's foreign indebtedness reached a peak in the late summer of 1938, threatening future imports of raw materials and foodstuffs. It was hardly surprising that military and civilian advisers were concerned about Hitler's plans for war.

III

Many of Hitler's officials thought that his timetable was far too short, and highly dangerous. They argued that an attack on Czechoslovakia could not be localized and would expose Germany to a war against the western powers that she could not win. General Beck was among the most outspoken of the military critics. Cautious by nature, conservative tactically, and very much the old-style general staff officer in thought and manner, Beck, aggrieved by Hitler's reorganization of the *Wehrmacht* command which undermined his position, felt Hitler was being deprived of the advice of his most senior generals. From May until August, 1938, he bombarded General Brauchitsch, the new commander in chief who had replaced Fritsch, with a series of warning memoranda, all highly critical of 'Case Green'. Though Beck shared Hitler's view that Germany required *Lebensraum* in Europe and in the colonies, and that Czechoslovakia was a danger-spot that had to be removed, by war if necessary, he thought that an attack on Czechoslovakia in the autumn of 1938, as currently planned, would bring in the western powers, who could draw on American assistance, and even intervention, while neither Italy nor Japan would act in concert with Germany. Rarely seeing Hitler, Beck hoped his memorandum of 5 May would be passed on by Brauchitsch. In mid-July, the frightened and subservient commander-in-chief ventured to present an edited version to Hitler who 'exploded in fury', particularly outraged by Beck's assessment of France's superiority in ground forces. As chief of the general staff, Beck accompanied Brauchitsch to the 28 May meeting, where Hitler explained his intention 'to smash Czechoslovakia at the first opportunity'. Two days later, Beck prepared a second protest against the risks that Hitler was taking. He insisted that the Czech defence could last three weeks, perhaps more, and that Britain and France would intervene. Beck again returned to the charge on 3 June, in a memorandum in which he vehemently condemned the revised 'Green' directive with the 1 October deadline as militarily unsound and advised the general staff to decline all responsibility for it. Unable to reach Hitler directly and dependent on Brauchitsch, a man who saw himself only as the executor of the Führer's instructions, Beck enlisted the support of his fellow officers in the general staff. For the annual general staff exercise in the spring of 1938, he chose a hypothetical attack on Czechoslovakia, in which the French would come to Prague's assistance, mount an offensive on Germany's western frontier, and break through the German lines, inflicting a disastrous defeat on the *Wehrmacht*. Not all who attended the concluding conference in May agreed with Beck's assessment of the war game. Schmundt, Hitler's adjutant, and Hans Jeschonneck, soon to become, at the relatively young age of 40, Göring's chief of staff of the *Luftwaffe*, both privately criticized the exercise with its old-fashioned tactics and neglect of air power, as well as Beck, its equally out-dated interpreter. Some of the younger officers may well have shared their views. It was unfortunate that Beck combined his operational and strategic critiques of the invasion plan, for while the war game suggested that the former was questionable, the latter arguments were well based. If, as seems likely, Hitler was told of Beck's address, it could only have confirmed the contempt with which he regarded his senior officers. 'What sort of generals are these, whom I, the head of state, have to force into making war?', he is claimed to have said. 'I don't ask my generals to understand my orders, but to obey them.'[35] He made no effort, however, to replace Beck who continued to participate in the planning for the campaign.

Similarly, General Wilhelm Adam, the respected German commander in the west, stressed the inadequacy of the western fortification in any war against France and Britain. There was an open confrontation with Hitler at the end of June. Adam complained of an insufficiency of supplies, and spoke disparagingly of Fritz Todt, the creator of the *Autobahns*, and Konstantin Hierl from the State Labour Service, who had been assigned by Hitler to take over parts of the construction work. As in the case of Beck, despite his highly critical views, Adam was not dismissed (or indeed executed), in striking contrast with Stalin's methods. The question of command on the West Wall remained unsettled. Hitler was concerned, however, to prevent Adam's pessimism from infecting others. He dictated a long and detailed 'Memorandum on the Question of our Fortifications', sent to the high commands of the *Wehrmacht* and three services. It made the case for a decentralized system of small fortifications that would give the army better protection than large fortifications. Given his absolute authority, the Führer was in an impregnable position and work on the West Wall proceeded according to his orders.

It says a great deal for Beck's courage that he continued to look for ways to stop the rush to war. On 16 July, he produced his fourth and last memorandum for Brauchitsch, again arguing that a victory over

[35] Quoted in Messerschmidt, 'Foreign Policy', 659.

Czechoslovakia in only a few days was impossible and that France and Britain would intervene. Beck's warnings were aimed more at the OKW than at Hitler. He proposed that a meeting of commanding generals be called, and went on to suggest that the military commanders resign, should their warnings not be heeded. He later raised the possibility of collecting all the better elements in Germany, civilians, officers, and reasonable party officials, in order to confront the SS and radical party leaders, and 're-establish orderly conditions' in the Reich. There was to be no *Putsch* and Hitler would remain but the Nazi system would be reformed. This belief in a 'positive' National Socialism both hindered the development of a real opposition movement and revealed Beck's own limitations as a possible leader. When Hitler scheduled a conference of key commanders and staff officers on 15 August, Beck prevailed upon Brauchitsch to assemble the leading generals for a meeting on 4 August. This was an extraordinary and unique event in the history of the Third Reich. Beck's memorandum was read to the assembled officers and General Adam described the hopelessness of the situation on the West Wall. The generals all doubted the feasibility of Hitler's plans, given the existing state of German armaments. There was no dissent from the view that war should be avoided. There was less unanimity on the question of confronting Hitler. The weak-kneed Brauchitsch concluded that all present were opposed to a war against the European Great Powers, but no further action was proposed or taken.

More was involved than a lack of courage—would any other country's general staff have resigned?—or a concern for future careers. Hitler and the military establishment shared too many goals for a divorce to be effected in 1938. Too many steps had already been taken in the direction of a European war. Moreover, the whole position of the army in the Hitler state precluded any questioning of Hitler's political judgments. This was the point made by Erich von Manstein, one of Germany's most intelligent generals and a great admirer of Beck, his former chief. In a letter designed to dissuade Beck from resigning, Manstein insisted on the difference between the military and the political responsibilities involved in deciding whether and when the Germans should solve the question of Czechoslovakia. 'I believe that the decision *whether* a Western military intervention is to be expected is for the political leadership alone', he wrote to Beck. 'There must be clear understanding between the political and military leaders about the consequences of so risky a step, but the final responsibility is the Führer's alone. After all, so far he has always judged the political situation correctly.'[36]

[36] Quoted in Taylor, *Munich*, 695 (Manstein to Beck, 21 July 1938. Italics in original.)

Reports of the meeting were not totally without effect. On 10 August, Hitler called together a group of about twenty of his more important junior generals and gave a long explanation of why he had decided to deal with Czechoslovakia. He insisted that neither Britain nor France would go to war for Czechoslovakia, that Poland and Hungary were waiting to 'pluck the carcass', and that the Red Army, since the purges, was in no condition to fight. In the discussion that followed, the mention of Adam's claim that the West Wall could not be held for more than three weeks against a French attack caused Hitler to erupt. Such liberties were not permitted when Hitler met with his senior commanders on 15 August. The Führer was in his most confident mood, fearing only that he might be removed before fulfilling his mission of making Germany the most powerful nation in Europe. He said that armies were never strong enough to suit their leaders, and that success depended on rightly gauging the politico-military balance. So far he had always been right in his assessments; the other powers would not intervene. He dismissed British threats as a bluff, as their efforts at compromise showed. He assured his officers that the British would keep out as long as Germany showed no sign of weakening. Hitler's performance may not have reassured all his listeners but the number of objectors among the generals, some of whom would join a vague and ill-considered plot against Hitler in September, was balanced by those, mainly the younger generals, who believed, in the 'genius of the Führer'. During the summer months, the great majority of the generals, who fell into neither category, came to accept Hitler's assessment, reassured by reports from military and diplomatic sources that the western powers wanted to avoid war, and by intelligence information casting doubts on French military capabilities. On 21 August, Beck's resignation was accepted; he agreed not to make it public. His successor, General Halder, was also critical of Hitler's plans, but his ability to act was severely circumscribed and his opposition was to take a conspiratorial form. While Hitler was aware of the presence of the doubters among his senior officers, in practice the *Wehrmacht* did not speak with a single voice, and so provided no threat to his authority.

It was not only the military who expressed their doubts about Hitler's war plans. Ernst von Weizsäcker, the state secretary at the Foreign Ministry and a diplomat of the old school of German imperialists, regarded a European war over the Sudeten question as unthinkable, and believed that Czechoslovakia would fall to Germany through 'a chemical process', a combination of internal dissolution and the application of economic pressure. His critical memorandum for Ribbentrop only resulted in instructions that the Foreign Ministry should tell 'all and sundry; that if necessary we would run the risk of a full-scale war with the Western

Powers even now and win it, too'.[37] Deeply concerned by the financial effects of the speeded up rearmament programme, Schwerin von Krosigk, the Reich's finance minister who had been in touch with Weizsäcker, tried, without success, to schedule a meeting with Hitler. In the last days of August, he prepared a detailed memorandum for the Führer, outlining the effects of the country's financial difficulties on its diplomacy. He explained that due to the extraordinary acceleration of rearmament, the Reich was facing an immediate cash crisis. It was out of the question to print money, but the prospects for raising a loan were made exceedingly difficult by the prevailing 'war and inflation psychosis', and the general feeling that the Reich was 'steering towards a serious financial crisis... precipitated by the drive to war'.[38] Schwerin's real point was to warn Hitler that Britain would fight and that Germany did not have the economic means to engage in a war against it. The ex-Rhodes scholar wrote: 'The fact that England is not ready for war militarily, does not prevent England fomenting it. For she possesses two great trump cards. One is the soon expected active participation of the United States of America' and the other was its knowledge of Germany's 'financial and economic weaknesses'. With this in mind, Britain and France would fight a war of attrition, not battling against the West Wall, but after Germany's early military success, wait while their enemy became weaker and weaker 'and finally lose our military advantage due to deliveries of armament and airplanes by the US'. Germany should postpone war, complete her armaments, create a balance between military and economic preparations, and then deliver the '*coup de grâce*' to Czechoslovakia without the disastrous confrontation with Britain and France. By the time Schwerin finished his memorandum, Beck had resigned. Despite the finance minister's key position in the administration, his warnings, like those of Schacht and the directors of the *Reichsbank*, were disregarded.

Whether Hitler was as confident of fighting an isolated war as he claimed is open to question. His operational plans put a high premium on surprise and speed. His uneasiness increased as the time for action approached. He could not totally ignore the doubts of his officers, and found it difficult to read the British situation. The May crisis had shaken his assumptions of British indifference. In mid-July, he used the trip to London of his military adjutant, Fritz Wiedemann, initiated by Göring, to allay British fears about German intentions and to hold out the promise of Anglo-German conversations once the Czech question was settled. Hitler carefully briefed his adjutant. Wiedemann was to tell

[37] *DGFP*, Ser. D, Vol. II, No. 288 (Memorandum by Weizsäcker, 12 July 1938; ibid. No. 304, p. 504. Record of a conversation of Weizsäcker and Ribbentrop, 21 July 1938).

[38] IMT EC419, See quotations in Tooze, *The Wages of Destruction*, 272.

Halifax that if the Sudeten question was not settled peacefully, 'it will one day be solved by force'.[39] Wiedemann was to name March 1939 as the deadline for resolving the Czech crisis. Halifax received Wiedemann informally at home. The latter held out the promise of a future Göring visit, and suggested that Hitler might give an assurance that Germany would observe the peace for a definite period, if there were no 'incidents' requiring German intervention. Halifax welcomed the possibility of talks in principle, following careful preparations, and suggested that a no-force declaration over Czechoslovakia or some other overt German act, might improve the existing situation. The two-hour conversation ended, according to Wiedemann's notes, with Halifax sending his greetings to Hitler, and saying that 'I, as English Foreign Minister, aim to get so far in my lifetime that one day the Führer will be seen entering Buckingham Palace at the side of the King of England' amid 'the acclamations of the English people'.[40] Chamberlain, who at first had seen the warnings to Hitler in May as an Anglo-French triumph, quickly abandoned any hope that threats would work. Reassured by Wiedemann that there was no immediate danger to the peace, the prime minister looked forward to a future visit from Göring and told the cabinet on 20 July that they would discuss all outstanding questions between the two countries, including colonies. The Commons was similarly encouraged to think that the war party in Germany had received a check, and that there might be a better prospect for peaceful resolution. On 26 July the prime minister told the Commons, shortly before it adjourned until the beginning of November, that the atmosphere was 'lighter' and the state of tension of six months earlier had relaxed. Not for the first or the last time, the prime minister was sadly deceived. The Wiedemann visit was not a bid for a future settlement of differences but a way of calming British anxiety over Czechoslovakia.

On the same occasion, Chamberlain told the Commons that 'an experienced person' would go to Czechoslovakia to investigate the Sudeten problem and to suggest means for bringing the negotiations to a successful conclusion. For Chamberlain, the solution to the Czech crisis was to put pressure on Paris and Prague and keep Hitler 'guessing' about British intentions. In response to Hitler's threatening language, in June Halifax had already raised the idea of sending a 'wise British subject' to speed up the Henlein–Czech talks and act as a mediator. He had informed both Newton in Prague and Phipps in Paris of this idea. The French were not to be told until the arbiter was selected. The man chosen was the 68-year-old industrialist, Lord Runciman, a former

[39] *DGFP*, Ser. D, Vol. VII, Appendix III, pp. 628, 633.
[40] *DGFP*, Ser. D, Vol. VII, Appendix III, pp. 631, 633.

cabinet minister in the Baldwin government, who had reached the end of his political career and was hardly thought to be a high flier. The idea behind the mission was to get Beneš to make sufficient concessions to the Sudeten leaders to prevent Hitler from losing his patience and resorting to force. Runciman, himself, rejected Halifax's offer twice before accepting, and insisted that he should be known as a 'mediator' and not as an 'arbiter'. He complained that 'the Government were pushing me out in a dinghy in mid-Atlantic'.[41] The mission arrived in Prague on 3 August. It was to spend the first two weeks in a round of conferences and dinners with Beneš, Hodža, Krofta, and the representatives of the Sudeten German Party, which included both a 'political' and a 'social' staff, an astute move for the Runciman party felt much more at ease with their Sudeten German landowning hosts than with the 'cruder' bourgeois Czechs.

IV

During all these months, the Russians kept a low diplomatic profile. Even before the May crisis there had been visits between Czech and Soviet military men in March and Soviet purchases of Czech armaments, particularly artillery. There were deliveries of planes to Czechoslovakia, overflying Romanian territory both during the summer months and in mid-September. The approval of the flights was given by the Romanian General Staff, possibly due to a Czech threat of an embargo on further arms deliveries to Bucharest.[42] There appears to have been some form of *rapprochement* between the Romanians and Russians after the blow-up occasioned by the defection of the Soviet chargé d'affaires in Bucharest in February 1938. Conversations with the French and Soviets in Geneva indicated that the Romanians would turn a blind eye to deliveries of planes to Prague, and were not averse to this form of assistance. At the same time, however, they assured the Germans, who were monitoring the flights, that Romania would not grant rights of passage to Russian troops. Moreover, in the summer of 1938, the Romanians authorized a further barter agreement of petroleum and cereals, in exchange for German war materials, in the hope of building up their own air industry. The Soviets, of course, were not obliged to come to Czechoslovakia's assistance unless the French acted first; this safeguard had been included in the Czech–Soviet agreement of 1935, at the insistence of the Czechs. There was no way that the Soviets

[41] Quoted in Taylor, *Munich*, 658.

[42] Rebecca Haynes, *Romanian Policy Towards Germany, 1936–1940* (Basingstoke and London, 2000), 54.

could directly assist the Czechs, except through Poland or Romania. The first option was ruled out by the Poles; the second by the Romanian government's refusal to allow Soviet troops to cross its borders, quite apart from logistic difficulties, and its caution about angering the Germans.[43] Litvinov, for his part, repeatedly warned the Soviet *polpred* in Prague that he should be extremely careful in his conversations with the Czechs. He wrote to Alexandrovsky on 11 August:

Of course, we are extremely interested in the preservation of Czechoslovakia's independence, in the hindrance of the Hitlerite drive to the South-East, but without the Western powers it is doubtful whether we would be able to do anything serious, and those powers do not consider it necessary to seek our assistance, ignore us and decide everything concerning the German–Czechoslovak conflict among themselves... We are not aware of Czechoslovakia herself ever pointing out to her Western 'friends' the necessity of bringing in the Soviet Union.[44]

The Soviets continued to follow a 'wait and see' policy. The defeat of the Japanese at Lake Khasan on the border between the Soviet Union and Japanese-occupied Manchuria in the summer of 1938 had relieved the pressure on Moscow, but had been followed by a severe purge in the Far East which had left the Soviet army weakened. There was no sign that Stalin was prepared to act independently or sanction a repetition of the Comintern performance in Spain. Soviet intelligence probably reported Hitler's decision to move against Czechoslovakia, and his 1 October deadline, but almost everything was done to avoid encouraging Czech resistance by promises of future Soviet support. Most Soviet statements were linked with prior French fulfilment of its obligations to Czechoslovakia. When approached about military co-operation during August by the Czechs, Litvinov replied that the Soviets would not help unless France did so also. Senior Czech officers arrived in Moscow in late August at Moscow's invitation, but were given a cool reception by the Russian military authorities, though contracts for

[43] For Soviet–Romanian contacts, see Hugh Ragsdale, *The Soviets, the Munich Crisis, and the Coming of World War* II (Cambridge, 2004), 85; Andreas Hillgruber, *Hitler, König Carol und Marshall Antonescu: Die deutsch–rumänischen Beziehungen 1938–1944,* 2nd edn. (Wiesbaden, 1965), 20; DDF, 2nd ser., Vol. XI, No. 457. Haynes, *Romanian Policy Towards Germany*, 54–55, stresses Romanian unwillingness to upset the Germans. Carley, M. J. ' "Only the USSR Has... Clean Hands": The Soviet Perspective on the Failure of Collective Security and the Collapse of Czechoslovakia, 1934–1938 (Part 1)', *Diplomacy and Statecraft*, 21: 2 (2010). Crucial Romanian documents have been found by Michael Carley which underline Romania's unwillingness to act until France was prepared to fulfil its obligations to Czechoslovakia.

[44] Quoted in Steiner, 'The Soviet Commissariat of Foreign Affairs and the Czechoslovakian Crisis in 1938', 759.

planes and military equipment may have been signed. As usual, Stalin left for his long summer break in late August; there was no press comment on foreign affairs between 1 and 20 September, and Litvinov was exceedingly careful in his responses to queries about Russian policy. On 2 September, the French chargé d'affaires in Moscow asked Litvinov what assistance the USSR would give Czechoslovakia, given its difficulties with Poland and Romania. Litvinov immediately asked Stalin for instructions. Though we do not have Stalin's reply, Litvinov subsequently told Payart that it would be left to France to act first and that after such action, the Soviet Union would fulfil its obligations with 'every means at its disposal'. He returned to his previous suggestion of a conference of powers, followed by a strong statement, and suggested military consultations between France, Britain, and the Soviet Union. He also reminded Payart that Romania's foreign minister had told Bonnet that his country would close its eyes to Soviet over-flights.[45] Litvinov, not without reason, feared that what he had said would be misrepresented in Paris. When Bonnet raised the same questions in Geneva on 11 September, he received exactly the same answers as those given to Payart. Yet in London, Bonnet emphasized Litvinov's demand for proceeding via the League of Nations and played down his offers of consultation. The French foreign minister told Litvinov that Britain had vetoed the idea of a three-power meeting; in fact, he had never informed the British about the proposal, preferring to give the impression that the Soviet Union was not fully committed to Czechoslovakia. He had fully understood what the Russians were offering but had no intention of alerting the British.

V

Even as Hitler intensified the preparations for 'Case Green', he was still uncertain of Britain's non-engagement. Though he repeatedly assured the military that Britain and France would not intervene, he hesitated as the date for action approached. There were many comments—to Mussolini, Henlein, and various German officers—that he would move even if France and Britain acted. By 8 September, according to an entry in Jodl's diary, Hitler apparently no longer believed that the western powers would stay out of the conflict, but he intended to launch his attack nevertheless.[46] There were signs of irresolution, not unusual for Hitler, as the time approached for final decisions. For instance, he was extremely reluctant to set a date for 'X-day', despite the rising concern

[45] *DDF*, 2nd ser., Vol. X, No. 534.

[46] Jodl diary, 8 September 1938, quoted in Messerschmidt, 'Foreign Policy', 664.

of those generals responsible for launching the surprise attack. It is difficult to believe, however, particularly after the May *débâcle,* that as the elaborate military and diplomatic preparations continued he would have pulled back had Chamberlain's unexpected request for a meeting not arrived on 14 September. Hitler's uncertainty suggests that the Chamberlain government's policy of 'keeping Hitler guessing' was not totally unsuccessful. The real question was whether a more forthright warning to Hitler would have proved a more effective deterrent.

There were further confrontations between the Führer and his generals. Hitler probably knew nothing of the military plotting against him, but his habitual contempt for the general staff made him increasingly impatient and dismissive of the objections brought to his notice. Late in August, he travelled in his special train to make an inspection of the western defences. When General Adam explained that only about a third of the work could be finished in 1938, and again stressed the probability of western intervention, Hitler shouted and swept aside the general's warnings. There was a disputatious meeting with Brauchitsch and Halder (who was central to the operational planning of the campaign even while plotting to avert it and to remove Hitler from power if necessary) on 9 September at Nuremberg. Hitler was visibly nervous about the possible failure of the pincer attack intended to cut Czechoslovakia in two; it was too uncertain and might result in a Verdun-like battle and a slow 'bleeding to death'. The generals had to listen again to Hitler's objections to their proposals, and though his own recommendation for an all-out attack on the western end of Czechoslovakia, using all the German armoured and motorized divisions was accepted, it was only as an addition to their own deployment plans and even then in a modified form. The whole encounter was regarded as a defeat for the angry and humiliated generals, condemned to take orders from a former corporal. General Keitel, the head of the *Wehrmacht* high command, who thought that Hitler could get what he wanted in Czechoslovakia without a war, was so perturbed by the much talked-about resistance of his officers to the Führer's plans, and by Göring's constant belittling of the army's efforts, that, on returning to Berlin, he called his departmental and section chiefs together and warned them that no criticism, reservations, or expressions of pessimism would be tolerated in the OKW.

But if it was the case, as Chamberlain wrote to his sister on 3 September, 'that the fate of hundreds of millions depends on one man, and he is half mad', there was nothing maniacal about the way that Hitler set the diplomatic stage for the attack on Czechoslovakia.[47] He was not unduly concerned when President Beneš, bowing to British and

[47] NC18/1/1066, Neville to Ida, 3 September 1938.

French pressure, informed the Sudeten German negotiators that he would accept the eight points put forward by Henlein in his Carlsbad speech. Henlein, carrying a letter from Runciman, who agreed to his trip, was received at the Berghof on 1 September, and told to have the Sudeten Germans provoke incidents on the following Sunday. Nor was Hitler thrown off balance when, on 4 September, Beneš effectively granted all the Sudeten German demands, to be written on a blank sheet of paper by the Sudeten representatives (the 'Fourth Plan'). When Henlein and the other SdP leaders went off to consult with Hitler, they were given new orders to cut off the negotiations and stage incidents throughout the country. The necessary pretext was easily found on 7 September when a SdP deputy was struck by a Czech policeman during an attack on the police at Moravska Ostrava. Within hours of Hodža presenting the 'Fourth Plan' to the head of the SdP negotiating committee, the Sudetens suspended the negotiations. Even while recognizing that the incidents were deliberately staged, Hodža accepted the SdP terms, presented by Runciman, for settling the Moravska Ostrava affair. Talks were to be resumed on 13 September, the day after the ending of the Nuremberg party rally. Hitler had other plans, and the SdP was to prove his loyal and effective instrument for their implementation.

The diplomatic preparations for the attack on Czechoslovakia were carefully thought out. Hitler had no wish to take the Italians into his confidence, but Mussolini, well briefed by his military attaché in Berlin and by SIM, the Italian intelligence agency, was fully aware of what was being planned. Already during the May crisis, he had been told that German military action had only been postponed. The Hungarians, too, reported that Czechoslovakia would be broken up by 1 September and that the German-Hungarian action would take two weeks. During June, Italian Army planners suggested that Libya offered opportunities for 'rewarding land offensives' against either Tunisia or Egypt and made specific proposals. In late July, General Pariani met with the Hungarian war minister and army chief of staff to discuss a *guerra di rapido corso* against Britain, France, and Russia in order to prevent them from encircling or breaking up the Axis powers. He was in no hurry; the next meeting with the Hungarians was planned for November.

Though Attolico, the Italian ambassador in Berlin, could get no answer from Ribbentrop as to what Hitler intended to do, conversations at the Wilhelmstrasse in mid-July and warnings from the German general staff left little doubt that the critical moment in the Czech crisis was fast approaching. On 19 August, the German military attaché in Rome warned Ciano of an attack on Czechoslovakia by the end of September. Ciano feared that France would then 'set fire to the powder barrel' and Italy would have no alternative but to fall behind Germany with all our resources. The Duce is decided on action.'[48] Though Mussolini was irritated by Hitler's unwillingness to reveal the details of his plans, when on 9 September Göring proposed that the two dictators meet before 25 September, an allusion to the German timetable, the Duce suggested an October meeting instead. During the next weeks, the Italian navy began to prepare for a surprise war in the Mediterranean and specific instructions were sent to naval and submarine commanders. At the same time, Mussolini's sources reported that neither the British nor the French were taking any special naval or military measures and the French went out of their way to reassure the Italians that no action against Italy was planned. Though naval planning continued on the assumption that the Czech crisis could easily lead to war, Mussolini refused to call for a major mobilization of the fleet.

By mid-September, Mussolini had ruled out a localized war. Everything would depend on Hitler. If Germany took action against Czechoslovakia on its own, it would not succeed; France, Britain and Russia would intervene. The result would be a hard and long war. If, however, Hitler accepted a compromise, 'Czechoslovakia would fall into his hands like a ripe fruit as happened with Austria'.[49] Still reassured by the absence of any unusual British or French military measures, the Italian leader, possibly to bring more pressure on the two governments, publicly identified himself with the Axis cause. On 15 September, he published an article, 'Letter to Runciman' in *Il Popolo d'Italia*, demanding self-determination for all ethnic groups in Czechoslovakia. Speeches in Trieste, Treviso and elsewhere were strongly critical of the Czechs and resounded with calls for justice for the Germans, Hungarians, and Poles. On 17 September, Mussolini told Ciano that if a struggle broke out between Germany, Prague, Paris and Moscow, Italy would remain neutral, but if Britain entered the war, 'we would throw ourselves into the flames'. It was only after the Godesberg meeting (22–23 September) that General Keitel told the Italian ambassador in Berlin that the Führer had set a deadline of 1 October for military action and that Hitler finally sent the Prince of Hesse to inform Mussolini about the probability of war and the 1 October deadline, regardless of what the western powers did. The Italian leaders felt that they had to act more decisively; the heads of all three services were ordered to start a mobilisation that would initially ensure Italy's 'armed neutrality'.[50] General Pariani carried out his instructions but on 27 September, recommended a series of more

48 Galeazzo Ciano, *Diario*, 1937–1943, 167.
49 Quoted in Gooch, *Mussolini and his Generals, 1937–1943*, 167.
50 Gooch, *Mussolini and his Generals*, 438.

far-reaching measures, defensive and offensive, that could be taken against France and Britain if they went to war, while admitting that Italy was in no position to implement them immediately. Mussolini could hardly have been surprised; he was very well informed about Italy's military weakness and knew that the colonies in North and East Africa could not sustain a war without considerable additional support. As the prospect of a general conflict seemed imminent, Mussolini and Ciano took increasing alarm. It was hardly surprising that Chamberlain's appeal for a last minute Italian intervention with Hitler was warmly received in Rome. Mussolini was already in Munich when the now irrelevant orders for further mobilization and troop movements were issued.

In the spring and summer of 1938, the Polish authorities assumed that France would not fight if Czechoslovakia was attacked by Germany. Beck believed that Hitler would prevail and that Germany would absorb the Sudeten German territories. In the short term, much could be gained by co-operating with Hitler. The stripping of Czechoslovakia, which Beck had long argued was an artificial creation, provided a unique opportunity for Poland. The Poles could annex Teschen, that bit of Silesia over which the two countries had been arguing since the peace conference and the 1920 decision to partition it. They looked forward, too, to Hungarian action in Ruthenia (Carpatho-Ukraine), and the creation of a common Polish–Hungarian border that would provide the base for a Balkan bloc, giving Poland greater security. Such hopes nourished Beck's more grandiose ambitions for a Polish-led regional group extending from Scandinavia to the Adriatic, a 'third Europe', as he explained to Ciano in March 1938. Nor was this simply fantasy, as Beck's trips to the Baltic and Scandinavian countries during the summer months suggested. Informal talks took place in Warsaw and Berlin over a possible extension of the 1934 treaty. Józef Lipski, the acute, unflappable, and well-informed Polish ambassador to Germany, was briefed in Warsaw on 13 September on the Polish price for 'neutrality': a recognition of the German–Polish frontier as final, the extension of the 1934 agreement, and a written commitment on Danzig, along the lines of Hitler's assurances to Lipski in November 1937. Whether Hitler would have sanctioned a freezing of the 1934 status quo is highly doubtful but nothing further transpired before Chamberlain's flight to Berchtesgaden. However ambitious Beck might have been, he recognized the dangers of pouncing on Czechoslovakia. Since *Anschluss*, the Francophiles in the Polish army were nervous about Warsaw's pro-German proclivities and fearful of moving too far from France. Consequently, Beck moved in two directions simultaneously, demanding from the Czechs concessions paralleling those given to the Germans on the grounds of self-determination, and assuring the French that, if there was a general war over Czechoslovakia, Poland would either join France or remain neutral. Hitler counted on Beck's opportunism. He did not feel compelled to offer any formal assurances. While he thought in terms of a short war, Poland's ultimate loyalty to France was not an immediate barrier to his plans for the rapid settlement of the Czech question.

Hitler's discussions with the Hungarian leaders were less satisfactory. In May 1938, the strongly pro-German government in Budapest fell and the new premier, Béla Imrédy, took a fresh look at Hungary's diplomatic situation. If Hungary participated in a military action against Czechoslovakia, it could be attacked by Yugoslavia and Romania. If the crisis escalated into a general war, Germany might be defeated and Hungary would be again on the losing side. Imrédy, an Anglophile and more cautious than his predecessors, nevertheless, shared their revisionist ambitions. If there was a carve-up of Czechoslovakia, he felt that Hungary should have its share. His government sought assurances from Belgrade that Yugoslavia would be neutral should Hungary move against Czechoslovakia. The Yugoslav prime minister said one thing in Berlin and Rome, and the contrary in Prague and Paris. As the Axis governments assumed that the Hungarians had no alternative but to orient their policy towards the Axis, they preferred to nurse their newly created, if competitive, links with Belgrade, rather than encourage Budapest. As a consequence, Hungarian attempts to get either Hitler or Mussolini to guarantee Yugoslav neutrality failed though the summer crisis brought the Hungarians and the Italians closer together. In an effort to achieve some kind of *modus vivendi* with Yugoslavia and Romania, Imrédy began to negotiate with the Little Entente powers, taking up the discussions of the previous year. On the eve of his departure for Berlin, Admiral Horthy was told that the campaign against Czechoslovakia would begin at the end of September or the beginning of October. It was ironic that the Little Entente agreement at Bled (Yugoslavia), when the Hungarians finally won recognition of their rights to arms equality in exchange for a declaration of non-aggression, was announced on 22 August 1938 when the Hungarian leaders were already meeting with Hitler. Informal agreements were initialled between Hungary on the one hand and Romania and Yugoslavia on the other to protect minority rights. Because of difficulties with the Czechs over this issue, that agreement was deferred until the question was settled.

News of the Bled meeting was hardly welcomed in Berlin. Hitler took umbrage at Hungary's 'wait and see' policy and suspected, too, that the Yugoslavs preferred a policy of balance, to open alignment, with Germany. Ignoring Hitler's offer of Slovakia and Carpatho-Ukraine if Hungary promptly joined in the attack, Horthy warned the Führer that the West would not remain indifferent, and that Britain would form a coalition that ultimately would defeat Germany. The regent, not without some reluctance, refused to be drawn any further. Hitler was outraged by the rejection of his offer of a military alliance, and told Imrédy that he expected nothing from Hungary, but added a warning: 'He who wanted to sit at table must at least help in the kitchen.'[51] Horthy appears to have had second thoughts about compromising Hungary's territorial claims, and convinced Kanya and Imrédy to abandon their objections. Hitler secured an undertaking that Budapest would be prepared to take part in the military campaign against Czechoslovakia. Despite intensified military preparations in Hungary, and a declaration that the Bled agreement did not apply to Czechoslovakia, the Kanya government still sought to avoid any military engagement, hoping that it could capitalize on the early incursions of the *Wehrmacht* into Czechoslovakia and march into Slovakia and Carpathian-Ruthenia, without firing a shot. Following the announcement of Chamberlain's trip to Germany, the Hungarians stepped up their diplomatic efforts in London to ensure that Hungary's territorial demands were recognized. Assured of British good-will, Imrédy felt free to disregard German and Polish demands for decisive military action against Czechoslovakia. Hitler would remember Hungarian unwillingness to come into the kitchen. Their share of the spoils would be less than they had hoped.

VI

Signals from London during the summer continued to be mixed. Even while insisting that Beneš make concessions to the Sudeten Germans, the British warned the Germans that, should a European war break out, the danger of British intervention was not 'negligible'. Various warnings reached London about a possible German attack on Czechoslovakia, but Chamberlain dismissed them. The cabinet had scattered for the holidays. Chamberlain returned to London early in August (to seek treatment for sinusitis) and was able to confer with Halifax who had stayed at the Foreign Office. Anti-Nazi Germans insisted that a firm British warning would cause either a backdown by Hitler, or a *coup* against him. One of the most important warnings came from Ewald von Kleist-Schmenzin of the German general staff, but Chamberlain was disposed to discount much of what he said comparing Kleist to 'the Jacobites at the court of France in King William's time'.[52] Kleist returned empty-handed to Berlin on 24 August, having found no one prepared to wage a preventive war. German diplomats, among them the Kordt brothers as well as Hans von Herwarth

51 *DGFP*, Ser. D, Vol. II, No. 383.
52 *DBFP*, 3rd ser., Vol. II, Appendix IV, (i) and (ii), pp. 683–686.

and Albrecht von Kessel, each warned of the dangers of appeasing Hitler, and alerted the British to the anti-Nazi opposition in the highest ranks of the military and Foreign Ministry. In the background to this flood of warnings were the conspiratorial activities of a wide circle of plotters, who hoped that resistance from the 'Allies', above all from Britain, at the critical moment, would open the way to the overthrow of the regime without the need for a civil war in Germany. Some of the conspirators aimed at a temporary military dictatorship that would introduce a constitutional monarchy and the formation of parliamentary government. Nationalists of the pre-Hitler era sought the return of the lost territories and a guarantee of the hegemonic position of Germany on the continent, as the price for their action. Such aims alienated some former British sympathizers. Vansittart turned against Carl Goerdeler, the ex-mayor of Leipzig, and one of his closest contacts with the German civilian opposition, claiming that Goerdeler differed from Hitler only in method.[53] Downing Street and Whitehall were equally sceptical of the possibility of a military *coup*. In fact, there was no single opposition, but individuals and groups with the shared intention of checking or unseating Hitler but acting independently and with different ultimate aims in mind. The German officers, who had the most detailed plans, had only limited support in the *Wehrmacht*, which remained basically loyal to Hitler.

Quite apart from the general scepticism about the German opposition, the British government had a choice of options. It could either, as Vansittart and the German opposition leaders were urging, issue a strong warning to Hitler that might compel him to stand down, or, as Nevile Henderson advised, settle the problem of Czechoslovakia through negotiation, because any warnings to Hitler, as issued during the May crisis, would force him into the hands of the extremists and lead to war. A rather feeble message concocted by Halifax and Horace Wilson, Chamberlain's main confidant, along the former lines, was despatched to Hitler on 11 August; Ribbentrop was annoyed that he had been bypassed and Hitler made no reply. As a consequence of Kleist's representations, the prime minister and foreign secretary suffered 'some feeling of uneasiness'. Halifax was ready to consider something capable of 'the most innocent interpretation, to keep H. guessing and strengthen the hand of his generals—if that sort of thing is really true.'[54] Nevile

[53] Most members of the 'opposition' shared the anti-Semitic views common to their class and profession. There were only few exceptions, including Hans Adolf von Moltke. See Hans Mommsen, *Germans Against Hitler: The Stauffenberg Plot and Resistance in the Third Reich* (London, 2008).

[54] *DBFP*, 3rd ser., Vol. II, Appendix IV (ii) p. 686.; NC7/ll/31, cited in R. A. C. Parker, *Chamberlain and Appeasement*, 154.

Henderson was ordered back from Berlin to London. Throughout the crisis, Henderson's despatches and recommendations reflected his antipathy towards the Czechs, and his strong belief that the whole Czech problem was not worth the effort expended on it. Convinced that a war with Germany would be the ultimate disaster and had to be avoided at any cost, Henderson opposed any attempt at deterrence. Warnings would strengthen the position of the extremists like Goebbels, Himmler, and the SS, who were urging the Führer to go to war. Henderson's presence at the 'meeting of ministers', hastily summoned for 30 August, reinforced the Halifax–Chamberlain line that the government should continue to keep Germany guessing and try to forward the success of Runciman's mission, though illusions on that score must have been few. Only a small number of ministers objected to the course proposed, and then only mildly. The most critical, Duff Cooper, the first lord of the Admiralty, suggested that ministers ought to show that they were thinking of the possibility of using force, and outlined some preparatory measures that the fleet might take. The cabinet unanimously decided not to threaten Hitler if he went into Czechoslovakia. No decision was reached on what Britain would do if Hitler resorted to force; the prime minister urged that 'nothing should be done in the nature of pinpricks'.[55] Every care was taken to avoid alarming the public; various members of the cabinet left London, including Chamberlain. A day or two before the cabinet met, Chamberlain discussed a new idea with Horace Wilson. If the Runciman effort failed, the prime minister would fly to Germany to see Hitler. 'Plan Z', as it was called, was revealed only to Halifax, Simon, and Henderson. It was to go into effect at the last moment, just before the German troops marched. Chamberlain told the king of his proposal and received his approval.

The Nuremberg party rally was to open on 5 September. Despite his opposition to any 'threat', Halifax grew increasingly nervous. Churchill visited him on 31 August and urged a joint warning from Britain, France, and the Soviet Union backed by some well-publicized naval measures. Halifax proposed a speech that would both admonish the Czechs and warn the Germans. The idea proved unacceptable to either Chamberlain, Henderson, or Newton, the British minister in Prague. Another suggestion by the prime minister of a private warning to Hitler that Britain would stand by France was also dropped. Warnings from Theodor Kordt on 6 September that Hitler would 'march' on 19 or 20 September led to Chamberlain being summoned back from Scotland. Unfortunately for those urging a warning to Hitler, on 7 September *The Times* ran a leading article recommending that the Czechoslovak

[55] TNA: PRO, CAB 23/94, notes of the meeting of ministers, 30 August 1938.

government should consider the cession of the Sudetenland. Halifax and Geoffrey Dawson, the *Times* editor, were old friends and in agreement over the Czech situation. Halifax was already considering a plebiscite in the Sudetenland if other possibilities failed. An official denial followed but Dawson knew that Halifax was not really upset by the article. As so often happens in a crisis, fewer and fewer people were consulted by the prime minister. As was customary, Chamberlain, Halifax, Simon, and Hoare gathered, usually attended by Wilson, Cadogan, and Vansittart, to settle matters before going to the cabinet. 'Plan Z' was discussed by this group on 8 September; only a few other ministers were informed. Cadogan approved but Vansittart fought the visit as hard as he could, likening it to Emperor Henry V's trip to Canossa.[56] Parliament was in recess until 28 September but the Labour Party executive meeting at Blackpool issued a public declaration that Britain would join France and the Soviet Union to resist any attack on Czechoslovakia. Intelligence reports of German troop concentrations on the borders resulted in Halifax approving a warning to Berlin, to be forwarded to Henderson at Nuremberg. That warning was never delivered; the British ambassador argued that it would drive Hitler 'off the deep end'. Henderson's message was discussed by the 'inner group' of ministers. Chamberlain, backed by Simon and Hoare, overruled Halifax. On 12 September, the cabinet agreed that no formal warning should be sent. Only Duff Cooper protested at the withdrawal of the message on the sole advice of Henderson. Everyone waited for Hitler's speech at Nuremberg on 12 September.

Chamberlain had prejudged the situation. He had already decided that Hitler would accept a non-military solution to the Czech crisis, but might resort to war if threatened. As he prepared for his flight to Germany, only the second he had ever taken, a new assessment from the chiefs of staff made much of Anglo-French unpreparedness. They claimed that Czechoslovakia would be quickly overrun, that France would not be able to launch an offensive against the Siegfried Line, and that the Anglo-French air forces were too inferior in strength to risk starting an air war. It was agreed, however, that no knock-out blow was to be feared as the German air force would be busy with Czechoslovakia. Though General Ismay, secretary to the chiefs of staff, admitted that a German success would increase her prestige and 'general war potential', he insisted that the improvement in Britain's air defences would be critical and that 'if war with Germany had to come, it would be better to fight them in say six to twelve months time'.[57] The chiefs of

56 Taylor, *Munich*, 671.

57 TNA: PRO, CAB 21/544, memorandum by Ismay, 20 September 1938.

staff's report simply buttressed Chamberlain's position; he had already decided on 'Plan Z'. It was useful mainly as a means to persuade the 'weaker brethren'—Oliver Stanley, Duff Cooper, De la Warr, and Elliot—to accept his proposed course of action. On 14 September, the cabinet endorsed Chamberlain's decision to fly to Germany. The next day, ministers discussed the details of what should be proposed to Hitler. They assumed that there would be one or more plebiscites in the Czech border lands, and that these would probably lead to an eventual transfer of territory to Germany. As Czechoslovakia would be left defenceless, Chamberlain suggested an international guarantee in which Britain would join. Discussion centred on the plebiscite; cabinet ministers wanted the process of dismemberment to be slow and orderly. No one objected to Chamberlain's trip.

Right up until the last day of the Nuremberg party rally, Hitler kept his cards close to his chest. There were warnings from the German ambassador in Paris, Johannes von Welczek, that a German attack on Czechoslovakia would force a reluctant France to come to the assistance of its ally, and that Britain would then join in. Admiral Canaris, returning from Italy, reported that the Italians were advising against war. Hitler erroneously attributed Italian hesitations to a conflict between Mussolini and his generals, similar to that which he was enduring. Germans and foreigners alike waited for Hitler's speech on 12 September. Full of invective against Beneš and the Czechs, the Führer spoke of a duel between himself and the Czech president. Taunting Beneš, to the apparent delight of the crowd, Hitler made no specific demands beyond 'justice' for the Sudeten Germans, and set no time limits for the redress of their grievances. He said nothing of what would happen if his demands were not met. There were appreciative words for Chamberlain's attempts at peace-making. The speech was the signal for demonstrations and riots throughout the Sudetenland, and the Prague government was forced to declare martial law. A partial mobilization increased the number of troops along the border to some half a million men. Order was restored within forty-eight hours. This suited neither Hitler nor the German Sudeten Party. Karl Frank, speaking for Henlein, set out the terms for a resumption of negotiations in the form of an ultimatum. While demanding the ending of martial law, the Sudeten leaders refused to come to Prague to discuss the maintenance of public order, as Hodža insisted. Early on 14 September, before Chamberlain's decision to fly to Germany was known, the Foreign Office official, Frank Ashton-Gwatkin journeyed to the Sudetenland to restore contact. The Sudeten German leaders insisted that their four-point ultimatum should be accepted without conditions. Faithful to Hitler's instructions, Henlein now demanded that any new talks must include the promise of a plebiscite, the first time that the demand was made publicly. Ashton-Gwatkin refused to acknowledge that the Sudeten negotiations had been a farce. He reported that Henlein did not wish to break off relations with the Runciman mission, and that they had parted friends. The Runciman mission left for London on 16 September. Henlein and his colleagues crossed the border into Germany, set up their new headquarters and began to organize the Sudeten German Legion. In Paris, a frightened Bonnet was convinced that the question of peace or war was a matter of minutes instead of days. The cooler Daladier suggested a conference of Germany, France, and Britain. The British prime minister was not prepared to have the French cramp his style; he intended to handle Hitler alone.

VII

French diplomacy becomes more comprehensible when seen in its wider context. On 13 April, Daladier had been given the emergency powers that had been denied to Blum and brought in a series of decrees intended, as he told the Chamber, to provide for the security of the country, both internal and external. Industrial production was at its lowest point since 1928. The number of strikes equalled those of the summer of 1936; workers were faced with the prospect of longer hours just as employers were opposing wage increases and demanding the abolition of the forty-hour week, the symbol of what had been won under the Popular Front government. In the charged social climate of the day, Daladier's first steps were modest, still trying to balance between conflicting claims, but needing to restore employer confidence in the economy. The devaluation of 4 May was followed within three weeks by a massive return of capital to France, but the growing resistance of the workforce to any extension of the working week, the toughening stance of the employers on wages, and the intensifying international crisis cut short this flow. Daladier was preoccupied with the need to mobilize French finance and industry in the interests of rearmament. The difficulties of the task led him to align the state more directly with the 'owners of capital'. Reports of German work on the West Wall and the closure of a number of defence factories for the summer holidays lay behind his broadcast on 21 August, calling on the nation to get back to work, and his announcement of the suspension of the forty-hour week in defence plants and firms engaged on rearmament orders. His actions signalled the beginning of a prolonged wage struggle with the unions. Employers used the new decrees to provoke labour, in many cases choosing an arrangement of hours that meant the sacrifice of the newly won weekend. Strikes and occupations of the factories were ruthlessly suppressed. While the government measures were not sufficient to restore financial confidence or to kick-start the process of industrial mobilization, the political pendulum had swung in the employers' direction. As the Sudeten crisis moved into its critical stage, 'social fear and the fear of war coincided'.[58]

As the summer drew on, with awareness of the German timetable but no information from the British, and no solution emerging in Prague, those politicians and officials who stayed behind in Paris became apprehensive. Few at the *Quai d'Orsay* believed that the solution to the Sudeten question lay in Prague. On 12 July, Daladier publicly reaffirmed France's 'solemn agreements' with Czechoslovakia, but on 20 July, Bonnet told the Czech minister in Paris that France would not aid Czechoslovakia. The warning must have been a shock, for in Prague the French minister, Victor de Lacroix, though following his instructions, had not concealed his own dismay at the line taken by the British. He distrusted Runciman, and believed that the pressure on Beneš only encouraged the Sudetens and the Germans. François-Poncet in Berlin also believed the Runciman mission was doomed to failure, and that Hitler would accept no compromise. It was through Lacroix and François-Poncet that the *Quai* kept abreast of what the British were doing. The first official note from the British about the Runciman mission came at the end of August. On 25 August, Bonnet sent Massigli to talk to Gamelin, who, as always, seemed entirely calm, insisting that 'our system is ready, it's only necessary to press a button to start it'.[59] On 2 and 5 September, the first steps were taken to implement the defensive *couverture* procedures. Bonnet was extremely nervous, but publicly stated that France would remain faithful to the pacts and treaties she had concluded.

The French had excellent intelligence on the German plans and current activities. They were aware of the fatalistic mood of the German population towards what seemed like an inevitable war. The intelligence services also knew of the discontent in the German high command and the plans for a possible *coup*. Like their British counterparts, these reports were not taken seriously. François-Poncet also received messages from emissaries of the German army 'urging France to be firm and unyielding and declaring that in case of war the Nazi regime would collapse'.[60] The ambassador told Phipps that he had not sent these messages on to Paris, lest they encourage the warmongers in France as

[58] Robert Frank[enstein], *Le prix du réarmament français, 1935–1939* (Paris, 1982), 193.

[59] Maurice G. Gamelin, *Servir*, vol. II (Paris, 1946), 341.

[60] Halifax Mss., FO 800/311, Phipps to Halifax, 31 October 1938. The full text is found in G. L. Weinberg, *The Foreign Policy of Hitler's Germany: Starting World War II, 1937–1939* (London, 1980), 397, fn. 84.

well as Beneš. In late August, the *Deuxième Bureau* expected the German attack to come at the end of September, for it had concluded that Hitler was determined to go to war and would not be deterred by a policy of firmness. 'Hitler will be satisfied with nothing less than the complete dismemberment of Czechoslovakia and its removal as a factor in international politics.'[61] The *Bureau* also argued that the attack on Czechoslovakia was only Hitler's first step in gaining the raw materials and foodstuffs that Germany needed in order to wage a long war for the domination of Europe, inevitably including a German assault on France. This view was widely held, but as the crisis accelerated, attention became focused on the immediate present and not on the future. The problem was not seen as one of putting off war today to fight tomorrow, but to avert war today.

The focus on France rather than Czechoslovakia did not arise from any disregard of the question of honour; Daladier, though not Bonnet, was particularly sensitive on the issue of French obligations to Czechoslovakia. Nor was it because the French failed to understand what would be lost to France, in terms of her own security, if Germany took Czechoslovakia. Given the unreliability of Poland, considered likely to come in on the German side if there was war, and the hostile appraisal of Soviet intentions, which, it was believed, would stay out of any Franco-German conflict and, in any case, was unlikely and unable to aid the Czechs, Czechoslovakia was the most vital link in what remained of France's two-front strategy. The issue, however, was no longer what Czechoslovakia could do to defend France, but what France would have to do to defend Czechoslovakia. Six weeks after *Anschluss*, Gamelin had informed the British war minister that it was 'impossible for France to give military assistance to Czechoslovakia'.[62] While the Czech army was judged to be well-trained and highly motivated, *Anschluss* had undermined the country's strategic position. Germany could now strike simultaneously into western Czechoslovakia from Silesia and Austria. The Czech fortifications were in no way the equivalent of the Maginot Line, and had to cover a long border, with the south-western frontier practically open. Much of the country's industry was located near the German border, was owned by Sudeten Germans, and depended on German raw materials for production. Furthermore, Czech weakness in the air in the face of overwhelming German air superiority, magnified French doubts about the country's survival time. For their part, the French had no planes to spare. The general staff therefore concluded that there was little France could do

[61] SHD-DAT, 7N, 2522–2, Liaision hebdomadaire, 23 August 1938.

[62] Quoted in Robert Young, 'French Policy and the Munich Crisis of 1938: A Reappraisal', *Canadian Historical Association Historical Papers* (1970), 192.

to save Czechoslovakia, which they felt could not hold out for more than a month. As the crisis accelerated, the military assessments became more pessimistic. On 21 September, Gamelin, who admittedly adjusted his estimates according to his audience, told Daladier that Czechoslovakia could not resist Germany for more than a few days.[63]

The real question was not how long Czechoslovakia could survive, but how France would fare in a war with Germany. Though the military balance of power was only one factor in the government's decision to abandon the Czechs, German strength and French weakness was one of the commonest arguments used to justify the French desertion. On 24 August, General Joseph Vuillemin, the newly appointed chief of staff of the air force, returned from his short official visit to Germany as the guest of the *Luftwaffe*, a trip that had taken place against the advice of François-Poncet and the French air attaché in Berlin. Though Vuillemin knew that the Germans intended to impress him with the overwhelming strength of the *Luftwaffe*, in order to forestall any action in support of Czechoslovakia, his bleak and highly pessimistic report of the disparity between the two air forces only confirmed his views, expressed two months before the German invasion of Austria, that the French air force was completely out-classed in every respect. Throughout September, apart from official warnings, Vuillemin pressed his defeatist views on anyone prepared to listen. The panic created in some political circles was magnified by the fear that Germany would bomb the defenceless Paris at the start of the war. Vuillemin's reports on Germany's massive air superiority were confirmed by no less an authority than Colonel Charles Lindbergh, who stopped in Paris and dined with Guy La Chambre at the American ambassador's home on 9 September. Guy La Chambre, who had replaced Pierre Cot as minister for air, had secured the funding needed to use newly available production capacity, but 'Plan V', introduced in March 1938, and approved three days after *Anschluss*, could not address the disparity in the air between France and Germany until the spring of 1939, despite a rise of expenditure from 21% to 41% of total defence spending. The exaggerated view of German air prowess, and the exposed weakness of the French air force, explains why the air chiefs warned the government that war had to be averted. During the first six months of 1938, the entire French aircraft industry produced an average of 50 military aircraft a month. In September, the French air force had only 27 modern aircraft, with no modern bombers, and only a few fighters that could compare with the German Messerschmidts. France had 1,126 planes but only 700 were considered operational. This picture of weakness simultaneously coloured the French view of German air

[63] *DDF*, 2nd ser., Vol. XI, No. 273 (Gamelin to Daladier, 21 September 1938).

Table 10.1 German Air Strength, 1936–1939

	Deuxième Bureau Estimate	German Air Strength (serviceable aircraft)	Accuracy of French estimate (actual = 100)
Mar.1936	900	1300 (1000)	69
Jan.1937	1600	1900 (1600)	84
Jun.1938	3247	3200 (1669)	101
Sep.1939	4561	3825 (2893)	119

Sources: Peter Jackson, *France and the Nazi Menace* (Oxford, 2000), 401. Richard Overy, 'German Air Strength, 1933–1939: A Note', *Historical Journal*, 27: 2 (1984), 465–471.

strength. The *Deuxième Bureau* estimated during the summer that the *Luftwaffe* had 2,760 operational aircraft (1,368 bombers and 524 fighters) of which more than 80% were the product of the renovation programme of 1937 and consequently superior to any French aircraft in service.[64]

The mistakes were not quantitative but qualitative, arising from an inability to judge what percentage of the *Luftwaffe* was operational and modern. There was also a considerable over-estimation of Germany's productive capacity. Estimates by the *Deuxième Bureau* that the monthly production figures were expanding rapidly were misleading. There was a major crisis in the German aircraft industry in the spring and summer of 1937 that resulted in a massive cost-cutting programme, cuts in the industry's expansion programmes, and a major lay-off of employees. Neither in 1937 nor in 1938 were the estimates for the production of aircraft met.[65] The drop in production in 1937 was due mainly to the modernization of the *Luftwaffe*, when all the planes associated with the air war of 1939 came into service.[66] The *Luftwaffe* suffered severely from the scarcity of raw materials, particularly iron and steel, resulting from the speed-up of the German rearmament effort after the May crisis. These difficulties coincided with the many uncertainties associated with changes in the bomber fleet, as well as the production problems resulting from the introduction of the Messerschmitt 109.[67] French analysts were inclined to accept Göring's assertion that the shortages of raw material and labour would not interfere with air rearmament, and to assume that the totalitarian system and the efficiency of German

[64] Peter Jackson, *France and the Nazi Menace: Intelligence and Policy Making, 1933–1939* (Oxford 2000), 270–271.

[65] Lutz Budrass, *Flugzeugindustrie und Luftrüstung in Deutschland, 1918–1945* (Düsseldorf, 1998), 485.

[66] See Appendices A-2 and A-3, which give precise production figures for the most important of these aircraft (Do-17, He-111, Bf-199).

[67] Militärgeschichtliches Forschungsamt (ed.), *Germany and the Second World War*, Vol. I, ed. Wilhelm Deist (Oxford, 1990), 500.

production methods, so different from those of France, would iron out any major difficulties. Instead, the lack of any concept of a co-ordinated production plan for the industry crippled production. The new system of production, introduced in 1938, was based not on the principles of a planned economy but on the basis of the entrepreneurial ability of Koppenberg of Junkers to organize the industry.[68] Warned that the French air force was completely outclassed, and that the *Luftwaffe* would be used primarily for strategic bombing, and told that it was absolutely essential that Britain should agree to deploy a 'significant portion of its air power on French soil', it was hardly surprising that Daladier and most of his cabinet took a catastrophic view of any future air war.

French intelligence also reported numerous German weaknesses; deficiencies in equipment, arguments within its general staff, the inability of the German forces to pierce the French defensive system, and the weaknesses of the West Wall. Why then did the general staff make so much of its inability to mount an offensive? Why should Gamelin, who knew that it would take a year or more to make the West Wall a real barrier against a French attack, have predicted a 'modernized Battle of the Somme' should an attack be attempted? The military leadership's fear of war in 1938 arose more from the sense of French inadequacy, than from the exaggerated impression of German strength. The unwillingness to launch an offensive rested on the strategic thinking that dominated French military planning throughout the inter-war period, in particular on the assumption, sometimes queried but never abandoned, that the next war would be a long war of attrition. It would be a war that France would have to fight against a more populous enemy with superior industrial resources. In such a war, France would first stand on the defensive, and only after the enemy assault was blunted and massive superiority achieved, would she launch her own counter-offensive. Prepared for a defensive war but not for a short offensive campaign (it did not possess a mobile strike force), the army was ill-organized for a partial mobilization of its forces, and ill-prepared to mount an *offensive à l'outrance*. It could, of course, mount local and limited tactical offensives but Gamelin doubted their efficacy. As the army operations bureau concluded in a study prepared after *Anschluss,* the French army was not capable of launching a swift offensive into Germany without 'a complete reorganization of our army and the restructuring of our military policy'.[69] No such revolution was possible.

[68] Budrass, *Flugzeugindustrie und Luftrüstung*, 473. See Tooze, *The Wages of Destruction,* and his discussion of the post-Munich situation.

[69] AN, Fonds Daladier, 496 AP 35, f. 5, 'Notes sur une action offensive pour soutenir la Tchécoslovaquie'.

Since the general staff was so strongly opposed to attacking Germany, it emphasized all the obstacles to such action. The best route through the Low Countries and into the Ruhr was foreclosed by Belgian and Dutch neutrality, while an attack through the Rhineland was difficult, either because of the terrain or the strength of the German fortifications. In London as in Paris, Gamelin insisted that France could not defeat Germany by itself. French and Czechoslovak forces could offer a '*couverture*', but this would not save Czechoslovakia or win the war. Gamelin never advised the government whether it should fight or not; this was a political decision that the civilians had to take.

The defensive mentality of the general staff hardly encouraged a warlike attitude in 1938, but too much can be made of the military's conservatism and rigidity of thought. This was not unique to the French military establishment. There were glaring mistakes, of course, such as the failure to appreciate how tanks could be used as independent offensive weapons rather than merely for infantry support (the de Gaulle-Reynaud argument), and the insufficient attention paid to the use of aircraft in co-ordination with land forces. Even Gamelin's present-day defenders admit that he was 'excessively academic in his strategic analysis' and 'exaggeratedly qualified and cautious in his prescriptions'.[70] The fact remained that the French army was not ready for war and her industries were in no position to cope with even a limited rearmament programme. Not only was much of French industry sclerotic, employing outdated and inefficient methods, and suffering severe shortages of skilled labour, machine tools, and the raw materials for war production, but the financial and economic effects of the late but long-lasting depression had encouraged neither investment nor expansion. A month before Munich, France's index of industrial production reached its lowest level of the decade. The Blum rearmament programme of 1936 was already overstraining the country's industrial base in 1938. The necessary reorganization of the aircraft industry took time and would not produce results until 1939. Gamelin's efforts to mechanize and motorize the army were crippled partly through problems of design, but also by the inability of industry to turn out the required vehicles. Only one of the projected three light armoured mechanized divisions was actually operational in 1938, and the planned heavy armoured division was far from ready. More money was allotted to the services in 1938 than in 1937 (over the objections of the Ministry of Finance) but there was a serious time gap between the receipt of funds and the production of weapons. There was no ministry for armaments and no co-ordinating minister.

[70] Martin S. Alexander, *The Republic in Danger*, 390.

In principle, Daladier should have exercised these powers but, being overburdened, he either delegated them to others or abandoned them to the army administration. The French rearmed within the framework of a peace economy believing that there was still time to deal with the German menace. Daladier's decrees and Reynaud's new measures late in 1938, while successful in stimulating the civilian economy, were not intended to put France on a war footing. Daladier's political shift to the right appeared to line up the government with management against labour. France's financial difficulties also directly affected her capacity to rearm. With the franc weakened by devaluation and the flight of capital and gold, the French needed exports to purchase the raw material imports that they lacked, i.e. crude oil (mainly from the United States), one-third of their coal, most of their rubber, and many minerals from the British Empire. French manufacturers were encouraged to expand their exports which were given precedence over defence output.

Daladier was also faced with a deeply fractured society. The Czechoslovakian crisis only served to magnify these divisions, even when they failed to follow traditional political lines. Public opinion was highly volatile, hardening after Godesberg, fearful and anxious when war appeared inevitable, relieved by Munich, and dividing again along pre-crisis lines in the weeks that followed. On the left, only the Communists spoke with a single voice, consistently opposing compromise and demanding that the USSR be included in an anti-German bloc. The Communist attitude pushed others into the appeasement camp. The Socialists were divided between the pacifists and the so-called *belliciste* wing led by Léon Blum; but Blum, a severe critic of Munich after the event, changed his position during the course of the crisis. The Radicals spoke with many voices; the party contained those who, like Daladier, were not pacifists but who accepted the need to negotiate with Hitler, or, like Bonnet, fully prepared to capitulate to Hitler in order to save the peace. But the party also had critics of appeasement like Jean Zay, Edouard Herriot, and Paul-Boncour. The right and right-centre parties represented a wide spectrum of opinion ranging from those who favoured the abandonment of all France's central European responsibilities, to the group who wanted to block German expansion but not at the price of an alliance with Moscow, and to those who were strongly Germanophobe but not in favour of war. Only members of the extreme right argued that nothing was worth taking the risk of war. These views had more to do with opposition to the Popular Front, hatred of the Soviet Union, and anti-Semitism than with pro-German sympathies. Included in the ranks of the right were the friends of Prague who, while deploring war, which every Frenchman viewed with horror, thought that if Britain and France stood together, Germany would stand down. 'Pertinax' (André Géraud) in *L'Europe nouvelle*, was one of the few journalists of the day who was critical of Britain and Chamberlain, and who argued for the incorporation of the Soviet Union in an anti-German front. There was no possibility of leading a united country to war in 1938.

The overwhelming sentiment in France was for peace, though not necessarily for peace at any price. It could hardly have been otherwise in a country that had lost one and a half million soldiers in the war, a higher percentage of losses than suffered either by Germany or Britain. Most of the political leaders of France had served on the Western Front: Bonnet and Daladier were recipients of the *croix de guerre*. There was hardly a village in France that did not have its war memorial. Few families in France escaped the impact of the war. The peasantry were overwhelmingly pacifist; millions of ex-servicemen were horrified at the thought of another war. On the eve of Munich, the powerful syndicate of teachers launched a peace appeal to the country, and in three days secured 150,000 signatures in its petition against war. Anti-war sentiment reached its peak at the time parliament reassembled on 4 October. Yet the unanimity of relief at the news of Munich soon dissipated. There were few who believed that France had to accept German dictation, or were prepared to acquiesce in the Reich's domination of Europe. The question in September 1938 was not one of the surrender of France to Germany, but whether Czechoslovakia should be the occasion for war. However strong the pacifist current, only a tiny minority were resolved on peace at any price. Though the mobilization was an organizational disaster, one million men were called up without any major protests. Police reports revealed that most of the public, believing that war was inevitable, were prepared to serve. According to the infant French opinion poll organization, the response, in the aftermath of the Munich crisis, to the question, 'Do you approve the accords of Munich?', was 57% 'yes', 37% 'no', and 6% 'no opinion'. Moreover, 70% of the respondents believed that Britain and France should resist all future demands from Berlin, and a similar percentage disapproved of the use of colonial concessions as a way of buying German goodwill.[71] The overwhelming majority that voted in favour of Munich did not believe that they were voting in favour of a policy of surrender to Germany, or for the abdication of France's claim to be a Great Power.

In the end, the main deterrent to action during September 1938 was the 1914–1918 war. That experience had taught the French that they could not beat the Germans in any contest where they stood alone. Nazi

[71] Yvon Lacaze, *L'opinion publique française et la crise de Munich* (Paris, 1991), 583 for figures.

rearmament made allies more and more essential. With Poland threatening to attack Czechoslovakia, Romania uncertain, Italy in the Axis camp, and the Soviet Union unreliable, this left only Britain. At no time between *Anschluss* and Munich did the British give the French a guarantee of military support: Chamberlain believed that he could come to an arrangement with Hitler and move towards that European settlement of which he so often spoke. The conversations of the Anglo–French military attachés in the summer of 1938 involved, as the British intended from the start, only a limited exchange of information. Better co-ordination was established for handling the technicalities of moving the two British infantry divisions to France, and an agreement was made to base an RAF bomber force on French soil in case of war. Little else emerged in the way of concrete planning. General Gamelin's efforts to get Britain to provide the armoured corps he wanted for Belgium, met with no success at all. Joint naval staff talks only began on the eve of Munich. The elusive alliance was still not within sight.

Daladier's policy was based on a deep sense of French inadequacy in the face of the German threat. France appeared far more in need of Britain's backing than the other way round. For Daladier, appeasement was a policy of expediency. He was reported to have told General Gamelin: 'Je ne crois pas que, dans la situation où nous nous trouvons, on ait pu faire autre chose.'[72] In a sense, Daladier's sacrifice of Czechoslovakia was part of the price paid to secure the British alliance thought necessary to French survival. It was hardly a bargain of which to be proud. Hitler was consequently in the driving seat during the last two weeks of September with Chamberlain as his only adversary; an uncomfortable and depressed Daladier played a secondary role. To have stood up to Hitler would have been to disregard the divisions in the country, and to reject the warnings of his advisers, military and civilian, of German omnipotence and French weakness. As a long-serving minister of defence, Daladier was well aware of the country's military situation. He was, in part, responsible for that unfortunate state of affairs. If it was politically expedient 'to ensure that Britain had the lion's share of responsibility for the abandonment of Czechoslovakia', it must be said that Daladier believed that France was in no condition to fight, and could not fight a successful war in the future, unless in alliance with Britain.[73]

The French followed their own path to Munich, but it was one laid out by the British. It was the British who had taken and kept the initiative in their effort to dissuade Hitler from resorting to war. It was not that the

[72] Gamelin, *Servir*, Vol. II, 359.

[73] Anthony Adamthwaite, *Grandeur and Misery: France's Bid for Power in Europe, 1914–40*, 214.

French were pulled in the British wake, but that their own unpreparedness for war made it imperative to stick close to London. Should France fight alone to safeguard her considerable strategic interests in the east, and maintain her honour, she might well face defeat. If she abandoned Czechoslovakia, France could still survive and might secure the alliance with Britain essential to her future safety. Throughout 1938, the British were imperious and condescending in their treatment of France. It was assumed in London that with no vital British interests to defend in Czechoslovakia, the danger was that France might help her ally, and bring Britain into an unwanted conflict. There was little thought about British dependence on the French army and only the most superficial conversations between their respective general staffs.

VIII

Munich represented not just a high point in Chamberlain's policy of appeasement but also the moment when Britain was militarily isolating herself from the continent. She was preparing to defend the home islands against what was considered the most immediate threat to their safety, an air attack from Germany. How strange it was that just when the British were prepared to accept German domination of central Europe, the Czech crisis pulled Britain back into eastern affairs. Because the British did not want war in 1938, many reasons, some undoubtedly justified, were marshalled to show why Britain could not fight. It is necessary, however, to recall how many British subjects, and indeed foreigners as well, viewed Britain and the British Empire (for the two were always linked) as *the* Great Power with only the Americans as a world rival. Neville Chamberlain's policies in 1938 cannot be understood unless one appreciates the power and prestige of the country that he represented. An assumption of strength as well as weakness lay behind his efforts not just to settle the Czech problem but, in consultation with Hitler, to establish a new and peaceful status quo in Europe. The British Empire was the largest in the world. Britain's battle and merchant fleets ruled the waves. The country had made a rapid recovery from the global depression, and though it had slipped in the comparative tables of economic and financial strength, Britain was still a major player both as investor and trader. It had a functioning and effective democratic government resting on a firm social base. The Fascist and Communist parties were small and of no real political importance. The government enjoyed a safe majority in the Commons (435 seats, of which 388 were Conservative, compared to the Labour Opposition's 145) and looked forward to victory in the 1940 elections. As France's strength ebbed and its political situation appeared unstable, those continental governments who were alarmed at the spectre of German and Italian expansionism, or the threat of Soviet imperialism, sought British assistance, usually in vain. No one in the cabinet questioned Britain's right to meddle in Prague's affairs, despite all previous disclaimers of interest. The Czechoslovakian crisis confirmed Britain's long-held claim to be the peace-keeper of Europe. The demonstration of British influence in September infuriated Hitler; its governess-like tone irritated friend and foe alike.

If Britain was expected to act as a Great Power in 1938, these same events revealed its vulnerability. Just as Chamberlain had succeeded in shaping Britain's foreign and strategic policies along the lines he thought would preserve the peace at the least cost to Britain, Hitler embarked on a series of initiatives that challenged the assumptions that underlay the prime minister's grand design. There was no sign from Berlin that the Führer was prepared to negotiate over Czechoslovakia, or that he had any interest in future arrangements for the peace of Europe. Britain was rearming so that Hitler would prefer to talk rather than fight. Chamberlain told the Commons during the defence debate of 7 March 1938: 'the building up of our defensive forces . . . has made a deep impression upon foreign nations . . . The sight of this enormous, this almost terrifying power which Britain is building up has a sobering effect, a steadying effect, on the opinion of the world.'[74] *Anschluss* suggested otherwise. British strategy did not change. The meetings with the French in April 1938 left little room for doubt that there was no intention to engage in a land war in defence of the security of France. Why should Britain fight for Czechoslovakia? The chiefs of staff did not believe in using the threat of military action as a deterrent, for such a threat would not succeed. Nothing could be done to stop Germany from invading and defeating Czechoslovakia, except by engaging in a long war against Germany which could become unlimited and world-wide. While Chamberlain was not fundamentally motivated by strategic factors, the emphasis on British unpreparedness for such a war, and German strength, provided strong support for the policies he intended to adopt.

British rearmament was based on the assumption that Germany would not be prepared for war until 1942, but even had British rearmament been further advanced, Chamberlain would have opted for a diplomatic rather than a coercive solution to the Czech crisis. The government had chosen a policy that depended on the country's ability to survive a knock-out blow from the air, and to win the subsequent war of attrition. This meant British rearmament was directed to a defensive strategy and a two-stage war in which the major emphasis was on protecting the home islands. The development of radar, and the fighter

[74] *Hansard*, HC Deb, 7 March 1938, Vol. 332, Cols. 1565–1566.

force, made it more than possible that the bombers would not get through. A strong defence would make it easier to promote conciliation. It is true that all the services felt that the funds allotted to rearmament were too restricted, and the pace of rearmament too slow. On 24 March, after *Anschluss*, Chamberlain announced to the Commons that 'in the present circumstances acceleration of existing plans has become essential' and that 'rearmament work must have first priority in the nation's effort', but he presented no proposals for enabling the government to give priority to rearmament. Chamberlain's speech mentioned specifically only 'the Royal Air Force and Anti-Aircraft defences' and, in fact, it was only the aircraft industry that went on to a two-shift system, though without any compulsory assignment of labour.[75] What was not revealed publicly was that the government was in the process of abandoning the pursuit of parity in bombers, as promised by Baldwin in 1934, and looking instead to the establishment and extension of the Chain Home system, the bases needed for the early warning system (radar), and for the build-up of the new fighter force of Hurricanes and Spitfires (which were also cheaper than bombers). The decision to proceed with the development of the Chain Home system was taken on 28 July 1937; its extension north to Scapa Flow and west to Bristol was authorized in April 1938. The threat of massive retaliation to ward off the knock-out blow gave way to a more defensive strategy.

The 1938 spring debates in the cabinet over the defence estimates, took place against a background of rising parliamentary dissatisfaction with the air programmes. Winston Churchill led the critical chorus, but his complaints were taken up by Labour, a fair number of Liberals, and even some Tories. The 12 May debates in both the Lords and the Commons turned into a powerful indictment of the government's air programme. With the latter unwilling to admit that it had executed a u-turn and abandoned air parity, opponents focused attention on the disparity between German and British aircraft production, 300 a month for the latter as against 500 to 600 for the Germans. There was a call for a full enquiry into the Air Ministry, averted by Chamberlain's dismissal of Lord Swinton, the air minister, and his replacement by Sir Kingsley Wood, one of his most loyal supporters. Wood, though knowing nothing about airplanes, turned out to be a quick learner and an excellent administrator. He set about reorganizing the production of aircraft, combining firms into a number of 'production groups' and limiting the types of aircraft in production. Wood's efforts would be seen in the mounting production figures in the spring of 1939.

[75] *Hansard*, HC Deb, 24 March 1938, Vol. 333, Cols. 1410–1411.

Apart from the acceleration of the air programme, there was no sign before the September crisis of a major reconsideration of defence spending, despite the more sympathetic public attitude towards rearmament. It was still intended, even with the two year increase in the air estimates, to keep to the overall five-year £1,650 million limit adopted in 1937. The Munich crisis found the British with serious deficiencies in both its Bomber and Fighter Commands and lacking in many of the other basic essentials of air defence. The bomber squadrons available to support the French air force (372 aircraft) consisted mainly of medium bombers, and had only just become operational, and so lacked reserves of aircraft, crews or spares. The situation in Fighter Command was worse: only 406 aircraft, of which 238 were obsolete or approaching obsolescence, and only one squadron of Spitfires (fourteen aircraft) which possessed a margin of speed over existing German bombers, was operational. If (and everything depended on that 'if') the Germans had mounted an air attack on Britain in September, Lord Inskip's parliamentary private secretary told Harold Nicolson, 'our air force would have been wiped out in three weeks and our pilots would have gone to certain death'.[76]

This unpreparedness went hand in hand with an exaggerated estimate of German air strength, and erroneous assumptions about German air doctrines. The existing disparity in the respective sizes of the two air forces discouraged the military from making any attempt to deter Hitler by threatening war. On 23 September, the Foreign Office, using air intelligence figures, correctly estimated Germany's total first-line strengths as 2,909 planes as against Britain's 1,550. In fact, if the French and Czechoslovakian air forces were added to the British figures, the combined total was considerably higher than that of Germany.[77]

The British estimated that the Germans had 1,233 first-line bombers, a figure which, like the French figures, exaggerated the number of the *Luftwaffe*'s serviceable aircraft as well as the capabilities of its planes. The range of the German bomber force and the number of bombs that could be carried and dropped, were wildly inflated. British air intelligence predicted in August 1938 that the existing German bomber force could make 720 sorties against England in a single day and deliver 945 tons of bombs. It would be capable of inflicting 50,000 casualties in a twenty-four-hour period.[78] Even the air staff refused to accept this 'calculus of destruction'. Nonetheless, throughout the September crisis, the air staff continued to stress the dangers of German bombing and the

[76] Harold Nicolson, *Diaries and Letters, 1930–1939*, vol. 1 (London, 1969), 381.
[77] Figures from Wesley K. Wark, *The Ultimate Enemy: British Intelligence and Nazi Germany, 1933–1939* (London, 1985), 69.
[78] Wark, *Ultimate Enemy*, 66–67.

TABLE 10.2 Comparison of Air Strengths, Munich Crisis

	Total first-line	First-line bombers
Germany	2909	1223
Great Britain	1550	200
France	1349	260
Czechoslovakia	628	100
Belgium	198	12

Source: W. K. Wark, *The Ultimate Enemy: British Intelligence and Nazi Germany, 1933–1939* (London, 1985), 69.

inadequacies of the British defence. Time was needed to complete the radar chain and build up Fighter Command. Ironically, just as air intelligence and the Foreign Office were warning of the vast disparity between the German and British air forces, General Helmuth Felmy, the head of a special *Luftwaffe* staff created to look, for the first time, at the problems of an air attack against Britain, reported on 22 September that a 'decisive war against England appears to be ruled out with the means now available'.[79] Existing German bombers did not have the range to reach Britain from bases in Germany, and their crews lacked the necessary training for overseas operations.

If the imbalance in the air was the most decisive strategic factor in dissuading the chiefs of staff from any attempt at deterrence, the widespread belief in German preparedness for war encouraged a general reluctance to consider fighting at the present time. As in Paris, the sheer scale of German rearmament so impressed the British that the numerous reports by the intelligence services of German weaknesses—i.e. the lack of raw materials and skilled labour, the operational shortcomings of the rapidly expanded army and air force, and the doubts of the German general staff about the country's readiness for war—were down-graded. The fact that in five years Nazi Germany had created, almost from nothing, an army equivalent in numbers to that of the German army of 1914, dwarfed intelligence about Germany's inability to mobilize and equip it to engage in a European war. British military intelligence correctly estimated in July 1938 that the German regular army would consist of 46 divisions. The number of first-line reserves and *Landwehr* divisions was considerably exaggerated, however, and during the course of the crisis these figures were further inflated, particularly the number of motorized and armoured divisions that Germany could put in the field. The assessments of the Air Ministry

[79] Quoted in Wark, *Ultimate Enemy*, 68.

and War Office were reinforced by reports from the Industrial Intelligence Centre, a key contributor to the British intelligence assessment process, whose contacts reported that German industry was already operating in conditions of 'partial mobilization', and that state direction would circumvent any economic difficulties impeding the fulfilment of the government's programmes. After the German test mobilization in August 1938, the War Office concluded that the Germans could launch 'at will a sudden and overwhelming onslaught on Czechoslovakia without fear of effective interference from the West during this operation'.[80] This warning was repeated twice during the first nine days of September. Neither information about the thin German *couverture* of the western frontier, nor about the numbers of the French and Czech forces, altered this assessment. Correctly enough, the War Office doubted whether the French would use their numerical superiority to launch an offensive, but it also dismissed encouraging reports from its own military attaché in Prague about the Czech willingness and readiness to fight. Britain's major task, it was agreed, was to win time for rearmament.

The prime minister's own reading of the situation rested, not on the imbalance of military forces between Britain and Germany, but on his conviction that he could persuade Hitler to accept a peaceful solution to the Czech crisis, and agree to the wider proposals for co-operation Chamberlain had in mind. He had few doubts that he could succeed, and while he was indeed successful, he failed to grasp the full implications of his 'success', which produced results entirely different from those he had in mind.

[80] Ibid., 107.

11

The Munich Settlement

I

When the 69-year-old Chamberlain took his plane trip to see Hitler on 15 September, he did not think he was 'going to Canossa'. There was, indeed, a considerable arrogance in his assumption that he could tell Hitler what he should or should not do, without being willing to take any corresponding risks. If the Führer was annoyed by the prime minister's intervention, he was also impressed by Chamberlain's sudden descent on Berchtesgaden. Chamberlain wrote to his sister that the German leader 'looks entirely undistinguished'. The prime minister was pleased with the way the conversation went, though its course was entirely different from what he had anticipated. Prepared to talk of Anglo-German relations, he found that Hitler was only interested in getting an 'instant solution' to the Sudeten problem and did not care 'whether there was a world war or not'.[1] Pressed by Chamberlain to make some gesture towards negotiation so that his journey had some point, Hitler agreed that the acceptance of the principle of secession would be enough to begin talks. On returning to London the following day, Chamberlain first met, as would become his usual procedure, with his 'inner cabinet': Halifax, Simon, Hoare, with Vansittart, Cadogan, and Horace Wilson in attendance, Lord Runciman later joined them. The next morning, 17 September, an emergency full meeting of the cabinet was held. Runciman officially presented his report, speaking out of both sides of his mouth. Finally disillusioned with Henlein, who had taken in so many Englishmen, including Vansittart and Churchill, the so-called mediator still blamed the Czechs for most of the current troubles. Just before a second cabinet meeting held after lunch, Halifax remembered to invite Daladier and Bonnet (Phipps had strongly advised that the latter should be present) to come immediately to London. It was more or less accepted by the cabinet that the Sudeten Germans should be given immediate self-determination, but that the principle should

[1] R. A. C. Parker, *Chamberlain and Appeasement*, 162–163.

be applied in an orderly fashion. Ministers also considered the possibility of guaranteeing the new frontiers, a startling departure in British diplomacy with regard to Eastern Europe. No one raised any objections to taking on these new responsibilities.

On 18 September, Daladier and Bonnet arrived accompanied by Léger, Charles Rochat, the chief of the *Quai d'Orsay's* European section, and Jules Henry, Bonnet's *chef de cabinet*. Formal talks began soon afterwards. Daladier, upset by France's loss of control and yet relieved that Chamberlain had assumed the major burden of responsibility, had been worried about the lack of contact with London since Chamberlain's return. Bonnet, on the contrary, had recovered his balance and experienced no regrets about ceding primacy to Britain. Daladier came with secret news from Beneš that the president would agree to a cession of territory and a transfer of population, subject to safeguards for the existing inhabitants, should it become necessary. The handwritten note, presented by Jaromir Necas (a cabinet minister in the Beneš government) to his friend Léon Blum, was absolutely secret and was to be used only as a last resort. Some four to six thousand square kilometres were involved and a transfer of a minimum of one and a half to two million Sudeten Germans. Daladier claimed that he told Chamberlain privately; the French premier was 'singularly embarrassed' by the offer and it was never actually discussed. Daladier arrived, too, with repeated warnings from Vuillemin, right up to the moment of his departure, about the dangers of war, and with a not unduly pessimistic report from the French high command. France could mount an offensive within ten or twenty days of the start of war, the officers claimed, though an important part of Czechoslovakia would have to be lost before the German army could be finally defeated. Daladier knew, too, that Halifax had refused to give France any guarantee of support should she go to war to assist Czechoslovakia.

The Anglo-French meetings were a one-sided affair. Daladier made his usual speech, questioning whether by accepting Hitler's demands he would be satisfied and peace secured and then agreeing that they should be accepted. He was opposed to a plebiscite and would have preferred a transfer; otherwise the Poles, Hungarians, and even the Romanians would help Hitler destroy Czechoslovakia. After much evasive talk on both sides, Daladier finally asked whether Britain was prepared to accept Hitler's terms. More sparring followed, but the British decision was clear and Daladier was expected to accept it. The hosts were somewhat scornful of their guests, particularly Daladier, whose 'voice trembling with carefully modulated emotion' spoke of French honour and obligations.[2] After lunch, Daladier totally capitulated, agreeing to the cession of territory and asking only that Britain join an international guarantee of the new Czechoslovak boundaries. This would make it easier for the French to convince the Czechs to accept the new plan and for Daladier to sell the idea to his cabinet. After a discussion of the guarantee, Chamberlain offered the French their 'gift' and the draft message to be presented to Beneš. Girard de Charbonnières described the scene at dinner at the French embassy that evening when, before sitting down to eat, Daladier began a long monologue:

> Well, gentlemen. No, I am not proud. I do not know what you think, you others, but I, I will say it again, I am not proud. For after all there is no doubt; the Czechs, they were our allies, we had commitments with them, and for those commitments, what I have just done is not to keep them. Yes, take it as you will, I have not honoured the signature of France, and that is not good.

Daladier pleaded that he could not take the risk that Hitler might be bluffing: France could not go to war. Georges Bonnet, 'his profile showing the great dull, glazed eye of a dead fish', assured the premier that nothing else could have been done. Alexis Léger, in a soft voice, claimed that the British would honour their guarantee, and that it was better to let the three and a half million inhabitants go, nearly a quarter of Czechoslovakia's population, but mainly German, and have the remaining territory guaranteed by Britain and France. Daladier, citing French behaviour towards its ally, questioned the value of the guarantee. He twisted and turned, but all knew he had already surrendered. The members of the French embassy present were unimpressed but no one said anything in criticism.[3]

At the final joint conference on a day of meetings that ended only at midnight, the British draft was accepted and the joint proposals sent off to the French and British representatives in Prague. Daladier insisted that nothing should be done until the French cabinet met. The Prague government was told that districts mainly inhabited by the Sudeten Germans should be transferred to Germany and that, recognizing the great sacrifice involved, France and Britain would join in an international guarantee of the new boundaries. The next morning, 19 September, the full British cabinet met and was told what had been done. They agreed, without difficulty, to the Anglo-French plan. The affirmative answer from Paris came at the end of

[2] David Dilks (ed.), *The Diaries of Sir Alexander Cadogan*, 100.

[3] Guy de Girard de Charbonnières, *La plus évitable de toutes les guerres*, 159–163.

their meeting. At the *Quai d'Orsay*, René Massigli had prepared a strong memorandum on the 'Garantie internationale à la Tchécoslovaquie', warning of the limitations of an international guarantee and citing the consequences to France should Czechoslovakia be sacrificed in the interests of preserving an uncertain peace.[4] It had little effect on Bonnet's thinking. Daladier's awareness of French weakness and his fear of going it alone precluded any alternative policy, whatever his compunctions about deserting an ally whose importance to France was fully recognized. A severe financial crisis and an outflow of funds from France, checked only by Chamberlain's trip to Berchtesgaden, was a timely reminder of the fragility of the French economy.

At 2 p.m. the British and French ministers in Prague, 'like two angels of death', arrived to see Beneš. Newton made it clear that the alternatives were a British guarantee of Czechoslovakia's national security, or a Czech war alone with the Third Reich. Beneš was left to consult his cabinet, but was warned that a quick response was necessary as Chamberlain planned to meet Hitler on 21 September. It was at this point that Beneš called in the Soviet minister, Alexandrovsky, and put two questions to him; the nature of the second of these has been much disputed. Beneš first asked whether, if the French were faithful to their treaty obligations, would the Soviet Union provide assistance against the Reich. According to Alexandrovsky, the second query was whether the Soviet Union would assist Czechoslovakia as a member of the League of Nations, on the basis of Articles 16 and 17 of the Covenant. Beneš' memoirs record a different question: 'What will the attitude of the Soviet Union be if France refuses to fulfil her obligations?' Speedy replies were necessary as general mobilization might have to be declared by the evening of the 29th. The answers, as recorded by Alexandrovsky, were both in the affirmative. Beneš remained mistrustful of Soviet intentions. He told his secretary, whom Alexandrovsky had informally urged to argue against capitulation: 'I know. They naturally play their own game. We cannot trust them completely either. If they get us into it, they will leave us twisting in the air.'[5] The president summoned Klement Gottwald, the head of the Czech Communist party, but got no information from him beyond an assurance that the Soviet Union always fulfilled its commitments. It may well be that Beneš hoped that an affirmative answer from Moscow would assist a divided cabinet to reject the Anglo-French demands, on the chance that Britain and France

[4] *DDF*, 2nd ser., Vol. XI, No. 223.

[5] Igor Lukes, *Czechoslovakia between Stalin and Hitler*, 224.

would reconsider their policies. Without the possibility of military assistance from France, it is highly unlikely that Beneš would have relied on the Soviet Union as his sole source of support. In any case, neither the Czech ministerial decision to reject the western powers' recommendation nor the later and more significant one to accept the Anglo-French ultimatum, had much to do with the Soviet replies.

In the evening of 20 September, Krofta handed the Czech refusal to Newton and Lacroix, the British and French ministers in Prague. The Czechs responded by reporting that they would resort to arbitration on the basis of the German–Czech arbitration treaty of 1925. In reporting the Czech refusal, the two ministers claimed that Beneš and his government would give way if given a clear and final warning that Czechoslovakia would be left to its fate if the Anglo-French proposals were rejected. Lacroix wired Bonnet that Hodža had suggested such a declaration and had insisted that it was 'the only way of saving the peace'.[6] Newton too reported that a solution had to be imposed upon the government, 'as without such pressure many of its members are too committed to be able to accept what they realize to be necessary'.[7] Bonnet telephoned the French legation in Prague to instruct Lacroix that the Czechs should be told that France would refuse because a Czech rejection would disrupt Anglo-French solidarity and France could not offer effective assistance without Britain. Lacroix, unlike Newton, made a simple if less brutal statement to the Czechs, but its substance was the same. Beneš insisted on written confirmation, clearly wanting the French to shoulder the blame for the Czech surrender. The two ministers arrived back at the Castle after two in the morning and stayed until four. Newton was commanding; Lacroix tearful but firm. In the end, it was clear that this was an ultimatum. Even so, the Czechs delayed, and it was only at 5 p.m. in the afternoon on 21 September that the Prague government finally capitulated to the Anglo-French demands.

As Hitler had planned, the Polish and Hungarian ministers presented their demands in Prague on the evening of 21 September, soon after the decision to accept the Franco-British ultimatum. The Hungarians were cautious and uncertain; their claims for Slovakia and the Carpatho-Ukraine, contested by the autonomists and separatists in both regions, might set off the war that they believed Hitler wanted, and which they feared he might lose. There were also worries about Yugoslavia. The Hungarian leaders had been summoned on 20 September to Berchtesgaden. Hitler was less than gentle with them, and reproached Imrédy and Kanya for their apparent indecision. Imrédy apologetically blamed

[6] *DDF*, 2nd ser., Vol. XI, No. 232 (20 September 1938).

[7] *DBFP*, 3rd ser., Vol. II, No. 979 (Newton to Halifax, 20 September 1938).

his government's delay on the speed of Hitler's actions. He promised that Hungary would demand a plebiscite, make the necessary military preparations, and refuse to guarantee any proposed borders until their demands were settled. Signs of Hungarian half-heartedness provoked another lecture from Hitler before the men departed. That evening, the Hungarians decided to present their demands to Prague, and on the next day they would institute a partial mobilization of reservists. Representations were made in Paris and in London. Nonetheless, the Berchtesgaden talks heightened Hungarian alarm about the possible consequences of helping in the preparations for the Czech dinner. Hitler had far less difficulty with the Poles. Józef Lipski, the Polish minister, came to Berchtesgaden later on the same day. He was courteously received, and there were no lectures. Hitler warned that the British proposals (the Germans were intercepting telephone calls between Prague and their embassies and so knew the details of the Anglo-French offer) would involve a new delineation of frontiers, and not the plebiscite he wanted. He might have to accept these terms if his own claims were to be recognized. What then should be done about the Polish and Hungarian demands? Lipski outlined the geographical borders of the Teschen region that Poland would demand and assured Hitler that force would be used if it proved necessary. It was agreed that neither Germany nor Poland would guarantee the new borders until all claims were settled. For the Czechs (and for the USSR) the Polish threat was obviously far more important than that of Hungary. Polish neutrality was essential for any plausible defence of Czechoslovakia against Germany. The Polish minister in Prague assured the Czechs that if the disputed area in the Teschen region were ceded to Poland, there would be no further problems between the two states.

By the evening of 21 September, the news of the Prague government's capitulation spread, and crowds gathered around the Castle, pushing towards the door leading to the presidential suite and apartment, until stopped by the state police. Elsewhere in the city, too, people demonstrated, demanding arms and mobilization. Gottwald and the Communists were active but the protest movements were genuinely spontaneous. A general strike was called. Beneš, who seems to have slept all through the clamour outside his apartment, quickly took charge the next morning, and within a few hours received Hodža's resignation and replaced him with General Jan Syrovy, whose main claim to fame was service in one of the Masaryk legions in Russia. He had, as Beneš knew, no political experience or ambition, but the appointment of a military man reassured the protesters. The workers disbanded and returned to their factories. Beneš was now fully in control of the government and his decisions were all that counted. He appeared strangely calm and confident; on the evening of 22 September, in his broadcast to the nation, he spoke of a 'plan for all eventualities'. Whether this was any more than a last-minute bid to secure a role for Czechoslovakia in the decisions about her fate remains open to question. 'If the gentlemen want to play up the minority question here [in Czechoslovakia] I will give it to them in the whole of Europe—and then we cannot lose.'[8]

Chamberlain and Hitler had agreed to meet at Godesberg on 22 September, at the Dreesen hotel where the Führer had launched the 'Night of the Long Knives' in June 1934. Chamberlain was optimistic about securing peace for Europe. Opinion, however, both in England and France, hardened as the German demands and their acceptance became generally known. There were fears in London, clearly voiced by Orme Sargent, that Hitler would raise the price for agreement. At the last pre-Godesberg cabinet meeting on 21 September, a consensus emerged that there should be no further concessions beyond what had been given already. Halifax reported on the pressure from the Polish and Hungarian representatives, who were besieging the Foreign Office and the *Quai d'Orsay* with their demands. The cabinet decided that if Hitler pressed their claims, Chamberlain should break off the talks and come back to London. As Chamberlain prepared to fly off again to Germany, there was as yet no plan in place for the transfer of territories and population, and no decision about who would monitor them. Halifax preferred German troops to Henlein's *Freikorps,* but hoped that Beneš would settle the problems of keeping order. During the night of 20–21 September, the Henlein *Freikorps*, an undisciplined rabble of Sudeten German enthusiasts, had mounted raids, aided by the Germans, across the border at Asch and at Eger and Franzensbad. Czech soldiers were told not to respond, but Prague informed the British and French governments. The German high command was appalled at this premature action, which could spoil what remained of its hopes for a surprise attack. There had been no slackening of the preparations for 'Plan Green' during these days. Carefully monitored by French observers, German army units were beginning to assemble at their appointed assault areas. Hitler himself intervened to restrict the *Freikorps* operations and bring its activities under German army supervision.

At Godesberg on 22 September, Hitler totally disregarded what Chamberlain was prepared to offer. Asked whether the Anglo-French terms had been accepted by Prague, Chamberlain replied that they had. Now Hitler said that he was sorry, but these proposals were no longer of use. The Czechs could not be trusted and he intended to

[8] Lukes, *Czechoslovakia between Stalin and Hitler*, 232–233.

move right away; there could be no discussion of details, properties, commissions, refugees, or the like. A 'frontier line must be drawn at once... [along] the language frontier' and all Czech forces and civil agencies removed. The area evacuated would be occupied by German troops and the plebiscites would be held after the German occupation. There could be no guarantees or non-aggression pacts until Polish and Hungarian claims were settled. The prime minister was deeply shocked. He understood that Hitler meant instant military action, and not the orderly transfer of territories that was intended to prevent war. The prime minister pointed out that 'in fact he had got exactly what the Führer wanted... In doing so, he had been obliged to take his political life into his hands... Today he was accused of selling the Czechs, yielding to dictators, capitulating, and so on. He had actually been booed on his departure today.'[9] Hitler was argumentative and threatening but Chamberlain refused to give up his pursuit of an agreement even after he left the Dreesen hotel. There was an exchange of letters and an equally disappointing second meeting. As Chamberlain had requested, Hitler presented his demands in a memorandum and drew up a map showing the areas to be transferred. At the late-night encounter between the two men, neither the changes in wording nor the postponement of the occupation date from 26 September until 1 October (30 September was, in fact, the earliest possible date for a German attack) disguised the fact that Hitler had scuppered Chamberlain's hopes for an orderly resolution of the crisis at Prague's expense. Hitler would occupy the territories he had designated as German and treat their inhabitants as he wished. At best, Chamberlain kept the door open for further talks.

A very weary prime minister arrived back in London the next day, lunched with Halifax and conferred with his inner cabinet. Their dismay was palpable, for the prime minister advocated acceptance of the memorandum. 'I was completely horrified—he was quite calmly for total surrender', Cadogan wrote in his diary. 'More horrified still to find that Hitler has evidently hypnotized him to a point. Still more horrified to find P.M. has hypnotized H. [Halifax] who capitulates totally.'[10] Chamberlain insisted that he had acquired some degree of personal influence over Hitler, and that the Führer was speaking the truth when he claimed that this was only a racial matter. When the cabinet met late in the afternoon, Chamberlain put forward the same arguments, assuring his colleagues that the 'object of his [Hitler's] policy was racial

[9] *DBFP*, 3rd ser., Vol. II, No. 1033 (Notes of a conversation between Mr Chamberlain and Herr Hitler at Godesberg on 22 September 1938).

[10] Dilks (ed.), *Diaries of Sir Alexander Cadogan*, 103.

unity and not the domination of Europe'.[11] He reminded them what a great tragedy it would be if the opportunity for reaching an agreement with Germany was lost. He spoke of the horrors of confrontation, and particularly of what German bombing would do to the thousands of unprotected homes he saw below him as he flew back over London. Either because he sensed the divisions in the cabinet, or in order to avoid precipitate action (Duff Cooper insisted on immediate general mobilization while others recommended partial mobilization), the prime minister suggested that nothing be decided until the next morning. Meanwhile, the French were again invited to London.

Litvinov, reacting to Chamberlain's second trip to see Hitler, tried to get Stalin to take a tougher line. On 23 September, he wrote from Geneva to Stalin, 'should we not declare even partial mobilization and conduct a campaign in the press that would be such as to force Hitler and Beck to believe in the possibility of a major war involving ourselves?'[12] On the same day, he saw De La Warr, an opponent of Chamberlain's appeasement policies, and R. A. Butler, an under-secretary of state at the Foreign Office, both of whom were representing Britain in Geneva. Each side tried, unsuccessfully, to find out what the other was planning. Litvinov, who again urged a conference of Great Powers outside of Geneva, pleaded ignorance of any Soviet military moves as he had been absent from Moscow for two weeks. His superiors quickly blocked any move, pointing out that it was highly doubtful that France and Britain would agree to a joint conference since they had hitherto ignored the USSR. According to Czech sources, Chamberlain was appalled at De La Warr's approach to Litvinov, and warned of the dangers of a Russian military presence in central Europe. Alexandrovsky, who had strongly pressed the Czech case for Soviet assistance, was repeatedly warned by Potemkin, the deputy commissar of foreign affairs, to avoid encouraging any illusions in Prague. Stalin had clearly refused to go beyond the assurances already given to Beneš. The Soviet Union would abide by the terms of the mutual security pact if France acted, and would assist as a League member if Czechoslovakia appealed under Articles 16 and 17 of the Covenant. Litvinov took the same public line in Geneva.

Even before the return of Chamberlain from Godesberg, a number of ministers and officials on both sides of the Channel had become restive and even disaffected. The news of Sudeten German *Freikorps* incursions into Czech territory had led to decisions in London and Paris to lift the

[11] Quoted in Parker, *Chamberlain and Appeasement*, 169.

[12] Quoted in Jonathan Haslam *The Soviet Union and the Struggle for Collective Security in Europe*, 187.

advisory ban on Czech mobilization. This had infuriated Hitler, and was hardly welcome news to the hard-pressed Chamberlain in Godesberg. In Prague, there was jubilation. The order for mobilization went out on the evening of 23 September and many Czechs would later recall 'that beautiful night' with considerable nostalgia. Some 1,250,000 men were mobilized with great efficiency and a minimum of confusion, yet half the Sudeten German men deserted to Germany, and a smaller percentage of Poles and a fraction of reservists of Polish extraction, failed to turn up.[13] Hitler's memorandum outlining the Godesberg terms, forwarded by the British, arrived in Prague in the evening of 24 September. While it was being studied, news came that the French government was calling up reservists. There was optimism, too, in the Czech Foreign Ministry, about the Soviet reaction to what was in every sense a *de facto* German ultimatum. Fierlinger, the over-enthusiastic Czech minister in Moscow, misleadingly reported that Soviet military representatives were coming by air to Prague, and passed on rumours of a Soviet–Romanian agreement on a land corridor. Stalin was not only unwilling to take any further steps in Prague, but probably shared the views of those who believed that the western powers were determined to exclude the USSR from their deliberations, and would seek an agreement with Germany that would leave the Soviet Union isolated. He was, however, prepared to take a tougher line with the Poles. Early signs of Polish irredentism had led to a reorganization of the Kiev and Byelorussian commands, and defence minister Voroshilov's decision in September to order manoeuvres in the Soviet–Polish frontier region. On 22 September, Foreign Minister Krofta told Alexandrovsky that Poland was concentrating its forces all along the frontier in preparation for an attack and asked whether the USSR would warn the Poles that the Soviet–Polish Non-Aggression Pact would cease to operate if Poland attacked Czechoslovakia. At four in the morning on 23 September, Potemkin summoned the Polish chargé d'affaires to receive that warning. The Poles were infuriated but not deterred from increasing their pressure on Prague. Between 21 and 24 September, the Soviets instituted a partial mobilization of their forces, involving some 330,000 men.[14]

[13] Lukes, *Czechoslovakia between Stalin and Hitler*, 237.

[14] Figures and detailed breakdown in David Glantz, *The Military Strategy of the Soviet Union* (London and Portland, OR, 1991), 69–70; see also Hugh Ragsdale, *The Soviets, the Munich Crisis and the Coming of World War II* (Cambridge and New York, 2004), 113–126; Haslam, *Soviet Union and the Struggle for Collective Security*, 189. See, too, Z. Steiner 'The Soviet Commissariat of Foreign Affairs and the Czechoslovakian Crisis in 1938: New Material from the Soviet Archives', *Historical Journal*, 42: 3 (1999), 770, and M. J. Carley ' "Only the USSR has . . . Clean Hands": The Soviet Perspective on the Failure of Collective Security and the Collapse of Czechoslovakia', forthcoming article (see fn. 43, p. 582).

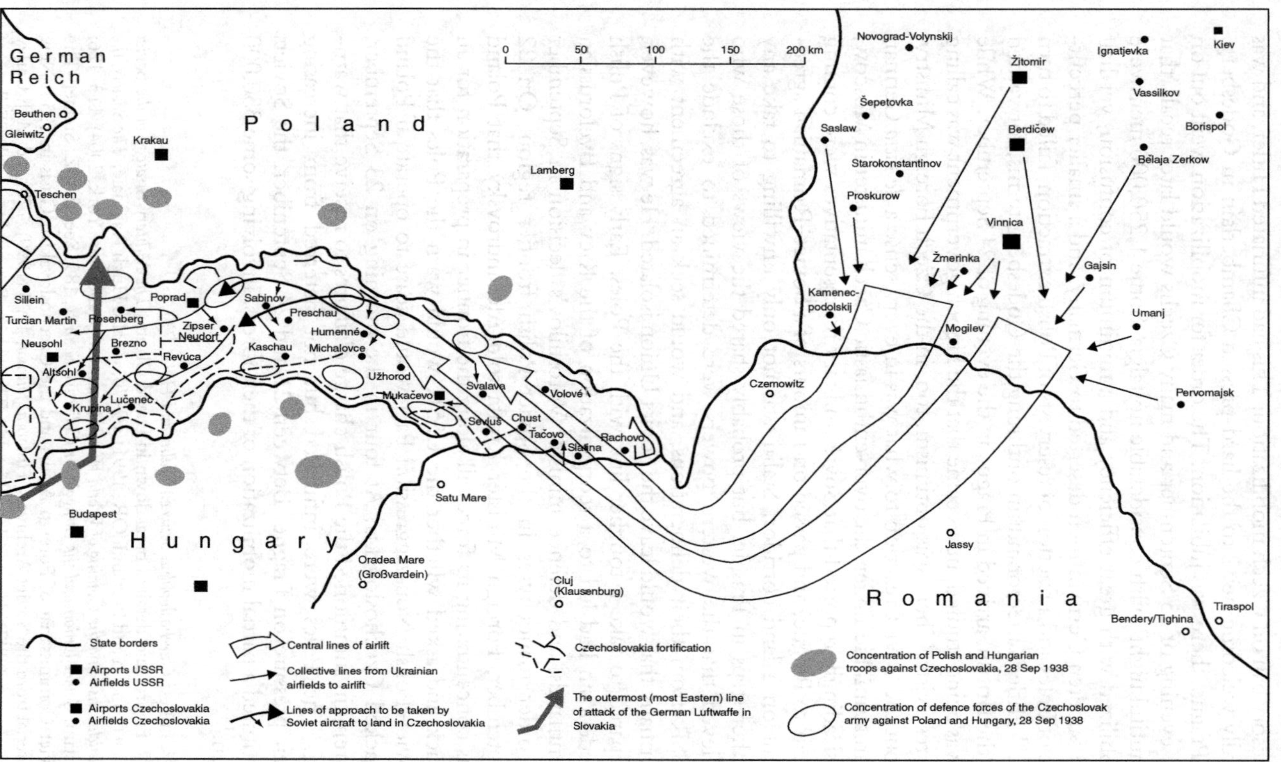

Map 7. Potential Soviet Aerial Support for Czechoslovakia, September 1938

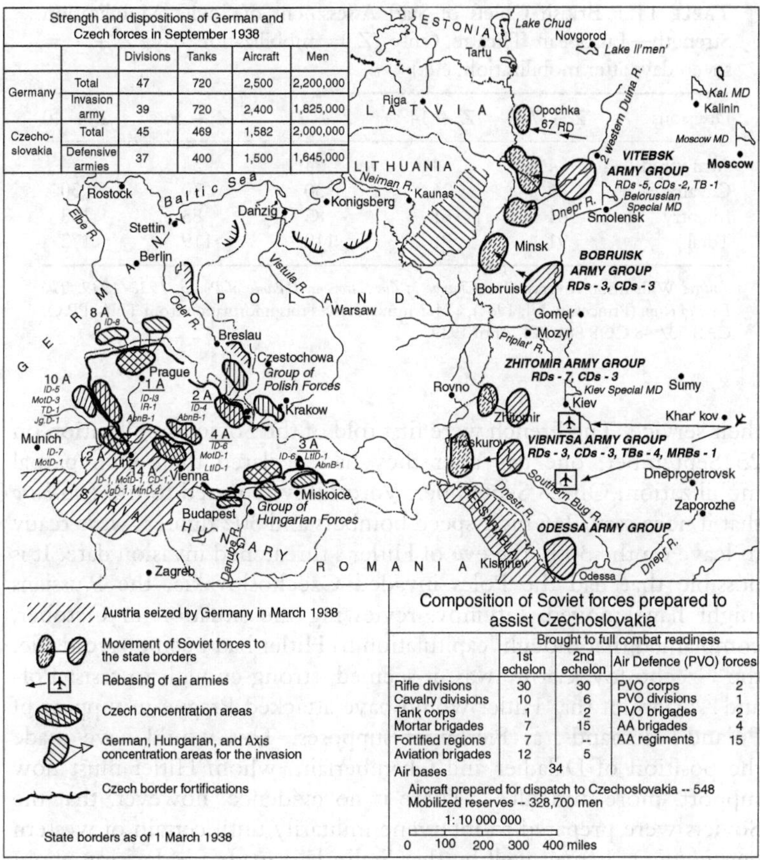

Strength and dispositions of German and Czech forces in September 1938

		Divisions	Tanks	Aircraft	Men
Germany	Total	47	720	2,500	2,200,000
	Invasion army	39	720	2,400	1,825,000
Czechoslovakia	Total	45	469	1,582	2,000,000
	Defensive armies	37	400	1,500	1,645,000

Composition of Soviet forces prepared to assist Czechoslovakia

Brought to full combat readiness	1st echelon	2nd echelon	Air Defence (PVO) forces	
Rifle divisions	30	30	PVO corps	2
Cavalry divisions	10	6	PVO divisions	1
Tank corps	1	2	PVO brigades	2
Mortar brigades	7	15	AA brigades	4
Fortified regions	7	--	AA regiments	15
Aviation brigades	12	5		
Air bases	34			

Aircraft prepared for dispatch to Czechoslovakia -- 548
Mobilized reserves -- 328,700 men

Map 8. Soviet Military Mobilization, September 1938

Most of the troops were deployed along the Polish frontier, but one army group was stationed on the Romanian border.[15] The deployments, mainly from the Kiev and Byelorussian military districts, included infantry, cavalry and tank corps, fighter planes and light bombers. At the same time, all military districts were ordered to hold back from discharging soldiers and NCOs who had completed

[15] Ragsdale, *The Soviets, the Munich Crisis and the Coming of World War II*, 167.

Table 11.1 British Chiefs of Staff Assessment of Soviet Mobilization Strength—European Theatre Only (Z = mobilization day; Z + 7 = seven days after mobilization, etc.)

Divisions	Z + 7	Z + 14	Z + 21	Z + 36	Z + 40
Armoured	4	4	4	4	4
Cavalry	26	26	30	30	30
Infantry	61	61	85	85	138
Total	91	91	119	119	172

Source: Williamson Murray, *The Change in the European Balance of Power, 1938–1939: The Path to Ruin* (Princeton, NJ, 1984), 124. Murray derives this information from TNA: PRO, CAB 53/ 48 COS 881 (JP), April 1939.

their service. The French were first told of the Soviet mobilization on 25 September, one day after they had declared their own partial mobilization. On 28 September, Voroshilov reported to the *Politburo* that if necessary, 246 high-speed bombers and 302 fighters were ready to leave on the 30th, the eve of Hitler's threatened invasion date. It is possible that had the Poles invaded Czechoslovakia, the Russians might have moved. Litvinov, reviewing the situation in October, complained that though 'capitulation to Hitler had been unavoidable, the Czechoslovak army was, it seemed, strong enough to resist Poland . . . I doubt that Hitler would have attacked Prague in support of Poland's demands, as Fierlinger supposes. This would have made the position of Daladier and Chamberlain, whom Hitler must now support, more difficult.'[16] There is no evidence, however, that the Soviets were prepared to intervene militarily until certain of western engagement. It may well be that Stalin had made no decision about what the USSR would do either if France honoured its commitment to Czechoslovakia or if Czechoslovakia had fought alone. It was not unusual for the Soviet leader to postpone such decisions until forced by events to act. Quite apart from the physical barriers to any movement of Soviet troops, most of the sources confirm the impression of Stalin's extreme caution and unwillingness to engage the Soviet Union in the 'second imperialist war'. If the French had acted the situation might have been different.

On 25 September, Masaryk informed the Foreign Office that his government found the contents of the German memorandum unacceptable, and would resist them. Seen from Prague, there were

[16] Quoted in Steiner, 'The Soviet Commissariat and the Czechoslovakian Crisis in 1938', 771.

good reasons why Beneš might have thought that the balance of forces after Godesberg was shifting in favour of Czechoslovakia. This would explain his buoyant mood between 23–26 September, as reported by Alexandrovsky, one of the very few foreign diplomats who saw Beneš continually during these critical days. On the day the British received the Czech rejection of the German terms, the British cabinet, for the first time in this crisis, overruled the prime minister. Halifax, who had already warned Chamberlain at Godesberg by telephone that the 'mass of public opinion' felt that the limits of concession had been reached, was the key defector. His disagreement was 'a horrible blow' to the prime minister, for Halifax was a much respected figure in the party whose loyalty to Chamberlain was essential for the continued acceptance of the appeasement policies. The foreign secretary was the one man in the cabinet who could pose a credible threat to Chamberlain's leadership. The arguments of Alexander Cadogan, whose exceptionally revealing and highly charged diary fills in the background of the story, had caused the usually unflappable Halifax a sleepless night and resulted in his 'tentative and reluctant' rejection of Chamberlain's advice. 'So long as Nazi-ism lasted, peace would be uncertain. For this reason he did not feel that it would be right to put pressure on Czechoslovakia to accept', Halifax explained. 'We should lay the case before them. If they rejected it he imagined that France would join in, and if the French went in we should join with them'.[17] Halifax's volte-face was critical. For the first time, the British cabinet actually considered the possibility of going to war. Chamberlain passed a note to Halifax during the meeting warning that 'if they [the French] say they will go in, thereby dragging us in, I do not think I could accept responsibility for the decision'.[18] The prime minister now placed his hopes in French pusillanimity. An earlier telegram dispatched on 24 September arrived from a badly frightened ambassador, who insisted that the British government 'should realize [the] extreme danger of even appearing to encourage [the] small, but noisy and corrupt, war group here. All that is best in France is against war, *almost* at any price . . . '.[19] This news gave substance to Chamberlain's hopes. But Phipps's warning, instead of strengthening the prime minister's hand, merely undercut his own reputation at the Foreign Office by convincing senior officials that their ambassador had imbibed too many of Bonnet's defeatist views and was failing to provide

[17] TNA: PRO, CAB 23/95, Cabinet 43(38), 25 September 1938.

[18] Note from N. Chamberlain to Halifax, in Cabinet, 25 September 1938, quoted in Andrew Roberts, *'The Holy Fox': A Biography of Lord Halifax* (London, 1991), 117.

[19] *DBFP*, 3rd ser., Vol. II, No. 1076 (Phipps to Halifax, 24 September 1938. Italics in original).

a balanced picture of opinion in France. Phipps was instructed on 25 September to ascertain the views of a wide range of French military and political figures, and to ask the British consuls in France to report to London on the state of opinion in their different consular districts. There were other signs of opposition in London to giving space to Hitler's demands. Winston Churchill in newspaper articles, and Clement Attlee in a letter to Chamberlain, demanded that the Germans should be warned that an invasion of Czechoslovakia would bring Britain, France, and the Soviet Union into a war against them.

If Chamberlain expected to use France's timidity to buttress his position, he was to be disappointed. Ambassador Bullitt reported to Roosevelt from Paris on 26 September that Daladier had told him that 'if Hitler should send one soldier across the Czechoslovakian frontier he would attack Germany at once'.[20] The premier, backed by a majority in his cabinet, had decided to reject the demands in Hitler's memorandum. New classes of reservists were mobilized, bringing the total number of troops mobilized to 1.5 million men, and the government declared itself ready to decree a general mobilization. By the time the French came to London, in response to the British invitation after Godesberg, they had received official confirmation of the Soviet mobilization. In the meeting with the French, Chamberlain and Simon, the latter in his best trial-lawyer mode, cross-examined Daladier on what France would do if Germany invaded Czechoslovakia. Though he had no concrete proposals to make, Daladier insisted that 'in the event of unprovoked aggression, France would fulfil her obligations'. Gamelin was asked to come to London the next day to explain the French military position. At a midnight meeting, Chamberlain tried, but failed, to convince his cabinet colleagues that Daladier and Bonnet were indecisive and their statement of military plans 'evasive'. Only a minority of the cabinet backed the prime minister. Even at this late hour, after a long and emotion-packed day, Chamberlain had a new proposal to make. He would send Sir Horace Wilson to Berlin with a letter for Hitler, asking for modifications of the Godesberg terms, and suggesting the creation of a German–Czech commission with a British representative in order to find ways for an orderly transfer of the Czech territory to Germany. If the appeal failed, there was to be a warning that a German invasion of Czechoslovakia, if followed by French action in support of the Czechs, would bring Britain into the war against Germany. By separating the appeal and the warning, and by placing both in the hands of Wilson, Chamberlain opened the way

[20] Bullitt to Washington, 26 September 1938, quoted in William Bullitt (ed.), *For the President, Personal and Secret: Correspondence between Franklin D. Roosevelt and William C. Bullitt*, 290–292.

Table 11.2 French Superiority by the Fifth Day of Mobilization, September 1938

	Germany	France
Divisions in the West	10 infantry (5 regular; 1 Landwehr; 4 reserve)	60 (54 infantry (4 in the Maginot Line); 3 mechanized infantry; 3 cavalry)
Divisions elsewhere	6 infantry (3 in East Prussia; 3 strategic reserve / screening Silesia against Poland)	40

Source: Williamson Murray, *The Change in the European Balance of Power, 1938–1939: The Path to Ruin* (Princeton, NJ, 1984), 240–242.

for implementing his own, rather than the cabinet's policies. He was still relying on conciliation rather than coercion.

The next morning, Monday 26 September, the British and French again met. Gamelin was his usual cool and calm self. He pointed out that if taken together, the French, Czech, and British military forces were still greater than those of the Germans. If Italy alone entered the war on the German side, he explained, then he could put into operation an already prepared plan for France to remain on the defensive along the Maginot Line, and launch an offensive across the Alpine border into the valley of the Po. After defeating the weak Italian forces, the French would march on to Vienna. It was the old dream of the land bridge to assist Czechoslovakia which, as Gamelin admitted, was only a dream, for he did not expect that the Italians would fight. In a more formal way, when he joined the Anglo-French leaders, he declared that the army would launch an attack in about five days at points already determined, and that the air force would bomb industrial targets near the frontier.

Germany and Czechoslovakia had some thirty-four divisions facing each other while France had twenty-three divisions on its frontier compared to eight for Germany. He made no mention of a French offensive, only an attack to draw German troops off from Czechoslovakia. In his subsequent conference with the British army and air ministers and the chiefs of staff, Gamelin sketched his intention to advance until his troops met serious opposition, when they would return to the Maginot Line. Because of superior German air power, he would have to wait four or five days so that Paris and the principal French towns could be evacuated. The British did not find his account reassuring. The question of Poland was also raised; Gamelin did not think Russia could help very much, but the Polish attitude was the 'key' to the whole situation. French military intervention would be decisive only if Poland and Hungary remained neutral, allowing Czech forces to hold the line in Moravia. Bonnet later told the British that Beneš had agreed to the cession of Teschen to the Poles. It was decided to issue a *démarche* at Warsaw, condemning any aggressive military action against Czechoslovakia. The British soldiers were not reassured and made no offers of military or aerial assistance.

At midday on 26 September, the British cabinet met and heard that Daladier had agreed to Horace Wilson's mission and to the messages he was instructed to convey to Hitler. It gave its unanimous approval to the decision and discussed emergency defence measures and preparations for war. Halifax later telegraphed Wilson in Berlin instructing him to make it clear to Hitler that the French would support Czechoslovakia with offensive action if it were attacked, and that this would bring in Britain: 'it should be made plain to Chancellor [Hitler] that this is inevitable alternative to a peaceful solution'. Without consulting the prime minister, Halifax also issued a press statement, warning that if a German attack was made on Czechoslovakia, 'the immediate result must be that France will be bound to come to her assistance, and Great Britain and Russia will certainly stand by France'.[21] Chamberlain was much put out by Halifax's action; he regarded public threats to Hitler as highly dangerous. His ministers, on the other hand, reminded of the accusations that if Britain had clearly stated its intention to go to war in 1914, peace might have been preserved, wanted Hitler to be left in no doubt as to the government's position. The Halifax statement proved to be the strongest that the British issued during the whole month of September. Bonnet, to the fury of the French embassy in London, claimed that the statement was spurious.

In Paris, the news of Godesberg brought a stiffening of opposition to Hitler, but also alarm and even panic. As the news spread, the great flight from Paris began. On Sunday, 25 September, the roads to the south and west of the capital were jammed with cars. Train stations were packed and extra trains put on to relieve the congestion. People in massive numbers lined up at the banks to withdraw their savings. There were enormous cancellations of subscriptions to defence bonds, which threatened the continuing financing of rearmament. Mobilization procedures, confused and bungling, with men in the wrong place and without equipment, placed additional strains on the government's finances. Strict restrictions were imposed on funds leaving the country, in order to avoid the bankruptcy of the Treasury. Already calling on emergency advances from the Bank of France to meet its expenses, the government appeared on the brink of financial disaster. As during the Rhineland crisis, the financial situation in France mitigated against a conflict with Germany.

[21] *DBFP*, 3rd ser., Vol. II, No. 1111 (Halifax to Henderson (Berlin), 26 September 1938, and Halifax communiqué, 26 September 1938, in footnote to No.1111).

France's depositors and fund holders were registering their opposition to war. The divisions of opinion in France persisted. The Assembly was not in session, but the partisans and adversaries of war mobilized their adherents and appealed to the public. Former prime minister Pierre-Étienne Flandin, a vehement opponent of war, plastered the Paris billboards with posters denouncing the 'clever devices' mounted by the 'occult forces' that were making war inevitable. Some former advocates of resistance, like Herriot and Blum, began to waver, but others made their views known in the pages of *L'Epoque*, *L'Ordre* and, of course, in *L'Humanité*. In the cabinet, too, the extreme pro-appeasement group, Bonnet and his circle, which included the Radical finance minister Marchandeau, were opposed by the equally convinced anti-appeasers, Georges Mandel, Paul Reynaud, César Campinchi, and Jean Zay. There were others, mainly moderate Radicals close to Daladier, inclined to appeasement but with reservations. *Bellicistes* could be found across the political spectrum, but they were scattered and represented a minority on the eve of Munich.

Whatever the weaknesses of France, and they were real and many, and the divisions in the body politic, on 27 September it appeared that the Daladier cabinet would have to stand by Czechoslovakia. On that morning, Bonnet, who had done everything possible to conceal or minimize the British pledge of support, wrote to the council of ministers: 'It is impossible to make war. I am against general mobilization. At any price, it is necessary to make an arrangement. I face intense opposition from the majority of my colleagues. The question of my resignation is unquestionably raised.'[22] Daladier and Gamelin conferred; the general warned that if the Germans seized Czechoslovakia, they would add thirty divisions to their force and enlarge their economic base. He concluded that 'even if peace is preserved by our holding aloof, in ten years France would be no more than a second class power'.[23] His advice, however, with regard to sending unofficial communications to the Czechs and Poles, was hardly that of a chief of staff on the eve of war. Daladier and Bonnet also conferred about the question of mobilization. At the cabinet meeting that followed, ministers agreed to call up additional classes of reservists but refused to order a general mobilization. They supported continuing efforts to solve the crisis peaceably and agreed to wait and see what happened with Chamberlain's new appeal. If Daladier thought that the new measures might convince Hitler to accept the pre-Godesberg settlement, he also played a waiting game hoping that the British might find a way out of his oppressive dilemma.

[22] *DDF*, 2nd ser., Vol. XI, No. 400 (27 September 1938).
[23] Maurice Gamelin, *Servir*. Volume II (Paris, 1946), 353.

Horace Wilson's mission to Germany was Chamberlain's last-minute bid to save the peace. At five in the afternoon on 26 September, accompanied by Nevile Henderson, he presented Hitler with Chamberlain's proposals for an international conference, to be attended by Germany, Czechoslovakia, and other powers, a possibility already raised with Masaryk and Beneš. The meeting was stormy. At its conclusion, Hitler insisted he would receive a Czech representative only if it were understood that the memorandum would have to be accepted as it stood. The territory demanded should be handed over and freed from Czechs on 1 October, and the Czech reply had to be received by Wednesday, 28 September. Even in the face of this tirade, Wilson did not present the 'warning' to Hitler, but arranged a meeting for the next morning. That evening, Hitler delivered his much awaited speech to a packed *Sportpalast* audience of Nazi party enthusiasts. Broadcast live and transmitted abroad, it was listened to by every German family with its own radio, or with access to the public loudspeakers in the streets. Hitler was a master of the spoken word; recordings resonate with his anger, punctuated by cheers and 'Sieg Heils' from his audience. He spoke for over an hour. There was a violent personal attack on Beneš ('two men stand arrayed one against the other: there is Mr. Beneš and here stand I'), flattering words for Poland, an approving nod towards Chamberlain, reassurances for France, and flattery for Mussolini. It was a clever as well as a highly emotive performance; anger and menace were balanced with soothing assurances directed at Chamberlain, and promises that 'when this problem is solved there is for Germany no further territorial problem in Europe'. After the Czech minority problems were settled, 'I have no further interest in the Czech state . . . We want no Czechs!'[24] Wilson paid his second visit to Hitler soon after midday on 27 September and finally issued the British warning but, as requested by Chamberlain, 'more in sorrow than in anger'. He referred to the prime minister's assurance that if the Germans agreed not to use force, the British government would ensure that Czechoslovakia carried out its promises 'fairly and fully' and with 'great promptitude'. Wilson's further attempts to water down the 'special message' only served to provoke Hitler's anger. If the memorandum was rejected, the Führer would 'smash' Czechoslovakia and in six days 'we will all be at war with one another'.[25] A few hours later, Wilson returned to London with little to show.

[24] Hitler's speech, 26 September 1938, cited from *Documents on International Affairs, 1938*. Volume II (London, 1943), 249–260.
[25] *DBFP*, 3rd ser., Vol. II, No.1129.

II

All was not going quite as smoothly for Hitler as these encounters suggested. In the first place, because he was reluctant to fix a firm date for the attack, there was a good deal of uncertainty and a certain slackness in the army's command structure. Units sent to their combat headquarters on 26 September were recalled, and sent back to the rear so as not to precipitate a premature conflict, but then, on the next day, sent back again to their combat deployment areas. Hitler knew of the weaknesses in Germany's military position, and the doubts of his military advisers; these increased his irritability and nervousness as the day for decision approached. Göring's opposition to war as well as Goebbels's objections, could not be totally dismissed. This was equally true of the hesitations of his senior officers. The rebel generals, Halder, Witzleben, and Brockdorff, believed, even as the planning for the attack went forward, that war with the western powers would end in disaster. It was highly unlikely that the plotters could have succeeded even if the Munich conference had not been held. Action had to be taken during the two day interval between Hitler's order to attack, and its implementation, in order to rally the army and the public to the rebel side. Taking Berlin would not have been enough; success depended on the spread of the revolt to the rest of Germany. This involved expert timing and a degree of planning beyond the capabilities of the generals, to say nothing of the absence of the basic structure needed for success. There was another signal that infuriated Hitler but caused concern. On the afternoon of the 27th, with X day, the assault on Czechoslovakia, less than forty-eight hours away, Hitler ordered a 'propaganda march' of motorized troops through central Berlin. The march down the Wilhelmstrasse was intended both to arouse the Berliners, and impress foreign diplomats and journalists. Hitler watched from the Reich Chancellery. There were about two hundred people assembled below. The tanks rolled; the people remained silent; no one cheered the Führer. Elsewhere the crowds were thin; people averted their eyes, turned their backs or ducked into doorways. On the diplomatic front, too, Hitler was coming under considerable pressure. General Franco made clear his deep concern about a European war, and left neither the Germans nor the Italians in any doubt that he would be reluctant to join the Axis in war, and would try to negotiate the neutrality of Spain should war break out. Both Hitler and Mussolini were indignant about Franco's complaints and his unacceptable lack of gratitude for their efforts in Spain. Still, there was little they could do to change his mind. Nor was Hitler impervious to President Roosevelt's intervention; his rambling reply was composed or edited on the night of the *Sportpalast* speech and sent on 27 September. In the final analysis, however, it was Britain's policy that was critical for Hitler. The Führer was still uncertain about British intentions and this anxiety may account for his decision to send Chamberlain a written reply to his proposals after the final interview with Horace Wilson. Repeating his demands for an immediate occupation of the Sudetenland, and accusing the Czechs of using the occupation proposal to secure British and French support in the hope of a general conflagration, Hitler left it up to Chamberlain to decide whether the prime minister wished to continue his efforts, for which Hitler was grateful, to bring the Prague government to its senses. It barely opened the door for further discussions.

Horace Wilson arrived back in London during the afternoon of 27 September, accompanied by the British military attaché, Mason-Macfarlane. During that 'frightful afternoon' (Cadogan's words), a small group of ministers met to discuss what to do, after receiving news of Wilson's second unhappy meeting with Hitler. Various people joined in. Military and Dominions spokesmen declared their opposition to war. The chiefs of staff again insisted that nothing could be done to save Czechoslovakia, and that the French should be warned off taking offensive action against Germany without first consulting London. Nevertheless, when Admiral Sir Roger Backhouse, Chatfield's successor as chief of the naval staff, insisted that the fleet would have to be mobilized well in advance of the outbreak of hostilities, Chamberlain reluctantly agreed. Mobilization should be ordered the next morning, but without any publicity. After the meeting, the military chiefs gathered to produce a new appreciation, the last one before Munich. From the military point of view, they wrote, 'the balance of advantage is definitely in favour of postponement. This is probably an exception to the rule that "no war is inevitable", for it will almost certainly come later. Our real object is not to save Czechoslovakia—that is impossible in any event—but to end the days of the Nazi regime. This is not our selected moment, it is theirs; we are in bad condition to wage even a defensive war at the present time; the grouping of the powers at the moment makes well nigh hopeless the waging of a successful offensive war.'[26] The hastily prepared paper was ready for the late evening cabinet. It made no difference to the decisions reached there. At the Foreign Office, Halifax and Cadogan were preparing a new proposal, which Cadogan called a 'timetable'. It provided for the German occupation of the Cheb and As regions in western Bohemia, outside the

[26] Chiefs of staff memorandum, 27 September 1938, quoted in B. Bond (ed.), *Chief of Staff: The Diaries of Lieutenant-General Sir Henry Pownall. Volume I, 1933–1940* (London, 1972), Appendix II, 380–383.

fortified line, by 1 October. There would be meetings of German and Czech plenipotentiaries over which the British would preside, and the creation of an International Boundary Commission on 3 October. On 10 October, German troops would enter the zones for which the plenipotentiaries had completed the arrangements for the hand-over and by 31 October German troops would enter the remaining areas within the frontiers determined by the Boundary Commission. This became the basis of the Commission idea adopted at the Munich conference. A joint guarantee of the new borders would follow as quickly as possible. Cadogan secured Halifax's authority to send telegrams off to Paris, Prague, and Berlin proposing the new 'timetable'.

Before Chamberlain's 8 p.m. broadcast to the nation on 27 September, the prime minister, Halifax, Cadogan, and Wilson gathered in the latter's room to consider Chamberlain's telegram to Beneš. Horace Wilson had prepared a draft of 'complete capitulation' urging the Czechs to accept Hitler's memorandum. Both Halifax and Cadogan took strong exception to the draft. The exhausted Chamberlain admitted, 'I'm wobbling about all over the place', and went in to broadcast.[27] His speech was a plea for peace: 'How horrible, fantastic, incredible it is that we should be digging trenches and trying on gas masks here because of a quarrel in a faraway country between people of whom we know nothing. It seems still more impossible that a quarrel which has already been settled in principle should be the subject of war.' Chamberlain assured his listeners that the call-up of men for anti-aircraft defences, and for ships, were only 'precautionary measures' and did not mean that 'we have determined on war'. 'You know', he told his audience, 'that I am going to work for peace to the last moment'.[28] At 9.30 p.m. that evening the cabinet met. The prime minister read out a telegram from Henderson advising that Czechoslovakia should be told to make the best terms it could with Berlin. After reports of equivocal Dominions opinion, Horace Wilson recounted the story of his meetings with Hitler. The cabinet turned down his proposal that the Czechs should withdraw their forces immediately from the specified areas to be ceded to Germany, but approved asking Prague to accept the new timetable as the only alternative to invasion and destruction and the possibility of a general conflict which would entail an incalculable loss of life. The Czechs were warned that whatever the result of the conflict, there was no possibility that 'Czechoslovakia could be restored to her frontiers of today'.[29] Phipps was to tell

[27] Dilks (ed.), *Diaries of Sir Alexander Cadogan*, 107 (Tuesday, 27 September 1938).

[28] N. Chamberlain's speech, 27 September 1938, quoted in *Documents on International Affairs, 1938*. Volume II, 270–1.

[29] *DBFP*, 3rd ser., Vol. II, No. 1138 (Halifax to Newton (Prague), 27 September 1938).

the French not to take offensive action without discussion with London. In Berlin, Henderson gave the 'timetable' to Weizsäcker to present to Hitler. The state secretary commented that the plan was 'out of date'; Henderson himself characterized it as 'quite useless'.

By 27 September, there was an overpowering sense of impending war. In London and elsewhere in the large cities, the feverish digging of trenches and air raid shelters and the filling of sandbags was indicative of the public mood. The distribution of gas masks to the whole population (except for babies, for whom masks had not yet been made), begun the previous weekend, continued, and instructions on protection against air raids were posted to every house in the country. Steps were taken to complete plans for the evacuation of children from large towns. The general impression was one of outrage over Hitler's Godesberg demands, but also a fear of war, above all fear of bombing. Air bombardment and the possibility of gas attacks had been discussed for a decade. Newsreels in cinemas of bombings in China, Ethiopia, and Spain, seen by about half the adult population, heightened popular anxieties. It hardly mattered to the 'man in the street' that the military did not believe that chemical bombs would be used or that they would be effective. Nor could the public have known that no 'bolt from the blue' was expected in September 1938. When Chamberlain invoked the sight of bombed-out houses after Godesberg, he was reacting to this general apprehension of bombing rather than to the opinion of his military advisers. Indeed, the Germans were simply incapable of mounting an aerial campaign of any substance against Britain in 1938, or indeed, in 1939. There was an appearance of outward calm and resignation. Vita Sackville-West, writing to her husband, Harold Nicolson, about being fitted for gas masks and digging trenches in the calf-orchard at Sissinghurst reported: 'Everyone is calm, resolute and cheerful. One hears more jokes than ever, although they all realize quite well what it means. I do respect the English for all their faults.'[30]

The Czechs prepared themselves for a German attack. That evening, the Czechs cabled their representative in Geneva requesting that Germany be identified as the aggressor as soon as their troops moved against Czechoslovakia. Both Bonnet and Halifax, without much hope of success, agreed to try out the idea of an International Commission and the revised 'timetable'. Beneš accepted the proposal knowing that Hitler had no interest in the fate of the Sudeten Germans, and was not concerned with an orderly transfer of territories. Once Czech mobil-

[30] Harold Nicolson, *Diary*, Vol. I, 3rd impression (London, 1966), 362 (entry for 27 September 1938).

ization had begun and war was anticipated, Beneš indulged in flights of fancy, asking Alexandrovsky many 'practical questions' about the forms of Soviet assistance to Czechoslovakia. 'I confess', Alexandrovsky wrote, 'to having a heavy feeling because I could tell Beneš nothing, especially regarding his 'practical questions'.[31] In Britain, the sudden escalation of the crisis took the public by surprise. Chamberlain and his closest advisers had used every means to keep newspapers and the BBC from publishing or broadcasting programmes that would provoke Hitler's anger or undermine confidence in the prime minister's peace efforts. Chamberlain's broadcast to the nation on 27 September was clearly intended to allay the public's apprehension. The most vocal of the anti-appeasers spoke up. Churchill made statements to the press on 26 September urging a joint Anglo-French-Soviet warning to Germany that an invasion of Czechoslovakia would mean war. He was supported by Lord Robert Cecil, speaking for the League of Nations Union, and by his own small group of personal adherents. The leaders of the Labour party made clear their opposition to the dismemberment of Czechoslovakia, and the need to warn Hitler that Britain, France, and Russia would unite to resist a German attack on Czechoslovakia. On 27 September, Churchill was briefly received by Chamberlain and Halifax, and was reassured about the government's attitude. Parliament was to meet two days later and it was important for the prime minister to have his most important critic mollified. Anthony Eden was less forthright. On 25 September, the former foreign secretary had sent Halifax a message urging the rejection of the Godesberg proposals, but he showed no disposition to join the Churchill 'adullamites'. While the prime minister was undoubtedly concerned by Halifax's defection, and the toughening of the cabinet attitude, he still believed he could avoid what was for him an unnecessary and useless war.

Godesberg, too, had stirred the Americans to consider some form of intervention. By August, the previously inactive president had become highly critical of Anglo-French moves to pressure Czechoslovakia, and considered ways to promote a stronger line against Hitler. Though exasperated by the defeatism of his own ambassador in London, Joseph Kennedy, the president remained suspicious of British intentions. Henry Morgenthau, the secretary of the Treasury, records Roosevelt complaining to him and Cordell Hull, the secretary of state, that 'Chamberlain was "slippery"; you could not trust him under any circumstances and that Chamberlain was playing the usual game of the British—peace at any price—and would try to place the blame on the United States for

[31] Quoted in Steiner, 'The Soviet Commissariat of Foreign Affairs and the Czechoslovakian Crisis in 1938', 772.

fighting or not fighting . . . '.[32] Faced by a barrage of confusing reports on the European situation, and confronted with the divergent views of his advisers, Roosevelt decided to watch and wait. Some light was cast on his views, always difficult to decipher, when he summoned Sir Ronald Lindsay, the British ambassador, to a secret meeting on the night of 19 September. He spoke appreciatively of Chamberlain's efforts which, if successful, he 'would be the first to cheer'. What really interested him was how the British and French would fight Germany, if, as seemed likely, peace could not be maintained. He urged a defensive rather than an offensive war, a strategy based on the isolation and exhaustion of Germany by blockade, and it would be accompanied by a bombing offensive that would undermine the German will to resist. The president told Lindsay that he might be able to persuade Americans to recognize the blockade and even avoid an arms embargo if there was no declaration of war. If an embargo was imposed, the Allies could import munition parts from the United States into Canada for shipment to Europe.[33] The president's proposals were intended to avoid Congressional debate and maintain and exercise American influence in Europe, at the least possible domestic cost. They had little effect on British policy. His message was not actually seen by the Foreign Office departments until after Munich and was probably only circulated at first to Chamberlain, Halifax, and Cadogan. It evoked little interest in London. As so often, Roosevelt's suggestions struck the British as impractical and raised more problems than they solved. Nothing in the conversation changed their view that the Americans would not intervene in Europe's affairs. In fact, Chamberlain had no wish to involve the Americans. He felt that he was perfectly capable of handling Hitler himself and, as in 1937, believed that Roosevelt's interference would only complicate his task. Nevertheless, though Chamberlain and Halifax may have been indifferent to the presidential initiative, the secret conversation confirmed the hopes that, if another European war broke out, the Americans, at some point, would be drawn in on the Anglo-French side. This combination of short-term doubt and long-term hope would become increasingly important once Chamberlain's policies were challenged.

Roosevelt believed that American intervention would make a difference. Hitler's threatening behaviour at Godesberg, the toughening of

[32] Morgenthau diary, 31 August and 1 September 1938, quoted in Barbara R. Farnham, *Roosevelt and the Munich Crisis: A Study of Political Decision-Making* (Princeton, NJ, 1997), 95–97.

[33] *DBFP*, 3rd ser., Vol. VII, Appendix IV, (v), pp. 627–629. Lindsay (Washington) to Halifax, 20 September 1938.

the British and French positions as reported to him by Bullitt and Kennedy, and the rising fear that war was imminent made it difficult for Roosevelt to stand aside. By the morning of 25 September, the chief State Department officials, who four days earlier had agreed that there was nothing to do 'except steer clear and keep quiet', had changed their minds and decided to draft a presidential appeal.[34] The draft, which Roosevelt continued to revise until midnight, was sent to Hitler, Beneš, Chamberlain, and Daladier at 1 a.m. on 26 September, though it was really aimed only at Hitler. 'The fabric of peace on the continent of Europe, if not throughout the rest of the world, is in immediate danger', the president declared. 'The consequences of its rupture are incalculable... On behalf of the 130 millions of people in the United States of America and for the sake of humanity everywhere I most earnestly appeal to you not to break off negotiations looking to a peaceful, fair, and constructive settlement....'[35] The message was so cautiously phrased—the United States eschewed 'political entanglements' but could not escape the consequences of a general war—that it is hard to believe that the president really expected something to come of it. It was, at best, a cautious gesture. The German leader's *Sportpalast* speech seemed to bring war closer and his written reply to Roosevelt's message, sent on the same day was, as the president told his cabinet on 27 September, 'truculent and unyielding'. Germany's new proposals, Hitler claimed, only involved the prompt fulfilment of what had been agreed before Godesberg. 'It does not rest with the German Government, but with the Czechoslovakian Government alone, to decide whether it wants peace or war.'[36] Hitler's attitude contrasted sharply with that of the British and French who expressed their gratitude for the president's message but who hardly expected any follow-up.

Following reports reaching Roosevelt on 27 September, that Hitler intended to march into Czechoslovakia at 2 p.m. the next day if his terms were not met, the president decided to try again. Alarmed at the prospect of war, he instructed the State Department to make inquiries in London, Paris, and also in Rome, about the possibility of an international conference, following a suggestion made by Bullitt and endorsed by Daladier. A special personal message was sent to Mussolini asking for his assistance in securing an agreement by negotiation. In the afternoon, the president had his cabinet listen to Chamberlain's 'moving speech' before discussing the European situation. 'The contrast between the two just bit into us—the shouting and violence of Hitler, and the

[34] Quoted in Farnham, *Roosevelt and the Munich Crisis*, 111, footnote 70.
[35] *FRUS*, 1938, I, 657–658 (Roosevelt to Hitler, 26 September 1938).
[36] *FRUS*, 1938, I, 669–672 (Hitler to Roosevelt, 27 September 1938).

roars, through their teeth, of his audience of "Krieg, Krieg"', Roosevelt told Arthur Murray two weeks later, 'and then, the quiet, beautiful statement of Chamberlain's'.[37] The cabinet was prepared to aid the Allies in every way possible while keeping the United States clear of involvement in war. Roosevelt resolved to act without waiting for the answers from Chamberlain and Daladier. After dinner at the White House, smoking incessantly and 'shooting questions' at his highly nervous State Department advisers, the president finished the drafting of his telegram to Hitler. It was despatched to Berlin just after 10 p.m. that evening. Roosevelt urged Hitler to continue negotiations and suggested that the talks be expanded to include 'all the nations directly interested in the present controversy'. There was no reference to American participation in the proposed conference, to be held at a neutral spot in Europe, and to guard against possible domestic repercussions the president again stressed that the United States had 'no political involvements in Europe'. Roosevelt warned Hitler, however, that the American people demanded that 'the voice of their government be raised again and yet again to avert and to avoid war'.[38] The president's proposal was treated as front page news in London and appeared alongside the news of Chamberlain's radio address and the announcement of the fleet mobilization. What Roosevelt intended has long been debated. The timing of his message suggests that he believed Chamberlain and Daladier were prepared to stand up to Hitler and that his telegram, along with Chamberlain's earlier radio speech, would convince Hitler to negotiate along the lines of the pre-Godesberg arrangements. If his recommendation was rejected and war occurred, at least the record would be clear, and there would be no doubt as to Hitler's responsibility.

The idea of a conference of five powers was also on the British agenda. Chamberlain had already raised the possibility on 25 September when Masaryk, the Czech minister, presented his government's rejection of the Godesberg demands. On 27 September, Lord Perth, the ambassador in Rome, suggested that Mussolini be asked to act as peacemaker. The Foreign Office agreed that Ciano should be told of the 'timetable' proposal and asked to use his influence with Hitler to accept it. By his own account, Dino Grandi, the Italian ambassador in London, ordered by Ciano to keep away from any involvement in the Czech question, reappeared and mobilized his clandestine contacts—Sir Joseph Ball, one of Chamberlain's few personal allies, and Adrian Dingli, the Maltese lawyer associated with the Italian embassy. Undoubtedly exaggerating his own influence, Grandi claimed to have used Sir Ronald

[37] Arthur Murray, *At Close Quarters* (London, 1946), 95.
[38] *FRUS*, 1938, I, 684–685 (Roosevelt to Hitler, 27 September 1938).

Graham, a former British ambassador in Rome, to convey the mediatory proposal that led to Chamberlain's eleventh-hour plea to Mussolini. More accurately, Graham recalled a joint visit to the Foreign Office 'where before their intercession, "very likely the policy of bringing in your great Duce had already been decided".'[39] Perth presented the British invitation for the Duce to assume the role of mediator at 10 a.m. in the morning of 28 September. At the same time, two messages drafted by Chamberlain were sent off, one to Hitler proposing that the prime minister should come to Berlin for a five-power conference to discuss arrangements for the transfer of the Sudeten territories, and the other his personal appeal to Mussolini to urge Hitler to accept this proposal. The prime minister also reaffirmed his guarantee that the Czech promises would be carried out.

In this way, Mussolini, undoubtedly relieved by the conference idea, suddenly found himself in the position that he most coveted. His assistance was being solicited on all sides (the French also appealed to Mussolini but were ignored) to save Europe from war. This was a strange dénouement to the long Czech crisis which the Duce had exploited for his own purposes. Finally informed after Godesberg by the Prince of Hesse about the German plans, including Hitler's 1 October deadline, Mussolini began to think concretely of an imminent war. Though he still doubted that the western powers would move, the Duce promised Hitler that Italy would come into the war as soon as Britain did. He discussed the possibility of a Ciano–Ribbentrop meeting to clarify the conditions of Italian intervention, and scheduled an exchange between Italian and German generals in Munich on 29 September. There were, however, signs of considerable unease in Rome. Ciano was particularly nervous. Already worried about events in Spain, where it seemed possible that Franco might accept a negotiated peace leaving the Italians with little to show for their efforts, and knowing that the Italian people were hostile towards Germany and had no stomach for war, Ciano had no wish to become involved in a conflict over a question in which Italy had no interest. Mussolini shared his fears, knowing that Italy was not prepared for war. As long as he believed that Britain and France would not fight, the Duce could engage in sabre-rattling from the sidelines but when war seemed probable, he drew back.

When, on 28 September, Perth came with Chamberlain's plea for Mussolini's intervention, Ciano seized the opportunity and rushed over

[39] Quoted in Alan Cassels, 'Fascist Italy and Mediation in the Munich and Danzig Crises, September 1938 and August 1939', in Alessandro Migliazza and Enrico Decleva (eds.), *Diplomazia e storia delle relazioni internazionali: studi in onore di Enrico Serra* (Milan, 1991).

to the Palazzo Venezia. Mussolini moved swiftly. The Italian ambassador in Berlin was instructed to ask Hitler for a twenty-four-hour delay in issuing the mobilization orders scheduled for 2 p.m. that day. Later at the embassy, Perth received Chamberlain's personal message to Mussolini describing his last appeal to Hitler and his offer to go to Berlin for a five-power conference. The Duce agreed to support the proposal for a conference of four and telephoned Attolico in Berlin. At the time that Attolico made the first of his four appearances at the Chancellery, Hitler was closeted with François-Poncet who was offering him, with Henderson's approval, a better deal (Prague had not been informed) than had been outlined in the previous 'timetable'. Hitler could occupy the whole Egerland instead of only that portion lying outside the Czech fortifications. Göring and Neurath, who had come in from his country estate on his own initiative, urged Hitler to find a peaceful way out. Ribbentrop, on the contrary, was urging war. He quarrelled with Göring and repeatedly interrupted François-Poncet. Attolico then arrived on the scene with the Duce's request for a twenty-four-hour delay. Having secured Hitler's consent, he hurried off explaining that he expected another message from Mussolini at noon. Hitler's reply to the French offer was put off until the afternoon. Göring and Neurath used the interval to again plead for a peaceful resolution. Attolico reappeared with Mussolini's second message just before Nevile Henderson came in with Chamberlain's communication to Hitler. The latter waited until the Italian returned, with the now superfluous copy of the British conference proposal which Attolico had gone to fetch, before agreeing to the conference on the condition that Mussolini would attend.

Having made his decision, Hitler sat down to lunch with a large and assorted group of military men and civilians. Weizsäcker recorded that the general feeling of relief was obvious. News of the conference also put an end to the idea of the *putsch*; the conspirators had postponed action until sure that Hitler would launch his war. According to Erich Kordt's testimony at Nuremberg, the conspirators discussed the possibility of a *coup* on 28 September but General Halder, who knew that the actual order to attack would not be given until the following day, preferred to wait another day. Mussolini's unexpected turn-about over intervention seems to have been one of the decisive factors in Hitler's decision to cancel the mobilization order and to send out the invitations to the conference. Contemporaries have stressed Hitler's seeming closeness to Mussolini. The Führer went out of his way to underline his solidarity with the Duce, both before and during the conference. He joined Mussolini at Kufstein, just over the old Austro-German border, and the Italian leader made the rest of his railway journey in Hitler's special coach, listening to the Führer's exposition of his plans to eliminate Czechoslovakia and his intention that the two dictators should fight 'side-by-side' against France and Britain. It was Mussolini who, after opening remarks from Hitler and Daladier at the conference, produced the proposals, drawn up by the Germans, which formed the basis of the discussions in Munich.

When he went to the Commons on 28 September to open what was expected to be a lengthy debate on the European situation, Chamberlain was unaware of Hitler's decision. While he was speaking, Sir John Simon interrupted Chamberlain to show him Hitler's message, hastily brought from the Foreign Office. The German chancellor invited Mussolini, Daladier, and Chamberlain to confer with him the following morning in Munich. Tumultuous cheering came from both sides of the House. Churchill shook the prime minister's hand. According to Harold Nicolson, Churchill said: 'I congratulate you on your good fortune. You were very lucky.'[40] The cabinet assembled at Heston airport the next morning to wish Chamberlain Godspeed. 'When I was a boy, I used to repeat "if at first you don't succeed, try, try, try again". That is what I am doing.' The prime minister then raised the literary tone by quoting Hotspur's speech in *Henry IV*, 'Out of this nettle, danger, we pluck this flower, safety.' It was not long after Munich that the Foreign Office tag, 'If at first you can't concede, fly, fly, fly again', made the rounds of London.[41] Other less respectable sallies followed but this was not the mood at Heston on 29 September, or at the airport on Chamberlain's return, or in Britain for the next few days.

III

The hastily assembled gathering at the *Führerbau* on 29 September, the Munich conference, was, in William Strang's words, a 'hugger-mugger' affair, the seating impromptu, no agenda, no pads or sharpened pencils, or any of the usual paraphernalia of an international conference. Accounts of what happened and what was said are in conflict; indeed, there is no agreement on exactly who was present, hardly surprising since though the first session was held *in camera*, during the second and third sessions streams of the officials attending each head of state wandered in and out with documents that had to be redrafted and translated. In effect, Hitler got the substance of his Godesberg demands. The evacu-

[40] H. Nicolson, *Diary*, vol. I, 371 (28 September 1938).

[41] For FO jibe, see Kenneth Young (ed.), *The Diaries of Sir Robert Bruce Lockhart: Volume I, 1915–1938* (London, 1973), 402. Chamberlain's words at Heston airport, 29 September 1938, are quoted in Telford Taylor, *Munich: The Price of Peace* (London, 1979), 15.

ation of the Sudetenland would now be in five stages, and not all at once. The 'predominantly German' areas of Czechoslovakia were to be ceded to Germany. Specified zones were to be occupied between 1 and 7 October in four stages. The remaining territory would be ascertained 'forthwith' by the international commission, on which the Czechs would be represented, and would be occupied by 10 October. The international commission also would decide which areas without clear German majorities would require plebiscites by the end of November. Due to the later decisions of the international commission, more territory was actually yielded than previously demanded, but the German occupation was spread over a period of ten days. In order to circumvent Daladier's efforts at the conference to preserve for Czechoslovakia some of its fortifications, as Gamelin hoped, Hitler agreed to the face-saving formula that the international commission could recommend to the four powers minor modifications in the 'strictly ethnological determination' of the zones to be transferred without plebiscites. A German–Czech commission would examine the means of facilitating the exchange of populations; individuals were to have the right to opt in or out of the transferred areas. In an annexe to the agreement, Britain and France would stand by their offer of an international guarantee of the new frontiers of Czechoslovakia; Germany and Italy would give a guarantee when the question of the Polish and Hungarian minorities had been settled. An additional declaration, which was a British revision of an Italian draft, stated that if the problems of the Polish and Hungarian minorities in Czechoslovakia were not settled within 3 months, there would be another meeting of the four Munich powers.

The conference did not break up until after midnight, and though the agreement was dated 29 September, it was actually signed the next day. After the proceedings, Chamberlain talked privately with Hitler. Daladier was told nothing about the prime minister's approach. After discussing the abolition of bombing and bomber aircraft, the Spanish Civil War, the world economy, and Germany's economic interests in south-east Europe, Chamberlain invited Hitler to sign a joint statement that he had prepared, and which William Strang, the Foreign Office official accompanying him at Munich, had redrafted at the hotel. The statement cited the Munich agreement and the Anglo-German naval treaty 'as symbolic of the desire of our two peoples never to go to war with one another again'. The two men were pledged to use 'the method of consultation . . . to deal with any other questions that may concern our two countries . . . '.[42] Chamberlain thought this document was his real

[42] *DBFP*, 3rd ser., Vol. II, No. 1228 (note of a conversation between the prime minister and Herr Hitler, 30 September 1938).

triumph at Munich. He believed he had succeeded in establishing an Anglo-German understanding and secured the prospect of a future arms limitation agreement.

The Czech representatives sat waiting for news of their country's fate. The results were a devastating blow to Beneš and to Jan Masaryk, the minister in London who had hoped for a change in British policy. Beneš appears to have inwardly resigned himself to his country's fate. A delegation of generals, including General Syrovy and the chief of staff, Ludwik Krejči, who had returned to Prague from his headquarters in Moravia, pleaded with the president not to make any more concessions. They assured him that the nation was united and that the army wanted to fight. Beneš dismissed their arguments that the former allies would be forced to enter the conflict. He was 'not prepared to lead the country into a slaughterhouse for some empty gesture'.[43] Some political leaders, too, both of the right and the left, urged Beneš to act, even without the promise of French support. Beneš decided otherwise. At three in the afternoon on the day of the Munich conference, the two Czech emissaries, Hubert Masařik and Vojtech Mastny, left Prague for Munich. Driven from the airport to the Regina Hotel (where the British delegation was staying) in a police car accompanied by the Gestapo, they waited without news until 7 p.m., when Ashton-Gwatkin of the Foreign Office briefly warned them of what would befall their country. When eventually they came to Chamberlain's suite in the hotel, the prime minister, tired but 'pleasantly so', assured Mastny and Masařik that the agreement was the best result achievable. Daladier, who, according to some accounts, had put up some defence of the Czech frontier claims ('without much conviction', Ciano recalled), sat silent while a copy of the agreement was read out by Dr Mastny. Asked by Masařik whether a response was expected, Léger replied that the four statesmen 'had not much time' and 'no longer expected an answer from us; they regarded the plan as accepted'.[44]

Beneš learned of the terms of the agreement on the morning of 30 September. He felt betrayed by the western powers, particularly by France, and blamed their defection on their fear of Communism. He told a small audience that the Munich agreement was signed by four powers, two of them Czechoslovakia's 'friends'.[45] But much of the Czech anger was focused on Beneš himself. Just before arranging for a meeting of the coalition parties on 30 September, the president

[43] Lukes, *Czechoslovakia between Stalin and Hitler*, 251.

[44] Masaryk's account, quoted in Dr Hubert Ripka, *Munich: Before and After* (London, 1939), 226.

[45] Lukes, *Czechoslovakia between Stalin and Hitler*, 261.

called Alekandrovsky and sought Soviet advice on whether he should capitulate or fight. However, by noon, the Soviet representative was told that the answer to his message to Moscow was no longer necessary. The members of the government had agreed that they would have to accept the Four Power Act. Beneš addressed the nation at 5 p.m. Crowds again gathered at the Castle. If, as Gottwald claimed at the end of December, the Communist party leadership intended to stage a *coup*, they were given no such opportunity, for the crowd was broken up by the state police. Whatever their anger, the government's decision was accepted without any counter-action. By 2 October, with the *Wehrmacht* pouring into the Sudetenland, there were demands for Beneš' resignation. On 5 October, there followed a cabinet reshuffle in which foreign minister Krofta was replaced by Frantisek Chalkovsky, an opponent of Beneš and the current minister to Italy. He immediately began to court his would-be masters in the hope of safeguarding what was left of Czechoslovakia.

What is one to write about Beneš' decision? The alternatives were stark enough and both unacceptable. The president believed, as he wrote in his 1948 memoirs, *Munich Days*, that it would have been highly irresponsible to risk a war that was bound to be lost. He not only dismissed the hypothesis that if Czechoslovakia had fought, the British and French would have come to its rescue, but was convinced, not without reason, that the leaders of both countries would blame Czechoslovakia's destruction on his stubborn refusal to grant the Sudeten Germans their rightful claim to self-determination and would wash their hands of the matter. In *Munich Days*, he commends the Soviet Union for its willingness to fulfil its legal obligations. His later opinions about the possibility of Soviet assistance were mixed; the most that could have been expected was something similar to the Soviet role in the Spanish Civil War, which would only have been a different sort of catastrophe for Czechoslovakia.[46] Always inclined to over-optimism, Beneš may well have believed that by surrendering he could preserve the nation, however mutilated. Assuming that Hitler would next turn on Poland, and using self-determination as his excuse, he thought the Germans would have no interest in the rump state or in challenging the newly concluded guarantee. In the inevitable war that would have to be fought between Germany and the western democracies, Beneš was sure that the former would be defeated and that he could then regain for his country what had been lost at Munich. There was something in his over-confident and proverbially optimistic character that inclined the

[46] Edward Taborsky, 'President Edvard Beneš and the Crises of 1938 and 1948', *East Central Europe/L'Europe Du Centre-Est*, 5: 2 (1978), 205–206.

president to rest too heavily on his own judgment and diplomatic dexterity, always seeking some 'plan' to save the situation. When the latter failed he found it difficult to face the consequences. Unlike Poland, whose leaders decided to fight in 1939, Czechoslovakia escaped the worst of the terrible German onslaught and occupation. There was, however, always the possibility that had the Czechs fought in 1938, the French would have been trapped by their treaty obligations and the British forced to back them. The Soviet Union might have joined in the collective action. Public opinion might have shifted under the impact of the German aggression. It would have been a long shot at best, and Beneš was not a gambler. In the end he chose capitulation over war as the lesser of two evils. His present-day countrymen are still arguing whether his choice was the right one.

The Soviets took great umbrage at later Czech charges of desertion. Alexandrovsky, in his summary report to Litvinov, speculated that Beneš' requests for help were 'a manoeuvre for laying the blame for Czechoslovakia's capitulation and ruin on the USSR as well'. In the four other capital cities, and in Washington, there was a heartfelt sense of relief. Chamberlain, Daladier, and Mussolini each returned home to a hero's welcome. Both Chamberlain and Daladier were cheered in Munich, much to Hitler's discomfiture. Descending from his aircraft back in London, the British prime minister told the waiting crowd that the settlement of Czechoslovakia was only the 'prelude to a larger settlement in which all Europe may find peace'. On the way from Heston to Buckingham Palace, where he appeared on the balcony with the king and queen, the streets were 'lined from one end to the other with people of every class, shouting themselves hoarse, leaping on the running board, hanging on the windows, and thrusting their hands into the car to be shaken'.[47] Later at 10 Downing Street, he appeared at the window to proclaim that for the second time in history, 'there had come back from Germany to Downing Street peace with honour. I believe it is peace for our time', words that some claim he immediately regretted and that he was to retract later in the Commons.[48] There is every reason to believe that Chamberlain meant this at the moment of speaking, however carried away by the emotions of the hour. Roosevelt, enormously relieved to hear of Hitler's invitation to Munich, sent his famous two word message to Chamberlain: 'Good man.' If Daladier somewhat exaggerated his fears about his reception in Paris, his despondent mood, and feeling that

[47] Robert Self (ed.), *The Neville Chamberlain Diary Letters*, Vol. 4 (Aldershot, 2005), 351 (To Hilda, 2 October 1938).

[48] Keith Feiling, *The Life of Neville Chamberlain* (London, 1970), 381.

France had only achieved a temporary reprieve, was undoubtedly genuine. One had only to compare Daladier's downcast countenance with Bonnet's smiles in their car on the return from the airport after Munich. It is possible that if the British cabinet had opted for war after Godesberg, or the Czechs had fought, Daladier would have honoured the Czech treaty. What is clear is that Munich represented for Daladier the means of escape from an intolerable situation. Daladier knew that appeasement was a policy of expediency: France had won an essential reprieve from a war that the premier knew it was in no state to fight. On 3 October, Bullitt reported to Hull that Daladier was predicting that 'within six months France and England would be face to face with new German demands'.[49] The great diversity of views across the political spectrum now disappeared momentarily. Champetier de Ribes, minister for the *anciens combattants*, organized a massive demonstration in Paris on 2 October, that would not be equalled until Charles de Gaulle made his triumphal re-entry into the capital in 1944.

While Mussolini, too, was cheered by great crowds from the Brenner to Rome as 'the angel of peace', the mood was otherwise with Hitler. Throughout the conference, except when in conversation with Mussolini, he had appeared ill at ease, irritable and impatient, clearly taking no pleasure in the proceedings. He was particularly put out with Chamberlain, a 'haggling shop-keeper'. ('I know no weekends and I don't fish', he told Mussolini when they lunched privately, after the conference.) Despite an avalanche of praise, Hitler had unfinished business, both immediate and future, to consider. The first meeting of the international commission was held in Berlin at five o'clock on 30 September, under the chairmanship of Weizsäcker. It soon became apparent that the occupation of the Sudeten areas would be carried out according to the orders of the *Wehrmacht* high command. Still, Hitler was left dissatisfied, angry at the Anglo-French intervention, at Mussolini's desertion, at the opposition of his subordinates to war, at the enthusiasm of his own people for peace and the peace-makers, and, above all, angry at his own retreat from military action. Munich represented the triumph of appeasement. Hitler was cheated of the war he so much wanted. He had bowed to the Anglo-French threat that they would move against Germany if Hitler's forces crossed the Sudeten frontier. He had accepted a negotiated settlement that fulfilled his public but not his private aims. When Chamberlain left Munich on 30 September, Hitler was alleged to have said: 'If ever that silly old man comes interfering here again with his umbrella, I'll kick him

49 *FRUS*, 1938, I, 711–712. Bullitt to Hull, 3 October 1938.

downstairs . . .'.[50] The joint declaration he had signed at Chamberlain's request meant nothing to him. Yet Chamberlain thought he had won, and that his policy had succeeded. His triumph sent out the wrong signals, above all to Hitler, who concluded that the method of consultation was an inconvenient nuisance. As the next weeks would show, the Führer was determined on his war and would not endure a second Munich. What a strange conclusion to the Munich conference.

Why was the USSR not at the Munich conference? The simple reason was that no one wanted it there. Neither Chamberlain nor Daladier had any confidence in Stalin. At no time did they wish to admit the Soviet Union into their circle, or to consider seriously its possible contribution to an anti-German front. This was partly due to the purges, which were assumed to have seriously damaged its military strength, but also to the widespread mistrust of the Bolshevik government and distaste for their system and ideology. This was accentuated by the importance of the French Communist party, and the political impact of any contact with Moscow on domestic politics. Repeatedly during the previous months, Chamberlain in particular, but others as well, argued that a war over Czechoslovakia would benefit only the USSR. It is curious, though not without importance, that while Chamberlain discounted the ideological factor in his search for an agreement with Hitler (though he regarded Nazism as a wholly repugnant creed), he could not abide the possible spectacle of Bolshevism moving across Europe. Whatever the tensions between Britain and France, the two countries were tied together for better or worse. There could be no such linkage between either country with the USSR, even in the most attenuated form.

The Soviet view of the western powers, both in ideological and in practical terms, was equally antagonistic and suspicious. All of Litvinov's efforts to promote a collective stand against Hitler had failed. Chamberlain's decision to fly to Berchtesgaden on 13 September, confirmed the view of those who believed not only that the western powers were intent on excluding the USSR from their deliberations, but were prepared to seek an agreement with Germany over Czechoslovakia that would leave the Soviet Union isolated. Russia's exclusion from Munich gave new point to Stalin's conviction that the Soviet Union had to play its own hand in a hostile capitalist world while preparing for the inevitable war which would come sooner rather than later.

IV

'Munich' has established a permanent place in the vocabulary of modern diplomacy. It has added a new and pejorative dimension to definitions of

[50] Ivone Kirkpatrick, *The Inner Circle* (London, 1959), 135.

the word 'appeasement' now found in almost every modern Anglo-American dictionary. The 'lessons of Munich' have become a 'notorious cliché', repeatedly cited by statesmen on both sides of the Atlantic as a reminder of what happens when democracies fail to stand up to dictators. Yet there was little consensus at the time as to the wisdom of appeasing Germany at Munich and there remains intense disagreement about the subject among historians today. While some see Chamberlain's flight to Germany as a dramatic gesture by a 69-year-old man that succeeded in postponing the outbreak of war by a year, others condemn Munich as an act of moral cowardice that saved Hitler's Reich from defeat and delayed a conflict which the western Allies were in a better position to fight in 1938 than in 1939.

The battle of the history books has, at least, made it possible to distinguish between the myths of Munich and the realities of the European situation in 1938. I have tried in these chapters to focus again on the events of September in the hope of reconstructing the scene as perceived by the participants and assessing its contemporary importance. From the time of Chamberlain's decision to fly to Germany until his return from Munich, more was involved than the future of Czechoslovakia. At the very first meeting between the two leaders, Chamberlain conceded the German right to occupy the regions inhabited by the Sudeten Germans. The subsequent quarrels, as the prime minister tried to explain to his ministers, were over whether Germany would seize the demanded territories immediately or accept a staggered occupation according to a pre-arranged timetable. Yet behind the Czech problem from the start of the crisis was always the question of Hitler's real intentions and the appropriate Anglo-French response to his demands. At the time of the Godesberg meeting, the British government, for the first time, faced the possibility of war with Germany. It was this which made the Munich settlement a defining moment, not only for the unhappy Czechs but for the Germans and for Britain and France. The decisions reached at the Munich Conference represented the apex (or nadir point) of the Anglo-French attempts to reach an accommodation with Hitler in order to avoid war and save their countries from destruction. What followed was Hitler's violations of the Munich agreements, the failed Anglo-French search for an alternative to appeasement, the Polish crisis, and the decisions for war. Those months represented the short fuse that led to the opening of the European war. Munich was decisive for Hitler; he was determined never again to be deterred by others from his decision to fight. At the same time, both western governments were forced to contemplate the probability of an impending struggle. Such a reality check altered the frame of reference within which decisions were reached. For many in London, though not for all, appeasement had lost its *raison d'être*. Nor should it be forgotten that Munich had consequences for other Great Powers not involved in the talks, among which the Soviet Union and the United States must be counted.

Though Daladier and his advisers played their role in the events that led up to Munich, there is considerable justification for viewing the two week crisis as an extraordinary duel between Hitler and Chamberlain. For Hitler, who had discounted British interference, Chamberlain's arrival at Berchtesgaden was an unwelcome interruption to his planned military intervention in Czechoslovakia. Unable to bully the British prime minister, Hitler had to face the possibility that Britain and France would respond to the German invasion of Czechoslovakia by declaring war. On 26–27 September, if Hitler had wanted war, he could have had it. For Chamberlain, the Munich agreements represented the culmination of his diplomatic efforts to negotiate a settlement that would satisfy Hitler's legitimate grievances in order to avoid a war that he felt would be disastrous for Britain and for Europe.

Chamberlain's peace saving efforts had begun before he assumed the prime ministership and were part of an on-going process that had started almost as soon as the Versailles treaty was signed. Successive British governments during the inter-war years believed that peace and prosperity depended on Germany's return to Great Power status and its re-integration into the concert of Europe. Many believed, well into the 1930s, that it was France rather than Germany that was obstructing the peaceful and necessary revision of the peace treaties. The advent of Hitler had not changed these assumptions. Hitler's rapid attacks on the remnants of the peace settlements forced a revision of these views. British rearmament in the 1930s increasingly aimed at insuring against a future threat from Germany. But it was also intended to allow the British government to deal with the Nazi regime from a position of strength. Hitler moved more quickly and effectively than either the British or French anticipated. While proclaiming his fervent desire for peace, he either temporized or rejected offers of compromise. Until Munich and even after, both the Chamberlain and Daladier governments continued on the double path of rearmament and appeasement. Chamberlain, in particular, was convinced that this double act would convince Hitler that negotiation was preferable to war.

The British attachment to the settlement of international quarrels 'through rational negotiation and compromise' had a long historical pedigree.[51] It dated back not just to 1919 but to the mid-nineteenth

[51] Paul Kennedy, *Strategy and Diplomacy, 1870–1945* (London, 1983), 16. There are many such definitions of appeasement and they continue to change.

century and was seen by British statesmen and by the electorate as an appropriate and rational policy that had served Britain well at home and abroad. It reflected long-standing assumptions that peace was better than war and that even a victorious war could come at an unacceptable price. Such beliefs had been reinforced by the experiences of the Great War, still a living presence in the memory of the Munich generation. This was what A. J. P. Taylor meant when he wrote, 'Munich was a triumph for all that was best and most enlightened in British life.'[52]

What was striking about Chamberlain's actions in September 1938 was not his willingness to compromise with Hitler at Czechoslovakia's expense. This was in keeping with earlier British policies. It was rather his daring decision to fly to Germany and deal with the German chancellor in face-to-face talks. He did so in the conviction that he could achieve a settlement of the Sudeten problem, improve Anglo–German relations and lay the foundations for peace in Europe. Well before the Prague crisis, Chamberlain had been irritated by the dilatory tactics of the Foreign Office in coming to terms with the dictators, and was convinced that he could handle these problems far better by himself. In October 1937, he wrote privately of 'the far-reaching plans which I have in mind for the appeasement of Europe and Asia and for the ultimate check to the mad armaments race.'[53] The prime minister's hubristic ambitions and self-confidence were extraordinary. This stiff, reserved, and unimaginative statesman had understood that a dramatic flight to Germany would impress Hitler (and the British public) and would force him to parley. Though at times the prime minister thought the German dictator half mad, he also believed that, if handled properly, Hitler would be amenable to rational argument and could be persuaded to accept a negotiated agreement. Chamberlain did not go to Germany to win time for rearmament; he went to prevent war and to lay the basis for a future continental peace.

Chamberlain's air trips to Germany and the two week duel with Hitler marked a new chapter in the conduct of diplomacy. It was not just that air travel had speeded up the diplomatic clock and made such exchanges possible but that the meetings between the two men, 'actually inaugurated modern summitry, with that oft-derided figure, Chamberlain, as its unlikely impresario'.[54] The personal encounters had little in common with Lloyd George's conference diplomacy, or with the

[52] A. J. P. Taylor, *The Origins of the Second World War* (London, 1961), 189. Taylor later claimed this was meant ironically.

[53] David Reynolds, *Summits: Six Meetings that Shaped the Twentieth Century* (London, 2007), 48.

[54] Ibid., 5. I owe to Professor Reynolds the whole idea of seeing these exchanges as the first of the twentieth-century summits.

Locarno tea parties of Briand, Austen Chamberlain, and Stresemann. And they had nothing at all to do with the Council sessions of the politically defunct League of Nations which took no part in the crisis. The one-to-one exchanges differed, too, from the twentieth century summits that followed in that there were no agendas or formal minutes kept, no staffs of experts to advise their political leaders, and no back-up papers to guide them. Chamberlain went to Germany without his foreign secretary and without his own interpreter, relying instead on Hitler's translator and note taker, Paul Schmidt. The conference at Munich was an *ad hoc* affair with people wandering in and out. The differing lists of those in attendance clearly illustrate its disorganization. The earlier Hitler–Chamberlain meetings were 'personal summits' in the true sense of the term.

Personal encounters concentrate power in the hands of the participants. It surprised no one that Hitler made his own decisions, kept the initiative throughout, and, almost to the very end, disregarded the warnings from some of his most senior military and civilian advisers. But Chamberlain, too, enjoyed a surprising degree of independence given the British constitutional and political structure. Chamberlain, alone, made the decision to go to Berchtesgaden and sought cabinet approval only at the last moment. He played on the drama of the moment; the rolled umbrella was one of his props. Chamberlain repeatedly reported first to his 'inner cabinet' rather than to the more critical full cabinet. The notorious 'piece of paper' the joint statement offered for Hitler's signature after the Munich conference had not been given cabinet approval. The exception to Chamberlain's relatively free hand was the cabinet revolt over the Godesberg terms, followed by further efforts to limit the prime minister's freedom of manoeuvre. Yet at the most critical moment, Chamberlain used his own personal confidant, Sir Horace Wilson, not just to deliver the cabinet rejection of the Godesberg terms but to keep open the channels of communication.

Chamberlain understood that his intervention was a high-risk strategy. Not only did he believe that Hitler might go to war, he also agreed with his civilian and military advisers that Britain was in no position to fight. There was virtual consensus in Whitehall that little could be done to protect Czechoslovakia against attack and that no peace treaty, even after a terrible war, could restore Prague to its 1919 position. The prime minister was convinced that 'no state, certainly no democratic state, ought to make a threat of war, unless it was both ready to carry it out and prepared to do so'.[55] Significantly, under crisis conditions, Britain's

[55] TNA: PRO, CAB 29/34, Cabinet, 30 August 1938.

leaders assumed a worst-case scenario. The expectation of a future German bombing campaign, the number of aircraft and bombs, and the resulting casualty figures were all grossly exaggerated. The Air Staff insisted that the RAF could not match the *Luftwaffe*. The radar chain and the ground control scheme were incomplete and only a third of the barrage balloons, anti-aircraft guns, and searchlights were in place over London. It was assumed that Britain was at least two years behind the corresponding German air programme. Little was expected from the Czech army though the British military attaché in Prague provided a very positive assessment of the Czech defences. There was no substantive joint planning with the French. The main British concern was not to strengthen French resolve but instead to prevent Daladier from taking any precipitate action.

Chamberlain undoubtedly reflected the opinion of most British men and women, when on the evening of 27th September, he spoke of 'a quarrel in a far-away country between people of whom we know nothing'.[56] While acknowledging the hardening of the political and public mood, he still believed that the country wanted peace. There was no credible 'war party' in Britain, and no possible leader who could replace him. Vansittart, Duff Cooper, Churchill, and others who argued that only the strongest and clearest action could prevent Hitler from invading Czechoslovakia, accepted that Hitler might call Britain's bluff and force it into war or humiliation. In this sense, they were 'warmongers' but while accepting the risk, they believed that a resolute stand by Britain and France might force Hitler to back down and possibly wreck his regime. Chamberlain and the majority of his cabinet and advisers were too cautious and fearful to run the risk of war, particularly when uncertain of Hitler's intentions.[57] Even those critical of the cabinet's weakness were relieved (and an overwhelming majority of the Commons cheered) when Hitler agreed to a conference in Munich. The final negotiations were left in the prime minister's hands.

In a sense, Chamberlain succeeded. Hitler stepped back from a war which he could have unleashed. It was a step which he later regretted. In so doing, according to one historian of the Nazi period, he may have 'saved his regime from disaster'.[58] Hitler blinked. Chamberlain had gained his major objectives. It proved to be a short-run victory. The whole point of Chamberlain's meetings with Hitler was to establish a

[56] Neville Chamberlain, *The Struggle for Peace* (London, 1939), 274–376, quoted in Reynolds, *Summits*, 78.

[57] See John Robert Ferris, 'Vansittart, Intelligence and Appeasement', in John Ferris (ed.), *Intelligence and Strategy: Selected Essays*, 82–84.

[58] Adam Tooze, *The Wages of Destruction,* 374.

personal relationship with the Führer and to make an accurate assessment of his motives and objectives. Yet Chamberlain's reading of Hitler's intentions was fatally flawed. Like Roosevelt and Churchill in their later dealings with Stalin, the prime minister thought he had created a bond with Hitler and had won his respect. Chamberlain told his colleagues that he 'had now established an influence over Herr Hitler, and that the latter trusted him and was willing to work with him'. If so, there was 'a wonderful opportunity to put an end to the horrible nightmare of the present armament race'.[59] Having placed so much emphasis on the importance of his personal diplomacy the prime minister would suffer a severe loss of reputation at the time of his death in 1940. The 'guilty men' image of Munich was born.

Just as important as the prime minister's excessive self-confidence was his misplaced assumption that Herr Hitler must share his own abhorrence of war. By nature, Hitler was willing to take risks which Chamberlain would not contemplate. There was a more basic difference between the two leaders, and it was one which Chamberlain never fully grasped. Hitler was preparing for war, not just war with Czechoslovakia but war with the western powers. The question was one of timing. Hitler would have preferred to avoid war with Britain (and France) until a later date, ideally, 1943 to 1945. But he was willing to move earlier if the external circumstances changed. Chamberlain not only wanted to avoid war in 1938; he hoped to avoid war in the future. His obsession with preserving the peace marred his judgment. Admittedly, Chamberlain later regretted his hasty reference to 'peace for our time'. As he assured the Commons, Britain would not stop rearming until it was clear that the dictators would stop the arms race. Coming back from Munich, his hopes were high. He was to wait in vain for some sign that Hitler shared them.

Daladier did not fall victim to Neville Chamberlain's illusions. He knew he had betrayed France's ally and weakened his country's strategic position in the East. This awareness explains his despair the evening after the conference with the British and his expectations of a hostile public reception on his return from Munich. French policy was based on considerations of *realpolitik*. French military leaders did not believe France could mount a successful offensive against Germany. The French army, which retained the structure it had been given during the military reorganization of 1927–1928, was the product of a different era of European politics and profoundly unsuited to the kind of aggressive offensive action that was required in 1938. Massive inferiority in the air

[59] Quoted in Parker, *Chamberlain and Appeasement*, 169.

and the sluggish output of new aircraft meant that the French air force could offer scant protection against a German bombing campaign. It had no offensive options. Like the British chiefs of staff, the French high command was convinced that Czechoslovakia could not withstand a determined German onslaught for an extended period. The assumption was that its well-equipped and well-trained army would be outnumbered and overwhelmed while its air force was hopelessly outclassed by the *Luftwaffe*. With the Little Entente in disarray, Poland (and Hungary) harbouring ambitions to participate in the break-up of their neighbour, there could be no eastern front without Soviet participation. But neither Bonnet nor Gamelin believed that the Soviet Union would offer concrete support to Prague. Nor did they solicit such assistance. Distrust of Moscow, an underestimation of its military power (despite reports from the French military attaché in Moscow), and awareness of British hostility to Soviet participation ruled out any reliance on the Russians.

The French domestic situation hardly encouraged audacity. Internal difficulties restricted Daladier more than they did Chamberlain. At the time of the Czech crisis, France's financial situation was perilous, and its rearmament effort restricted by backlogs in the production of planes, tanks, and motorized vehicles. There were also bitter disputes between government, employers, and trade unionists over the retention of the Popular Front gains, above all the statutory forty-hour week. All of this helps explain France's one-sided relationship with Britain in September 1938. This state of affairs, considered desirable by Bonnet but 'inescapable' by Daladier, meant that the French would follow in the British wake. Daladier knew that the British had strong doubts about defending Czechoslovakia and were equivocal about supporting France if it went to its ally's defence. London repeatedly resisted efforts to coordinate future war policy. Yet without British assistance, France could not face Germany in the war of attrition which provided its only hope of victory. Honour was compromised and strategic and economic assets lost to avoid defeat. Daladier never believed that the Munich agreements would open a new chapter in relations with Germany. He had hopes, however, that if war was postponed, he could use the time to strengthen the Anglo-French partnership and to speed up the French rearmament effort.

It is now known that Germany was not ready for war in 1938. The West Wall was still a construction site and the Germans had limited forces available to defend it. General Beck may have been wrong about the length of the Czech campaign and the predicted speed of a French attack in the west but his basic strategic assessment was accurate. The German army not only needed a rapid victory over the Czechs but had to deliver a swift and decisive blow against France. Even if the French army could not mount a successful offensive against Germany, it could certainly have mounted a strong enough defence to force the German army to accept a war of attrition. Influential German military and civilian leaders argued that in such a war France and Britain would have the upper hand, particularly if, as they expected, the United States would back the Allied efforts with material assistance. Beck spoke of a 'world coalition' against Germany that would include Britain, France, the United States, and the Soviet Union.

Nor could Germany have mounted a strategic bombing campaign against Britain. It might even have had some difficulty in bombing French cities. Contrary to Anglo-French expectations, the German air force was still being mainly prepared to support the German land armies. It possessed neither the bombers nor the infrastructure for a strategic bombing campaign. As British and French intelligence correctly reported, the Reich was already facing economic and financial problems resulting from the acceleration and expansion of its armament programme. As Hitler publicly recognized in January 1939, Germany would have 'to export or die'. Yet with the American recession of 1937 and the Reich's rising defence requirements, exports were in steady decline. The Reich, according to Schwerin von Krosigk, the Reich finance minister, was 'steering towards a serious financial crisis'.[60] Like Beck and Colonel Georg Thomas, the financial minister argued that Germany would be at a serious disadvantage in any prolonged war. It would be better to wait, complete the German armaments programme and create a 'balance between military and economic preparations' before going to war against Britain and France.

It is difficult to judge whether Hitler's military opponents would have successfully implemented their plans to arrest Hitler and the Nazi leadership and take over the Reich. I have my doubts. It is even less probable that the anti-war feeling in Germany would have resulted in any open opposition to war in 1938. Nevertheless, it is true that Hitler would have begun the war under inauspicious conditions with so many influential voices opposing a premature war for which Germany was not prepared. The diplomatic situation seems to have only indirectly affected Hitler's calculations. He seems to have paid little attention to the Soviet Union even though the possibility of an enemy in the East posed the threat of encirclement and a two-front war. Had Britain and France marched, it is unlikely that the Poles would have moved against Czechoslovakia. The alliance with France would have become a necessary condition of their security. The Hungarians, too, already very reluctant to take military action, might have had even more doubts

[60] Quoted in Tooze, *Wages of Destruction*, 272. For further discussions see 267–273.

about its alignment with Germany. For Hitler, Mussolini's support was of more importance than any military or naval assistance Italy might offer. Assured by his intelligence sources that the French would not move to save the Czechs and by his own agents and even the French authorities that France would not launch any attacks on Italy, Mussolini felt free to proclaim his loyalty to the Führer and declare his intention to march with the Germans if the war was expanded. When British and French intervention seemed probable, though he still might have stood with Hitler, he and his bellicose military chiefs were forced to recognize that the Italians could not face a war against either. The Duce had good reason after Godesberg to welcome the idea of a conference and the peaceful resolution of the conflict.

On balance, it would have been possible for Chamberlain to have stayed at home and the British, along with the French, to have threatened Germany with war if Hitler sent his troops into Czechoslovakia. An alternative policy of firmness might have forced Hitler to reconsider. For such a policy to have carried weight, however, the British would have had to open staff talks with the French and, in doing so, would implicitly have threatened action. If Hitler had taken up the challenge, the probable result might have been a stalemate but not the obliteration of Britain's cities nor the destruction of France. Like so many counterfactual scenarios, the arguments for war in 1938 seem much stronger in retrospect than they did at the time. It is possible that Czechoslovakia would have held out longer than anticipated; the proposed pincer movement had its critics, including Hitler. Much would have depended on the speed with which the French army could have launched an offensive against the German forces behind the West Wall. If the French, as seems probable, had been forced on to the defensive, a war of attrition might have ensued. No one could predict what its consequences would have been. The British could have done little. Naval power might have been used offensively against Italy but the imposition of a successful blockade against Germany would have taken time. It is highly probable that with the outbreak of war, political divisions in Britain and France might have been resolved. War anxiety and fears of bombing might well have diminished. The Allied populations, like their German counterparts, would have rallied to support their governments, but a war of attrition takes its toll.

Neither side was in a position to win a decisive victory. Apart from the possible success of the conspiracy against Hitler, the short-term prospects for Germany might well have been less bleak than the dissidents assumed. Under war conditions, far more is possible than when operating under peacetime constraints, even in Germany, where economic mobilization was already far advanced. There are many imponderables in the international situation that have to be considered. Would war have brought all the Commonwealth nations into the war given their support for the appeasement of Germany? It is not at all clear that the United States would have moved to assist the Allied countries in the short- or even longer-term future. While Godesberg acted as a catalyst in strengthening Roosevelt's belief in the German threat to American security, he was still thinking in terms of stiffening Anglo-French resistance to Hitler's demands, hoping their efforts would succeed without the active participation of the United States in any European or global conflict. The president, moreover, remained politically cautious and conscious of the need to tailor his policies to the main currents in American opinion. He could push against these limits but was not prepared to challenge them. Without 'a clear and present danger' to American security, he would have had a fierce battle to amend the Neutrality Acts. The isolationist winds were still exceedingly powerful in 1938.

No historian can predict with any degree of certainty what Stalin would have done had France honoured its obligations to Czechoslovakia. He might have sent aircraft to Prague but would he have done anything more? Neither the Poles nor Romanians were likely to have modified their objections to the movement of Soviet forces across their countries, though the Romanians might well have opened its airspace to allow for the delivery of Soviet planes. They too, were waiting to see what the French would do. In the autumn of 1938, neither Stalin nor the Western leaders were thinking in terms of a coalition war against Germany. It is perfectly possible, though this is pure conjecture, that Stalin would have played a waiting game until the situation became clearer and that the British and French would have tried to avoid 'supping with the devil' unless the fortunes of war had turned decisively against them.

With hindsight, the case for war is considerably strengthened when the balance of forces and the role of the Soviet Union in September 1938 is compared with that of a year later. In many respects, it was Germany rather than the Allied powers that gained most from the delay. But decisions for war are rarely the result of counting men, weapons, and aircraft. Statistics provide only part of the answer. Given their misperceptions of German power and the divided state of public opinion, one can understand why Britain and France chose to sacrifice Czechoslovakia to avoid what they believed would be the start of another war in Europe. There still remained the hope that, with concessions, Hitler would abandon the idea of military action. The scales were weighted towards appeasement. Unlike Hitler, Chamberlain and Daladier would not take risks. To understand the Munich settlement does not, however, excuse

Chamberlain's fundamental misjudgement concerning Adolf Hitler's intentions. The Munich story does not provide an object lesson in the costs of giving way to dictators. It does highlight the dangers of untrammelled conviction and self-confidence on the part of statesmen engaged in personal summitry. For Hitler, too, drew the wrong conclusions from these meetings as became clear in August 1939.

V

The Munich conference raised major questions for each of the leaders present. For Hitler, the British intervention was unexpected and unwanted. He now had to consider what Britain's future role would be as he prepared his plans for expansion in the East. His first reaction was one of anger; he had allowed himself to be bluffed and so missed an opportunity for a military victory at very little cost. For the present, he could set about preparing for further moves in Czechoslovakia without consideration of the British and French reactions. Further moves involved another escalation in German war production despite warnings of inflationary pressures from his financial advisers. Mussolini had good reason to be proud of his performance at Munich. He had not wanted a general war in September 1938 though he had assured the Germans that he would be with Hitler should such a conflict occur. Hitler left the Duce in no doubt on their train ride to the conference that he intended to have a war with Britain and France sometime in the future. For Mussolini, the question of timing was important; Italy was in no condition to take on either power. He could well have considered using the favourable diplomatic situation to divide Britain and France in order to secure some of the imperial gains he sought without actually concluding an alliance with Germany.

For Britain, the most important unanswered question was that of Hitler's future intentions. Chamberlain believed or, at least, hoped, that Hitler would be satisfied with the fulfillment of his declared aims and would come to the negotiating table to end the nightmare of the accelerating arms race. Even at his moment of triumph, the prime minister was far too intelligent and too rational not to have considered the alternative reading of Hitler's aims. He had saved the peace, which was his overriding aim, and secured Hitler's signature to a proposed future settlement of their differences. As his subsequent actions showed, he was 'hoping for the best but preparing for the worst' with more emphasis on the former than on the latter. Almost all the prime minister's advisers, including those critical of his policies, believed that the country was not ready to fight in September 1938 and needed time for further rearmament. Godesberg, after all, had brought this possibility very close. Many agreed with the prime minister that the defence of a doomed country was neither a vital British interest nor worth the incalculable costs of war. The widespread feelings of relief and gratitude for the prime minister's efforts had not obscured, however, the doubts about whether there would be peace during their lifetimes. The aftermath of Munich would result in a growing gap between the prime minister, his foreign secretary, and his still far from united critics in the Commons. Chamberlain was still the hero of the hour in the months after Munich but Hitler's actions would soon create a growing sense of revulsion and unease.

Daladier knew that France's security position had been severely compromised at Munich though it would take some time before he saw what could be done to improve it. The one consolation prize on which he set his mind was the conclusion of the long-sought-for British alliance. At first, Daladier, like Bonnet (and the British Foreign Office), considered abandoning Eastern Europe to the Germans, though he soon had second thoughts. While still considering his seemingly limited options, he turned to strengthening the French economy in preparation for the rearmament measures that were so desperately needed. In the autumn of 1938, after eight years of stagnation, the economy began to recover. Government measures led to a revival of business confidence and increased arms spending further stimulated the economy. The September panic began to subside but divided counsels on what should or could be done precluded any firm decisions. Soon after Munich, the public mood began to shift in the direction of a tougher stance towards Germany, undoubtedly strengthened by the signs of economic recovery. It may be that in both countries, the over-riding fear of war, that had for so long shaped public policy, reached its peak in September 1938. Could there have been a second crisis on this emotional scale? The sense of escape could not entirely blunt the doubts and uncertainties that Munich left in its wake. Hitler's triumph undoubtedly brought closer the perception of what the costs of appeasement might be.

Books

Andrew, C. M., *Secret Service: The Making of the British Intelligence Community* (London, 1985).

—— and Gordievsky, O., *KGB: The Inside Story* (New York, 1990).

—— and Mitrokhin, V., *The Sword and the Shield: The Mitrokhin Archive and the Secret History of the KGB* (New York, 1999).

—— and Dilks, D. (eds.), *The Missing Dimension: Governments and Intelligence Communities in the Twentieth Century* (London, 1984). See D. Dilks and J. Stengers.

Aster, S., *1939: The Making of the Second World War* (London, 1973).

Beer, S., *Der 'unmoralische' Anschluss: Britische Österreichpolitik zwischen Containment und Appeasement, 1931–34* (Vienna, 1988).

Bellstedt, H. F., *'Apaisement' oder Krieg: Frankreichs Aussenminister Georges Bonnet und die deutsch–französische Erklärung vom 6. Dezember 1938* (Bonn, 1993).

Bernhardt, W., *Die deutsche Aufrüstung, 1934–1939: Militärische und politische Konzeptionen und ihre Einschätzung durch die Allierten* (Gütersloh, 1939).

Berstein, S., *L'Histoire du Parti radical* (Paris, 1980).

Bialer, U., *The Shadow of the Bomber: The Fear of Air Attack and British Politics, 1932–1939* (London, 1980).

Bischof, G., Pelinka, A., and Lassner, A. (eds.), *The Dollfuss/Schuschnigg Era in Austria: A Reassessment* (New Brunswick, NJ, 2003). See A. Lassner.

Bolech, D., *L'accordo di due imperi: L'accordo Italo-inglese del 16 aprile 1938* (Milan, 1977).

Botz, G., *Nationalsozialismus in Wien: Machtübernahme, Herrschaftssicherung, Radikalisierung 1938/39*, rev. edn. (Vienna, 2008).

Boyce, R. W. D. (ed.), *French Foreign and Defence Policy, 1918–1940: The Decline and Fall of a Great Power* (London, 1998). See P. Jackson and Y. Lacaze.

—— and Robertson, E. M. (eds.), *Paths to War: New Essays on the Origins of the Second World War* (New York, 1989). See S. Aster and N. Jordan.

Braddick, H. B., *Germany, Czechoslovakia and the Grand Alliance in the May Crisis, 1938* (Denver, CO, 1969).

Brook-Shepherd, G., *The Anschluss* (London, 1963).

Brügel, J. W., *Tschechen und Deutsche, 1918–1938* (Munich, 1967).

—— *Czechoslovakia before Munich: The German Minority Problem and British Appeasement Policy* (Cambridge, 1973).

Celovsky, B., *Das Münchener Abkommen, 1938* (Stuttgart, 1958).

Charmley, J., *Chamberlain and the Lost Peace* (Chicago, IL, 1989).

—— *Churchill's Grand Alliance* (New York, 1995).

Cienciala, A. M., *Poland and the Western Powers, 1938–1939* (London, 1968).

Cockett, R., *Twilight of Truth: Chamberlain, Appeasement and the Manipulation of the Press* (London and New York, 1989).

Colloque international sur les relations franco-allemandes (eds.), *Relations franco-allemandes, 1933–1939* (Paris, 1976).

Colvin, I., *The Chamberlain Cabinet* (London, 1971).

Cowling, M., *The Impact of Hitler: British Politics and British Policy, 1933–1940* (Cambridge, 1975).

Crowson, N. J., *Facing Fascism: The Conservative Party and the European Dictators, 1935–1940* (London, 1997).

Deutsch, H. C., *Hitler and his Generals: The Hidden Crisis, January–June 1938* (Minneapolis, MN, 1974).

Dockrill, M. L., *British Establishment Perspectives on France, 1936–1940* (Basingstoke, 1999).

Doise, J. and Vaïsse, M., *Diplomatie et outil militaire, 1871–1991*, second edn. (Paris, 1992).

Doughty, R. A., *The Seeds of Disaster: The Development of French Army Doctrine, 1919–1939* (Hamden, CT, 1985).

DULLIN, S., *Des hommes d'influences: les ambassadeurs de Staline en Europe, 1930–1939* (Paris, 2001).

DUTAILLY, H., *Les problèmes de l'armée de terre française, 1935–1939* (Paris, 1984).

EDMONDSON, C. E., *The Heimwehr and Austrian Politics, 1918–1936* (Athens, GE, 1978).

FABER, D., *Munich: The 1938 Appeasement Crisis* (London, 2008). Read after completion of chapter.

FARNHAM, B. R., *Roosevelt and the Munich Crisis: A Study of Political Decision-Making* (Princeton, NJ, 1997).

FRANK[ENSTEIN], R., *Le prix du réarmament français, 1935–1939* (Paris, 1982).

FUCHSER, L. W., *Neville Chamberlain and Appeasement: A Study in the Politics of History* (New York, 1982).

FUNKE, M. (ed.), *Hitler, Deutschland und die Mächte* (Düsseldorf, 1976).

GEDYE, G. E. R., *Betrayal in Central Europe: Austria and Czechoslovakia, the Fallen Bastions* (New York, 1939).

GIRAULT, R. and FRANK, R. (eds.), *La puissance en Europe, 1938–1940* (Paris, 1984).

GLANTZ, D. M., *The Military Strategy of the Soviet Union: A History* (London and Portland, OR, 1992).

GOLDSTEIN, E. and LUKES, I. (eds.), *The Munich Crisis, 1938: Prelude to World War II* (London, 2000). All the essays are pertinent to these chapters.

GOOCH, J., *Mussolini and his Generals: The Armed Forces and Fascist Foreign Policy, 1922–1940* (Cambridge, 2007).

HAIGHT, J. M. Jr., *American Aid to France, 1938–1940* (New York, 1970).

HASLAM, J., *The Soviet Union and the Struggle for Collective Security in Europe, 1933–1939* (London, 1984).

—— *The Soviet Union and the Threat from the East 1933–41: Moscow, Tokyo and the Prelude to the Pacific War* (London, 1992).

HENKE, J., *England in Hitlers politischem Kalkül* (Boppard am Rhein, 1983).

HERMAN, J., *The Paris Embassy of Sir Eric Phipps: Anglo–French Relations and the Foreign Office, 1937–1939* (Brighton, 1998).

HILDEBRAND, K., WERNER, K. F. and MANFRASS, K. (eds.), *Deutschland und Frankreich, 1936–1939: 15. Deutsch–französisches Historikerkolloquium des Deutschen Historischen Instituts Paris (Bonn, 26.–29. September, 1979)* (Munich, 1981).

HILL, C., *Cabinet Decisions on Foreign Policy: The British Experience, October 1938 – June 1941* (Cambridge, 1991).

IMLAY, T., *Facing the Second World War: Strategy, Politics and Economics in Britain and France 1938–1940* (Oxford, 2003).

Imperial War Museum and Comité d'histoire de la Deuxième Guerre Mondiale (eds.), *Les Relations Franco-britanniques de 1935 à 1939*, Comité d'Histoire de la 2ème Guerre Mondiale (Paris, 1975).

JACKSON, P., *France and the Nazi Menace: Intelligence and Policy Making, 1933–1939* (Oxford, 2000).

KINDERMANN, G.-K., *Hitler's Defeat in Austria, 1933–1934* (London and Boulder, CO, 1988).

KITCHEN, M., *The Coming of Austrian Fascism* (London, 1980).

KOMJATHY, A. and STOCKWELL, R., *German Minorities and the Third Reich* (New York, 1980).

KNOX, M., *Mussolini Unleashed* (Cambridge, 1982).

KREISSLER, F. (ed.), *Fünfzig Jahre danach—Der Anschluss von innen und außen gesehen* (Vienna, 1989).

LACAZE, Y., *L'opinion publique française et la crise de Munich* (Bern, 1991).

—— *La France et Munich: étude d'un processus décisionnel en matière de relations internationales* (Bern, 1992).

LAMMERS, D. M., *Explaining Munich: The Search for Motive in British Policy* (Stanford, CA, 1966).

LE GOYET, P., *Munich: 'Un traquenard'?* (Paris, 1988).

LOW, A. D., *The Anschluss Movement, 1931–1938, and the Great Powers* (Boulder, CO, and New York, 1985).

LUKES, I., *Czechoslovakia between Stalin and Hitler: The Diplomacy of Edvard Beneš in the 1930s* (New York and Oxford, 1996).

—— and GOLDSTEIN, E. (eds.), *The Munich Crisis, 1938: Prelude to World War II* (London: 1999).

LUZA, R., *Austro-German Relations in the Anschluss Era* (Princeton, NJ, 1975).

MACDONOGH, G., *1938: Hitler's Gamble* (London, 1998).

MEYERS, R., *Britische Sicherheitspolitik, 1934–1938: Studien zum außen—und sicherheitspolitischen Entscheidungsprozess* (Düsseldorf, 1976).

MIDDLEMAS, K., *Diplomacy of Illusion: The British Government and Germany, 1937–1939* (London, 1972).

MILLETT, A. R. and MURRAY, W. (eds.), *Military Effectiveness. Volume II: The Interwar Period* (Boston, MA, 1988).

MOMMSEN, W. J. and KETTENACKER, L. (eds.), *The Fascist Challenge and the Policy of Appeasement* (London, 1983). See J. Dunbabin, R. Frankenstein, R. Girault, W. Michalka, and R. M. Smelser.

MÜLLER, K.-J., *Das Heer und Hitler: Armee und nationalsozialistisches Regime, 1933–1940* (Stuttgart, 1969).

—— *The Army, Politics and Society in Germany, 1933–1945: Studies in the Army's Relations to Nazism* (Manchester, 1987).

MURRAY, W., *The Change in the European Balance of Power, 1938–1939: The Path to Ruin* (Princeton, NJ, 1984).

—— *German Military Effectiveness* (Baltimore, MD, 1992).

—— and MILLETT, A. R. (eds.), *Calculations: Net Assessment and the Coming of World War II* (New York, 1992).

NAMIER, L., *Diplomatic Prelude, 1938–1939* (London, 1948).

NIEDHART, G. (ed.), *Kriegsbeginn 1939: Entfesselung oder Ausbruch des Zweiten Weltkriegs?* (Darmstadt, 1976). See K. Hildebrand and A. Hillgruber.

NOGUÈRES, H., *Munich or the Phoney Peace* (London, 1965).

OVERY, R. J., *War and Economy in the Third Reich* (Oxford, 1994).

PARKER, R. A. C., *Chamberlain and Appeasement: British Policy and the Coming of the Second World War* (Basingstoke, 1993).

PAULEY, B., *Hitler and the Forgotten Nazis: A History of Austrian National Socialism* (London, 1981).

—— *From Prejudice to Persecution: A History of Austrian Anti-Semitism* (Chapel Hill, NC, 1997).

PEDEN, G. C., *British Rearmament and the Treasury, 1932–1939* (Edinburgh, 1979).

PETSCHAR, H., *Anschluss: 'Ich hole Euch heim': Eine Bildchronologie* (Vienna, 2008).

PEUKERT, D. J. K., *Inside Nazi Germany: Conformity, Opposition, and Racism in Everyday Life* (New Haven, CT, 1982).

PONS, S., *Stalin e la guerra inevitabile, 1936–1941* (Turin, 1993). Translated as *Stalin and the Inevitable War* (London, 2002).

—— and Romano, A. (eds.), *Russia in the Age of Wars, 1914–1945* (Milan, 2000).

PRESTON, A. (ed.), *General Staffs and Diplomacy before the Second World War* (London, 1978).

PROST, A., *In the Wake of War: 'Les Anciens Combattants' and French Society* (Providence, RI, and Oxford, 1992).

RAGSDALE, H., *The Soviets, the Munich Crisis and the Coming of World War II* (Cambridge, 2004).

Relations militaires franco-belges de mars 1936 au 10 mai 1940, Travaux d'un Colloque d'Historiens Belges et Français (Paris, 1968).

ROBBINS, K., *Munich 1938* (London, 1968).

ROBERTS, G., *The Soviet Union and the Origins of the Second World War: Russo-German Relations and the Road to War, 1933–1941* (Basingstoke, 1994).

ROBERTSON, E. M., *Hitler's Pre-War Policy and Military Plans, 1933–1939* (London, 1963).

SALEWSKI, M., *Wehrmacht und Nationalsozialismus, 1933–1939* (Munich, 1978).

SALERNO, R., *Vital Crossroads: Mediterranean Origins of the Second World War, 1935–1940* (Ithaca, NY, 2002).

SALMON, P., *Scandinavia and the Great Powers, 1890–1940* (Cambridge, 1997).

SCHIRMANN, S., *Les relations économiques et financières franco-allemandes, 24 décembre 1932 – 1 septembre 1939* (Paris, 1995).

SCHMIDL, E., *Der 'Anschluss' Österreichs': Der Deutsche Einmarsch im März 1938* (Bonn, 1994).

STOURZH, G. and ZAAR, B. (eds.), *Österreich, Deutschland and die Mächte: Internationale und Österreichische Aspekte des 'Anschlusses' vom März 1938* (Vienna, 1990).

TAYLOR, T., *Munich: The Price of Peace* (London, 1979).

THIELENHAUS, M., *Zwischen Anpassung und Widerstand: Deutsche Diplomaten, 1938–1941* (Paderborn, 1984).

TOSCANO, M., *The Origins of the Pact of Steel* (Baltimore, MD, 1967).

ULAM, A. B., *Expansion and Coexistence: Soviet Foreign Policy, 1917–1973*, second edn. (New York, 1976).

VAN LANGENHOVE, F., *La Belgique en quête de sécurité, 1920–1940* (Brussels, 1969).

VON KLEMPERER, K., *German Resistance against Hitler: The Search for Allies Abroad, 1938–1945* (Oxford, 1992).

WARK, W. K., *The Ultimate Enemy: British Intelligence and Nazi Germany, 1933–1939* (London, 1985).

WATT, D. C., *How War Came: The Immediate Origins of the Second World War, 1938–1939* (London, 1989).

WEINBERG, G. L., *The Foreign Policy of Hitler's Germany: Starting World War II, 1937–1939* (London, 1980).

—— *Der gewaltsame Anschluss 1938: Die deutsche Außenpolitik und Österreich* (Vienna, 1988).

WENDT, B.-J., *München 1938: England zwischen Hitler und Preußen* (Frankfurt am Main, 1965).

—— *Großdeutschland: Aussenpolitik und Kriegsvorbereitung des Hitler–Regimes* (Munich, 1987).

YOUNG, R. J., *In Command of France: French Foreign Policy and Military Planning, 1933–1940* (Cambridge, MA, 1978).

Articles and Chapters

ADAM, M., 'La Hongrie et les accords de Munich, 1938', *Revue d'histoire de la deuxième guerre mondiale* 33 (1983).

ADAMTHWAITE, A., 'The British Government and the Media, 1937–1938', *Journal of Contemporary History*, 18: 2 (1983).

ALEXANDER, M., 'Die außenpolitische Stellung und die innere Situation der CSR in der Sicht des Auswärtigen Amtes in Berlin; 1918–1933', in Hoensch, J. K. and Kováč, D. (eds.), *Das Scheitern der Verständigung: Tschechen, Deutsche und Slowaken in der Ersten Republik (1918–1938)* (Essen, 1994).

ALEXANDER, M. S., 'Did the Deuxième Bureau Work? The Role of Intelligence in French Defence Policy and Strategy, 1919–1939', *Intelligence and National Security*, 2 (1991).

—— 'In Lieu of Alliance: The French General Staff's Secret Co-operation with Neutral Belgium, 1936–1940', *Journal of Strategic Studies*, 4 (1991).

ASTER, S., 'Appeasement Before and After Revisionism', *Diplomacy & Statecraft*, 19: 3 (2008).

BECK, R. J., 'Munich's Lessons Reconsidered', *International Security*, 14: 2 (1989).

BÉDARIDA, F., 'Le "gouvernante anglaise"', in Rémond, R. and Bourdin, J. (eds.), *Édouard Daladier, chef de gouvernement, avril 1938 – septembre 1939* (Paris, 1977).

BEN-ARIE, K., 'Czechoslovakia at the Time of "Munich": The Military Situation', *Journal of Contemporary History*, 25 (1990).

BLASIUS, R. A., 'Weizsäcker contra Ribbentrop: "München statt des großen Krieges"', in Knipping, F. and Müller, K.-J. (eds.), *Machtbewusstsein in Deutschland am Vorabend des Zweiten Weltkrieges* (Paderborn, 1984).

BUFFOTOT, P., 'La perception du réarmement allemand par les organismes de renseignement français de 1936 à 1939', *Revue historique des armées*, 3 (1979).

—— 'The French High Command and the Franco-Soviet Alliance, 1933–1939', *Journal of Security Studies*, 5: 4 (1982).

BURDIN-BAKER, V., 'Selective Inattention: The Runciman Mission to Czechoslovakia, 1938', *East European Quarterly*, 24: 1 (1991).

BUTTERWORTH, S. B., 'Daladier and the Munich Crisis: A Reappraisal', *Journal of Contemporary History*, 9: 3 (1974).

CARLEY, M. J. '"Only the USSR has... Clean Hands": The Soviet Perspective on the Failure of "Collective Security" and the Collapse of the Czech Revolution, 1935–1938', Part I *Diplomacy and Statecraft*, 21, 2010. Pt II forthcoming.

CASSELS, A., 'Fascist Italy and Mediation in the Munich and Danzig Crises, September 1938 and August 1939', in Decleva, E. and Magliazza, A. (eds.), *Diplomazia e storia delle relazioni internazionali: studi in onore di Enrico Serra* (Milan, 1991).

CIENCIALA, A. M., 'Poland and the Munich Crisis, 1938: A Reappraisal', *East European Quarterly*, 3 (1969).

—— 'The View from Warsaw', in Latynski, M. (ed.), *Reappraising the Munich Pact: Continental Perspectives* (Washington, DC, 1992).

CORNWALL, M., 'A Fluctuating Barometer: British Diplomatic Views of the Czech–German Relationship in Czechoslovakia 1918–1938', in Schmidt-Hartmann, E. and Winters, S. B. (eds.), *Great Britain, the USA and the Bohemian Lands 1848–1938* (Munich, 1991).

—— 'The Rise and Fall of a "Special Relationship"?: Britain and Czechoslovakia, 1930–1948', in Brivati, B. and Jones, H. (eds.), *What Difference did the War Make?* (Leicester, 1993).

CROZIER, A. J., 'British Foreign Policy and Germany, 1935–1938', *European Studies Review*, 6 (1976).

DILKS, D., 'Intelligence and Appeasement', in Dilks, D. (ed.), *Retreat from Power*, Vol. I (London, 1981).

—— '"We Must Hope for the Best and Prepare for the Worst": The Prime Minister, the Cabinet and Hitler's Germany, 1937–1939', *Proceedings of the British Academy*, 73 (1987).

DÜLFFER, J., 'Der Beginn des Krieges 1939: Hitler, die innere Krise und das Mächtesystem', in Bracher, K. D., Funke, M., and Jacobsen, H.-A. (eds.), *Nationalsozialistische Diktatur, 1933–1945: eine Bilanz* (Bonn, 1983).

DULLIN, S., 'Les diplomates soviétiques des années 1930 et leur évaluation de la puissance de l'URSS', *Relations internationales*, 91 (1997).

DUTTER, G., 'Doing Business with the Nazis: French Economic Relations with Germany under the Popular Front', *Journal of Modern History*, 63: 2 (1991).

FACON, P., 'La visite du Général Vuillemin en Allemagne, 16–21 août, 1938', *Revue historique des Armées*, 2 (1982).

—— 'Le Haut Commandement aérien français et la crise de Munich', *Revue historique des armées*, 3 (1983).

—— 'Le Haut Commandement aérien français et le problème du réarmament, 1938–1939: une approche technique et industrielle', *Revue historique des Armées*, 3 (1989).

FAIR, J. D., 'The Chamberlain–Temperley Connection: Munich's Historical Dimension', *The Historian*, 48 (1985).

Ferris, J. R., 'Indulged in All Too Little? Vansittart, Intelligence and Appeasement', *Diplomacy and Statecraft*, 6: 1 (1995).

—— 'Intelligence and Diplomatic Signalling during Crises: The British Experience of 1877–78, 1922 and 1938', *Intelligence and National Security*, 21: 5 (2006).

Geyer, M., 'The Crisis of Military Leadership in the 1930s', *Journal of Strategic Studies*, 4 (1991).

Goldman, A. L., 'Two Views of Germany: Nevile Henderson vs. Vansittart and the Foreign Office, 1937–1939', *British Journal of International Studies*, 6: 3 (1980).

Haight, J. M., Jr., 'France, the United States and the Munich Crisis', *Journal of Modern History*, 32 (1960).

Holland, R. F., 'The Federation of British Industries and the International Economy, 1929–1939', *Economic History Review*, 2nd series, 34 (1981).

Jackson, P., 'French Military Intelligence and Czechoslovakia, 1938', *Diplomacy and Statecraft*, 5: 1 (1994).

—— 'La perception de la puissance aérienne allemande et son influence sur la politique extérieure française pendant les crises internationales de 1938 et 1939', *Revue historique des armées*, 39: 4 (1994).

—— 'Intelligence and the End of Appeasement', in Boyce, R. (ed.), *French Foreign and Defence Policy, 1918–1940: The Decline and Fall of a Great Power* (London, 1998).

Jordan, N., 'Maurice Gamelin, Italy and the Eastern Alliances', *Journal of Security Studies*, 14: 4 (1991).

—— 'Léon Blum and Czechoslovakia, 1936–1938', *French History*, 5: 1 (1991).

Jukes, G., 'The Red Army and the Munich Crisis', *Journal of Contemporary History*, 26 (1991).

Kennedy, P. and Imlay, T., 'Appeasement', in Martel, G. (ed.), *The Origins of the Second World War Reconsidered: A. J. P. Taylor and the Historians*, 2nd edn. (London, 1999).

Kindermann, G.–K., 'Der Feindscharakter Österreichs in der Perzeption des Dritten Reiches', in Stourzh, G. and Zaar, B. (eds.), *Österreich, Deutschland und die Mächte: internationale und österreichische Aspekte des "Anschlusses" vom März 1938* (Vienna, 1990).

Knipping, F., 'Frankreich in Hitlers Außenpolitik, 1933–1939', in Funke, M. (ed.), *Hitler, Deutschland und die Mächte* (Düsseldorf, 1976).

Lacaze, Y., 'Daladier, Bonnet and the Decision-making Process during the Munich Crisis, 1938', in Boyce, R. (ed.), *French Foreign and Defence Policy, 1918–1940: The Decline and Fall of a Great Power* (London, 1998).

Lammers, D. M., 'Fascism, Communism and the Foreign Office, 1937–1939', *Journal of Contemporary History*, 3 (1971).

—— 'From Whitehall after Munich: The Foreign Office and the Future Course of British Policy', *Historical Journal*, 16: 4 (1973).

Lassner, A., 'The Invasion of Austria in March 1938, Blitzkrieg or Pfusch', *Contemporary Austrian Studies*, 8 (2000).

—— 'The Foreign Policy of the Schuschnigg Government 1934–1938: The Quest for Security', in Bischof, G. and Lassner, A. (eds.), *The Dollfuß/*

Schuschnigg Era in Austria: Contemporary Austrian Studies 11 (New Brunswick, NJ, 2003).

—— 'Austria between Mussolini and Hitler: War by Other Means', in Bischof, G. and Lassner, A. (eds.), *Austian Foreign Policy in Historical Context: Contemporary Austrian Studies* 14 (New Brunswick, NJ, 2006).

LUKES, I., 'Did Stalin Desire War in 1938?: A New Look at Soviet Behaviour during the May and September Crises', *Diplomacy and Statecraft*, 2: 1 (1990).

—— 'Benesch, Stalin und die Comintern: vom Münchner Abkommen zum Molotow–Ribbentrop Pakt', *Vierteljahrshefte für Zeitgeschichte*, 3 (1993).

—— 'Stalin and Beneš at the End of September 1938: New Evidence from the Czech Archives', *Slavic Review*, 52: 1 (1993).

—— 'The Czechoslovak Partial Mobilisation in May 1938: A Mystery (Almost) Solved', *Journal of Contemporary History*, 31: 4 (1996).

MCDONOUGH, F., 'Chamberlain and the Czech Crisis of 1938: A Case Study in the Role of Morality in the Conduct of International Relations', in Nemecek, J. (ed.), *Mnichovská dohoda: cesta k destrukci demokracie v Evrope* (Prague, 2004).

MILLS, W. C., 'Sir Joseph Ball, Adrian Dingli, and Neville Chamberlain's "Secret Channel" to Italy, 1937–1940', *International History Review*, 24: 2 (2002).

'MUNICH, 1938: Mythes et réalités', *Revue des Études Slaves* (Paris), 52: 1–2 (1979).

MURRAY, W., 'German Air Power and the Munich Crisis', *War and Society: A Yearbook of Military History*, 2 (1977).

—— 'Munich 1938: The Military Confrontation', *Journal of Strategic Studies*, 2 (1979).

—— 'Appeasement and Intelligence', *Intelligence and National Security*, 4 (1987).

NEVILLE, P., 'Nevile Henderson and Basil Newton: Two British Envoys in the Czech Crisis 1938', *Diplomacy and Statecraft*, 10: 2–3 (1999).

—— 'Sir Alexander Cadogan and Lord Halifax's "Damascus Road" Conversion over the Godesberg Terms of 1938', *Diplomacy and Statecraft*, 11: 3 (2000).

—— 'The Foreign Office and Britain's Ambassadors to Berlin, 1933–39', *Contemporary British History*, 18: 3 (2004).

NEWMAN, M., 'The Origins of Munich: British Policy in Danubian Europe, 1933–1937', *Historical Journal*, 21: 2 (1978).

NUREK, M., 'Great Britain and the Scandinavian Countries before and after the Signing of the Munich Agreement', *Acta Poloniae Historica*, 59 (1989).

OVERY, R., 'German Air Strength, 1933–1939: A Note', *Historical Journal*, 27: 2 (1984).

PARKER, R. A. C., 'British Rearmament, 1936–1939: Treasury, Trade Unions and Skilled Labour', *English Historical Review*, 96 (1981).

PEDEN, G. C., 'A Matter of Timing: The Economic Background to British Foreign Policy, 1937–1939', *History*, 1 (1984).

PORCH, D., 'Military Intelligence and the Fall of France, 1930–1940', *Intelligence and National Security*, 1 (1989).

PRAZMOWSKA, A., 'Poland's Foreign Policy: September 1938–September 1939', *Historical Journal*, 29: 4 (1986).

Pronay, N. and Taylor, P. M., '"An Improper Use of Broadcasting": The British Government and Clandestine Radio Propaganda Operations against Germany during the Munich Crisis and after', *Journal of Contemporary History*, 19 (1984).

Ragsdale, H., 'The Munich Crisis and the Issue of Red Army Transit across Romania', *Russian Review*, 57: 4 (1998).

—— 'Soviet Military Preparations and Policy in the Munich Crisis: New Evidence', *Jahrbücher für Geschichte Osteuropas*, 47 (1999).

Rathkolb, O., 'The Anschluss in the Rearview Mirror, 1938–2008: Historical Memories between Debate and Transformation', in Bischof, G. et al. (eds.), *New Perspectives on Austrians and World War II: Contemporary Austrian History* 17 (New Brunswick, NJ, and London, 2009).

Robertson, E., 'Hitler's Planning for War and the Response of the Great Powers, 1938 to Early 1939', in Koch, H. (ed.), *Aspects of the Third Reich* (London, 1985).

Rose, N., 'The Resignation of Anthony Eden', *Historical Journal*, 25: 4 (1982).

Sakmyster, T. L., 'The Hungarian State Visit to Germany of August 1938: Some New Evidence on Hungary in Hitler's pre-Munich Policy', *Canadian Slavic Studies*, 3: 4 (1969).

—— 'Hungary and the Munich Crisis: The Revisionist Dilemma', *Slavic Review*, 32 (1973).

Salerno, R. M., 'The French Navy and the Appeasement of Italy, 1937–1939', *English Historical Review*, 112: 445 (1997).

Sasse, H. G., 'Das Problem des diplomatischen Nachwuchses im Dritten Reich', in Dietrich, R. and Oestreich, G. (eds.), *Forschungen zu Staat und Verfassung: Festgabe für Fritz Hartung* (Berlin, 1958).

Schulte, A., 'Hitler und Chamberlain in Godesberg, 1938', *Godesberger Heimatblatt*, 11 (1973).

Scott, W. E., 'Neville Chamberlain and Munich: Two Aspects of Power', in Krieger, L. and Stern, F. (eds.), *The Responsiblity of Power: Essays in Honour of Hajo Holborn* (New York, 1967).

Soutou, G.-H., 'La perception de la puissance française par René Massigli en 1938', *Relations internationales*, 33 (1973).

Steiner, Z., 'The Soviet Commissariat of Foreign Affairs and the Czechoslovakian Crisis in 1938: New Material from the Soviet Archives', *Historical Journal*, 42: 3 (1999).

Steininger, R., '12 November 1918 – 12 March 1938: The Road to Anschluss', in Steininger, R., Bischof G., and Gehler, M. (eds.), *Austria in the 20th Century* (New Brunswick, NJ, 2002).

Stourzh, G., 'Die Außenpolitik der österreichischen Bundesregierung gegenüber der nationalsozialistischen Bedrohung', in Stourzh, G. and Zaar, B., Österreichische Akademie der Wissenschaften. Veröffentlichungen der Kommission für die Geschichte Österreichs (eds.), *Österreich, Deutschland und die Mächte: Internationale und österreichische Aspekte des Anschlusses*, Vol. 16 (Vienna, 1990).

Strang, G. B., 'War and Peace: Mussolini's Road to Munich', in Lukes, I. and Goldstein, E. (eds.), *The Munich Crisis, 1938: Prelude to World War II* (London, 1999).

—— 'The Spirit of Ulysses? Ideology and British Appeasement in the 1930s', *Diplomacy & Statecraft*, 19 (2008).

STRONGE, BRIGADIER, H. C. T., 'The Czechoslovak Army and the Munich Crisis: A Personal Memorandum', *Yearbook of Military History*, 1 (1975).

TABORSKY, E., 'President Beneš and the Crises of 1938 and 1948', *East–Central Europe/Europe du Centre–Est*, 5: 2 (1978).

THOMAS, M., 'Appeasement in the Late Third Republic', *Diplomacy & Statecraft*, 19 (2008).

TÖPFER, M. L., 'American Governmental Attitudes towards the Soviet Union during the Czechoslovak Crises of 1938', *East European Quarterly*, 14: 1 (1980).

VAÏSSE, M., 'La perception de la puissance soviétique par les militaires françaises en 1938', *Revue historique des armées*, 3 (1983).

—— 'Der Pazifismus und die Sicherheit Frankreichs', *Vierteljahrshefte für Zeitgeschichte*, 4 (1985).

VITAL, D., 'Czechoslovakia and the Powers, September 1938', *Journal of Contemporary History*, 1: 4 (1966).

VOGEL, R., 'Chamberlain and Appeasement', in Farrell, B. P. (ed.), *Leadership and Responsibility in the Second World War: Essays in Honour of Robert Vogel* (Montreal, 2004).

WALDENEGG, G. and BERGER, C., 'Hitler, Göring und der Anschluss Österreichs an das Deutsche Reich', *Vierteljahrshefte für Zeitgeschichte*, 2 (2003).

WALLACE, W. V., 'The Making of the May Crisis of 1938', *The Slavonic and East European Review*, 41 (1963).

—— 'A Reply to Mr. Watt', *The Slavonic and East European Review*, 44 (1966).

WARK, W. K., 'Three Military Attachés at Berlin in the 1930s: Soldier-statesmen and the Limits of Ambiguity', *International History Review*, 4 (1987).

WATT, D. C., 'The May Crisis of 1938: A Rejoinder to Mr. Wallace', *The Slavonic and East European Review*, 44 (1966).

—— 'Hitler's Visit to Rome and the May Weekend Crisis: A Study in Hitler's Response to External Stimuli', *Journal of Contemporary History*, 9 (1974).

—— 'Churchill and Appeasement', in Blake, R. N. W. and Louis, Wm. R. (eds.), *Churchill* (Oxford, 1993).

WEINBERG, G. L., 'The May Crisis 1938', *Journal of Modern History* 29: 3 (1957).

—— 'Munich after 50 years', *Foreign Affairs*, 67: 1 (1988).

—— 'German Foreign Policy and Austria', in Weinberg, G. L. (ed.), *Germany, Hitler and World War II: Essays in Modern German and World History* (Cambridge, 1995).

—— 'Germany, Munich and Appeasement', in Weinberg, G. L. (ed.), *Germany, Hitler and World War II: Essays in Modern German and World History* (Cambridge, 1995).

YOUNG, R. J., 'French Policy and the Munich Crisis of 1938: A Reappraisal', *Canadian Historical Association Historical Papers* (1970).

—— 'Le haut commandement français au moment de Munich', *Revue d'histoire moderne et contemporaine*, 24 (1977).

—— 'Reason and Madness: France, the Axis Powers and the Politics of Economic Disorder, 1938–1939', *Canadian Journal of History*, 20 (1985).

Zorach, J., 'Czechoslovakia's Fortifications: Their Development and Role in the 1938 Munich Crisis', *Militärgeschichtliche Mitteilungen*, 2 (1976).
—— 'The British View of the Czechs in the Era before the Munich Crisis', *Slavonic and East European Review*, 57: 1 (1979).

Theses

Lassner, Alexander N., 'Peace at Hitler's Price: Austria, the Great Powers, and the Anschluß, 1932–1938', Ph.D. diss., Ohio State University, 2001. I have not read this thesis but have been advised of its importance.
Wilkinson, S., 'Perceptions of Public Opinion: British Foreign Policy Decisions about Nazi Germany, 1933–1938', Ph.D. diss., Oxford, 2000.

PART II

The Road to Hitler's War, 1938–1939

In the nightmare of the dark
All the dogs of Europe bark,
And the living nations wait,
Each sequestered in its hate.

W. H. Auden, 'In Memory of W. B. Yeats', February 1939

12

The Fog of Peace: Strategic Choices after Munich

I

The sense of relief engendered by the Munich agreements soon disappeared. Instead of being the 'prelude to a larger settlement in which all Europe might find peace', as Chamberlain hoped, Hitler initiated a war of nerves that engulfed the chancelleries of Europe. In a matter of weeks, there was again talk of war, and each of the participants in the Munich conference accelerated his rearmament programme. Hitler and Mussolini took the initiative; each planned for future aggression. The former intended not only to secure what he felt he had lost through the intervention of Chamberlain and Daladier, but to accelerate the military build-up needed to achieve his more extended ambitions in Europe. Mussolini believed the moment ripe to separate Britain and France, and begin his expansionist campaign by demanding territorial concessions from France in East Africa. While Chamberlain had every intention of building on what had been achieved at Munich, he was forced, by his cabinet colleagues and military advisers, to sanction an enlarged rearmament budget which he feared would undermine the economic well-being of Britain and unleash the very armaments race that he hoped to avoid. *Kristallnacht* proved a powerful blow to the prime minister's hopes of separating Hitler's domestic and foreign policy in the public mind. The sheer brutality of the Nazi attack on the Jews shocked the British nation, and raised uncomfortable questions about future arrangements with Germany. There was cross-party condemnation of the Nazi methods, and criticism of the British government's level of intervention. Chamberlain was not impervious to the impact of this response. The French, with the most to lose if Germany and Italy renewed their attacks, began to stir. Daladier recovered his courage and embarked on a programme of domestic reform, intended to result in a more resolute policy should the attempts at conciliating the dictators fail. In the new year, the British accepted what they had refused to concede since 1919, the promise of military support for France and joint staff talks. It was but the first step in what became a radical transformation in British policy, and a new Anglo-French strategy to avoid the war that neither country wanted.

It is easy to understand why Hitler considered Munich a major defeat: he had been forced to settle for his ostensible aims, not his real ones. He had been prevented from launching the rapid war that would have given him Czechoslovakia, with all the domestic advantages that an easy victory would have brought. For a man driven by his own sense of mortality and belief in his own unlimited power, the set-back, however temporary, was intolerable. In later years, he was to claim that Munich was the greatest error of his career. Reflecting in his Berlin bunker in February 1945 on the causes of the German failure, he lamented:

> What we ought then to have done was to have struck at once. We ought to have gone to war in 1938. It was the last chance we had of localizing the war. But they gave way all along the line and . . . ceded to all our demands. Under such conditions it was very difficult to seize the initiative and commence hostilities. At Munich we lost a unique opportunity of easily and swiftly winning a war that was in any case inevitable. Although we ourselves were not fully prepared, we were nevertheless better prepared than the enemy. September 1938 would have been the most favourable date.[1]

Hitler stepped back for reasons he immediately regretted. The behaviour of Chamberlain and Daladier at Munich convinced him that the 'little worms' would not have fought—they were bluffing. The more he thought about Munich, the angrier he became. Britain, and Chamberlain in particular, had deprived him of the fruits of victory by subjecting him to the ignominy of an international agreement. The praise lavished on the British prime minister, even within Germany, enraged him. At a speech soon after the conference, at Saarbrücken on 9 October, Hitler paid tribute to Mussolini, Germany's 'one true friend', and gave voice to his anger. 'It would be a good thing if in Great Britain people would gradually drop certain airs which they have inherited from the Versailles epoch', he declared. 'We cannot tolerate any longer the tutelage of governesses!'[2] The Führer's public comments were accompanied by a violent press campaign against the 'Churchill–Eden–Duff Cooper clique' and British rearmament. His private remarks about Chamberlain, that 'desiccated stick', became common knowledge in London.

[1] François Genoud (ed.), *The Testament of Adolph Hitler: The Hitler–Bormann Documents, February–April 1945*, trans. by R. H. Stevens, with an introduction by H. R. Trevor-Roper (London, 1961), 84–85.

[2] Hitler's speech at Saarbrücken, 9 October 1938, in *Documents on International Affairs, 1938*, Vol. II (London, 1943), 337–340.

It was necessary to put matters right as quickly as possible. Ever since he had taken power, Hitler had appeared publicly as the man of peace. His intentions were always to lead the German people to war, but until the German army was ready for the European struggle he rarely showed his bellicose side in public. Steps were now taken to make the German people 'war-worthy'. In the weeks after Munich, the German press was ordered to stress the need for increases in armaments. On 10 November, Hitler spoke to a gathering of 400 invited journalists: 'It was only out of necessity that for years I talked of peace. But it was now necessary gradually to re-educate the German people psychologically and make it clear that there are things which *must* be achieved by force.'[3] Congratulated on their propaganda work, the journalists were told that the 'pacifist record' was played out. Believing that Germany might have to fight in the West before moving East, work on the West Wall was intensified and a gigantic programme of rearmament announced by Göring on 14 October included a five-fold increase in the *Luftwaffe*, orders for large amounts of offensive weapons, particularly heavy artillery, tanks for the army, and an acceleration in naval construction. Almost a quarter of Germany's steel production was allotted to the *Wehrmacht* to complete the build-up already begun. Within four years, the *Luftwaffe* was to reach a strength of 21,000 aircraft. In addition to the 7,000 Ju88 medium bombers planned five months earlier, there were to be over 800 heavy four-engined bombers and longer-range fighter escorts and interceptors. The navy was to launch a huge building programme so that it could compete with the British fleet within six years. In December, it was agreed to construct six giant battleships followed by a fleet of 249 U-boats and eight long-range cruisers.[4] The fiscal and economic implications of this enormous programme were staggering.

To fulfil these goals, coming on top of the accelerated programme which followed the May crisis, those responsible for implementing the programme realized that it would be necessary to reorganize the German economy. In October and November, an effort was made to co-ordinate the Reich's armaments schedules and to work out a common strategy between Göring, the leaders of the *Wehrmacht*, and Ribbentrop's Foreign Ministry. Not unexpectedly, given the competitive nature of the Reich's bureaucracies, the effort failed.[5] The October plans were, in any case, entirely utopian. Neither the air force nor the

[3] Speech in J. Noakes and G. Pridham (ed.), *Nazism, 1919–1945, Volume III: Foreign Policy, War and Racial Extermination: A Documentary Reader*, reprint (Exeter, 1995), 721–724.

[4] Adam Tooze, *The Wages of Destruction*, 288.

[5] See the discussion in Tooze, *The Wages of Destruction*, 292–293.

naval targets were within the realm of the possible. Yet at the end of October, the *Luftwaffe* general staff submitted a programme based on Göring's requirements. Monthly aircraft production figures were actually dropping, as shortages of skilled workers and raw materials created bottle-necks in production, but drafts were prepared for the new procurement programmes. If the projected wartime *Luftwaffe* was to be kept ready for action for a lengthy period after the start of the war, it would be necessary to import 85% of the world's total oil production to fill as yet non-existent storage tanks.[6] Meanwhile the *Luftwaffe*, with Britain added to the list of enemies, needed to develop new planes, new operational plans, and new training programmes, all of which existed only in the most embryonic form. The naval figures were similarly beyond Germany's reach. On 27 January 1939, Hitler signed a special decree giving the navy's requirements priority over both the other two services, a directive only successfully challenged by Göring at the end of August 1939. Yet the 'Z' programme, given the shortages of dockyard space and the absence of skilled labour and raw materials, could not be fulfilled in peacetime. The fuel oil requirements for mobilization alone far outstripped what Germany could produce domestically or could meet through the advanced storage of fuel. Oil was the German Achilles heel. Even in peacetime, German production of fuels of all kinds covered less than half the amount the country was consuming. In wartime, requirements would more than double, depending on the extent of the German military operations.

Not unexpectedly, the programmes ran into serious financial difficulties. 'By the end of the year', Adam Tooze has argued, 'the Reich found itself facing both a cash-flow crisis and a severe squeeze on its foreign exchange account, blocking any substantial progress toward Hitler's target of tripling armaments production'.[7] The heads of the *Reichsbank*, knowing that they could not cover the huge budgetary deficit, warned that if an inflationary disaster was to be avoided, the total *Wehrmacht* spending would have to be cut. Hitler was not interested in the bankers' fears. Schacht and two of his colleagues were dismissed on 20 January 1939 and Schacht replaced by the more compliant Walther Funk. In June, all formal limitations on the expansion of the money supply were removed. In practice, if not in theory, Germany had abandoned the gold standard and monetary restrictions on rearmament were lifted. The *Wehrmacht* did not get all that it wanted but the large-scale military spending of 1938 was maintained. To ease the

[6] Militärgeschichtliches Forschungsamt (ed.), *Germany and the Second World War. Volume I: The Build-up of German Aggression*, ed. Wilhelm Deist (Oxford, 1990), 500–501.

[7] Tooze, *Wages of Destruction*, 295.

cash-flow problem, the New Finance Plan of March 1939 compelled suppliers of goods and services to accept payment of at least 40% of their contract value in the form of tax credits, to be offset against tax liabilities in the future. The Reich had secured a low-interest loan to cover the costs of the Four-Year Plan. Even then, the results were far less satisfactory than had been hoped. Apart from a squeeze on the liquidity of the Reich's contractors, there was still a large financial gap between spending, and tax revenues and safe long-term borrowing. The budgetary shortfall had to be covered by short-term credit from the *Reichsbank*, a practice that amounted to printing money.

These measures, freeing the rearmament programmes from domestic financial constraints, did not solve the problem of the balance of payments and the shortages of foreign currency needed to buy raw materials. To correct the deteriorating balance of trade situation, Germany would have to launch a major export campaign. In early November, the *Wehrmacht* was told that export orders would take priority over all other contracts. In his infamous speech to the Reichstag on 30 January, when Hitler warned of the destruction of European Jewry, he also appealed for German discipline and resolve in the light of the nation's economic difficulties. As the 'one-time victorious powers' (referring to the United States as well as Britain) would not allow 'an expansion of *Lebensraum* for our *Volk,* we must export in order to be able to purchase food from abroad. Since these exported goods use up raw materials which we ourselves do not possess we must export yet more goods to secure these raw materials for our economy.'[8] Unable to expand territorially, Germany had no choice but to 'export or perish'. Hitler made clear that this was a national emergency, which required a unified National Socialist leadership and the co-operation of all Germans. The new export programme had already been initiated. Exports were given the highest priority, and a massive cut-back in steel allocations to the army and air force was announced at the end of November. The army faced cuts in its steel ration which were put back almost to 1937 levels; ammunition production, weapons programmes, and tank production were all affected. The *Luftwaffe* production schedules of 1938–1939 were maintained only by reducing the targets for 1939 and 1940, and shifting more and more output to 1941 and 1942. The range of aircraft included in production plans was reduced, so as to concentrate on fewer models. The armaments slump of 1939, whose full effects would be felt in the spring, was far more dramatic than that of 1937, and far more dangerous, given the growing possibility of war. Only the navy was exempt from

[8] Max Domarus (ed.), *Hitler: Speeches and Proclamations 1932–1945*, Vol. 3 (London, 1990), 1443–1444.

Table 12.1 Military Spending as Percentage of National Income, 1933–1941

	Britain	Germany	Soviet Union	USA
1933	3	2		
1934	3	4		
1935	2	6		
1936	5	11		
1937	7	12	8	
1938	8	17		
1939	16	25		1
1940	48	44	20	1
1941	55	56		13

Source: These figures were kindly provided by Dr Adam Tooze.

the sudden contraction of available resources. Its relatively small steel requirements continued to rise, and its construction programmes did not suffer from shortages of materials. In any case, Plan Z, in giving priority to a whole new generation of giant battleships and the dockyards needed to construct them, would take many years to complete.[9]

While it is important to stress the growing gap between the German rearmament programme and the ability of the German economy to meet it, it must be understood that Germany had a formidable war machine coming into existence. During 1938, the German military was consuming 17% of national production, twice the level of Britain or France and with a productive base larger than either of theirs. In 1939, the German percentage figure increased to almost 20%.

Anschluss and occupation of the Sudetenland added seven divisions to the *Wehrmacht*. Germany was fully prepared to fight a short war and could easily defeat Poland. On land, at least, its defensive position was rapidly improving, though it was still unclear how it could win the war against Britain and France, a problem which preoccupied Hitler's domestic critics. This did not prevent the Führer from thinking of such a conflict even as he laid plans for the elimination of Czechoslovakia.

II

The pace of Nazi radicalization began to quicken. The Jews were the victims. A new wave of anti-Semitic violence, far worse than that of 1933 and 1935, started in the spring of 1938 and gained momentum

[9] All this information is from Adam Tooze, *Wages of Destruction*, 302–304.

during the summer and autumn. The March events in Vienna inspired the Nazi leaders to take action in the cities of the 'Old Reich'. A flood of discriminatory restrictions and occupational bans was carried out by Nazi party members, accompanied by attacks on Jewish property and on individual Jews. Sparked by Goebbels's summer campaign for the 'racial cleansing' of Berlin, it was only stopped because of Hitler's concern for Germany's image during the Munich conference. The violence spread to Frankfurt, Magdeburg, and other towns and cities. The conference over, the pressure to exclude Jews from the economy and speed up their emigration mounted as did the outbursts of violence in different parts of Germany. Adolf Eichmann, the architect of the Vienna expulsions, had suggested earlier that a pogrom would hasten the Jewish exodus from Germany. Goebbels was soon given the opportunity to act.

The assassination on 7 November of a German diplomat in Paris by a 17-year-old Jew, Herschel Grynszpan, provided the needed occasion. Grynszpan was driven to despair by the deportation of his parents to Poland, just two among thousands of other Polish Jews recently sent back by the Gestapo. Goebbels prepared the way for retribution by making the murder front-page news. On 9 November 1938, at a meeting of the party's 'old guard' at the Old Town Hall in Munich, Goebbels and Hitler conferred. The Führer, Goebbels recorded in his diary, decided that 'the Jews should for once get to feel the anger of the people'.[10] The SA was unleashed, and most Germans stood by as a series of attacks were made on Jews and Jewish property during the night of 9–10 November, known as *Kristallnacht* or 'the night of broken glass'. What began in Munich spread to the rest of the country. The 'action' was called off the next day after Goebbels had spoken with Hitler. About a hundred synagogues were demolished and several hundred others burned. Some 8,000 shops were destroyed and countless apartments vandalized. Individual Jews were attacked and beaten; over ninety were killed and others committed suicide. The SS made a late entrance, arresting some 26,000 of the wealthier Jews who were taken off to concentration camps to be released when they promised to emigrate. Göring was quick to re-assert his authority. On 12 November, he set out his policy of planned expropriation. 'Demonstrations' were to stop. Jews were to surrender all their property to the state in return for compensation, which was to be kept as low as possible. The Reich, and not individuals, as happened in Austria, was to be the beneficiary. The Jewish community, as compensation for the death of Rath, was to pay a fine of one billion Reichsmarks while repairing all the damage

[10] *Die Tagebücher von Joseph Goebbels*, part I, vol. 6, p. 180; quoted in Ian Kershaw, *Hitler, Vol. II: Nemesis, 1936–1945* (London, 2000), 138.

Table 12.2 Emigration from Germany, 1933–1938

Year	Number of emigrants during the year	Total from 1933 onwards
1933	37,000	37,000
1934	23,000	60,000
1935	21,000	81,000
1936	25,000	106,000
1937	23,000	129,000
1938 (first half)	14,000	143,000

Source: Werner Rosenstock, 'Exodus 1933–1939: A Survey of Jewish Emigration from Germany', *Leo Baeck Institute Yearbook*, 377.

done (insurance claims were forfeited to the Reich). The German government had already made a financial killing from the earlier expropriation of Austrian and German Jewry; in the next months all the sources of Jewish wealth were in its hands. The amounts provided momentary relief at a time when the Reich's finances were under extreme pressure but apart from impoverishing the Jewish community and making emigration more difficult, the total amount was hardly a major item in the Reich budget.

On 12 November, Göring ordered the cessation of all Jewish business activity. By 1 January, Jews had to sell all their enterprises, land, stocks, jewels, art works, and valuables. New decrees excluded them from the general welfare state and cut them off from all forms of public life, theatres, cinemas, cabarets, concert halls, museums, libraries, and sports facilities. Jewish children were excluded from German schools. Though these and other measures were intended to isolate, demean, and impoverish the Jewish community, their main purpose was to drive the Jews out of Germany. With the possibility of war looming, forced emigration rose to the top of the Reich's anti-Semitic agenda. After the initial flood of Jews leaving Germany in 1933, the annual number leaving dropped to about 20,000–25,000 a year.

At that rate, it would take a long time for Germany to become *judenrein*. The enactment of the Nuremberg Laws in November 1935, disenfranchizing and segregating Jews, brought another upsurge of flight, but the laws were seen by some Jews, as well as Germans, as establishing a permanent framework of discrimination that would end the previous reign of arbitrary terror. Many Jews believed that the worst was over; a surprising number who had left Germany actually returned. It was only in late 1937 that the German Jewish population began to understand that the liquidation of Jewish economic life and enforced

Aryanization were at the centre of the Nazi anti-Semitic programme. *Anschluss* was a wake-up call, but it was *Kristallnacht* that sounded the alarm and began an unregulated flood of refugees from Germany to any country that would take them. The Reich authorities, though anxious for the Jews to leave, were unwilling to forego the financial benefits to be gained from Jewish emigration or to use their own limited foreign exchange reserves to facilitate their expulsion. There were some 500,000 Jews left in Germany in the autumn of 1938. In so far as *Kristallnacht* was intended to speed up the emigration of the Jews, it succeeded in its purpose. The flood of those wanting to leave became a torrent. Flight was difficult, both the leaving of Germany and the finding of a place of refuge was a tortuous process with obstacles raised at both ends. The German Jews were the most assimilated in Europe; they could not avail themselves of the refugee organizations set up by Orthodox Jewry and Zionists, which proved to be the most effective of the voluntary groups assisting emigration and settlement. Apart from the children, the majority of those adults who fled Austria and Germany were under forty, healthy, and prosperous. But Jews were not wanted either by the Germans or by the overwhelming majority of the world's nation-states. The international response was muted indignation, but very little action. At Munich, the British and French accepted the principle that a national frontier should be re-drawn to place ethnic Germans under German rule, and that non-Germans should be removed from the annexed territories. This represented one of the unfortunate legacies of the nationalities settlements of 1919. The hopes of the peace-makers that the League of Nations would correct any resulting injustices were entirely misplaced, as the international mechanisms for dealing with refugees were almost totally shattered by the Jewish refugee crisis (see pp. 177–8).

Kristallnacht had an additional purpose. It was specifically intended to stifle the euphoria in Germany created by Munich, and to focus attention on the ever-present internal enemies of the Reich. The assault on the Jews, however, provoked a chorus of disapproval among Germans, despite their passivity during the attacks, and world-wide condemnation. Senior Nazis, like Göring and Speer, were more upset by the wanton destruction of property, German as well as Jewish, than by the treatment of the Jews. The reaction outside Germany was sharpest in the United States and in Britain. President Roosevelt recalled the American ambassador from Berlin (though diplomatic relations were maintained) and the 15,000 German and Austrian refugees on visitors' visas were allowed to stay in America. Only the intervention of Cordell Hull prevented the United States Treasury from imposing severe punitive tariffs on German exports. Strong parliamentary criticism from both sides of the Commons closed the door to negotiations with Germany. Lord Halifax used the growing public abhorrence of the Nazi regime to legitimize his opposition to continuing the talks and the cabinet fully supported him. Official protests were rejected, however, in favour of private representations and reports of the parliamentary debates, which were forwarded to Berlin to underline the British message. From London, Ambassador Dirksen warned of the negative effects of the pogrom on British opinion, but Ribbentrop as well as Himmler and Heydrich felt there was no need to worry about foreign reactions to German treatment of their own Jews, and blamed the Jewish-controlled press for the adverse comment. Their response only confirmed Hitler's assumptions about Jewish power.

Ignoring the expressions of indignation at home and abroad, Hitler made no direct reference to what had happened either at the time or later, not even to his 'inner circle'. The day after *Kristallnacht*, disregarding the previous day's events, he publicly commented on the dangers inherent in an exaggerated attempt to maintain peace. Despite his public distancing from the events of 9 November, *Kristallnacht* made a profound impression on him. Thinking in terms of the forthcoming war, the connection between the Jews and the German defeat in 1918, discussed in the last chapter of *Mein Kampf*, took on a new relevance. In Hitler's distorted mind, the German Jews were part of the 'world Jewish conspiracy' and had to pay the price for the actions of their race in threatening the existence of the Reich. The United States was increasingly seen as the centre of the concerted Jewish action against Germany, and President Roosevelt was depicted as the tool of 'world Jewry'. Roosevelt's State of the Union address on 4 January, with its veiled but unmistakable attack on Nazi practices, set off a vicious anti-Semitic and anti-American press campaign.[11] Crude cartoons hammered home the image of an American president surrounded by his Jewish advisers. While the Roosevelt administration never placed the persecution of the Jews at the centre of its policy towards Germany, anti-Semitism became increasingly important in the Nazi view of America.

Hitler's ruminations on the Jewish question took on an implicit genocidal form in his over two-hour speech delivered to the Reichstag on 30 January 1939, celebrating the sixth anniversary of his appointment to the chancellorship. Centred on Germany's economic difficulties and the need for a new chapter in Nazi economic policy, numerous references were made to the 'Jewish world enemy' determined to 'exterminate' the German people. The Reichstag was treated to sardonic references to Anglo-American demands for German monetary assistance

[11] Tooze, *Wages of Destruction*, 281–284.

to facilitate Jewish emigration. Half way through his speech, Hitler warned that although the 'Jewish world enemy' had been defeated within Germany, the Jews now confronted it from abroad, spreading scandalous propaganda through their control of the media in order to drive 'millions among the masses of people into a conflict that is utterly senseless for them and serves only Jewish interests'. For the first time since the 1920s, Hitler returned to the open threat of mass murder of the 'Jewish race in Europe'.[12]

Hitler was not to forget this awesome prophecy that took on proportions that even he might not have imagined possible in 1939. In at least four subsequent speeches broadcast on radio and published in the German and world press, Hitler repeated his prophecy. He did so twice again in speeches to Nazi officials, read in his absence on 15 February 1942 and 24 February 1943. And in his final reflections in 1945, Hitler referred once more, with evident satisfaction, to his earlier prediction. 'I told them that, if they precipitated another war, they would not be spared', he said, 'and that I would exterminate the vermin throughout Europe, once and for all'.[13]

III

In the weeks after Munich, Hitler's impatience with the restraints on his freedom of action was directed not just at Britain, but at the settlement itself. Though the Germans got more than was promised at Munich, Hitler viewed the international commission as a burdensome irrelevance. With Weizsäcker as the chairman and the Germans in the driving seat, the representatives of the three other powers agreed to the transfer of all territories with a 51% German–Czech ratio based on the last pre-war census of 1910, which was far more favourable to German claims than the 1930 census proposed by the Czechs. Once again, the latter were summoned and forced to accept a *fait accompli*. Subsequent territorial changes resulted in a further 30,000 Czechs and 6,000 Germans passing under German rule. Hitler was far from satisfied: he would have liked to have moved militarily against Czechoslovakia almost immediately. While caution prevailed, the future tasks of the *Wehrmacht*,

[12] Domarus (ed.), *Hitler: Speeches and Proclamations, 1931–45*, Vol. 3, 1449. See Herf, *The Jewish Enemy*, 52. For full quotation see my earlier reference, p. 17.

[13] Genoud (ed.), *The Testament of Adolf Hitler*, 66.

outlined in a military directive signed by Hitler on 21 October 1938, included the liquidation of the remainder of the Czech state, and the occupation of Memel, the Baltic port under Lithuanian control since the *coup* of 1923, but enjoying autonomous status guaranteed by international statute. Overawed by Hitler's correct appraisal of the west in September, the *Wehrmacht* generals no longer debated strategic questions. They put their trust in Hitler's judgment and accepted their exclusion from strategic planning, preparing only for the next specified campaign. During the winter, Hitler addressed selected groups of officers, intending to inculcate in his men a sense of racial superiority and ideological correctness that would turn them into enthusiastic followers. He exhorted his listeners to have confidence in his ideas which were 'carefully thought out and unalterable', while shedding little light on what they were. The *Wehrmacht* leadership neither questioned the effects of Hitler's changing priorities on their planning, nor protested against the regime's unrealistic rearmament demands. The anti-Hitler military opposition was left despondent and paralysed.

The signs that Hitler was thinking in terms of a war in the west before turning East, pre-date the September crisis, but Chamberlain's intervention and obstruction concentrated his mind. He was determined never again to be manoeuvred into an international conference and told what he could or could not do. Britain and France would have to be defeated to prevent them from interfering with the future conquest of *Lebensraum* in the east. Poland would be brought within the German orbit to destroy the Franco-Polish alliance, and Germany's economic domination over Eastern Europe extended to broaden the country's raw material base. To move against his western foes, he needed the military alliances with Italy and Japan which Ribbentrop assured him were within easy reach. Some insight into Hitler's strategic thinking in the autumn of 1938 can be found in General Keitel's 'Notes for *Wehrmacht* discussions with Italy', sent to Ribbentrop at the end of November 1938 when the latter was promoting the German–Italian–Japanese military alliance. The 'basic military–political' aim was: 'War by Germany and Italy against France and Britain, with the object of first knocking out France. That would also hit Britain, as she would lose her bases for carrying on the war on the Continent and would then find the whole power of Germany and Italy directed against herself alone.' Belgium, Holland, and Switzerland were to be kept neutral, Spain and Hungary were expected to show 'benevolent neutrality', the Soviet Union would be 'hostile', and Poland and the Balkans would be of 'doubtful attitude'. Germany would concentrate on breaking through the Maginot Line and eliminating France from the war. The naval war would be directed against British and French communications in the North Sea and the Atlantic. An air offensive would be directed against Britain, and the German air and naval forces would combine to cut off its sea routes. The Italians were to carry out diversionary operations against the two western powers, and ward off attacks against Germany's southern and eastern flanks.[14] So much for Chamberlain's hopes for the 'larger settlement in which all Europe may find peace'.

IV

For that is what the British prime minister believed he had put in train at Munich. During those incredibly intense and stressful days—three trips to Germany involving uncomfortable air, train, and car journeys, and multiple meetings that went on past midnight—Chamberlain had kept two aims in mind. The first was to prevent war, and the second was to reach an understanding with Germany resolving all points of difference. He had achieved the first goal; he believed that he had laid the basis for the second. He continued to assume that Hitler spoke the truth when he said the 'object of his policy was racial unity and not the domination of Europe', and did not anticipate further demands. Even accounting for the heady mixture of fatigue and triumph that marked his return from Munich, he appears to have thought that the paper that bore his name and Hitler's was a promise of peace for the future. The prime minister came back hoping that the way was clear for an agreement with the 'Dictator Powers' that would stop the armaments race.

He had a less easy time in the Commons than he expected, given the outpouring of gratitude and good wishes—20,000 letters and telegrams between late September and early October—that followed his return. Despite an overwhelming majority in the government's favour, 366 votes to 144, there were important 'doubters', even in the Conservative ranks. Only Duff Cooper resigned from the cabinet, but thirty Conservative MPs abstained from voting and twelve of these, including Churchill, remained seated during the division on Munich, as a further protest against the government's policies. Apart from that of the prime minister, it was Churchill's speech that was most widely reported even in the Chamberlainite press. Labelling Munich as 'a total and unmitigated defeat', Churchill warned that

> this is only the beginning of the reckoning. This is only the first sip, the first foretaste of a bitter cup which will be proffered to us year by year unless by a supreme recovery of moral health and martial vigour, we arise again and take our stand for freedom as in the olden time . . . [I]n future the Czechoslovak State

[14] *DGFP*, Ser. D, Vol. IV, No. 411 (Keitel to Ribbentrop, 30 November 1938).

cannot be maintained as an independent entity. You will find that in a period of time which may be measured by years, but may be measured only by months, Czechoslovakia will be engulfed in the Nazi regime.[15]

Churchill's prophetic words, so tragically confirmed within months, established his position as the central voice of opposition to the policy of appeasement. Hitler's repeated denunciations only enhanced that reputation. Those sharing Churchill's views embraced a wide variety of politicians, spread across the political spectrum. However vocal and individually influential, Chamberlain's opponents did not constitute a solid block of opposition, nor did their views reflect majority opinion. The prime minister's position in his party and in the Commons seemed unassailable. Eden and Churchill each harboured hopes of joining his cabinet. While the prime minister was sensitive enough to the unease in the Commons to stress the need for rearmament, as demanded by his own supporters, he had no wish, and could not be compelled, to broaden the base of his cabinet either by bringing Eden back or admitting Churchill, viewing the latter as his most formidable political rival as well as an obstacle to negotiations with Hitler. Chamberlain found the Commons debate 'a pretty trying ordeal', and complained that 'all the world seemed to be full of my praises except the House of Commons'.[16] He looked forward to an early general election, in which his foreign policy performance would provide the *pièce de résistance*, enabling him to ignore the doubters and get on with disarmament. Despite the efforts made to popularize the case for appeasement, and they extended both to the press and the BBC and included censorship of the most blatant kind, the change in public feeling after *Kristallnacht* was palpable. In the by-elections held before the end of 1938, the Conservative majorities were hardly those expected from a grateful electorate. The party actually lost two seats, one to an independent candidate, the journalist and broadcaster Vernon Bartlett, who fought on an anti-appeasement platform. The government intervened to prevent newspapers from detailing the work of the International Commission, and dodged queries about the promised international guarantee to Czechoslovakia. The gulf between the prime minister and his colleagues, revealed after Godesberg, was never fully bridged. Contrary to Chamberlain's intentions, the cabinet insisted on reconsidering the current rearmament programmes. Their demands were backed by the Foreign Office and service ministries, who viewed Munich primarily as a means of postponing war. Chamberlain's response was at best equivocal. 'Ever

[15] *Hansard*, HC Deb, 5 October 1938, Vol. 339, Col. 373.

[16] Quoted in R. A. C. Parker, *Chamberlain and Appeasement*, 184.

since he had been chancellor of the exchequer, he had been oppressed with the sense that the burden of armaments might break our backs', Chamberlain told the cabinet on 3 October. 'This had been one of the factors which had led him to the view that it was necessary to try and resolve the causes which were responsible for the armament race'.[17] During October and November, as the services presented their demands for increased defence estimates, and pressure mounted for the establishment of a Ministry of Supply, the prime minister dragged his feet.

Chamberlain's efforts to build on Munich were, in the first instance, undermined by Hitler himself. The latter's speeches, rumours of his ambitions in the Ukraine and in south-east Europe, evidence of German rearmament, and the impact of *Kristallnacht,* meant the prime minister had to accept Halifax's conclusion that the road to Berlin was temporarily blocked. There could be no question of resuming the colonial negotiations broken off at the time of the *Anschluss*. Leo Amery, the colonial secretary, argued that any cession of territory to Germany, or even a discussion of it, was more likely to lead to war than peace. While the German people might want peace, Chamberlain judged, it was not at all certain that the same was true of 'the crazy persons who had managed to secure control of the country'.[18] Any attempt to forward the peace process in Berlin would depend on a change of German policy. Chamberlain turned his attention to Mussolini. Though he suffered some doubts about the meeting in view of the public mood, he still hoped that a visit to Rome and a 'heart-to-heart talk' with the Duce could help the latter 'escape from the German toils'. Totally misjudging Mussolini, the prime minister thought he could enlist the Duce in his thwarted campaign to make Hitler see reason.

For Édouard Daladier, Munich was a humiliation. When he met Hitler there for the first time he knew, as he had already said in London, that the German chancellor's 'purpose was to establish his domination over Europe'. Little redeemed his conduct at Munich. Czechoslovakia was France's ally and little was done to save it. French impotence had been graphically revealed. Its strategic interests and extensive financial investment had been sacrificed, and the Germans were the beneficiaries. Daladier's tumultuous reception in Paris stunned him. Responding to the hurrahs of the crowd, he commented to Léger, 'The people are crazy.' All that mattered to those who cheered his triumphal drive into Paris was that peace was saved. Daladier knew that the reprieve was

[17] Cabinet meeting, 3 October 1938. TNA: PRO, CAB 23/95.

[18] Quoted in D. Dilks, '"We Must Hope for the Best and Prepare for the Worst": The Prime Minister, the Cabinet and Hitler's Germany, 1937–1939', *Proceedings of the British Academy*, 73 (1987), 334.

temporary. Nonetheless, he defended the settlement in his report to the Chamber of Deputies. The debate that followed was short, and the vote overwhelmingly in favour of the agreement, with 535 votes for the government and seventy-five opposed (including the seventy-three Communist deputies). The anti-appeasers in the Daladier cabinet sat silent. Most of France was overwhelmingly *munchois*, with only the Communists resolutely in opposition. All the newspapers, with the exception of *L'Humanité*, welcomed the outcome. At the same time, according to the prefectorial and police reports, many Frenchmen believed that war would come, an idea they accepted without enthusiasm, but with some measure of support. The political mood altered as the sense of deliverance faded. In the aftermath of Munich, Daladier, always hesitant about taking decisions, sought advice, and postponed making any choice between the alternatives proposed by his advisers. Apart from seeking to strengthen the ties with Britain, on which everyone was agreed, the premier kept an open mind as to what France should do next. His attention was concentrated instead on the problems of French finances and the economy. At the 4 October meeting of the Chamber of Deputies, Daladier demanded and received full financial and economic plenary powers to implement a state of 'permanent mobilization'. In contrast to the Munich vote, the division figures were 331 votes against seventy-eight, 203 deputies abstained (mainly from the Socialist parties). The parties of the centre-right and moderate-right supported Daladier. This vote heralded his shift to the right and the destruction of the electoral basis of the Popular Front coalition. Bonnet remained as foreign minister but the subsequent success of the government's domestic policies encouraged Daladier to take a more active part in charting French foreign policy.

V

The diplomatic initiative, after Munich, rested with the Führer. Only the most deluded observer could have expected that he would remain inactive. Hitler's recourse to Ribbentrop to carry out his orders created some confusion during the next few months. The ignorant, haughty, and fundamentally dishonest German foreign minister, who had few friends in Berlin or at the German Foreign Ministry, was challenged by foreign policy initiatives from Goebbels and Göring. Nor was he much liked by Hitler, who kept him at a distance and rarely invited him to Berchtesgaden. Ribbentrop had to rely on an intermediary, an ex-Dienstelle official, Walther Hewel, Hitler's cellmate at Landsberg in 1923. Hewel, a highly entertaining companion with a fund of comic Ribbentrop stories, shared the prevailing Wilhelmstrasse view of the foreign minister, but was too lightweight a figure, or perhaps too shrewd an operator, to meddle in political affairs. As a consequence, Hitler, who, in any case, despised the diplomatic service, depended on his own instincts and on digests of the foreign press for his understanding of the outside world. Nonetheless, he allowed Ribbentrop a good deal of freedom, and encouraged him to rush around Europe, hoping to deliver the diplomatic alignments needed for the forthcoming war.

Even as Hitler pushed forward his preparations for war, he had to finish what was left unsettled at Munich. At the time of the 21 October directive ordering the destruction of Czechoslovakia, Hitler spoke of mid-March as his target date. The military orders were accompanied by covert financial and political support for Slovak independence, for Slovakia was to play the same role as the Sudetenland before Munich. The expectation was that Czechoslovakia would collapse through internal disintegration. When the moment was ripe, German troops would be sent in for the final act. This could be done without any planned mobilization, so as not to alert the Czechs or produce a forceful reaction from the western powers. The Czechs were bullied and humiliated; Hitler's old anti-Czech sentiments were compounded by his annoyance that the prey had escaped his trap. The Prague government accepted almost every German demand in the vain hope that submission would secure a semi-autonomous position for the truncated state. Hitler soon realized that neither Britain nor France would take the guarantee of the Czechoslovakian settlement seriously. Whether from a sense of helplessness, fatigue, or guilt, or a combination of all three, little was done in London or Paris either to strengthen the guarantee, or to offer sufficient financial and economic assistance to stabilize Czechoslovakia. The financial assistance that was given was not expected to encourage Czech resistance to Hitler's demands. The true position was spelled out in a German *note verbale* addressed to the two western powers on 28 February 1939, much of which was written by Hitler himself. As the French ambassador in London commented, 'Decoded, this message means that the western powers no longer have any right to look in the direction of Central Europe.'[19] There were moves in London to assist political refugees, that is, the Sudeten Germans and old Reich refugees. Many went on to Canada which was given 'landing money' to facilitate their entry. Before and after the German march into Prague, both official and private arrangements were made to bring out Czech refugees. The Jews were put at the very bottom of their priority lists, though this was the group that the Gestapo most wanted to leave.

[19] Quoted in Telford Taylor, *Munich: The Price of Peace*, 922.

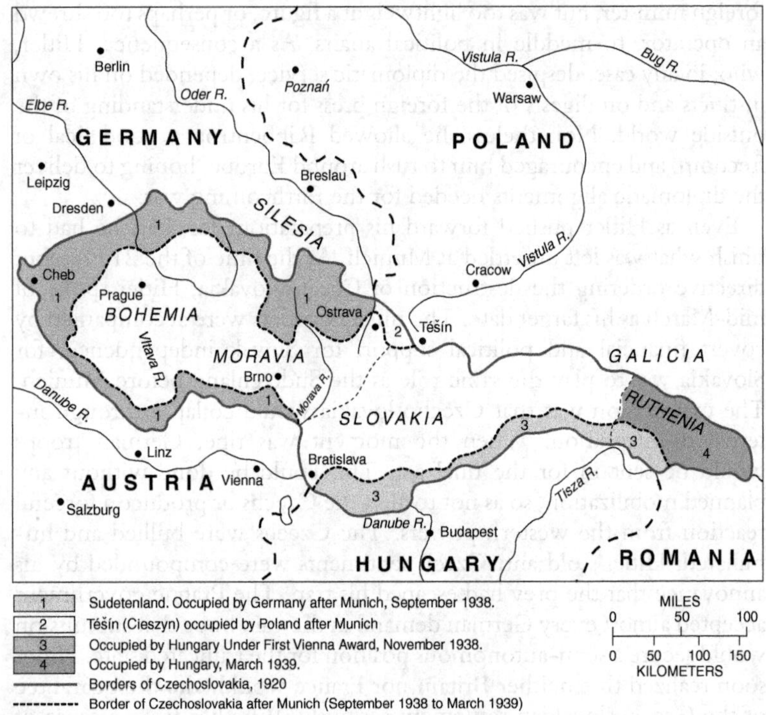

Map 9. The Dismemberment of Czechoslovakia, 1938–1939

Hitler anticipated that the Poles and Hungarians would assist in the destruction of Czechoslovakia; the former would take Teschen and the latter Slovakia and Ruthenia (Carpatho-Ukraine). The Poles played their part as expected; an ultimatum was sent to Prague on 1 October demanding cession of part of Teschen within twenty-four hours, and the rest in ten days. The Czechs quickly capitulated. This was not the case with the Hungarians, whose claims to a large part of Slovakia and to all of Ruthenia, a mountainous and undeveloped part of Czechoslovakia separating Hungary from Poland, were far more extensive than those of the Poles. Hungarian demands provoked varied reactions from its interested neighbours. The Slovaks, who had no wish to return to Hungarian rule, disputed fiercely over which territories should be ceded to Budapest. The Italians championed the Hungarian claims in Slovakia, hoping to create a Balkan bloc under Italian influence, as did the Poles, who sought the long-desired common Polish–Hungarian border. After Hitler rejected the Hungarian demand for all of Slovakia, attention was focused on Ruthenia, a poor and undeveloped region containing half a million Ruthenian peasants, 100,000 Magyars, 80,000 Jews, and some Romanians. Poland and the USSR both backed the Hungarians, mainly for fear of a revival of Ukrainian nationalism in their own territories. This was one of the few common bonds between these two states. The Romanians, on the contrary, as the chief beneficiary of the Hungarian peace treaty, pleaded with the Germans not to satisfy Budapest's claims. If Ruthenia, the eastern most tip of Czechoslovakia bordering on Romania, was given to Hungary, Bucharest would lose its direct route to central Czechoslovakia. Arms coming from Germany or Czechoslovakia would have to go through hostile Hungarian territory. An enlarged Hungary, moreover, might claim Transylvania, depriving Romania of one of the fruits of the 1919 peace treaty. Not even a Polish offer of a territorial bribe could modify Romanian opposition to the aggrandizement of Hungary. Having lost their Czech allies, the Romanians sought to cultivate Hitler. King Carol of Romania travelled to Berchtesgaden to begin commercial and political talks with the Germans. He expressed his strong opposition to Hungary's annexation of Ruthenia, but Hitler carefully avoided committing himself.

Various clandestine German organizations were active in Ruthenia; some of their activities dating back to the collapse of the independent Ukraine in 1918. These agencies favoured a semi-autonomous Ruthenia from which they could operate freely against Poland and the Soviet Union. The *Wehrmacht* and Foreign Ministry, traditionally anti-Polish, strongly opposed a common Polish–Hungarian border and any further Hungarian gains. Hitler appears to have decided by 8 October that he would not allow the Hungarians to occupy Ruthenia. Why had he changed his mind after positively encouraging the Hungarians at the time of Munich? Contrary to those who were urging retention of the region for nationalist purposes, he was not inclined to foster Ukrainian nationalism in a region that he hoped one day to populate with German farmers. Nor was he thinking, in the autumn of 1938, about using Ukrainian nationalism as a weapon against the Soviet Union. The Ukraine was not yet on Hitler's menu, despite rumours to the contrary. Possibly he was thinking of how the competing aspirations could be used to forward the wooing of Warsaw and contribute to the destruction of Czechoslovakia. For the moment, Ruthenia would remain as an autonomous unit within the rump state. Hitler could wait, preparing to extract a reward for what he might have given freely to Hungary, had he not been thwarted at Munich. In other words, Ruthenia was merely another diplomatic pawn to be used in the future.

Hitler insisted that Czechoslovakia and Hungary submit their dispute to German–Italian arbitration. While Ciano pressed Hungary's claims for Ruthenia and the common Hungarian–Polish border, Ribbentrop demanded that the Hungarians give way to Prague. Hitler ultimately intervened, and it was agreed that the foreign ministers of Germany, Italy, Czechoslovakia, and Hungary should meet in Vienna on 3 November 1938. The Vienna award, the result of this meeting, gave Hungary much, though not all, of what it had demanded in Slovakia and the southern strip of Ruthenia. The thwarted Hungarians expressed their appreciation of Ciano's efforts, but planned for an invasion of Ruthenia. Budapest's solicitations of support for military action from Rome and Warsaw, found the Italians cool and the Poles offering only verbal encouragement. Thanks to Hungarian bungling, the raid planned for 21 November never took place. An angry Hitler issued an ultimatum warning that any action taken against Ruthenia would be regarded as an unfriendly act. The result was just what Hitler wanted. Polish support for Hungary, and its own territorial demands in Slovakia, alienated the Slovaks. The Italians abandoned Hungary, and allowed the Germans to determine the future timetable. In December, Ciano paid a visit to Budapest in an attempt to mollify the Hungarians, still hoping that a bloc between Italy, Hungary, and Yugoslavia might emerge as a counterweight to Germany. The Germans, who annexed a small but strategically important piece of Slovak territory, now posed as the defenders of the Slovaks and Ukrainians against Hungary and Poland. Hitler could proceed without interference from Italy, and without reference to either Britain or France. He had also struck a blow, though the Polish politicians were slow to gauge its impact, at any Polish attempt to act as an arbiter in central Europe, and had acquired a useful carrot in the negotiations over Danzig and the 'Polish Corridor'. The Hungarians had no alternative. If they wanted their share of the Czech spoils they had to fall in line with Hitler's policies and wait for him to fulfil the promise of acquisitions. It was only on 12 March 1939, three days before his march into Prague, that Hitler instructed Budapest to seize its promised rewards. By the time the Hungarians took over, the German occupation of the Czech rump state (composed of Bohemia and Moravia), and their indirect control over Slovakia, more than compensated for any advantages Hungary and Poland might have gained from their participation in the Czech carve-up.

Hitler was playing a much larger Polish game in which Ruthenia was only one small piece. Poland was the vital link between the destruction of Czechoslovakia and the future war in the west. Using Ribbentrop as his intermediary, the Führer wanted to broker an agreement with Colonel Beck, Poland's all-powerful foreign minister, that would bring Danzig and the Polish Corridor back to the Reich but keep Poland as a friend. Such an arrangement, concluded before the liquidation of Czechoslovakia, would allow Hitler to plan his campaign against the west, with his rear covered and at a time of his own choosing, that is, before Britain and France rearmed. Negotiations began in mid-November; many subjects were discussed, including Polish participation in the Anti-Comintern pact, but the central issue was the status of Danzig. Ribbentrop insisted that it had to return to Germany; Beck refused to compromise. He thought that there was time for bargaining, as the Germans would need Polish goodwill to fulfil their plans to move against the Soviet Union. The Polish leaders thought that Hitler would modify Ribbentrop's position, assuming that the foreign minister was playing his own hand. They could not have been more mistaken. Hitler was impatient. He had been annoyed by the re-affirmation of the Polish–Soviet Non-Aggression Pact on 26 November, and by Polish support for the abortive Hungarian *coup* in Ruthenia. He was irritated, or so he claimed, by Polish mistreatment of the German minorities in the Teschen territory, particularly as he had imposed press silence over Polish abuse of the Germans in Upper Silesia and in other parts of Poland. He held back, too, on the annexation of Memel, though Lithuanian authorization of elections in December were bound to result in an overwhelming pro-German vote. The Memel question would have to wait until Hitler knew more about the Polish situation. He probably expected that the Poles would yield, so that he could take Danzig peacefully. But his courting of Poland went hand-in-hand with a Führer order, issued late in November, for the occupation of Danzig by German troops. The operation was to be a surprise raid and not part of a war against Poland. It would, if necessary, take place simultaneously with the seizure of Memel. Just in case the Poles reacted, Hitler ordered intensified work on the eastern fortifications.

On the Polish side, Beck thought there were grounds for discussion without compromising Polish rights in Danzig, where Nazi propaganda was becoming more blatant, and the Nuremberg-like laws against the Jews were being enforced. While worried by the German-backed campaign, Beck did not actually believe that Hitler wanted a confrontation; he judged that a compromise over the status of the Free City could be found. No progress was made before 5 January 1939 however, when Beck, in Berlin to meet with Ribbentrop, was taken off unexpectedly to see Hitler at Berchtesgaden. The Führer stressed the importance of a territorial settlement for the two countries' future, but insisted on the return of Danzig. On the next day, Beck told Ribbentrop that there was no possibility of an agreement along these lines, and warned that the actions of the Nazi regime in Danzig could provoke a crisis. Ribbentrop again raised the question of Polish adhesion to the Anti-Comintern pact, stressing that this would not necessarily mean common military action against the Soviet Union. In return, he offered co-operation over the Ukraine. Beck, though adamant in his refusal to compromise on Polish rights in Danzig, was seriously alarmed, and on his return to Warsaw proved more amenable to the demands from the Francophiles that he repair the diplomatic bridges to the west, particularly to France. Little could be expected from Britain, where the Foreign Office regarded the disputes over Danzig as a barrier to the improvement of relations with Germany. When Ribbentrop finally made his much-heralded trip to Warsaw in January 1939, he was left in no doubt that Poland would never allow Germany to take Danzig. He returned to Berlin with nothing to show, much to the delight of his rivals, who, whether they favoured the 'little solution' of a military *coup* against Danzig, or the larger scheme favoured by Göring, of enlisting Polish assistance for the war against the Soviet Union, were all united in their disparagement of Ribbentrop. Still clinging to the hope of securing something from Beck, Ribbentrop persuaded Hitler that negotiations should continue. Hitler, in his mammoth 30 January Reichstag speech, referred to the German–Polish friendship 'as one of the reassuring factors in the political life of Europe'.[20] Assuming that Beck would give way to the combination of carrot and stick, Hitler could consider the implementation of far more ambitious plans.

Simultaneously with the Polish talks, Ribbentrop tried to bring the negotiations for a tripartite pact with Italy and Japan to fruition. Hitler had alerted Mussolini on their train trip to Munich of his expectation of war with Britain and France, with the Duce at his side. Ribbentrop had handed Ciano a draft of the tripartite treaty during the conference, without eliciting any expressions of enthusiasm from the Italian. While the two foreign ministers were still arguing about the Hungarian claims in Ruthenia, Ribbentrop announced to Ciano that he would like to come to Rome in October. Anticipating the purpose of his trip, Ciano was well prepared for the renewed German effort to secure an alliance. During his stay, 27–28 October, Ribbentrop told the Italians that Hitler was convinced there would be war in four or five years' time. Britain and France had detailed military agreements, and it was time that the Axis powers had the same. Ciano was no more impressed with the message than he was with the messenger: 'I distrust Ribbentrop's initiatives. He is vain, frivolous and loquacious. The Duce says you only have to look at his head to see that he has a little brain. And he is very tactless.'[21] Ciano easily persuaded Mussolini to postpone any

[20] Quoted in D. C. Watt, *How War Came*, 71.
[21] Galeazzo Ciano, *Diario, 1937–1943* (Milan, 1946, 1998), 200.

discussions about an alliance which, in any case, would be highly unpopular in Italy because of Nazi treatment of German Catholics.

Mussolini was much buoyed up by his recent 'triumph' at Munich and the simultaneous courting of Italy by both the French and British. The former had agreed to accredit their new ambassador to the 'King of Italy and Emperor of Ethiopia', thereby recognizing Italian sovereignty over Ethiopia, and the latter, Ciano was assured, would implement the Easter Accords in mid-November.[22] Mussolini risked little in turning his back on Ribbentrop's alliance proposal. Nonetheless, the combination of admiration, jealousy, and fear that characterized Mussolini's attitude towards Hitler, made him cautious. He undoubtedly wanted to be on Hitler's side in the next European war, but he was also afraid of the Führer's dynamism. It might take the Germans into the Adriatic, already marked out for the Roman empire, and could even endanger Italy itself. He needed to move quickly before Hitler's triumphs reduced the Italian bargaining position in Europe.

While underlining the Fascist identity of interests with National Socialism, Mussolini also considered the fulfilment of his own expansionist goals in the Balkans and in the Mediterranean. More promising for an extended Italian role in the Balkans than Ciano's hopes for a bloc against Germany, was the foreign minister's unfolding plan for the occupation of Albania, and for the assassination of King Zog in the spring of 1939. Intending to conciliate the Yugoslavs by offering Salonika (a Greek city) as compensation, Mussolini gave Ciano the green light on 14 November. At the same time, he intended to pursue his territorial ambitions at French expense. André François-Poncet, transferred from Berlin to Rome in the hope that he could establish good personal relations with Mussolini, arrived in early November, ending the two-year absence of a French ambassador to Italy. He was not received by the Duce until the end of the month, and was given a very cold reception. Convinced that France was weak and could be diplomatically isolated, and hopeful that Italy would finally enjoy the fruits of the Spanish campaign, Mussolini considered a war against France. First, he sought British ratification of the Easter Accords, agreeing to withdraw 10,000 volunteers from Spain as a gesture, but warning that Britain had to respond or face the consequences. Chamberlain, anxious to court the Duce and much worried by the Japanese moves towards the South China Sea and south Pacific, was happy to agree. Ever hopeful that Mussolini might be enlisted to restrain Hitler, the

[22] The Anglo-Italian agreement (Easter Accords) of April 1938 provided for the mutual recognition of the status quo in the Mediterranean and British recognition of Italian sovereignty over Ethiopia in return for the withdrawal of Italian forces from Spain.

prime minister asked only for a diplomatic breathing space because of the possible public reaction to yet another act of appeasement. On 16 November, the Anglo-Italian accords came into effect, and a few weeks later it was agreed that Chamberlain and Halifax would visit Rome early in the new year. Mussolini had already outlined for Ciano his intention to push his demands for Djibouti, Tunisia, Corsica, and Suez, though the timetable was uncertain. For immediate purposes, he would mount a major anti-French propaganda campaign, partly in the hope of blocking any Franco-German *rapprochement* resulting from Ribbentrop's forthcoming visit to Paris.

On 30 November, Ciano spoke before the Chamber of Fasces and Corporations in Mussolini's presence. At the end of his speech, he referred to the 'natural aspirations of the Italian people'. There was a storm of acclamation and shouts of 'Tunis, Corsica, Nice, Savoy', a staged performance whatever Ciano's claims to the contrary. That evening, Mussolini laid out his 'programme' for the *Gran Consiglio del Fascismo*, the regime's highest organ: 'Albania will become Italian... Then, for the requirements of our security in this Mediterranean that still confines us, we need Tunis and Corsica. The [French] frontier must move to the Var [River]. I do not aim for Savoy, because it is outside the circle of the Alps. But I have my eye on the Ticino, since Switzerland has lost its cohesive force and is destined one day, like so many small nations, to be demolished. All this is a programme. I cannot lay down a fixed timetable. I merely indicate the course along which we shall march.'[23] Mussolini was delighted by Ciano's Chamber speech, as 'he always is when he smells gunpowder', and told him he would set aside the Mussolini–Laval agreement of 1935 and synchronize Italian demands with Germany's colonial claims.

On 17 December, François-Poncet was informed that the Franco-Italian agreement was superseded. Neither strong French resistance to the Italian demands, nor a somewhat equivocal British reaction, deterred the Duce. The French informed the Italians and the British that France would not yield territory to Italy. Chamberlain insisted that his visit to Rome must go ahead, but in the Commons underlined the cordiality of Anglo-French relations and warned against any Italian change in the status of Tunis. Privately, the prime minister thought that once the clamour died, the French should accept some of the less objectionable of Mussolini's demands. He believed that Mussolini wanted the Anglo-Italian friendship to develop to redress the Italian trade balance, and to find a way to escape from Spain. He wrote to his sister that Mussolini 'dislikes and fears the Germans and welcomes

[23] Quoted in MacGregor Knox, *Mussolini Unleashed* (Cambridge, 1982), 38–39.

anything which will make him less dependent on them'.[24] His reading of Mussolini's position was entirely wrong. On the very day that the Easter Accords were signed, Ciano went to the Palazzo Venezia to report to Mussolini. 'All this is very important', came the reply, '. . . [but] it does not alter our policy. In Europe the Axis remains fundamental. In the Mediterranean we will collaborate with the English as long as we can. France remains outside—our claims upon her have now been defined.'[25] Mussolini did not expect the British to convince Daladier to turn over Nice, Savoy, and Corsica to Italy, but he counted on Chamberlain to stand aside.

In keeping with his hopes to move against France, Mussolini decided at the end of 1938 to commit Italy to a military alliance with Germany. On New Year's Day, Ciano was told of the Duce's decision to transform the Anti-Comintern pact into a tripartite alliance. The triumphant Ribbentrop was informed the next day. His sense of elation was premature, as Japan now became the stumbling block. On 4 January, Prince Konoe, the Japanese prime minister, resigned, frustrated by his inability to find a way out of the China quagmire, and disappointed by the response to his announcement of the 'New Order' in East Asia. He had been unable to forge any consensus about the scope of the military alliance to be concluded with Germany and Italy. Under the new premier, Baron Hiranuma, a weak appointee known for his reticence (the 'Japanese Calvin Coolidge'), the cabinet debate developed into a struggle between, on the one hand, the army leadership and a faction in the Foreign Ministry who wanted to extend the scope of the three-power alliance to include Britain and France as well as the Soviet Union as enemies, and, on the other, the foreign minister, and the more conservative officials in the Foreign Ministry, who favoured a limited treaty aimed at the Soviet Union. The navy was equally cautious about antagonizing the Russians and the Anglo-Americans simultaneously. The China war had already created friction with the Americans, who in July 1938, had inaugurated a 'moral embargo' on the export of aeronautical equipment and who, in November, issued a strong protest about the closing of the 'open door' in China. The cabinet debate in Tokyo developed into a struggle between the army and navy. A compromise reached in mid-January proved unacceptable to Berlin as well as to the pro-alliance Japanese ambassadors in Berlin and Rome. Matters were left in an inconclusive state with the cabinet unable to resolve its differences.

[24] Robert Self (ed.), *The Neville Chamberlain Diary Letters,* Vol. 4, 372 (To Ida Chamberlain, 8 January 1938).

[25] Ciano, *Diario*, 213 (16 Nov. 1938).

Mussolini's ambitions in the Mediterranean pushed him further towards Germany. Neither the difficulties with Tokyo, nor Chamberlain's visit to Rome, nor even a secret French emissary, Paul Baudouin, sent by Daladier and Bonnet at the end of January to establish more conciliatory relations with the Duce, dimmed his enthusiasm for expansion. Within weeks of Chamberlain's visit, Italo-German naval talks began, and the Italian army and air force renewed plans for an attack on Egypt and Suez from Libya. The navy, acutely conscious of its inferiority to the Anglo-French naval forces, raised strong objections. Marshal Badoglio, the chief of staff, pressed the naval case, and, to the fury of both the army and the air force chiefs, convinced Mussolini to reconsider his plans. The Duce abandoned the idea of an attack on Egypt and, on 3 February, told the *Gran Consiglio* that although war with France was inevitable, it would have to wait until Italian military and economic preparations were completed at the end of 1942. Moments of clarity, and doubts about Italian capabilities, did not check Mussolini's imperial dreams. Colonial concessions from France were only to be the first step in Italy's 'March to the Sea'. His extended remarks were part of a document prepared for the *Gran Consiglio* on 4 February, designed to 'orient' Italian policy in the near and far future. Mussolini explained that Italy was a prisoner within the Mediterranean, and would have to break the 'bars of the prison', Corsica, Tunis, Malta, and Cyprus. Once Italy escaped, its task was 'to march to the ocean', either the 'Indian Ocean, joining Libya with Ethiopia through the Sudan, or the Atlantic through French North Africa'. In either case, Italy would have to deal with Anglo-French opposition, and needed Germany to cover 'Italy's shoulders on the continent'.[26]

Mussolini was delighted by Franco's promise, after repeated prompting from Rome and Berlin (and Tokyo), to adhere to the Anti-Comintern pact, though not until after the end of the civil war. The Spanish conflict was at last drawing to some sort of conclusion. In November, the Nationalists, backed by the CTV (the Italian force) and Italian aircraft, finally defeated the Republicans at the Ebro and Mussolini and Ciano, though accustomed to Franco's devious ways, hoped that once he moved into Catalonia, the war would end. Mussolini agreed to send arms and supplies rather than new 'volunteers' to Franco, who was pressing for additional assistance. It would be the Italian-led Nationalist forces that would take Barcelona at the end of January. Primed by his Spanish victories and spurred on by a stream of anti-Italian articles in the French

[26] MacGregor Knox, *Mussolini Unleashed*, 39–40. Professor Knox calls this document 'a sort of Mussolinian *Mein Kampf*'. See Reynolds Salerno, *Vital Crossroads: Mediterranean Origins of the Second World War, 1935–1940*, 106.

press, Mussolini's animosity towards France became ever more vocal. Anticipating a future attack on Tunisia, in early February the Duce ordered an immediate doubling of Italy's Libyan garrison. The French estimated that even with British support, their forces would be at a numerical disadvantage. While increasing the pressure on France, Mussolini sought Hitler's backing. Given the Japanese hesitations, he told Ciano, a military alliance with Germany alone would be 'sufficient to meet the array of Anglo-French forces, and at the same time would not appear to be anti-English or anti-American'.[27] He wanted German support both for his campaign against France, and for his more immediate Albanian venture, scheduled for the first week of April, Easter week. Sceptical about the 'phlegmatic and slow Japanese', he pressed for a bilateral alliance. Though of less interest to Hitler than the anti-British tripartite alliance, and unpopular with the German generals who had little confidence in the Italian army, Hitler was prepared to agree. Ribbentrop accepted the Italian proposals for staff talks. At the same time, the Duce declared his disinterest in the Hungarian–Slovak conflict, and turned a deaf ear to Hungarian requests for moral and material support. With the tripartite Anti-Comintern alliance still in the balance, and the Polish negotiations at an impasse, Hitler appeared to be marking time. A peaceful lull in European affairs set in during the latter part of February.

VI

The British were not blind to what was happening in Germany. With some reluctance and not without dispute, the Chamberlain government came to accept that Hitler's open belligerence required a closer British partnership with France. This critical change in policy owed much to the activity of the French, who embarked on a programme of economic and military recovery, and showed increasing impatience with the demands of the Axis powers. They succeeded in making their influence felt in London, but this was not a partnership of equals. France was the supplicant, and the need for British assistance was more pressing than in 1914, given the absence of the old Russian alliance. Britain continued to set the pace, tone, and direction of the western democracies' engagement with the dictator states. In terms of practical politics, Chamberlain's margin of diplomatic manoeuvre began to shrink.

With no signs of encouragement coming from Hitler during the winter of 1938–1939, Chamberlain shifted his diplomatic focus to Mussolini. He went off to Rome on 10 January with the clear intention

[27] Quoted in Mario Toscano, *The Origins of the Pact of Steel* (Baltimore, MD, 1967), 127. Note the contradictory references to England.

of wooing the Duce. During the four-day meeting, Mussolini did most of the talking, defending German policy and attacking France. Refusing to join any general guarantee of the borders of Czechoslovakia, he offered little in the way of encouragement. With a blindness that could only have come from a considerable faith in his own powers of persuasion, Chamberlain believed that it was a 'wonderful meeting' which had improved the chances of peace. Mussolini drew very different conclusions. He judged his visitors to be 'the tired sons of a long line of rich men, and they will lose their empire'.[28] Rome was well informed of what was transpiring in London. Having broken the British diplomatic code, the Italians had also secured access to the British ambassador's despatch box and to the embassy safe, a breach of security discovered only when their spy, a Chancery servant, stole the ambassador's wife's tiara instead of secret documents. Mussolini never intended that the Chamberlain visit should have any consequences, and had already decided to opt for the military alliance with Germany. After the visitors' departure, Ciano telephoned Ribbentrop to tell him the visit was a fiasco ('big lemonade'), and laid plans for renewed press attacks against France.

Temporarily thwarted in his peace-building efforts, Chamberlain tried to keep the doors open for future negotiation. This explains why he resisted a major rearmament programme as demanded by the 'weaker brethren' in his cabinet, backed by Halifax, and by all three service chiefs. It was not that Chamberlain doubted the necessity of further remedying the deficiencies in Britain's defences, above all in the air, as revealed during the September crisis. Rather, he was not prepared to follow up the Munich agreement with an armaments programme that would provoke the very arms race that he wanted to avoid. In his view, conciliation and rearmament were two sides of the same coin, and the purpose of the latter was to make Britain safe from attack, and not to threaten the Axis powers. Together with Sir John Simon, his loyal chancellor of the exchequer, he could still exercise a considerable influence over the rearmament process, to limit expenditure and to defeat demands for a Ministry of Supply with compulsory powers. The cabinet agreed to establish a Ministry of National Service that would compile a voluntary register of manpower reserves. Though the Treasury felt increasingly embattled, it had set the overall amount to be spent on defence and could still challenge the share demanded by each service. There was little difficulty with the navy's relatively modest demands for new escort vessels, minesweepers and carrier-based aircraft.

[28] Ciano, *Diario*, 238 (11 January 1939).

Provision was made to accelerate existing programmes, but given the shortages of skilled labour, the room for improvement was limited. The first battle came with the Air Force. The estimated costs of the new RAF programme proposed in late October 1938, nearly £350 million, looked staggering to the Treasury and provoked an immediate response from Simon who claimed that the costs would gravely endanger the country's financial stability. The air chiefs were asking both for an enlarged fighter force, and a heavy bomber fleet that could act both as a deterrent and as an offensive striking weapon. The latter, they claimed, might provide the war-winning strategy once the initial German attack was repulsed. While the chancellor of the exchequer agreed to the full programme of fighters, increasing Britain's fighter strength by thirty percent, the bomber programme was cut to what was necessary to maintain an adequate flow of production and prevent large-scale dismissals in the aircraft factories. Chamberlain backed Simon; he was converted to the emphasis on fighters over bombers, not just on the grounds of cost, but because they represented a defensive strategy that would not antagonize Hitler. Even this limited expansion could not be implemented immediately. Aircraft factories were already heavily engaged in fulfilling existing production schedules and were facing shortages of skilled labour and materials. Without compulsory powers, which neither ministers, industrialists, nor the unions favoured, the government had to depend on persuasion and voluntary agreements. The secretary for air, Sir Kingsley Wood, was able to facilitate large-scale planning by making greater use of sub-contracting that allowed work to go where labour was available. Existing firms were combined into a number of production groups concentrating on specific types of aircraft. Production figures improved. In the first six months of 1939, Britain produced 3,753 aircraft as compared to 1,045 in the same six-month period in 1938.

The army continued to be the 'poor relation' of the three services, the third in line in the order of defence priorities. After some £70 million of cuts to its funding during 1937–1938, Munich provided a salutary shock. It would have been impossible to send more than two ill-equipped divisions to France, and they would have lacked the tanks, guns, ammunition reserves, and even the winter clothing needed for a European engagement. No single armoured division was ready to fight (a situation that continued until after war broke out). The Territorial Army was so badly equipped that its divisions would not be able to train adequately when called up. The new proposals, which it was claimed would only enable the army to fulfil its designated tasks, involved an additional expenditure of £81 million (cancelling out the previous savings made on the army), and provoked a fierce debate at the highest levels of decision-making. Sir Samuel Hoare, the home secretary, led the opposition in the December discussions, insisting that the army's principal role was the anti-aircraft defence of Britain, and that the new funding pointed to a continental commitment which had been specifically rejected. Halifax was more sympathetic to the military's demands, and warned that it was necessary to reassure the French of British land support if it was to continue to resist Germany. Halifax's backing for the increased expenditure further distanced him from the prime minister. When pressed by the secretary of war to take a more realistic view of the army's needs, Chamberlain apparently commented that 'as our Army was so small was it worth worrying whether it was ready or not?'[29] An alliance between the army and navy chiefs of staff led to the approval of the army's expansion programme, but no further action was taken until reports of French disaffection and rumours of an imminent German attack on Holland decisively altered the situation in the army's favour in early 1939.

The Chamberlain–Simon efforts at penny-pinching had a serious purpose. There were genuine worries about Britain's financial health, 'the fourth arm of defence'. At the end of 1938, Britain's adverse balance of trade stood at £70 million. Unemployment figures rose to 1.9 million in December, the highest for 1938, and rose again to over two million in January 1939. There was a continuing drop in the value of sterling during 1938, while total gold reserves were reduced by one-quarter in 1938 and by the same proportion in the first half of 1939.[30] Simon feared that if the financial restraints on rearmament were removed, Britain's monetary reserves would be exhausted, and 'we should have lost the means of carrying on a long struggle altogether'.[31]

Apart from avoiding measures that would antagonize Hitler, Chamberlain searched for ways to approach him. One possibility was to pursue the economic agreement that had been mentioned in his post-conference exchanges with Hitler. It was widely reported that the German economy was under severe strain, and that Hitler would be forced to decide soon whether to continue to rearm at the cost of an internal crisis, or to moderate the pace of rearmament and seek peaceful means to secure his goals. There was also a domestic side to the search for an Anglo-German economic agreement. The general contraction of world trade meant that Britain's staple industries, still the major producers of her export income, were facing a particularly difficult struggle to

[29] B. Bond (ed.), *Chief of Staff: The Diaries of Lieutenant-General Sir Henry Pownall*, vol. I, 172.

[30] Parker, *Chamberlain and Appeasement*, 284.

[31] Quoted in David Dutton, *Simon: A Political Biography* (London, 1992), 262.

maintain overseas markets. British business interests demanded government protection of home markets against foreign goods and assistance in markets abroad in Europe and in central and Latin America where Germany was seen as the main and most unprincipled competitor. Two foreign trade debates in the Commons, at the end of November and in mid-December 1938, focussed on opposition arguments for a more *dirigiste* form of economy, and even for the adoption of German methods to protect British trade. Neither Chamberlain, the Treasury, nor the Board of Trade would countenance such measures; they hoped that economic co-operation with Germany would improve the conditions for world trade, and open the door for some form of political settlement. They were prepared to explore the possibilities of easing the situation by extending the Anglo-German Payments Agreement of 1934, which had been revised in 1938 after *Anschluss,* and provided the official framework for regulating economic relations between the two countries.[32]

Despite difficulties on both sides, the agreement had worked fairly well before 1938. The Germans had won a moratorium on their Standstill debts, and on the much larger volume of other medium- and long-range debts to Britain. They could spend 55% of the sterling earned on exports to buy imports with 10% reserved for debt service. Earned sterling not used for either ('free exchange') could be used for purchases elsewhere. British creditors and traders benefited from the agreement. Germany quickly paid off its heavy commercial debts and continued to pay interest in full to British holders of Dawes and Young loans. While there was little hope that the Germans would liquidate their debts, British bankers were getting cash payments on the Standstill and on other medium- and long-term loans. British exporters also benefited, mainly from the import–export ratio provisions in the agreement. There was a marked increase in German purchases of British goods, particularly coal, the major export, but also in cotton, textiles, and the herring trade. In 1938, Germany was, after India, Britain's best

[32] For the terms of 1934 Payments Agreement see pp. 96–97. In 1938, the Germans threatened to write off Austria's international obligations, including the Austrian reconstruction loans. By threatening to impose a unilateral clearing on Germany, the British forced the Germans to retreat. There was to be a full transfer on the Austrian loans but interest rates on German debts to Britain would be reduced. A sliding scale was created for British exports, a large proportion of which were to be of finished goods. As a result, it was calculated that the Germans would be paying £1 million more per year to Britain than under the 1934 agreement. The agreement was welcomed in London not only because of the commercial advantages but because it was seen as a victory for the supposed moderate Nazis and a check to the 'warmonger party'. Neil Forbes, *Doing Business with the Nazis: Britain's Economic and Financial Relations with Germany, 1933–1939* (London, 2000), 115–119.

single customer, taking exports to the value of £20.6 million, just ahead of the United States and Argentina. Britain was supplying not only a margin of free exchange but the best market in which to spend it.[33] Contrary to Schacht's claims (which the British took seriously) that Germany was denied access to British colonial raw materials, the volume of some German purchases, rubber, copper, sisal, and cocoa, from selected colonies, actually increased with British bankers, shippers, and insurers providing the services used to acquire them.[34]

Neville Chamberlain, Frederick Leith-Ross, the government's chief economic adviser, and Montagu Norman, the governor of the Bank of England, were not only strong supporters of the Payments Agreement, but hoped that Germany's need for foreign exchange could be used to wean Berlin away from autarchy and back to the world economy. By offering positive inducements to co-operation, the British believed they could strengthen the influence of 'moderates' like Schacht and Göring, who were thought to favour a return to liberal trading practices and a modification of the German rearmament programme. Much was expected of Schacht, whose leadership of the *Reichsbank* was regarded as a guarantee of continued co-operation in the pursuit of liberalization. Schacht and Norman were close personal friends and there were institutional links between the *Reichsbank* and the Bank of England.

Efforts were made in the autumn and winter of 1938–1939 to forward Anglo-German co-operation. The British suggested that the payment agreements should be altered to give Germany more free exchange, to be used for additional imports from south-east Europe, thus freeing the Balkan states from the clearings so that they could purchase goods on the world market. The visiting German delegation presented the Board of Trade with a list of German exports on which the *Reichsgruppe Industrie* (RI), the organization representing the main German exporters, wanted

[33] Forbes, *Doing Business with the Nazis*, 124.

[34] David Meredith 'British Trade Diversion Policy and "Colonial Issues" in the 1930s', *Journal of European Economic History*, 25: 1 (1996), 56. There were a number of commodities where sales to Germany were smaller in volume in the Ottawa period, 1932–1938 as compared to the gold standard years, 1925–1931. But against these declines must be set the increases in products from other colonial sources. It is true that Britain restricted foreign imports to its colonies and in reducing Germany's sales to Britain's colonies reduced Germany's purchasing power. This would not have been a problem if the Germans were willing to use foreign exchange earned elsewhere to purchase colonial produce but this was precluded by the regime's strict exchange controls. The British acknowledged some of the German complaints and pressed for a League of Nations enquiry into the problem of international access to raw materials in colonies. Leith-Ross and others continued to feel that the British actions in 1931–1932 had seriously hurt Germany and that Britain, having recovered quickly from the worst of the depression, should make amends.

TABLE 12.3 Exports from British Colonies to Germany, Selected Commodities 1925–1931 and 1932–1938 (annual averages)

Colony	Commodity	Exports 1925–1931		To Germany 1925–1931	As percentage	Exports 1932–1938		To Germany 1932–1938	As percentage
Cyprus	Asbestos	7,839	tons	1,944	24.8	6,866	tons	291	4.2
	Copper					89,824	tons	65,271	72.7
Gambia	Groundnuts	63,059	tons	11,967	19	55,062	tons	7,493	13.6
	Palm kernels	696	tons	249	35.8	672	tons	238	35.2
Sierra	Palm kernels	61,726	tons	29,248	47.4	73,281	tons	25,906	35.4
Leone	Piassava fibre	2,379	tons	1,759	73.9	3,459	tons	795	23
Gold Coast	Cocoa	222,000	tons	50,000	22.5	254,000	tons	59,000	23.1
	Palm kernels	6,152	tons	3,658	59.5	6,421	tons	3,518	54.8
	Copra	1,280	tons	718	56.1	1,495	tons	428	28.6
	Rubber (wild)	744	000 lbs	181	24.4	604	000 lbs	32	5.3
Nigeria	Groundnuts	128,714	tons	55,143	42.8	220,857	tons	29,000	13.1
	Palm kernels	255,857	tons	115,714	45.2	315,286	tons	116,143	36.8
	Palm oil	123,857	tons	10,286	8.3	131,429	tons	9,000	6.8
	Cocoa	47,507	tons	10,629	22.4	82,686	tons	15,393	18.6
	Raw cotton	13,349	000 lbs	285	2.1	15,590	000 lbs	3,167	20.3
	Rubber (wild)	4,099	000 lbs	1,970	48.1	4,290	000 lbs	1,291	30.1
N. Rhodesia	Copper	3,221	tons	256	7.9	127,406	tons	44,602	35
	Zinc	12,863	tons	3,102	24.1	13,940	tons	1,074	7.7

Source: D. Meredith, 'British Trade Diversion Policy and the "Colonial Issue" in the 1930s', *Journal of European Economic History*, 25 (1996), 57.

reduced tariffs. It was suggested that talks on market arrangements be opened between the RI and the Federation of British Industries (FBI). Further attempts to encourage liberalization through the expansion of the German export markets came to nothing, and were rejected by the Germans in early 1939.

At the end of November 1938, Chamberlain agreed that Norman and Schacht should exchange views. Schacht arrived in London in December, anxious to counteract the hostile mood in the City, partly provoked by *Kristallnacht,* but also by growing dissatisfaction with German exchange and trade practices. Schacht, who met Chamberlain, Oliver Stanley, the president of the Board of Trade, as well as Norman, Leith-Ross, and others, enquired about a British loan or a reduction in interest rates on foreign debts, to cushion the German economy from the impact of restoring a free system of currency. He also raised the possibility of facilitating Jewish emigration by accepting an increase in German exports to obtain more foreign currency. While none of his suggestions evoked much enthusiasm, Schacht made a good impression on the British officials and on the merchant bankers. In the new year, Montagu Norman, using the occasion of a private visit to Schacht, talked with the *Reichsbank* directors about a possible remodelling of the Payments Agreement 'on more liberal principles', as well as about Schacht's scheme for facilitating Jewish emigration. The trip aroused a great deal of adverse comment in London and was strongly criticized by the Foreign Office.

Both before and after Munich, John Magowan, the knowledgeable commercial counsellor in the Berlin embassy, not only criticized these efforts but queried the political as well as the commercial assumptions behind the Payments Agreement. Magowan insisted that any modification of the agreement providing Germany with more foreign currency would result in additional purchases of the raw materials needed for rearmament. The Germans were already applying an import–export ratio of 71%, and the steep rise in its imports was due to the purchase of commodities used for rearmament. Magowan claimed that Germany was 'practically at war with Britain', and demanded that security issues, rather than commercial interests, should be given greater weight in determining economic relations with Berlin. His views, seconded by the military attaché in Berlin, Mason-McFarlane, were not well received in Whitehall, and in the winter of 1939, he carried on a solitary campaign to show how Germany had reconstituted its imports to secure materials for rearmament.

The implementation of the Payments Agreements was undoubtedly providing the credits and the raw materials—coal, steel, scrap-iron, copper—needed for Germany's war industries. Given Germany's financial difficulties, and its need for foreign exchange for imports, it would have been better to have increased the squeeze on German credits. What is noticeable is that at no time, despite intelligence about Germany's financial and economic difficulties, was there any move in London to take advantage of Germany's weakness. Insofar as is known, Desmond Morton, the head of the Industrial Intelligence Centre (IIC), who was fully aware of the German financial difficulties, never suggested any such possibility.[35] Both the continuing attachment to *laissez-faire* principles, and the persistent hope for a return to a liberal international trading system, precluded official action. Apart from the arms trade, where the government did intervene, there was relatively little government interference with firms engaged in Anglo-German trade.

It is true that the balance sheet was not quite so favourable to the Germans as Magowan's arguments implied. Without much chance of the repayment of Germany's debts 'in a reasonable time', the British creditors were benefiting from the servicing of the Standstill and other long-term debts which gave them one-quarter return from the proceeds of German exports. If a unilateral clearing had been imposed, Germany would have been severely hurt, but the leading merchant banks in London would have lost their substantial cash payments. Moreover, as Desmond Morton argued, Britain's imports from Germany included machine tools and machinery that were not easily obtained elsewhere.[36] It appears that the Treasury and the Board of Trade clung to the Payments Agreement in the hope that the remnants of the old liberal order of multilateral trade that Britain had helped to destroy in 1931 could be restored, and that Germany would re-engage with the world trading community. In fact, during 1939, as Germany's foreign trade contracted, an increasing percentage of the British credits were used, not to finance the movement of goods, but as working capital in Germany. In the summer of 1939, there were still some £36 million owed to British creditors who, sensing that war was close, tried unsuccessfully to get some form of cash payment. The Payments Agreement remained in force until after the outbreak of war.

Until the very last months of peace, the hope that some form of economic co-operation could lead to political negotiations was never totally disregarded. Schacht's dismissal as *Reichsbank* president in January 1939, and his replacement by Walther Funk, a known Nazi ideologue, sent shockwaves through the British government and the City. But the

[35] Information from Gill Bennett, *Churchill's Man of Mystery: Desmond Morton and the World of Intelligence* (Oxford and New York, 2007). See also Forbes, *Doing Business with the Nazis*.

[36] Forbes, *Doing Business with the Nazis*, 125.

conclusion of a coal cartel agreement on 28 January, even if only after a British threat to subsidize coal exports, and Hitler's speech two days later with his reference to Germany's need to 'trade or perish', kept hopes alive. The German 'overtures', and encouraging messages from Ambassador Henderson in Berlin, boosted Chamberlain's confidence that the prospects for peace were improving. Plans were made to send the president of the Board of Trade to Berlin in March. In anticipation of his visit, Frank Ashton-Gwatkin, from the Foreign Office economics department, was sent to report on the situation in Germany. His February memorandum presented a mixed picture of conditions in the country. He found the situation 'not brilliant' but certainly 'not disastrous', and he reported that most Germans did not think the country was heading for an 'economic collapse'.[37] Göring, Funk, and Dr Helmuth Wohlthat, the latter just back from a visit to Romania, had specific proposals in mind and were anxious to begin conversations with the British. Admittedly Ribbentrop was less than enthusiastic and warned Ashton-Gwatkin that Germany had unfinished business in central Europe which England must not mix in. The Foreign Office official recommended pursuing the discussions, but recognized that political difficulties might prevent any settlement.

In mid-February, the Duke of Coburg, in a speech supposedly written by Hitler, told the Anglo-German society in Berlin, that the coal cartel agreement was welcome and claimed that he looked forward to further talks and friendly relations between the two countries. In his own subsequent speech at Blackburn, a city in the heart of a highly depressed area, Chamberlain took up Hitler's 30 January address and Coburg's olive branch. Declaring that international tension was the main cause of unemployment, and if tension was lessened, trade would flourish and unemployment be reduced, the prime minister suggested that the best way to improve Anglo-German relations was through economic discussions, which would lead to arms limitation and the guarantee of peace. Chamberlain's confidence had revived; he believed that the recent alarms of a German attack on Western Europe had been taken far too seriously, and that the prospects for peace in Europe were actually improving.

At the same time as these exchanges, the government encouraged contacts established between British industrial combinations and their German counterparts. Anxious to offset the effects of the 'Roosevelt recession' and Germany's 'unfair' export policies, without resorting to active intervention, the Board of Trade responded to FBI (Federation of British Industries) pressure and parliamentary critics by recommending

[37] *DBFP*, 3rd ser., Vol. IV, Appendix II, p. 598.

new cartel arrangements, and the tightening of existing agreements, in preference to the use of subsidies or clearing arrangements. The talks between the British FBI and the German RI, begun in the autumn of 1938, were supported both by the Board of Trade in London and the Ministry of Economics in Berlin. The discussions culminated in the Düsseldorf agreement, concluded on 16 March 1939, one day after German troops entered Prague. The twelve-point programme provided a framework for formal discussions between industrial groups about the fixing of market prices and, in some cases, for the division of third country markets. About fifty British industrial groups, representing some 30% of Britain's export industries, indicated their willingness to negotiate under the new guidelines. It was hoped that multilateral cartel arrangements could be re-established with government support. Provisions were made for an appeal for government backing, if any trading partner refused to conform with the agreements.

It was hardly surprising that this provision provoked strong criticism in Washington, where, even after the November 1938 Anglo-American trade agreement, there was considerable suspicion that Britain's 'trade alliance' with Germany had an anti-American purpose. The Americans dismissed the British government's claims that these industrial agreements were of a private nature. The Labour Opposition also attacked the agreement. They were particularly incensed by the 16 March FBI invitation to their German counterparts to attend a meeting in June to arrange ways for monitoring the new arrangements. The government's unwillingness to denounce the agreement was taken as a sign that the diplomatic protests against the German action in Czechoslovakia were not seriously meant. The FBI negotiators disregarded the political overtones. Sir Guy Locock, director of the FBI wrote, 'We decided that political differences have nothing to do with industries, and we are going to carry on our programme exactly as planned.'[38] The American view that 'the business of business is business' was not really applicable to the situation in 1939, although this appears to have been the view of the British negotiators. Cartel arrangements arose out of specific market interests and were designed to regulate production and consumption to the benefit of each party. German industrialists, some of whom refused to believe that there was a serious prospect of a general war, were interested in expanding export markets, and cartels were a useful avenue of approach. British industrialists were anxious that Germany's use of export subsidies and bilateral

[38] Quoted in R. F. Holland, 'The Federation of British Industries and the International Economy, 1929–1939', *Economic History Review*, 2nd series, 34 (1981), 298.

trade agreements should not adversely affect their markets or contract the purchasing power of primary producers in the empire. It was hoped that the new agreements would counteract these unwelcome practices. The talks had their own internal dynamic and the coincidence of dates between their conclusion, and the German action in Czechoslovakia, was accidental. Nevertheless, in Berlin, the Ministry of Economics monitored the talks and made the Reich government's wishes clear, and though the Board of Trade refused to give the FBI political guidance, it too had a considerable stake in the success of the exchanges. The Germans were reassured by the talks, which they felt showed that Britain had a continuing interest in accommodation. In March, Göring in particular tried to use the economic carrot to detach Britain from France and would again resort to offers of economic co-operation in the summer of 1939. On the British side, too, for Chamberlain and Halifax, who was increasingly pessimistic about the possibilities of *détente*, the prospect of an economic agreement appeared to keep open an avenue of approach to the so-called moderates in Berlin. Though the head of the Board of Trade Oliver Stanley's visit to Berlin was cancelled after the occupation of Prague, it was still hoped that commercial contact would be resumed.

It is noticeable that in the post-Munich papers cited earlier, suggesting what might be done with regard to Germany, there was barely a mention of economic policy. There was 'almost a fatalistic view of the respective strengths of Germany and the UK' and little interest in trying to capitalize on Germany's weaknesses.[39] In December 1938, Desmond Morton insisted, as he had done earlier, that 'to dismiss any possibility of using economic weapons against Germany was to miss an important trick'[40] He went on to argue that 'the statement sometimes made that, with the aid of the resources of South-Eastern Europe, the Reich is now blockade-proof, does not accord with the facts.'[41] Even when IIC information went to the cabinet or CID, there is no indication that it was acted upon. The many lengthy and detailed reports sent to the military and civilian authorities between Munich and the outbreak of war, though received with interest, had little impact on their actual decisions.

[39] Information from Gill Bennett who had also pointed out that the SIS contribution to the post-Munich debate noted that the Germans were cultivating self-sufficiency but that the British should 'see what really legitimate grievances Germany had and what surgical operations are necessary to rectify them'. Information sent on 12 November 2007. Citation is to 18 September 1938, TNA: PRO C 14471/42/18, FO 371 21659.

[40] Bennett, *Churchill's Man of Mystery*, 186.

[41] Cited in Bennett, *Churchill's Man of Mystery*, 187.

Doubts were raised about giving the Germans a free hand in south-eastern Europe, as the full implications of their economic hegemony in the east came to be considered within the framework of an impending war. Even before Munich, it had been agreed that Britain should act in Turkey and Greece to counteract the German economic stranglehold. Turkey was of key importance in maintaining Britain's position in the Mediterranean and in the Middle East, where British interests were under severe pressure because of the Palestinian and Arab difficulties. (The Arab revolt in Palestine began in May 1936.) Ankara was seen mainly through a Middle East perspective and the maintenance of the lines of communication to India. Halifax was able to convince the cabinet 'that Turkey has become, not the main, but the only obstacle to the *Drang nach Osten*'.[42] Greece, too, was regarded as an important hindrance to German progress towards the eastern Mediterranean. There were many British ties with Greece, but since General Ioannis Metaxas had assumed dictatorial powers in Athens in the summer of 1936, the Germans were playing an increasingly important part in the strengthening of the Greek army and had become in return its main market for tobacco, Greece's chief export. The Foreign Office noted that 'if the defence of Egypt is a criteria, then first in importance comes the consolidation of British influence in Turkey and Greece'.[43] In May 1938, the Turks, who had been trying for some time for an economic *rapprochement* with Britain to counter-balance its heavy economic dependence on Germany (78% of its trade transaction took place through clearings), were granted a £16 million credit for industrial products and arms. It was to be treated as a special case and no further initiatives were taken in south-eastern Europe for fear of antagonizing the Germans.

Responding to Britain's loss of influence and Germany's economic domination of the region, in June 1938 Halifax established an inter-departmental committee on south-eastern Europe to consider the extension of a British economic presence. The committee met twice during the summer of 1938, but none of its recommendations for the purchases of Yugoslav and Hungarian products, Romanian oil and wheat, or Greek tobacco were followed up. In late September, the Bucharest government, already negotiating with the Germans over cereals and oil under the clearings, offered the British 300,000 tons of wheat and other products in return for foreign exchange to service its foreign loans.

[42] Quoted in Lawrence R. Pratt, *East of Malta, West of Suez: England's Mediterranean Crisis, 1936–1939* (Cambridge 1975), 147.

[43] Quoted in Pratt, *East of Malta, West of Suez*, 148. See discussion of Greece in Mogens Pelt, *Tobacco, Arms and Politics: Greece and Germany from World Crisis to World War, 1929–1941*, 214–219.

Stirred to action by the announcement of Walther Funk's tour of the Balkans, Halifax persuaded the cabinet in October to purchase 200,000 tons of wheat though the transaction was both 'uneconomic and unbusinesslike'.[44] This was only a gesture intended to keep a small foothold in Romania, and Chamberlain was assured that the purchase would not be at German expense. In its first interim report to the cabinet on 21 November, the committee recommended only the most limited reductions in British tariffs, and suggested that the government either grant credits on a non-commercial basis, or encourage private British combines to purchase more Romanian oil or Greek tobacco. Following the former recommendation, the cabinet made an allocation of £10 million worth of credit guarantees for non-commercial purposes. Much can be learned about British priorities from the Committee of Imperial Defence's ranking of important customers: (1) Belgium and Holland; (2) Egypt; (3) Portugal and Turkey; (4) Iraq; (5) Greece; (6) Saudi Arabia; (7) Afghanistan; (8) Yugoslavia; (9) Romania; and (10) Bulgaria.

When King Carol of Romania visited London on his way to Berlin in mid-November 1938, he tried to convince Chamberlain and Halifax to consider requests for credits. An offer of £1 million from the authorized £10 million was made, mainly for the construction of grain silos. Further wheat purchases were considered, and in early March, because of Romanian pressure, it was decided to send Leith-Ross with a commercial mission to visit both Romania and Greece. By this time, the Romanians were engaged in far-reaching talks with the Germans and the German trade negotiator, Helmuth Wohlthat, was visiting Bucharest to arrange the details. Meanwhile, Greece's economic dependence on German purchases of its tobacco deepened. In London, it was feared that the Greeks would follow the Romanian example and give way to Germany's political and economic demands. Efforts were made, though with minimum success, to convince the Imperial Tobacco Company to introduce Greek tobacco on to the British market so as to break the German monopoly. In December, as a gesture, Greece was given a £2 million credit for arms purchases in Britain. This hardly impinged on the Greek–German trade in war materials and military technology. All these were hard-won *ad hoc* measures, but at least there were some at the Foreign Office and elsewhere who were beginning to question the wisdom of giving Germany a free economic hand in south-east Europe.

[44] Quoted in Andrew Roberts, '*The Holy Fox': A Biography of Lord Halifax* (London, 1991), 136.

VII

Whatever the differences between Chamberlain and Halifax in the autumn of 1938, and the prospects for renewed talks with Germany, the foreign secretary did not challenge Chamberlain's policies. Halifax offered no real alternative to the policy of 'conciliation and rearmament', though he was more enthusiastic about the latter than the prime minister. Halifax was deeply loyal to Chamberlain, and would neither resign from the cabinet nor join the dissidents. Part of his problem was an inability to suggest any alternative programme and the failure of his advisers to provide meaningful options. Senior officials at the Foreign Office were agreed that Munich had been a humiliating experience, and all argued that Britain must intensify its rearmament efforts for its own self-defence. Beyond that, the limited amount of consensus that existed within the department over future policy hardly amounted to a change of direction. Most recommended that Britain should withdraw from central and Eastern Europe, recognize German economic and political predominance in the region, and concentrate its own efforts on the 'defence of the west', including its traditional interests in the Mediterranean and the empire. Cadogan, the permanent under-secretary wrote 'We must cut our losses in central and eastern Europe—let Germany, if she can, find there her "*Lebensraum*" and establish herself if she can, as a powerful economic unit.'[45] With minor variations and with only limited hopes for success, most officials proposed a comprehensive settlement based on colonial concessions, an undertaking to stabilize the frontiers of Europe ('for what that might be worth', Cadogan noted), a limitation of armaments, and an improvement of economic prospects. Halifax, generally receptive to the advice of his senior officials, concurred with the prevailing view. 'It is one thing to allow German expansion in Central Europe, which to my mind is a normal and natural thing', he wrote to Ambassador Phipps in Paris, 'but we must be able to resist German expansion in Western Europe or else our whole position is undermined. It would be fatal to us to be caught again with insufficient strength.'[46] He shared the Foreign Office sense of resignation with regard to Eastern Europe, and believed that to contest the German position would only provoke Hitler and make any settlement of differences impossible. Cadogan admitted that 'everyone has weighed in with bright, or dark ideas and I am getting more and more muddled. Only

[45] David Dilks (ed.), *The Diaries of Sir Alexander Cadogan*, 119. See also Donald Lammers, 'From Whitehall after Munich: The Foreign Office and the Future Course of British Policy', *Historical Journal*, 4 (1975).

[46] *DBFP*, 3rd ser., Vol. III, No. 285 (Halifax to Phipps, 1 November 1938).

thing to do is to go ahead on my line of a frank challenge to Germany to state her grievances . . . I can think of nothing better.'[47] While Chamberlain disliked the idea of a division of Europe into contending blocs and still hoped for a general agreement with Hitler, he was thinking along the same lines as suggested by his diplomatic advisers.

VIII

The decisive change in British policy between Munich and Prague was not in south-east Europe, but in its policy towards France. This was due as much to the French as to any action by Germany. The Daladier government was quick to show its dissatisfaction with the state of Anglo-French relations after Munich. One of the premier's rationalizations of his behaviour at Munich was the hope that by accepting British leadership, he could secure the alliance that was the *sine qua non* of French security. On 23–24 November, Chamberlain and Halifax went off to Paris to meet with their French counterparts. Neville Chamberlain hoped to 'give the French people an opportunity of pouring out their pent-up feelings of gratitude and affection' and to strengthen Daladier and encourage him to do something at last to put his country's defences in order and to pull his people into greater unity.[48] The trip was more than a 'thank-you' visit.[49] Chamberlain wanted to make sure that the French would stay in line in Eastern Europe and continue to back his policies of appeasement, now centred on Italy. There was to be no repetition of the Czech situation, where France had almost dragged Britain into war. The French, for their part, wanted compensation for the loss of Czechoslovakia's thirty-four divisions. Daladier spoke of the need for greater support from Britain in case of a German attack. 'It was not enough to send two divisions after three weeks', he said. 'More divisions should be sent and as far as possible they should be motorized.'[50] Daladier's attempt to initiate serious staff talks were stillborn. Chamberlain insisted that Britain, rather than France, would be Hitler's first target and that it was his government's 'first duty' to make Britain safe. Daladier's claim that French aircraft production would rise from eighty to four hundred a month in six months' time only confirmed Chamberlain's pessimistic view of France's air defences, and raised doubts about the French premier's sense of reality. Halifax proposed

[47] Dilks (ed.), *The Diaries of Sir Alexander Cadogan*, p. 123 (7 November 1938).

[48] NC 18/1/1075 Neville Chamberlain to Hilda, 6 November 1938.

[49] M. Dockrill, *British Establishment Perspectives on France, 1936–1940* (Basingstoke, 1999), 116.

[50] *DBFP*, 3rd series, Vol. III, No. 325 (Record of Anglo-French Conversations, 24 November 1938).

that the guarantee of Czechoslovakia should be a joint one coming into force only as the result of a decision by three of the four Munich signatories. Daladier and Bonnet protested but, as usual, after a show of indignation, the British formula was accepted. The entire encounter was shadowed by a feeling of dissatisfaction, reflecting the distance between the still hopeful Chamberlain and the deeply depressed Daladier. Halifax feared that, in their current mood, the French might be driven to a settlement with Germany.

During the next weeks Bonnet's recommended policies met with British approval. Like his colleagues, the French foreign minister advocated faster rearmament and an alliance with Britain, but he also insisted that France had to recognize German hegemony in the east and 'restructure' its obligations in Eastern Europe, so as not to be drawn into a war where French security was hardly at risk. Once the eastern treaties were renegotiated, the way would be opened for a Franco-German understanding. The senior officials in the *Quai d'Orsay*, while critical of their foreign minister's methods, agreed that in view of France's weakness some form of readjustment was necessary. The most outspoken anti-Munich diplomats were moved to less influential positions. René Massigli, the *Quai d'Orsay's* political director, was sent as ambassador to Ankara in a manner that left little doubt that the appointment was a way of getting him out of Paris. Léger remained in place. Munich, for him, was an evil necessity but a necessity nonetheless. Differently from Bonnet, he thought that France had won a respite that could be used to revive the economy and put a major rearmament programme into effect. Like a good civil servant, he carried out his chief's orders. Léger replaced the ousted officials with more amenable collaborators. They, too, believed that Hitler was determined on a policy of conquest but, while acknowledging that changes had to be made, were unwilling to abandon the east to the Germans.

Bonnet sought a radical revision of France's alliance system. His efforts to re-define and narrow the Polish treaty met with fierce resistance from Warsaw. In dispute with the Germans over Danzig, and concerned about Soviet intentions, they could not afford to weaken the French link. There were divided opinions in Paris about the Soviet Union. On the one hand, believing that France was too weak to construct an eastern barrier against German expansion, there was much to be said for abandoning the Franco-Soviet alliance. On the other hand, warnings of the dangers of Soviet isolation, and even the possibility of a Soviet–German *rapprochement*, suggested that the alliance still served an important purpose. Bonnet, more ambitious than his officials, had hopes of a reconciliation with Germany. He wanted a non-aggression pact, or something similar to the agreement made between Hitler and Chamberlain in September 1938. A visit by Ribbentrop to Paris was repeatedly postponed, in part because of the anger created by *Kristallnacht* (9–10 November, 1938). When it did take place in early December, at German request, the Jewish members of the cabinet were not invited to the reception. In the pact signed on 6 December, the two countries recognized the Franco-German border as 'definitive', and asserted that there were no territorial differences between them. They agreed to mutual consultations over questions of interest to both parties. As far as Bonnet was concerned, he hoped the accord would lead to a further *rapprochement* and possibly discourage Hitler from premature moves in Eastern Europe that would make it difficult for France to implement its policy of retreat. Ribbentrop expected little from the declaration beyond lulling the French into complacency. He assured an alarmed Mussolini that the pact had little significance.

Bonnet followed up the talks by initiating a series of commercial discussions. As in London, the 'economic appeasers' in France thought that a more benevolent attitude towards Germany's economic difficulties might prevent the seizure of its neighbours' lands and resources. Already in July 1937, the Popular Front government had concluded an agreement intended to increase German trade with France and its empire, and encourage the exchange of German coke for French coal. France became Germany's largest supplier of iron ore, an essential requirement for German armament production. In return, France was supplied with all the coke (and more) than it needed to purchase. The trade agreement resulted in an expansion of French exports to Germany and a slight diminution of German exports to France. New economic negotiations were initiated after Munich and, following the conclusion of the Franco-German accord, Bonnet sent representatives to Berlin in order to translate what he believed to be the new political understanding into commercial bargains. 'I must insist very strongly with you', Bonnet wrote to the minister of commerce, Fernand Gentin, on 18 February 'that these questions receive as soon as possible a solution that will translate the policy of *rapprochement* announced by the Franco-German declaration of December 6 into facts.'[51] The only gains were a new agreement in January 1939 and, in March, an arrangement to regulate French commerce with the Sudetenland. Daladier's patronage of the talks and support for a trade mission to Berlin, had, like Chamberlain's similar efforts, political objectives. By giving Germany freer access to raw materials without offering colonial concessions, it was hoped to underwrite the moderates in Berlin. For Bonnet, economic co-operation was a

[51] Quoted in Gordon Dutter, 'Doing Business with the Nazis: French Economic Relations with Germany Under the Popular Front', *Journal of Modern History*, 63 (1991), 323.

way of showing French goodwill towards German requirements, and would demonstrate the positive advantages of co-operation. The agreements were limited in scope and benefited both sides; the French exchanged agricultural products for much needed industrial goods. These efforts did not die with the German march into Prague, but the attempt to use commercial arrangements for political purposes was undercut by the changed political atmosphere in Paris. In Berlin, the Franco-German declaration and the economic overtures, like the British initiatives, were seen as evidence that despite the 'noise of press and popular opinion, the serious political classes were united in their desire to avoid war and to find some grounds for accommodation with the changing reality of European power'.[52]

Paradoxically, Bonnet's attempts to withdraw from an over-extended position in the east, and the pursuit of an economic accommodation with Germany, occurred simultaneously with an 'economic counter-offensive' in the Balkans, particularly in Yugoslavia and Romania. An agreement was reached with Belgrade in February, increasing French quotas on Yugoslav timber, corn, pigs, and sheep, though the French Agricultural Ministry blocked any concessions on wheat purchases. A stream of warnings alerted the French authorities to the danger of German military action to seize the rich Ploesti oilfields in Romania. An Anglo-French blockade could deprive them of all imports from Venezuela and the United States, making the Romanian oilfields critical for the German war effort. In early February 1939, the Paris embassy in Berlin informed the *Quai d'Orsay* that seizing control of the Romanian oilfields was 'one of the most frequently debated questions within the Nazi leadership'.[53] At the same time, the Romanians told the French that they were being threatened with increasing German subversion, and pleaded for economic assistance. Daladier and Bonnet tried to reverse the contraction of French influence by increasing French oil imports, but were unable to overcome the opposition of powerful agricultural interests. Resistance to increased agricultural quotas, lack of money for subsidies, and shortages of arms to export to Romania, thwarted agreement until the end of March 1939. Unlike the Germans, the French government was reluctant to take on private interest groups whose objectives differed from their own; the private French oil companies in Romania were a case in point. The plain fact was that

[52] Richard Overy, 'Strategic Intelligence and the Outbreak of the Second World War', *War in History*, 5: 4 (1998), 457, citing *DGFP*, Ser. D, Vol. IV, Nos, 281, 380, 367.

[53] Quoted in Peter Jackson, 'France and the Guarantee to Romania, April 1939', *Intelligence and National Security*, 10: 2 (1995), 260.

France was in no position to compete with Germany on the economic level in south-east Europe. If the German economic onslaught was to be checked, the initiative would have to come from Britain, even though this region traditionally fell within France's sphere of influence. Bonnet claimed there was no contradiction between the recognition of Germany's dominant position in south-eastern Europe, and French protection of its existing interests, but the economic spotlight on the Balkans weakened his case for a political withdrawal from Eastern Europe. Even before the German occupation of Prague, but particularly after, German economic domination of the Balkans undermined his efforts at appeasement and strengthened the hand of those preferring to create an eastern barrier against German expansion.

It was Daladier who, after a period of uncertainty and indecision, emerged as the key policy maker. Ultimately, he was the one who decided that France should take a firmer stand against both Axis powers. After the Munich shock, Daladier's first efforts were to put in hand the economic steps essential for rearmament, and address the problems of the French air force that he believed had made Munich necessary. In partnership with Paul Reynaud, the new finance minister, he removed the remaining 'interventionist' measures blamed for the economic malaise of the country. The Reynaud decrees lifted price controls and restrictions on the employment of workers, introduced cuts in rates for overtime work and, above all, heralded the end of the forty-hour week, the symbol of what the workers had achieved under the Popular Front regime. Only defence spending was increased. The new programme inevitably brought a confrontation between labour and employers, with the government backing the latter. A campaign of repression defeated the strikes that followed, and decisively aligned the propertied classes with the Daladier government. France enjoyed a massive repatriation of capital: between November 1938 and August 1939, 26 billion francs worth of investment returned to swell the coffers of the Bank of France.[54] The pace of rearmament quickened, though within the limits of the funds available. Daladier was preoccupied with the French weakness in the air. The gap between France and the Axis powers, inflated by French intelligence, and the knowledge that the

[54] Robert Frank[enstein], 'Réarmement français, finances publiques et conjoncture internationale, 1935–1939', *Bulletin de la Société de histoire moderne*, 9 (1981), 11–18; Alfred Sauvy, *Histoire économique de la France entre les deux guerres*, vol. II (Paris, 1967), 338–339. The return of gold, much of it from London, left France in September 1939 with a gold reserve of 2,833 tons, more than double the reserves of August 1914 (1,203 tons). Robert Frank[enstein], *Le prix du réarmement français*, 205.

French aircraft industry was still in no position to reduce this imbalance, spurred the government to seek foreign sources of assistance. At a meeting of the CPDN on 5 December, the Air Ministry demanded a further 2.5 billion francs over its 1939 budget allocation, to buy American planes. With neither the army nor the navy willing to accept reductions in their demands, and with Gamelin insisting that their needs should have priority, an impasse was reached. Daladier prevailed, and it was agreed that an order for 1,000 planes, for July 1939, should be placed with the United States. Quite apart from the strength of American isolationist opinion, the limited productive capacity of the American aircraft industry and the need for time to develop new prototypes restricted what could be achieved, even with the major expansion of the industry initiated by Roosevelt. The combined opposition of the American air force and army chiefs as well as protests from Congressmen about American involvement in European affairs checked Roosevelt's initiatives. The crash of a Douglas plane with French officers aboard created a major scandal. It was mainly due to the president's backing that, in February 1939, Jean Monnet, the French representative, concluded the purchase of 555 planes costing $60 million, with a delivery date well after the July 1939 deadline. Options were placed for Pratt and Whitney engines, but the French were warned that the order could not be completed until July 1940. To save dollars and ease the shortage of engines, French orders were also placed in Holland, Czechoslovakia, Switzerland, and Britain. In all, the total funding allotted to the Air Ministry nearly quadrupled, from 6.64 billion francs in 1938 to 23.9 billion francs in 1939; 48% of the total defence budget was earmarked for the air force.[55]

Reynaud feared that this spiralling defence bill would lead to renewed pressure on the franc, and warned the Chamber of Deputies' financial commission in March 1939: 'The situation will always be difficult so long as France's military expenditure is incontestably disproportionate to our resources.'[56] However, it was not only restricted funds that explained why more was not accomplished by way of rearmament. Industrial production improved significantly during 1939, raising French morale and contributing to the cabinet's willingness to take a firmer stand against the Axis powers. Output rose in coal mining, chemicals, steel, and textiles; the index of industrial production jumped

[55] Frank, *Le prix du réarmement français*, 295–296 and 306.

[56] Quoted in Talbot Imlay, *Facing the Second World War*, 273. See Imlay's argument that Reynaud's laissez-faire views and anti-labour policies retarded French industrial mobilization.

from seventy-six in October 1938 (1929 = 100) to ninety in June 1939, the first time it had reached that level since 1928.[57] Output in the aircraft industry also showed a marked improvement, from an average of thirty-seven planes a month during 1938 to more than a hundred in March 1939, as earlier reforms worked their way through the industry. Not only had the percentage of the state's expenditure on defence risen dramatically, but much of it was devoted to the production of modern weapons, tanks, anti-aircraft guns, artillery, and aircraft. The problem was that France started rearmament later than either Germany or Britain, and from a smaller and less efficient industrial base. No Ministry of Supply or its equivalent was created, nor any attempt made to direct labour or to retrain skilled labour for defence industries. Whereas in Britain steps were taken to encourage voluntary co-operation between employers and unions, in France labour hostility engendered by the government's support for the 'employer offensive' persisted even as the unions lost power. Except with respect to the air force, little thought was given to what would happen if the concept of the long war proved as illusory for France as had that of the short war in 1914.

While Daladier had no doubt about the need to revitalize the economy, he was more uncertain about the direction of French foreign policy after Munich. There was general agreement in the defence establishment on the need for a strengthened relationship with Britain, but on little else. Should the eastern European alliances be retained as a counterweight to Germany, or should the focus be shifted to the Mediterranean? Gamelin vacillated between the two options. In October he submitted a bleak appreciation of the strategic situation that suggested a 'new orientation of our military policy', shifting the centre of French concern from eastern Europe to the Mediterranean. He informed Daladier that three of the four service chiefs favoured such a change. By December, having recovered from the shock of Munich, Gamelin was urging the construction of an eastern bloc of Poland, Romania, Yugoslavia, and Turkey that could draw on material support from the Soviet Union. In an unusually emotional note to Daladier on 19 December, he asserted that 'the fate of human civilization, that of all democratic powers' depended on France's resolve to resist the *Drang nach Osten*.[58] Intelligence chiefs were even more outspoken in their opposition to Bonnet's strategy, warning that it

[57] Imlay, *Facing the Second World War*, 71.

[58] For this and later quotations see Peter Jackson, 'Intelligence and the End of Appeasement', in Robert Boyce (ed.), *French Foreign and Defence Policy, 1918–1940: The Decline and Fall of a Great Power* (London, 1998), 236, 245.

would not only provide Germany with access to the natural resources of the region but deprive France of a potential reservoir of much needed manpower. The head of air force intelligence claimed in early January that 'if Britain and France did not make a stand in the east, Germany would crush Poland, overrun Romania, seize the Ukraine', and become 'the unchallengeable mistress of Europe and the world'. Not all the advice Daladier received was so unequivocal. Louis Aubert, one of his most trusted advisers, acknowledged that the German acquisition of resources would permit her to turn against France, but recommended that the government should concentrate its diplomatic activity and military and naval strength in the Mediterranean, where Italy represented the weakest point of the Axis and where it would be easier to promote an Anglo-French *entente*. For much of October and November, Daladier suffered from his usual indecision, compounded by the depressing memory of Munich and his bitterness at Chamberlain's personal diplomacy. Talks between the British and French chiefs of staff in November made little progress, and drove home how little France had achieved at Munich in the way of a *quid pro quo*. In the end, Daladier made no decisive choice. He gave his approval to the Franco-German agreement of 6 December, but neither renounced nor strengthened France's commitments in the east, and refused to give Bonnet a green light in the German direction. Given the state of France's defences and the absence of the British alliance, he chose to adopt a waiting game in eastern Europe, and sought greater scope for action in the Mediterranean.

Faced with German–Italian co-operation at Munich, and subsequent intelligence reports on the inadequacy of Italian war preparations, Daladier was prepared to respond publicly to Mussolini's winter blustering. He received contradictory advice: Bonnet and François-Poncet, the French ambassador in Rome, urged that an agreement should be reached with Mussolini. Some *Quai d'Orsay* officials, Gamelin, and above all, the naval chief of staff, Admiral Darlan, opposed any kind of territorial concession to the Italians. The main danger was that a belligerent policy towards Italy would antagonize Chamberlain. As the Duce's propaganda campaign and actions in North Africa became more openly hostile, support for a tougher line increased. Even the conciliatory Bonnet refused to enter into any negotiations that would go beyond the issues covered by the 1935 accord. In early January, Daladier visited Corsica, Tunis, and Algeria, and declared that France would never surrender either an acre of her territory, or any of her rights. The French reinforced Djibouti and the eastern frontier of Tunisia. Evidence, in the form of decrypted Italian diplomatic cables, made it clear that Mussolini was intent on converting the Mediterranean into an

Italian sea, at French expense. There were further efforts at negotiating with Mussolini. Hoping that Franco's capture of Barcelona, at the end of January, would put him in a more benevolent mood, Paul Baudouin, the former general manager of the Bank of Indo-China, was sent by Daladier and Bonnet as a secret emissary to open talks. News of the talks leaked and a wave of criticism in the left-wing press followed, leading Daladier, already mistrustful of Mussolini's intentions, to cut short the conversations. The French knew that the Italian economy was strained to the point of breakdown, and that the population was pacific and anti-German. According to the *Deuxième Bureau*, Italy would constitute a 'deadweight for Germany', and if involved in a long war would face an internal crisis.[59] Despite the Italian reinforcements of the Libyan garrison, Gamelin did not doubt that any Italian attack in North Africa could be successfully thwarted, and that France could go on the offensive against Italy. The latter possibility, however, had to be weighed against the need to guard against a German attack on France's north-eastern frontier.

Further efforts, which continued right up to the outbreak of war and beyond, to open a dialogue with Mussolini failed due to the latter's belligerence. As Bonnet's influence on Italian policy began to wane, the continuing deterioration in relations with Rome gave Admiral Darlan a fresh opportunity to press for an aggressive war policy, including the bombardment of the Italian mainland and air and ground assaults on Tripoli and Italy's north-western frontier. Few were willing to support these proposals, which even Darlan acknowledged would depend on British assistance, and would require a reduction of the troops needed to fight Germany. Daladier was concerned, too, that given the imminent prospect of Franco's victory in Spain, if France engaged with Italy, Spanish troops would cross the Pyrenean frontier. The premier opted for a compromise between Darlan's aggressive war plans and Gamelin's preferred more passive methods, such as inciting domestic unrest in Italy, and 'asphyxiating' Italy by closing Suez and Gibraltar. At the meeting of the CPDN on 24 February, Daladier proposed that France should mount an assault against Libya if Italy moved against either Tunisia or Djibouti, but rejected Darlan's proposed attacks on the Italian mainland. On the same day, France accepted the long-awaited invitation from London for staff talks. Attitudes had changed a great deal in a mere three months. A German mis-information campaign gave the French the opportunity to press more forcefully their case for a British continental army.

[59] Quoted in Peter Jackson, 'Intelligence and the End of Appeasement', 243.

IX

There was no absence of warnings that Hitler was planning a further foreign adventure for the spring of 1939. The difficulty was in knowing in which direction he would strike. It was impossible to obtain more detailed information due to the confused situation in Berlin, where the unexpected resistance of the Warsaw government had left Hitler with a number of possible options. Three different directives were given to the *Wehrmacht*: preparations for smashing the remnants of the Czech state, a 'peaceful' occupation of Czechoslovakia without mobilization, and an occupation of Danzig. None necessarily involved a war in the west. In Paris, there was general agreement that Hitler would move East. French intelligence had long predicted that Hitler would try to secure the natural resources of Eastern Europe and the Balkans before making his bid for the domination of Europe. The post-Munich assessments made by the *Service de Renseignement*, which gathered clandestine information for the army and air force intelligence departments, warned in a general fashion of a possible German attack in the east in early 1939. The *Deuxième Bureau* predicted only that Hitler would pursue his 'programme of hegemony', and make Poland his next target. In London, too, intelligence sources predicted that Hitler would move East; in December came reports that the Germans would set up an independent Ukraine, under their control. On extended leave in London from October until February, and already suffering from the cancer that would cause his death in 1942, Ambassador Nevile Henderson's absence from Berlin allowed his staff to send chilling accounts of the German preparations for war, and manifestations of ill-will towards Britain. Much of their information, as well as other reports reaching the Foreign Office, was derived from anti-Hitler officers and conservative dissidents who re-emerged after Munich. As before, it was a heterogeneous assortment of diplomats, exiles, anti-Nazis living in Germany and, potentially the most influential of all, the military, including serving officers on the general staff, the army staff, the Air Ministry, and the *Abwehr*. All provided intelligence about Hitler's intentions to strike in the spring. Britain's own Secret Intelligence Service (SIS) and Vansittart's private 'detective agency', reported on Germany's war preparations and its domestic situation. The reports emphasized the acceleration of German rearmament, and the severe strains imposed on the German economy, resulting in considerable unrest among ordinary Germans.

Early in January, accounts began to appear in London that Hitler intended to strike westwards. Embassy officials in Berlin, commenting on the difficulties of simultaneously meeting Germany's need for exports and for armaments, concluded that if Germany was going to settle her accounts with Britain, she might be driven to act before the economic situation got worse. Gladwyn Jebb summed up the situation: 'all our sources are at one in declaring that he [Hitler] is barely sane, consumed by an insensate hatred of this country, and capable both of ordering an immediate aerial attack on any European country and of having his command instantly obeyed'.[60] It appears that the winter rumours of a move against the west originated with Hans Oster, deputy to the *Abwehr*'s chief, Admiral Canaris, or someone in a similar position. Oster was a sophisticated and sardonic figure whose deep repugnance for the barbarism and crudity of the Nazi élite, and Hitler in particular, was concealed by a somewhat dandyish front. He was well-placed to know just what would alarm the British, and how to plant the necessary disinformation to encourage a tougher British line towards Hitler. By the time the Chamberlain party returned from their trip to Rome, they were faced with a mass of intelligence predicting an all-out air attack on London, an invasion of Holland to secure air bases, or an attack on Switzerland to bypass the Maginot Line. While the prime minister thought it far more likely that Hitler would go east rather than west, he admitted that it was just possible that the Germans were planning to punish Britain, should it interfere with Hitler's eastern ambitions. Steps were put in motion to hasten the air defence measures. Significantly, these rumours did not appear in the French weekly intelligence reports in either December or January. Nonetheless, the French also began a lobbying campaign, warning of a likely German attack on Holland, Belgium, or Switzerland, as part of their attempt to exert greater pressure on London for the creation of a substantial British Expeditionary Force. In this aim, Paris was abetted by estimates from the War Office, which, knowing that an attack on the Low Countries would be regarded as affecting a vital British interest, hoped to secure the promise of an enlarged continental force. While Halifax was sceptical of the reports, as was Chamberlain, ministers agreed by late January that Britain would have to proceed as if they were true.

The chiefs of staff concluded that the strategic importance of Holland and her colonies was so great that a German attack had to be considered as an attack on Britain. There were moral implications, too. The failure to intervene in Holland would 'undermine our position in the eyes of the Dominions and the world in general. We might thus be deprived of support in a subsequent struggle between Germany and the British Empire.' The chiefs of staff had accepted that nothing could be done

[60] Dilks (ed.), *The Diaries of Sir Alexander Cadogan*, 139.

to save Holland, but recommended that a field force should be dispatched in the hope of encouraging France to support Belgium. They admitted, too, that British intervention would almost inevitably bring in Italy and possibly Japan. With only France as a possible ally, 'if we were compelled to enter such a war in the near future we should be confronted with a position more serious than the Empire had ever faced before'.[61] The ultimate outcome might well depend on the intervention of other powers, in particular the United States. Yet despite these depressing prospects, the chiefs of staff, in sharp contrast to their advice before Munich, recommended British intervention. Both they and the cabinet were influenced by the constant stream of reports that had flowed from the British ambassador and military attaché in Paris during the months following Munich, warning that without any clear backing from Britain, in the form of a commitment to send an expeditionary force to the continent shortly after war broke out, France might refuse to actively resist German expansion in Eastern Europe, and strike a deal with Germany. The cabinet, meeting on 1 February, endorsed a series of far-reaching decisions. Britain would assure France that it would go to war if Germany invaded either Holland or Switzerland, if the French gave mutual pledges in return. The cabinet also authorized joint staff planning with the French and Belgian governments, though this constituted a 'far more binding commitment' than had been contemplated previously. The planners would consider a war against Germany, in combination with Italy, and would cover all likely theatres of war, particularly the Mediterranean and Middle East. Periodic liaison should be established between their respective general staffs, a development previously stoutly resisted. Though it was understood that these proposals were 'almost tantamount to an alliance, nevertheless the step must be taken'. In February, the British transmitted their declaration of support for France and the offer of staff talks to Paris.

The hasty British diplomatic initiatives of these few days, taken despite Foreign Office scepticism about likely German action, suggest how nervous Halifax and Cadogan had become. The 'war scares' of 1938–1939 were taking their toll. A message was sent to Roosevelt, asking the president to issue a public warning before Hitler's Reichstag speech of 30 January, if Chamberlain did the same. Halifax also appealed to the Belgians, and urged that they hold talks with the Dutch and the French. Both ploys came to nothing. Roosevelt would not go beyond his January State of the Union message, for he judged the American climate too isolationist for anything more, and was already engaged in congressional battles over appropriations. King Leopold, for his part, dismissed

[61] Both quotations are from TNA: PRO, CAB 24/282/7041.

the rumour of a German attack, and rejected all suggestions that might call Belgian neutrality into question. Chamberlain's speech in Birmingham on 28 January was, according to Cadogan, 'quite good enough', though it was not a warning but an appeal to Hitler. The prime minister spoke of the strictly defensive character of British rearmament, and expressed the hope that his government could secure international peace. Chamberlain gave special emphasis to what he considered his key sentence: 'I feel that the time has now come when others should make their contribution'.[62] Horace Wilson sent the text in advance to Hitler at Berchtesgaden, and Chamberlain was convinced that the so-called moderation of Hitler's speech two days later was a response to his appeal. Hitler's speech was not entirely reassuring. The Führer informed the world of his solidarity with Italy if the latter were attacked. He again denounced Churchill, Eden, and Duff Cooper, but he did hold out an olive branch of sorts to London. He thanked Chamberlain for assisting in the Munich settlement, stressed Germany's need to trade, and claimed that colonies were not a problem that would cause war. His statement that he 'looked forward to a long period of peace' was received with loud applause. Cadogan was concerned that Chamberlain might take too optimistic a view of the situation. On 6 February, using a draft prepared by Halifax and Vansittart, again an influential figure, the prime minister gave a forceful answer to a parliamentary question about Anglo-French solidarity in case of an Italian attack on France.

> It is impossible to examine in detail all the hypothetical cases which may arise, but I feel bound to make plain that the solidarity of interest, by which France and this country are united, is such that any threat to the vital interests of France from whatever quarter it came must evoke the immediate co-operation of this country.[63]

If such a declaration had been made in 1934, or even in 1919, many of the subsequent problems in European affairs might have been averted. Only a threat to one of Britain's age-old interests had moved the cabinet to take action.

As a result of the scare over Holland, not only had the cabinet agreed to staff talks, but the chiefs of staff accepted the army's demands that a field force be equipped for continental service. At a special cabinet meeting on 5 February, Chamberlain, together with Simon, fought a rearguard action to trim the army's budget and keep the lid on defence spending. The prime minister hoped that once the position was explained to the French, they would realize what a gigantic effort the

62 Quoted in Parker, *Chamberlain and Appeasement*, 195.
63 *Hansard*, HC Deb, 6 February 1939, Vol. 343, Col. 623.

British were making and would see that, in the common interest, it might not be best for Britain to expand its land forces. Halifax, however, stressing the sensitivity of the French on the question of Britain's continental commitment, argued that Britain could risk borrowing the needed funds for rearmament. Either war would come soon or the Nazi regime would collapse. On 22 February, the greater part of the army programme was approved. Ministers, including Hore-Belisha, the secretary for war, were still thinking of a limited, if well-equipped expeditionary force. The French could count on four Regular Army infantry divisions and the two mobile divisions but there was no promise to commit the Territorial Army divisions. Neither Chamberlain nor the chiefs of staff showed any great sense of urgency about starting the proffered staff talks. The former was clearly reluctant to formalize relations with France, while the latter feared that high-level talks would attract publicity and provoke Hitler to take precipitate action. The chiefs of staff recommended that Britain play for time until rearmament was more advanced. The talks with the French should be confined to the planning level, and conversations with the Dutch and Belgians should be postponed to a later stage. But neither Chamberlain's reluctance to change course, nor the still limited size of the field force, should obscure the importance of the British shift of perspective in the winter of 1939. The idea of a war of limited liability had been abandoned, and Britain was preparing a first army equipped for service on the continent, and a second army equipped for service in the colonies or elsewhere overseas. This involved a much higher scale of equipment and reserve forces. As it turned out, the Anglo-French staff talks only began on 29 March, by which time the international situation had already changed for the worse.

After a series of alarms, a quiet lull set in during the latter part of February 1939. During this respite, the search for peaceful alternatives to confrontation continued, though few were as optimistic as earlier. Not everyone was convinced that war with Germany was inevitable. As the dire predictions of German action failed to materialize, Chamberlain recovered his confidence. Buttressed by reports from Henderson, who had returned to Berlin, he told his sister on 19 February that 'all the information I get seems to point in the direction of peace and I repeat once more that I believe we have at last got on top of the dictators. Of course that doesn't mean I want to bully them.'[64] His hopeful attitude was not shared by either Halifax or Cadogan. The rapid increase in the defensive power of the RAF convinced the prime minister that Hitler would not risk provoking a European war; on the contrary, Germany's

[64] Self (ed.), *Diary Letters*, 382 (To Hilda, 19 February 1939).

economic difficulties would compel Hitler to opt for a policy of peace and disarmament. On 9 March, Chamberlain told the parliamentary lobby correspondents that 'the foreign situation is less anxious and gives me less concern for possible unpleasant development than it has done for some time'.[65] The next day, asked by Chamberlain to discourage the view that war was inevitable, Samuel Hoare told his Chelsea constituents that if the 'peoples of Europe were able to free themselves from the nightmare that haunts them, and from an expenditure on armaments that beggars them, could we not then devote the inventions and discoveries of our time to the creation of a golden age? . . . Five men in Europe, if they worked with a singleness of purpose and a unity of action, might in an incredibly short space of time transform the whole history of the world.'[66] His many qualifications were ignored; the note of optimism struck a welcome chord. It was an unfortunate speech.

[65] Quoted in Roberts, *The Holy Fox: A Biography of Lord Halifax*, 141.

[66] Quoted in D. C. Watt, *How War Came*, 163–164. Unlike so many other historians, Watt notes the 'ifs and buts'.

13

Black Sun: Aggression and Deterrence

I

At 9 a.m. on 15 March 1939, the first advanced German troops entered Prague. That same morning, Hitler boarded a train and after a long journey by rail and car, through continuous blizzards, arrived at the Hradčany Palace after six in the evening. He stayed for two days and returned home via Vienna to a tumultuous reception. The remaining Czech territories of Bohemia and Moravia were restored to 'their ancient historic setting' and made a German protectorate. The final plans to complete the elimination of Czechoslovakia had been put in place in early February—seven army corps were prepared to march, though neither internal resistance nor foreign intervention was anticipated—but the country's disappearance did not take place quite as Hitler had intended. The first steps towards its dissolution were successful though it proved difficult to recruit Slovak leaders to undermine the state. Subsequent Czech action caused the German script to go wrong. Despite Hitler's bullying and threats, the Slovakian Assembly in Bratislava declared independence, but refused his demands that they request German 'protection'. Finally, under enormous pressure, the Slovak government, led by Father Tiso, requested a very limited form of protection. The Führer's reply on 16 March simply ignored the qualifications. The deed was done, and German troops quickly arrived to guarantee Slovakia's 'independence'. Slovak recalcitrance made the task of crushing Prague a little more difficult. A German press campaign, making much of staged incidents in the country, was launched on 12 March, as German troops were already moving towards the border in the expectation that all would go well in Slovakia, and the occupation could begin at once. Lacking a Slovak invitation, Hitler had to deal directly with the Czechs. The elderly and infirm President Emil Hacha came to Berlin to negotiate, and, after hours of waiting, was finally received by Hitler at 1.15 in the morning of 15 March. He was treated to one of Hitler's vintage harangues, revealing yet again what a thoroughly despicable human being the dictator was. Hacha had no weapons with which to fight, not even the kind of strong popular backing that Tiso could marshal. He knew that German troops had already crossed the border. The president grovelled, hoping to save some vestige of his country's independence. Instead, Göring informed the Czech representatives that he would be sorry to bomb beautiful Prague, but it would be a salutary lesson for France and Britain. Hacha either fainted or had a minor heart attack and was revived by Hitler's doctor. He phoned Prague to urge that there should be no resistance. After a further hour and a half of bullying, Hacha signed the prepared draft, placing 'the fate of the Czech people in the hands of the Führer'. As the beaten Czechs left, Hitler embraced his private secretaries, still waiting at this late hour should their services be required. 'Children', he said, 'this is the greatest day of my life. I shall enter history as the greatest German of them all'.[1]

Hitler was not finished. On Sunday, 12 March, he summoned the Hungarian minister in Berlin and told him he was about to smash Czechoslovakia and was withdrawing protection from Ruthenia. The Hungarians were warned to seize it quickly or not at all, as others, above all the Poles, were interested in the region. Horthy was delighted; his long wait was finally over. Hungarian troops marched across the border on 14 March. Ruthenian nationalists took on the invading Hungarians in what was a short and hopeless engagement. Ruthenians became Hungarians. Now in a position to threaten the Poles from the south, Hitler intended to outflank them from the north. He had held his hand over Memel all through the autumn, hoping that the Poles would yield Danzig. The situation had changed. On 20 March, the foreign minister of Lithuania was summoned to Berlin and given the same treatment as Tiso and Hacha. He stubbornly refused to cede Memel, as Ribbentrop demanded, or obtain the consent of his government by telephone, but under the threat of an air bombardment of their capital, the Lithuanians gave in. Memel was handed to the Germans on 23 March. Hitler went to see his latest acquisition aboard the pocket battleship *Deutschland*; the crossing was rough and the Führer was seasick.

The occupation of the remainder of Czechoslovakia paid high economic and military dividends. By 1 June, 40,000 Czech skilled workers had been recruited for work in Germany. Seized army stores were sufficient to equip or complete the equipment of twenty divisions. Three German armoured divisions sent against France in 1940 were equipped with tanks, guns, and trucks made in Czech factories. Czechoslovakia's most important armament firms, including the huge Škoda works, along with other iron, steel, and coal industries, were taken over

[1] Quoted in D. C. Watt, *How War Came*, 154.

by the *Hermann Göring Reichswerke*. The new industrial acquisitions in Austria and Czechoslovakia were to provide the industrial base for the build-up of the war-oriented economy. With the Reich's industrial accretions of 1938–1939, Germany enjoyed 15% of the world's industrial production and, was second only to the United States among the industrial powers. Through a series of treaties, almost all economic activity in Slovakia was brought under German control, providing minerals and supplies of foodstuffs to the resource-poor Reich.

The creation of the Protectorate inaugurated a new phase in the establishment of Germany's economic hegemony over south-eastern Europe. The Reich authorities, searching for supplies of raw materials, hoped to enlarge the German dominated economic area that might ease its present and future situation. The Germans extended their control over the Balkan economies through the transfer or purchase of industrial shares. The German–Romanian economic treaty of 23 March 1939 was seen as a major breakthrough, assuring Germany of the oil and grain it needed. It was intended as the model for similar long-term treaties with Yugoslavia, Bulgaria, Hungary, Greece, and Turkey, in order to create 'a German-controlled clearing system extending over the whole of the Southeast'.[2] The Romanian treaty was based on a five-year plan under which Romania was to supply designated agricultural products and raw materials (oil being the most important), while the Germans would export the plants and machinery needed for production and processing. Joint Romanian–German companies would accelerate the exploitation of Romanian mineral wealth, and implement a large-scale petroleum programme. In return, Germany would equip the Romanian forces with arms and aircraft. While the Germans did not establish a monopolistic position in Romania (trade agreements were concluded with France on 31 March and with Britain on 11 May), the treaty tied Romania into the extended German trading system, and was viewed as a victory for Foreign Minister Gafencu's pro-German policies.

A similar effort was made to draw Yugoslavia into the Reich's economic orbit. Germany succeeded in securing an ever-increasing volume of Yugoslav trade in 1938–1939, outdistancing all other rivals as they acquired the former Viennese investments in Croatia, and took up the Czech investments in Yugoslavia's machinery, armament, sugar and textile industries. The German interest in Belgrade was mainly economic rather than political. The regent, Prince Paul, was more

[2] Quoted in David E. Kaiser, *Economic Diplomacy and the Origins of the Second World War*, 267.

concerned with Italian irredentism than with German expansion. Worried by deficiencies in arms and aircraft, he sought supplies wherever he could find them, soliciting both German and western aid. The prince played a complex game, but his country was too enmeshed in the German net to avoid economic subservience. Hitler courted him shrewdly, avoiding threats or fist-shaking during the monarch's all-important trip to Berlin in June 1939. Every effort was made to stress German friendliness towards the country. Hitler's conciliatory approach and 'studied restraint', against the background of marching troops and air displays, had its effect. While the prince was not overawed, and resisted Ribbentrop's attempts to secure his adherence to the Anti-Comintern Pact or to leave the League of Nations, he returned to Belgrade with enhanced respect for German power if not reassured about Hitler's intentions with regard to Yugoslavia.

There were limits to what the Germans could achieve. In the first place, imports from the region could only meet a fraction of the requirements of the German war economy. The limited productive capacity and agricultural backwardness of the Balkan states restricted their export capacities, particularly as the Reich was unable to supply them with the raw materials needed for industrial development and armaments. The system of exchanging arms for raw materials and agricultural products began to break down, as Germany's own requirements took precedence. The speed-up of the German rearmament programme intensified the German need for raw materials but restricted its ability to export in a shrinking world market. Germany still had to get most of its agricultural produce from northern Europe and overseas sources. Nor were the Balkan states anxious to become German satellites or allies in the war which many assumed was coming. Their leaders recognized the dangers of the German *Großwirtschaftsräume* and tried to redress the economic balance by seeking credits and arms from the western powers, the United States, and Sweden. As will be discussed (see pp. 952–3) the British and French proved either unwilling or unable to meet their needs and the Americans, Swedes, and Swiss demanded hard currency, but despite Germany's well-entrenched position, the states were still able to avoid German economic exploitation. On 8 March, Hitler claimed that Germany's economic problems would be solved by 1940, once Poland was conquered and Hungary, Romania, and Yugoslavia came under German control.[3] It remained to be seen how far countries like Romania and Yugoslavia could preserve their neutrality and avoid alignment with either power bloc.

[3] *FRUS*, 1939, I, 672 ff (March 1939).

Table 13.1 Value of German Trade with Eastern Europe, 1928, 1933–1939 (in million Reichsmarks)

	1928	1933	1934	1935	1936	1937	1938	1939
Austria								
Imports from	232.1	57.6	66.3	71.1	76.6	93.3	17.3	n/a
Exports to	425.7	120.7	106.7	107.9	108.5	122.7	29	n/a
Bulgaria								
Imports from		31.3	33.7	41.4	57.6	71.8	95.7	110
Exports to		17.7	19.3	39.9	47.6	68.2	61.6	97.8
Czechoslovakia								
Imports from	538.3	121.7	162.3	121.4	111.9	141.4	188.8	89.9
Exports to	649.4	160.1	148.4	130	139	151	161.1	86.9
Greece								
Imports from		53.4	55.3	58.5	68.4	76.4	101	92.1
Exports to		18.7	29.3	49.1	63.5	113.1	121.2	85.5
Hungary								
Imports from	71.9	34.2	63.9	77.9	93.4	114.1	186.2	222.5
Exports to	154	38.1	39.6	62.9	83	110.5	146.4	228.7
Romania								
Imports from	188.1	46.1	59	79.9	92.3	179.5	177.8	209.5
Exports to	173	46	50.9	63.8	103.6	129.5	168.6	216.7
Yugoslavia								
Imports from	66.6	33.5	36.3	61.4	75.2	132.2	172.2	131.5
Exports to	117.6	33.8	31.5	36.9	77.2	134.4	144.6	181.3
Poland and Danzig								
Imports from	377.9	77.1	78.1	75.5	74	80.8	140.8	97.8
Exports to	499.3	82.4	55.1	63.3	73.9	99.7	155.2	101.2
Estonia								
Imports from	33.3	8.4	8.2	13.1	13.8	23.7	24.3	28.3
Exports to	41.2	7.1	7.3	11.4	17.6	19.9	22.3	25.7
Latvia								
Imports from	66.3	17.5	21.1	31.1	33.2	45.7	43.6	44.1
Exports to	78.9	17.2	18.8	27.9	31.2	28.4	43	49.8
Lithuania								
Imports from	54.7	22.1	15.1	2.6	9.1	17.2	27.8	28.2
Exports to	52.6	19.7	14.7	6.7	7.3	20.4	24.3	29.3
Total German trade								
Imports	14,051.2	4,203.6	4,451.1	4,158.7	4,217.9	5,468.4	6,051.7	4,796.5
Exports	12,054.8	4,871.4	4,166.9	4,269.7	4,768.2	5,911	5,619.1	5,222.2

Sources: David E. Kaiser, *Economic Diplomacy and the Origins of the Second World War: Germany, Britain, France, and Eastern Europe 1930–1939* (Princeton, NJ, 1980), 319. Militärgeschichtliches Forschungsamt (ed.), *Germany and the Second World War*, Vol. 1, ed. Wilhelm Deist (Oxford, 1990), 349.

Table 13.2 Foreign Share of German Imports Immediately before the War (%)

	Overall	Foodstuffs	Raw Materials
Reliable Imports			
Italy	4.5	6.5	2.9
Czechoslovakia	2.4	1.0	2.6
Hungary, Romania, Yugoslavia, Bulgaria and Greece	9.9	17.2	5.3
Scandinavia and Finland	11.4	11.2	11.5
Baltic States	1.8	2.2	1.3
Belgium, Holland and Switzerland	9.1	6.2	7.5
Russia	0.9	0.1	1.9
Total	*40.0*	*44.4*	*33.0*
Defaulting or Doubtful Imports	60.0	55.6	67.0

Sources: Opinion of Tomberg of the War Economy and Armaments Office, January 1940. Militärgeschichtliches Forschungsamt (ed.), *Germany and the Second World War*, Vol. 1, ed. Wilhelm Deist et al. (Oxford, 1990), 352.

II

Even while digesting the dividends arising from the destruction of Prague, Hitler continued his efforts to bully the Poles into yielding Danzig and the Polish Corridor. The Czech *coup* and the occupation of Memel should have intimidated Warsaw, but the Poles appeared more concerned with the suddenness of the German move and their failure to consult over Slovakia rather than with the actual disappearance of their neighbour. Polish troops joined the Hungarians moving into Ruthenia; the long-desired common border was in sight. There was considerable alarm over Memel. Quite apart from the possibility that Germany might use Lithuania in any conflict with Poland, the city's former autonomous status, guaranteed by international statute, presented a clear parallel with Danzig. The future of Danzig had become the major issue between Germany and Poland. In late March, the Germans made it clear that they intended to get their way over the control of the territory but the Poles refused to accept the absorption of Danzig into the Reich. There was even a political assurance that Warsaw would remain committed to an anti-Soviet policy, though no offer to join the Anti-Comintern Pact. It was Ribbentrop, who in his blundering fashion, brought the dispute to crisis point. On 26 March, he threatened the Polish ambassador; any Polish aggression against Danzig would be treated as aggression against Germany. While the Poles intended to demonstrate that they could not be treated like the Czechs, there was no sign that they were going to invade Danzig. As rumours about the extent of German demands circulated, anti-German riots broke out, and the Polish press echoed and stoked the public anger, giving full coverage to the prevailing hostility towards Germany. Ribbentrop had gone too far. The Führer, while impatient with the Poles, did not yet want to solve the Danzig problem by force, and so push Poland into Britain's arms. He told General Brauchitsch, the commander-in-chief, that he was not thinking of solving the Polish question, 'for the time being', but that the general staff should study the problem. This order was the genesis of what became 'Case White', the attack on Poland, probably prepared around 27–28 March. Preparations were made for military operations, but implementation would depend on how the situation developed. Given the heady atmosphere in Poland, Beck could give only one answer to Ribbentrop's threats: Poland would regard as a *casus belli* any German attempt to alter the status of Danzig by unilateral action. The Poles would not give way to Berlin.

III

The Prague *coup* took London by surprise. Chamberlain's immediate response in the House of Commons was cautious and muted; it did not reflect the sense of outrage felt in the country over this blatant disregard of the promises made at Munich, and the violation of Hitler's solemn assurances that he did not want to incorporate Czechs into the Reich. Even the Dominion governments, appeasement-minded in September 1938, denounced Hitler's actions, which made a mockery of the Munich agreement and the principles of self-determination. Chivvied by the cabinet and pushed by Halifax, Chamberlain used a speech to his constituents in Birmingham on 17 March to dwell on Hitler's dishonesty, and to make clear the government's intention to review its policies, to turn to France and the Commonwealth, and to interest itself in south-east Europe. Still, half the speech was devoted to a defence of appeasement. 'The facts as they are today cannot change the facts as they were last September', he told his listeners. 'If I was right then, I am still right now.' It was not the defence of his policies but the warning 'that no greater mistake could be made than to suppose that, because it believes war to be a senseless and cruel thing, this nation has so lost its fibre that it will not take part to the utmost of its power in resisting such a challenge if it ever were made', that produced the most enthusiastic applause.[4] In sharp distinction to the public reaction to the German march into Prague, there was little response to the occupation of Memel beyond words of sympathy. The Chamberlain government would not take on

[4] Neville Chamberlain, *The Struggle for Peace* (London, 1939), 414, 420.

any obligations in the Baltic beyond those stemming from its membership in the League of Nations. Symbolic gestures of disapproval, such as the interruption of the Anglo-German trade talks, hardly matched the public mood. Further measures resulted from the intervention of the Romanian diplomat, Vergil Tilea, who on 17 March erroneously warned Halifax of an imminent German action against Romania. Supporting evidence, some contested at the time, emerged to back his claim.[5] Coming as it did immediately on top of Hitler's Czech *coup* and only one day after an appeal from King Carol in Bucharest for some sign that Britain and France had not lost all interest in south-eastern Europe, the Foreign Office reacted feverishly to Tilea's news. A series of

[5] Much more is now known about the 'Tilea affair'. King Carol, while wanting to hasten the commercial negotiations with Germany that resulted in the 23 March accord, took alarm at the German and Hungarian actions in Czechoslovakia. In keeping with his hopes of maintaining an equilibrium between the Great Powers, he sought to alert the British and French to the danger of having only one arbiter left in Europe. The Romanian ministers in London and Paris were instructed to speak to the respective foreign ministers. Tilea, even before receiving instructions, had already warned the Foreign Office that his government had reason to believe that within a few months Germany would reduce Hungary to vassalage and 'disintegrate' Romania. An anonymous caller on the morning of the 17th, now identified as Adrian Dumitrescu, general manager of the industrialist Nicolae Malaxa, was instructed to tell Tilea about the extent of Germany's economic and political demands on Romania. Malaxa, part of Carol's unofficial 'camarilla' feared that the new agreement would undercut his freedom to operate independently, despite his close links with German firms. It was after this phone call and the reception of Gafencu's instructions received the same day that Tilea spoke to Halifax of 'something very much like an ultimatum' and asked for British support. Though the king and Gafencu were committed to economic co-operation with Germany, others in Bucharest, such as the minister president, Armand Călinescu, were more pro-western and dubious about ties with Berlin. In fact, the German negotiator, Wohlthat, had been instructed by the Reich Foreign Ministry not to make any political commitments though, as Göring's negotiator, he may have been authorized to offer a guarantee. It is possible that sometime after Wohlthat returned to Bucharest (the negotiations had stalled and he left the capital) on 10 March, he linked the concessions to a political agreement but Gafencu, who had been seeking a guarantee, turned it down because of the international tension and Britain's reaction to Tilea's warning. Subsequent western pressure on the Romanians led Wohlthat to change the drafts of the agreement, which originally contained secret clauses and even possibly a political guarantee. Gafencu ordered Tilea, whom he claimed had gone far beyond his instructions, to return home but the minister stayed on in London, seeking a British loan for arms, and pressing for the formation of an anti-German bloc, because his fears of a German military threat were real. On 17 March, the day on which Tilea told the British about the German 'ultimatum', King Carol invited Göring to the anniversary celebration in May of King Carol I's birth. On 23 March, the Germans agreed to Carol's demand that fifty wagon-loads of arms, which were ordered from Czechoslovakia before the German invasion, should be delivered. Gafencu's pursuit of guarantees both from Germany and from Britain and France, were intended to secure Romania's position of equilibrium between the Reich and the West. All these details are from Rebecca Haynes, *Romanian Policy towards Germany, 1936–40*, 76–90.

telegrams were dispatched to Warsaw, Ankara, Athens, and Belgrade, asking what their attitude would be if Germany attacked Romania. The Soviets were asked whether, if requested, they would assist Romania, for Britain could do little to provide aid without Soviet and Polish co-operation.

Gafencu, the Romanian foreign minister, immediately denied that there had been any 'economic ultimatum', and King Carol assured the British ambassador in Bucharest that 'while there was much in the German proposals that was unpalatable . . . no sort of exception could be taken to the manner in which they had been presented and pressed'.[6] Tilea continued to insist that the ultimatum story was true; continuing intelligence reports that German motorized forces were moving east and southwards beyond Prague, gave weight to British fears of a 'mad dog act'. Though Chamberlain at Birmingham was prepared to warn the German leader, he had no wish to anger him, and in fact sent a personal appeal to Mussolini on 20 March to work for peace, hoping he would calm and restrain the volatile Führer. The following day, the cabinet retreated from the impulsive Foreign Office enquiries on behalf of Romania, which might have been seen as a call for an eastern alliance against German aggression, and recommended instead a joint four-power declaration by Britain, Poland, France and the Soviet Union, that if the political independence of any power was threatened, they would consult together on what steps should be taken to 'offer joint resistance'. The latter words were added at the insistence of the French ambassador, Charles Corbin, who had found Chamberlain's original proposal impossibly vague. Considering that the chiefs of staff reported on 18 March that it was necessary to face Germany with a two-front war in order to check her, Chamberlain's 'bold and startling' initiative was hardly either.

The British enquiries in Eastern Europe were met with considerable suspicion. Yugoslavia, it seemed, would remain neutral until the last moment, and if strongly pressed would co-operate grudgingly with Germany and Italy. Beck declared that he would consult with the Romanians, but he would not provoke Berlin by joining any anti-German grouping that accepted support from the Soviet Union. The Greeks would wait to see what the other members of the Balkan League (Greece, Turkey, Romania, and Yugoslavia), particularly Yugoslavia, would do. The Turkish leaders were sympathetic but they, too, wanted to know exactly what action Britain intended to take. Litvinov, suspicious that the British wanted to engage the Soviet Union without any

[6] Quoted in Rebecca Haynes, *Romanian Policy Towards Germany*, 78.

promise of their own involvement, made his customary offer: the calling of a conference at which delegates from Romania, Poland, Britain, France, and the Soviet Union would discuss common action. He interpreted British unwillingness to consider his conference idea as proof that no serious action was intended.

Decisions in London were being reached in a charged atmosphere. On 21 March, the day that the French president, Albert Lebrun, arrived on an official state visit, the cabinet decided to bring the regular anti-aircraft units to readiness should Hitler, reported to be in a towering rage, lash out in a wild act of aggression. During the visit, annoyed by Chamberlain's questions about the French production of aircraft, Bonnet pressed Halifax about Britain's military contribution in a future war, and urged that Britain adopt some form of national service. Not ready to tackle the question of conscription, the cabinet agreed on 29 March to double the size of the Territorial Army, but turned down the War Office's demand for adding another 50,000 men to the existing six regular divisions. There was a growing awareness of the need to keep Hitler from overrunning Eastern and south-eastern Europe. The British military, like their French counterparts, now stressed the importance of threatening Hitler with a two-front war. What remained in question was where to turn for the necessary support. The chiefs of staff asserted that action in the east could only be pursued with the assistance of Poland and the Soviet Union, and argued that the latter's support, even with Poland neutral, would be the more decisive. Others shared the view of Chamberlain and Halifax that attention should be focused on Poland and Romania, and that the Soviet Union was of less importance, as it had neither the intention nor the ability to offer decisive assistance. The prime minister had no doubt that if a choice had to be made between Poland and the Soviet Union, it should be for the former. He was convinced that the USSR was an 'unreliable friend', and incapable of real action. As he told a Labour party delegation on 23 March, 'the key to the position is not Russia, which has no common frontier with Germany, but Poland which has common frontiers with both Germany and Romania'.[7] To give substance to his argument that Europe should not be divided into opposing ideological blocs, Chamberlain constructed a list of those countries, in addition to Poland and Romania (Finland, Yugoslavia, Italy, Spain, Portugal, and some South American republics), who would dislike association with the Soviet Union or would be alienated should Britain form such an association. As he confessed to his sister Ida, he had 'the most profound distrust of Russia' and 'her motives, which seem to me to have little connection

[7] Quoted in Watt, *How War Came*, 180.

with our ideas of liberty'.[8] Nor did he change his mind when, on the evening of 22 March, still committed to some form of collective action, Litvinov agreed that the Soviet Union would sign the proposed four-power declaration as soon as France and Poland had accepted it. Not for the first or last time, Chamberlain's ideological antipathies, which he refused to allow to influence his policies towards Germany, coloured his approach to the USSR.

Across the Channel, even Bonnet, by mid-March, accepted that only an eastern front, along with the British alliance, would prove an effective deterrent in the light of the failure of attempts at appeasement. While Daladier and Gamelin felt that it was necessary to include the Soviet Union in any eastern front, for Bonnet, Poland and Romania were the key participants, though he recognized that the Soviet Union had a role to play, if only to provide the war supplies required by its two neighbours. On 18 March, he urged Bucharest to accept Soviet assistance. When his advice was rejected, he asked Jacob Surits, the Soviet representative in Paris, whether the USSR would make the first gesture, only to be told that the Soviets would do nothing unless France took the lead. By the time Bonnet met with Halifax on 21 March, he was aware of the difficulties of obtaining Polish and Romanian agreement to Soviet participation in any multinational declaration. It was, he told Halifax, 'absolutely essential to get Poland in. Russian help would only be effective if Poland were collaborating'. While 'the time had come to call a halt to Germany', France did not 'want to have to bear the burden of war alone. British help on land would at first be very small. If, in an eastern war, there was no help from Poland or from any other eastern country, France would be in a bad position.'[9] Poland was the key, and she must not be given any pretext for running out on account of Soviet involvement. Warnings from ambassadors Lord Perth and François-Poncet in Rome, of the likely negative effect on Mussolini if it appeared that Britain and France were about to launch an ideological crusade against the dictatorships, further weakened any advocacy of Soviet inclusion.

On the afternoon of 23 March, at a Foreign Office reception for the French, the possibility of a guarantee to Poland was raised, if she would commit herself to the assistance of Romania. It was agreed that Soviet participation could be sought after an understanding was reached with Poland. But the next day, Count Raczynski, the Polish ambassador in London, told Halifax that Poland could not associate itself with the Soviet Union in a public declaration. Poland intended to preserve her neutrality between Germany and Russia, and no Russian army would be welcomed on Polish soil whatever its purpose might be. Instead, he

[8] NC 18/1/1091, 26 March 1939. [9] *DBFP*, 3rd ser., Vol. IV, No. 458.

offered a secret Anglo-Polish agreement to guarantee British aid in case of an attack on Danzig or on Poland. Halifax stalled, for he preferred a public demonstration of common resolve. He feared, correctly, that Beck might use such an agreement to strike a more favourable bargain with Hitler. The cabinet remained divided over the relative merits of Poland and the Soviet Union as partners in a coalition intended to deter Hitler, but Chamberlain and the pro-Polish faction ultimately prevailed. It was agreed in principle to go ahead with the offers of support for Poland and Romania, if each promised to assist the other. If the position was consolidated, Turkey and Greece could be rallied to the common course and, at some convenient moment, the Soviet Union would be approached to secure its benevolent neutrality. After a further ministerial debate, the four-power declaration was dropped in favour of a reciprocal guarantee to Poland. As Halifax put it: 'we had to make a choice between Poland and Soviet Russia; it seemed clear that Poland would give greater value'.[10] Neither the British nor the French could secure much information about the Polish–German talks over Danzig. Beck had long inspired distrust in both capitals, and with his habitual secretiveness, he decided not to reveal the nature of the German demands to either government. In the absence of hard information, rumours and reports from 'well-informed' sources circulated freely. Diplomatic intelligence and press reports coming into London warned of rising tension in Danzig, and the possibility of an imminent German attack on the city or even against Poland itself. There was further misinformation from anti-Hitler informants that a German drive into the Baltic was imminent, probably leaked in order to provoke Britain into taking action to check Hitler. Ian Colvin, a *News Chronicle* journalist recently expelled from Germany, warned Halifax and Chamberlain that Hitler would attack Poland unless Britain threatened to attack Germany. He gave detailed information about Hitler's future plans, probably leaked by someone on Brauchitsch's staff who wanted to provoke the British.

Already in a high state of alarm bordering on panic over German intentions and anxious about opinion at home, the British government could not face the possibility of a German *coup* without taking some form of preventive action. On 30 March, at an emergency cabinet meeting, Halifax proposed a 'clear declaration of our intention to support Poland if Poland was attacked by Germany'. The next day, Arthur Greenwood, the Labour spokesman, raised the question in the Commons. Telegrams, drafted by Chamberlain and amended by Halifax and Cadogan, went to Paris and Warsaw. Kennard, the British ambassador

[10] TNA: PRO, CAB 27/628, 38, 27 March 1939.

in Warsaw, was in the process of pressing the unwanted four-power declaration on the Polish foreign minister. Upon receiving the new offer of support, Beck, as he told a friend, made up his mind 'between two flicks of the ash off his cigarette'.[11] After telephoning the president and Marshal Rydz-Śmigły, he accepted the guarantee. Kennard was taken aback by the British offer and suggested that it might be watered down in case the Poles were tempted to take some rash action in Danzig.

In this manner, Britain became tied to Poland. The decision for war or peace was entrusted to another country and, in effect, was placed in the hands of a man who was not trusted in London or Paris. Indeed, no one was sure that Poland would choose to resist German expansion or agree to join a coalition to deter Hitler. It was only a temporary measure intended to cover the period while Britain and France constructed an eastern front, bringing together the states of central and south-eastern Europe that could be threatened by Germany. Nevertheless, it was seen, as Chamberlain said, as the 'the actual crossing of the stream'.[12] The British were committed to go to war should Germany attack Poland. It was a political guarantee that had no military backing, for it was aimed at preventing Hitler from risking war rather than preparing the way for a war against him. This is why military considerations and the USSR were of secondary interest. No one on the British side expected that Poland could defend itself against Germany; the only argument concerned the length of its resistance. The chiefs of staff admitted that nothing could be done in the west to stop Germany from overrunning and absorbing Poland and Romania. They stressed the importance of including the Soviet Union in any East European arrangements. The Soviets, however, were not given the text of the guarantee to Poland until a few hours before its announcement, for fear of offending Poland. Subsequent correspondence throws a sharp light on the Soviet sense of outrage. 'Chamberlain is prompting Hitler to direct his aggression to the Northeast', Litvinov wrote to Maisky, the peppery ambassador in London, on 4 April. 'Chamberlain is counting on us to resist occupation of the Baltic area and expecting that this will lead to the Soviet–German clash he had been hoping for.'[13] The German occupation of Memel had raised great apprehensions in Moscow, for it exposed the Soviet Union to a direct attack through the Baltic states, by-passing Poland. Chamberlain's reference to Moscow's understanding and appreciation of the

[11] Quoted in L. B. Namier, *Diplomatic Prelude, 1938–1939* (London, 1948), 107.

[12] Robert Self, *Neville Chamberlain: A Biography*, 357.

[13] Quoted from Geoffrey Roberts, 'The Alliance that Failed: Moscow and the Triple Alliance Negotiations, 1939', *European History Quarterly*, 26: 3 (1996), 389.

principles of the British action, intended to soothe the Opposition benches, hardly accorded with Litvinov's letter to Maisky. 'It is intolerable for us to be in the situation of the man who is invited to a party and then asked not to come because the other guests do not wish to meet him. We would prefer to be crossed off the list of guests altogether.'[14] A secret initialled Anglo-Polish document summarizing the talks left the British free to negotiate with Romania, the Balkan *entente*, and the Soviet Union. Britain's primary purpose was to deter Hitler through a demonstration of collective resolve, but the government had only its guarantee of Poland and the latter's reciprocal engagement, which in turn made it more difficult to build a more inclusive coalition. It restricted Britain's negotiating space and enhanced Beck's power. It is not certain that Chamberlain, who made the announcement of the guarantee to a cheering Commons, fully understood the implications of what had happened. He told his sister Hilda that the declaration dealt only with Poland's independence and not with its territorial integrity: 'And it is we who will judge whether that independence is threatened or not.'[15] This analysis did not accord with the popular perception of Britain's commitment, as was demonstrated by the storm of criticism in the Commons and in the press following articles which echoed the prime minister's line. When Beck came to London on 3 April British ministers hoped to clarify the position in Danzig as well as to discuss the creation of an anti-German bloc. They were to be disappointed. Beck was intent on negotiating the Danzig question directly with Germany, and refused to commit Poland to the support of Romania or any other possible victim of German aggression. Like Chamberlain, Beck did not believe that war was inevitable, and thought that a policy of resoluteness would convince Hitler that Poland could not be conquered like Czechoslovakia. It is doubtful whether Chamberlain was displeased by Beck's resistance to the inclusion of the Soviet Union in any anti-German front.

The offer of the guarantee was more than a panicked response to the German threat to Poland. It had behind it the realization of the futility of Munich and the sacrifice of Czechoslovakia. With his march into Prague, Hitler had destroyed any moral justification for his actions. Ever since Godesberg, Halifax and the Foreign Office had been trying to draw a line beyond which Hitler should not be permitted to go. Early in the year, that line had been drawn in Western Europe, but officials were already preparing to take some form of parallel action in the east

[14] Roberts, 'The Alliance that Failed', 389.

[15] Robert Self (ed.), *The Neville Chamberlain Diary Letters*, 401 (to Hilda, n.d. [1–2 April 1939]).

before the 'ultimatum' to Romania. The government, divided and apprehensive, was moving in the same direction as the public. It may well be that the changing public mood and its possible effects on the political fortunes of the Chamberlain government encouraged the cabinet to take a stiffer stand. Not even last-minute reports denying that Hitler was considering military action against Poland caused Halifax to reverse his decision. The guarantee was enthusiastically received right across the political spectrum. Charles Corbin, the French ambassador in London, was astonished at the warmth of its public reception. He wrote to Bonnet on 4 April that this new orientation in British foreign policy 'represents a complete break with its traditional principles, and marks an importance that one is able, without exaggeration, to call historic'.[16]

The French cabinet agreed with alacrity to join in the British guarantee to Poland. Intelligence reports received in Paris at the end of March also predicted an imminent German attack on Poland. Already incensed at Italian demands for French territory, and convinced that Germany and Italy were working together, the Daladier government viewed the Prague *coup* as the start of 'a very serious crisis in the near future menacing France directly'.[17] Daladier's tougher line was largely the result of the improved relationship with Britain, but owed much to his strengthened domestic position. He was enormously popular and was being showered with approving letters for his stand against Mussolini. The Chamber of Deputies, in session during the Polish crisis, demanded energetic measures, and except over the question of the Soviet Union, backed the government. If, once again, Britain set the diplomatic pace, the revival of French self-confidence allowed the Daladier government to exercise a greater influence on British policy in Eastern Europe than it had previously.

IV

Chamberlain and Halifax still hoped that Italy could be detached from Germany. Such illusions were nourished by Mussolini's 'mediating' role at Munich, and strengthened by reports of the Duce's anger at Hitler's Prague *coup*. A major debate over the issue of Italy had already started in the winter. At the Admiralty, the new first sea lord and chief of the naval staff, Admiral Sir Roger Backhouse, read the Mediterranean situation very differently from Chamberlain and Halifax. He argued that Italy was firmly attached to Germany, and would seek to establish itself in the Mediterranean at Britain's expense. Looking for an offensive role for the

[16] Quoted in J.-B. Duroselle, *La décadence, 1932–1939*, 405.
[17] A. Adamthwaite, *Grandeur and Misery: France's Bid for Power in Europe 1914–1940*, 220.

navy that would open the Treasury's purse strings, the naval advocates of an 'Italy first' strategy argued that if the British lost the Mediterranean, they would lose the war. In their view, it was Italy, rather than Germany, that posed the more immediate threat to the British Empire and, as the weaker of the two powers, should be knocked out of the war at its onset. This was, of course, the same strategic approach as proposed by Admiral Darlan and adopted in an amended form by the French on the eve of the staff talks with Britain. The new strategy, however, found little favour among the chiefs of staff or at the Foreign Office, and was opposed by navalists who remained faithful to the 'fleet to Singapore' strategy, which placed a premium on naval action in the Far East. There was pressure from British representatives in East Asia, and from Ambassador Craigie in Tokyo, for a demonstration of naval power at Singapore, to warn the Japanese against threatening British interests and to dissuade them from concluding an alliance with Germany and Italy. The Admiralty refused to commit a squadron to the Far East on the grounds that the fleet was needed in the Mediterranean. The British tried again to shift the burden of responsibility in the Pacific to the Americans, who appeared to be taking a stronger line in Tokyo. Chamberlain appealed to Roosevelt to agree to send the American fleet to Honolulu, should Britain become involved in a war with Germany. Apart from a decision that the fleet should return to the Pacific in mid-April, one month early, no concrete American action followed. Nonetheless, on 20 March, Chamberlain assured J. A. Lyons, the Australian prime minister, that 'Britain and the navy intended to prevent any major operations against Singapore, Australia, New Zealand or India', though he admitted that the size and composition of the fleet would depend on the circumstances of the moment.[18] The dilemma of balancing the naval requirements of a war in the Mediterranean and a war in the Far East remained unresolved. It was decided that Britain should consider the French position before coming to any conclusions.

Both the Mediterranean and the Balkan scene changed when Mussolini invaded Albania on Good Friday, 7 April. King Zog and his wife, with their 2-day-old infant, jewels, and much of the country's gold, took refuge in Greece, hardly an enthusiastic host. Mussolini had been badly upset by Hitler's surprise occupation of Prague.[19] His sense of ruffled *amour propre*, combined with soothing assurances of friendship from Berlin following the *coup*, and the welcome fall of Madrid to Franco in late March, inspired the Duce to carry out a *fait accompli* of

[18] TNA: PRO, Prem 1/309, Chamberlain to Lyons, 20 March 1939.

[19] King Zog spent the war years in Britain, occupying a floor in the Ritz Hotel in London paid for, presumably, with the gold he took with him from Tirana.

his own. It would redress the balance of power in the Italian direction and contain any German threat to domination of the Adriatic. Ciano's long-laid plans for annexation, dating to the post-*Anschluss* period, came to fruition at last. Even so, the attack was badly bungled; material rewards, most of which were already in Italian hands, were negligible. The costs in terms of munitions were high. Nonetheless, Mussolini indulged in dreams of grandeur, in which the conquest of Albania would (in the words of an ingratiating Dino Grandi) 'open the ancient paths of the Roman conquests in the east to the Italy of Mussolini' and threaten Britain 'with the loss in advance of its naval bases, and our complete domination of the Eastern Mediterranean'.[20] In May, Mussolini, Ciano, and Pariani considered attacks on Greece, Romania, and Croatia. Should a European war come, the Italian seizure of Greece would 'help drive the British from the Mediterranean basin'.[21]

The British and French reacted differently to this act of Italian brigandage, which caught them both by surprise. The former were left anxious over the implications for the Balkan 'dam' they hoped to build against the dictator powers. Greece and Turkey were needed to check a German drive through south-eastern Europe, to deter Mussolini and to protect vital British naval defences in the eastern Mediterranean. Both General Metaxas, and the Turkish president, Ismet Inonu, fearful of Italian ambitions, had for some time sought closer ties with Britain, to secure further credits and arms as well as to strengthen the unity of the Balkan pact, if possible by including Bulgaria. Effective engagement had previously stalled because of political and economic hesitations in London, but Mussolini's *coup* broke the log-jam. With the news of the Albanian occupation, the Greeks appealed to London, warning that the Italians were about to attack Corfu, an important would-be British naval base, and would then turn on Greece. The small group of ministers still in London over the Easter weekend were at first reluctant to allow a 'comparatively minor question' to wreck the prospect of weaning Italy from the Axis, just as Rome was completing the promised withdrawal of troops from Spain. Chamberlain, returning hurriedly from Scotland, opposed any action against Italy. There was nothing to be done about Albania, though Mussolini should be warned off further aggression. The prime minister wanted only a general statement of support for the *status quo* in the Mediterranean and a reaffirmation of the Easter agreement, but there was strong cabinet pressure for unilateral declarations of British

[20] Quotation from MacGregor Knox, *Mussolini Unleashed, 1939–1941: Politics and Strategy in Fascist Italy's Last War*, 41. See J. Gooch, *Mussolini and His Generals: The Armed Forces and Fascist Foreign Policy, 1922–1940*, 468.

[21] Quoted in Knox, *Mussolini Unleashed*, 41.

support for Greek and Turkish independence. The Commons would expect no less. The Albanian affair was seen as an Italian 'insult' directed personally against the prime minister. Somewhat surprised at the strength of anti-Italian feeling, Chamberlain agreed to offer the Greeks a guarantee along the lines of the Polish precedent. More was demanded. Halifax wanted a guarantee for Turkey. The service chiefs pointed out that Turkey was the 'key' to the situation in the eastern Mediterranean, and would need to be assured of British firmness even if this meant the promise of political and military backing to a Balkan bloc of Turkey, Greece, Romania, and Bulgaria, despite the latter's unreliability. Chamberlain objected, preferring to wait to see if the Balkan states were prepared to resist aggression, and whether Turkey would assist Romania and Greece. Under intense pressure from his cabinet colleagues and from Conservative dissidents demanding action, he retreated. Unwilling to abandon his preferred policy of patience with the Axis powers, and still hoping for Mussolini's co-operation, Chamberlain found himself unable to resist demands for a demonstration of British resolve. The new moves were intended to encourage the Balkan states and Turkey, the linchpin in any Balkan deterrent, to agree to assist each other in case of further Axis aggression. It could be extended to include Romania, Yugoslavia, and Bulgaria.

There was no difficulty in reaching agreement about the guarantee to Greece, though the chiefs of staff immediately warned that Britain would not be able to defend the long and exposed Greek coastline. Turkey was the more important factor in any strategic calculations. As the 'gate-keeper of the Dardanelles', Turkey controlled the door from the Black Sea to the Mediterranean and could play a vital role in isolating Italy. It could also help contain a German drive into the Balkan peninsula. As the only member of the Balkan pact who had not shared in the territorial carve-up of Bulgaria, it was in a good position to woo Sofia, taking the pressure off Romania and strengthening the pact's deterrent value. Enjoying good relations with the USSR, Turkey provided a useful link with Moscow. The Turkish leaders had their own price for co-operation; they would not enter into new commitments unless assured of British willingness to underwrite Turkish security.

The Romanians, too, were anxious to secure Anglo-French guarantees of their territorial integrity as a counter-balance to their agreements with Germany. In this way, Bucharest could continue to balance between the power blocs. Carol and Gafencu had, however, no interest in a western pact of mutual assistance that would leave Romania defenceless against any German move. Such a pact would make military sense only if the Soviet Union was involved, and few in Bucharest were prepared to call for Soviet assistance except under the most dire circumstances.

Unsolicited Anglo-French declarations of support, however, could be used to check Germany without provoking hostile counter-action in Berlin or Budapest, and would allow Bucharest to follow a policy of neutrality between Germany and its western opponents. Similarly, the Romanians were not anxious to turn their anti-Soviet alliance with Poland into an alliance against Germany, knowing that Poland would not defend Romania's western borders for fear of upsetting the Hungarians. These local antagonisms, inherited from the peace treaties, were as much a part of the Balkan situation as the fear of German domination. 'Greece was, of course', Halifax told the cabinet, 'infinitely more important to us than Romania'.[22] Aware of Romania's military weakness and discouraged by Beck's opposition to extending the Polish–Romanian treaty, the British had no wish to meet the Romanian request of 9 April for a further self-standing, unilateral, and unconditional guarantee like that given to Poland. The British still hoped that Romania could be included in a defensive coalition in which other powers would guarantee its security. Bucharest would have to wait. Again, what was most significant about all these British efforts at dam-building in the Balkans, dependent as they were on the co-operative action of the states involved, was their shared intention to prevent war rather than preparing for fighting such a war.

Gafencu, scheduled to visit Ankara, Warsaw, and Berlin, arrived in London on 9 April and put the case for a freely offered guarantee. Halifax was discouraging; such a guarantee would make it more difficult to bring Romania, Poland, and Turkey into a broader coalition. Chamberlain was equally negative, arguing that it should be left to the Poles and Turks to guarantee the Romanians. Tilea went to work; warning Churchill, Labour's Hugh Dalton, as well as the *Daily Telegraph* military correspondent, and Lord Lloyd, the head of the British Council with a special interest in the Balkans, that if guarantees were given only to Greece and Turkey, Romania would settle with Germany. The British refusal would have been sustained if it had not been for French intervention. On 29 March, Daladier, convinced that Mussolini was intent on carrying out his expansionist programme at France's expense, temporarily closed the opened door of Franco-Italian negotiations with a powerful radio speech reiterating his unwillingness to make any concessions to the Italians. The French, misled by false intelligence, believed that the Italian attack on Albania was part of a more concerted move on the part of the Axis powers in the direction of war. Daladier described it as 'only the prelude to a big Italo-German offensive from

[22] TNA: PRO, CAB 27/624.

the North Sea to Egypt'.[23] On 8 April, just after the Albanian invasion, reports again arrived that operational plans were underway for an invasion of Poland at the end of the month, along with the seizure of the Romanian oil fields, and air raids on Paris and London. None of this was true. Nonetheless, coming at the same time as Mussolini's seizure of Albania, and warnings of impending Italian action against Corfu, Egypt, and Gibraltar, the *Quai d'Orsay* took the bait. It appeared that Italy and Germany were about to launch simultaneous offensives. The Permanent Committee of National Defence, meeting on 9 April, ordered preparatory measures for a war against Italy. On 11 April, the Romanians appealed in Paris for a unilateral guarantee. As Daladier believed that Hitler would try to secure Romania's oil in advance of war, he wanted to respond at once. He was so alarmed at the thought of an imminent German–Hungarian attack on Romania, or, at the least, of Romania being drawn completely into the German orbit, that he would wait only twenty-four hours for the British to participate. Bypassing Bonnet, who argued that a Romanian guarantee would seriously weaken France's bargaining position *vis-à-vis* Poland and the Soviet Union, Daladier urged London to act, and warned on 12 April that France would act alone in the absence of their agreement. Halifax characterized the French demand as 'unfortunate and ill-considered', despite British intelligence warnings that Romania, rather than Poland, would be the next German target. To offer a guarantee to Bucharest would leave Britain with a series of isolated bilateral or unilateral guarantees, without any framework to connect them. This hardly constituted the trip wire London wanted to construct. There was renewed pressure from Bucharest. Gafencu claimed that he would be offered a political guarantee when he visited Berlin on the 18 April and that the Germans would ask for exorbitant concessions in return. The Romanian case was strengthened by a series of Hungarian *démarches* warning of measures taken to counter the movement of Romanian troops towards the western frontier. Gafencu used these to demonstrate the dangers of a war in the Balkans. The British gave way to the French. On 13 April, the cabinet agreed to offer unilateral guarantees to both Greece and Romania, arguing that the preservation of the unity of the Anglo–French front overrode all other considerations. The French embassy in London concluded with some satisfaction that 'London has been accustomed for so long to see Paris follow the English watch-word that there was complete surprise to see us maintain our point of view.'[24]

[23] Quoted in A. Adamthwaite, *France and the Coming of the Second World War*, 308.

[24] Quoted in Peter Jackson, 'France and the Guarantee to Romania', *Intelligence and National Security*, 10: 2 (1995), 265.

As war came closer and the French assessed their strategic situation, attention became focused on Germany's economic position, especially its shortages of raw materials. Germany's problems held out some promise of success in an otherwise bleak strategic situation. France's future war plans, defensively oriented in the first instance, were based on a successful blockade that would deprive Germany of the materials vital to its war effort. Romanian oil was one of the critical factors in that balance sheet. French preoccupation with German imports of Romanian oil continued, not only throughout the immediate pre-war period but well into the war itself, though neither its own nor the British efforts to restrict the flow of oil to Germany were successful. Between April and August Germany took over 38% of Romania's oil, while French and British imports accounted for only 9.95% and 9.51% respectively. The French marginally increased their monthly imports of oil, but British and British Empire imports actually dropped. Germany more than doubled its monthly imports from 60,000 to 140,000 tons.[25] In late March, the French began to consider plans to sabotage or destroy the Romanian oil fields. France and Britain had hoped to attach Romania to their deterrent bloc in Eastern Europe; instead, their unilateral guarantees strengthened the neutralist current in Bucharest by reinforcing the impression that Romania could balance between the Great Powers. The Romanians continued to court the Allied powers in the post-guarantee period, but their main aim was to use the guarantees to preserve their freedom of action with regard to Germany, rather than to give weight to the western deterrent strategy. King Carol and his government would not join an anti-German front; instead, they assured Hitler of Romanian friendship and neutrality, while telling the British that Romania would be on the Anglo–French side if war came. Gafencu made clear his dislike of the Anglo–Turkish declaration in May, and his objections to making any territorial adjustments to bring Bulgaria into a Balkan bloc. Anglo-French hopes for a 'peace front' were rapidly disappearing.

It is doubtful that even if the British and French had been able to supply Romania with the credits and armaments that it needed, they could have changed the situation. In late March, the French concluded a new commercial agreement with Bucharest (and with Belgrade), offering more generous quotas on agricultural products in exchange for Romanian oil. Yet trade continued its downward trend. In May, the British offered a £5 million credit and a new wheat purchase agreement, but the sum was too small to offset Romania's dependence on Germany, and neither Britain nor France were prepared to offer the

[25] Figures from Ion Calafeteanu, 'Les relations économique germano-roumaines de 1933–40', *Revue d'histoire de la deuxième guerre mondiale*, 140 (1985), 31.

aeroplanes, anti-tank and anti-aircraft guns the Romanian government wanted, particularly given their doubts about its reliability. The Germans sought a further trade agreement with the Romanians but found the latter stiff bargainers well placed to take advantage of the Reich's need for oil.

For the British, the 13 April offer of a guarantee to Turkey against an Italian attack in return for an alliance and support in the Balkans was far more valuable than the Romanian guarantee. The latter move, however, seems to have convinced the Turkish leaders that the British were serious about a defensive front in the Balkans. They agreed to a public declaration and secret negotiations for an alliance that would eventually be made public. What made the subsequent talks difficult were the different aims of the two countries. The primary Turkish concern was with the Italian threat; the British were focused on the Balkans and were loath to take on new obligations in the Mediterranean. The Turks, before joining an anti-German coalition, needed to strengthen their defences on the Balkan frontiers and assure themselves of Soviet friendship. This meant credits and equipment from Britain and France to replace what had been ordered from the Reich. Ankara wanted both a Black Sea security pact with Moscow, and an Anglo-Soviet agreement assuring Turkey of both Soviet and British friendship. On 6 May, the Turks accepted the British declaration providing for mutual assistance in case of war in the Mediterranean. On 9 May, the day on which Germany and Italy announced their 'pact of steel', the British asked that the Anglo-Turkish declaration be enlarged to include consultation to ensure 'the stability of the Balkans'. When the declaration was read to the Turkish assembly, the foreign minister emphasized that it stood independent of any obligations arising from the Balkan *entente*. Both Yugoslavia and Romania, under German pressure, complained about the reference to the Balkans, and accused the Turks of violating the spirit of the Balkan pact by concluding a unilateral agreement with an outside power. Contrary to British hopes, the Turks refused to offer a guarantee to Romania for fear of alienating the USSR. The situation in the Balkans remained unresolved. The Balkan 'dam' was full of holes.

Having secured the Anglo-Turkish declaration, Halifax was content to let the Balkan situation simmer. The British showed little interest in offering the credits or military equipment requested by the Turkish authorities. They were offered only token amounts of anti-aircraft guns and obsolete light bombers and, at the end of June, a derisory defence credit of £10 million sterling. Further demands in July met with a cold reception. As late as 24 August, the deputy chiefs of staff in London warned that without arms credits for Turkey, 'we were in danger of losing her as an ally'.[26] British dilatoriness was connected not only with its own needs but also with the policy debate over the Mediterranean. Having given up the idea of an early attack on Italy, there were again good reasons for conciliating Mussolini. There was no real risk of losing Turkish support in the Balkans. While peace was maintained, the British were prepared to accept the risk; once war was declared, compensatory steps would have to be taken. The French, preoccupied with war in the Mediterranean, might have been expected to act with greater dispatch but here, too, there were delays and obstruction. The prospects for French participation in the Anglo-Turkish declaration had collapsed at the last moment over the fate of the Sanjak of Alexandretta, a region lying between Syria and Turkey that was still under French control. The Turkish majority had long demanded the withdrawal of the French, particularly after Syria was granted some measure of self-government in 1936, but the powerful French colonial lobby had blocked any form of retreat. It was only after much wrangling that a Franco-Turkish treaty was finally concluded on 23 June and Alexandretta reverted to Turkey. During this time, the French considered the possibility of sending an Anglo-French expeditionary force to Salonika after war began, but there was no enthusiasm among the British for such a proposal. Having reverted back to the Singapore strategy, there were few advocates either for an 'Italy first' or a Balkan campaign. The French were more forthcoming and proposed to London that they should co-operate in providing the financial assistance the Turks demanded. The marked lack of haste in cementing relations with Ankara suggests that the British were content with the knowledge that the Turks were benevolently inclined and would not join the Axis powers. This was sufficient for the purposes of deterrence. While they were still negotiating with the Soviet Union, the British and French tried to use the talks as a means of assuring Turkish attachment to the west. The Turks had, in fact, offered to intercede in Moscow to speed up the negotiations, but the western allies were prepared to let matters rest. The conclusion of the Nazi–Soviet pact would bring swifter allied action (see pp. 962–5.)

V

One did not need the wisdom of Solomon to realize that if the Anglo-French deterrent was to have teeth it required the participation of the

[26] Quoted in Sidney Aster, *1939: The Making of the Second World War* (London, 1973), 148.

Soviet Union. A two-front war, as both the British and French military chiefs came to realize, required, at the very least, Soviet assistance to Poland and Romania. By May, the military were advocating direct Soviet military intervention in Eastern Europe. Chamberlain, and the more changeable Halifax, did not believe that Soviet participation in the 'peace bloc' was essential to its success. On the contrary, the prime minister argued that the main object of the Soviet Union was to egg on the capitalist powers to 'tear each other to pieces', and so fight her battles for her.[27] An alliance with the Soviet Union, in Chamberlain's view, would rule out *détente* and settlement with the Axis powers. Like Beck, the prime minister thought that the Danzig question was negotiable and the question of Poland's military weakness irrelevant. Not all officials shared the prime minister's sanguinity that the existing guarantees were sufficient to 'check' Hitler and bring him back to a more reasonable frame of mind. Since the start of 1939, Vansittart, William Strang, head of the key Central department, and Lawrence Collier of the Northern department, had been urging Halifax to test the Soviet waters. Soon after the new Russian-speaking (the first to be appointed) ambassador to the USSR, Sir William Seeds, took up his post, it was decided to send Robert Hudson, from the Ministry of Overseas Trade, to Moscow, ostensibly to discuss commercial questions, but in fact to get some idea of what the Soviet leaders were thinking. Hudson arrived in the Soviet Union only after the Prague crisis, and was received by a sceptical Litvinov on 23 March. The latter wrote to Stalin that: 'In view of the rejection of all our previous offers, we have no intention of making any new offers and it is up to others to take the initiative . . . In particular, we are ready now as we always have been, to co-operate with Britain. We are prepared to look at any concrete suggestions.'[28] As Litvinov knew, Hudson was not authorized to make any such offer and the talks produced no concrete results. They ended badly when, at the last minute, the British tried to delete any reference to the discussion of political matters in the joint communiqué.

The dropping of the joint declaration, and the decision to opt for Poland rather than the Soviet Union, hardly smoothed the course of Anglo-Soviet relations. When Maisky pressed Halifax for further information on Chamberlain's reference to 'direct and indirect' aggression in his Commons statement on Poland, the foreign secretary ignored the question, and only assured the ambassador that Britain wanted a broad coalition to protect the peace, and that this would

[27] Quoted in Maurice Cowling, *The Impact of Hitler: British Politics and British Policy, 1933–1940* (Cambridge, 1975), 302.

[28] DVP, Vol. XXII, No. 157 (Litvinov to Stalin, 20 March 1939).

not be formed without the Soviet Union. At the same time, neither Halifax nor his officials were prepared to consider Maisky's suggestion that Litvinov be invited to London to facilitate negotiations. 'Personally', Cadogan minuted, 'I regard association with the Soviet as more of a liability than an asset. But I should rather like to ask them what they propose, indicating that we don't want a lesson in "moral issues", but some practical indication of what they propose should be done.' Halifax concurred '. . . of course we want if we can—without making a disproportionate amount of mischief. . . —to keep them in with us'.[29] Halifax reverted to the idea of a unilateral Soviet declaration of support to any of its European neighbours that resisted aggression. It was hardly a proposal that would elicit support in Moscow. When, on April 17, Litvinov, in what turned out to be his final effort to breathe life into his collective security policy, sent off a proposal for a tripartite political agreement and a Soviet military alliance against Germany, Cadogan found it 'extremely inconvenient'. It would alienate friends and provoke enemies, while its military advantages were 'problematical'. Cadogan feared that the 'left' would make capital out of a refusal, and there was the risk, 'a very remote one', of a Soviet non-intervention agreement with Germany.[30] There followed a three-week interval during which there was a fierce debate in Whitehall over the response to the Soviet offer. By the time the British sent their reply on 6 May, Litvinov was no longer in office.

The French, in keeping with the tougher Daladier–Gamelin line after Munich, were more active in soliciting Soviet co-operation. Intelligence and military sources concurred that neither Romania nor Poland could resist a German attack for any length of time without outside assistance. France's inability to supply Poland with arms and tanks, though Warsaw was given priority over all other foreign claimants, or to provide additional credits beyond an advance on the Rambouillet credits, strengthened the case for a Soviet alliance. Though a French staff paper in February 1939 mentioned the possibility of 'carefully executed offensives' on the north-eastern frontier, France, as became clear during the Anglo-French talks in May, remained wedded to a defensive strategy in the west, and Gamelin's assurances to the Poles, that France would launch a significant offensive action against the Siegfried Line fifteen days after mobilization, were almost worthless. In April, Bonnet began to press Surits, the Soviet ambassador in Paris, for closer Franco-Soviet

[29] Quotations cited in Michael Jabara Carley, 'End of the "Low, Dishonest Decade": Failure of the Anglo-Franco-Soviet Alliance in 1939', *Europe–Asia Studies*, 45: 2 (1993), 317–318.

[30] Quoted in Ian Colvin, *The Chamberlain Cabinet* (London, 1971), 200.

co-operation, but Litvinov, who viewed the French as junior partners in the *entente*, was unresponsive. Surits reported on the toughening mood in Paris, the turn-about in French public opinion, and the almost total cessation of press attacks on the USSR. He claimed that the old French arrogance was gone and that the French were supplicants, 'people who need us, not . . . people whom we need'. While he recommended negotiations, he warned Litvinov not to assume any obligations without reciprocal guarantees.[31] On 14 April, Bonnet proposed an exchange of letters promising Soviet aid and assistance if France went to war with Germany as a result of assisting Poland or Romania. Surits suggested that the proposal might have a better chance of acceptance if there were a measure of reciprocity. The very next day, Bonnet produced a more complete text offering a reciprocal arrangement, and suggested that the two countries discuss how to make their mutual assistance effective. The British showed little liking for the French proposal; Bonnet preferred to temporize and let London take the lead.

From the very start of the talks with the Soviet Union, there was a whole succession of difficulties that stood in the way of success. Some related to the attitudes and fears of Russia's neighbours. Poland, Romania, Finland, and the Baltic states shared the deepest suspicion of the USSR and wanted neither its guarantees nor promises of assistance. In London and Paris, too, the suspicions of Soviet intentions that had for so many years coloured relations with Moscow, were not easily overcome. The negotiations intensified rather than diminished the uneasiness among the less committed participants to an agreement. It was necessity, and the fear of a Nazi–Soviet pact, that convinced the majority of statesmen on both sides of the Channel that talks had to be opened and pursued. Most had as little trust in Stalin as the Soviet leader had in them.

VI

The first months of 1939 were a time of breath-taking activity. What started as the first moves towards the creation of an Anglo–French alliance at the start of the year, ended in April with the reappearance of Britain and France in eastern Europe, and the giving of guarantees to Poland, Greece, Romania, and Turkey. The catalyst was Hitler's march into Prague and the destruction of the Munich agreement. Hitler had abandoned his lip-service to self-determination, and made clear his intention to challenge whatever restraints still existed to the fulfilment of his ambitions in the east. In a minor but equally disruptive move,

[31] Quoted in Carley, 'Low, Dishonest Decade', 319.

Mussolini decided that he, too, could now give substance to his Mediterranean dreams. His ambitions pushed him further into Hitler's increasingly dangerous embrace. Faced with Hitler's unwillingness to parley, his open aggression, and mounting activity in south-east Europe, there had to be an Anglo-French response. In both countries, the public mood was changing. A combination of shame, fear, and anger precluded further concessions to Nazi Germany. The British still retained the initiative, but the toughening of French policy and opinion had its effect on British attitudes. A change took place during these months but one must be careful not to read history backwards. Though angered by the guarantees to Poland, Hitler still assumed that Britain and France would not resist German expansion; they would not fight for Danzig and the Polish Corridor. He still believed that he could force the Poles to submit to his will without resorting to war. War planning had only begun. Nor did the British or the French believe that war was inevitable. Rather, by showing the dictators that they intended to support those countries under threat, they would force the Axis leaders to think again about taking risks. It was a warning that the trip-wire had been moved from western to eastern Europe. But the barrier was weak, and had no military back-up. This was due as much to the policies of the guaranteed countries, as to British and French intentions.

Unprepared for war, each of the Munich participants believed that there were powerful reasons why their opponents would not risk war. Hitler assumed that Britain and France were still too weak militarily, and the latter too politically divided, to obstruct German moves in the east. Intelligence reports on their inability to construct a military front among the smaller Balkan states, confirmed this impression. The German ambassador in London, Herbert von Dirksen, reported that the British intended through 'armament and the formation of a coalition, to compel Germany to achieve her further demands through negotiation', rather than to risk world war.[32] This was not far from the truth. The British and French anticipated and feared a further German move in the east. Information about its economic difficulties and domestic unrest was both frightening and reassuring. Domestic problems might lead to a 'mad-dog act' but, faced with Allied rearmament and the new guarantees, Hitler might prefer to negotiate rather than fight. The French, more immediately vulnerable to Axis aggression than the British, were prepared to take a tougher line than their trans-Channel neighbour. They suspected that Mussolini was tied to Hitler and refused to follow

[32] Quotations, including citation from Dirksen Papers, doc. 29, 175, from Richard Overy, 'Strategic Intelligence and the Outbreak of the Second World War', *War in History*, 5: 4 (1998), 461.

Chamberlain's lead in Rome, and were more prepared to take soundings in Moscow. France's economic recovery and its new ties with Britain increased Daladier's self-confidence. The European skies had definitely darkened but the future was still uncertain. It was accepted that Hitler intended to deal with Poland but how and when this would be done was still unclear. The Anglo-French leaders continued to speculate about Hitler's intentions. Given their own abhorrence of war, they still hoped that he would step back from the abyss.

Bibliography for Chapters 12 and 13

Books

ALEXANDER, M. S., *The Republic in Danger: General Maurice Gamelin and the Politics of French Defence, 1933–1940* (Cambridge, 1992).

—— and PHILPOTT, W. J. (eds.), *Anglo-French Defence Relations Between the Wars* (Basingstoke, 2002). See M. S. Alexander and W. J. Philpott.

ANDREW, C., *Secret Service: The Making of the British Intelligence Community* (London, 1985).

BARIÉTY, J., GUTH, A., and VALENTIN, J.-M. (eds.), *La France et l'Allemagne entre les deux guerres mondiales* (Nancy, 1987). See K.-J. Müller and R. Poidevin.

BARNETT, C., *The Collapse of British Power* (London, 1972).

BELL, C. M., *The Royal Navy, Seapower and Strategy between the Wars* (London, 2000).

BENNETT, G., *Churchill's Man of Mystery: Desmond Morton and the World of Intelligence* (London, 2007).

BIALER, U., *The Shadow of the Bomber: The Fear of Air Attack and British Politics, 1932–1939* (London, 1980).

BOND, B., *British Military Policy between the Two World Wars* (Oxford, 1980).

BOUVIER, J. and ASSELAIN, J.-C. (eds.), *La France en mouvement, 1934–1938* (Seyssel, 1986).

BOYCE, R. (ed.), *French Foreign and Defence Policy: The Decline and Fall of a Great Power* (London, 1998). See M. Alexander, J. Jackson, P. Guillen, Y. Lacaze, and R. Boyce.

—— and ROBERTSON, E. (eds.), *Paths to War: New Essays on the Origins of the Second World War* (London, 1989). See R. Overy, N. Jordan, and C. MacDonald.

BUDRASS, L., *Flugzeugindustrie und Luftrüstung in Deutschland, 1918–1945* (Düsseldorf, 1998).

BURLEIGH, M., *Germany Turns Eastwards: A Study of Ostforschung in the Third Reich* (Cambridge, 1988).

CARR, W., *Arms, Autarky and Aggression: A Study in German Foreign Policy, 1933–1939* (London, 1972).

CARROLL, B. A., *Design for Total War: Arms and Economics in the Third Reich* (The Hague, 1968).

CATTERALL, P. and MORRIS, C. J. (eds.), *Britain and the Threat to Stability in Europe, 1918–1934* (London, 1994). See M. Dockrill and A. Dobson.
CHAPMAN, H., *State Capitalism and Working-Class Radicalism in the French Aircraft Industry* (Berkeley, CA, 1991).
CHARMLEY, J., *Chamberlain and the Lost Peace* (London, 1989).
Colloques Internationaux du Centre de la Recherche Scientifique, *Les Relations Franco-Allemandes, 1933–1939* (Paris, 1976). See Ch. Bloch, J. Bariéty, A. Kupferman, E. Campus, H. A. Batowski, R. A. C. Parker, A. Adamthwaite, and F. L'Huillier.
—— *Les Relations Franco–Britanniques de 1935 à 1939* (Paris, 1975). See P. Fridenson and J. Lecuir, R. Wheatley, and D. C. Watt.
COWLING, M., *The Impact of Hitler: British Politics and British Policy, 1933–1940* (Cambridge, 1975).
CROWSON, N. J., *Facing Fascism: The Conservative Party and the European Dictators, 1935–1940* (London, 1997).
CROZIER, A. J., *Appeasement and Germany's Last Bid for Colonies* (Basingstoke, 1988).
DAUNTON, M., *Just Taxes: The Politics of Taxation in Britain, 1914–1979* (Cambridge, 2002), especially chapter 5.
DEIST, W. (ed.), *The German Military in the Age of Total War* (London, 1984).
DILKS, D., *Retreat from Power: Studies in Britain's Foreign Policy of the Twentieth Century*, Vol.1: 1906–1939 (London, 1980).
DOCKRILL, M., *British Establishment Perspectives on France, 1936–1940* (London, 1999).
—— and MCKERCHER, B. (eds.), *Diplomacy and World Power: Studies in British Foreign Policy, 1890–1950* (Cambridge, 1996). See B. McKercher and D. C. Watt.
DOISE, J. and VAÏSSE, M., *Diplomatie et outil militaire, 1871–1991,* 2nd edn. (Paris, 1991).
DÖSCHER, H.-J., *Das Auswärtige Amt im Dritten Reich: Diplomatie im Schatten der 'Endlösung'* (Berlin, 1987).
DOUGHTY, R. A., *The Seeds of Disaster: The Development of French Army Doctrine, 1919–1939* (Hamden, CT, 1985).
DREIFORT, J., *Yvon Delbos at the Quai d'Orsay: French Foreign Policy during the Popular Front* (Lawrence, KA, 1973).
DRUMMOND, I. M., *British Economic Policy and the Empire* (London, 1972).
—— *Imperial Economic Policy, 1917 to 1939: Studies in Expansion and Protection* (London, 1974).
DÜLFFER, J., *Weimar, Hitler und die Marine: Reichspolitik und Flottenbau, 1920–1939* (Düsseldorf, 1973).
DUROSELLE, J.-B., *La décadence 1932–1939* (Paris, 1979).
DUTAILLY, H., *Les problèmes de l'armée de terre française, 1935–39* (Paris, 1980).
FORBES, N., *Doing Business with the Nazis: Britain's Economic and Financial Relations with Germany, 1931–1939* (London, 2000).
FRANK[ENSTEIN], R., *Le prix du réarmement français, 1935–1939* (Paris, 1982).
FRENCH, D., *Raising Churchill's Army; The British Army and the War against Germany, 1919–1945* (Oxford, 2000).

FRENCH, D., *British Way in Warfare, 1688–2000* (London, 1990).
FRIDENSON, P. and LECUIR, J., *La France et la Grande-Bretagne face aux problèmes aériennes 1935 - mai 1940* (Vincennes, 1976).
FUCHSER, L. W., *Neville Chamberlain and Appeasement: A Study in the Politics of History* (London, 1982).
FUNKE, M. (ed.), *Hitler, Deutschland und die Mächte* (Düsseldorf, 1976). See H.-A. JACOBSEN, J. Dülffer, and W. Michalka.
GANNON, F. R., *The British Press and Germany 1936–1939* (Oxford, 1971).
GIBBS, N. H. *Grand Strategy,* I, *Rearmament Policy* (London, 1976).
GILLARD, D., *Appeasement in Crisis: From Munich to Prague, October 1938 – March 1939* (Basingstoke, 2007).
GIRAULT, R. and ROBERT, F. (eds.), *La puissance en Europe, 1938–1940* (Paris, 1984) See A. Adamthwaite, C.-R. Ageron, S. Berstein, J. Delmas, and Z. Steiner.
GOOCH, J., *Mussolini and his Generals: The Armed Forces and Fascist Foreign Policy, 1922–1940* (Cambridge, 2007).
GORDON, G. A. H., *British Seapower and Procurement between the Wars: A Reappraisal of Rearmament* (Annapolis, MD, 1988).
GOURVISH, T. (ed.), *Business and Politics in Europe, 1900–1970: Essays in Honour of Alice Teichova* (Cambridge, 2003).
GRENZEBACH JR., W. S., *Germany's Informal Empire in East-Central Europe: German Economic Policy toward Yugoslavia and Rumania, 1933–1939* (Stuttgart, 1988).
HAIGHT, JR., J. M., *American Aid to France, 1938–40* (New York, 1970).
HARRIS, J. P., *Men, Ideas and Tanks: British Military Thought and Armoured Forces, 1903–1939* (Manchester, 1995).
HASLAM, J., *The Soviet Union and the Struggle for Collective Security in Europe, 1933–1939* (London, 1984).
HAYES, P., *Industry and Ideology: IG Farben in the Nazi Era* (Cambridge, 1987).
—— *From Co-operation to Complicity: Degussa in the Third Reich* (Cambridge, 2004).
HAYNES, R., *Romanian Policy towards Germany, 1936–1940* (Basingstoke, 2000).
HENKE, J., *England in Hitlers politischem Kalkül, 1933–1939* (Boppard am Rhein, 1973).
HERMAN, J., *The Paris Embassy of Sir Eric Phipps: Anglo-French Relations and the Foreign Office, 1937–9* (Brighton, 1998).
HILDEBRAND, K., *The Foreign Policy of the Third Reich* (Berkeley, CA, 1973).
—— SCHMÄDEKE, J., and ZERNACK, K. (eds.), *1939: An der Schwelle zum Weltkrieg* (Berlin, 1990).
—— and WERNER, K. F., (eds.) *Deutschland und Frankreich 1936–1939* (Munich 1981). See H. Dutailly, W. Deist, C. Christienne, P. Buffotot, K. A. Maier, J.-L. Crémieux-Brilhac, H.-J. Schröder, and A. Hillgruber.
HILL, C., *Cabinet Decisions on Foreign Policy: The British Experience, October 1938–June 1941* (Cambridge, 1991).
HINSLEY, F. H., *British Intelligence in the Second World War: Its Influence on Strategy and Operations*, Vol. 1 (London, 1979).

HOMZE, E., *Arming the Luftwaffe: The Reich Air Ministry and the German Aircraft Industry, 1919–1939* (Lincoln, NE, 1976).
HOWARD, M., *The Continental Commitment: The Dilemma of British Defence Policy in the Era of the Two World Wars* (London, 1972).
IMLAY, T. C., *Facing the Second World War: Strategy, Politics, and Economics in Britain and France, 1938–40* (Oxford 2003).
IRVING, D., *The Warpath: Hitler's Germany, 1933–1939* (London, 1978).
JACKSON, J., *The Popular Front in France: Defending Democracy* (Cambridge, 1988).
JACKSON, P., *France and the Nazi Menace: Intelligence and Policy Making, 1933–1939* (Oxford, 2000).
JAMES, H., *The Deutsche Bank and the Nazi Economic War Against the Jews* (Cambridge 2001).
JORDAN, N., *The Popular Front and Central Europe: The Dilemmas of French Impotence, 1918–1940* (Cambridge, 1992).
KAISER, D. E., *Economic Diplomacy and the Origins of the Second World War: Germany, Britain, France and Eastern Europe, 1930–1939* (Princeton, NJ, 1980).
KENNEDY, P., *The Rise and Fall of the Great Powers: Economic Change and Military Conflict from 1500 to 2000* (New York, 1987).
KETTENACKER, L. and MOMMSEN, W. (eds.), *The Fascist Challenge and the Policy of Appeasement* (London, 1983). See A. Adamthwaite, R. Frank, and R. Girault.
KIER, E., *Imagining War: French and British Military Doctrine between the Wars* (Princeton, NJ, 1997).
KIESLING, E. C., *Arming against Hitler: France and the Limits of Military Planning* (Lawrence, KA, 1996).
KOBRAK, C. and HANSEN, P., *European Business, Dictatorship and Political Risk, 1920–1945* (New York, 2004). See N. Forbes and M. Wilkins.
KOCH, H. W. (ed.), *Aspects of the Third Reich* (London, 1985). See E. M. Robertson, H. Trevor-Roper, W. Michalka, and B. H. Klein.
KNOX, M., *Mussolini Unleashed* (Cambridge, 1982).
—— *Common Destiny: Dictatorship, Foreign Policy, and War in Fascist Italy and Nazi Germany* (Cambridge, 2000).
KYNASTON, D., *The City of London*, Vol. 3: *Illusions of Gold, 1914–1945* (London 2000).
LANGHORNE, R., *Diplomacy and Intelligence during the Second World War: Essays in Honour of F. H. Hinsley* (Cambridge and New York, 1985). See B. Lee, D. Boadle, and R. Bosworth.
LEVINE, H. S., *Hitler's Free City: A History of the Nazi Party in Danzig, 1925–1939* (Chicago, IL, and London, 1973).
LITTLEFIELD, F. C., *Germany and Yugoslavia, 1933–1941: The German Conquest of Yugoslavia* (New York, 1988).
LUKES, I., *Czechoslovakia between Stalin and Hitler: The Diplomacy of Edvard Beneš in the 1930s* (Oxford, 1996).
MAIOLO, J., *The Royal Navy and Nazi Germany, 1933–1939* (London, 1998).
—— *Cry Havoc. The Arms Race and the Second World War, 1931–1941* (London, 2010).
MARGAIRAZ, M., *L'Etat, les finances et l'économie: Historie d'une conversion, 1932–1952*, 2 vols. (Paris, 1991).

MASON, T. W., *Social Policy in the Third Reich: The Working Classes and the 'National Community'*, ed. Jane Caplan (Providence, RI, and Oxford, 1993).

MAY, E. R., *Knowing One's Enemies: Intelligence Assessment before the Two World Wars* (Princeton, NJ, 1984). See D. C. Watt, R. J. Young, M. Geyer, M. Knox, and J. Erickson.

—— *Strange Victory: Hitler's Conquest of France* (New York, 2000).

MCDONOUGH, F., *Neville Chamberlain, Appeasement and the British Road to War* (Manchester, 1998).

MICAUD, C., *The French Right and Nazi Germany, 1933–1939: A Study of Public Opinion* (Durham, NC, 1943).

MICHAELIS, M., *Mussolini and the Jews: German–Italian Relations and the Jewish Question in Italy, 1922–1945* (Oxford, 1978).

MICHALKA, W., *Ribbentrop und die deutsche Weltpolitik, 1933–1940: außenpolitische Konzeptionen und Entscheidungsprozesse im Dritten Reich* (Munich, 1980).

MIDDLEMAS, K., *Diplomacy of Illusion: The British Government and Germany, 1937–1939* (London, 1973).

Militärgeschichtliches Forschungsamt (ed.), *Germany and the Second World War, Vol. I: The Build-up of German Aggression*, ed. Wilhelm Deist et al. (Oxford, 1990).

—— *Germany and the Second World War, Vol. II: Germany's Initial Conquests in Europe*, ed. Klaus A. Maier et al. (Oxford, 1991).

MILLETT, A. R., and MURRAY WILLIAMSON, M (eds.), *Military Effectiveness*, Volume II: *The Interwar Period* (Boston, MA, 1988). See R. A. Doughty, R. Spector, B. Bond and W. Murray, B. R. Sullivan, and M. Messerschmidt.

MORRIS, B., *The Roots of Appeasement: The British Weekly Press and Nazi Germany during the 1930s* (London, 1991).

MÜLLER, K. J., *Das Heer und Hitler: Armee und nationalsozialistisches Regime, 1933–1940*, 2nd edn. (Stuttgart, 1980).

MURRAY, W., *The Changes in the European Balance of Power, 1938–1940: The Path to Ruin* (Princeton, NJ, 1984).

—— and MILLETT, A. R. (eds.), *Calculations: Net Assessment and the Coming of World War II* (New York, 1992). Almost all chapters are relevant.

NEILSON, K., *Britain, Soviet Russia and the Collapse of the Versailles Order, 1919–1939* (Cambridge, 2006).

NEVILLE, P., *Appeasing Hitler: The Diplomacy of Sir Nevile Henderson, 1937–39* (Basingstoke, 2000).

NEWMAN, S., *March 1939: The British Guarantee to Poland: A Study in the Continuity of British Foreign Policy* (Oxford, 1976).

NEWTON, S., *The Profits of Peace: The Political Economy of Anglo-German Appeasement* (Oxford, 1996).

OVENDALE, R., *'Appeasement' and the English Speaking World: Britain, the United States, the Dominions and the Policy of 'Appeasement', 1937–1939* (Cardiff, 1975).

OVERY, R. J., *Göring: 'The Iron Man'* (London, 1984).

—— *War and the German Economy in the Third Reich* (Oxford, 1994).

PARKER, R. A. C., *Chamberlain and Appeasement: British Policy and the Coming of the Second World War* (Basingstoke, 1993).

—— *Churchill and Appeasement* (London, 2000).

Passmore, K., *From Liberalism to Fascism: The Right in a French Province, 1928–1939* (Cambridge, 1997).

Peden, G. C., *British Rearmament and the Treasury, 1932–1939* (Edinburgh, 1979).

—— *The Treasury and British Public Policy, 1906–1959* (London, 2000).

—— *Arms, Economics and British Strategy: From Dreadnoughts to Hydrogen Bombs* (Cambridge, 2007).

Posen, B. R., *The Sources of Military Doctrine: France, Britain and Germany between the World Wars* (Ithaca, NY, 1984).

Powers, B. D., *Strategy without Slide-rule: British Air Strategy, 1914–1939* (London, 1976).

Prażmowska, A., *Britain, Poland and the Eastern Front, 1939* (Cambridge, 1987).

—— *Eastern Europe and the Origins of the Second World War* (Basingstoke, 2000)

Price, C., *Britain, America and Rearmament in the 1930s: The Cost of Failure* (Basingstoke, 2001).

Prost, A., *Les anciens combattants et la société française*, 3 vols. (Paris, 1977).

Rémond, R. and Bourdin, J. (eds.), *Édouard Daladier, chef de gouvernement* (Paris, 1977).

Reynolds, D., *The Creation of the Anglo-American Alliance, 1937–1941: A Study in Competitive Cooperation* (London, 1981).

—— *In Command of History: Churchill Fighting and Writing the Second World War* (London 2004).

Robbins, K., *Appeasement* (Oxford, 1988).

Rohe, K. (ed.), *Die Westmächte und das Dritte Reich, 1933–1939* (Paderborn, 1982). See G. Schmidt, B.-J. Wendt, C. A. MacDonald, K. Schwabe, and G. Ziebura.

Ruggiero, J., *Neville Chamberlain and British Rearmament: Pride, Prejudice, and Politics* (Westport, CT, 1999).

Salerno, R., *Vital Crossroads: Mediterranean Origins of the Second World War, 1935–1940* (Ithaca, NY, 2002).

Schirmann, S., *Les relations économiques et financières franco-allemandes, 24 décembre 1932–1 septembre 1939* (Paris, 1995).

Schmidt, G., *The Politics and Economics of Appeasement: British Foreign Policy in the 1930s* (Leamington Spa, 1986).

Sharp, A. and Stone, G. A. (eds.), *Anglo–French Relations in the Twentieth Century: Rivalry and Cooperation* (London, 2000). See G. A. Stone.

Shay, R. P., *British Rearmament in the Thirties: Politics and Profits* (Princeton, NJ, 1979).

Shorrock, W. J., *From Ally to Enemy: The Enigma of Fascist Italy in French Diplomacy, 1920–1940* (Kent, OH, 1988).

Siegel, M., *The Moral Disarmament of France: Education, Pacifism and Patriotism, 1914–1940* (Cambridge, 2004).

Smith, M., *British Air Strategy between the Wars* (Oxford, 1984).

Soucy, R., *French Fascism: The Second Wave, 1933–1939* (New Haven, CT, 1995).

TOMBS, R. and I., *That Sweet Enemy: The French and the British from the Sun King to the Present* (London, 2006).
TOOZE, A., *The Wages of Destruction: The Making and Breaking of the Nazi Economy* (London, 2006).
TOSCANO, M., *The Origins of the Pact of Steel* (Baltimore, MD, 1967).
TURNER, H. A, *General Motors and the Nazis: The Struggle for Control of Opel, Europe's Biggest Carmaker* (London, 2005).
VINEN, R., *The Politics of French Business, 1936–1945* (Cambridge, 1991).
WARK, W. K., *The Ultimate Enemy: British Intelligence and Nazi Germany, 1933–1939* (London, 1985).
WATT, D. C., *How War Came: The Immediate Origins of the Second World War, 1938–9* (London, 1989).
WEINBERG, G. L., *The Foreign Policy of Hitler's Germany*, Vol. 2: *Starting World War II, 1937–1939* (Chicago, IL, 1980).
WENDT, B.-J., *Economic Appeasement: Handel und Finanz in der britischen Deutschlandpolitik 1933–1939* (Dusseldorf, 1971).
YOUNG, R. J., *In Command of France: French Foreign Policy and Military Planning, 1933–1940* (Cambridge, MA, 1978).

Articles and Chapters

ADAMTHWAITE, A., 'France's Government Machine in the Approach to the Second World War', in Shamir, H. (ed.), *France and Germany in an Age of Crisis* (Leiden, 1990).
ALEXANDER, M. S., 'Les réactions à la menace stratégique allemande en Europe occidentale: la Grande Bretagne, la Belgique et le "cas Hollande", décembre 1938 – février 1939', *Cahiers d'histoire de la Seconde Guerre Mondiale*, 7 (1982).
—— 'In Defence of the Maginot Line: Security Policy, Domestic Politics and the Economic Depression in France', in Boyce, R. (ed.), *French Foreign and Defence Policy, 1918–1940: The Decline and Fall of a Great Power* (London, 1998).
—— 'Le Général Gamelin, chef d'état, major général de l'armée, et les gouvernements (1935–1940)', in Duhamel, E., Forcade, O., and Vial, P. (eds.), *Militaire en République, 1870–1962: Les officiers, le pouvoir et la vie publique en France* (Paris, 1999).
BARTOV, O., 'Martyrs' Vengeance: Memory, Trauma, and Fear of War in France, 1918–1940', in Blatt, J. (ed.), *The French Defeat of 1940: Reassessments* (Providence, RI, and Oxford, 1998).
BÉDARIDA, F., 'La "gouvernante anglaise"', in Rémond, R. and Bourdin, J. (eds.), *Édouard Daladier, chef de gouvernement* (Paris, 1977).
BUFFOTOT, P., 'The French High Command and the Franco-Soviet Alliance, 1933–1939', *Journal of Strategic Studies*, 5: 4 (1982).
CALAFETEANU, I., 'Les relations économiques, germano-roumaines de 1933–40', *Revue d'histoire 2ème Guerre*, 140 : 31 (1985).
CARLEY, M. J., 'End of the "Low, Dishonest Decade": Failure of the Anglo-Franco-Soviet Alliance in 1939', *Europe–Asia Studies*, 45: 2 (1993).

Cassels, A., 'Fascist Italy and Mediation in the Munich and Danzig Crises, September 1938 and August 1939', in *Diplomazia e storia delle relazioni internazionali: Studi in onore di Enrico Serra* (Milan, 1991).

Cowson, N., 'Conservative Parliamentary Dissent over Foreign Policy during the Premiership of Neville Chamberlain: Myth or Reality', *Parliamentary History*, 14: 3 (1995).

Dutter, G., 'Doing Business with the Fascists: French Economic Relations with Italy under the Popular Front', *French History*, 4: 2 (1990).

—— 'Doing Business with the Nazis: French Economic Relations with Germany under the Popular Front', *Journal of Modern History*, 63: 2 (1991).

Forbes, N., 'Managing Risk in the Third Reich: British Business with Germany in the 1930s', in Kobrak, C. and Hansen, P. (eds.), *European Business, Dictatorship and Political Risk, 1920–1945* (New York, 2004).

—— 'The City, British Policy and the Rise of the Third Reich, 1931–1937', in Mitchie, R. and Williamson, P. (eds.), *The British Government and the City of London in the Twentieth Century* (Cambridge, 2005).

—— 'Multinational Enterprise, Corporate Responsibility, and the Nazi Dictatorship: The Case of Unilever and Germany in the 1930s', *Contemporary European History*, 16:2 (2007).

Frank, R., 'Réarmament français, finances publiques et conjoncture internationale, 1935–1939', *Bulletin de la Société d'Histoire Moderne*, 9: 1 (1981).

—— 'L'entrée des attachés financiers dans la machine diplomatique, 1919–1945', *Relations internationales*, 32 (1982).

Geyer, M., 'The Dynamics of Military Revisionism in the Inter-war Years: Military Politics between Rearmament and Diplomacy', in Deist, W. (ed), *The German Military in the Age of Total War* (Leamington Spa, 1985).

Goldman, A. L., 'Two Views of Germany: Nevile Henderson vs. Vansittart and the Foreign Office, 1937–39', *British Journal of International Studies*, 6: 3 (1980).

Gorman, L., 'The *Anciens Combattants* and Appeasement: From Munich to War', *War and Society*, 10: 2 (1992).

Henke, J., 'Hitlers England-Konzeption: Formulierung und Realisierungsversuche', in Funke, M., *Hitler, Deutschland und die Mächte: Materialen zur Außenpolitik des Dritten Reiches* (Düsseldorf, 1976).

Hillgruber, A., 'Der Faktor Amerika in Hitlers Strategie, 1938–1941', in Michalka, W. (ed.), *Nationalsozialistische Außenpolitik* (Darmstadt, 1978).

Imlay, T., 'Retreat or Resistance: Strategic Reappraisal and the Crisis of French Power in Eastern Europe, September 1938 to August 1939', in Mouré, K. and Alexander, M. S. (eds.), *Crisis and Renewal in France, 1918–1962* (New York, 2001).

—— 'Paul Reynaud and France's Response to Nazi Germany, 1938–1940', *French Historical Studies*, 26 (2003).

—— 'Democracy and War: Political Regimes, Industrial Relations and Economic Preparations for War in France and Britain up to 1940', *Journal of Modern History*, 79 (2007).

Jackson, P., 'La perception de la puissance aérienne allemande et son influence sur la politique extérieure française pendant les crises internationales de 1938 à 1939', *Revue historique des armées*, 39: 4 (1994).

JACKSON, P. 'Intelligence and the End of Appeasement, 1938–1939', in Boyce, R. (ed.), *French Foreign and Defence Policy, 1918–1940: The Decline and Fall of a Great Power* (London, 1998).

—— 'La politisation du renseignement en France, 1933–1939', in Soutou, G.-H., Frémeaux, J., and Forcade, O. (eds.), *L'exploitation du renseignement en Europe et aux États-Unis des années 1930 aux années 1960* (Paris, 2001).

—— 'Post-War Politics and the Historiography of French Strategy and Diplomacy before the Second World War', *History Compass*, 4: 5 (2006).

—— and MAIOLO, J., 'Strategic Intelligence, Counterintelligence and Alliance Diplomacy in Anglo-French Relations before the Second World War', *Militärgeschichtliche Zeitschrift*, 65: 2 (2006).

JORDAN, N., 'The Cut-price War on the Peripheries: The French General Staff, the Rhineland and Czechoslovakia', in Boyce, R. and Robertson, E. M. (eds.), *Paths to War: New Essays on the Origins of the Second World War* (London, 1989).

LAMMERS, D., 'Fascism, Communism and the Foreign Office, 1937–9', *Journal of Contemporary History*, 6: 3 (1971).

—— 'From Whitehall after Munich: The Foreign Office and the Future Course of British Policy', *Historical Journal*, 16: 4 (1973).

MACDONALD, C. A., 'Economic Appeasement and the German 'Moderates', 1937–1939: An Introductory Essay', *Past and Present*, 56 (1972).

—— 'Deterrent Diplomacy: Roosevelt and the Containment of Germany, 1938–1940', in Boyce, R. and Robertson, E. M. (eds.), *Paths to War: New Essays on the Origins of the Second World War* (London, 1989).

—— 'Britain, France and the April Crisis of 1939', *European Studies Review*, 2 (1972).

MARKS, F. W., III, 'Six between Roosevelt and Hitler: America's Role in the Appeasement of Nazi Germany', *Historical Journal*, 28: 4 (1985).

MEREDITH, D., 'British Trade Diversion Policy and the "Colonial Issue" in the 1930s', *Journal of European Economic History*, 25: 1 (1996).

MICHALKA, W., 'From the Anti-Comintern Pact to the Euro-Asiatic Bloc: Ribbentrop's Alternative Concept to Hitler's Foreign Policy Programme', in Koch, H. W. (ed.), *Aspects of the Third Reich* (London, 1985).

MILWARD, A., 'The Reichsmark Bloc and the International Economy', in Hirschfeld, G. and Kettenacker, L. (eds.), *Der 'Führerstaat': Mythos und Realität: Studien zur Struktur und Politik des Dritten Reiches* (Stuttgart, 1981).

MINNITI, F, 'Le materie prime nella preparazione bellica dell' ltalia, 1935–1943, Parts I and II, *Storia Contemperanea* (1986).

OVERY, R., 'Hitler's War and the German Economy', in Boyce, R. and Robertson, E. M. (eds.), *Paths to War: New Essays on the Origins of the Second World War* (London, 1989).

PARKER, R. A. C., 'British Rearmament, 1936–1939: Treasury, Trade Unions and Skilled Labour', *English Historical Review*, 96: 379 (1981).

—— 'The Pound Sterling, the American Treasury and British Preparations for War, 1938–1939', *English Historical Review*, 98: 387 (1983).

PEDEN, G. C., 'The Burden of Imperial Defence and the Continental Commitment Reconsidered', *Historical Journal*, 27: 2 (1974).

—— 'A Matter of Timing: The Economic Background to British Foreign Policy, 1937–1939', *History*, 225 (1984).

POIDEVIN, R., 'La tentative de rapprochement économique entre la France et l'Allemagne, 1938–1939', in Bariéty, J., Guth, A., and Valentin, J. M. (eds.), *La France et l'Allemagne entre les deux guerres mondiales* (Nancy, 1987).

PRAŻMOWSKA, A., 'Poland's Foreign Policy: September 1938 – September 1939', *Historical Journal*, 29: 4 (1986).

RÉMOND, R., 'L'image de l'Allemagne dans l'opinion publique française de mars à septembre 1939', in Hildebrand, K. and Werner, K. F. (eds.), *Deutschland und Frankreich 1936–1939* (Munich, 1981).

ROCK, W. R., 'The British Guarantee to Poland, March 1939: A Problem in Diplomatic Decision-making', *South Atlantic Quarterly*, 65 (1966).

SALERNO, R. M., 'The French Navy and the Appeasement of Italy, 1937–1939', *English Historical Review*, 112: 445 (1997).

SCHRÖDER, H.-J., 'Das Dritte Reich, die USA und Lateinamerika, 1933–1941', in Funke, M. (ed.), *Hitler, Deutschland und die Mächte* (Düsseldorf, 1976).

STAFFORD, P., 'The Chamberlain–Halifax Visit to Rome: A Reappraisal', *English Historical Review*, 98: 386 (1983).

—— 'The French Government and the Danzig Crisis: The Italian Dimension', *International History Review*, 6: 1 (1984).

STRANG, G. B., 'Two Unequal Tempers: Sir George Ogilvie-Forbes, Sir Nevile Henderson and British Foreign Policy, 1938–9', *Diplomacy and Statecraft*, 5: 1 (1994).

—— 'Once More Unto the Breach: Britain's Guarantee to Poland, March 1939', *Journal of Contemporary History*, 31: 4 (1996).

TEICHOVA, A., 'East-Central and South-East Europe', in Mathias, P. and Pollard, S. (eds.), *The Cambridge Economic History of Europe*, Vol. VIII, second edn. (Cambridge, 1989).

—— 'Bilateral Trade Revisited: Did the Southeast European States Exploit National Socialist Germany on the Eve of the Second World War?', in Glätz, F. (ed.), *Modern Age—Modern Historian: In Memoriam György Ránki, 1930–1988* (Budapest, 1990).

THOMAS, M., 'To Arm an Ally: French Arms Sales to Romania', *Journal of Strategic Studies*, 19 (1996).

VIDAL, G., 'Le Parti Communiste français et la défense nationale (septembre 1937 – septembre 1939)', *Revue historique*, 630 (2004).

WADDINGTON, G., 'Hassgegner: German Views of Great Britain in the later 1930s', *History*, 81: 261 (1996).

WARK, W. K., 'Three Military Attachés in Berlin in the 1930s: Soldier, Statesmen and the Limits of Ambiguity', *International History Review*, 9: 4 (1987).

—— 'Something Very Stern: British Political Intelligence, Moralism and Strategy in 1939', *Intelligence and National Security*, 5: 1 (1990).

WENDT, J., 'Südosteuropa als "Informal Empire" Deutschlands, 1933–1939: das Beispiel Jugoslawiens', *Jahrbücher für die Geschichte Osteuropas*, 23 (1975).

YOUNG, R. J., 'The Aftermath of Munich: The Course of French Diplomacy, October 1938 to March 1939', *French Historical Studies*, 8 (1973).

—— 'The Strategic Dream: French Air Doctrine in the Inter War Period, 1919–1939', *Journal of Contemporary History*, 9 (1974).

—— 'La guerre de longue durée: Some Reflections on French Strategy and Diplomacy', in Preston, P. (ed.), *General Staffs and Diplomacy before the Second World War* (London, 1978).

—— 'Reason and Madness: France, the Axis Powers and the Politics of Economic Disorder, 1938–1939', *Canadian Journal of History*, 20 (1985).

Theses

HUCKER, D., 'The Role of Public Opinion in the Formulation of British and French Foreign Policy, 1938–1939', Ph.D. diss., University of Wales, Aberystwyth, 2007.

14

Darkening Skies: Peace Talking and War Planning in Britain and France

I

To understand the Anglo-French reactions to Hitler's policies during the first half of 1939, it is necessary to look away from the diplomatic chessboard and to view the broader scene. On both sides of the English Channel, the months following the Munich conference saw a striking change of perception and a toughening of both the official and public mood. It was almost as if the danger of war, not as immediate as in September 1938 but in the foreseeable future, served to strengthen the conviction that the two governments should prepare for a showdown with Nazi Germany. The change had much to do with the failure of the Munich conference to bring about any improvement in the prevailing atmosphere of fear and apprehension. At a deeper level, there was a shift in public attitudes towards the prospect of war and a greater degree of confidence among the military planners that they could withstand the initial German thrust and put their war-winning strategies into practice

The growing popular hostility towards Nazi Germany was due, in the first instance, to what was happening in Germany. *Kristallnacht* shocked the British and French publics and the march into Prague convinced people on both sides of the Channel that Hitler's justifications for his *coups* were worthless. The acceptance of the idea of war in the not too distant future was connected, too, with the acceleration of the war preparations of the governments. The very frequency of the reminders in Britain to 'take your gas mask with you' accustomed people to accepting the possibility of bombardment while providing some assurance that steps were being taken for their protection. The clearest sign of the public distancing from Munich was Chamberlain's awareness that any open gesture of appeasement would meet with disapproval. His letters to his sisters vividly record his growing sense of isolation in the Commons, where his party enjoyed such an overwhelming majority.

The prime minister's main fear, quite apart from any political threat to his leadership, was that the inclusion of Churchill in his cabinet would give the wrong signals to Hitler and shut the door to future negotiations. On black days, Chamberlain admitted that events allowed 'my enemies to mock me publicly' and confessed to feeling 'dispirited and alone'.[1] In private, he still believed that continued rearmament and the offer of future talks would bring Hitler to the negotiating table. In public, he was forced to conceal his efforts to keep the possibility of dialogue open. In June 1939, Lord Chatfield was told when preparing a speech that 'the prime minister himself wishes to use as little as possible in political speeches the word "appeasement" which is now open to considerable misconstruction'.[2]

The shift in British public feeling occurred despite the continued efforts by Chamberlain and Halifax to clamp down on press critiques of Hitler and Mussolini. The government's efforts at press control, as well as the self-imposed restraints on criticism of the prime minister in the mainstream Conservative newspapers, could not conceal the changing mood. The *News Chronicle* published a poll at the beginning of October 1938 showing that 37% of the population was dissatisfied with Chamberlain as prime minister and that 72% wanted an increase in rearmament. More revealing were the results of a poll that the paper's editor forwarded to Chamberlain but did not publish out of a sense of public duty: 86% of those interviewed did not believe Hitler when he claimed to have no further territorial ambitions. During the summer months, the prime minister's standing recovered. Opinion surveys showed that the majority of those men (women were also asked) polled were satisfied with Chamberlain's leadership and believed that the risk of war had decreased since the previous autumn, though they wanted Churchill included in his cabinet. In July, an overwhelming majority (76%) believed that if Germany and Poland went to war over Danzig, Britain should fulfil its pledge to fight on Poland's side.[3] While public opinion polls, particularly at this date, provided only crude indicators of popular views, nonetheless, all pointed to a 'sea-change' in feeling that ruled out an early election and made Chamberlain ever more circumspect about revealing his thoughts about the right road to peace. The summer by-elections pointed in a similar direction. The turnout was

[1] Keith Feiling, *The Life of Neville Chamberlain*, 401–402.

[2] R. A. C. Parker, *Chamberlain and Appeasement*, 292.

[3] George Gallup (ed.), *The Gallup International Public Opinion Polls: Great Britain, 1937–1975*, vol. 1 (New York, 1976), 21. See Daniel Hucker, 'The Role of Public Opinion in the Formulation of British and French Foreign Policy, 1938–9', unpublished Ph.D. thesis, University of Wales at Aberystwyth, 2007, vol. II.

generally low, national press coverage relatively scant and the electorate apathetic. Conservative candidates referred to the government's desire to settle differences between nations by 'discussion and cooperation' but underlined its determination to oppose, by war if necessary, attempts to impose settlements by force. Labour candidates criticized the government for its failure to adopt the policies of collective security and argued that war was not inevitable if the right policies were followed. There was still a small minority of politicians and peers, mainly attached or sympathetic to the Conservative party, who even after Prague, clung to ideas of negotiating with Hitler but most of these and other German sympathizers had abandoned their illusions.

As the summer holidays loomed, there was a general feeling that the government was doing all that was necessary to strengthen the 'peace front' and was taking in hand the preparations necessary for the safety of the home islands. Members of Parliament were somewhat uneasy despite the announcement just before the 31 July adjournment debate that Britain and France would begin immediate military talks with the Soviet Union. Parliament was to recess on 4 August and not to meet again for another eight weeks, a date accepted only after a very unpleasant debate that showed how dubious the Commons was about such a long adjournment. 'It's a very hard thing', Churchill told the Commons in his speech of protest, 'for the Government to say to the House, "Begone! Run off and play. Take your gas masks with you."' Members laughed at the familiar admonition. The debate continued in a courteous manner, until after three and a half hours, Chamberlain intervened: 'The question is whether you trust the Government or distrust the Government. If you distrust them, and show it by your vote, very well; it is a vote of no confidence in the Government, and no confidence in the prime minister in particular.'[4] Chamberlain won his vote but he rightly sensed the dissatisfaction in the Commons, even in his own party. While MPs may have been troubled, they, like most of Britain, went on holiday without anticipating an immediate crisis. The upper classes enjoyed the usual summer social whirl; receptions, parties, and banquets were as, if not more, lavish than usual, tinged perhaps by a sense of the 'last fling' before this whole way of life might vanish. Only a very few, such as the senior history master at Rugby, took their holidays early in anticipation of the outbreak of war. British school children were sent to Germany on an exchange visit. The daily BBC wireless programmes in August began with the introit anthem, 'Blessed are the peacemakers' followed by 'A Safe Stronghold our God is Still'. Many thought that Hitler was bluffing over Danzig and that the very knowledge that he would face Britain if he

[4] *Hansard,* HC Deb, 2 August 1939, Vol. 350, Cols. 2381–2525.

attacked Poland would force him to stand down. The announcement of the Nazi–Soviet pact banished such ideas. War now seemed inevitable.

There was a similar 'sea-change' in France though it evolved slowly after Munich. Daladier's policies began to win widespread approval and public resistance to policies of conciliation was growing. An opinion poll in February showed that 70% of those interviewed said that 'France and Britain should resist any new aggression by Hitler.'[5] The government's propaganda campaign in the press, on the air waves and in the movie houses actively played on the prime minister's growing popularity and focused on the strength of France and its empire, which could offer compensation for France's inferiority to Germany in population and industrial resources. *Pathé-Journal* and the French subsidiaries of American film companies produced 'shorts' such as the thirteen-minute coverage of Daladier's celebrated trip to Corsica, Tunis, and Algeria and the prize winning documentary *Sommes-nous défendus?* These confidence and unity building exercises in turn made it more difficult for the government to retreat in the face of Axis provocation. The Prague *coup* was more than a catalyst; in some ways it represented the high watermark in French resolve. The Chamber debate on 17 March was the only time in the inter-war period when all speakers called for a policy of '*fermeté*'. Hitler's action helped to alter the anti-war attitudes of the veterans' associations and peasantry. The two most powerful veterans' organizations, so profoundly pacifist in the past, now called for strong leadership and a united France. A strong demand for an anti-totalitarian policy appeared in a written appeal to the government signed by many of the bishops of France. Writing to President Roosevelt on 23 March, Ambassador Bullitt commented on the 'quiet resolution' of the two classes of French reserves mobilized over the last three days and the calmness of their families. People were convinced 'that words were useless, and that Hitler could be stopped by nothing but force. As a result, there is curious "serenity" from one end of France to the other. There is no vacillation or mourning.'[6] The revival of confidence and Daladier's growing authority was sustained in part by the return to prosperity. It helped, too, that though he supported an alignment with the Soviet Union, thereby winning Communist support for policies promoting national defence, Daladier's powerful domestic anti-Communism was welcomed by many Socialists and the parties of the right. Frenchmen

[5] Jean-Baptiste Duroselle, *La décadence, 1932–1939*, 179. After Munich, 57% had approved of the settlement, 37% were opposed. Jean-Louis Crémieux-Brilhac, *Les Français de l'an 40*, Vol. 1, *La guerre oui ou non?* (Paris, 1990), 65.

[6] Orville H. Bullitt (ed.), *For the President: Personal and Secret*, 332.

like Flandin, Marcel Déat, and François Piétri, who were in regular touch with the German embassy, told their German contacts that the majority of the French people were resolved to meet a 'fresh *coup de force* by every means, even by means of war'.[7] Patriotism had a strong edge of xenophobia; the treatment of the Spanish refugees was scandalous and Jewish refugees in France found their welcome less than warm. On 14 July, 35,000 troops marched along the Champs Elysées; Lord Gort, the chief of the imperial general staff, took the salute alongside General Gamelin. Hore-Belisha, the British secretary of state for war, attended, as did an unofficial but highly welcome guest, Winston Churchill. Marchers from the Royal Navy, the Royal Marines, the Foot Guards in full dress uniform, and an RAF fly past were much noted in the Paris press, as was the strong colonial presence. 'An unforgettable day', a French writer later recalled, 'every kind of dream was permissible, illusions strong as ever, fears vanished'.[8] The rudimentary public opinion polls tell a similar story of strengthening resolve. In July, 76% of those questioned believed that France should fight if Germany seized Danzig and only 17% answered 'no'.[9] When Marcel Déat, whose article 'Mourir pour Dantzig?', published on 4 May 1939 in *l'Oeuvre*, had encouraged the Germans to hope that the French and British would not support Polish resistance to their demands, returned to the charge on 10 May in a piece entitled, 'Négocier pour Dantzig', he was strongly denounced by the Communists, Socialists and most of the right-wing press. Police reports indicated that only the extremist sections of French opinion, such as 'the far right anti-Semitic organisations, integral pacifists or isolated groups of far left socialist revolutionaries' opposed the government's firm line against the dictators.[10]

It is difficult to depict the mood in France in the summer of 1939. There is no doubt of the general support for Daladier's foreign policy and for the negotiations with the Soviet Union. There were summer fêtes and balls in Paris and people enjoyed the splendid weather. There was also, particularly in some political and intellectual circles, a sense of impending doom, brilliantly depicted in Jean Renoir's film *La Règle du Jeu* (banned in September as too defeatist). Beneath the demonstrations

[7] *DGFP*, Ser. D, Vol. VI, No. 481 (6 June 1939).

[8] M. Destrem, *L'été 39* (Paris, 1969), 95, cited in John Lukacs, *The Last European War, September 1939–December 1941* (Garden City, NY, 1976), 39.

[9] Christel Peyrefitte, 'Les premier sondages d'opinion', in René Rémond and Janine Bourdin (eds.), *Edouard Daladier, chef du governement* (Paris, 1977), 271; Crémieux-Brilhac, *La Guerre Oui ou Non*, 65.

[10] Hucker, 'The Role of Public Opinion in the Formulation of British and French Foreign Policy, 1938–9', 218.

of national unity and backing for Daladier there remained deep political divisions. The French labour movement had no love for the Daladier government; there would be no *Union Sacrée* as in 1914. Daladier's special powers nonetheless evoked only 'formal criticism' and the decree proroguing Parliament until 1 June 1942 was passed with virtually no opposition on 30 July. It may be that the government's fears of a resurgence of pacifist and defeatist sentiments lay behind Reynaud's radio broadcast of 29 July exhorting the French people not to 'abandon the spirit of sacrifice, cease to believe in France, or once again fall back on facile ideas' and Daladier's imposition of tighter control over the press, radio, and cinema in the summer of 1939.[11] Questions remain about the depth of the premier's own determination. Current revisionism has not wholly restored Daladier's reputation on the eve of the war and it is not easy to dismiss the charges made by contemporary critics, admittedly writing during the '*drôle de guerre*', that he was a man 'embarrassed by his irresolution' and 'without a compass, buffeted between those whom he consulted, showing at short intervals quite opposite tendencies, concluding often in the sense of the last heard'.[12] Bonnet, admittedly a supporter of the Soviet alliance that would strengthen deterrence and contribute to the peace, was kept in office mainly for political reasons though Daladier complained of his intrigues and was well aware of his pro-appeasement sympathies. In the final crisis, the premier wavered and took advice.

The great summer departure from Paris took place as usual. Observers claimed that the mood was calm, if somewhat fatalistic, for many thought that war would have to come eventually. The news of the Nazi–Soviet pact brought the holidays to an abrupt end. Between 21 and 27 August, 900,000 men were called to the colours. The government cancelled the first Cannes film festival scheduled for 1 September and the Communist party called off '*la fête de l'Humanité*' fixed for 3 September. The roads were crowded with people returning home but there was no panic.

II

The second feature of this immediate pre-war period that distinguishes it from the autumn of 1938 was the changed attitude of the military establishments in both countries. Official and popular opinion

[11] Cited in Hucker, 'The Role of Public Opinion in the Formulation of British and French Foreign Policy', 226.

[12] Jules Jeanneney, *Journal Politique (septembre 1939–juillet 1942)*, ed. J.-N. Jeanneney (Paris, 1972), 20 (entry for 21 October 1939).

reinforced each other in similar directions. The service chiefs moved from the extreme pessimism of the previous September to a more balanced view of the strategic situation and an even somewhat optimistic appraisal of the chances of victory. The new assessments reflected and reinforced the more determined attitudes of the body politic. Military and intelligence analysts, however circumscribed by their professional milieux, almost unconsciously respond to more general currents of opinion. The growing sense that a European war could not be long avoided encouraged a reconsideration of the balance of forces. Reasons were found—indeed, almost had to be found—to abandon the worst case scenarios of 1938 and to explain why the balance was no longer so disproportionately tilted in the Axis direction. Attention was focused on how the war should be fought rather than on why it should be avoided. When the service chiefs looked at their enemies with war in mind, they began to question whether they were as formidable as they had seemed several months earlier. The revised appraisals had little to do with new sources of information; they were the consequence of the altered framework within which the old data was interpreted. The same body of evidence, with some updating, used to support the policy of retreat in September 1938 was now used to prove that Britain and France could face war in 1939, though 1940 would be preferable. The expanded and accelerated rearmament programmes engendered confidence in the future though the intelligence services in both countries noted the increasing disparity in land and air forces between the Germans and the western powers and warned of the contribution made by the annexed territories to the German rearmament programme.

The major European strategic appreciation for 1939–1940 produced by the British chiefs of staff sub-committee during February 1939 was far less pessimistic than its predecessors. Even while enumerating Germany's advantages, questions were raised about the effectiveness of the Nazi war machine. The review projected a more confident picture of Britain's ability both to withstand an initial German attack and to engage in a protracted war. Much of the report was devoted to the economic aspects of the coming war. It dwelt on the gap between Germany's massive rearmament drive and its shortages of raw material and foreign exchange. It called attention to the opposition to war in Germany, so clearly demonstrated at the time of Munich, and the possibility that German morale might crack if the situation seriously deteriorated. Diplomats in the Berlin embassy and the Secret Intelligence Service (SIS) disagreed. Military intelligence underlined the weaknesses of Germany's long-term economic and financial situation. Even when correct, such information, of course, could shed very little light on how Hitler was responding to this litany of difficulties. The markedly different tone had more to do with the change in perspective rather than the reports of German shortages and shaky morale.

It was accepted that there had been little improvement in the numerical ratio of forces; in some respects, it had worsened. The British army, only recently committed to a continental role and faced with the anticipated disruptions of conscription, lacked guns, including heavy anti-tank guns, and tanks. Production figures began to improve, particularly during the second half of 1939. Estimates that the Germans could raise a wartime army of between 121 and 130 divisions with 2.5 million effectives were hardly reassuring news.[13] The chiefs of staff judged that the German army would be larger and better equipped than in 1914 and would be superior to what France could put in the field. Confidence in an eventual Allied victory depended on the unexamined belief in the staying power of the French army and the heightened perception of German economic weakness and vulnerability to blockade.

The last pre-war British air intelligence report, produced in early 1939, showed that Germany possessed more than double the number of first-line aircraft (4,210 versus 1,998) and long-range bombers (1,750 versus 832) as the RAF.[14] Again, the figures were not seriously out of line. Germany had 4,093 first-line aircraft available on 1 September 1939, with a bomber fleet 1,542 strong.[15] The more balanced view of the situation in the air stemmed from improvements made on the defensive side and from a more critical assessment of the German situation. Fighter Command had replaced most of its bi-planes with monoplanes with retractable undercarriages in 1938–1939. The new RAF machines were capable of intercepting the fastest German bombers.[16] Hurricane and Spitfire fighters were reaching the RAF in increasing numbers, the radar chain was being extended and considerable improvements had been made in air raid protection schemes (ARP). The latter was of key importance since it was thought, erroneously, that the German air force would give priority to strategic bombing. The airmen were also encouraged by the increase in Britain's productive capacity, which by September 1939 would overtake the German monthly output of aircraft.

[13] The estimated strength of the German army in September 1939 was 2,758,000 effectives in 103 divisions.

[14] Wesley K. Wark, *The Ultimate Enemy: British Intelligence and Nazi Germany, 1933–1939*, 73.

[15] Militärgeschichtliches Forschungsamt (ed.), *Germany and the Second World War*, Vol.1, ed. Wilhelm Deist, 503. See Appendices A-2 and A-3.

[16] G. C. Peden, *Arms, Economics and British Strategy: From Dreadnoughts to Hydrogen Bombs* (Cambridge, 2007), 110.

Table 14.1 British Aircraft Deliveries, 1939–1940

	Bombers	Fighters	General reconnaissance
Last six months of 1938	404	253	22
First six months of 1939	827	680	18
Last six months of 1939	1010	644	43
First six months of 1940	1415	1504	237

Note: Despite the decision to concentrate on fighters, the production of bombers continued partly because of the wishes of the Air Ministry but also because of the already existing productive base for bomber production.

Source: Talbot Imlay, *Facing the Second World War: Strategy, Politics, and Economics in Britain and France, 1938–1940* (Oxford, 2003), 369.

Using difficult to secure estimates of current production schedules, it was argued that the Germans would find it difficult to sustain or expand their rate of future production given the shortages of materials and skilled labour.

The British still saw themselves as a naval power as much as anything else, and by the mid-1930s felt they had numerous weaknesses in this respect, as well as opportunities to grow. The *King George V* programme was seen as a crash solution to some of these problems. Between 1937 and 1939, the British easily outbuilt any other power at sea, pulling up their relative positions with regard to Germany, Italy, and Japan, or all three of them together. The *King George V* battleships lay at the core of this surge in strength, though the British also built more aircraft carriers and cruisers than anyone else. There were originally to be five such battleships (1937 programme) but the number had been cut to four. In 1939, all the *King George V* ships were quickly coming on stream. Together with the improvements in Fighter Command, this naval surge increased British confidence and encouraged hopes that they could do even better in the two areas most central to the country's security, power and strategy.

It is true that the Admiralty was shocked (though it knew something about plan 'Z') by the German claim to a 100% ratio in submarines made in December 1938. Though the German fleet could not challenge Britain's naval supremacy, there was a good possibility that the two nations would soon be at war. Higher priority had been given to building major warships than to anti-submarine vessels on the correct grounds that the latter could be built quickly if the need arose. The Admiralty, too, thought it could rely on ASDIC (underwater sound detection apparatus) and the new radar systems to assist in the sea war. In the spring of 1939, there were naval and U-boat scares, now known to be manufactured by the *Abwehr*, which threw the naval chiefs off balance. Yet even before the Tientsin crisis in June–July 1939 refocused attention on the Far East, the Admiralty had continued to think in terms of its global strategy and the building of the two-ocean fleet that would allow Britain to engage its two main naval competitors (Germany and Japan). Demands for a crash programme to secure the industrial plant to lay down three instead of two battleships annually from 1940 was first postponed and then dropped at the outbreak of war. Time ran out. There was, however, no question of British superiority over Germany. In fact, at the start of the war, the Royal Navy controlled all the waterways vital to the British war effort.

The strategic situation, as reported by the British intelligence services, still left the immediate military advantage with the Axis powers. Any military confrontation would be highly dangerous, especially if Japan intervened. The service chiefs wanted to postpone war until 1940 when British defences would be much improved. The events of March forced the services to speed up their timetables. The chiefs of staff hoped that an eastern front would help deter Hitler and give them time; most were converted to the inclusion of the Soviet Union. Should deterrence fail, Germany would then be faced with a two-front war that would reduce the chances of an aerial attack and the possibility of an early victory. British armament production was clearly improving and there was still some slack in the system that could be exploited.[17] The more favourable projection of future German weakness encouraged confidence. The chiefs of staff became accustomed to thinking in terms of an imminent war rather than some far-off eventuality. This realization opened the public purse despite sterling depreciation and exchange losses. Military strategy and not financial policy was determining the pace of rearmament.[18]

The new French 'policy of firmness' was adopted during the winter despite the awareness of the increasing gap in the Franco–German land and air forces. Rather than encouraging a policy of withdrawal and isolation, the increasing danger only made the reconstitution of an eastern front more imperative. Factors omitted or downgraded in the pre-Munich period were given a central place in calculating the continental balance of power and contributed, as in London, to a sense of limited optimism. The French intelligence services recorded the strains in the body politic that, under war conditions, might shake the stability

[17] Peden, *Arms, Economics and British Strategy*, 144.

[18] Defence expenditure rose from £262.1 million in 1937/8 to £382 million 1938/9 to an estimated £750 million in 1939/40. Figures in Peden, *Arms, Economics and British Strategy*, 136–137.

and coherence of German (and Italian) society. While no commentator believed that Germany was on the verge of a domestic crisis, French intelligence emphasized the strains that the rearmament effort was placing on the German population, strains that would be greatly increased under blockade conditions. Much was made of Germany's worsening balance of trade and payments and its lack of raw materials which would undermine its long-range prospects of victory. The French saw in Hitler's 30 January speech an admission of economic weakness and highlighted the importance of General George Thomas's 7 February warning to the German commanders against anticipating a 'lightning war'. The French welcomed his prediction that a long war was 'less favourable but much more likely', and his emphasis on the financial and raw material difficulties that the Reich would face.[19] In April and May, the French intelligence services again reported on the German economic difficulties which the mobilization measures during the Czechoslovakian crisis had considerably worsened. In June, it was noted that since the previous year, Germany's balance of trade and balance of payments had further deteriorated and that production in all sectors but defence had declined. While the Germans would neither abandon rearmament nor autarky, its current policies might well drive the economy over the brink. Right up to the outbreak of war there were reports of considerable unrest in Germany and disenchantment with Nazi policies. Ruhr industrialists, formerly staunch allies of the regime, even hoped that war 'would result in the seizure of power by the army'.[20] The French predicted, too, that in a long war, working class morale might collapse and the workers turn against their government. Such illusory hopes were a major feature in French strategic thinking.

The emphasis on Germany's financial and economic weakness, along with France's own economic revival, fed the renewed sense of confidence. For immediate purposes, the situation was hardly encouraging but, even here, the service chiefs found grounds for hope. In the air, it was accepted that Germany was more powerful in relative terms, both quantitatively and qualitatively, than in September 1938. Intelligence officers nonetheless reported that the German airmen suffered from a lack of training and practical experience and predicted that German planes would soon become obsolete and prove difficult to replace. French production figures were rising; its output of fighter aircraft (almost no bombers were produced) would soon equal that of Germany. The first fighters and reconnaissance aircraft purchased in America

[19] Quoted in Peter Jackson, *France and the Nazi Menace*, 351–352.
[20] Ibid., 355.

arrived in September. With regard to the army, a combination of blind confidence in inherited doctrines and an increased emphasis on the limitations of the *Wehrmacht* appeared to compensate for Germany's undoubted quantitative superiority. The French believed, though appraised of the new German doctrines of mobility, that neither speed nor mobility would overcome superior French firepower. 'Continuous fire' would blunt any German attack. The Spanish Civil War experience, it was thought, had confirmed the superiority of concentrated firepower over armoured vehicles. Gamelin and the general staff could not conceive of a German breakthrough unless the French were caught off guard. In a sense, this was what happened in 1940. Given the inherent advantage of defensive forces, the French felt they could rely with confidence on the Maginot Line, on their preparations for fixed battles, and on the strength of their anti-tank guns and heavy artillery. Tanks were designed mainly to support ground troops and not to be used *en masse*. The French had motorized units; they were intended to move the French troops forward, above all into Belgium, before the Germans arrived. Behind its continuous defensive system, still not extended in the north and north-east, France would continue to rearm until it could safely move from a defensive to an offensive position against a weakened German army.

There was a new awareness of the weaknesses in the *Wehrmacht*. The *Deuxième Bureau* pointed out, and the *Wehrmacht* leadership would not have disagreed, that the German army was short both of officers and reserve officers and that its reserve forces had neither the training nor the arms needed for war. Only the *Marine* painted a wholly pessimistic assessment of its situation. Like its campaign to make Italy the first target of the war, this was, in part, a way to gain more funds, an effort which succeeded in April 1939. Darlan again pushed for a naval campaign against Italy in the summer of 1939 but again without success.

As both the British and French intelligence bureaus noted, it was impossible to apply the rules of democratic countries and a free market economy to conditions in Nazi Germany. Nonetheless, Daladier and Chamberlain believed that Hitler would be reluctant to engage in war. The French prime minister thought that a policy of firmness would convince the dictator to step back. Chamberlain was afraid that a strategy of containment might force Hitler to take retaliatory measures to prove that he was neither weak nor frightened. A tough policy might precipitate the war that the prime minister was so anxious to avoid. Different interpretations were also placed on the German financial and economic difficulties. Chamberlain still thought that economic concessions might help deter Hitler from further aggression and strengthen the influence of the 'moderates' though his views were not shared by others in the cabinet and Foreign Office. The French had recognized the dangers of the German success in south-eastern Europe but lacked the means to recover the ground it had lost.

Daladier and Bonnet believed that the Soviet alliance was essential for deterring Hitler and preserving the peace. Chamberlain did not. The announcement of the Nazi–Soviet pact was a far greater shock to the French cabinet than to the British. Already divided between 'resisters' and 'pacifists', Mandel, Reynaud, Sarraut, Campinchi, and Zay insisted that France had to uphold the guarantee to Poland while Bonnet, Marchendeau, and Anatole de Monzie, as well as some outside politicians, were prepared to renounce their promises to Poland. There were no such parallel arguments in London. Undoubtedly, British firmness at this time helped to convince Daladier that France had no alternative but to do the same. Though rarely publicly articulated in either capital, the Allies expected much from the Americans, whom they believed would tip the balance in the economic war. President Roosevelt's failure to secure the revision of the Neutrality Acts in the summer of 1939 was hardly a good omen. As the 'cash-and-carry' provision of the Neutrality Act had lapsed on 1 May 1939, neither Britain nor France would have access to American arms in wartime even if they could pay the bill. In the hope that the arms embargo would be lifted, a joint Anglo–French purchasing mission was established in London. It was only after the war started, on 4 November, that a special session of Congress replaced the embargo with a 'cash-and-carry' provision.

The intelligence assessments in both countries strengthened their mutual belief in the kind of war they intended to fight. Both states would stand on the defensive at the start of the war. Radar and fighters would protect Britain against a German aerial 'knockout blow'. The French army, if it failed to contain the German armies outside France, would retreat to the impregnable Maginot Line. It was still assumed that the Allied powers were in a better position than Germany to fight the subsequent *guerre de longue durée* given access to the resources of their empires and to the industrial power of the United States. It was claimed that 'time was on our side' and that in a battle of attrition, naval power and blockade would undermine the German ability to sustain the war. There was undoubtedly an overriding wish on both sides of the Channel to find a way that would avoid the 1914–1918 bloodbath. Reliance on blockade to deliver victory was based on what many historians now believe to have been an exaggerated belief in its effectiveness in the 1914–18 war. Given their faith in the efficacy of economic warfare in wartime, the British made arrangements for the creation of a wartime Ministry of Economic Warfare; the French, somewhat more slowly, initiated their own plans for a *Ministère du Blocus*. In May 1939, a

Franco-British Committee was established to coordinate economic efforts. The French were all too aware of their deficiencies in raw materials and the lack of shipping needed for transporting such supplies. Some steps were taken towards creating machinery to control planning, purchase, allocation, and supply, but no comprehensive or coordinated system emerged prior to the war. Both governments were warned that German control over Eastern Europe would strengthen its capacity to counter the blockade and that a German–Soviet alliance would open the abundant natural resources of the USSR to Germany. The difficulty lay in preventing either from happening.

The separate Anglo-French efforts to assist Romania and Yugoslavia in the spring of 1939 failed to stem the German economic steamroller and Britain's earlier abandonment of her Baltic interests meant that the Scandinavian countries were prepared to forego British offers to avoid incurring German wrath. In June, the British Industrial Intelligence Centre (IIC) took a more pessimistic view of the immediate future and predicted that Germany might be able to maintain its industrial activity for fifteen to eighteen months after the outbreak of war just from the resources at its command. The bumper harvest of 1938 and the foodstuffs available from the Baltic and Balkans would increase its reserves of food supplies. The British had moved too late and too slowly and the French had neither the funds nor the arms needed to re-establish its former position that the 'surrender' at Munich had almost demolished.

It was left to the British and French financial authorities to challenge prevailing assumptions about the superior capacity of the Allies to fight a long war against Germany. Both Britain and France were devoting higher proportions of their national incomes to defence than in 1937–1938 but their respective finance ministers warned that neither country was financially strong enough to sustain the current pace of rearmament over any length of time.

Britain was heavily dependent on imports of food and raw materials; 25% to 30% of the price of armaments produced in British factories represented the cost of imported raw materials.[21] It has been argued that far more could have been done to strengthen the sterling bloc making Britain less dependent on the United States and much less vulnerable to the loss of gold.[22] The question remains whether the Dominions would have accepted a ban on their trading elsewhere (Canada had already broken ranks with a trade agreement with the United States in 1935) and, moreover, whether the Dominions could

[21] Peden, *Arms, Economics and British Strategy*, 133.

[22] Christopher Price, *Britain, America and Rearmament in the 1930s: The Cost of Failure* (Basingstoke, 2001), 95–131, 183.

TABLE 14.2 French Military Expenditure, 1936–1939

	Army	Navy	Air	Colonies	Military element in civilian ministries	Total
1936	11941	5358	4090	937	382	22708
1937	13423	5247	4648	812	393	24523
1938	15527	6143	6645	961	177	29453
1939	53668	9897	23904	915		88384

Source: Robert Frank[enstein], *Le prix du réarmement français, 1935–1939* (Paris, 1982), 304.

TABLE 14.3 Percentage of Gross National Product Devoted to Military Expenditure (Great Britain, Germany, France, 1935–1940)

	Great Britain	Germany	France
1935	3.3	7.4	5.8
1936	4.2	12.4	6.3
1937	5.6	11.8	7.1
1938	8.1	16.6	8.6
1939	21.4	23	23
1940	51.7	38	

Source: G. C. Peden, 'A Matter of Timing: The Economic Background to British Foreign Policy, 1937–1939', *History*, 69: 225 (1984), 25.

TABLE 14.4 British Defence Expenditure as Percentage of National Income, 1933–1939

	National income = gross national product net of capital consumption (£m)	Defence departments' expenditure adjusted from financial years to calendar years (£m)	Defence expenditure as percentage of national income
1933	3650	106.65	2.92
1934	3910	112.37	2.87
1935	4078	131.18	3.22
1936	4308	173.79	4.03
1937	4556	243.11	5.34
1938	4754	352.37	7.41
1939	4907	634.9	12.94

Sources: col. 1—B. R. Mitchell, *British Historical Statistics* (Cambridge, 1988), 829; col. 2—*Statistical Abstract for the United Kingdom 1924–1938* (Cmd. 6232), PP 1939–40, x, 367, and (for 1939 only) Robert P. Shay, *British Rearmament in the Thirties* (Princeton, NJ, 1977), 297.

have (or would have) supplied the materials and industrial imports, such as machine tools, that Britain needed. There is little evidence, for instance, that Canada, the dominion most suited to assist Britain, was willing to become its peacetime arsenal.[23] France, though more self-sufficient for food, was even more dependent on raw materials and manufactured goods for war production. It would have to rely, moreover, on the British mercantile navy to transport war materials to France.

Neither government wished to create a war economy in peacetime. It was only on 22 March 1938, after *Anschluss*, that the British cabinet abandoned its 'business as usual' approach to rearmament and another twelve months before War Office orders enjoyed priority over normal trade.[24] In the same month, the Chamberlain government began conversations with representatives from the trade unions and industry. Major problems of dilution (the substitution of semi-skilled for skilled workers) were not resolved until August 1939 and some persisted well into the war. In its preoccupation with preserving its financial and economic strength for the long war, the government had been reluctant to put the country on a semi-war footing. Matters were not helped by Treasury warnings that inflation could only be avoided by assuming dictatorial government powers such as existed in Germany. This was not within the realm of possibility in peacetime Britain. As the international situation deteriorated and Britain's pace of rearmament quickened, the pressure on sterling mounted. Rather than impose exchange controls (which the Bank of England had requested earlier) the government tried to maintain the value of the pound by using its gold reserves. As a result, the reserves were being rapidly reduced. In early January, 1939, the Bank of England transferred some £200,000,000 of gold, valued at the old statutory price of eighty-five shillings per ounce, to the Exchange Equalization account in an attempt to impress the market that the fund had ample resources to meet the crisis. The Bank was left with £126,000,000, an amount roughly equivalent to what the Bank of England had in its possession when it abandoned the gold standard in 1931.[25] The Treasury warned the cabinet that if the gold losses of the previous months continued it would become 'a serious economic anxiety even in peace' and would gravely affect Britain's staying power in war. Acknowledging that the Johnson Act made it impossible to borrow in the United States, the Treasury spokesman concluded that 'unless, when the time comes the United States are prepared either to

[23] Michael Hennessy, 'The Industrial Front: The Scale and Scope of Canadian Industrial Mobilization during the Second World War', in Bernd Horn (ed.), *Forging a Nation: Perspectives on the Canadian Military Experience* (St Catherine's, Ont., 2002), 137.

[24] Peden, *Arms, Economics and British Strategy*, 137.

[25] Price, *Britain, America and Rearmament in the 1930s*, 145–146.

lend or to give us money as required, the prospects for a long war are becoming increasingly grim'.[26] He admitted that Britain was in a worse position to fight a long war than in 1914, 'subject to the question whether the United States was prepared to help us with finance'.[27] Ministerial morale could hardly have been improved by the Treasury's assessment of the German financial effort for rearmament which made it clear that the Reich, without any source of overseas finance and with already high taxation, 'could keep up her expenditure on armaments indefinitely', a view, by the way not shared by the more orthodox German financial authorities.[28] Kingsley Wood wondered whether Britain ought not to adopt German methods.

In July, the Treasury again warned that Britain's financial power would be dissipated before war broke out. Treasury officials questioned the assumption, which they had done so much to encourage, that the western powers enjoyed greater 'staying power' than the enemy. Sir John Simon, the chancellor of the exchequer, glumly informed the cabinet that Britain's prospects would be 'exceedingly grim' unless it could obtain American loans and gifts on a massive scale. The losses of gold and fall in the value of the pound not only restricted the length of time, from six to nine months, that the present rate of spending could be maintained but would directly affect how long Britain could fight the war. As in January, Lord Halifax thought that the Treasury took 'too gloomy a view' and predicted that 'the position of Germany was very likely to be even more difficult in regard to the conduct of a long war'. If the war continued for some time, he believed that 'the United States would be sufficiently favourable to us to enable us to win the war'.[29] Given the circumstances of the summer of 1939, this prescient prediction was based on hope. Oliver Stanley, the president of the Board of Trade, argued that Britain and Germany were already engaged in war and that the time was coming when fighting would have to begin: 'The point would ultimately come when we should be unable to carry on a long war', he said. 'There would, therefore, come a moment which, on a balance of our financial strength and our arms strength, was the best time for war to break out.'[30] Britain could then go on a full war-time footing.

During these months, as war fears increased the pressure on sterling, nothing was done to stop the haemorrhaging of gold, mostly to the United States, where it was used by the American Treasury to help

[26] Quotations from TNA: PRO, Cab. 24/287, CP 149 (89) Cabinet. Note on the Financial Situation. See references in Richard Rosecrance and Zara Steiner, 'British Grand Strategy and the Origins of World War II', in R. Rosecrance and A. A. Stein (eds.), *The Domestic Bases of Grand Strategy* (Ithaca, NY, and London, 1993), 136.

[27] Price, *Britain, America and Rearmament in the 1930s*, 170.

[28] Ibid., 173–174.

[29] Ibid., 156.

[30] Quoted in Parker, *Chamberlain and Appeasement*, 285.

reflate the economy just beginning to recover from the 'Roosevelt depression' of 1937–1938. While the Americans may not have pressured the British Treasury to maintain the over-valued pound, they did nothing to help alleviate the situation, which was to their advantage. Unwilling to impose exchange controls or to devalue, which would have raised import prices, or engage in a stiff deflation, particularly in an election year, the Treasury continued to use gold to prop up the pound as the pound-dollar ratio slipped. The British war chest shrank from a current value of £594 million in gold on 31 March to £470 million on 22 August.[31] More might have been done earlier to slow this drain; export controls were only imposed with the outbreak of war. It was not just the government's preoccupation with the 'fourth arm of defence' and the anticipated war of attrition that explains the slowness with which the government moved before the spring of 1939 but also residual if fading hopes that war might still be avoided, at least for the present, and that Britain would have time to re-arm.[32]

France's current financial position was somewhat stronger than that of Britain. The government's policies had restored investor confidence and French capital returned from abroad in record amounts. On the eve of the war, the Bank of France had forty-eight billion francs in gold, eleven billion more than in September 1938 and close to the fifty million thought essential as a war chest.[33] The difficulty lay with the swelling defence budget. Decree laws in March and April relieved the service ministries from having to submit estimates to parliament. By September 1939, military spending accounted for 135% of government revenue (includes deficit spending) as compared to 48% the year before. In March, Reynaud warned Daladier that the heavy military spending might compromise the economic turnabout and in June, he wrote to the premier that 'France's financial resources were not without limits.'[34] Reynaud warned the parliamentary commission on finance that military spending was disproportionate to France's financial resources'.[35] Far more urgently than the British, the French needed to

[31] Chart in R. A. C. Parker, 'The Pound Sterling, the American Treasury and British Preparation for War', *English Historical Review*, 98: 387 (1983), 263. Foreign currency holdings fell from £16 million to £7 million over the same period.

[32] Readers should note the continuing debate on the British government's financial strategies and the degree to which financial and economic factors provide a defence for British appeasement policies. For a recent statement of the two positions, see Peden, *Arms, Economics and British Strategy*, chapter 3, particularly 133–135, and Price, *Britain, America and Rearmament in the 1930s* (Basingstoke, 2001).

[33] Talbot C. Imlay, *Facing the Second World War*, 271.

[34] Ibid., 273; Robert Frank[enstein], *Le prix du réarmament français, 1935–1939* 206–217.

[35] For full quotation, see p. 717.

buy aircraft in America and, like Britain, were prevented from raising loans in the United States by the Johnson Act. After shipping gold in February 1939 to pay for a consignment of Martin and Douglas bombers, Reynaud and Daladier sought other ways to gain access to the American money market. Reynaud suggested a lump sum payment of ten billion francs in gold, about 10% of the Bank of France's gold holdings, against the French war debt. Knowing that this sum was too small to satisfy Congress, Reynaud offered the Americans various French overseas possessions, the Clipperton Islands, the French interests in the New Hebrides, and 'any other French possession that we [the United States] might fancy in either the Caribbean or the Pacific'.[36] Roosevelt told Monnet, the French negotiating agent, that the French should keep their cash reserve for 'a little while' and that the French possessions would either be a headache or practically worthless compared to the total debt they owed. Both Daladier and Léger admitted in conversations with Ambassador Bullitt in the summer of 1939 that only an alliance with the Soviet Union and the revision of the Neutrality Act giving the Allies access to American military supplies would prevent Hitler from attacking Poland. Neither came to fruition in the summer of 1939 but the latter was soon in sight. In December, overriding objections from both Simon and Reynaud, René Pleven, a French representative from the Anglo-French Coordinating Committee, was despatched to Washington to negotiate for the warplanes both countries wanted. Like some ministers and officials in London, Daladier looked to Washington to make up its shortages in aircraft or other essential resources.

To relieve the pressure on the French finances in the summer of 1939, Reynaud advocated a programme based on cuts in non-military spending and measures that would encourage industrialists to use returned capital for investment purposes and so expand their production. The government held back on issuing mobilization directives to industrialists and made no move to coordinate war production. Calls for a peacetime Armaments Ministry were ignored; the service departments thought such a move would disrupt production and also because the government did not want to interfere with the running of the economy. Apart from the nationalized war industries, any steps for the coordination of the private war sector were left to the industrialists. Some moves were made but without government pressure, were of a limited nature. Some firms speeded up production by increasing the hours of work. As the government favoured industry over labour and the trade unions were weak

[36] William R. Keylor 'France and the Illusion of American Support' in Joel Blatt (ed.), *The French Defeat of 1940: Reassessments* (Providence, RI, and Oxford, 1998), 239.

(the Communist unions did not want to delay rearmament) industrial workers carried a disproportionate share of the economic burden of rearmament.[37]

British and French perceptions of German economic and financial weakness were entirely correct but it proved difficult, if not impossible, for the Allies to judge whether Hitler would be constrained by such considerations or whether, as some predicted, they would force him to go to war. Chamberlain clung to the hope that Hitler would see reason; others in London feared some 'mad dog act' that would result in a war for which they were not yet ready to fight. However good or faulty western intelligence on German rearmament might have been, no one could do more than speculate on how Hitler would assess the German situation.

During the post-Prague months, while constructing their peace front intended to deter Hitler, the two western governments began planning for war. Two sets of military discussions were held between 29 March–4 April and 24 April–4 May 1939 in order to work out the details of cooperation. A third set, which went on at intervals throughout the summer of 1939, cleared up outstanding details and was followed up by a series of conferences between local commanders in the Mediterranean and Middle East as well as in Singapore. A close relationship was established at the senior level despite hesitations on the British side, especially about providing information. The fear of leaks was perhaps understandable given that the French general staff was sparing in its own briefings to French politicians on similar grounds. The common policy developed in the early stages of the staff talks envisioned the war being fought in three phases. During the first phase, land forces would remain on the defensive and a naval blockade would be instituted against the Axis. If the Low Countries were invaded, the Anglo-French armies would go as far forward into Belgium as circumstances permitted. In the second phase, the entente powers would still remain on the defensive towards Germany although bombing attacks on economic and industrial targets might weaken its resistance. It was agreed to follow a restricted bombing policy as long as the two countries remained greatly inferior in offensive air strength to the Germans. Only military targets 'in the narrowest sense of the term' would be bombed and attacks would be confined to those objectives unlikely to involve the loss of civilian life. There would be offensives into north and east Africa to knock Italy out of the war and a possible attack on continental Italy if forces could be released from the western front. It would only be during the third and

[37] Frank, *Le prix du réarmament français*, 273–288.

last phase of the war that an Anglo-French offensive with massive numerical superiority would be launched against Germany.

How to deal with a German attempt to outflank the Maginot Line was clearly of critical importance. To the north, the French would either reinforce the Belgians on their eastern frontier (the Meuse-Albert canal line) or go as far as the Scheldt river. Everything depended on cooperation with a Belgian government that was pledged to strict neutrality and with whom no official military contacts were permitted. Gamelin, in his anxiety to distance the eventual war zone as far from northern France as possible, took an enormous gamble by pinning his hopes on secret exchanges with the chief of the Belgian general staff, General van den Bergen, whom he trusted would convince the king and his ministers to abandon neutrality and issue an appeal for assistance in time for the French troops to advance to the Albert Canal and River Meuse. If the appeal came too late, the French would have to fight an encounter battle with the Germans from an undefended line, the very eventuality that Gamelin wished to avoid. The French were anxious to secure the collaboration of British bombers with their own army and air force in order to delay any German advance into Belgium. The RAF, intent on its own strategic bombing role, insisted that the bulk of the British air force would be needed at home. As to the Dutch, neither the British nor the French contemplated assisting their army except in the most unlikely situation where an eastern front would draw off enough German forces to make this practical. Some attention was also paid to a German attack through Switzerland. Franco-Swiss talks during 1938–1939 arranged that French forces would be allowed to enter Switzerland and would link up with the Swiss army in a line running between Basle and Berne. Initiated by the French, these exchanges were made far easier because the senior Swiss military figures were strong Francophiles. The British, who were not told of the talks, were assured that the French had the matter well in hand and could comfortably meet a German outflanking manoeuvre from the south.

The British remained unwilling to go too far along the road of joint planning; they did not want to commit troops to the French battle line in the same manner as in 1914. The War Office planned that the first two divisions of the expeditionary force would be despatched to France within thirty-three days of mobilization. A third division would arrive three months after mobilization, with the rest of the force arriving much later. The first British armoured division would not be ready to take the field until about eight months after the outbreak of war. The French knew that the initial British land effort would be more limited than in 1914 and that their troops would be slower in arriving. While they demanded and won a faster deployment of troops, the French army would have to carry the brunt of any German offensive through the first phase of the war. Gamelin was particularly disappointed by Britain's failure to supply the small armoured and mechanized field force that he wanted. No one raised the question of whether the French army could contain the German advance. There were few doubts in France about the country's defensive capabilities. The French High Command invested heavily in modernizing the army and developing tanks and motorized units after 1935–1936 but they underestimated or even rejected the possibility of a rupture in the *front continu*. No plans were made to fight a war of movement should Germany achieve a major breakthrough. In the late spring of 1939, senior officers were confident of the morale of their troops and the preparedness of the Maginot Line. The British, as junior military partners, never questioned their assurances. British intelligence work was mainly concentrated on potential enemies; information about France, generally from French sources, was accepted uncritically. The French army manoeuvres of 1938 had been cancelled and war broke out before the 1939 manoeuvres took place. There was no opportunity to check the impressions of the post-Munich period when some doubts were raised about the French army's efficiency. Given their belief that in modern war an offensive could not succeed unless it had a superiority of three to one over the defence in the zone of impact, the British not only failed to consider how tanks and close air support could strengthen their own offensive capacity but thought that the French were in an impregnable position, despite their weakness in the air. Closer contact with the French army leaders in the summer of 1939 provided a favourable impression of the army's morale. Few senior British officers anticipated the French collapse and no plan was prepared to deal with such an eventuality until May 1940.

III

Both delegations of military planners assumed that Hitler would attack first in the east. Not much was expected from Polish resistance. During the second set of Anglo-French staff talks, it was agreed that no effort should be made to defend Poland which, it was predicted, would collapse in the early stages of the conflict with Germany. It was merely hoped that the Poles might hang on long enough to give the Allies time to build up their position in the west. Gamelin's cynicism or realism was revealed when he spoke privately to General Gort in mid-July. '[W]e have every interest in the war's beginning in the east and becoming a general conflict only little by little. We will thus have the time necessary to put on a war footing all Franco-British forces', he told his British counterpart. 'The sacrifice of the Poles, would lead to the immobilization, to our advantage, of important German forces in the east.'[38] It was to lengthen the period of Polish resistance that the western powers sought Soviet assistance. The Soviet air force, using Polish facilities, could reduce the effect of a German aerial attack and, in the absence of British and French supplies, provide Poland with the armaments and industrial goods it needed. Yet despite all the talk in London and Paris of a 'second front' and the need for Soviet assistance to Poland, there was no discussion of what was required or expected of the USSR in the event of its intervention against Germany. The French army chiefs gave little thought to what Soviet military intervention would involve. The British were somewhat shocked when the Anglo-French staff talks revealed how little the French intended to do but, as became clear by the end of the summer, they were not inclined to do anything themselves. No proposals for fighting in the east were made. Considerable pressure was put on Beck to be reasonable over Danzig but no generosity was shown towards Polish demands for military and financial assistance. No one was willing to tell the Poles that 'the fate of Poland will depend upon the ultimate outcome of the war and that this in turn, will depend upon our ability to bring about the eventual defeat of Germany'.[39]

Beck continued to seek the Danzig solution that Hitler had no intention of offering, but he and his military advisers were misled into thinking that they could count on Allied assistance if their efforts failed. Beck's mistaken gamble that the Germans would negotiate meant that he was slow to follow up the April guarantee with further talks with the French and British. He did not even stop in Paris on his way back from the London talks of 4–6 April, and Bullitt found him 'most hostile to France'.[40] The Polish ambassador in Paris was finally instructed to ask that the 1921 Franco-Polish pact be harmonized with the Anglo-Polish accord. The resulting political protocol was approved on 12 May. Bonnet agreed to an additional secret article taking note that Poland considered Danzig a vital national interest but then delayed signing the agreement on the grounds that London had not accepted any formal commitment on Danzig. As the military protocol, signed on 19 May, was made dependent on the conclusion of the political accord, neither came into effect before the outbreak of war.

It was only after the occupation of Prague that Polish attention had shifted from the war in the east to that in the west. As a result, Poland

[38] Quoted in Martin Alexander, *The Republic in Danger*, 311.

[39] Quoted in Anita Prazmowska, *Britain, Poland and the Eastern Front, 1939* (Cambridge, 1987), 86.

[40] Quoted in A. Adamthwaite, *France and the Coming of the Second World War*, 319.

entered the war with no overall plan for mobilization, supply or defence in the west, and with most of its supply bases still in eastern Poland. Polish hopes centred on being able to hold out for the time needed by the Allies to mobilize and start their offensive. Gamelin promised the Polish representatives that France would take limited offensive action from the third day of mobilization and would commit the bulk of the French forces from the fifteenth day of mobilization. According to his post-war memoirs, he warned the Polish military authorities that an 'offensive' did not mean an attack on the Siegfried Line and that 'bulk' meant only the striking forces available in north-eastern France, thirty-five to thirty-eight divisions. On behalf of the French air force, General Vuillemin pledged 'vigorous action' at the beginning of a conflict with Germany. Five bomber groups, admittedly with obsolete planes, were to fly across Germany to reinforce the weak Polish air force.

All the French involved in these talks contributed to this misleading charade. Gamelin had no intention of launching a major offensive against Germany; the instructions given to General Georges on 31 May spoke only of a careful, graduated, step-by-step engagement with the German forces in the Saarland between the Rhine and the Moselle. Vuillemin knew that the French air force would do nothing. It would take a further six months without any serious operations at all before the Anglo-French forces could approach parity with the *Luftwaffe* and he was not going to risk his precious planes to assist Poland. Rightly or wrongly, however, the Polish negotiators left Paris convinced that they would receive help whenever the war with Germany began. Bonnet, 'congenitally uncandid', played a particularly deceitful game. His interest in the guarantees and the talks with the Soviets was limited to the pursuit of deterrence. He did not intend to make a German attack on Poland the cause of France's entry into war. Bonnet's behaviour was devious but Gamelin's was hardly more creditable. He, unlike Bonnet, thought that France should fight if Poland was attacked but deliberately misled the Poles as to his intentions.

Both the British and the French sent military missions to Poland, the latter on 23 August, but neither was given instructions to arrange for military cooperation of any kind. The British chiefs of staff did consider some form of air action against Germany, including the possibility of establishing forward bases in Poland, but the issue was side-tracked at the Anglo-Polish staff talks in Warsaw in late May. The British delegates found the Poles highly optimistic about their ability to withstand the Germans and sanguine about the reactions of their other neighbours. They expected that the Russians would be neutral, or even benevolently neutral, and while admitting that they would require Soviet material assistance should Germany attack Poland, refused to enter into talks in peacetime. The British delegation returned to London urging financial and material assistance to Warsaw. The delegation report was not discussed by the CID until two months later, on 24 July. The chiefs of staff agreed, somewhat reluctantly, that establishing air bases in Poland to bomb Germany at the outset of the war was better than doing nothing at all, but neither they nor the civilian ministers wanted to set off a reciprocal bombing campaign. The final decision was postponed until further talks were held with France and Poland. In acrimonious exchanges with the French at the very end of August, the British adopted an even narrower view of air action than their allies, who again tried to get the British to commit their planes to the western front and to offer some form of air assistance to Poland. The British military chiefs narrowed the earlier list of permissible targets and decided that bombing should be directed only to warships at sea. Action during the Polish campaign was to be limited to flying reconnaissance planes and dropping propaganda leaflets over Germany. Without British co-operation, the French refused to take any aerial action on their own.

The British signals to the Poles, like those of the French, encouraged false optimism. In mid-July, concerned about the deteriorating situation in Danzig and the possibility that the Poles might overreact to German provocation, General 'Tiny' (six feet, four inches tall) Ironside, the Inspector-General of Overseas Forces and the man many thought would command the future British Expeditionary Force, was sent to Warsaw. Handsome, personable, an excellent linguist, and a cavalry man to boot, if not noted for his intellectual capacities, Ironside enjoyed a great personal success. Beck assured him that the Poles would not attack the Germans unless Poland itself was invaded but would give no promise to consult London before taking military action. Unfortunately, the visit convinced Beck that in case of war, Britain would use its air force to attack Germany and that Ironside's recommendations for military assistance to Poland would produce results.

The Poles, to be sure, gave the western powers a misleading impression of the strength of their army and air force. Such a foolhardy approach could only soothe guilty consciences in London and Paris. The Allied countries thought that, even without their assistance, the Poles were capable of putting up a considerable fight (possibly even for four months) before their army would be defeated. Little attention was paid to Poland's material or financial needs. The French would offer further loans only as part of an Anglo-French package in which Britain would take the major share and would not authorize arms deliveries, particularly not tanks which were so desperately needed at home. Gamelin still hoped the Soviet Union would make up the Polish deficiencies. The British concentrated on countries vital to the defence of the British Isles and empire. Egypt, Greece, and Turkey, among others, took precedence over Poland. As it was assumed that no assistance to Poland or indeed to Romania would materially increase the ability of either country to defend itself, Britain's limited resources were better used elsewhere. Chamberlain was, in any case, more interested in avoiding Polish provocation of Germany than in its future defence. The Anglo-Polish loan talks went nowhere and only embittered the Poles, who resented the paltry sum that Britain was offering and the intrusive conditions that were attached. Beck refused what he considered a demeaning offer hardly worthy of Poland's 'Great Power' status. He fatally exaggerated the importance of Poland in the western view of the strategic balance as, in his eyes, it was essential for the Allies that Poland should fight if attacked by Germany. The Anglo-Polish loan talks were resumed only on 1 September at Poland's request; the earlier British offer was accepted and the agreement signed on 7 September, too late for the battle of Poland. The Poles continued to believe that the British and French would honour their guarantees.

Once Stalin finally opted for the German alternative in August, Poland's fate was sealed but the cards were stacked against Poland well before the Moscow talks began. Whether Beck could have got more from Britain and France if he had been less arrogant and more honest in his presentation of Poland's requirements is open to question. Those two governments suffered, as did Beck, from the same late awakening to the imminent danger of war and had little equipment to spare. The conversations with the Poles underlined their continuing commitment to deterrence in the first instance but also, should deterrence fail, to defensive strategies in which Poland played only a transitory part. By writing off Poland from the very start of the war, the Allies gave the Germans the opportunity to complete their first campaign without any opposition on their part and forfeited any advantages that might have resulted from a breakthrough in the west. Such an attack might, for instance, have just made Stalin pause before committing his troops to eastern Poland.

The most important contribution the Poles made to the ultimate Allied victory was not their eventual short stand against the Germans but their work in laying the theoretical foundations for the decryption of the 'Enigma' machine cipher used by the Germans for their high-level communications. Although at the end of 1938, the Germans had developed a new version of the Enigma machine that defeated the Poles, the Polish decision to share their information with French and British cryptographers on 25 July 1939 and to transfer two of their reconstructed Enigma machines to the French in August provided the basis for the wartime cryptological triumph so important for Britain's survival and the German defeat.

IV

The British and French not only intended to stay on the defensive against Germany at the start of the war but also dismissed the possibility of an early offensive against Italy. The latter question was directly addressed during the first stage of the staff talks when the French representatives argued that an early offensive against Italy at the start of the war would relieve the pressure on Poland. They recommended an Allied attack on Libya from both Tunisia and Egypt and a simultaneous attack on Italian sea communications in the central Mediterranean. The Mediterranean strategy proposed by Admiral Sir Roger Backhouse and Admiral Drax in the post-Munich period of an early attack on Italy was abandoned (see pp. 741–742) The dominant voices among British naval planners did not believe that the Italians posed any threat to the shipping routes outside the Mediterranean or that an Italian attack on Egypt and Suez was possible. They made clear that Britain would have to defend its vital interests in the Far East as its global position depended on the maintenance of the Singapore base. The issue was discussed in greater detail during the second stage of the talks, along with a consideration of the consequences of the east European guarantees. The French navy wanted the Allies to remain on the defensive in the Far East, relying on the Americans and Russians to contain Japan, until Italy was defeated and the Mediterranean made secure. The British naval authorities, on the contrary, were adamant about the importance of British interests in the Far East and the need to be able to counter Japanese aggression through naval action. There were divided counsels in Paris about such action; Gamelin and Vuillemin came to prefer a neutral Italy in the hope of reducing the number of battlefronts. The army staff, moreover, wanted to deploy the African troops defending the well-protected Tunisian/Libyan border and others garrisoned in North Africa in mainland France rather than squander them in avoidable operations against the Italians. In any case, the British were not interested. Without much debate, on 18 July, the chiefs of staff concluded that little pressure could be put on Italy with the forces available and that unless a decisive defeat of Italy could be obtained before the Germans attacked Poland, the German forces would not be deflected from their objective. They recommended that even if Italy declared war, the Allies should remain on the defensive, divert their shipping around the Cape, do nothing provocative and rely on their ability to close the entrances to the Mediterranean to strangle Italy economically.

Nor were the British really interested in French suggestions of a possible pre-emptive Salonika campaign. Since May, when he was informed of a possible Italian move from Albania into Macedonia and Greece, General Gamelin started to take a greater interest in General Weygand's proposals for a preventive French occupation of Salonika. The French high command, reverting to earlier ideas of a Balkan front, believed that an Allied expeditionary force to Salonika might discourage Italian action in the eastern Mediterranean and open the supply route to the east. Any such action would depend mainly on the involvement of Turkish and Greek troops and on British naval cooperation. Though it never won official approval and the navy thought the idea highly impractical, Gamelin was slowly converted to Weygand's project. If the Turks could be persuaded to take the lead in a Balkan pact (and Mussolini's blustering over claims to the Dodecanese in the early summer suggested that Ataturk might agree) then the prospect of opening up a wider front in south-east Europe became feasible. With this in view, the French were far more assertive than the British in the summer tripartite talks with the Turks. Despite British disinterest in the proposal, the day after the announcement of the Nazi–Soviet pact Gamelin offered Weygand, possibly, in part, to get his rival out of Paris, the command of the French forces in the Levant with the task of 'coordinating eventual Allied operations'. At the last two pre-war meetings of the Anglo-French staff officers in August, the French again urged that local commanders in the Mediterranean and Middle East, consider the possibilities of the Salonika move. The speedy defeat of Poland and the fear of a German invasion of Romania kept the project alive in Paris throughout the autumn and winter of 1939–1940.

Would it have been more advantageous for the Allies to have moved against Italy at the start of the war rather than encouraged its non-belligerency? As Hore-Belisha, the secretary of state for war, pointed out at the time, a neutral Italy 'would sustain Germany, whereas as an ally she would constitute a drain on German resources'.[41] The balance of naval power in the Mediterranean was in the Allied favour in 1939. The British and French together had six battleships and an aircraft carrier in the Mediterranean; the Italians had four operational battleships with two additional ships expected in the summer of 1940. Due, in part to Mussolini's veto, they had no aircraft carrier, nor any escort vessels needed to keep the sea lanes open. The Italians did enjoy a decisive superiority in submarines (105 to 77), something which worried the French because of their potential to stop troopships coming from North Africa.[42] Through intelligence sources, both open and covert, the Allied

[41] Quoted in MacGregor Knox, *Mussolini Unleashed, 1939–1941: Politics and Strategy in Fascist Italy's Last War* (Cambridge and New York, 1982), 45.

[42] Figures from John Gooch, *Mussolini and his Generals: The Armed Forces and Fascist Foreign Policy, 1922–1940* (Cambridge, 2007), 476, 480–481. Also see R. Salerno, *Vital Crossroads: Mediterranean Origins of the Second World War, 1935–1940* (Ithaca, NY, and London, 2002), 123. Two additional 42,000 ton battleships would come into service in the summer of 1940.

governments knew about Mussolini's military and economic weaknesses and the uncertainties of Italian control over Libya and East Africa. British hesitations about a Mediterranean offensive had more to do with fears of a three-front war, highlighted in June by the Tientsin crisis, than from any high regard for the forces of its opponent.

The exposed British position in the Middle East also encouraged a conciliatory attitude towards Mussolini. In 1938, three of the British army's five divisions were tied up in Palestine. It took a considerable military effort to contain the Arab rebellion (assisted by the Italians) which was only crushed during the winter of 1938–1939. The revolt had damaged Britain's relations with the Arab states. Not only were the British lines of communication at risk, but so were British supplies of oil from Iran and Iraq, essential if Britain was to reduce its dependence on American oil supplies. Italian threats to Egypt led to demands for the reinforcement of the British garrison stationed there.[43] The dynamic if imperious high commissioner, Sir Miles Lampson, was so preoccupied with the Italian menace and a possible anti-British uprising that he demanded that London end its commitment to a Jewish national homeland. Such fears indirectly contributed to the decision to restrict Jewish immigration to Palestine in May 1939. The attack on Albania and the Italian reinforcement of Libya created a state of panic in Cairo. There were urgent pleas from Lampson and from the senior military representatives in Egypt that additional troops be sent from Palestine and India. The chiefs of staff thought Lampson a nuisance and over-anxious but they agreed that part of the Egyptian garrison in Palestine should return to Egypt.[44] They were cautious, however, about other reinforcements and reluctant to send troops from India. In mid-July, at Britain's request, the French strengthened their own forces in Syria to offset British military weakness in Egypt. British forces in Egypt took up war positions on 28 August in case the Italians decided on a surprise attack but the danger was thought to be slight. In fact, though the Italian forces in Libya vastly outnumbered the British troops defending Egypt, they were virtually untrained, lacking in equipment, and faced not only the British but a French army in Tunisia. Whatever may have been the over-blown ambitions of the Italian military establishment, only the collapse of France and the removal of the Tunisian threat made an Italian attack feasible.

[43] See Steven Morewood, *The British Defence of Egypt, 1935–1940* for the most authoritative discussion of the Egyptian strategic situation.

[44] S. Morewood, *The British Defence of Egypt*, 119, 124, 166; Michael J. Cohen, 'British Strategy in the Middle East in the Wake of the Abyssinian Crisis, 1936–29', in Michael J. Cohen and Martin Kolinsky (eds.), *Britain and the Middle East in the 1930s: Security Problems, 1933–1939* (Basingstoke, 1992), 36.

Chamberlain's continuing belief, at least partly shared by Halifax, that Mussolini could be detached from Hitler and enlisted in the battle for deterrence remained a decisive factor in British policy towards Italy before the outbreak of war. The conclusion of the 'Pact of Steel' on 22 May 1939 made no difference to the prime minister's thinking about the Axis relationship. He and Halifax, relying on Sir Eric Phipps's close working partnership with Bonnet in Paris, brought considerable pressure to bear on Daladier. The French had repeatedly tried to open conversations with Mussolini and did so again in September but the Duce was not interested. It was hardly surprising that Daladier refused to budge. He was convinced that he and Chamberlain had been bluffed and deliberately misled at Munich and that Italian offers of an agreement were a trap to destroy British solidarity with France in North Africa. Daladier had the backing of many of his ministers and a good deal of public support both from the left and right. Phipps was recalled to London in June, under cover of the Anglo-French talks with the Russians, to discuss Anglo-French differences over Italy and Spain, where despite British and Portuguese insistence, the Daladier government refused to return the Republic's gold reserves without further progress on the repatriation of the 400,000 Spanish Civil War refugees who had fled to France. At Bonnet's suggestion, Chamberlain wrote personally to Daladier. When Phipps presented the letter on 14 July, he told the premier that Chamberlain thought that war or peace probably depended on his reply. In his note, Chamberlain insisted that Mussolini was the 'one man who can influence Hitler to keep the peace'. He flattered Daladier, claiming that it was because 'no French minister in recent times has had his people so solidly behind him' that he was in a position to allow Italy to formulate proposals in order to break the 'dangerous deadlock'.[45] The tone of Daladier's reply on 24 July was cordial but firm. He pointed out that the Italy of 1939, allied to Germany by a military accord of an aggressive character, was not the Italy of 1935 and was determined on a 'maximum programme of expansion in the Mediterranean and in Africa'.[46] While Daladier made no formal approach to the Duce, he did not actually publicly challenge him. Chamberlain was not prepared to abandon his own efforts. On 5 July, he sent a personal message to Mussolini asking that he restrain Hitler from a *coup* in Danzig. In answer, the British ambassador in Rome was lectured about Italian fidelity to the German alliance and told that Poland was responsible for the Danzig problem. Another approach was suggested by the high commissioners of Australia and South Africa on 3 August but Loraine, considerably more tough-minded than his

[45] *DBFP*, 3rd ser., Vol. VI, No. 317. [46] *DBFP*, 3rd ser., Vol. VI, No. 428.

predecessor, and doubtful whether Mussolini could be detached from Hitler, disliked the idea which would be interpreted as a sign of weakening British support for Poland. He preferred, and Chamberlain and Halifax agreed, to keep Mussolini 'uncomfortable' by maintaining a policy of silence.

The announcement of the Nazi–Soviet pact in August resolved the Anglo-French divisions over Italy. On 22 August, General Ismay, the secretary to the CID, sent off an urgent appeal to the French asking that no drastic action be taken against Italy, even if Rome was technically neutral but biased towards Germany, 'which [is] likely to have the effect of bringing her in against us'.[47] On 23 August, the day Ismay's letter was received in Paris, Daladier, at Bonnet's prompting, called a special meeting to decide what France would do should Germany attack Poland. Gamelin persuaded his colleagues that a hostile Italy would decrease the duration of Polish and Romanian resistance, close the supply routes to eastern Europe, and weaken France's position on the western front. Gamelin telephoned Ismay to say that France was 'in full agreement' with his views.

V

It was when the British and French military authorities began to plan for cooperation outside of Europe that the differences between their imperial positions emerged. The two empires could not be compared in size, value, and importance but there was also a sharp contrast in the way the two national governments regarded their imperial obligations. Britain was a global and maritime power whose interests in Europe were balanced by concerns for its rich but geographically scattered empire. France was a European land power focused almost exclusively on the German threat to metropolitan France for whom the colonies, however valuable, were adjuncts to France's continental position. This fundamental contrast was reflected in their defence priorities and the disposition of their military forces.

Both countries, it is true, witnessed a revival of imperial sentiment after Munich. In the British case, this partly resulted from economic interest but was also due to a sense of embattlement and isolation in a hostile world. Imperial sentiment was fuelled by highly popular imperial film spectaculars, American as well as English (*The Sun Never Sets*, *Gunga Din*, and *Stanley and Livingstone* were all shown in 1939), and more directly by the schools, by royal and national celebrations, and by government propaganda. Empire Day was one of the highlights of the

[47] Quoted in Reynolds M. Salerno, 'The French Navy and the Appeasement of Italy, 1937–1939', *English Historical Review*, 112 (1997), 102.

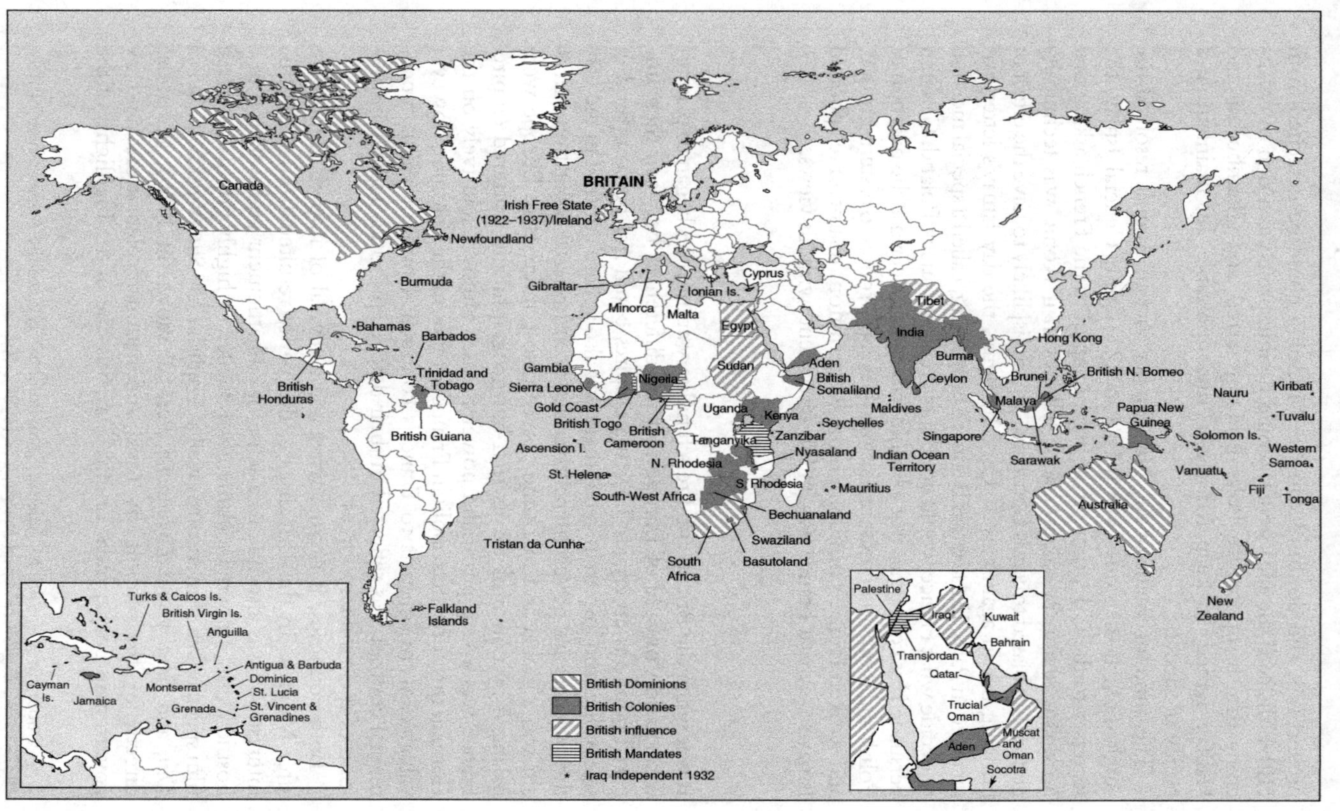

Map 10. The British Empire in the 1930s

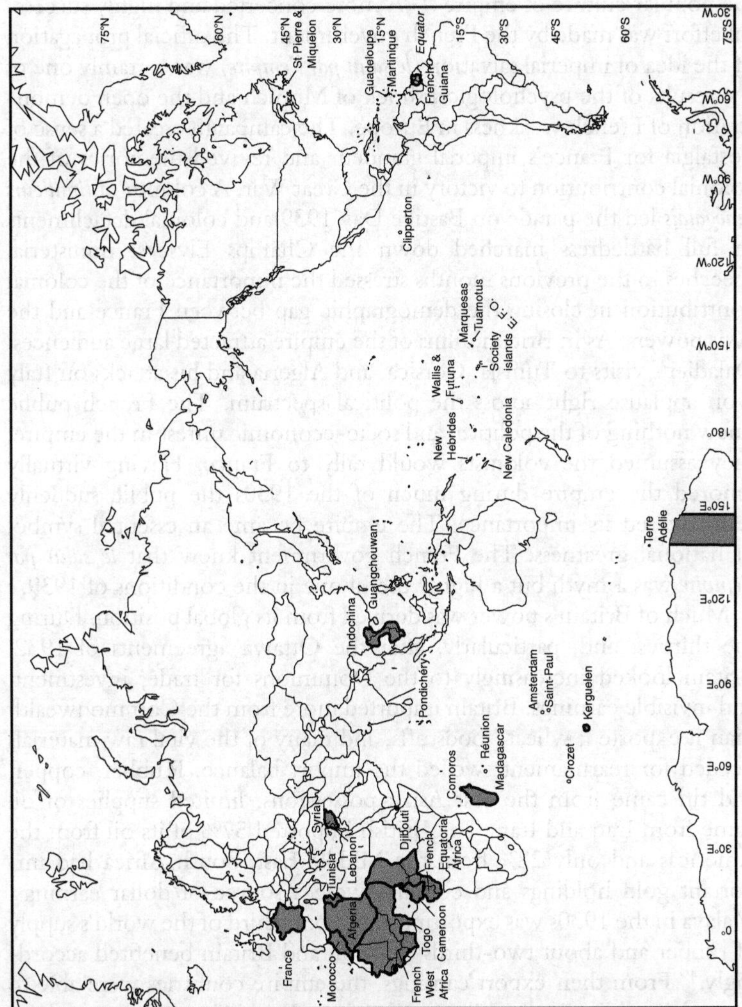

Map 11. The French Empire in the 1930s

school year, a half holiday gave point to its importance. Classroom maps depicted the British Empire in red; the rest of the world was reduced in size and coloured dully brown. The government used the BBC (there were nine million British wireless licenses in 1939), the press, and sponsored exhibitions to popularize the empire and to disseminate imperial ideas. The result, particularly of the outpouring of films with an 'Imperial' context, was to create an 'extraordinary Indian summer in the popular culture of empire'.[48] A more concerted and highly successful effort was made by the French government. The official propagation of the idea of imperial salvation (*le salut par l'empire*) was certainly one of the results of the psychological shock of Munich and the open demonstration of French weakness in Europe. The campaign created a sense of nostalgia for France's imperial grandeur and revived memories of the colonial contribution to victory in the Great War. A column of *tirailleurs sénégalais* led the parade on Bastille Day 1939 and colonial detachments in full battledress marched down the Champs Elysées; ministerial speeches in the previous months stressed the importance of the colonial contribution in closing the demographic gap between France and the Axis powers. As in Britain, films of the empire attracted large audiences. Daladier's visits to Tunisia, Corsica, and Algeria and his attacks on Italy won applause right across the political spectrum. The French public knew nothing of the political and socio-economic unrest in the empire; they assumed the colonists would rally to France. Having virtually ignored the empire during much of the 1930s the public suddenly rediscovered its importance. The empire became an essential symbol of national greatness. The French government knew that *le salut par l'empire* was a myth but a highly useful one in the conditions of 1939.

Much of Britain's power was derived from its global position. During the thirties, and, particularly, after the Ottawa agreements of 1932, Britain looked increasingly to the Dominions for trade, investment, and invisible earnings. Britain imported more from the Commonwealth than it exported; wheat, foodstuffs, and many of the vital raw materials needed for rearmament swelled the import balance. Rubber, copper, and tin came from the east Asian possessions; limited supplies of oil came from Iraq and Iran. The British imported 57% of its oil from the Americas and only 22% from the Middle East. South Africa had important gold holdings and colonies were a source of dollar earnings. Malaya in the 1930s was exporting about one-third of the world's supply of rubber and about two-thirds of its tin and Britain benefited accordingly.[49] From their export earnings, the empire countries were able to meet debt obligations while income from British investments and repayments on overseas loans helped Britain's adverse balance of payments.

[48] John M. Mackenzie, 'The Popular Culture of Empire in Britain'; in Judith Brown and Wm. Roger Louis (eds.), *The Oxford History of the British Empire:* Vol. IV, *The Twentieth Century* (Oxford, 1999), 225.

[49] G. C. Peden, 'The Burden of Imperial Defence and the Continental Commitment Reconsidered', *Historical Journal*, 27: 2 (1984), 422.

TABLE 14.5 Value of Imports to Britain (in £million)—Analysis by Country Source

	1938	1939
Total	919.5	885.5
British countries	371.5	358.1
Foreign countries	548	527.4
France and Northern Europe	262.2	240.6
Rest of Europe	46	42.7
Africa	63.4	68.7
India and Western Asia	79.4	76.5
Rest of Asia	44.2	38.8
Oceania	120.7	105.6
North America	199.3	199.4
Central America and West Indies	34.7	34.3
South America	69.6	78.9
Argentine Republic	38.5	46.8
Australia	71.8	62
Belgium	18.6	18.8
Brazil	7.7	8.8
Canada	78.7	80
Ceylon and Dependencies	12.4	10.7
Denmark incl. Faroe Islands	37.9	36.4
Dutch East Indies	6.4	5.9
Dutch West Indies	14.7	13.9
Egypt	11.6	12.1
Eire	23	25.3
Finland	19.3	14.6
France	23.6	26.9
Germany (incl. Austria in 1939)	30.1	19.4
India	49.9	48.5
Burma	6	5.1
Malaya (British)	12.2	9.9
Netherlands	29.3	30.2
New Zealand	46.9	41.8
Nigeria (incl. Cameroons under British mandate)	6.3	7.2
Northern Rhodesia	4.1	6
Soviet Union	19.5	8.2
Sweden	24.5	25.6
United States of America	118	117.3
Union of South Africa	14.6	15.9

Source: Central Statistical Office, *Statistical Digest of the War* (London, 1951), 165.

Britain's ability to wage a war of attrition depended on the manpower and material support of its empire. During the Great War, the Indian army and forces from Canada, Australia, New Zealand, South Africa, and Ireland served in France; Indian troops served in the Middle East and in East Africa; South African troops in German

South-West Africa.[50] It was widely anticipated that Britain would again draw on these forces in any future conflict. Even before the outbreak of war, the Indian Army was being used to provide reinforcements for the Middle East and Far East.[51] The change in strategic priorities in 1938–1939 only highlighted the importance of keeping the sea lanes open and strengthening the overseas garrisons so that they would not have to call on reinforcements from Britain.[52] It became essential to build up a field force in Egypt and to create an imperial mobile strategic reserve for the Middle East. The safety of the Suez Canal, the 'jugular vein of the empire', was crucial both for the Middle East and Far East if the fleet was not to be compelled to take the long Cape route to Singapore. Troops had to be provided to strengthen the small forces scattered around the globe to deal with local discontents or possible conflicts with Italy or Japan.

The Indian Army was asked to provide much of this military power.[53] In 1938, Indian troops were earmarked for Egypt, Singapore, Persia, Aden, and Iraq. In 1939, 'Force Heron' was summoned from India for use in Egypt, 'Force Wren' was scheduled to go to Burma, 'Force Emu' was on call for Singapore, and Indian artillery for Kenya.[54] The Indian Army, paid for by the Government of India, was increasingly used not just to keep order in India and along its frontiers but to defend British interests in other parts of the world.

The pre-war imperial balance sheet was a mixed one.[55] As the Commonwealth countries were practically independent states with their own foreign policies (when they wished) and diplomatic establishments, there was no certainty that they would again join Britain in war as they had in 1914. At the time of the Chanak crisis in 1922, with the exception of

[50] For break-down of numbers and also for a balanced analysis of the nature and mixed consequences of this engagement see Robert Holland, 'The British Empire and the Great War, 1914–1918' in Brown and Louis (eds.), *Oxford History of the British Empire: The Twentieth Century* (Oxford, 1999).

[51] Brian Bond, *British Military Policy Between the Two World Wars* (Oxford, 1980), 257–258.

[52] John Gallagher, *The Decline, Revival and Fall of the British Empire* (Cambridge, 1982), 136.

[53] In 1938, the Indian Army establishment consisted of 5,500 British troops (about one-third of the British army), 20,000 Gurkas and 120,000 Indians (of whom some 51,000 were Muslims, 46,000 Hindus and 23,000 Sikhs). Figures from Gallagher, *Decline, Revival and Fall*, 137.

[54] John Gallagher and Anil Seal, 'Britain and India between the Wars', *Modern Asian Studies*, 15: 3 (1981), 412.

[55] There is, to my knowledge, no statistical approach to this subject as compared to Patrick K. O'Brien, 'The Costs and Benefits of British Imperialism, 1846–1914', *Past and Present*, 120: 1 (1988), 163–200. O'Brien concluded that the costs of empire were probably greater than the benefits. The economic evidence, he found, lends 'rather strong empirical support to Cobdenite views of Britain's imperial commitments from 1846 to 1914' (p. 199).

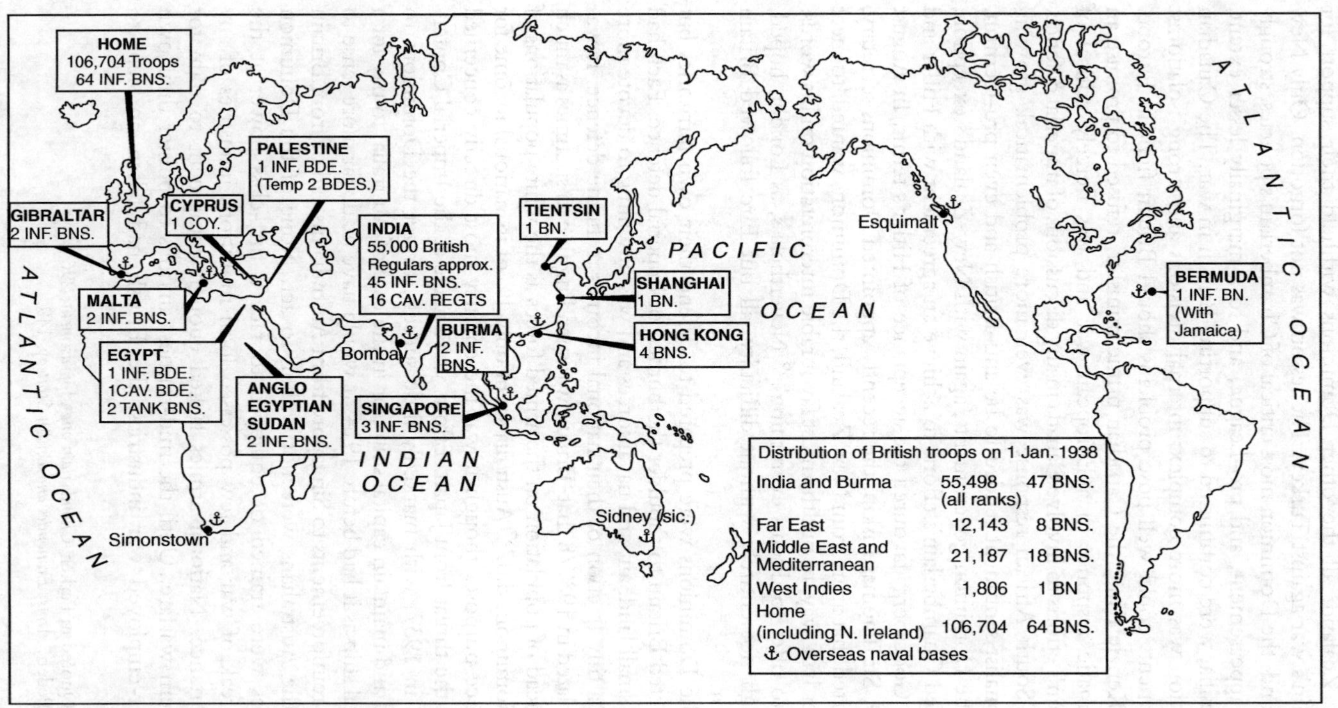

Map 12. Distribution of British Troops, 1 January 1938

New Zealand, all the other Dominions withheld their support for Britain's war against Turkey. The lesson was not forgotten. Only New Zealand, the Dominion most critical of Chamberlain's policies, strongly anti-appeasement, and pro-League, and to a marginally lesser extent, Australia, were committed to supporting Britain in war. The Canadian situation was more complex; internal divisions and strong isolationist sentiments could well pose problems should Britain fight in Europe. MacKenzie King, the Canadian prime minister, refused to promise an automatic response to a European war and was fiercely critical of Britain's efforts to involve Canada in any discussions of imperial defence. The South African response was even more problematical; growing nationalist sentiment tended to be anti-British and even pro-German. All the Dominion governments, again with New Zealand's exception, backed Chamberlain's efforts to achieve an agreement with Hitler and after Godesberg, favoured the acceptance of Hitler's terms. In August 1939, Sir Thomas Inskip, the recently appointed Dominions secretary, reported that apart from New Zealand, the Dominions wanted 'to meet Hitler half-way, to put the most favourable interpretation on his words, and to offer to discuss everything'.[56] Nevertheless, as London hoped, though not entirely without difficulty, all but Eire followed Britain to war.

The Dominions were prepared to defend their own territories but expected Britain to shoulder the burden of imperial defence. Each had only small land, air, and naval forces and was unwilling to devote more than a tiny fraction of their national incomes to home defence. It was calculated in 1937/8 that 'Britain was spending five to six times as much per head of population on the armed forces as the white populations of the dominions did.'[57] Australia spent only 1% of its national income for defence purposes though it was the country most directly concerned with the threat from Japan. Efforts were made at the Imperial Conference in 1937, with markedly little success, to get the Dominions to build and maintain capital ships, or in the case of Australia, to pay for a capital ship as it had before 1914. It would have made far more sense to send reinforcements to Singapore from Australia instead of from Britain but the Australians were not willing to act. None of the Dominion armies were trained or equipped to face a first-class power at the outbreak of war and few possessed local munitions industries of any importance. National armies lacked enough equipment to train for modern warfare. Until the mid-thirties, anxious to bolster their own under-employed war industries, the British had taken no steps to

[56] Quoted in Parker, *Chamberlain and Appeasement*, 296.
[57] Peden, *Arms, Economics and British Strategy*, 149.

encourage the establishment of rival firms. Thereafter, it was cheaper and more efficient to expand the British industrial base or to buy American goods than to invest in Dominion industrial development. A scheme was mooted in June 1939, to manufacture bombers in Canada which had a small aircraft industry. Its object was to secure a future insurance policy should Britain's aircraft factories be damaged by bombing. There was the hope, too, as Chamberlain explained, that if Canada became interested in selling aircraft to Britain 'the aloofness of that dominion from imperial defence might be reduced'.[58] The Dominions would not or could not have supplied the materials Britain needed for rearmament.[59] When, during 1940–1941, Canada became the main source of war materials for Britain, this was possible only because of the special arrangements made with the United States.

The Indian army, though large and expensive, was only equipped to keep internal order and to fight frontier wars. Between the wars, it had become increasingly conservative and militarily obsolete: 'Nodding plumes and gleaming lances were no longer enough; automatic weapons would have to be brought in.'[60] Even this obsolete army was costing more than half the budget of the Government of India. Financially stretched and precluded from raising taxes because of the internal political strife, Delhi demanded that London assume part of the costs of the necessary upgrading of the Indian Army. As the Indian army was thinned down (the number of British troops was cut by some 10,000 providing a possible reserve for other imperial duties) and re-equipped, the British Treasury was forced to assume a part of the costs. According to an agreement reached in 1939, the British government was to pay for all defence expenditure that was not purely Indian. By the end of the war, some 2.25 million Indians were serving in the armed forces. The British owed the Government of India £1,000 million, a figure which rose later to £1,500 million.

The burden of imperial defence fell on Britain at a time when disturbances in the empire required military interventions and when it faced three potentially hostile foreign powers in three different parts of the globe. Despite consultations and regular imperial conferences, there was no common imperial defence strategy and no imperial force as such. The various parts of the globe painted red created a false sense of power: 'The British Empire was sustained in large measure by the convenient belief held by non-British people that armed forces could be summoned

[58] Peden, 'The Burden of Imperial Defence', 419.

[59] Michael Hennessy, 'The Industrial Front: The Scale and Scope of Canadian Industrial Mobilization during the Second World War', in Bernd Horn (ed.), *Forging a Nation: Perspectives on the Canadian Military Experience* (St. Catherine's, Ont., 2002), 137.

[60] Gallagher, *The Decline, Revival and Fall of the British Empire*, 137.

up at will for the immediate deployment in any part of the world.'[61] In peacetime, at least, the different parts of the empire did not constitute a 'power system'. Professor George Peden has convincingly argued that most of Britain's resources were directed to the defence of the United Kingdom rather than to the overseas territories and that there was no significant diversion of these resources before 1940.[62] By 1939, however, men and equipment, the latter admittedly old and sometimes obsolete, had to be dispatched to the Middle and Far East though hardly in the numbers wanted by the local authorities. Britain's leaders repeatedly argued that there was no foreseeable time when Britain's defences would be strong enough to safeguard its territory, trade, and interests against three powers simultaneously. The country's diplomatic, strategic, and military policies after 1935 were shaped by this worst-case scenario, a simultaneous war against three enemies in three different battle theatres. The interlocking of these challenges made them even more insoluble. This was, of course, the rationale for the effort to reduce Britain's commitments and the number of potential enemies. As the threat from Germany loomed ever larger, the vulnerability of the empire contributed to the policies of appeasement. Britain suffered from a bad case of 'imperial overstretch'.[63] The empire posed a strategic dilemma for which there was no real solution. Nor could the French, with their eyes on Germany, provide much assistance, despite its reliance on the British Empire for its survival in a war of attrition. The Admiralty insisted that the navy alone was able to meet the most serious dangers faced by the home islands, that is, the destruction of its overseas trade and the loss of its eastern empire. The naval chiefs argued that 'war in one hemisphere would ultimately have to be fought in both' and that to focus only on Germany was strategically unsound.[64] The disposition of the fleet would depend on the competing claims of the North Sea, the Mediterranean, and the Pacific. Even without the two-ocean fleet it wanted, the Admiralty was still preparing to send a fleet to Singapore in the summer of 1939. The army, though engaged in augmenting the home army and preparing to raise a continental field force, had to

[61] Keith Jeffrey, 'The Second World War', in Brown and Louis (eds.), *Oxford History of the British Empire: The Twentieth Century*, 306.

[62] Peden, 'The Burden of Imperial Defence', 405–423. Professor Peden challenges the arguments of Michael Howard and Corelli Barnett that the defence of the British Empire forced a diversion from a continental commitment. He also argues, contrary to Barnett, that any diversion of military effort to imperial defence that did take place need not have militated against technical innovation.

[63] The phrase used to such good effect by Paul Kennedy, *The Rise and Fall of the Great Powers: Economic Change and Military Conflict from 1500 to 2000* (London, 1988).

[64] Christopher M. Bell, *The Royal Navy, Seapower and Strategy between the Wars* (Basingstoke, 2000), 110.

maintain British soldiers in India, Egypt, Sudan, Palestine, Singapore, Hong Kong, Shanghai, Jamaica, Malta, Gibraltar, and later Cyprus. As local commanders complained, such forces were too small and under-equipped to engage a major enemy. The air force, still producing more bombers than fighters in 1939 and convinced that a strategic bombing campaign (for which it lacked the necessary aircraft) would prove a war-winning strategy against Germany, not only had aircraft stationed in Egypt, India, Iraq, Palestine, Malta, Aden, and Singapore, but expected to augment its squadrons in Egypt and Singapore. Some plans for increasing overseas squadrons were vetoed in order to concentrate on enlarging the RAF in Britain but the protection of the home islands and the empire was seen as integrally linked. The need for future imperial assistance remained a continuing concern particularly as the future role of the United States remained problematic.

The French situation was somewhat different. Imperial defence was an unaffordable luxury for a country struggling to meet the German challenge. Next to the German threat, one of the most respected historians of the French empire has written, France's overseas possessions came a very poor second.[65] The colonies had supplied men and material for France in the 1914–1918 war. Some 800,000 colonials had served either on the Western Front or as workers in the factories of metropolitan France. It was not uncommon in the mid-1930s to speak of a 'nation of one hundred million', a compensation for the disparity between the French and German military-age populations. The main concern of the French high command in 1938–1939 was to see that this imperial reserve of manpower could be brought to the mainland in case of war. French trade and investment with its colonies increased during the 1930s. In 1938, the empire accounted for 27% of total French overseas trade; by 1940, some 45% of French overseas investment went to empire projects. Ultimately, the effects on the metropolitan economy were negative but before the war, the empire was considered a major asset in a highly competitive world. The colonies became heavily dependent on France as their only possible market.

The empire existed to serve the needs of France. Imperial troops were to come to the assistance of France but not the reverse. Not only was the metropolitan army exempted from imperial duties but increasingly the French colonial forces were assigned a future European role to the exclusion of their imperial obligations.[66] The organization of the French

[65] Martin Thomas, *The French Empire between the Wars: Imperialism, Politics and Society* (Manchester and New York, 2005), 314–317.

[66] Martin Thomas, 'At the Heart of Things? French Imperial Defense Planning in the Late 1930s', *French Historical Studies*, 21: 2 (1998), 333.

TABLE 14.6 Percentage Represented by France's Trade with the Colonies

	Imports		Exports	
	1937	1938	1937	1938
Food stuffs	67.1	74.4	37.6	35.3
Raw materials	11.3	11.4	11.1	11.2
Manufactures	2.3	2.8	38.9	35.2
Percentage of total trade	23.8	27	28.8	27.3

Source: Martin Thomas, 'Economic Conditions and the Limits to Mobilization in the French Empire, 1936–1939', *Historical Journal*, 48: 2 (2005), 475.

military force into three armies, with the metropolitan army by far the most important, reflected current thinking.[67] The metropolitan army alone was the measure of French strength against Germany and it absorbed the major proportion of the French defence budget. The two imperial armies were expected to deal with local difficulties and to defend the territories against foreign attack. There was no regular army strategic reserve that would be sent to assist them. The weakness of the French air force precluded overseas support; few fighter planes could be spared for colonial defence. The main purpose of the French navy, despite its offensive ambitions, was to keep the western Mediterranean open for the transport of African troops to France. It was hoped to mobilize and put in place some three hundred thousand empire troops and a further two hundred thousand empire war workers during the first year of the war.

Imperial planning was patchy and ill-coordinated. What colonial funds were available went to the Maghreb (Morocco, Algeria, and Tunisia) where an integrated air defence system was created, anti-aircraft batteries were installed in the Mers-el-Kébir base at Oran and Bizerta, the two principal North African ports, and raw material stockpiles were created. There was a heavy investment in frontier fortifications along the Tunisian–Libyan border to guard against an Italian attack. The French high command considered a pre-emptive strike against Spanish Morocco, subject, of course, to metropolitan needs. In the spring of 1939, when joint Allied planning became a reality, the French reconsidered their defence needs, and Daladier and Gamelin were prepared to consider launching joint offensive actions against Italian Libya. When Mussolini opted for non-belligerency, imperial defence planning shifted to the Levant and the movement of the bulk of the Levant army to Salonika.

Beyond the Mediterranean littoral, imperial defence was patchy and no integrated imperial defence system emerged. In the absence of French

[67] Thomas, 'At the Heart of Things', 351–352.

funding, schemes for improving the defensive infrastructure in individual colonies and efforts to create unified regional commands were only partially implemented. The Indochina Federation, France's second most important captive market after North Africa, an important source of rubber, coal, zinc, and tungsten, and, along with the Maghreb, an important reservoir of revenue for France's war chest, was left without any possibility of French reinforcements.[68] As discussed previously, the authorities in Paris knew that the colony could not be defended.[69] Some measures were introduced to strengthen the colony's defensive position and to increase its self-sufficiency if the links with France were cut but these were token moves to retain France's imperial presence. The Japanese moves into southern China in late 1938 posed a major threat to Saigon while the occupation of Hainan and the Spratly Islands in February–March 1939 placed the Japanese forces in a strategic position to accelerate their southern advance whenever they wished. Whatever the considerable economic value of holding Indochina, it was not of sufficient strategic importance to warrant the diversion of French major naval or air forces from Europe or to send reinforcements to fight against overwhelmingly superior Japanese forces. The local colonial authorities, moreover, had grave doubts about the viability of Britain's main fleet to Singapore strategy. Though rarely discussed at ministerial or general staff level, the French believed that the British were relying far too heavily on the naval defences of the Singapore base and measures against possible landings on the eastern side of Singapore island, and had failed to create the mobile and fixed defences needed to protect Singapore until the British fleet arrived. Whatever their criticism of the British strategy, the French naval staff, the best informed about British planning, had no forces of their own to send to the Far East. The regional staff talks held in Singapore between 22–27 June 1939 were inconclusive. The French representatives believed that Singapore would have to be massively reinforced to withstand a prolonged attack yet they could offer no reinforcement plans of their own. The historian, John Dreifort, has summed up the strategic dilemma: 'The British naturally tended to emphasize the role of naval defence in stopping Japan, but Admiral Sir Percy Noble had no fleet. The French stressed military operations to check Japan but they had no army.'[70]

[68] Martin Thomas, *The French Empire between the Wars*, 315, 331, 337. Along with the Maghreb territories, Indochina became 'the principal colonial cash cow for the French war economy in 1939–1940'. Martin Thomas, 'Economic Conditions and the Limits to Mobilisation in the French Empire, 1936–1939', *Historical Journal*, 48: 2 (2005), 493.

[69] See p. 482–3.

[70] John Dreifort, *Myopic Grandeur: The Ambivalence of French Foreign Policy Towards the Far East, 1919–1945*, 164.

VI

It was paradoxical that just as the Admiralty had rejected the 'knock-out Italy first strategy' because of the need to send the fleet to Singapore, the Tientsin crisis of June–July 1939 exposed the weakness of its Far Eastern position. The crisis was part of a more general Japanese offensive against the western imperialist powers in anticipation of the change in the world order that would allow Japan to establish its hegemony in the east. Though locked in disagreement about joining the Axis military alliance, the Japanese leaders were prepared to capitalize on the Allied difficulties in Europe. By the spring of 1939, the Japanese navy was within striking distance of the Philippines, Singapore, and Indochina. The Admiralty was unwilling to send ships out 'to show the flag', as they were needed in the Mediterranean. The relationship with the Americans in the Pacific was critical to any resolution of Britain's problems. At the request of the Foreign Office in March 1939, the president agreed to resume the January 1938 naval talks, demanding, however, the strictest secrecy as the first steps were being taken to revise the Neutrality Acts. Elaborate precautions were taken to keep the conversations secret and only the president and Sumner Welles were kept informed of their progress. Commander T. C. Hampton of the Royal Navy arrived in Washington in mid-June to inform the Americans about modifications in Britain's Far Eastern naval strategy if Japan decided to take advantage of Britain's difficulties in Europe. Hampton warned the Americans that if Japan took aggressive action in the Far East, the Admiralty did not know whether it could send a fleet to the Far East or what its composition would be. Admiral Leahy, the American chief of naval operations, thought that in case of a European war, the president would move the fleet to Hawaii as a warning to Japan. Leahy, expressing his personal opinion, suggested that if there was a wartime alliance against Germany, Italy, and Japan, the US fleet would move a sufficient number of ships (a minimum of ten) to Singapore to defeat the Japanese fleet if Britain sent an adequate token fleet including some capital ships as well. Exchanges of signal books and cipher books had already taken place and other steps were proposed so that the two fleets could cooperate. The talks were strictly private and no official record was kept.

British defence policy in south-east Asia rested on Singapore and the launching of a naval blockade against Japan. There were, however, increasing doubts about whether the base could be defended and whether the British could dispatch a large enough fleet early enough to deal with a Japanese threat. Chamberlain's assurances to the Australian prime minister, Joseph Lyons, on 20 March 1939 could hardly have satisfied him. In their summer conversations, the British and French representatives privately conceded that there was little that could be done if Japan intervened in a European war except to act defensively until the arrival of reinforcements. Similarly vulnerable were the Dutch East Indies; the Dutch looked to the British for assistance in their defence. Without means of their own to protect their possessions, they sought closer cooperation with London; but while recognizing the importance of the east Indies for the safety of Singapore, the British did not want to take on new and definite commitments that they could not fulfil. Dutch policymakers warned that in case of a war between Britain and Japan, Holland would preserve absolute neutrality, a 'fantastic' hope in the view of a Foreign Office official. The Dutch territories might have been considered 'Britain's Achilles' heel' but if Japan seized them, there was nothing Britain could do.

It was in north China rather than in the South Seas that the Japanese tested Britain's resolve to defend its interests. The Japanese challenge to the British concession at Tientsin, a port about eighty miles south-east of Peking, began in the late autumn of 1938, accelerated in the spring of 1939, and reached its climax at the end of June. The western concessions were prickly thorns in the Japanese side, inhibiting the efforts of the puppet Peking government to establish its domination over the north China economy. To bring pressure on the British and French, the Japanese had imposed a makeshift blockade on the concession in mid-December 1938; it was temporarily relaxed in early February and then re-enforced during the first week of March. On 9 April, the manager of the Japanese sponsored Federal Reserve Bank in Tientsin was murdered while watching the film *Gunga Din* in the British concession. Through a mixture of indecision, complacency, and slipshod communications between British officials in Tientsin, Tokyo, and London, the four Chinese suspects remained interned in the concession for weeks rather than being handed over to the local authorities. The Japanese government responded by ordering a total blockade of the concessions starting on 14 June. Supplies of food and fuel were interrupted, business obstructed, and all concession residents, males and females, were subjected to body searches at bayonet point. The Japanese demands went far beyond the surrender of the accused Chinese 'assassins'; they effectively required Britain's acquiescence in the construction of their 'New Order' in East Asia. As Cadogan admitted, the British had 'bungled' and faced a potentially dangerous crisis at a moment when the Danzig problem was claiming British attention.

Lurid stories appeared in the British press about terrified children and the indignities suffered by women under the mocking eyes of the Japanese. The government responded by opening diplomatic exchanges with the Japanese in Tokyo but also raising the possibility of retaliation and the sending of a battle squadron to the Pacific. The commander-in-chief of China Fleet asked for a squadron of two or three capital ships, a cruiser squadron, and a destroyer flotilla. It should be remembered that at the beginning of June, there had been another shift of power at the Admiralty and the new first sea lord and deputy chief of naval staff favoured a return to the old orthodoxy of sending the main fleet to Singapore rather than concentrating on an early blow to Italy. Throughout July, discussions continued over the sending of the fleet and reinforcing Malaya with aircraft and troops (the latter mainly from India). Sir Robert Craigie, the British ambassador, and Arita Hachiro, the Japanese foreign minister, had found a formula that could lead to a negotiated settlement but the situation remained tense. On 2 August, Lord Halifax informed the cabinet that 'the situation in the Far East was now causing him more anxiety than the position in any other part of the world'.[71] In the Commons, Chamberlain warned that the world should not assume that Britain was incapable of establishing its decisive naval superiority over Japan in the Pacific. It appeared that Britain would stand up to Japan and the latter would have to retreat.

The idea of a pre-emptive strike was soon dropped. The Admiralty warned the government that with so many capital ships in dry dock for modernization, it could send seven (after offering only two) capital ships to the Far East but only if they were withdrawn from the Mediterranean. It was estimated that the Japanese could send nine capital ships south towards Singapore. Other means of coercing Japan were examined but the cupboard looked bare. Chamberlain insisted that Britain could not retaliate against Japan with sanctions, as urged by the Foreign Office, without being prepared to fight and wanted a negotiated settlement. The Americans informally supported the strong British position but Cordell Hull as well as Grew, the American ambassador in Tokyo, insisted on separate representations in Tokyo. Halifax informed Ambassador Kennedy in London that Britain had no intention of creating another 'Munich' in the Far East but he hoped that Washington would 'help to ensure that Britain was not embarrassed in the Far East'.[72]

British ministers acknowledged that a Tientsin settlement would involve a serious loss of prestige. The chiefs of staff argued that there was no alternative given the negative effects of a reduction of British naval power in the Mediterranean. The Anglo-Japanese talks in Tokyo had begun on 15 July in a highly charged atmosphere punctuated by anti-British demonstrations. The four Chinese suspects were handed over to the Japanese for interrogation; they were subsequently found guilty and presumably

[71] TNA: PRO, CAB 24/100, CC40 (39)4.
[72] G. Kennedy, *Anglo-American Strategic Relations and the Far East, 1933–1939*, 46.

killed. More widely, though Arita wanted a settlement, Britain was forced to recognize Japan's special position in China and acknowledge that the Japanese forces had the right to maintain peace and order in the areas they had occupied. The Chinese regarded the final Anglo-Japanese declaration, the 'Craigie–Arita agreement' (24 July), as a British surrender to Japanese demands. Craigie, who had long insisted that the negotiations with the Japanese were necessary and had opposed joint Anglo-American action as counter-productive, believed that the Sinophile Foreign Office had mishandled the whole situation and that only a surrender could open the way to the promotion of peaceful relations with Tokyo. Having done nothing openly to assist the British, the Americans made their displeasure known. British weakness confirmed Hull's view that separate rather than joint action better suited American interests.

Suddenly, on 26 July, without any warning to the British, President Roosevelt gave notice of the American abrogation of the Japanese–American commercial treaty of 1911. The presidential notification, coming two days after the signing of the Arita–Craigie agreement, was generally interpreted as a warning that the Japanese could not expect to enjoy a free hand in China. It was, in part, a presidential response to the administration's defeat over amending the Neutrality Acts. On 11 July, the Senate Foreign Relations Committee had decided to defer consideration of the Act until the next session of Congress in January 1940. Left without any effective means of influencing the European situation, this presidential demonstration of American resolve was intended to show the dictators that the United States was a global player whose interests could not be ignored.

There was a strong negative reaction to the Craigie–Arita accord in the British press, in Liberal and Labour circles, and even among ministers and defence chiefs who had recognized its necessity. Britain was, after all, a 'great imperial power' that did not have to submit to insults. Japan was bogged down in China and could not produce a speedy victory. In its effect, the crisis had provoked a limp official reaction that was totally out of keeping with the tougher public mood at home. Within a month of the Craigie–Arita declaration, undoubtedly encouraged by Roosevelt's action, the government's resolve stiffened despite divided counsels in London. The Foreign Office, arguing that the British could not afford to antagonize the Americans, opposed any further agreements with Tokyo. Though Arita was willing to accept a limited agreement, on 21 August the Craigie–Arita conversations were suspended at Britain's request. Ambassador Craigie fought a losing battle when he argued that, in the face of the danger of a Japanese–German alliance, Britain should give way to the Japanese to keep the talks going. Only a *détente* with Japan, he argued, could preserve Britain's future position in the Orient. His advice that the one million pounds in silver used to back the Chinese currency should be deposited in the vaults of a bank in Tientsin and kept under seal until the end of the war was rejected. When (false) rumours reached Roosevelt that the British were thinking of closing the Burma Road, he commented, or so Sumner Welles reported, that if true, the American position would become one of 'trying to lend its moral support to a power which is deliberately intent on suicide'.[73] Severe flooding at Tientsin eased the political situation in the region and British women and children were evacuated from the concession. The Zhukov offensive in Nomonhan, the disputed area adjoining Outer Mongolia, launched by the Soviet army in August forced the Japanese to retreat across the Mongolian border. Coming together with the announcement of the Nazi–Soviet pact on 23 August, these staggering blows left the Japanese bewildered and off balance. The British were rescued from the possibility of a simultaneous war against Germany and Japan (intelligence sources threw doubt on the possibility), though they were still trapped in the same set of interlocking strategic dilemmas.

The Tientsin crisis showed what the Foreign Office had long argued, that Britain could not defy Japan without the active support of the Americans. In one of his last interviews with Sumner Welles, the highly professional Lindsay lashed out at his own government for giving in over Tientsin, fearful of its effects on Anglo-American relations. Admittedly, Roosevelt told the new British ambassador, Lord Lothian, that if there was no fundamental realignment of Japanese policy towards China after the Russo-German agreement, 'he had two more methods of pressure "in the locker"'. The first was to send aircraft carriers and bombers to the Aleutian Islands, about 700 miles from Japanese northern islands. The second was to move the American fleet to Hawaii.'[74] There were hopes in London but not certainty that such promises were more than flights of presidential rhetoric.

VII

Anglo-American relations remained difficult right up to and after the outbreak of war. The British were under siege in both Europe and in East Asia. The Americans faced 'no clear and present danger' in either region. In East Asia, cooperation with the British navy against Japan was useful but the Americans were free to play their own diplomatic hand. In Europe, after Munich, despite Roosevelt's occasional public interventions, Anglo-American relations were often competitive as well as

[73] Quoted in Parker, *Chamberlain and Appeasement*, 238.

[74] Roosevelt–Lothian conversation 30 August 1939 quoted in G. Kennedy, *Anglo-American Strategic Relations and the Far East*, 249–250.

complementary, and the president remained cautious about open demonstrations of support. At the same time, he was critical of British pusillanimity. In a much cited letter written on 15 February, he commented: 'What the British need today is a good stiff grog, inducing not only the desire to save civilization but the continued belief that they can do it. In such an event they will have a lot more support from their American cousins.'[75] The creation of the 'peace front' still left open the question of Chamberlain's intentions. Roosevelt's suspicions were undoubtedly fed by alarmist messages from Ambassador Bullitt, an old friend who so often acted as Daladier's spokesman. Joseph Kennedy, the appeasement minded American ambassador in London, was not part of Roosevelt's inner circle and his influence, fortunately for the British, was limited.

There were some hopeful signs. The first part of Roosevelt's annual address to Congress in January 1939 warned against the illusion of neutrality by legislation and the assumption that any country was safe from war. 'There are many methods short of war, but stronger and more effective than mere words', he told Congress, 'of bringing home to aggressor governments the aggregate sentiments of our own people'.[76] The president had come to believe that the United States could not safely exist in an Axis-dominated world and that Britain and France were America's first line of defence. It was important to stress the global threat to American security. Roosevelt spoke of the Nazi threat in Latin America and possible aerial action. There were also checks to any assistance to the Allies. On 23 January 1939, a Douglas bomber crashed in California with an official of the French Air Ministry on board. The revelation that foreigners were being given access to American planes and perhaps to military secrets as well caused a furore, particularly among the Congressional isolationists. Forced to defend his policy, Roosevelt was less than candid with his critics and he was pressed further than he wished to go. In assuring members of the Senate military affairs committee that the deal to sell military aircraft to France for cash was lawful, Roosevelt went on to say, in confidence, that America would have to become engaged in Europe and that the safety of the Rhine frontier must necessarily interest the United States. A leak to the press claimed that Roosevelt had said that 'America's frontier is on the Rhine'. The storm that followed forced the president to declare that American foreign policy had not changed in any way and to retreat from

[75] Quoted in David Reynolds, *The Creation of the Anglo-American Alliance 1937–1941: A Study in Competitive Co-operation* (London, 1981), 43–44.

[76] Samuel I. Rosenman, *The Public Papers and Addresses of Franklin D. Roosevelt, 1933–1939*, Vol. 1939 (New York, 1941), 3.

the fight for neutrality revision.[77] Despite the presidential retreat, he could only have been pleased by the results of the latest Gallup poll which showed strong public support for doing everything short of war to help Britain and France if Germany went to war against them. Sixty-two percent also thought that if Germany and Italy defeated Britain and France, they would then make war on the United States. The problem for Roosevelt was how to proceed when there was no clear threat to America's national interests. Though he wanted to stiffen Anglo–French resolve and to strengthen their efforts at deterrence, he did not want the US to be involved in any European conflict.

The British tried to find the right way to handle the Americans. Fully aware of the strength of American isolationism, though it varied according to region and ethnic identification, London found it difficult to judge to what degree it restricted Roosevelt's efforts. The Foreign Office was aware, too, of the president's belief that the Allied powers were unduly timorous in their handling of Hitler. Roosevelt repeatedly brushed aside suggestions that Britain had neither the power nor the wealth to defend its global responsibilities. The British had to court both the president and the American public if they were to count on active assistance. Yet officials were unwilling to launch a propaganda campaign which, as Lindsay insisted, would prove self-defeating. As a result, the British Library of Information, the public front of Britain's publicity effort, was a back-up organization for the American media. Well into the war, publications and lecturers targeted élite opinion rather than a mass audience.

It may be true that isolationist sentiment was stronger in Congress than in the electorate, but as Roosevelt travelled only rarely (others, including his wife, reported on the mood of the nation), he was particularly sensitive to Washington opinion. With control over foreign policy shared between the president and Congress and each believing in the critical importance of public opinion, however ill-defined, American foreign policy appeared erratic and unpredictable. The Washington scene presented entirely different problems than those associated with the European states, whether dictatorial or democratic, with which Britain had to deal. The president himself was an enigma. 'You know I am a juggler', Roosevelt would tell Henry Morgenthau in May 1942, 'and I never let my right hand know what my left hand does'.[78] There was a detectable pattern in Roosevelt's thinking after Munich and after Prague but his private con-

[77] See the discussion with extracts in Barbara R. Farnham, *Roosevelt and the Munich Crisis: A Study of Political Decision-Making* (Princeton, NJ, 1997), 198.

[78] Warren F. Kimball, *The Juggler: Franklin Roosevelt as Wartime Statesman* (Princeton, NJ, 1991), 7.

versations could be misleading and the experienced and cautious Lindsay was always chary of anticipating any follow up. Roosevelt was neither a Wilsonian idealist nor a realist in the Machiavellian mode, though his policies had a good dose of the latter. Public statements were often deliberately ambiguous and his pragmatism sometimes bordered on the devious. It is understandable why Lindsay found it so difficult to judge whether the lack of presidential action was due, as Roosevelt so often claimed, to the strength of isolationist feeling or was the consequence of the president's own indecision and cautious, political approach to foreign policy questions. Sceptics in London wondered how long it would take the president to 'educate' the American people and whether that education would not come too late for the European democracies. Matters were not helped by Roosevelt's 'debonair' administrative style that left the institutionally orderly British disoriented. Lord Halifax complained that dealing with the Americans was 'like hitting wads of cotton wool'. Departments, often divided in their own sympathies, enjoyed a measure of independence that had no real equivalent in Britain. Cordell Hull, the secretary of state, had his own foreign policy agenda not always shared with that of the president or with his own subordinate, Sumner Welles, Roosevelt's personal protégé and often the main channel of communication with the British ambassador. Roosevelt encouraged bureaucratic rivalries adding to the confusion of foreign observers.

In London, Neville Chamberlain never abandoned his suspicions of the Americans nor his personal dislike of Roosevelt. The lessons of the president's 'desertion' at the World Economic Conference of 1933 left a lasting impression on him. He was far too intelligent to underestimate the importance of the United States, but he continued to believe that American assistance, if actually provided, would come at a high price and that could be detrimental to Britain's global position. American policy in 1938–1939 confirmed the prime minister's suspicions that the Roosevelt administration was not above capitalizing on Britain's economic and financial difficulties. The American agreements with Canada and the tough American stance in the negotiations over the trade agreement of 1938 were specifically aimed at weakening the Ottawa preferential system with which Chamberlain was identified. There was rivalry, too, for trade outside the empire as American bankers and exporters re-entered the world markets. Cordell Hull, the great proponent of multilateral trade agreements, was highly suspicious of Britain's bi-lateral agreements with Nazi Germany. American investment and trade with Germany began to revive, though, of course, within far narrower limits than in the Weimar period. Subsidiaries of American firms, including General Motors, Standard Oil, DuPont, and IBM, like their British equivalents, expanded their operations in

Germany, participating in their rearmament and Aryanization campaigns despite severe restrictions on profits and the ban on the removal of funds from Germany. Chamberlain clearly understood what was at stake; his motivation at concluding the Anglo-American trade agreement was political. He was willing to sacrifice imperial economic benefits for American goodwill. Just as the decision to avoid a 'Munich' in the Far East was intended as a signal to the Americans of British resolve, so the sharing of intelligence about Britain's production of planes and prior notification of the guarantee to Poland was a way of improving Anglo-American relations. The prime minister was, however, wary of taking any steps that would mortgage his country's economic and financial future to the Americans or would encourage American inroads on the British Empire. Admittedly, it was not easy to do business with Roosevelt or the Americans. One can well understand why Chamberlain was unwilling to cede to the president the larger role in European politics that closer links, even if they could be forged, would inevitably bring. Past experience hardly encouraged confidence that presidential interventions were useful or productive.

However welcome the appearance of Anglo-American amity, Chamberlain and Halifax did not share Vansittart's view that wooing the Americans was Britain's 'only chance'. They did not believe that the British had to go to Washington with a begging bowl and had no intention of so doing. It must be remembered, too, that even in the summer of 1939, Chamberlain still had some hopes that Hitler would see reason. It was just possible that offers of financial cooperation, resources, and market sharing agreements might pave the way to political *détente*. Anglo-American interests were not identical and the elements of rivalry and competition that had marked their earlier relations continued to exist. Chamberlain recognized the need to cultivate good relations with the Americans as long as the price was not too high.

It proved easier for the French to deal with the Americans though their illusions of American support were cruelly exposed in 1940. They desperately needed 'clouds of planes' and Daladier was determined to have them despite his minister of finance's objections and even some doubts on the part of his air force advisers who preferred their own technologically advanced fighters. Payment was a problem, especially in view of the still unpaid $3 billion war debt and the provisions of the Johnson Act. The French proposed an immediate payment of ten billion francs in gold (10% of France's total gold holdings), as well as offering French islands in the Caribbean or in the Pacific. Roosevelt was not interested. More was involved than the payment for the planes. Daladier already knew that, given the undeveloped state of the American aircraft industries, relatively few planes would be delivered before 1940. The

French were willing to pay a considerable price for American goodwill. The emotional Bullitt, responding to Daladier's promptings, warned Roosevelt that 'if the Neutrality Act remains in its present form, France and England will be defeated rapidly'.[79] The British were less willing to offer sweeteners to the Americans for hypothetical gains. When a debts-for-bases settlement was raised, the Admiralty suggested terms that made any practical proposal impossible. The Colonial Office refused to sacrifice any part of the British Empire. Roosevelt's subsequent suggestion, the transfer of a site for a naval base and a 200-mile neutrality zone around the Americas patrolled by the Americans was considered 'inherently impractical'. The British agreed to Roosevelt's request for the lease of land for bases on the islands of Trinidad, St. Lucia, and Bermuda but Whitehall found the scheme 'typically Rooseveltian' while the president found the British response 'characteristically nit-picking and insensitive to his own domestic constraints'.[80]

In the end, it proved singularly difficult to judge whether Roosevelt's caution was due to his fears of an isolationist backlash or to his own reservations about committing America too far. He had to accept the more balanced rearmament programme demanded by the military and recommended an appropriation of $525 million to be spent by June 1940, of which $300 million was to be spent on the air force. The Prague *coup* undoubtedly helped the passage of this defence bill. Yet the president felt obliged to stay out of the bitter Congressional battle over amending the Neutrality Acts, leaving his natural internationalist supporters in a state of disarray. Though encouraged by public opinion polls that showed increased support for sending food and war material to the democracies in wartime, the president and his secretary of state resorted to futile behind-the-scenes manoeuvres. The restless president decided to launch a peace initiative. The so-called peace plan of 14 April was a rather naïve and geographically muddled proposal that had originated with the German opposition. The suggestion that Hitler and Mussolini should guarantee the integrity of thirty-one specified European and Middle Eastern states, many of which had no border with either Germany or Italy and did not feel threatened by the dictators, gave Hitler a welcome opportunity to display his considerable rhetorical skills at Roosevelt's expense before the Reichstag on 28 April. The initiative may well have been directed as much to the American public to alert them to the European situation as to the dictators. The presidential offer to sponsor a conference on disarmament in return for an offer of equal access to raw materials was turned into a devastating attack on American policy, past and

79 Bullitt, *For the President, Personal and Secret*, 369.
80 Reynolds, *Anglo-American Alliance*, 65.

present. Officials in London and Paris were doubtful, if not scathing, about the president's initiative. Far more politically acute and successful was Roosevelt's invitation to George VI and his consort to visit the United States, the first such visit by a reigning British monarch. The president took enormous pains to make the visit in June 1939 a success as a symbol of Anglo-American friendship. He set out to personalize the British monarchy in a way that would appeal to the American people without provoking the isolationists and to make the most of his talent for personal diplomacy. Eating hot dogs at Hyde Park guaranteed positive press coverage. The Foreign Office remained far more sceptical than the inexperienced George VI of demonstrations of Roosevelt's bellicosity towards the dictators, his promise that America would enter the war if London was bombed and his fanciful plans for assistance. Roosevelt was pleased with the visit; he believed he had forged a new link with the British at a time when he did not trust their political leadership and had little sense of kinship with the prime minister. He correctly judged, more accurately than those in London, the importance of filling the reservoirs of popular goodwill whatever the absence of short-term practical results.

The president's efforts to see the Neutrality Acts revised came to a crashing defeat during July, due to a combination of isolationism, Republican party partisanship, and anti-Roosevelt feeling in the Democratic party. The British were understandably bitter at this example of presidential incompetence and Congressional short-sightedness which would leave them unable to buy arms even if they had the funds to do so. The members of Congress, an infuriated Chamberlain complained, 'are incorrigible. Their behaviour over the Neutrality Legislation is enough to make one weep, but I have not been disappointed for I never expected any better behaviour from these pig-headed and self-righteous nobodies.'[81] The presidential appeals, on 4 August to the Soviets, on 23 August to King Victor Emmanuel, and on the next day to Hitler and the president of Poland were futile gestures mainly directed to convincing the American public that Hitler bore the responsibility for the war. The French wanted Roosevelt to summon a conference; Kennedy reported that the British wanted pressure on the Poles to make concessions. The president did neither. In a 'fireside chat' two days after the outbreak of war, Roosevelt assured his countrymen that 'this nation will remain a neutral nation'. Whatever his sympathies and various schemes of providing back-up and material assistance to the Allies, he intended to keep the country out of war.[82] He would help the British and French to contain Hitler by offering

[81] Quoted in Reynolds, *Anglo-American Alliance*, 57.

[82] MacKenzie King, who had accompanied the royal couple to Hyde Park and was convinced that Roosevelt would do everything possible to assist Britain short of

diplomatic and material assistance but they would have to do the job. The British and French leaders, as well as many in Berlin, knew that the American role would be critical to the economic war which they all anticipated. But neither the British nor the French could place too much faith in American backing or on the fulfilment of the bulk of the president's promises. Their caution proved well-judged.

VIII

As late as the summer of 1939, the British, especially Neville Chamberlain, and the French clung to the hope that war could be avoided or at least postponed. This persistence can only, in part, be explained by the belief that the Soviet alliance would be concluded and deterrence would work. Chamberlain did not attribute overwhelming importance to its conclusion and continued to fear that such an agreement would provoke Hitler. Daladier and Bonnet believed that the alliance was essential for French safety but the former recognized that ultimately, with or without an eastern front, France could not separate itself from Britain. In a revealing letter to his sister on 23 July, Chamberlain explained his position:

> One thing is I think clear, namely that Hitler has concluded that we mean business and that the time is not ripe for the major war. Therein he is fulfilling my expectations. Unlike some of my critics I go further and say the longer the war is put off the less likely it is to come at all as we go on perfecting our defences, and building up the defences of our allies ... You don't need offensive forces sufficient to win a smashing victory. What you want are defensive forces sufficiently strong enough to make it impossible for the other side to win except at such a cost to make it not worthwhile yet, they will presently come to realise that it never will be worthwhile. Then we can talk ... Meanwhile there is I think a definite detente.[83]

Convinced that Hitler had put Danzig in cold storage, Chamberlain wanted to assure the German 'moderates' that they had a good chance of getting reasonable consideration and treatment from Britain if they gave up ideas of 'forceful solutions'. He thought that Hitler had got the

committing the United States to war, was 'disgusted' and 'really ashamed' by Roosevelt's prompt and comprehensive declaration of neutrality. See David Reynolds, 'The President and the King' reprinted in Reynolds, *From World War to Cold War: Churchill, Roosevelt, and the International History of the 1940s* (Oxford, 2006), 144. The British were not so misled.

[83] Robert Self (ed.), *The Neville Chamberlain Diary Letters*, Vol. 4 (to Ida, 23 July 1939).

message but that it could be made more palatable if these warnings were accompanied by offers to negotiate.

Just as the prime minister's private efforts to renew contact with Berlin served mainly to muddy the waters and convince Hitler that Britain would not fight, so the many German attempts to alert the British to Hitler's real intentions and the danger of imminent war either failed in their purpose or proved counter-productive. In the spring and summer of 1938, the members of the old German 'opposition', acting independently of each other and often at cross purposes, tried to get the British government to take a more determined stand. Carl Goerdeler was particularly active both in London and Paris. In fact, the Foreign Office, SIS, and Vansittart's 'private detective agency' had all relied, in varying degrees, on Goerdeler, their link with the German opposition, during the winter of 1938–1939 even while repudiating his authority.[84] His visit to England at the end of May proved to be the last as his far-fetched peace plans were dismissed as irrelevant. More important were the attempts of Admiral Canaris and his even more committed anti-Nazi deputy, Colonel Oster, of the *Abwehr* to warn the British of the dangers of a Nazi–Soviet pact and a German attack on Poland. Some of the visitors were associated with the secretary of state at the Foreign Ministry, Ernst von Weizsäcker, who thought a war with Britain and France would be disastrous for the Reich. 'Amateur diplomatists', men like the Swedish industrialist, Axel Wenner-Gren and Birger Dahlerus, were encouraged by Göring to initiate talks in London, mainly in the hope of bringing back the agreement with Britain that Ribbentrop had failed to achieve. Many of these visitors were received in the highest political and social circles in England but their warnings and recommendations, with some exceptions, had little effect on British policy-makers, while their reports, if they reached Hitler, only convinced him that England wanted peace and would not come to Poland's assistance in its final hour.

More significant than most but ultimately futile was the visit of Gerhard von Schwerin, an officer of the German general staff who headed the 'Foreign Armies West' section in military intelligence. During his visit at the end of June, he met a wide variety of influential politicians, officers, and officials at the Foreign Office and made an excellent impression. Told of Britain's enhanced defence capabilities and determination to stand by Poland, the German staff officer insisted that Britain should actually *do* something to show its hand. For instance, RAF units should be immediately dispatched to France, Churchill

[84] John R. Ferris, ' "Now that the Milk is Spilt": Appeasement and the Archive on Intelligence', *Diplomacy and Statecraft*, 19: 3 (2008), 549.

should be brought into the government, and the alliance with the Soviet Union concluded. Whereas his earlier warning had been dismissed and his motives questioned, this time his pleas did not fall on deaf ears. It may have been due partly to his urging that in early July a major press campaign to bring Churchill into the cabinet was launched by Lord Astor, J. L. Garvin of the *Observer*, and Lord Camrose, the owner of the *Daily Telegraph*, the voice of patriotic Conservatism. Despite the press barrage in which other papers joined (but not *The Times*), Chamberlain refused to give way. The inclusion of Churchill or Eden in his government would give the wrong signals to Hitler and Mussolini. Aware of the shift in public opinion, Chamberlain enlisted Sir Joseph Ball, his confidant, and head of the Conservative Research Department, to run a campaign in *Truth*, a magazine controlled by Ball, denigrating Churchill and discrediting the so-called 'glamour boys' pressing for his inclusion in the cabinet. Schwerin returned to Germany promising to inform everyone that the British were in earnest but warned that 'unwelcome intelligence' was difficult to get into the heads of the army and the state.

Many of the emissaries were distrusted either because of their views or because they were servants of the Nazi state. In late April or early May, Weizsäcker and some of his officials worked out a scheme by which the rump of Czechoslovakia, namely Bohemia and Moravia, would be restored to independence in return for a solution of the Danzig and Polish Corridor questions. This suited the state secretary who was an old-fashioned German nationalist and was revolted by the irrational expansionism of Hitler and Ribbentrop. His purpose throughout was to preserve the peace and not to challenge the regime. He proposed that Adam Trott, a handsome former Rhodes Scholar with a wide circle of friends in London and Oxford, should go to Britain in early June. Trott dined with Lord Halifax, Lord Lothian, soon to go as ambassador to Washington, and Sir Thomas Inskip at Cliveden and later saw Chamberlain. In 1939, Trott's position was clothed in ambiguity, despite his later role in the resistance and the ultimate penalty he paid for his opposition to Hitler in August 1944. Though anti-Nazi and socialist in his political sympathies, he was a passionate nationalist and territorial revisionist, quick to take offence at slights to the honour of his country. He feared a fratricidal war of the kind that destroyed the Greek cities and thought that the British, through a combination of pressure and gestures of goodwill towards Germany, could ward off such a calamity. He was unwilling to meet Churchill whom he thought a 'warmonger' and championed Göring's role as a mediator in Anglo-German relations. Trott's rather confused and half-baked ideas and his espousal of territorial expansionism put him at odds with his friends at Balliol and All Souls, most of whom had become fierce critics of appeasement.

A second Trott visit to London and Oxford in mid-June only heightened their suspicions. Trott's camouflaged account of the visit which he hoped Ribbentrop, and even Hitler, would read, highlighted British concerns about German policy in Czechoslovakia and suggested that acceptable territorial changes could be made. His expectations were not fulfilled; he did not see either Ribbentrop or Hitler and the former blocked his visit to Göring, on whom Trott placed so many hopes. Hitler received a shortened version of Trott's paper.

The members of the Weizsäcker circle kept up their campaign of warnings throughout the summer but their message was obscured by their own revisionism and by their official positions as representatives of the Reich. Among the many warnings to the Foreign Office of a forthcoming Nazi–Soviet pact were the messages from the Kordt brothers, diplomats more committed to the checking and toppling of Hitler than their respected mentor and protector, Weizsäcker. Their warning of a Nazi–Soviet agreement and a war to follow was passed on to Halifax and Chamberlain but as they were active diplomats, they were suspected of being loyal servants of the Reich. Vansittart was one of the few to take their warnings seriously. Weizsäcker used their services again in mid-August to warn the Foreign Office of the forthcoming invasion of Poland and to alert the British to Italian hesitations about supporting Germany. Again, these interventions, intended to stiffen the British backbone, had little effect on policy making.

These failures resulted, in part, from the plethora of intelligence coming into London and the inability of the authorities to properly assess their meaning. Only the first steps were taken in the summer of 1939 to create a more efficient assessment system. The sheer number of visitors, some of whom were actually implementing the very policies they were trying to undermine, created confusion and aroused suspicion. The attitudes of Weizsäcker and Canaris, for instance, were equivocal at best and the proposals of their emissaries were hardly different in substance from what the British believed Hitler was offering. Even the most sympathetic listener felt that everything was being left to the British to accomplish. There was no offer to remove or assassinate the Führer, the suggestion made by the courageous if erratic Mason-Macfarlane, the British military attaché in Berlin, but rejected by his more legally minded superiors. Most important of all, despite the multitude of intelligence coming to London, it proved difficult to judge Hitler's intentions correctly. Uncertainty about Hitler's plans and his willingness to implement them and the fear of 'guessing wrong or bluffing too far helped to queer their [British policy makers] pitch'.[85]

[85] Ferris, 'Appeasement and the Archive on Intelligence', 557.

By the summer of 1939, however, it became difficult to believe that there could still be doubts about Hitler's intention to go to war.

Yet as the Allied powers pushed ahead with the Moscow talks, Chamberlain and Daladier clung to the belief that deterrence would succeed. They feared that if Hitler was threatened without leaving the way open for compromise, the Allied powers would bring on the very catastrophe they sought to avoid. Planning for war had moved into a higher gear but still the two leaders found it difficult to accept that time had run out. Neither Chamberlain, the man of peace, nor Daladier, the ex-soldier of 1914–1918, wanted war. Their electorates had reluctantly accepted that only war would stop Hitler's further moves into Europe but most hoped that the peace would last. War could only bring catastrophe and the collapse of the hopes of all right thinking men and women. Hitler had never shared this aversion to war. For him, war was the ultimate goal of all politics and the primal condition of life. The fixation on the idea of struggle as an end in itself was a leitmotiv that ran throughout his political life. He had achieved a position in Nazi Germany where his decision was the only one of any importance. All did not go quite as he intended during the summer of 1939 but in the end, he launched the attack which he knew would bring Britain and France into conflict with Germany. He did so deliberately for pragmatic and for ideological reasons which neither Chamberlain nor Daladier could really grasp.

Books

Adams, R. J. Q., *British Politics and Foreign Policy in the Age of Appeasement, 1935–1939* (Stanford, CA, 1993).

Adamthwaite, A., *France and the Coming of the Second World War, 1936–1939* (London, 1977).

—— *Grandeur and Misery: France's Bid for Power in Europe, 1914–1940* (London, 1995).

Aldrich, R. and Connell, J., *France's Overseas Frontier: Départements et Territoires d'Outre-Mer* (Cambridge, 1992).

Alexander, M., *The Republic in Danger: General Maurice Gamelin and the Politics of French Defence 1933–1940* (Cambridge, 1992).

Andrew, C., *For the President's Eyes Only: Secret Intelligence and the American Presidency from Washington to Bush* (London, 1995).

Becker, J.-J. and Berstein, S., *Histoire de l'anticommunisme* (Paris, 1987).

Beckett, F., *Enemy Within: The Rise and Fall of the British Communist Party* (London, 1995).

Bennett, E. M., *Separated by a Common Language: Franklin Delano Roosevelt and Anglo-American Relations, 1933–1939: The Roosevelt–Chamberlain Rivalry* (San Jose, CA, 2002).

Berstein, S., *Histoire du Parti radical, tome 2: Crise du radicalisme 1926–1939* (Paris, 1982).

Betts, R., *France and Decolonisation, 1900–1960* (Basingstoke, 1991).

Biondi, J.-P., *La mêlée des pacifistes 1914–1945* (Paris, 2000).

Blatt, J. (ed.), *The French Defeat of 1940: Reassessments* (Providence, RI, and Oxford, 1998). See O. Bartov, M. J. Carley, and W. R. Keylor.

Blumenthal, H., *Illusion and Reality in Franco-American Diplomacy, 1914–1945* (Baton Rouge, LA, 1986).

Boyce, R., The Great Interwar Crisis and the Collapse of Globalization (Basingstoke, 2009).

Branson, N., *History of the Communist Party of Great Britain, 1927–1941* (London, 1985).

Brinkley, A., *The End of Reform: New Deal Liberalism in Recession and War* (New York, 1995).

Brochand, C., *Histoire générale de la radio et de la télévision en France*, vol.1 (Paris, 1994).

Brown, J. M. and Louis, Wm. R. (eds.), *The Oxford History of the British Empire, Vol. IV: The Twentieth Century* (Oxford, 1999). See D. K. Fieldhouse, R. Hyam, and A. Clayton.

Burk, K., *Old World, New World: The Story of Britain and America* (London, 2007).

Cain, P. J. and Hopkins, A. G., *British Imperialism: Crisis and Deconstruction, 1914–1990* (London and New York, 1993).

—— *British Imperialism, 1688–2000* (Basingstoke, 2002).

Cairns, J. C. (ed.), *Contemporary France: Illusion, Conflict and Regeneration* (New York, 1978).

Ceadel, M., *Pacifism in Britain, 1914–1945: The Defining of a Faith* (Oxford, 1980).

—— *Semi-detached Idealists: The British Peace Movement and International Relations, 1854–1945* (Oxford, 2000).

Chafer, T. and Sackur, A. (eds.), *French Colonial Empire and the Popular Front: Hope and Disillusion* (London, 1999).

Charmley, J., *Lord Lloyd and the Decline of the British Empire* (London, 1987).

Clarke, P. and Trebilcock, C. (eds.), *Understanding Decline: Perceptions and Realities of Economic Performance* (Cambridge, 1997).

Clayton, A., *The British Empire as a Superpower, 1919–1939* (London, 1986).

Compton, J. V., *The Swastika and the Eagle: Hitler, the United States, and the Origins of the Second World War* (Boston, MA, 1967).

Cohen, M. and Kolinsky, M. (eds.), *Britain and the Middle East in the 1930s: Security Problems, 1935–1939* (Basingstoke, 1992).

Cross, C., *The Fascists in Britain* (London, 1961).

Crowson, N. J., *Facing Fascism: The Conservative Party and the European Dictators, 1935–1940* (London, 1997).

Dann, U. (ed.), *The Great Powers in the Middle East, 1919–1939* (New York, 1988). See G. Sheffer, and D. C. Watt.

Dennis, P., *Decision by Default: Peacetime Conscription and British Defence, 1919–1939* (London, 1972).

Diplomacy and Statecraft, Vol. 19, No. 3 (2008). See also under articles.

DOENCKE, J. D. and STOLER, M. A., *Debating Franklin D. Roosevelt's Foreign Policies, 1933–1945* (Lanham, MD, and Oxford, 2005).

DRUMMOND, I. M., *Negotiating Freer Trade: The United Kingdom, the United States, Canada, and the Trade Agreements of 1938* (Waterloo, Ontario, 1989).

—— *Imperial Economic Policy, 1917–1939: Studies in Expansion and Protection* (Toronto, 1997).

DUMETT, R. E. (ed.), *Gentlemanly Capitalism and British Imperialism: The New Debate on Empire* (Harlow, 1999).

EADEN, J. and RENTON, D., *The Communist Party of Great Britain since 1920* (Basingstoke, 2002).

FARNHAM, B. R., *Roosevelt and the Munich Crisis: A Study of Political Decision-Making* (Princeton, NJ, 1997).

FERRIS, J., *Intelligence and Strategy: Selected Essays* (London and New York, 2005).

FIELDHOUSE, D. K., *Western Imperialism in the Middle East, 1914–1958* (Oxford, 2006).

FUCHSER, L. W., *Chamberlain and Appeasement: A Study in the Politics of History* (New York, 1982).

GASSERT, P., *Amerika im Dritten Reich: Ideologie, Propaganda und Volksmeinung, 1933–1945* (Stuttgart, 1997).

GIRAULT, R. and FRANK, R. (eds.), *La puissance en Europe, 1938–1940* (Paris, 1984). See A. Adamthwaite, C.-R. Ageron.

—— *Turbulente Europe et nouveaux mondes, 1914–1941* (Paris, 1988).

GRAHAM, B. D., *Choice and Democratic Order: The French Socialist Party, 1937–1950* (Cambridge, 1994).

GRIFFITHS, R., *Fellow Travellers of the Right: British Enthusiasts for Nazi Germany, 1933–1939* (London, 1980).

HAGGIE, P., *Britannia at Bay: The Defence of the British Empire against Japan, 1931–1941* (Oxford, 1981).

HAIGHT, J. MCVICKAR, *American Aid to France, 1938–1940* (New York, 1970).

HILDEBRAND, K. and WERNER, K. F. (eds.), *Deutschland und Frankreich, 1936–1939* (Munich, 1981).

HOISINGTON, W. A. JR., *The Casablanca Connection: French Colonial Policy, 1936–1943* (Chapel Hill, NC, 1984).

HOLLAND, R. F., *The Pursuit of Greatness: Britain and the World Role, 1900–1970* (London, 1991).

HORN, B. (ed.), *Forging a Nation: Perspectives on the Canadian Military Experience* (St. Catharine's, Ont., 2002). See M. Hennessy.

HYAM, R., *Britain's Declining Empire: The Road to Decolonization, 1918–1968* (Cambridge, 2007).

IMLAY, T. C., *Facing the Second World War: Strategy, Politics, and Economics in Britain and France, 1938–1940* (Oxford, 2003).

—— and DUFFY TOFT, M. D. *(eds.), Fog of Peace and War Planning: Military and Strategic Planning under Uncertainty* (London and New York, 2006). See T. C. Imlay, and J. Ferris.

INGRAM, N., *The Politics of Dissent: Pacifism in France, 1919–1939* (Oxford, 1991).

Iriye, A., *The Globalizing of America, 1913–1945* (Cambridge, 1993).
Irvine, W. D., *French Conservatism in Crisis: The Republican Federation of France in the 1930s* (Baton Rouge, LA, and London, 1979).
Jackson, J., *The Politics of Depression in France, 1932–1936* (Cambridge, 1985).
—— *The Popular Front in France: Defending Democracy, 1934–1938* (Cambridge, 1988).
Jackson, P., *France and the Nazi Menace: Intelligence and Policy Making, 1933–1939* (Oxford, 2000).
Jeanneney, J.-N., *L'Argent caché: milieux d'affaires et pouvoirs politiques dans la France du XXe siècle* (Paris, 1981).
Jordan, N., *The Popular Front and Central Europe: The Dilemmas of French Impotence, 1918–1940* (Cambridge, 1992).
Kahn, D., *Seizing the Enigma: The Race to Break the German U-Boat Codes, 1939–1943* (London, 1992).
Kennedy, D. M., *Freedom from Fear: The American People in Depression and War, 1929–1945* (Oxford and New York, 1999).
Kennedy, G. and Neilson, K. (eds.), *Far-flung Lines: Studies in Imperial Defence in Honour of Donald Mackenzie Schurman* (London, 1997). See G. Kennedy.
Kier, E., *Imagining War: French and British Military Doctrine between the Wars* (Princeton, NJ, 1997).
Kiesling, E., *Arming Against Hitler: France and the Limits of Military Planning* (Lawrence, KA, 1996).
Kuisel, R. F., *Capitalism and the State in Modern France* (Cambridge, 1981).
Marseille, J., *Empire coloniale et capitalisme français: histoire d'un divorce* (Paris, 1984).
Martin, J., *L'Empire triomphant, 1871–1936*: Vol. II. *Maghreb, Indochine, Madagascar* (Paris, 1990).
Masson, P., *La Marine française et la guerre, 1939–1945* (Paris, 1991).
McIntyre, W. D., *The Rise and Fall of the Singapore Naval Base, 1919–1942* (London, 1979).
McKercher, B. J. C., *Transition of Power: Britain's Loss of Global Pre-Eminence to the United States, 1930–1945* (Cambridge, 1999).
Méadel, C., *Histoire de la radio des années trente: du sans-filiste à l'auditeur* (Paris, 1994).
Middlemas, K., *Diplomacy of Illusion: The British Government and Germany, 1937–1939* (London, 1972).
Morris, B., *The Roots of Appeasement: The British Weekly Press and Nazi Germany during the 1930s* (London, 1991).
Mortimer, E., *The Rise of the French Communist Party, 1920–1947* (London, 1984).
Murfett, M. H., *Fool-Proof Relations: The Search for Anglo-American Naval Cooperation During the Chamberlain Years, 1937–1940* (Singapore, 1984).
Namier, L. B., *Diplomatic Prelude, 1938–1939* (London, 1948).
Neville, P., *Neville Chamberlain: A Study in Failure?* (London, 1992).
—— *Appeasing Hitler. The Diplomacy of Sir Nevile Henderson, 1937–1939* (Basingstoke, 2000).
Nicholas, S., *The Echo of War: Home Front Propaganda and the Wartime BBC, 1939–1945* (Manchester, 1996).

OFFNER, A. O., *American Appeasement: United States Foreign Policy and Germany, 1933–1938* (Cambridge, 1969).
OMISSI, D., *Air Power and Colonial Control: The Royal Air Force 1919–1939* (Manchester, 1990).
PARKER, R. A. C., *Chamberlain and Appeasement: British Policy and the Coming of the Second World War* (London, 1993).
—— *Churchill and Appeasement* (London, 2000).
PEDEN, G. C., *British Rearmament and the Treasury, 1932–1939* (Edinburgh, 1979).
—— *Arms, Economics and British Strategy: From Dreadnoughts to Hydrogen Bombs* (Cambridge, 2007).
PETERS, E. R., *Anthony Eden at the Foreign Office, 1931–1938* (Aldershot, 1986).
PUGH, M., *'Hurrah for the blackshirts!': Fascists and Fascism in Britain between the Wars* (London, 2005).
RÉMOND, R. and BOURDIN, J. (eds.), *Edouard Daladier, chef du gouvernement* (Paris, 1977).
REYNOLDS, D., *The Creation of the Anglo-American Alliance, 1937–1941: A Study in Competitive Co-operation* (London, 1981).
—— *Britannia Overruled: British Policy and World Power in the Twentieth Century* (Harlow, 1991).
—— *From Munich to Pearl Harbor: Roosevelt's Foreign Policy and the Origins of the Second World War* (Chicago, IL, 2001).
—— *In Command of History: Churchill Fighting and Writing the Second World War* (London, 2004).
ROCK, W. R., *Appeasement on Trial: British Foreign Policy and its Critics, 1938–1939* (Hamden, CT, 1966).
—— *Chamberlain and Roosevelt: British Foreign Policy and the United States, 1937–1940* (London, 1988).
RUGGIERO, J., *Neville Chamberlain and British Rearmament: Pride, Prejudice, and Politics* (Westport, CT, 1999).
SCHMIDT, G., *The Politics and Economics of Appeasement: British Foreign Policy in the 1930s* (Leamington Spa, 1986).
SELF, R., *Britain, America and the War Debt Controversy: The Economic Diplomacy of an Unspecial Relationship, 1917–1941* (London and New York, 2006).
SHAY, R. P., *British Rearmament in the Thirties: Politics and Profits* (Princeton, NJ, 1977).
SIEGEL, M. L., *The Moral Disarmament of France: Education, Pacifism, and Patriotism, 1914–1940* (Cambridge, 2004).
STERNHELL, Z., *Ni droite, Ni gauche: l'idéologie fasciste en France* (Paris, 1983).
THOMAS, M., *The French Empire between the Wars: Imperialism, Politics and Society* (Manchester and New York, 2005).
THOMPSON, A., *The Empire Strikes Back: The Impact of Imperialism on Britain from the Mid-Nineteenth Century* (Harlow, 2005).
THOMPSON, N., *The Anti-Appeasers: Conservative Opposition to Appeasement in the 1930s* (Oxford, 1971).
THORPE, A., *The British Communist Party and Moscow, 1920–1943* (Manchester, 2000).
THURLOW, R. C., *Fascism in Britain: A History, 1918–1985* (Oxford, 1987).

TOMBS, R. and I., *That Sweet Enemy: The French and the British from the Sun King to the Present* (London, 2006).

VAÏSSE, M. (ed.), *Le Pacifisme en Europe: des années 1920 aux années 1950* (Brussels, 1993). See F. G. Dreyfus, J. Giraux, and E. Hermon.

WALL, I., *French Communism in the Era of Stalin* (London, 1983).

WARK, W. K., *The Ultimate Enemy: British Intelligence and Nazi Germany, 1933–1939* (London, 1985).

WEBER, E., *The Hollow Years: France in the 1930s* (London, 1995).

YOUNG, R. J., *In Command of France: French Foreign Policy and Military Planning, 1933–1940* (Cambridge, MA, 1978).

Articles and Chapters

AGERON, C.-R., 'La perception de la puissance française en 1938–1939—le mythe impérial', in Girault, R. and Frank, R. (eds.), *La puissance en Europe, 1938–1940* (Paris, 1984).

ALEXANDER, M. S., 'Preparing to Feed Mars: Anglo-French Economic Co-ordination and the Coming of War, 1937–1940', in Alexander, M. S. and Philpott, W. J. (eds.), *Anglo-French Defence Relations between the Wars* (Basingstoke, 2002).

ALEXANDROFF, A. and ROSECRANCE, R., 'Deterrence in 1939', *World Politics*, 29 (1977).

ASTER, S., 'Appeasement: Before and After Revisionism', *Diplomacy and Statecraft*, 19: 3 (2008).

BUFFOTOT, P., 'La perception du réarmement allemand par les organismes de renseignement français de 1936 à 1939', *Revine historiques des armées*, 3 (1979).

—— 'The French High Command and the Franco-Soviet Alliance, 1933–1939', *Journal of Strategic Studies*, 5: 4 (1982).

CORNWALL, M., 'The Rise and Fall of a "Special Relationship"? Britain and Czechoslovakia, 1930–1948', in Brivati, B. and Jones, H. (eds.), *What Difference Did the War Make?* (Leicester, 1993).

COSTIGLIOLA, F., 'Broken Circle: The Isolation of Franklin D. Roosevelt in World War II', *Diplomatic History*, 32: 5 (2008).

CROZIER, A. J., 'Imperial Decline and the Colonial Question in Anglo-German Relations, 1919–1939', *European Studies Review*, 11 (1981).

DARWIN, J., 'Imperialism in Decline? Tendencies in British Policy Between the Wars', *Historical Journal*, 23 (1980).

FERRIS, J. R., '"Now that the Milk is Spilt": Appeasement and the Archive on Intelligence', *Diplomacy and Statecraft*, 19: 3 (2008).

GEYER, M., 'The Crisis of Military Leadership in the 1930s', *Journal of Strategic Studies*, 14: 4 (1991).

GIRAULT, R., 'The Impact of the Economic Situation on the Foreign Policy of France, 1936–1939', in Mommsen, W. and Kettenacker, L. (eds.), *The Fascist Challenge and the Policy of Appeasement* (London, 1983).

GRANATSTEIN, J. L., and BOTHWELL, R., 'A Self-Evident National Duty: Canadian Foreign Policy, 1935–1939', *Journal of Imperial and Commonwealth History*, 3: 2 (1975).

GRAYSON, R. S., 'Imperialism in Conservative Defence and Foreign Policy: Leo Amery and the Chamberlains, 1903–39', *Journal of Imperial and Commonwealth History*, 34: 4 (2006).

HAIGHT, J. MCVICKAR Jr., 'Roosevelt as Friend of France', in Divine, R. A. (ed.), *Causes and Consequences of World War II* (Chicago, IL,1969).

HARRIS, J. P., 'Two War Ministers: A Reassessment of Duff Cooper and Hore-Belisha', *War & Society*, 6: 1 (1988).

HINSLEY, F. H. et al, 'The Polish, French and British Contributions to the Breaking of the Enigma: A Revised Account', in Hinsley, F. H. et al. (eds.), *British Intelligence and the Second World War*, Vol. IV (London, 1988).

HODGSON, G., 'Sir Nevile Henderson, Appeasement and the Press: Fleet Street and the Build-up to the Second World War', *Journalism Studies*, 8: 2 (2007).

IMLAY, T. C., 'Paul Reynaud and France's Response to Nazi Germany, 1938–1940', *French Historical Studies*, 26: 3 (2003).

—— 'Democracy and War: Political Regime, Industrial Relations, and Economic Preparations for War in France and Britain up to 1940', *Journal of Modern History*, 79 (2007).

—— 'Preparing for Total War: Industrial and Economic Preparations for War in France between the Two World Wars', *War in History*, 15 (2008).

—— and HORN, M., 'Money in Wartime: France's Financial Preparations for the Two World Wars', *International History Review*, 27: 4 (2005).

—— 'Retreat or Resistance: Strategic Reappraisal and the Crisis of French Power in Eastern Europe, September 1938 to August 1939', in Mouré, K. and Alexander, M. S. (eds.), *Crisis and Renewal in France, 1918–1962* (New York and Oxford, 2002).

—— 'France, Britain and the Making of the Anglo-French Alliance, 1938–9', in Alexander, M. S. and Philpott, W. J. (eds.), *Anglo-French Defence Relations between the Wars* (Basingstoke, 2002).

JACKSON P. and MAIOLO, J., 'Intelligence in Anglo-French Relations before the Outbreak of the Second World War', in Alexander, M. S. and Philpott, W. J. (eds.), *Anglo-French Defence Relations between the Wars* (Basingstoke, 2002).

JORDAN, N., 'The Cut-Price War on the Peripheries: The French General Staff, the Rhineland and Czechoslovakia', in Boyce, R. and Robertson, E. M. (eds.), *Paths to War: New Essays on the Origins of the Second World War* (London, 1989).

KAHN, D., 'How I Discovered World War II's Greatest Spy', *Cryptologia*, 34: 12–21 (2010).

MAIOLO, J. A., '"I believe the Hun is cheating": British Admiralty Technical Intelligence and the German Navy, 1936–1939', *INS*, 11: 1 (1996).

MARGUERAT, P., 'Positions économiques de la France dans la zone de la petite entente au cours des années trente', in Friedländer, S., Kapur, H. and Reszler, A. (eds.), *L'Historien et les relations internationales* (Geneva, 1981).

McKercher, B. J. C., 'National Security and Imperial Defence: British Grand Strategy and Appeasement, 1930–1939', *Diplomacy and Statecraft*, 19: 3 (2008).

Murfett, M. H., 'Living in the Past: A Critical Re-examination of the Singapore Naval Strategy, 1918–1941', *War and Society* 11: 1 (1993).

Overy, R. J., 'Air Power and the Origins of Deterrence Theory Before 1939', *Journal of Strategic Studies*, 15: 1 (1992).

—— 'Strategic Intelligence and the Outbreak of the Second World War', *War in History*, 5:4 (1998).

Parker, R. A. C., 'The Economics of Rearmament and Foreign Policy: The United Kingdom Before 1939', *Journal of Contemporary History*, 10: 4 (1975).

—— 'British Rearmament, 1936–1939: Treasury, Trade Unions and Skilled Labour', *English Historical Review*, 96: 379 (1981).

Peden, G. C., 'A Matter of Timing: The Economic Background to British Foreign Policy, 1937–1939', *History*, 69: 225 (1984).

—— 'Winston Churchill, Neville Chamberlain and the Defence of Egypt', in Hattendorf, J. B. and Murfett, M. H. (eds.), *The Limitations of Military Power: Essays Presented to Professor Norman Gibbs on his Eightieth Birthday* (Basingstoke, 1990).

Pithon, R., 'Opinions publiques et représentations culturelles face aux problèmes de la puissance: le témoignage du cinéma française (1938–1939)', *Relations internationales*, 33 (1983).

Rémond, R., 'L'image de l'Allemagne dans l'opinion publique française de mars 1936 à septembre 1939', in Hildebrand, K. and Werner, K. F. (eds.), *Deutschland und Frankreich, 1936–1939* (Munich, 1981).

Salerno, R. M., 'The French Navy and the Appeasement of Italy, 1937–1939', *English Historical Review*, 112 (1997).

Sencourt, Robert, 'The Foreign Policy of Neville Chamberlain', *Quarterly Review*, 292 (1954).

Smith, M., 'Rearmament and Deterrence in Britain in the 1930s', *Journal of Strategic Studies*, 1: 3 (1978).

—— 'A Matter of Faith: British Strategic Air Doctrine before 1939', *Journal of Contemporary History*, 15: 3 (1980).

Strang, G. B., 'Two Unequal Tempers: Sir George Ogilvie-Forbes, Sir Nevile Henderson and British Foreign Policy, 1938–1939', *Diplomacy and Statecraft*, 5: 1 (1994).

—— 'The Spirit of Ulysses? Ideology and British Appeasement in the 1930s', *Diplomacy and Statecraft*, 19: 3 (2008).

Thobie, J., 'Le nouveau cours des relations franco-turques et l'affaire du Sandjak d'Alexandrette, 1921–1939', *Relations internationales*, 19 (1979).

Thomas, M., 'To Arm an Ally: French Arms Sales to Romania, 1926–1940', *Journal of Strategic Studies*, 19: 2 (1996).

—— 'At the Heart of Things? French Imperial Defense Planning in the Late 1930s', *French Historical Studies*, 21: 2 (1998).

—— 'Imperial Defence or Diversionary Attack? Anglo-French Strategic Planning in the Near East, 1936–40', in Alexander, M. S. and Philpott,

W. J. (eds.), *Anglo-French Defence Relations between the Wars* (Basingstoke, 2002).

—— 'Appeasement in the Late Third Republic', *Diplomacy and Statecraft*, 19: 3 (2008).

THOMPSON, J. A., 'Conceptions of National Security and American Entry into World War II', *Diplomacy & Statecraft*, 16 (2005).

WARK, W. K., 'Three Military Attachés at Berlin in the 1930s: Soldier-Statesmen and the Limits of Ambiguity', *IHR*, 9: 4 (1987).

YOUNG, R. J., 'The Strategic Dream: French Air Doctrine in the Interwar Period, 1919–1939', *Journal of Contemporary History*, 9 (1974).

—— 'French Military Intelligence and the Franco-Italian Alliance, 1933–1939', *Historical Journal*, 28: 1 (1985).

—— 'A. J. P. Taylor and the Problem with France', in Martel, G. (ed.), *The Origins of the Second World War Reconsidered: A. J. P. Taylor and the Historians*, 2nd edn. (London, 1999).

15

Unleashing the Dogs of War

Hitler's intention to settle the 'Polish question' through military action became 'virtually immutable' after the Anglo-French guarantees in March. The western guarantees infuriated Hitler but did not deter him. What looked like deterrence to Britain and France was seen by the Führer as a threat to the fulfilment of his ambitions. Whatever the fixity of his purpose and his willingness to gamble even when the stakes were high, there was nevertheless a highly rational and calculating streak in Hitler's make-up. He believed that Britain was Germany's most dangerous adversary and the main obstacle to his programme of expansion. Despite his contempt for the men of Munich and his fury at their intervention in German affairs, he never underestimated British strength. He did not want war with Britain but he would not tolerate its interference in Poland nor accept a new negotiated settlement. Most of his actions in the months after the Prague *coup* were directed at preparing, diplomatically as well as militarily, for the Polish campaign. Germany's adverse diplomatic and armament situation after Prague tempted him to take the offensive even if this meant war with Britain and France. His decision to seek an alliance with the Soviet Union, surely an unwelcome move but a necessary one if Germany was not to be confronted with a two-front war, shows how determined he was to pursue his objectives by war.

On 10 February 1939, he told a group of officers that he would launch a war in the not too distant future. As only he could lead the German people in this struggle, it would have to be fought in his lifetime. He would seek European domination first and then world hegemony but the former conflict had to be launched before other nations rearmed and expanded and would be in a position to thwart the creation of a German-centred empire. Even when moved by his own rhetoric, Hitler was often shrewd in his strategic assessments. In his view, the immediate situation favoured Germany; the ambitions of Italy and of Japan would put the already declining British and French empires under increasing pressure. Like Mussolini, Hitler believed that the western powers had lost the will to rule and their own countries were the natural inheritors of their empires, though Germany and Italy would have to claim their inheritance through war.

I

When Hitler spoke to his officers in February, he still thought he could convince the Poles to acknowledge Germany's hegemonic position in Europe and accept a satellite role. The German demands for Danzig and the Polish Corridor were only window-dressing as the Poles were quick to realize. When and why did Hitler change his mind and opt for a military solution? The Polish rejection of his offer of 21 March, the partial mobilization of 23 March, and the British guarantee convinced him that the Poles would not serve as faithful subordinates. The first time Hitler publicly referred to the idea of solving the 'Polish question' by military means was in an instruction to the commander-in-chief of the army on 25 March when he ordered the start of planning for operations against Poland (known as 'Case White'). In subsequent instructions to his generals, though he left open the possibility that the Poles would yield, his mind was increasingly focused on the final outcome of the war with Poland. 'Case White' was not the 'necessary prerequisite' for the war with the western powers. He clearly hoped to separate the timing of the two wars.

On 28 April came Hitler's denunciation of the German-Polish Non-Aggression Pact and the Anglo-German Naval Agreement of 1935. On the following day, after outlining his terms for a settlement of the Danzig and 'Polish Corridor' questions to the Reichstag, he withdrew from the public platform and lapsed into silence. The first plans for the military operations were submitted on 26 or 27 April and the definitive OKH planning finished on 15 June. The army command wanted to eliminate Poland as quickly as possible for, despite Hitler's assurances to the contrary, they feared intervention by the western powers and a war on two fronts. On 23 May, Hitler, in rambling fashion, told his senior commanders and closest military advisers that he had decided to attack Poland at the first suitable opportunity. It was necessary to isolate Poland diplomatically to assure military success but if the west intervened, 'it will be better to attack the west, and incidentally liquidate Poland'. Hitler's subsequent musings about the war with Britain reflected his rising anger with its continued interference in continental affairs. He acknowledged that Britain would be a formidable opponent that could only be conquered from the air if her fleet was annihilated first. Though a long war might be necessary, much could be achieved by a surprise attack and the delivery of a shattering blow—'only possible if we do not "slide" into war with England on account of Poland'.[1] The thrust into Holland and Belgium would be followed not by an advance on Paris but on the Channel ports to provide launching sites for the bombing and blockade of Britain. Hitler's timing for the forthcoming war varied, 1940–1941, while Britain's anti-aircraft defences were still deficient, or 1944, when the new German armaments programme would be completed. There was no reference to the United States but a mention of the Soviet Union, which might 'disinterest itself in Poland'. He told his listeners, some of whom, in view of Germany's need for raw materials, were urging the conclusion of a German–Soviet trade agreement, that economic relations with Moscow would depend on an improvement in political relations. The conclusion of a French–British–Soviet alliance, he warned, would force him to attack Britain and France with a 'few annihilating blows'. It is hardly possible that Hitler could have believed that this was possible. The Führer was watching the progress of the Moscow talks and by mid-May was weighing up the pros and cons of negotiating with the Soviet Union.

Hitler had confirmed that the war against Poland was to be launched. As his officers were planning only for that war, they left the meeting with some sense of relief that nothing more ambitious was contemplated. For, though receptive to the idea of war with Poland and the recovery of the lost lands, they were deeply sceptical about Germany's ability to take on Britain and France. Much had been accomplished in preparing Germany's war machine but there was still much to do. The army, for instance, was well on its way to producing the 103 divisions projected in 1936 but at the outbreak of war, some thirty-four of Germany's 105 divisions were still under-equipped and only 10% of new recruits in the replacement training units had any weapons at all. The *Wehrmacht* was not a mechanized army but relied heavily on horses for transport. The vast majority of German soldiers would go to war on foot.

It would take at least two years before the air force could face a conflict with Britain with any degree of confidence. The *Luftwaffe* schedules had been badly disrupted. The Junkers 88 programme was preserved but well-tested and effective aircraft had to be dropped to make room for the new, untried models. In the summer of 1939, there were further cuts in the allocation of aluminium, needed for airframe production, and of copper, threatening future production plans.[2] In May and June 1939, and again in August, officers warned that the *Luftwaffe* could only achieve a partial success against Britain and would only become a real threat to the British

[1] All quotations from *DGFP*, Ser. D, Vol. VI, No. 433. This is not a verbatim account but notes taken by Rudolf Schmundt, Hitler's adjutant, written some months later.

[2] For the details of the effects see Adam Tooze, *The Wages of Destruction*, 302–303.

TABLE **15.1** German Army Expansion, 1936–1939[3]

Type of Division	1936	1937	1938	1939
Infantry	36	34	38	38
Motorized/Mechanized		5	8	8
Armoured/Panzer	3	3	5	6
Reservist/Landwehr		7	27	51
Total after mobilization	39 effectives unavailable	49 effectives unavailable	78 effectives unavailable	103 2.76 million

in 1941. Even the fulfilment of the planned mass production of the Ju-88 would not assure *Luftwaffe* success in an air war against England. Admiral Raeder, who had offered to resign in early 1939 in the face of armament demands he could not meet, knew that the 'Z' plan had to be modified even while the naval armament priority lasted. It ended in August. German surface ships were so few and weak that when war broke out, Raeder claimed that, even if fully committed, 'they would only be able to show that they know how to die with honour'.[4]

TABLE **15.2** German Production of Aircraft and Ammunition, 1937–1939[5]

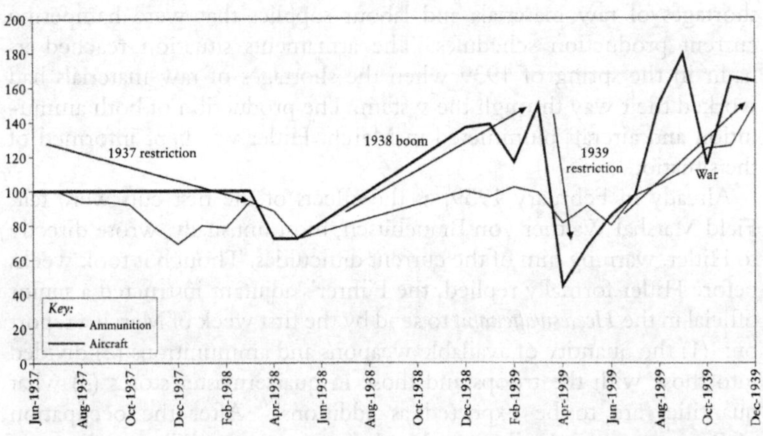

Source: Reproduced from Adam Tooze, *The Wages of Destruction: The Making and Breaking of the Nazi Economy* (London, 2006), 305.

[3] Militärgeschichtliches Forschungsamt, *Germany and the Second World War*, Vol.1 ed. Wilhelm Deist et al. (Oxford, 1990), 503 and 691.

[4] Lutz Budrass, *Flugzeugindustrie und Luftrüstung in Deutschland*, (Düsseldorf, 1998), 558.

[5] Deist et al., 480.

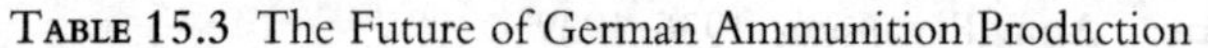

Table 15.3 The Future of German Ammunition Production

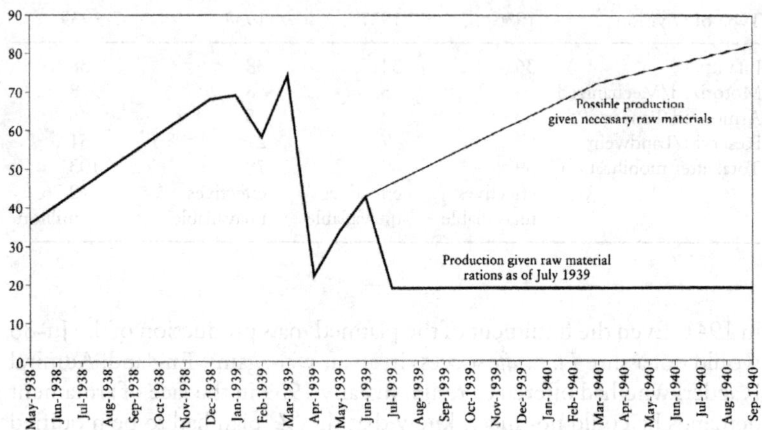

Source: Reproduced from Adam Tooze, *The Wages of Destruction: The Making and Breaking of the Nazi Economy* (London, 2006), 314.

However docile, Hitler's military leaders were acutely aware of the shortages of raw materials and labour supplies that were hampering current production schedules. The armaments situation reached its nadir in the spring of 1939 when the shortages of raw materials had worked their way through the system. The production of both ammunition and aircraft plummeted in March. Hitler was kept informed of the situation.

Already in February 1939, as the effects of the first cuts were felt, Field Marshal Walther von Brauchitsch, most unusually, wrote directly to Hitler, warning him of the current difficulties. Though it took weeks before Hitler formally replied, the Führer's adjutant instructed a senior official in the *Heereswaffenamt* to send by the first week of March a report on: '(1) the quantity of available weapons and ammunitions (2) divided into those with the troops and those in quartermaster stores (3) what quantities are to be expected as additions'.[6] After the occupation of Prague, on 15 April, Brauchitsch again sent the Führer a letter of complaint and a gloomy assessment, accompanied by thirty pages of statistics and charts, of the situation created by the shortages of steel and of rod iron. A few months later, he again complained, to both Hitler and

[6] Quotes in Tooze, *Wages of Destruction*, 311.

General Keitel, the chief of the *Wehrmacht* high command, this time about the lack of non-ferrous metals, particularly copper. Contrary to what has sometimes been claimed, Hitler was interested in the details of Germany's armament position and kept himself closely informed. As the war with Poland drew closer, he demanded a breakdown of the armaments situation as of 1 April and 1 October 1940, using the same formula as had been required for 1939. The army's weapons procurement office returned an extremely pessimistic appraisal of future production schedules. Worried about Hitler's reaction, the head of the office asked his staff to re-check the figures, particularly the exceedingly low forecast given for infantry ammunition. A more thorough explanation of the calculations, based on projections of the summer steel and copper allocations, confirmed the earlier negative judgment.

As many in London were predicting, the German armaments economy was reaching the limits of what could be done under peacetime conditions. The country was already devoting more than 20% of its national income to military expenditure and the *Wehrmacht*'s share of critical war materials was hovering between 20% and 30% of that total. There was little room for expansion while maintaining the existing 'wartime economy at peace'. German exports, after a brief surge, declined and did not recover before the outbreak of war. Reserves of gold and the foreign exchange position were under extreme pressure and there were few opportunities available to secure foreign loans. Final decisions had to be made in the very near future. On 24 May, Major-General Thomas, the head of the Office of War Economy, joined the chorus of Cassandras. He presented a careful and highly pessimistic analysis of the balance of forces to an assembled group of foreign ministry officials. Thomas concluded that Britain, France, and the United States would outspend Germany and Italy in 1939–1940 by a margin of at least a billion Reichsmarks. A comparative analysis in macroeconomic terms yielded even more negative results. Whereas Germany in 1939 was already devoting 23% of its income to the military, the figure for France was 17%, Britain, 12%, and the United States only 2%. Even without America, the Anglo-French alliance would enjoy a significant advantage over Germany in any European arms race; with the United States included, the German position would be far worse. Throughout his presentation, Thomas assumed that Britain could count on 'the entire Empire and the United States as an armoury and reservoir of raw materials'.[7] As will be described later, Thomas

[7] Tooze, *Wages of Destruction*, 310. The argument as well as the quotations are based on Tooze's book, chapter 9.

returned to the charge on 27 August, again confronting Hitler with his figures but provoking only the most negative response.

Thanks to Adam Tooze's work, we know that Hitler had all the information he required about the massive set-back to Germany's armaments programme. He knew, too, about the difficulties of expanding the existing German raw material base. Many of the German generals did not believe that Germany was prepared for war against Britain and France in 1939. The plans for in-depth mobilization, which they believed essential for victory, were still in the earliest stages of implementation. General Thomas summed up the situation on 3 September at a meeting of the three services called by the OKW:

> The position is clear. The total mobilization of the economy has been ordered . . . a whole number of programmes are still at this time in progress, which should actually have been ready by the outbreak of war; the giant explosives plan; the programme for munitions production; the substitution of scarce materials; the Ju-88 programme; the building up of the oil industry; the expansion of Buna, aluminium and magnesium production; the construction of fortified airfields; further necessary building on the *Westwall* and the construction of public air-raid shelters.[8]

These were projects due for completion during the next four or five years. Whatever the military thought about the forthcoming conflict, planning for the war with Poland continued without major protest. The senior commanders either accepted Hitler's assurances that Poland would be isolated or, if they had doubts, they suppressed them. It was only in late August that Hitler felt it necessary to publicly bolster their confidence by which time he was able to call on the non-aggression pact with the Soviet Union to ease both the strategic and economic situations. There were no signs of open dissent and no military conspiracies. Personnel changes and new assignments had weakened the position of the former opponents to Hitler. Most were disillusioned and depressed by Munich and Hitler's foreign policy successes. General Halder, a possible leader of some future resistance group, did not think that opposition or a *coup d'état* had any chance of success. Individual general staff officers tried to alert the western powers to the dangers that lay ahead; the British and French were well informed of the progress of German military planning. In general, however, the attack on Poland met with general approval in military circles; the solution of the Polish Corridor and Danzig problems was overdue and fell within the military conception of Germany as a Great Power.

[8] Quoted in R. J. Overy, *War and Economy in the Third Reich*, 198.

Hitler's first goal was to isolate and demoralize the Poles. The *Auswärtiges Amt* was instructed to break off all diplomatic relations with Warsaw. Weizsäcker's anti-Polish sentiments made him an enthusiastic accomplice. At the end of March, he informed the Danzig authorities of Germany's intention to follow a policy of pressure on Poland to the 'point of destruction'. After the German offer to the Poles in March, there was no further official communication between Berlin and Warsaw; Hitler did not want to receive any proposals for compromise from Warsaw or any offers of outside mediation in the quarrel. He was anxious to keep matters in his own hands so as not to be forced into negotiations or premature action. The tension in Danzig city was built up gradually: 'incidents' multiplied, particularly along the border between Danzig and Poland. The local police force became a small army. A good-sized SA force was raised and equipped with smuggled German arms; Goebbels's speeches fanned the chauvinist flames of pro-Nazi Danzigers. The intention in this war of nerves was to provoke Warsaw into taking 'aggressive action', thereby providing an excuse to send troops into Poland. Everything was being done to centre attention on Danzig, the weakest link in the British and French guarantee. By the middle of June, the date of the German attack was scheduled for late August. The campaign had to be completed before the autumn rains turned the Polish flatlands into a quagmire totally unsuitable for tanks. Lithuania and the newly created puppet state of Slovakia would be asked to join the Germans from the north and south. In mid-June, an announcement was made that a German light cruiser would visit the Free City between 25 and 28 August to commemorate the dead of the *Magdeburg*, sunk by the Russians in 1914. An old, retired battleship used for training purposes, the *Schleswig-Holstein*, was used instead. It duly arrived in Danzig harbour on 25 August. It would fire the first shots in the European war, at 4.45 a.m. on 1 September.

The miscalculating Beck kept open the Polish door to negotiations and tried not to alienate the Germans any further. There were indications that the Germans might negotiate; the economic agreement of September 1938, for instance, remained in force. Hitler's denunciation of the Polish–German non-aggression pact forced a reconsideration of Beck's strategy. While he still hoped for negotiations, he was prepared to warn Hitler of Poland's determination to fight if conciliatory efforts failed. Just before Beck left for vacation, he spoke of preventing the escalation of the Danzig conflict, claiming that the present situation had arisen because of 'Chamberlain's actions at Munich, France's attitude towards the Czechoslovak issue and Ribbentrop's stupidity'.[9]

[9] Anita Prażmowska, *Britain, Poland and the Eastern Front, 1939*, 71.

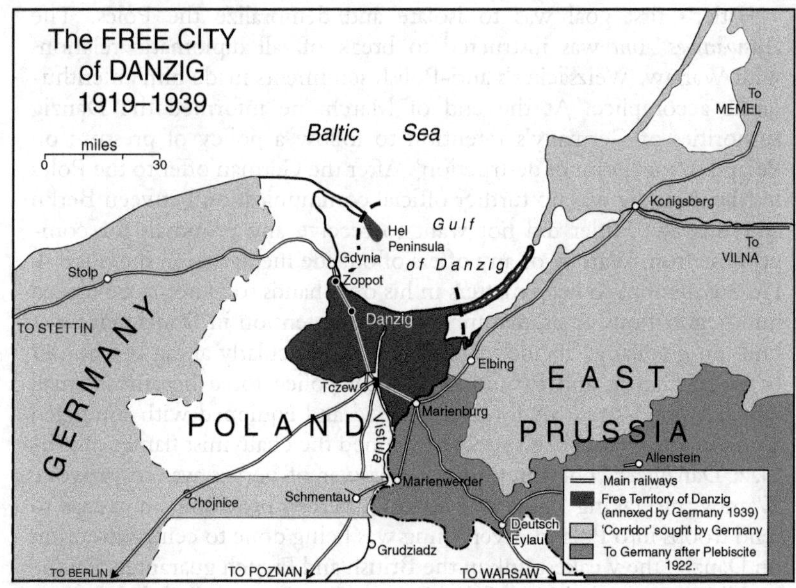

Map 13. The Free City of Danzig, 1919–1939

The under-secretary at the Polish Foreign Ministry informed the German ambassador that the Danzig crisis had to be defused and essential Polish rights acknowledged if Polish–German relations were to improve, but he also assured him that Poland was not involved in the western talks with Moscow. Poland would continue its previous policy of balancing between Germany and the Soviet Union. The British, whose interference and promptings were much resented, were given the same message. Poland would not resign its rights in Danzig or accept a *fait accompli* but would continue to negotiate the existing dispute. Any German attack on Danzig would be viewed as an attack on Poland's independence and territorial integrity. Beck intended to keep the conduct of relations with Germany in his own hands. With the fate of Czechoslovakia in mind and knowing that Halifax feared that Polish intransigence over Danzig might set off a European war, there was little incentive to consult London or allow the British to take over the talks with Berlin. Nor were the Poles willing to accept the mediation of the League's Danzig High Commissioner, Carl Burckhardt, a man whom Beck believed was in the German pocket and whom he distrusted and disliked. Offers by the Italians, the Japanese, and the pope to assist in the settlement of the dispute were similarly rejected. Beck still thought that war could be averted; he nurtured the illusion that Hitler was not yet ready to engage in conflict and would not fight for Danzig. Beck's stiff attitude had much to do with the unhelpful behaviour of the British and French whose attempts to separate the question of Danzig from the larger question of Polish–German relations fuelled his anxieties of a new 'Munich' at Polish expense. There was a streak of pure hubris and a misplaced sense of Polish power, given the wretched state of its army, in Beck's behaviour. For the Polish leader, there was no alternative to standing firm and calling Hitler's bluff.

In early July, the Germans heated up the 'war of nerves' and Danzig became the centre of international attention. Rumours were rife, including false reports (some spread by Göring anxious to discredit Ribbentrop) of an impending *coup*. Göring was not opposed to war with Poland but wanted to see Britain neutralized before action was taken. Few knew better how unready Germany was for a European struggle and how damaging it would be to his highly enjoyable existence if the *Luftwaffe* and the economy were put to the test. He posed as the man of peace, intending to convince the British that the German demands on Poland were justified and the blame for the escalating crisis lay with the hysterical Poles. Through a series of private interlocutors sent to London in the summer, he tried to detach Britain from France with promises of economic and industrial cooperation and the recognition of Britain's imperial interests.

There were stories, subsequently denied by Weizsäcker, that Hitler would visit Danzig on 20 July and that the free city would announce its adhesion to the Reich. Ribbentrop's personal representative in Paris (and the future Reich ambassador to Vichy) Otto Abetz, spread the news. Daladier took alarm and warned the German ambassador, who came rushing back to Paris, that any modification of the status quo in Danzig would bring the Franco-Polish agreement into action. To Ribbentrop's fury, Abetz was quietly expelled from France and two French journalists were arrested on charges of spying. Both men were found guilty of taking money to spread Nazi propaganda, Madame Bonnet was indirectly implicated, and Bonnet himself offered his resignation on 18 July though the exact cause was not clear. The foreign minister had toned down Daladier's sharp *démarche* in response to the false news but it, nevertheless, provoked a brutal and contemptuous reply from Ribbentrop, already in a highly nervous state because of his temporary loss of credibility. His unqualified assurances to Hitler that Britain and France would never fight were being contradicted by members of his own diplomatic staff as well as by Göring. Ribbentrop warned the French that the German army would march and annihilate Poland in response to any action or provocation. He accused Bonnet of going back on his supposed promise in December that France would disinterest herself in Germany's relations with her eastern neighbours. Bonnet's mild answer, denying the charge and intended primarily to calm the troubled waters, was unconvincing as a defence of French policy. The British were more circumspect about the *coup* rumours and had refused to make the public declaration over Danzig that Daladier requested. After a momentary panic, the Poles decided that there was no need to take alarm.

Despite 'incidents' in Danzig and in the Polish borderlands, the next two or three weeks of July were relatively quiet. There was a slow-down in the militarization of Danzig and in the build-up of German troops along the border. Even the German anti-Polish press campaign went into a lower gear. Albert Forster, the German gauleiter in Danzig, who was expected to play a Henlein-type role there, travelled back and forth to meet Hitler to inform him of the local situation. Despite the calm, both the French and British ambassadors reported on the growing number of reservists being called up in Germany and the curious way in which troop movements were announced and disguised. A more acute and balanced observer than Nevile Henderson, who was fiercely critical of Polish behaviour, the French ambassador, Robert Coulondre noted that the German general staff was acting as if a fixed date for action was settled. He thought that action would take place in August, after the harvest was gathered. There were some hopeful signs. The French *chargé*, who headed the French embassy in Berlin when Coulondre went on leave, informed the *Quai d'Orsay* that Hitler seemed to be hesitating and had lost confidence in Ribbentrop who had misled him about Britain. A strong Halifax speech on 29 June at Chatham House, and Chamberlain's warning in the House of Commons on 10 July that what happened in Danzig could not be considered 'as a purely local matter', was noted at the Wilhelmstrasse. Weizsäcker complained to Henderson that public warnings 'only made it more difficult for Herr Hitler to heed them' but admitted that he did not know which reports were actually read by the German leader.[10] Hitler went off to the Berghof on the Obersalzberg. The relaxation in tension, a deliberate German manoeuvre, was intended to pave the way for the final denouement which was to convince both the German people and the British that Poland's unacceptable behaviour was the cause of the German attack. This was also true of Forster's assurances to Carl Burckhardt in Danzig. The latter, who was already convinced that nothing could be done to stop Hitler from realising his demands, sought British help in calming the crisis. London duly pleaded with Beck for restraint and circumspection. The Polish leader was rightly suspicious; he

[10] Henderson to Halifax, 15 July, 1939, *DBFP*, 3rd Series, Vol. VI, No. 332.

doubted whether there had been any change in German policy and suspected that the German gesture was a ploy intended to divide Britain and Poland. There was no indication that the Danzig Senate intended to behave more reasonably; on the contrary, old difficulties over Polish customs and frontier guards in Danzig resurfaced. On 2 August, the under-secretary at the Polish Foreign Ministry told the British ambassador that he anticipated a crisis towards the end of August that could pass within a few hours from 'the political to the military phase'. He also admitted that the reports of military preparations in Danzig were somewhat exaggerated and thought that the Germans would hesitate before 'going to the length where a serious crisis must develop'.[11]

By early August, the mood had darkened. The German press campaign had resumed; it was expanded to include German demands to the entire Corridor, Posen, and parts of Upper Silesia. Much was made of the maltreatment of the German minority in Poland. In conjunction with the 25th anniversary of the outbreak of the 1914 war, notice was taken of Germany's improved defence position in case of a general conflict. German opinion, according to foreign journalists, was divided. Whereas some thought a war with Poland inevitable, others believed that Hitler would again triumph without a resort to arms. In Danzig, the dispute over the rights of inspection by Polish customs officials accelerated into a 'war of notes', the Danzig Senate acting throughout in close cooperation with the Reich government. Beck decided that the Senate's refusal to recognize the authority of some Polish border customs officials was the issue on which he would make his stand and, without consulting the British or French, successfully intimidated the Senate into backing down.

To Hitler's fury, the world press made much of the Senate's retreat. The Polish ambassadors in London, Paris, and Washington, in Professor D. C. Watt's words, 'positively glowed with confidence'. The German response, however, delivered to the Polish *chargé d'affaires* in Berlin on 9 August, was an unambiguous threat. Another ultimatum or threat of reprisal would lead to the 'aggravation' of Polish–German relations. The Polish reply was delivered in Warsaw the following day: in effect, the Germans were told to mind their own business. It was only after the event that Beck asked Halifax whether the British could take any action to reinforce the Polish stand. While Beck seemed to think that war might still be avoided, others presented a more frightening picture of Hitler's intentions. On 8 August, the Hungarian foreign minister was warned that 'unless Poland will see reason at the very last moment', the Polish army and the Polish state 'will be destroyed'.[12] No wonder the

[11] Sir H. Kennard to Viscount Halifax, 2 August 1939, *DBFP*, 3rd Series, Vol. VI, No. 519.
[12] *DGFP*, Ser. D, Vol. VI, No.784.

poor man took fright and hastened to counter the pro-Polish sympathies of his government. Three days later, with a minimum of ceremony, High Commissioner Burckhardt, accompanied by Forster, was flown to Salzburg and faced a furious Hitler at Berchtesgaden. The Führer could wait only if the Poles would leave Danzig calm and relieve the sufferings of the German minority in Poland. If there was the slightest incident, he would smash the Poles without warning and wipe Poland off the map. After telling Burckhardt that he could only laugh at the military strength of England and France and that nobody was going to scare him with the Russians, he said that he was prepared to conclude a pact with the British and suggested that a German-speaking Englishman could come to Berlin. 'Everything that I undertake is directed against Russia; if the West is too stupid and too blind to grasp this, I will be obliged to come to an understanding with the Russians, to defeat the West, and then after its downfall to turn with my assembled forces against the Soviet Union', he insisted.[13] The Führer, despite his 'cast iron convictions' that the western powers would not fight, was still trying to localize his coming war. Burckhardt conveyed Hitler's message to the British and French, as members of the League's Danzig committee. Beck, who was not consulted, was cautioned to exercise restraint. The French and probably the Soviet intelligence services were already reporting the date for the German offensive as late August.

II

Until mid-July, when Hitler took up the Soviet negotiations again, his diplomatic preparations for war were conducted in a low-key fashion and indeed there were weeks of almost total inaction. Hitler felt it necessary, after the Prague *coup*, to restore relations with Mussolini. Quite apart from those special feelings for Mussolini that persisted even when Italy was a lost cause, Hitler knew that any alliance with Italy depended on Mussolini's good will. To be sure, the German high command had little use for the Italian army and was only concerned that Italian needs should not interfere with German rearmament. Nothing that had happened in Spain had changed the German view. General Brauchitsch, who visited Italy and Libya after the talks between the German and Italian chiefs of staff in April 1939, had such a negative opinion of the Italian forces that he strongly opposed the alliance negotiations. Admiral Raeder was perhaps less contemptuous of the Italian fleet, the best prepared of the three services. As the Germans had neither the available ships nor the intention to share the patrolling of

[13] Carl J. Burckhardt, *Meine Danziger Mission, 1937–1939* (Munich, 1960), 348.

the Mediterranean, they had to rely on the Italian navy to check the western powers. Once Hitler had decided to attack Poland, there were good reasons for following up the earlier German initiatives for an alliance especially when it appeared that the Japanese would not agree to join an enlarged Anti-Comintern pact. At the least, Mussolini would discourage western meddling in Polish affairs and assist in the isolation of Poland.

The courting of Mussolini began almost immediately after Hitler's entry into Prague. The Duce had been hurt by Hitler's last-minute announcement of the *coup*. An irate Ciano wanted to denounce the Axis but Mussolini, with designs on the eastern Mediterranean and in south-eastern Europe, had every reason to move closer to Hitler. Concerned that the Germans might take up the Croatian cause and spoil his plans for Yugoslavia, Mussolini temporized. The Germans moved swiftly to apply balm to Mussolini's bruised ego. Ribbentrop, in an unctuous letter to Ciano intended for Mussolini, renewed the German promise to recognize Italy's exclusive rights in the Mediterranean, Adriatic, and adjacent zones. Mussolini, after reading Ribbentrop's letter, found the promise interesting, 'provided we can believe in it' but added, 'We cannot change our policy now. After all we are not prostitutes.'[14] Others among the Italian leadership were more scathing about the value of the German promises. In response, Mussolini prepared his own *fait accompli*, the invasion of Albania. Mussolini, indeed, indulged in further dreams of grandeur. In May, he started planning for the future invasion of Greece and Yugoslavia. Hopes for assistance as well as fears of isolation in the face of the hostile western reaction to the Albanian *coup*, pushed the Italians further in the direction of Germany. In the face of many warnings of the German attack on Poland, Mussolini planned for his own adventures. He was, unfortunately, encouraged by his military advisers. Ciano, writing in his diary after a meeting of the Council of Ministers on 29 April, complained that 'There has been a good deal of bluffing in the military sphere, and even the Duce himself has been deceived—a tragic bluff.'[15] On 8 May, the Duce summoned his generals to Palazzo Venezia and was given a very optimistic view of Italy's military prospects in a war, assurances which quite obviously coloured General Pariani's speech to the Chamber of Deputies two days later when he assured deputies that Italy was well prepared for the *Guerra di rapido corso*, a gross exaggeration.[16] The army was desperately short of everything from boots to motor cars. It consisted mostly of unreformed

[14] Galeazzo Ciano, *Diario 1937–1943* (Milan, 1946, 1998), 269 (20 March 1939).

[15] Ciano, *Diario*, 290 (29 April 1939).

[16] John Gooch, *Mussolini and His Generals*, 470–472. The idea was to prepare for a war of rapid movement.

infantry divisions not fit for combat in the field. In speeches to the Chamber of Deputies later in May, Cavagnari gave an equally upbeat picture of the naval situation, claiming that the navy had massed sufficient reserves 'even for a conflict of long duration'.[17] Notwithstanding the optimism of his service chiefs, Mussolini was fully aware of Italy's unpreparedness for war and the weakness of its financial and industrial structure. Instead of following a policy of circumspection, the Duce proceeded to conclude a military alliance that committed Italy to march with Germany without securing any real compensating safeguards.

The steps taken towards what Mussolini christened the 'Pact of Steel' predated the occupation of Albania. On 29 March, Daladier, convinced that Mussolini was intent on carrying out his expansionist programme at French expense, closed the hardly opened door of negotiations with a powerful radio speech reiterating his unwillingness to make any concessions to Italy. The Japanese were still debating the terms of the draft treaty for the German–Italian–Japanese alliance. On 2 April, the Germans rejected the new Japanese proposals as too narrowly conceived and sent them back to Tokyo for reconsideration. Though less concerned about the Japanese reservations, Ciano supported Ribbentrop's demand that the clause allowing the Japanese to reassure the British, French, and Americans that the pact was not directed against them should be removed. The whole idea of the pact was, for Ribbentrop (and Hitler) to bring the British to heel. Subsequent to the answers to the Japanese draft, on 5–6 April, Generals Pariani and Keitel met in Innsbruck. The Germans, in order to placate Mussolini after Prague, had initiated the contacts. The *Wehrmacht* chief of staff pledged German support for Italy in any future conflict. Under orders from Mussolini, Pariani referred to the possibility of an isolated war between France and Italy that would only require German material assistance. Keitel, hardly wanting Germany dragged into a conflict of Mussolini's making, denied that such a war could be localized. Pariani's unfortunate reference, repeated again when Ciano met Ribbentrop in Milan a month later, led the Germans to believe that, given Italy's aggressive plans against France, Mussolini would support them whatever the circumstances or timing of their action. The two chiefs of staff agreed that war against the western powers was inevitable but needed to be postponed until their countries were properly prepared. Pariani spoke of three or four years. Keitel warned that everything in Germany was being subordinated to the preparations for war and that once a certain level of efficiency was achieved, the Germans would launch a short campaign, but he said nothing about the operational plans to attack Poland. Pariani omitted to

[17] Gooch, *Mussolini and his Generals*, 474.

say anything about Albania. The two men parted company having misunderstood each other. Keitel believed that they had concurred that a war must be short since Italy was even less well placed to endure a long war than Germany. Pariani believed they had taken into account both types of war and had agreed to give one another reciprocal economic as well as military support. Sometime between 11–20 May, Pariani sent Mussolini an appreciation of Italy's strategic options that foresaw a quick war against France, which he thought the Axis could win.[18]

Göring arrived in Rome on 14 April and was officially received by Mussolini and Ciano. He assured the Duce that Germany did not wish to make an exclusive claim to south-east Europe or to act unilaterally on economic matters. It would recognize the Italian sphere of influence in Croatia. He obtained Mussolini's blessing for an approach to the Soviet Union and appeared to convince him that any war launched against France would entail British intervention. Göring strongly hinted that Hitler would settle the Polish question during 1939 and specifically linked the need to isolate Warsaw with the *rapprochement* with Moscow. The Duce summed up his impression of the discussions: Germany and Italy 'still needed two to three years in order to join in a general conflict well armed and with the prospect of victory'.[19] The conclusion of the pact was followed by attempts to give substance to the collaboration between the military, naval, and air staffs but the exchanges were limited in scope, as Hitler wished, and hardly encouraged hopes that the Italians would make substantial material or strategic gains from their new alliance.

Ribbentrop had taken up the possibility of a belated alliance with Italy because neither the Polish nor the Japanese situations were developing along the lines he wanted. He needed a diplomatic success to impress Hitler. Ciano, worried by reports from his ambassador in Berlin about German action against Poland and possible German intervention in the Balkans, invited Ribbentrop to Italy for exploratory talks. The foreign minister's hesitation in setting a date was due to renewed hopes that the Japanese would accept the extended pact. On 4 May, the Japanese reconfirmed their refusal to go beyond an anti-Soviet alliance. Faced with the navy's strong opposition to any anti-British or anti-American action, the Hiranuma government refused to consider an extension of the alliance. As this rejection blocked Ribbentrop's hopes to immobilize the British in preparation for the war against Poland, he had to change tactics. On 5 May, he left for a meeting with Ciano in Milan. The German foreign minister arrived with a memorandum containing a critical assessment of Italian policies and capabilities and two draft treaties

[18] See Gooch, *Mussolini and his Generals*, 471.

[19] Quotation from Mario Toscano, *The Origins of the Pact of Steel*, 249.

which were never shown to Ciano. Ribbentrop took great pains to court the Italians and to avoid the bombast of his previous visits. He reassured Ciano about German intentions towards Poland and towards Romania and Greece, leaving him under the impression that though a local war against Poland could not be ruled out, it would not take place immediately and no major war would result. The Italians assumed that Germany, like Italy, required a long period of preparation for war. Mussolini wanted a period of peace of not less than three years and military accords that 'would operate almost automatically', a demand that Ribbentrop put to excellent use to make the resulting treaty as binding as possible.[20] Ciano, who had long distrusted and disliked Ribbentrop, was, nevertheless, partly disarmed by his assurances. On this occasion, Ribbentrop proved too clever by half and Ciano not clever enough.

III

The bargain was struck. Mussolini, wanting to make a diplomatic splash and to impress the French, urged that a public announcement be made of the imminent conclusion of the alliance. Hitler gave his assent. Ciano left the drafting of the treaty entirely to Ribbentrop without providing any statement of the Italian terms. The Italian foreign minister admitted that the treaty, which bore no resemblance to the cautious and limited Wilhelmstrasse drafts 'contains some real dynamite' but suggested no changes of substance. Presented to the Italians on 12 May, it was an offensive alliance directed against Britain and France without any of the usual window dressing. Article III stipulated immediate help regardless of whether the conflict had been provoked by one of the partners. This weakened from the start the provisions made for consultation. Mussolini gave his approval; he could now ignore a papal suggestion of 3 May for a five-power conference to discuss both the Franco–Italian and German–Polish controversies (in any case, he despised the pope) and could take a tougher line with the French. Ribbentrop was decorated with the Order of the Annunziata, making him one of twenty-four honorary cousins of the king of Italy, infuriating the jealous Göring. The Duce saw the alliance as a demonstration of Axis unity. He knew that it brought the danger of war with the western powers closer but he was blinded by the prospect of alliance with the strongest military power in Europe. By their own lights, the Italians were acting rationally but were seriously miscalculating. Even Ciano's customary laziness about details hardly explains why most of the trump cards were given to Hitler. There was nothing in writing about the three year period of peace or anything said about Poland. The Italians had

[20] C. J. Lowe and F. Marzari, *Italian Foreign Policy, 1870–1940* (London, 1975), 332.

not even secured in return the implementation of Hitler's 1938 promise to transfer the German-speaking population of the South Tyrol to Germany. War broke out before any agreement was signed and only a virtual ultimatum and an Italian undertaking to reimburse the ethnic Germans at a highly favourable exchange rate secured a German signature to the agreement on 21 October 1939.[21]

The 'Pact of Steel' was signed in Berlin on 22 May. Ribbentrop again assured Ciano that Germany wanted a long period of peace and would preserve the *status quo* in the Balkans. Hitler confirmed that 'Mediterranean policy will be directed by Italy' and was enthusiastic about making Albania 'a stronghold which will inexorably dominate the Balkans'.[22] One day after the signing, Hitler told his generals of his decision to attack Poland. Mussolini was not informed. He knew nothing of the distinctions Hitler drew between the local war against Poland and the more ambitious war against the western powers. Many items of intelligence were reaching Rome and Mussolini felt uneasy. On 30 May, Mussolini sent Hitler a memorandum describing war with the democracies as inevitable but stressing that Italy would not be ready for combat until 1943. The Führer assured the Duce that he was totally in accord with the contents of the memorandum but made no formal commitment. Hitler had told his generals on 23 May that he would attack Poland as soon as possible.

The news from Moscow may have been the reason for Mussolini's memorandum. On 6 May, Hans von Herwarth of the German embassy in Moscow informed his Italian colleague that the Nazi leadership was seeking an alliance with the Soviets. The Soviet *chargé d'affaires* and NKVD *rezident* in Rome apparently substantiated this information in his many conversations with Ciano. On 13 June, Mussolini and Ciano told the German ambassador that they knew of 'certain steps' being taken with Moscow and warned that this might endanger the Axis. By late June, rumours were circulating about the impending Nazi–Soviet agreements, including Polish partition, within informed European circles. The Hungarians, who wanted Italian support for their claims on Transylvania, kept the Italians well informed of Hitler's plans. By early June, the Duce had told Ciano that 'war was now inevitable and would explode in August.'[23] Despite his knowledge of Hitler's plans to attack Poland and the German overtures to the Soviet Union, Mussolini made

[21] The South Tyrol dispute was to push Mussolini to authorise the rapid reinforcement of the northern frontier and provoked his warning to the Dutch and Belgian ambassadors in late December 1939 that the Germans were about to invade their countries.

[22] Ciano, *Diario*, 299 (21–23 May 1939).

[23] Quoted in Brian R. Sullivan, 'Italy', in Neville Wylie (ed.), *European Neutrals and Non-Belligerents during the Second World War*, 133.

no attempt to restrain Hitler during the ensuing months but rather proceeded with his own planning for moves in the Balkans.

For the Duce, the alliance with Germany was a powerful offensive military alliance directed against the democracies. Immediately after the pact was signed, the Duce told his military chiefs that 'war between the plutocratic and egotistically conservative nations and the populous and poor nations is inevitable. On this premise, we need to prepare ourselves.'[24] The alliance was a green light for Mussolini's own programme of expansion. During the preparatory period, he could exploit Italy's stronger diplomatic position in the Mediterranean and Balkans. He began at once to dabble in Croatian separatism for control of Albania and Croatia was the necessary prerequisite for Italy's war in the Mediterranean. 'Immediately on the outbreak of war, we must seize the Balkans and the entire Danubian basin. We will not be content with declarations of neutrality; we will occupy these territories and exploit them for military, alimentary and industrial supplies. This operation which should be swift', he told his three service chiefs, 'and carried out with extreme decisiveness, not only would knock out the "guarantees" for Greece, Romania and Turkey but would provide us with security [in our rear]'.[25] Knowing that war was imminent, the Duce speeded up his plans for a 'parallel war', intending to move into Croatia, Greece, and Romania. There were discussions with the Hungarians, known to Admiral Horthy, and planning began for the moves into Romania and Greece though no operational plans were concluded. Mussolini and Pariani seem to have ignored the Italian army's total unpreparedness for such offensives.

IV

Hitler knew that the alliance with Italy was not really a substitute for a German–Italian–Japanese front against Britain. It would, at least, discourage London and Paris from intervening on Poland's behalf and make more difficult any moves to detach Italy from Germany. Mussolini, indeed, was openly hostile towards both Britain and France. When the Duce finally received Percy Loraine, the new British ambassador, on 27 May, he delivered a blistering attack on Britain's policies. Loraine stood his ground but warned Halifax that the 'die is cast and that the only argument is the visibility of overwhelming physical strength'.[26] Frozen out, Loraine ultimately saw Mussolini only twice and made little

[24] Quoted in Reynolds Salerno, *Vital Crossroads: Mediterranean Origins of the Second World War 1935–1940* (Ithaca and London, 2002), 126.

[25] Quoted in Salerno, *Vital Crossroads*, 127.

[26] *DBFP*, 3rd ser., Vol. V. No 653.

headway with his instructions 'to burn no bridges which one day the Italians might wish to re-cross'.[27] The even more unpopular François-Poncet could make no progress in restarting the talks with Ciano. A stinging speech from Daladier on 12 May insisting that there would be no concessions ended the would-be talks before they began, though it did not end French efforts to reach the Italians. At the end of May, Mussolini told Ciano that he had no intention of easing relations with France and was determined to annex Tunisia and Corsica. However, the strident German tone about Danzig in June and the realization that, once again, there was no consultation with Rome, began to worry the Italians. The Italian ambassador in Berlin, primed by Germans alarmed by the increasing influence of the 'hawks' in Berlin, sent off a series of warnings to Ciano. At first, the Italian foreign minister, distracted by the death of his father at the end of June and not informed of all of Mussolini's war plans, ridiculed Attolico's fears and dismissed the ambassador's prediction of an attack on Danzig before 14 August. Ciano and Mussolini decided that the German–Polish dispute would end in a compromise and agreed that the meeting between the two dictators scheduled for the first week of August could be postponed until the following month.

Mussolini, with that strange combination of self-assurance and doubt when it came to dealing with Hitler, became increasingly uneasy. On 24 July, he launched a new idea, a proposal for an international conference that would deal with the Danzig problem. Even so, he assured Hitler that if Germany were to mobilize, Italy would do the same and at the same time. In a secret communication intercepted by the British, he told Hitler 'clearly and unmistakably' that though he would like to postpone the war, 'if the Führer really thinks that today is the proper moment, then Italy is one hundred percent ready'.[28] Two days later, Ribbentrop rejected the conference idea. On 31 July, Hitler intervened and cancelled the Brenner meeting.

It was only in the first week of August that Ciano, just back from two weeks in Spain, and Mussolini, faced with a variety of worrying reports that the western democracies would back Poland by force and that the British, French, Greeks, and Turks would seize the Dodecanese, defend Salonika against Italian attack, overrun Bulgaria, attack Libya, and invade northern Italy, took fright. The two men were convinced that the war with Poland could not be localized and that a general war would

[27] *DBFP*, 3rd ser., Vol. V, No. 593; quoted in John Herman, *The Paris Embassy of Sir Eric Phipps* (Brighton, 1998), 163.
[28] *DDI*, 8th ser., Vol. XII, No. 662.

be 'disastrous' for everybody. The Germans were ominously silent. Mussolini demanded that Ciano and Ribbentrop meet.

Ciano went off to meet Ribbentrop, at the latter's lovely country home near Salzburg confiscated from a Jew murdered by the Gestapo, and then went on to Berchtesgaden to see Hitler. The foreign minister returned from his three day visit (11–13 August) a very frightened man, 'completely disgusted with the Germans, their leader, with their way of doing things. They have betrayed and lied to us. Now they are dragging us into an adventure which we do not want and may compromise the regime and the country as a whole.'[29] Ciano was left in no doubt that the Germans intended to attack Poland and would defeat, annihilate, and annex her in the same way as they had Austria and Czechoslovakia. He asked, 'Is it only Danzig that you want?' 'No', replied Ribbentrop. 'We want much more than that. We want war.'[30] Hitler made the same points the next day at Berchtesgaden. He worked himself into a rage over 'Polish brutalities', culminating in declaring his determination to 'liquidate' the situation before 15 October. He dismissed Ciano's fears that the western powers would intervene but spoke of their defeat at the hands of the Axis should they do so. Neither the Russians, with whom talks had begun, nor the Americans, who were more isolationist than ever, would take any part. All protestations were swept aside, as was Mussolini's idea for an international conference; a diplomatic solution that hardly suited the Führer's purpose. To sweeten the bitter pill, Hitler suggested that Italy might settle its accounts with Yugoslavia by seizing Croatia. Thanks to German informants, the British knew the truth about the meeting but proved unwilling to give the cautionary warnings that the Kordt brothers wanted.

There followed days of intense activity, anguish and despair, as the angry and humiliated Ciano, assisted by Attolico, the ambassador in Berlin, used every conceivable argument to persuade Mussolini to stand aside from this suicidal war. The Duce was like a weather vane on a windy day. 'Honour' compelled him to march alongside the Germans. If, as he believed (he had good intelligence sources and Loraine was unambiguous in his warnings) the western powers would fight for Poland, common sense dictated a policy of neutrality. If, however, by some chance they did not fight, as Hitler's partner, Italy would be assured of its share of the spoils. Should the Allies compel Italy to go to war, Italy would first secure the defences of its borders at home and in the colonies, and then, after a brief pause, prepare an attack on Greece with the object of seizing Salonika. Should circumstances permit, after

[29] Ciano, *Diario*, 327 (13 August 1939).

[30] Quoted in D. C. Watt, *How War Came*, 426.

fomenting disorder in Yugoslavia, the Italians would take control of Croatia to secure the use of its material resources.[31] Though Marshal Badoglio warned that the Allies would move against the Italians in North Africa, Mussolini thought the gains in the Balkans would be worth the losses in North Africa. Before the end of August, the army had revised its plans for offensive operations against Greece and Yugoslavia and planning proceeded for counter-offensives in Tunisia, Egypt, Djibouti and British Somalia, and in the Aegean.[32] In mid-August, nonetheless, the realities of the situation caused both Pariani and Cavagnari to retreat. The former warned that Italy could not launch an offensive in the Balkans on its own while Cavagnari admitted that he had no workable naval strategy for a war against England and France. Marshal Badoglio repeated his warnings of Italy's vulnerability to French attack. Ciano increased his efforts to persuade Mussolini against involving a totally unprepared Italy in a war with Britain and France against the will of the overwhelming majority of Italians. He had the support of Vittorio Emanuele III, who had attended the late August manoeuvres of the army of the Po in late August and had found its preparedness 'pathetic'. Warnings from the minister of currency and exchange as well as the complaints from the service chiefs about inadequate stocks of raw materials added weight to Ciano's admonitions. On 17 August, Ribbentrop was told that the Italians did not believe that a conflict with Poland could be localized and that Italy was in no condition to engage in war. Nothing was actually settled. While the debate was raging, the Hungarian foreign minister, Count Csáky, suddenly appeared in Rome, to propose an alliance with the Axis that he hoped would save Hungary from a German invasion or 'friendly occupation'. The Hungarian people, he claimed, hated the Germans and Horthy called them 'buffoons and brigands'. Mussolini was not impressed, though Csáky, was prepared to offer the throne of Hungary to the Duke of Aosta, the cousin of the Italian king. Mussolini's reaction may have been due to Badoglio's highly negative view of the military value of the Hungarians.

Caught between 'the fear of war and the fear to reveal his fear of war', Mussolini refused to caution Hitler that Italy would not follow Germany to war.[33] Of all the Great Powers, Italy was the least equipped to engage in conflict yet no European state spent proportionately more on military and pacification campaigns during the 1930s. Most of the money allotted to the armed services was consumed by the wars in

[31] For details of Mussolini's conversation with Marshal Badoglio on 16 August, see Gooch, *Mussolini and his Generals*, 484–485.

[32] Salerno, *Vital Crossroads*, 135.

[33] Quoted in Lowe and Marzari, *Italian Foreign Policy, 1870–1940*, 340.

Ethiopia, Spain, and Albania and in the pacification of Italian East Africa (some 77 billion out of a total of 116 billion lire between 1935 and 1940). Little was left for the much needed modernization programmes.[34] The Ethiopian and Spanish wars left the army and air force stripped of essential equipment and with serious supply and transport problems. Still predominately an agricultural country, a good part of the Italian armament industry was technologically backward and incapable of turning out the large numbers of modern arms, motorized vehicles, and aircraft required to replace what was lost in fighting and keep pace with the other rearming nations. The army was desperately short of trained officers and NCOs. The air force suffered from a shortage of trained pilots, spare parts, petrol, and modern aircraft; the outdated biplane was only abandoned in favour of all-metal mono-wing fighters in mid-1939. The navy, which had suffered least in the campaigns in Ethiopia and Spain, and was supposedly the best equipped of the three services for action, could do little more than provide protection for the fast transport convoys moving between eastern Sicily and coastal Libya. It could not take the offensive in the Mediterranean.[35] Despite the drive for autarky, Italy continued to suffer from an acute shortage of raw materials and had to import coal, iron, and other mineral ores as well as oil, for which hard currency and high prices had to be paid. Continental imports of oil covered only a small percentage of what was used each year in peacetime and none of the armed services had extensive reserves in store. Italy had sufficient forces and resources to mount small wars, though even these had been badly fought. It was not ready to fight in the big league.

Mussolini was aware of the deficiencies of his services. The manoeuvres of the newly created Sixth Army in August 1939 were a public disgrace. The very best units in the Italian army provided a highly embarrassing spectacle of outmoded equipment and incapable direction for the outraged king and foreign military attachés who struggled to hide their discomfort. The Duce's confidence in securing Italy's place in the Mediterranean and Balkans depended on avoiding any major conflict until 1943 or 1944 and on German acceptance of the future division of the spoils. Mussolini had many moments of self-deception but he was lucid enough to recognize that Italy needed both time and German assistance to spring outside its cage.

[34] Brian Sullivan, 'The Italian Armed Forces, 1918–1940', in Allan R. Millett and Williamson Murray (eds.), *Military Effectiveness* (London, 1987), 171, 191. The Ethiopian war consumed 39 billion lire worth of military equipment, Spain some seven to nine billion (including 7.7 million shells, 319 million rounds of small arms ammunition, 7,400 motor vehicles, 1.8 million uniforms).

[35] Salerno, *Vital Crossroads*, 134.

Mussolini vacillated in August, when it became clear that Hitler was going to accelerate his timetable for war, not just out of 'honour' but from the temptation of winning the glittering prizes that he had so long sought. Ciano struggled to prevent any promise to the Germans of unconditional support and to rescue Italy from the entanglements of the pact that he had so enthusiastically signed. He told his father-in-law that 'The Germans—not we—have betrayed the alliance in which we were associates not servants. Rip up the pact, throw it in Hitler's face and Europe will recognize you as the natural leader of the anti-German crusade.'[36] It was a revolution in Italian policy that Mussolini could not accept. Ciano did extract a personal letter from Mussolini to Hitler that, despite its complicated chicaneries, was a statement of Italian neutrality should Germany attack Poland and Britain and France intervene. Ciano's efforts to meet Ribbentrop to deliver the message revealed the news that the German foreign minister was about to go to Moscow to sign a political pact with the Soviets. Mussolini's message of caution to Hitler remained undelivered. Opportunism triumphed, at least temporarily.

Hitler appears not to have been unduly concerned about the signs of Italian wobbling and showed no inclination to alter his timetable. This may have been a mark of his ultimate confidence in Mussolini's loyalty or of the strength of his belief that Britain and France would not fight. By this time, too, he was looking to the Soviet Union. The German high command continued to take a dim view of cooperation with the Italians. Joint discussions between the service chiefs neither progressed very far nor brought satisfaction to either side. No precise information was exchanged and no move made to create joint staffs. It was only on the very eve of the attack on Poland that Hitler had to face the possibility of an Italian scuttle.

V

Hitler assured the Italians and his own military commanders that Britain and France would not intervene in Germany's war with Poland. The same message was repeated by Ribbentrop over and over again. Hitler's relative passivity with regard to the Anglo-French-Soviet talks until mid-July suggests that he did not believe that they would succeed. Once his own talks with Moscow began, his confidence with regard to isolating Poland was strengthened. He was convinced that, in the last resort, the western democracies would not unleash a general war. He had been warned, both in public and private, that the western powers would stand by their guarantee to Poland. Chamberlain, in the

[36] Ciano, *Diario*, 331 (21 August 1939).

Commons and outside, declared that 'no undertaking by Hitler would be of any use; and that the resumption of negotiations between London and Berlin depended on a demonstration of Hitler's resolve to abandon the use of force'.[37] The message was somewhat less clear than these statements suggested. All through the summer months, Chamberlain and Daladier clung to the hope that war could be avoided or at least postponed.[38] Chamberlain and Halifax assumed that the guarantee to Poland and subsequent warnings were sufficient to convince Hitler not to resort to force. The prime minister believed that anyone threatened with the prospect of war with the British Empire would draw back. At the same time, because he wanted to keep the door open to negotiation, his warnings were accompanied by offers of future talks to negotiate the differences between Britain and Germany. After a secret meeting between Ralph Makins, a Foreign Office official, and Carl Burckhardt in Geneva on 11 June, Makins reported that Weizsäcker believed that 'the best chance for peace was that England should maintain a solid front, "un silence menaçant". Otherwise Herr von Ribbentrop would again succeed with his thesis that the British would not march. He thought that 'the door to negotiations should be kept ajar, but only just'.[39]

Unfortunately for all concerned, the so-called 'menacing silence' failed to convince Hitler of Britain's resolve to act. Official exchanges between London and Berlin were limited; the British waited for a sign that never came and Hitler refused to provide any opportunity for British meddling in Polish affairs. The prime minister's speeches in any case sounded more equivocal in Berlin than in London. The official British reply to Hitler's speech of 28 April denouncing the Anglo-German naval agreement was only sent to Berlin on 23 June. The British specifically denied Hitler's contention that the agreement had been made in exchange for a German 'free hand' in Eastern Europe but held out an olive branch. If the Germans wanted to negotiate another agreement, the British government was prepared to receive proposals. Chamberlain told the cabinet that he did not think a naval agreement would be useful as there was no assurance that the agreement would be kept.

Still, the door was not shut. The message that negotiations were possible should Hitler make some gesture to restore international confidence was repeated through 'discreeter channels'. A progression of British visitors to Germany, authorized or encouraged by Horace Wilson,

[37] *Ironside Diaries 1937–1940*, 77, quoted in Sidney Aster, *1939: The Making of the Second World War*, 217.

[38] Quoted in Sidney Aster, 'Guilty Men: The Case of Neville Chamberlain', in Robert Boyce and Esmonde M. Robertson (eds.), *Paths to War* (Basingstoke and London, 1989), 254–255.

[39] *DBFP*, 3rd ser., Vol. VI, No. 36.

Chamberlain, or both, conveyed the government's wish to find grounds for agreement. Their interventions served to soften the impact of firmer official statements, especially since some of the visitors conveyed false impressions of British policy. In May, Henry Drummond-Wolff, an ex-MP and a member of the Council of Empire Industries Association, made a private visit to Berlin. Briefed by Horace Wilson, he saw Wohlthat and a Foreign Ministry economic official and hinted at concessions in south-east Europe and a British loan to cover Germany's foreign exchange problems. At the end of July, the industrialist, E. W. Tennant, a friend of Ribbentrop, and long-time publicist of good Anglo-German relations, went off to Fishl, Ribbentrop's country home near Salzburg. Sharing a train journey with Walther Hewel, Ribbentrop's liaison officer with Hitler, he learned that Hitler was convinced that the Jews had so much power in the British government that there was 'nothing to be done but to fight it out'.[40] Tennant, already disillusioned with Hitler and suspicious of his future intentions, assured his German hosts of Britain's pacific intentions and hopes for an Anglo-German settlement. His memorandum of 31 July sent to Chamberlain explained his view:

> The united, dynamic, very young German nation is something tremendous which is definitely there, and we should, I feel, make more effort to understand it, work with it and accept it. It is now too late to attempt to dam up this terrible force. The last chance of doing this would have been at the time of the march into the Rhineland. We can now only try to guide them and this we can only begin to do if we get on to more friendly terms.[41]

Tennant was not untypical of the group of the older enthusiasts who had been shocked by the march into Prague and who now believed that war might be inevitable but still hoped there was some possibility of peace. Arthur Bryant, the popular historian and enthusiastic Germanophile, who had few such fears, also saw Hewel during a private visit to Germany in July. Bryant's adulatory views of Hitler and Nazi Germany reflected the opinions of only a tiny minority of Germanophiles still active in the summer of 1939. Hewel promised to pass on Bryant's positive picture of Britain's future German policy and the possibilities of peace to Hitler. When reviewing Bryant's report on these exchanges, Chamberlain found the author 'naïve' and many of Hewel's recommendations for improved relations 'obviously' impossible. More damaging, because Hitler was personally involved, was the visit of Lord

[40] R. A. C. Parker, *Chamberlain and Appeasement*, 265–266.

[41] Richard Griffiths, *Fellow Travellers of the Right: British Enthusiasts for Nazi Germany 1933–1939* (Oxford, 1983), 364. This was not his view at the time of the Rhineland crisis.

Kemsley, the newspaper proprietor and owner of the *Sunday Times* and *Daily Sketch* to Germany in late July. Kemsley and Otto Dietrich, Hitler's press chief, agreed to exchange newspaper articles on the respective policies and attitudes of their countries. Bryant was to prepare the first British contribution. Dietrich arranged a meeting for Kemsley with Hitler at Bayreuth on 27 July. The Führer spoke vaguely but agreed that each country should put its demands on paper and that this could lead to a general discussion. With only Cadogan informed, Chamberlain, Horace Wilson, and Halifax prepared a draft answer for Kemsley to send to Dietrich for Hitler's perusal. Chamberlain penned an additional sentence emphasizing the need for Hitler to do something to restore confidence before any steps could be taken. The efforts to preserve secrecy proved unnecessary for Hitler never responded. These initiatives, no single one important in itself, confirmed Hitler's belief that Britain did not want war and would try to avoid it. He shut out those messages that he did not wish to hear. The case for coercive deterrence was hardly helped by Nevile Henderson's presence in Berlin. The ambassador just could not accept that his 'mission' might fail and continued his efforts all through the summer to seek grounds for accommodation. His lack of sympathy for the Poles hardly reinforced the British case for firmness.

Some visitors to Britain in the summer of 1939 were not members of the German opposition circles but advocates of Anglo-German cooperation, associated in some way with Herman Göring. Axel Wenner-Gren, a wealthy Swedish businessman, well-acquainted with Göring, was referred to Chamberlain by the Conservative chief whip. He met the prime minister on 6 June. He suggested that Göring would welcome new proposals on Poland and that Britain should offer colonies in return for German assurances of peace. Chamberlain insisted that confidence would have to be restored before discussions could begin and that Hitler would have to take the initiative. Göring proved cool to the suggestions and no approach to Hitler was made. The second of the 'diplomatic interlopers' was a more important figure. Helmuth Wohlthat, the deputy head of the Four-Year Plan who had carried off the successful Romanian treaty, knew Schacht and had excellent contacts in the City of London. A frequent visitor to London in connection with conferences on refugees and whaling, he secured Göring's permission to informally raise the possibility of an Anglo-German agreement with Horace Wilson. On 6 and 7 June and again on 18 and 31 July, he saw Wilson who seems to have told him that the German government had to take measures to reduce tension before any discussions could begin. Wohlthat's report to Göring, however, stressed the benefits that would flow from cooperation, especially easier access to world markets through colonial developments and joint economic planning. The subject was taken up again when Wohlthat returned to London in July as head of the German delegation to the International Whaling Conference. He again saw Horace Wilson and Robert Hudson, the self-important and ambitious political head of the Department of Overseas Trade. The latter seems to have ranged far and wide and speculated on the fruits of Anglo-German co-operation. Delighted by his own performance, Hudson was indiscreet at an evening dinner party and the next morning, reports appeared in the *Daily Telegraph* and *News Chronicle* of a huge British loan to the Germans in return for international control of German rearmament after a conference settling the Danzig question in Germany's favour. An uproar in London followed. There was a denial in the *Sunday Times* on 23 July and a somewhat evasive admission by Chamberlain in the Commons that Wohlthat had seen Wilson but that no loan was under consideration and Hudson was speaking privately. The prime minister was furious with Hudson, whom he suspected of not telling the whole truth but did not wish to add to his own troubles by dismissing him. Despite the harm done in Moscow where the worst gloss was put on the Hudson–Wohlthat talks, Chamberlain optimistically concluded that Hitler knew that Britain meant business and that 'the time was not ripe for a major war'.[42] He could not have been more mistaken.

Wohlthat's report to Ribbentrop, prepared on 24 July and written with the assistance of Dirksen, the German ambassador in London, was a compilation of many proposals extending from a no resort to force declaration, revision of the Treaty of Versailles, and an arms limitation agreement, to proposals for common policies on materials and markets and loans for the *Reichsbank*. All these recommendations were attributed to Horace Wilson. Ribbentrop only sensed the danger of a diplomatic crisis at the end of the month. By the summer of 1939, Ambassador Dirksen had concluded that Britain would go to war over Poland. In assisting Wohlthat, he had hoped to convince his chief that Britain would compromise but only if negotiations were conducted in the normal way. Instead, Ribbentrop used his assurances that Chamberlain was open to negotiation as confirmation of his own judgement that Britain would not fight. On 14 August, Dirksen left London for his summer leave. Like the German ambassador in Paris, he was told not to return to his post. Neither Ribbentrop nor Hitler saw him; they did not wish to hear his message. An intercepted, indiscreet, exchange with the Italian ambassador in Berlin ended his career and he retired to his estates in East Prussia.

[42] Quoted in Watt, *How War Came*, 401.

The third interloper, Birger Dahlerus, another Swedish businessman, an associate of Wenner-Gren and a long-time friend of Göring, played his part in the final weeks of the Danzig crisis. Though warned by Göring that approaches from parties, 'which we can trace to England or believe have come from England, are seen as a sign of weakness on the part of England', Dahlerus came to London at the end of July and met Lord Halifax who encouraged his plans to arrange a secret meeting between Göring and a group of British businessmen. The meeting was not a success; the head of the Four-Year Plan reacted negatively to the businessmen's exposition of British opinion and his angry reply ended with proposals that were in the nature of an ultimatum. Nothing was suggested that the Foreign Office could take up. It was thought that the meeting had not done much good but had caused little harm. Göring's account of the meeting, sent to Hitler, only confirmed his master's view that Britain would seek any alternative to war. Dahlerus played his major role in late August when the unsuspecting Swedish go-between was used by Göring in his power struggle with Ribbentrop to get the British to abandon the Polish guarantee. During these weeks, Dahlerus benefited from Chamberlain's and Halifax's reluctance to face the reality of war. Never quite taken seriously, he encouraged the British leaders to think that the situation was not hopeless and that Hitler might compromise when in fact he was determined on war.

Whatever might have been the muddied signals, Hitler was aware of the high degree of risk involved in counting on British acquiescence in an attack on Poland. It is true that he trusted his instincts, confirmed by their behaviour at Munich, that men like Chamberlain and Daladier would not lead their states to war. The worn-out democracies had no stomach for conflict. Ribbentrop, often in Hitler's presence during these weeks, stoked his misplaced confidence. But Ribbentrop had failed to deliver on his promised triple alliance and the talks between Britain, France, and the Soviet Union continued raising the spectre of a second front. During the summer months, too, Hitler became convinced that Chamberlain as well as Roosevelt was coming under the influence of the Jews and that the rise of anti-Nazi feeling in Britain could be attributed to the Jewish control over the media. The realities of the situation, that both the British and Americans were trying to control the influx of Jewish refugees and that there was a much noted growth of anti-Semitic feeling in both countries, made no impression on the German leader. It was the fear that Britain and the Soviet Union would strike a bargain and the exigencies of his military timetable that led Hitler to Moscow.

A massive propaganda campaign demonized the Poles; in July and August, there was a relentless agitation against the Polish atrocities. 'The terrible treatment and mistreatment of the German population by fanatic Polaks has aroused the greatest animosity', a district committee report for July–August noted, 'and one repeatedly hears people remark that it is time the Führer intervened'.[43] Much was made in Germany of the country's 'encirclement', a popular catchword. Britain as well as Poland became hate objects. Victor Klemperer, a professor of comparative philology, defined as a Jew but married to a Christian, noted in his diary on 27 June 'The propaganda campaign against England more vociferous every day, even more vociferous than against Poland; every day new emphasis on the absolute defencelessness and helplessness of England, its humiliation by Japan, its prostration before Russia, its songs of hate against Germany.'[44] Hitler's great popularity in the summer of 1939 owed much to his bloodless foreign policy successes and to the expectation that Poland would be added to the list. Curiously enough, given his instructions to the press chiefs after Munich that the German people had to be made 'war worthy', little was done to psychologically prepare the population for war until the massive late summer propaganda campaign.

There were few signs of the tension and depression that characterized the weeks before Munich. Hitler's previous 'successes' at Munich and Prague justified German faith in the Führer. After Prague, congratulations showered down on Hitler from classrooms, universities, and churchmen of both confessions. School children called him 'General Bloodless'. Hitler's fiftieth birthday was a celebration of the apostle of peace; few expected a European war. At most, some anticipated a localized war against Poland that could be easily won, a kind of '*Blumenkrieg*' ('flower war') as in 1938. During the second half of August, the popular mood darkened and anxieties increased but the great majority of Germans still believed that the British were bluffing and would not fight for Poland as they had not fought for Czechoslovakia.

'Trust in the Fuhrer' ran one *Kreisleitung* report, 'and pride in German policy among the population is boundless. Everyone is sympathetic.'[45] After his Reichstag speech of 28 April, Hitler avoided public appearances. The endless rallies, parades, and military demonstrations, intended to demonstrate German invincibility, were used both to inspire

[43] Quoted in Marlis G. Steinert, *Hitler's War and the Germans: Public Mood and Attitude during the Second World War,* ed. and trs. By Thomas E. J. de Witt (Athens, OH, 1977), 42.

[44] Victor Klemperer, *I Shall Bear Witness: The Diaries of Victor Klemperer, 1933–41* transl. Martin Chalmers (London, 1998), 290.

[45] Quoted in R. J. Overy, 'Hitler's War Plans and the Economy', in Overy, *War and Economy in the Third Reich*, 201.

confidence and underline the dangers faced by the Reich. The intensified pace of rearmament, it is true, created, as a later report sent to the Bank of England from Berlin in October 1939 stated, 'plenty of minor grumbling but no serious discontent'.[46] Reports from party and government officials characterized the public mood as 'calm and reliable' despite many accounts of local dissatisfaction. Shortages in the shops and poor quality goods, along with high taxes and forced savings programmes, had already cut into consumption levels. Butcher shops and greengrocers ran short of meat and produce, ostensibly because food had to be stored for the army. Workers complained against the Four-Year Plan regulations; labour was directed to jobs, movement was restricted, and strict wage controls kept wage rates at depression levels. A report from the governor of the Pfalz on 10 August noted 'heavy resentment among large segments of the population, in particular, the workers, employees, and civil servants, over the unjustifiably high food prices'.[47] Domestic housing construction had almost come to a standstill. It appears, however, that this did not lead to any opposition that the state could not handle. Contrary to what was reported by British and French intelligence services, there was no political threat to the stability of the regime and no questioning of the preparations for war which were having an increasing impact on the civilian population.[48] The state possessed unlimited powers of persuasion and coercion; the natural leaders of resistance were in prison or had fled and the mass of workers were either resigned or apathetic. People concentrated on the problems of everyday life and did not challenge the system. In so far as the German population reflected on Germany's enhanced position in the world and the still more extraordinary future which Hitler and his dedicated followers promised, present privations were the necessary cost for future victory. Hitler's dreams had become part of the reality of everyday life. There was no question about the loyalty of the masses to the regime and, above all, to the Führer, who embodied the will of the nation.[49]

For Hitler, war was more than a natural part of the international order. War was central to his thought and actions. The 'compulsion to wage war' was embedded in the fanaticism of the leader, and his most fervent

[46] Quoted in R. J. Overy, 'Hitler's War Plans and the Economy', 225. Quotation in fn. 64.

[47] Quoted in Steinert, *Hitler's War and the Germans*, 31.

[48] See the debate 'Germany, "Domestic Crisis" and War in 1939' between David Kaiser, Tim Mason and Richard Overy, *Past and Present* 116 (1987) and 122 (1989); Tim Mason, *Nazism, Fascism and the Working Class* (Cambridge, 1995), 33–52, 104–130, 205–322. Also see comment by Tooze: 'In 1939 there was no crisis in the Third Reich, either political or economic', in *Wages of Destruction*, 321.

[49] For a thought provoking exploration of these issues, see Michael Geyer, 'The Nazi Pursuit of War' in Richard Bessel (ed.), *Fascist Italy and Nazi Germany: Comparisons and Contrasts* (Cambridge 1996).

supporters in the expanding ranks of the SS. It was only through war that the trauma of war and defeat could be overcome and that Hitler could achieve the position of the Reich to which it was entitled. He was obsessive about his ultimate goals, whether the war in the East or the removal of the Jews. He was also acutely aware of his own mortality and the passage of time. The question of timing was important. On 11 April, Hitler signed the orders for 'Operation White', the possible attack against Poland. Military preparations had to be completed and plans ready for action by 1 September 1939 in order to move before the bad weather set in. On 4 May, the Japanese refused to join the tripartite pact. On 31 May, the Italians informed Hitler they would not be ready for war for two or three years. By this time, the British and French were engaged in alliance negotiations with the Soviet Union. Time was beginning to run out. Hitler was a driven man; he would have his war with Poland. He was, however, well aware of the factors, both at home and abroad that could affect the timing of his war and the chances of success. He continued to play on the Allied reluctance to go to war. Why should they go to war for Danzig? To increase the pressure on Britain and to counter the possibility of an Allied settlement with the Soviet Union, Hitler turned to Moscow as a short-term tactic. The decision was an ideological and strategic defeat in terms of Hitler's future ambitions. It was also an example of 'inspired opportunism'. An agreement with the USSR might convince the British to abandon the Polish guarantee, and if this manoeuvre failed, Germany could go to war against the western powers without the fear of an eastern front. When his final efforts to isolate Poland failed, fanaticism, ideology, and calculation led to Hitler's decision to launch his attack.

Books

ADAMTHWAITE, A., *Grandeur and Misery: France's Bid for Power in Europe, 1914–1940* (London, 1995).

ALTRICHTER, H. and BECKER, J. (eds.), *Kriegsausbruch 1939* (Munich, 1989).

BUDRASS, L., *Flugzeugindustrie und Luftrüstung in Deutschland* (Düsseldorf, 1998).

CARROLL, B. A., *Design for Total War: Arms and Economics in the Third Reich* (The Hague, 1968).

CHILDERS, T. and CAPLAN, J. (eds.), *Re-evaluating the Third Reich* (New York, 1993). See P. Hayes, H. JAMES, T. Mason.

DESTREM, M., *L'été 39* (Paris, 1969).

DI NOLFO, E. et al. (eds.), *L'Italia e la politico di potenza in Europa, 1938–1940* (Milan, 1985).

FUNKE, M. (ed.), *Hitler, Deutschland und die Mächte: Materialien zur Außenpolitik des Dritten Reiches* (Düsseldorf, 1976). See H.-A. Jacobsen, J. Dülffer, M. Geyer, L. Schwerin von Krosigk, H.-J. Schröder, J. Henke, G. Wollstein.

GASSERT, P., *Amerika im Dritten Reich* (Stuttgart, 1997).

GOOCH, J., *Mussolini and His Generals: The Armed Forces and Fascist Foreign Policy, 1922–1940* (Cambridge, 2007).

HENKE, J., *England in Hitlers politischem Kalkül, 1933–1939* (Boppard, 1972).

HILDEBRAND, K., SCHMÄDEKE, J., and ZERNACK, K. (eds.), *1939: An der Schwelle zum Weltkrieg: Die Entfesselung des Zweiten Weltkrieges und das internationale System* (Berlin, 1990). See K. Hildebrand, E. Jäckel, G. L. Weinberg, O. Groehler, and M. Steinert.

—— and WERNER K. F. (eds.), *Deutschland und Frankreich, 1936–1939* (Munich, 1981). See section on 'Die Situation im September 1939', contributions by J.-L. Crémieux-Brilhac and A. Hillgruber.

HILLGRUBER, A., *Die Zerstörung Europas: Beiträge zur Weltkriegsepoche 1914 bis1945* (Frankfurt am Main, 1988).

HOFER, W., *Die Entfesselung des Zweiten Weltkrieges: eine Studie über die internationalen Beziehungen im Sommer 1939* (Frankfurt am Main, 1954).

HOMZE, E. L., *Arming the Luftwaffe: The Reich Air Ministry and the German Aircraft Industry, 1919–1939* (Lincoln, NE, 1976).

KLEY, S., *Hitler, Ribbentrop und die Entfesselung des Zweiten Weltkrieges* (Paderborn, 1996).

KNIPPING, F. and MÜLLER, K.-J. (eds.), *Machtbewusstsein in Deutschland am Vorabend des Zweiten Weltkrieges* (Paderborn, 1984).

KNOX, M., *Mussolini Unleashed, 1939–1941: Politics and Strategy in Fascist Italy's Last War* (Cambridge, 1982).

—— *Common Destiny: Dictatorship, Foreign Policy and War in Fascist Italy and Nazi Germany* (Cambridge, 2000).

MALLET, R., *The Italian Navy and Fascist Expansionism, 1935–1940* (London, 1998).

—— *Mussolini and the Origins of the Second World War* (Basingstoke, 2003).

MASON, T., *Social Policy in the Third Reich: The Working Class and the 'National Community'* (Providence, RI, 1993).

—— *Nazism, Fascism and the Working Class* (Cambridge, 1995).

MCKERCHER, B. J. C. and LEGAULT, R., *Military Planning and the Origins of the Second World War in Europe* (Westport, CT, 2001). See A. Cassels.

MICHALKA, W., *Der Zweite Weltkrieg: Analysen, Grundzüge, Forschungsbilanz* (Munich and Zurich, 1989). See G. Schreiber, W. Deist, J. Dülffer, M. Funke. Most of the essays in Part I and many in Part II are relevant.

MÜLLER, K.-J., *Das Heer und Hitler: Armee und nationalsozialistisches Regime, 1933–1940* (Stuttgart, 1969).

MURRAY, W., *The Change in the European Balance of Power, 1938–1939* (Princeton, NJ, 1984).

NIEDHART, G. (ed.), *Kriegsbeginn, 1939: Entfesselung oder Ausbruch des Zweiten Weltkrieges* (Darmstadt, 1976).

OVERY, R., *War and Economy in the Third Reich* (Oxford, 1994), especially chapters 6 and 7.

ROHE, K. (ed.), *Die Westmächte und das Dritte Reich 1933–1939: Klassische Großmachtrivalität oder Kampf zwischen Demokratie und Diktatur* (Paderborn, 1982). See C. A. MacDonald and K. Schwabe.

SIROIS, H., *Zwischen Illusionen und Krieg: Deutschland und die USA, 1933–1941* (Paderborn, 2000).

STEINERT, M., *Hitlers Krieg und die Deutschen: Stimmung und Haltung der deutschen Bevölkerung im Zweiten Weltkrieg* (Düsseldorf, 1970).

STRANG, G. B., *On the Fiery March: Mussolini Prepares for War* (Westport, CT, 2003).

TOOZE, A., *The Wages of Destruction: The Making and Breaking of the Nazi Economy* (London, 2006).

WATT, D. C., *How War Came: The Immediate Origins of the Second World War* (London, 1989).

WEINBERG, G. L., *The Foreign Policy of Hitler's Germany: Starting World War II, 1937–1939* (Chicago, IL, 1970).

—— *A World at Arms: A Global History of World War II* (Cambridge, 1994).

—— *Visions of Victory: The Hopes of Eight World War II Leaders* (Cambridge, 2005), especially chapter 1.

WENDT, B.-J., *Großdeutschland: Außenpolitik und Kriegsvorbereitung des Hitlerregimes* (Munich, 1987).

WYLIE, N. (ed.), *European Neutrals and Non-belligerents during the Second World War* (Cambridge, 2002).

Articles and Chapters

BARTOV, O., 'From Blitzkrieg to Total War', in Fulbrook, M. (ed.), *Twentieth-Century Germany: Politics, Culture and Society, 1918–1990* (London and New York, 2001).

BAUMGART, W., 'Zur Ansprache Hitlers vor den Führern der Wehrmacht am 22. August 1939: eine quellenkritische Untersuchung', *Vierteljahrshefte für Zeitgeschichte*, 16 (1968).

—— 'Zur Ansprache Hitlers vor den Führern der Wehrmacht am 22. August 1939: Erwiderung', *Vierteljahrshefte für Zeitgeschichte*, 19 (1971).

DEIST, W., 'The Road to Ideological War: Germany 1918–1945', in Murray, W., Knox, M. and Bernstein, A. (eds.), *The Making of Strategy: Rulers, States, and War* (Cambridge, 1994).

DÜLFFER, J., 'Der Beginn des Krieges 1939: Hitler, die innere Krise und das Mächtesystem', *Geschichte und Gesellschaft*, 2: 4 (1976).

GEYER, M., 'German Strategy in the Age of Machine Warfare, 1914–1945', in Paret, P. (ed.), *Makers of Modern Strategy* (Princeton, NJ, 1986).

—— 'Restorative Elites, German Society and the Nazi Pursuit of War', in Bessel, R. (ed.), *Fascist Italy and Nazi Germany: Comparisons and Contrasts* (Cambridge, 1996).

GREENWOOD, S., 'The Phantom Crisis: Danzig, 1939', in Martel, G. (ed.), *The Origins of the Second World War Reconsidered: A. J. P. Taylor and the Historians*, 2nd edn. (London, 1999).

GOOCH, J., 'Fascist Italy', in Boyce, R. and Maiolo, J. A. (eds.), *The Origins of World War Two: The Debate Continues* (Basingstoke, 2003).

HILLGRUBER, A., 'Der Faktor Amerika in Hitlers Strategie, 1938–1941', in Michalka, W. (ed.), *Nationalsozialistlische Außenpolitik* (Darmstadt, 1978).

KAISER, D., MASON T. and OVERY R., 'Debate: Germany, "Domestic Crisis" and War in 1939', *Past and Present*, 122 (1989). Original article by Overy in

Past and Present, 116 (1987) followed by Tim Mason's and David Kaiser's replies, and Overy's response in *Past and Present*, 122 (1989).

KNOX, M., 'Conquest, Foreign and Domestic, in Fascist Italy and Nazi Germany', *Journal of Modern History*, 56 (1984).

MASON, T., 'Innere Krise und Angriffskrieg, 1938–39', in Forstmeier, F. and Volkmann, H.-E. (eds.), *Wirtschaft und Rüstung am Vorabend des Zweiten Weltkrieges* (Düsseldorf, 1975).

OVERY, R., 'Hitler's War Plans and the German Economy', in Boyce, R. W. D. and Robertson, E. M. (eds.), *Paths to War: New Essays on the Origins of the Second World War* (London, 1989).

—— 'Strategic Intelligence and the Outbreak of the Second World War', *War in History*, 5 (1998).

PINOCCHIO, G. P., 'The Cat and the Fox: Italy between Germany and the Soviet Union, 1939–1940', in Wegner, B. (ed.), *From Peace to War: Germany, Soviet Russia and the World, 1939–1941* (Oxford, 1977).

RITSCHL, A. O. (2001), 'Nazi Economic Imperialism and the Exploitation of the Small: Evidence from Germany's Secret Foreign Exchange Balance', *Economic History Review*, 54: 2 (2001).

SULLIVAN, B., '"Where One Man, and Only One Man, Led": Italy's Path from Non-alignment to Non-belligerency to War, 1937–1940', in Wylie, N. (ed.), *European Neutrals and Non-Belligerents during the Second World War* (Cambridge, 2002).

ÜBERSCHÄR, G. R., 'General Halder and the Resistance to Hitler in the German High Command, 1938–40', *European History Quarterly*, 18: 3 (1988).

WEINBERG, G. L., 'Hitler and England, 1933–45: Pretence and Reality', *German Studies Review*, 8 (1983).

16

Red Clouds: The Soviet Union and the Nazi–Soviet Pact, 1939

I

At the start of 1939, the Soviet Union was on the periphery of the European stage; six months later, Moscow was at its centre with the western powers and the Germans competing for its favour. The summer courtships were hardly built on trust and a major factor in the wooing was to prevent a marriage with the rival. It was a match that Hitler won, although Stalin and the Russian people paid a very high price for their mistaken choice of partners. The change in Moscow's status had relatively little to do with Soviet action. After Munich, Soviet confidence was at a low ebb and Litvinov's policies discredited. Stalin's much-cited speech to the XVIII Party Congress on 10 March 1939 was a reaction to the sense of Soviet exclusion from Great Power politics but was, at the same time, a public reaffirmation of the country's strength and ability to defend its borders. Though most of the speech was directed against the western powers, it was not really a signal to the Germans that the USSR was ready to open negotiations. It was rather an assertion of the Soviet freedom of choice in the face of checks to previous attempts at collective security. As part of his ringing indictment of the western policies of non-interference and neutrality, Stalin, not for the first time, insinuated that Britain and France were exaggerating the internal disorders of the USSR and the weakness of its forces in the hope of encouraging the Germans to push eastwards and start a war with the Bolsheviks.

Stalin's long-standing belief that the western powers, and Britain in particular, sought to entangle the Soviet Union and Nazi Germany in a conflict, the mirror image of Chamberlain's suspicions about the Soviet Union, coloured his thinking right up to the outbreak of war and beyond. Assured by some of his intelligence agents that Nazi aggression was directed westward, Stalin was able to minimize the danger of the German threat to the Ukraine and to present the recent warnings about Hitler's intentions as part of a western plot. He dismissed as 'lunatic' anyone who dreamt of detaching the Ukraine from the Soviet Union, taking some time in his speech to ridicule the idea of uniting the 'elephant', the Soviet Ukraine, with the 'little goat', the so-called Carpathian Ukraine. While lashing out at the 'suspicious noises' made by the western press, he nevertheless attacked those 'mentally ill' Germans who harboured such illusions, revealing some doubts about his own denials. In a more affirmative vein, Stalin set out to convince the 'congress of survivors' (those not purged) of Soviet power and strength. He spoke of the country's increasing economic, political and cultural power, its moral and political unity (no reference to the Terror), and the strength of the Red Army and navy. Stalin was less direct when he turned to the question of what was to be done in the face of a situation where the 'non-aggressive states', i.e. England and France, were willing to let the 'aggressors' do their 'dirty work undisturbed'. He proposed the careful and cautious consideration of the options while the nation relied on its own power to protect its borders. The USSR wanted to establish peaceful relations and an expansion of trade with all countries that did not stand against Soviet interests as well as those states sharing a common border with the Soviet Union who did not attack, directly or indirectly, the Soviet frontiers. At the same time, Stalin promised Soviet support for those nations who were victims of aggression and who fought for their independence. The USSR, he warned would-be enemies, was unafraid of the 'aggressors' threats' and capable of responding with 'double force' to any attack on its frontiers. Stalin was suggesting both that the Soviet Union could reach an agreement with the 'aggressor states' and that she was prepared to fight them. The Soviet choice depended on the actions of the other states. 'We must be cautious', Stalin warned his listeners, 'and not allow our country to be drawn into conflict by the war-mongers who are used to having others pull the chestnuts out of the fire for them'.[1] Believing in the inevitable war between the capitalist powers, Stalin, relying on the strength and unity of the Soviet state, intended that the USSR should not be engaged in that struggle.

The ambiguities in Stalin's speech did not pass unnoticed. Members of the foreign department of *Izvestiia* discussed what the speech might mean. One employee detected a hint of a change in relations with Germany only to have his suggestion dismissed by all the others present. Schulenburg, the German ambassador in Moscow, noted the absence of the usual denunciations of the authoritarian states and the emphasis on the iniquities of Britain, France, and the United States. Yet, like the British and French ambassadors, he denied that the speech represented a

[1] GK, doc. no. 177 for original speech. For British report on Stalin's speech see *DBFP*, 3rd ser., Vol. IV, No. 93.

break with current Soviet policy. There were persistent rumours of a German–Soviet agreement, most recently in February 1939 when the news of the Soviet trade negotiator's (Schnurre) forthcoming visit to Moscow was leaked to the French press. They were taken seriously enough for both the British and the French to attempt to mollify the USSR. Nor was Stalin's attack on the 'non-aggressive powers' unexpected. After all, even Litvinov, who was most conspicuously associated with collective security, had made clear his loss of confidence in the western willingness to stand up to Hitler. Despite a series of reports from Surits in Paris and Maisky in London, commenting on the hardening of attitudes toward Nazi Germany and the shift of opinion away from appeasement in their respective capitals, the commissar did not expect any change in their direction. Secret intelligence, not always accurate and often framed to suit the anticipated reaction in the Kremlin, fed Litvinov's and Stalin's suspicions that Britain's chief aim was to encourage the Germans to move eastwards in order to bring about a German–Soviet conflict. In the post-Munich period, Litvinov appeared unwilling to take any initiative. Whether this was because of Stalin's orders, his own inclination, or both cannot be determined. Five years of failed efforts took their toll. 'We are still prepared to engage in real co-operation, if it suits the others', he wrote to Surits, 'but we can survive without it and therefore would not exert ourselves to achieve it'.[2]

Regardless of what Stalin told the party faithful, the USSR was in an exposed position. Though she had the largest army in Europe, some 1.2 million men in 1939, she faced two strong military adversaries, Germany and Japan, each of whom had single-handedly defeated her in the not-forgotten past. Stalin was well-informed, unlike the British and French, of the details of the Polish–German stand-off. He knew, too, from the Sorge network in Tokyo that the negotiations for a military alliance between Germany, Italy, and Japan had stalled over the Japanese refusal to extend the anti-Soviet pact to include military action against the western powers and that the Japanese were unprepared for a sustained conflict with Russia. We do not know how Stalin interpreted this intelligence, which freed the USSR from the immediate threat of a two-front war, but did not necessarily lift the possibility of local Russo–Japanese clashes nor remove apprehensions of either a Polish–German settlement or a military conflict in the West. There were renewed difficulties with Japan along the Outer Mongolian border where the Japanese forces were again testing Soviet resolve. On 25 April, the Kwantung army command issued new 'Principles for the Settlement of Soviet–Manchurian Border Disputes' to its corps commanders.

[2] GK, doc. no. 149, Litvinov to Surits, 10 February 1939.

Commanders were allowed to determine the borders where existing lines were indistinct and were permitted to temporarily invade Soviet territory or to decoy Soviet soldiers and 'get them into Manchukuoan territory'.[3] Once again, the Kwantung army was successfully flouting the decisions of the central Tokyo command.

The Soviet armed services were just emerging from the worst of the Terror though the purges continued, on a reduced scale, until 1941. The army suffered not only from the after-effects of the Terror but from the greater powers given to untrained political officers attached to almost every unit regardless of size. The execution in 1937 of Tukhachevsky and other leading generals who had encouraged innovation and their replacement by less experienced officers was hardly a stimulus to modernization. Nonetheless, progress was made not only in expanding the army and navy and in armaments production but also in improving the available weaponry, including aircraft and tanks. After the decision to pull out of Spain in November 1938, it was possible to digest the military lessons of that conflict. It was acknowledged that the current generation of Soviet fighters and bombers was no match for the new generation of German aircraft. New Soviet aircraft designs were rushed into production: the TB-7, an advanced four-engine bomber; two twin-engine bombers, the DB-3 and the Pe-2; and three high-performance fighters, the I-22, I-26, and Mig-I (I-6I).[4] The Soviets learned, too, that their light tanks were vulnerable to small-calibre anti-tank guns and that Tukhachevsky's decision to design tanks for specialized purposes had created organizational difficulties in the field. The decision to build the medium T-34, the tank that would outgun and outfight even the best German armour in 1941, and the heavy KV-1 with interchangeable engines was taken only in August 1939. The experience in Spain initiated a continuing debate about the strategic role of the bomber and about the type of tank required for European warfare, as well as about the best usage of both.

The size of the Red Army continued to increase; the number of men and women more than doubled under the Second Five-Year Plan. Between 1937 and 1940, the rate of growth accelerated, the number of regular forces personnel trebled. In part, the extraordinary expansion in 1939–1940 was due to the absorption of the territorial units into the regular army. On the negative side, the army was seriously short of

[3] Jonathan Haslam, *The Soviet Union and the Threat from the East, 1933–1941: Moscow, Tokyo and the Prelude to the Pacific War* (Basingstoke, 1992), 129.

[4] Earl F. Ziemke, 'Soviet Net Assessment in the 1930s', in Williamson Murray and Alan R. Millett (eds.), *Calculations Net Assessment and the Coming of World War II* (New York and Toronto, 1992), 200–201.

Table 16.1 Personnel of the Soviet Regular Armed Forces ('000s)

	Series A	Series B
1926/27	586	
1931	562	
1932	638	
1933	885	
1934	940	
1935	1067	
1936	1300	
1937	1433	1683
1938	1513	
1939		2099
1940	4207	

Source: Mark Harrison and R. W. Davies, 'The Soviet Military–Economic Effort during the Second Five-Year Plan, 1933–1937', *Europe–Asia Studies*, 49: 3 (1997), 373.

officers and the military schools proved incapable of either turning out the numbers required or providing the kind of instruction needed for preparing men for war. The effects were felt after the outbreak of the German–Russian war.

In the winter of 1935–1936, Stalin decided that he wanted to build a great ocean-going fleet. His decision led to the redefining of the navy's responsibilities and a change from constructing light surface vessels to building capital ships. Plans were drawn up in 1936 for a naval force that would include battleships, heavy cruisers, light cruisers, destroyers, submarines, and many support vessels. In January 1937, Stalin began to reorganize both the naval high command and the defence industry and appointed men to work out the new construction plans. They, as well as many of their successors, were victims of the naval purges which continued up to 1940.[5]

Progress was slow. At the end of 1937, the Soviet surface fleet still relied mainly on the rebuilt and modernized vessels of the Imperial navy. The submarine programme was more successful; though the projected

[5] In addition to the chief of the naval forces and such senior officers as the commanders of the Pacific, Baltic, Black Sea, and Northern fleets, arrested between January and June 1938 and executed before 1940, 'eight leaders of central administrations, five chiefs of staff of fleet and flotillas, fifteen other flag officers, fourteen chiefs of brigades, seventeen commanders of divisions and chief of staff of units, twenty-two commanding officers... became victims of the purges'. Technicians too, were among the victims. Quotation and citations from Jürgen Rohwer and Mikhail Monakov, 'The Soviet Union's Ocean-Going Fleet', *International History Review*, 18: 4 (1996), 855.

Table 16.2 Ships Entering Service with the Soviet Navy, 1930–1940 (units and tons)

Year	Surface Ships			Submarines			Combined tonnage	
		tons			tons			
	units	total	per ship	units	total	per ship	total	% of 1937
1930	1	600	600	1	934	934	1534	22
1931	1	600	600	5	4690	938	5290	75
1932	5	3000	600	0	0	0	3000	43
1933	1	600	600	15	10845	723	11445	163
1934	3	1452	484	34	7828	230	9280	132
1935	3	1463	488	32	13777	431	15240	217
1936	13	7360	566	46	25110	546	32470	462
1937	6	2156	359	9	4869	541	7025	100
1938	16	40474	2530	14	8800	629	49274	701
1939	14	32018	2289	14	8845	632	40893	582
1940	8	45058	5632	24	16390	683	61448	387

Source: Mark Harrison and R. W. Davies, 'The Soviet Military–Economic Effort during the Second Five-Year Plan, 1933–1937', *Europe–Asia Studies*, 49: 3 (1997), 375.

numbers could not be reached, with 143 submarines the Soviet force was one of the strongest in the field. Despite the purges, a new plan was approved by the *Politburo* in early 1938 and yet another in the summer of 1939, after a new commissar and chief of the navy had been appointed. It included a revised programme for expanding the northern Baltic, Black Sea, and Pacific fleets, the last still the most important. Stalin, like Hitler, liked battle cruisers and, though the number of battleships was reduced, the number and tonnage of battle cruisers was increased. Whereas the total cost of shipbuilding in the Second Five-Year Plan had been 6,796,000,000 roubles, the total for the Third Plan was 14,351,000,000 roubles. It was estimated that 130,000 men would be needed.[6] On Stalin's orders, the details of the programme were kept secret and not even the fleet commanders were informed. The projections and plans for the capital ships had to be approved by Stalin personally.

The main problem was Russia's relative technological and industrial backwardness which dated back to Tsarist times. The flight of technicians after the revolution and the subsequent purges of their successors made it imperative to solicit foreign technical assistance, whether by overt or covert means. The Soviets wanted not only capital ships and

[6] Figures from Rohwer and Monakov, 'The Soviet Union's Ocean-Going Fleet', 857.

weapons but the most technologically advanced designs in order to catch up with the leading naval powers. Even when negotiations with foreign countries were satisfactorily concluded, the Soviets found they were often sold second-rate designs. It was in the hope of gaining access to British technical expertise, and to its leading naval construction firms, that Stalin opened negotiations for an Anglo–Soviet naval arms limitation treaty in 1936–1937. The British needed the bilateral treaty, for a Soviet refusal would mean that the Germans would also refuse such a treaty, bringing an end to British hopes of an arms control regime that would avoid a new naval arms race. Both the Soviet and German treaties were signed in July 1937.[7] Despite Soviet hopes for purchases, the Admiralty successfully limited arms sales and naval officers ensured that the Russians were not given any up-to-date technology. The Soviet purchasers turned to the United States and were, at first, encouraged by President Roosevelt, who welcomed future support against Japan. In 1938, despite the technical and economic difficulties, the Soviet shipyards began work on two battleships in the 60,000-ton range. Two more were added in 1939 and 1940 along with two 35,000-ton battle cruisers.[8] Considerable progress was made but Soviet capabilities continued to lag well behind its naval aspirations.

Soviet war production rose very rapidly in the late 1930s. The increase in the rates of production of aircraft, tanks, artillery, infantry armament, and ammunition was striking. In 1938, there was an improvement in industrial production and a larger increase took place in 1939.[9] By 1940, the effort to switch to armaments was so intense that it put a great strain on all the rest of the economy.[10]

In order to accommodate the new armament programmes, a higher percentage of the state budget was allocated to defence, 18.7% in 1938, 25.6% in 1939, and 43.3% in 1941. By 1940, almost one-third of the budget was earmarked for defence, consuming more roubles than the entire state budget of 1934. The increase in allocation was due partly to the belief in the increased danger of war but also to technological

[7] Despite the British ratification of the London Naval Treaty and the bilateral treaties that followed, the whole system of naval arms control collapsed as both the Japanese and Germans built beyond the treaty limits.

[8] Jürgen Rohwer and Mikhail S. Monakov, *Stalin's Ocean-Going Fleet, Soviet Naval Strategy and Shipbuilding Programmes, 1935–1953* (London and Portland, OR, 2001), 95; Ziemke, 'Soviet Net Assessment', 201.

[9] Annual rate of growth (in %) 1936: 29; 1937: 11; 1938: 16; 1940: 12. Both the good and modest growth rates are exaggerated. Figures from *Promyshlennost' SSSR: statisticheskii sbornik* (Moscow, 1957), 31.

[10] I am indebted to Professors R. W. Davies and Mark Harrison of the Centre for Russian and East European Studies, University of Birmingham, UK, for assistance and for reference to statistical information.

TABLE 16.3 Soviet Tank and Armament Production and Procurement, 1930–1940: Alternative Figures (physical units)

	Tanks			Guns		Rifles	
	production previously published	Tanks production from Gosplan	procurement by NKO*	production previously published	procurement by NKO*	production previously published	procurement by NKO*
1930	170	0	170	952	952	126	126
1931	740	493	740	1966	1911	174	174
1932	3038	3039	3038	2574	2574	224	224
1933	3509	3849	3509	4638	4638	241	241
1934	3565	3559	3565	4123	4123	303	303
1935	3055	2994	3055	4383	4383	222	221
1936	4800	3935	4804	4324	5235	403	403
1937	1559	1558	1559	5473	5443	578	567
1938	2271	2270	2271	12340	12687	1175	1171
1939	2950	2986	2986	17348	16459	1503	1497
1940	2794	2696	2790	15300	13724	1461	1461

Note: *NKO = People's Commissariat of Defence.
Source: Mark Harrison and R. W. Davies, 'The Soviet Military–Economic Effort during the Second Five-Year Plan, 1933–1937', *Europe–Asia Studies*, 49: 3 (1997), 405.

Table 16.4 The Number of Weapons in Military Procurement, 1930–1940 (Valued as Typical Weapons of 1937; million roubles and %)

	Total	Armament	Ammunition	Tanks	Aircraft
1930	551	75	17	17	160
1931	1002	129	20	99	196
1932	2145	192	24	344	317
1933	3230	242	37	487	619
1934	3241	235	26	475	727
1935	2327	188	42	355	329
1936	3779	262	81	515	684
1937	4014	333	98	241	1348
1938	6881	778	218	351	1874
1939	9873	1045	311	448	2952
1940	11552	1057	430	450	3512

Source: Mark Harrison and R. W. Davies, 'The Soviet Military–Economic Effort during the Second Five-Year Plan, 1933–1937', *Europe–Asia Studies*, 49: 3 (1997), 406.

changes that made armament production far more expensive for all the major powers. Non-defence production and the non-defence work of the armaments industries were cut. The production of civilian aircraft and motor vehicles almost ceased. Mobilization planning went into high gear and an overall scheme was developed.

There was every sign that as the preparations for war intensified, Stalin's main aim in 1939 was to avoid involvement in the imminent conflict. Litvinov's policies of building up a coalition against Germany to avoid war had suffered a severe check and the balance of European power seemed to be moving in Hitler's direction. Litvinov was on the defensive, politically and personally. Though he had lost confidence in the British leadership, he had not changed his view that Nazi Germany presented the greater threat to Soviet independence, nor had he abandoned his opposition to an expansion of German–Soviet trade that would assist German rearmament. In this continuing differentiation between the capitalist powers, he stood out from those who, in more doctrinaire terminology, saw the USSR as surrounded by hostile capitalist states, whether Fascist or otherwise, and who all presented a threat to its existence. Litvinov found himself isolated and it was widely rumoured that he would be the next victim on the NKVD list.[11]

Litvinov was necessarily cautious. The Soviet response to the German invasion of truncated Czechoslovakia was muted. The party congress was still in session when Hitler entered Prague; Litvinov hardly needed any reminder of the line Stalin had set. Yet he consulted Stalin before

[11] See p. 463.

replying to the British inquiry about the Soviet response to the Romanian 'ultimatum'. He caustically reminded Seeds, the British ambassador, on 18 March, that the Soviet government, too, was interested in knowing in advance the position of other countries and that the Romanians had not approached him. He proposed, instead of an answer to the British query, the immediate convocation, preferably in Bucharest, of an international conference for joint consultations on how to deal with the crisis. In the post-Prague weeks, while the British were putting together their 'peace front', Litvinov waited for a concrete offer that would allow the Soviet Union to co-operate with the British on full and equal terms. Without any real confidence in Chamberlain's proposed four-power declaration (20 March), he nevertheless quickly offered to sign if France and Poland promised their signatures. He suggested, too, that the invitation be extended to the USSR's neighbours, Finland, the Baltic states, and the Scandinavian countries. There was no British answer; anticipated Polish and Romanian objections had buried the project. When the Soviets were faced, at the last minute, with the news of the guarantee to Poland, Litvinov's reaction was mixed. He was angry and outraged but he also saw future advantages for Moscow. On 1 April, an irate Litvinov told Seeds that the Soviets neither understood nor appreciated the British guarantee to Poland and expressed his doubts whether Britain would fight for Danzig or the Corridor. Seeds' attempted defence of the guarantee as only an interim arrangement was brushed aside and Litvinov declared that all his efforts for Anglo–Soviet co-operation had been 'summarily dropped'. The 'Soviet government would stand aside—a course which might possibly be in their best interests'.[12] Notwithstanding his anger, Litvinov was still trying to assess the new situation and Maisky continued to press Halifax for information about the British position. Neither Litvinov nor Maisky were reassured by Halifax's insistence that the guarantee was only the first of a two-stage approach and that after the quadripartite defence bloc was formed, the British government would try to create a united front of peace-loving powers. Litvinov pointed out to Maisky that the guarantee to Poland would strengthen its position in negotiations with Hitler. An agreement might be reached over Danzig and the 'Corridor' in exchange for Lithuania, and Hitler would be free to move in the Baltic region, leading to the Soviet–German clash that Chamberlain wished. Maisky reinforced this suspicious appraisal of Chamberlain's intentions, claiming that the British prime minister was merely temporizing until, when circumstances changed, he could return to a policy of appeasement.

[12] *DBFP*, 3rd ser., Vol. IV, No. 597.

Little more was expected from the French who, in any case, were thought to follow the British line. Litvinov regarded Bonnet as an 'even more incorrigible appeaser then Chamberlain'.[13] He had little interest in Bonnet's attempt to get the Russians to commit themselves to supplying Poland and Romania in case of a German attack. Nor was he convinced by the French offer of a tripartite declaration without Poland. At no point did Bonnet actually say what assistance France would give to either of the two countries. On 11 April, Daladier instructed the French military attaché to inform the Soviet General Staff that the French were prepared to jointly study what aid might be given Poland and Romania, and asked the USSR to immediately detail what war material could be supplied. The Soviet staff replied that the matter should be handled by the People's Commissar of Foreign Affairs. After four years of failed efforts to get military talks going, this was hardly an offer that the military would pursue or that Litvinov was willing to follow up. The latter again suggested a conference of powers directly interested but Daladier thought it unnecessary and asked Bonnet to pursue 'this very simple matter' directly with the Soviet Foreign Ministry.[14] Despite Surits's positive assessment of the French feelers, Litvinov did not believe that there had been any change in British or French policy towards the Soviet Union. On the contrary, he suspected that the new guarantees might prove to be the prelude to the formation of an anti-Soviet coalition.

Litvinov realized that the guarantees actually strengthened Soviet security on all its European borders with the exception of the Baltic region. On 4 April, he wrote to Merekalov, the Soviet *polpred* in Germany: 'We know very well that it is impossible to restrain and stop the aggression in Europe without us and, later it will be necessary to pay us well for our assistance. That is why we are remaining calm during the upheaval surrounding the apparent change in English policy.'[15] Having been ignored in September by both Germany and the western powers, the Soviet Union could now play a pivotal role in Europe. If Germany attacked Poland, the western powers were pledged to come to its assistance, and if war came Hitler would be compelled to deal with Britain and France before turning on the USSR. The Soviet Union could stand aside and build up her defences and Stalin would have achieved his purpose without engaging in war. Seeds telegraphed

[13] Albert Resis, 'The Fall of Litvinov: Harbinger of the German–Soviet Non-Aggression Pact', *Europe–Asia Studies*, 52: 1 (2000), 40.

[14] Resis, 'The Fall of Litvinov', 41; *DDF*, 2nd ser., Vol. XV, No. 476.

[15] Sabine Dullin, 'Les diplomates soviétiques des années 1930 et leur évaluation de la puissance de l'URSS', *Relations internationales*, 91 (1997), 355.

the Foreign Office on 13 April that under the present circumstances, Russia 'can quite properly be tempted to stand aloof and in case of war confine its advertised support of the victims of aggression to the profitable business of selling supplies to the latter'.[16] He warned, too, of the '"possible" danger that if Germany reached the Soviet frontier, there would be a German offer of Bessarabia, parts of Poland, Estonia and Latvia in order to pursue Hitler's aims in the West'. Seeds was told that the British interest was in keeping Soviet Russia in play and avoiding the 'natural tendency of the Soviet Government to stand aloof'.[17] The diplomatic situation had changed. It could be anticipated in Moscow that the Soviet Union would be courted by both capitalist blocs. If the British were to make good their guarantee to Poland, they would need Soviet assistance and, as Litvinov suggested, co-operation would come at a high price. By the same token, Hitler, however contemptuous of Soviet military power, would have to neutralize the USSR in order to avoid a two-front war. With Britain's March guarantees, the USSR won back its room for manoeuvre.

The road was still a twisting one. The Soviets still might have preferred a single multilateral system of collective security, an anti-Nazi grand alliance, as the best guarantee of a temporary peace. Stalin was not at all convinced that Britain would stand by its guarantee, or that Beck would continue to resist German pressure. There could be an Anglo-German settlement at Soviet expense. Even after the conclusion of the Nazi–Soviet pact and indeed after the outbreak of war, the ever-suspicious Stalin continued to fear a second Munich. Like so many others, he had no confidence in Beck. The Polish–Soviet agreement of 26 November 1938 had been made in the hope of encouraging the Poles to stand up to Hitler but it was not discounted that Beck would use it to improve his negotiating hand in Berlin as he had done in 1934 and that the Poles would reach a compromise with Hitler. The danger existed, too, that with an easy advance into Poland blocked, Hitler would move into Finland and the Baltic. The Latvian and Estonian rejection of Moscow's March warnings and further difficulties with Finland in the spring heightened Soviet concerns about the exposure of Leningrad. The Poles or British could strike a bargain with Hitler in the Baltic. Litvinov in mid-April, and Molotov in June and July, would place the question of Finland and the Baltic states at the centre of the alliance discussions.

16 *DBFP*, 3rd ser., Vol. V, No. 52.

17 Quoted in Keith Neilson, *Britain, Soviet Russia and the Collapse of the Versailles Order*, 283.

The Italian occupation of Albania heightened Anglo-French fears of Axis activity in the Balkans. On 11 April, Halifax told Maisky of the British intention to guarantee the frontiers and independence of Greece and to offer some form of guarantee to Turkey. Litvinov, in objecting to these moves that fell far short of the collective security arrangements the Soviets sought, carefully kept the door open to further talks. On 14 April, Maisky told Halifax that the Soviet Union was prepared to take part in giving assistance to Romania but first wanted to know how Britain envisaged such aid. This was, of course, more than Halifax (or Romania) wanted; the British foreign secretary preferred a unilateral Soviet declaration of support that would strengthen the deterrent without raising the awkward question of implementation. Surits made a parallel approach to the more responsive Bonnet who offered to extend the Franco-Soviet alliance. Seeds's warning to Halifax of a possible Soviet neutrality pact with Germany coincided with the latter's all-important telegram asking the Soviet government to make a public declaration 'on their own initiative' that 'in the event of any act of aggression against any European neighbour of the Soviet Union which was resisted by the country concerned, the assistance of the Soviet Government would be available, if desired . . . A positive declaration by the Soviet Government at the present moment would I believe, have a steadying effect upon the international situation.'[18] The Soviets interpreted this to mean that the British did not want to face Hitler with a united front for fear of provoking the Germans and were interested only in a deterrent that would bring him to the negotiating table. Worse still from the Soviet standpoint were the various reservations attached to the so-called unilateral guarantee that would leave the decision to call for assistance, as well as its form, to the power attacked. This hardly suited Soviet requirements. On the same day, 14 April, in Paris, Bonnet suggested that France and Russia supplement their mutual assistance treaty of 1935 with an exchange of secret letters in which the two countries would agree to assist each other if either found itself at war with Germany as a result of coming to aid Poland or Romania. Surits dismissed the offer though, in fact, it did offer some measure of reciprocity and went beyond what Halifax was asking. The British quickly intervened in Paris and the French stayed their hand.

On 15 April, Litvinov urged Stalin to set out the Soviet Union's minimal conditions for an agreement. If the Soviets wanted to gain something from the western powers, he wrote, 'we also have to start gradually revealing our wishes. We cannot expect that the other side would offer us exactly what we want.'[19] In what turned out to be his

[18] *DBFP*, 3rd ser., Vol. V, No. 170.
[19] *DVP*, Vol. XXII, Book 1, No. 224 (Litvinov to Stalin, 15 April 1939).

final effort to secure some kind of agreement with Britain and France, Litvinov prepared a counter-proposal, listing the Soviet *desiderata*. His memorandum was sent to Stalin, Molotov, the defence commissar, Voroshilov, and the deputy chairman of Sovnarkom, Lazar Kaganovich, who together constituted a *Politburo* foreign affairs committee.[20] From this point on, most of the day-to-day management of foreign affairs rested with this committee, with Stalin taking the major role. The *Politburo* committee found the Litvinov counter-proposal incomplete and set about revising its contents. When despatched by Seeds to London on 18 April, the Soviet offer consisted of eight articles, three of which constituted the non-negotiable core of the Soviet case until the abortive end of the negotiations. First, the three powers would conclude a five- to ten-year agreement to give each other immediate assistance, including military assistance, in case of aggression in Europe against any one of the signatories. Second, the three powers would give help, including military assistance, to the Eastern European states between the Baltic and the Black Sea bordering on the USSR in case of aggression against any one of them. Third, the three countries would discuss and conclude an agreement at the earliest possible date on the extent and forms of the military assistance to be given in order to fulfil their obligations. The counter-proposals, some of which were drafted by Stalin and Molotov, expanded on the contents of Litvinov's memorandum.

The Kremlin refused to respond to Halifax's suggestion of Soviet unilateral guarantees. Instead, on 17 April, counter-proposals were sent to London and Paris. On 19 and 21 April, in response to the Halifax–Maisky meeting and the Soviet reply, meetings were held in Stalin's office. Litvinov, accompanied by Potemkin, saw Stalin for an hour and ten minutes in the presence of Molotov, Voroshilov, Mikoyan, and Kaganovich. They were joined briefly by Boris Shtein, called back from Helsinki where he was negotiating for territory for Soviet bases. Lavrenti Beria, who had replaced Yezhov as head of the NKVD in late 1938, also joined the group for the last forty minutes. On 21 April, Maisky, summoned from London, and Merekalov, from Berlin, attended the meeting. Surits was not there, and as the French ambassador in Moscow, Naggiar, was away between February and late May because of illness, negotiations with the French were being conducted in Paris.

The British discussed the Soviet counter-proposal with the French; on 19 April Cadogan minuted that the new Soviet offer was 'extremely

[20] Sabine Dullin, *Des Hommes D'Influences: Les ambassadeurs de Staline en Europe, 1930–1939* (Paris, 2001), 260–264.

inconvenient'. At a later meeting with Maisky on 29 April, when Halifax claimed that he had no definitive reply to the Soviet proposal, he assured Maisky that Soviet fears that they would be committed to helping Poland and Romania while Britain and France remained aloof were 'a mistaken conclusion'.[21] A few days later, Maisky was reported to be in a 'rather truculent mood' and would consider nothing but British acceptance of the Soviet offer of 17 April. In conversation with others, Maisky referred to the post-Munich isolationist tendency in Moscow, and hinted that there were divided views in the Soviet government. Halifax was sufficiently concerned to consider going to Geneva.

Surits found Bonnet more forthcoming; the foreign minister responded positively to all the points made with the exception of the clause pertaining to the Baltic states. He claimed, however, that the Soviet memorandum was too complex to allow for immediate adoption, and renewed his offer of a three-power agreement to guarantee the independence of Poland and Romania. An element of reciprocity was introduced but Bonnet absolutely refused to extend the tripartite guarantees to cover the Baltic states.

There was another player to be considered. At the Kremlin meeting on 21 April, Stalin had asked Merekalov: 'Will the Germans start a war against us or not?'[22] According to his notes, the Soviet ambassador to Germany replied that Hitler would seize Poland in the autumn of 1939, bringing Germany to the Soviet border. The Germans would then try to secure Soviet neutrality while they dealt with France. When that task was finished, they would in two or three years launch the inevitable war against Russia. No discussion followed Merekalov's report and he was told by Stalin that he was free to leave. Stalin must have considered his options. Having regained a measure of manoeuvrability, his interest was to stay in this position and not ally with either side as long as this was possible. It may be that he feared that, with the new British guarantees, the Soviet Union would find itself faced with a *fait accompli* before it had provided for its safety. Or he might have thought that as Britain and France had more need of the Soviet Union than the latter needed them, it was a good time to explore the western option. It is also possible that Stalin was willing to give Litvinov one more chance to prove his usefulness before dismissing the commissar. He was, after all, prepared to pursue all possible roads, including that of isolation, which such spokesmen as Andrei Zhdanov had publicly supported only days before the April offer. If the British had immediately picked up on the Litvinov initiative, Stalin might have kept him in place for entirely

[21] Neilson, *Britain, Soviet Russia and the Versailles Order*, 286.
[22] Albert Resis 'The Fall of Litvinov', 48.

pragmatic reasons. With the British rejection of the Soviet counter-proposals, Litvinov, after so many years of failure, was no longer useful.

II

There were simultaneous stirrings of another kind. Mention has already been made of the Soviet annoyance and disappointment at the cancellation of the Schnurre visit and the return to the policies of official reserve towards Germany. The credit talks continued in Moscow under Schulenburg's direction until stopped by Hitler in March. The Führer was thinking about his future war plans. After Prague, it is hardly credible that Hitler did not consider the possibility of improving relations with the USSR. He purposely left unsettled a number of questions that had a bearing on his attitude towards Moscow. On 25 March, he told General von Brauchitsch that he did not intend a German occupation of the Ukraine and would leave open the question whether an independent Ukraine should be established at some later date. Two days after he signed the plan to invade Poland, the phrase 'it may become necessary to occupy the Baltic states up to the border of the former Courland [Lithuania and southern Latvia] and encorporate them in the Reich' was deleted. The propaganda war against the Soviet Union was still on hold. Hitler was beginning to think seriously about a move towards Moscow but had not made up his mind.

During the month of April, clandestine contacts were opened between the Soviets and the Germans. As in 1935 and 1937, these could well have involved an NKVD agent attached to the Soviet embassy in Berlin and members of a group around Göring and Koch, the gauleiter of East Prussia. Ribbentrop was worried enough about their activities to instruct Peter Kleist of his private office (the *Büro Ribbentrop*) to improve his contacts with the Soviet embassy. Kleist gave such an enthusiastic account of his meeting with Georgi Astakhov, the Soviet *chargé d'affaires* and possibly an NKVD agent, that he was told to break off the exchanges. These soundings, which were multiplied as the Russians realized that they were not the axis of the new Anglo–French 'security' arrangements, moved to the official level on 17 April when the *polpred*, Merekalov, just before returning to Moscow, had his first meeting with Weizsäcker since his official reception. The reports of the meeting sent by each of the two men make it clear that neither wanted to be seen taking the initiative and that neither was fully apprised of the attitude of his own government. The meeting was called because of difficulties arising out of Soviet orders placed at the Škoda works. Each man claimed that the other had opened the subject of political relations between the two countries. According to Merekalov, the German state secretary initiated the general discussion, referring to the German talks with Poland, blaming Britain for the tense international atmosphere, and assuring the Soviet representative that Germany did not want to attack anyone. Weizsäcker said he was 'ready and willing to exchange opinions on the general political situation and to respond to every question of interest'.[23] Astakhov, who accompanied the Soviet ambassador, reported to Moscow that before leaving, Merekalov asked Weizsäcker what he thought about Soviet–German relations. 'Now they could not be better', Astakhov quoted Weizsäcker as light-heartedly saying, adding in a more serious tone, 'you know that between us there are contradictions of an ideological character. But, at the same time, we sincerely want to develop economic relations with you.'[24] Weizsäcker's report to Ribbentrop, on the contrary, claims that Merekalov took the initiative and on the question of ideological differences insisted that these had hardly influenced the Soviet–Italian relationship and 'did not disturb [relations] with Germany' either. According to Merekalov, as far as Russia was concerned, 'there was no reason why she should not live on a normal footing with us. And out of normal relations could grow increasingly improved relations.'[25] The two men circled around each other, setting the pattern for German–Soviet exchanges until the end of July. There was no official follow-up to this exchange and its importance should not be exaggerated. Merekalov returned to Moscow, made his report and disappeared. He survived detention, was released after fifteen years and died only in 1983.[26]

Stalin, without an official reply from London but probably informed by his sources in London of British objections to the alliance talks, was preparing to dump Litvinov. On 27 April 1939, Litvinov and Maisky were summoned to the Kremlin. Maisky recalled: 'For the first time I saw how relations had taken shape between Litvinov, Stalin and Molotov. The atmosphere was about as tense as it could get. Although outwardly Stalin appeared at peace, puffing at his pipe, I felt that he was extremely ill-disposed towards Litvinov. And Molotov became violent, colliding with Litvinov incessantly, accusing him of every kind of mortal

[23] *DVP*, Vol. XXII, Book 1, No. 236; cited in Jonathan Haslam, 'Soviet–German Relations and the Origins of the Second World War: The Jury is Still Out', *Journal of Modern History*, 69 (1997), 793.

[24] Quoted in Geoffrey Roberts, *The Soviet Union and the Origins of the Second World War*, 70. He cites *DVP* 1939, Vol. I, Doc. 236. Also, I. Fleischauer, *Pakt: Hitler, Stalin i Initsiativa Germanskoi Diplomatii, 1938–39* (Moscow, 1991), 126–127, providing a somewhat different citation.

[25] *DGFP*, Ser. D, Vol. VI, No. 215.

[26] Information from D. C. Watt, *How War Came*, 230.

sin.'[27] Molotov's differences with Litvinov dated back to 1931, for he had repeatedly questioned the latter's attempt to ally the USSR with the western powers. The hatred between the two men persisted even after Litvinov's return to grace in 1941. On 3 May, after a fortnight of silence, Seeds told Litvinov that the British had not yet reached a decision. That evening the Narkomindel building was surrounded by NKVD troops. As morning broke, Litvinov was informed by Molotov, Malenkov, and Beria that he had been dismissed.

The tough, intelligent, obstinate, and inflexible Molotov, intensely loyal to Stalin, was appointed commissar for foreign affairs. It was hardly a pleasant experience to do business with him. A hard man, who shared with Hitler his vegetarianism and abhorrence of alcohol, Molotov spoke no foreign language and had never been outside the Soviet Union. He was not, however, an amateur with regard to foreign affairs. Usually present during Litvinov's often extended conversations with Stalin, he had many times previously acted as Stalin's spokesman on foreign policy. Stalin trusted him in so far as he trusted anyone. He was the only man from 1939 onwards, as we know from Stalin's appointment diary, who was almost in constant attendance when Stalin received various functionaries at the Kremlin from the early evening until late at night. Stalin telegraphed the senior Soviet representatives abroad that there had been a conflict between comrade Molotov and comrade Litvinov, who was accused of being disloyal to the party, and that Litvinov had asked to be relieved of his duties. The press announcement on 4 May, of course, made no reference to such a conflict. The axe also fell on Litvinov's closest advisors. Among those arrested were Nazarov, Litvinov's personal secretary, Hershelmann, the head of the general secretariat, Gnedin, the chief of the press department, and Plotkin, the director of the juridical department. According to the often unreliable Gnedin's memoirs (he was liberated during the Khrushchev thaw), they were interrogated and tortured during May and June in order to collect evidence for a public trial of Litvinov.[28] Gnedin was asked to testify to Litvinov's support for war and to the existence of an espionage ring within the Narkomindel that was tied to Radek and Bukharin. It has been tentatively suggested that by publicly accusing Litvinov and his collaborators of espionage, Stalin might have hoped to reassure Hitler about the change in Soviet policy.[29] The idea of a trial was abandoned in October 1939. With Molotov came the 'new men'. Potemkin, away in

[27] Quoted in Haslam, *The Soviet Union and the Threat from the East,* 129.
[28] Sabine Dullin, 'Le rôle de Maxime Litvinov dans les années trente', *Communisme,* 42/43/44 (1995), 88.
[29] Ibid., 89.

Ankara after a trip through the Balkans, retained his post as first deputy commissar for the West, but two new appointments were made. Semen Lozovsky, formerly head of the disbanded Profintern (the Red International of Trade Unions) became first deputy commissar for the East, and Vladimir Dekanozov, chief of the foreign department of the NKVD, was made third deputy commissar in order to finish carrying out the cleansing of the commissariat. If the younger entrants to the Foreign Ministry were diplomatic neophytes, they had come to maturity in the hard school of the Terror and could be expected, as under Litvinov, to march as directed.

Molotov's first task was to assure the outside world that there was no change in Soviet policy. In a sense this was true. The negotiations with Britain and France were resumed. The unyielding Molotov accomplished what Litvinov was unable to achieve. He got the western powers to negotiate on the Soviet terms and in time to accept most, but not the essential and all-important Polish agreement, of the original offer of 17 April. There was, however, a difference in the Soviet situation that cannot be ignored. First and foremost, Litvinov's dismissal meant that Stalin, a man who distrusted everybody and was suspicious of all foreign statesmen, tightened his control over foreign affairs. Molotov, as the outside world would learn, would make no move that did not carry his leader's imprimatur. Quite apart from their personal antagonisms, Litvinov and Molotov were publicly identified with alternative lines of diplomacy. It was not without significance that on 5 May, according to Schnurre, Astakhov indirectly asked the Germans whether the dismissal of Litvinov might cause 'a change in our attitude towards the Soviet Union'.[30] Germany's leading diplomatic and military experts on the Soviet Union were recalled for discussions with Hitler and Ribbentrop. For their part, the British anticipated a possible Soviet retreat into isolation and neutrality despite the many warnings that this might bring the Russians into the German orbit. It is not clear whether Stalin had yet decided to follow up the German contacts or to wait to see if he could forge a military alliance with the western powers whose military strength he judged to be superior to that of Nazi Germany. It was in the Soviet interest to stay in its non-aligned position as long as possible providing Stalin with the considerable bargaining power and preserving the manoeuvrability he had won with the British guarantee to Poland.

[30] *DGFP*, Ser. D, Vol. VI, No. 332.

III

The debate among historians about the background to the Nazi–Soviet pact continues and no final answers have emerged. We just do not know when Stalin decided to opt for a double-track policy or at what point he decided that talks with the British and French were not going anywhere. DVP documents suggest 29 July is the key date. There is no doubt that during May, alongside the difficult exchanges with Britain and France, there were talks between the Russians and the Germans. Which side took the initiative is still in dispute. The key point is that not much progress was made. The British reply to Litvinov's proposal came on 8 May; once again Halifax proposed that the USSR make a unilateral Soviet declaration paralleling the western guarantees. Bonnet was convinced, rightly, that the Russians would never accept such a one-sided arrangement and wanted to take up the Soviet offer of a tripartite alliance. Despite warnings from sources in Berlin that 'something was brewing in the East', Bonnet, though convinced that only a western alliance with the Soviets would deter Hitler, let Halifax set the leisurely pace in the talks with Moscow. There were a multitude of signals reaching London about German intentions and the possibility of a Russo-German *rapprochement*. They came from diplomatic and military sources in Berlin, including Lt. Colonel Count Gerhard von Schwerin, a German general staff officer, who warned that it was essential for Britain to take a firm stand against Hitler, and the opposition spokesman, Carl Goerdeler. On 14 May, Molotov rejected the British proposals. He demanded a tripartite mutual assistance pact, the extension of the guarantees to cover Estonia, Latvia, and Finland and a concrete military accord. He refused to go to Geneva to meet Halifax as Seeds suggested. Maisky, and not Potemkin, whom the British would have preferred, represented the USSR at the Council meeting.

During the next ten days there was a fierce debate in London and the pressures on Chamberlain and Halifax, who still opposed an alliance, mounted. Chatfield, the minister for co-ordination of defence and in touch with the chiefs of staff, reversed his earlier stand and argued that it would be dangerous to have the Soviets neutral in a war. A Soviet–German pact would be disastrous. Halifax and Cadogan also came around to the idea of alliance talks, albeit somewhat reluctantly. The Soviets turned down another attempt to make the unilateral declaration proposal more attractive by offering a pledge of an alliance once war broke out and even military staff conversations before that happened. Daladier and Bonnet, assisted by Léger, buttonholed the British foreign secretary on his way to Geneva. In Geneva, Maisky was not to be put off. The choice was clear, as the British foreign secretary gloomily conceded: either the breakdown of the negotiations or a triple alliance. Halifax bowed to the inevitable. In the Foreign Policy Committee, only 'Rab' Butler, the parliamentary under-secretary for foreign affairs, supported the prime minister in his continuing opposition to the alliance talks and, as Chamberlain admitted, 'he was not a very influential ally'. In the Commons, the alliance supporters mounted a strong and well-informed attack on Chamberlain's position. Churchill, their most influential spokesman, was carefully prepped by Maisky. The press overwhelmingly favoured the alliance, with *The Times* one of the few exceptions. At a *News Chronicle* policy conference on 19 May, it was agreed that 'in view of the almost unanimous feeling of public opinion in favour of an alliance with Russia ... we should continue to press the Government to lose no time in concluding their negotiations with that country'.[31] Finally, on 24 May, Chamberlain was overruled by his ministerial colleagues and, despite a threat of resignation, agreed to open talks for a 'triple pact'. Chamberlain's case against the alliance was further undermined when it became known as a consequence of the staff talks that the French would remain on the defensive and do nothing to draw off the weight of the German attack on Poland. Though Chamberlain was forced to bow to the cabinet majority, he continued to argue 'that the alliance would definitely be a lining up of opposing blocs and an association which would make any negotiation or discussion with the totalitarians difficult if not impossible'.[32] Even at this point, with the assistance of Horace Wilson, he engineered a 'most ingenious' way out of his difficulties by linking the alliance with the consent of threatened third states and with Article 16 of the League Covenant. He rashly informed the Commons that the new British proposals would make an early agreement possible.

Molotov had other ideas; he received Seeds and Payart, the French *chargé d'affaires*, sitting at a large desk on a raised platform and dismissed the new British proposal, whose terms he already knew. He referred to the interminable delays of the League and the ability of a small state like Bolivia to block action while the Soviet Union was being bombed. His repeated references to Bolivia made it almost impossible for Seeds to defend the British offer. Neither the ambassador's efforts at this meeting nor at a late-night interview on 30 May convinced Molotov that the British were serious about an alliance. Quite apart from the difficulties that he accused Chamberlain of creating, Molotov raised the key issue of

[31] Quoted in Richard Cockett, *Twilight of Truth: Chamberlain, Appeasement and Manipulation of the Press* (London, 1989), 116.

[32] Quoted in R. A. C. Parker, *Chamberlain and Appeasement*, 230.

those eastern states that did not want Soviet assistance against German occupation collapsing under German attack or, like Czechoslovakia, 'inviting' German troops into their country in response to threats. Seeds replied that his government would not impose guarantees of protection on independent states against their will. Already it was clear that the USSR and the western powers had different aims in mind; the former was thinking in terms of a war with Germany, while the latter were concerned with preventing that war from happening. On 31 May, Molotov addressed the Supreme Soviet and presented a review of the negotiations with the Allied powers, stressing the Soviet requirements for an effective defensive front and underlining the need for reciprocity which the western proposals did not yet offer. In the same speech, he gave the first positive public signal addressed to Berlin since March 1936, indicating that the Soviet government 'would not abstain' from economic relations with such countries as Germany and Italy and that credit negotiations with Germany might resume. He also used the occasion to issue a warning to Finland, which had refused to supply any information with regard to the fortifications of the Åland islands, and to raise the question of Japanese violations of the Manchurian border. The Japanese ambassador had been warned previously that Soviet patience was at its limit but the attacks and the Soviet counter-attacks along the Mongolian–Manchurian border continued.

Talks with the western powers were still high on the Soviet agenda and the Supreme Soviet formally endorsed the government's policy. On 2 June, Molotov handed Seeds and Naggiar a revised version of the British proposals. The countries to be guaranteed were to be named and would include Belgium, Greece, Turkey, Romania, and Poland as well as Latvia, Estonia, and Finland. The military agreement should be concluded as quickly as possible so as to come into force simultaneously with the political agreement. Neither side should make a separate peace. These provisions, in a somewhat different form, echoed those of Litvinov's April offer. The British began their usual lengthy process of internal consultation. Worried by the slow pace of the negotiations in Moscow, Halifax suggested that the British send their legal adviser to the Soviet capital but Cadogan convinced him to bring back Seeds instead. Unfortunately, Seeds took ill and William Strang was sent to Moscow, disappointing the Soviets who, like many in Britain, thought that a more senior person would be selected. Anthony Eden offered himself and, to Chamberlain's horror, Lloyd George suggested that Churchill should go. Strang was a first-rate negotiator but hardly known outside the Foreign Office. His energetic intervention in the Metropolitan-Vickers case during his previous assignment in Moscow hardly endeared him to those Soviet authorities who survived to remember the incident.

Strang favoured an alliance but as an official his private opinions were beside the point. He proved an excellent back-up for the hard-pressed Seeds, caught between the convoluted instructions sent by Halifax and the blunt and unmoving Molotov. Bonnet instructed Naggiar, who returned to Moscow in early June, to remain in the background. The French would take the initiative only if the British failed to get an agreement. On 7 June, Chamberlain gave the House of Commons a brief résumé of the talks and spoke of one or two difficulties to be resolved, especially giving guarantees to states that did not want them. He announced the departure of a Foreign Office official for Moscow.

From the beginning of May, contacts between the Germans and Russians resumed but like the earlier Merekalov–Weizsäcker conversations, they were still tentative and inconclusive. Stalin had in his possession a copy of a long report, dated 9 May, from Peter Kleist, Ribbentrop's advisor, probably intercepted by a Soviet agent, clearly stating Germany's ultimate intention to expand into the Soviet Union for ideological and economic reasons. Kleist pointed out that Germany would be militarily prepared to act against Poland by August and that the Polish war would be localized as neither Britain nor France had the forces to intervene. The memorandum cited German interest in the annexation of the Ukraine and in penetrating the Baltic states through peaceful means, separating them from the Soviet Union and ensuring their subservience to Germany. Alerted to the dangers that lay ahead, Stalin necessarily moved with caution. On 5 May, following Litvinov's dismissal, Schnurre told Astakhov, the main Soviet spokesman in Merekalov's absence, that the Škoda contracts would be honoured. The Soviets did not read too much into this concession, which they believed was theirs by right. Another Wilhelmstrasse official, Baron von Stumm, the deputy head of the press department, raised the question of improving German–Soviet relations. According to Astakhov, there were no grounds for taking such friendly remarks or the absence of anti-Soviet outbursts in the press as indicating any real German change of mind. As the Germans had caused the deterioration of Soviet–German relations, it was up to them to undertake any real improvements. Astakhov, possibly on his own initiative, informed the Germans that Moscow would welcome an amelioration of relations but that Germany would have to offer some inducement. Astakhov's reports reflected his personal distrust of the Germans.

Nonetheless, it was in May that Hitler, after a meeting with Gustav Hilger, the commercial attaché at the German embassy in Moscow, decided that something could be done with the Russians. Ambassador von der Schulenburg, who returned to Berlin for a week of consultations with Ribbentrop, was instructed to see Molotov and suggest the resumption of the trade talks, but to proceed with caution so as not to alarm the Japanese whom the German foreign minister still hoped might agree to the tripartite pact. At a key meeting with Molotov on 20 May, before the British decision to go ahead with the alliance talks, von der Schulenburg suggested that the credit negotiations should be resumed and that 'the famous' Schnurre would be sent to Moscow to expedite them. Molotov, remembering the earlier fiasco, was not prepared to play games. 'We have reached the conclusion that for the economic talks to succeed', he told von der Schulenburg, 'an appropriate political basis would have to be created'.[33] The ambassador reported to Berlin that he thought that Molotov was playing for time, did not want to engage himself with the Germans at the moment, and would leave any political initiative to the Germans. von der Schulenburg was instructed 'to sit tight' and wait for the Russians to speak more plainly. Meanwhile, Soviet agents were feeding the Germans with reports about the Anglo-Soviet talks, which were intended to play on German anxieties. Weizsäcker, in a cancelled telegram, explained that the Soviet negotiations with Britain showed that the Russians were afraid of German aggression against the USSR though 'such intentions are far from our mind' and that the Germans, too, were 'naturally mistrustful of the Comintern's attitude'. It was necessary, therefore, 'to restore mutual confidence and put this to a practical test'. Weizsäcker proposed that the economic negotiations should be followed by an official avowal of a return to normal political relations.[34] Uncertain of what Molotov actually meant by his comment to von der Schulenburg, Weizsäcker sought clarification from Astakhov on 30 May. The Soviet representative, who appears not to have been informed of the Schulenburg–Molotov conversation, referred to the 'extraordinary rumours' being spread in Berlin about Soviet–German relations including a story of a military alliance, with the Czech general and former minister of defence, Syrovy, acting as the go-between. Astakhov was generally elusive and once again reported to Moscow that the Germans were testing the possibility of negotiations in the hope of preventing the Soviet *rapprochement* with Britain. They would commit themselves to nothing and had not even used the term, 'improvement of relations'. Weizsäcker encouraged Ribbentrop; Astakhov had assured him that the Soviet government was still faithful to the view that a *rapprochement* with Germany 'need not involve ideological considerations'. The state secretary concluded that Molotov was prepared to accept a German approach.[35]

[33] *DVP*, Vol. XXII, Book 1, No. 326. Also quoted in Roberts, *The Soviet Union and the Origins of the Second World War*, 76.

[34] *DGFP*, Ser. D, Vol. VI, No. 441.

[35] *DGFP*, Ser. D, Vol. VI, No. 529.

On 31 May, Molotov's report to the Supreme Soviet referred to the conclusion of business arrangements with Germany and Italy. He reiterated his warnings to the Japanese ambassador about the attacks along the Mongolian frontier. The fear of war in the Far East shadowed the Soviet European negotiations. Victor Sorge, the accomplished Soviet spy in Tokyo, had a serious motorcycle accident on 13 May and radio transmissions to Moscow were considerably reduced, leaving the Soviet authorities without their usual source of information just as the fighting around Khalkhin-Gol (Nomonhan) was becoming serious. Even when Sorge resumed his activities, his chiefs in Moscow (he was attached to the Red Army's Department Four) expressed scepticism about his optimistic appraisal of the Japanese intentions. He wrote in 1942, during his imprisonment, that 'The Soviet Union . . . held the deepest suspicion that Japan was planning an attack on the Soviet Union. This suspicion was so strongly held that the Moscow authorities sometimes found my analyses to the contrary unacceptable. Two specific instances of this were during the Nomon-Han battle and the great mobilization of the summer of 1941.'[36]

Detailed information from Peter Kleist, forwarded to Stalin on 19 June, revealed that Hitler was determined to solve the Polish problem at all costs even at the risk of fighting a two-front war. Stalin learned, too, that Hitler would not be deterred by the possibility of an Anglo-Soviet bloc. Hitler counted on Moscow to 'conduct negotiations with us, as she had no interest whatever in a conflict with Germany, nor was she anxious to be defeated for the sake of England and France'. Kleist went on to report that Hitler believed that 'a new Rapallo stage should be achieved in German–Russian relations and that according to the precedent of the German–Polish agreement, it would be necessary to conduct a policy of *rapprochement* and economic collaboration with Moscow for a limited period of time. In the opinion of the Führer, the amicable relations which would prevail during the next two years between Germany and Russia should be devoted to the settlement of problems in western Europe.' The Baltic states 'would not be subjected to German military pressure, neither during the time of our conflict with Poland, nor in the following two year period'.[37] This intelligence was confirmed by intercepts of von der Schulenburg's telegrams to Berlin.

[36] Quotation from Sorge's memoir in Chalmers Johnson, *'An Instance of Treason': Ozaki Hotsumi and the Sorge Spy Ring,* expanded edition (Stanford, CA, 1990), 152.

[37] Military archives, op. 9157, d.2. II, 350–360, quoted in Gabriel Gorodetsky, *Mif Ledokola* (Moscow, 1995), 59. Kindly translated by Gorodetsky for the author.

It would appear that, on the German side, Hitler was thinking in terms of a short-term agreement with the Soviet Union. The possibilities opened up by the Schulenburg-Molotov conversation were undoubtedly considered in both camps. According to German sources, the Soviet government tested the ground through an intermediary, Parvan Draganov, the Bulgarian minister in Berlin. Astakhov, writing to Moscow on 14 June, claimed that Draganov tried to convince him that an alliance with Britain would be disadvantageous to the USSR and that a comprehensive agreement with Germany was possible. It may be that Draganov, who had many contacts with those German army generals who favoured a return to Rapallo, was representing their views. The Germans needed Soviet raw materials for rearmament yet imports from the USSR continued to decline. The figures showed a further drop in the value of imports from 50 million RM in 1938, an already low amount, to only 6 million RM for the first quarter of 1939.[38] When, on 17 June, Astakhov met von der Schulenburg, in Berlin on leave, the latter tried unsuccessfully to draw him out about Soviet intentions. The *chargé* knew very little about what was going on in Moscow, and sought clarification from Molotov with regard both to the Anglo–Soviet talks and as to the attitude he should adopt towards the German authorities. The commissar was not prepared to share his thoughts with his representative, who was later to suffer the same fate as so many other faithful servants of the USSR. Recalled to Moscow in August 1939, a few days before Ribbentrop's arrival in the Soviet capital, he was given a subordinate post at the Museum of the People of the USSR, although the Germans wanted him to be named as ambassador to Germany.

Both Hitler and Stalin were still playing a 'wait and see' game. It was only after Ciano's visit to Berlin to celebrate the new 'pact of steel' that Ribbentrop learned that the Japanese had decided to reserve their position if war broke out in Europe. Concerned with what he thought to be the imminent conclusion of an Anglo–Soviet agreement and prompted by Weizsäcker, Ribbentrop moved on the Russian front. With Hitler's permission, he authorized Weizsäcker to sound out Astakhov and instructed von der Schulenburg to approach Molotov in Moscow. The German ambassador told Molotov that he was authorized by Hitler and Ribbentrop to say that Germany not only wanted to normalize but to improve its relations with the Soviet Union. Molotov was unimpressed: 'If that is all the ambassador can offer, even after his visit to Berlin, it is obvious that he is a great optimist who considers that there is

[38] *DGFP*, Ser. D, Vol VI, No. 530. Information with regard to Draganov from Stoicho Moshanov, *Moiiata Misiia v Kairo* (Sofia, 1991) and was given to me by Dr V. Dimitrov.

nothing wrong with Soviet–German relations.'[39] The commissar was not assuaged by Germany's non-aggression treaties with Latvia and Estonia that Schulenburg claimed were proof of German goodwill towards Russia. He reminded the ambassador of the ease with which Germany had abrogated the non-aggression pact with Poland; treaties were not sacrosanct for Germany. Even the economic talks stalled. Gustav Hilger, the economics counsellor at the Moscow embassy, contacted Anastas Mikoyan, the Soviet trade commissar, and a visit by Julius Schnurre was tentatively arranged. At the end of June, however, possibly connected with the negotiations with Britain and France, the Russians pulled back. Mikoyan insisted that the political difficulties between the two countries would have to be solved before Schnurre's visit. For the moment, Hitler appears to have grown tired of the whole affair. He called off the economic discussions in Moscow and temporarily suspended any further political overtures.

In mid-June, Strang arrived in Moscow with the new British proposals for the alliance. These did not meet Molotov's demand for guarantees for states that did not want them. The commissar not only rejected the new draft but accused the British and French of treating the Soviet government as being 'naïve and foolish people'. He wanted no consultation but an automatic guarantee to keep the border states out of the German reach. If the western powers refused to guarantee Estonia, Latvia, and Finland, it might be best for the three powers to agree only to defend each other against direct attack. The negotiations appeared to be going nowhere as Molotov rejected new western proposals and made new demands. The frustration on the western side mounted in the face of Molotov's inflexibility. In the background were continuing reports that the Germans were seeking an agreement with the Soviet Union. Vansittart penned agitated warnings based on information from his private sources but Cadogan thought them suspect and that 'Van' was too easily upset. Even Sir Nevile Henderson wrote from Berlin on 13 June: 'I feel intuitively that the Germans are getting at Stalin.'[40] Chamberlain was not alone, however, in believing that a 'real alliance' between Germany and the Soviet Union was impossible. British suspicions tended to be intermittent and low-key. It was difficult to evaluate the incoming intelligence and almost impossible to sort the wheat from the chaff. Much that was received was related to the commercial talks between Germany and the Soviet Union. Other intelligence was thought to be 'misinformation', instigated either by the Germans or

[39] GK, no. 442.

[40] Quoted in Christopher Andrew, *Secret Service: The Making of the British Intelligence Community* (London, 1985), 424.

by the Soviets to further their own purposes. Frank Roberts of the Central department thought it 'in the Russian interest to frighten us with the bogy of an agreement with Germany'.[41]

Once the talks in Moscow were in progress (the trade talks were publicly announced on 22 July), western officials assumed that Stalin was too shrewd and far-thinking to prefer the uncertainties of a bargain with Hitler, the eternal anti-Bolshevik, to the assurance of western assistance in a European war against Germany. On 24 May, Colonel Gauché, the head of the *Deuxième Bureau*, informed the French high command that though Germany was probably making overtures to the USSR, the Russians were 'not considering a pact with Germany' and these overtures were 'almost certainly without effect'.[42] Even in late July when the intensive German–Soviet talks began, neither the British nor the French intelligence services appear to have picked up any information about the negotiations. Since the start of the year, a young German diplomat attached to the German embassy in Moscow, Hans von Herwarth, kept his tennis partner, Charles Bohlen of the United States embassy, continuously and accurately informed of the details of the intermittent German courtship of the Soviets and conveyed similar information to the Italian embassy as early as 6 May.[43] Much of this information was reaching the authorities in Paris and London whatever the seeming lack of definite intelligence.[44]

It was only at the eleventh hour when, on 17 August, the Americans told the British the news derived from Herwarth's conversation with Bohlen, that the political basis of the German–Soviet pact had been agreed. It was sent by airmail to London but arrived at the Foreign Office only on 22 August possibly due to the intervention of the Soviet mole in the Communications department of the Foreign Office. As Laurence Collier, the head of the Northern department, admitted after the pact was signed, by putting themselves in the Soviet position the British had concluded, wrongly, that 'isolation, rather than a *rapprochement* with Germany' was the most probable Russian alternative to an alliance with the western powers. The problem in London, as in Paris, was not the absence of evidence that an agreement might be concluded but the conviction that it was unlikely to materialize.

41 Ibid., 425.

42 SHD-DAT, 1N 44–7, 'Compte-rendu de la réunion des Chefs d'état-Major du 24 Mai'.

43 See Brian R. Sullivan, ' "Where One Man, and Only One Man, Led": Italy's Path from Non-Alignment to Non-Belligerency to War, 1937–1940', in Neville Wylie (ed.), *European Neutrals and Non-Belligerents during the Second World War* (Cambridge, 2002), 132.

44 See Brian R. Sullivan, ' "Where One Man, and Only One Man, Led"', in Wylie (ed.), *European Neutrals and Non-Belligerents*, 133 and fn. 37 with full references.

Given the information the western powers had at their disposal, the agreement could not have come as a surprise.

By the end of May, the Soviet–western talks were at an *impasse*. Molotov, more outspoken and less urbane than Litvinov but taking the same line as his predecessor, demanded 'guarantees of protection' for states—particularly the Baltic states and Finland—which did not want them. On 31 May, Molotov told the Supreme Soviet that 'Soviet Russia was unwilling to pull other people's chestnuts out of the fire.'[45] Between the Soviet proposals of 2 June and 1 July, the British and French made three separate proposals to Molotov. Each was rejected and counter-proposals presented. There was a growing sense of exasperation in London but the cabinet majority believed that the talks had to continue even at the cost of further retreats. Maisky reported from London that the British could not risk the breakdown of the talks because the public would have found failure incomprehensible. The Soviet embassy as well as the *Tass* representatives made sure that the electorate was aware of the dilatoriness of its own government. Possibly more important than public pressure was the belief, shared by Halifax, that only an alliance with the Soviet Union would give substance to the policy of deterrence. As a consequence, Molotov was never actually threatened with an ultimatum. The Soviets knew exactly what they wanted and Molotov stuck to his brief. There were three key points at issue: Soviet insistence that Finland and the Baltic states be included in the guarantee, the acceptance of the Soviet definition of 'indirect aggression', and the Soviet demand that the political and military agreements be concluded simultaneously. The British gave way on the first and last points, prodded in each instance by the French, but fought against accepting the second which would have allowed the Soviet Union to interfere with the independence of neighbouring states. The Foreign Office was repeatedly warned by the Finnish and Baltic representatives against acceptance. Molotov refused to budge. It was only by securing the maximum concessions from the British that Stalin and the sceptics could be convinced that the alliance was worth having. The real test, however, as the anticipated date of German action against Poland drew near, was whether the western powers would conclude the defensive alliance that Stalin wanted. Much of June was spent arguing over which states were to be guaranteed and the Soviet demand for joint assistance against both direct and indirect aggression. The French, alerted by intelligence reports to the probability of a German action in Danzig in late August, urged that the British give way. By the end of the month, the British were driven to agree to the Soviet proposed list of

[45] Neilson, *Britain, Soviet Russia and the Versailles Order*, 297.

states but insisted that they be named in a secret protocol. If their offer was rejected, Britain would try for a simple tripartite mutual guarantee without any provision for assisting other countries. Chamberlain was more sanguine about the possibility of failure than his foreign secretary and found his colleagues excessively nervous of the consequences. He remained, as before, sceptical of the real value of Russian assistance.

The prospects for success were hardly encouraging. Neither side trusted the other; each was accused of not really wanting a pact and of using 'bazaar techniques' (Maisky's description). As the difficulties over the Baltic states continued, Molotov's position became more unyielding. The USSR wanted an absolute guarantee of Soviet security. This meant the right to move troops into any neighbouring state—Poland was crucial—whether they were wanted or not. In London, the Soviet demands were seen as highly threatening to the future independence of the border states. Whatever might have been British reservations about fighting to preserve their independence, it was another matter to open these states, against their will, to the possibility of Soviet occupation in order to deter Hitler. The British were afraid that Stalin would use the cover of the alliance to pursue his own territorial ambitions. After a war in which the Soviet Union, among the victors, paid the highest human price and whose troops occupied half of Europe, the Americans and British conceded what the Chamberlain cabinet was unprepared to give in 1939. British tactics proved clumsy and counter-productive but their resistance to Molotov's demands, given their reading of Soviet intentions, can be defended. Seeds was criticized by Hoare and Chamberlain for appearing 'feeble and weak-kneed'. The problem was not with poor Seeds or even with the divisions of opinion in London. Apart from the prime minister, who clung to the policies of the past, others in the cabinet were unwilling to pay the Soviet price for strengthening the deterrent. Only some believed that, if the deterrent failed and war came, Britain would need the Soviet Union's assistance to defeat Hitler's Germany. If the French had recognized the value of the Soviet Union's participation in an eastern front as the necessary prerequisite to the success of their long war strategy, planners were unwilling to examine the actual issues of Soviet involvement too closely.[46] There was, therefore, considerable hesitation about putting small and independent nations at risk knowing that they did not want Soviet assistance. The real problem was the weakness of the British position. While Seeds and Strang were negotiating with the 'tiresome' Molotov, there was a blow-up in the Far East in mid-June and the British, after a flurry of

[46] Talbot C. Imlay, *Facing the Second World War*, 45.

diplomatic activity involving the Americans as well as the Japanese, chose to compromise over Tientsin rather than to risk the possibility of a conflict with Japan. Britain was clearly under pressure both in Europe and in the Far East while the Russians, in part because of the Anglo-French guarantees to Poland, could afford to wait and insist that their terms be accepted. One can hardly blame Halifax for losing his patience. On 23 June, he asked Maisky 'point blank' whether the Soviets really wanted a treaty at all and complained that, 'throughout the negotiations the Soviet Government had not budged a single inch and we had made all the advances and concessions'. Maisky replied, 'of course'; he later admitted that the Soviets should not have set their 'irreducible minimum' initially but should have asked for more than they wanted so as to subsequently offer concessions. Halifax concluded the interview on a bitter note: 'I said that saying No to everything was not my idea of negotiation and that it had a striking resemblance to Nazi methods of dealing with international questions.'[47] Unwilling to see the talks fail, the British gave way, slowly and grudgingly, in the face of Molotov's refusal to compromise over the border states. The possibility that the Russians would engage with the Germans was a powerful incentive to reach an agreement with Moscow.

The British objections and hesitations fed Stalin's suspicions of their ultimate intentions. There were public signs of Soviet distrust. On 29 June, an article by Zhdanov appeared in *Pravda* under the headline, 'The English and French Governments do not want an Agreement on Terms of Equality with the USSR'. Zhdanov's concerns about Leningrad had made him particularly anxious about the slow progress of the talks and Britain's unwillingness to guarantee the Baltic states. The concurrent visit of the chief of the German army staff, Franz Halder, to Estonia and Finland revived Stalin's fears that Finland might become the 'springboard' for anti-Soviet moves for either of the two main 'bourgeois-imperialist groupings'. Zhdanov accused the British and French of complicating the negotiations in order to disrupt them, claiming that they did not want a real agreement or one acceptable to the USSR and that 'the only thing they really want is to talk about an agreement and, by making play with the obstinacy of the Soviet Union, to prepare their own public opinion for an eventual deal with the aggressors'.[48] He made much of the speed of the Soviet reactions in contrast to the dilatory procedures of the English and the French to buttress his argument. There were good reasons why Molotov could react with speed to any western proposal. The Soviets had a highly useful 'man in place', almost

[47] Quotations from Neilson, *Britain, Soviet Russia and the Versailles Order*, 304.
[48] *DBFP*, 3rd ser., Vol. VI, No. 193.

certainly John Herbert King, a member of the Foreign Office communications department and a Soviet spy reactivated in the spring of 1939. King had access to the diplomatic traffic between London and the British diplomatic missions abroad and could alert Moscow as to what could be expected. He or some other source was used to transmit information, when, and in the form, the Soviets wanted, to the German embassy in London. At the end of June, the German embassy reported to Berlin that the Soviet government was conducting the pact negotiations without enthusiasm and would not be disappointed by their failure. The Soviets were intercepting British communications and benefited from such informants as Donald Maclean, attached to the British embassy in Paris, an Italian agent in Rome who regularly burgled the safe of the British embassy, and reactivated agents in other key European listening posts.

On 1 July, the new Anglo-French draft was handed to the commissar. It was proposed that the countries to be guaranteed against direct aggression should be named in a secret protocol and that the list include, as well as Finland and the Baltic states, Switzerland, the Netherlands, and Luxemburg, the last added to satisfy the French. Molotov accepted the idea of a secret protocol but balked at the inclusion of the new countries protesting that neither the Netherlands nor Switzerland had recognized the USSR. He also suggested that the words 'direct or indirect' aggression should be inserted into the treaty. Two days later, in a formal reply, he agreed to include the Netherlands and Switzerland on the condition that Poland and Turkey conclude treaties of mutual assistance with the USSR and that the definition of 'indirect aggression' as an 'internal *coup d'état* or a reversal of policy in the interests of the aggressor' be included in the secret protocol. He was demanding exactly what the British did not want and, in the case of Poland, could not offer.

There were immediate, if different, reactions from London and Paris to Molotov's demands. Chamberlain and Halifax were prepared to revert to the limited tripartite pact. Other members of the cabinet, led by Hoare and Stanley, held out for a trade-off, the dropping of the Netherlands and Switzerland if the Soviet Union abandoned its definition of 'indirect aggression'. Bonnet telephoned from Paris. He wanted a general agreement that included, above all, provision for the defence of Poland and Romania. France would consider the simple tripartite pact only if everything else failed and only after Seeds and Naggiar referred back to their capitals. The ambassadors and Strang saw Molotov on 8 and 9 July. The commissar refused to consider the inclusion of the three newly named states unless Turkey and Poland concluded pacts of mutual assistance with the Soviet Union. He insisted on the inclusion of both 'direct' and 'indirect' aggression in the secret protocol but reformulated the definition of indirect aggression. At the next meeting, he again altered the definition to enlarge the signatories' freedom. Action would be taken if any of the named states allowed its territory or its armed forces to be used by the aggressor either under threat or without threat. Molotov again raised the earlier Soviet demand that the political and military agreements be signed and come into force simultaneously.

Once more, the bargaining resumed. The French, but not the British, were ready to accept the Soviet proposal dealing with indirect aggression. Halifax was prepared to trade off the simultaneous signing of the military and political agreements, which was unacceptable to the French, for the dropping of Molotov's definition of indirect aggression. The French offered, as a way of reassuring the Russians, to send representatives of the chiefs of staff to start technical negotiations in Moscow. They hoped that these would not need to involve Poland or Romania though Naggiar, their ambassador, repeatedly reminded Bonnet that the co-operation of both was vital for the success of the talks. The Soviet Union 'would not compromise itself against Germany without "precise and concrete military guarantees"'.[49] Molotov knew of the Anglo-French exchanges and their differences but was determined to have the 'i's dotted and 't's crossed before committing the USSR to an alliance. To Chamberlain's delight, Halifax was getting 'fed up' with Molotov. 'If we do get an agreement, as I rather think we shall', the prime minister wrote to his sister, 'I'm afraid I shall not regard it as a triumph. I put as little value on Russian military capacity as I believe the Germans do.'[50] The foreign secretary instructed Seeds to warn Molotov, at a time of his own choosing, that 'our patience is well-nigh exhausted' and that he should not presume that the British would yield every time the Soviet government put forward a new demand.[51]

The exchanges in Moscow on 17 July were unsatisfactory. Molotov was pleased that the western powers had dropped their demand to include the Netherlands and Switzerland in the guarantee and agreed to consider, though doubtful, their proposed formula for consultation with states not actually named in the secret protocol. At this point Molotov's interest had shifted to the question of a single politico-military agreement. He asked the ambassadors whether their governments were willing to open military conversations. Naggiar answered in the affirmative; Seeds insisted on prior agreement on the political articles in dispute. The Soviets would have to move on the question of indirect

[49] Michael J. Carley, 'End of the "Low, Dishonest Decade": Failure of the Anglo-Franco-Soviet Alliance in 1939', *Europe–Asia Studies*, 45: 2 (1993). 324.

[50] Quoted in Parker, *Chamberlain and Appeasement*, 240.

[51] *DBFP*, 3rd ser., Vol. VI, No. 298.

aggression. Molotov complained of misrepresentations in the British and French press, items in fact emanating from the *Tass* representative in London as part of the Soviet campaign to increase public pressure on the western governments. Molotov was somewhat misled by Maisky, an enthusiast for the alliance, who, in reporting that public opinion would force the London cabinet to yield, encouraged his chief's intransigence. Maisky and Surits fuelled Soviet fears that the Chamberlain government would try to come to terms with Hitler before concluding the alliance with the Soviet Union. Whatever reassurance the Soviets might have drawn from Chamberlain's Commons statement on 10 July that a seizure of Danzig would not be considered as a local matter but as a threat to the independence of Poland, was undone by the sensational and exaggerated account of the exchanges between Robert Hudson and Helmuth Wohlthat which appeared in the *News Chronicle* on 22 July. The subsequent denials and explanations only confirmed Stalin's suspicions that the British were not to be trusted and that the 'Chamberlain clique', Lloyd George's phrase quoted by Maisky, was manoeuvring to secure an agreement with Germany. Seeds and Naggiar urged their governments to begin the military talks.

There may well have been a connection between Molotov's insistence on the start of military talks and the renewed Soviet–German contacts. Hitler began to recalculate his strategic situation. The failure to secure the Japanese military alliance and the approaching August date for the Polish campaign may have been the catalyst, or it may have been the fear, assisted by the Soviet misinformation campaign, that Moscow was nearing an agreement with the western powers. Though Hitler still hoped that an Anglo-German understanding could be reached once the Polish question was settled, an Anglo-Soviet alliance would pose a danger to his plans for a campaign against Poland. It could mean a premature European war. 'This summer's decision between peace and war will, it is considered here, depend on whether the doubtful negotiations in Moscow bring Russia into the orbit of the western powers', Weizsäcker noted on 29 July. 'If they do not, the depression in that quarter will be such that we can do what we like with Poland.'[52] Hitler was worried enough to suggest that if the Moscow negotiations were successful, he would call off the Polish operation and hold a 'party rally of peace'. This would not have happened, but clearly without a German-Italo-Japanese alliance to threaten the British, the conclusion of an Anglo-Soviet agreement would have been a blow to his plans. Hitler was really not interested in what Helmuth Wohlthat discussed

[52] Leonidas E. Hill (ed.), *Die Weizsäcker–Papiere* (Frankfurt am Main, Berlin and Vienna, 1974), 157.

with Robert Hudson on 20 July. Offers of colonies, peaceful revision of Germany's eastern frontiers, and declarations to refrain from the use of force were hardly what Hitler had in mind just weeks before the start of the Polish campaign. An arrangement with Britain could be made only after Poland was 'smashed'. A settlement with Russia, though it went against all of Hitler's instincts, would detach Britain from Poland and give Germany a free hand to move East.

Accounts as to who took the initiative to restart the trade talks differ but whether it was the Germans or the Russians is relatively unimportant. The key point was that the talks were resumed and that Moscow left the Germans in no doubt that they wanted something more than a commercial agreement. The Soviet deputy trade representative in Berlin, Barbarin, sought out Schnurre and told the somewhat surprised German official on 18 July that if their discussions resulted in a clarification, he was empowered to sign a treaty in Berlin. On 21 July, the British, after a series of communications from the French embassy in London and an impassioned plea from Bonnet to Halifax, agreed to the simultaneous conclusion of the military and political agreements and to immediate military conversations if the breakdown of the current talks appeared imminent. By this time, Halifax knew that discussions of some kind were taking place between the German and Soviet governments. He was not prepared, however, to abandon the fight against the Soviet stand on indirect aggression and rejected the French appeal to concede the point. Chamberlain favoured calling the Soviet bluff, but Halifax, while he disliked the idea, agreed to begin the military talks. 'We are only spinning out the time before the inevitable break comes', Chamberlain wrote to his sister, 'and it is rather hard that I should have to bear the blame for dilatory action when if I wasn't hampered by others I would have closed the discussions one way or another long ago'.[53] On the evening of the same day the cabinet agreed to military talks, Moscow Radio carried an announcement of the Barbarin–Schnurre negotiations.

Molotov, in his meeting with the Anglo-French representatives on 23 July, pushed aside the whole problem of 'indirect aggression' that had been the subject of acrimonious debate for three weeks. Such questions could easily be solved, he said, once the military agreement was concluded. Pessimistic about the possibility of success, Seeds hoped that the drawn-out negotiations would tide the Entente powers over the next dangerous months before the autumn rains began. On 25 July, the British

[53] Quoted in Robert Self (ed.), *The Neville Chamberlain Diary Letters*, Vol. 4, 432 (to Ida, 23 July 1939).

and French, the latter with considerable relief, agreed to authorize the new conversations. Without dropping the problem of indirect aggression, the British arranged to send a military delegation to Moscow. Halifax complacently assumed that the talks in themselves would prevent the Soviet Union from negotiating with Germany. He showed no sense of urgency despite knowing, as did the far more anxious Bonnet, that the *Reichswehr* was preparing for action during the second half of August. The story of the subsequent weeks is well-known. The British military mission was headed by Admiral Plunkett-Ernle-Erle-Drax, a name too easily mocked. Under the circumstances, Drax was not a wise choice. An extremely able naval officer and aide to the king and one of those pushing for offensive action against Italy in the Mediterranean, he carried weight in Admiralty circles but was an unknown figure in Moscow. He might have been more acceptable if accompanied by an army officer of high rank, at least equivalent to that of General Ironside, who had just returned from his much touted trip to Poland. Instead, Major General T. G. G. Heywood, an ex-military attaché, was sent. The French selected General Joseph Doumenc, one of their most senior serving generals, to head their mission. Stalin did his homework; he told Molotov and Beria: 'They're not being serious. These people can't have the proper authority. London and Paris are playing poker again, but we would like to know if they are capable of carrying out European manoeuvres.' 'Still, I think the talks should go ahead', Molotov said, looking him in the eye. 'Well, if they must, they must', Stalin concluded blandly.[54] There was the farce of sending Drax without written credentials and with instructions to 'go slowly'. And there was the barely defensible decision to send the two missions on an old, slow, commercial vessel, the *City of Exeter*. Whatever may have been the greater impatience of the French and their complaints, they followed in the British wake. General Gamelin's instructions to General Doumenc, though non-specific, made it clear that he hoped he would get a 'military accord that provided the broadest help possible from the Soviets'. Doumenc's draft accord, composed while en route to Russia, envisaged the passage of Soviet land and air forces across the Vilna Corridor (into Eastern Poland).[55] Knowing that the subject of Polish–Soviet co-operation was taboo in Warsaw, neither Halifax nor Bonnet, already having difficulties with Beck, wanted to raise the subject. The British and French missions arrived in Moscow on the afternoon of 11 August.

Another poker game was also in progress but hidden from public view. On the day after the Moscow announcement of the resumption of

[54] Quoted in Dimitri Volkogonov, *Stalin: Triumph and Tragedy* (London, 1988), 349.
[55] Imlay, *Facing the Second World War*, 45.

the Soviet–German trade talks, Weizsäcker cabled Schulenburg, advising him that Hitler wanted an agreement with the USSR as soon as possible. The ambassador was 'to pick up the threads again'.[56] On 24 July, in Berlin, Schnurre outlined to Astakhov a three-stage plan for the improvement of German–Soviet relations: an agreement on trade and credit, on culture and press relations, and finally a settlement of the political questions. Two days later, at a dinner in a Berlin restaurant with Astakhov and Barbarin, the head of the Soviet trade mission, Schnurre, briefed by Ribbentrop, compared what England and Germany could offer to the Soviet Union. He insisted there was no problem between Germany and the Soviet Union from the Baltic to the Black Sea or in the Far East that could not be solved. As was so often the case, the German and Soviet accounts of the evening differ but Schnurre did warn his superiors that he thought Moscow was undecided and would pursue tactics of 'delay and postponement' towards both Germany and Britain. Astakhov was becoming convinced that the Germans really meant business but he had no idea of what his masters had decided. On 28 July, Molotov assured the *chargé* that he had done the right thing in limiting himself to forwarding Schnurre's remarks. The Russians were waiting for more detailed and practical offers. Given the Soviet distrust of all the capitalist governments, Stalin could well have feared another Munich. An agreement with Nazi Germany was a gamble that might expose the USSR to the worst of all possible worlds. On 2 August, Ribbentrop saw Astakhov but offered little beyond what Schnurre had said earlier apart from a gentle hint about an understanding over the fate of Poland. It was only on 3 August that Schulenburg was able to secure an appointment with Molotov. The ninety-minute meeting was not entirely pleasant. While the ambassador offered the Soviets the possibility of arrangements in the Baltic and in Poland, he was reminded of the Anti-Comintern pact and Germany's encouragement of Japanese aggression against the Soviet Union. The German ambassador warned his government that it would require a 'considerable effort' to reverse the Soviet course.

The Far Eastern question was certainly a factor in Stalin's calculations. It should be remembered that the Soviets were aware of the long-standing links between the Poles and the Japanese. The Japanese attacks on the Mongolian frontier in May had been repulsed but on the 26–27 June, after a pause while Sino-Japanese action switched to the Yangtse valley, the Japanese air force renewed its assaults. Sorge sent reassuring messages from Tokyo that German–Japanese military action against the Soviet Union was unlikely. Germany was preoccupied with Poland and

[56] *DGFP*, Ser. D, Vol. VI, No. 700.

the struggle with Britain and France. The German armed forces would not be ready for war until 1941 at the earliest. The Japanese high command, however, proved unable to rein in the Kwantung army. On 2–3 July, after acquiring considerable reinforcements, the Japanese launched a successful attack on the border and invited foreign observers to see how weak the Soviets were. By this time, Stalin was distinctly worried. On 5 July, he ordered a reorganization of the Red Army in the Far East and dispatched a personal letter to Chiang Kai-shek, painting a very positive picture of the Soviet negotiations with Britain and France and urging Chiang to take the offensive against Japan. The Chinese leader would not be pushed. By mid-July, the Red Army reorganization was complete and the 57th special corps in Mongolia was reformed and re-equipped as the First Army Group under the command of Georgii Zhukov, a protegé of Timoshenko who had escaped the purges. Aware that the Kwantung army was preparing a general offensive for 24 August, Zhukov, with a force vastly superior to that of the Japanese, launched a massive attack, one of the first to combine tanks, artillery, aircraft, and infantry in one operation, on 20 August. Due in part to Zhukov's exceptional skills and to the Red Army's operational superiority, it was a highly successful operation boosting the army's morale.

The situation in the Far East before the Khalkhin-Gol victory encouraged Stalin to see what his wooers could offer. The British had decided against soliciting Soviet assistance against Japan and appeared to be giving way to the Japanese over Tientsin. Ambassador Craigie advised that an agreement with Moscow would undermine the position of the moderates in Tokyo. Shigemitsu Mamoru, the new Russophobe Japanese ambassador, who had come to London from Moscow, told Rab Butler that an Anglo-Soviet agreement in the Far East would throw Japan into the arms of Germany. As the diplomatic intercepts revealed that the Japanese ambassador was opposing closer Japanese–German relations, his warnings with regard to Russia were taken seriously. While the British excluded any consideration of Japan during the tripartite pact talks, Ribbentrop and Schnurre, on the contrary, specifically linked the European and Far Eastern questions in late July and early August. At the critical meeting between Molotov and Schulenburg on 15 August, the former specifically asked whether Germany could exert influence on these matters or whether it was inadvisable to raise the question at this point. Though Schulenburg had no instructions on the question, he informed Molotov that Ribbentrop had told him that he could bring his own 'not insignificant influence' to bear on Japan's position.

During the first two weeks of August, the Germans increased their pressure on the Soviet representatives but waited for Moscow to react.

Molotov (i.e. Stalin) appeared interested, but Soviet suspicions ran deep and the Russians wanted to know exactly what Hitler was willing to offer. On 8 August, in a letter to Molotov, Astakhov summarized the state of 'negotiations'. He was still distrustful of Germany's longer-range intentions once the Soviet Union was neutralized in any German–Polish war. It appeared that in return for Soviet disinterest in the fate of Danzig and former 'German Poland', the Germans would declare their lack of interest in the Baltic countries, with the exception of Lithuania, in Bessarabia, and in Russian Poland and would give up their aspirations in the Ukraine. Molotov replied that he was interested but that such discussions required considerable preparation and that he would like them to take place in Moscow. Hitler agreed; he informed Ciano at Salzburg on 12 August that the Kremlin was prepared for negotiations to be held in Moscow but he had not decided whether the German ambassador or a special envoy should conduct the talks.

The Führer needed to move quickly. While he knew from military intelligence reports that neither the British nor the French were in a position to offer military aid to Poland, he had to assure others in Berlin that they need not fear British intervention. The German military timetable was tight. For logistical reasons, the Germans would not be ready to act before 26 August and yet the Polish campaign had to be over by early October before the autumn rains began. Hitler's generals pressed for an early decision on the date of the attack; at the very latest, it should be on the 23 August. Finally, German intelligence reported that concealed mobilization in Poland had been introduced on 25 July. It would be necessary to start the process of German mobilization on 21 August. German plans to disrupt the enemy mobilization and defeat the Polish forces west of the Vistula, San, and Narew rivers before the Poles were fully mobilized might have to be abandoned. Soviet assistance might be useful to cut off the Polish retreat. On 14 August, after meeting with his generals who were waiting for a decision on 'Operation White', Hitler decided that Ribbentrop should go to Moscow if he could see Stalin. The all-important meeting between Molotov and Schulenburg took place on 15 August. Molotov was impressed with Ribbentrop's offer but still demanded to know exactly what form of political co-operation the Germans had in mind. He referred to the so-called 'Schulenburg plan', mentioned earlier by Ciano to the Soviet *chargé d'affaires* in Rome, that involved German intervention in the Japanese–Soviet conflict, a German–Soviet non-aggression pact, a joint guarantee of the Baltic states, and a wide-ranging economic agreement between the two countries. Schulenburg was embarrassed; the so-called plan was the result of talks with the Italian ambassador in Moscow and had no official sanction. At the end of their meeting,

Molotov, in what was clearly a pre-planned question, asked whether the German government had come to a conclusion about a non-aggression pact with the USSR. Schulenburg promised to seek guidance from Berlin. One can assume that once Molotov asked this question, Stalin was already seriously considering the German option. As the supplicants, the Germans had to say what they were prepared to pay for Soviet neutrality. To increase the tension in Berlin, on 14 and 17 August, the German embassy in London was told that the Anglo–Soviet talks were going well and that the Poles were about to open staff talks with the Russians. Hitler was now in a great hurry; Stalin took his time.

On 12 August, a hot and sultry day, the two western delegations met with the Soviet team led by Marshal Voroshilov backed by all the Soviet military chiefs. The opening did not go well. After Voroshilov announced that he was empowered to sign any military agreement, he asked the heads of the French and British delegations for their credentials. He wanted a discussion of detailed military plans and closely questioned the heads of the western delegations after their general exposés of their respective positions. On 14 August, during the fourth meeting of the delegations, Voroshilov asked whether either government had made arrangements with the other states of Eastern Europe, particularly Poland, for the movement of Soviet troops across their countries. Neither Drax nor Doumenc could make any kind of commitment. The Soviet marshal insisted that until the Russians knew whether Soviet forces could move through the Wilno Gap and Polish Galicia and whether they would be allowed to use Romanian territory if that country was attacked, the continuation of the talks was useless. The detailed exchanges continued but only revealed how wide was the gap between the two sides. The Russians asked about the strength of the British and French forces, what plans had been made to fight the Germans, and how the western forces would be deployed. The British were thinking in terms of deterrence and neither the British nor the French were prepared to discuss military co-operation in wartime. Marshal Voroshilov's exposition of the Soviet position made it entirely clear that the Soviets would offer only an 'after you' approach to co-operation with the west. If the aggressors attacked Britain and France, he told the negotiators, the USSR would engage a force equal to 70% of the Allied forces directly engaged in combat. If Germany attacked Poland and Romania, the USSR, if France and Britain secured rights of passage and operations in Poland, Romania, and if possible Lithuania, would match the Anglo-French effort against Germany. If the Germans attacked the Soviet Union, the western powers would commit 70% of their forces. Despite the numerical details, the discussions had a distinct air of unreality about them.

The critical point for the Soviets, as Naggiar had warned his government weeks earlier, was Poland. Would the Poles consent to the passage of Soviet troops? The Russians may have thought that if the Allies were really serious, they would just override the Polish veto. The French delegation was particularly alarmed and sent urgent messages back to Paris. Bonnet did what he could with Beck and the Romanians, but neither diplomatic pressure nor representations to the Polish chiefs of staff had any effect. Russian proposals for 'corridors' in Galicia and in the vicinity of Wilno had no chance of Polish acceptance. On 19 August, Beck declared that 'Poland cannot allow the question of use of its territory by foreign troops to be discussed.'[57] He argued that prior agreement would lead Hitler to an immediate declaration of war and that the Soviets could not be relied upon for assistance of any military value. The real fear, of course, was that should Soviet forces enter Poland, they would never leave. There would be abundant opportunities for Bolshevik mischief among the country's minorities. The British seconded the French efforts at Warsaw while also advising the Poles to try to compromise their difficulties with Germany.

Until the middle of August 1939, Soviet military intelligence had been unable to supply any reliable or exact information on Germany's plans for war in the autumn of 1939. This was clear from a paper, prepared by the analysts of the RU (the Red Army military intelligence organization) and the general staff, 'Considerations by the Soviet side for the negotiations with the military missions of Great Britain', which was submitted to Stalin by the chief of the general staff, Shaposhnikov, on 4 August. Though five different possible ways in which the war might begin were discussed, two were considered the most probable, either a German attack on France through Belgium and the Netherlands or an attack upon Poland. Even if it is assumed that for the sake of the negotiations, the Red Army leadership was stressing a blow in the West in order to bring pressure on the British and the French, it seems highly improbable that a document prepared for 'internal use only' would place this possibility at the top of its list, given the traditional order in which the possible variants of war were set out in general staff documents. Stalin was less well served by military intelligence in 1938–1939 than he was earlier. The purges had badly disrupted the RU, and it was only at the end of 1939 and the beginning of 1940 that it was able to re-establish the 'residencies' and networks of agents it had previously employed in Germany and in other countries of central and Western Europe. Undoubtedly, intelligence did reach the RU from the autumn

[57] *DDF*, 2nd ser., Vol. XVIII, No. 68.

of 1938 until the spring of 1939, most of it showing that the main aim of German policy was to destroy the USSR. There was, however, intelligence that pointed in the opposite direction, such as Kleist's report that Hitler was thinking of a revival of the Rapallo connection. Little reached Stalin that could enable him to determine whether Hitler intended to move West or East.[58] Most assumed an attack on Poland.

A great deal depended on Stalin's impressions of Anglo-French intentions. Nothing that transpired during the military talks brought any assurance that the western powers were determined on war if Hitler attacked and were prepared to fight alongside the Russians. On the contrary, the talks reinforced Stalin's suspicions that the British would strike a deal with Hitler. Despite further western concessions, excluding British acceptance of assistance in case of 'indirect aggression', the talks again stalled. On 17 August, the same day that Voroshilov adjourned the military talks until the 21 August, Schulenburg and Molotov met. The former offered the Russians a non-aggression pact for twenty-five years, a joint guarantee to the Baltic states and German services as mediator between the USSR and Japan. Molotov's answer was probably written by Stalin. The Russians were prepared to match the change in Germany's policies. Once the trade pact was signed, they were ready to sign a non-aggression pact with a special protocol defining the two countries' interests. The two men were moving closer but not fast enough for Hitler who was warned by his embassy in London of the progress in the Anglo-Soviet talks. The German ambassador in London, Dirksen, told his masters that the British would honour the Polish guarantee and be drawn automatically into a German–Polish conflict. On 19 August, with Schulenburg warning that Berlin could not wait, Molotov presented a draft pact that was to come into force only after ratification, giving the Russians additional time. It would last for five years. The special protocol, providing for the demarcation of spheres of influence in Poland and the Baltic area, was to form an integral part of the pact. Molotov suggested that Ribbentrop should come to Moscow (the trade agreement was signed on 19 August) on 26–27 August. This was not good enough for Hitler in view of his military plans. He sent a special letter to Stalin on 19 August, part carrot and part stick, demanding that Ribbentrop should arrive the very next day or at the latest on 23 August. The letter was sharp, almost an 'ultimatum'; Stalin marked in thick blue pencil Hitler's 'advice' to accept the draft agreement as a 'crisis may

[58] This information comes from an article by Vladimir Pozniakov, 'The Enemy at the Gates: Soviet Military Intelligence in the Inter-War Period and its Forecasts of Future War, 1921–41', in Silvio Pons and Andrea Romano (eds.), *Russia in the Age of Wars, 1914–1945* (Milan, 2000), 215–233.

occur any day'. It would be wise, Hitler wrote, for Stalin 'not to lose any time'.[59] Two hours after its receipt, Stalin agreed to receive the German foreign minister on 23 August. Hitler had speeded up the clock and Stalin had immediately responded. Most unusually, the Soviet leader would personally conduct the negotiations. Hitler ordered champagne for all, though he drank none. 'That will really land them in the soup', he declared, referring to the western powers.[60]

On 21 August, Voroshilov proposed an adjournment *sine die*, Drax and Doumenc asked for three to four days' delay. This was the last time the delegations met. The French, in desperation, authorized Doumenc to give an affirmative answer in principle to the Soviet question about Poland. The British refused to follow suit. On the morning of 22 August, *Tass* announced Ribbentrop's visit. General Doumenc's last-minute effort with Voroshilov that evening was useless. The transparency of the French offer of a convention envisaging the passage of Soviet troops through Polish and Romanian territory was obvious and was now beside the point. The British and French were apparently unaware of the rapid progress of the German–Soviet talks. On 25 August, after the Nazi–Soviet pact was announced and Britain had reaffirmed her obligations to Poland, Voroshilov, Drax, and Doumenc agreed that the western negotiators should go home.

IV

In itself, the Nazi–Soviet pact did not differ in form from any previous non-aggression treaties except in one particular. The usual provision that allowed either party to opt out if the other committed aggression against a third party was omitted. Stalin rejected the profession of eternal friendship that Ribbentrop had added as a preamble to the Soviet draft. The public terms were simple. If either power was involved in hostilities with another power, the other would not support that power. Nor would either join any group of powers directed in any way against the other signatory. In effect, the Russians were to be neutral in the forthcoming conflict and the Germans were not to attack them or their areas of interest. The pact came into force on signature and not on ratification. The secret protocol, whose existence Soviet officials continued to deny until the late 1980s, was

[59] Quoted in Gabriel Gorodetsky, *Grand Delusion: Stalin and the German Invasion of Russia* (New Haven, CT, and London, 1999), 7.
[60] Ian Kershaw, *Hitler: Nemesis, 1936–1945*, 205.

a division of spheres of influence highly favourable to the Russians. Poland was divided along the line of the rivers Narev, Vistula, and San. A small Polish state remained in existence separating the two Great Powers. Its future would be settled by joint agreement. Russia was to have a free hand in Estonia, Latvia, and Finland, Germany in Lithuania. Stalin declared his 'interest' in Romania's Bessarabia to which there was no German objection. Whether the secret protocol would turn into an actual territorial division of Eastern Europe with Germany depended on future contingencies. The pact signed, toasts followed. Stalin drank to Hitler's health; Ribbentrop drank to Stalin's. The German foreign minister went into a tirade against the British. Though Stalin echoed him, he warned Ribbentrop that Britain would wage war 'craftily and stubbornly'. The meeting ended (we have only the German version) with Stalin's promise that the Soviet Union would not betray Germany.

This review of the Soviet negotiations with the western powers and Germany suggests that Stalin was not intent on a Nazi–Soviet pact from their inception. But it suggests, too, that Stalin was fully prepared to explore other options simultaneously with the talks with Britain and France. It was not the case that the Soviets were merely responding to German overtures and the exigencies of the moment. Although it was Hitler who drove the Nazi–Soviet pact to its conclusion, he had picked up the signals from Moscow that an approach might be welcome. Had Stalin not turned towards Hitler, the Germans could hardly have prevented the conclusion of the tripartite pact. It is difficult to pin-point the time when Stalin shifted his focus from London to Berlin but it was a conscious decision that reflected the realities of the Soviet situation. Stalin's main interest at the time was in the security of the Soviet Union and neither in its revolutionary nor territorial expansion. Convinced that the Soviet Union was encircled by hostile states, he would try to avoid involvement in the 'second imperialist war' and prepare the best position possible to exploit its consequences.

Would Stalin have concluded the pact with Hitler if the British had been less dilatory and more determined to conclude an alliance with Moscow? It would have been difficult, given the guarantee to Poland, but not impossible to have overridden Beck's veto. There were, however, basic and fundamental differences between what the two sides wanted. The barriers to agreement were not mainly ideological but practical. The western powers wanted the tripartite pact as a deterrent to avoid war with Germany. They were not thinking of fighting the war with the Soviet Union as an equal partner. To have moved faster and more convincingly, they would have had to accept that war was inevitable and that Soviet assistance was necessary for its prosecution. The

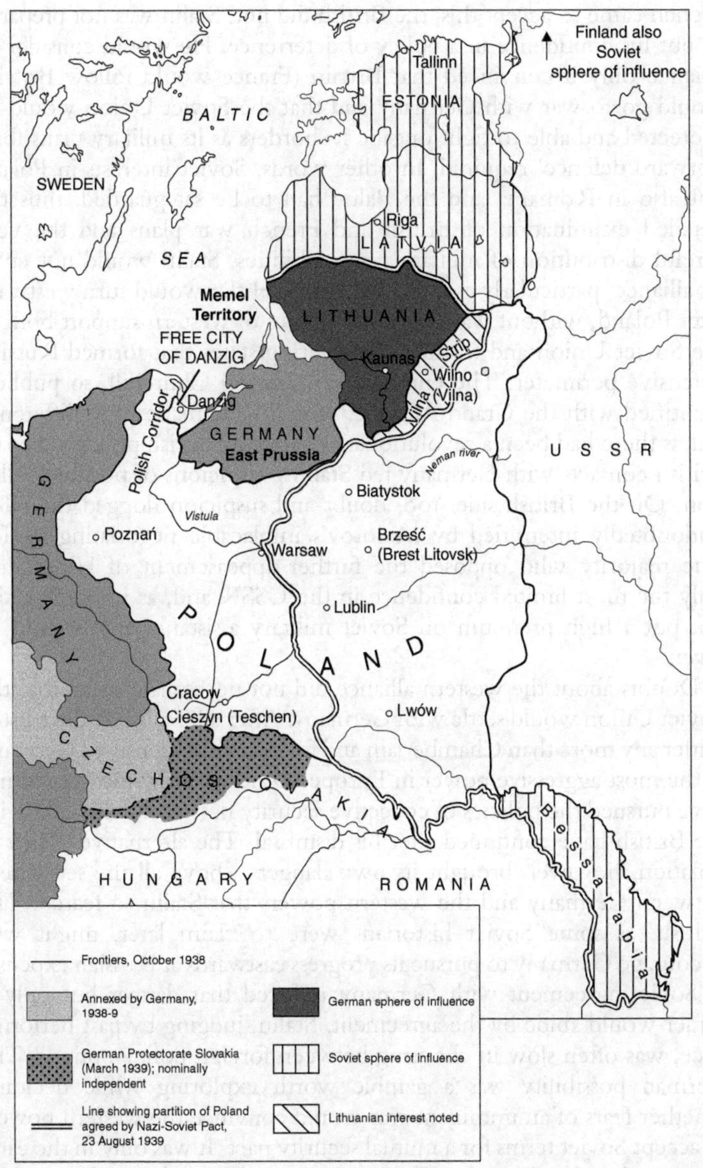

Map 14. The Nazi–Soviet Pact, 23 August 1939

French came to accept this; the British did not. Stalin was not prepared to put his confidence in a policy of deterrence. He would consider an alliance only if convinced that Britain (France would follow Britain) would go to war with Germany and that the Soviet Union would be protected and able to fight outside its borders as its military plans for a 'forward defence' required. In other words, Soviet interests in Poland but also in Romania and the Baltic had to be safeguarded, thus the detailed examination of British and French war plans and the very careful distribution of military responsibilities. Stalin would not enter an alliance, particularly as he believed that Hitler would turn westward after Poland, without watertight guarantees of western support both to the Soviet Union and to the neighbouring states that formed Russia's defensive perimeter. The entrance of Winston Churchill, so publicly identified with the Grand Alliance, would have made little difference unless there had been a revolutionary change in British policy. The late British contacts with Germany fed Stalin's suspicions of possible collusion. On the British side, too, doubt and suspicion dogged the talks, undoubtedly intensified by Molotov's implacable negotiating tactics. The majority who opposed the further appeasement of Hitler, had only the most limited confidence in the USSR and, as important, did not put a high premium on Soviet military assistance if it should be given.

Doubts about the western alliance did not necessarily mean that the Soviet Union would settle with Germany. After all, Stalin hardly trusted Hitler any more than Chamberlain and for years had identified Germany as the most aggressive power in Europe. Otherwise Litvinov could not have pursued the policies of collective security nor would the talks with the British have continued after his dismissal. The alternative policy of isolation, however, brought its own dangers, above all the settlement between Germany and the western powers that Stalin so feared. The British, as some Soviet historians were to claim later, might well encourage Germany to pursue its progress eastwards at Russian expense. A Soviet agreement with Germany reduced that danger but only if Hitler would abide by the agreement. Stalin, judging by past performance, was often slow in choosing between foreign policy options. The German possibility was a gamble worth exploring while deciding whether fears of an imminent war would convince the western powers to accept Soviet terms for a mutual security pact. It was only in the early summer that the German offer became a practical reality and even then Stalin moved cautiously. Once convinced that Hitler's offer was seriously meant, Stalin could weigh its advantages against what the western powers would offer. When informed that Hitler would attack Poland regardless of any agreement with Moscow, Stalin had to act. On purely pragmatic and *realpolitik* grounds, the German terms offered the USSR a greater measure of security than the western offers. It allowed the Soviet Union to remain neutral and held out the promise of a more protected position in Poland and the Baltic. The USSR would win a breathing space in Europe as well as in the Far East.

There is little, if any, evidence that Stalin considered that the pact with Germany should be the prelude to world revolution. It was only on 7 September, in the face of the unexpectedly rapid advance of the German troops into Poland, that Stalin demanded that the Comintern abandon the strategy of the Popular Front and fight against the war and not Fascism. The instructions to the key British, French, and Communist parties went out later in the month, suggesting that the change in Comintern tactics, like parallel Soviet military and diplomatic moves, was an indication of Stalin's anxieties about the speed of the German advance. The Communist parties were later instructed that they should act to prevent the spread of the war into Turkey and south-eastern Europe. Stalin made it clear to Dimitrov, the president of the Comintern, that it was not ideological considerations that had led him to the pact though he justified the division of Poland in a characteristically doctrinaire way: 'what harm would have been caused if, as a result of the dismemberment of Poland, we had extended the socialist system to new territories and populations?'.[61] Dimitrov was specifically warned by Stalin and Zhdanov at their 25 October meeting against having any illusions about the revolutionary potential of the war situation. '[I]n the First Imperialist War the Bolsheviks overestimated the situation', he was told. 'We all rushed ahead and made mistakes! This can be explained, but not excused, by the conditions prevailing then. Today we must not repeat the position held by the Bolsheviks.'[62] Dimitrov's orthodox revolutionary aspirations were firmly quashed in the interests of the Soviet Union's more mundane concern to stay out of the European war.

There are powerful arguments for Stalin's *realpolitik* irrespective of any ideological presumptions. The distinction between the pragmatic and ideological sources of Soviet foreign policy appears artificial however useful such labels may appear as tools of analysis. Stalin had always been convinced that there was a basic conflict between Soviet goals and those of the capitalist powers. Collaboration with any of the capitalist states was fraught with danger. Unlike Litvinov, Stalin saw little difference between dictatorships and democracies in their relations with Moscow. Within this framework, the Soviet Union could pursue any number of possibilities as it had since Lenin's day.

[61] Quoted in Gorodetsky, *Grand Delusion,* 8. [62] Ibid.

But ideological assumptions distorted perception and clouded judgment. For Stalin, Britain's hesitations about extending the guarantees to states that did not want such guarantees arose only from its hesitations about rendering assistance to the USSR. Stalin could hardly have discounted Hitler's anti-Bolshevism and his drive for *Lebensraum* in the East. Hitler's drive for a *judenfrei* Germany hardly concerned him, but he accepted that necessity had provided the Soviet Union with a window of opportunity. We do not know how long Stalin believed it could last, but Hitler's terms provided the Soviet Union with a breathing space and an enhanced strategic position. At best, the capitalist powers would fight each other to exhaustion leaving the Soviet Union in a commanding position at the peace table. All the other scenarios were fraught with danger; if war came and either the Allies or Nazis won an early victory, either could turn on the USSR. It may have been easier to do business with Hitler than with Chamberlain but there is every indication that Stalin knew he was taking a risk.

British attitudes towards the Soviet Union were shaped by a parallel combination of ideological dislike and practical calculations. For some, indeed possibly for most, British ministers, Bolshevism represented an antithetical and dangerous force. Clandestine operations continued both in Britain and in the empire. There was, according to many politicians and diplomats, more to be feared from Soviet Communism than Nazism and Fascism. But Nazi Germany was the more immediate and more powerful threat, and British pragmatism and *realpolitik* encouraged a turn to Moscow. Public opinion favoured an agreement with the Soviet Union, important at a time when Chamberlain was under pressure in parliament. Neither Chamberlain nor Halifax thought of himself as an ideologue. Yet, in retrospect, it is clear that neither was suited to deal with men like Hitler or Stalin. They played by different rules. If Chamberlain thought he could convince Hitler to rejoin the European order, he found after Prague that he was sadly deluded, though he still had hopes that the German people would see the light. The reaction to the dissolution of Czechoslovakia meant an increasing reluctance in London to yield the border states either to Hitler or to Stalin, quite apart from the arguments from expediency. It is certainly true that Chamberlain detested Bolshevism but he had no use for Nazism and was repelled by *Kristallnacht* and what followed whatever his personal feelings about Jews. He did not believe that Stalin was negotiating in good faith and, more important, did not think the Soviet Union would either strengthen the western deterrent or prove a valuable ally in wartime. Though the military chiefs were now supporting the conversations, they still had doubts about the offensive capacities of the Soviet military, weakened further by the purges. The British were unwilling to give hostages to secure an agreement with Stalin; the price was too high. The opposition of Poland, Romania, Finland, and the Baltic states only reinforced both the moral and practical barriers to an agreement. In the last resort, neither Chamberlain nor Halifax were prepared to sup with this devil. Nor did they think it necessary. If Daladier and Bonnet were more desperate and so more willing, they knew that France's fate was tied to that of Britain and followed London's lead.

V

Even after the conclusion of the Nazi–Soviet pact, Stalin remained uncertain of what would follow. He was unsure whether Britain and France would stand by their guarantee or come to terms with Germany. If the Soviet Union moved westward into Poland and an agreement was made between Germany and the western powers, the USSR could find itself at war with either or with both. He had resisted, at first, Hitler's pressure for a move into the territory assigned to the USSR, but the rapidity of the German advance placed the Soviet Union in a dangerous position. The Germans might go beyond the assigned line into the territories intended for Russia; German troops, facing continued Polish opposition after their initial victories, were soon fighting in the promised Soviet sphere. Any Polish–German armistice or Germany–western agreement would endanger the Soviet Union. The Soviet decision to invade Poland was taken on 9 September and implemented on 17 September. Two days later, Stalin informed the Germans that he wanted no Polish rump state, and proposed a rearrangement of the boundary between the Soviet and German spheres of influence. In addition to other changes, he offered to trade a substantial portion of central Poland between the Vistula and Bug rivers in exchange for Lithuania, amending the earlier pact to close the corridor leading to Leningrad. Population exchanges meant that those of German descent in the Baltic states, now in the Soviet sphere, could 'return' to Germany. Though the Soviet Union had large stretches of east Poland, where the Belorussians and Ukrainians were in the majority, they had no Polish state and fewer Poles on their side of the new border.

The Nazi–Soviet Non-Aggression Pact of 23 August and the Nazi–Soviet agreement of 29 September represent different stages in the evolution of Soviet policy. As a result of the September agreement, the security of the Soviet Union rested not on its neutrality but on territorial acquisitions and 'spheres of influence' in eastern Europe. The northerly area of Poland on the Soviet side of the dividing line was given to Lithuania, now part of the Soviet sphere. Western Belorussia and the western Ukraine were merged with the corresponding Soviet Republics

Table 16.5 Soviet Raw Material Deliveries to Germany under the Nazi–Soviet Pact, 1939–1941

	Tons
Oil	865,000
Wood	648,000
Manganese ore	14,000
Copper	14,000
Grain	1,500,000
Rubber	15,400

Note: See appendices A5 and A6.
Source: Richard Overy, *Russia's War* (London, 1998), 53.

after staged plebiscites organized by the NKVD. Mass deportations followed and the treatment of the deportees was as inhuman and brutal as experienced by the Soviet victims of the Great Terror. Not long after the incorporation of the new territories into the Soviet Union, extreme pressure was brought on the Baltic states to surrender their sovereignty to Soviet hegemony. At the same time, Stalin moved decisively in the German direction, out of a combination of fear and calculation. He joined in Hitler's campaign for peace, gave new instructions to the Communist parties abroad, and agreed 'to engage in mutual consultations in regard to necessary measures' if the war continued.[63] Stalin explained to Ribbentrop in September that though he knew that Germany did not intend to involve the USSR in war as she required no assistance: 'if Germany will be in the condition to request help, it can be certain that the Soviet people will help it and will not let it perish. The USSR is interested in a strong Germany and will not let it be beaten.'[64] Stalin agreed to provide Germany with large amounts of raw materials—e.g. grain, iron ore, oil—in return for manufactured products, technical designs and equipment, and other products and was prepared for the Soviet Union to act as the German purchasing agent with third parties. The deal was hammered out in February 1940. The Soviet Union, in addition to sending Germany most of its animal feed imports, supplied 74% of its phosphates needs, 67% of its asbestos, 40% of its chrome ore supplies, 55% of its manganese, 40% of its nickel imports, and 34% of its imported oil.[65] It was a much-needed boost for

[63] Quoted in Adam Ulam, *Expansion and Coexistence: Soviet Foreign Policy 1917–73*, 2nd edn. (New York, 1976), 284.
[64] Quoted in Sylvio Pons, *Stalin e la guerra inevitabile* (Turin, 1993), 282.
[65] Tooze, *The Wages of Destruction*, 321.

the resource-poor German war economy. The Russians also did well out of the deal though the Germans were often less than forthcoming in supplying what the Russians demanded.

There was direct assistance to Germany in the naval sphere including the provision of a naval base near Murmansk for German submarines. Even if the territorial acquisitions of 1939–1940 were a way of ensuring Soviet security, Stalin was also shifting the goal posts. He had returned to earlier doctrines, believing that the Soviet Union could benefit from the collapse of the Versailles system and the anticipated war between the capitalist powers. As long as he did not provoke Hitler, the pact would hold. The Soviet Union could build up its military forces and claim a favourable position at the future peace table. That he did not differentiate between the aims of the capitalist powers and thought Britain, whose power he grossly exaggerated, a more immediately dangerous enemy than Germany, would cost his country dear in 1941.

Would Hitler have postponed or even abandoned the war with Poland if the western negotiations with the USSR had succeeded? This question cannot be answered. Common sense suggests that it would have been an 'act of desperation' to have attacked Poland in the face of an Anglo-French-Soviet alliance. In August, faced with the Anglo-Polish alliance and the Italian desertion, Hitler had a moment of hesitation. Yet, for reasons to be fully explored in the final chapter, Hitler felt that this was the right moment to launch his war. The Nazi–Soviet pact provided just the reassurance that his gamble would pay off.

Books

Ahmann, R., *Nichtangriffspakte: Entwicklung und operative Nutzung in Europa 1922–1939. Mit einen Ausblick auf die Renaissance des Nichtangriffsvertrages nach dem Zweiten Weltkrieg* (Baden-Baden, 1988).

Altrichter, H. and Becker, J. (eds.), *Kriegsausbruch 1939* (Munich, 1989).

Bartel, H., *Frankreich und die Sowjetunion 1938–1940: ein Beitrag zur französischen Ostpolitik zwischen dem Münchner Abkommen und dem Ende der Dritten Republik* (Stuttgart, 1986).

Carley, M. J., *1939: The Alliance that Never Was and the Coming of World War II* (Chicago, IL, 1999).

Charmley, J., *Chamberlain and the Lost Peace* (London, 1989).

Coox, A. D., *Nomonhan: Japan against Russia, 1939* (Stanford, CA, 1986).

Crowe, D. M., *The Baltic States and the Great Powers: Foreign Relations, 1938–1940* (Boulder, CO, 1993).

Davies, R. W., Harrison, M., and Wheatcroft, S. G., *The Economic Transformation of the Soviet Union, 1913–1945* (Cambridge, 1994).

DUROSELLE, J.-B., *Les relations germano–soviétiques de 1933 à 1939* (Paris, 1954).
—— *La décadence, 1932–1939* (Paris, 1979).
—— *L'abîme* (Paris, 1986).
ERICSON III, JOHN, *Feeding the German Eagle: Soviet Economic Aid to Nazi Germany 1933–1941* (Westport, CT, 1999).
FLEISCHHAUER, I., *Der Pakt: Hitler, Stalin und die Initiative der deutschen Diplomatie* (Berlin, 1990).
*FORCADE, O., *La République secrète: Histoire des services spéciaux français de 1918 à 1939* (Paris, 2008). Read after completion of chapter.
GIRAULT, R. and FRANK, R. (eds.), *La Puissance en Europe 1938–1940* (Paris, 1989).
GLANTZ, D. M., *The Soviet Conduct of Tactical Maneuver: Spearhead of the Offensive* (London, 1991).
—— *The Military Strategy of the Soviet Union: A History* (London and Portland, OR, 1992).
—— *Stumbling Colossus: The Red Army on the Eve of World War* (Lawrence, KA, 1998).
GORODETSKY, G., *Soviet Foreign Policy, 1917–1991: A Retrospective* (London, 1994).
—— *Grand Delusion: Stalin and the German Invasion of Russia* (New Haven, CT, and London, 1999).
HARRISON, M., *Soviet Planning in Peace and War, 1938–1945* (Cambridge, 1985).
—— (ed.), *Guns and Roubles: The Defense Industry in the Stalinist State* (New Haven, CT, 2008).
HASLAM, J., *The Soviet Union and the Struggle for Collective Security in Europe, 1933–1939* (London, 1984).
—— *The Soviet Union and the Threat from the East, 1933–1941: Moscow, Tokyo and the Prelude to the Pacific War* (Basingstoke, 1992).
HILL, C., *Cabinet Decisions on Foreign Policy: The British Experience, October 1938 – June 1941* (Cambridge, 1991).
ILIC, M. (ed.), *Stalin's Terror Revisited* (Basingstoke, 2006).
IMLAY, T. C., *Facing the Second World War: Strategy, Politics, and Economics in Britain and France, 1938–1940* (Oxford, 2003).
KHLEVNYUK, O., *Le Cercle du Kremlin. Staline et le Bureau politique dans les années 1930: les jeux du pouvoir* (Paris, 1996).
MURRAY, W., *The Change in the European Balance of Power: The Path to Ruin* (Princeton, NJ, 1984).
NEILSON, K., *Britain, Soviet Russia and the Collapse of the Versailles Order, 1919–1939* (Cambridge, 2006).
NEKRICH, A., *Pariahs, Patriarchs, Predators: German–Soviet Relations, 1922–1941* (Chichester and New York, 1997).
OBERLÄNDER, E. (ed.), *Hitler–Stalin–Pakt 1939: Das Ende Ostmitteleuropas?* (Frankfurt am Main, 1989). See under articles for specific references though almost all contributions are useful.
PONS, S., *Stalin e la guerra inevitabile, 1936–1941* (Turin, 1993). Translated as *Stalin and the Inevitable War, 1936–1941* (London, 2002).

—— and ROMANO A. (eds), *Russia in the Age of Wars, 1914–1945* (Milan, 2000).

READ, A., and FISHER, D., *The Deadly Embrace: Hitler, Stalin and the Nazi–Soviet Pact, 1939–1941* (London, 1988). Still readable but needs updating.

Les relations franco–britanniques de 1935 à 1939 (Paris, 1973).

ROBERTS, G., *Unholy Alliance: Stalin's Pact with Hitler* (London, 1989).

—— *The Soviet Union and the Origins of the Second World War: Russo-German Relations and the Road to War, 1933–1941* (Basingstoke, 1995).

ROHWER, J. and MONAKOV, M., *Stalin's Ocean-Going Fleet, Soviet Naval Strategy and Shipbuilding Programmes, 1935–1953* (London and Portland, OR, 2001).

SANTAMARIA, Y., *1939: Le pacte germano-soviétique* (Brussels, 1999).

SHAW, L. G., *The British Political Elite and the Soviet Union, 1937–1939* (London, 2003).

TOOZE, A., *The Wages of Destruction: The Making and Breaking of the Nazi Economy* (London, 2006).

ULAM, A. B., *Expansion and Coexistence: Soviet Foreign Policy, 1917–1973*, 2nd edn. (New York, 1976).

WATT, D. C., *How War Came: The Immediate Origins of the Second World War, 1938–1939* (London, 1989).

WEBER, R. W., *Die Entstehungsgeschichte des Hitler–Stalin–Paktes 1939* (Frankfurt am Main, Berne, and Cirencester, 1980).

WEGNER, B. (ed.), *From Peace to War: Germany, Soviet Russia and the World, 1939–1941* (Providence, RI, 1997). See chapters cited below.

WEINBERG, G. L., *Germany and the Soviet Union* (London, 1954).

—— *The Foreign Policy of Hitler's Germany: Starting World War II, 1937–1939* (Chicago, IL, 1980).

YOUNG, R., *In Command of France: French Foreign Policy and Military Planning, 1933–1940* (Cambridge, 1938).

Articles

AHMANN, R., 'Soviet Foreign Policy and the Molotov–Ribbentrop Pact of 1939: An Enigma Reassessed', *Storia delle relazione internazionali*, 5: 2 (1989).

—— 'Der Hitler–Stalin Pakt: Nichtangriffs- und Angriffsvertrag?' in Oberländer, E. (ed.), *Hitler–Stalin–Pakt 1939: Das Ende Ostmitteleuropas?* (Frankfurt am Main, 1989).

—— 'The German Treaties with Estonia and Latvia of 7 June 1939: Bargaining Ploy or an Alternative to German–Soviet Understanding?', *Journal of Baltic Studies*, 20: 4 (1989).

ARUMAE, H., 'Noch einmal zum sowjetisch–deutschen Nichtangriffspakt', in Oberländer, E. (ed.), *Hitler–Stalin–Pakt 1939: Das Ende Ostmitteleuropas?* (Frankfurt am Main, 1989).

CARLEY, M. J., 'End of the "Low, Dishonest Decade": Failure of the Anglo-Franco-Soviet Alliance in 1939', *Europe–Asia Studies*, 45: 2 (1993).

—— 'Down a Blind Ally: Anglo-Franco-Soviet Relations, 1920–1939', *Canadian Journal of History*, 29: 1 (1994).

CARLEY, M. J., 'Prelude to Defeat: Franco-Soviet Relations, 1919–1939', *Historical Reflections*, 22 (1996).

DAVIES, R. W., 'The Soviet Economy and the Launching of the Great Terror', in Ilic, M. (ed.), *Stalin's Terror Revisted* (Basingstoke, 2006).

—— 'Preparation for Mobilization of the Soviet Economy in the 1930s', in Harrison, M. (ed.), *Guns and Roubles: The Defense Industry in the Stalinist State* (New Haven, CT, 2008).

DOERR, P. W., 'The Changkufeng/Lake Khasan Incident of 1938: British Intelligence on Soviet and Japanese Military Performance', *Intelligence and National Security*, 5: 3 (1990).

DULLIN, S., 'Le rôle de Maxime Litvinov dans les années trente', *Communisme*, 42/43/44 (1995).

—— 'Litvinov and the People's Commissariat of Foreign Affairs: The Fate of an Administration under Stalin, 1930–39', in Pons, S. and Romano, A. (eds.), *Russia in the Age of Wars, 1914–1945* (Milan, 2000).

ERICKSON, J., 'Threat Identification and Strategic Appraisal by the Soviet Union, 1930–1941', in May, Ernest R. (ed.), *Knowing One's Enemies: Intelligence Assessment before the Two World Wars* (Princeton, NJ, and Guildford, 1984).

FLEISCHHAUER, I., 'Soviet Foreign Policy and the Origins of the Hitler–Soviet Pact', in WEGNER, B. (ed.), *From Peace to War: Germany, Soviet Russia and the World, 1939–1941* (Providence, RI, 1997).

GREGORY, P. and HARRISON, M., 'Allocation under Dictatorship: Research in Stalin's Archives', *Journal of Economic Literature*, 43: 3 (2005).

HARRISON, M., 'The Dictator and Defense', in Harrison, M. (ed.), *Guns and Roubles: The Defense Industry in the Stalinist State* (New Haven, CT, 2008).

HASLAM, J., 'Soviet–German Relations and the Origins of the Second World War: The Jury is Still Out', *Journal of Modern History*, 69: 4 (1997).

HAUNER, M., 'The Soviet Threat to Afghanistan and India, 1938–1941', *Modern Asian Studies*, 15: 2 (1981).

HOVI, K., 'Der Hitler–Stalin–Pakt und Finnland', in Oberländer, E. (ed.), *Hitler–Stalin–Pakt 1939: Das Ende Ostmitteleuropas?* (Frankfurt am Main, 1989).

IMLAY, T. C., 'France and Britain and the Making of the Anglo-French Alliance, 1938–1939', in Philpott, W. and Alexander, M. (eds.), *Anglo-French Defence Relations between the Wars, 1919–1940* (London, 2002).

KATZ, B. C., 'Purges and Production: Soviet Economic Growth, 1928–1940', *Journal of Economic History*, 35: 3 (1975).

KENNEDY, G., 'Becoming Dependent on the Kindness of Strangers: Britain's Strategic Foreign Policy, Naval Arms Limitation and the Soviet Factor, 1935–7', *War in History*, 11 (2004).

KHLEVNIUK, O., 'The Objectives of the Great Terror, 1937–38', in Cooper, J. and Perrie, M. (eds.), *Soviet History, 1917–1953: Essays in Honour of R.W. Davies* (London and New York, 1995).

—— 'Economic Officials in the Great Terror, 1936–1938', in Ilic, M. (ed.), *Stalin's Terror Revisited* (Basingstoke, 2006).

KOCHO-WILLIAMS, A., 'The Soviet Diplomatic Corps and Stalin's Purges', *Slavic and East European Review*, 86: 1 (2008).

Lukes, I., 'Benesch, Stalin und die Comintern: Vom Münchener Abkommen zum Molotow–Ribbentrop Pakt', *Vierteljahrshefte für Zeitgeschichte*, 41 (1993).

Maiolo, J. A., 'Anglo-Soviet Naval Armaments Diplomacy before the Second World War,' *English Historical Review*, 123 (2008).

Manne, R., 'The British Decision for Alliance with Russia, May 1939', *Journal of Contemporary History*, 9 (1974).

Narinsky, M., 'Le Kremlin, le Komintern et la politique extérieure de l'URSS, 1939–1941', *Communisme*, 49–50, (1997).

Neilson, K., 'Stalin's Moustache: The Soviet Union and the Coming of the War', *Diplomacy and Statecraft*, 12 (2001).

—— 'Arms Control and the Anglo-Soviet Naval Agreement of 1937', in Hamilton, K. and Johnson, E., *Arms and Disarmament in Diplomacy* (London and Portland, OR, 2008).

Pozniakov, V., 'The Enemy at the Gates: Soviet Military Intelligence in the Inter-war Period and the Feasibility of Future War, 1921–1941', in Pons, S. and Romano, A. (eds.), *Russia in the Age of Wars, 1914–1945* (Milan, 2000).

Prażmowska, A., 'The Eastern Front and the British Guarantee to Poland of March 1939', *European History Quarterly*, 14: 2 (1984).

—— 'Poland's Foreign Policy, September 1938 – September 1939', *Historical Journal*, 29: 4 (1986).

Rauch, G. von, 'Der deutsch–sovietische Nichtangriffspakt vom August 1939 und die sowjetische Geschichtsforschung', in Niedhart, G. (ed.), *Kriegsbeginn, 1939: Entfesselung oder Ausbruch des Zweiten Weltkrieges* (Darmstadt, 1976).

Resis, A., 'The Fall of Litvinov: Harbinger of the German–Soviet Non-Aggression Pact', *Europe–Asia Studies*, 52: 1 (2000).

Roberts, G., 'Infamous Encounter? The Merekalov–Weizsäcker Meeting of 17 April 1939', *Historical Journal*, 35: 4 (1992).

—— 'The Fall of Litvinov: A Revisionist View', *Journal of Contemporary History*, 27 (1992).

—— 'The Soviet Decision for a Pact with Nazi Germany', *Soviet Studies*, 45: 1 (1992).

—— 'The Alliance that Failed: Moscow and the Triple Alliance Negotiations, 1939', *European History Quarterly*, 26: 3 (1996).

Robertson, E. M., 'German Mobilisation Preparations and the Treaties between Germany and the Soviet Union of August and September 1939', in Boyce, R. W. D. and Robertson, E. (eds.), *Paths to War: New Essays on the Origins of the Second World War* (London, 1989).

Schroeder, P. W., 'Alliances, 1918–1945: Weapons of Power and Tools of Management', in Knorr, K. (ed.), *Historical Problems of National Security* (Lawrence, KA, 1976).

Strang, G. B., 'John Bull in Search of a Suitable Russia: British Foreign Policy and the Failure of the Anglo-French-Soviet Alliance Negotiations, 1939', *Canadian Journal of History*, 41: 1 (2006).

Thurlow, R. C., 'Soviet Spies and British Counter-Intelligence in the 1930s', *Intelligence and National Security*, 19 (2004).

Uldricks, T., 'A. J. P. Taylor and the Russians', in Martel, G. (ed.), *The Origins of the Second World War Reconsidered: The A. J. P. Taylor Debate after 25 Years* (London and Boston, MA, 1986).

—— 'Soviet Security Policy in the 1930s', in Gorodetsky, G. (ed.), *Soviet Foreign Policy: A Retrospective, 1917–1991* (London, 1994).

—— 'Debating the Role of Russia in the Origins of the Second World War', in Martel, G. (ed.), *The Origins of the Second World War Reconsidered: A. J. P. Taylor and the Historians*, 2nd edn. (London, 1999).

Varey, D. K., 'The Politics of Naval Aid: The Foreign Office, the Admiralty, and Anglo-Soviet Technical Co-operation, 1936–7', *Diplomacy and Statecraft*, 14: 4 (2003).

Waddington, G. T., 'Ribbentrop and the Soviet Union, 1937–1941', in Erickson, J. and Dilks, D. (eds.), *Barbarossa: The Axis and the Allies* (Edinburgh, 1994).

Wark, W., 'Something Very Stern: British Political Intelligence—Moralism and Strategy in 1939', *Intelligence and National Security*, 5 (1990).

Watson, D., 'Molotov's Apprenticeship in Foreign Policy: The Triple Alliance Negotiations in 1930', *Europe–Asia Studies*, 52 (2000).

—— 'The Politburo and Foreign Policy in the 1930s', in Reese, E. A. (ed.), *The Nature of Stalin's Dictatorship: The Politburo, 1934–1953* (London, 2004).

Watt, D. C., 'The Initiation of the Negotiations Leading to the Nazi–Soviet Non-Aggression Pact: A Historical Problem', in Abramsky, C. (ed.), *Essays in Honour of E. H. Carr* (London, 1974).

—— 'Francis Herbert King, A Soviet Source in the Foreign Office', *Intelligence and National Security*, 4 (1988).

Yegorova, N. I., 'Stalin's Conception of Maritime Power: Revelations from the Russian Archives', *Journal of Strategic Studies*, 28 (2005).

17

Escape from War or Persecution? The Smaller Powers and the Jews

Could any European country escape the coming war? Many of the smaller states sought to do so through the bolthole of neutrality, though political, geographic, and economic factors meant that it was a strategy that could succeed only for the few.[1] As for non-national groups, most prominently, the mass of Jewish refugees that Nazi policies produced wherever their reach extended, there was even less chance of fleeing from their already haunted existence. Former avenues of escape, such as emigration to Palestine, were being closed off as the decade drew on, just as they were most needed. For all but the Great Powers, the possibilities of choice were limited, as events no longer lay within their ability to control.

A. The Smaller Powers

I

The choice between peace and war lay with the Great Powers, whose statesmen paid little attention to the wishes of their smaller neighbours. Since 1935, the international response to the Italian invasion of Abyssinia showed clearly that Europe's fate lay outside the hands of the League or the small states. The 'former neutrals' from the First World War—Denmark, the Netherlands, Norway, Spain, Sweden, and Switzerland—had responded to the failure of the League sanctions policy with a joint declaration on 1 July 1936 castigating the League for its inconsistent application of the Covenant and announcing that until the international community agreed to abide by the rule of law, they would not consider themselves bound by Article 16. The return to neutrality was a symptom of the collapse of the 1920s experiment in internationalism, not a cause, for with the exceptions of Switzerland

[1] With the exception of Eire and Luxembourg, I have chosen only to discuss those small powers that have appeared previously in this study. Italy, possibly the most important European 'non-belligerent', has been covered in earlier chapters.

and Spain, the former neutrals remained within the League but the latter existed only in an emasculated form, which afforded little protection. The neutrality that took shape in Europe from 1936 was not some 'lofty refuge', isolated from the world's events, but rather a strategy that hopefully would allow the small states to engage in international affairs without running the risk of alienating powerful neighbours. Most sought 'independence' or 'non-alignment'. With the Czech crisis of 1938, the latter tended to harden into neutrality, which it was believed might still provide room for independent action. In the face of Hitler's increasingly aggressive foreign policy, immediate security requirements took precedence over longer-term considerations. Some believed that opting for neutrality instead of making common cause with the western powers would protect them from attack. A few gravitated towards the Axis camp without actually entering it, hoping to avoid intervention. As Churchill typically put it in early 1940, each one 'hopes that if he feeds the crocodile enough, the crocodile will eat him last'.[2] Turkey was exceptional in that it did not seek neutrality but alliances with Britain and France though their slow response and the Nazi–Soviet pact put neutrality back on the diplomatic menu.

States chose neutrality, hoping rightly or wrongly that they could stand aside from the war. It was still assumed that the rules of the international community, above all the rules of war, would be observed by the belligerents. A surprising number of governments were able to exercise some degree of control over their own destinies. Decisions were often influenced by domestic factors. In many cases, neutrality was the one option which the majority of the body politic would accept. It was often used to create unity or to strengthen the bonds of statehood. Even where leaders were not constrained by public opinion, decisions could well be influenced by tradition, past practices, and geography as well as the policies of the other powers, both friends and foes. The situation in 1939, however, was no longer a fluid one and the bi-polarization of the European scene restricted the options of statesmen everywhere.

The opening of the war in 1939 proved to be only the preamble to what became a far wider European and ultimately a global war but it provides the historian with a snapshot view of the behaviour of the smaller powers that has its importance for what followed. It has been argued that 'neutrality had tended to encourage aggression of the strong against the weak' and so helped to undermine the European balance of

[2] Broadcast by Churchill, 20 January 1940, cited in Martin Gilbert (ed.), *The Churchill War Papers*, vol. I (London, 1993), 673.

power.[3] To some extent, however, the move towards neutrality was not only a response to fears of aggression but also to the failures of the Great Powers to make the Geneva system work or to offer alternative options for keeping the peace. Many states sought, as they had in the 1920s, a Great Power protector only to find, until 1939, that Britain and France were reluctant to take on the task, and were even failing to meet the German economic challenge in the hope of turning Hitler away from war in the west. States which thought that voluntary co-operation with Hitler might protect them from attack hesitated for fear of Allied action or, as in the case of Hungary and Bulgaria, for fear of ending again on the losing side of a new European war. No state in Eastern Europe was willing to entrust its fate to the Soviet Union though some hoped that the enmity between Berlin and Moscow might provide some form of protection for the future.

There were attempts to strengthen security through common action but multilateral arrangements weakened under the pressure of events. The 'Oslo group', forged in 1930, consisting of the Scandinavian countries, the Netherlands, Belgium, and Luxembourg, was from the start a loose grouping. Norway was particularly reluctant to engage in any firm regional political, economic, or security organization. It proved difficult to extend economic co-operation but leaders remained in contact. All its members wanted to avoid involvement in the coming war, but their divergent political and strategic objectives and the failure of either Belgium or Sweden to provide effective leadership and Dutch unwillingness to enter into tighter arrangements, undercut whatever bargaining power the group might have had. In 1934, the Baltic States, Estonia, Latvia, and Lithuania, created a mutual defence bloc. Even here, different enemies weakened regional solidarity; Estonia and Latvia were focused on the Soviet Union and Lithuania, the first regional victim of Hitler's aggression, on Germany. In south-east Europe, the Balkan Entente, established in 1934, and consisting of Turkey, Romania, Yugoslavia, and Greece, tried to ensure the maintenance of the Balkan status quo. Two separate problems weakened the bloc: Bulgaria remained outside the grouping and had territorial claims against all its members but Turkey. None of the powers victorious in the Great War were willing to cede the lands they had won. Members of the Balkan Entente had different enemies; Italy, for the most part, but also Germany, with or without Hungary, and the Soviet Union, with geography being a major factor. Military co-operation between the Balkan powers was restricted to talks between staffs and subsequently, only meetings between military attachés.

[3] Neville Wylie, 'The Neutrals', in R. Boyce and J. Maiolo (eds.), *The Origins of World War Two: The Debate Continues* (Basingstoke, 2003), 176.

By the summer of 1939, the Balkan Entente countries had largely dissipated its capability for regional action.

As war approached, members of these regional groupings hoped that neutrality would keep war from their door. Most waited to see what the major powers would do and, in particular, what the outcome of the Anglo-French-Soviet negotiations would be. In some capitals, there was an unnatural sense of calm during the summer months. Little was known about the discussions between Germany and the Soviet Union and the announcement of the Nazi–Soviet pact took many, but not all, by surprise. Its effect was to give added weight to the choice of neutrality as the most viable policy. The only significant gesture from the smaller powers was the peace appeal issued by King Leopold of Belgium following the meeting of foreign ministers of the Oslo states in Brussels on 23 August. Predictably, it had no effect; polite replies were received from Britain, France, and other countries but none at all from Germany or Italy. Each member of the Oslo group was quick to proclaim its neutrality. Despite all the obvious dangers, it appeared as the best alternative to the risks of engagement.

II

Regional contiguity did not necessarily dictate common policy. The case of Ireland was exceptional. It was the only member of the British Commonwealth that did not follow Britain into war, yet it shared a border with Britain and was dependent on London for protection. Neutrality was a policy based on both principle and pragmatism. It provided an affirmation of independence and strengthened the cohesion of the state. It also served Ireland's security needs. The state had only a small army, about 6,000 soldiers and airmen and 13,000 men in the largely untrained Volunteer Force. It had no navy, hardly an air service worth the name and no air defence system. From the time of the Anglo–Irish treaty of 6 December 1921, it was assumed that Britain would defend Ireland from outside air and naval attack. The Irish government had been quick to join the League of Nations, despite initial British disapproval and the implied dilution of its absolute neutrality. It joined in the sanctions against Italy even in the face of public and church hostility. As was the common reaction, the League's political shortcomings led to Irish disenchantment and a loss of faith in collective security.

The British set out to include Ireland in their defence system. In the 1921 negotiations, they had demanded and won special provisions for Britain's strategic needs. The settlement provided for Britain's retention of naval and communications facilities along Ireland's southern and south-western coasts, and the right to claim, in times of war or strained relations with a foreign power, harbour and other facilities needed for defence. The Irish government publicly acknowledged that an independent and neutral Ireland would never pose a threat to Britain's security interests.

In a remarkable agreement concluded in the spring of 1938, in return for the settlement of a financial dispute and the resumption of normal trade (after a six year so-called economic war), Britain agreed to unconditionally relinquish its 1921 defence rights. Though the Irish authorities reiterated their promise to do nothing that would threaten British security, London was no longer to have any naval bases in Ireland or any right to demand them. This renunciation undoubtedly facilitated Irish neutrality when war broke out. There was no serious build-up of Irish military forces and steps were taken, mainly through contacts between the intelligence services, to quiet British concerns about possible sabotage and IRA co-operation with Nazi Germany. Unlike so many other countries opting for neutrality, Ireland successfully defended its position, maintaining diplomatic relations with both Britain and Germany throughout the war. The Americans proved more difficult than the British. Success, particularly before 1941, was due to Eamon de Valera's adroit diplomacy, and his wide public support but also to German indifference and British restraint. The Irish were fortunate in both respects.

III

The neutrality of Belgium, the Netherlands, and Luxembourg had been guaranteed by the Great Powers in the 19th century. Only the Belgians, responding to the failure of their traditional policies during the Great War, had broken ranks with the past by entering into a military alliance with France on 7 September 1920. Responding mainly to domestic political pressures, on 6 March 1936, one day before Hitler marched into the Rhineland, the Belgians opted for a policy of 'independence'. In the summer of 1936, the Belgian political leaders announced their support for an 'exclusively and fundamentally Belgian foreign policy', and on 14 October, King Leopold spelled out the objectives of the 'new policy of independence'. The latter was seen by many as the 'policy of the king'. At the same time, the Belgian parliament insisted that the declaration of 'independence' was matched with a commitment to increased defence spending.

Belgium was a country torn apart by divisions, between the Flemish nationalists and the Walloons, between French and Flemish speakers, between and within parties. There was even a German-speaking minority, sympathetic to Nazism, in the lands annexed from Germany in 1919. Break-away groups from the Catholic party, the Francophone Catholic Rexists and the Flemish nationalist VNV (Flemish Nationalist Union) posed major threats to ruling coalitions from the extreme right and though the Catholic party recovered in the elections of 1939, the VNV still polled a considerable vote in Flanders. The economic crisis made collaboration between the parties more difficult and the coalition governments even weaker. A general sense of crisis led to general disillusionment with parliamentary government as such. The new king, Leopold III, had strong authoritarian tendencies and was a major influence in the turn to 'independence'. Independence was a policy that had wide appeal across the political spectrum. The term could be variously interpreted and could embrace those on the left anxious not to abdicate their role in the wider battle between democrats and fascists and those, who like King Leopold, wanted to withdraw from any form of partisanship. The anti-neutralists were a tiny minority even in 1939, when the dangers from Nazi Germany were clear. There was a direct line between the decisions of 1936 and the Belgian proclamation of neutrality on the same day as the British and French declarations of war.

Those Belgians who thought that 'independence' would provide an element of greater flexibility in foreign affairs were soon disappointed. Within two years, 'independence' had become 'strict neutrality'. The Anglo–French attempts to conciliate Hitler in 1937–1938 only convinced the Belgians that they had chosen the right policy. Though the French had taken umbrage at the Belgian action, General Gamelin remained sanguine about Belgian action when war came, counting on his covert and indirect contacts with the Belgian chief of staff, General Edouard van den Bergen. The British were more sympathetic to the Belgian position; the chiefs of staff believed that Belgian neutrality would free Britain from the entanglements of military commitments as well as act as a check on the over-hasty French. They, too, opened secret channels of communication with van den Bergen though the information exchanged, mainly about Belgium's defence plans, tended to be one way.

As the prospect of war drew nearer, the Belgians clung more tightly to the policy of 'strict neutrality'. Despite rumours, the product of a German opposition disinformation campaign, of a possible German invasion of the Low Countries in early 1939, the government rejected the possibility of staff talks with the western powers. Senior officers agreed that it would be impossible for Belgium to remain neutral if Holland was invaded but a move into the Anglo-French camp would invite the German action they were trying to avoid. Continuing suspicion of France and lingering doubts about the seriousness of Britain's new continental commitments coloured official attitudes. Many doubted whether the Allied powers were capable of offering effective assistance. Neutrality became more rigidly enforced. General van den Bergen found it difficult to provide new intelligence and the Allies were reluctant to press the general for fear of harming his position. King Leopold's forlorn appeal for peace in August failed to elicit backing beyond northern Europe and made no impact on Berlin. His clumsy offer of mediation with Queen Wilhelmina of the Netherlands in September caused only irritation in the belligerent capitals. The steadfast defence of 'strict neutrality' involved a certain amount of calculated blindness. The government found it easier to embrace an increasingly restrictive concept of neutrality than to admit failure and accept the domestic political consequences of restoring links with France. When war broke out, the sovereign and the Belgian people were at one, support for neutrality among the population extended from the conservative Catholic right to the Communists on the left, still disoriented by the signing of the Nazi–Soviet pact. The debate concerning the Belgian decision and its role in the Allied defeats of 1940 still continues. It may have been a dangerous and unrealistic choice of options but the British and French were not blameless in the sequence of events that led to Belgium's ostrich-like behaviour.

The Netherlands followed a parallel but separate path to absolute neutrality. When war broke out in September 1939, the Dutch reacted in much the same way as they had in 1914, with the minister-president announcing that the policy of independence would be maintained 'fully and undiminished'. It was a policy that had served the Dutch well during the 1914–1918 war. The Dutch position as neutrals had strong moral overtones that persisted even after the outbreak of the 1939 war. It was felt that the country had stood out as a beacon of light and civilization in war-torn Europe. The Netherlands had joined the League of Nations somewhat reluctantly. Some opposed membership because the Covenant was an integral part of the Peace Treaties which were considered unduly harsh towards Germany and would spell disaster for peace in Europe; others feared that the League would prove to be a French vehicle. In the end, the Dutch joined, in part to counter Belgian designs on its territory, but also because of its long identification since the time of Grotius with the principles of international law.[4] The Netherlands took considerable pride in the presence of the International Court of Justice (1921) in The Hague. Even when taking a more active international role in order to protect itself and the Dutch East Indies against foreign aggression, Dutch diplomats portrayed neutrality 'as a position of elevated morality'. Possession of the Dutch East Indies

[4] J. J. C. Voorhoeve, *Peace, Profits and Principles: A Study of Dutch Foreign Policy* (Leiden, 1985). I owe this reference and others to Anne-Isabelle Richard, research student at the University of Cambridge.

re-enforced the perception of the Netherlands as a 'middle power', more important than Belgium (despite the Congo) or Denmark and therefore in a rather different position than the other small nations. The security situation of the islands changed in the 1930s as the Japanese embarked on a more aggressive policy. There was an acute awareness at The Hague that there was no way the Netherlands could defend the colony, particularly when the British refused to take on the burden of defence. It may be that despite the passivity of Dutch policy, the potential threat from Japan gave added weight to the conciliatory attitude towards Germany in the later thirties in the hope that Berlin would act as a restraint on Tokyo. Though conscious of its exposed position, the Dutch still adhered to their faith in a policy of independence and non-alignment.

As with the Oslo Conference nations, the failure of the League in the Ethiopian crisis led the Netherlands to revert to its more traditional pre-war policy of absolute neutrality. Defended both on pragmatic and moral grounds, this return encouraged an insular, provincial, and self-righteous outlook that tried to ignore the storms outside the Dutch boundaries. The chief positive change during the 1930s was an improvement in Dutch–Belgian relations. The Oslo Convention (1932) and the Ouchy agreement served to promote economic cooperation. The new friendship, undoubtedly assisted by the Belgian return to neutrality, did not lead to any joint military measures that might have improved their respective security situations.

Political and economic circumstances reinforced the belief in neutrality as both a moral and a realistic policy. During the 1930s, the Netherlands was ruled by confessional cabinets, which were strongly anti-Communist. The French alliance with the Soviet Union (which the Dutch refused to recognize) and the Anglo-French negotiations in Moscow in August 1939 were seen as repugnant and dangerous. No government would associate itself in any way with Moscow. There was a short-lived National Socialist movement in the Netherlands. The depression hit the country late but harder than most of its neighbours. Successive governments, headed by Hendrikus Colijn, had an almost emotional attachment to free trade and the gold standard and it was not until 1936 that the Netherlands finally abandoned gold. The result was economic stagnation and a social and political crisis leading to a chorus of protest against the immobilism of the government. The National Socialist Movement, which began as a middle-class and anti-parliamentary protest movement, won almost 9% of the vote in 1935. Its victory led to radicalization; it became increasingly reactionary and anti-Semitic and soon lost part of its middle-class membership. Colijn was far more successful than the head of the Dutch National Socialist Movement (NSB) in presenting himself as a 'strong man' and issued a decree banning civil servants from joining the NSB. A broadly based anti-fascist movement was created, establishing a 'political cordon sanitaire' that forced the NSB leader back to the margins of politics. Its share of the electorate was halved in the parliamentary elections of 1937 as compared to those of 1935.[5] Under the threat of war, a new and broader parliamentary coalition was created but though the socialists participated (for the first time) in the government, it still rested on the old confessional-liberal majority.

While there may have been little liking for Nazi doctrines in the Netherlands, Germany was its main trading partner, particularly when the British Empire markets became less accessible. Germany took a substantial proportion of the country's exports, almost half of which were agricultural products. In the late 1930s, Germany's economic importance exerted a considerable influence over all the Dutch cabinets. The experience in the 1914–1918 war convinced most Dutchmen that there was a strong link between the maintenance of neutrality and the security and well-being of the state. In wartime, it was hoped that the Netherlands could use its neutral position to bargain with both Germany and Britain so that the latter's blockade would not result in the impoverishment of the country. During 1939–1940, the Netherlands struggled to defend its neutrality as the belligerents sought not only to safeguard their own economic interests but to damage those of their enemies.

Given the general aversion to military spending and the distrust of the armed service, the Netherlands was left without any significant defence forces. Colijn had raised defense spending from 1.1% of GNP in 1934 to 2.2% in 1938, hardly an amount that would make a substantial difference. After January 1939, in response to the false rumours of a German attack, the country was assured of British assistance, but neither side believed this would provide adequate protection in case of invasion. The British chiefs of staff agreed that the preservation of the territorial integrity of the Netherlands was of vital strategic interest to Britain, but pointed out that 'there is no hope of preventing Holland from being overrun, and that the restoration of her territory would depend upon the later course of the war'.[6] Alignment with France and Britain would not have offered effective protection; an alliance would have furnished Germany with a pretext for

[5] This material is taken from Martin Conway and Peter Romijn, 'Belgium and the Netherlands', in Martin Gerwarth (ed.), *Twisted Paths: Europe 1914–1945* (Oxford, 2007), 103–104.

[6] Quoted in Bob Moore, 'The Netherlands', in N. Wylie (ed.), *European Neutrals and Non-Belligerents During the Second World War*, 83.

attack. Given its indefensible position, in Europe and in the Dutch East Indies, and the prevailing mood in the country, many Dutch historians have questioned whether there was any alternative policy available to a conservative, confessional, and passive government faced with a strongly pro-neutrality electorate.

In 1914, the Netherlands had ordered a rapid mobilization of the armed services in order to demonstrate the country's readiness to defend its neutrality. Though the first steps were taken on 22 August with the announcement of the Nazi–Soviet pact, the government held back on mobilization. The prime minister gave his approval to King Leopold's call for peace. It was mainly due to pressure from Queen Wilhemina, who was in many ways more resolute than her prime minister or the majority of his cabinet, that on 24 August the armed forces took up their battle positions. Four days later, the government decided on general mobilization and began to make defensive preparations to show their determination to defend its neutral position. There was a large measure of wishful thinking in the Dutch attitude towards the war. The observance of neutrality precluded any formal ties with potential allies; unofficial military and intelligence contacts with Belgium, France, and Britain were no substitute for more detailed or more long-term planning. For too long, successive governments trusted the policies that had served the country so well in the Great War would again protect the country from attack.

Luxembourg was totally isolated in the summer of 1939. International agreements in 1864 guaranteed the independence and sovereignty of this perpetually demilitarized state, though they had not prevented the German invasion and occupation of the country on 2 August 1914. The object of fierce Franco-Belgian quarrels in 1919, the Grand Duchy formed an economic union with Belgium (1921), the seemingly less dangerous partner of the two. It also joined the League of Nations, an assertion of its independence, though winning reservations with regard to military sanctions and without altering its constitution to allow for membership. Once Joseph Bech became president (1924–1937) and then foreign minister (1937–1953), he assumed full control of the Grand Duchy's foreign policy and became a familiar and active figure at Geneva, identified with the search for collective security and disarmament. Luxembourg allied with the states imposing economic sanctions (with some reservations) on Italy and was later represented at the meetings of the Committee on Non-Intervention in London as an observer nation and without taking any part in its debates. The Rhineland crisis, followed by Belgium's withdrawal from the French alliance in March 1936, undermined the

Grand Duchy's strategic position. With the credibility of the League fatally damaged and without defences of its own, it was totally exposed to an attack. Bech immediately sought new guarantees of his country's independence and neutrality. He would have preferred a multilateral guarantee but was forced to seek separate agreements with possible friends and foes.

In July 1936, Bech turned to the French, who showed little interest in guaranteeing a disarmed country that was completely dependent on the actions of its neighbours. He subsequently opened talks with the Belgians and the British, hoping to find support for a new Rhineland pact that would include Germany, Britain, the Netherlands, France, and Britain, but was given little encouragement in any capital. The British preferred a Franco-German bilateral guarantee and when this proved unattainable, refused to extend the 1937 guarantees given by Belgium to Luxembourg. In April 1938, the Belgians disclaimed all responsibility for the Grand Duchy. As the French wanted to preserve the right to send troops into Luxembourg if attacked by Germany, they preferred not to recognize its neutrality. Without any other option available, talks were opened with Germany in the hope of securing a guarantee along the lines of those given to Belgium. The negotiations seemed to prosper but were purposely drawn out as the Germans waited for a French response to Bech's enquiries for similar action. The French finally agreed to respect the independence and territorial integrity of Luxembourg but made no mention of its neutrality. The Germans insisted that Luxembourg should abstain from any action taken by powers hostile to the Reich. In April 1939, France suddenly cut off all contacts unwilling to limit their freedom of military action, though the British appeared willing to make the occupation of Luxembourg a *casus belli* if the French did the same. The separate talks with France and Germany in 1938–1939 led nowhere.

Luxembourg was a natural haven for fleeing refugees. Their arrival provoked a xenophobic and anti-Semitic response, resulting in the closure of its borders in 1938. Though the Grand Duchy contained a cohesive and pro-Nazi German community, there was no influential Nazi party before 1940. The actual percentage of collaborators (3% of a total population of 299,000 inhabitants) was matched by a similar percentage of active resisters. Like the Netherlands, Luxembourg was heavily dependent on German trade, and could not afford to abandon it. There were few alternatives to waiting on events despite rising doubts whether the traditional policies would protect the Grand Duchy's independence in the ruthless world of 1939.

Luxembourg was only a spectator in the diplomatic game. For the first time, in 1939, the national budget included an item for the surveillance of the frontiers. On 27 August, the government affirmed its impartiality in case of war and spoke of its conviction that the belligerents would respect the inviolability of its territory. Separate and independent communications from Germany and France confirmed their respective recognition of the Grand Duchy's neutrality. The president of the country spoke publicly of his confidence in the force of international law. In private, neither he nor Bech were sanguine about the future.

Statesmen in all three countries, even Bech who considered himself a realist, indulged in some form of 'wishful thinking' or 'ostrich-like behaviour', but neither the British nor the French had offered much in the way of positive support until 1939. In each of the three countries, the public supported the governments' policies. For differing reasons, all responded to the threat of German attack by placing their trust in the rules of international behaviour, which Hitler had already openly breached. Statesmen and people alike wanted to stay out of the approaching war at almost any cost. 'Absolute neutrality' appeared as the only available option.

IV

The Nordic (Denmark, Sweden, Norway, and Finland), Scandinavian (Denmark, Norway, and Sweden), and Baltic (Latvia, Estonia, and Lithuania) countries shared an over-optimistic belief that it would be possible to stand aside in case of war. Yet, with the exception of Sweden, all suffered occupation by either Germany or the Soviet Union. Once it became clear that the League of Nations could not safeguard their independence, governments sought alternative ways to do this. In the mid-thirties, they all began to spend more on defence. As they started from very low standards of military preparedness, none could really rely on their military forces to ward off outside attack. It proved singularly difficult to create regional military pacts. The limits of both Nordic and Baltic solidarity were clearly shown in their responses to the German offers of non-aggression pacts on 28 April 1939. Finland, Sweden, and Norway rejected the offer; Denmark, Estonia, and Latvia accepted them. The Norwegian foreign minister believed that with the progress of military technology (the long range of modern aircraft reducing the need for advanced bases) there was actually less reason for a belligerent attack on Norway than in the last war. Denmark, on the other hand, felt defenceless and sought to placate its over-mighty German neighbour. When the Nordic states met in Oslo on 31 August 1939, no plans were made to tighten their military links. The only result was the 'renewal of the well-known declarations on strict neutrality towards all third countries'.[7] After September 1939, the survival of each depended on the credibility of their respective claims to neutrality.

There was no official political Nordic co-operation in the 1930s although in the latter half of the decade there were regular meetings of foreign ministers and sometimes prime ministers that continued until October 1939. The Oslo bloc representatives also conferred regularly, for the last time in August 1939. In the spring of 1938, the Swedish foreign minister spoke informally of establishing a military pact but Denmark and Norway rejected participation. The former, in particular, was caught between Britain and Germany, with 90% of exports and 60% of imports involving the two Great Powers. Britain was the dominant trading partner but 'Germany was no less indispensable, not least as a counter-balance to Britain.'[8] Strategically, Germany posed the greater threat. This was the *raison d'être* for accepting the proffered non-aggression pact with Germany in May–June 1939. The overriding aim was to keep out of the war and this meant inspiring confidence in Berlin that Denmark would remain neutral. No steps were taken to upgrade the Danish defensive system which was in worse shape than in 1914. On 3 September, Denmark proclaimed its absolute neutrality. Relying on the German confirmation of its non-aggression treaty, other countries were warned not to engage in any action incompatible with this principle.

The Norwegians, on the contrary, felt that they had little to fear from Germany which would benefit far more from their neutrality, in terms of raw materials and access to the oceans via Norwegian territorial waters, than from involving Norway in war. Like Denmark, it was caught between Germany and Britain. Though the British assumed that Norway lay within its sphere of influence, the Norwegian government did not want to become involved in a British blockade of Germany. Oslo was not sure whether Britain would come to its assistance if the Germans took reprisals. Relying on the Anglophile sympathies of the king, the leaders of the armed forces, and the business community, the British Foreign Office underestimated the extent to which isolationism, neutralism, and

[7] Bogdan Koszel, 'The Attitude of the Scandinavian Countries to Nazi Germany's War Preparations and its Aggression on Poland', in John Hiden and Thomas Lane (eds.), *The Baltic and the Outbreak of the Second World War* (Cambridge, 1991), 130. See also Patrick Salmon, *Scandinavia and the Great Powers, 1890–1940*. 338–340 for Britain's decision not to include Denmark among the states that London wanted to guarantee in the abortive alliance negotiations with the Soviet Union.

[8] Hans Kirchhoff, 'Denmark, September 1939 – April 1940', in Wylie (ed.), *European Neutrals and Non-Belligerents During the Second World War*, 37.

the growing fear of Germany might undermine its unspoken assumptions about Norwegian support. The British knew that Norway played a critical role in assisting the transport of Swedish iron ore to Germany and few had doubts about the importance of this trade to the German preparations for war. Belated British attempts to draw closer to Norway in 1939 were rejected both by the king and by the main political leaders who had come to believe that safety lay in a policy of strict neutrality. The Norwegian mistrust of Britain's future intentions, however, went hand in hand with an equally powerful faith that in the last resort, Britain would always be willing and able to defend Norway and that the Royal Navy would stop a German invasion. After 1937, Norway began to spend significant sums on armaments in the hope that the country would be strong enough to hold out until the British help arrived. Much of the money remained unspent by April 1940 as it proved difficult to find sources for military purchases. In the months before the war, as well as after, everything was done to preserve the country's neutrality so as not to provoke any action by either London or Berlin.

The positions of Sweden and Finland were more complex. When in the spring of 1938, Sweden took the initiative in pushing for Nordic military co-operation, only the Finns responded. Finland had been part of Sweden for some 500 years until 1809, and traditional feelings of solidarity were strong. The two governments entered into a bilateral arrangement for military co-operation. Finland was focused on the USSR but while most Swedes shared its anti-Bolshevik sympathies, they were unwilling to compromise their neutrality by moving too far in an anti-Soviet direction. Sweden's social democratic government, too, was rather suspicious of the relations between the Finnish bourgeois-conservative élite and the Germans. These differences came to the fore over the defence of the demilitarized Åland Islands that lay between the two countries. The Swedish–Finnish agreement to defend the islands had been signed in January 1939, but failed to come into force. When the Soviets rejected the agreement in Geneva in May, the Swedes withdrew from the arrangement about which they had never been overly enthusiastic. As the possibility of war came closer, the Swedish government sought to avoid any defence commitment at all, leaving the Finns only with the illusion of future backing against Soviet demands.

The news of the Anglo-French-Soviet talks seemed ominous to both Finland and Sweden. The Soviet demand for a guarantee of Finland threatened to divide that country from the other Nordic countries, above all, from Sweden. With Finland guaranteed by the Great Powers, and recognized as being within the Soviet sphere of influence, a common Nordic neutrality policy would become impossible. Though the announcement of the Nazi–Soviet pact was a shock, it was received in Sweden with a considerable sense of relief. Unlike the Anglo-French-Soviet negotiations, the new alignment would not separate Finland from its Nordic neighbours (the existence of the secret protocol was unknown). It would also remove the immediate prospect of a Great Power war in the Baltic and a preventive *coup* against the Åland Islands by any one of the belligerents. For Sweden, at least, the situation seemed more favourable than it had been at the time of the Munich agreement.

Apart from the overriding goal of remaining outside of the conflict, Sweden's primary concern was to secure sufficient supplies of food and fuel in order to avoid domestic unrest by negotiating long-term trade agreements with both sides. It was essential to balance carefully between Germany and Britain. A large proportion of Swedish trade was with the former, including the supply of commodities that Germany desperately needed—above all, iron ore. The Germans had made it clear that it would continue to respect Swedish neutrality only as long as iron ore shipments were continued without interruption. In April 1939, the Germans secured a promise from Stockholm that Sweden would take no part in any effort to cut off the iron ore supplies to Germany. The British, fully apprised of the importance of these deliveries, feared that Sweden would resist their efforts to impose a blockade. In fact, the Swedes proved more circumspect in their trade policies than London anticipated. Their pro-German policies in 1914–1918 had led to Allied reprisals; this time, Stockholm hoped to avoid such a situation by a more even-handed policy. As far as possible, trade with the belligerents would be carried on at the same level and in the same proportions as in peacetime but only if both sides recognized Swedish neutrality and continued to supply its economic requirements. The British were far from happy with this decision and drew up a number of plans for covert action, either in Sweden in order to stop production, or in Norwegian territorial waters to intercept supplies going to Germany. Despite the difficulties of balancing between London and Berlin, the Swedes believed there were grounds for optimism if they carefully manoeuvred between the two Great Powers.

Finland had re-oriented its policy away from the Baltic States (though Finland's defence co-operation with Estonia lasted up to 1939), and towards Scandinavia, and Sweden in particular, in facing the Soviet threat. From the Finnish perspective, the loss of Swedish backing for some form of military co-operation in 1939 was critical, though they may have retained hopes of informal co-operation. Admittedly, after long negotiations in August, the Swedes announced that they would pass on any surplus military supplies to Finland and one other Nordic country if both would stay neutral in case of war. It may be that Finland refused to negotiate seriously with the USSR partly based on the hope that Sweden would come to their aid if attacked by the Russians.

In the spring of 1939, Finland was under renewed pressure from the Soviet Union seeking reassurance that the Finns would not allow their territories to be used to launch an attack on the USSR. In March 1939, Litvinov proposed that Finland should lease Suursaari (Hogland) and a number of other small islands in the Gulf of Finland to Russia, but the Finns refused to cede any part of their territory. Though suspicious of Soviet intentions, they were convinced that, due to the purges, Moscow would not consider war for some years yet. At the same time, with the Soviet Union very much in mind, they continued to co-operate with Estonia, preparing a joint defence against future Soviet action. From 1930 until 1939, the two states developed a highly secret intelligence and military relationship. Joint plans were drawn up to close off the narrowest point of the Gulf of Finland by laying mines and rebuilding the Tsarist naval batteries on either side of the Gulf. In the summer of 1939, two secret defensive exercises were arranged, concentrating on repelling a hypothetical Soviet naval attack from the east. Co-operation had to be kept secret. The Finnish decision after 1935 to align with the Scandinavian powers expressly ruled out too close a relationship with the Baltic states, while Estonian neutrality was buttressed by its excellent relations with Germany and its distance from any anti-German combination. By September 1939, the joint blockade plan had been tested both in war games and in practical exercises, but it all came to naught when Estonia surrendered its bases to the Soviet Union in the autumn of 1939 and agreed to sign a mutual security pact. The blockade idea did not escape the notice of the Soviets. An effective blockade in the mouth of the Gulf of Finland would bottle up the Soviet fleet and make it impossible to operate against German ships in the Baltic. As the Finns and Estonians were building on a defence line established by the Imperial Russian General Staff for use against the Germans, Stalin undoubtedly had the old strategy in mind when, in the autumn of 1939, he demanded that specific areas in the two countries be yielded to Moscow.[9] Finland would face Russia alone when war broke out on 30 November 1939.

[9] This information comes from a Finnish study by Jari Leskinen, *Vaiettu Suomen Silta: Suomen ja Viron salainen sotilaallinen yhteistoiminta Neuvosoliiton varalta vuosina 1930–1939* (Helsinki, 1997), with an English summary on pp. 450–459. I am indebted to Dr Kristina Spohr-Readman for bringing the book to my notice and for assistance in preparing this section.

Latvia and Estonia were more afraid of the USSR than of Germany. Arguing that the new non-aggression treaties with Germany balanced their non-aggression treaties with the Soviet Union (renewed in 1934) and so strengthened their respective positions as neutral states, both governments accepted the German demand for an unrestricted neutrality clause valid even in the case of German aggression against another power. The treaties not only improved Germany's strategic and economic position, but were viewed in Berlin as a considerable propaganda victory. The non-aggression treaty with Lithuania (22 March 1939), which followed the German seizure of Memel, had already isolated the country and left it open to German dictation. Taken together, the new treaties would prevent any Baltic move towards an anti-German coalition, and would allow Germany to find substitute sources for the foodstuffs she would lose as a result of a war with Poland. While neither Latvia nor Estonia formally agreed to give the Germans priority in trade, the Germans assumed, and the British feared, that this would be the case. Unlike the prevailing opinion in the Scandinavian states, there was a slow spread of pro-National Socialist sentiment mainly among the Germans living in the two Baltic states, adding to Soviet concerns about 'indirect aggression' in the summer talks with Britain and France. In the early contest between Germany and the Soviet Union for power in the Baltic, it was the former that was the more successful. This explains, in part, why the Soviets were so insistent that the Baltic States be included in any Allied guarantee during the alliance negotiations. All this changed dramatically with the signing of the Nazi–Soviet pact. When Ribbentrop went to Moscow, the Soviets insisted that the line separating the German–Soviet spheres of influence should be drawn so that Estonia and Latvia came under Moscow's control, bringing the USSR's strategic frontier 200 miles further west. The later secret protocol concluded on 28 September brought Lithuania, along with half of Poland, into the Soviet orbit.

V

The Swiss clung to the concept of neutrality and were able to remain outside the conflict all through the war. In no other country was 'neutrality so deeply engrained or so critical to the political fabric and the survival of the state'.[10] It was only by promoting consensual policies at

[10] Neville Wylie, 'Switzerland: A Neutral of Distinction?', in Wylie (ed.), *European Neutrals and Non-Belligerents*, 332.

home and avoiding any engagements abroad that the weak federal government could accommodate the diverse national, ethnic, and religious interests of its disparate population. It is also true that respect for Swiss independence, affirmed in 1815, had become an accepted part of the European consensus and that all the states, whatever their form or ideology, would not easily infringe Switzerland's neutrality. There had been a considerable debate about joining the League of Nations. The federal government had never really been comfortable with this form of 'partial' or 'differential' neutrality, though Swiss citizens were active members of the League's secretariat and took the lead in expanding the boundaries of international action. Yet a small country, perched between the Axis powers on the one side and the French on the other, could not escape the more extreme tensions of the mid-thirties. There was a change of policy after which the confederation had to make a number of uncomfortable choices, some of which struck at the core of it status as a neutral state. Foreign policy had been driven by two objectives, the first centred around the promotion of international peace and security through the League of Nations, which Switzerland had joined only with the promise of exemption from carrying out any military operations ('differential neutrality'). The second strategy, which took shape during the early 1930s, was to rely on Italy to assist the Swiss balancing act between its two largest neighbours, France and Germany. The centrality of these two objectives made the Ethiopian crisis, rather than the remilitarization of the Rhineland, the definitive moment in Swiss diplomacy in the years leading up to the war. The crisis exposed Switzerland's commercial dependence on good relations with all its neighbours, and rapidly exposed the fragility of its support for the League when membership entailed participation in economic sanctions. By the time the 'midsummer of madness' was over the Swiss attachment to an independent foreign policy based on absolute neutrality was firmly established. Forced to choose between Rome and Geneva, the Swiss showed no hesitation in opting for the former in March 1938. Swiss pro-Italian policy, it should be said, was the brainchild of its long-standing Swiss–Italian foreign minister Giuseppe Motta. This was only the first step to Switzerland's departure from the League of Nations in the same year and its return to a position of 'integral' neutrality in foreign affairs. Not only was Switzerland freed of any obligations to the discredited League, but it could set about coming to terms with its Fascist neighbours. Few in Switzerland welcomed the decline of the League system of security, but the events of the next years meant that Berne had to convince the dictators of Switzerland's total commitment to neutrality.

While integral neutrality obliged the Swiss government to avoid any overt bias in its external relations and to encourage an atmosphere of unity in the country and detachment from ideological conflicts (with the possible exception of its anti-Bolshevism), the pro-Allied sentiment in the country, and the distaste in some quarters for the domestic Nazi policies, complicated relations with Berlin. By 1938, Swiss consumers were regularly boycotting German goods, and Switzerland's 4–2 victory over Germany in the football World Cup of that year was met with an outburst of uncontained glee. The task of balancing was further complicated by the inescapable fact that, notwithstanding Italy's occasional irredentist claims over the Swiss canton of Ticino, Germany alone posed a physical threat to Switzerland. Swiss safety depended on German respect for its neutrality. There was, however, a Francophone element in the Swiss army, led by the future commander-in-chief, Henri Guisan, which was prepared to initiate secret military discussions with the French in 1936. Agreement was reached on a set of contingency plans that envisaged large-scale Franco-Swiss military co-operation in the event of a German invasion of Switzerland. Their defence plans were so far advanced that by the summer of 1940, the French ambassador in Berne had to take direct action to prevent the staff of his military mission from triggering the movement of French forces across the border to take up pre-arranged positions in Switzerland's defence line. The Berne government, on the other hand, sought to underline Switzerland's distance from the raging nationalist and racialist fevers consuming the continent. The federal authorities took measures to heighten Swiss self-awareness and to emphasize the unique position of a neutral Switzerland in a continent at war. For Berne, the protection of neutrality became the over-riding Swiss concern. Nevertheless, the Swiss—more than other countries—devoted considerable effort towards civil defence measures in the lead-up to the war: they allocated space for food production and comparatively sophisticated, if embryonic military–civil structures to maintain civilian morale at the outbreak of the war. When considering 'neutral' defence measures, they were preparing for a concept of defence that extended well beyond the border fortifications. Having suffered during the First World War due to economic dislocation and blockade, they were determined to avoid the same fate again. It had been this that had undermined their claims to sovereignty after 1914, rather than the military threat of the belligerents. In the end, the defeat of France would change the whole diplomatic equation though not Switzerland's adherence to the age-old principle of neutrality.

VI

It might have been expected that the Germans and Italians could count on Spain's benevolent neutrality, if not its active support, in any future war. By 1939, the *Caudillo* had emerged completely triumphant in Spain; his ties to Germany and especially Italy were undeniable in light of the massive military assistance he had received. Yet he continued his customary policy of giving priority to his own interests whatever the pressures applied. It was only after a considerable delay that the victorious Spanish leader agreed to join the Anti-Comintern Pact and it was not until 27 March 1939, well after he had secured both British and French *de jure* recognition of Spain, that he actually signed the treaty. The public announcement took place on 6 April. The canny dictator continued to play a double game, assuring his partners that Spanish adhesion represented an act of real solidarity, while telling the British that it was merely a gesture of ideological loyalty.

On the economic side, too, Franco kept to his careful course. The wartime bargains with Berlin meant that Spain would provide much-needed minerals such as iron ore, copper, pyrites, and wolfram to Germany, and would accept German participation in some of Spain's extractive plants. However, the Spanish leader successfully blocked the German efforts to secure more long-term economic concessions, and managed to make inroads on their already established position. Franco was not going to mortgage Spain's economic future to the Axis. A German delegation visited Spain in June 1939 with the intention of normalizing trade relations by abolishing the Hisma–Rowak system and persuading Franco to increase the proportion of exports needed for German rearmament. In August 1939, the *Reichsstelle für Wirtschaftsausbau* [the State Office of Economic Expansion] concluded that Spain's considerable mineral wealth made her 'an especially valuable partner' and 'a natural addition to south-eastern Europe, indispensable to the *Großraumwehrwirtschaft* [Greater War Economy]'.[11]

The Germans fared far better than the Italians who had postponed the payment of the major part of the Nationalist debt until after the end of the civil war, and consequently received almost nothing. Mussolini, in August, complained to the German ambassador that his country had been 'bled white' by the Spanish Civil War, which had eaten into Italy's foreign exchange reserves, compounding the problem of buying foreign raw materials.[12] Franco's shrewd handling of his debts to the Axis powers did not prevent him, in the heady days after victory, from identifying closely with the dictators. He was particularly, and uncharacteristically, effusive towards Mussolini, who accepted verbal gratitude

[11] Glyn Stone, *Spain, Portugal and the Great Powers, 1931–1941*, 97.

[12] Glyn Stone, 'The European Great Powers and the Spanish Civil War, 1936–1939', in Robert Boyce and Esmonde M. Robertson (eds.), *Paths to War: New Essays on the Origins of the Second World War*, 206.

in place of more substantial recompense. On 31 March, Franco signed a treaty of friendship with Germany that committed each power to avoid 'anything in the political, military and economic fields that might be disadvantageous to its treaty partner or of advantage to its opponent' and on 8 May, took Spain out of the League of Nations.[13]

When the 'Pact of Steel' was concluded in May, Spanish troops were sent to the Gibraltar area in an open anti-British demonstration and were used to reinforce the Spanish side of the frontier between the French and Spanish zones in Morocco. Berlin and Rome knew that Franco had plans to establish a new Spanish empire in Africa. Though the Spanish Army was reduced almost by half in the summer of 1939, Franco still had 500,000 men under arms, however poorly equipped. His military forces were to be divided between the Pyrenees and Gibraltar in order to counter any French or British moves. The Spanish leader was also preparing to enlarge his navy and develop his air force but this had to be for sometime in the future. In early August, Franco sent troops and ordered the construction of new fortifications near the French border. He set up a Gibraltar command backed by a division. He also advised Admiral Canaris that he intended to assist the German navy in its Atlantic operations by offering various kinds of logistic support. In fact, Spain was far too economically impoverished and its inhabitants much too exhausted for even the contemplation of future war. On 19 July, Franco struck a more realistic note when Ciano reported that 'Franco considers that a period of peace of at least five years is necessary, and even this figure seems to many observers optimistic. If, in spite of what is foreseen and in spite of goodwill, a new and unexpected fact should hasten on the testing time, Spain repeats her intention of maintaining very favourable—even more than very favourable—neutrality towards Italy.'[14] He could hardly promise more. The country was crippled and its coffers empty. The *Caudillo* had to deal with Republican stragglers, guerrilla wars, and even a possible rebellion. An immediate outbreak of war involving Germany and Italy could lead to a French invasion of Spanish Morocco as the French had planned. Spain could not sustain a war either at present or in the near future and 'a direct assault on Gibraltar was unthinkable'.[15] Though the Germans knew that Franco had no choice but to opt for a policy of neutrality, they had good reason to believe that it would be neutrality of the benevolent kind.

[13] Paul Preston, *Franco: A Biography* (London, 1993), 326.

[14] Quoted in Elena Hernández-Sandoica and Enrique Moradiellos, 'Spain', in Wylie (ed.), *European Neutrals and Non-Belligerents*, 246 fn.

[15] Preston, *Franco*, 336.

The British and French followed a cautious course in dealing with Franco after granting *de jure* recognition in February. The French concluded a new agreement with the Spanish, the Bérard–Jordana agreement, to settle the disputes between the two countries and appointed Marshal Pétain as ambassador in Burgos, signalling their intention to improve relations with Franco. The Anglo-French military leaders insisted on the strategic importance of securing Spanish neutrality. It proved difficult, however, to capitalize on Spanish economic weakness and the British faced an uphill battle not helped by their unwillingness to guarantee a loan on the open market in the summer of 1939. The British task was made no easier by the French refusal to return either the Spanish gold in their possession or the captured war materials as covered by the Bérard–Jordana agreement without substantial progress on the resettlement of the Spanish refugees interned in France. The British pushed Daladier hard to settle with Franco but the matter was not concluded until the end of July. The gold was returned though not the captured war material, which included modern Czech anti-aircraft guns and motor equipment much coveted by the French. More than 200,000 Spanish refugees claimed asylum in France (see pp. 247–8). In the end, Spanish neutrality owed very little to the British and French efforts to improve relations; Spain's impoverished condition was the decisive factor both before and after the start of the war. On 4 September, Franco announced Spain's 'strict neutrality' in the conflict. The German ambassador was informed, but was told that Spain was nevertheless 'willing to assist as far as she possibly could'.[16] It did not take long before this assistance, propaganda, intelligence, and logistic support began, but the imposition of the Allied naval blockade balanced by British offers of a loan and supplies of corn, industrial products, and desperately-needed fuel put limits on Spain's pro-Axis orientation. With its borders exposed and its armed forces still in disarray, Franco responded favourably to the Allied carrot-and-stick policy while still identifying with the Axis cause. The public alignment with Germany (not withstanding the Nazi–Soviet pact) and Italy did not mean a rupture with Britain and France but the balance would depend on Spanish recovery and on the circumstances of the war.

The case of Portugal was somewhat different. Salazar had supported the Francoists and had rendered important services, men, material, and transit rights to the Nationalist forces. During the civil war, relations with Britain were strained and the Germans made much of their opportunities to cultivate both political and economic ties with Lisbon. The Italians and,

[16] *DGFP*, Ser. D, Vol. VII, No. 524.

more aggressively, the Germans, mounted propaganda campaigns; visits of organizations with common aims were encouraged. The Germans tried, too, to weaken Britain's dominant economic position in Portugal and to contest its established role in supplying the Portuguese armed services. Fortunately for the British, Hitler had refused to consider their offer of colonial territories in March 1938, subjecting a large proportion of the Portuguese empire to limitations on Portugal's sovereignty and ceding other parts to Germany. Hitler's acceptance might well have driven Salazar, temporarily at least, into the German arms.

The British (hostile Franco-Portuguese relations precluded any French initiative) were not inactive; a British military mission spent six months in Lisbon in 1938 and, backed by export credits of £1 million, persuaded Salazar to purchase a variety of arms from Britain. It proved difficult to fulfil these orders because of prior claims, but the appointment of permanent service attachés to the British embassy in Lisbon helped to mitigate the negative results (see pp. 199–200 for details). In fact, Salazar could not move far from London; the alliance with Britain (the old alliance of 1386 had been renewed in the Treaty of Windsor in 1899) was central to Portugal's independence and Salazar's position. The Royal Navy provided security for the communications and trade routes between Portugal and its colonies in Asia, equatorial Africa, and in Southern Africa (Angola and Mozambique). Britain was, moreover, Portugal's main trading partner and its chief source of foreign investment. Finally, whatever the ties between the authoritarian leaders (and there were many differences) Salazar knew that Franco might well cast his eye on its smaller neighbour and that he would need British backing against such a threat. If Spain tied itself to the Axis powers, there was a distinct danger that Portugal would be forced to follow suit, whatever the costs. Portugal, like Britain, had a vested interest in Spanish neutrality and this provided a basis for collaboration. The Portuguese, as they informed the British minister, could provide useful information about Franco's policies and reinforce their efforts to keep Spain neutral.

The clashes with Britain during the Spanish Civil War and the changes in the international situation had opened up new possibilities for Portugal to improve its negotiating position and Salazar made the best of these opportunities. Well before the outbreak of war, he repeatedly alerted London to the damage a hostile Spain, backed by the Axis powers, could inflict on British interests and underlined the important role that a neutral Portugal could play in keeping Spain from entering the war. At the same time, he refused to give a pledge of unconditional support to the British. He assured the Germans that Portugal was under no obligation to give assistance to Britain, even in a defensive war. The British, he rightly believed, wanted to ensure the neutrality of the Iberian peninsula, and Portuguese neutrality would serve their interests. Britain had no wish to assume any new obligations towards Portugal unless Spanish adhesion to the Axis powers made Lisbon's co-operation essential for the security of Gibraltar and for the maintenance of the Atlantic sea lanes.[17] Portugal opted for neutrality, and not non-belligerency as it had in 1914, because it wanted to create a certain distance from Britain in order to exploit the circumstances of the moment in securing the best terms possible from London. Salazar aimed, above all, at keeping Portugal out of the war for intervention could easily ruin the country. Within the confines of its traditional friendship with Britain, he hoped to exact a price for Portuguese neutrality.

VII

In south-east Europe, the last months of peace were a time of continuous diplomatic activity. Those states already tied to Germany, if mainly through economic dependence, tried to avoid political subservience and to resist any involvement in war. Yugoslavia and Romania, but even Hungary and Bulgaria, moved warily, as war became more certain. Even the Turks, after the announcement of the Nazi–Soviet pact, had to re-think their position for they had always insisted that any alliance with Britain and France would have to be paralleled by an agreement with Moscow.

Romanian and Yugoslav efforts to maintain policies of 'equilibrium' or balance between the power blocs have been described in Chapter 7. Both countries faced similar problems in the early summer of 1939. The possibility of Axis aggression and attacks from the Hungarians, on the one hand, and the fear that neither France nor Britain would defend the Balkan status quo, on the other, pointed to a cautious policy of avoiding too close an identification with either side. Another problem emerged with the continuing talks between the western allies and the Russians in Moscow. Domestic difficulties in both Romania and Yugoslavia added to the necessity of following flexible policies in an increasingly inflexible continental situation.

[17] Fernando Rosas, 'Portugal', in Wylie (ed.), *European Neutrals and Non-Belligerents*, 272.

The Romanians, under continuous threat from Italy and Hungary, kept a careful eye on the talks with Moscow. Despite Bucharest's deep distrust of Moscow and the ever-present issue of Bessarabia, the Romanians did not oppose the discussions as such. If attacked by Germany, Soviet arms, but not its troops, would be welcome. It was important, however, to avoid any provocation that could bring about the German invasion that Bucharest so feared. As the Moscow talks continued and King Carol and his advisers became convinced that the western allies would strike a bargain with Stalin, there were second thoughts. During the last week of July, they decided that should the Turkish–Soviet negotiations succeed, they would use the Turks to approach Moscow for a non-aggression pact. False reports that the Germans were using the Danzig crisis as a cover for an attack on Romania, possibly originating with the Germans who wanted to distract attention from Poland, began to circulate early in July. Berlin, in fact, was trying to contain Hungary's territorial appetites and to avoid any collision with Romania. A second wave of similar reports of a Hungarian–German attack circulated at the beginning of August, causing a Romanian mobilization and a visit to Ankara by an alarmed King Carol who was cruising in the Black Sea. The Turkish authorities promised immediate mobilization if Romania was attacked and pressed the king to approach the Soviet Union. Carol agreed to enter a non-aggression pact if the Russians recognized Romanian sovereignty over Bessarabia. The shrewd president of Turkey, Ismet Inönü, a master hand at patient negotiation, promised to intervene in Moscow but was sceptical of success unless the Romanians would allow Soviet troops to cross their country. Later in August, when the Hungarians backed down and the war scare subsided, the Romanians recovered their nerve and raised their conditions for a Russian pact. They were now hoping for an international conference, along Munich lines, where their territorial claims arising from the peace settlements would be confirmed.

The conclusion of the Nazi–Soviet pact increased the sense of Bucharest's political and military isolation from the West. It appeared that Germany and Russia were now the 'arbiters' of the fate of Eastern Europe. The Romanians needed the Reich to act as a mediator with, and even a barrier against, the Soviet Union. Gafencu used the previous pledges of Romanian neutrality as a way to gain German support for the country's territorial integrity. It was pointed out to the Germans that they would need an independent Romania in order to keep the mouth of the Danube free and open to German shipping.

The Romanian foreign minister was still trying to save something from the earlier policies of 'balance'. There were divisions over how to define

Romania's diplomatic position once war broke out. Some Romanians feared that a declaration of neutrality might jeopardize Romania's right to call for western assistance under the Anglo-French guarantee if invaded. A declaration of neutrality, too, might compromise Romania's position at the peace conference.[18] Romanian politicians assured the Germans that the country would remain neutral but at first resisted Reich pressure for an official declaration. The Germans were told that Romania would remain neutral in a Polish–German war, even if the Allied powers intervened. King Carol assured the German air attaché that he had rejected British plans to sabotage the oil fields in the case of war. By the 6th, there had been a change of mind. It may have been the Yugoslav declaration of neutrality on 5 September, or the German warnings to the Hungarians, who had moved troops up to the Romanian border, that they were not to move against the Romanians that influenced their decision. On 6 September, the Crown Council voted for a formal declaration of neutrality, though some would have preferred a more decided pro-German orientation and possible German guarantees of Romania's borders. During discussions in Berlin, great emphasis was laid on Romania's need for a powerful Germany to protect it against Soviet revisionism. This theme would become even more important with the division of Poland.

Hitler preferred a neutral but friendly Romania to a belligerent one, partly for fear that, as was being planned, the western powers would blow up the oil fields. If not totally assured of King Carol's support, he had won deliveries of oil that his forces needed. As shown earlier (see pp. 729–730, 746–748), in mid-August there was pressure on both sides to give substance to their commercial agreements. The Romanians wanted their promised but delayed arms deliveries while the Germans were desperate for oil. The latter were forced to agree to speed up the deliveries of Heinkel fighters and other war materials. Thereafter, the Romanians proved highly co-operative, releasing oil supplies well over the negotiated quantities in return for war materials that had yet to be delivered. The Romanians hoped to use the oil negotiations to secure German backing against a potential Soviet threat.

The policy of equilibrium had given way to one of neutrality but the Romanians still tried to conciliate both sides. Where possible, concessions and counter-concessions were the rule. The British and French retained control of the oil fields and their operations on the international market brought hard currency into Romania. They were, of course, dependent on Bucharest to maintain the status quo. As soon as war

[18] Rebecca Haynes, *Romanian Policy towards Germany, 1936–1940*, 107.

broke out, secret contingency measures were worked out between the British and the Romanians for destroying the oil wells and installations, should the Germans invade the country. For the Romanian leaders, it became a matter of defining their country's interests in the rapidly changing political–military situation. For immediate purposes, Romanian neutrality favoured Germany, but future policy, in so far as it could be decided in Bucharest, would depend on the exigencies of the moment.

Prince Paul of Yugoslavia had been relentless in his attempts to find a way out of Yugoslavia's exposed position, but the German and Italian moves in the spring of 1939 undermined his policy of balance. *Anschluss* had brought the Greater Reich right up to Yugoslavia's borders while the creation of an independent Slovakia, under German sponsorship, in March 1939, set an example for the Croats and Slovenes. Italy's seizure of Albania gave Mussolini his long-desired position to move against Belgrade. Both Hungary and Bulgaria, particularly the former, were waiting to make good their revisionist claims. And the Yugoslavs were still desperately short of aircraft and arms to defend themselves. The Italian move into Albania made it essential to keep a policy of non-alignment.

Yugoslavia's situation was complicated both by Prince Paul's attachment to Britain and by Hitler's promises to Mussolini, for it was Italy rather than Germany that posed the major threat to Yugoslavia. Whatever his personal sympathies, Britain's unwillingness to provide material support and the continuing Italian danger to Yugoslavia meant that the prince regent had to follow a policy of 'balance'. Aleksandar Cincar-Marković, the Yugoslav foreign minister, believed it was necessary to continue courting the Germans and Italians. On a visit to Berlin in April, he assured Hitler and Ribbentrop that Yugoslavia would not take sides in any hostile action against the Axis powers. Cincar-Marković did manage to secure promises of arms credits from Göring and the delivery of over one hundred aircraft. Ciano was told that Yugoslavia would not accept guarantees from the western states but would pursue a policy of 'benevolent neutrality'.[19] At the same time, though Prince Paul was anxious to secure credits and arms deliveries from wherever he could, he refused to declare an 'Axis-friendly' neutrality in case of war. Hitler's efforts to convince the prince regent that he would restrain Mussolini did not impress him. The Führer's careful handling of the Yugoslav ruler during his early June visit to Berlin—Prince Paul's first since coming to power in 1934—failed to pay any political dividends whatever the economic

[19] Dragoljub R. Zivojinovic, 'Yugoslavia', in Wylie (ed.), *European Neutrals and Non-belligerents in the Second World War*, 220.

pay-offs. Despite their efforts to make the visit a success and to impress their guests during their eight day visit, Prince Paul resisted the German pressure to leave the League of Nations and join the Anti-Comintern Pact as a mark of solidarity. The prince left Berlin determined to maintain his country's independence but convinced that war was imminent and that Hitler was secretly negotiating with the Soviet Union.

The Yugoslavs were necessarily cautious. They responded positively to German–Italian anger over the Anglo-Turkish declaration of 12 May, objecting strongly to the reference to Balkan security and threatening to leave the Balkan Entente because the Turks were compromising its neutrality. Axis pressure on Belgrade was renewed when the Franco-Turkish declaration, published in June, included both a Turkish obligation to assist Britain and France in their execution of the guarantees to Greece and Romania and a reference to measures to ensure stability in the Balkans. Cincar-Marković assured Ribbentrop that he would not follow Turkey's lead but would try to forge a neutral coalition that would include Hungary, Bulgaria, Romania, and Greece without Turkey. The foreign minister's overture to Hungary was rejected; Budapest was not ready to abandon its claims for Transylvania against Romania. A meeting at Bled on 9 July with Georgi Kiosseivanov, the prime minister and foreign minister of Bulgaria, who was anxious to weaken Germany's stranglehold over his country but not at the cost of abandoning Bulgaria's territorial demands, produced an agreement on a policy of independence and neutrality but nothing more.[20] Cincar-Marković informed Ribbentrop that even if his proposed neutral coalition failed, Yugoslavia would not take an anti-German position. He claimed that Belgrade was already distancing itself from the Balkan Entente and had refused to take on the presidency of the next session of the Council of the League of Nations. In return, he asked for military credits. The Germans were sceptical; they knew from various sources that the Anglophile Prince Paul was seeking western support and that he had been offered credits to be spent on arms and military equipment. Just before going to Paris in June seeking credits for arms and military equipment, the Yugoslav finance minister convinced the Germans to sign a protocol to the existing German–Yugoslav arms credit increasing deliveries of war materials though the Germans proved slow in delivering on their promises.

Prince Paul had his own scenario, only part of which became known to the Germans and Italians. Believing that war would come soon, he thought it essential that the difficult Serb–Croat talks, started in

[20] Quoted in Alfredo Breccia, *Jugoslavia, 1939–1941: Diplomazia della Neutralità* (Rome and Milan, 1979), 150.

December 1938, in which he played a leading part, should succeed if the Italians were not to have an easy target for their intrigues. The prince regent wanted to get the Italians out of Albania and ward off an Italian attack on Salonika. Already in May, the Yugoslav chief of staff began consultations with his Greek counterpart despite the latter's traditional unwillingness to participate in an Italian–Yugoslav war. The prince regent had an even more radical plan. In July, he sent General Petar Pešić to consult with the French and British chiefs of staff. He was to explain that though Yugoslavia would be forced to declare her neutrality on the outbreak of war, it would join the western allies as soon as the Mediterranean and Adriatic came under Allied control. The Yugoslav army would be ready to intervene at the most opportune moment.[21] General Gamelin proved more sympathetic than the British (Pešić saw General Gort, the chief of the imperial general staff, Lord Halifax, and Lord Chatfield). Pešić found the two governments had different views both over the Salonika campaign and the question of Yugoslav neutrality. Though encouraged by Gamelin, who wanted a swift Yugoslav entry into the war, a joint Salonika campaign, and an early attack on Italy, Pešić was not impressed by the French situation. There were too many uncertain factors in France's strategic calculations and given the state of the French army, there was far too much optimism in their plans.[22] The British were considerably cooler, having little interest in a Salonika campaign and an early campaign against Italy. Prince Paul also had information from General Weygand, via the French minister in Belgrade, that the Allies would require a period of at least three months between the decision to open the Salonika front and the deployment of troops during which time the Balkan countries would have to hold the front themselves. Prince Paul could not have been overly optimistic when he paid a so-called 'private' visit to London (17 July–4 August) to see his son at school. Though he was warmly received and much fêted, he found, as General Pešić had warned, that the British had little interest in a Balkan campaign. Chamberlain and Halifax were, in fact, pressing Daladier to come to an agreement with Mussolini. Lord Halifax evaded the prince's question as to whether Britain could be confident of finishing off the Italian fleet should war come by claiming that strategic questions did not fall within his area of responsibility.[23] Nor, despite

[21] D. C. Watt, 294.

[22] See Irina Nikolic, 'Anglo-Yugoslav Relations, 1938–1941', Ph.D. thesis, University of Cambridge, 2001, 102–103. Dr Nikolic has used the Pešić report in *Cvetkovic*, unpublished autobiography, Hoover Institution Archives, Stanford, CA, which gives a rather different and much more critical view of the situation than the one found in Watt, *How War Came*, 295.

[23] Watt, *How War Came*, 296.

Halifax's encouraging noises was there a positive response to Prince Paul's complaints about the delayed deliveries of aircraft and armaments for which the Yugoslavs had been petitioning since September 1938. What was finally offered, after a fierce bureaucratic battle in London, was little more than a gesture. After intense lobbying by Lord Halifax, Belgrade was given in June credit guarantees of up to £1 million for commercial purposes and a half million, later raised to £1 million for armaments. Yet Yugoslavia remained at the bottom of the Balkan queue for arms. When at the end of June, the situation was reviewed, the decision was taken to authorize the despatch of only half the aircraft already allotted to Belgrade, some Blenheim aircraft, and 1,000 second-hand Hotchkiss guns. It had been decided in London that nothing could be done for Yugoslavia and whatever equipment could be spared should be used to satisfy more important petitioners. The French had been more forthcoming. On 14 July, the Yugoslav minister of finance concluded an agreement with Daladier for a massive shipment of guns of all varieties, tanks, trucks, and mobile workshops using the arranged 200 million franc loan from the Bank of Seligmann in Paris. This still left the Yugoslavs woefully short of what they believed they needed.

Hitler was much perturbed by Prince Paul's visit to London and possibly thought more had been accomplished than was the case. He was particularly incensed by the news that Prince Paul was to be made a member of the Order of the Garter. Information that Yugoslavia's gold reserves had been shipped to Britain and the United States only convinced him that Yugoslavia was an 'uncertain neutral'. There were renewed Axis demands in July that Yugoslavia leave the League of Nations and make an open declaration of support. Calming statements from Cincar-Marković had little effect. In meetings with the Hungarian and Italian foreign ministers on 8 and 12 August, Hitler and Ribbentrop stressed Belgrade's untrustworthiness. The Italians were strongly encouraged to seize Croatia and Dalmatia. It was 'like throwing some dog a bone'.[24] The Italians were already conspiring with the Hungarians and Mussolini was making plans, of which Hitler knew little, for a 'Balkan parallel war'. There was little certainty about what Yugoslavia would do when war came. Hitler was still angry about his failure to solicit a clear promise of support from the prince regent. He did not expect Belgrade to remain neutral for long, and he encouraged Mussolini in his already formulated plans to seize Croatia and Dalmatia. The Yugoslavs had watched the Hungarian visits to Rome and

[24] Brian R. Sullivan, 'Italy', in Wylie (ed.), *European Neutrals and Non-Belligerents*, 141.

Berlin and the Italian military preparations with considerable anxiety. Troops were sent to Slovenia and Croatia, where both the Germans and Italians were stirring up separatist feelings. Again and again, the Germans were assured that Yugoslavia would remain neutral in war. There was, nonetheless, a perceptible Yugoslav move towards the Balkan Entente and unconcealed expressions of sympathy for the western powers among the political elite in Belgrade.

The announcement of the Nazi–Soviet pact came as a shock offset only by the conclusion of a Serb–Croat agreement (*Sporazum*) on 23 August due to Prince Paul's intervention. He had instructed the Serbian minister president, Dragiša Cvetković, to conclude an immediate agreement with the Croatians even at the expense of accepting some of their more extreme demands. This was a possible way to block Italian (and German) fishing in the Yugoslav waters. A new government was formed, headed by Cvetković and Vladko Maček, the head of the Croatian peasant party but its durability and the unity of the state was still open to question.

As in Romania, against these political setbacks, the Germans were eventually able to consolidate their control over Yugoslavia's mineral wealth. It was only in May 1939 that they began to move on the negotiations initiated by Prince Paul at the start of the year for a long-term credit to purchase bombers, fighters, and anti-aircraft artillery. Hard bargaining on both sides resulted in a protocol that was less favourable than the Germans wanted. Though signed on 5 July, the Germans were dissatisfied and held back the deliveries of planes and arms. German pressure on Belgrade for raw materials intensified. On 24 August, an agreement was reached for a 200 million mark credit for German military equipment, though the delivery problems of the past continued. The Yugoslavs desperately tried to find alternative sources of supply but the British and French had no spare equipment to offer and the Swedes, Belgians, and Americans demanded cash for arms. The Italian declaration of non-belligerence relieved some of the pressure though Prince Paul rightly distrusted Mussolini and warned Hitler that Yugoslavia would fight if Italy entered the war and moved towards Salonika, the port essential for supplies to reach Yugoslavia. Hitler was pleased and somewhat surprised by the Yugoslav proclamation of neutrality on 5 September and its declaration that it would follow this policy in all conflicts that did not involve Yugoslav independence and political integrity. Given the poor state of its military forces and its exposure not only to Italian enmity but to threats from its revisionist smaller neighbours, there were good reasons for opting for neutrality and winning time for further rearmament. Once war broke out, Prince Paul would again approach the Allied powers for arms and for a Balkan campaign. Nevertheless, on 5 October, a new secret protocol gave the Germans the full substance of their economic demands assuring them access to the only available sources of needed minerals outside the Soviet Union. The Yugoslavs had to make immediate payment, mainly in raw materials, for the aircraft and artillery they received in return. Though Hitler may have wanted more from Belgrade than they were willing to provide, neutrality had not blocked the flow of materials required by Germany.

VIII

Even with regard to Hungary and Bulgaria, generally considered German pawns, Hitler faced new difficulties on the eve of the Polish war. Both the Hungarians and the Bulgarians made their peace with Berlin though the former refused to take part in any action against Poland. The Germans were content with private assurances that neither state would act against them and would not 'anticipate events', i.e. not attack Romania. The Hungarians were to follow the Italian example and opt for 'non-belligerency'. The Germans needed only Slovak participation in the Polish campaign for German troops were to be sent to Slovakia in order to invade Poland from the south. Monsignor Tiso was given little choice. The rumours that Slovakia might lose her independence to Hungary only increased his willingness to accept Hitler's offer on 23 August to guarantee Slovakia's frontiers with Hungary and help her recover the territories lost to Poland.

The Führer wanted Hungary, which shared a common border with Poland, to avoid any action that would upset the Balkan status quo. Having taken sub-Carpathian Ruthenia (Carpatho-Ukraine) at Hitler's invitation, he believed the Hungarians should have been content. Nevertheless, Admiral Horthy and Count Pál Teleki, the prime minister, who replaced the openly pro-Nazi Béla Imrédy in February, were cautious about tying Hungary too tightly to Germany. Teleki shared Horthy's conviction that the democracies would defeat Germany in a war of attrition and was anxious not to be on the losing side again. As the Poles were Hungary's only friends in Europe, Teleki, a devout Catholic, would not countenance Hungarian participation in a German war with Poland. But the Hungarians needed German underwriting. Both Teleki and Horthy were strong revisionists and their territorial demands complicated relations with all their neighbours, especially Romania which felt particularly vulnerable. The Hungarians hoped to 'straddle the fence' between the Axis and the western powers, making use of Hitler's need to secure their loyalty to advance their territorial claims. They thought that once Hungary regained her lost territories, the victorious powers would not be able to muster either the moral authority or the physical strength to dislodge the ill-equipped but courageous Hungarian army. The Hungarians were not above conspiring with the Italians in their efforts to regain Transylvania. In late May, unknown to Ciano, the Hungarian military attaché in Rome opened conversations with the Italian army chief of staff, Alberto Pariani, for a Balkan campaign that would involve assaults on Greece and Romania. As a consequence of their appetites, the Hungarians were almost universally distrusted. Under such circumstances, they had to nurse their contacts with Berlin and Rome. The Hungarian economy was tied to that of Germany, the country's best customer. Its agricultural surplus was sold to the Germans and its fledgling precision and communications industries were linked to their German counterparts. The Hungarian share in the carve-up of Czechoslovakia, presented to the public as an independent and even an anti-German action, had helped to advance Hitler's plans for Poland. Almost all Budapest politicians, however, whatever their political orientation, were opposed to assisting Germany against Poland. Hitler, who met with the Hungarians on 29 April and 1 May, stressed German strength, Poland's suicidal obstinacy, British and French weakness, and the Japanese ability to keep the Americans from playing any military role in Europe. Teleki was troubled but he could not antagonize Hitler particularly after the strong showing of the extreme right in the late May elections and its relentless pro-Axis campaign.

The real crisis came in July when the Germans and Italians demanded an open show of loyalty to the Axis. On 22 July, Count Teleki wrote identical letters to Hitler and Mussolini declaring that Hungary would align its policies with the Axis as long as such action was compatible with its sovereignty. Two days later, at Horthy's request and against Count Csáky's advice, a second letter was sent stating that 'Hungary could not, on moral grounds, be in a position to take armed action against Poland.'[25] Hitler was furious; the Hungarians were again showing themselves to be untrustworthy and ungrateful clients. Csáky came to Berchtesgaden on 8 August and was bullied by Hitler. Without consulting Budapest, the foreign minister told the Germans to forget Teleki's letter. Official confirmation of his action came the next day. Cancellation did not mean, however, that Hungary would participate in a war against Poland. The decision to stand aside was made somewhat easier when the Italians opted for non-belligerent status and offered to act as intermediaries between Budapest and

[25] C. A. Macartney, *October Fifteenth: The History of Modern Hungary, 1929–1945*, Vol. I (London, 1956), 358–359.

Berlin. In an unofficial secret message sent to Lord Halifax at the end of August, Teleki explained that Hungary would adopt a neutral position in a European war but could not declare its formal neutrality because of its special position with regard to Germany. The Germans warned Hungary against attacking Romania and Ciano moved to convince Berlin of Hungary's loyalty. On 1 September, the Hungarians presented a statement of loyalty to the German alliance to Ribbentrop but refused to join the war against Poland. Even after the German attack on Poland, Teleki and his government continued their planning for an offensive against Romania. In a letter to Mussolini on 2 September, they raised the possibility of an international conference of arbitration that would include the Hungarian claims on Romania. The idea had a short life in so far as the Germans wanted to use the Hungarian railway line to transport their troops to Poland. While vaguely raising the possibility of territorial revision, they again warned the Hungarians against attacking the Romanians. On 9 September, a high level meeting in Budapest concluded that Hungary 'would not participate in any military measure connected with the war against Poland'.[26]

A short-lived refusal to allow German forces to move into the Hungarian–Polish border area allowed some 70,000 Polish refugees (the numbers are disputed) to cross the Polish–Hungarian border, outraging Hitler and confirming his deep distrust of Horthy whom he denounced as 'friendly to the Jews, hostile to the Germans, and infinitely egotistical'.[27] The display of Hungarian sympathy towards the fleeing Poles, among whom were many Polish officers, was noted in the Allied capitals and created some sympathy for Hungary's ambitions, for there was no let-up in the Hungarian hopes for territorial revision at Romanian expense. As they had told both the Germans and the British, there was no official Hungarian declaration of neutrality but the Teleki government, while pledged to co-operation with Germany, tried to avoid new commitments to Berlin and kept the lines open to the western powers. This seemed the best way to secure territorial revisions without engaging in the European war.

IX

There appeared, at first, little reason for Berlin to woo Bulgaria but King Boris and Georgi Kiosseivanov, the premier-foreign minister, did not want to tie their country too closely to Germany. Like the

[26] Tibor Frank, 'Hungary', in Wylie (ed.), *European Neutrals and Non-Belligerents*, 162.

[27] Quoted in Thomas Sakmyster, *Hungary's Admiral on Horseback: Miklos Horthy, 1918–1944* (Boulder, CO, 1994), 434.

rulers of Romania and Yugoslavia, the shrewd and cautious king thought the western powers would prevail in a war with Germany and, knowing the terrible costs of defeat, had no wish to be on the losing side. Personal preference, as well as domestic pressures pointed to a policy of neutrality and a strong commitment to the return of the lost territories, southern Dobrudja from Romania, Macedonia from Yugoslavia, and Aegean Thrace from Greece. If war came and Bulgaria was engaged on its western front, then Romania might offer neutrality or even benevolent support in return for the lost lands. Kiosseivanov, less dedicated to the return of the lost lands than the king and concerned with the overwhelming German domination of Bulgarian trade (well over half its imports and exports and taking nearly all of its important tobacco crop), was in contact with the Turks and prepared to be wooed by the Balkan Entente powers. Due to western pressure, in July 1938, Metaxas, the Greek dictator acting as president of the Council of the Balkan Entente, signed a treaty of friendship and non-aggression that recognized Bulgaria's right to rearm but met none of Sofia's territorial wishes. It was only after the British offers of guarantees to Turkey and Romania that the situation changed in the Bulgarian favour with the western states and the Germans as suitors. Turkey, Britain, and the Soviet Union each urged Bulgaria to join the Balkan Entente. The Turks, the natural link between Bulgaria and the Balkan Entente powers, tried to broker a Romanian cession of a part of Dobrudja as the price to be paid, but the Romanians rejected the deal. Already faced with the loss of Turkey and highly uncertain of Yugoslavia, the Germans put greater pressure on the Bulgarians to declare themselves more openly in favour of the Axis powers. Some attempt was made to link their participation in the Anti-Comintern Pact with the granting of an armaments credit. Though this military initiative was checked by the Foreign Ministry, the German ambassador in Sofia urged Kiosseivanov in March to follow a more public pro-German line. The prime minister, while claiming that he was already pursuing a pro-German line, refused to declare himself in such an open way. The Germans retreated and the Bulgarians were granted the armaments credit in April in return for Kiosseivanov's vague assurances and some economic concessions.

A directive sent by Kiosseivanov to all Bulgarian representatives abroad in April 1939 throws a sharp light on the Bulgarian position. Although arguing that Bulgaria wanted the revision of its borders and consequently would not join the Balkan Entente, the government emphasized that it would try to follow an independent policy without committing itself to anyone. At the same time, it was acknowledged that Germany dominated Bulgaria's trade and was its main source of armaments since other countries would not sell weapons on credit. There was a danger 'that Germany might attempt to set political conditions on us'.[28] It was clear in 1939 that Bulgaria had only two choices, either an alliance with Germany or neutrality. The king and government preferred the latter but might not have the freedom to choose.

As part of the attempt to pressure the Bulgarians, Kiosseivanov was invited to Berlin. During his stay, 6–7 July, he seems to have had a relatively easy time. He assured the Germans that the Bulgarians were maintaining their revisionist claims against Romania but also against Greece and looked for German support and the arms needed to help themselves. Kiosseivanov told Ribbentrop 'quite categorically that Bulgaria would never join a combination of Powers which ran contrary to German Interests'.[29] Hitler promised that the Bulgarians would get all the arms they wished and there was no mention of the Anti-Comintern pact. Ribbentrop assured Kiosseivanov that there was no conflict of interest or any barriers to a German–Soviet understanding. The Bulgarians already knew of the exchanges in which the Bulgarian minister in Berlin acted as an intermediary between the German Foreign Ministry and the Soviet *chargé d'affaires*. While giving welcome private assurances to the Germans, neither the king nor his minister committed himself to any promise to collaborate only with the Axis powers.

Kiosseivanov was determined to foster the *rapprochement* with Yugoslavia. The joint statement of their mutual interest in independence and neutrality did not go down well in Berlin. News of the visit of the president of the Bulgarian parliament and his meetings in London with George VI, Lord Halifax, and Sir Frederick Leith-Ross, the government's chief economic adviser, was even more unwelcome. Kiosseivanov denounced Stoica Mokanov and, on his return home, the latter claimed his visit was purely formal and that the British failed to understand Bulgaria's situation, or its fear of Turkey. The charade was intended to reassure the Germans. During the first weeks of August, there were reports intended for German ears suggesting that Bulgaria was under siege, anticipating an ultimatum to join the Balkan Pact, and expecting British aircraft to arrive in Salonika or even a Soviet naval attack on Bulgaria's Black Sea coast. The Germans, however sceptical of these supposed threats, speeded up the promised arms deliveries, which

[28] Quoted in Vesselin Dimitrov, 'Bulgaria', in Wylie (ed.), *European Neutrals and Non-Belligerents*, 202.

[29] Quoted in C. A. Macartney and A. W. Palmer, *Independent Eastern Europe* (London, 1966), 406.

was their purpose. The Bulgarian visit to London paid dividends; an Anglo-Bulgarian credit agreement was signed, and the credits were extended to cover Egypt and Palestine where Bulgarian tobacco was more acceptable to smokers than in Britain.

The Nazi–Soviet pact was welcomed by most Bulgarians but not by King Boris. Many Bulgarians were traditionally pro-Russian and the combination of the two ex-enemies held out hopes for Bulgaria's territorial claims. The Bulgarian Communist party had been outlawed in 1924 but the Bulgarian Workers' Party was a real political force. The king did not share the general sense of relief which greeted the announcement of the pact. He had been a strong supporter of Britain's appeasement policies and had hoped that the western powers would settle with Moscow. He feared that the Germans might concede Bulgaria to the Soviet sphere of influence and sought assurances from Berlin. While trying to calm King Boris's apprehensions, there were hints that Germany would not be able to support Bulgaria if it came into conflict with Moscow.[30] The king continued to hope that the Polish war could be localized and repeatedly pressed British and French diplomats to stop the war and arrange an agreement with Germany if they wished to avoid 'universal destruction'.[31] King Boris was too shrewd to follow an anti-Soviet policy against the wishes of so many of his countrymen and set about improving relations with Moscow. Bulgaria declared its official neutrality on 15 September 1939.

X

As far as the Germans were concerned, by the summer of 1939 both Greece and Turkey were in the western camp. It was thought possible, nonetheless, that Metaxas, the dictator of Greece since his royal appointment in August 1938, might steer a neutral course. There were strong traditional and more recent ties between Greece and Britain. The present king, George II, was an Anglophile, having spent twelve years of his exile in Britain, and, on his return to power in 1935, had made the British ambassador his special confidant. Greece relied on British naval power. It was dependent on its sea imports for its food, raw materials, and other commodities. The substantial Greek merchant fleet earned most of its money from the carrying trade with Britain and was insured in London. Nevertheless, the Germans had established an important presence in the country. Encouraged by Metaxas, they had played a major role in the economic regeneration of the country and in the re-equipment and modernization of the army, of special concern to the Greek leader.

[30] Dimitrov, 'Bulgaria', 203. [31] Ibid.

Metaxas's dictatorship was somewhat different from that of Hitler's but brutal in its own way. He admired many aspects of the National Socialist regime, had no quarrels with Nazism, and welcomed the expanded German economic role in Greece. The Germans dominated Greece's foreign trade and took more than 70% of the tobacco crop, its major export. In return, they supplied the Greeks with arms and with the machine tools and equipment required for the armament industries. Due to the co-operation between the German armaments firm, Rheinmetall-Borsig and the Greek Power and Cartridge Company, assisted by Göring's patronage, Greece became a major exporter of arms to the Balkan states, Republican Spain (Göring was happy to supply both sides), Nationalist China, and to the Middle East. Armament exports provided valuable hard currency that was used for purchases elsewhere. Greece's economic dependence on Germany continued right up to and after the outbreak of the war. As the Metaxas regime became more authoritarian and George II identified himself with the dictatorship, British influence in Athens declined. The British Minister, having tried unsuccessfully to convince the king to distance himself and even dismiss Metaxas, had to be replaced in 1939 as he was no longer an effective representative.

A good deal of the Greek defence effort was directed against Bulgaria and Metaxas looked mainly to Turkey to keep Bulgarian revisionism in check. The more dangerous threat, however, came from Italy. After the Albanian occupation, the dictator had welcomed the British 13 April guarantee but, as earlier, preferred an alliance with Britain that would have deterred Mussolini and provided protection should deterrence fail. Neither the British cabinet nor the chiefs of staff were prepared to make such an offer, which would have provoked the Italians and burdened Britain with the almost impossible task of defending Greece's exposed land frontiers and coastline. Even while seeking a clearer British commitment to Greece and pressing for credits and arms, Metaxas sought to maintain good relations with Berlin, assuring Göring that Greece would continue to follow a strictly neutral course. There was a short-lived *rapprochement* with Italy in the early summer, and an exchange of letters, rather than the renewal of the 1928 pact of friendship that Mussolini wanted, expressing the hope that in the future 'circumstances would permit a closer relationship between the two countries'.[32] Metaxas had sought British guidance and approval of these exchanges. Though the Italians removed their troops from the Albanian–Greek border, Metaxas rightly remained highly suspicious of Mussolini's intentions and would not move far from Britain. At the same time, without the prospect of a

[32] John Koliopoulos, *Greece and the British Connection, 1935–1941*, 114.

British alliance, he had no wish to alienate or provoke the Germans, who, even apart from their position in the Greek economy, could act as a restraining influence on Italy. There was some reason, therefore, for the Germans to hope that Greece might remain neutral if it was not attacked.

The British had recognized the dangers of Greek economic dependence on Germany but despite the efforts of the British minister in Athens and Lord Halifax in London, it proved exceedingly hard to arrange either a credit (holders of Greek bonds wanted payment first) or an increase in tobacco imports, given the resistance of the Imperial Tobacco Company and the unwillingness of the British public to smoke the Greek product. It was only after a sustained battle that Lord Halifax and the Foreign Office convinced the cabinet in the spring of 1939 to give Greece a £2 million credit to buy arms. The credit agreement was signed on 12 July 1939 but little could be done about increasing Greek tobacco imports until after the war had begun. Again, despite repeated efforts on the part of Leith-Ross, the military authorities refused to place orders with the Greek Powder and Cartridge Company while Vickers turned down a request to consider investing in the company to prevent it falling under full German control. Again, it was only after the start of the war that British attitudes changed.

Even as war approached, Metaxas remained cautious and continued to assure the Germans that Greece would remain neutral. Without an alliance with Britain, there could be no open declaration of support for the western powers. The Greeks, despite Italy's non-belligerency, continued to stress their neutrality in all their dealings with Berlin. The Greek declaration of neutrality was somewhat ambiguous for it had little choice but to adopt a position of benevolent neutrality towards Britain. Basically, the Anglo-Greek relationship was an unequal one between a Great Power and a small country. The British expected little from Greece and would make no firm commitments. The obligations to defend the exposed country seemed greater than the benefits Britain would receive. Unlike the French, the British had little interest in a Balkan front. Greek expectations of future British support, on the contrary, were high. Metaxas was convinced that circumstances would force Britain to take Greece under its protection if it were attacked. For the first six months of the war, at least, the two governments drew closer and agreements were concluded that extended British economic support both for the Greek government and for private Greek ship-owners.

Turkey was in a special category but thought to be in the Allied camp. Until 1939 the German interest in Ankara was mainly economic. Turkey produced 16% of world chromium, which imparted firmness to iron and steel and was therefore vital to armament production. By

1937, Germany drew over half her chromium supplies from Turkey. When Britain concluded a £16 million credit agreement with Turkey in May 1938, including £6 million for armaments, Germany stepped in with a 150 million Reichsmarks counter offer in January 1939. As it turned out, this was not ratified, but Berlin sought to woo Ankara in other ways, especially by buying agricultural products above world market prices. Politically, Hitler was remarkably complacent about Turkey before the spring of 1939. There was no German ambassador in Ankara for five months between late November 1938 and late April 1939 when Papen was sent out to bully and cajole the Turks.

The Anglo-Turkish declaration (12 May 1939) stirred the Germans into taking action. Responding to the Turkish alignment with the West, Hitler ordered the cancellation of a Turkish order for heavy howitzers from the Škoda works for which payment had already been made. Further economic intimidation followed, including a semi-ultimatum of 21 August proposing the cancellation of all arms contracts and the credit agreement of January 1939. The Turks stood firm, informing Berlin that after the German breaches of existing agreements, all Turkish economic and technical missions in Germany would be withdrawn. The economic cost to Ankara was considerable; the Germans took a major share of Turkish imports and exports. Though the Turkish trade was a small item for the Germans, their dependence on Turkish chrome was serious enough to persuade Hitler to reverse his decision on the arms contracts and to court the Turks by assurances that he would not take action in the Balkans. Still hoping that Britain would compensate Turkey for its losses of arms, Ankara decided not to renew the German–Turkish clearing agreement, which regulated the exchange of chrome and agricultural produce in return for German armaments, when it expired on 31 August 1939.

Because of its geo-strategic position, Turkey was of greater importance to Britain than to Germany. The Montreux Convention of 1936 had prohibited warships from entering the Turkish Straits in peacetime but, like Suez, they remained open at all times to merchant shipping irrespective of nationality. This allowed Italy to draw raw materials, especially Romanian oil, from the Black Sea region, which were vital to its economy. Should Turkey become a belligerent on the Allied side, this lifeline would be curtailed. From the British perspective, too, Turkey represented an excellent buffer to protect the Middle East from attack from the north. Along with Iraq and Palestine, it provided defence in depth for the protection of Suez, the Iranian oil fields and the overland route from Basra to Palestine.

Yet despite its importance, Britain and France remained largely indifferent to Turkish needs until the events of spring 1939 when they were keen to involve Ankara in their guarantees of Greece and Romania. This was matched by Turkey's sudden realization of its vulnerability in the uncertain international climate. Italian domination of the Mediterranean was as much a danger to Turkey as to Britain. The Straits were expected to be a focal point of conflict; the Soviets had been approached but had given little guidance as to their future attitude. The Anglo-Turkish declaration (12 May 1939) followed by the complementary Franco-Turkish declaration (24 June) provided for collaboration in the event of the war extending to the Mediterranean. Complications soon fractured this appearance of unity. The Turks were unwilling to support Greece unless it was attacked by Bulgaria (a most unlikely eventuality) or by a third power acting in concert with Bulgaria. Moreover, the German reaction to these declarations made it essential that Turkey should get more material support from the allies. The Turks found it difficult to move beyond the Allied declarations. The British dragged their feet over the military convention and proved unwilling to meet the Turkish demands for financial and military assistance. There was a fundamental disjunction between the aims of the two countries. The British were mainly interested in the façade of an alliance that would deter the Axis from military intervention in the Balkans and enlist the support of the Balkan powers in the maintenance of the regional status quo. The Turkish government wanted an alliance that would provide it with assistance in case of war. The British viewed the negotiations with the Soviet Union as a means of giving weight to the eastern deterrent. For the Turks, an agreement with Moscow was an essential condition of their security in the Caucasus–Black Sea area. If they were engaged elsewhere, the Soviets could easily cast their eyes on Istanbul and the Straits.

It was mainly due to the French, particularly the French military with visions of another Salonika campaign, that, at the end of August, the three powers agreed on a proposed tripartite military convention based on a Franco-Turkish draft. It comprised a series of operational proposals, covering the Dardanelles, Salonika, and the Aegean littoral, and Turkish action against Bulgaria, most of which would require extensive preparations and a high level of Allied support. Even though the British came to accept the agreement concluded between General Huntzinger, the French army commander designate for the Middle East in case of war, and Marshal Çakmak, the head of the Turkish army, they remained reluctant to provide the assistance that the Turks demanded as part of the price for an alliance. The British could spare little military equipment and faced pressures on sterling and extensive financial commitments. The defence credits offered and promised to Ankara were only a small proportion of what the Turks claimed they needed. Members of the Turkish military mission in London, moreover, were treated as 'ignorant natives, suddenly offered a shopping spree at Harrods and unable to judge for themselves what was genuinely necessary and what was not'.[33] When faced in July with Turkish threats of devaluation and the establishment of a compensation fund, the British finally proposed joint Anglo-French discussions on financial support for Ankara. The French had been far more forthcoming in offering the Turks military equipment but the French Treasury proved as reluctant to act as the British. An agreement to meet some of the Turkish needs was reached at the end of August as war loomed.

Until very late in the day, the British never thought it imperative to secure an alliance with Turkey. It would become important only if Italy was an enemy and London hoped for Italian neutrality. An alliance would be useful as a deterrent, but it was difficult to see how it would operate against Germany 'without a parallel agreement with Russia and the consolidation of the Balkans on the side of the western Allies'.[34] Both of these would be difficult to achieve and their costs might prove too high. The Turks, for their part, needed considerable assistance to replace what would be lost from severing the German connection and could not contemplate a war with the Axis powers unless allied with the Soviet Union or assured of its friendship. Saraçoğlu, the Turkish foreign minister, believed that the allies would bring the Moscow negotiations to a successful conclusion and hoped to follow it up with a Turkish agreement with the Soviets. Caught between fears of Russia and Germany and doubts about British backing, the Turks were already considering whether their best suit was to preserve their neutrality. Hanging over them was the knowledge that in 1914 Turkey chose the wrong side and lost its remaining empire in consequence. Uncertain whether Britain would come to its aid if war spread to the Balkans and assured by Germany that it did not intend to invade south-east Europe, official opinion in Ankara shifted towards the idea of a neutral bloc encompassing Bulgaria, Greece, Romania, Turkey, and Yugoslavia, but excluding Italy. Meanwhile, Turkish attention was focused on Moscow. At the end of July, Molotov proposed a bilateral agreement as had been mooted in May and assured the Turks that rumours of a Russo-German settlement were baseless. Russian pressure increased; in early August they requested an emissary be sent as soon as possible to Moscow to conclude an alliance.

[33] Watt, *How War Came*, 306.

[34] Quotation from Brock Millman, *The Ill-Made Alliance: Anglo-Turkish Relations, 1939–1940* (Montreal and Kingston, 1998), 175.

On 10 August, Saraçoğlu was given plenipotentiary powers to negotiate a non-aggression pact in Moscow. The news of the Nazi–Soviet pact was more than a shock; it aroused real fears about future Soviet intentions. The visit was postponed until later in September.

It was now the British who wanted immediate ratification of the Tripartite Alliance only to find the Turks reluctant to give more than an assurance that Turkey would do nothing without first consulting Britain and France. Extreme Soviet demands, which the Turks rejected, increased the pressure on all three parties to consummate their alliance and the Tripartite Treaty was finally concluded on 19 October 1939. Turkey was promised military aid if it because the victim of direct aggression by a European power, or if it became embroiled in a Mediterranean conflagration. For its part, Turkey pledged to assist Britain and France if engaged in a Mediterranean conflict as a result of aggression by a European power or arising from the guarantees to Greece and Romania. In a secret protocol, disclosed to Moscow, it was made clear that these obligations would not require Turkey to make war on the Soviet Union. Hovering over the Turkish authorities were the historical traumas of continued Russian encroachments against the crumbling Ottoman Empire with Constantinople and the Straits as the ultimate prize. Faced with the reality of war and without a Russian agreement, Turkey and the other Balkan states were less willing and less able to consider active participation in the war against Germany. The idea of a neutral bloc returned to the top of the Balkan menu only to be discarded once more because of old grievances and quarrels. The past was always present in Balkan politics.

XI

Hitler did not get all that he wanted in south-eastern Europe but neither were the western powers able to create a bloc which would act as a deterrent or the base for another front, as the French had hoped, in case of war. There were more uncertainties than Hitler would have liked and some signs of resistance to his plans for domination. Mussolini's ambitions in the region were a problem but Hitler expected the Italians to march with him when the final showdown came and knew relatively little of the Duce's plans for local wars in the Balkans. Hitler did not want such conflicts while he dealt with Poland. He knew that neither Romania nor Hungary would assist Poland, and with the possible exceptions of Greece and Turkey, assumed that none of the other powers would ally with Britain and France. Even before the outbreak of war, ethnic and territorial disputes prevented the creation of a regional neutral grouping to preserve the independence of its members. Due to the late Anglo-French decision to create a bloc in the region and the limited ability of either country to offer the credits and arms that the Balkan states required, Hitler was able to capitalize on Germany's well-established economic base in the region. Romania, Yugoslavia, and Hungary were particularly targeted for the reserves of oil and chrome, manganese, copper, lead, and bauxite needed by the *Wehrmacht*. It is important to emphasize once again that south-eastern Europe supplied only a small percentage of Germany's estimated import needs. The economic authorities had already decided that only the actual occupation of the Balkan countries would allow Germany to exploit the resources of the region. In February, when the first preliminary decisions about Poland were taken, talks had begun with the Soviet Union about initiating new commercial discussions. After the 19 August Nazi–Soviet credit agreement was signed, Hitler assured his commanders-in-chief that in the event of Anglo-French intervention in the Polish conflict, 'we need not be afraid of a blockade' as 'the east will supply us with grain, cattle, coal, lead, zinc'.[35] As he prepared for his Polish campaign, and before his diplomatic revolution, Hitler was content to have quiet in the Balkans.

XII

Countries exhibited an almost dizzying variety of behaviour, which hardly conformed to either balance of power principles or to doctrines of 'offensive realism'. Hardly equipped for war, leaders had to think in terms of national survival, political and economic, even if they stayed out of the impending struggle. Some indulged in wishful thinking. Others followed policies based on illusions, the Nordic and Scandinavian states imagined that the war would be fought on the European mainland, leaving sufficient time to co-ordinate their defensive measures. Spain and Portugal, the former far too exhausted to fight, hoped that by clever diplomacy, they might exploit the needs of the Germans and British to improve their negotiating positions. The Balkan situation proved particularly complex given Mussolini's overt and covert planning and the increasing importance of the Soviet engagement in the region.

Important, too, were the experiences of the Great War. In the case of the Dutch, historical experience as well as moral precepts favoured a

[35] Quoted in Militärgeschichtliches Forschungsamt (ed.), *Germany and the Second World War*, vol. 1, ed. Wilhelm Deist (Oxford, 1990), 358.

policy of absolute neutrality. In south-eastern Europe, much depended on whether the country had been among the victors or losers in the earlier struggle, and the strength of irredentist feeling. The battles over territorial revision were as sharp and pervasive as the immediate dangers of the impending war in Poland.

It was not just the international environment that left the small powers with restricted options; their domestic situations imposed tight constraints on how they could respond to the changing political and strategic picture. Though it is true that the normative structures and sources of soft power in the international community in 1939 were simply insufficient to provide these states with anything like the kind of support they needed to sit out the coming conflict, few of these statesmen, however authoritarian, could ignore the domestic context within which they had to operate.

A few states chose neutrality because they believed that international laws had established the nation's right to declare itself neutral and that the rules of neutrality would be observed in wartime. Neutrality had an honourable history yet it inevitably involved compromise. During the course of the war, some of the 'successful neutrals', notably Sweden and Switzerland, made compromises with one or the other of the belligerents in ways that tarnished their reputations. These were seen to be the necessary price for survival. Later generations would come to question their judgements. What may have seemed a self-evident moral choice in wartime came to appear less defensible when judged in the light of hindsight. The proponents of 'small state realism' had their answer; national survival must come first. This defence has raised uncomfortable dilemmas for their present descendants. The war would change perspectives and behaviour but only a few states, because of geography, resources, astute leadership, and luck, or a combination of all these factors, could remain outside of the conflagration.

General Works

LEITZ, C., *Nazi Germany and Neutral Europe during the Second World War* (Manchester, 2000).

NEVAKIVI, J. (ed.), *Neutrality in History La neutralité dans l'histoire* (Helsinki, 1993). See particularly P. Salmon.

ROULET, L.-E. (ed.), *les etats neutres européens et la Seconde Guerre Mondiale* (Neuchâtel, 1985).

VAN ROON, G., *Small States in Years of Depression: The Oslo Alliance 1930–1940* (Assen, 1989).

WATT, D. C., *How War Came: The Immediate Origins of the Second World War 1938–1939* (London, 1989).

WATT, D. C., 'Britain and the Neutrals: Some Considerations', in L.-E. Roulet (ed.), *Les états neutres européens et la Seconde Guerre mondiale* (Neuchâtel, 1985).

WYLIE, N. (ed.), *European Neutrals and Non-Belligerents during the Second World War* (Cambridge, 2002).

Greece

KOLIOPOULOS, J. S., *Greece and the British Connection, 1935–1941* (Oxford, 1977).

MAZOWER, M., *Greece and the Interwar Economic Crisis* (Oxford, 1991).

PELT, M., *Tobacco, Arms and Politics: Greece and Germany from World Crisis to World War, 1921–1941* (Copenhagen, 1998).

—— 'The Establishment and Development of the Metaxas Dictatorship in the Context of Fascism and Nazism, 1936–41', *Totalitarian Movements and Political Religions*, 2: 3 (2001).

Ireland

*CROWE, C. et al. (eds.), *Documents on Irish Foreign Policy*, Vol. 5: *1937–1939* (Dublin, 2006), and Vol. 6: *1939–1941* (Dublin, 2008). Read after completion of manuscript.

DICKEL, H., 'Irland als Faktor der deutschen Außenpolitik von 1933–1945: Eine propädeutische Skizze', in FUNKE, M. (ed.), *Hitler, Deutschland und die Mächte: Materialien zur Aussenpolitik des Dritten Reiches* (Düsseldorf, 1976).

KENNEDY, M., *Ireland and the League of Nations, 1916–1946: International Relations, Diplomacy and Politics* (Dublin, 1996).

—— and SKELLY, J. M., *Irish Foreign Policy, 1919–1966: From Independence to Internationalism* (Dublin, 2000).

O'DRISCOLL, M., *Ireland, Germany and the Nazis, 1919–39: Politics and Diplomacy* (Dublin, 2004).

—— and KEOGH, D. (eds.), *Ireland in the Second World War: Neutrality and Survival* (Cork, 2004).

O'HALPIN, E., *Defending Ireland: The Irish Free State and its Enemies* (Oxford, 1999).

—— 'Irish Neutrality in the Second World War', in Wylie, N. (ed.), *European Neutrals and Non-belligerents during the Second World War* (Cambridge, 2002).

RAYMOND, R. J., 'Irish Neutrality and Anglo-Irish Relations, 1921–1941', *International History Review*, 9 (1987).

SALMON, T. C., *Unneutral Ireland: An Ambivalent and Unique Security Policy* (Oxford, 1989).

Low Countries

ALEXANDER, M., 'In Lieu of Alliance: The French General Staff's Secret Cooperation with Neutral Belgium, 1936–1940', *Journal of Strategic Studies*, 14: 4 (1991).

ARON, R., *Leopold III: ou, le choix impossible* (Paris, 1977).

BOND, B., *Britain, France and Belgium, 1939–1940*, 2nd edn. (Oxford, 1990).

KAYSER, S., 'La neutralité luxembourgeoise dans l'entre-deux-guerres, 1918–1940', *Galerie*, 14: 4 (1996) and 15: 1 (1997).

—— 'Joseph Bech aux affaires étrangères—de 1926 à 1954, le recherché de garanties internationales pour le Grand-Duché de Luxembourg', *Galerie*, 17: 4 (1999).

KIEFT, D. O., *Belgium's Return to Neutrality* (Oxford, 1972).

KONINCKX, C., *Leopold III, roi et diplomate: la politique belge et les initiatives de paix pendant l'entre-deux-guerres, 1934–1940* (Anvers, 1997).

KOSSMANN, E. H., *The Low Countries 1780–1940* (Oxford, 1978).

KRIER, E., 'Die Außenpolitik des Dritten Reiches gegenüber Luxemburg', in Funke, M. (ed.), *Hitler, Deutschland und die Mächte: Materialien zur Aussenpolitik des Dritten Reiches* (Düsseldorf, 1976).

LADEMACHER, H., 'Die Niederlande und Belgien in der Außenpolitik des Dritten Reiches 1933–1939—Ein Aufriß', in FUNKE, M. (ed.), *Hitler, Deutschland und die Mächte: Materialien zur Aussenpolitik des Dritten Reiches* (Düsseldorf, 1976).

MOORE, B., 'The Posture of an Ostrich? Dutch Foreign Policy on the Eve of the Second World War', *Diplomacy and Statecraft*, 3: 3 (1992).

—— 'The Netherlands', in Wylie, N. (ed.), *European Neutrals and Non-belligerents during the Second World War* (Cambridge, 2002).

STEINER, Z. (ed.), *The Times Survey of Foreign Ministries of the World* (London, 1982).

VAN LANGENHOVE, F., *L'élaboration de la politique étrangère de la Belgique entre les deux guerres mondiales* (Brussels, 1980).

Scandinavia

FRITZ, M., 'Swedish Iron Ore and German Steel', *Scandinavian Economic History Review*, 21: 2 (1973).

KIRCHHOFF, H., 'Denmark, September 1939 – April 1940', in Wylie, N. (ed.), *European Neutrals and Non-belligerents during the Second World War* (Cambridge, 2002).

LEVINE, P. A., 'Swedish Neutrality during the Second World War: Tactical Success or Moral Compromise?', in Wylie, N. (ed.), *European Neutrals and Non-belligerents during the Second World War* (Cambridge, 2002).

LOOCK, H.-D., 'Nordeuropa zwischen Außenpolitik und "großgermanischer" Innenpolitik', in Funke, M. (ed.), *Hitler, Deutschland und die Mächte: Materialien zur Aussenpolitik des Dritten Reiches* (Düsseldorf, 1976).

MAIER, K. and STEGEMANN, B., 'Securing the Northern Flank of Europe', in Militärgeschichtliches Forchungsamt (ed.), *Germany and the Second World War,* Vol. 2, *ed. Klaus A. Maier et al. (Oxford, 1991).*

SALMON, P., 'British Plans for Economic Warfare against Germany, 1937–1939: The Problem of Swedish Iron Ore', *Journal of Contemporary History*, 16 (1981).

—— *Britain and Norway in the Second World War* (London, 1995).

—— *Scandinavia and the Great Powers, 1890–1940* (Cambridge, 1997).

Salmon, P., 'Norway', in Wylie, N. (ed.), *European Neutrals and Non-belligerents during the Second World War* (Cambridge, 2002).

South-eastern Europe

Breccia, A., *Jugoslavia 1939–1941: diplomazia della neutralità* (Rome and Milan, 1978).

Broszat, M., 'Deutschland—Ungarn—Rumänien', in Funke, M. (ed.), *Hitler, Deutschland und die Mächte: Materialien zur Aussenpolitik des Dritten Reiches* (Düsseldorf, 1976).

Crampton, R. J., *A Short History of Modern Bulgaria* (Cambridge, 1987).

Dimitrov, V., 'Bulgarian Neutrality: Domestic and International Perspectives', in Wylie, N. (ed.), *European Neutrals and Non-belligerents during the Second World War* (Cambridge, 2002).

Förster, J., 'Germany's Acquisition of Allies in South East Europe', in Militärgeschichtliches Forschungsamt (ed.), *Germany and the Second World War,* Vol. 4, *ed. H. Boog et al. (Oxford, 1998).*

Frank, T. (ed.), *Dreaming Peace, Making War: The Budapest Conversations of John F. Montgomery, 1935–1941* (New Haven, CT, 1999).

—— 'Treaty Revision and Doublespeak: Hungarian Neutrality, 1939–1941', in Wylie, N. (ed.), *European Neutrals and Non-belligerents during the Second World War* (Cambridge, 2002).

Haynes, R., *Romanian Policy towards Germany, 1936–1940* (Basingstoke, 2000).

Hoppe, H.-J., 'Deutschland und Bulgarien, 1918–1945', in Funke, M. (ed.), *Hitler, Deutschland und die Mächte: Materialien zur Aussenpolitik des Dritten Reiches* (Düsseldorf, 1976).

Hoptner, J. B., *Yugoslavia in Crisis, 1934–1941* (New York, 1962).

Juhász, G., *Hungarian Foreign Policy, 1919–1945* (Budapest, 1979).

Lampe, J. R., *Yugoslavia as History: Twice There Was a Country* (New York and Cambridge, 1996).

Leitz, C., 'Arms as Levers: Materiel and Raw Materials in Germany's Trade with Romania in the 1930s', *International History Review,* 19: 2 (1997).

Lungu, D. B., *Romania and the Great Powers, 1933–1940* (Durham, 1989).

Macartney, C. A., *October Fifteenth: A History of Modern Hungary, 1929–1945,* 2nd edn. (Edinburgh, 1961).

Nikolic, I. A., 'Anglo-Yugoslav Relations: 1938–1941', Ph.D. thesis, University of Cambridge, 2001.

Pavlowitch, S. K., *Yugoslavia* (London, 1971).

—— *A History of the Balkans, 1804–1945* (New York, 1999).

Pearton, M., *Oil and the Romanian State* (Oxford, 1971).

—— 'Romanian Neutrality, 1939–1940', in Wylie, N. (ed.), *European Neutrals and Non-belligerents during the Second World War* (Cambridge, 2002).

Schreiber, G., 'Germany, Italy and South East Europe: From Political and Economic Hegemony to Military Aggression', in Militärgeschichtliches Forschungsamt (ed.), *Germany and the Second World War,* Vol. 3, *ed. Schreiber, G. et al. (Oxford, 1995).*

Schröder, H.-J., 'Der Aufbau der deutschen Hegemonialstellung in Südosteuropa 1933–1936', in Funke, M. (ed.), *Hitler, Deutschland und die Mächte: Materialien zur Aussenpolitik des Dritten Reiches* (Düsseldorf, 1976).

Stefanidis, X., 'Greece, Bulgaria and the Approaching Tragedy, 1938–1941', *Balkan Studies*, 2 (1991).

Tilkovsky, L., 'The Late Inter-War Years and World War II', in Sugar, P. F. (ed.), *A History of Hungary* (London, 1990).

Zivojinovic, D. R., 'Yugoslavia', in Wylie, N. (ed.), *European Neutrals and Non-belligerents during the Second World War* (Cambridge, 2002).

Spain and Portugal

Clarence-Smith, G., *The Third Portuguese Empire, 1825–1975* (Manchester, 1985).

Hernández-Sandoica, E. and Moradiellos, E., 'Spain and the Second World War, 1939–1945', in Wylie, N. (ed.), *European Neutrals and Non-belligerents during the Second World War* (Cambridge, 2002).

Leitz, C., 'Nazi Germany's Struggle for Spanish Wolfram during the Second World War', *European History Quarterly*, 25 (1985).

—— *Economic Relations between Nazi Germany and Franco's Spain, 1936–1945* (Oxford, 1996).

Nogueira, F., 'Portugal: The Ministry for Foreign Affairs', in Steiner, Z. (ed.), *The Times Survey of Foreign Ministries of the World* (London, 1982).

Pike, D. W., *Franco and the Axis Stigma* (London, 2008).

Preston, P., *Franco: A Biography* (London, 1993).

Resa, F., 'Portuguese Neutrality in the Second World War', in Wylie, N. (ed.), *European Neutrals and Non-belligerents during the Second World War* (Cambridge, 2002).

Smyth, D., *Diplomacy and the Struggle for Survival: British Policy and Franco's Spain* (Cambridge, 1986).

Stone, G., *The Oldest Ally: Britain and the Portuguese Connection, 1936–1941* (London, 1994).

—— *Spain, Portugal and the Great Powers, 1931–1941* (Basingstoke, 2005).

—— 'The Official British Attitude to the Anglo-Portuguese Alliance, 1910–1945', *Journal of Contemporary History*, 10 (1975).

Tusell, J., *Franco, España y la Segunda Guerra Mundial: Entre el Eje y la Neutralidad* (Madrid, 1995).

Switzerland

Bourgeois, D., *Le Troisième Reich et la Suisse* (Neuchâtel, 1974).

Kreis, G., *Auf den Spuren von 'La Charité': die schweizerische Armeeführung im Spannungsfeld des deutsch–französischen Gegensatzes* (Basel, 1977).

Urner, K., *Let's Swallow Switzerland: Hitler's Plans against the Swiss Confederation* (Langham, IL, 2002).

Wylie, N., *Britain, Switzerland and the Second World War* (Oxford, 2003).

Wylie, N., 'Switzerland: A Neutral of Distinction?', in Wylie, N. (ed.), *European Neutrals and Non–belligerents during the Second World War* (Cambridge, 2002)

Zimmermann, H., 'Die "Nebenfrage Schweiz" in der Außenpolitik des Dritten Reiches', in Funke, M. (ed.), *Hitler, Deutschland und die Mächte: Materialien zur Aussenpolitik des Dritten Reiches* (Düsseldorf, 1976).

Turkey

Ackermann, J., 'Der begehrte Mann am Bosporus: Europäische Interessenkollisionen in der Türkei (1938–1941)', in Funke, M. (ed.), *Hitler, Deutschland und die Mächte: Materialien zur Aussenpolitik des Dritten Reiches* (Düsseldorf, 1976).

Curtwright, L. H., 'Great Britain, the Balkans and Turkey in the Autumn of 1939', *International History Review*, 10: 3 (1988).

Marzari, F., 'Western–Soviet Rivalry in Turkey, 1939', *Middle Eastern Studies*, 7 (1971).

Millman, B., *The Ill-Made Alliance: Anglo-Turkish Relations, 1934–1940* (Montreal and London, 1998).

—— 'Turkish Foreign and Strategic Policy, 1934–1942', *Middle Eastern Studies*, 31: 3 (1995).

Schönherr, K., 'Neutrality, Non-belligerence or War: Turkey and the European Powers' Conflict of Interests, 1939–1941', in Wegner, B. (ed.), *From Peace to War* (Oxford, 1997).

Seydi, S. and Morewood, S., 'Turkey's Application of the Montreux Convention in the Second World War', *Middle Eastern Studies*, 41: 1 (2005).

Soysal, I., 'The 1936 Montreux Convention 60 Years Later', in Turkish Straits Voluntary Watch Group (ed.), *Turkish Straits: New Problems, New Solutions* (Istanbul, 1995).

Weisband, E., *Turkish Foreign Policy 1943–1945: Small State Diplomacy and Great Power Politics* (Princeton, NJ, 1973).

The Persecution of the Jews

In a chilling sentence, Albert Speer wrote in his post-war autobiography that hatred of the Jews 'seemed so self-evident that it did not make an impression on me'.[36] What was happening in Germany to the Jews was well-known outside of the country. As early as 21 March 1933, the British ambassador in Berlin had told the foreign secretary that the Jews were being singled out for ill treatment and abuse. His many and full reports on the behaviour of the Reich government for which he held Hitler responsible left the Foreign Office in no doubt as to what was happening in Germany. Similar accounts were sent by

[36] Albert Speer, *Erinnerungen* (Frankfurt, 1969), 126.

diplomats to their home capitals in Rome, Paris, and Washington, DC. The treatment, and forced expropriation and expulsion of Austria's 180,000 Jews was widely reported. *Kristallnacht* stirred the world's conscience; the reaction was strongest in the United States and Britain but there were loud voices of protest elsewhere. After that terrible night, the process of isolating and excluding Jews, as defined by the Nuremberg Laws, from the 'national community' proceeded at an ever faster rate. Deprivations and humiliations followed each other in almost dizzying succession. The dehumanization process was well-advanced before the outbreak of war and Jews taken to Buchenwald concentration camp often did not reappear. One sign of Hitler's more sinister intentions was his warning during the course of his 30 January 1939 speech that if war came, the result would be 'the annihilation of the Jewish race in Europe'. Rhetoric or reality? Other parts of the speech drew more attention.

The Jews began to leave Germany after the Nazi seizure of power. In 1933, some 37,000 Germans of Jewish faith left the country, some for political rather than explicitly racial reasons.[37] Like the Armenian and White Russian émigrés in the 1920s, they had no national homeland to receive them and the economic depression made emigration more difficult as governments feared the new arrivals would swell the unemployment rolls and their already over-burdened welfare systems. During the early years, most of those who left were educated, able-bodied, and affluent, though the Reich made it impossible for them to take more than a small proportion of their personal funds and imposed a heavy 'flight tax' on those leaving. While anxious to be rid of their 'parasites', the Nazis did not want to release the foreign exchange needed to fulfil foreign visa requirements. After the first flight in 1933, only 23,000 Jews left in 1934, 21,000 in 1935, 25,000 in 1936, and 23,000 in 1937, hardly figures that satisfied the more radical Nazi party members or sufficient to make Germany *judenfrei* in the foreseeable future. Neither the enactment of the Nuremberg Laws in 1935, forbidding marriage or sexual relations outside of marriage between Aryans and Jews, nor the new Reich Citizenship Law, passed at the same time, depriving Jews of German citizenship, led to massive

[37] According to the German official statistics, there were 439,683 'Volljuden' of 'Mosaic faith', 0.77% of the total German population. The most commonly used figure is 525,000, of whom 99,000 were of foreign birth. There are endless difficulties with the statistics as the definition of a Jew varied considerably and even the designation of one grandparent of Jewish blood was much disputed. As assimilation in Germany was common practice, inter-marriage and conversion had led many Jews to forget or deny their Jewish roots. In May 1939, the German census recorded that the number of 'race Jews' and *Mischlinge* (Jews of mixed parentage) was 233,000. The drop in numbers was not only due to emigration but also to the consistent excess of deaths over births.

Table 17.1 Main Countries of Jewish Immigration in 1937

Country of Immigration	Meldestelle	Estimate—Number	Estimate—Percentage
Europe (excl. Repatriates)	4653	5000	21
Europe (Repatriates)	653	1000	4
Europe Total	5306	6000	25
Palestine	2950	3680	15
USA	6665	8800	38
Argentina	1357	1640	7
Brazil	745	850	4
Other South American countries	1247	1600	7
South America Total	3349	4090	18
South Africa	447	500	2.2
Australia	252	300	1.3
British Empire Total	699	800	3.5
Other countries overseas	115	130	0.5
Total	19084	23500	100

Source: Werner Rosenstock, 'Exodus 1933–1939: A Survey of Jewish Emigration from Germany', *Leo Baeck Institute Yearbook*, 1 (1956), 382.

increases in emigration. On the contrary, many Jews, like some Germans, hoped that the new laws, by defining more clearly the lines between Aryans and Jews, would halt the frequent acts of violence and, while isolating and degrading Jews, would leave them undisturbed within the bounds set by thc Reich. Some who left Germany decided to return, believing that the worst was over. Among those who fled in 1933, most stayed in Europe, many in France, still hoping that conditions in Germany would improve and that they could go back. In the next years, an increasing number went to countries overseas, some to Palestine, but in 1936 and 1937, in greater numbers to the United States, Argentina, Columbia, and other Latin American states. By mid-1938, about 150,000 Jews had left.[38]

There was only one early initiative launched in Germany to exchange Jews for foreign currency, the Haavara transfer of 1933. This was an agreement between the Reich authorities and a group of Zionist businessmen living on an orange plantation just outside Tel Aviv, that allowed German Jews to make payments into a fund in Berlin in return for certificates providing them with sufficient Palestinian pounds to secure visas for emigration to the mandate.[39] The funds deposited in

[38] All figures are from David Vital, *'A People Apart': A Political History of the Jews in Europe, 1789–1939* (Oxford, 1999), 828.

[39] The British mandate restricted immigration for those without financial means: those with 1,000 Palestinian pounds (£1,000) were granted free entry until the adoption of the White Paper in May 1939 restricting the Jewish emigration into Palestine.

Table 17.2 Main Countries of Jewish Immigration, January–June 1938

Country of Immigration	Jan.–Jun. 1938: Number	Jan.–Jun. 1938: Percentage
Europe (excl. Repatriates)	2359	21.2
Europe (Repatriates)	673	6
Europe Total	3032	27.2
Palestine	1201	10.8
USA	4348	39.1
Argentina	983	8.8
Brazil	56	0.5
Columbia	630	5.7
Uruguay	240	2.2
Other South American countries	238	2.1
South America Total	2147	19.3
South Africa	130	1.2
Australia/ New Zealand	203	1.8
British Empire Total	333	3
Other countries	69	0.6
Total	11130	100

Source: Werner Rosenstock, 'Exodus 1933–1939: A Survey of Jewish Emigration from Germany', *Leo Baeck Institute Yearbook*, 1 (1956), 385.

Berlin were used to buy German goods for export to Palestine and the Jews were reimbursed with Palestinian pounds when the goods were sold. Every Reichsmark exported by a German–Jewish emigrant was matched by a compensating export order. In total, some 60,000 Jews were able to use this scheme to settle in the mandate between 1933 and 1939. Payments to the Reich under the Transfer Agreement totaled £8 million or approximately $40 million. There were doubts about the scheme, both in Germany and in Palestine. A group of radical young officers, including Adolph Eichmann, in charge of the newly formed (1935) Jewish Affairs Division of the SS, feared that encouraging German Jews to go to Palestine would accelerate the formation of a Jewish state with dangerous consequences for Germany. For some Jews, the Transfer Agreement was an unacceptable surrender to expediency and compromised the Jewish boycott of German goods instituted in 1933 in response to the Reich's anti-Jewish legislation. Though the value of the boycott is still debated, the Germans took it seriously enough for supporters to press forward. Towards the end of 1938, the agreement, by common consent, was allowed to peter out. The moral issues raised by the agreement, passionately debated at the annual Zionist Congresses, lost all relevance as the realities of the German situation crowded in.[40]

[40] See the discussion in Vital, *A People Apart*, 879–881.

Table 17.3 Distribution of Jewish Emigrants in 1938

Palestine		44000
USA		27000
South America		26150
Argentina	13000	
Brazil	7500	
Uruguay	1500	
Columbia	1400	
Peru	250	
Chile	1000	
Other countries	1500	
British Empire		9400
South Africa	7600	
Australia	1000	
Other Commonwealth countries	800	
Other countries overseas		800
Total		107350

Source: Werner Rosenstock, 'Exodus 1933–1939: A Survey of Jewish Emigration from Germany', *Leo Baeck Institute Yearbook*, 1 (1956), 387.

What was seen as a period of 'relative quiet', though punctuated by intensified propaganda campaigns and increased ghettoization, came to an end with Hitler's speech at the Party Rally on 13 September 1937, the greater part of which was devoted to attacking the Jews. A new series of laws and decrees followed, aimed at the total separation of the Jews from the rest of German society. It was, however, *Anschluss* and the outrages against the Jews in Vienna on 11–12 March 1938, and the subsequent actions of the occupiers, abetted by many Austrians, which sounded loud alarm bells among German Jews and caught international attention. The official foreign response was hardly encouraging for those forced to flee. Austria's two neighbours, Yugoslavia and Hungary, closed their doors completely. France, Switzerland, the Netherlands, and Belgium tightened their immigration restrictions. In Britain, the government introduced visa qualifications for Austrian refugees. Somewhat unexpectedly, though there had been continuous pressure from Jewish organizations, President Roosevelt, a 'chameleon' with regard to Jews and Jewish refugees, seized the initiative, combined the German and Austrian quotas to let in more refugees, and invited 32 governments and 39 private charitable organizations to attend a nine day conference at Evian-les-Bains (6–14 July) to discuss the problem of German and Austrian 'political refuges'. Faced with strong Congressional and public pressure against any relaxation of the American immigration laws, he declared that 'no country would be expected or asked to receive a greater number of emigrants than

Table 17.4 German Jewish Immigrants into Palestine, 1933–1939

Year	Total	German	Percentage
1933	27289	6803	25
1934	36619	8479	23
1935	55407	7447	13
1936	26976	7896	29
1937	9441	3280	35
1938	11222	6138	55
1939		10200	

Note: From 1938 includes Austrian and in 1939 Czech Jews.

Source: John Hope Simpson, *Refugees:A Review of the Situation since September 1938* (London, 1939).

is permitted by existing legislation'.[41] Even within these limits, it became clear that no country was prepared to take positive action. The delegates agreed that the victims would not be referred to as 'Jews' but as 'political refuges' though no one doubted that over 85% of the people concerned were Jews. The British refused to discuss Palestine, where the greatest number of German Jews had gone previously, and argued that with the possible exception of Kenya, its colonial empire had no space for refuges. Most Dominion representatives were hostile towards the admission of Jews; the prime minister of Canada, W. L. MacKenzie King, was convinced that the Jews would pollute Canada's 'bloodstream' and instructed his delegate not to promise anything. The Australian representative assured his listeners that Australia had no real racial problem and was not desirous of importing one by any scheme of large-scale foreign immigration. The head of the French delegation announced that France could no longer be a haven for the oppressed; it had already reached saturation point with over four million foreigners in its midst. He sharply criticized America's restrictive immigration policies that had left thousands of refugees stranded in France. Representatives from the Latin American nations, which had previously absorbed a number of refuges, expressed their sympathy but argued that they, too, could not absorb any more Jews. The conference was little more than an international façade which allowed delegates to disguise the unwillingness of their so-called civilized governments to act. Openly anti-semitic speeches provided the Nazi press with a field day. Many delegates claimed, however, that the real barrier to immigration was the Reich's unwillingness to allow the Jewish refugees to take their personal assets with them. As Secretary of State Hull admitted:

[41] Ouoted in Dalek, *Franklin Roosevelt and American Foreign Policy*, 167.

'The little that was achieved bore no relationship to the hopes that were aroused.'[42] In this sense, the meeting was almost a total failure. The one positive action by the conference was the creation of an inter-governmental committee on refugees (IGCR) of official and non-official representatives to coordinate matters of relief and resettlement The director, George Rublee, a Washington lawyer, was delegated to negotiate with Germany about the fate of those wanting to leave. Rublee quickly found that the British government was uninterested in his work and that the task of finding places of settlement for Jewish refugees proved as difficult as negotiating with the Germans. Only Generalissimo Rafael Trujillo of the Dominican Republic formally offered to take large numbers of settlers and actually supplied land. After denouncing the Evian conference and pointing out that no country anywhere was prepared to admit the German Jews, the Germans at first refused to discuss co-operation with the new committee. Yet, such was the need for foreign currency that, in the autumn of 1938, talks began between Rublee and the officials of the Third Reich. In November, Hermann Göring authorized Schacht and the Austrian economics minister to work out a scheme by which the wealth of Austrian and German Jewry, now under Reich control, could be used to raise a foreign currency loan of at least 1.5 billion Reichsmarks to be subscribed by 'international Jewry' and foreign governments. Schacht opened discussions with Rublee and with the British but nothing came of these efforts before his dismissal in early 1939. The talks continued: Helmuth Wohlthat, from the Economics Ministry took over the negotiations for Germany and an agreement was reached with Rublee that each side should act independently so that no contract had to be signed and the western nations were not implicated in the Nazi extortion. The Rublee–Wohlthat agreement never came to fruition. There was, contrary to Hitler's belief, no 'global network of Jewish high finance' and neither the Jewish communities abroad nor any foreign government was prepared to pay this form of financial blackmail. The IGCR tried to avoid the Germans securing major financial gains. Its members also wanted to prevent other nations, Poland with its 3.3 million Jews, Romania, and Italy from expelling their Jews on similar terms. No decisions were taken and further action was delayed. Under considerable pressure from President Roosevelt, warned by his embassy in Berlin that lives were actually in danger, the leading American Jewish organization agreed in May to establish a Co-ordination Foundation to

[42] Quoted in Richard Breitman and Alan M. Kraut, *American Refugee Policy and European Jewry, 1933–1945* (Bloomington, IN, 1987), 61.

raise private money to fund the departure and settlement of Jewish refugees, primarily to countries outside the United States. On the German side, after Schacht's resignation, the hardliners improved their position and demanded the removal of German Jewry almost immediately and not in three to five years. Reinhard Heydrich, the Gestapo chief, took over the new Reich Office for Jewish Emigration in February 1939 and instructed his officials to promote emigration by all possible means, regardless of the Rublee agreement. Poor Jews were to be given priority, presumably to stir up anti-Semitic reactions abroad. The Co-ordinating Foundation was only set up in July 1939. The ICGR was still without places for settlement. Success depended not only on German compliance, which seemed increasingly unlikely, but also on the co-operation of countries that had already served notice that they would not host any additional refugees. With the exception of the Dominican Republic, the IGCR was unable to find any place where the 'unwanted' could be sent. When governments reacted positively, they offered the colonial possessions of other countries, such as Portugal, for settlement rather than their own.

Kristallnacht turned what the international community had hoped would be a well-ordered exodus into an uncontrollable flood. *Kristallnacht* created world-wide indignation; the horror of these 'barbarities', Chamberlain's description, produced official and private expressions of disapproval. The British prime minister moved quickly, insisting that action be taken to bring in refugees on temporary visas. He wrote to his sister: 'I am horrified by the German behaviour to the Jews. There does seem to be some fatality about Anglo-German relations which invariably blocks every effort to improve them'.[43] Dirksen warned of the negative effects of *Kristallnacht* on British opinion but Ribbentrop, as well as Himmler and Heydrich, felt that there was no reason to worry about the foreign reaction to the treatment of the Jews. A Jewish-controlled press was blamed for the adverse comment. The question was a domestic one and no interference would be tolerated. The anticipated approaches from foreign governments for 'controlled emigration' never came.

Despite the expressions of sympathy for the German Jews, no concerted action followed the German pogrom. The League of Nations appeared impotent. Already in December 1935, in his letter of resignation, the high commissioner for refugees affairs, the American James G. MacDonald, urged the League to intervene directly on behalf of the Jews in Germany rather than concentrate its activities on dealing with

[43] Robert Self (ed.), *The Neville Chamberlain Diary Letters*, Vol. 4 (Aldershot, 2005), 363 (To Ida, 13 November 1938).

those expelled.[44] His advice fell on deaf ears; only his plea that his independent office be placed under the League's jurisdiction was followed. The next appointee, 'an elderly gentleman with a distinguished military career', Sir Neil Malcolm, now a League official, would have nothing to do with the domestic policies of Germany. The few initiatives he took were quickly checked by the secretary general of the League of Nations, Joseph Avenol, who took an exceedingly narrow view of what the League should attempt. The princely sum of £2,000 was given for Malcolm's operations and he was forbidden from soliciting outside funds. In late 1938, all the League offices dealing with refugees were brought together under the high commissioner for refugees. The last incumbent in the post, Sir Herbert Emerson, was an ailing, ex-India Civil Service official. Though more sympathetic than Malcolm, he was able to do little. The most qualified candidate for the post, Sir John Hope Simpson, had been deliberately passed over for fear of having a second MacDonald in place.[45] Emerson also became the director of the IGCR when George Rublee resigned after the Americans had approved his plan, a supposedly improved version of the original German proposal. Neither the high commissioner nor his office had the prestige or the backing needed to negotiate effectively with the Reich government. Nor was there any evidence that the Germans would have kept their part of Rublee–Wohlthat bargain whatever the financial incentives. The IGCR was quietly 'put to sleep' (President Roosevelt's phrase) when the war broke out.

The occupation of Czechoslovakia added thousands more to the list of fleeing refugees. The Nazi leadership responsible for the Jews began to use more draconian methods to get rid of their Jews. The Gestapo dumped groups of refugees over the borders into France and Switzerland where they were not wanted. Refugees were loaded onto ships that wandered from port to port to seek safety; only Shanghai took refugees without passports. It received some 10,000 refugees by May 1939. The story of the voyage of the *St. Louis* from Hamburg to Cuba was unique only in the amount of publicity it generated.[46] The Jews, denied entry to

[44] See pp. 677–80 on *Kristallnacht*, pp. 177–8 on League of Nations.

[45] Simpson's book, *Refugees: A Review of the Situation since September 1938* (London, 1939), provided one of the best statistical analyses of the Jewish refugee problem at the time and has been used in later accounts as well.

[46] The 935 passengers, mostly Jews, had applied for American visas. The Cuban government had already collected a considerable sum from its European 'tourists' who wanted to stay in Cuba while waiting for the American visas. New and harsher conditions were introduced and when the refugee ship docked, the authorities were ordered not to honour the 'tourist' letters or to allow the refugees to disembark. Attempts by the Joint Distribution Committee and subsequently a group of New York financiers to raise

Cuba and to the United States, their final destination, were finally rescued from a return to Germany through the efforts of the (Jewish American) Joint Distribution Committee which, offering very substantial financial guarantees, got the British, French, Dutch, and Belgian governments to accept the Jews. Corrupt German officials demanded money or goods in return for agreeing to apply the all-important rubber stamp needed for emigration papers. The Germans only continued to express an interest in the Rublee Plan in order to encourage the departure of the Reich Jews. With war approaching, there was mounting pressure to export the Jews by any means possible. The expulsion campaign was seen as essential not only for the protection of the Reich in wartime but as the necessary prerequisite for the German racial reordering of Europe that had always been at the heart of Hitler's ideological programme. The acceptance or appeal of this programme to the vast majority of Germans still raises difficult questions. Accounts are necessarily impressionistic. It appears that the individual response to the government's efforts varied considerably. There were party enthusiasts and avid anti-Semites ('An anti-Semite' 'is someone who hates Jews more than is necessary'—attribution contested) in all sections of the population who welcomed these moves against an old enemy. Others benefited from the exclusion of Jews and the discriminatory measures against them and closed their eyes to the human costs. There were also individual acts of humanity and small gestures of support. But whether because of traditional anti-Semitism, the fierce and constant daily indoctrination, ingrained habits of obedience, or fear, the majority of Germans on the eve of the war, appear to have been indifferent, if not assenting, or enthusiastic, about the Reich's treatment of the Jews. It may be that Hitler intended to use the remaining German Jews as hostages to extract as much money and foreign exchange from the international community as possible or, as suggested in his 30 January speech, that he hoped to use the captive Jews as a means of deterring the United States from entering the war. Other readings suggested more unthinkable possibilities. If only a minority of Germans grasped the full implications of Hitler's obsessive concern with the Jews, the vast majority appear to have accepted the Nazi racial programme without protest.

whatever sums of money the Cuban government required produced no agreement. The State Department refused to intervene; the American ambassador was not allowed to raise the question and President Roosevelt failed to respond to a telegram from the St. Louis passengers. The refugees were on their way back to Hamburg when the JDC successfully intervened.

National interests, political, economic, and strategic, often tinged with home-grown and widespread anti-Semitism, limited what was actually done elsewhere. The refugee problem was not restricted to the Reich; countries such as Poland, Romania, and Hungary, had implemented anti-Semitic laws that convinced some Jews to leave the countries of their birth. On the eve of the war, the Polish government was discussing with the French the possibility of using French Madagascar as a place to deport their unwanted Jewish minority. As in Germany, anti-Semitism in most Eastern European countries was linked to radical nationalism, and the Jews, even when acculturated, were seen as impediments to the realization of full nationhood. The immediate pressure, in the spring and summer of 1939 came, however, from the German and Austrian Jews for whom life had been made intentionally unendurable, as well as from those unfortunate refugees who had sought sanctuary in Czechoslovakia. Governments took alarm at what they saw as a flood of Jews trying to enter their countries. Some established escape routes were blocked off just when they were most desperately needed. The most notable volte-face took place in France, which in 1937 had the largest German refugee population in Europe. Daladier, whether anti-Semitic as some French writers claim or not, had long viewed the refugees as a security problem. Under his influence, a decree of May 1938 prohibited the expulsion of refugees already in France but increased the authority of border guards to refuse entry. In the spring of 1939, new decrees required refugees to perform military service or do forced labour. The border became effectively closed and legal immigration almost stopped completely. Other countries followed the French example. Belgium, the Netherlands, and Switzerland made entry more difficult and by mid-1939, a large number of Latin American countries were practically closed to new entrants.

Some liberalization took place on the eve of the war as individuals and private organizations redoubled their efforts to bring the refugees out of the Reich. Britain, Belgium, the Netherlands, and above all, the United States, found ways to increase their intake. Under American pressure, Argentina and Brazil temporarily reopened their doors. Chile took in almost 15,000 immigrants from Germany and Austria, ninety percent of whom arrived between May and August 1939. Australia, which prior to the annexation of Austria had taken very few Jewish refugees, by September 1939 had admitted well over 7,000 Jews.[47] The most marked change took place in Britain, whose pre-1937 record was poor (5,000 refugees hosted by 1937), given that the Anglo-Jewish

[47] Figures from Werner Rosenstock, 'Exodus 1933–1939: A Survey of Jewish Emigration from Germany', *Leo Baeck Institute Yearbook*, 1 (1956), 389–390.

community faithfully honoured its 1933 commitment to cover all the charges for the accommodation and maintenance of refugees in Britain. Not only did the London government feel a special responsibility for the Czech refugees (political refugees were given priority; the Jewish refugees came at the end of the rescue queue), but the new policies in Palestine encouraged a more generous entry policy at home. The Home Office authorized the admission of thousands of refugees, especially children and domestic servants, the latter a wonderfully flexible category. More than 50% of the entry in 1938–1939 were women, a large number, regardless of their backgrounds, were assigned to British families as domestic servants. Some Jewish children scheduled to go to Palestine were allowed to enter Britain. A special programme under the direction of the Council for German Jewry, the Quakers, and other Christian groups, arranged for the entry to Britain of approximately 10,000 children under the age of 18. Private groups provided the funding and supervised their placement.[48] Encouraged by the British example, similar action was taken by the Netherlands (2,000 children), Belgium (800), and France (700). Whereas at the time of the Evian Conference Britain had received 8,000 refugees, by the outbreak of war there were some 40,000 Jewish immigrants from Germany and Austria in the country, as well as some 7,000 from Czechoslovakia. Many, indeed most, were expected to move on to the United States but the war intervened and the majority were given residence in the United Kingdom. The United States proved more hospitable; the period from March 1938 until September 1939 marked the most liberal phase of American immigration policy with about 20,000 Germans admitted monthly under the quota system. The overwhelming majority were Jews or refugees of Jewish descent.

The most tragic closure took place in Palestine. It was a critical blow not only to the German Jews but also to those of Poland, Romania, Greece, Latvia, and Lithuania where Zionist organizations were active. Jewish emigration had already exacerbated Arab–Jewish relations in the mandate and in 1936 a serious Arab revolt began which attracted wide support in the Middle East, particularly in Saudi Arabia and Iraq. From a tiny minority in the mandate, the Jews soon constituted some 25% of its total population and were viewed as a serious political and economic threat by the majority Arabs. The British-appointed Royal Commission (the Peel Commission) sent to investigate the Palestinian situation in 1936 published its report in July 1937, suggesting a partition of Palestine with a small Jewish state of some 2,000 square miles to be established alongside a larger Arab state. In the

[48] Ibid., 222–223.

interim, in order to relieve Arab fears, Jewish immigration was to be restricted to 12,000 entries a year for the next five years, a slashing cut to the average annual arrival of the previous years. The Zionists were divided in their response but proved willing to negotiate; the Arabs totally rejected the proposal. A pan-Arab Congress in Syria in May 1937 had already claimed Palestine as part of the Arab homeland and, in the autumn, after further serious disturbances in the mandate, the Grand Mufti, accepted by most Arabs as the leader of the Palestinian Arabs and known to be sympathetic to Germany, was exiled from Palestine to Lebanon. Frightened for their own position in Lebanon and Syria, where pro-Arab sentiments were strong, the French refused to expel him and did little to control the political agitation. The continuing rebellion and the adverse reaction of the Arab states led to second thoughts in London and a retreat from the idea of partition. After the Munich crisis, with Palestine in administrative chaos, the Foreign Office was adamant that it was essential for Britain to restore good relations with the Arabs, already being strongly courted by the Italians and Germans who were helping to fund the Arab agitation. A round table conference held in London achieved nothing beyond confirming Jewish fears that immigration would be severely cut and would eventually depend on Arab consent. Militant Jews resorted to terrorist tactics. A White Paper, published in London on 17 May 1939, which remained the formal basis of British policy throughout the war, promised that Palestine would become an independent country within ten years with Arabs and Jews sharing power. Jewish immigration was limited to no more than 10,000 immigrants annually for the next five years and after that, only with Arab consent. In some areas, transfers of Arab land would be prohibited and elsewhere, it would be restricted. Simultaneously, in order to appease American opinion, proposals were made to settle some Jews in British Guiana. The secretary of state for India warned that Muslim opinion in India had taken up the Arab cause providing further reasons for restricting Jewish emigration. These restrictions came at a time when the European Jews had become desperate to leave and when few alternative places of settlement were available.

The expanded entry of Jews into the United States and Britain during the spring and summer of 1939 created its own problems. An April 1939 *Fortune* magazine poll claimed 83% of all Americans opposed an increase in the quotas. A bill introduced in February 1939 (Wagner–Rogers Bill) to bring into the United States 20,000 German refugee children failed to secure the necessary support in the Senate and the House Immigration Committee never reported the bill out. The rush to adjourn for the summer ended any chance of passage. In London, the Home Office was particularly worried by the build-up of Jews waiting to go to the United States. In July the British government proposed to speed up the flow of German refugees from countries outside Germany by adding government money to private funds but other governments had to participate as well. The British offer, as well as the prospect of settlement in British Guiana, opened up a new possibility. Washington was not interested; any discussion of the refugee problem would only complicate the task of revising the neutrality legislation. The British dropped the project when war broke out. In both countries, opinion polls recorded a rise in anti-refugee and anti-Jewish feeling. In Britain, fears were expressed that the refugees might include Nazi spies, an idea that would affect government attitudes and policies after war broke out.

Why were so many countries hostile to admitting refugees? Why should the humanitarian impulse which had been so strong in the 1920s, leading to the settlement of millions of refugees, including over one million Russians, have been so diminished when it came to the fleeing Jews? Why should the League of Nations have practically abdicated its earlier role in rescuing the 'unwanted'? To be sure, there was the question of numbers and the knowledge that there could be no return. Between June 1938 and June 1939, 120,000 people left Germany, a number approximately equal to that of the previous five years.[49] And yet, when compared to present-day figures of refugee flight, the number seems absurdly small. At the time, private organizations were overwhelmed and governments took fright. Apart from the Society of Friends (Quakers), though some Catholic and Protestant voluntary groups tried to raise funds, most of these organizations were Jewish. The papacy had not responded to *Kristallnacht* and was silent in the months that followed. In what would become a major leitmotiv in future papal policy, its main concern was with those Jews who had been baptized and were, in terms of Catholic doctrine, indistinguishable from other Catholics. While Catholic theologians might distinguish between the traditional and doctrinal religious hostility towards the Jews who would not acknowledge the coming of Christ and the racial anti-Semitism of the Nazi regime, such distinctions were ignored by the majority of Catholics.

Ever since the Concordat was concluded between the papacy and the Nazi regime in July 1933, there had been a stream of complaints from Cardinal Pacelli, the former papal nuncio to Germany and subsequently

[49] For figures see Claudena M. Skran, *Refugees in Inter-war Europe: The Emergence of a Regime* (Oxford, 1995), 245–255. The figure does not include Jewish refugees from Czechoslovakia. It has been estimated that 20,000 Jewish people flooded out of Germany and Austria between March 1938 and September 1939. Adam Tooze, *The Wages of Destruction*, 281.

the Vatican secretary of state in Rome, about Nazi violations of the agreement. A new level of intimidation against the Catholic Church began at the end of 1935 when Goebbels and the Propaganda Ministry accused Catholic organizations of corruption. The campaign created further demonstrations of Catholic hostility towards the Nazis and even open protests in the strongly Catholic rural area of southern Oldenburg. In January 1937, a delegation of senior German bishops and cardinals, including the leading critics of Nazi policy towards Catholics, Cardinals, Bertram, Faulhaber, and Bishop Galen of Münster, went to Rome to denounce the Nazis for their violations of the Concordat. Encouraged by the pope, Cardinal Faulhaber drafted a new papal encyclical, '*Mit brennender Sorge*' edited and extended by Pacelli, summing up the long list of Vatican complaints about Nazi violations of the Concordat. It included an indirect condemnation of the Nazis' racial policies.[50] Most unusually, the encyclical was in German and not in Latin. It was smuggled into Germany where it was reprinted and distributed, taking even the Gestapo by surprise. The encyclical was read out on 21 March 1937 in almost every Catholic pulpit in Germany and caused an uproar in official circles. As a consequence, the Nazi campaign against the Catholic Church and its organizations was intensified and ultimately succeeded in driving the Church out of public life and severely reducing its influence and activity. The Catholic community remained loyal subjects of the Reich and, though individuals might protest against the party's anti-Christian actions, Hitler, himself, was never blamed.[51]

'*Mit brennender Sorge*' was cautiously worded so as not to condemn the regime. National Socialism was nowhere named nor was there any mention of the Jews. The Vatican did not want to provoke a Nazi repudiation of the Concordat. There was still the slim hope that the existing situation for the Catholic Church might improve. Pacelli was a *Realpolitiker* who feared the consequences of any open conflict with the Nazi authorities. No such considerations and qualifications applied to Pius XI's condemnation of Communism, '*Divini redemptoris*', issued on 19 March 1937, which was sharply critical of 'atheistic Soviet Communism' and referred specifically to the persecutions in Russia, Mexico, and Spain. In June 1938, Pius XI asked the Jesuits to compose an encyclical on the questions of nationalism and racism. Two members of the order prepared drafts, which were given to the Jesuit General at the end of September 1938. One of the drafts was far more outspoken than any utterance of the papacy.

[50] The wording of the relevant section is found in Richard J. Evans, *The Third Reich in Power*, 243.

[51] Ibid., 248.

[T]he so-called Jewish question is in its essence a question neither of race, nor nation, nor affiliation to the state, but it is a question of religion, and since Christ, a question of Christianity... Today the Church sees only with indignation and pain how the Jews are treated on the basis of legislation which is contrary to the law of nature and does not deserve the honourable name of law.[52]

'*Societatis unio*' was buried by the new pope and never saw the light of day. No other encyclical even indirectly referring to the Jews was issued. In January 1939, Cardinal Pacelli requested local bishops to set up committees to help some Catholic Jews emigrate from areas where they were being oppressed.[53]

On 10 February, after a long illness, Pius XI died. Unusually, in a conclave of only a single day, Pacelli was declared pope on 2 March 1939. The new head of the Church made it clear from the start that he alone would handle the German question. Subsequent to his elevation, a new period of détente began in Nazi–Catholic Church relations. However ascetic Pius XII may have been in matters spiritual, in temporal matters, as was clear during his time as papal legate in Germany, he was a diplomat of the old school. Like Pius XI, he was more concerned with the threat of Bolshevism than that of Nazism. The Concordats with Mussolini and Hitler remained the only guarantee of the semi-independence of the Catholic Church. Sitting in Rome created an uneasy atmosphere for those most concerned with the continued exercise of papal power. The new pope began his pontificate as he had begun his Munich nunciature, with a peace initiative, proposing in April 1939 that the governments of France, Germany, Great Britain, Italy, and Poland attend a five-power conference to settle European tensions. About the Jews, he said and did nothing.[54]

There is little question that the fact that these refugees were Jews made rescue and settlement more difficult. There were few countries where there was not public manifestations of the dislike and fear of the Jews. The roots of anti-Semitism were deep and well-watered long before Hitler came to power. Given the tense state of relations between

[52] Text in Gerhard Besier, *The Holy See and Hitler's Germany*, trans. W. R. Ward (Basingstoke, 2007), 179–180.

[53] John S. Conway, 'The Vatican, Germany and the Holocaust', in Peter C. Kent and John F. Pollard (eds.), *Papal Diplomacy in the Modern Age* (London, 1994), 110–112. S. J. P. Blet, *Pius XII and the Second World War* (New York, 1997), 10–13. See Hubert Wolf, *Pope and Devil: The Vatican's Archives and the Third Reich*, (Cambridge, MA, and London, 2008), 270, for evidence that Mussolini urged Pius XI to take 'effective measures' including excommunication, against Hitler on 10 April 1938. I am indebted to Prof. Stewart A. Stehlin for assistance with regard to the papal position.

[54] The Vatican has announced that it will open its papers on the Holocaust to scholars, which will certainly lead to further discussions of Pius XII.

the western powers and the Nazi government, the Jewish problem was viewed as only one more source of difficulty and far from the most pressing. Official expressions of disapproval, as after *Kristallnacht*, were rare and condemned by many as damaging to relations with Germany or even counter-productive for the Reich Jews. No figure like Fridtjof Nansen, the instigator of so many refugee rescue schemes in the 1920s, appeared on the international stage to provide the moral leadership so visibly missing in Geneva. Well-known humanitarians, expected to take the lead in countering public hostility to the entrance of Jewish refugees, were either silent or, in some cases, opposed to the lifting of restrictive quotas. Bureaucratic indifference or domestic rivalries further complicated the efforts of the mainly Jewish organizations trying to bring out the refugees. Some consular officials proved exceptional in their efforts to facilitate emigration; Henry Foley, the British passport control officer in Berlin was an outstanding example. Most officials carried out their instructions in the face of lengthening queues of supplicants. In such an atmosphere, it proved impossible to arrange a co-ordinated response to the rising tempo of German efforts to expel its Jews. It was, of course, easier for individuals and organizations to rescue 'distinguished Jews' than the thousands who might compete for jobs or who could become charges on the state. The Jewish organizations were themselves divided on what could or should be done and were acutely aware that overstepping the bounds of the possible might set off hostile official and public reactions that would only restrict their efforts.

By the start of the war, the 1933 German Jewish population of approximately 525,000 had dropped to well under half. In 1938, 180,000 Jews lived in Austria; by July 1939, 97,000 had fled. Those who remained were too old, too poor, or unable to obtain exit visas or find sponsors. Some lacked the courage or the energy to begin a new life in an unknown country, or were simply unable to believe that their country was no longer their homeland. 'Terrible that it's war again', the dismissed professor of Romance languages, Victor Klemperer, who expected to be shot or put in a concentration camp, wrote in his diary on 3 September, 'but yet one is so patriotic, when I saw a battery leaving yesterday, I wanted more than anything to go with them'.[55] The German Jews were the most assimilated in Europe; many thought of themselves as Germans rather than as Jews. Orthodox Jews and Zionists had more opportunities to leave than those who became Jews through official designation. Only the terror of what could happen convinced parents to send their children out of the Reich while they stayed behind.

[55] Victor Klemperer, *I Shall Bear Witness: The Diaries of Victor Klemperer 1933–1941* (London, 1998), 295.

The outbreak of war found some still agonizing over what to do but others waiting for the stamp that would allow them to leave, or the visa or letter of sponsorship that was the only passport to escape.

The western powers did not confront Hitler because of the Jews. The refugee problem was never given a high priority in the capitals of the West. Few statesmen believed that the abuse of human rights was the concern of the international community. Hitler had turned back the international clock; the League's refugee regime could not respond to his challenge. The fact that the abuser was one of the most powerful nations in Europe and that its victims were Jews helped to seal the latter's fate. Admittedly, though neither Roosevelt nor Chamberlain had any personal liking for Jews, both were appalled by the Nazi treatment of the Jewish minority.[56] Yet each had more pressing problems on his mind than the fate of the Jews. Neither was going to add to the difficulties of preserving the peace by taking up the problem of the Jews. President Roosevelt's failure to follow up Evian with a call for a more liberal immigration policy at home suggests that the 'Jewish dilemma did not command a very high priority in his mind'.[57] Chamberlain, in the midst of a political and diplomatic battle to make deterrence work, hardly referred to the Jews in his summer letters to his sisters. If the Jews were not a major issue for Roosevelt or Chamberlain, and of no interest to the unsympathetic Daladier or Beck or the even more deeply anti-Semitic Stalin, this was not true of Hitler. He had convinced himself that Roosevelt was the 'fulcrum of a world Jewish conspiracy for the ruination of Germany and the rest of Europe'.[58] He and other leading Nazis believed that the Jews in London and Paris were establishing their ascendancy over their respective governments and creating the war psychosis in each capital. They assumed that there was a political actor, called Jewry or international Jewry, determined to launch a war to establish their world power. Hitler had spoken of the Jews as the 'world enemy' determined to destroy the Aryan states at the Nuremberg Party rallies of September 1937 and 1938. After January 1939, German propaganda became more apocalyptic with the United States and President Roosevelt as one of the main targets. The government-controlled *Völkischer Beobachter* ran stories headlined, 'The Hebrew Posters for F. D. Roosevelt' and 'USA under Jewish Dictatorship'.[59] The 'Word of

[56] Louise London, *Whitehall and the Jews, 1933–1948: British Immigration Policy, Jewish Refugees, and the Holocaust* (Cambridge, 2000), 106.

[57] Robert Dallek, *Franklin D. Roosevelt and American Foreign Policy, 1932–1945*, 168.

[58] Tooze, *The Wages of Destruction*, 284.

[59] Jeffrey Herf, *The Jewish Enemy: Nazi Propaganda During World War II and the Holocaust* (Cambridge, MA, 2006), 105–107, 281–283.

the Week' wall posters which appeared everywhere in Germany and were changed weekly repeated the same theme. The lead article in *Die Judenfrage* of 18 September 1939, written in response to Chaim Weizmann's assertion that Jews stood on the side of Britain and of democracy against Nazi Germany, concluded: 'The Führer's clear assertion that international and plutocratic Jewry is guilty for the outbreak of the war had been confirmed very quickly. Immediately after England's entry into the war, the Jewish world organizations have placed themselves at its disposal . . . Today we know whom we are facing in England, the world enemy number 1; international Jews and the power-hungry hate-filled world Jewry.'[60] Hitler was not immune to his own propaganda. Obsessed with the international Jewish conspiracy that was closing around the Reich, he felt he had to launch his war before it was too late.[61] While Britain and France struggled to preserve the peace, Hitler set his sights on what began and remained a racially motivated war.

Books

(This bibliography is obviously highly selective.)

Abella, I. M., and Troper, H., *None is Too Many: Canada and the Jews of Europe, 1933–1948* (New York, 1983).

Adam, U. D., *Judenpolitik im Dritten Reich* (Düsseldorf, 1972).

Anderl, G. and Rupnow, D., *Die Zentralstelle für jüdische Auswanderung als Beraubungsinstitution* (Vienna, 2004).

Bajohr, F., *'Aryanisation' in Hamburg: The Economic Exclusion of Jews and the Confiscation of their Property in Nazi Germany* (Oxford, 2002).

Bankier, D. (ed.) *Probing the Depths of German Anti-Semitism: German Society and the Persecution of the Jews, 1933–1941* (Jerusalem, 2000). See W. Z. Bacharach, F. Bajohr, U. Büttner, A. Fischer, W. Gruner, and M. Wildt.

Bauer, Y., *My Brother's Keeper: A History of the American Jewish Joint Distribution Committee, 1929–1939* (Philadelphia, PA, 1974).

Baumann, A. and Heusler, A. (eds.), *München 'arisiert': Entrechtung und Enteignung der Juden in der NS-Zeit* (Munich, 2004).

Besier, G., *The Holy See and Hitler's Germany*, trans. W. R. Ward (Basingstoke, 2007).

Blet, S. J. P., *Pius XII and the Second World War* (New York, 1997).

Bolchover, R., *British Jewry and the Holocaust* (Cambridge, 1993).

Botz, G., *Wohnungspolitik und Judendeportation in Wien 1938 bis 1945: zur Funktion des Antisemitismus als Ersatz nationalsozialistischer Sozialpolitik* (Vienna, 1975).

[60] Herf, *The Jewish Enemy*, 61–2. Weizmann was a British Jew who was head of the World Zionist Organization and could speak only in this context.

[61] Tooze, *The Wages of Destruction*, 663–664, where this argument is developed.

Braham, R. (ed.), *Jewish Leadership during the Nazi Era: Patterns of Behavior in the Free World* (New York, 1985).

Brechtken, M., *'Madagaskar für die Juden': Antisemitische Idee und politische Praxis 1885–1945* (Munich, 1997).

Browning, C. R., *The Path to Genocide: Essays on the Launching of the Final Solution* (Cambridge, 1992).

—— *The Origins of the Final Solution: The Evolution of Nazi Jewish Policy, September 1939–March 1942* (Lincoln, NE, 2004).

Bruns-Wüstefeld, A., *Lohnende Geschäfte: Die 'Entjudung' der Wirtschaft am Beispiel Göttingens* (Hannover, 1997).

Burrin, P., *Hitler and the Jews: The Genesis of the Holocaust* (London, 1989, 1994).

Bottum, J. and Dalin, D. (eds.), *The Pious War* (New York, 2004).

Caron, V., *Uneasy Asylum: France and the Jewish Refugee Crisis, 1933–1942* (Stanford, CA, 1999).

Chadwick, O., *Berlin and the Vatican during the Second World War* (Cambridge, 1986).

Conway, J., *The Nazi Persecution of the Churches, 1933–1945* (London, 1968).

Cornwell, J., *Hitler's Pope: The Secret History of Pius XII* (New York, 1999).

*Dean, M., *Robbing the Jews: The Confiscation of Jewish Property in the Holocaust, 1933–1945* (Cambridge, 2008).

Feilchenfeld, W. et al. (eds.), *Haavara-Transfer nach Palästina und Einwanderung deutscher Juden 1933–1939* (Tübingen, 1972).

Fichtl, F. et al., *'Bambergs Wirtschaft Judenfrei': Die Verdrängung der jüdischen Geschäftsleute in den Jahren 1933 bis 1939* (Bamberg, 1998).

Fischer, A., *Hjalmar Schacht und Deutschlands 'Judenfrage': Der 'Wirtschaftsdiktator' und die Vertreibung der Juden aus der deutschen Wirtschaft* (Cologne, 1995).

Friedländer, S., *Nazi Germany and the Jews*, Vol. 1: *The Years of Persecution, 1933–1939* (New York, 1997).

Genschel, H., *Die Verdrängung der Juden aus der Wirtschaft im Dritten Reich* (Göttingen, 1966).

Graml, H., *Anti-Semitism in the Third Reich* (Cambridge, MA, 1992).

Herbst, L. and Weihe, T. (eds.), *Die Commerzbank und die Juden 1933–1945* (Munich, 2004).

Herf, J., *The Jewish Enemy: Nazi Propaganda During World War II and the Holocaust* (Cambridge, MA, 2006).

Herzig, A. and Lorenz, I. (eds.), *Verdrängung und Vernichtung der Juden unter dem Nationalsozialismus* (Hamburg, 1992). See especially G. Kratzsch.

Hildesheimer, E., *Jüdische Selbstverwaltung unter dem NS-Regime: Der Existenzkampf der Reichsvertretung und Reichsvereinigung der Juden in Deutschland* (Tübingen, 1994).

James, H., *The Deutsche Bank and the Nazi Economic War against the Jews* (Cambridge, 2001).

Kaplan, M. A., *Between Dignity and Despair: Jewish Life in Nazi Germany* (New York, 1998).

KIEFFER, F., *Judenverfolgung in Deutschland—eine innere Angelegenheit? Internationale Reaktionen auf die Flüchtlingsproblematik 1933–1939* (Stuttgart, 2002).

LONDON, L., *Whitehall and the Jews, 1933–1948: British Immigration Policy, Jewish Refugees, and the Holocaust* (New York, 2000).

LUDWIG, J., *Boykott—Enteignung—Mord: Die 'Entjudung' der deutschen Wirtschaft* (Hamburg, 1989).

MARRUS, M. R., *The Holocaust in History* (Hanover, NH, 1987).

MATARD-BONUCCI, M.-A., *L'Italie fasciste et la persécution des juifs* (Paris, 2007).

MEYER, B., *'Jüdische Mischlinge': Rassenpolitik und Verfolgungserfahrung 1933–1945* (Hamburg, 1999).

NICOSIA, F. R., *The Third Reich and the Palestine Question* (London, 1985).

PÄTZOLD, K. and RUNGE, I., *Pogromnacht 1938* (Berlin, 1988).

READ, A. and FISHER, D., *Kristallnacht: Unleashing the Holocaust* (London, 1989).

SHAW, S., *Turkey and the Holocaust: Turkey's Role in Rescuing Turkish and European Jewry from Nazi Persecution 1933–1945* (London, 1993).

SHERMAN, A. J., *Island Refuge: British Refugees from the Third Reich, 1933–1939* (London, 1973).

SIMPSON, Sir J. H., *Refugees: A Review of the Situation since September 1938* (London, 1939).

SKRAN, C. M., *Refugees in Inter-war Europe: The Emergence of a Regime* (New York and Oxford, 1995).

STEHLIN, STEWART A., *Weimar and the Vatican, 1918–1933: German–Vatican Relations in the Inter-War Years, 1918–1933* (Princeton, NJ, 1993).

STEINBERG, J., *All or Nothing: The Axis and the Holocaust, 1941–1943* (London, 1990).

VITAL, D., *A People Apart: The Jews in Europe, 1789–1939* (Cambridge, 1999).

WASSERSTEIN, B., *Britain and the Jews of Europe 1939–1945* (London and New York, 1979).

WELS, C. B., *Aloofness & Neutrality* (Utrecht, 1982).

WHITEMAN, D. B., *The Uprooted: A Hitler Legacy: Voices of Those Who Escaped before the 'Final Solution'* (New York, 1993).

WOLF, HUBERT, *Pope and Devil. The Vatican Archives and the Third Reich* (Cambridge, MA, and London, 2010).

WYMAN, D. S., *The Abandonment of the Jews: America and the Holocaust, 1941–1945* (New York, 1984).

Articles

BARKAI, A., 'Die deutschen Unternehmer und die Judenpolitik im "Dritten Reich"', *Geschichte und Gesellschaft*, 15 (1989).

—— 'German Interests in the Haavara-Transfer Agreement 1933–1939', *Leo Baeck Institute Yearbook*, 35 (1990).

BARTOV, O., 'Eastern Europe as the Site of Genocide', *Journal of Modern History*, 80 (2008).

CONWAY, J. S., 'The Vatican, Germany and the Holocaust', in Kent, P. C. and Pollard, J. F. (eds.), *Papal Diplomacy in the Modern Age* (London, 1994).

HAGEN, W. W., 'Before the "Final Solution": Toward a Comparative Analysis of Political Anti-Semitism in Interwar Germany and Poland', *Journal of Modern History*, 68 (1996).

HAYES, P., 'Big Business and "Aryanization" in Germany 1933–1939', *Jahrbuch für Antisemitismusforschung*, 3 (1994).

KOPPER, C., 'Die "Arisierung" jüdischer Privatbanken im Nationalsozialismus', *Sozialwissenschaftliche Information für Unterricht und Studium*, 20 (1991).

KWIET, K., 'To Leave or Not to Leave: The German Jews at the Crossroads', in Pehle, W. H. (ed.), *November 1938: From 'Reichskristallnacht' to Genocide* (New York, 1991).

LAAK, D. van, 'Die Mitwirkenden bei der "Arisierung". Dargestellt am Beispiel der rheinisch–westfälischen Industrieregion, 1933–1940', in Büttner, U. (ed.), *Die Deutschen und die Judenverfolgung im Dritten Reich* (Hamburg, 1992).

MILLMAN, B., 'Turkish Foreign and Strategic Policy, 1934–1942', *Middle Eastern Studies*, 31: 3 (1995).

MILTON, S., 'The Expulsion of Polish Jews from Germany, October 1938 to July 1939: A Documentation', *Leo Baeck Institute Yearbook*, 29 (1984).

MOSER, J., 'Depriving Jews of their Legal Rights in the Third Reich', in Pehle, W. H. (ed.), *November 1938: From 'Reichskristallnacht' to Genocide* (New York, 1991).

NICOSIA, F. R., 'Ein nützlicher Feind: Zionismus im nationalsozialistischen Deutschland 1933–1939', *Vierteljahrshefte für Zeitgeschichte*, 37 (1989).

RABINOVICI, D., 'Expediting Expropriation and Expulsion: The Impact of the "Vienna Model" on Anti-Jewish Policies in Nazi Germany, 1938', *Holocaust and Genocide Studies*, 14 (2000).

ROSENSTOCK, W., 'Exodus 1933–1939: A Survey of Jewish Emigration from Germany', *Leo Baeck Institute Yearbook*, 1 (1956).

RUBINSTEIN, W. D., 'Winston Churchill and the Jews', *Jewish Historical Studies*, 39 (2004).

SHERMAN, A. J., 'A Jewish Bank during the Schacht Era: M. M. Warburg & Co., 1933–1938', in Paucker, A. et al. (eds.), *The Jews in Nazi Germany, 1933–1945* (Tübingen, 1986).

STEHLIN, S. A., 'Pius XII, the Second World War, and the Jews', paper delivered at the German Historical Institute London, 14 March 2006.

STRAUSS, H. A., 'Jewish Emigration from Germany: Nazi Policies and Jewish Responses', *Leo Baeck Institute Yearbook*, 25 (1980).

THOMAS, M., 'Imperial Defence or Diversionary Attack? Anglo-French Strategic Planning in the Near East, 1936–1940', in Alexander, M. S. and Philpott, W. J. (eds.), *Anglo-French Defence Relations between the Wars* (Basingstoke, 2002).

VOLLNHALS, C., 'Jüdische Selbsthilfe bis 1938', in Benz, W. (ed.), *Die Juden in Deutschland 1933–1945: Leben unter nationalsozialistischer Herrschaft* (Munich, 1988).

WETZEL, J., 'Auswanderung aus Deutschland', in Benz, W. (ed.), *Die Juden in Deutschland 1933–1945: Leben unter nationalsozialistischer Herrschaft* (Munich, 1988).

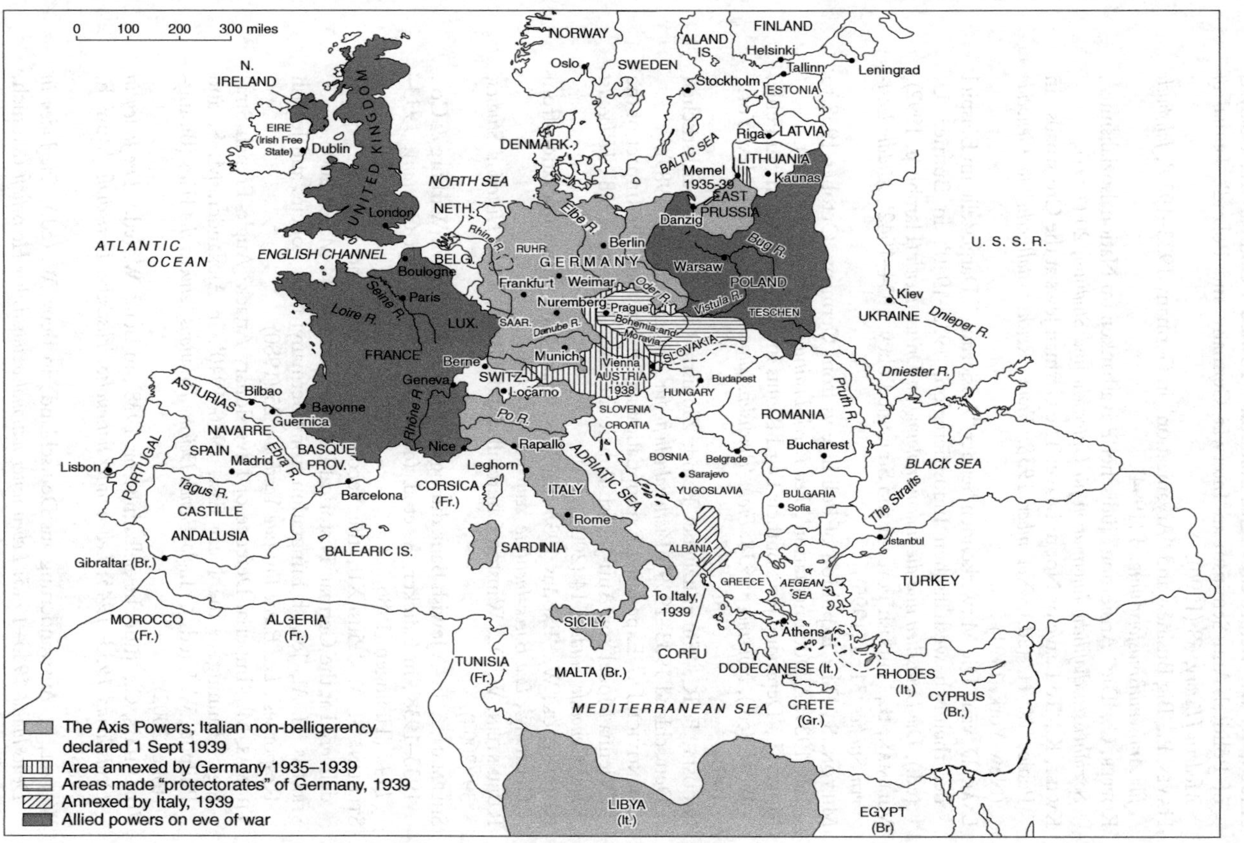

Map 15. Europe on the Eve of War, 1939

18

The Nightmare of the Dark: The Decisions for War

I

The signing of the Nazi–Soviet non-aggression pact during the night hours of 23–24 August was the start of the final act in the pre-war tragedy. From Hitler's point of view, Germany was now ready for its quick victory over Poland. Should Poland not be provoked into attacking Germany as he hoped, the SS, under Hitler's orders, planned for a simulated attack. A small group of senior officials selected 250 experienced, middle-aged, Polish-speaking SS soldiers to operate in Polish uniforms at three points along the German–Polish frontier in Upper Silesia. Concentration camp prisoners (*Konserven* or 'canned goods'), also dressed in Polish uniforms, were to provide the corpses to give authenticity to the scene for the cameras. All that remained to be done while the fuse burned towards its appointed end was to avoid mediation and separate the western powers from Poland. The Führer's address on 22 August, when Hitler was already certain of the outcome of the Moscow talks, was full of confidence. It was time to act; Germany had no other choice. 'In two or three years all these fortunate circumstances will no longer exist', he told his senior officers. 'No one knows how long I may live.' With the news of the Nazi–Soviet pact confirmed he could assure his anxious generals about the effect of any blockade.[1] Hitler hoped that the Nazi–Soviet treaty would lead to Britain's neutrality but was prepared to move against the western powers should they honour the Polish guarantee. Hitler's only fear was 'that at the last moment some *Schweinhund* will present me with a mediation plan'. Although in the morning he dismissed his opponents as 'little worms', in the afternoon, after a simple lunch, he admitted that there could be a 'life-and-death struggle'. 'A long period of peace would not be good for us', he declared.[2] The orders for the attack on Saturday morning, 26 August, would be issued later.

[1] See J. Noakes and G. Pridham (eds.), *Nazism, 1919–1945, Vol. 3. Foreign Policy, War and Racial Extermination* (Exeter, 1995), 740.

[2] Quotations from Joachim Fest, *Hitler* (London, 1974), 883–885.

When the British cabinet met for the first time on 22 August, no discussion was necessary before a revised and strengthened letter from Chamberlain was sent to Henderson to be delivered personally to Hitler. Referring to the July 1914 crisis when Britain was accused of not making its position clear, Chamberlain's letter left no room for doubt about Britain's determination to stand by Poland. The reported agreement between Germany and the USSR made no difference. In all of this, neither the politicians nor the electorate applied those criteria of strategic assessment employed by modern day theorists. There was no question that Britain would stand by its obligations to Poland whatever the consequences. In that sense the situation was entirely different from that of September 1938. When Henderson presented Chamberlain's short but decisive message to Hitler, he was subjected to a two-hour tirade. The Führer spoke of the terrible sins committed by Poles against Germans and the blame attached to Britain for supporting Poland. Hitler claimed that he was not interested in direct Anglo-German talks and doubted whether the British were either. As the ambassador, who had gone well beyond his instructions in attempting to mollify Hitler, left the room, the Führer's mood changed. He slapped his leg, laughed and predicted that Chamberlain's cabinet would fall that night. At their second meeting, when Henderson received Hitler's written answer to Chamberlain, the German leader spoke more calmly but the threat to go to war was undisguised. He told the ambassador that Germany and Britain would never be able to come to an agreement and that he preferred a war when he was 50 than when he would be 55 or 60. Nonetheless, on 24 August, Chamberlain, with full cabinet approval, told the House of Commons that Britain would fight if necessary for 'an international order' based on the observance of 'mutual international undertakings' and 'the renunciation of force in the settlement of differences'. Britain's defence of the European balance of power would coincide with its 'high moral purpose'.[3]

The French position was more equivocal. Far more hope had been invested in the negotiations with the Soviet Union and the conclusion of the Nazi–Soviet pact was a very heavy blow. There were significant divergences in the views of both politicians and officials. On the one hand, Reynaud and Mandel led a group of *durs* within the cabinet who, along with Léger and the majority of *Quai d'Orsay* officials, insisted that France must fulfil its commitments in the event of a German attack on Poland. On the other hand, Bonnet and Anatole de Monzie, minister of public works, along with other ministers and parliamentarians, opposed

[3] R. A. C. Parker, *Chamberlain and Appeasement*, (Basingstoke, 1993) 331.

war and hoped it could be averted by another international conference. Daladier and Gamelin, too, still hoped for a last-minute reprieve but were resigned to going to war against any further German aggression. Failure to do so, Gamelin had counselled Daladier, would be to surrender France's status as a great European power.

The cabinet met on 22 August, its first meeting since the end of July. Daladier insisted a new effort would be made to induce the Poles to allow the passage of Soviet troops. Calls for full mobilization were rejected (France already had one million men under arms) as was a plea for negotiations with Italy. At a special war council the next day, called in response to the Nazi–Soviet pact, Bonnet tried to secure from Gamelin an admission that the army was not ready for war. This time the service chiefs were not prepared to repeat their Munich role and Bonnet was almost alone in his advocacy of the withdrawal of the commitment to Poland. Gamelin assured the council that the French forces were ready; Admiral Darlan, too, announced that the navy was ready and was superior in almost all categories to both the German and Italian fleets. Air minister Guy La Chambre, meanwhile, insisted that 'The situation of our aviation must not weigh on the government's decision as it did in 1938.'[4] Three days later, Vuillemin informed La Chambre that Britain and France would need six months before they were ready for war since the German and Italian air forces 'still dominate by a great deal' those of the two powers.[5] The meeting ended with the decision to continue the preliminary measures in anticipation of a general mobilization.

French confidence was genuinely higher than at the time of Munich. Daladier, taking his cue from Gamelin, believed that if Poland could resist long enough for the French army to complete its preparations for a defensive war, France could withstand the onslaught of a German offensive. He believed that in a war of attrition, the superior economic and financial resources of the Allied empires would defeat the Germans. Daladier, it is true, clung to the hope that something might still be salvaged from the talks with the Soviets. He was prepared, moreover, as he told the cabinet on 24 August, to urge the Poles to negotiate over Danzig, a position that Gamelin, not to mention Bonnet and his circle of like-minded colleagues, fully endorsed. Daladier sought to avoid what, like most Frenchmen and women, he viewed as a catastrophe. Unlike Bonnet, however, he never considered deserting Poland. During the last days of the crisis he wavered, as did Gamelin, but was forced to recognize that France had no alternative but to go to war. Political

[4] *DDF*, 2nd ser., Vol. XVIII, No. 324.

[5] Quotation in Talbot C. Imlay, *Facing the Second World War*, 47.

considerations were as important as strategic ones. The French finally had the elusive alliance with Britain in hand; if the latter remained loyal to its alliance with Poland, the French could do no less. The country could not have endured a second Munich without abandoning all claims to be a major power. Neither Daladier nor Gamelin was prepared for such an eventuality and the revival of confidence in the preceding months made such an abdication politically difficult.

The Polish response to the news of Ribbentrop's trip to Moscow was to accelerate the mobilization that had been going on since mid-August. The new measures that were implemented on 23 August amounted to general mobilization in the 'Corridor', Great Poland, and Upper Silesia. Further mobilization measures followed on 27 and 28 August but orders were given that the Polish troops should not allow themselves to be provoked. It seems likely that between 22 and 28 August, despite the growing alarm, there were still some doubts in Warsaw whether war with Germany was imminent. Beck believed that a peaceful solution could be negotiated. The signing of the Anglo-Polish alliance on 25 August confirmed Polish assumptions that the western guarantee would be honoured though the political agreement with the French, the necessary authorization for the implementation of the military alliance, remained unsigned until 4 September. Beck was aware of the reluctance of his guarantors to fight for Poland but he thought that if the Allied powers remained firm in the face of Hitler's threats, war might not, in fact, be necessary. Intent on keeping the alliances with the western powers intact, he proved more flexible in the face of their demands to talk with the Germans than his more determined colleagues. It was not until the evening of 28 August that the situation was judged serious enough to advise the president to order general mobilization. On the morning of 29 August, the army commanders were told to move their troops to jumping off positions. The order for general mobilization was cancelled that same afternoon after appeals from the British and French ambassadors that such war preparations would wreck the possibility of a peaceful settlement. On 30 August, mobilization was again ordered for the following day and, after some delay, the already mobilized troops moved into their assigned positions. When the German attack began, only one-third of the Polish troops of the first echelon were ready for action.

Hitler, though determined on war, was prepared to give the British another chance to acquiesce in his plans for Poland. On 25 August, he summoned Henderson to the Reich Chancellery and made his 'last offer' for an understanding with Britain. Polish provocation was intolerable and Germany had to end the 'Macedonian conditions' on its eastern frontier. When this was accomplished, he would be willing to personally guarantee the existence of the British Empire and place the power of the Reich at its disposal. He would offer a formal acknowledgement of Germany's western border in return for the right to move east without restriction. He would accept, moreover, a reasonable limitation on armaments and ask only for limited colonial concessions to be negotiated by peaceful means. Once the Polish question was resolved, he would settle down and conclude his life as an artist. The 'offer' arrived in London as the Anglo-Polish alliance treaty was signed. By then, Hitler already had confirmed the order to attack Poland at dawn on the next day. Two messages temporarily upset his equilibrium during that Friday afternoon. The first was the news of the signing of the Anglo-Polish treaty. The second was Mussolini's reply to Hitler's message justifying the conclusion of the Nazi–Soviet agreement and warning that the attack on Poland was possibly hours away.

Common sense seemed to have prevailed in Rome only at the very last minute. The British had kept the Italians fully informed of the details of their policy during August, in sharp contrast to the continued silence from Hitler. Mussolini appeared to take the announcement of the Nazi–Soviet pact calmly, but Ciano responded by trying to convince his chief that the German alliance should be denounced. The Duce wavered, retreating again into his weather-vane mode. He would not disown the alliance but he knew it could not be honoured. Given the present state of Italy's war preparations, Mussolini told Hitler in his message on 25 August, intervention would take place only if Germany could immediately deliver the armaments and war materials needed to withstand an Anglo-French offensive against Italy. Hitler asked for the Duce's understanding and support, but privately referred to his 'disloyal Axis partner'. The point was driven home on the following day when the list of Italian military requirements, requested by Hitler, proved so extensive that the Germans at first thought it must be a joke. 'It's enough to kill a bull', Ciano wrote in his diary, 'if a bull could read it'.[6]

On the evening of 25 August, Hitler cancelled the attack on Poland. Some *Abwehr* and SS units had already moved and the damage had to be repaired. Neither the Anglo-Polish alliance nor the Italian defection could have come as a surprise but there was a moment of shock. Hitler had no intention of abandoning the attack. Postponement brought some practical advantages. It would give Hitler a final opportunity to divorce the Allied powers from Poland and to stage the Polish 'provocations' intended to mobilize home and foreign opinion behind the German cause. In military terms, too, the loss of the surprise element was more

[6] Galeazzo Ciano, *Diario 1937–1943* (Milan, 1946, 1998), 334 (26 August 1939).

than counterbalanced by the opportunity to send more troops to the eastern front so as to provide the quick victory needed in case of a French offensive. Hitler's action was temporary. Mobilization went on and the military build-up continued. Military opponents to the war took heart from Hitler's retreat and a few even imagined that Hitler had suffered a political setback. There was a revival of opposition planning for his overthrow and a simultaneous *coup d'état*. Other officers, after the 25 August pull-back, hoped that, as in the case of Austria and Czechoslovakia, Hitler would again pull off a triumph in Poland without outside intervention. There were war hawks in the Führer's entourage: Ribbentrop, who kept physically close to Hitler throughout these days and repeatedly assured him that the Allied powers would not fight, SS leaders, anxious to fan Hitler's distrust of the general staff in order to increase their own influence, and generals Jodl and Keitel, the staunchest of Hitler's military supporters, who insisted that the *Wehrmacht* was loyal. 'Operation White' was rescheduled for 1 September. Hitler assured his military chiefs and Mussolini that he would fight on two fronts if necessary yet made numerous efforts between 26 and 31 August to strike a bargain with the British.

During these days, there was an endless stream of communications between Berlin and London as Hitler tried to separate Britain from Poland while the British sought to get Hitler to substitute negotiation for military action. To add further confusion to the scene, Göring used the services of a long-time friend, the naïve and loquacious Swedish businessman Birger Dahlerus, to encourage the British to think that there was still a chance of peace between Germany and Poland. Göring's real intention was to best Ribbentrop and present the Führer with the much desired prize of British neutrality. Shuttling back and forth between London and Berlin, Dahlerus benefited from the unwillingness of Chamberlain and Halifax to fully shut the door. Never quite taken seriously, the Swede encouraged the British leaders to think that the situation was not hopeless and that Hitler would compromise when, in fact, he was determined on war. At yet another level of conspiracy, the German state secretary, Weizsäcker, assisted by Attolico, the Italian ambassador in Berlin, and the ex-ambassador to Italy, Ulrich von Hassell, entered the arena to try to get the Poles to send a representative to Berlin in order to prevent the outbreak of war. They wrongly believed that if Hitler could get what he wanted through negotiation, he might abandon his military plans.

Almost all the diplomatic sparring took place between Germany and Britain. The other states were sidelined. Other than Daladier's personal letter to Hitler on 26 August, again sent from one ex-serviceman to another, stressing the horrors and costs of war and pleading for a peaceful resolution of the conflict with Poland, the French left the diplomatic initiative to the British. Following its 24 August meeting, the French cabinet did not reassemble until 31 August. What action was taken in the interval consisted mainly of Bonnet's efforts to avoid war by pressuring the Poles and by promoting Italian mediation. There was a counter-campaign conducted by Coulondre, the French ambassador in Berlin, and the most senior officials at the *Quai*, led by Léger, to convince Daladier to '*tenir, tenir, tenir*' in the belief that Hitler was hesitating and would retreat if the western powers stood firm. Once Mussolini reneged on intervention, he, too, played the part of bystander. Restless and upset at his own and Italy's impotence, he vacillated between suggestions to Hitler that a political settlement was still possible and the painting of imaginary pictures for his subordinates of all the advantages that would come to Italy should the Reich and the Allies fight a long and exhausting war. Hitler showed no interest in Mussolini's offer to act as his messenger in London. The Duce would launch a proposal for a general conference on 31 August, but the final flurry of Italian activity, encouraged by Bonnet, did little more than keep the telephone lines engaged. On 31 August, too, fearing that Italian war preparations might alarm Britain, Ciano assured the British that the Italians would never start a war against Britain and France. The Japanese had no part to play at all. Their consternation at the conclusion of the Nazi–Soviet pact was undisguised. The German desertion at a time when they had just suffered a military defeat at the hands of the Soviet Union was a stunning blow to the Hiranuma government. The Japanese prime minister referred to the 'inexplicable new conditions' that had arisen in Europe when he resigned on 28 August. The blatant violation of the Anti-Comintern pact gave rise to a wave of anti-German feeling and a sense of betrayal that was slow to ebb. The Japanese were in a state of shock during the last days of Europe's peace.

There were some initiatives from the neutral powers; none affected the central drama. Responding to the news of the Nazi–Soviet negotiations and appeals from Daladier for a conference in Washington, Roosevelt sent a message on 23 August to Italy's King Victor Emmanuel asking him to take up the president's April proposals when, in return for an Italian and German promise not to attack certain designated countries, he offered to convene a conference on disarmament and trade in which the United States would participate. On the 24th, he asked both Hitler and the president of Poland to refrain from hostilities for a set period while they solved their problems through negotiation, arbitration, or conciliation and indicated his willingness to serve as mediator if both sides agreed to respect the other's independence and territorial integrity. These messages were mainly for American domestic consumption;

Roosevelt was anxious to 'put the bee on Germany', so that there could be no question about who was responsible for the outbreak of war. The president sent Hitler a second message on the following day; the Poles had accepted direct negotiation or conciliation and many lives would be saved if Hitler did the same. The Führer answered only on 31 August when he claimed that Polish intransigence rendered the president's appeal invalid. According to the appeasement-minded Joseph Kennedy, the American ambassador in London, the British wanted American pressure on the Poles to make voluntary concessions to save the peace. In Washington, this message was seen as a British manoeuvre to get the Americans to arrange for a new Munich. Kennedy had misrepresented the British request so that it appeared that Chamberlain was prepared to have the Poles make unilateral concessions. In some Washington quarters, suspicions of the British persisted until 3 September. The president, however, took steps to reassure the anti-appeasers in London, confirming on 31 August the tacit understanding between Britain and the United States that the latter would assume the main responsibility for restraining Japan in case of a Far Eastern war. For the most part, Roosevelt and the State Department could only watch and wait. The failure of the president's efforts to revise the Neutrality Act in July weakened his hand but did not affect the German belief that the Americans would deliver the arms needed by the Allied powers

There were two other attempts at mediation. The Pope, following Halifax's recommendation, made an appeal for peace on 19 August to a group of pilgrims visiting the Vatican and broadcast a second appeal on the Vatican radio on 24 August. The position of the papacy was far from clear. More conciliatory by nature than his predecessor, and as papal legate to Nazi Germany one of the architects of the Concordat, Pius XII made every effort to maintain normal relations with the Führer. As was clear in his response to the German persecution of the Jews, his main, indeed often his exclusive, concern was to protect the safety of the Catholic Church in Germany and elsewhere. Nonetheless, Pius XII was deeply afraid of war and harboured strong suspicions about Hitler's real intentions. The papal appeal of 24 August was primarily directed to the Italians whom he felt should keep their distance from Germany. The papacy also backed the British and French efforts to warn the Poles against taking any provocative action. In one of his most misguided moves, the Pope had the papal nuncio in Warsaw, despite the latter's protestations, present Mussolini's scheme for the Polish abandonment of Danzig. The Polish leaders, of course, recognized the Italian source of the offer but, in any case, faced on 31 August with Hitler's list of demands, showed no interest in the papal suggestion. Pius XII made one more futile effort, appealing to Germany, Poland, France, and Italy to avoid any step that would aggravate the existing situation. When, on the next morning, the Germans began their attack on Poland, that most loyal daughter of the Church, the Vatican refused to make any comment despite appeals from Britain and France.

The only other significant gesture was the peace appeal issued by the King of the Belgians on 23 August following the meeting of foreign ministers of the 'Oslo states' (Belgium, Netherlands, Luxemburg, Finland, Denmark, Norway, Sweden). Predictably, King Leopold's initiative had little effect. The reports of the conference had created some anxiety in Berlin where on 26 August the Ministry of Economics decided to send two senior diplomats to warn the Oslo states that in the event of war, trade with Germany had to be maintained if their neutrality was to be respected. The governments concerned thought they could isolate themselves from the conflict and that if they maintained their neutral rights without distinguishing between the belligerent powers, they would be safe from attack. On 28 August, Queen Wilhelmina and King Leopold, at the former's suggestion, made a joint offer of their good offices to Britain, France, Poland, Germany, and Italy. Hitler was not interested. The Dutch and Belgians retreated behind their paper-thin walls.

II

In the diplomatic duel fought during the last week of August, Hitler tried to bully, bribe, and trick the British into abandoning the Polish alliance. Even before the official British rejection of his 'last offer' was received, Hitler gave his approval to the attempts of Göring's envoy Dahlerus to broker an agreement with Britain. Hitler proposed a pact with Britain; Germany was to get Danzig and the corridor and Poland was to have a free port in Danzig, a corridor to Gdynia and a German guarantee of her frontiers. There would be an agreement about Germany's colonies, guarantees for the German minority, and a German pledge to defend the British Empire. It was a combination of old and new offers designed to tempt the British. In London, Dahlerus saw Halifax, Chamberlain, and Cadogan. His message encouraged the exceedingly thin British hopes that negotiations might be possible. While the Foreign Office and cabinet were still working on an official answer to Hitler's 25 August offer, Cadogan and Dahlerus put together a private message to be conveyed to Hitler. Britain would honour its guarantees. It recommended direct negotiations between Germany and Poland with any agreement to be guaranteed by the powers. Britain was anxious for an understanding with Hitler but there could be no talks until the present situation was honourably settled. Dahlerus took the message off to Berlin, arriving back at midnight on 27/28 August. Later that night, Göring called on Hitler and secured his ostensible agreement to the British demand for direct negotiations between Germany and Poland and the idea of an international guarantee of Poland. On that same day, 28 August, the orders were given that the attack on Poland should begin on 1 September. Chamberlain's official reply to Hitler's offer convinced the Führer to pursue the Dahlerus–Göring line. The Foreign Office and cabinet had worked hard and long over the weekend (25–27 August) to salvage something from Hitler's unacceptable bid for an alliance without compromising Polish independence. Foreign Office officials intervened to correct the 'worst errors' in the too deferential initial draft. The cabinet met on Saturday and Sunday and again on Monday, 28 August, to get the balance right. In essence, the British terms were the same as had been given privately to Dahlerus. Hitler's bribe was rejected. He was told that Britain would stand by its obligations to Poland. Having first secured Beck's agreement, Chamberlain proposed that there should be direct Polish–German negotiations and, if they were successful, an international guarantee of Poland. Henderson, who had returned to London to present Hitler's 'last offer', flew back to Berlin with the prime minister's answer, which he presented that evening. The Führer agreed to discuss an exchange of minorities with the Poles and would think about political negotiations. He insisted on having Danzig and the 'Corridor' and demanded additional frontier rectifications in Silesia. He became excited only when Henderson, as instructed, told him that it was not a question of Danzig and the Corridor but of British determination to meet force with force. Hope revived in London. With British encouragement, Mussolini urged his ally to negotiate; Hitler replied that he had agreed to receive a Polish negotiator. The Poles had already made a move, on 27 August, to suggest that they would be interested in negotiations. Two days later, after consulting the president and Rydz-Śmigły, Beck decided there would be no talks in Berlin but only in a town near the frontier or in a railway carriage. Beck would not repeat the experiences of Schuschnigg and Hacha.

In London, all through 29 August, Halifax waited expectantly for Hitler's promised answer. The foreign secretary thought, as did his officials, that Hitler was in difficulty. He had made a poor bargain in concluding a deal with the Soviet Union in place of Japan, Italy, and Spain and now had to get out of this situation. 'Halifax thought it very important to get into negotiation', his private secretary noted, 'and then be very stiff and then Hitler would be beat'.[7] The foreign secretary had

[7] John Harvey (ed.), *The Diplomatic Diaries of Oliver Harvey, 1937–1940*, 309.

misjudged the situation in Berlin. The Dahlerus intervention provided Hitler with a new opportunity to isolate Poland diplomatically. He explained the nature of his plot to General Halder, the chief of the army staff, on the afternoon of 29 August. Halder recorded in his diary: 'Führer has hope of driving a wedge between England, French and Poles. Underlying idea: Bombard with demographic and democratic demands. Then came the actual timetable: 30 August: Poles in Berlin. 31 August: Blow up. 1 Sept.: Use of force.'[8] The timetable was short; at most, Hitler would delay the attack by one day for otherwise he believed, and was encouraged to believe by his anxious generals, that he would have to abandon the campaign. Very much on edge, Hitler told Henderson that he would accept the British proposal of direct German–Polish negotiations but demanded that a Polish representative be produced in Berlin within twenty-four hours. The totally unrealistic deadline suggests that he would move regardless of what took place in London but wanted to avoid any possibility of being trapped into negotiations as had happened in 1938. Göring played down the time limit though he insisted that someone would have to come from Warsaw to receive the proposals. It may be that Hitler was thinking in terms of establishing an alibi that would convince the German people that he had offered the Poles moderate terms and that they had insisted on war. In actual fact, Hitler proved too impatient to wait for the deadline set for Polish compliance. He gave the order for the German army to take up its positions at 6.30 a.m. on 31 August even before the efficient German intelligence service intercepted a message of Beck's on 29 August that made clear the Poles would not negotiate on German terms. Almost at that very same moment, Hitler signed 'Directive Number 1 for the Conduct of the War'.

This was war by calculation and not by miscalculation. Since the 23 August, Hitler was fully aware of the probability of British involvement but willing to take the risk. The immediate situation was advantageous. The *Wehrmacht* enjoyed a temporary advantage over its enemies; Roosevelt had failed to secure the revision of the Neutrality Act and the Soviet Union would support the German aggression. All these advantages could disappear in the near future. Hitler might well have assumed that Germany had 'nothing to gain by waiting' and that his Jewish-inspired opponents would soon close the net around him.[9] It is possible that he could have secured the territorial concessions that he demanded from Poland if this had been his aim but he wanted far more. 'In two months Poland will be finished', he told Weizsäcker on

[8] Quoted in Fest, *Hitler*, 599.

[9] Adam Tooze, *The Wages of Destruction*, 324–325.

29 August, 'then we shall have a great peace conference with the western powers'.[10] Hitler's War Directive No. 1 ordered the greatest possible restraint *vis-à-vis* the western powers. The responsibility for the opening of hostilities should rest with them.

Both the British and French governments nourished the illusion that Hitler's last minute 'offers' were a sign of weakness intended to cover his retreat and that there might be a compromise on Danzig and the Corridor. Reluctant to go to war, their leaders were prepared to explore any possibility, however slight, that might preserve the peace. This meant advising the Poles to avoid provocative action and to enter into direct negotiations with Hitler on the assumption that such talks should be genuine and not 'dictation' on the Czechoslovak model. The British misperceptions in this respect had much to do with Chamberlain's basic misunderstanding of Hitler's intentions but also with Halifax's admittedly diminishing belief that the differences between Germany and Poland could be resolved through negotiation and were not of a nature to make war necessary. Rational to a fault, Chamberlain could not imagine that anyone in his right mind (and there was always the possibility that Hitler was mad) would actually want war. To the very end, this stiff, controlled, and stubborn man sought to convince himself that some way existed to avoid the looming catastrophe. Chamberlain was as blind to Hitler's true nature as he was to the intense loyalty of most Germans to their Führer. Halifax, who tended to panic in moments of crisis, remained surprisingly calm and detached during the last week of August as he took on the major negotiating role. Immersing himself in the drafting and redrafting of the answers to Hitler, Halifax became so involved in the conduct of daily business that he neither grasped the extent of Hitler's deviousness nor sensed the rising anger of his colleagues at the prolongation of the talks. He repeatedly and rightly assured his subordinates that there would be no 'second Munich' but failed to respond to the surge of emotion that made the very idea of making any kind of concession to Hitler repugnant and unacceptable. Tarred with the appeasement brush, the continuing talks raised fears of a 'sell-out' among some cabinet ministers as well as MPs, who shared and reflected the country's mood. People only wanted to know whether Hitler would stand down.

Only some desperate hope not to overlook any possibility of avoiding war explains why Halifax and Chamberlain were prepared to follow up the demands made by Hitler in his meeting with Henderson on 29 August. Ministers were divided. Told that the message when 'stripped of its verbiage' revealed a man 'trying to extricate himself from a difficult

[10] E. V. Weizsäcker, *Memoirs* (London, 1951), 208.

position' and assured by Chamberlain that there would be no yielding on the question of the Polish representative, which smacked too much of Prague, the cabinet settled for another try. Chamberlain sent off a conciliatory personal message to Hitler welcoming the continuing exchanges as evidence of the desire for an Anglo-German understanding. The Foreign Office sent off official messages to Berlin and to Warsaw. The British would support the negotiations between Germany and Poland and the international guarantee but reserved their position as to the nature of the proposals. As immediate negotiations were hardly practicable, the Foreign Office proposed a military standstill and a temporary *modus vivendi* for Danzig. The message was intended to be firm but not provocative. News of so-called disturbances in Germany and Dahlerus's report that Göring was hopeful contributed to some degree of optimism. On 30 August, 'a wave of hopefulness' swept the City and the Paris bourse. That night, however, a calamitous encounter between Henderson and Ribbentrop brought matters to a head.

Substituting for his master and aping the latter's bullying tactics, Ribbentrop told Henderson that as the Poles had not sent a representative, the German proposals were irrelevant. Germany's sixteen demands on Poland, drafted at the German Foreign Ministry, were rattled off at top speed by Ribbentrop, who then refused to hand over the actual text. The angry and distraught Henderson tried to salvage something from the debacle, though once again his solution was to put pressure on the Poles. Seizing on Ribbentrop's denial that the 30 August deadline was an ultimatum, he demanded that Lipski, the Polish ambassador, meet with Ribbentrop and sent Dahlerus to confront him. The Swedish intermediary, whom Lipski did not even know, urged the ambassador to see Göring, sign whatever he wanted, and then everyone could go 'shoot stags together'. Dahlerus had the German text from Göring and read out the sixteen demands. Lipski pretended not to understand but had taken in their import and warned Warsaw that neither Beck nor any other representative should be sent to Berlin. His warnings were unnecessary. The infuriated Dahlerus telephoned London to say that the sixteen points were 'extremely liberal' and that the Poles were being obstructive. Halifax disagreed. He remained firm but still thought that Hitler might retreat and that if the German–Polish negotiations could be started, they just might succeed. Resisting Henderson's pleas that Beck be forced to send a plenipotentiary, he only asked Beck to enter into direct conversations with the Germans. Beck had already instructed Lipski to see Ribbentrop at midday on 31 August; the German foreign minister delayed receiving him until 6.30 p.m. Lipski was forthwith dismissed when he said that he had no authority to negotiate on the German proposals. As Hitler had already issued his orders to the *Wehrmacht*, the conversation was virtually pointless. The Polish embassy's telephone link to Warsaw was cut.

However useless these final efforts might appear in retrospect, some ministers in London and Paris still clung to the hope that war might be avoided. There were reports reaching London of open disaffection in Germany, general staff discontent, and rumours of a military revolt or a 'Palace Revolution'. At 9 p.m. on 31 August, Berlin Radio announced that the Poles had refused to open negotiations and broadcast the text of the sixteen demands. Cadogan wrote in his diary at midnight: 'It *does* seem to me Hitler is hesitant and trying all sorts of dodges, including last-minute bluff. We have got to stand firm.'[11] Some of this misplaced optimism was due to the shuttle diplomacy of Dahlerus, which continued until minutes before the eventual British ultimatum ran out. The pacific and encouraging messages he brought from Göring still fostered the illusion that Hitler was open to persuasion. At the least, the possibility could not be dismissed. Henderson, too, played his part in keeping the Anglo-German dialogue going, though he had lost much of his credibility at the Foreign Office. One cannot help but have some sympathy for this terminally ill, deeply fatigued, and much-tried man, who could hardly believe that he was being treated by Hitler and the despised Ribbentrop in such a brutal manner. A representative of the old school of diplomacy, he simply could not stand up to their hammering tactics and lost his self-control. His reports were delayed, confused, and even inaccurate. He was unbelievably careless in his use of the embassy telephone, naturally tapped by the Germans. Most important of all, though he understood the dangers of Hitler's volatile moods, and the strength of his hold over the German people, he failed to convey to London an accurate picture of the situation in Berlin. He imagined almost to the very end that if the situation was properly handled, Hitler could be dissuaded from war. His desperation made him easy prey for those who, for the worst (Göring) or best (Weizsäcker) of reasons, wanted to force the Poles into negotiations. Henderson showed, it is true, as little sympathy towards the Poles as he had towards the Czechs in 1938 but he was not pro-Nazi. His only concern was to get the German–Polish negotiations started so as to avert war. In this, he was hardly out of step with Halifax though he was prepared to push the Poles further than the foreign secretary was willing to sanction. Given his previous efforts at appeasement, he was not the best person to convince Hitler that the British would stick to the Polish guarantee. He was not to blame for Chamberlain's and Halifax's failure to understand Hitler's determination to have his war. The French ambassador in Berlin proved

[11] David Dilks (ed.), *The Diaries of Alexander Cadogan*, 206.

far tougher in his dealings with the Germans (he had been previously ambassador in Moscow). Coulondre was highly mistrustful of Henderson and more sympathetically inclined towards Lipski. His advice that Hitler would step back if the Allies stood firm was ill-judged but it strengthened Daladier's hand in the cabinet. In the end, the diplomats were only the servants of their respective governments.

III

The German attack on Poland began at 4.45 a.m. on 1 September with the shelling of the Polish armaments dumps on the island of Westerplatte by the cruiser *Schleswig-Holstein*. The bombardment was preceded by a faked Polish attack on the German radio station of Gleiwitz mounted by the SS and two other staged incidents. There was no German declaration of war. These carefully planned manoeuvres were intended to convince the German people and the outside world that a German 'policing operation' was necessary. It was hardly worth the effort that went into their planning for few even in Germany were convinced by the charade. The same day, Danzig, which by now had become a secondary matter in the eyes of the world, was incorporated into the Reich. There was some uncertainty in London and Paris about what was actually happening in Poland on that morning but the news of the attacks and the bombings of Polish cities was soon confirmed. The Poles expected that the Anglo-Polish treaty would come into force and Halifax confirmed this view when the Polish ambassador came to the Foreign Office. Though war had begun for Poland, it was not to begin for the British until 11 a.m. and for the French at 5 p.m. on 3 September. The delay was not to the credit of either government, nor was their subsequent inaction.

The Italian, French, and British governments all contributed to the delayed reaction to the German attack. On 31 August, Ciano, warned that unless something new came up there would be war in a few hours, called Halifax and suggested that Mussolini would approach Hitler if he could offer him the 'fat prize' of Danzig. After some consideration, Halifax rejected the proposal. Then Ciano suggested that Mussolini might convene a conference for 5 September to consider the revision of the Treaty of Versailles. Chamberlain's first reaction was to insist that both sides would have to demobilize before any such conference could be called. Halifax still felt that the key was to begin the German–Polish negotiations. If they were initiated, no conference would be necessary; if not, war would follow and any conference would be superfluous. In Paris, Bonnet favoured accepting the idea of a conference; Daladier, briefed by Léger, angrily dismissed the Italian proposal as a new Munich.

The French cabinet met on the evening of 31 August, its first meeting for a week. Bonnet pressed the ministers to accept the Italian offer of mediation but Daladier, turning his back on his foreign minister throughout the meeting, warned that the proposal was a 'ploy'. 'Are we going to agree to cut up Poland and dishonour ourselves?' he asked his cabinet colleagues. 'The lesson of Munich is that the signature of Hitler is worth nothing'.[12] At this point, apparently by coincidence, an earlier missive arrived from Coulondre in Berlin who, in emotive language, urged that France must 'hold fast' to its commitment to resist German aggression. Daladier read the note to the cabinet. President Lebrun turned to Bonnet. 'You see, my dear colleague', he observed, 'this is the unanimous opinion of our diplomats. We must hold fast.'[13] A press communiqué implied that the Italian offer had been rejected but Bonnet and his confederates proceeded as if they had won. They sent off to London on 1 September a positive French reply to the Italian offer and proposed that the Poles join the conference. As Europe hovered on the brink of war, France appeared to be pursuing two distinct contradictory lines of policy. Official statements proclaimed France's commitment to fulfil its obligations to Poland while behind the scenes, Bonnet was engaged in an increasingly desperate attempt to secure Italian mediation.

The news of the German attack on Poland did not stop the Bonnet group. The Italian ambassador was told that the cabinet had accepted the Italian proposal for a conference. Bonnet moved to collect more general support. When the cabinet met on 1 September, it was decided that general mobilization, which would take 16 days, should begin the next day and that the National Assembly should be convened to vote seventy-five billion francs in supplementary military credits. Bonnet demanded that the Italian offer be accepted but the cabinet, which kept no records, apparently did not debate the issue further. Still, Bonnet informed Ciano that France would accept the Italian proposal on condition that Poland was invited. Ciano, though encouraged, was already sceptical about German acceptance. When Hitler saw Attolico, the Italian ambassador, on the evening of 31 August, he rejected the possibility of Italian mediation and agreed that 'everything was now at an end'.[14] This did not prevent Ciano, prodded by Bonnet, from refloating the conference idea. On 1 September, with great effort, the Duce was able to extract a note from Hitler absolving Italy from its responsibilities under the Pact of Steel. At the afternoon meeting of the Grand Council, the Italians opted

[12] Quoted in Jean-Baptiste Duroselle, *La décadence, 1932–1939* (Paris, 1979), 481.
[13] Quoted in Elisabeth du Réau, *Édouard Daladier, 1884–1970* (Paris, 1993), 363.
[14] *DGFP*, Ser. D, Vol. VII, No. 478.

for 'non-belligerency', a word that Mussolini felt had a stronger ring than 'neutrality' and was more in keeping with Italy's role as a Great Power. Despite Mussolini's equivocation, the Italians had clearly reneged on their alliance with Berlin.

The British, too, were deliberating about what should be done. As Halifax and others were still hoping on 31 August that Hitler would negotiate and would hardly go to war because of the non-appearance of the Polish negotiator, the German attack took them by surprise. On the morning of the attack, officials rejected two separate mediation proposals from Dahlerus and Henderson, making it clear to the former (and consequently to Göring) that only the immediate suspension of hostilities and the withdrawal of German troops from Polish territory would prevent the outbreak of war. Before the cabinet met, Halifax sent a message to Rome thanking Mussolini for his offer of mediation but regretting that German action made it impossible to move along those lines. At the morning cabinet meeting, ministers dithered. Halifax, expecting that Britain, in contrast to Nazi Germany, would follow the normal procedures of issuing an ultimatum and a declaration of war before embarking on hostilities, was still reluctant to take the final step. There were other waverers; a variety of reasons were found why the note sent to Hitler should not include a time limit though some ministers believed that they had drafted an ultimatum. Some fear of taking the final step to war, given the nightmares about its consequences, may explain these last-minute hesitations. What was to be done in the case of an unfavourable German reply to the British demand that the Germans withdraw their troops from Poland was left undecided. Full mobilization was declared and, as had been decided on the previous day, the long-planned evacuation of children and women from London and other cities began. The military authorities were considerably alarmed at these simultaneous actions but, thanks to the elaborate plans already prepared and to the experiences of the semi-mobilization of September 1938, both the evacuation and the mobilization went smoothly. Parliament was summoned for that evening. Chamberlain made a dignified statement expressing British determination 'to set our teeth and enter upon this struggle' and was supported by the spokesmen for the Labour and Liberal parties. Harold Nicolson noted in his diary that the prime minister was 'evidently in real moral agony and the general feeling in the House is one of deep sympathy for him and of utter misery for ourselves'.[15] It was generally felt both in the Commons and in the country that Britain would stand by her pledge to Poland. As Chamberlain had told the cabinet that morning, 'our

[15] Nigel Nicolson (ed.), *Harold Nicolson: Diaries and Letters*, Vol. I (London, 1966), 417.

consciences were clear and there should be no possible question now where our duty lay'.[16] In the evening, the prime minister invited Winston Churchill to join the cabinet as minister without portfolio. As Chamberlain had long predicted, as war came closer, Churchill's political position grew stronger and with war momentarily expected, he could not be denied his cabinet place whatever the prime minister's personal feelings. The Conservative dissident, publicly identified with opposition to Hitler's Germany, had to be taken in. No public announcement was made and Churchill heard nothing from the prime minister during the course of the next day. Anthony Eden was also approached to join the government but without a cabinet seat, an indication of how his stock had fallen since February 1938, while Churchill's had risen dramatically.

This demonstration of unity and determination was soon disrupted. Outwardly, the French were moving in step with the British. On 1 September their respective ambassadors in Berlin each informed Ribbentrop that his country would, without hesitation, fulfil its obligations to Poland unless the German aggression ceased immediately and German troops were promptly withdrawn from Poland. Bonnet was so involved in the Italian negotiations that he instructed his ambassador to associate himself with Henderson's *démarche*, which as Coulondre ironically remarked, made his task that much easier. At midnight, Bonnet published in *Havas,* the official French news agency, an equivocal but purposely misleading official communiqué indicating that the French had given a positive response to an Italian proposal for resolving Europe's difficulties. Bonnet, in his own mind, was seeking any means to restore peace. He had even inquired of Warsaw whether Poland would attend a conference. Given that Poland had already been attacked and Warsaw had been bombed twice, it is hardly surprising that Beck should find the enquiry irrelevant. The Polish ambassador in Paris was outraged. To add to the confusion, conflicting signals were coming from Paris and from the French embassy in London. The gap between the British and the French positions was soon to be exposed.

On 2 September, German bombers flew where they wished over Poland, attacking civilian as well as military targets. The German forces were soon deep into Polish territory. Still no action was taken in London or Paris. Asked when the French would implement their alliance, Bonnet told the Polish ambassador that if no reply was received from Berlin, then parliament, meeting that afternoon, would vote for an ultimatum with a deadline, which might be twenty-four or forty-eight hours. Bonnet, lying through his teeth, blamed the British for the delay.

[16] Quoted in Parker, *Chamberlain and Appeasement*, 337.

The irate but desperate Polish ambassador personally complained to Daladier who promised to expedite matters. Despite the ambassador's second visit to Bonnet later that day, the protocol to the Franco-Polish alliance, required before the military agreements became valid, was still left unsigned.

Bonnet was playing his own game. He convinced Ciano that Britain as well as France would support a conference. New Italian proposals for an armistice and a conference were sent to Berlin. The Germans stalled, while the British and French ambassadors insisted that nothing could be done until the German troops were withdrawn from Poland. Ciano telephoned Halifax to explain what was happening in Berlin and to say that Hitler wanted until noon the next day, 3 September, to reply. Halifax was ready to give the conference proposal a chance but only if the German armies were evacuated from Poland. Word was rushed to the Commons that Chamberlain would make a statement later that day. The MPs were restive; rumours were circulating about the *Havas* statement and the unsatisfactory interview between the Polish ambassador and Bonnet. The mere announcement of an impending statement from the prime minister stirred widespread fears that Chamberlain and Halifax were contemplating some new form of Munich settlement.

Halifax had a difficult morning. He had already received disturbing news from Paris that the French were dragging their feet and that Bonnet was trembling before the prospect of war. Halifax advised his ambassador to try to infuse some 'courage and determination' into the French foreign minister. Phipps telegraphed that nothing could be done until the French parliament met that afternoon but that the French wanted to present simultaneous declarations of war. Phipps's last message before the Assembly met brought the unwelcome news that the French wanted a forty-eight hour limit on any ultimatum so that mobilization and evacuation could take place before any German action. At 4 p.m., Bonnet called Halifax, reviewing what the British had already heard from Ciano, and claiming that the essential point was not the withdrawal of the German troops but Polish representation at the forthcoming conference. He also raised the issue of the forty-eight hour delay. Halifax replied that these matters would be considered at the hastily called cabinet meeting that afternoon.

The French parliament convened at 3 p.m. on 2 September. Daladier's speech to the National Assembly, modelled on that of French premier Viviani in 1914, was well received. In sharp contrast to the situation in Britain, where the Chamberlain government was compelled to stand firm by the combined pressure from its own and the opposition parties, Daladier was unsure of his political backing. He wanted to show that every effort was being made to prevent the outbreak of war. The funds requested were to enable France to face the obligations of the international situation but he did not ask for a declaration of war. In fact, the word 'war' did not appear in the text of either of the requests for military credits. Debate was cut off in both the Chamber of Deputies and in the Senate so that the opponents of war never had the chance to put their case. The anti-war party was small and the credits were passed unanimously in both houses but Daladier was not confident enough to let opponents be heard. Daladier's presentation left open the possibility of either a conference or war. When the French cabinet met that evening, Daladier agreed that the Italian offer should be followed up. Crucially, however, the premier insisted that no conference could take place until Germany had withdrawn its troops. He maintained this position despite protests from Bonnet and de Monzie who claimed the demand was unrealistic. The premier, along with the majority of his colleagues, was convinced of the wisdom of a forty-eight hour delay. In this, he was influenced, no doubt, by Gamelin, who, haunted by the fear of an all-out German attack while the French mobilized, demanded the respite. Gamelin also seems to have convinced himself that the Germans had completed their fortifications in the West and that there were sufficient German forces to mount a counter-attack.[17] Apart from these military considerations, there were also hopes that the extra time might permit a negotiated settlement. The cabinet, with three dissenters, agreed to accept Bonnet's proposal to use the time delay to explore the Italian offer but only if the Germans evacuated Poland. By this time, the Italians had already withdrawn their mediation offer because of Britain's demand for an immediate German withdrawal and the knowledge that Hitler would not accept the French terms.

While the French were debating the mediation idea and the forty-eight hour delay, Chamberlain and Halifax were still discussing the Italian proposal. At the cabinet meeting on the afternoon of 2 September, Halifax was inclined to agree to a conference on 5 September if Hitler withdrew his troops from Poland. He and the prime minister had 'provisionally' agreed to wait for Hitler's reply to the British warning until noon or even midnight on the next day (Sunday, 3 September). Chamberlain noted the French request for a time delay. The cabinet reacted very differently from its French counterpart; there could be no further delay. All the other ministers insisted that the promises to Poland must be kept and that war should begin at midnight. Chamberlain and

[17] For two (significantly varying) estimates of German and French forces in September 1939, see Ernest R. May, *Strange Victory: Hitler's Conquest of France* (New York, 2000), 476, and Peter Jackson, *France and the Nazi Menace*, 402.

Halifax were authorized to settle the terms of the ultimatum with the French and to prepare the statement to be made in parliament that evening. Cadogan telephoned Bonnet and warned him that if Hitler did not withdraw his troops by midnight, Britain would declare war. If the troops were withdrawn and the Germans and Poles wanted the participation of other powers in their discussions, the British would not object. Bonnet refused to consider war at midnight and explained that the French ministers would decide on the questions of troop withdrawals and timing by 8 or 9 p.m. He insisted that France needed the forty-eight hour time limit to evacuate its civilians and mobilize its forces. He pretended that no Polish representations had been made. A few hours later, with no answer from Paris with regard to the withdrawal of the German troops or the length of time to be included in the ultimatum, and with Chamberlain's statement in the Commons approaching, Phipps, as instructed, told Bonnet that the forty-eight hour delay was unacceptable. Bonnet claimed, again untruthfully, that the Poles would be content with twenty-four hours. Halifax meanwhile spoke to Ciano, insisting that while he hoped the Italians would do their best in Berlin, the British would not favour any conference while German troops remained in Poland. Ciano doubted whether Hitler would accept such terms and decided that nothing more could be done. Mussolini made some further efforts with Hitler but, on 3 September, the Führer delivered his final refusal to parley. He was sure that 'even if we now march down separate paths, Destiny will yet bind us one to the other. If National Socialist Germany were to be destroyed by the Western Democracies, Fascist Italy also would face a hard future. I personally was always aware that the futures of our two regimes were bound up, and I know that you, Duce, are of exactly the same opinion.'[18] In this respect, Hitler proved entirely right.

The Commons had filled to hear the government statement at 6 p.m. on 2 September. It would prove one of the stormiest parliamentary scenes in the twentieth century. When Chamberlain rose to speak, everyone expected that he would say that war would soon commence. Cabinet ministers thought he would announce that war would begin at midnight. Instead he began by saying that there was as yet no answer from Hitler and that the delay might have been caused by consideration of the Italian proposal for a conference. No ultimatum was mentioned and no announcement of war at midnight though he referred to talks with the French over the time limit within which the Germans could withdraw from Poland. There was fury in the House and fear that there

[18] Quoted in H. James Burgwyn, *Italian Foreign Policy in the Interwar Period, 1918–1940*, 206.

was to be another Munich. When the deputy leader of the Opposition, Arthur Greenwood, rose to speak, not only did his own people cheer but there was a second and even greater wave of support from the government benches. 'Speaking for the working class', he began. 'Speak for England', shouted Leo Amery, the ultra-right Tory and arch imperialist.[19] Such was the mood of the House that a division would have brought the government down. When Chamberlain spoke again, very briefly, it was to insist that Britain had to work alongside France and to assure MPs that the French were not weakening. His statement was feeble and ill-received. Greenwood told the prime minister as they left the House that unless there was an ultimatum to Germany before 11 a.m. tomorrow, 'neither you nor I nor anyone else on earth will be able to hold the House of Commons'.[20] Surprisingly, Churchill did not speak, though he let off steam later that night when he called the French embassy and demanded that France act. Chamberlain's cabinet ministers were infuriated by the prime minister's speech. What followed was a unique rebellion of cabinet ministers that left him no alternative but to move without the French. Over a dozen of the protesting ministers demanded that in no circumstances should the expiry of the ultimatum go beyond twelve noon the next day. Chamberlain pleaded the disadvantage of declaring war without France, but ministers insisted that if the French did not agree to the noon deadline, Britain should act alone. Not content with Chamberlain's promise that he and Halifax would do their best with the French, they met again later that evening, refusing to disperse until they knew that an ultimatum, expiring before noon the next day, would be sent to Germany.

The Germans made one final fruitless effort. At 8 p.m. on that eventful evening, Ribbentrop (through an intermediary) invited Sir Horace Wilson to come secretly to Berlin; Wilson was not flattered by the German invitation. The real action was going on elsewhere. Chamberlain had been much shaken by his reception in the Commons. He summoned the seemingly unflappable Halifax, who had gone home from the Lords to change into black tie for dinner at the Savoy, and told him to come to 10 Downing Street. They were joined by Cadogan, Wilson, Simon, and Corbin, the French ambassador, who was told that the events in the House and Britain's naval security made a delayed ultimatum unacceptable. Corbin defended the honour and actions of his government and tried to explain the military reasons for the French delay. Unable to move him, Chamberlain spoke directly with Daladier

[19] The official record of the parliamentary debate does not cite interventions and there are different versions given in contemporary accounts.

[20] Quoted in D. C. Watt, *How War Came*, 90, 580.

and Halifax with Bonnet. The prime minister told Daladier that Britain was unable to wait any longer and that an ultimatum would be presented at 8 a.m. the next morning. Daladier refused to advance the French deadline unless British bombers were immediately sent to France, a request made by Gamelin who knew that it made no strategic sense at all and appears to have been looking for some reason to delay. Halifax warned Bonnet that if France could not act with Britain on the 8 a.m. timetable, Britain would act alone as long as the French government gave an assurance that they would follow suit within twenty-four hours. The unhappy Corbin returned to his embassy, already besieged by newsmen, knowing that the two countries would go to war separately and that it would appear that France was being dragged into war by Britain. At 11.20 p.m., the British ministers were summoned to a cabinet meeting at Downing Street. It was pouring with rain; the decision to send an ultimatum to Germany was taken against a background of thunder and lightning. Henderson would present the British ultimatum at 9 a.m.; it would expire at 11 a.m. that Sunday. Chamberlain was calm, even 'icy-cold', for like Halifax he had felt the lash of the ministers' revolt. He asked whether anyone disagreed with the decision. No one spoke. 'Right, gentlemen', he said. 'This means war.'[21] At this moment there was a clap of thunder and the cabinet room was lit up by 'a blinding flash of lightning'.

IV

At 9 a.m. on 3 September, Henderson, dressed in full ambassadorial uniform, went to Ribbentrop's office where he was met by Paul-Otto Schmidt, the foreign ministry translator, as his chief once again avoided an unwelcome duty. Schmidt brought the ultimatum to the Chancellery where Hitler and Ribbentrop received him. Hitler sat frozen at his desk while Schmidt translated the ultimatum. 'What happens next?', Hitler asked Ribbentrop, who was standing by the window.[22] Ribbentrop replied that an ultimatum from the French would arrive in the next few hours. As Schmidt left through the crowded antechamber, he was mobbed by the anxious members of Hitler's cabinet and other party officials. His announcement of war was greeted by total silence. Ribbentrop was determined to have the last word. After the expiry of the British ultimatum, he summoned Henderson to the Foreign Ministry and presented the German memorandum rejecting the British ultimatum and restating the German case. The two men did not shake hands.

[21] Quoted in Watt, *How War Came*, 588.
[22] Ian Kershaw, *Hitler: 1936–1945: Nemesis*, 223.

In Britain, people stayed close to their radios until a programme offering tips for making meals out of tinned soups was interrupted and listeners told to stand by for 'an important announcement'. At 11.15 a.m., Chamberlain spoke by radio to tell the nation in a resigned and melancholy voice that it was now at war with Germany. As he later told the Commons, 'everything I have worked for, everything that I have hoped for, everything that I have believed in during my public life, has crashed into ruins'.[23] A few minutes later, the sirens went off in London. People dutifully went off to the shelters. The alarm had been set off by a solitary aircraft returning from Le Touquet. All the British Dominions followed the mother country with the exception of Eire, which opted for neutrality. There had been a swing away from the neutralist positions of 1938, though some of the High Commissioners still thought that war might be averted. Differently from 1914, the Dominions were now free to decide the questions of war and peace for themselves. Australia and New Zealand declared war on 3 September without consulting their parliaments; the Canadians summoned their parliament which passed its war declaration on 10 September. The case of South Africa was more difficult. The Germanophile premier, General James Herzog, who wished to remain neutral, found himself outnumbered in the cabinet by only one vote. His deputy, General Smuts, carried the war motion in the South African parliament by a small majority. The governor-general refused Herzog's request for a dissolution of parliament and new elections (which might well have returned a majority for neutrality) and asked Smuts to form a new government. War was declared on 6 September. In India, the viceroy declared war immediately and without consultation with Indian leaders, a move that was much resented and severely criticized in the sub-continent. As the British government always assumed, war in Europe, whether it started in the East or West, was bound to have global ramifications. For the moment, with neither Italy nor Japan as belligerent powers, British intelligence had already reassured the government on this point, as well as information that Spain would take no action against France or Britain, the Chamberlain government had succeeded in two of its major aims though relief was tempered by continuing uncertainty about their future roles.

At midnight on 2/3 September, with his policy in tatters, a resigned Bonnet telegraphed Coulondre to present his *démarche* at midday (three hours after the British) with a time limit of 5 a.m. on Monday, 4 September. After second thoughts, Bonnet shortened the time limit

[23] Watt, *How War Came*, 601–602.

to 5 p.m. on Sunday. Ernst von Weizsäcker was sent to receive Coulondre at noon but a half hour later, Ribbentrop met with the French ambassador. Coulondre presented the French ultimatum and announced that France would go to war because of her obligations towards Poland. 'Ah well!', said Ribbentrop, 'France will be the aggressor.'[24] Coulondre appealed to the verdict of history but refused to engage in debate. He shook hands with Weizsäcker but not with the German foreign minister.

Britain and France were now at war with Germany. In the afternoon of 3 September, four proclamations were read to the German people on the wireless, blaming the British for their policy of encirclement, which had led to the war. It was not the British people who were responsible but the Jewish plutocratic and democratic upper class 'who were trying to destroy Germany'.[25] The new military directives for the conduct of the war issued on 3 September ordered the exercise of the greatest restraint against the West. Offensive operations should be left to the western powers. Only the navy was allowed to take action against Britain. The Germans should not open the air war; the fighting power of the *Luftwaffe* 'must be conserved for the decision against the western Powers after the defeat of Poland.'[26] No German action against either country followed. But as soon as the Polish campaign was over and in response to his fears that the American Neutrality Acts would be repealed, Hitler began to argue for an immediate attack on the West, setting 12 November as the date for the *Wehrmacht*'s assault on the French border. It was not the pleas of his generals, concerned with the condition of their troops, but bad weather that forced delay

Meanwhile the German war against Poland was vigorously pursued. As the Allied planners had agreed months before, nothing was done to assist the Poles who were caught in the middle of their mobilization. No French action was taken to relieve the Poles as had been promised in May. When pressed by the Polish ambassador, Gamelin replied evasively and falsely that the French were engaging the Germans on the ground (apart from a small diversionary tactic) and in the air. The British sent 29 planes to attack German shipping (seven were lost). Other air activities related to the dropping of millions of leaflets over Germany, explaining the causes of the war and asking the German people to end it. The secretary of state for air, defending the decision not to bomb German industrial targets in the Ruhr reminded his critics that the suggested targets were private property. Poland fought alone, courageously and even, given its strategic and massive material inferiority, effectively. The

[24] Duroselle, *La décadence*, 492.
[25] Max Domarus (ed.), *Hitler: Speeches and Proclamations*, Vol. III (London, 1990), 1783.
[26] Ibid., 1789.

Table 18.1. German and Polish Forces in September 1939

	Total men	Armd./ mot. Divs.	In. Divs.	Mtn. Divs.	Cav. Brigs.	Total divisions (brigades)	Armd. vehicles	Artillery pieces	Aircraft	Ships
Germany	1.5m	15	37	1	1	53 (1)	3600	6000	1929	40
Poland	1.3m	1 brig.	37		11	37 (12)	750	4000	900	50

Source: Militärgeschichtliches Forschungsant (ed.), *Germany and the Second World War*, Volume II, ed. Klaus Maier et al. (Oxford, 1991), 101.

outcome of the Polish campaign was never in doubt; defeat was a foregone conclusion and only the speed of the German advance, using its panzer and motorized infantry divisions and aerial supremacy to good effect, took the onlookers, including Stalin, by surprise. On 17 September, the Red Army crossed the Polish frontier.

The invasions were only the beginning of the Polish agony: Poland was to pay heavily and long for its resistance to Hitler, far more than the Czechs who had surrendered without fighting. Like the Czechs and with even more reason, the Poles felt that the western powers had deserted them. Even the meagre supplies of guns, ammunition and planes promised in August and September did not reach Poland until after its defeat.

V

All the efforts made by the British and the French and even the Poles to avoid war had come to nought and in the end, the one leader who had actually wanted war was the one who got his wish, though it was not the war he had wanted nor the one for which Germany was prepared. For Chamberlain and Daladier, as for their electorates, war could only bring the collapse of the hopes of all right thinking men and women. This is the only explanation of their last-minute irresolution and dithering. In the end, there were no powerful and stirring calls to war, merely the expiry of unanswered deadlines. Except in Poland, where the fighting had already begun, there was a muted reaction to the outbreak of war. Europeans over the age of forty had hoped to avoid a second catastrophe in their lifetimes. The lessons of the Great War were not forgotten; its length, costs, and aftermath seared the memories of its survivors and those who followed. The fear of bombing raids and of mechanized warfare added to the nightmares of the past. Historians have abandoned the traditional view that the people of Europe greeted the outbreak of war on 1914 with wild enthusiasm. The pictures of cheering crowds in Europe's capitals give a false impression of mass bellicosity and eagerness to fight. Nevertheless, the contrasts in mood between 1914 and 1939, whether in Berlin, London, or Paris were striking. The romantic vision of war, still alive in 1914, had been permanently tarnished by the experience of its reality. Most adults, regardless of nationality, anticipated that the next conflict would be long and arduous, involving whole populations and widespread destruction. There were some, and not just in Germany, who welcomed the opportunity of winning honour and glory and who revelled in the experience of war. After all, Hitler and Mussolini, the latter with considerably less success, had done much to prepare their countrymen for service to leader, party, and state. Both men saw war as the expression of the best in man and country. Yet even in Germany, the actual outbreak of war created shock and bewilderment among some sections of the population. One looked in vain for cheering crowds. As Hitler made his way from the Reichs Chancellery to the Opera Kroll on 1 September to explain to the Reichstag why Germany was at war, the streets of Berlin were abnormally quiet and the crowds were thin. His speech was a lacklustre affair and the applause less enthusiastic than on less important occasions. Despite the massive propaganda campaign against the Poles, there were few signs of popular enthusiasm for the Polish war and considerable anxiety about its possible escalation. The press had been instructed in July to warn readers that the war of nerves would develop into a serious crisis but to provide assurances that there would be no war. A natural solution would be found, 'in the form of a nervous collapse, which will then make the use of weapons superfluous. The English position is basically the same as in September.'[27] The conclusion of the pact with Stalin reinforced popular hopes that war would be avoided. The mood grew more sombre after 25 August as the visible war preparations began to alarm the population. In Berlin, the huge and sudden call-up of reservists, the cancellation of rail transport for civilian travellers and, above all, the restrictions placed on foodstuffs and the introduction of ration cards caused considerable anxiety. The last revived memories of the rigours of 1917 and the possibility of worse to come.

Professor Gerhard Ritter, the German historian, who stayed in his country throughout the war, denied any trace of 'the so-called "war enthusiasm"'.[28] A number of diarists as well as police reports note that the people appeared 'calm and self-possessed' but also 'stunned', their faces showing 'astonishment' and 'depression'. Explicit comparisons

[27] Quoted from an instruction to the press of 5 July 1939, in Marlis Steinert, *Hitler's War and the Germans*, 42.

[28] G. Ritter, *The German Resistance: Carl Goerdeler's Struggle against Tyranny*, transl. R. T. Clark (London, 1958), 139.

with 1914 were made by all, with common observations and conclusions. William L. Shirer, the American correspondent recorded 'no excitement, no hurrahs, no cheering, no throwing of flowers, no war fever, no war hysteria'. Joining a group in Berlin listening to the announcement of the British declaration of war, he reported 'when it was finished, there was not a murmur'. Later he noted: 'Everybody against the war. People talking openly. How can a country go into a major war with a population so dead against it?'[29] Karl Wahl, the gauleiter of Swabia, travelling around Germany, recalled that 'nothing on the journey reminded me of 1914; no enthusiasm, no joy, no cheering. Wherever you went there was an uncanny quiet, not to say depression.'[30] After listening to Hitler's broadcast, a German soldier, Bernt Engleman, drove into Düsseldorf. 'No crowds had gathered', he later recalled. 'We saw no trace of rejoicing, certainly none of the wild enthusiasm that Germans had shown when war broke out in August 1914. Here and there small groups of people clustered around the newsstands, talking quietly among themselves, depressed and anxious. No one waved to us soldiers or pressed bouquets into our hands... "They don't believe it yet", Pliechelko [his companion] said. "They probably thought everything would turn out all right this time too".'[31] Contemporary diarists stress the fear and anxiety with which the news of the European war was received.[32] Walter... (1889–1964), a teacher and member of the NSDAP wrote: 'And despite all propaganda not the slightest appearance of enthusiasm. Dull, depressed faces everywhere. For we elderly are still under the impression of experiencing the Great War. The danger of air attacks, the economic situation multiply the pressure on the atmosphere of the nation'.[33] Ernest... (1890–1981), Oberpostinspector in Freiburg, who had travelled to the United States and enjoyed using English phrases, wrote on 27 August: 'Since yesterday, mobilization is running! I do not believe in a war—and if it does come to one, then everything will have gone for a burton for half a century... and H. was a great butcher.' W. Horst, born 1924 and apprenticed as a bricklayer, noted in his diary: 'Despite being flooded daily by continuing Nazi propaganda the fact that Germany is starting a war has

[29] William L. Shirer, *Berlin Diary: The Journal of a Foreign Correspondent, 1934–1941* (London, 1943), 154.

[30] Militärgeschichtliches Forschungsamt (ed.), *Germany and the Second World War*, vol. I, ed. Wilhelm Deist (Oxford, 1990), 11.

[31] Bernt Engelmann, *In Hitler's Germany* (London, 1988), 151–152.

[32] All of these extracts are from photostated diaries sent to me by the Tagebucharchiv Emmendingen, an absolute treasure-trove of private diary material. I am very grateful for their assistance. In some instances, surnames have been omitted.

[33] Last names omitted by the archivists.

shaken us deeply. I immediately had to think of the saying of my grandmother... "Remember, the worst thing that can happen in life is war".'[34] Whatever the shock or apathy expressed in these diary extracts, there was no question that the German people would loyally follow Hitler into war. Nineteen-year-old Käte von..., who had just completed her grammar school education, wrote about her fascination with war and with Adolf Hitler. 'From now on he wants to wear the soldier's dress and not take it off until the fighting has come to a victorious ending or not at all. Just like Frederick the Great!!' It may be that this general impression of the German reluctance to go to war is as over simplified as the war enthusiasm of 1914. There were good reasons why Germans might have feared war in 1939, but many, particularly among the young, had been well indoctrinated and probably not only accepted but welcomed war and never considered the possibility of defeat.[35] No opposition was expected, no anti-war demonstrations were anticipated and none took place. Life went on as normal during the next few days. There was no rush out of Berlin and the operas, theatres, and cinemas were open and full. As the news of the military successes in Poland began to arrive, the general anxiety began to dissipate and expressions of support for the war became more common. Rumours of peace began to circulate even before the Polish campaign was over.

In Britain, there was relief mixed with apprehension. There were a few, the 'realists' and 'defeatists', mainly found in upper class circles, as well as some pacifists on both the left and right, who argued that Britain should stand aside. Lord Rothermere, the newspaper proprietor, a long-time admirer of Mussolini and respectful of Hitler, in an unposted letter to Chamberlain dated 2 September, urged the prime minister not to fight. 'Whether victorious or not, Britain will emerge from such a conflict with her social and economic fabric destroyed. That may well mean a revolution of the Left in these islands, which might be more deadly than the war itself... And for what? Not a reconstructed Poland, for that is now a palpable impossibility.'[36] The opponents of war were but a small and politically insignificant part of the population. Though actually taken by surprise by the German attack on Poland, once the Polish campaign began, the overwhelming majority accepted the

[34] Engelmann, *In Hitler's Germany*, 151–152.

[35] See Michael Geyer, 'Restorative Elites, German Society and the Nazi Pursuit of War', in Richard Bessel (ed.), *Fascist Italy and Nazi Germany: Comparisons and Contrasts* (Cambridge, 1996), 156–7, for a nuanced interpretation of this possibility.

[36] N. J. Crowson, *Fleet Street, Press Barons and Politics: The Journals of Collin Brooks, 1932–1940* (London, 1998), 291.

necessity of war. Few thought war would be a heady adventure or come to a quick end, but there were strong feelings that British honour was engaged and that Hitler would have to be beaten. Total calm was the exception, but there was no panic. The left-wing British weekly, *The New Statesman and Nation*, recorded the country's response in an ironic, self-deprecating verse.

> I see the nation's keeping cool
> The public calm is fine
> The crisis can't shake England's nerves
> It's playing hell with mine.[37]

The general impression was one of reserve and individual hopes to conceal any feelings of fear, above all of bombing. Expressions of gloom were accompanied by those of relief that something definite had happened. 'My nerves have completely gone', Tom Harrisson, the founder of Mass Observation, recalled a young woman from Lancashire saying, 'we've been waiting a whole year, not knowing if there'll be a war or not. I want a knock at Hitler.'[38] Guy Chapman, M.C., author of two superb books of war memoirs, wrote in his personal notebook: 'It was a relief. We had waited in suspense too long. We had been shamed and humiliated. We have regained self-respect'.[39] On 1 September, a blackout order came into effect across the country and the evacuation of the children, the old, the blind, and the infirm began. In all, three million people were moved, the greatest internal migration in British history. The barrage balloons floating over London were reassuring; people who had lost their gas masks collected new ones. Many of those with gardens equipped themselves with Anderson shelters, fourteen corrugated iron sheets that could take four to six people. Whitehall had decided that there were to be no mass shelters that would encourage 'shelter mentality'. The movie houses and theatres were closed but were soon reopened. The last days of peace were not a crisis in the psychological sense of the previous September. Apart from the purchasing of extra foods and commodities needed for the blackout, there was no great run on the shops or any signs of mass buying. A year earlier, people had crowded to church; on 3 September 1939, only the usual congregations assembled. The main sign of war fever was a marked increase in

[37] *The New Statesman and Nation*, Vol. XVIII, No. 445, 2 September 1939, last verse of poem entitled 'Nerves'.

[38] Tom Harrisson, *Living Through the Blitz* (London, 1976), 29.

[39] Guy Chapman, notebooks for 1939–1940, in author's possession.

the number of marriages. The absence of panic may have been due to the experiences of Munich or to the long period of anxious waiting. A speaker on the BBC suggested that wireless broadcasts over a long period of persistent international tension had convinced the British people that Hitler was the cause of the crisis and that a war had to be fought against him. While the declaration of war in 1914 had seemed to come 'from the blue like a thunderbolt', the road to war in 1939 had been long and stressful and the wireless had kept the public, 'farmers, cottagers, factory hands, assistant clerks', informed of every turn and twist along the way.[40] Most people, however apprehensive of the anticipated consequences, had few doubts that Britain would prevail. Few shared Chamberlain's misplaced hopes that fighting would not be necessary and that Germany would collapse from within. Nor were there many who were as pessimistic as Alexander Cadogan: 'We shall fight to the last and may win—but I confess I don't see how'.[41] Most of Britain went to war in expectation of victory, but without any expectation that the war would be anything but arduous, complex, and costly.

There could be no joy at war in France, not in a country where 1.3 million Frenchmen had been killed and at least another 300,000 permanently invalided during the Great War. The schools of France were seedbeds of pacifism and anti-military sentiment. France's military leaders, with but few exceptions, wished to put off the fighting as long as possible. The well-informed, highly intelligent, and unflappable Gamelin had to believe that, once the French had mobilized, any German attack against the Maginot Line would result in 'one long cemetery'. Did his extraordinary composure and imperturbability disguise a fundamental uneasiness about the immediate situation? In France, as well as in Britain and Germany, the Munich crisis took the emotional edge off the public reaction in August. Resignation had replaced alarm but there could be little enthusiasm about what had to be. The common and popular phrase: '*il faut en finir*' said it all. The French entered the war calmly. There was a general sang-froid but no patriotic songs or grandiloquent speeches, no demonstrations and no flowers. The prefect of Rhone reported that it was 'something between resolution and resignation'.[42] From all over France came reports that morale was excellent and the mood calm. If there was a sense of fatality, there was also a belief that the war was necessary. There were very few reports during the last weeks of

[40] Talk reproduced in *The New York Times*, Magazine section, 10 September 1939.
[41] Dilks (ed.), *The Diaries of Alexander Cadogan*, 214 (6 September 1939).
[42] Quoted in Jean-Louis Crémieux-Brilhac, *Les Français de L'an 40*, Vol. I (Paris, 1990), 57. This is just one of many reports quoted by Crémieux-Brilhac.

August or first weeks of September of defeatist sentiment or anti-war protests. The Communists in the Chamber on 2 September had applauded Daladier and Herriot and voted for the military credits. Daladier had moved swiftly: the Communist journals were seized and publications stopped on 25–26 August. Both the evacuation from Paris and the mobilization went smoothly. It was only after reading the afternoon papers on 1 September that Parisians began to leave, by car and train, in large numbers. Georges Sadoul, a well-known post-war historian of the cinema, was in Paris. It was the last night before his call-up. 'Around the column of the Bastille turned a crowd of cars of all kind, their headlights off, mattresses on their roofs, which were fleeing from the threatened city.'[43] Even this spontaneous evacuation, following the sixth official evacuation request, showed fewer signs of the panic that had characterized the exodus of the previous September. It was more or less over by 6 September and the remainder of the Paris population settled down to the war. The mobilization went according to plan and was far more efficiently carried out that in 1938. The reservists assembled quietly; the prevailing mood appears to have been confident determination mixed with 'exasperated resignation'.

L'Illustration underlined the contrast between the start of the two wars when it provided a picture of the reservists leaving from the Gare de l'Est with a commemorative portrait hanging overhead of the departures of August 1914. William Bullitt, the American ambassador, the German military attaché, and a variety of foreign correspondents each commented on the extraordinary sense of calm. Janet Flanner, writing in the *The New Yorker*, reported that there were 'no flags, flowers, or shrill shouts of "Vive la patrie!"'. The men departing seemed 'intelligent, not emotional': 'If it's got to come, let's stop living in this grotesque suspense and get it over with once and for all.'[44] Such accounts, of course, say nothing of those on the right and left who were totally out of sympathy with the government, or of the many factory workers who considered Daladier their enemy. Few of the latter opposed the war. There were some in political and intellectual circles who were defeatists. And many more who, like the French writer, Simone de Beauvoir, in private letters and in personal exchanges, feared the disasters that would arise out of a new war and the destruction of the world as they knew it. France might not survive a second blood-letting. Even that long-time opponent of appeasement, Geneviève Tabouis, the foreign editor of *L'Oeuvre*, warned that 'tomorrow, all this will have disappeared, our beloved

[43] Georges Sadoul, *Journal de Guerre (2 septembre 1939–20 juillet 1940)* (Paris, 1977), 15.

[44] Quoted in Robert J. Young, *France and the Origins of the Second World War* (Basingstoke, 1996), 128.

Paris will exist no longer'.[45] But warnings of defeat and destruction were not plastered on the walls of Paris. As in Britain, though people went to war reluctantly, most thought France would emerge victorious. In late August and early September, there were few forebodings of national defeat.

The Poles were the only ones actually fighting the Germans in September 1939. In that country, too, some immediately drew parallels with the earlier European war. The Polish author, Zofia Nałkowska, wrote 'Once again [one is] experiencing something that will later seem inconceivable. I do not fear nor am I surprised, just sad. Something enormous is happening once again—twenty-five years later. Quick rearrangement.'[46] Those commanding the Polish troops near the East Prussian border had few illusions. Lt. General W. Anders, commander of the Novogrodek Cavalry Brigade in 1939, wrote in his autobiography: 'To me, as to most other soldiers, it was clear as I waited there, not far from the battlefield of Grunwald, where in 1410 Poland achieved her brilliant victory over the Teutonic Knights, that the military position of Poland in the coming war would be very difficult; if not hopeless. With only cavalry and light armour to face the German forces pouring over the frontier, there was only one outcome possible.' According to Anders: 'Our defences were flimsy, for, after weeks of unaccountable vacillation, it was only in August that we had been permitted to dig in and to erect barbed-wire entanglements. Even the general mobilization, ordered and announced on August 28, only three days before the outbreak of war, had suddenly been cancelled . . . due to the *démarche* made by the British, American and French Ambassadors.' Anders noted that this was a different kind of war. Journeying through burning villages to take up his command with an infantry division already in retreat 'Once I saw a group of small children being led by their teacher to the shelter of the woods. Suddenly there was the roar of an aeroplane. The pilot circled round, descending to a height of 50 metres. As he dropped his bombs and fired his machine-guns, the children scattered like sparrows. The aeroplane disappeared as quick as it had come, but on the field some crumpled and lifeless bundles of bright clothing remained.'[47] Younger Poles were less prescient. Władysław Bartoszewski, a politician and professor of history (later twice foreign

[45] Quoted in Crémieux-Brilhac, *Les Français*, 55.

[46] Zofia Nałkowska, *Dzienniki v 1939–1944: Opracowanie wstęp i komentarz Hannah Kirchner* (Warsaw, 1996), 29. References to Polish materials provided by Professor Norman Davies and Professor Ola Kubinski.

[47] Lt. General W. Anders, *An Army in Exile* (London, 1949), 1–3. Anders was later C-in-C of the Polish forces in the USSR and then Commander, Second Polish Corps in Italy.

minister of Poland), was a 17-year-old high school student at the outbreak of war. 'The enthusiasm of the nation confirmed the state leaders in the opinion that by accepting the war they were doing the right thing... We thought that the war would be won quickly. They threaten us, shout, provoke but if they dare attack, they will certainly lose. The frame of mind was optimistic, even more so, because no-one foresaw the possibility of an alliance between the Germans and the USSR. If it comes to war, we will win it. Why? Among other reasons, because we are right.'[48] Aleksandra Piłsudska, the widow of Jozef Piłsudski, confirms the feverish haste and unfinished preparations for the defence of Warsaw. 'The optimism of the last few months', she wrote, 'gave way to determination'.[49] Some Poles felt betrayed. Stanisław Grabski, an economist, politician, and professor of law at Lvov University in 1939, recalls: 'I went back to Lvov from Warsaw with the worst presentiments. For there, I had learned that we completely lacked modern heavy tanks... that we possessed barely a few dozen aeroplanes capable of standing up to the German aeroplanes, that we lacked even sufficient numbers of rifles for mobilizing all of the trained year-groups of infantry. But all those shortages were scrupulously hidden from public opinion. They attempted to shout down anyone who mentioned them. And Minister Beck affirmed that there would be no war; and believing his affirmation, instead of hastily buying modern fighting equipment for the gold which we possessed... we sold the apparently magnificent anti-tank armaments produced by us in order to increase our supply of gold. Unceasingly the question bothered me: stupidity or treason?'[50] Jarosław Iwaszkiewicz, one of the major Polish writers of his time, felt similarly downbeat. 'Yesterday, the first day of the war demoralized me completely', he wrote on 2 September, 'Podkowa [a suburban town near Iwaszkiewicz's village] was bombed while the girls [his daughters] were out mushroom picking and we could not call them back home. But apart from fearing for myself and them, [I have] a feeling of terrible disgust, despair and disillusionment. The beastliness of our enemy and the devastation of the country, which has just begun to rebuild itself.'[51] The Poles, like so many elsewhere, had hoped, until the very eve of war, that they would escape the hurricane. No one was prepared for surrender to Hitler's demands but there remained many unanswered questions. It would be fifty years before Poland came out of the dark.

[48] Władysław Bartoszewski, *Wywiad rzeka* (Warsaw, 2006), 30.

[49] Aleksandra Piłsudska, *Wspomnienia* (Warsaw, 1989), 14.

[50] Stanisław Grabski, *Pamietniki*, Vol. II (Warsaw, 1989), 302–303.

[51] Jarosław Iwaszkiewicz, *Dzienniki 1911–1955* (Warsaw, 2007), 141.

Table 18.2 German, Polish, and Soviet Losses in September 1939

	Polish German	Polish Soviet	German	Soviet	Polish
Killed	70,000	50,000	11,000	700	
Wounded	133,000		30,000	1,900	
Missing			3,400		
Prisoners	700,000	30,000			
Escaped abroad					150,000
Armoured vehicles	700		300		
Guns			370		
Other vehicles			5,000		
Aircraft	330		560		

Source: Militärgeschichtliches Forschungsamt (ed.), *Germany and the Second World War*, Vol. II (Oxford, 1991), 124.

VI

This was Adolf Hitler's war. He despatched his soldiers knowing that he would have to fight Britain and France as well as Poland. This was war by premeditation and not by accident. Hitler had long considered the possibility that he might have to fight the western powers, and during 1938 his accelerated armament preparations were directed to preparing for this conflict. He knew that Germany would not be ready for this hegemonic struggle, whose difficulty he never underestimated, before 1942 or 1943 but his decision to act would depend on outside circumstances. He had told his military chiefs that the war against Poland would be 'a precautionary complement' to his main objective, the war against the Allied powers. On 23 May he had explained that if Poland could not be isolated, it would be necessary to 'fall upon the West and finish off Poland at the same time' but later spoke of a long war against Britain, a 'life and death struggle for hegemony that would take place after the Polish campaign'.[52]

After the order on 3 April 1939 to prepare for the military campaign in Poland, everything was done to find out whether Britain (and France) would stand by their guarantees to Poland when she was attacked. A mass of intelligence was siphoned through the bureaucratic struggles and rivalry between Ribbentrop and Göring. More important was Hitler's own views of the 'umbrella men', and 'little worms' he had met at Munich. There was, too, his belief that the British Empire was on the wane in the Far East, in the Mohammedan world, and in the Mediterranean. He assured his commanders in chief on 22 August that Britain and France had undertaken

[52] *DGFP*, Ser. D. Vol. VI, pp. 224–225.

obligations that neither could fulfil. The British had not even assisted the Poles to rearm. While assuming that the western powers would not intervene, Hitler sought through diplomatic means to avoid their action. He backed Ribbentrop's efforts to secure a tripartite military alliance with Italy and Japan. When it became clear that the Japanese would not join and that the Italians would not be ready to fight until 1943, he picked up the Soviet card which had been on his table since May. Hitler had watched the western talks with the Russians; at first, he did not think they would succeed. With the approaching 1 September deadline in sight and knowing the Moscow talks were stalled, Hitler pressed his suit. Given his obsessive and enduring hatred of 'Judeo-Bolshevism' and the home reaction to such a *volte-face,* it could not have been an easy decision to seek an agreement with Stalin. The stakes were high. Such a pact would deter the western Allies from supporting Poland. If deterrence failed, Germany would be saved from a two-front war and would gain access to critical war materials such as oil, grain, manganese, and rubber. 'With this I have knocked the weapons out of the hands of these gentlemen', Hitler boasted. 'Poland has been manoeuvred into the position that we need for military success . . . Tremendous revolution in the whole European political situation.'[53]

General Halder and other members of the German High Command had considered the possibility of western intervention and a French offensive. They wrongly assumed that the French would not mobilize before the eve of the war but predicted that France would be able to launch an offensive two weeks after mobilization and would enjoy a large measure of superiority in men, tanks, guns, and aircraft if they attacked the Siegfried Line. Halder does not seem to have been unduly troubled by this state of affairs. Anticipating that the Polish campaign would take only two weeks, he and his colleagues judged that the French would have only a very brief period in which to break through the German lines and exploit their advantage before the German troops could be moved from the east to the west.[54] General Halder appears to have assumed that the French offensive could be stopped. In fact, the French exaggerated the strength and number of the German divisions' defending the Siegfried Line and, in any case, General Gamelin had no intention of carrying out such an attack at the start of the war. Hitler had plans only for the war with Poland; he had no strategy for fighting the western powers.

[53] Quoted in Richard Overy, 'Strategic Intelligence and the Outbreak of the Second World War', *War in History*, 5: 4 (1996), 476.

[54] Alan Alexandroff and Richard Rosecrance, 'Deterrence in 1939', *World Politics*, 29 (1977), 415–416.

Hitler's efforts at deterrence failed. On the 25th, the Anglo–Polish treaty was signed in London and Hitler was informed that Mussolini would not enter the war. The order to begin the Polish operation on the 26th was cancelled. Hitler had some additional days to bring further pressure on the Allied coalition. It was clear on the next day that he would go to war regardless of what Britain or France might do. A number of explanations have been offered to explain why he did not pull back as he had in 1938; for Germany was not ready to fight the western powers. It is highly possible that, after the Munich retreat which he so regretted, he was not going to step back again. Intent on war, he would go ahead regardless of the costs. It may be, as Adam Tooze has so impressively argued, that he judged there was nothing to be gained by waiting.[55] Hitler's efforts to develop a wartime programme of preparation for war with the western powers had failed. The German armament situation in the summer of 1939 was squeezed by the perennial balance of payments problems at a time when all the other Great Powers had embarked on major rearmament programmes. Hitler had been warned by his financial and military advisers that Germany, faced with Britain and France, backed by the British Empire and the United States, could not win a war of attrition and that the gap between their power positions would increase. As he had told his military leaders at Berchtesgaden on 22 August, the economic pressures were such that Germany could 'only hold out for a few more years'. It was better to move before its enemies had fully rearmed. The Soviet pact provided a window of opportunity. This temporary marriage of convenience had altered the strategic balance of power in Germany's direction. Hitler would have an accomplice and not an enemy in the East and could avoid some of the consequences of the British blockade. Whether, as Adam Tooze argues, it was Hitler's fear of the influence of World Jewry personified by President Roosevelt that provided the final push to war is open to argument. There is no question of Hitler's assumptions about the extent of Jewish power but the case for his immediate fears of Jew-led America remains unproven. In the end, we just do not know what drove Hitler to take what could only be a massive gamble. He knew that time was not on Germany's side.

Domestic pressures did not force Hitler to go to war. There was no political or economic crisis in Germany in the summer of 1939. People grumbled and complained as consumer goods disappeared. Some foodstuffs were in short supply and, with no new construction permitted, there was an acute shortage of housing. Workers disliked and even protested against new measures of reallocation and tighter labour regu-

[55] Tooze, *The Wages of Destruction*, 662–664.

lations but these complaints did not take the form of political dissent. Whatever might be the daily difficulties and the boredom of constant rallies and exhortations, the Germans took pride in the accomplishments of the Reich, its technological wonders, and its new standing in Europe and the world, which were attributed to Hitler's leadership. It was not just a question of education, propaganda, and militarization. Whatever the fears of bombing and the deprivations and costs of war, the bonds between the Führer and his people were strong and never threatened. British and French intelligence had got the story wrong.

Few in Britain at the start of the summer expected to be at war with Germany at its end. The dramatic change in British policy in the winter and spring of 1939 heralded the abandonment of appeasement in favour of a more active policy of deterrence. The moves towards France strengthened Britain's new continental strategies. Hitler's march into Prague destroyed the moral case for concessions to Germany. The speedy and ill-considered guarantees to Poland and Romania (due to France), was an admission that the previous policies had failed. In so far as appeasement had been a way of winning time for rearmament, that time had run out. Britain was already tooling up for war. The guarantees to Poland and Romania were radical steps, too radical for some, given that Germany had not yet posed a threat to either. They were not followed up, however, by the only move that would have given them substance in the absence of any Allied military back-up. As Hitler knew from his intelligence sources, the western powers had not really built a 'peace front' against aggression. By guaranteeing Poland, Britain had strengthened Beck's negotiating hand and made it more difficult to negotiate an agreement with Moscow. In an either/or situation, Poland or the Soviet Union, the British opted for the former, instinctively resistant to the idea of lining up with the Soviet Union.

By May, the Foreign Office and the chiefs of staff had been converted to the idea of a Soviet alliance. The reasons were both positive and negative: only the Soviet Union could provide the material support for Poland that would make an eastern front militarily viable while a Nazi–Soviet agreement could spell strategic disaster. The British, prodded by the French, who had gone beyond thinking of a deterrent and had to face the prospect of war, as well as rumours of a Nazi–Soviet pact, were forced to accept the need for Soviet military support for Poland. The military talks stalled; the Poles would not consider the entry of Soviet troops into Poland, and the last-minute efforts to force Beck's hand did not convince the Soviet negotiators. Given that the Allied powers had no plans for an offensive in the west, they had little to offer that could match Hitler's cards. The Nazi–Soviet pact ruled out an eastern front. Those who still thought war could be avoided could only use the threat of war to force Hitler to negotiate. Neither the British nor the French had a short-term strategy to deal with the German decision for war.

Almost to the very end, Chamberlain and Halifax struggled to keep open the possibility that Hitler might relent. During the spring and summer months, opposition groups, whether in the Conservative, Liberal, or Labour parties had come to view Nazi Germany as a repellent and dangerous regime with which it was impossible to deal. This view of Germany dwarfed even the deep-seated dislike of Soviet Communism, resulting in the massive support for an alliance with the Soviet Union across party lines and in the country at large. There were no political alliances between the different opposition groups but they shared the assumption that Germany would have to be resisted regardless of the cost. Chamberlain had recognized the strength of this feeling and had given way, particularly with regard to the Soviet alliance though he never accepted its necessity. It may well be that even in August, unlike most back-benchers, he still did not regard Germany as an implacable enemy that had to be fought and defeated. This explains the confused sequence of events during the last days of peace. It would have been difficult, if not impossible, for either Chamberlain or Halifax to have considered any step that would have qualified British support for Poland. There were fears, however unjustified, that there might be a second Munich. In the end, most unusually, public feeling as expressed in parliament, hastened the declaration of war.

There are many more questions about the support of the Soviet alliance and '*une politique de fermeté*' in France than in Britain. Right through the summer months, sections of the right remained lukewarm about the pact with Moscow though few were forthright in their condemnations of the negotiations.[56] While the majority may have accepted the policy of firmness, some recoiled from the idea of war should the policy fail. There were undoubtedly defeatists. France's internal weaknesses and its political and ideological divisions did not encourage optimism. In the army (Colonels Gauché and Coulson) and in the *Quai d'Orsay* (Alexis Léger), leading figures expressed strong doubts about the possibility of victory. Still a subject that arouses debate, it seems highly probable that it was mainly on the left that politicians and their supporters viewed the coming war in ideological, anti-Nazi terms. The announcement of the Nazi–Soviet pact had a greater impact on French than on British opinion. The right immediately demanded measures against the PCF and the government responded, even before the Communist party had announced its official position. The collapse of hopes for an eastern front was a harsh strategic blow. Though the

[56] See the arguments in Crémieux-Brilhac, *Les Français*, 65–67; Talbot Imlay, *Facing the Second World War*, 164–166.

French military chiefs refused to back Bonnet's call for the abandonment of the Poles at the meeting on 23 August, they had invested heavily in securing Soviet support for Poland. Most spoke with more confidence about France's position than they felt. The cabinet remained divided as Bonnet tried to avoid war through Italian intervention. If these arguments are accepted, there appear to have been good reasons for Daladier's careful handling of the war credit issue in the Chamber of Deputies on 2 September. The French leaders went to war because they felt they had very little choice. Few believed that Hitler would stop with Poland. With a German victory in the east, France's strategic situation could only deteriorate further. With the British alliance in place, the French would not have to fight alone and could anticipate the possibilities of a long-war strategy. The only alternative to war was to accept France's relegation from the ranks of the Great Powers. Few would accept such a voluntary abdication.

Four countries were at war. Hitler's war against Poland had been expanded at his choice to a war involving Britain and France. Stalin would seize his part of the booty but then concentrate on the preparations for some future conflict. In fact, Poland fought alone and the British and French waited as Hitler considered his next moves. It was a very different start to the war that began in 1914 and whose memory was to cast a long shadow over Europe for the next twenty years. Any analysis of the strategic situation in the summer of 1939 might well have suggested that neither side should have gone to war. Hitler could not mount a successful offensive against France and Britain and had no plans to do so. He knew that Germany could not win a war of attrition. The French and British could not have defeated Germany in a short war and never entertained the possibility. There were doubts, in both London and Paris, about their ability to win the anticipated war of attrition without a considerable American engagement. Yet the countries went to war. It may be that Hitler believed that there was nothing to be gained and much to be lost by waiting. For the Allied governments, the future strategic balance appeared no better than in September 1938 and might be worse. Such strategic considerations, while hardly irrelevant, were only part of the story.

War had long been on Hitler's agenda; vision, obsession and calculation led him to take what he knew was a gamble. One can only guess what impulse, what trait of character, what fears and unwillingness to accept a second retreat led him to initiate his premature war. The British and French decisions to fight arose not just from their profound distrust of Hitler which had grown with each month after Munich. It was taken because the situation that had long been feared, German domination of the European continent, now became a reality. Neither country was willing to live alongside a triumphant Nazi Germany. The line had been drawn and was crossed. For France, the question was one of survival as a great power; most men and women believed that their country was strong enough to avoid that fate. In the eyes of the public, Britain was a great power and had to act as one. It was, as Hitler had so often insisted, a matter of will rather than a careful weighing of the military and economic balances. Some could not see how the war would be won. They placed their hopes on the French army, on Britain's capacity to rearm and the support of the Empire. Chamberlain hoped that the German people would see the folly of Hitler's decision and turn against their 'half-mad' leader. Others trusted that the Americans would provide the backing that would make the difference between victory and defeat. Most did not think in terms of balances; they just assumed that Britain and its empire would prevail. It was fortunate for many of us that it was this assumption of victory and not its calculation that determined the choice for war.

CONCLUSION

I

These many pages analysing the behaviour of the inter-war statesmen must, if they are to have any value, offer light on why a catastrophic war was followed just over twenty years later with another even more destructive conflict that reshaped the patterns of international politics still more dramatically and in a form that lasted for almost fifty years. One must start by again stressing how deeply and irrevocably the Great War itself altered the map of Europe and the bases of national and international life. It was a catalyst for changes that dated back well before 1914; the years of fighting introduced new elements of thought and practice that speeded up the dissolution of the pre-war structures. This involved far more than the end of four empires and the creation of more new states than at any time since the Peace of Westphalia, more even than the extension of inter-state politics to include non-European players. It encouraged the development of new ideas and instruments of government and of new technologies that would change not only warfare but peacetime existence. It engaged, physically moved, and even empowered millions of men and women on an unparalleled scale. Some of the changes and developments lasted despite victory or defeat and the peace treaties that ended the war. Some of the causes of the Great War were not addressed by the peacemakers; others were handled inadequately and remained unresolved. Prominent among them was the presence in the middle of Europe of a country with enormous potential power but with a territorial and resource base that failed to fulfil all of its ambitions. Many Germans did not accept the reality of defeat and the Armistice had bequeathed the peacemakers a perhaps insoluble strategic problem by leaving Germany basically intact. For other countries, particularly for France, the length and nature of the conflict altered the very concept of war, its glamorous image shattered forever. The destructiveness of 1914–1918 permeated every level of society and the unacceptable casualty lists of the Western Front lay behind the efforts of the former Allied governments to avoid another war even at considerable cost. For the next twenty years, that human price provided the backdrop for the activities of most, though not all, of Europe's leaders. Few though could have foreseen in 1919 the descent into barbarism that was to come.

The outbreak of war in 1939 seemed to give a terrible retrospective weight to Marshal Foch's grim prophecy of 1919 about the Treaty of Versailles: 'This is not peace. It is an armistice for twenty years'. Yet, as this account of the inter-war years has sought to show, it was not the peace treaty that caused the Second World War. The Versailles regime did not achieve its main purpose, which was to create an international structure that would keep the peace. But Hitler neither came to power in 1933 nor did he wage war in 1939 because of the peace of 1919. It is true that there were many connections between the two wars, but it was a twisted road that led from one to the other. One of the key elements of this two-volume account, compensation perhaps for its great length, is that it treats Europe's history during each of the two inter-war decades as equally meaningful. It approaches the 1930s neither as a clean slate nor exclusively in 'pre-war' terms. The conflict that began in 1939 was very much Hitler's war, but the context in which it arose and the specific choices that brought Europe to its new cataclysm make sense only if one appreciates that the framework of European international relations had already been established in the 'post-war' decade of the 1920s. While a new ideological chasm would open during the 1930s, its contours were shaped by the existing backdrop.

The Great War cast its shadow over both interwar decades. Yet the two were different in both the spirit and objectives of the main protagonists. The men and women of the 1920s were trying to reconstruct a shattered world, some looking back and others forward, as they sought to re-establish or create anew the basic structures of national and international life. Domestic and international reconstruction went on simultaneously, with the latter often the victim of national pressures. The victor powers were in the ascendant in post-war Europe and their leaders sought to maintain their positions. But the peace settlements were open-ended, the war was too close for gaping wounds to heal and there were too few major players in Europe—in fact, only three, Britain, France and Germany—to create a new balance of power or to sustain the full burden of political stabilization. Many of the sources of tension between France and Germany could not be resolved and Britain proved either unwilling or unable to balance the system alone, though its power and influence was still considerable. Yet, by mid-decade, some progress had been made and there were hopes that systemic change could be managed without recourse to outright conflict. Despite their differences, Aristide Briand, Austen Chamberlain, and Gustav Stresemann shared common values and similar assumptions about the workings of the international regime. At the very least, they had a common interest in preserving existing 'liberal democratic' governments at home and the reconstructed global fabric abroad. Notwithstanding the continuing struggle for power within Europe, none of the three European leaders wanted to destroy the existing rules and conventions that made peaceful co-existence possible and all were acutely aware of the high costs of diplomatic failure. Each had some reasons for optimism. Few of the adjustments made to encourage peaceful change had been at Britain's expense and, despite the American challenge, it still had the world's largest navy and remained a major global investor and trader. The French failed to prevent a readjustment of the Versailles system in Germany's favour but France still possessed a substantial military advantage over its potentially more powerful neighbour and enjoyed a period of economic growth. The Weimar government, though battered, was still in place at the time of Stresemann's premature death in 1929; both the parliamentary regime and the Locarno structure owed much to his efforts.

Other powers and leaders, less content with the status quo on the continent, need not have undone the nascent Locarno consensus. For the most part, the revisionist states in Eastern Europe during the 1920s were too weak militarily and too absorbed in their domestic difficulties to challenge the peace settlements. The beneficiary states were able to secure Great Power protection, mainly from France, to safeguard their gains. Poland and Czechoslovakia suffered from the weakening of French support after Locarno and their own failure to work together but they were not directly challenged during the decade either by Germany or the Soviet Union (after the Russo–Polish war of 1920). The rumblings in south-eastern Europe did not lead either to war or to further territorial adjustments. Nor, however, were there any signs of increasing economic and political cooperation. Mussolini harboured revisionist ambitions in the Adriatic and in Africa, but Italy remained the 'least of the Great Powers' and, though successful at home, neither he nor his country had the resources to give substance to his dreams. The Duce's ambitions could be accommodated, or at least contained, within the reconstructed European order, particularly as he vacillated between wanting to preserve the status quo in central Europe and extending Italian power into the Balkans.

The one major exception among the Great Powers was the Soviet Union and, even here, *realpolitik* dictated a temporary retreat from revolutionary tactics if not from revolutionary goals. Most European governments viewed Bolshevism as an alien, dangerous, and destructive creed. The actions of the Comintern and domestic Communist parties were closely monitored and, in the case of the latter, sometimes outlawed. The Soviet Union was a pariah state even when attempts were made, as in the case of Weimar Germany, to use Moscow as a bargaining counter in the European game. The other peripheral Great Power, the United States, not only shared the ideological assumptions of the democratic liberal states but was also a major exponent of liberal capitalism. Through most of the post-war decade, it was courted by the European powers, particularly by Germany, for its financial wealth and as the best source for loans and investments. American financial and commercial power proved a mixed blessing: American capital broke the reparations log-jam and made the 1925 Locarno settlement possible but the private and unregulated flow of investment funds into Europe, the flood of American exports, its high and rising tariffs, and demands for war-debt payments acted as destabilizers on the European economy. The United States, meanwhile, remained aloof from Europe's security problems; the retreat from Wilsonian internationalism did not preclude a role in the disarmament process but, except in the Far East, there was no offer to participate in any kind of security system. While the Americans posed no threat to the European political equilibrium, they provided little assistance for its maintenance or advancement.

Admittedly, the 'Wilsonian moment' was a brief one. The dreams of 'self-determination', whether for the minorities in the newly created states of Eastern Europe or for those in the expanded European empires, were left unfulfilled as the dominant nationalities and the imperial powers retained or consolidated their control. The early moves towards creating democratic and representative governments in Eastern Europe stalled and regional alignments were plagued not only by nationalist sentiments but by economic competition. Either through the use of force or the offer of concessions, Europe's colonial powers were able to maintain their empires. The Commonwealth emerged as a symbol of British pragmatism.

The tremors elsewhere were real and success came at a price. The undercurrents set in motion by the war and President Wilson's rhetoric did not disappear but they remained below the surface of international politics. The most prominent new experiment in internationalism fell similarly short of fulfilling the hopes invested in it. The League of Nations acted as an adjunct to the traditional means of settling disputes but failed to substitute 'collective security' for the discredited balance of power mechanism. It successfully handled the small change of diplomacy and was capable of addressing disputes between countries that did not touch on Great Power interests, though even there the results were mixed. But its dependency upon the dominant European states and their willingness to exercise military and political power on its behalf left the

League isolated and ultimately moribund as the internationalist impulse steadily diminished amidst the conflicting pulls between national and international needs. Public pressure for disarmament may have remained strong in Britain and France, and in most of the smaller countries. With the opening of the World Disarmament Conference in 1932 public enthusiasm for the disarmament cause reached a new peak, yet even here the realities of national security and the uncertainties of international politics made progress impossible and resulted only in another prominent failure for internationalism. Among the revisionist states, secret or overt rearmament had already begun and during the mid 1930s it once again appeared near the top of the international agenda.

If the Great War provided a shock and transforming impulse in all the states of Europe, both in terms of national and international politics, the Great Depression was a mighty aftershock, the effects of which persisted well into the late 1930s. For the war and its aftermath had destroyed the traditional patterns of international finance and trade producing dislocations and maladjustments that made the world economic structure particularly vulnerable to crises and less able to contain them when they occurred and spread. The destruction of the gold standard and the rise of the United States as the world's chief creditor and lender transformed the financial scene. Governments and bankers alike believed that only a return to gold and the resurrection of an idealized gold standard would bring stability and prosperity. While the United States returned to gold in 1919, augmenting its large gold reserve, other nations struggled to stabilize their currencies, initiating a long, difficult, and staggered process of adjustment before achieving this goal. The gold exchange system, developed after 1923 to partly replace the shattered pre-1914 system, placed a heavy burden on supposedly independent central banks and on governments expected to adjust their domestic economies to prop up the foreign exchanges, the latter almost an impossibility given their enlarged electorates and the pressures for social welfare programmes. The replacement of London with two, and later, three, gold centres (New York, London, and then Paris) encouraged the switching of funds and led to greater volatility in the system. The latter brought neither the accommodation nor the cooperation needed for success; the fixed exchange rates of the system deepened the downturn in the economic cycle after it began.

The war and peace vastly increased the levels of international indebtedness. War debts and reparations acted as political and financial destabilizers and the American refusal to link the two further exacerbated problems of payment which became the centre of domestic distributional and inter-state conflicts. The Americans were, by far, the chief international lenders, followed by Britain and France. Unlike Britain in the pre-war period, even apart from its protective tariff, due to an agricultural surplus, an advanced technological/industrial base and modern managerial skills, the United States offered only a limited market to its foreign exporters and debtors. Since much of the American capital outflow, particularly to Germany, was private, it was unregulated, adding yet another element of instability to the financial system. The war expanded the American role as a major exporter of industrial goods as well as agricultural products, creating competitive conditions for European producers both in continental and overseas markets. The poor and mainly agricultural Eastern European countries could not compete with American and Canadian grain exports. Almost all, except Czechoslovakia, as a result of both political and economic circumstances, became heavily dependent on foreign investment and foreign loans, usually at high interest rates. Some capital was used to pay interest but much was used for non-productive purposes. Given the break-up of the former empires, nationalist sentiments, and new tariff walls, many of these states no longer traded with their neighbours but sought markets further afield. Both with regard to loans and markets, these states were dangerously exposed to international currents over which they had no control.

As a result of the war, too, Europe suffered a severe check in economic growth (perhaps as much as by eight years) though some states were more adversely affected than others. The United States and Japan, as well as countries on the periphery of the international economy, were the chief beneficiaries. The distortion of traditional production and trading links hastened shifts that had begun before 1914. Britain, in particular, was faced with the loss of some traditional markets and suffered from war-induced excess capacity. Whether the causes of the depression and the banking and finance crisis of 1931 were systemic or otherwise, the war and peace created hastened changes that made the whole economic system far more fragile and unstable while the return to gold added a further degree of inflexibility that made adjustment difficult. The consequences of this unprecedented depression were worldwide. They accelerated the collapse of those admittedly fragile political, economic, financial, and diplomatic global structures that had been put in place to encourage the strengthening of the international system. It made the 'have-not' states more aggressive and the responses of the 'have' states more cautious. It placed a heavy, and in some countries insupportable burden on existing governments and opened the way to strengthened or new authoritarian regimes: it was not only in Germany that democracy gave way to dictatorship. The depression and the responses to it nourished the ideological divisions of the 1930s, weakening the possibilities for peaceful adjustment and compromise. Anti-liberal forces were strengthened as the radical right, and right-wing movements, grew in size and influence at the expense of the centre and left. The depression and unemployment provided Hitler with the opportunity to create a national mass party at the expense of the moderate forces within the Weimar Republic. The Communists, too, gained in power within Germany but their mistaken tactics against the Social Democrats helped to ensure Nazi successes. The Soviet Union, relatively unaffected by the depression, attracted new supporters but, particularly in Eastern Europe, peasants looked to the radical right rather than to Moscow. The effects of unemployment and extreme rural distress encouraged this right-wing orientation; the radical right-wing movements offered a diet of nationalism, anti-Semitism, and anti-Bolshevism which conservative governments found necessary and easy to embrace. Already a battered faith in the 1920s, liberalism and *laissez-faire* policies lost further ground in the 1930s, both domestically and in international affairs. The centre held in those countries where constitutionalism and democratic forms had deep roots, as in Britain, France, Scandinavia, the Low Countries, and Switzerland. Despite challenges, the traditional frameworks remained in place and political change was accommodated within those structures. France was able to withstand the attacks from the right. Though the Communist party gained in membership and importance, its leadership backed (but did not participate in) Blum's Popular Front government. The Soviet support for Popular Front governments, in some countries at least, contributed to their survival. Almost everywhere, however, liberalism came under pressure as the extremes benefited from the weakening of the middle parties. In an atmosphere of fear and suspicion, multilateral diplomacy gave way as each state sought to defend its interests through independent action.

The effects of the depression encouraged not only the emergence of authoritarian and interventionist governments but led to the shattering of the global financial system. Britain, the symbolic leader of the old international financial and trading order, led the way in abandoning the gold standard and renouncing free trade in favour of imperial preference. The United States, too, abandoned gold and adopted domestic measures to promote economic recovery with only an occasional effort at international action. Most European states followed the British example and left gold, though at different times, and partly in response to the 'beggar-thy-neighbour' tactics of those who had preceded them. Germany, Hungary, and most of the East European states acted individually to end convertibility into gold or other currencies, tightened their control over foreign exchange and markets, and embarked on defensive economic policies—often at cost to their neighbours. Trade barriers went up, channelling commerce into newly created blocs or bilateral clearings. The collapse of the old system did not lead to anarchy as some predicted but often to fierce competition between competing blocs, further underlining the distance between the 'have' and 'have not' nations and providing the rationale for demands for territorial expansion and settlement.

There was no way that any peace treaty coming after the Great War could have covered the fissures that such an earthquake had opened or contained the vapours released by its eruptions. Cracks in the reconstructed international system were still clearly visible during the last years of the post-war decade. The admittedly slender hopes that the 'Conference on the Liquidation of the War' held at The Hague in August 1929 would mark the end of the post-war era proved illusory as the physical impact of the depression, in a very literal sense, drove open those gaps until in some places they were irreparable. Well before Hitler took power in Germany in January 1933, the 'lights' of the previous years—reconstruction, internationalism, multilateralism, and disarmament—had dimmed and the dark undercurrents of explosive nationalism, authoritarian rule, autarchy, and militarism had surfaced. The failure of the World Disarmament Conference not only crushed the hopes of many supporters of the League of Nations and the disarmament movements but also strengthened the ranks of those who opted for appeasement or some form of pacifism. Pressures for collective action gave way to policies of self-defence, neutrality and isolation. Against such a background, the balance of power shifted steadily away from the status quo nations in the direction of those who favoured its destruction. It is crucial to realize, however, that whatever the damage done, the reconstruction of the 1920s was not inevitably doomed to collapse by the start of the 1930s. Rather, the argument here is that the demise of the Weimar Republic and the triumph of Hitler proved the motor force of destructive systemic change.

II

Hitler came to power at a time when almost all the European nations were grappling with the problems of the depression and when the international system was in disarray. It was a turbulent and hence ideal moment for a man of Hitler's megalomaniac ambitions. He was a uniquely charismatic leader with a clear vision of his future goals, though far less certain of how to achieve them. From before the time that he took power, he believed that Germany needed new lands for settlement and food if it was to challenge the other great empires and that these had to be won by war. The creation of a new racial Reich depended on the prior removal of the Jewish 'parasites' in Germany who had so often thwarted the ambitions of the Aryan *Volk*. Hitler was able to project these ideas in ways that won the support of an overwhelming majority of Germans. At home and abroad, he proved a master political tactician, posing as the man of peace while planning for war and allowing others to implement the policies towards the Jews that he had approved and sanctioned. Yet Germans were neither duped nor taken by surprise by Nazi policies. Military and industrial leaders knew that a major war was in the making. Few in Germany, given the endless propaganda and educational programmes that turned the stereotyped Jew into a real hate figure, could have been ignorant of the government's intention to rid Germany of its unwelcome inhabitants. Hitler's visions indeed reflected the hopes and fears, the anxieties and resentments, of most Germans. Oratory, propaganda, organization, and violence were used to spread the message but it reached a receptive audience. No historian yet has adequately explained why Hitler triumphed so easily and so completely in this well-educated, culturally advanced, and highly industrialized society.

From the time he took power, Hitler was intent on preparing the Reich for war. The new chancellor immediately assured his officers that rearmament must take priority over all other tasks; this was not merely an attempt to win over the military establishment. Building on already existing programmes, decisive steps were taken in the summer of 1933; by the end of the year Germany had left the World Disarmament Conference and the League of Nations. The country faced even more acute financial problems than those slowing rearmament in other countries, yet at each crisis, when choices had to be made, Hitler demanded greater and faster armament programmes. As the costs grew higher, rearmament absorbed an ever-increasing share of the German national budget, greater by far than any other country with the exception of the Soviet Union. These efforts, as well as the other costs of reducing unemployment, threatened to derail the regime in 1934 and were soon to practically exhaust Germany's reserves of gold and foreign exchange, exacerbating its perennial balance of payments problem. Shortages of imported raw materials created setbacks to production plans, the most dramatic and dangerous in the spring of 1939. Having squeezed the consumer sector as far as thought possible, Hitler's response to Germany's difficult situation was to launch his war, in spite of, or perhaps because of, the long-term impossibility of matching the combined production of the western industrial powers. The costs to the German people of Hitler's plans were high and did not go unnoticed. Yet grumbling did not evolve into political opposition while identification with and involvement in the war machine brought their own satisfactions. What German would not be proud of their country's technical advances and the new respect with which it had to be treated? The campaign against the Jews may have brought individual protests but was generally accepted and, by some, enthusiastically endorsed. Foreign observers noted the militarization of Germany; some publicly condemned the Nazi treatment of the Jews. The former affected official assessments of German power and led to exaggerated estimates of its military strength; the latter was regarded with distaste but left to one side as falling within the domestic jurisdiction of the Reich.

The speed with which Hitler consolidated his power and began to implement his programme allowed him to seize the initiative in European affairs. The democratic powers faced constraints that Hitler felt free to ignore. The gap resulting from Nazi Germany's early start in its rearmament was further accentuated by the Anglo-French misreading of Hitler's intentions as well as their failure to work together. The British, still recovering from the shock of 1931 and the abandonment of free trade, were cautious as they set about repairing their defences. They, too, needed imports to feed the nation and to rearm. Like the Germans, they suffered from a negative balance of payments and fears of inflation. But the National government was particularly concerned to sustain the recovery after 1931 and to avoid any steps that might upset the political and economic balance, which was the source of its strength and of the popularity of the government. This concern with financial stability and economic recovery gave added weight to Treasury fears that rapid rearmament would result in inflation and undercut Britain's 'fourth arm of defence'. The retention of Britain's financial assets was judged essential for victory in the war of attrition for which the government planned. While the British spent just over 7% of their national income on defence as late as 1938, the Germans were spending well over double that amount. In the belief, moreover, that an improvement in world trade was essential for British prosperity and for the European peace, policy-makers hoped that Germany would abandon its autarkic policies and rejoin the world market. This seemingly rational view encouraged a lenient attitude towards the Nazi economic expansion into south-eastern Europe until 1939. There were repeated attempts, moreover, to open up markets for the German Reich in order to relieve the pressures on its economy. It was only late in the day that the British and French woke to the dangers of the German economic hold over Eastern Europe. By then, it was a matter of too little and too late; faced with their own rearmament requirements, neither had capital or arms to spare. The late arrival of the depression in France and its effect on the political as well as the economic situation delayed or even blocked French rearmament. The economic crisis weakened the French response to the German danger and influenced its behaviour at times of crisis. Munich was a case in point. Budget deficits hardly encouraged diplomatic initiatives or dramatic gestures. Blum's Popular Front government in 1936, despite its political, economic, and social difficulties, introduced a long-range defence programme. But his successors fruitlessly tried to balance the national budget and so cut back on armament orders when they should have been expanded. It was not until the Daladier government of 1938–1939 that France embarked on the major rearmament programme that was essential for its survival in war. Again like the British, some Frenchmen hoped that by meeting the Reich's economic demands it would be possible to turn Hitler away from territorial expansion. Such illusions were based on a false assessment of Hitler's persona and of his intentions. Because the British and French were so aware of the financial and economic limitations within which they operated, they expected Hitler to react similarly. The mirror image proved fallacious.

Hitler's preoccupation with rearmament had its effects on the policies of many of the states in Eastern Europe, most of which were severely hit by the depression and by the drying up of the inflows of foreign capital. Faced with extreme rural distress, these agricultural countries desperately sought foreign markets for their grain, meat, and other raw materials. They were more than ready to enter into the clearing arrangements that Germany proposed. No other government offered such markets and certainly not at the higher than world prices that Germany was ready to pay. These states could supply only a small percentage of what was required and Germany still had to buy from hard currency countries but their exports were important in the battle to feed the German population and to keep the armament industries functioning. Some states, particularly Romania and Yugoslavia, were able to strike excellent bargains because of Germany's need for oil and rare minerals. They secured not only arms and industrial goods but even foreign exchange in return for their exports. Nonetheless, Romania, Yugoslavia, Bulgaria, Hungary, Greece, and Turkey were drawn into the German economic net. Some of these governments, even those considered Germany's satellites, might have preferred to balance between the revisionist and democratic blocs. In addressing their security problems, such states spent increasing sums on rearmament and sought safety, if they could, in neutrality and non-engagement rather than in cooperation. Yet all, with the exception of Greece and Turkey, found it necessary and even advantageous to continue supplying Germany after war broke out.

Ultimately, Germany, which was only a middle-sized country whose inhabitants were already highly taxed and enduring relatively low standards of living, could not sustain a war that would engage opponents of far larger populations and greater industrial power. In the short run, however, Hitler could ignore the burden on the population and the danger to the financial and economic stability of the state to prepare for the immediate wars that he hoped to conclude before the British and French were fully armed. The former, aware of their more threatened position during the 1930s, continued to rely on the 'soft power' of prestige, negotiation, and conciliation, while building up their defensive capacities. Though conscious that the French army was their shield in any land war with Germany, they did little to strengthen it. Only when deterrence failed were they forced to accept the failure of their efforts. The French, faced with a far more complex and divisive political, ideological, and social situation than the British, aggravated by the late arrival of the depression and the worsening of their European security structure, sought various ways to fashion an appropriate response to their exposed position but with limited success. The gains made by the Axis powers presented a direct threat to French security, yet, with good reason, the memories and fears of the costs of war ran even deeper through every level of French society than in Britain. Since 1919, but with increasing urgency in the 1930s, the French sought a military alliance with Britain, whatever doubts it had about its military utility, as the best and most politically acceptable safeguard to its future. The conclusion of that alliance in 1939 undoubtedly was a major reason for the decision for war.

III

Whether National Socialist, Fascist, Liberal, Communist, or militant militarism, belief systems separated the nations from one another and added to the difficulties of inter-state communication and mutual comprehension. Once Hitler took power, ideology was bound to become an even more important and more divisive factor in the conduct of international politics than it had been in the 1920s. Nazism's concept of racial *Lebensraum* directed against the Soviet Union could hardly be ignored in Moscow. The Soviet response to the Nazi challenge was to seek collaboration with the western powers and to encourage the creation of united or popular anti-Nazi fronts in the interests of protecting Russian national interests. Despite its efforts, ideological antipathies played their part in the western failure to conclude agreements with Moscow. For many contemporaries (and for some commentators today) the Spanish Civil War was a 'microcosm of Europe's ideological battle-lines'.[1] Though contained, the conflict led to a polarization of political attitudes along ideological lines that extended far beyond the

[1] David Reynolds, *From Munich to Pearl Harbor*, 20.

confines of Spain and the European continent. Foreign intervention in the Spanish fighting created the illusion that this was a conflict between Communism and Fascism–Nazism. This gave substance to Hitler's claims that he was leading a crusade against 'Judeo-Bolshevism' and its unchecked spread throughout Western Europe. Among conservative and right-wing forces in western countries and in Eastern Europe, the Spanish Civil War strengthened fears of a rising Bolshevik wave, blocking the construction of a common and expanded front against German and Italian aggression. This over-simplified picture of what was happening in Spain was reinforced not just by Nazi–Fascist propaganda but by the behaviour of the opposing forces in the conflict. Even such an exponent of *realpolitik* as Winston Churchill, who favoured a 'Grand Alliance' against Nazi Germany, took temporary umbrage at the Soviet intervention in Spain. While polarization led many Liberals, Socialists, and trade unionists in the democracies to identify with the Republicans and even to accept the need for rearmament, the so-called ideological conflict in Spain brought Germany and Italy closer together and made it more difficult for the British and French to build a dam against Axis aggression.

Even when combined with *realpolitik* policies, ideological assumptions affected the way statesmen and their advisers saw the world about them. It mattered that Chamberlain hated war and believed that wasteful arms races led to conflict. He assumed that others shared his views. Hitler's belief in Social Darwinism, in *Lebensraum*, and the Aryan race, and Mussolini's dreams of a revived Roman Empire, a new Italy, and a new Italian, gave shape to the policies they adopted. Again and again during the course of this book, I have called attention to the shaping force of the ideological assumptions of those in power. Core beliefs, not only about the nature of international politics but also about the human condition, to an important extent created reality as it was perceived by statesmen who enjoyed remarkable autonomy in deciding the most important issues of the time. This was true not only of Hitler, Mussolini, and Stalin but also of Chamberlain and Daladier, despite the constitutional and popular constraints within which the latter two men operated. The age of mass politics did not bring about the democratization of the direction of foreign affairs. Japan was unusual in that below the emperor no single figure of authority emerged and the old military and naval élites, in competition with each other, retained their influence. A whole complex of factors determined decision-making at the top; military and economic strength were not the sole determinants of action. Other factors, exerting an equal if not stronger force affected the very definition of power as well as the choice of strategic options. Personality, beliefs, national and racial stereotypes, and historical experience all entered into the diplomatic equation. In almost every state, the information provided by diplomatic, military, intelligence, and other professional advisers contributed to the decision-making process. This advice, however influential, was rarely unanimous, simple, coherent, or free from bureaucratic constraints and rivalries. Its importance varied from time to time and from crisis to crisis, but in all cases it was interpreted and understood through the prism of the core beliefs of the leading statesmen.

Intelligence in particular was vital to the formulation of national policy. In the case of the dictatorships, information and intelligence was often shaped to accord with Hitler's, Stalin's, or Mussolini's views. Unwanted intelligence could be ignored or reinterpreted. For the democratic powers, there was a distinct difference in the application and use of intelligence between the 1920s and 1930s. In the earlier decade, good intelligence had buttressed their dominant strategic position within Europe. In the 1930s, as this balance shifted, the status quo powers needed more than good intelligence. They had not only to acquire estimates of enemy capabilities but also to accurately assess and predict the intentions of the aggressors. As John Ferris has insightfully noted, 'A reactive power needs better intelligence than a strong and active one. It must know the active power's intentions, the latter merely its own mind. The situation breeds tendencies such as uncertainty, guessing as to the active party's aims and the means to influence them, and worse case planning. Between 1933 and 1939 the status quo powers needed outstanding intelligence. They did not have it.'[2] Too many variables distorted the picture; the coordination of intelligence left much to be desired, and statesmen varied widely in their appreciation of its importance. The result in the Allied camp was an exaggerated view of German strength until very late in the decade and then a sudden change of perspective as the probability of war increased.

Expert advice was in any case never value-free or cut off from the prevailing currents of contemporary opinion. It is thus difficult to accept the view of those 'realist' theorists who argue that Great Powers (or rather their leaders) are rational actors, aware of their external environment and making strategic decisions about how to survive in it. Some international theorists believe that the structure of the international system determines the behaviour of the states, whether seeking to protect their security or aiming at hegemony in order to survive. One

[2] John Ferris, 'Intelligence', in Robert Boyce and Joseph A. Maiolo (eds.), *The Origins of World War Two: The Debate Continues* (Basingstoke, 2003), 322–323. See also his more extended and highly important essay, 'Image and Accident: Intelligence and the Origins of the Second World War, 1933–1941', in John Ferris, *Intelligence and Strategy* (London and Newark, NJ, 2005), 99–137.

cannot, however, ignore the domestic context in which decisions are reached. Power, in terms of comparative standing within the international system, does not necessarily explain the state's behaviour. Whether Germany was led by Bismarck, Wilhelm II, or Hitler made a vital difference to its policies. The Führer's programme was not determined solely by the distribution of European power and the Reich's international position. Japanese behaviour must be seen in terms of the unique role of the emperor and the army–navy rivalry as well as the popular appeal of militant nationalism. The racial factor can hardly be ignored when considering European perceptions of Japan and China. In each case, room must be left for the irrational and the accidental, which produce unforeseen and inexplicable consequences. The excessive concentration on the international environment offers only a partial indicator of how states, or rather their statesmen, have behaved in the past or are likely to behave in the future. This form of reductionism, while providing a useful perspective on international politics, necessarily distorts reality and makes historical analysis more, rather than less, difficult.

A perceptual gap prevented statesmen from understanding each other's policy. It stemmed mainly from differences in ideology and affected the way statesmen understood the mechanisms of power politics. It proved more difficult for some in London and in Paris, for instance, to understand the nature of Nazism than that of Stalinism. Without sympathy with either creed, a fundamental misunderstanding of National Socialism contributed to Chamberlain's differential treatment of Nazi Germany and the Soviet Union. Protected by a successfully functioning political system and an inherited set of beliefs as to how the global system should operate, as well as a certain insularity despite Britain's imperial reach, some senior British policymakers failed to come to terms with the popular appeal of the new ideological movements, whether in Europe or in East Asia. They looked for rational explanations of phenomena that lay outside their practical experience. Chamberlain dangerously misunderstood Hitler's intentions. The perceptual gap was widened because self-confident men like Hitler, Stalin, or, indeed, Chamberlain, were unwilling to change their minds on basic issues of policy. Even more fundamentally, while the democratic leaders felt they were playing a common game with one set of rules, in fact everyone was playing a different game with the same pieces. The results were repeated crises and a war that did not go as any of them had anticipated.

The leaders of the democratic states were, in the short run, the most disadvantaged in this respect. They assumed that all those playing the game shared and accepted certain essential principles. All should, and hence would, agree that peace was preferable to war and that negotiation was more productive than fighting. These views were hardly appropriate for dealing with the Nazis, the Fascists, or the militarist Japanese leadership. This argument requires emphasis as we have become accustomed to the disasters and atrocities of our own day and routinely anticipate irrational behaviour. Men like Chamberlain and Daladier, as well as their foreign ministers, because of their personalities, upbringing, education, and beliefs barely understood a leader like Hitler. They, like so many others of the old élites, belonged to a world where statesmen made sensible choices, where rules and conventions were observed, and where men avoided bluff and reckless behaviour. The cataclysm of 1914–1918 had left the French and British leaders with the visceral horror of another war. Hitler suffered no such qualms. This lent his apocalyptic and vengeful vision an almost irresistible dynamism. Few had the insight or imagination to comprehend its meaning. Reason and logic were almost helpless in the face of what Chamberlain all too rightly regarded as near lunacy. Only Stalin might have understood the German dictator but he became the victim of his own miscalculations and self-delusions. It would ultimately take the almost archaic romanticism of a Winston Churchill to grasp and counter the Führer's visionary ambitions. Western leaders expected that their signals would be understood by their opponents; they were not, contributing to the failure of deterrence. Hitler allowed no escape from the unwelcome decision that had to be taken. By his own actions, he foreclosed alternative possibilities until it appeared that war was the only available choice. Surrender to Hitler in September 1939 would have brought only further catastrophes in its wake. For Britain and France, this was a necessary war.

IV

The road to war was one mapped out by the actions of the German leader. But, as this account has attempted to show, the significance of this path goes beyond any simple enumeration of the 'steps' or crises leading to the eventual conflict. While this volume has provided a sequential rendering of the history of the period, the interpretation is not one of inevitability but stresses the contingent nature of much of Hitler's successes. This is clear in the extent to which his decisions and the reactions of other statesmen were conditioned by the totality of Europe's international relations, rather than simply a narrow focus on Hitler's behaviour. The diplomatic system became increasingly atomized between 1933 and 1938. Nation-states, both large and small, began to follow their own independent trajectories as they struggled to find their place in a weakened international order. The ties between would-be allies remained weak and existing regional groupings either came under increasing strain or fell apart. It was only in 1939 that the British finally offered the alliance and staff talks that France had for years so often sought in vain. The Germans and Italians played a double game with each other, particularly with regard to Britain. German domination did not prevent Mussolini from considering parallel wars while Hitler engaged the British and French. If Italy failed to benefit from the strategic shift as much as Germany and Japan, it was because of its undeveloped economic base and the squandering of its troops and material in Ethiopia and Spain. Nazi Germany was unable to create the Triple Alliance with Italy and Japan as an anti-British grouping until 1940 because of disagreements over their respective enemies. It was, in part, Ribbentrop's failure in this respect that persuaded Hitler to temporarily abandon his life-long aversion to the Soviet Union and seek an alliance with Moscow. The would-be aggressors were the main beneficiaries of this fragmentation that allowed them to capitalize on the disunity of their opponents. They were aided immeasurably by the already existing structural weaknesses in the European order. At the time when Hitler began to push aggressively at the boundaries hemming in Germany, there was little left in terms of systems of peacekeeping, multilateral cooperation, trust in the League of Nations or even continent-wide trade networks considered worthy of stern defence, to resist him from the very first instance.

Yet the most critical shifts in Europe took place only in the last twelve months of peace, from October 1938 to September 1939. The new European settlement agreed at Munich altered matters dramatically as it created a new balance in the Continent's international politics, however temporarily. Hitler was not to be deflected again from his desire for war, but now it could only come at the price of certain British intervention. In response to Hitler's repeated assaults on the Munich 'settlements', the British and French governments abandoned appeasement for deterrence and accelerated their preparations for war. Deterrence failed even before the Nazi–Soviet pact was signed. After Munich, too, Hitler was not to be deterred despite the growing fears of Anglo-French intervention. Whether the Anglo-French actions came too late, and whether more could have been done to prevent this 'unnecessary war' (Churchill's famous description), is still the subject of active debate. For both the British and French, it would have taken an enormous psychological leap to have moved earlier from peace to war. Without a clear and immediate danger to national existence, both governments looked for alternative possibilities and found reasons for so doing. Chamberlain, in particular, felt that if war could be postponed, it might be avoided. Yet only a serious threat of war would have deterred Hitler in the Rhineland, over *Anschluss*, or over the Sudetenland. The Godesberg and Prague crises may have been the necessary precursors for the stand over Poland. It was only at this late date that both countries became convinced that Hitler was determined on European domination. For the British, and consequently the French, the engagement with Eastern Europe that followed from Munich's repudiation by Hitler was the shift that produced the war as it broke out in September 1939. Even in the final crisis, however, it may well be that the British public was more resolute and the French more resigned to war than were their leaders. As one reviews the many arguments for British appeasement, and the debate has lost none of its potency, it is hard to excuse the blindness of British policymakers towards France and their long-term indifference towards Eastern Europe. Even after seventy years, one cannot be sure how Hitler (or Mussolini) would have reacted if Britain and France had stood together earlier, if Britain had raised a continental army before 1939 (Dunkirk was an *Allied* failure), or paid Stalin's high price for an alliance. Given Hitler's unpreparedness for a European war, the British under-used their power. Even given what was known, Chamberlain could have taken a stronger line. If war had come in 1938, it is highly doubtful whether Germany would have achieved the kind of victory won in 1940. The Chamberlain government was reluctant to take risks and France would not act without Britain. Hitler was a gambler; Chamberlain was not.

Seeking others to share the burden of containing Hitler ('buck-passing') proved less than successful. Italy, though wooed, was a disappointment. Chamberlain continued to think he could detatch Mussolini from Hitler well after Daladier had given up this illusory possibility. It was not due to the Allied efforts that Italy remained neutral. Both governments tried to enlist the assistance of the United States. Securing the promise of material support was far from easy. Like the Republicans in the 1920s, the Roosevelt administration sought to remain outside of the security struggles in Europe and preferred to follow an independent, if parallel, policy to that of Britain in East Asia. Some in London, including Chamberlain, were reluctant to cede to the Americans too large a role in European affairs for fear of the price that might be demanded in return. The prime minister never felt that he needed to approach the Americans with a begging bowl as Robert Vansittart had once suggested. British and American interests differed and clashed; the latter proved exceedingly tough negotiators where trade and finance were concerned. American policy hardly encouraged reliance on its goodwill. The difficulties of dealing with the erratic Roosevelt, whose attitudes and policies appeared ambiguous at best and who repeatedly promised more than he delivered, quite apart from the strength of American isolationism, served to limit what could be expected from

Washington. From the time of the Anti-Comintern Pact in 1936, Roosevelt had been conscious of the global dangers posed by the 'have not' powers. He thought, however, in terms of an international rather than an American response. As the international situation deteriorated he increasingly urged Britain and France to stand up to Hitler, making no secret of his belief that Britain lacked the will to do so. Insofar as he sought to strengthen their resolve, especially after Munich, he was admittedly limited in what he could do by America's undeveloped defence industries, by the Johnson Act, and by his futile peacetime efforts to revise the Neutrality Acts. The president was chary of using his political capital, already under attack, in an open fight with the Congressional isolationists. Faced with contradictory advice and aware of the need to 'educate' the American public, he moved with extreme caution. Though in 1939 opinion polls showed overwhelming support for the Allied powers, the president and the electorate were at one in insisting the United States should not become involved in Europe's wars. The Allied powers, especially France, desperate for American aircraft, found ways in peacetime to tap the undeveloped American industrial arsenal but orders were limited in number and size and the promised delivery times late in 1939 or in 1940. While many of Hitler's advisers predicted that the United States would provide the war materials the Allies required and so win the arms race with the Reich, the democracies could not realistically base their policies on such assumptions. War did not bring any change in the president's determination to avoid military involvements abroad. If the British hoped for more open American support in East Asia, and there were important, if secret, moves towards naval cooperation, the Chamberlain government, with vital imperial interests at stake in East Asia, had to tread carefully between hostile acts that might provoke Japan and appeasing Tokyo at the risk of alienating the Americans. While accepting that Britain and France would have to fight Hitler with, at best, limited American assistance, the British government knew that the maintenance of Britain's East Asian position depended on the continuation of the Sino-Japanese war and American underwriting.

It was still possible in September 1938 to leave the Soviets out of the Munich settlement and to treat Moscow's overtures with suspicion, if not outright hostility. On the defensive, and fearing attacks from a German–Polish–Japanese bloc, Stalin backed Litvinov's approaches to the western powers as a valuable insurance policy. But the commissar met with only limited success in Paris and failure in London. From the French point of view, possible Soviet participation in an eastern front had to be weighed against objections to the activities of the French Communist party at home and British objections to ties between Paris and Moscow. An understanding with Britain was the more important prize. In any case, there were real doubts about the offensive capacity of the Red Army, even before the purges, while the existing ties to Poland, France's only ally in the east, could not be easily abandoned. There were equally formidable barriers in London to an agreement with Moscow. Suspicion of the Comintern and Communist party activities, doubts about Soviet military power, the constant hope that a settlement with Nazi Germany would preserve the peace without need for an arrangement with Moscow, repeatedly thwarted efforts at détente or agreement. The assumption that the ideological antipathies between Berlin and Moscow would prevent a Nazi–Soviet agreement coloured Anglo-French attitudes towards any *rapprochement* with the Russians. On both sides, there were grounds for suspicion. If in London there were fears that talks with the Soviets would close the door to a settlement with Hitler and alienate many of the smaller European nations, Allied moves towards Berlin fed Soviet suspicions that the democracies would settle with Hitler at Soviet expense. Munich confirmed the seeming failure of Litvinov's policy. After Munich, those favouring the alternative security option of an arrangement with Germany voiced their opinions publicly. Yet tentative approaches on both sides failed to make progress. It was thought, as Litvinov and the Soviet ambassadors in Paris and London warned, that the Soviets would retreat into a position of isolation while building up their military strength for the conflict that was to come.

It was only in the spring and summer of 1939 that the Soviet Union moved into the centre of European politics as the Anglo-French guarantee to Poland changed the strategic situation and made the USSR a vital element in the military balance. Stalin was wooed both by the western powers (against Chamberlain's wishes) and by Hitler, who became increasingly anxious to conclude his bargain before the attack on Poland. Stalin's late choice in favour of Nazi Germany, explicable in terms of the options he was offered and the intelligence at his command, was a pragmatic and realistic move but reflected, too, his continuing fear of a new Munich and a possible western attack on the Soviet Union. Hitler offered the best chance of providing the breathing space and the territorial safeguards that Stalin believed Moscow required. The Russian dictator anticipated both a longer Polish–German and Allied–German war than what actually followed. The events of 1939–1940 shortened the timetable for Soviet military preparations and threatened Stalin's hopes of a central position at some future peace conference. The defeat of France was a terrible shock. In Berlin, the Nazi–Soviet pact provided Hitler with a last-minute but highly persuasive argument for launching the war that he was not yet ready to fight. Germany was now guaranteed against a two-front conflict and protected against the worst consequences of the Anglo-French blockade. Would Hitler have been deterred, even temporarily, from invading Poland if he had been faced with an Anglo-French-Soviet alliance? It seems at least possible. At the time, both Hitler and Stalin considered the Nazi–Soviet pact a master act of *realpolitik*.

In the last months of peace, the Allied powers were faced with diminishing options. Though their leaders clung to the hope, encouraged by a variety of diplomatic and intelligence reports, that Hitler would see reason and stand down, the failure of deterrence and the ultimately unsuccessful talks with the Soviets left the initiative with the German leader. To have left Germany triumphant in central Europe would have exposed France, and consequently Britain, to the possibility of defeat. To count on a Russo-German war that might have exhausted both parties was to have courted disaster either in the interim or in the future. For Chamberlain, war was a defeat. His near fatal misreading of Hitler's intentions continued—writing to his sister on 10 September 1939: 'But I believe he did seriously contemplate an agreement with us, and that he worked seriously at proposals (subsequently broadcast) which to his one-track mind seemed almost fabulously generous. But at the last moment some brainstorm took possession of him—maybe Ribbentrop stirred it up—and once he had set his machine in motion, he couldn't stop it.'[3] Chamberlain clung to the hope that Britain would not have to *fight*. For Churchill, by contrast, invited to join the war cabinet, Nazi Germany and Nazism were existential threats that had to be defeated at whatever cost: 'We are fighting to save the whole world from the pestilence of Nazi tyranny and in defence of all that is most sacred to man', he announced the day war was declared.[4] Not all shared this ideological view of Nazism. Some in the Allied capitals thought that Hitler would retreat in the face of the Allied threats of war. But the overwhelming feeling in both countries once Hitler invaded Poland left few doors open for further diplomacy. Differently from July 1914, public pressure helped to push the government to war. The French choice for war or peace was more stark. The Nazi–Soviet pact was a severe strategic blow. Even Bonnet, hardly a *belliciste,* had hoped that an agreement with Russia would give substance to the Allied policy of deterrence. As in London, Daladier and his ministers hoped that by standing firm, Hitler would be persuaded to negotiate. In contrast to the situation in London, the divisions in the French cabinet persisted and Bonnet found supporters for his idea of a conference under Mussolini's

[3] Quoted in Keith Feiling, *The Life of Neville Chamberlain* (London, 1947), 417.
[4] Quoted in Talbot Imlay, *Facing the Second World War,* 229–230.

auspices even after German troops entered Poland. Although Daladier had united the parties of the right and right–centre on a policy of 'firmness', the fear of war and defeat was strong and there were some on both the right and left who were unwilling to face the reality of combat. The actual advent of war promoted unity. The overwhelming majority of the French people supported the call to arms. The stakes for France were high. Speaking on 2 September, Daladier insisted that France's vital interests were involved and that flushed with victory and the spoils of Europe, 'the aggressors will soon turn against France with all their force'.[5] There was no English Channel to protect France.

Hitler gambled and, in the end, lost. This was his war; he sent his soldiers into Poland knowing that he would have to fight Britain and France. As Donald Watt has concluded, 'what is extraordinary in the events which led up to the outbreak of the Second World War is that Hitler's will for war was able to overcome the reluctance with which everybody else approached it. Hitler willed, desired, lusted after, war, though not the war with France and Britain, at least not in 1939. No one else wanted it, though Mussolini came perilously close to talking himself into it.'[6] With Poland prepared to fight, Britain and France took up Hitler's challenge. They were Great Powers and not prepared to relinquish their positions without a battle. Their electorates expected no less. The fear of war was strong and the forebodings many. What followed before the wars in Europe and East Asia came to an end proved far more destructive of the European future than even the most prescient of Cassandras could have imagined.

[5] *Journal officiel de la République française*, Chambre de députés, *Debats parlementaires*, 2 September 1939, 1952.

[6] Donald Cameron Watt, *How War Came*, 610.

EPILOGUE

Despite the efforts to avert it, whether cynical, well-intentioned, naïve, or desperate, the first days of September 1939 brought the return of the nightmares of 1914. Yet, at least at first, they did not bring the all-encompassing Armageddon so many feared. The opening months of this new war involved only five European nations and engaged only three in actual fighting. Poland was quickly defeated, as first the German armed forces overran its defenders from the West and then, from the middle of the month, Soviet forces invaded from the East. By the first days of October the fighting was over, with some 100,000 Polish soldiers dead, and the country divided between its executioners. The Soviets grabbed their prize and retired to the sidelines. Over the following months, Moscow proved willing to supply the German war machine while hastening its own preparations for an impending conflict. A series of new economic agreements underpinned a massive exchange of Soviet raw materials for German manufactured products and technical expertise. Soviet goods would provide the economic foundation for Germany's ability to attack in the West: 'there would be enough oil for her tanks, enough manganese for her steel industry, and enough grain for her soldiers and workers'.[1] Such an attack, once again at the time of Hitler's choosing, was only possible, however, because the events of September 1939 brought no aggressive response in the West. The two powers committed to defending Poland against unprovoked aggression, Britain and France, declared war but did little else.[2] Long-standing military thinking in both Paris and London called for an initial defensive strategy to check the German advance. It was only after a massive superiority of forces had been built up, and Germany weakened by a naval blockade, that offensive operations were to be mounted. This meant a long war unless, as Chamberlain hoped, short-term economic pressure would convince the German people to

[1] Gerhard L. Weinberg, *A World at Arms: A Global History of World War II* (Cambridge, 1994), 63.

[2] The British Empire also entered the war; the Commonwealth countries at different times.

abandon their leader and the war. Though Poland would inevitably be overrun, it would ultimately have its independence restored following the Allied triumph. Despite the promises made to the Poles, there were no plans for an Allied advance into Germany or a bombing campaign.

The British nightmare of a three-front war did not materialize, at least not in 1939. The Italians failed to move, restrained by their obvious and appalling military weakness. To Hitler's intense irritation, Mussolini maintained Italy's 'non-belligerence' ('neutrality' sounded too pacific) yet his basic policy remained an adherence to the Axis and entry into the war as soon as Italy was ready. There appeared no other way to achieve his imperial ambitions. Japan stayed out of the conflict as it wrestled with the implications of the Nazi–Soviet pact. For the moment, it abandoned plans for an attack on the Soviet Union, though the army leaders began to think of stealing the navy's strategic clothes and opting for a strike southwards. In the rest of Europe, most countries did everything possible to maintain their neutrality, while abetting or resisting the German war effort in varying degrees. The most important neutral was, of course, the United States. Opinion was near unanimous that Germany was to blame for the war and that a Franco-British victory was desirable, but also that America should not get involved. Determined not again to send troops to Europe, Roosevelt pondered the problem of how to supply the British and the French with the war materials they required. Despite the president's efforts, only a modest start was made on expanding the American defence industries while Republican isolationists were still powerful enough to restrict revisions to the neutrality legislation. Sumner Welles, assistant under-secretary of state, was sent on a presidential mission to Rome, Berlin, Paris, and London in February 1940 to sound out the prospects for a negotiated peace. He reported that there was no question of either Hitler or Mussolini considering a negotiated peace and that, while he found the French demoralized and apathetic, the British were determined to fight to the last. Anthony Eden and, in particular, Winston Churchill were convinced that no other solution was possible than the 'outright and complete defeat of Germany [and] the destruction of National Socialism'.[3]

After the initial bloodshed in Poland, the war mostly went quiet. The only other significant fighting before the spring of 1940 was, like the Polish war, a localized affair: the winter conflict between the Soviet Union and Finland (November 1939 – March 1940) did not bring in the Allied powers though both the French and, at moments, the British considered intervention. The Finnish appeal to the League of Nations

[3] Quoted in David M. Kennedy, *Freedom from Fear: The American People in Depression and War, 1929–1945* (New York, 2005), 437.

led to the expulsion of the Soviet Union, one of the last political actions taken by that tragic organization. The humiliating failure of the Allied attempts to prevent the German occupation of Denmark and Norway, launched in April and completed by June, made clear the extent not only of Allied weakness but also the fraudulence of the German attitude towards neutrality. On 10 May 1940 German troops invaded Holland and Belgium. Over the next six weeks they completely defeated the French and British armies. Winston Churchill's post-war volume covering 1940 was called *Their Finest Hour*; the French translation was titled *L'Heure Tragique*, supposedly to head off the criticism it evoked in France. Some 340,000 troops (220,000 British and 120,000 French) were evacuated at Dunkirk between 27 May and 4 June; Paris fell on 14 June and on the same day German troops broke into the Maginot Line. Only one week later a Franco-German armistice was agreed, signed in the same railway carriage as the German capitulation of November 1918. Hitler had accomplished in a mere six weeks what the German imperial army had failed to do in over four years of intense fighting.

The fall of France was unexpected, astonishing, and far from inevitable. Both Hitler and Guderian, one of the architects of Germany's military victory, believed that the Sedan breakthrough was 'almost a miracle'. While the actual number of divisions, tanks, and aircraft may have been less decisive to the outcome of the campaign than the actions of individuals and the role of organizational culture, even the numerical figures hardly suggested a French defeat. Not counting the Belgian and Dutch divisions, the number of German and Allied troops was almost equal.[4] On the German side, the *Wehrmacht* possessed 157 divisions, of which 135 were deployed in *Fall Gelb* (Operation Yellow) (only ten were Panzer divisions). The French army possessed 117 divisions manning the frontier with Germany and Belgium and the British sent thirteen divisions but three were not combat-ready and two were outside the British Expeditionary Force sphere of control. The two sides had about an equal number of tanks but the French tanks were qualitatively better than those of the enemy. In the air, the Germans maintained their earlier numerical advantage; the British kept back a part of their airforce and the French had only begun their transition. Few new planes were in front-line squadrons in 1940 and maintenance crews found servicing them difficult.[5] In air operations, the two sides were closely matched but the French air force and the RAF failed to cooperate adequately in any

[4] For the most accurate figures, see Karl-Heinz Frieser, *Blitzkrieg-Legende: Der Westfeldzug 1940* (Munich, 1995).

[5] Williamson Murray, unpublished manuscript. See also Williamson Murray, *The Luftwaffe, 1933–1945: Strategy for Defeat* (Washington and London, 1996).

combined operation, giving the advantage to the Germans. Yet the *Luftwaffe* lost 1,129 aircrafts (plus 299 from accidents) during the battles over Holland, Belgium, and France, aircraft that would not subsequently be available for the Battle of Britain.[6]

How does one explain the defeat of France in May 1940? There was no overwhelming superiority of German forces. The French fought hard, particularly in the latter stages of the campaign, and the casualty figures were high. The question continues to haunt the present generation of French men and women. A majority of French historians have argued, both in the past and at present, that a deep malaise in French society affected both its civilian and military leadership. The Third Republic was a country in decline; French politics reflected the decadence and corruption of its society. More recently, this 'decline and decadence' thesis has been challenged, led by British, Canadian, and American, but also some French, scholars. They have examined the real constraints within which the French had to operate and have reassessed, more favourably than in the past, the political and military response to the demographic, economic, geographic, and diplomatic obstacles that they faced. This interpretation has moved away from morally charged theories of societal malaise, which explain little, to focus on the more tangible causes of the 1940 defeat: the intelligence failure to predict the German breakthrough in the Ardennes, the rigidities in French military thinking during the 1930s, and the dismal record in Anglo-French cooperation before and during the war. This change of perspective has raised its own problems; the devastating indictment of French political, diplomatic, military, and cultural failures captured in Marc Bloch's *L'étrange défaite*, written in the immediate aftermath of the debacle, has lost little of its power and immediacy. Yet with its emphasis on the difficult choices facing France's leadership in the pre-war decade and its depiction of the failures of 1940 as Allied rather than exclusively French, the new literature has successfully challenged the assumption that a French defeat was preordained and that its roots lay in the decadence, lethargy, and corruption of the Third Republic.

To many, not only in France, the war seemed to be over. The appearance of a quick victory convinced Mussolini to act. Italy formally joined the war on 10 June but made no serious moves to attack French or British positions, the Duce believing that the fruits of victory would fall into his lap. Seeking to reap the benefits of his deal with Hitler, Stalin

[6] Patrick Facon, *L'armée de l'air dans la tourmente: La bataille de France, 1939–1940* (Paris, 1997), 256–280. Facon provides a nuanced analysis of the impact of these losses on the Battle of Britain, acknowledging that various French scholars have exaggerated the extent of their impact. For figures, see Williamson Murray, *The Luftwaffe*, 40.

increased the level of Soviet cooperation with Germany, anticipating in return support for Soviet plans against the Baltic states and Finland. The British, meanwhile, were expected in Berlin to follow the French example and acknowledge the totality of the Allied defeat. Instead, they decided to fight on alone. Yet neither of the two antagonists could move effectively against the other. The *Luftwaffe* had failed to provide the victory Hitler required; the Germans did not have the heavy bomber fleet necessary to achieve the mastery over south-east England required for an invasion. The Battle of Britain was a critical British victory. German plans had to be temporarily abandoned. The German surface fleet could not take on the Royal Navy though the U-boat campaign gained momentum. Still, the British hung on, refusing to negotiate. The Norwegian debacle had led to the fall of Neville Chamberlain's government and the appointment of Winston Churchill as prime minister. Once it was clear that France had fallen but a major part of the British army had been saved, his coalition war cabinet rejected the possibility of a negotiated peace on the correct assumption that no acceptable terms offered by Hitler could possibly be trusted.[7] Britain would fight on. Still, it was not at all clear how the war was to be won. The British, as one Foreign Office official admitted, had to rely on hope. They could not move against Nazi Germany. It was impossible to contemplate re-entry into Europe. Scattered bombing raids improved morale but did little actual harm to German war preparations. There was no strategic bombing force to destroy German cities. The country was dependent on supplies from Canada, and, above all, the United States, to re-equip its forces. British defiance increased the prospects of both American assistance and a war of attrition. Though after the election in November 1940, and the passage of the Lend-Lease bill, Roosevelt stepped up his efforts to get supplies to Britain, he was still unwilling to join the conflict. This was, for Churchill, the *sine qua non* of a British victory. The blockade set some limits on German economic expansion but could do little with regard to German imports of Swedish iron ore, Romanian oil, or the flow of Soviet supplies to the Reich.

It was difficult to predict how long this stalemate would have continued. There was some movement in the other theatres of war. Angry about the lack of consultation with Berlin and worried about German movements in the Balkans, the Italians invaded Greece on 18 October 1940 without informing Hitler. The attack went nowhere and only German intervention prevented an Italian defeat. Italian failures in

[7] For Churchill's doubts, see David Reynolds, 'Churchill and the British "Decision" to Fight on in 1940', in Richard Langhorne (ed.), *Diplomacy and Intelligence during the Second World War: Essays in Honour of F. H. Hinsley* (Cambridge, 1985), 147–67.

North and East Africa, where British imperial troops triumphed, also required German intervention and an expansion of its sphere of operations. In terms of the Anglo-German war, these were side-shows. Meanwhile, Germany's defeat of France, the Netherlands, and seemingly Britain, had produced real war enthusiasm in Tokyo. The leadership, undoubtedly encouraged by the Germans (the Berlin–Rome–Tokyo pact had been signed on 27 September 1940), was convinced that now was the moment for Japan to seize territory in South-East Asia from the defeated or weakened colonial powers, even at the risk of confrontation with America.

Unbeknown to the British, and hardly expected, there was a possible improvement in their future position being discussed in Berlin. On 31 July 1940, while considering his plans for the invasion of Britain, Hitler told his chiefs of staff of his intention to 'smash' the Soviet Union. Almost immediately, the *Wehrmacht* was instructed to expand the army to 180 divisions by the spring of 1941. These directives were not operational decisions; only the circumstances of the next months gave substance to Hitler's *idée fixe*. It was only either at the end of 1940 or at the start of 1941 that the decision became irreversible. Historians differ in their interpretation of what actually led Hitler to act but there is general agreement that he thought in terms of a *blitzkrieg* war against the Soviet Union and appears to have believed that the defeat of Russia would be the key to victory in the West. The short Russian campaign was seen by many in Berlin as a far easier task than the risky operation across the English Channel. After it was accomplished and the Soviet Union destroyed, Britain would be forced to capitulate and it would then be the turn of the United States. The expansion of the conflict across and even outside of Europe was integral to the purpose of launching the war, and indeed to the ideological premises of National Socialism. Far from having come to a quick end, the war was in fact about to expand enormously in its scale, scope, and human cost.

It was the defeat of France that turned 'a European conflict into a world war and helped reshape international politics in patterns that endured for nearly half a century, until the momentous events of 1989'.[8] The fall of France ended the European war and wrecked the possibility of any return to a European balance of power. It destroyed the ability of the great European nations to determine the global order. Each of the Axis powers were encouraged to embark on aggressive policies which were to bring the Soviet Union and the United States into what became in 1941 a global conflict. While the survival of Britain

[8] David Reynolds, '1940: Fulcrum of the Twentieth Century?', International Affairs, 66: 2 (1990), 328.

prevented a total German victory, only the entry of the Soviet Union and the United States ensured the destruction of Nazi Germany and, for the most part, dictated the outcome of the world war and the shape of the post-war settlement. As had been predicted by Alexis de Tocqueville, in 1835, Russia and the United States had become the two World Powers. Europe would never regain the place or influence that it still enjoyed in 1919. Global politics replaced the European-oriented politics of the past. France's defeat also proved a turning point in the history of European imperialism. It opened the 'decisive phase of Britain's imperial crisis'.[9] The Italians were encouraged to move in the Mediterranean and threaten British control over Egypt and Suez. The Japanese advanced into French Indo-China, which would serve as an advanced base for the invasion of British Malaya and the Dutch East Indies, both overrun in the winter of 1941–1942. As Britain could not provide for their defence and was, itself, under siege, Canada, Australia, and New Zealand moved closer to the United States. After May 1940, when Indian cooperation became more vital, first in the Middle East, and, after the Japanese invasion of Malaya, for the very future of British India, the Congress party twice refused the offer of Dominion status at the end of the war. A series of defeats in different theatres of war between June 1940 and October 1942 'set in motion a rapid, cumulative and irreversible transformation of the pre-war structure of British world power'.[10] The fall of Singapore on 15 February 1942 was more than a defeat for Britain; it accelerated the collapse of the structures of European world rule as they had been renewed in 1919.

Germany attacked the USSR on 22 June 1941, with Hitler convinced that the Soviet state would disintegrate under a few thunderous hammer blows. It almost did. Torn between his fears of a German attack and the unprepared state of the Red Army, Stalin pursued a policy of appeasement towards Germany while speeding measures for defence. As the German forces gathered for the attack, the Soviet dictator disregarded almost every conceivable warning that Germany was about to invade. He could not admit that he had miscalculated. Always suspicious of British intentions, he dismissed Churchill's warnings of the forthcoming invasion, more equivocal in the manner of their presentation than was later claimed, in the belief that it was a manoeuvre to get the Soviet Union engaged in a war with Germany. Any German offensive, he was convinced, would come only after a period of negotiations and increasing diplomatic and military pressure. The

[9] John Darwin, *The Empire Project: The Rise and Fall of the British World System, 1830–1970* (Cambridge, 2009) 499.
[10] Darwin, *The Empire Project*, 501.

cost of his stubbornness, even in the face of the alarms of his own generals, was immeasurable. The first days of the war saw literally hundreds of thousands of Soviet soldiers killed, wounded, and captured and much of the Red air force destroyed on the ground. But the quick victory Hitler intended did not materialize; in its place came years of unparalleled brutality and destruction as the greater part of the fighting during the remainder of the war took place on the Eastern Front. It would be the Soviet armies, with decisive material assistance from the West, that would destroy the *Wehrmacht*.

Japan attacked the United States on 7 December 1941 knowing that it could not achieve a decisive military victory. The Japanese leaders anticipated a German victory over the Soviet Union and Hitler was urging a southern attack. A weakened Britain could not defend its empire. At a time when the Japanese were preparing to take advantage of the global crisis to stop the flow of Western (mainly American) supplies to China and to achieve its autarkic goals, the Americans adopted a stronger line towards Tokyo. Roosevelt and Hull hoped through diplomacy and sanctions to deter Japan from moving north or south. The Japanese leadership were prepared to fight to achieve their goals, believing that initial naval victories against the United States would be followed by a stalemate and a negotiated peace recognizing Japan's position in China and its new gains. The leadership was convinced that this was the time to fight, while the global situation was highly favourable and before the Americans completed their naval rearmament. Their plan was fatally flawed, for an unprovoked attack in peacetime destroyed from the outset the possibility of a negotiated peace and, by so doing, ensured Japan's ultimate defeat. There were miscalculations and misperceptions on both sides. Just as Tokyo believed rightly that the United States would deal with the German threat first but wrongly that it would condone Japanese expansionism, the Americans misjudged the extent of the Japanese commitment to an empire that would end its economic insecurity and confirm its leadership in East Asia. During 1941, assuming that Japan would not go to war against a power it could not defeat, Washington tightened the 'economic noose' around Japan's neck and sent out diplomatic and economic warnings. Divisions in Washington turned a flexible sanctions policy into a virtual freeze on bilateral trade and a *de facto* oil embargo. Already concerned that Japan would be cut off from the raw material imports needed to make war, Tokyo was faced with this grim reality. It was to solve the strategic dilemma that General Hideki Tōjō abandoned the traditional naval strategy against the United States and opted for an attack on Pearl Harbor, hoping that an enfeebled and disheartened Washington would negotiate and turn its attention to

Germany. The Americans, too, were the victims of their own miscalculations and, almost to the end, thought the Japanese would back down and accept their terms.

Finally, Germany declared war on the United States, Hitler recalling the rubber-stamp Reichstag especially for the purpose on 11 December, making a German victory impossible. Assuming that war with America was inevitable and, indeed, that it had already begun, Hitler's main fear had been that Japan would settle with the United States. Though not forewarned of the coming attack, the German leader quickly seized what he saw as the opportunity to cement the alliance with Japan and bring its powerful navy into the war. Japan could now fight the Americans on Germany's behalf until the USSR and Britain were defeated and Germany could prepare for the 'war against the continents'. It was an irrational act. Hitler was gambling on the ability of the *Wehrmacht* to bring a quick victory. Roosevelt obtained declarations of war from Congress in return. Whether this would have been possible without Hitler's declaration of war is a moot point. With the United States now in the conflict and the Germans engaged with the Red Army, there was only one possible outcome. As Churchill recalled the moment of America's entry into the war in his memoirs: 'So we had won after all! . . . All the rest was merely the proper application of overwhelming force'.[11]

As the limited European struggle became a global war, there was no way that Germany could triumph against its adversaries, but it would still take over three more years and overwhelming losses before it was conquered. In the meantime, Hitler almost won his racial war. The killings had already begun in Poland and, on 30 January 1941, Hitler reiterated his pledge of two years earlier to finish the role of Jewry in Europe. Formal decisions taken on 20 January 1942 in the Berlin suburb of Wannsee to implement a 'Final Solution of the Jewish Question' were intended to assure, as Reinhard Heydrich explained, that all eleven million Jews in Europe should 'fall away'. The Nazis ultimately managed to murder almost six million Jews, a figure so large and so horrific that its reality still remains near impossible to comprehend. Too many, and not just in Germany, willingly assisted them. While the war's immeasurable costs and the destruction were not restricted to Europe, it is clear in retrospect that it marked the end of the Continent's global ascendancy. The demise of European dominance was a gradual process that began before 1914 and ended after 1945, yet only the bloodletting of two massive wars ensured the transfer of power away from Europe to

[11] Winston S. Churchill, *The Second World War*, Vol. III: *The Grand Alliance* (London, 1950), 539.

the United States and the Soviet Union and to the near collapse of the European empires. Europe would never again be at the centre of world politics, nor could it ever again claim the superior moral position that had buttressed its prestige in so many non-European regions. Hitler's war transformed the global scene in ways that neither he nor his reluctant opponents could have anticipated. The Continent is still to recover from this second hecatomb. It was as Yeats had prophesized in 1921:

> Things fall apart; the centre cannot hold;
> Mere anarchy is loosed upon the world,
> The blood-dimmed tide is loosed, and everywhere
> The ceremony of innocence is drowned;
> The best lack all conviction, while the worst
> Are full of passionate intensity.
>
> W. B. Yeats, 'The Second Coming'

When the fighting finally ended, a new world, dark in its own way, loomed.

APPENDIX A
STATISTICAL TABLES

Table A-1. US$ Conversion Tables, 1929–1941

	$/GBP	GBP/$	Fr./$	RM/$	Lira/$	Yen/$	Swiss Fr./$	Rouble/$
1929	4.88	0.2	25.39	4.18	19.1	2.04	5.14	1.94
1930	4.86	0.21	25.24	4.19	19.09	2.02	5.16	1.94
1931	3.37	0.3	25.49	4.23	19.57	2.23	5.13	1.9
1932	3.28	0.3	25.62	4.2	19.57	4.82	5.2	1.93
1933	5.12	0.2	16.34	2.68	12.16	3.25	3.3	1.93
1934	4.95	0.2	15.16	2.47	11.71	3.47	3.09	4.96
1935	4.93	0.2	15.15	2.47	12.38	3.48	3.08	5.04
1936	4.91	0.2	21.42	2.46	19.01	3.51	4.35	5.9
1937	5	0.2	29.46	2.48	19.01	3.44	4.32	5.29
1938	4.67	0.21	37.99	2.47	19.01	3.68	4.42	5.3
1939	3.93	0.25	44.9	2.49	37.25	4.27	4.46	5.3
1940	4.04	0.25	49.19	2.49	43.18	4.27	4.31	5.3
1941	4.04	0.25	44.94	2.5	52.78	4.27	4.31	5.3

Sources: 'Global Financial Data', database; R. L. Bidwell, *Currency Tables* (London, 1970).

Table A-2. German Output of Modern Bombers and Fighters 1936–1939 (by quarters)

	Bombers			Fighters
	Do 17	He 111	Ju 88	Bf 109
III 36	21	0	0	0
IV 36	39	0	0	3
I 37	90	36	0	21
II 37	90	112	0	33
III 37	89	97	0	155
IV 37	126	96	0	118
I 38	94	134	0	235
II 38	45	140	0	319
III 38	205	196	0	179
IV 38	116	223	0	198
I 39	181	194	2	359
II 39	221	351	9	303
III 39	212	334	24	476
IV 39	157	248	75	394
1936	60	0	0	3
1937	395	341	0	327
1938	460	693	0	931
1939	771	1127	110	1532
	Bombers		Fighters Bf 109	
1936	60		3	
1937	736		327	
1938	1153		931	
1939	2008		1532	
Grand Total	3957		2793	

Source: Bundesarchiv/Militärarchiv Freiburg, RL 3/976: Fertigungsablauf Bomber-Jäger, 19.9.1941. Sent to author by Lutz Budrass, author of *Flugzeugindustrie und Luftrüstung in Deutschland 1918–1945* (Düsseldorf, 1998).

Table A-3. German aircraft production, 1934–1939

	1934	1935	1936	1937	1938	1939	1934/5
Hertel Figures	1817	3307	5248	5749	5316	7582	Ju52/He70
Antoine Figures	1961	3101	5161	5947	5401	7957	
Antoine figures %							
Bomber	2	2	6	20	27	30	17
Light fighter	7	7	5	5	18	20	7
Heavy fighter & Dive bomber	1	1	2	6	5	12	1
Reconnaissance	17	17	6	3	4	5	17
Other	70	72	81	66	46	33	58
Antoine figures							
Bomber	39	62	310	1189	1458	2387	
Light fighter	140	222	258	297	972	1591	
Heavy fighter & Dive bomber	28	44	103	357	270	955	
Reconnaissance	334	529	310	178	216	398	
Other	1420	2246	4180	3925	2484	2626	

The Hertel figures were an estimation made for the US Airforce in 1953 by Walter Hertel, an ex-senor official of the RLM. The Antoine figures are more contemporary and were compiled from monthly data in the RLM in 1943. The differences between them are not great and can be explained by assigning aircraft to different categories, such as the Ju % transport appears as an auxiliary bomber up until 1937. The table clearly shows that before the major changeover to new types of aircraft which would be used in the war, such as the He 111 and the Me 109, the bulk of production was devoted to training aircraft.

Source: Antoine, Herbert: *Die Deutsche Luftfahrtindustrie in Zahlen 1933–1945, Statistisches und Persönliches* Manuskript Anfang 1943. (Forschungsstelle Luftfahrtindustie, Ruhr-University Bochum) Hertel, Walter: *Die Flugzeugbeschaffung in der Deutschen Luftwaffe*, 2 Bde., (Bibliothek des Militärgeschichtlichen Forschungsamtes, Lw 16/1 u. 2.) Sent to author by Lutz Budrass, author of *Flugzeugindustrie und Luftrüstung in Deutschland 1918–1945* (Düsseldorf, 1998).

Table A-4. Comparative Strengths of the Principal Naval Powers before September 1939

	UK	USA	Japan	France	Italy	Germany	Russia
Battleships	12	15	9	5	4	2	3
Battle cruisers	3			1		2	
Pocket battleships						3	
Aircraft carriers	7	5	5	1			
Cruisers	62	32	39	18	21	6	4
Destroyers	159	209	84	58	48	17	34
Escorts	38			25	32	8	
Submarines	54	87	58	76	104	57	170

Sources: S. Roskill, *Naval Policy Between the Wars*, Vol. 1, 577; Jürgen Rohwer and Mikhail S. Monakov, *Stalin's Ocean-Going Fleet* (London, 2001), 90–102. Except for Soviet Union—figures reproduced here are for August 1939.

Table A-5. Major Soviet Exports to Germany in Thousands of Tons, 1939–1941 (Soviet Figures)

	1939 (Sep.–Dec.)	1940	1941 (Jan.–June)
Grains	5.7	897.7	707.7
Timber	90.1	975.8	161.7
Textiles	8.1	98.2	65.1
Rags	2.1	6.0	1.9
Meats	0.3	3.8	1.4
Animal skins	0.6	1.1	0.1
Pulses	8.4	35.9	36.5
Oil Seed Cake	0.0	26.2	15.6
Fat Vegetable Oils	0.0	8.9	0.5
Oil	1.4	657.4	282.9
Manganese	3.4	107.1	54.7
Chromium	0.0	23.4	0.0
Asbestos	1.8	13.6	3.2
Phosphates	10.3	163.6	28.4
Glycerine	0.0	3.7	0.2
Other	13.9	10.4	2.4
Total	**146.1**	**3032.8**	**1362.3**

Source: Edward E. Ericson, *Feeding the German Eagle: Soviet Economic Aid to Nazi Germany, 1933–1941* (Westport, CT, 1999), 198.

TABLE A-6. Major German Exports to the Soviet Union, 1938–1941

	1938	1939	1940	1941 (6 months)
Coal	0.0	0.0	3845.9	1273.6
Machines	4.6	9.1	19.4	40.2
Finished Iron: Tools	2.5	0.8	14.3	8.4
Unfinished Iron: Tubing	15.9	15.7	98.7	61.4
Motor Vehicles & Planes	0.0	0.0	0.4	3.0
Chemicals: Unfinished	2.6	0.5	1.7	2.1
Electrical Goods	0.1	0.6	3.3	3.5
Optical Equipment	0.2	0.1	0.2	0.3
Metals	0.5	0.1	3.7	3.1
Naval Equipment	0	0	6	5

Source: Edward E. Ericson, *Feeding the German Eagle: Soviet Economic Aid to Nazi Germany, 1933–1941* (Westport, CT, 1999), 199.

APPENDIX B
PRIME MINISTERS AND FOREIGN MINISTERS OF SELECTED EUROPEAN POWERS

Czechoslovakia

Prime Minister	Period of Office
Jan Malypetr	31 Oct. 1932 – 6 Nov. 1935
Milan Hodža	9 Nov. 1935 – 22 Sep. 1938
Jan Syrový	22 Sep. 1938 – 1 Feb. 1939
Rudolf Beran	1 Feb. 1939 – 13 Mar. 1939
Alois Eliáš	27 Apr. 1939 – 28 Sep. 1941

Foreign Minister	Period of Office
Edvard Beneš	16 Nov. 1918 – 18 Dec. 1935
Milan Hodža	18 Dec. 1935 – 28 Feb. 1936
Kamil Krofta	28 Feb. 1936 – 4 Oct. 1938
František Chvalkovský	4 Oct. 1938 – 1939

France

Prime Minister	Period of Office	Foreign Minister
Joseph Paul-Boncour	18 Dec. 1932 – 28 Jan. 1933	Joseph Paul-Boncour (31 Dec. 1932 – 30 Jan. 1934)
Édouard Daladier	31 Jan. 1933 – 26 Oct. 1933	Joseph Paul-Boncour
Albert Sarraut	26 Oct. 1933 – 23 Nov.1933	Joseph Paul-Boncour
Camille Chautemps	26 Nov. 1933 – 27 Jan. 1934	Joseph Paul-Boncour
Édouard Daladier	30 Jan. 1934 – 7 Feb. 1934	Édouard Daladier
Gaston Doumergue	9 Feb. 1934 – 8 Nov. 1934	Louis Barthou (to 9 Oct. 1934) Pierre Laval (from 13 Oct. 1934)
Pierre-Étienne Flandin	8 Nov. 1934 – 31 May 1935	Pierre Laval
Fernand Bouisson	1 Jun.1935 – 4 Jun. 1935	Pierre Laval
Pierre Laval	7 Jun. 1935 – 22 Jan. 1936	Pierre Laval
Albert Sarraut	24 Jan. 1936 – 4 Jun. 1936	Pierre-Étienne Flandin
Léon Blum	4 Jun. 1936 – 21 Jun. 1937	Yvon Delbos
Camille Chautemps	22 Jun. 1937 – 14 Jan. 1938	Yvon Delbos
Camille Chautemps	18 Jan. 1938 – 10 Mar. 1938	Yvon Delbos
Léon Blum	13 Mar. 1938 – 8 Apr. 1938	Joseph Paul-Boncour
Édouard Daladier	10 Apr. 1938 – 20 Mar. 1940	Georges Bonnet (10 Apr. 1938 – 13 Sep. 1939) Édouard Daladier (13 Sep. 1939 – 21 Mar. 1939)
Paul Reynaud	21 Mar. 1940 – 16 Jun. 1940	Paul Reynaud (to 18 May 1940) Édouard Daladier (18 May 1940 – 5 June 1940) Paul Reynaud (5–16 June 1940)
Philippe Pétain	16 Jun. 1940 – 12 Jul. 1940	Paul Baudouin

Germany

Reichskanzler	Period of Office	Foreign Minister
Kurt von Schleicher	3 Dec. 1932 – 30 Jan. 1933	Konstantin Freiherr von Neurath
Adolf Hitler	30 Jan. 1933 – 30 Apr. 1945	Konstantin Freiherr von Neurath (to 4 Feb. 1938) Joachim von Ribbentrop (4 Feb. 1938 – 30 Apr. 1945)

Italy

Prime Minister	Period of Office	Foreign Minister
Benito Mussolini	31 Oct. 1922 – 25 July 1943	Benito Mussolini (31 Oct. 1922 to 12 Sep. 1929), Dino Grandi (12 Sep. 1929–20 July 1932), Benito Mussolini (20 July 1932–1936), Galeazzo Ciano (10 June 1936–8 February 1943), Benito Mussolini (1943)

Union of Soviet Socialist Republics

Chairman of the All-Russian Central Executive Committee

30 Mar. 1919 – 15 July 1938	Mikhail Kalinin

Chairman of the Council of People's Commissars

19 Dec. 1930 – 6 May 1941	Vyacheslav M. Molotov
6 May 1941 – 5 Mar. 1953	Joseph Stalin

Secretary-General of the Communist Party

3 Apr. 1922 – 5 Mar. 1953	Joseph Stalin

Foreign Ministers

27 July 1930 – 3 May 1939	Maksim M. Litvinov
3 May 1939 – Mar. 1949	Vyacheslav M. Molotov

United Kingdom (Britain)

Prime Minister	Period of Office	Foreign Secretary
James Ramsay MacDonald	5 Nov. 1931 – 7 June 1935	Sir John Simon (5 Nov. 1931 – 7 June 1935)
Stanley Baldwin	7 June 1935 – 28 May 1937	Sir Samuel Hoare (7 Jun. 1935 – 18 Dec. 1935) Anthony Eden (from 22 Dec. 1935)
Neville Chamberlain	28 May 1937 – 10 May 1940	Anthony Eden (to 20 Feb. 1938), Edward Frederick Wood, Viscount Halifax (21 Feb. 1938 – 22 Dec. 1940)

United States of America

Presidents	Period of Office
Herbert Hoover	4 Mar. 1929 – 4 Mar. 1933
Franklin Delano Roosevelt	4 Mar. 1933 – 12 Apr. 1945

Secretary of State	Period of Office
Henry Lewis Stimson	28 Mar. 1929 – 4 Mar. 1933
Cordell Hull	4 Mar. 1933 – 30 Nov. 1944

APPENDIX C
CHRONOLOGY OF INTERNATIONAL EVENTS, 1933–1941

1933

28 Jan.	Kurt von Schleicher resigns as German chancellor
30 Jan.	Adolf Hitler appointed German chancellor
16 Feb.	Little Entente Pact of Organization
27 Feb.	Reichstag fire
24 Feb.	League adopts Lytton report
5 Mar.	Reichstag elections
14 Mar.	Mussolini proposes Four Power Pact
24 Mar.	Enabling Law in Germany
27 Mar.	Japan leaves League of Nations
20 Apr.	United States abandons Gold Standard parity
3 July	Joseph Avenol appointed Secretary-General of the League of Nations
12 June–25 July	Second World Economic Conference in London
15 July	France, Germany, Great Britain, and Italy sign 'Pact of Four'
14 Oct.	Germany leaves World Disarmament Conference and League of Nations

1934

26 Jan.	German–Polish Non-Aggression Pact, to expire in ten years
9 Feb.	Greece, Romania, Turkey, and Yugoslavia conclude Athens Pact of the Balkans to protect status quo
6 Feb.	Right-wing riots in Paris
12 Feb.	General strike in France
12–16 Feb.	Civil war in Vienna and suppression of Socialists
17 Mar.	Rome Protocol signed between Austria, Hungary, and Italy
15 May	Ulmanis *coup* in Latvia
14–16 June	Mussolini and Hitler meet in Venice
30 June	Hitler's 'Night of the Long Knives'
25 July	Failure of National Socialist putsch in Vienna and assassination of Austrian chancellor, Engelbert Dollfuss
30 Jul.	Kurt Schuschnigg chancellor of Austria
2 Aug.	Reichspräsident Hindenburg dies in Germany. Reichspräsident's office amalgamated with that of Reich chancellor. Hitler's official title becomes 'Führer'
12 Sep.	Cooperation Treaty between Estonia, Latvia, and Lithuania

18 Sep.	Soviet Union enters the League of Nations
9 Oct.	Assassination in Marseilles of King Alexander of Yugoslavia and French foreign minister, Louis Barthou
19–22 Oct.	Treaty of Cooperation between Hungary and Poland negotiated in Warsaw
1 Dec.	Assassination of Kirov
5–6 Dec.	Wal Wal incident in Ethiopia

1935

5 Jan.	French–Italian Agreement
13 Jan.	Plebiscite in Saarland
17 Jan.	Saarland returns to Germany
16 Mar.	German military conscription introduced
11–14 Apr.	Stresa Conference
2 May	Franco-Soviet Pact signed
12 May	Death of Marshal Piłsudski
16 May	Russo-Czech mutual assistance treaty signed
18 June	Anglo-German naval agreement
27 June	British Peace Ballot results published
15 Sep.	Nuremberg Laws against Jews in Germany
3 Oct.	Italy invades Ethiopia
11 Oct.	League of Nations imposes sanctions on Italy
6–7 Dec.	Hoare–Laval plan

1936

20 Jan.	Accession of King Edward VIII in Britain
7 Mar.	Hitler re-militarizes Rhineland and denounces Locarno Pact
21–24 Mar.	Conference in Rome between representatives of Austria, Hungary, and Italy to co-ordinate policy in the Danube region
3 May	Popular Front government in France
5 May	Ethiopian War ends
11 July	Austro-German Treaty
17 July	Spanish Civil War begins
20 July	Montreux Convention gives Turkey effective control over Straits
21 July	Litvinov and Titulescu conclude Russo-Romanian protocol regarding mutual assistance pact in Montreux
1–16 Aug.	Olympic Games in Berlin
5 Aug.	Dictatorship of General Metaxas established in Greece
26 Sept.	Dismissal of Yagoda and replacement by Ezhov; beginning of large-scale purges in the USSR
1 Oct.	Franco declared head of state in Spain
1 Oct.	Devaluation of French franc
25 Oct.	Rome–Berlin Axis Agreement signed
1 Nov.	Mussolini proclaims existence of Rome–Berlin Axis
18 Nov.	Germany and Italy officially recognize Franco's government in Spain
25 Nov.	Anti-Comintern Pact (Nazi Germany and Japan)
11 Dec.	Abdication of King Edward VIII after constitutional crisis

1937

2 Jan.	Anglo-Italian Accord on maintaining Mediterranean status quo
14 Mar.	Pope Pius XI publishes encyclical *Mit brennender Sorge*
19 Mar.	Pope Pius XI publishes encyclical (*Divini Redemptoris*) condemning Communism
25 May	World Exhibition opens in Paris
7 July	Sino-Japanese undeclared war begins
11 July	Stalin begins purge of Red Army generals
25–28 Sep.	Mussolini's visit to Berlin
5 Oct.	President Roosevelt's 'quarantine speech'
6 Nov.	Italy joins German–Japanese Anti-Comintern Pact
26 Nov.	Hjalmar Schacht relieved of his post as minister for economic affairs in Germany
11 Dec.	Italy leaves the League of Nations

1938

12 Feb.	Hitler and Schuschnigg meet at Obersalzberg
24 Feb.	Joachim von Ribbentrop replaces Konstantin Freiherr von Neurath as German foreign minister
12–13 Mar.	*Anschluss*
3–9 May	Hitler's visit to Rome
20 July	British government proposes Runciman mission to Czechoslovakia
3 Aug.	Anti-Semitic legislation introduced in Italy
20–29 Aug.	Non-Aggression Pact between Hungary and Little Entente (Bled)
15 Sep.	Chamberlain–Hitler meeting at Berghof
20–21 Sep.	German–Hungarian talks regarding the co-ordination of their territorial demands against Czechoslovakia
22–23 Sep.	Godesberg meeting
29 Sep.	Munich Agreement between France, Germany, Great Britain, and Italy
2 Nov.	First Vienna Award grants parts of Slovakia to Hungary
9–10 Nov.	Anti-Semitic pogroms in Germany (*Kristallnacht*)

1939

24 Feb.	Hungary joins Anti-Comintern Pact and Rome–Berlin Axis
12 Mar.	Pope Pius XII crowned
14 Mar.	Slovak parliament declares independence of Slovakia under leadership of Josef Tiso
14–15 Mar.	Germany occupies Czechoslovakia
16 Mar.	Hitler proclaims Bohemian–Moravian protectorate
23 Mar.	German–Romanian economic agreement
23 Mar.	Germany occupies Memel
28 Mar.	Spanish Civil War ends
31 Mar.	British–French guarantee for Poland
31 Mar.	French–Romanian economic agreement
7 Apr.	Italy seizes Albania
3 May	Molotov appointed commissar for foreign affairs replacing Litvinov
11 May	British–Romanian economic agreement
22 May	German–Italian Pact of Steel

23 Aug.	Soviet–German Non-Aggression Pact
31 Aug.	German ultimatum to Poland
1 Sep.	Germany invades Poland
3 Sep.	Britain and France declare war on Germany
5 Sep.	Independent Slovakia joins attack on Poland
7 Sep.	Romania declares neutrality
17 Sep.	Soviet attack on Poland
24 Sep.	Resumption of diplomatic relations between USSR and Hungary
28 Sep.	Capitulation of Poland
29 Sep.	Partition of Poland by Germany and USSR
5 Oct.	Pact of mutual assistance between USSR and Latvia
Oct.	Soviet troops occupy Latvia, Lithuania, and Estonia
30 Nov.	USSR attacks Finland
14 Dec.	USSR expelled from League of Nations

1940

8 Apr.	Germany invades Denmark and Norway
10 May	Germany invades Belgium, Luxembourg, and the Netherlands
10 May	Churchill replaces Chamberlain as prime minister of Britain
27 May	Romanian–German economic agreement
10 June	Italy declares war on France and the United Kingdom (effective 11 June)
14 June	German troops enter Paris
16 June	Philippe Pétain prime minister of France
16 June	Soviet occupation of Baltic states
17 June	Pétain asks for armistice
18 June	De Gaulle's first radio appeal from London for 'Free France'
22 June	France signs Armistice with Germany
24 June	Franco-Italian armistice signed in Rome
1 July – 19 Aug.	Italian offensive against British forces in North Africa
3 July	British Royal Navy destroys part of French fleet at Oran
30 Aug.	Second Vienna Award: Hungary gains Northern Transylvania from Romania
31 Aug.	Sean Lester becomes (last) secretary general of the League of Nations
27 Sep.	Tripartite Pact between Germany, Italy, and Japan
2 Oct.	Warsaw ghetto established
23 Oct.	Hitler–Franco meeting at Hendaye, France
24 Oct.	Hitler–Pétain meeting at Montoire, France
28 Oct.	Italy invades Greece
20 Nov.	Hungary joins Tripartite Pact (Germany, Italy, Japan)
23 Nov.	Romania joins Tripartite Pact

1941

5–27 Mar.	Coup against pro-German Regent in Yugoslavia
6 Apr.	Germany invades Yugoslavia and Greece
17 Apr.	Capitulation of Yugoslavian army
3 May	Italy annexes parts of Slovenia
22 June	Germany invades USSR
27 June	Hungary declares war on USSR

29 June	Germany occupies Lithuania
7 July	United States occupy Iceland
1–2 July	Germany occupies Latvia
July–Aug.	Germany occupies Estonia
14 Aug.	Atlantic Charter signed by Roosevelt and Churchill
14–16 Oct.	Beginning of systematic deportation of German Jews to concentration camps
6 Dec.	United Kingdom declares war on Finland and Romania
7 Dec.	Japanese attack on Pearl Harbor
7 Dec.	Hungary declares war on United Kingdom
8 Dec.	United Kingdom and the United States declare war on Japan
11 Dec.	Germany and Italy declare war on United States
12 Dec.	Bulgaria and Romania declare war on United States
13 Dec.	Hungary declares war on United States

GENERAL BIBLIOGRAPHY
Volume 2

Manuscript and Primary Sources

Work in these archives for this volume has been highly selective. Few private collections have been seen in their entirety. Only general categories of Foreign Office and Ministry papers have been cited, except when used in the text.

Britain

Private papers

Stanley Baldwin	Cambridge University Library
Alexander Cadogan	Churchill College, Cambridge: ACAD National Archives, Kew: FO800/293
Austen Chamberlain	Birmingham University Library: AC National Archives, Kew: FO800/263
Neville Chamberlain	Birmingham University Library: NC
Winston Churchill	Churchill College, Cambridge: CHAR
Duff Cooper Papers	Churchill College, Cambridge: DUFC
Hugh Dalton Papers	British Library of Political Science and Economics, London
Admiral Reginald Drax	Churchill College, Cambridge: DRAX
Anthony Eden	Birmingham University Library: AE
Lord (Maurice) Hankey	Churchill College, Cambridge: HNKY
Thomas Inskip	Churchill College, Cambridge: INKP
Sir Hugh Montgomery Knatchbull-Hugessen	Churchill College, Cambridge: KNAT
Owen O'Malley	In author's possession, bulk are held in Dublin, Ireland
Sir Eric Phipps	Churchill College, Cambridge: PHPP National Archives, Kew: FO794/16
Lord (John) Simon	Bodleian Library, Oxford: MSS. Simon National Archives, Kew: FO800/285–291

Lord Templewood (Samuel Hoare)	Cambridge University Library
Lord (Robert) Vansittart	Churchill College, Cambridge: VNST
Viscount Weir	Churchill College, Cambridge: WEIR

The National Archives: Public Record Office, Kew

Cabinet Office: CAB

CAB24	Cabinet Papers
CAB27	Cabinet Committees
CAB53	Chiefs of Staff Committee

Foreign Office: FO

FO371	Foreign Office: General Correspondence
FO800/264–271	Sir Nevile Henderson Papers
FO800/272–279	Orme Sargent Papers
FO800/293	Alexander Cadogan Papers
FO800/296	Lord Cranborne Papers
FO800/309–328	Viscount Halifax Papers
FO954	Office Papers of Sir Anthony Eden

Prime Minister's Office: PREM

Records of the Public Records Office: PRO

PRO30/69	James Ramsay MacDonald Papers

Treasury: T

France

Private papers

Papiers d'Agents-Archives Privées dans les Archives du Ministère des Affaires Étrangères, Paris:

Papiers Réné Massigli

Papiers 1940:

Papiers Georges Bonnet

Papiers Édouard Daladier

Papiers Henri Hoppenot

Papiers Alexis Léger

Archives Nationales, Paris

Papiers Joseph Paul-Boncour

Papiers Édouard Daladier

Papiers André François-Poncet

Papiers Paul Reynaud

Papiers Victor-Henri Schweisguth

Archives du Ministere des Affaires Étrangères, Paris

Série Z, Europe 1918–1940

Allemagne

Printed Official Sources

Belgium

Documents diplomatiques belges, 1920–1940

Tome 3: période 1931–1936 (Brussels, 1964).

Tome 4: période 1936–1937 (Brussels, 1964).

Tome 5: période 1938–1940 (Brussels, 1966).

Britain

Documents on British Foreign Policy, 1919–1939

Series II: *1929–1938*, 21 vols. (London, 1946–1984).

Series III: *1938–1939*, 10 vols. (London, 1947–1961).

British Documents on Foreign Affairs: Reports and Papers from the Foreign Office Confidential Print, Part II: From the First to the Second World War

Series A: *The Soviet Union, 1917–1939*, 17 vols. (Frederick, MD, 1984–1992).

Series B: *Turkey, Iran, and the Middle East, 1918–1939*, 35 vols. (Frederick, MD, 1985–1997).

Series C: *North America, 1919–1939*, 25 vols. (Frederick, MD, 1986–1995).

Series F: *Europe, 1919–1939*, 67 vols. (Bethesda, MD, 1990–1996).

Series J: *The League of Nations, 1918–1941*, 10 vols. (Frederick, MD, 1992–1995).

Series K: *Economic Affairs, Cultural Propaganda, and the Reform of the Foreign Office, 1910–1939*, 4 vols. (Bethesda, MD, 1997).

Parliamentary Debates (Official Reports)

House of Commons, Fifth Series, vols. 274–366: 1933–1940.

House of Lords, Fifth Series, vols. 86–117: 1933–1940.

Gilbert, M., *Winston S. Churchill, Vol. 5: Companion. Pt. 1: Documents, The Exchequer Years, 1922–1929*; *Pt. 2: Documents, The Wilderness Years, 1929–35*; *Pt. 3: Documents, The Coming of War, 1936–1939* (London, 1979–82). 3 vols.

France

Chambre des Députés, Débats Parlementaires: Journal officiel de la République française

16e législature (1932–1936).

17e législature (1936–1940).

Sénat, Débats Parlementaires:
Journal officiel de la République française

16e législature (1932–1936).
17e législature (1936–1940).

Documents diplomatiques français, 1932–1939
2ème série: *1936–1939*, 19 vols. (Paris, 1963–1986).

Germany

Akten zur Deutschen Auswärtigen Politik, 1918–1945
Serie C: *1933–1937*, 6 vols. (Göttingen, 1971–1981).
Serie D: *1937–1941*, 13 vols. (Baden-Baden/Frankfurt am Main, 1950–1970).
Documents on German Foreign Policy, 1918–1945
Series C: *1933–1937*, 6 vols. (London, 1957–1983).
Series D: *1937–1945*, 13 vols. (London, 1949–1964).
Office of Chief of Counsel for the Prosecution of Axis Criminality, *Nazi Conspiracy and Aggression*, 8 vols. (London, 1946–1950).

Italy

I documenti diplomatici italiani
Settima serie: *1922–1935*, 16 vols. (Rome, 1953–1990).
Ottava serie: *1935–1939* (publication continuing), 13 vols. (Rome, 1952–).
MUSSOLINI, BENITO, *Opera Omnia*, ed. Susmel, Edoardo and Duilio, vols. 25–29: *24 Mar. 1931 – 12 June 1940* (Rome, 1954–1959).

Switzerland

Commission Nationale pour la Publication de Documentation diplomatiques Suisses, nationale Kommission für die Veröffentlichtung diplomatischer Dokumente der Schweiz, *Documents diplomatiques suisses—Diplomatische Dokumente der Schweiz—Documenti diplomatici svizzeri*, vols. 7–13: 11 Nov. 1918–31 Dec. 1940 (Bern, 1979–1991).

USA

Department of State, *Papers Relating to the Foreign Relations of the United States*, vols. for 1933–1940 (Washington, DC, 1933–1940).
The Public Papers and Addresses of Franklin D. Roosevelt, 1938–1950, ed. Samuel I. Rosenman, 13 vols. (New York, 1939–1950).
Franklin D. Roosevelt and Foreign Affairs, January 1933 – January 1937, ed. Edgar B. Nixon, 3 vols. (Cambridge, MA, 1969).
Franklin D. Roosevelt and Foreign Affairs, January 1937 – August 1939, ed. Donald B. Schewe, 11 vols. (New York, 1979).

—— *The Roosevelt Letters: Being the Personal Correspondence of Franklin Delano Roosevelt*, 3 vols., ed. E. Roosevelt (London, 1949–1952).

USSR

Degras, Jane (ed.), *The Communist International, 1919–1943: Documents and Commentary*, 3 vols. (London, 1956–1965).

Dokumenty po istorii miunkhenskogo sgovora, 1937–1939 (Moscow, 1979).

Dokumenty vneshnei politiki, SSSR
7 noiabria 1917 g.–31 dekabria 1938 g., 21 vols. (Moscow, 1957–1977).

Dokumenty vneshnei politiki 1939 god, 2 vols. (Moscow, 1992).

God krizisa: dokumenty i materialy, 2 vols. (Moscow, 1990).

Gromyko, A. A. et al. (eds.), *Soviet Peace Efforts on the Eve of World War II (September 1938 – August 1939): Documents and Records* (Moscow, 1973).

Ministry of Foreign Affairs of the USSR, *Documents and Materials relating to the Eve of the Second World War: The Dirksen Papers (1938–9)* (Moscow, 1948).

Royal Institute of International Affairs, *Soviet Documents on Foreign Policy, 1917–1941*, ed. Jane Degras, 3 vols. (London, 1951–1953).

League of Nations

Official Journal, (London, Geneva, Lausanne, 1933–1940), 8 vols.

Memoirs, Diaries, Letters, and Autobiographies

Britain

Amery, Leopold C. M. S., *My Political Life, 1953–1955*, 3 vols. (London, 1953).

—— *The Empire at Bay: The Leo Amery Diaries, 1929–1945*, ed. John Barnes and David Nicholson (London, 1988).

Angell, Sir Norman, *After All* (London, 1951).

Ashton-Gwatkin, Frank, 'Thoughts on the Foreign Office, 1918–1939', *Contemporary Review*, 188 (1955), 374–378.

Atholl, Duchess of [Katharine Marjory StewertMurray], *Working Partnership* (London, 1958).

Attlee, Clement, *As It Happened* (London, 1954).

Avon, Lord (Anthony Eden), *The Eden Memoirs*, 3 vols. (London, 1960–5).

Baldwin, Stanley, *This Torch of Freedom: Speeches and Addresses* (London, 1935).

Balfour, Arthur James, *Opinions and Argument from Speeches and Addresses of the Earl of Balfour, 1910–1927* (London, 1927).

Balfour, Harold, *Wings over Westminster* (London, 1973).

Bartlett, Vernon, *And Now Tomorrow* (London, 1960).

Bernays, Robert, *The Diaries and Letters of Robert Bernays, 1932–1939: An Insider's Account of the House of Commons*, ed. Nick Smart (Lampeter, 1996).

Boothby, Balinron [Robert J. G. Boothby], *Boothby: Recollections of a Rebel* (London, 1978).

BRACKEN, BRENDAN, *My Dear Max: The Letters of Brendan Bracken to Lord Beaverbrook, 1925–1958*, ed. Richard Cockett (London, 1990).

BRIDGEMAN, WILLIAM, *The Modernisation of Conservative Politics: The Diaries and Letters of William Bridgeman, 1904–1935*, ed. Philip Williamson (London, 1988).

BROCKWAY, ARCHIBALD FENNER, *Inside the Left: Thirty Years of Platform, Press, Prison, and Parliament* (London, 1942).

BROOKS, COLLIN, *Fleet Street, Press Barons and Politics: The Journals of Collin Brooks, 1932–1940*, ed. N. J. Crowson (Cambridge, 1998).

BUTLER, SIR HAROLD BERESFORD, *Confident Morning* (London, 1950).

BUTLER, R. A., *The Art of the Possible* (London, 1971).

CADOGAN, SIR ALEXANDER, *The Diaries of Sir Alexander Cadogan, 1938–1945*, ed. David Dilks (London, 1971).

CECIL, ROBERT, *Peace and Pacifism* (Oxford, 1938).

—— *All the Way* (London, 1949).

CHAMBERLAIN, SIR AUSTEN, *Down the Years* (London, 1935).

CHAMBERLAIN, NEVILLE, *The Struggle for Peace* (London, 1939).

—— *The Neville Chamberlain Diary Letters*, ed. Robert Self, 4 vols. (Aldershot, 2000–2005).

CHANNON, SIR HENRY, *'Chips': The Diaries of Sir Henry Channon*, ed. Robert Rhodes James (London, 1999).

CHATFIELD, 1ST BARON [Admiral of the Fleet Alfred E. M. Chatfield], *The Navy and Defence* (London, 1942).

CHURCHILL, WINSTON S., *The Second World War*, Volume 1: *The Gathering Storm* (London, 1948).

—— *His Complete Speeches, 1897–1963*, ed. Robert Rhodes James, 8 vols. (London, 1974).

CITRINE, WALTER M., *Men and Work: An Autobiography* (London, 1964).

COCKBURN, CLAUD, *Cockburn Sums Up: An Autobiography* (London, 1981).

COLLIER, LAURENCE, *Flight from Conflict* (London, 1944).

COLVILLE, JOHN, *Footprints in Time: Memories* (London, 1976).

—— *The Fringes of Power: Downing Street Diaries, 1939–1955* (London, 1985).

CRAIGIE, SIR ROBERT, *Behind the Japanese Mask* (London, 1946).

CROZIER, WILLIAM PERCIVAL, *William P. Crozier: Off the Record. Political Interviews*, ed. A. J. P. Taylor (London, 1973).

DALTON, HUGH, *The Fateful Years: Memoirs, 1931–1945* (London, 1957).

—— *The Political Diary of Hugh Dalton, 1918–1940*, ed. Ben Pimlott (London, 1986).

DAVIDSON, J. C. C., *Memoirs of a Conservative: J. C. C. Davidson's Memoirs and Papers, 1910–1937*, ed. Robert Rhodes James (London, 1969).

DELMER, SEFTON, *Trail Sinister* (London, 1961).

DOMVILE, ADMIRAL SIR BARRY EDWARD, *By and Large* (London, 1936).

DOUGLAS, BARON [Marshal of the Royal Air Force William Sholto Douglas], *Years of Combat* (London, 1963).

DRAX, R. P. 'Mission to Moscow', *Naval Review*, Pt. 1, Vol. XI, no. 3 (1952); Pt. 2, Vol. XI, no. 4 (1952); Pt. 3, Vol. XII, no. 1 (1953).

DUFF COOPER, ALFRED, *Old Men Forget* (London, 1953).

—— *The Duff Cooper Diaries: 1915–1951*, ed. John Julius Norwich (London, 2005).

DUFF, SHEILA GRANT, *The Parting of Ways: A Personal Account of the Thirties* (London, 1982).

DUGDALE, BLANCHE, *Baffy: The Diaries of Blanche Dugdale, 1936–1947*, ed. Norman Rose (London, 1973).

EINZIG, PAUL, *In the Centre of Things: An Autobiography* (London, 1960).

FRANCIS-WILLIAMS, BARON [FRANCIS WILLIAMS], *Nothing So Strange: An Autobiography* (London, 1970).

FULLER, MAJOR-GENERAL JOHN F. C., *Memoirs of an Unconventional Soldier* (London, 1936).

GLADWYN, BARON (Hubert Miles Gladwyn Jebb), *The Memoirs of Lord Gladwyn* (London, 1972).

GOLLANCZ, VICTOR, *Reminiscences of Affection* (London, 1968).

GORE-BOOTH, BARON [SIR PAUL HENRY GORE-BOOTH], *With Great Truth and Respect* (London, 1974).

GREENE, SIR HUGH CARLETON, *The Third Floor Front* (London, 1969).

HALIFAX, LORD, *The Fulness of Days* (London, 1957).

HAMILTON, MARY AGNES, *Remembering My Good Friends* (London, 1944).

HANKEY, MAURICE, *Diplomacy by Conference: Studies in Public Affairs, 1920–1946* (New York, 1946).

HARRISSON, TOM, and MADGE, CHARLES, *Britain by Mass Observation* (London, 1939).

HARVEY, SIR OLIVER, *The Diplomatic Diaries of Sir Oliver Harvey, 1937–1940*, ed. John Harvey (London, 1970).

HAYTER, SIR WILLIAM, *A Double Life: The Memories of Sir William Hayter* (London, 1974).

HEADLAM, CUTHBERT, *Parliament and Politics in the Age of Baldwin and MacDonald: The Headlam Diaries, 1923–1935*, ed. Stuart Ball (London, 1992).

—— *Parliament and Politics in the Age of Churchill and Attlee: The Headlam Diaries, 1935–1951*, ed. Stuart Ball (Cambridge, 1999).

HENDERSON, SIR NEVILE, *Failure of a Mission: Berlin, 1937–1939* (London, 1940).

—— *Hippy, In Memoriam: The Story of a Dog* (London, 1943).

—— *Water Under the Bridges* (London, 1945).

HODGSON, SIR ROBERT MACLEOD, *Spain Resurgent* (London, 1953).

HOLLIS, SIR LESLIE CHASEMORE, *One Marine's Tale* (London, 1956).

HOME, 14TH EARL OF [Alexander Frederick Douglas-Home], *The Way the Wind Blows* (London, 1976).

IRONSIDE, WILLIAM EDMUND, *The Ironside Diaries, 1937–1940*, ed. Colonel Roderick MacLeod and Denis Kelly (London, 1962).

ISMAY, BARON (General Hastings Lionel Ismay), *Memoirs* (London, 1960).

JAY, DOUGLAS, *Change and Fortune* (London, 1980).

JONES, SIR RODERICK, *A Life in Reuters* (London, 1957).

JONES, THOMAS, *A Diary with Letters, 1931–1950* (Oxford, 1954).

KELLY, SIR DAVID VICTOR, *The Ruling Few: Or, The Human Background to Diplomacy* (London, 1953).

KENNEDY, A. L., *The Times and Appeasement: The Journals of A. L. Kennedy, 1932–1939*, ed. Gordon Martel (Cambridge, 2000).

KEYNES, J. M. (ed.), *The Collected Writings of John Maynard Keynes* (London, 1972).

KILLEARN 1ST BARON [Miles Wedderburn Lampson], *The Killearn Diaries, 1934–1946*, ed. Trefor Ellis Evans (London, 1972).

—— *Politics and Diplomacy in Egypt: The Diaries of Sir Miles Lampson, 1935–1937*, ed. M. E. Yapp (Oxford, 1997).

KILMUIR, 1ST VISCOUNT [David Patrick Maxwell Fyfe], *Political Adventure* (London, 1964).

KIRKPATRICK, IVONE, *The Inner Circle* (London, 1959).

KNATCHBULL-HUGESSEN, HUGH, *Diplomat in Peace and War* (London, 1949).

LANSBURY, GEORGE, *My Life* (London,1928).

LAWFORD, VALENTINE, *Bound for Diplomacy* (London, 1963).

LEE, JENNIE [Baroness Lee of Ashridge], *This Great Journey: A Volume of Autobiography, 1904–1945* (London, 1963).

LEEPER, SIR REGINALD WILDIG ALLEN, *When Greek Meets Greek* (London, 1950).

LEITH-ROSS, SIR FREDERICK, *Money Talks: Fifty Years of International Finance* (London, 1968).

LIDDELL-HART, SIR BASIL HENRY, *Memoirs*, 2 vols. (London, 1965–6).

LINDLEY, SIR FRANCIS OSWALD, *A Diplomat off Duty* (London, 1928).

LOCKHART, ROBERT HAMILTON BRUCE, *The Diaries of Sir Bruce Lockhart*, vol. 1, ed. Kenneth Young (London, 1973).

LONDONDERRY, 7TH MARQUESS OF [Charles Stewart Henry Vane-Tempest-Stewart], *Ourselves and Germany* (London, 1938).

MACDONALD, MALCOLM John, *People and Places: Random Reminiscences* (London, 1969).

MACLEAN, FITZROY, *Eastern Approaches* (London, 1991).

MACMILLAN, HAROLD, *Memoirs, Volume 1: Winds of Change, 1914–1939* (London, 1966).

MARTIN, KINGSLEY, *Editor: A Second Volume of Autobiography, 1931–1945* (London, 1968).

MAUGHAM, 1ST VISCOUNT [Frederic Herbert Maugham], *At the End of the Day* (London, 1954).

MCDONALD, IVERACH, *A Man of 'The Times': Talks and Travels in a Disrupted World* (London, 1976).

MCFADYEAN, SIR ANDREW, *Recollected in Tranquillity* (London, 1964).

MINNEY, R. J., *The Private Papers of Hore-Belisha* (London, 1960).

MORGAN, GENERAL J. H., *Assize of Arms: Being the Story of the Disarmament of Germany and Her Rearmament, 1919–1939* (London, 1945).

MOSLEY, SIR OSWALD, *My Life* (London, 1968).

MUGGERIDGE, MALCOLM, *Chronicles of Wasted Time*, 2 vols. (London, 1972–1973).

NICOLSON, HAROLD, *Harold Nicolson: Diaries and Letters, 1930–1939*, ed. Nigel Nicolson (London, 1966).

O'MALLEY, SIR OWEN ST. CLAIR, *The Phantom Caravan* (London, 1954).

PARMOOR, 1ST BARON [Charles Alfred Cripps], *A Retrospect: Looking Back Over a Life of More than Eighty Years* (London, 1936).

PARROTT, SIR CECIL, *The Tightrope* (London, 1975).

PETERSON, SIR MAURICE, *Both Sides of the Curtain* (London, 1950).

PHIPPS, SIR ERIC, *Our Man in Berlin: The Diary of Sir Eric Phipps, 1933–1937*, ed. Gaynor Johnson (London, 2008).

PIGGOTT, F. S. G., *Broken Thread* (London, 1950).

PONSONBY, SIR CHARLES EDWARD, *Ponsonby Remembers* (London, 1964).

POWNALL, SIR HENRY, *Chief of Staff: The Diaries of Lieutenant-General Sir Henry Pownall*, Volume 1, *1933–1940*, ed. Brian Bond (London, 1972).

PRICE, GEORGE WARD, *I Know These Dictators* (London, 1938).

PRITT, DENIS NOWELL, *The Autobiography of D. N. Pritt*, 3 vols. (London, 1965–1966).

RANDALL, SIR ALEC WALTER GEORGE, *Vatican Assignment* (London, 1956).

REITH, 1ST Baron [John C. W. Reith], *Into the Wind* (London, 1949).

RENDEL, SIR GEORGE, *The Sword and the Olive: Recollections of Diplomacy and the Foreign Service, 1913–1954* (London, 1957).

ROTHERMERE, 1ST VISCOUNT [Harold Sidney Harmsworth], *My Fight to Rearm Britain* (London, 1939).

—— *Warnings and Predictions* (London, 1939).

ROWSE, A. L., *All Souls and Appeasement* (London, 1961).

SAMUEL, 1ST VISCOUNT OF [Herbert Louis Samuel], *Memoirs* (London, 1945).

SELBY, SIR WALFORD H. M., *Diplomatic Twilight, 1930–1940* (London, 1953).

SHAKESPEARE, SIR GEOFFREY HITHERSAY, *Let Candles be Brought In* (London, 1949).

SIMON, VISCOUNT (John Simon) *Retrospect: The Memoirs of the Rt. Hon. Viscount Simon* (London, 1952).

SNOWDEN, 1ST VISCOUNT [Philip Snowden], *An Autobiography*, 2 vols. (London, 1934).

SPEARS, SIR EDWARD, *Assignment to Catastrophe*, 2 vols. (London, 1956).

STRANG, BARON [William Strang], *Home and Abroad* (London, 1956).

—— *The Moscow Negotiations* (Leeds, 1968).

STRONG, SIR KENNETH W. P., *Intelligence at the Top: The Recollections of an Intelligence Officer* (London, 1968).

SWINTON, 1ST EARL OF [Philip Cunliffe-Lister, Baron Masham], *I Remember* (London, 1951).

TALLENTS, SIR STEPHEN, *Man and Boy* (London, 1943).

TAYLOR, A. J. P. (ed.), *My Darling Pussy: The Letters of Lloyd George and Frances Stevenson, 1913–1941* (London, 1975).

TEMPERLEY, A. C., *The Whispering Gallery of Europe* (London, 1938).

TEMPLEWOOD, LORD [Samuel Hoare], *Nine Troubled Years* (London, 1954).

TENNANT, ERNEST W. D., *True Account* (London, 1957).

THOMAS, JAMES HENRY, *My Story* (London, 1937).

THOMPSON, SIR GEOFFREY, *Frontline Diplomat* (London, 1959).

TREE, RONALD, *When the Moon was High: Memoirs of Peace and War, 1897–1942* (London, 1975).

VANSITTART, BARON [Robert Gilbert Vansittart], *Lessons of My Life: The Autobiography of Lord Vansittart* (London, 1943).

—— *The Mist Procession* (London, 1958).
WELLESLEY, SIR VICTOR, *Diplomacy in Fetters* (London, 1944).
WHEELER-BENNETT, SIR JOHN W., *Knaves, Fools and Heroes: In Europe between the Wars* (London, 1974).
WILLIAMSON, PHILIP and BALDWIN, EDWARD, *Baldwin Papers: A Conservative Statesman, 1908–1947* (Cambridge, 2004).
WINTERBOTHAM, FREDERICK WILLIAM, *The Nazi Connection* (London, 1978).
WINTERTON, 6TH EARL [Edward Turnour], *Orders of the Day* (London, 1953).
WOOLF, LEONARD SIDNEY, *Downhill All the Way: An Autobiography of the Years 1919–1939* (London, 1967).

France

AURIOL, VINCENT, *Hier... demain*, 2 vols. (Tunis, 1944).
BARTHÉLEMY, JOSEPH, *Mémoires d'un ministre du Maréchal* (Auch, 1948).
BAUDOUIN, PAUL, *Neuf mois au gouvernement* (Paris, 1957).
BEAUFRE, GENERAL ANDRÉ, *Mémoires, 1920–1940–1945* (Paris, 1969).
BÉLIN, RENÉ, *Du secrétariat de la CGT au gouvernement de Vichy: Mémoires, 1933–1942* (Paris, 1978).
BÉRARD, ARMAND, *Un ambassadeur se souvient*, tome I: *Au temps du danger allemand* (Paris, 1976).
BÉRAUD, HENRI, *Les derniers beaux jours, 1918–1940* (Paris, 1953).
BEUVE-MÉRY, HUBERT, *Réflexions politiques, 1932–1952* (Paris, 1951).
BIDAULT, GEORGES, *Resistance: The Political Autobiography of Georges Bidault*, transl. Marianne Sinclair (London, 1967).
BLOCH, MARC, *L'étrange défaite: témoignage écrit en 1940* (Paris, 1946).
BLONDEL, JULES FRANÇOIS, *Ce que mes yeux ont vu, de 1900–1950* (Arras, 1964).
—— *Au fil de la carrière: Récit d'un diplomate, 1911–1938* (Paris, 1960).
BLUM, LÉON, *L'exercice de pouvoir* (Paris, 1937).
—— *L'histoire jugéra* (Montreal, 1945).
—— *L'Œuvre de Léon Blum*, 4 vols. ed. Robert Blum (Paris, 1951).
BONNET, GEORGES, *La crise européenne, mai–septembre 1938* (Paris, 1938).
—— *Défense de la Paix*, tome I: *De Washington au Quai d'Orsay*; tome II: *Fin d'une Europe: de Munich à la guerre* (Genève, 1946).
—— *Le Quai d'Orsay sous trois Républiques, 1870–1961* (Paris, 1961).
—— *Vingt ans de vie politique, 1918–1938: de Clemenceau à Daladier* (Paris, 1969).
—— *Dans la tourmente, 1938–1948* (Paris, 1971).
BONTE, FLORIMOND, *De l'ombre à la lumière: souvenirs* (Paris, 1965).
BOURRET, GENERAL VICTOR, *La tragédie de l'armée française* (Paris, 1947).
BRASILLACH, ROBERT, *Notre avant-guerre: mémoires* (Paris, 1941).
BRINON, FERNAND de, *Mémoires* (Paris, 1949).
BÜHRER, GENERAL JULES E., *Aux heures tragiques de l'Empire, 1938–1941* (Paris, 1947).
CHAMBRUN, COMTE CHARLES PINETON DE, *Traditions et souvenirs* (Paris, 1952).
CHARLES-ROUX, FRANÇOIS, *Huit ans au Vatican, 1932–1940* (Paris, 1947).
CHASTENET, JACQUES, *Quatre fois vingt ans* (Paris, 1974).

Chautemps, Camille, *Cahiers secrets de l'armistice, 1939–1940* (Paris, 1963).

Claudel, Paul, *Journal*, 2 vols. (Paris, 1968–1969).

—— *Mémoires improvisés* (Paris, 1969).

Comert, Pierre, 'Lettres d'il y a trente ans sur Munich', *Politique aujourd'hui* (January 1969).

Cot, Pierre, *Le procès de la République*, 2 vols. (New York, 1944).

Coulondre, Robert, *De Staline à Hitler: Souvenirs de deux ambassades, 1936–1939* (Paris, 1950).

Daladier, Édouard, *In Defence of France* (London, 1939).

—— 'Munich: vingt-trois ans après', *Le Nouveau Candide* (September–October, 1961).

Dampierre, Robert de, 'Dix années de politique française à Rome (1925–1935)', *Revue des deux Mondes*, 21 (1953), 14–38; 21 (1953), 258–283.

Daridan, Jean, *Le chemin de la défaite, 1938–1940* (Paris, 1980).

Darlan, Alain, *L'Amiral Darlan parle* (Paris, 1953).

Daudet, Léon, *Souvenirs politiques* (Paris, 1974).

Déat, Marcel, *Mémoires politiques* (Paris, 1989).

Drieu la Rochelle, Pierre, *Chronique politique, 1934–1942* (Paris, 1943).

Duclos, Jacques, *Mémoires*, tome I, *Le chemin que j'ai choisi: De Verdun au parti Communiste;* tome II, *1935–1939: Aux jours ensoleillés de Front populaire* (Paris, 1968–1969).

Fabre-Luce, Alfred, *Journal de la France, 1940*, tome I: *mars 1939 – juillet 1940* (Paris, 1941).

—— *Histoire de la révolution européenne, 1919–1945* (Paris, 1954).

Fabry, Jean, *De la Place Concorde au cours de l'Intendance* (Paris, 1942).

—— *J'ai connu, 1934–1945* (Paris, 1960).

—— 'D'Édouard Herriot à Raymond Poincaré', *Écrits de Paris*, 194 (1961), 54–64.

Faucher, General Louis, 'Some Recollections of Czechoslovakia', *International Affairs*, 18 (1939), 343–360.

Faure, Paul, *De Munich à la cinquième République* (Paris, 1949).

Flandin, Pierre-Étienne, *Discours: Le ministère Flandin, novembre 1934 – mai 1935* (Paris, 1937).

—— *Politique française, 1919–1940* (Paris, 1947).

François-Poncet, André, *Souvenirs d'une ambassade à Berlin, septembre 1931 – octobre 1938* (Paris, 1946).

—— *The Fateful Years* (London, 1949).

—— 'Il y a trente ans: ce que fut Locarno', *Historia*, 107 (1955), 401–410.

—— 'Hitler et Mussolini', *Historia*, 105 (1955), 121–130.

—— 'J'ai assisté à la conférence de Munich', *Historia*, 142 (1958), 239–248.

—— *Au Palais Farnèse: souvenirs d'une ambassade à Rome, 1938–1940* (Paris, 1961).

Gamelin, Maurice, *Servir*, 3 vols. (Paris, 1946–1947).

Garnier, Jean-Paul, *Excellences et plumes blanches, 1922–1946* (Paris, 1961).

Gauché, Maurice, *Le Deuxième bureau au travail, 1935–1940* (Paris, 1953).

Gaulle, Charles de, *Lettres, notes et carnets, tome II: 1919–juin 1940* (Paris, 1980).

GAULLE, PHILIPPE DE, *Mémoires accessoires*, vol. 1, *1921–1946* (Paris, 1997).
—— *De Gaulle, mon père: entretiens avec Michel Tauriac*, 2 vols. (Perrin, 2003–2004).
GENEBRIER, ROGER, 'Édouard Daladier, président du Conseil', in Rémond, R. and Bourdin, J. (eds.), *Édouard Daladier, chef de gouvernement: avril 1938 – septembre 1939* (Paris, 1977), 75–84.
—— *Septembre 1939: La France entre en guerre* (Paris, 1982).
GIRARD DE CHARBONNIÈRES, GUY DE, *La plus évitables de toutes les guerres* (Paris, 1985).
HERRIOT, ÉDOUARD, *Jadis*, tome II: *D'une Guerre à l'autre, 1914–1936* (Paris, 1948).
JACOMET, ROBERT, *L'armement de la France, 1936–1939* (Paris, 1945).
JEANNENEY, JULES, *Journal politique de Jules Jeanneney: septembre 1939 – juillet 1942*, ed. Jeanneney, J.-N. (Paris, 1972).
JOUVENEL, BERTRAND de, *D'une guerre à l'autre*, 2 vols. (Paris, 1940–1941).
—— *Un voyageur dans le siècle, tome I: 1903–1945* (Paris, 1979).
KAYSER, JACQUES, *De Kronstadt à Khrouchtchev: voyages franco-russes, 1891–1960* (Paris, 1962).
LAGARDELLE, HUBERT, *Mission à Rome* (Paris, 1955).
LANIEL, JOSEPH, *Jours de gloire et jours cruels: 1908–1958* (Paris, 1971).
LAROCHE, JULES, *La Pologne de Pilsudski: Souvenirs d'une ambassade, 1926–1935* (Paris, 1953).
LA ROCQUE, COLONEL ANNET FRANÇOIS DE, *Au service de l'avenir* (Paris, 1948).
LAVAL, PIERRE, *The Unpublished Diary of Pierre Laval* (London, 1948).
LAZAREFF, PIERRE, *De Munich à Vichy* (New York, 1944).
LE GOYET, COLONEL PIERRE, *Munich: 'un traquenard'?* (Paris, 1988).
LEBRUN, ALBERT, *Témoignage* (Paris, 1945).
LÉMERY, HENRY, *D'une république à l'autre: souvenirs de la mêlée politique, 1894–1944* (Paris, 1964).
MASSIGLI, RENÉ, 'De Versailles à Locarno', *Revue de Paris*, 64 (1957), 24–39.
—— *La Turquie devant la guerre: Mission à Ankara, 1939–1940* (Paris, 1964).
MAUROIS, ANDRÉ, *Mémoires* (Paris, 1970).
MAURRAS, CHARLES, *La seule France: Chronique des jours d'épreuve* (Lyon, 1941).
MINART, COLONEL JACQUES, *Le drame du désarmement français, 1918–1939* (Paris, 1959).
MOCH, JULES, *Rencontres avec Léon Blum* (Paris, 1970).
—— *Le front populaire: grande espérance* (Paris, 1971).
MONICK, EMMANUEL, *Pour mémoire* (Paris, 1970).
MONNET, JEAN, *Memoirs*, trans. R. Mayne (London, 1977).
MONTIGNY, JEAN, *Heures tragiques de 1940: La défaite* (Paris, 1941).
—— *Le complot contre la paix, 1935–1939* (Paris, 1966).
MONZIE, ANATOLE DE, *Ci-devant* (Paris, 1941).
NAVARRE, GENERAL HENRI, *Le service des renseignements, 1871–1944* (Paris, 1978).
NOËL, LÉON, *L'agression allemande contre la Pologne: une ambassade à Varsovie* (Paris, 1946).
—— *Les illusions de Stresa: L'Italie abandonée à Hitler* (Paris, 1975).
—— *La Guerre de 39 a commencé 4 ans plus tôt* (Paris, 1979).
—— *La Tchécoslovaquie d'avant Munich* (Paris, 1982).

—— *Polonia Restituta: la Pologne entre deux mondes* (Paris, 1984).

Nollet, General Charles, *Une expérience de désarmement: cinq ans de contrôle militaire en Allemagne* (Paris, 1932).

Painlevé, Paul, *Paul Painlevé: Paroles et écrits* (Paris, 1936).

Paul-Boncour, Joseph, *Entre deux guerres, tome II: Les lendemains de la victoire, 1919–1934* (Paris, 1945).

—— *tome III: Sur les chemins de la défaite, 1935–1940* (1946).

Pertinax, (André Géraud), *Les Fossoyeurs: défaite militaire de la France*, 2 vols. (New York, 1943).

Puaux, Gabriel, *Mort et transfiguration de l'Autriche* (Paris, 1966).

Queuille, Henri, *Journal de guerre, 7 septembre 1939 – 8 juin 1940* (Paris, 1993).

Raphaël-Leygues, Jacques, *Chroniques des années incertaines, 1935–1945* (Paris, 1977).

Requin, Édouard, *D'une guerre à l'autre, 1919–1939* (Paris, 1949).

Reynaud, Paul, *La France a sauvé l'Europe*, 2 vols. (Paris, 1947).

—— *Au cœur de la mêlée, 1930–1945* (Paris, 1951).

—— *Mémoires*, tome I: *Venu de ma montagne* (Paris, 1960).

Rueff, Jacques, *Œuvres complètes: I, De l'aube au crépuscule; Autobiographie de l'auteur* (Paris, 1977).

Saint-John Perse (Alexis Léger), *Œuvres complètes* (Paris, 1982).

Sainte-Suzanne, Raymond de, *Une politique étrangère: le Quai d'Orsay et Saint-John Perse à l'épreuve d'un regard, novembre 1938 – juin 1940* (Paris, 2000).

Serrigny, Bernard, *Trente ans avec Pétain* (Paris, 1959).

Stehlin, General Paul, *Témoignage pour l'histoire* (Paris, 1964).

Tabouis, Geneviève, *Ils l'ont appelée Cassandre* (New York, 1942).

Tardieu, André, *L'année de Munich: notes de semaine, 1938* (Paris, 1939).

Thorez, Maurice, *Fils du people* (Paris, 1938).

Tournelle, G. de la, 'À Dantzig de décembre 1934 à septembre 1939', *Revue d'histoire diplomatique*, (1978), 321–347.

Villelume, Paul de, *Journal d'une défaite, 23 août 1939 – 16 juin 1940* (Paris, 1976).

Weiss, Louise, *Mémoires d'une Européenne*, 3 vols. (Paris, 1972–1974).

Weygand, Maxime, *Mémoires*, 3 vols. (Paris, 1950–1957).

Zay, Jean, *Carnets secrets de Jean Zay (Munich à la guerre)*, (Paris, 1942).

—— *Souvenirs et solitude* (Paris, 1945).

Germany

Below, N. von, *Als Hitlers Adjutant 1937–1945* (Mainz, 1980).

Boveri, M., *Wir lügen alle: Eine Hauptstadtzeitung unter Hitler* (Olten, 1965).

Breloer, H. (ed.), *Mein Tagebuch: Geschichten vom Überleben 1939–1947* (East Lansing, MI, 1965).

—— *Geheime Welten: Deutsche Tagebücher aus den Jahren 1939 bis 1947*, 2nd edn. (Cologne, 1999).

Brüning, H., *Memoiren 1918–1934*, 2 vols. (Munich, 1972).

—— *Briefe und Gespräche 1934–1945*, ed. Claire Nix et al. (Stuttgart, 1974).

CHROUST, P. (ed.), *Friedrich Mennecke: Innenansichten eines medizinischen Täters im Nationalsozialismus: Eine Edition seiner Briefe 1935–1947* (Hamburg, 1988).

DAHLERUS, BIRGER, *The Last Attempt* (London, 1948).

DIETRICH, OTTO, *12 Jahre mit Hitler* (Köln, n.d.).

—— *Mit Hitler in die Macht: Persönliche Erlebnisse mit meinem Führer*, 7th edn. (Munich, 1974).

DIRKSEN, HERBERT VON, *Moskau, Tokio, London: Erinnerungen und Betrachtungen zu 20 Jahren deutscher Außenpolitik 1919–1939* (Stuttgart, 1950).

DOENITZ, KARL, *Memoirs: Ten Years and Twenty Days* (London, 1959).

ENGEL, GERHARD, *Heeresadjutant bei Hitler 1938–1943*, ed. Hildegard von Kotze (Stuttgart, 1974).

GAY, P., *My German Question: Growing Up in Nazi Berlin* (London, 1998).

GOEBBELS, J., *Tagebücher 1924–1945*, ed. R. G. Reuth (Munich, 1987).

—— *Die Tagebücher von Joseph Goebbels*, 32 vols., ed. Elke Fröhlich im Auftrag des Instituts für Zeitgeschichte (Munich, 1993–2008).

GOLLWITZER, H., KUHN, K. and SCHNEIDER, R. (eds.), *'Du hast mich heimgesucht bei Nacht': Abschiedsbriefe und Aufzeichnungen des Widerstandes 1933–1945* (Munich, 1957).

GÖRING, HERMANN, *Reden und Aufsätze*, ed. Erich Gritzbach (Munich, 1938).

GROSCURTH, HELMUTH, *Tagebuch eines Abwehroffiziers 1938–1940* (Stuttgart, 1970).

HALDER, FRANZ, *Hitler als Feldherr: Der ehemalige Chef des Generalstabes berichtet die Wahrheit* (Munich, 1949).

HASSELL, ULRICH VON, *Vom Anderen Deutschland: Aus den nachgelassenen Tagebüchern 1938–1944* (Zurich, 1946).

—— *Die Hassell–Tagebücher 1938–1944*, ed. Friedrich Freiherr Hiller von Gaertringen (Berlin, 1989).

HEIBER, HELMUT (ed.), *Goebbels–Reden* (Düsseldorf, 1971).

HERWARTH, H. VON, *Against Two Evils* (New York, 1981).

HILGER, G., *Wir und der Kreml: deutsch-sowjetische Beziehungen 1918–1941: Erinnerungen eines deutschen Diplomaten* (Frankfurt, 1955).

HILL, LEONIDAS (ed.), *Die Weizsäcker–Papiere 1933–1950* (Frankfurt am Main, 1974).

HIMMLER, HEINRICH, *Die Schutzstaffel als antibolschewistische Kampforganisation* (Munich, 1936).

HITLER, ADOLF, *Reden und Proklamationen 1932–1945*, ed. Max Domarus (Munich, 1965).

—— *Mein Kampf* (Munich, 1933).

—— *Mein Kampf*, translated by Ralph Manheim, with introduction by D.C. Watt (London, 1972).

—— *Hitler's Table Talk, 1941–1944*, ed. H. Trevor-Roper (London, 1953).

HOFFMANN, HEINRICH, *Hitler Was My Friend* (London, 1955).

HOSSBACH, FRIEDRICH, *Zwischen Wehrmacht und Hitler* (Wolfenbüttel, 1949).

HÜRTEN, HEINZ (ed.), *Deutsche Briefe 1934–1938* (Mainz, 1969).

JANSSEN, KARL HEINZ, and TOBIAS, FRITZ, *Der Sturz der Generäle: Hitler und die Blomberg–Fritsch Krise 1938* (Munich, 1994 [1938]).

Kalshoven, Hedda, *Ich denk so viel an Euch: Ein deutsch–holländischer Briefwechsel 1920–1949* (Munich, 1995 [1991]).

Keitel, Wilhelm, *Memoirs* (London, 1965).

Kessler, Harry Graf, *Tagebücher, 1918–1937*, ed. Wolfgang Pfeiffer-Belli (Frankfurt am Main, 1961).

Kleist, P., *Zwischen Hitler und Stalin* (Bonn, 1950).

Klemperer, Klemens von (ed.), *A Noble Combat: The Letters of Sheila Grant-Duff and Adam von Trott zu Stolz, 1932–1939* (Oxford, 1988).

Klemperer, Victor, *I Shall Bear Witness: The Diaries of Victor Klemperer, 1933–41* (London, 1995).

Klepper, Jochen, *Briefwechsel, 1925–1942*, ed. Ernst G. Riemschneider (Stuttgart, 1958).

—— *Unter dem Schatten deiner Flügel: Aus den Tagebüchern der Jahre 1932–1942* (Munich, 1976).

Klöss, Erhard (ed.), *Reden des Führers: Politik und Propaganda Adolf Hitlers, 1922–1945* (Munich, 1967).

Kordt, E., *Nicht aus den Akten . . . Die Wilhelmstrasse in Frieden und Krieg: Erlebnisse, Begegnungen und Eindrücke 1928–1945* (Stuttgart, 1950).

Ley, Robert, *Soldaten der Arbeit* (Munich, 1938).

Löffler, P. (ed.), *Bischof Clemens August Graf von Galen: Akten, Briefe und Predigten 1933–1946, I: 1933–1939* (Mainz, 1988).

Mann, Thomas, *Diaries, 1918–1939* (London, 1984).

Meissner, Otto, *Staatssekretär unter Ebert, Hindenburg, Hitler*, 3rd edn. (Hamburg, 1950).

Moltke, H. J. von, *Briefe an Freya 1939–1945*, ed. B. Ruhm von Oppen (Munich, 1988).

Mommsen, H. and Gillman, S. (eds.), *Politische Schriften und Briefe Carl Friedrich Goerdelers* (Munich, 2003).

Müller-Waldeck, G. and Ulrich, R. (eds.), *Hans Fallada: Sein Leben in Bildern und Briefen* (Berlin, 1997).

Nadolny, R., *Mein Beitrag* (Wiesbaden, 1955).

Papen, Franz von, *Memoirs* (London, 1952).

—— *Der Wahrheit eine Gasse* (München, 1952).

Peterson, Agnes et al. (ed.), *Himmler: Geheimreden 1933 bis 1945* (Frankfurt am Main, 1974).

Raeder, Erich, *Mein Leben von 1935 bis Spandau 1955*, 2 vols. (Tübingen, 1957).

Rauschning, Hermann, *Hitler Speaks* (London, 1939).

Ribbentrop, Joachim von, *Zwischen London und Moskau: Erinnerungen und letzte Aufzeichnungen*, ed. Annelies von Ribbentrop (Leoni am Starnberger See, 1953).

—— *The Ribbentrop Memoirs* (London, 1954).

Ribbentrop, Rudolf von, *Mein Vater, Joachim von Ribbentrop: Erlebnisse und Erinnerungen* (Graz, 2008).

Richardson, H. F. (ed.), *Sieg Heil! War Letters of Tank Gunner Karl Fuchs, 1937–1941* (Hamden, CT, 1987).

Riefenstahl, Leni, *A Memoir* (New York, 1993).

Rosenberg, Alfred, *Letzte Aufzeichnungen: Ideale und Idole der nationalsozialistischen Revolution* (Göttingen, 1955).

Schacht, Hjalmar, *Abrechnung mit Hitler* (Berlin, 1949).

—— *My First Seventy-Six Years* (London, 1955).

Schirach, Baldur von, *Ich glaubte an Hitler* (Hamburg, 1967).

Schirach, Henriette von, *Der Preis der Herrlichkeit: Erfahrene Zeitgeschichte* (Berlin, 1975).

Schmidt, Paul, *Statist auf diplomatischer Bühne 1923–1945* (Bonn, 1953).

Schweppenburg, Leo Geyr von, *Erinnerungen eines Militärattachés* (Stuttgart, 1949).

Seraphim, H.-G. (ed.), *Das politische Tagebuch Alfred Rosenbergs aus den Jahren 1934/35 und 1939/40* (Munich, 1964).

Smith, B. and Peterson, A. F. (eds.), *Heinrich Himmler: Geheimreden 1933 bis 1945* (Berlin, 1974).

Sommerfeldt, Martin H., *Ich war dabei. Die Verschwörung der Dämonen 1933–1939: Ein Augenzeugenbericht* (Darmstadt, 1949).

Speer, Albert, *Inside the Third Reich: Memoirs* (New York, 1970).

Spitzy, R., *So haben wir das Reich verspielt* (Munich, 1988).

Strasser, Otto, *Hitler und ich* (Buenos Aires, 1940).

Thyssen, Fritz, *I Paid Hitler* (London, 1941).

Vogel, J. P., *Hans Pfitzner: Leben, Werke, Dokumente* (Berlin, 1999).

Wagner, E. (ed.), *Der Generalquartiermeister: Briefe und Tagebuchaufzeichnungen des Generalquartiermeisters des Heeres General der Artillerie Eduard Wagner* (Munich, 1963).

Walb, Lore, *Ich, die Alte—ich, die Junge: Konfrontation mit meinen Tagebüchern 1933–1945* (Berlin, 1997).

Wahl, K., *'Es ist das deutsche Herz.' Erlebnisse und Erkenntnisse eines ehemaligen Gauleiters* (Augsburg, 1954).

Warlimont, Walter, *Inside Hitler's Headquarters, 1939–1945* (London, 1964).

Weinberg, Gerhard L. (ed.), *Hitler's Second Book* (New York, 2003).

Weizsäcker, E. von, *Erinnerungen* (Munich, 1950).

Zoller, Albert, *Hitler privat: Erlebnisbericht seiner Geheimsekretärin* (Düsseldorf, 1949).

Italy

Alfieri, D., *Due dittatori di fronte* (Milan, 1948).

Aloisi, Baron P., *Journal: 25 juillet 1932 – 14 juin 1936* (Paris, 1957).

Anfuso, F., *Roma Berlino Salò (1936–1945)* (Milan, 1950).

—— *Da Palazzo Venezia al Lago di Garda* (Bologna, 1957).

Badoglio, P., *The War in Abyssinia* (London, 1937).

Balbo, I., *Diario 1922* (Milan, 1932).

Bastianini, G., *Uomini, cose, fatti: memorie di un ambasciatore* (Milan, 1959).

Bottai, G., *Diario 1935–1944* (Milan, 1982, 2001).

—— *Caro Duce: lettere di donne italiane a Mussolini, 1922–1943* (Milan, 1989).

Ciano, G., *Diario 1937–1943*, ed. R. De Felice (Milan, 1980).

—— *Ciano's Diary, 1937–1938*, ed. A. Mayer (London, 1952).

—— *Ciano's Diary 1939–1943*, ed. M. Muggeridge (London and Toronto, 1947).
DINGLI, A., *Diaries, 1938–1940* (copies from Robert Mallett).
FAVAGROSSA, C., *Perchè perdemmo la guerra: Mussolini e la produzione bellica* (Milan, 1946).
GAYDA, V., *Italia e Inghilterra: l'inevitabile conflitto* (Rome, 1941).
GRANDI, D., *Il mio paese* (Bologna, 1985).
GRAZZI, E., *Il principio della fine: l'impresa di Grecia* (Rome, 1945).
GUARIGLIA, R., *Ricordi, 1922–1946* (Naples, 1950).
MAGISTRATI, M, *L'Italia a Berlino (1937–1939)* (Milan, 1956).
SUVICH, F., *Memorie 1932–1936*, ed. G. Bianchi (Milan, 1984).

United States

BOHLEN, CHARLES E., *Witness to History, 1929–1949* (New York, 1973).
BOWERS, CLAUDE, *My Mission to Spain: Watching the Rehearsal for World War II* (New York, 1954).
—— *My Life: The Memoirs of Claude Bowers* (New York, 1962).
BULLITT, WILLIAM C., *For the President, Personal and Secret: Correspondence between Franklin D. Roosevelt and William C. Bullitt*, ed. Orville H. Bullitt (Boston, MA, 1972).
DODD, WILLIAM E. *Ambassador Dodd's Diary, 1933–1938*, ed. William E. Dodd Jr. and Martha Dodd (London, 1941).
DREXEL BIDDLE IV, ANTHONY J., *Poland and the Coming of the Second World War: The Diplomatic Papers of Anthony J. Drexel Biddle IV, United States Ambassador to Poland, 1937–1939*, eds. Philip V. Canistraro, Edward A. Wynot Jr., and Theodore P. Konaleff (Columbus, OH, 1976).
FREEDMAN, M., *Roosevelt and Frankfurter: Their Correspondence, 1928–1945* (Boston, MA, 1967).
GIBSON, HUGH, *Hugh Gibson, 1883–1954: Extracts from His Letters and Anecdotes from His Friends*, ed. Perrin C. Galpin (New York, 1956).
GREW, JOSEPH, *Turbulent Era: A Diplomatic Record of Forty Years*, Vol. 2 *(London, 1953)*.
HULL, CORDELL, *Memoirs*, 2 vols. (New York, 1948).
ICKES, HAROLD L., *The Secret Diary of Harold L. Ickes*, 3 vols. (New York, 1953–1954).
KENNAN, GEORGE F., *From Prague after Munich: Diplomatic Papers, 1938–1940* (Princeton, NJ, 1968).
—— *Memoirs, 1929–1960* (London, 1968).
—— *Sketches from a Life* (New York, 1989).
KENNEDY, JOSEPH P., *Hostage to Fortune: The Letters of Joseph P. Kennedy*, ed. Amanda Smith (New York, 2001).
KIMBALL, W., *Churchill and Roosevelt: The Complete Correspondence* (Princeton, NJ, 1984).
MACVEAGH, LINCOLN, *Ambassador MacVeagh Reports: Greece, 1933–1947*, ed. John Olatrides (Princeton, NJ, 1980).
MOFFAT, JAY PIERREPONT, *The Moffat Papers: Selections from the Diplomatic Journals of Jay Pierrepont Moffatt, 1919–1943*, ed. Nancy Harvison Hooper (Cambridge, MA, 1956).

MORGENTHAU JR., HENRY, *From the Morgenthau Diaries: Years of Crisis, 1928–1938*, compiled and edited by John Morton Blum (Boston, MA, 1965).
—— *From the Morgenthau Diaries: Years of Urgency, 1938–1941* (Boston, MA, 1965).
ROOSEVELT, ELEANOR, *This I Remember* (New York, 1949).
ROOSEVELT, ELLIOTT, *As He Saw It* (New York, 1946).
—— *A Rendezvous with Destiny: The Roosevelts of the White House* (New York, 1975).
ROSENMAN, SAMUEL I., *Working with Roosevelt* (London, 1952).
SCHLESINGER JR., ARTHUR M., *A Life in the Twentieth Century: Innocent Beginnings, 1917–1950* (Boston, MA, 2000).
SHIRER, WILLIAM L., *Berlin Diary: The Journal of a Foreign Correspondent 1934–1941* (London, 1941).
—— *This is Berlin: A Narrative History, 1938–1940* (London, 1999).
SHOTWELL, JAMES T., *The Autobiography of James T. Shotwell* (Indianapolis, IN, 1961).
STIMSON, HENRY L., *Democracy and Nationalism in Europe* (Princeton, NJ, 1934).
—— *On Active Service in Peace and War* (New York, 1947).
WELLES, SUMNER, *A Time for Decision* (London, 1944).
WILSON, HUGH R., *Diplomat between Wars* (New York, 1941).
—— *A Career Diplomat: The Third Chapter: The Third Reich*, ed. Hugh R. Wilson Jr. (New York, 1960).

USSR

BANAC, I. (ed.), *The Diary of George Dimitrov, 1933–1949* (New Haven, CT, 2003).
BEREZHKOV, VALENTIN M., and MIKHEYEV, SERGEI V., *At Stalin's Side: His Interpreter's Memoirs from the October Revolution to the Fall of the Dictator's Empire* (New York, 1994).
BERIA, S., *Beria, My Father* (London, 2001).
DALLIN, A. and FIRSOV, F. I. (ed.), *Dimitrov and Stalin, 1934–1943: Letters from the Soviet Archives* (New Haven, CT, 2000).
FISCHER, LOUIS, *Men and Politics: An Autobiography* (London, 1941).
HILGER, G. and MEYER, A. G., *The Incompatible Allies: A Memoir History of German-Soviet Relations, 1918–1941* (New York, 1953).
KHRUSHCHEV, NIKITA S., *Khrushchev Remembers*, trans. and ed. Strobe Talbott (London, 1971).
KUUSINEN, AINO, *Before and After Stalin* (London, 1974).
LARINA, A., *This I Cannot Forget: The Memoirs of Nikolai Bukharin's Widow* (New York, 1993).
LIH, LARS T., NAUMOV, OLEG, and KHLEVNIUK, OLEG V. (eds.), *Stalin's Letters to Molotov* (New Haven, CT, 1995).
LITVINOV, MAXIM M., *Against Aggression: Speeches by Maxim Litvinov* (London, 1939).
LUCIANI, GEORGES, *Six ans à Moscou* (Paris, 1937).
LYONS, EUGENE, *Assignment in Utopia* (New York, 1938).

Maisky, Ivan M., *Who Helped Hitler?* (London, 1964).
—— *Memoirs of a Soviet Ambassador* (Moscow, 1966).
—— *The Munich Drama* (Moscow, 1972).
Mandelshtam, N., *Hope Against Hope* (New York 1970).
—— *Hope Abandoned* (New York, 1974).
Molotov, Viacheslav, *Soviet Peace Policy: Four Speeches By V. Molotov* (London, 1941).
Orlov, A., *The Secret History of Stalin's Crime* (New York, 1953).
Resis, A. (ed.), *Molotov Remembers: Inside Kremlin Politics. Conversations with Felix Chuev* (Chicago, IL, 1993).
Serge, V., *Memoirs of a Revolutionary, 1901–41* (New York, 1984).
Witkin, Z., *An American Engineer in Stalin's Russia, 1932–34* (Berkeley, CA, 1991).
Zhukov, G. K., *The Memoirs of Marshal Zhukov* (New York, 1971).

Others

Beck, Józef, *Dernier rapport: politique polonaise, 1926–1939* (Neuchatel, 1951).
—— *Final Report* (New York, 1957).
Beneš, Edvard, *Memoirs: From Munich to New War and New Victory*, trans. Godfrey Lias (London, 1954).
—— *My War Memoirs*, trans. Paul Selver (Westport, CT, 1971).
Burckhardt, C. J. *Meine Danziger Mission, 1937–1939* (Munich, 1962).
Gafencu, Grigore, *Prelude to the Russian Campaign: From the Moscow Pact (August 21st, 1939) to the Opening of Hostilities in Russia (June 22nd, 1941)*, trans. E. Fletcher-Allen (London, 1945).
—— *The Last days of Europe: A Diplomatic Journey in 1939*, trans. E. Fletcher-Allen (London, 1947).
Grabski, Stanisław, *Pamietniki*, vol II (Warsaw, 1989).
Gripenberg, Georg Achates, *Finland and the Great Powers: Memoirs of a Diplomat* (Lincoln, NE, 1965).
Hodža, Milan, *Federation in Central Europe: Reflections and Reminiscences* (London and New York, 1942).
Horthy, Miklós, *Memoirs* (New York, 1957).
Hymans, Paul, *Memoires*, 2 vols. (Brussels, 1958).
Lipski, Józef, *Diplomat in Berlin, 1933–1939*, ed. W. Jędrzejewicz (New York, 1968).
Łukasiewicz, Juliusz, *Diplomat in Paris, 1936–1939*, ed. W. Jędrzejewicz (New York, 1970).
Osuský, Štefan, *The Way of the Free* (New York, 1951).
Pearson, Lester B., *Mike: The Memoirs of the Right Honourable Lester B. Pearson*, 3 vols. (Toronto, 1972–1975).
Piłsudski, Józef, *Erinnerungen und Dokumente. Von Josef Pilsudski, dem ersten Marschall von Polen, persönlich autorisierte deutsche Gesamtausgabe*; ausgewählt, bearbeitet und redigiert von Major Dr. Wacław Lipiński . . . und Generalkonsul J. P. Kaczkowski, mit einem Geleitwort von Ministerpräsident General Hermann Göring (Essen, 1935–1936).

RACZYŃSKI, EDWARD, *In Allied London* (London, 1962).
RIPKA, HUBERT, *Munich: Before and After* (London, 1939).
SZEMBEK, J., *Journal 1933–9* (Paris, 1952).
WIMMER, LOTHAR, *Expériences et tribulations d'un diplomate autrichien entre deux guerres, 1929–1938* (Neuchatel, 1946).

Biographies (Short titles sometimes cited)

Useful Collections of Biographical Material

BARNETT, C. (ed.), *Hitler's Generals* (London, 1990).
BOSBACH, F. and BRECHTKEN, M. (eds.), *Politische Memoiren in deutscher und britischer Perspektive* (Munich, 2005).
CAPET, A. (ed.), *Britain, France and the Entente Cordiale since 1904* (Basingstoke, 2006).
CRAIG, G. A. and GILBERT, F. (eds.), *The Diplomats, 1919–1939* (Princeton, NJ, 1953).
DUTTON, D. J. (ed.), *Statecraft and Diplomacy in the Twentieth Century: Essays Presented to P. M. H. Bell* (Liverpool, 1995).
FARRELL, B. P. (ed.), *Leadership and Responsibility in the Second World War: Essays in Honour of Robert Vogel* (Montreal, 2004).
JONES, K. P. (ed.), *U.S. Diplomats in Europe, 1919–1941* (Santa Barbara, CA, 1981).
KELLY, R. N. and CANTRELL, J. A. (eds.), *Modern British Statesmen, 1867–1945* (Manchester, 1997).
MACKINTOSH, J. P. (ed.), *British Prime Ministers in the Twentieth Century*, Vol. 1: *Balfour to Chamberlain* (London, 1977).
MAYNE, R., JOHNSON, D. and TOMBS, R. (eds.), *Cross-Channel Currents: 100 Years of the Entente Cordiale* (London, 2004).
NEILSON, K. and OTTE, T.G. (eds.), *The Permanent Under-Secretary for Foreign Affairs, 1854–1946* (New York, 2009).
OTTE, T. G. (ed.), *The Makers of British Foreign Policy: From Pitt to Thatcher* (Basingstoke, 2002).
PARKER, R. A. C. and BARNETT, C. (eds.), *Winston Churchill: Studies in Statesmanship* (London, 1995).
SMELSER, R. M. and ZITELMANN, R. (eds.), *The Nazi Elite* (Basingstoke, 1989).
UEBERSCHÄR, G. (ed.), *Hitlers militärische Elite* (Darmstadt, 1998).

Britain

Books

ADDISON, P., *Churchill on the Home Front, 1900–1955* (London, 1992).
ASTER, S., *Anthony Eden* (London, 1976).
AYERST, D., *Garvin of the Observer* (London, 1985).
BALL, S., *Winston Churchill* (London, 2003).
BARCLAY, SIR R., *Ernest Bevin and the Foreign Office, 1932–1969* (London, 1975).

Beckett, F., *Clem Attlee* (London, 2000).

Bédarida, F., *Churchill* (Paris, 1999).

Bell, P., *Chamberlain, Germany and Japan, 1933–4: Redefinining British Strategy in an Era of Imperial Decline* (Basingstoke, 1996).

Bennett, G., *Churchill's Man of Mystery: Desmond Morton and the World of Intelligence* (London and New York, 2007).

Best, G. F. A., *Churchill: A Study in Greatness* (London, 2001).

Billington, D. P., *Lothian: Philip Kerr and the Quest for World Order* (Westport, CT, 2006).

Birkenhead, F. W. F. S., *Halifax: The Life of Lord Halifax* (London, 1965).

Blake, R. N. W. and Louis, W. R. (eds.), *Churchill* (Oxford, 1993).

Bowle, J., *Viscount Samuel: A Biography* (London, 1957).

Boyle, A., *Only the Wind Will Listen: Reith of the BBC* (London, 1972).

Brendon, P., *Winston Churchill: A Brief Life* (London, 2001).

Briquebec, J., *Winston Churchill* (London, 1972).

Broad, C. L., *Winston Churchill, 1874–1952*, revised edition (London, 1952).

—— *Sir Anthony Eden: The Chronicles of a Career* (London, 1955).

—— *Winston Churchill: A Biography*, Vol. 2: *The Years of Achievement* (New York, 1963).

Brody, J. K., *The Avoidable War: Lord Cecil and the Policy of Principle, 1933–1935* (New Brunswick, NJ, 1999).

Brookshire, J. H., *Clement Attlee* (Manchester, 1995).

Burridge, T., *Clement Attlee: A Political Biography* (London, 1985).

Butler, E., *Mason-Mac: The Life of Lieutenant-General Sir Noel Mason-MacFarlane* (London, 1972).

Butler, J. R. M., *Lord Lothian, 1882–1940* (London, 1960).

Campbell-Johnson, A., *Viscount Halifax: A Biography* (London, 1941).

—— *Sir Anthony Eden: A Biography*, revised edn. (London, 1955).

Caputi, R.J., *Neville Chamberlain and Appeasement* (Selinsgrove, PA, 1999).

Carlton, D., *Anthony Eden: A Biography* (London, 1981).

—— *MacDonald versus Henderson: The Foreign Policy of the Second Labour Government* (London, 1970).

—— *Churchill and the Soviet Union* (Manchester, 2000).

Chadwick, O., *Britain and the Vatican during the Second World War* (Cambridge, 1986).

Charmley, J., *Duff Cooper: The Authorized Biography* (London, 1986).

—— *Lord Lloyd and the Decline of the British Empire* (London, 1987).

—— *Churchill: The End of Glory* (London, 1993).

Chastenet, J., *Winston Churchill et l'Angleterre du XXe siècle* (Paris, 1956).

Churchill, R., *The Rise and Fall of Sir Anthony Eden* (London, 1959).

Colville, J. R., *Man of Valour: The Life of Field-Marshal the Viscount Gort* (London, 1972).

Colvin, I., *Vansittart in Office* (London, 1965).

Colvin, I., *The Chamberlain Cabinet: How the Meetings in 10 Downing Street, 1937–9, led to the Second World War, told for the First Time from the Cabinet Papers* (London, 1971).

CROSS, C., *Philip Snowden* (London, 1966).
CROSS, J., *Sir Samuel Hoare: A Political Biography* (London, 1977).
—— *Lord Swinton* (London, 1983).
DANCHEV, A., *Alchemist of War: The Life of Basil Liddell-Hart* (London, 1999).
DE GROOT, G. J., *Liberal Crusader: The Life of Sir Archibald Sinclair* (London, 1993).
DELLAR, G. (ed.), *Attlee as I Knew Him* (1983).
DUTTON, D., *Austen Chamberlain: Gentleman in Politics* (Bolton, 1985).
—— *Simon: A Political Biography of Sir John Simon* (London, 1992).
—— *Anthony Eden: A Life and Reputation* (London, 1997).
—— *Neville Chamberlain* (London, 2001).
EGREMONT, M., *Under Two Flags: The Life of Major General Sir Edward Spears* (London, 1997).
ENRIGHT, D., *Winston Churchill: The Greatest Briton* (London, 2003).
FARRELL, A., *Sir Winston Churchill* (London, 1962).
FEILING, K. G., *The Life of Neville Chamberlain* (London, 1947).
FOOT, M., *Aneurin Bevan: A Biography*, 2 vols. (London, 1962–1973).
FUCHSER, L. W., *Neville Chamberlain and Appeasement: A Study in the Politics of History* (New York, 1982).
GARVIN, H. K., *J. L. Garvin: A Memoir* (London, 1948).
GILBERT, M., *Plough My Own Furrow: The Story of Lord Allen of Hurtwood as Told Through his Writings and Correspondence* (London, 1965).
—— *Winston Churchill* (Oxford, 1966).
—— (ed.), *Churchill* (Englewood Cliffs, NJ, 1967).
—— *Sir Horace Rumbold: Portrait of a Diplomat, 1869–1941* (London, 1973).
—— *Winston S. Churchill*, Vol. 4: *1917–1922* (London, 1975).
—— *Winston S. Churchill*, Vol 5: *1922–1939* (London, 1976).
—— *Churchill* (London, 1979).
—— *Winston Churchill: The Wilderness Years* (London, 1981).
—— *Winston S. Churchill*, Vol. 6: *Finest Hour, 1939–1941* (London, 1983).
—— *Prophet of Truth: Winston Churchill, 1922–1939* (London, 1990).
—— *Churchill: A Life* (London, 1991).
—— *In Search of Churchill: A Historian's Journey* (London, 1994).
—— *Winston Churchill and Emery Reves: Correspondence, 1937–1964* (Austin, TX, 1997).
—— *Churchill: A Life* (London, 2000).
—— *Churchill and America* (London, 2005).
GRIFFITHS, R., *Patriotism Perverted: Captain Ramsay, The Right Club and British Anti-Semitism, 1939–40* (London, 1998).
HAFFNER, S., *Churchill: Eine Biographie* (Berlin, 2001).
HAMILTON, M. A., *Arthur Henderson: A Biography* (London, 1938).
HARRIS, K., *Attlee* (London, 1995).
HERMAN, J., *The Paris Embassy of Sir Eric Phipps: Anglo-French Relations and the Foreign Office, 1937–1939* (Brighton, 1998).
HOWARD, A., *The Life of R. A. Butler* (London, 1987).
HYDE, H. M., *Baldwin: The Unexpected Prime Minister* (London, 1973).
—— *Neville Chamberlain* (London, 1976).

JAMES, R. R., *Churchill: A Study in Failure, 1900–1939* (London, 1970).
—— *Anthony Eden* (London, 1986).
JAROCH, M., *'Too Much Wit and Not Enough Warning'?: Sir Eric Phipps als britischer Botschafter in Berlin von 1933 bis 1937* (Frankfurt, 1999).
JENKINS, R., *Baldwin* (London, 1987).
—— *Churchill* (London, 2001).
JUDD, D., *Lord Reading: A Life of Rufus Isaacs, First Marquess of Reading, 1860–1935* (London, 1982).
KEEGAN, J., *Churchill: A Life* (London, 2002).
KERSHAW, I., *Making Friends With Hitler: Lord Londonderry and Britain's Road to War* (London, 2004).
KROCKOW, C. GRAF VON, *Churchill: Man of the Century* (London, 2000).
LEES-MILNE, J., *Harold Nicolson: A Biography*, 2 vols. (London, 1980–1981).
LEMONNIER, L., *Winston Churchill* (Paris, 1944).
LUKACS, J., *Churchill: Visionary, Statesman, Historian* (New Haven, CT, 2002).
LYSAGHT, C. E., *Brendan Bracken* (London, 1979).
MACLEOD, I. N., *Neville Chamberlain* (London, 1961).
MCDONOUGH, F. *Neville Chamberlain, Appeasement and the British Road to War* (Manchester, 1998).
—— *Hitler, Chamberlain and Appeasement* (Cambridge, 2002).
MCLACHLAN, D., *In the Chair: Barrington-Ward of 'The Times', 1927–1948* (London, 1971).
MANCHESTER, W., *The Caged Lion: Winston Spencer Churchill, 1932–1940* (London, 1988).
MICHIE, L. W., *Portrait of an Appeaser: Robert Hadow, First Secretary in the British Foreign Office, 1931–1939* (Westport, CT, 1996).
MIDDLEMAS, K. and BARNES, J., *Baldwin: A Biography* (London, 1969).
MORGAN, A. J., *Ramsay MacDonald* (Manchester, 1997).
MORGAN, K. O., *David Lloyd George: 1863–1945* (Cardiff, 1981).
MOWAT, C. L., *Lloyd George* (Oxford, 1964).
NAYLOR, J. F., *A Man and an Institution: Sir Maurice Hankey, the Cabinet Secretariat and the Custody of Cabinet Secrecy* (Cambridge, 1984).
NEVILLE, P., *Neville Chamberlain: A Study in Failure?* (London, 1992).
—— *Winston Churchill: Statesman or Opportunist?* (London, 1996).
—— *Appeasing Hitler: The Diplomacy of Sir Nevile Henderson* (Basingstoke, 2000).
O'HALPIN, E., *Head of the Civil Service: A Study of Sir Warren Fisher* (London, 1989).
OTTE, T. G., *Harold Nicolson and Diplomatic Theory: Between Old Diplomacy and New* (Leicester, 1998).
PARKER, R. A. C., *Chamberlain and Appeasement* (Basingstoke, 1993).
—— *Churchill and Appeasement* (London, 2000).
—— and BARNETT, C. (eds.), *Winston Churchill: Studies in Statesmanship* (London, 1995).
PEARCE, R. D., *Attlee* (London, 1997).
PELLING, H. M., *Winston Churchill* (Ware, 1999).

PETER, M., *John Maynard Keynes und die britische Deutschlandpolitik. Machtanspruch und ökonomische Realität im Zeitalter der Weltkriege, 1919–1946* (Munich, 1997).

PETERS, A. R., *Anthony Eden at the Foreign Office, 1931–1938* (Aldershot, 1986).

PETRIE, C., *The Life and Letters of the Right Hon. Sir Austen Chamberlain*, 2 vols. (London, 1939–1940).

PIMLOTT, B., *Hugh Dalton* (London, 1985).

PONTING, C., *Winston Churchill* (London, 1994).

POPE-HENNESSY, J., *Lord Crewe, 1858–1945: The Likeness of a Liberal* (London, 1955).

RANKIN, N., *Telegram From Guernica: The Extraordinary Life of George Steer, War Correspondent* (London, 2003).

READ, C., *Winston S. Churchill: Man of the Twentieth Century* (Leicester, 2002).

REES-MOGG, W., *Sir Anthony Eden* (London, 1956).

REYNOLDS, D., *In Command of History: Churchill Fighting and Writing the Second World War* (London, 2004).

ROBBINS, K., *Churchill* (London, 1992).

ROBERTS, A., *'The Holy Fox': A Biography of Lord Halifax* (London, 1991).

—— *Hitler and Churchill: Secrets of Leadership* (London, 2003).

ROCK, W. R., *Neville Chamberlain* (New York, 1969).

ROI, M. L., *Alternative to Appeasement: Sir Robert Vansittart and Alliance Diplomacy, 1934–1937* (Westport, CT, 1997).

ROLPH, C. H., *Kingsley: The Life, Letters and Diaries of Kingsley Martin* (London, 1973).

ROSE, N., *Vansittart: Study of a Diplomat* (London, 1978).

—— *Churchill: An Unruly Life* (Hemel Hempstead, 1994).

—— *Harold Nicolson* (London, 2005).

ROSKILL, S. W., *Hankey: Man of Secrets*, 3 vols. (London, 1970–1974).

ROTHWELL, V. H., *Anthony Eden: A Political Biography, 1931–1957* (Manchester, 1992).

RUGGIERO, J., *Neville Chamberlain and British Rearmament: Pride, Prejudice and Politics* (Westport, CT, 1999).

SENCOURT, R., *Winston Churchill* (London, 1940).

SELF, R., *Neville Chamberlain: A Biography* (Aldershot, 2006).

SHEPHERD, J., *George Lansbury: At the Heart of Old Labour* (Oxford, 2002).

SKIDELSKY, R., *Oswald Mosley* (London, 1975).

—— *Keynes: The Return of the Master* (New York, 2009).

SOAMES, M., *Clementine Churchill*, revised edn. (London, 2002).

SPÄTER, J., *Vansittart: britische Debatten über Deutsche und Nazis, 1902–1945* (Göttingen, 2003).

STEWERT, G., *Burying Caesar: Churchill, Chamberlain and the Battle for the Tory Party* (London, 1999).

STRAUCH, R., *Sir Nevile Henderson: Britischer Botschafter in Berlin 1937 bis 1939* (Bonn, 1959).

SWIFT, J., *Labour in Crisis: Clement Attlee and the Labour Party in Opposition, 1931–40* (Basingstoke, 2001).

Taylor, A. J. P., *Beaverbrook* (London, 1972).
Thorpe, D. R., *Eden: The Life and Times of Anthony Eden, First Earl of Avon, 1897–1977* (Pimlico, 2004).
Vernon, B. D., *Ellen Wilkinson, 1891–1947* (London, 1982).
Waterfield, G., *Professional Diplomat: Sir Percy Loraine of Kirkharle Bt., 1880–1961* (London, 1973).
Watts, D., *Ramsay MacDonald: A Labour Tragedy?* (London, 1998).
Williamson, P., *Stanley Baldwin: Conservative Leadership and National Values* (Cambridge, 1999).
Wrench, J. E., *Geoffrey Dawson and Our Times* (London, 1955).
Wrigley, C., *Arthur Henderson* (Cardiff, 1990).
—— *Lloyd George* (Oxford, 1992).
Young, G. M., *Stanley Baldwin: A Biography* (London, 1952–53).
Young, K., *Stanley Baldwin* (London, 1976).
Zebel, S. H., *Balfour: A Political Biography* (London, 1973).

France

Agulhon, Maurice (ed.), *Charles de Gaulle: du militaire au politique, 1920–1940*, (Paris, 2004).
Alexander, Martin S., *The Republic in Danger: General Maurice Gamelin and the Politics of French Defence, 1933–1940*, (Cambridge, 1992).
Aron, Robert, *Charles de Gaulle* (Paris, 1964).
Audry, Colette, *Léon Blum ou la politique du juste* (Paris, 1955).
Auffray, Bernard, *Pierre de Margerie (1861–1942) et la vie diplomatique de son temps* (Paris, 1976).
Barbier, Colette, *Henri Hoppenot (25 octobre 1891–10 août 1977): diplomate* (Paris, 1999).
Bariéty, Jacques (ed.), *Aristide Briand, la Société des Nations et l'Europe: 1919–1932* (Strasbourg, 2007).
Barré, Jean-luc, *Devenir de Gaulle, 1939–1943: d'après les archives privées et inédites du général de Gaulle* (Paris, 2003).
—— *Philippe Berthelot: l'éminence grise, 1866–1934* (Paris, 1998).
Barros, James, *Betrayal from Within: Joseph Avenol, Secretary-General of the League of Nations, 1933–1940* (New Haven, 1969).
Bauchard, Philippe, *Léon Blum: le pouvoir pour quoi faire?* (Paris, 1976).
Baudouï, Rémi, *Raoul Dautry (1880–1951): Le technocrate de la République* (Paris, 1992).
Beauvois, Yves, *Léon Noël: De Laval à de Gaulle via Pétain, 1888–1987* (Villeneuve d'Ascq, 2001).
Bellstedt, Hans F., *'Apaisement' oder Krieg: Frankreichs Aussenminister Georges Bonnet und die deutsch-französische Erklärung vom 6. Dezember 1938* (Bonn, 1993).
Berstein, Serge, *Léon Blum* (Paris, 2006).
Bouleaux-Jossoud, M. T., *Raymond Poincaré, 1860–1934* (Bar-le-Duc, 1960).

BOULIC, JEAN-YVES, and ANNIK LAVAURE, *Henri de Kerillis (1889–1958): l'absolu patriote* (Rennes, 1997).
BRUNET, JEAN-PAUL, *Jacques Doriot: du communisme au fascisme* (Paris, 1986).
BURRIN, PHILIPPE, *La dérive fasciste: Doriot, Déat, Bergery, 1933–1945* (Paris, 1986).
CHAIGNE, LOUIS, *Paul Claudel: The Man and the Mystic* (Westport, Conn., 1978).
CHAMBRUN, RENÉ DE, *Pierre Laval devant l'histoire* (Paris, 1983).
CHAUVY, GÉRARD, *Édouard Herriot, 1872–1957, et le radicalisme triomphant* (Lyon, 1996).
COBLENTZ, P., *Georges Mandel* (Paris, 1946).
COINTET, JEAN-PAUL, *Pierre Laval* (Paris, 1993).
—— *Marcel Déat: du socialisme au national-socialisme* (Paris, 1998).
COLE, HUBERT, *Laval: A Biography* (London, 1963).
COLTON, JOEL, *Léon Blum: Humanist in Politics* (New York: 1966).
COUTAU-BÉGARIE, HERVÉ and HUAN, CLAUDE, *Darlan* (Paris, 1989).
CRANE, RICHARD FRANCIS, *A French Conscience in Prague: Louis Eugène Faucher and the Abandonment of Czechoslovakia* (Boulder, 1996).
CROUY-CHANEL, ÉTIENNE DE, *Alexis Léger, ou, l'autre visage de Saint-John Perse* (Paris, 1989).
CROZIER, BRIAN, *De Gaulle*, vol. 1: *The Warrior* (London, 1973).
DALBY, LOUISE E., *Léon Blum: Evolution of a Socialist* (New York, 1963).
DALLOZ, JACQUES, *Georges Bidault, biographie politique* (Paris, 1992).
DEMEY, ÉVELYNE, *Paul Reynaud: mon père* (Paris, 1980).
DEMORY, JEAN-CLAUDE, *Georges Bidault, 1899–1983: biographie* (Paris, 1995).
DESTREMAU, BERNARD, *Weygand* (Paris, 1989).
DREIFORT, JOHN E., *Yvon Delbos at the Quai d'Orsay: French Foreign Policy during the Popular Front, 1936–1938* (Lawrence, Kansas, 1973).
DURAND, PIERRE, *Maurice Thorez, 1900–1964: le fondateur, essai biographique* (Pantin, 2000).
FERRO, MARC, *Pétain* (Paris, 1987).
FESTORAZZI, ROBERTO, *Laval–Mussolini, l'impossibile asse: la storia dello statista francese che volle l'intesa con l'Italia* (Milan, 2003).
GEORGES, BERNARD and TINTANT, DENISE, *Léon Jouhaux dans le mouvement syndical français, 1921–1954* (Paris, 1979).
GHEBALI, ÉRIC, *Vincent Auriol: le président citoyen, 1884–1966* (Paris, 1998).
GILBERT, JOSEPH, *Fernand de Brinon: l'aristocrate de la collaboration* (Paris, 2002).
GILLET-MAUDOT, M. J., *Paul Claudel* (Paris, 1966).
GLASNECK, JOHANNES, *Léon Blum: Republikaner und Sozialist* (Bern, 2003).
JACKSON, JULIAN, *Charles De Gaulle* (London, 2003).
JANSEN, SABINE, *Pierre Cot: Un antisfasciste radical* (Paris, 2002).
JEANNENEY, JEAN-NOËL, *François de Wendel en République: l'argent et le pouvoir, 1914–1940* (Paris, 1976).
—— *Georges Mandel: L'homme qu'on attendait* (Paris, 1991).
KAROUTCHI, ROGER and OLIVIER BABEAU, *Jean Zay (1904–1944): ministre de l'instruction du Front populaire, résistant, martyr* (Paris, 2006).
KRAKOVITCH, RAYMOND, *Paul Reynaud dans la tragédie de l'histoire* (Paris, 1999).

KEIGER, J. F. V., *Raymond Poincaré* (Cambridge, 1997).
KUPFERMAN, FRED, *Laval* (Paris 1987).
LA GORCE, PAUL-MARIE DE, *De Gaulle* (Paris, 1999).
LACHAISE, BERNARD, *Yvon Delbos, 1885–1956: biographie* (Périgueux, 1993).
LACOUTURE, JEAN, *Léon Blum* (Paris, 1977).
—— *De Gaulle* (Paris, 1984–1986).
LARCAN, ALAIN, *De Gaulle: Inventaire* (Paris, 2002).
LE GOYET, PIERRE, *Le mystère Gamelin* (Paris, 1975).
LÉGER, ALEXIS, *Briand* (Paris 1943).
MANIGAND, CHRISTINE, *Henry de Jouvenel* (Limoges, 2000).
MAYAFFRE, DAMON, *Le poids des mots: le discours de gauche et de droite dans l'entre-deux-guerres: Maurice Thorez, Léon Blum, Pierre-Étienne Flandin et André Tardieu, 1928–1939* (Paris, 2000).
MELTON, GEORGE E., *Darlan: Admiral and Statesman of France, 1881–1942* (Westport, 1998).
MONTDARGENT, ROBERT, *Gabriel Péri, la double loyauté: annexes et documents* (Pantin, 2002).
NOBÉCOURT, JACQUES, *Le Colonel de La Rocque (1885–1946), ou, Les pièges du nationalisme chrétien* (Paris, 1996).
PÉRI, GABRIEL, *Un grand Français: Gabriel Péri, une vie de combat pour la paix et la sécurité de la France*, ed. Marcel Cachin (Paris, 1947).
PLANTÉ, LOUIS, *Un grand seigneur de la politique: Anatole de Monzie* (Paris 1955).
PROST, ANTOINE (ed.), *Jean Zay et la gauche du radicalisme* (Paris, 2003).
PUYAUBERT, JACQUES, *Georges Bonnet (1889–1973): Les combats d'un pacifiste* (Rennes, 2007).
RAY, OSCAR, *The Life of Édouard Daladier* (London 1940).
RÉAU, ELISABETH DU, *Édouard Daladier, 1884–1970* (Paris, 1993).
RÉMOND, RENÉ, and JANINE BOURDIN (eds.), *Édouard Daladier, chef de gouvernement, avril 1938–septembre 1939* (Paris, 1977).
RENOUVIN, PIERRE, and RENÉ RÉMOND (eds.), *Léon Blum: Chef de Gouvernement, 1936–1937* (Paris, 1981).
RIOUX, JEAN-PIERRE, *De Gaulle: La France à vif* (Paris, 2000).
RIVES, JEAN, *Gaston Doumergue: du modèle républicain au sauveur suprême* (Toulouse, 1992).
ROUSSEL, ERIC, *Jean Monnet, 1888–1979* (Paris, 1996).
—— *Charles de Gaulle : Tome 1, 1890-1945* (Paris, 2007).
RUBY, MARCEL, *Jean Zay: député à 27 ans, ministre à 31 ans, prisonnier politique à 36 ans, assassiné à 39 ans* (Orléans, 1994).
—— *La Vie et l'œuvre de Jean Zay* (Paris, 1969).
SACOTTE, MIREILLE, *Alexis Léger/Saint-John Perse* (Paris, 1998).
SARRAZIN, BERNARD and D'AUVERGNE, JEAN, *Édouard Herriot* (Saint-Étienne, 1957).
SCHÄFER, CLAUS W., *André Francois-Poncet als Botschafter in Berlin (1931–1938)*, (Munich, 2004).
SERVENT, P, *Le mythe Pétain: Verdun, ou les tranchées de la mémoire* (Paris, 1992).
SHENNAN, ANDREW, *De Gaulle* (London, 1993).
SHERWOOD, JOHN M., *Georges Mandel and the Third Republic* (Stanford, 1970).

SIROT, STÉPHANE, *Maurice Thorez* (Paris, 2000).
TELLIER, THIBAULT, *Paul Reynaud: Un indépendent en politique, 1878–1966* (Paris, 2005).
THOMSON, DAVID, *Two Frenchmen: Pierre Laval and Charles de Gaulle* (Westport, Conn., 1975).
TOURNOUX, JEAN-RAYMOND, *Pétain et de Gaulle* (Paris, 1968).
ULRICH-PIER, RAPHAËLE, *René Massigli (1888–1988): Une vie de diplomate*, vol. I (Brussels, 2006).
VARENNE, FRANÇOIS, *Mon patron, Georges Mandel* (Paris, 1945).
VENDROUX, JACQUES, *Cette chance que j'ai eue (1920–1957)*, (Paris, 1974).
WARNER, GEOFFREY, *Pierre Laval and the Eclipse of France* (London, 1968).
WILLIAMS, CHARLES, *The Last Great Frenchman: A Life of General de Gaulle* (London, 1993).
WORMSER, G., *Georges Mandel: L'homme politique* (Paris, 1980).
WORONOFF, DENIS, *François de Wendel* (Paris, 2001).
YOUNG, ROBERT, *Power and Pleasure: Louis Barthou and the Third French Republic* (London, 1991).

Germany

ACKERMANN, J., *Heinrich Himmler als Ideologe* (Göttingen, 1970).
ARONSON, S., *Reinhard Heydrich und die Frühgeschichte von Gestapo und SD* (Stuttgart, 1971).
BALFOUR, M. and FRISBY, J., *Helmuth von Moltke: A Leader Against Hitler* (London, 1972).
BENTLEY, J., *Martin Niemoeller, 1892–1984* (Oxford, 1984).
BIRD, K. W., *Erich Raeder: Admiral of the Third Reich* (Annapolics, MD, 2006).
BLASIUS, R. A., *Für Großdeutschland – gegen den großen Krieg: Staatssekretär Ernst Freiherr von Weizsäcker in den Krisen um die Tschechoslowakei und Polen 1938–1939* (Wien, 1981).
BLOCH, M., *Ribbentrop* (London, 1992).
BRAMSTED, E. K., *Goebbels and National Socialist Propaganda, 1925–1945* (East Lansing, MI, 1965).
BUCHHEIT, G., *Ludwig Beck, ein preussischer General* (Munich, 1964).
BULLOCK, A., *Hitler and Stalin: Parallel Lives*, 2nd edn. (London, 1998).
BUTLER, E., *Marshal without Glory* (London, 1951).
CARR, W., *Hitler: A Study in Personality and Politics* (London, 1978).
CONRADI, P., *Hitler's Piano Player: The Rise and Fall of Ernst Hanfstaengl, Confidant of Hitler, Ally of FDR* (New York, 2004).
DEUERLEIN, E., *Hitler: Eine politische Biographie* (Munich, 1969).
DÜLFFER, J., 'Albert Speer: Cultural and Economic Management', in Smelser, R. M. and Zitelmann, R. (eds.), *The Nazi Elite* (Basingstoke, 1989).
FEST, J. C., *Hitler* (London, 1974).
—— *Speer: Eine Biographie* (Berlin, 1999).
—— *Speer: The Final Verdict* (London, 2001).
FINKER, K., *Stauffenberg und der 20. Juli 1944* (East Berlin, 1977).

FOERSTER, W., *Generaloberst Ludwig Beck: Sein Kampf gegen den Krieg* (Munich, 1953).

FRISCHAUER, W., *The Rise and Fall of Hermann Goering* (Boston, MA, 1951).

GALL, L., *Krupp: Der Aufstieg eines Industrieimperiums* (Berlin, 2000).

GRAML, H., *Zwischen Stresemann und Hitler: Die Außenpolitik der Präsidialkabinette Brüning, Papen und Schleicher* (Munich, 2001).

GRIECH-POLELLE, BETH A., *Bishop von Galen: German Catholicism and National Socialism* (New Haven, Conn., 2002).

HAMANN, B., *Hitlers Wien: Lehrjahre eines Diktators* (Munich, 1996).

HARTMANN, C., *Halder: Generalstabschef Hitlers 1939–1942* (Paderborn, 1991).

HEINEMAN, J. L., *Hitler's First Foreign Minister: Constantin Freiherr von Neurath* (London and Los Angeles, CA, 1979).

HOFFMANN, P., 'Generaloberst Ludwig Becks militärpolitisches Denken', *Historische Zeitschrift*, 234 (1981).

—— *Claus Schenk Graf von Stauffenberg und seine Brüder* (Stuttgart, 1982).

HÖVER, U., *Joseph Goebbels, ein nationaler Sozialist* (Bonn, 1992).

HUBATSCH, W., *Hindenburg und der Staat* (Göttingen, 1966).

JÄCKEL, E., *Hitler in History* (Hanover and London, 1984).

JAMES, H., 'Hjalmar Schacht', in Smelser, R. and Zitelmann, R. (eds.), *Die braunen Eliten* (Darmstadt, 1993).

JOACHIMSTHALER, A., *Hitlers Liste: Ein Dokument persönlicher Beziehungen* (Munich, 2003).

KERSHAW, I., *Hitler: 1889–1936: Hubris* (London, 1998).

—— *Hitler: 1936–1945: Nemesis* (London, 2000).

KLEY, S., *Hitler, Ribbentrop und die Entfesselung des Zweiten Weltkriegs* (Paderborn, 1996).

KOPPER, C., *Hjalmar Schacht: Aufstieg und Fall von Hitlers mächtigstem Bankier* (Munich, 2006).

KREBS, A., *Fritz-Dietlof Graf von der Schulenburg: Zwischen Staatsräson und Hochverrat* (Hamburg, 1964).

KRÖNER, B. R., *'Der starke Mann im Heimatkriegsgebiet': Generaloberst Friedrich Fromm: Eine Biographie* (Paderborn, 2005).

KUBE, A., *Pour le mérite und Hakenkreuz: Hermann Göring im Dritten Reich* (Munich, 1986).

LANG, J. VON, *Der Sekretär. Martin Bormann: Der Mann, der Hitler beherrschte* (Frankfurt am Main, 1980).

LUKACS, J., *The Hitler of History* (New York, 1997).

MARTENS, S., *Hermann Göring: 'erster Paladin des Führers' und 'zweiter Mann im Reich'* (Paderborn, 1985).

MASER, W., *Adolph Hitler: Legende, Mythos, Wirklichkeit*, 3rd edn. (Munich, 1973).

MEYER-KRAHMER, M., *Carl Goerdeler und sein Weg in den Widerstand: Eine Reise in die Welt meines Vaters* (Freiburg, 1989).

MICHALKA, W., 'Joachim von Ribbentrop: From Wine Merchant to Foreign Minister', in Smelser, R. M. and Zitelmann, R. (eds.), *The Nazi Elite* (Basingstoke, 1989).

Michels, H., *Ideologie und Propaganda: Die Rolle von Joseph Goebbels in der nationalsozialistischen Außenpolitik bis 1939* (Frankfurt am Main, 1992).

Moltke, F. von, Balfour, M., and Frisby, J., *Helmuth James von Moltke 1907–1945: Anwalt der Zukunft* (Stuttgart, 1972).

Müller, C., *Stauffenberg* (Düsseldorf, 1970).

Müller, K.-J. (ed.), *General Ludwig Beck: Studien und Dokumente zur politisch-militärischen Vorstellungswelt und Tätigkeit des Generalstabschefs des Deutschen Heeres 1933–1938* (Boppard, 1980).

Overy, R. J., *Goering* (London, 1984).

Paret, P., *An Artist Against the Third Reich: Ernst Barlach, 1933–1938* (Cambridge, 2003).

Pätzold, K., *Adolf Hitler: Eine politische Biographie* (Leipzig, 1995).

Pentzlin, H., *Hjalmar Schacht: Leben und Wirken einer umstrittenen Persönlichkeit* (Berlin, 1980).

Petzold, J., *Franz von Papen: Ein deutsches Verhängnis* (Munich, 1995).

Peuschel, H., *Die Männer um Hitler: Braune Biographien—Martin Bormann, Joseph Goebbels, Hermann Göring, Reinhard Heydrich, Heinrich Himmler und andere* (Düsseldorf, 1982).

Rainbird, Sean (ed.), *Max Beckmann* (New York, 2003).

Ramen, F., *Hermann Göring: Hitler's Second in Command* (New York, 2000).

Reuth, R. G., *Goebbels: Eine Biographie* (Munich, 1990).

Reynolds, N. E., *Treason was no Crime: Ludwig Beck, Chief of the German General Staff* (London, 1976).

Ritter, G., *Carl Goerdeler und die deutsche Widerstandsbewegung* (Stuttgart, 1955).

Scheurig, B., *Ewald von Kleist-Schmenzin: Ein Konservativer gegen Hitler* (Frankfurt am Main, 1994).

Schmidl, Erwin A., *März 38. Der deutsche Einmarsch in Österreich* (Vienna, 1987).

Schmidt, M., *Albert Speer: Das Ende eines Mythos. Speers wahre Rolle im Dritten Reich* (Munich, 1982).

Schöllgen, G., *Ulrich von Hassell 1881–1944: Ein Konservativer in der Opposition* (Munich, 1990).

Scholtyseck, J., *Robert Bosch und der liberale Widerstand gegen Hitler 1933 bis 1945* (Munich, 1999).

Schreiber, G., *Hitler. Interpretationen, 1923–1983: Ergebnisse, Methoden und Probleme der Forschung* (Darmstadt, 1984).

Seidler, F. W., *Fritz Todt: Baumeister des Dritten Reiches* (Munich, 1986).

Sereny, G., *Albert Speer: His Battle with Truth* (New York, 1995).

Smelser, R. M., *Robert Ley: Hitler's Labor Front Leader* (Oxford, 1988).

Smith, B., *Adolf Hitler: His Family, Childhood and Youth* (Stanford, CA, 1967).

—— *Heinrich Himmler 1900–1926. Sein Weg in den deutschen Faschismus* (Munich, 1979).

Stachura, P. D., *Gregor Strasser and the Rise of Nazism* (London, 1983).

Stauffer, P., *Zwischen Hofmannsthal und Hitler. Carl J. Burckhardt: Facetten einer außergewöhnlichen Existenz* (Zurich, 1991).

Steinert, M., *Hitler* (Munich, 1994).

STERN, J. P., *Hitler, the Führer and the People* (London, 1975).
STONE, N., *Hitler* (London, 1980).
STUDNITZ, CECILIA VON, Es war wie ein Rausch: Fallada und sein Leben (Düsseldorf, 1997).
THACKER, T., *Joseph Goebbels: Life and Death* (Basingstoke, 2009).
TURNER, H. A., *Hitler's Thirty Days to Power: January 1933* (New York, 1996).
VOGEL, J. P., *Hans Pfitzner: Leben, Werke, Dokumente* (Berlin, 1999).
WEITZ, J., *Hitler's Diplomat: Joachim von Ribbentrop* (London, 1992).
WHITING, C., *Heydrich: Henchman of Death* (London, 1999).
WIGHTON, CHARLES, *Heydrich: Hitler's Most Evil Henchman* (London, 1962).
ZITELMANN, R., *Adolph Hitler: Eine politische Biographie* (Göttingen, 1989).

Italy

BOSWORTH, R. J. B., *Mussolini* (New York, 2002).
CANNISTRARO, P. V. and SULLIVAN, B. R., *Il Duce's Other Woman* (New York, 1993).
DE FELICE, R., *Mussolini il duce: I. Gli anni del consenso, 1929–1936* (Turin, 1974).
—— *Mussolini il duce: II. Lo stato totalitario, 1936–1940* (Turin, 1981).
—— and MARIANO, E. (eds.), *Carteggio D'Anunzio–Mussolini (1919–1938)* (Milan, 1971).
FERMI, L., *Mussolini* (Chicago, IL, 1966).
GUERRI, G. B., *Galeazzo Ciano una vita 1930–1944* (Milan, 1979).
HIBBERT, C., *Benito Mussolini* (London, 1962).
MACK SMITH, D., *Mussolini* (London, 1981).
MILZA, P., *Mussolini* (Rome, 2000).
MORI, R., *Mussolini e la conquista dell'Etiopia* (Florence, 1978).
MOSELEY, R., *Mussolini's Shadow: The Double Life of Count Galeazzo Ciano* (New Haven, CT, 1999).
NELLO, P., *Dino Grandi, La formazione di un leader fascista* (Bologna, 1987).
—— *Un fedele disubbidiente. Dino Grandi da Palazzo Chigi al 25 luglio* (Bologna, 1993).
PIERI, P. and ROCHAT, G., *Pietro Badoglio* (Turin, 1974).
RIDLEY, J., *Mussolini* (London, 1997).
ROCHAT, G., *Italo Balbo* (Turin, 1986).
SEGRÈ, C., *Italo Balbo: A Fascist Life* (Berkeley, CA, 1987).

United States

ABBOTT, P., *The Exemplary President: Franklin D. Roosevelt and the American Political Tradition* (Amherst, MA, 1990).
ASBELL, B., *The F.D.R. Memoirs: As Written by Bernard Asbell* (Garden City, NY, 1973).
BEDTS, R. F. DE, *Ambassador Joseph Kennedy, 1938–1940: An Anatomy of Appeasement* (New York, 1985).
BENNETT, E. M., *Franklin D. Roosevelt and the Search for Security: American–Soviet Relations, 1933–1939* (Wilmington, DE, 1985).

Beschloss, M. R., *Kennedy and Roosevelt: The Uneasy Alliance* (New York, 1986).

Best, G. D., *Herbert Hoover: The Post-presidential Years, 1933–1964* (Stanford, CA, 1983).

Black, C., *Franklin Delano Roosevelt: Champion of Freedom* (London, 2003).

Brownell, W., *So Close to Greatness: The First Biography of William C. Bullitt* (New York, 1987).

Burke, B. V., *Ambassador Frederic Sackett and the Collapse of the Weimar Republic, 1930–1933: The United States and Hitler's Rise to Power* (Cambridge, 1994).

Burns, J. M., *Roosevelt: The Lion and the Fox* (New York, 1956).

—— *Roosevelt: The Soldier of Freedom* (New York, 1970).

Casey, S., *Cautious Crusade: Franklin D. Roosevelt, American Public Opinion, and the War against Nazi Germany* (Oxford, 2004).

Cassella-Blackburn, M., *The Donkey, the Carrot, and the Club: William C. Bullitt and Soviet–American Relations, 1917–1948* (Westport, CT, 2004).

Castle, A. L., *Diplomatic Realism: William R. Castle Jr. and American Foreign Policy, 1919–1953* (Honolulu, HI, 1998).

Cole, W. S., *Senator Gerald P. Nye and American Foreign Relations* (Minneapolis, MN, 1962).

—— *Charles A. Lindbergh and the Battle Against American Intervention in World War II* (New York, 1974).

—— *Roosevelt and the Isolationists* (Lincoln, NE, 1983).

Costigliola, F., 'John B. Stetson and Poland: The Diplomacy of a Prophet Scorned', in Jones, K. P. (ed.), *U.S. Diplomats in Europe, 1919–1941* (Santa Barbara, CA, 1981).

Current, R. N., *Secretary Stimson: A Study in Statecraft* (New Brunswick, NJ, 1954).

Dallek, R., *Democrat and Diplomat: The Life of William E. Dodd* (New York, 1968).

Dallek, R., *Franklin D. Roosevelt and American Foreign Policy, 1932–1945* (New York, 1979).

Doenecke, J. D. and Stoler, M. A., *Debating Franklin D. Roosevelt's Foreign Policies, 1933–1945* (Lanham, MD, 2005).

Duroselle, J.-B., *From Wilson to Roosevelt: Foreign Policy of the United States, 1913–1945* (Cambridge, MA, 1963).

Farnham, R. B., *Roosevelt and the Munich Crisis: A Study of Political Decision-making* (Princeton, NJ, 1997).

Farnsworth, B., *William C. Bullitt and the Soviet Union* (Bloomington, IN, 1967).

Ferrell, R. H., *American Diplomacy in the Great Depression: Hoover–Stimson Foreign Policy, 1929–1933* (New Haven, CT, 1957).

Flynn, G. Q., *Roosevelt and Romanism: Catholics and American Diplomacy, 1937–1945* (Westport, CT, 1976).

Freidel, F., *Franklin D. Roosevelt*, 4 vols. (Boston, MA, 1952–73).

—— *Franklin D. Roosevelt: A Rendezvous with Destiny* (Boston, MA, 1990).

Gellman, I., *Secret Affairs: Franklin Roosevelt, Cordell Hull, and Sumner Welles* (Baltimore, MD, 1995).

GLAD, B., *Key Pittman: The Tragedy of a Senate Insider* (New York, 1956).
GRAFF, F. W., *Strategy of Involvement: A Diplomatic Biography of Sumner Welles* (New York, 1988).
HAMBY, A. L., *For the Survival of Democracy: Franklin Roosevelt and the World Crisis of the 1930s* (New York, 2004).
HARPER, J. L., *American Visions of Europe: Franklin D. Roosevelt, George F. Kennan, and Dean G. Acheson* (Cambridge, 1994).
HEARDEN, P., *Roosevelt Confronts Hitler: America's Entry into World War II* (DeKalb, IL, 1987).
HEINRICHS, W., *American Ambassador: Joseph C. Grew and the Development of the United States Diplomatic Tradition* (Boston, MA, 1966).
—— *Threshold of War: Franklin D. Roosevelt and American Entry into World War II* (New York, 1988).
HERZSTEIN, R., *Roosevelt and Hitler: Prelude to War* (New York, 1989).
HODGSON, G., *The Colonel: The Life and Wars of Henry Stimson, 1867–1950* (New York, 1990).
HOOKER, N. H. (ed.), *The Moffat Papers* (Cambridge, MA, 1956).
ISRAEL, F., *Nevada's Key Pittman* (Lincoln, NE, 1966).
JENKINS, R., *Franklin Delano Roosevelt* (New York, 2003).
JOHNSON, C. O., *Borah of Idaho* (New York, 1936).
JOHNSON, N. M., *George Sylvester Viereck: German–American Propagandist* (Urbana, IL, 1972).
KAUFMANN, W. W., 'Two American Ambassadors: Bullitt and Kennedy', in Craig, G. A. and Gilbert, F. (eds.), *The Diplomats, 1919–1939* (Princeton, NJ, 1963), 649–681.
KOSKOFF, D. E., *Joseph P. Kennedy: A Life and Times* (Eaglewood Cliffs, NJ, 1974).
LEUCHTENBURG, W., *Franklin D. Roosevelt and the New Deal, 1932–1940* (London, 1963).
LOWITT, R., *George W. Norris: The Triumph of a Progressive, 1933–1944* (Urbana, IL, 1978).
MCELVAINE, R. S., *Franklin Delano Roosevelt* (Washington, DC, 2002).
MCKENNA, M. C., *Borah* (Ann Arbor, MI, 1961).
MARKS III, F. W., *Wind Over Sand: The Diplomacy of Franklin Roosevelt* (Athens, GA, 1988).
MORISON, E., *Turmoil and Tradition: The Life and Times of Henry L. Stimson* (Boston, MA, 1960).
PRATT, J. W., *Cordell Hull*, 2 vols. (New York, 1964).
RAUCH, B., *Roosevelt from Munich to Pearl Harbor: A Study in the Creation of a Foreign Policy* (New York, 1950).
ROSENBAUM, H. D. and BARTELME, E. (eds.), *Franklin D. Roosevelt, the Man, the Myth, the Era, 1882–1945* (Westport, CT, 1987).
SCHLESINGER Jr., A., *The Age of Roosevelt*, 3 vols. (Boston, MA, 1957–1960).
SCHMITZ, D. F., *Henry L. Stimson: The First Wise Man* (Wilmington, DE, 2001).
SMITH, J. E., *FDR* (New York, 2007).
SWIFT, W., *Kennedys Amidst the Gathering Storm: A Thousand Days in London, 1938–1940* (New York, 2008).

Thompson, J. A., *Woodrow Wilson* (London, 2002).
Tugwell, R. G., *The Democratic Roosevelt: A Biography of Franklin D. Roosevelt* (Garden City, NY, 1957).
—— *In Search of Roosevelt* (Cambridge, MA, 1972).
Welles, B., *Sumner Welles, FDR's Global Strategist: A Biography* (Basingstoke, 1997).

USSR

Bullock, A., *Hitler and Stalin: Parallel Lives* (London, 1991).
Broué, P., *Trotsky* (Paris, 1988).
Carswell, J., *The Exile: A Life of Ivy Litvinov* (London, 1983).
Cohen, S., *Bukharin and the Bolshevik Revolution: A Political Biography, 1888–1938* (New York, 1975).
Debo, R. K., 'Litvinov and Kamenev—Ambassadors Extraordinary: The Problem of Soviet Representation Abroad', *Slavic Review*, 34 (1975).
Deutscher, I., *Stalin: A Political Biography*, 2nd edn. (New York, 1960).
—— *Trotsky*, 3 vols. (New York, 1954–1963).
Fayet, J.-F., *Karl Radek (1885–1939): biographie politique* (Bern, 2004).
Fischer, L., *The Life and Death of Stalin* (London, 1953).
Gazur, E. P., *Alexander Orlov: The FBI's KGB General* (New York, 2002).
Jansen, M., and Petrov, N., *Stalin's Loyal Executioner: People's Commissar Nikolai Ezhov, 1895–1940* (Stanford, CA, 2002).
Lerner, W., *Karl Radek: The Last Internationalist* (Stanford, CA, 1970).
Khlevniuk, O. V., *Master of the House: Stalin and his Inner Circle* (New Haven, CT, 2009).
Knight, A., *Beria, Stalin's First Lieutenant* (Princeton, NJ, 1993).
Marie, J.-J., *Staline* (Paris, 2001).
Medvedev, Z. and R., *The Unknown Stalin: His Life, Death and Legacy*, trans. E. Dahrendorf (New York, 2004).
Meissner, H.-O., *The Man with Three Faces* (London, 1957).
Miner, S. M., 'His Master's Voice: Viacheslav Mikhailovich Molotov as Stalin's Foreign Commissar', in Craig, G. A. and Loewenheim, F. L. (eds.), *The Diplomats, 1939–1979* (Princeton, NJ, 1994).
Nove, A. (ed.), *The Stalin Phenomenon* (London, 1993).
Phillips, H. D., *Between the Revolution and the West: A Political Biography of Maxim M. Litvinov* (Boulder, CO, 1992).
Radzinsky, E., *Stalin* (London, 1996).
Sebag-Montefiore, S., *Stalin: The Court of the Red Tsar* (London, 2003).
—— *Young Stalin* (London, 2007).
Service, R., *Stalin: A Biography* (London, 2004).
—— *Lenin: A Political Life*, 2 vols. (London, 1985–1991).
Sheinis, Z., *Maxim Litvinov* (Moscow, 1990).
Tucker, R. C., *Stalin in Power: The Revolution from Above, 1928–1941* (New York, 1990).
Ulam, A. B., *Stalin: The Man and his Era* (New York, 1973).
Volkogonov, D. A., *Stalin: Triumph and Tragedy*, trans. H. Shukman (New York, 1991).

—— *Trotsky: The Eternal Revolutionary*, trans. H. Shukman (New York, 1996).
WHYMANT, R., *Stalin's Spy: Richard Sorge and the Tokyo Espionage Ring* (New York, 1998).
WILLOUGHBY, C. A., *Sorge: Soviet Master Spy* (London, 1952).

Others

ABLONCZY, B., *Pál Teleki (1874–1941): The Life of a Controversial Hungarian Politician*, trans. Thomas J. and Helen D. DeKornfeld (Boulder, CO, and Wayne, NJ, 2006).
BÁN, A., *Hungarian–British Diplomacy, 1938–1941: The Attempt to Maintain Relations*, trans. Tim Wilkinson (London and Portland, OR, 2004).
CZETTLER, A., *Pál Graf Teleki und die Außenpolitik Ungarns 1939–1941* (Munich, 1996).
DRÂGAN, I. C., *Antonescu: Marshal and Ruler of Romania, 1940–1944*, trans. Andrei Bantas (Bucharest, 1995).
JEDRZEJEWICZ, W. (ed.), *Piłsudski: A Life for Poland* (New York, 1982).
NETEA, V., *Nicolae Titulescu* (Bucharest, 1969).
SAKMYSTER, T. L. *Hungary's Admiral on Horseback: Miklós Horthy, 1918–1944* (Boulder, CO, and New York, 1994).
TITULESCU, N., *Romania's Foreign Policy: 1937*, ed. George G. Potra and Constantin I. Turcu (Bucharest, 1994).

INDEX

Note: Bold entries refer to maps and tables.

Abert, Louis 719
Abetz, Otto 841
Abwehr 721, 774, 820
Action Française 128
Adam, General Wilhelm 576, 577, 584
Addis Ababa, and Italian occupation of 130
Addison, Joseph 266
Aden 800
air forces, and comparison of strengths of 608
  see also French Air Force; Italian Air Force; *Luftwaffe*; Red Army; Royal Air Force (RAF); United States Army Air Forces
Åland Islands 936, 937
Alaska 481
Albania 359
  and British reaction to Italian invasion 743–4
  and French reaction to Italian invasion 745–6
  and Italy 368, 569
    invasion by 742–3
    occupation plans by 693
Alexander, King of Yugoslavia 77
Alexandretta 749
Alexandrovsky, Sergei 582, 613, 618, 623, 633, 643
Algeria 719, 806
Allen, Clifford 168
Aloisi, Pompeo 34, 88, 104, 126, 155
Amau Eiji 488
American Committee for Non-Participation in Japanese Aggression 543
Amery, Leo 115, 685, 1016
Amtag (Soviet trade organization) 208
Anders, Lt Gen W 1027–8
Anglo-Egyptian treaty (1936) 133
Anschluss 552, 553–4
  and British and French reactions 557
  and completion of 554
  and economic effects of 556
  and Hitler-Schuschnigg meeting 364
  and importance of 554
  as improvised affair 555
  and intention to annex denied by Germany 104
  and Mussolini's concerns over 27, 69
  and Soviet reaction 559
  and ultimatums to Schuschnigg 552–3
  and unlikelihood of foreign intervention over 360–2, 557
  see also Austria
Anti-Comintern Pact 262, 263, 476, 538
  and Germany 262, 263, 476, 484–5, 524, 540
  and Italy 240, 241, 316–17, 486, 524

Anti-Comintern Pact (*cont.*)
and Japan 262, 263, 476, 484–5, 538, 540, 695
and Spain 696, 942
and terms of 484–5
anti-Communism:
and France 415–16, 424, 768
and Franco's use of 184
and Germany 195
and Great Britain 914–15
and growth of 10
and Hitler 15, 445
and Netherlands 930
and Yugoslavia 290
anti-Semitism:
and Austria 554–5
and Great Britain 860
and growth of 10
and Hungary 372, 373, 981
and Italy 570–1
and Lueger's definition of 980
and nationalism 981
and Poland 367, 981
and Romania 405, 981
and United States 860
widespread in Europe 15
see also Hitler, Adolf; Jews; *Kristallnacht*
Antonescu, Marshall Ion 396
Antonescu, Victor 370, 395–6, 401
Antonov-Ovseenko, Vladimir 210
appeasement:
and definition of 647, 647n51
and France 308, 318–19, 323, 326, 330, 567
colonial appeasement 307, 324–5
economic appeasement 307, 323, 714, 1046
policy of expediency 603, 644
political and economic pressures for 347–8
and Great Britain 326–7, 330, 604, 1053
abandonment by 1032
Chamberlain's aims 683
Chamberlain's defence of 733
Chamberlain's diplomacy 339–40, 648–51, 654–6, 683
colonial appeasement 305–7, 310, 324, 325
Czechoslovakia 341–3
economic appeasement 301–5, 307, 308–10, 323–4, 390–1, 700, 702, 704, 706, 776–7, 1045
Eden on 149
efforts made to popularize 684
Hitler-Halifax meeting (1937) 336–9
imperial vulnerability 804
Japan 426, 479, 499, 508, 509, 811
motives for 292–3
opposition to 340, 683–4
peace groups 169
relationship with rearmament 297–8
Spanish Civil War 222
warnings from 'opposition' Germans 589–90
and Munich conference 645–6
and Soviet Union 492, 1064
Ardennes:
and failure to fortify 281, 322
and German breakthrough 1060, 1061
Argentina, and Jewish refugees 974, 982
Arita Hachiro 539, 810, 811
armaments trade:
and Germany 199
and Great Britain 200
and League of Nations' publications 171
and Nye Committee (USA) 110, 172
and public revulsion with 172
and Royal Commission on the Manufacture of and Trade in Armaments (1935-36) 172

armies, *see* British Army; French Army; Italian Army; Red Army; *Reichswehr*; *Wehrmacht*
Arrow Cross 372, 373
Ashton-Gwatkin, Frank 302, 390, 593, 594, 641, 706
Association pour la paix par le droit (APD) 168
Astakhov, Georgi 882, 883, 885
  and distrust of Germany 889
  and German-Soviet *rapprochement* 890
  and negotiations with Germany 905
  and talks with Draganov 892
  and talks with Schnurre 903
Astor, Lord 821
Ataturk, Mustafa Kemal 792
Attlee, Clement 33, 221, 624
Attolico, Bernardo 129, 585, 638, 851, 852, 1000
Auden, W H 670
Auriol, Vincent 206
Australia 515, 799, 802, 982, 1018
Austria 359
  and amnesty for Austrian Nazis 156
  and Anglo-French-Italian declaration on (1934) 76
  and anti-Semitism 554–5
  and attempted Nazi putsch 75
  and Austrian National Socialist Party 76, 156, 362
  and elections (1935) 267
  and France, response to German invasion 557
  and Germany:
    Austrian Nazis prepared for future role 156
    Austro-German agreement (1936) 156–7
    discussions with Italy about 314, 315, 316
    Hitler's cautious approach 264–5
    trade with 731
    visa tax imposed by 39
  and Great Britain 76, 362
  and Italy 75–6, 78, 155
    Anglo-French-Italian declaration on Austria (1934) 76
    Hitler supported by 554
    reduced interest of 157
    seeks German reassurance 104
  and Jews in 973, 976, 987–8
  and Rome Protocols (1934) 69
  and Schuschnigg's attempt to strengthen government 156
  and Soviet Union, response to German invasion 559
  and tariff preference proposals 403
  see also Anschluss
Austrian National Socialist German Workers' Party (NSDAP) 76, 156, 362, 554
Avenol, Joseph 107, 172, 520, 979
Azaña, Manuel 246

Backhouse, Admiral Sir Roger 630, 741–2, 791
Badoglio, Pietro 696
  and concerns over Austria 69
  and Ethiopian crisis 121, 127, 128
  and Franco-Italian military talks 108–9
  and Spanish Civil War 192, 194
  and warns of Italian vulnerability 853
balance of power:
  and British attitude towards 351–2
  and German recognition of British interest in 17, 317–18
  and impact of Ethiopian crisis 135–6
  and Soviet role in maintaining 415, 482
  and Spanish Civil War 185
Balbo, Italo 26, 192
Baldwin, Stanley 92
  and abdication crisis 302
  and air force strength 50
  and becomes prime minister 105

Baldwin, Stanley (*cont.*)
and bombing danger 87–8
and East Fulham by-election (1933) 45
and establishes cabinet committee on foreign policy 154
and Ethiopian crisis 114–15, 125, 126
and general election (1935) 120
on Hitler's Eastern ambitions 299
and League of Nations 106
and rearmament 84, 87
and Rhineland reoccupation 146, 148
and Spanish Civil War 202, 433
Balearic Islands 188–9
Balkan Conference 67, 68
Balkan Pact (Balkan Entente) 68
and Bulgaria 957
and factors weakening 925
and limitations of 407
and limited military cooperation 925
and reactions to 68
and Rhineland reoccupation 151
and suspicion of France 93
Balkans:
and avoidance of German economic exploitation 730
and cooperation between states 67–8
and extreme right-wing movements 9
and German economic domination 716, 729
and military conventions 68
see also individual countries
Ball, Sir Joseph 636, 821
Baltic Entente 393
Baltic states:
and defence spending 934
and extreme right-wing movements 9
and Germany:
Hitler's intentions 392
naval and intelligence contacts 393
Nazi-Soviet Pact provisions 910, 939
trade with 387, **388**, **389**, **731**
and Great Britain:
response to German trade effort 390
trade agreements 387
trade with **388**, **389**
and limits of regional solidarity 934
and mutual defence bloc 925
and occupation of 934
and Soviet Union:
Anglo-Soviet alliance negotiations 895
Nazi-Soviet Pact provisions 910, 939
pressures by to surrender sovereignty 916
revision of Nazi-Soviet Pact terms 915
see also Estonia; Latvia; Lithuania
Bank of China 500
Bank of England, and gold reserves 780
Bank of France 128, 348
Bank of Madrid 213
Bank of Spain 213
Banque Commerciale pour l'Europe du Nord (Commercial Bank for Northern Europe, BCEN) 213
Barbarin, Yevgeniy 901, 903
Barcelona 184
Barthou, Louis 48
and assassination of 77, 78
and attitude towards German rearmament 53–4
and becomes foreign minister 48–9
situation faced by 69–70
and Czechoslovakia 71
and Eastern Locarno Pact 71–2, 74
and European reconciliation 49
and Franco-Belgian relations 70
and Italy, talks with 76

and Mediterranean Locarno 75
and personality 49, 77
and Poland 71
and World Disarmament Conference 70
Bartlett, Vernon 684
Bartoszewski, Władysław 1028
Baudouin, Paul 696, 720
BBC:
and Anglo-Portuguese relations 200
and government pressure on 633
and popularization of imperial ideas 797
and public awareness of international situation 1025
Beauvoir, Simone de 1027
Beaverbrook, Lord 431
Bech, Joseph 932, 933, 934
Beck, Józef 34
and Czechoslovakia 587–8
and Danzig 265, 787, 839–41, 843
Polish-German negotiations 691–2
refuses to reveal details of negotiations 738
and distrust of 366
and French suspicions of 283
and Germany 366, 998
and Great Britain:
accepts guarantee from 739
calls for restraint by 842–3
decision for war entrusted by 739
and Jews, disinterest in 988
and meeting with Beneš 64–5
and Rhineland reoccupation 151
and Romania 394
and Soviet Union 71, 907
Beck, General Ludwig 44, 335, 652, 653
and lack of enthusiasm for Italian alliance 569
and mobile warfare 253
and rearmament 254
and reform of Nazi system 577
and resignation of 578
and warns against invasion of Czechoslovakia 575–7
Beckles, Gordon 21–2
Belgium:
and Anglo-French war plans 785
and disarmament 53
and divisions over defensive strategy 140–1
and France:
Anglo-French declaration on (1937) 322
divisions in attitude towards 140
informal military talks between 281, 322, 785, 928
military agreement between (1920) 70–1, 140, 141, 927
military talks between (1936) 151–2
rising Francophobia 141
unsettled relations between 70–1
and Germany 323
invaded by 1060
non-aggression pact proposal 319, 320
proposals for ensuring independence 320–1
and Great Britain 320
Anglo-French declaration on (1937) 322
reaction to policy of independence 280–1, 928
seeks security guarantee from 54, 71
staff talks between 149, 151, 322–3
and Jewish refugees 976, 981–2
and Luxembourg 933
and military reform 140–1
and Netherlands 930
and neutrality (policy of independence) 141, 279–81, 927, 928–9
British reaction 280–1
French reaction 279–80
and peace appeal by 1003

Belgium: (*cont.*)
and political divisions 927–8
and Rhineland reoccupation 147, 148–9
and urges Franco-German talks 47
Belorussia, and Soviet Union 915–16
Beneš, Edvard 35, 365
and Czech anger with 641
and France:
approves attempts to conciliate Germany 421
confidence in 406
Franco-Little Entente alliance talks 396
proposes alliance with Little Entente 290
rejects Anglo-French demands 614
visits Paris (1933) 64
and Germany:
believes détente possible with 406
downplays danger from 369
non-aggression pact talks 268
rejects Hitler's terms 622–3
and Great Britain:
accepts timetable proposal 632
rejects Anglo-French demands 614
and Hoare-Laval plan 132
and Italy 369
and Munich conference, accepts agreement 641–3
and *Munich Days* 642
and Poland:
reaction to German-Polish declaration (1934) 66
seeks understanding with (1934) 64–5
and Rhineland reoccupation 151
and Soviet Union:
asks about assistance from 633
Czech-Soviet mutual assistance pact (1935) 94–5
seeks to ascertain attitude of 613–14
and Sudeten Germans 267, 406, 561, 584–5, 611, 622–3
and Yugoslavia 367, 369
Bérard-Jordana agreement (Franco-Spanish) 944
Beria, Lavrenti 880, 884
Berliner Tageblatt, on Edward VIII 153
Berlin Pact of Non-Aggression and Neutrality (1926), and extension of (1933) 28
Berlin Radio 1008
Bermuda 817
Bernhardt, Johannes 187, 195, 196
Bertram, Cardinal Adolf 985
Bessarabia 370, 910
Bessonov, Sergei 447, 450–1
Béthouart, Marie-Emile 400
Bilbao 226
Bismarck, Prince von (German embassy counsellor in London) 42, 215
Bloch, Marc 1061
Blomberg, Field Marshal Werner von 37, 43, 334
and meets with Halifax (1937) 339
and opposes strengthening links with Japan 485
and questions Hitler's plans 333
and Rhineland reoccupation 142, 144
and Spanish Civil War 191
and World Disarmament Conference 42
Blum, Léon 128, 161, 627
and appeasement 308, 318–19
and Austria 557
and character 271
and colonial appeasement 307
and constitutionalism of 272
and Czechoslovakia, potential assistance to 558
and discussions with Schacht 258, 291
and domestic attacks on 272
and fall of government (1937) 326
and fall of government (1938) 558

and Germany, approach towards 278
and Little Entente, alliance proposals 397
and rearmament 273, 318
and Soviet Union 326, 419, 420
and Spanish Civil War 204, 205, 206, 234, 243, 558
Blum, Robert 395
Blyukher, General Vasily 538
Bodasakis-Athanasiadis, Prodromos 198, 378
Bogomolov, Dmitrii 496, 520
Bohemia 555, 630–1, 690, 727, 821
Bohlen, Charles 894
Bonnet, Georges:
and appeasement 326, 567
retreat from central Europe 343
and Austria 362
and becomes finance minister 347
and becomes foreign minister 559
and Czechoslovakia 572, 583, 595, 611–12, 627
and freeze on defence spending 348, 349–50
and Germany 713, 714–15, 1019
and Great Britain 240, 343, 567, 611, 625–6, 627, 632, 713, 736, 737, 886, 901–2, 1013, 1015, 1017
and Italy 567, 719
and Munich conference 644
and need for eastern front as deterrent 737
and offers resignation 841
and Poland 713, 737, 777
advocates withdrawal of guarantee 997
hopes to avoid war over 996–7, 1001
reaction to German invasion 1010, 1012–13, 1014, 1015
and rearmament 713
and restructuring of Eastern European obligations 713, 718–19
and Romania 737
and Soviet Union 713
alliance negotiations 889, 898
believes alliance to be essential 777, 818
considers tripartite alliance offer by 881, 886
military talks with 909
offers reciprocal arrangement with 752
talks with Surits 879
Boris III, King of Bulgaria 407, 956–7, 959
Bottai, Giuseppe 194–5
Bowers, Claude 207
Brauchitsch, General Walther von 882
and becomes commander in chief 334
and Czechoslovakia, invasion planning 572
and Italy, negative opinion of forces of 844
and Poland, invasion planning 733
and warns Hitler about armaments shortages 836–7
Brazil 374, 375, 982
Breiting, Richard 18
Bretton Woods agreement 175
Briand, Aristide 49, 1037
Bridges, Edward 297
Brinkmann, Rudolf 450
Brinon, Fernand de 40, 47, 117
British Army:
and Belgium, staff talks between (1936) 149, 151
and British Expeditionary Force 1060
and continental commitment 724–5
deployment of expeditionary force 785–6
and distribution of troops (1938) 801
and expansion of 699–700, 724–5, 736
conscription 772

British Army: (*cont.*)
Third Deficiency Programme (1936) 295
and Field Force 295, 344–5
and France:
joint staff planning (1939) 723, 725
staff talks (1936) 149, 151, 160–1
staff talks (1938) 719
staff talks (1939) 725
and imperial obligations 804–5
in Middle East 793
and planned expenditure 51, 52
disagreements over 699–700
and Territorial Army 295, 699, 736
and unpreparedness of 699, 772
British Council, and Anglo-Portuguese relations 200
British Empire **796**
and British responsibility for imperial defence 802–5
and declaration of war against Germany 1018
and distribution of troops (1938) **801**
and economic importance of 798
and Empire Day 795–7
and impact of Second World War 1064
and imperial obligations 795, 800
and lack of common imperial strategy 803
and revival of imperial sentiment 795–8
as source of manpower and material support 799–800
and uncertainty over support for Britain in war 800–2
see also Dominions
British Guinea 984
British Library of Information 814
Brittain, Vera 168
Brockdorff, General Walter von 629
Broqueville, Charles de 70
Broz, Josip (Marshal Tito) 214
Bruce Report (1939) 175
Brunete, battle of 226
Brüning, Heinrich 73
Brussels Nine-Power Conference (1937), and Sino-Japanese conflict 522, 524, 525–8
Bryant, Arthur 857, 858
Buchenwald concentration camp 973
Bukharin, Nikolai Ivanovich 211, 492, 559
Bulgaria 359
and Balkan Entente 957
and Germany **731**, 956–7, 958–9
and Great Britain 958, 959
and impact of Nazi-Soviet Pact 959
and isolation of 68
and Italy 261
and neutrality 956–9
and Romania 957
and Soviet Union 959
and territorial claims 957, 958
and Turkey 957
and Yugoslavia 367, 950, 958
Bulgarian Workers' Party 959
Bullitt, William 271, 292, 343, 421, 567, 1026
Bülow, Prince Bernard von 30
Bürckel, Josef 554
Burckhardt, Carl J 265–6, 366, 840, 842, 844, 856
Burma, and Indian Army 800
Butler, R A 618, 887, 904

Cadogan, Alexander 310, 329, 592, 858, 1015
and China 486–7, 502
and Czechoslovakia 565, 630–1
persuades Halifax to oppose further concessions 623
and disarmament 31
and Far East 479, 502, 809
and Germany 563, 711–12, 1025
and relative dangers of Communism and Fascism 438
and Soviet Union 751, 880–1, 886

Çakmak, General Fevzi 963
Călinescu, Armand 734n5
Calvo Sotelo, José 181, 186
Cameroons 306, 310, 324, 325
Campinchi, César 627, 777
Camrose, Lord 821
Canada 799, 802, 803, 1018
Canaris, Admiral Wilhelm 190, 191, 593, 820
Capa, Robert 183
Carol, King of Romania 288, 747, 947, 948
  and establishes personal dictatorship 405
  and Germany 382, 689, 735
  and Great Britain 399–400, 710, 734
  and National Christian party 405
  and non-alignment policy 289, 370
Carpathian-German Party (KdP) 267
Carranza, Fernando 196
Catholic Centre Party (Germany) 21
Catholic Church, and Nazi-Catholic relations 985, 986–7
  see also papacy
Cavagnari, Admiral Dominico 103, 104, 846, 853
Cecil, Viscount Robert 106, 169, 633
Cerrutti, Vittorio 26
Chalkovsky, František 642
Chamberlain, Austen 33, 299, 306, 1037
Chamberlain, Neville:
  and aims of 683
  and *Anschluss* 557
  and appeasement 326–7, 339–40
    colonial appeasement 306, 310, 324
    defence of 733
    economic appeasement 301–2, 303–4, 305, 307, 309, 310, 324, 403, 700, 702, 704, 706, 776–7
    limits use of word 766
  and assumption of British strength 604
  and becomes prime minister 234, 326
  as Chancellor of the Exchequer:
    air deterrent 295–6
    Defence Requirements Committee report (1934) 51, 52, 426, 507–8
    economic appeasement 301–2, 303, 305, 307
    influence of 131, 148, 295
    Japan 479, 499, 508, 509
    maintenance of economic stability 131, 297
    Third Deficiency Programme (1936) 294
    vetoes Yugoslav credit guarantee 399
  and Churchill 821, 1012
  and control of foreign policy 329, 340
  and convinced of German and Italian anxiety for agreement 222–3
  and Czechoslovakia:
    advocates acceptance of Hitler's demands 617–18
    Anglo-French discussions 342
    broadcasts to nation about crisis 631
    Hitler-Chamberlain talks at Berchtesgaden 610
    Hitler-Chamberlain talks at Godesberg 616–17
    loses support of Halifax 623
    overruled by Cabinet 623
    policy towards 563–4
    proposes modification of Hitler's terms 624–5
    rebuts French criticism of policy 565
    response to German *coup* (1939) 733
    Runciman mission 580–1
    seeks Italian assistance 636–8

Chamberlain, Neville (*cont.*)
suggests five-power conference 637
Wilson's mission to Germany 628
and deterrence:
air defence 51, 295, 296
belief in success of 823
economic concessions 776–7
Polish guarantee 738–9, 740
and diplomacy of:
caution 650
emphasis on personal relationship with Hitler 650–1
high-risk strategy 649
ideological antipathies 736–7
ideological assumptions 1048
misreading of Hitler 650–1, 655–6, 683, 1006, 1056
obsession with preserving peace 651
persists in believing war can be avoided 818–19, 856
rationality of 1006, 1050–51
response to public opinion 650
self-confidence 648, 651
and Eden, disagreements with 526, 535, 562
and Ethiopian crisis 115, 125, 131
and France:
asserts solidarity with 724
confronts over aircraft production 346
differences over Italy 564
exasperation with 351
limited staff talks with 564, 603
meets with Chautemps and Delbos (1937) 341
opposition to military commitment 344
visits Daladier (1938) 712–13
and Germany, *see* Hitler, and separate topics
and Hitler:
appeals to in Birmingham speech 724
fears effects of containment policy on 776
future intentions of 656
meetings between 610, 616–17
misreading of 650–1, 655–6, 683, 1050, 1056
optimism over future policy 725–6
responds to Kemsley's talks with 858
tells of determination to stand by Poland 996
and influence over strategy 295, 297
and Italy 234
clashes with Eden over 236
meets with Mussolini (1939) 697–8
misjudgement of Mussolini 685, 694–5, 698
reaction to invasion of Albania by 743–4
seeks agreement with 235–6, 240–1, 562, 693–4
seeks detachment from Germany 794–5, 1053
and Japan:
favours settlement with 426, 479, 499, 508, 509
Tientsin crisis 810
and Jewish refugees 978–9, 988
and Munich conference, *see* Munich conference
and Mussolini 685, 694–5, 697–8, 735, 794–5
and Poland:
Danzig 842
determination to stand by 996
guarantee to 739, 740
keeps door open for negotiations with Germany 856–7
last-minute attempts at agreement with Germany 1004
reaction to German invasion 1009, 1011–12, 1014–16

and political isolation 765–6, 767
and public opinion 650, 766
and rearmament:
acceleration of 606
concentration on air force 295–6
hostility towards army 700
influence over defence spending 51, 52, 294, 426, 507–8
maintenance of economic stability 313, 684–5
motives for 605
resistance to massive 698
see also Defence Requirements Committee (DRC); separate armed services
and Rhineland reoccupation 149
and Romania 745
and Sino-Japanese conflict 521, 522
and Soviet Union:
agrees to open alliance talks 887, 1033
alliance negotiations 889, 898
attitude towards 736–7, 750, 777
believes German-Soviet alliance impossible 893
doubts over alliance with 818
opposition to tripartite alliance with 886–7, 896, 899, 901
and Spanish Civil War 244
and United States 340
Anglo-American trade agreement (1938) 534, 816
antipathy towards 499, 815, 818
on behaviour of US Congress 818
clash with Eden over 526, 533–5
cultivates good will of 816
dislike of Roosevelt 815
naval appeal to 742
Neutrality Acts 818
rejects Roosevelt's peace plan 534
reluctance to involve in Europe 634, 1053
seeks support in Far East 504, 531, 742
trade talks 534
unreliability of 531
Chambre, Guy la 346, 597, 997
Chambrun, Charles de 41, 107, 124, 128, 282
Chanak crisis 800–2
Chang Hsueh-liang 495, 496–7
Chapman, Guy 1024
Charbonnières, Girard de 215, 565, 612
Chastenet, Jacques 452
Chatfield, Sir Ernle 508, 766, 886
Chautemps, Camille 46, 48, 234, 347
and appeasement 326
retreat from central Europe 343, 405
and Austria 362
and Great Britain 341
and rearmament, crisis in aircraft production 346
Chiang Kai-shek:
and army modernization 490
and arrest of 496–7
and German military assistance 262, 484, 485
and Japan, seeks agreement with 489–91
and negotiations with Chinese Communist Party 497, 498
and Nine Power (Brussels) Conference (1937) 525
and opposition to policies of 491, 492
and reaction to Anti-Comintern Pact 263
and Sino-Japanese conflict:
appeals for international mediation 516
Marco Polo Bridge incident 515–16
refuses to capitulate 541
rejects revised peace terms 528, 529

Chiang Kai-shek: (*cont.*)
Shanghai campaign 516–17
and Soviet Union:
military assistance from 230–1, 520
negotiations with 496
offensive urged by 904
and Tangku truce (1933) 488
Chiappe, Jean 48
Chile 374, 375, 982
Chilston, 2nd Viscount (Aretas Akers-Douglas) 427, 435, 451
Chilton, Sir Henry 202
China:
and arms supplied to **519**
and currency reform 501
and France 482
and Germany 484
arms deliveries ended 524, 540
military assistance to Kuomintang 262, 485, 519
and Great Britain:
economic interests of 477–8
Leith-Ross mission 500–1
and Italy 486
and Japan:
Amau declaration 488–9
anti-Japanese feeling 491
desire to create economic bloc in North China 501
establishment of autonomous provinces by 490
internationalist strategy 489
relations between (1933-35) 489–91
relations between (1936-37) 491–2
Sato's revised China policy 502–3
seeks agreement with 489–91
Tangku truce (1933) 488
and Kuomintang/Chinese Communist Party negotiations 497, 498
and National Salvation Association 491
and Soviet Union:
arrest of Chiang Kai-shek 496–7
Chinese Communist Party (CCP) 493–5
military assistance to Kuomintang 230–1, 496, 520
non-aggression pact (1937) 520
urges offensive by Chiang Kai-shek 904
and Tientsin crisis 809–12, 896–7
and United States:
open door policy 480–1
Silver Purchase Act (1934, USA) 500
trade with 481
and western assumptions about 486–7
see also Chinese Communist Party (CCP); Far East; Kuomintang; Sino-Japanese conflict
Chinese Communist Party (CCP) 490, 491
and arrest of Chiang Kai-shek 496–7
and Kuomintang, relations with 494, 495, 497, 498
and Soviet Union:
demands cooperation with Kuomintang 494, 495, 529
differences over warlords' rebellion 494–5
independence from 493–4
relations with 493–4
and united front tactics 494
Chinese Eastern Railway (CER) 492
Chou En-lai 497
Churchill, Winston 33, 299, 306, 427, 1059
and abdication crisis 302n46
and appointed prime minister 1062
and Czechoslovakia 683–4
Sudeten Germans 561
urges warning to Germany 591, 624, 633

and Ethiopian crisis 114
and France, attends military parade 769
and joins cabinet 1012
and Munich agreement, opposition to 683–4
and Nazism as existential threat 1056
on neutrality 924
and pressure for rearmament 50, 169, 606
and public and press campaign for inclusion in cabinet 766, 821
and Soviet Union:
favours alliance 431, 887
show trials 211
talks with Maisky 431
warns of German invasion 1064
and Spanish Civil War 203, 238, 434, 1048
and United States, on entry into war 1066
Ciano, Galeazzo 155
and Albania, occupation plans 693, 743
and *Anschluss* 317
and Anti-Comintern Pact 316
and aspirations of Italian people 694
and attempts to dissuade Mussolini from war 852, 853, 855
and Czechoslovakia 585–6, 637–8
and Germany 369
on betrayal by 852
dismisses warning of attack on Poland 851
fears over attack on Poland 851–2
German-Italian protocol (1936) 261
meeting with Hitler (1936) 190
meeting with Hitler (1939) 852
'Pact of Steel' (1939) 848–9
pressures Mussolini to denounce alliance with 999
reaction to Czech *coup* 845
reaction to invasion of Poland by 1009, 1013
relations with Ribbentrop 568, 692–3, 698, 846, 847–8, 852
and Hungary 371
and impact of Nazi-Soviet Pact 999
and Spanish Civil War 187
creation of *Ufficio Spagna* 192
German-Italian cooperation 190–1
military assistance 239
Nyon Conference (1937) 238
and Yugoslavia 316–17
treaty with (1937) 367–9
Cincar-Marković, Aleksandar 949, 950, 952
Clerk, Sir George 113, 205, 298, 364
Coburg, Duke of 706
code-breaking, and Enigma machines 790
Colijn, Hendrijus 930–1
collective security 3
and belief in 100
and Hoare's speech to League of Nations 111
and loss of confidence in 159
and public support for 113
and Soviet foreign policy 67, 134, 245, 414, 439, 442, 451, 452, 878
and undermined by Ethiopian crisis 131, 134–5
Collier, Laurence 340
and relative dangers of Communism and Fascism 437, 438
and response to German trade effort in northern Europe 390
and similarity of Soviet, German and Italian policy 430
and Soviet Union 426, 428, 433, 435, 750, 894

colonies:
and Far East, native-elite relations 487
and France 482–3, 526–7, 807
and Germany, tactical demand for 260, 325
and Great Britain, colonial appeasement 305–7, 324
and League of Nations' mandate system 175–6
and Netherlands 483, 809, 929–30
and Portugal 539
see also British Empire; French Empire
Colson, General Louis-Antoine 417
Columbia, and Jewish refugees 974
Colvin, Ian 738
Comert, Pierre 125
Comintern 1038–9
and Chinese Communist Party 493–5, 497, 498, 529
and debates on Soviet-German relations 452, 453
and France 416, 423, 913
and Great Britain 426, 913
and Japan, opposes appeasement of 492
and loss of influence 443
and Popular Front strategy 442–3
Stalin demands abandonment of 913
and purges of 464
and Spanish Civil War 209, 210, 211, 213, 214
Comité Permanent de la Defense Nationale (CPDN) 239–40, 346, 351, 717, 720
Comité Secret d'Action Révolutionaire 274
Committee of Imperial Defence (CID) 222, 322, 398, 708, 789
Communism, and limited appeal of 9
Communist Party of Germany (KPD) 19, 20–1, 28, 464
Communist Party of Spain (*Partido Communista de España*, PCE) 209, 214, 215, 218, 219, 228
concentration camps:
and Jews taken to 973
and Spanish Civil War refugees 248
Condor Legion 191, 219
Confederación Nacional de Trabajo (National Confederation of Labour, CNT) 228
Conféderation Général du Travail (CGT) 49
Conseil Supérieur de la Défense Nationale (CSDN, Supreme Council of National Defence) 37
Constantini, Francesco 104n6
Constantini, Secondo 104n6
Cooper, Duff 237, 297, 591, 592, 683
Corbin, Charles 216, 329, 341, 397, 420, 565, 735, 741, 1016–17
Corfu 743
Corsica 719, 851
Cot, Pierre 169
and disguises air production difficulties 346
and distrust of 345, 396
and domestic attacks on 272
and Poland 394
and Romania 401
and Soviet Union 291
air mission to 419
enthusiasm for military alliance with 418–19
Franco-Soviet talks (1933) 36
and Spanish Civil War 206
Coulondre, Robert 420, 422, 842, 1001, 1009, 1010, 1019
Craigie, Sir Robert 517–18, 536, 538, 543, 742, 904
and Anglo-German naval talks 87
and Tientsin crisis 810, 811
Craigie-Arita agreement 811

Croatia:
  and Italy 850, 853
  and Serbo-Croat talks 950–1, 953
Csáky, Count István 853, 955
Cuza, Alexander 405
Cvetković, Dragiša 953
Cyprus, and British forces in 805
Czechoslovakia 359, 688
  and counterfactual case for war over 654–5
  and France 565, 624
    abandoned by 597, 604
    Anglo-French demand to transfer territory 612–13
    Anglo-French discussions 341–3, 365, 564–5, 611–12
    Anglo-French policy 565–6
    Anglo-French ultimatum to 612–13
    approves attempts to conciliate Germany 421
    Beneš visits Paris (1933) 64
    factors influencing policy during crisis 594–604
    Franco-Little Entente alliance talks 396, 397
    potential assistance from 558
    promises to meet obligations 557–8
    rejects Anglo-French demands 614
    unlikelihood of military assistance from 596–7
    visit by Delbos (1937) 406
  and Germany 568, 583–4, 630, 728–9
    agrees to conference 638
    diplomatic and economic doubts over plans of 578–9
    diplomatic preparations for attack by 585
    Hitler's Nuremberg speech 593
    invasion planning by 334, 365, 560, 571, 572–3, 584, 616, 681
    non-aggression pact talks 267–8
    post-Munich bullying by 687
    reassured by over Austrian invasion 554
    trade with **731**
    transfer of territory 681
  and Great Britain 589–90
    accepts Henlein's view of Sudeten problem 561
    Anglo-French discussions 341–3, 365, 564–5, 611–13
    Anglo-French ultimatum to 612–13
    guarantee of new frontiers 611, 612
    policy of 563–5, 590–1, 626
    presses for concessions to Sudeten leaders 581
    rejection of Hitler's Godesberg terms 622–3
    rejects Anglo-French demands 614
    Runciman mission 580–1, 594, 595, 610
    supports self-determination for Sudeten Germans 610–11
    timetable for hand-over of territories 630–2
    see also Chamberlain, Neville; Great Britain
  and Hungary 372–3, 589
    demands cession of territory 688–9
    German-Italian arbitration of territorial demands (Vienna award, 1938) 689–90
    policy of 588–9
    territorial claims by 614–15
    territory seized by 690, 728
  and Italy 369, 568, 585–7, 638
  and Jewish refugees 980
  and mobilization 571–2, 593, 619
  and Poland:
    antagonism between 65, 66, 95
    backs Hungarian claims to Ruthenia 689
    policy of 587–8
    reaction to German-Polish declaration (1934) 66

Czechoslovakia (*cont.*)
seeks understanding with (1934) 64–5
territorial claims by 614, 615
territory ceded to 688
and rearmament 64
and refugees from 687
and Romania 401, 689
and Soviet Union:
arms supplies from 581
asks about assistance from 633
backs Hungarian claims to Ruthenia 689
Beneš seeks to ascertain attitude of 613–14
Czech-Soviet mutual assistance pact (1935) 94–5, 581
inability to directly assist 581–2
military assistance proposals 417–18
offers Anglo-French-Soviet consultations 583
response to German invasion 875–6
takes preparatory military measures to assist (1938) 619–22
'wait and see' policy of 582–3
and strategic weakness 596
and Sudeten Germans 266–7, 406, 560
Anglo-French demands 612–13, 614
Anglo-French ultimatum 612–13
concessions to 584–5
grants all demands to ('Fourth Plan') 585
Henlein's demands 560–1
Hitler's terms rejected 622–3
staging of incidents 585, 593
transfer of territory 681
and tariff preference proposals 403
and United States 633, 634, 635–6
and Yugoslavia 369
see also Little Entente

Dahlerus, Birger 820, 860, 1000, 1003–4, 1005, 1007, 1008
Daily Herald, on Hitler 21–2
Daladier, Édouard:
and anti-Communism 768
and appeasement 603, 644
and assumption of no imminent crisis 346–7
and Austria 557
and becomes prime minister (1938) 559
appoints Reynaud finance minister 716
French economic revival 716
goals of 567
and Czechoslovakia:
Anglo-French discussions (15 Sept 1938) 611–12
behaviour during September crisis 611–12
criticises British policy 565
May crisis 572
motives for defence of 566–7
potential assistance to 558
reaffirms agreement with 595
sensitivity to obligations to 596
and failure to modernize army 47
and Gamelin, relations with 281
and Germany 47, 624, 823
fear of air power of 599
pleads for peaceful resolution over Poland 1000–1001
resigned to war with 997
and ideological assumptions 1048
and indecisiveness of 25
and Italy 564
abandons talks with 720
adopts tougher line towards 719, 745, 846, 851
Anglo-French differences over 794
reaction to invasion of Albania by 745–6
and Jewish refugees 981, 988
and Munich conference 641, 643–4

defence of agreement 686
despair over 651, 657
humiliated by 685
motives for accepting British leadership 712
and Poland:
Danzig 841
pleads for peaceful resolution 1000–1001
prepared to go to war over 997–8
reaction to German invasion 1010, 1013–14
and policy of firmness 776
and popularity of 768
and rearmament 274–5, 349, 716–17
and refugees 981
and reputation on eve of war 770
and Soviet Union:
believes alliance to be essential 777, 818
doubts value of air assistance 419
military talks with 418, 419, 420
opposition to military talks 417
and Spanish Civil War 205, 243, 558
and uncertainty over foreign policy direction 718
Mediterranean and Eastern European strategy 718–19
and United States, purchase of aircraft from 816–17
and war economy 313
Dalton, Hugh 745
Danzig 840
and France 841–2
and German-Polish dispute 690–2, 732–3, 787, 839–44
and Great Britain 842
calls for Polish restraint 842–3
Hudson-Wohlthat talks 858–9
talks with Germany 856–60
and Hitler orders occupation of 691
and incorporation into Reich 1009
and Nazi activity in 30–1, 265–6, 365, 733, 839
see also Poland
Darányi, Kálmán 372
Darlan, Admiral Jean-François 204–5, 347
and strategic importance of Mediterranean 239
and warns of subservience to British policy 350
and assurances of naval readiness 997
and German colonialism 325
and Italy:
opposes concessions to 719
presses for aggressive policy against 720, 742, 776
and protests about level of naval spending 350
Darré, Walter 255, 392
Daudet, Leon 107
Davies, R W 466
Davignon, Jacques 323
Davies, Norman 38, 507, 521, 525
Dawson, Geoffrey 592
Déat, Marcel 769
De Bono, General Emilio de 32, 100, 116, 121
Decoux, Admiral Jean 204–5
Defence Requirements Committee (DRC)
and membership of 50
and naval strength 91
and need for French military support 293
and planned defence expenditure 51, 52
Chamberlain's intervention 51–2, 426, 507–8
and rearmament programme 293–5
and threat assessment by 50–1, 426
de Gaulle, General Charles 277

Dekanozov, Vladimir 885
De La Warr, Earl 618
Delbos, Yvon:
  and appeasement 318–19
    retreat from central Europe 343, 405
  and becomes foreign minister (1936) 272–3
  and Belgium 279
  and Czechoslovakia 342, 406, 421
  and Great Britain 292, 341
  and Little Entente, alliance proposals 396
  and Poland 405
  and Romania 405
  and Sino-Japanese conflict 526, 527
  and Soviet Union:
    coolness over relations with 291
    military talks with 418, 419, 420
  and Spanish Civil War 205, 237, 238
  and tour of Eastern Europe 341
  and Yugoslavia, refusal to abandon 404
democratization, and post-First World War decade 1039
Denain, Victor 52–3
Denmark:
  and Germany:
    non-aggression pact 934, 935
    occupied by 1060
    trade with 386, 388, 389
  and Great Britain, trade with 388
  and League of Nations 359
    criticism of 923
  and neutrality 393, 923, 935
deterrence:
  and failure of 1047, 1051, 1052, 1056
  and France:
    Eastern Pact 51
    need for Soviet participation 777, 886
  and Great Britain:
    active policy by 1032
    air defence 51, 87, 294, 295, 296, 699
    economic concessions 776–7
    Greek guarantee 744, 746, 960
    Henderson's opposition to 591
    Polish guarantee 738–9, 740
    Romanian guarantee 747
    search for Soviet participation 749–50, 774, 879, 895
    Turkey 749, 964
  and Soviet Union:
    anti-Fascist coalition 443
    mutual assistance pacts 439
    need for participation 749–50, 774, 777, 879, 886, 895, 1032–3
Deutschland incident (1937) 233
Deuxième Bureau (French military intelligence agency):
  and assessment of Nazi threat 24–5, 80, 276, 277–8, 286–7
  and Czechoslovakia 572, 596
  and estimate of German air strength 598
  and German activity in Yugoslavia 400
  and German rearmament 39, 312–13, 416
  and Italy 720
  and Poland 93, 721
  and prediction of outbreak of war 313
  and unlikelihood of German-Soviet agreement 894
de Valera, Eamon 927
Devèze, Albert, and military reform 140, 141
Die Judenfrage 989
Dietrich, Otto 858
Dimitrov, Georgi 209, 464, 529, 913
Dingli, Adrian 636
Dirksen, Herbert von 262, 484, 680, 753, 979

and believes Britain will go to war over Poland 859, 908
and end of career 859–60
and recalled by Hitler 335
and Sino-Japanese conflict 519
disarmament:
and failure of 9, 45
and France:
Anglo-French tensions 54
cuts in defence spending 25, 70
opposition to 52–3
proposals of (1934) 47–8
response to British proposals 52, 53–4
and Germany, Hitler's proposals 45, 50
and Great Britain:
public opinion 514
response to Hitler's proposals 45–6
and League of Nations, attempts to renew efforts by 172–3
and public opinion 167, 1040
and United States 37–8
see also pacifist organizations; World Disarmament Conference (1932-34)
Djibouti 76, 104, 105, 694, 719, 720, 853
Dollfuss, Engelbert 39, 69, 75
Dominican Republic 977, 978
Dominions:
and appeasement, support for 802
and British economic policy 778–80
and Chanak crisis 800–2
and Czech crisis 631, 733
and declaration of war against Germany 1018
and low military expenditure 802
and Rhineland reoccupation 159
and uncertainty over support for Britain in war 800–2
see also British Empire
Doumenc, General Joseph 902, 906, 909
Doumergue, Gaston 48, 52
Draganov, Parvan 892
Drax, Admiral Sir Reginald 791, 902, 906, 909
Dreifort, John 807
Drummond, James Eric (16th Earl of Perth) 106, 111, 122, 636, 637, 638
Drummond-Wolff, Henry 857
Dumitrescu, Adrian 734n5
Dunkirk, and evacuation from 1060
Dutch East Indies 483, 809, 929–30
Dutch National Socialist Movement (NSB) 930

Easter Accords (Anglo-Italian agreement, 1938) 562–3, 693–4
Eastern Locarno Pact:
and Franco-Soviet negotiations (1935) 80–1
and French policy 71–2, 74
and German opposition to 73
and Great Britain 427, 429, 436
and Polish opposition to 72–3
economic and financial policies, *see* entries under individual countries
Eden, Anthony 48, 328, 888, 1012, 1059
and appeasement 149
and Austria 362
and becomes foreign secretary 126
and becomes minister for League of Nations affairs 105
and Chamberlain, disagreements with 526, 535, 562
and China 501–2
and colonial appeasement, opposition to 306, 307, 309, 324
and Czechoslovakia 633
and economic appeasement 303–4, 308–9
and Ethiopian crisis 108, 113, 125
Hoare-Laval plan 123
oil sanctions 128, 129–30
'Zeila' plan 105

Eden, Anthony (*cont.*)
and France:
Franco-Little Entente alliance talks 398
meets with Chautemps and Delbos (1937) 341
warns of effects of Franco-Soviet military talks 421
and Germany:
Berlin talks with Hitler (1935) 86–7
desire to reach agreement with 146, 159, 161, 433
opposition to agreement with 340
and Italy:
clashes with Chamberlain over 236
opinion of Mussolini 105
as 'possible enemy' 235
and Japan 501–2
and Mediterranean Declaration (1937) 222, 223
and Poland, on Beck 366
and resignation of 526, 535, 562
and Rhineland reoccupation 142, 146, 147, 149–50
and Sino-Japanese conflict:
clarifies position on 525
League of Nations 520–1
mediation attempts over Shanghai 517
raises economic boycott with America 521
and Soviet Union 427
distrust of 432
meets with Stalin (1935) 429–30
vetoes loan proposal 432
and Spanish Civil War 433
armistice proposal 232
desire to extend non-intervention 223–4
Nyon Conference (1937) 238
on Soviet intervention 212
and Vansittart 328–9
and World Disarmament Conference 31–2, 38, 41
'MacDonald plan' (1933) 32
Edward VIII, King 152–3, 169, 302n46
Egypt:
and Anglo-Egyptian treaty (1936) 133
and British reinforcement of 793, 805
and impact of Ethiopian crisis 133
and Indian Army 800
and Italy 853
abandons idea of attack 696
threat from 793
Eichmann, Adolf 555, 677, 975
elections:
and Austria (1935) 267
and France (1936) 139, 145, 169, 415–16
and Germany:
plebiscite (1933) 43
plebiscite (1936) 150
plebiscite (1938) 555
Reichstag elections (1932) 19
Reichstag elections (1933) 21
and Great Britain:
East Fulham by-election 45
general election (1935) 120
Peace Ballot (1935) 106
post-Munich by-elections 684, 766–7
and Romania (1937) 405
and Saar plebiscite (1935) 83
and Spain (1936) 186, 201
Emerson, Sir Hubert 979
Engleman, Bernt 1022
Enigma code machine 790
Epp, Ritter von 260
Eritrea 100
Estonia 359
and Baltic states' mutual defence bloc 925
and Finland 938
and Germany:
naval and intelligence contacts 393
non-aggression treaty 893, 934, 939

trade with 270, **388–9**, **731**
and Great Britain 387, **388–9**
and neutrality 938, 939
and Soviet Union 939
mutual security pact 938
Nazi-Soviet Pact provisions 910
non-aggression treaty 939
Ethiopian crisis:
and France 107, 136
Anglo-French relations 109, 113, 118, 120, 122, 160
attempts to reach agreement with Italy 103, 120
dilemma faced by 109
divisions over 107–8, 119
Franco-Italian agreement over Ethiopia (1935) 78–9, 102
Hoare-Laval plan 122–5
opposes oil sanctions 110, 129, 130
pledges military support of Britain 116–17
reluctance to become involved 105, 107
threat to Franco-Italian relations 121
and Great Britain 135–6
Anglo-French relations 109, 113, 118, 120, 122, 160
concessionary approach urged by 101, 103
Hoare-Laval plan 122–5
League of Nations 111
Maffey report into impact of Italian invasion 104–5
naval demonstration 111–12
naval strength during crisis **114**
public opinion 106
refusal to sanction Italian attack on 89
reluctance to become involved 105
reluctance to risk war over 115
sanctions 108, 110, 128, 129–30, 131
'Zeila' plan 105
and impact of:
Egypt 133
European balance of power 135–6
German perceptions of British resolve 135–6
League of Nations 134–5
smaller countries 131–2
Soviet Union 134
Turkish control of Straits 132–3
and Italy:
annexation of Ethiopia 130
determined on military solution 100, 101–2
Franco-Italian agreement over Ethiopia 78–9, 102
Hoare-Laval plan 124
impact of sanctions 126
increasing British hostility 108
invades Ethiopia 112, 116
military planning 100
military success 128, 130
Mussolini attempts to divide Britain and France 120
naval strength **114**
objectives of 101, 120
prepared to risk conflict with Britain 108
rejects compromise solution 112
response to threat of oil sanctions 121
sanctions lifted 131
seeks clarification of French position 107
Wal Wal incident 101
and League of Nations 100, 115
appeals for intervention by 101, 102
damaged by 134–5
delayed action over 105
Hoare's speech on collective security 111
impact of crisis on smaller countries 131–2
Mussolini rejects compromise solution 112

Ethiopian crisis: (*cont.*)
rebuked by Haile Selassie 131
response to Italian invasion 112
sanctions 108, 109, 112, 120–1, 126, 129–30, 131
sanctions lifted 131
and United States 110
Evian conference (1938) 977
exchange rate system 1040
Eyre-Monsell, Sir Robert 87

Fabry, Jean 80
Falkenhausen, Alexander von 485, 519
Far East 475
and diplomatic representatives 476–7
and experts on 476, 477
and France 482–3
and Germany 484
and Great Britain:
Anglo-American naval cooperation 340, 532–3, 808
defence policy 808–9
difficult relationship with America 479–80, 481–2, 503
'fleet to Singapore' strategy 742, 791
naval weakness 514–15
policy options 499, 544
preference for Soviet-Japanese hostility 482
seeks to work with America 742
Singapore 479, 808
uncertainty over policy 498
vulnerability in 478–9
and inter-connection of regional and global crises 541, 544–5
and Italy 484, 486
and Netherlands 483
and relationship between colonial elites and native populations 487
and Soviet Union 477, 541–2
Changkufeng 538
concerns of 903–4
fear of war 891
German-Soviet negotiations 904
Nomonhan (Khalkhin-Gol) 904
reorganization of Red Army 904
and United States:
Anglo-American naval cooperation 340, 532–3, 808
investments of 481
neutralization proposal 504
open door policy 480–1
relations with Great Britain 479–80, 481–2, 503
suggests Anglo-American cooperation 503–4
and western assumptions about 486–8
see also China; Japan; Pearl Harbor; Sino-Japanese conflict; Tientsin crisis
Far Eastern Combined Bureau 504
Faulhaber, Cardinal Michael von 985
Federation of British Industries (FBI) 390, 704, 706
and Düsseldorf agreement (FBI-RI) 707
and mission to Manchukuo 509
Felmy, General Helmuth 608
Ferris, John 1049
Ferrostaal (German company) 377, 381
Fierlinger, Zdeněk 619, 622
Fifth Column, and Spanish Civil War 218, 247
film:
and France, propaganda 768
and Great Britain, imperial sentiment 795
Finland 359
and Anglo-French-Soviet talks 936–7
and Estonia 938
and Germany:
rejects non-aggression pact with 934

trade agreement 386
trade with 388
and Great Britain 391
military contacts 392
trade with 388
and League of Nations 131
and neutrality 393
and reorientation of foreign policy 937
and Soviet Union 938–9
Anglo-Soviet alliance negotiations 895
Nazi-Soviet Pact provisions 910
pressure from 938
warned by 888
winter war between 1059–60
and Sweden 936, 937–8
First World War (Great War):
and attitude towards neutrality 966–7
as catalyst for change 1036
and economic effects of 1040
and Great Britain, British Empire contribution to 799–800
and impact on French policy 602, 1047
and impact on inter-war years 1–2, 1020–21, 1034, 1036–7
and post-war reconstruction 1037–8, 1043
Fischer, Louis 229
Fisher, Sir Warren 50, 530–1
Flandin, Pierre-Ètienne 627, 769
and Anglo-French talks (1935) 82–3
and becomes foreign minister (1936) 128
and Ethiopian crisis 129, 130
and Rhineland reoccupation 140, 145, 146, 147–8, 149
and Stresa talks (1935) 89
Flanner, Janet 1026
Flemish Nationalist Union (VNV) 928
Foch, Marshal Ferdinand 1037
Foley, Henry 987
Foreign Enlistment Act (UK) 217
Forster, Albert 265, 266, 365, 366, 842, 844
Four-Power Pact (1933)
and British reaction to 33
and French reaction to 33–4
and German reaction to 34
and provisions of 33
and suggested by Mussolini 28, 32
motives 32–3
France:
and Albania, reaction to Italian invasion 745–6
and anti-Communism 415–16, 424
and anti-war feeling 26, 170, 184, 602, 1014
changes in 768–9
and appeasement 308, 318–19, 323, 326, 330, 567
colonial appeasement 307, 324–5
economic appeasement 307, 323, 714, 1046
policy of expediency 603, 644
political and economic pressures for 347–8
and Austria:
acquiescence over *Anschluss* 360–2
Anglo-French-Italian declaration on (1934) 76
response to German invasion 557
and Belgium:
Anglo-French declaration on (1937) 322
informal military talks between 281, 322, 785, 928
military agreement between (1920) 70–1, 140, 141, 927
military talks between (1936) 151–2
reaction to policy of independence 279–80
unsettled relations between 70–1

France: (*cont.*)
and Central and Eastern Europe:
Anglo-French discussions 341–3
considers retreat from 343, 350, 405
loss of prestige in 408
opposition to retreat from 718–19
restructuring obligations to 713
and Chiefs of Staff 137, 138, 652, 719
and China 482
and constraints on foreign policy 347
and cultural diplomacy 395
and Czechoslovakia:
abandonment of 597, 604
Anglo-French demands rejected by 614
Anglo-French demand to transfer territory 612–13
Anglo-French discussions 341–3, 365, 565–6, 611–12
Anglo-French ultimatum to 612–13
approves attempts to conciliate Germany 421
Barthou's visit to (1934) 71
Beneš visits Paris (1933) 64
Delbos visits (1937) 406
factors influencing policy during crisis 594–604
potential assistance to 558
promises to meet obligations to 557–8
reaffirms agreement with 595
rejects Hitler's terms 624
rumours of German invasion 571–2
unable to give military assistance to 596–7
and deterrence:
Eastern Pact 51
need for Soviet participation 777, 886
and disarmament:
Anglo-French tensions 54
cuts in defence spending 25, 70
opposition to 52–3
proposals for (1934) 47–8
proposed Daladier-Hitler meeting 40–1
response to British proposals 52, 53–4
and Eastern Locarno Pact 71–2, 74–5
Franco-Soviet negotiations (1935) 80–1
Polish opposition to 72–3
and economic and financial policies 276
Anglo-French economic coordination 777–8
budget deficits 46
capital flight 349
cuts in expenditure 348, 783
Czech crisis 626–7
dependence upon imports 780
devaluation 348, 594
economic depression 83
economic recovery 657, 775
economic warfare 777–8
fall in production 349
financial crisis (1935) 128
financial crisis (1937) 307, 325–6
financial reconstruction of central Europe 403
gold reserves 782, 783
impact of empire 805
impact of Rhineland reoccupation 145
lack of coordination of war production 600–1, 718, 783
repatriation of capital 716, 782
Reynaud decrees 716
seeks access to American money market 783
tax increases 348

tripartite exchange rate agreement (1936) 174–5, 278
and elections (1936) 139, 145, 169, 415–16
and emergency powers 594
and Ethiopian crisis, *see* Ethiopian crisis
and factory occupations 271, 594–5
Matignon agreements 272
and Far East 482–3
and First World War, impact on French policy 2, 602, 1047
and Germany:
armistice between 1060
change in attitude towards 765
defeated by 1060–61
economic cooperation 714–15
exaggerated respect for totalitarian efficiency 312–13
Franco-German pact (1938) 714
Hitler's peace overtures (1933-34) 47
Laval's overtures to (1935) 117–18
necessity of *rapprochement* with 278
overestimation of military capacity 138
reaction to Hitler's appointment as Chancellor 22, 24–6
reaction to Polish invasion 1010, 1012–14, 1015
Schacht-Blum conversations (1936) 258
trade agreement 714–15
ultimatum to 1019
uncertainty over expansionary intentions 313, 1045
unlikelihood of German-Soviet agreement 893–5
willingness to seek accommodation with 347
and Great Britain:
acquiescence in leadership of 340–1
Anglo-French plan for war 784–6
centrality to foreign policy position 278, 292, 566, 652, 697
differences over Italy 564, 794–5
economic coordination 777–8
Franco-Little Entente alliance proposals 397–8
military guarantee from 603, 723
mutual suspicion 92, 98, 116, 136
opposition to Franco-Soviet military collaboration 416, 419, 420, 430
staff talks (1936) 149, 151, 160–1
staff talks (1938) 564, 603, 719
staff talks (1939) 725, 784–7, 791–2
talks on Czechoslovakia 341–3, 564–5, 611–12
warn of German attack in West 722
and Hitler's attitude towards 18–19
and impact of Nazi-Soviet Pact 996, 997, 1034, 1056
and Indochina, Japanese threat to 482–3, 526–7, 807
and industrial unrest 271, 348–9, 594–5
and intelligence services:
adopt worse-case scenario 138, 312
application and use of intelligence 1049
assessment of Nazi threat 24–5, 80, 276, 277–8, 286–7
disparity of forces 771

France: (*cont.*)
divisions among Hitler's advisers 311–12, 595
estimate of German air strength 598, 775
expects German attack in East 721
fear of simultaneous German-Italian actions 746
German activity in Yugoslavia 400
German and Italian political strains 774–5
German rearmament 39, 416
German-Soviet *rapprochement* 894
German weaknesses 599, 775, 776
Italy 720, 792–3
Nazi-Soviet alignment 28
oppose retreat from Eastern Europe 718–19
overestimation of German military capacity 138, 312
predict German attack on Poland 741
prediction of outbreak of war 313
reports of Italo-German *rapprochement* 127
warns of German attack on Czechoslovakia 572, 596
and Italy:
anti-French campaign by 569–70, 694
critical importance of 130
disarmament proposals 41
failure to open dialogue with 720
failure to reach agreement with 567–8
Four-Power Pact (1933) 33–4
Franco-Italian agreement (1935) 78–80, 102
increasing distance between 282–3
Mediterranean Locarno project 75
military agreement between (1935) 80
military talks between 108–9
reaction to Anglo-Italian Easter Accords 563
reaction to invasion of Albania by 745–6
recognition of sovereignty over Ethiopia 693
refusal to accept French ambassador 283
talks between 31, 76, 77, 78
tougher line towards 719, 745, 846, 851
unhappiness with Italy's Austrian policy 69
and Japan 482–3
and Jewish refugees 976, 981
and Little Entente:
desires pact with 290, 291
failure of alliance talks with 395–8
lack of enthusiasm for alliance with 288
and Luxembourg 933
and military planning:
air and demographic weakness 566, 599
Anglo-French defence of Belgium 785
Anglo-French plan for war 784–6, 1058–9
Anglo-French staff planning (1939) 723
Anglo-French staff talks (1936) 151
Anglo-French staff talks (1938) 719
Anglo-French staff talks (1939) 784–7, 791–2
confidence in defensive capabilities 786, 997
debate over Mediterranean or Eastern European strategy 718–19

defeat in 1940 1061
defence of northern frontier 281–2
defensive caste of 276–7, 599, 776, 777
economic warfare 777–8
expectations of long war 599, 747, 773, 777
focus of 239–40
impact of Belgian independence 322
imperial obligations 805–7
Italian offensive dismissed 791, 792–3
lack of offensive capability 599, 652
mobilization Plan D (1935) 139
no defence of Poland 786–7
prepare for fixed battles 776
Salonika campaign proposal 791–2
Soviet Union 787
and mobilization 624, 1010, 1026
and Munich conference 643–4
approval of agreement 686
motives for accepting British leadership 712
public opinion 602, 686
reveals French impotence 685
and pacifism 602
and pacifist organizations 168, 169, 170, 171
and Paris:
flight from during Czech crisis 626
evacuation of 1026
and Poland:
accord between (1939) 787
air agreement talks 394
attempts to re-define alliance with 713
Danzig 841
divisions over guarantee to 777
failure to monitor war planning by 393–4
guarantee to 741
military mission to 788
military strength overstated by 789
no military effort to defend 786–7
prepared to go to war over 997–8
Rambouillet loan and arms agreement 283–6, 393, 394
reaction to German invasion 1010, 1012–14, 1015
reaction to German-Polish declaration (1934) 65–6
refuses to give security guarantee to 63
slowness in supplying equipment 394
suspicion between 71
and political divisions 169–70, 347–8, 601–2, 627, 770, 1034, 1056–7
impact of Spanish Civil War 205–6
and political paralysis (1932-34) 46–7
and Popular Front government 154–5
attacks on 272
economic policy 276
origins of 49
see also Blum, Léon
and propaganda, film 768
and public opinion 602
change in 765, 768–9
defeatism 1026–7
disaffection with government 46, 48, 128
expectation of victory 1027
hostility towards Germany 765
mood on eve of war 769–70
mood on outbreak of war 1025–7, 1057
opinion polls 769
post-Munich 657
and *Quai d'Orsay* (foreign ministry):
Austria 76, 557

France: (*cont.*)
Belgium 147, 280
Blum-Schacht talks 258–9, 278
Czechoslovakia 365, 395, 558, 571, 595, 613
disarmament proposals to Germany 47–8
Eastern Locarno Pact 71–3, 80
Ethiopian crisis 103, 119, 121
Far East 487, 526–7
Four-Power Pact (1933) 33–4
Halifax-Hitler talks 341
Italy 53, 76, 128, 282, 283, 343, 564, 719, 746
Little Entente 288, 290, 395, 398
Munich conference 713
pessimism in 350
Poland 64, 65, 80, 283, 284, 394, 996
Rhineland reoccupation 139, 143, 145, 158
seeks British security guarantee 146, 277
Soviet Union 74, 415, 416, 417, 420
Spanish Civil War 203, 204, 205, 206, 235, 240, 242
World Disarmament Conference (1932-34) 38, 41
Yugoslavia 369, 404
and rearmament 84, 221, 273
air force expansion 275, 775–6
aviation industry 597
constraints on 312, 313, 600–1, 718
crisis in aircraft production 346
Daladier 274–5, 313, 349, 594, 601, 716–17, 1046
economic and financial constraints 276, 313, 600, 601, 717, 782, 1045–6
freezing of expenditure 348, 349–50
increased industrial production 717–18
industrial organization shortcomings 275–6, 312, 402–3, 600
labour relations 275–6, 594–5, 716, 718
lack of coordination of war production 600–1, 718, 783
military expenditure 782
military expenditure (1932-37) **273**
military expenditure (1935-40) **779**
military expenditure (1936-39) **779**
nationalization of war industries 275
Popular Front government 312, 346, 1046
purchase of foreign aircraft 716–17, 782–3
re-establishment of two-year service 84, 275
relations with industrial suppliers 138, 275–6
Reynaud 277, 716, 717, 782
start of 138
and Rhineland reoccupation:
appeal to League of Nations 144–5
British 'Text of Proposals' 148–9
diplomatic planning for 139–40
lack of military planning for 138–9
response to 144–5, 146, 158
seeks British agreement on sanctions 147–8
unwillingness to respond militarily 145–6, 158
and Romania:
air assistance pact talks 401
attempts to improve military cooperation with 400–1
failure to reach trade agreement 287
guarantee to 746
inability to supply arms to 401–3

oil supplies 402, 747
sabotage of oil fields 747
trade agreement 715, 747
traditional links between 369–70
visit by Delbos (1937) 405
and Sino-Japanese conflict 526–7, 539
and social divisions 601–2, 627, 652
and Soviet Union:
air mission to 419
alliance negotiations 889, 893, 895–900, 901–2
barriers to agreement between 1054–5
believes alliance to be essential 777, 818
British opposition to military collaboration 416, 419, 420
considers tripartite alliance offer by 881
deterioration of relations between 424–5
different aims in negotiations 888, 910–12
difficulties in way of talks with 752
divided opinion over relations with 72, 291
divided opinions over value of alliance 713
evaluation of Red Army 417, 422
fear of German-Soviet *rapprochement* 420–1
Franco-Soviet mutual assistance pact (1935) 93–4, 415, 421, 430
Franco-Soviet negotiations (1933) 36, 67
impact of purges on relations 415, 459
impact of Spanish Civil War on relations 414
Laval distrusted by 415
military assistance proposals 417–18
military talks between 416–21, 422, 901–2, 906–7, 908, 909
negotiations between (1935) 80–1
opposition to military talks 416–17, 419–20, 422
press for closer cooperation with 751–2
pressure for military staff talks 291
response to military proposals by 418
response to Polish guarantee 877
revised alliance proposals from 888
staff talks 326
suspect interference in domestic matters 423
trade agreement 424
and Spain, Bérard-Jordana agreement 944
and Spanish Civil War, *see* Spanish Civil War
and Stavisky affair 48
and Stresa talks (1935) 88–9
and strikes 348–9, 594–5, 652, 716
and Switzerland, military talks with 785, 941
and 'Tardieu plan' 34–5
and trade policy:
Germany 714–15
imperial trade 805, 806
proposal to divert German trade 403–4
Rambouillet loan and arms agreement 283–6, 393, 394
Romania 715
south-east Europe 714–16
Yugoslavia 287, 401, 715
and Turkey 749
Anglo-French financial support 964

France: (*cont.*)
Anglo-French-Turkish alliance (1939) 965
Anglo-French-Turkish military convention 963
Franco-Turkish declaration (1939) 963
and United States:
attempts to secure support of 1053
expectations of 777
offers French possessions to 783
purchase of aircraft from 717, 782–3, 813, 816–17
seeks access to money market 783
and Western Pact policy 278, 319, 321
and World Disarmament Conference 36–9, 40–4
and Yugoslavia:
arms supplies to 401, 952
assurances from 404
attempts to improve military cooperation with 400–1
inability to supply arms to 402–3
increasing distance between 289–90
loss of influence in 395
military consultations between 951
reaction to Italian-Yugoslav treaty (1937) 369
refusal to abandon 404–5
trade agreement 287, 715
Franchet d'Esperey, Marshal Louis 289
Franco, General Francisco 181
and Anti-Comintern Pact 696, 942
and becomes *Generalísimo* of rebel armies 189
and brutality of 185, 227
and campaigns:
Alcazar 189
Basque 225–6, 232–3
Guernica 225–6
Madrid 189–90, 219
Teruel 245–6
and cautious military approach 224, 226
and consolidation of power 189
and Germany:
appeals for assistance from 187
economic relations with 942
treaty of friendship 943
and Italy, appeals for assistance from 187
and military victory 246
and Mussolini 942–3
and neutrality (1939) 629, 943, 944
and takes control of foreign assistance 189
and use of anti-Communism 184
François-Poncet, André 21, 26, 64, 143, 595–6, 693, 719
and attitude towards German rearmament 53
and Czechoslovakia 595
and Hitler, relations with 47, 117
and reaction to Hitler's appointment as Chancellor 22
and sent as ambassador to Rome 693
and unable to restart talks with Ciano 851
Frank, Karl 593
French Air Force:
and exaggerated view of German air power 597–9
and expansion of 275, 775–6
crisis in 346
and imperial obligations 806
and Poland 788
and rearmament:
purchase of foreign aircraft 716–17, 782–3, 816–17
reduction in spending on 349
and weakness of 138, 597, 651–2
see also Chambre, Guy la; Cot, Pierre

French Army:
and British lack of concern over weakness of 344
and *Corvignolles* 274
and dismal state of 138, 651
and *Division Cuirassée de Reserve (DCR)* 282
and Franco-Italian agreement (1935), strategic implications 102–3
and imperial armies 806
and military planning 139, 239–40, 276–7, 281–2, 599, 600, 625, 786
and modernization of 138, 275
failure of 600
and political neutrality of 273–4
and re-establishment of two-year service 84, 138
and Rhineland reoccupation, unwillingness to respond militarily 145–6, 158
and shortage of recruits 82–3
and unpreparedness of 600
see also Gamelin, General Maurice
French Communist Party (PCF):
and attacks on government 94
and foreign policy 348
and joins general strike 49
and measures against 1034
and support of Popular Front government 415, 455, 1042
French Empire 797
and French trade 805
and imperial defence 806–7
and imperial obligations 795
as manpower reserve 805
and revival of imperial sentiment 798
and subservience to French interests 805
as symbol of national greatness 798
French Navy:
and expansion of 275, 508
and imperial defence 325, 806
and Mediterranean, strength in 792
and reduction in spending on 349–50
and war readiness 997
see also Darlan, Admiral Jean-François
Friedrikson, L Kh 458
Fritsch, General Werner 312
and mobile warfare 253
and questions Hitler's plans 333
and resignation of 334
and Rhineland reoccupation 142, 144
Fromm, General Friedrich 254
Funk, Walther 335, 674, 705, 706, 710

Gafencu, Grigore 729, 734n5, 735, 745, 746, 947
Galen, Clemens August Graf von, Bishop of Münster 985
Gamelin, General Maurice 102, 120
and Anglo-French relations, vital importance of 139
and Austria 557
and Belgium, informal military talks with 281, 322, 785, 928
and condemns Laval's approach to Hitler 118
and Czechoslovakia 558
impossibility of military assistance to 596
plans in event of war 625
predicts swift fall of 597
and Italy:
military talks between 108–9, 121
opposes concessions to 719
and mechanized forces 281, 344, 600
and military planning:
defensive caste of 276–7
mobilization Plan D (1935) 139
preparedness of 276, 595
and Poland:
prepared to go to war over 997

Gamelin, General Maurice (*cont.*)
    Rambouillet loan and arms agreement 283, 284, 285
    sacrifice of 786–7
  and promises to keep army out of politics 273
  and Rhineland reoccupation 138–9, 144, 145–6, 158
  and Romania 400, 401
  and Salonika campaign 791–2
  and Soviet Union:
    opposition to military talks 416–17, 419–20
    military talks with (1939) 902
  and Spanish Civil War 203, 558
  and Yugoslavia 400–1, 951
Garvin, J L 821
Gauché, Colonel Maurice 287, 894
Gemlich, Adolf 15
Gentin, Fernand 714
George II, King of Greece 377, 378, 959, 960
George V, King of England 121, 127
George VI, King of England 232, 818
Geraud, André ('Pertinax') 25, 125, 601–2
German Navy:
  and expansion of 90, 254, 508, 574, 673, 675–6
    Plan Z 674, 676, 835
    raw material shortages 331
  and submarines:
    claims parity in 773
    Soviet Union provides base for 917
  and weakness at outbreak of war 835
Germany:
  and *Anschluss* 554, 556
  and anti-Bolshevism 195
  and anti-Semitism 676–7
  and armed services:
    Hitler's authority over 334–5
    subordination to National Socialist state 335, 577
  and Austria:
    Austrian Nazis prepared for future role 156
    Austro-German agreement (1936) 156–7
    denies intention to annex 104
    discussions with Italy about 314, 315, 316
    Hitler's cautious approach to 264–5
    Hitler-Schuschnigg meeting 364
    invasion of 552, 553–4
    trade with 731
    ultimatum to Schuschnigg 552–3
    unlikelihood of foreign intervention over *Anschluss* 360–2
    visa tax imposed on 39
  and Baltic states:
    naval and intelligence contacts 393
    Nazi-Soviet Pact provisions 910, 939
    trade with 387, 388, 389, 731
  and Belgium:
    declaration of independence by 323
    invasion of 1060
    non-aggression pact proposal 319, 320
    proposals for ensuring independence of 320–1
  and Bulgaria 731, 956–7, 958–9
  and Catholic Church:
    détente in relations (1939) 986–7
    intimidation of 985
    Mit brennender Sorge (With Burning Anxiety) 985–6
  and China 484
    ends arms deliveries to 524, 540
    military assistance to Kuomintang 262, 485, 519
  and colonial demands 309, 324
    Schacht's campaign 306–7

as tactical weapon 260, 325
and Czechoslovakia:
agrees to conference over 638
Beck warns against invasion of 575–7
calms British anxieties over 579–80
diplomatic and economic doubts over plans for 578–9
diplomatic preparations for attack 585
economic gains from occupation 728–9
elimination of 727–8
Hitler-Chamberlain talks at Berchtesgaden 610
Hitler reassures army over 578
Hitler's Nuremberg speech 593
Hitler's reply to Roosevelt's peace appeal 635
Hitler's terms rejected by 622–3
invasion planning 334, 365, 560, 571, 572–3, 584, 616, 681
invasion rumours 571–2
non-aggression pact talks 267–8
post-Munich bullying of 687
press campaign against 364
reassured over Austrian invasion 554
reply to Chamberlain's proposals 630
seeks Italian support over 568
trade with 731
transfer of territory 681
uncertainty over British intentions 583–4, 630
warns Italians of attack on 585–6
and Denmark:
non-aggression pact 934, 935
occupation of 1060
trade agreement 386
trade with 388, 389
and disarmament, Hitler's proposals 45, 50
and Eastern Locarno Pact, opposition to 73
and economic and financial policies:
autarchy 373
balance of payments problems 255, 373, 556, 675, 775, 1031, 1044
balance of trade 96–7, 384, 675, 775
Eastern Europe 269–70, 375–6, 379, 383–4, 385, 709, 710, 729–30, 1045, 1046
effects of *Anschluss* 556
export campaign 675
fears of inflation 656, 674, 1045
food supplies 376–7, 379
foreign currency shortages 253, 255, 268–9, 331, 675, 977
foreign exchange problems 96, 254–5, 305, 330, 376, 384, 575
Four-Year Plan (1936) 257–8, 574
gold reserves 837, 1044
Hitler's 'export, or die' speech 673, 675, 706
Hitler's role in 335
impact of rearmament 837
inability to sustain war of attrition 1046
international trade 97
Lebensraum 384–5
moratorium on debt repayments 96, 373
New Finance Plan 675
New War Economy Production Plan 574
political motivations 385–6
Rapid Plan (*Schnellplan*) 574–5
rearmament 673, 674–5
Schacht's 'New Plan' 96–7, 269
securing raw materials 196–8, 269–70, 379
steel rationing 330
subservience to rearmament 254–7

Germany: (*cont.*)
and economic crisis (1934) 96–7
and economic recovery 12, 97
and elections:
plebiscite (1933) 43
plebiscite (1936) 150
plebiscite (1938) 555
Reichstag elections (1932) 19
Reichstag elections (1933) 21
Saar plebiscite (1935) 83–4
and Enabling Law ratified (1933) 21
and Estonia:
naval and intelligence contacts 393
non-aggression treaty 893, 934, 939
trade with 270, **388–9**, **731**
and Ethiopian crisis, lessons learned from 135–6
and Far East 484
and Finland 386, **388**, 934
and First World War, impact on inter-war period 2
and France:
armistice between 1060
confident of no intervention over Poland 855–6
defeat of 1060–61
Franco-German pact (1938) 714
invasion of 1060
overestimation of German military capacity by 138, 312
peace overtures to (1933-34) 47
reaction to Polish invasion 1010, 1012–14, 1015
Schacht-Blum conversations (1936) 258
trade agreement 714–15
ultimatum from 1019
and German minorities abroad 264
Danzig 265–6, 366
Memel Germans 265
Sudeten Germans 266–7, 364
Upper Silesia 365–6
and Great Britain:
Anglo-German Naval Agreement (1935) 91–3, 391, 513
Anglo-German naval arms limitation treaty (1937) 873
Anglo-German Payments Agreement (1934) 96–7, 373, 701–2, 704–5
Berlin talks between (1935) 86–7
cartel arrangements 390–1, 706–8
coal cartel agreement 706
conciliatory approach of 141–2, 153–4, 155
conditions for cooperation 327
confident of no intervention over Poland 855–6, 858
declaration of war 1018
economic cooperation sought by 700–1, 702–8
Halifax-Wiedemann talks 579–80
Hitler-Chamberlain meeting at Berchtesgaden 610
Hitler-Chamberlain talks at Godesberg 616–17
Hitler denounces naval agreement 833
Hitler-Halifax meeting (1937) 336–9
Hitler offers bilateral talks (1935) 84
Hitler's campaign for friendship with 152–3, 259–60, 317
Hitler's 'last offer' of understanding with 998–9
Hudson-Wohlthat talks 858–9
informal attempts to reach agreement on Poland 856–60
last-minute attempts at agreement with 1003–9
naval talks (1935) 90–1
negotiations with 153–4
offers naval talks 87

private diplomacy 857–8
propaganda campaign against 861
reaction to *Kristallnacht* 679–80
reaction to Polish invasion 1009, 1011–12, 1013, 1014–17
rejects Henderson's proposals 556–7
Ribbentrop's assessment of policy of 317–18
seeks to separate from France 87
trade talks 702–4
trade with 302, 701–2, **703**
ultimatum from 1016–17
warnings from 'opposition' Germans 589–90

and Greece:
arms supplies to 960
establish presence in 959
intervention in 1062
maintenance of relations by 960–1
neutrality assurance from 961
trade with 377, 378, 709, 710, **731**, 960

and Hitler's appointment as Chancellor 10, 19–20
British reactions to 21–4
domestic reactions to 20, 29–30
élite reaction 30
French reactions to 21, 22, 24–6
Italian reactions to 26–7
Soviet Union's reaction to 27–9

and Hungary:
agrees to joint action against Czechoslovakia 372–3, 589
army contacts with 372
demand show of loyalty from 955
discussions over Czechoslovakia 588–9
economic relations with 955
non-belligerency in Polish campaign 954, 955–6
tensions between 371
trade agreement 269, 386
trade with 379–80, **731**

and intelligence services:
pandering to Hitler's views 1049
warnings to Britain 820–1

and Italy 155
absence of formal alliance 317
absolves from Pact of Steel responsibilities 1010–11
alliance negotiations 847–8
alliance proposals (1938) 692–3
Ciano-Ribbentrop meeting (1939) 852
commitment to military alliance by 695
conflicting interests 261–2
cooperation between 561
Danzig conference proposed by 851
does not consult about Poland 849, 851
German-Italian protocol (1936) 261
growing closeness between 314–16
impact of Spanish Civil War 185
lack of enthusiasm for alliance with 569
military alliance pressed by 697
military convention with 569
military pact conversations 568–9
military talks between 846–7
naval talks 696
non-belligerency chosen by (1939) 1011, 1059
opts for partnership with 262
'Pact of Steel' (1939) 794, 846, 847, 848–50
promises to recognise rights of 845
rapprochement between 129, 261
reaction to Polish invasion 1009, 1013

Germany: (*cont.*)
recognition of Ethiopian annexation 261
reneges on intervention 999
Rome-Berlin Axis proclaimed (1936) 157, 194
rumours of Nazi-Soviet pact 849
staff talks 697
talks over non-aggression pact 128–9
tensions over Austria 75–6
told of intentions in Poland 852
undelivered statement of neutrality from 855
warned of attack on Czechoslovakia 585–6
and Japan 484, 539–40
Anti-Comintern Pact 262, 263, 476, 484–5, 540
Hitler sanctions new talks with 262–3
racial views 487–8
recognition of Manchukuo 540
refuses to join tripartite pact 846, 863
talks between (1935) 262
and *Kristallnacht* 16–17, 671, 677, 679
American reaction 679
British reaction 679–80
domestic disapproval 679
stifling of post-Munich euphoria 679
and Latvia:
naval and intelligence contacts 393
non-aggression treaty 893, 934, 939
trade with 270, **388–9**, **731**
and League of Nations, departure from 42–3
and Lithuania:
Memel handed over by 728
Nazi-Soviet Pact provisions 910
non-aggression treaty 939
trade with **388–9**, **731**
and Luxembourg 933
and military planning:
Beck warns against invasion of Czechoslovakia 575–7
dealing with French offensive 1030–31
inability to mount strategic bombing campaign 653
invasion of Austria 553
invasion of Czechoslovakia 334, 365, 560, 571, 572–3, 584, 616, 681
invasion of Poland 733, 833, 839, 863, 905
Memel occupation 682
naval war with Britain 574
strength of forces **1020**
unpreparedness for war in 1939 652–3
War Directive No 1 1005, 1006, 1019
West Wall 573, 574, 576, 577, 578, 652, 673
and Munich conference 639–41
and Netherlands 386, 931, 1060
and 'Night of the Long Knives' 73–4
and Nordic states 386, 387, **388**, 389
and Norway **388**, 934, 1060
and 'opposition' in 589–90, 629, 638, 653
intelligence from 721
warnings to Britain 820–2
and papacy, Concordat between (1933) 985
and peace offer following Rhineland reoccupation 144
and Poland 587–8
assurances to (1933) 35
assurances to (1938) 366
breaks off diplomatic relations 839
British reaction to invasion 1009

confident of no Anglo-French intervention 855–6, 858, 860, 1030
Danzig 265, 266, 365, 366, 690–2, 732–3, 787, 839, **840**, 841–4
French reaction to invasion 1010
German-Polish non-aggression treaty (1934) 62–4, 65
Hitler cancels attack on 999
Hitler denounces Non-Aggression Pact 833
Hitler orders attack on 999, 1004, 1005
Hitler orders occupation of Danzig 691
invasion of 1009, 1012, 1020, 1058
invasion planning 733, 833, 839, 863, 905
losses in invasion of **1029**
Nazi-Soviet Pact provisions 910
negotiations between 690–1
propaganda campaign against 843, 861
provocation of 839
rapprochement with 62
rejects Italian mediation over 1010
relaxation of tension over Danzig 842
revision of Nazi-Soviet Pact terms 915
simulated attack 995, 1009
trade with 379, **731**
Upper Silesia 365–6
Westerplatte affair (Danzig) 30–1

and Portugal 199, 944–5
and propaganda campaigns:
against Britain 861
against Poland 861
and public mood:
on eve of war 861–2
on outbreak of war 1021–3
and public opinion:
acceptance of treatment of Jews 980–1, 1045
awareness of Nazi aims 1044
Hitler's popularity 12, 85, 96, 150, 314, 861, 1032, 1044
pride in German advances 1044–5
and rearmament 12, 30, 52, 96, 252–3
1938 programme 673
acceleration of 574
aircraft industry crisis 598
aircraft production **835**
aircraft production difficulties 598–9, 674, 834
ammunition production **835**, **836**
army equipment shortages 834
army expansion 44, 84–5, 195, 252–3, 330, 574, 673, 736, **835**, 837–8
balance of payments problems 255, 556, 675, 775, 1031, 1044
economic effects of 579, 653, 837
facilities acquired in Czechoslovakia 728–9
fears of inflationary effects 656, 674, 1045
financial difficulties 674–5
Four-Year Plan (1936) 195, 257–8, 330
impossibility of programme (1938) 673–4
introduction of conscription 84–5, 736
Luftwaffe expansion 86, 254, 330–1, 574, 598–9, 673, 674, 834, **835**, 1069–70
military expenditure (1933-38) **331**
military expenditure (1933-41) **676**
military expenditure (1935-40) **779**

Germany: (*cont.*)
naval expansion 90, 254, 331, 508, 574, 673, 674, 675–6, 835
New War Economy Production Plan 574
official announcement of *Luftwaffe's* existence 84
oil shortages 674
pessimism over future production 837–8
priority of 254–7, 1044
problems with 837–8
production increases **257**
Rapid Plan (*Schnellplan*) 574–5
raw material shortages 330–1, 385, 675, 730, 836–7, 1044
securing raw materials 269–70
see also individual armed services
and *Reichsbank*:
covering budgetary deficit 675
fears of inflationary impact of rearmament (1939) 674
Montagu Norman-Schacht conversations (1938) 704
Schacht's dismissal as president (1939) 705
trade policy 97
Walther Funk appointed president (1939)
warnings of financial and economic weakness 579
see also Schacht, Hjalmar
and Reichstag fire 20–1, 29
and Rhineland reoccupation **143**
Hitler's peace offer 144, 150
muted reaction to 152
occupation of 130, 136–7, 142–4
rejection of British 'Text of Proposals' 150
secures Italian support 137
and Romania:
alliance offered to 370
arms supplies to 402
economic treaty (1939) 729
oil supplies 380–1, 382, 715, 747, 948
rumour of German action against 734–5, 947
trade agreement 270, 376–7, 382, 581, 748
trade with 380–3, **731**, 948, 1046
and Sino-Japanese conflict 518–19, 539–40
arms supplies to China 519
ends arms deliveries to China 524, 540
mediation efforts 529
neutrality 519
support for Japan 524
and Soviet Union:
agreement offered to 903
agrees to negotiations in Moscow 905
approaches by (1935) 450–1
Berlin Pact of Non-Aggression and Neutrality (1926), extension of (1933) 28
clandestine contacts between (1939) 882
considers negotiating with 834, 863, 882
credit talks 882
credit treaty (1935) 447
decides on war with 1063
deterioration of relations between 454
draft pact presented by 908
economic agreements (1939) 1058
Far East in negotiations between 904
Hitler on improved relations with 891
Hitler rejects political talks proposal by (1937) 456
Hitler's urgency over reaching agreement 903, 908–9
illusory view of relations between 28

initiates contacts with 889–90
invasion of (1941, 'Operation Barbarossa') 1064–5
Litvinov on possible understanding between 459–60
Merekalov-Weizsäcker meeting 882–3
military contacts 27–8
military contacts cancelled 29
naval base provided by 917
negotiations between (1939) 904–6, 908
obstacles to approaches by 445
positive signals from 888
re-appraisal of relations by (1933) 35–6
rejects Baltic pact offered by 66–7
response to Hitler's Nuremberg speech (1936) 454
Ribbentrop authorises approach to Molotov 892–3
Stalin's motives for reaching agreement 910, 912–13
Surits' assessment of German policy 449–50
temporary suspension of approaches to 893
trade agreement (1934) 447
trade agreement (1936) 454
trade agreement (1939) 908
trade negotiations (1935) 447–9, 451
trade negotiations (1936) 454, 455–6
trade negotiations (1938) 458–9
trade talks resumed (1939) 901
trade with **448**, 892, 916–17
see also Nazi-Soviet Pact (1939)
and Spain 196–8, 942, 943
and Spanish Civil War, *see* Spanish Civil War
and state of emergency established 21
and Stresa talks (1935) 88
and Sweden **388**, 389, 934, 937
and Switzerland 941
and trade policy **388**
Anglo-German cartel arrangements 390–1, 706–8
Anglo-German coal cartel agreement 706
Anglo-German Payments Agreement (1934) 96–7, 373, 701–2, 704–5
Anglo-German talks 702–4
balance of trade 96–7, 384, 675, 775
Baltic states 387
changes in direction of trade **374**
clearing agreements 96, 269, 270, 375–6, 381
disengagement from western powers **375**
Düsseldorf agreement (FBI-RI) 707
Eastern Europe 269–70, 375–6, 379, 383–4, 385, 709, 710, 729–30, **731**, 1045, 1046
economic goals 384
export campaign 675
food supplies 376–7, 379, 381, 382
France 714–15
growth in Latin American trade 374–5
Hitler's 'export, or die' speech 673, 675, 706
as means of expanding influence 268–9
northern Europe 386, 387, **388, 389**
oil supplies 380–1, 382, 674, 715, 729
political motivations 385–6
Romania 748
Scandinavia 387, **388**, 389
securing raw materials 196–8, 269–70, 379
share of East European trade **374**

Germany: (*cont.*)
Soviet Union 447–9, 451, 454, 455–6, 458–9, 916–17
Spanish Civil War 196–8
Wirtschaftsraum 383, 384, 386, 392
and Turkey 377, 961–2
and United States:
debt default 96
declares war on 1065–6
offers mediation with Poland 1001–2
reaction to *Kristallnacht* 679
trade with 97, 815–16
and Weimar Republic, collapse of 10, 1043
and *Wilhelmstrasse* (foreign ministry):
Belgium 279
Czechoslovakia 572, 585
domestic weakness of French government 258
Far East 484, 485
German-Italian draft treaty 848
hostility towards Poland 35, 63, 365
loss of influence of 261, 524
Sino-Japanese conflict 518
staff encouraged to join Nazi party 30
view of Ribbentrop 686–7
and World Disarmament Conference 36, 37, 38, 40, 42–3
and Yugoslavia 367
approves Italian-Yugoslavian treaty (1937) 368
arms credits to 950, 953
assurances of neutrality from 953
conciliatory approach of 949
conciliatory approach to 730, 949–50
Hitler-Stojadinović talks (1938) 404
trade agreement 269, 270, 376, 380, 386, 953, 954
trade with 380, 383, 729–30, **731**, 1046
uncertainty over neutrality of 952
see also German Navy; Jews, in Germany; *Luftwaffe*; Nazi-Soviet Pact (1939); *Reichswehr*; SA (*Sturmabteilung*- Storm-troopers); *Stahlhelm*; *Wehrmacht*
Gestapo 677, 687, 980
Gibraltar 201, 805
Giral, José 186, 189, 204, 229
Glaise-Horstenau, Edmund von 552
Gnedin, Evgeny 884
Goebbels, Joseph:
and Catholic Church 985
and Danzig 839
and Hitler's appointment as Chancellor 20
and *Kristallnacht* 16, 677
and meets with Halifax (1937) 339
and racial cleansing of Berlin 677
and Rhineland reoccupation 144–5
Goerdeler, Carl 590, 820, 886
Goga, Octavian 405
gold standard:
and American and British abandonment of 9, 1042
and desire to return to 1040
and destruction of 1040
and return to 1041
Gömbös, Gyula 268, 371
Gomes, Dolores Ibarruri (*La Pasionaria*) 218
Göring, Herbert 450, 454
Göring, Hermann 28
and anti-Semitism:
expropriation of Jews 677–8
Kristallnacht 679
Rublee-Wohlthat agreement 977–8
and appointed head of Economics Ministry 196

and Austria 156–7, 314
invasion planning 553
and control of steel industry 331
and Czechoslovakia 268, 638, 728
and food crisis 376
and Four-Year Plan 257–8, 270
revision of 574
and Great Britain 338–9, 858, 860
and Italy, discussions with Mussolini 847
and 'Night of the Long Knives' 73
and Poland 841, 858
and Polish Corridor 266
and rearmament 255, 257
1938 programme 673
Junkers-88 bomber programme 574
and Reichswerke Hermann Göring 331
and Romania, offers alliance with 370
and Sino-Japanese conflict 524
and Soviet Union:
clandestine contacts with 882
normalisation of relations 455
trade negotiations (1936) 454, 455
and Spanish Civil War 188, 196, 198
see also Luftwaffe
Gort, General John 769, 951
Gottwald, Klement 214, 613, 615, 642
Grabski, Stanisław 1028
Graham, Sir Ronald 637
Grandi, Dino:
and concerns over revitalized Germany 26
and Czech crisis 636–7
and Great Britain 82, 103, 104, 235–6
and Non-Intervention Committee 215, 216
and Rhineland reoccupation 155
and supports Albanian invasion 743
Grant-Duff, Sheila 406
Great Britain:
and the Admiralty:
Anglo-American naval talks (1937-38) 532–3
Anglo-American naval talks (1939) 808
Anglo-German Naval Agreement (1935) 87, 90, 91–3, 513
Anglo-German naval arms limitation treaty (1937) 873
Anglo-Italian tensions during Ethiopian crisis 82, 111, 113, 117
Anglo-Soviet naval arms limitation treaty (1937) 873
'fleet to Singapore' strategy 810
German claims of submarine parity 773
'Italy first' strategy 741–2
Japan seen as the immediate threat (1934) 50
naval building programme (1936) 294, 507, 508, 514
New Standard Navy programme 513, 514
Second London Naval Conference (1935-36) 508–12
Second London Naval Treaty (1936) 512
Spanish Civil War 205, 232, 233, 237, 238
supports withdrawal from Eastern Europe 398
two-ocean fleet 91, 508, 513, 774
weakness of Far Eastern position 808, 810
and air defence 606, 772, 1024–5
and air power:
concerns over German strength 50
fear of bombing 87–8, 632
prominence in strategy 295–6
and Albania, reaction to Italian invasion 743–4

Great Britain: (*cont.*)
and anti-Semitism 860
and appeasement 326–7, 330, 604, 1053
abandonment of 1032
Chamberlain's defence of 733
Chamberlain's diplomacy 648–51, 654–6, 683
Chamberlain's wishful thinking 339–40
colonial appeasement 305–7, 310, 325
Czechoslovakia 341–3
economic appeasement 301–5, 307, 308–10, 323–4, 390–1, 700, 702, 704, 706, 776–7, 1045
Eden on 149
efforts made to popularize 684
of Japan 426, 479, 499, 508, 509, 811
motives for 292–3
opposition to 340, 683–4
peace groups 169
relationship with rearmament 297–8
Spanish Civil War 222
warnings from 'opposition' Germans 589–90
and assumptions of strength of 604
and Austria 76, 362
and Baltic states 387, **388**, **389**, 390
and Belgium:
Anglo-French declaration on (1937) 322
proposals for ensuring independence of 320
reaction to policy of independence 280–1, 928
security guarantee sought by 54, 71
staff talks between 149, 151, 322–3
three-power London meeting (1936) 299
and Board of Trade 304–5, 387, 499, 500, 503
economic cooperation with Germany 701, 702–4, 705, 706
FBI-RI talks 706–7, 708
and Bulgaria 958, 959
and cabinet committee on foreign policy 154
and Central and Eastern Europe:
abandonment of 299–300
Anglo-French discussions 341–3
ill-defined policy towards 318, 327–8
indifference towards 1053
propose four-power declaration 735–6
and Chiefs of Staff:
accept army's demand for continental field force (1939) 724
Anglo-French staff talks (1936) 151
Anglo-French staff talks (1938) 719
Anglo-French staff talks (1939) 725
Anglo-Italian tensions during Ethiopian crisis 111, 114, 118
Anglo-Polish staff talks (1939) 788–9
assessment of German army strength (1939) 772
avoidance of Eastern European war 299
Belgian neutrality 280, 300, 928
Czechoslovakia 605, 630
defensive strategy against Italy (1939) 791
demand avoidance of war until 1939 222
demand reduction of overseas commitments 301
Egypt 793

Far East 479, 483, 531, 810
Greece 744, 960
lack of support for 'Italy first' strategy 742
Netherlands 722–3, 931
objection to Anglo-French staff talks (1936) 149
opposition to continental commitment 50
outline of defence priorities (1937) 400
rearmament 297
Soviet Union 435, 622, 736, 739, 774, 1032
Turkey 748–9
and China:
committed to independence of 478
difficulty in defending interests in 478
economic interests 477–8
financial rehabilitation of 500–1
and civilian war preparations 632, 765, 772, 1011, 1024–5
and Colonial Office 570, 817
and Czechoslovakia:
accepts Henlein's view of Sudeten problem 561
Anglo-French demands rejected by 614
Anglo-French demand to transfer territory 612–13
Anglo-French discussions 341–3, 365, 611–12
Anglo-French policy towards 565–6
Anglo-French ultimatum to 612–13
Chamberlain advocates acceptance of Hitler's demands 617–18
Chamberlain overruled by cabinet 623
Chamberlain proposes modification of Hitler's terms 624–5
Chamberlain's broadcast to the nation 631
Chamberlain's Plan Z (meeting with Hitler) 591, 592, 593
Churchill urges warning to Germany 591, 633
criticism of 364–5
factors influencing policy during crisis 604–9
French criticism of policy towards 565
German invasion rumours 571–2
guarantee of new frontiers 611, 612
Halifax opposes further concessions 623
Hitler-Chamberlain talks at Berchtesgaden 610
Hitler-Chamberlain talks at Godesberg 616–17
Hitler's terms rejected by 622–3
pledge of support for 626
policy towards 563–5, 590–1
possible alternative policy towards 654–5
presses for concessions to Sudeten leaders 581
response to German *coup* 733
Runciman mission 580–1, 594, 595, 610
seeks Italian assistance over 636–8
self-determination for Sudeten Germans 610–11
suggests five-power conference 637
sympathy for Sudeten complaints 364
timetable for hand-over of territories 630–2
warnings from 'opposition' Germans 589–90
warning to Germany withdrawn 592
Wilson's mission to Germany 626, 628
and Denmark, trade with 388

Great Britain: (*cont.*)
and deterrence:
active policy of 1032
air defence 51, 87, 294, 295, 296, 699
economic concessions 776–7
Greek guarantee 744, 746, 960
Henderson's opposition to 591
naval power 91
need for Soviet participation 749–50, 774, 879, 895, 1032–3
Polish guarantee 738–9, 740
Romanian guarantee 747
Turkey 749, 964
and disarmament:
Anglo-French tensions 54
proposals for (1934) 49
public opinion 514
response to Hitler's proposals 45–6
and Eastern Locarno Pact 427, 429, 436
and economic and financial policies:
abandonment of gold standard 9, 1042
Anglo-French economic coordination 777–8
balance of payments problems 303, 1045
balance of trade 387, 392, 700
British Empire 798–9
dependence upon imports 778
dilution of labour 780
doubts over ability to finance long war 780–1
economic recovery 1045
economic warfare 777–8
exchange rate 780, 781, 782
failure to consider using against Germany 708
fears of inflation 294, 302, 780, 1045
German position in south-eastern Europe 709–10
gold reserves 700, 780, 781–2
imperial preference 1042
international trade 302–3
tripartite exchange rate agreement (1936) 174–5, 278
worry over impact of rearmament 297, 700
and Egypt, Anglo-Egyptian treaty (1936) 133
and elections:
East Fulham by-election (1933) 45
general election (1935) 120
Peace Ballot (1935) 106
post-Munich by-elections 684, 766–7
and Estonia 387, 388–9
and Ethiopian crisis, *see* Ethiopian crisis
and Far East:
Anglo-American naval cooperation 340, 532–3, 808
defence policy 808–9
'fleet to Singapore' strategy 742
holding operation in 544
naval appeal to America 742
naval weakness 514–15
policy options 499
preference for Soviet-Japanese hostility 482
relations with America 479–80, 481–2, 503
Singapore 479, 808
uncertainty over policy 498
vulnerability in 478–9
and Finland 388, 391, 392
and First World War, impact on inter-war period 2
and Foreign Office:
abandonment of Eastern Europe 300
Anglo-American trade talks (1937) 534
Anglo-French staff talks (1936) 151

Anglo-German Naval Agreement (1935) 87, 90, 92–3
Arabs 983
Ashton-Gwatkin's report on Germany 706
Belgium 281, 300
Chamberlain's dissatisfaction with 296–7, 302, 648
Czechoslovakia 266, 364, 365, 397, 563, 571, 630–1, 636
denies existence of 'moderate' German group 324
divided views on Germany (1933) 23, 24
Eastern Europe 327, 328, 362, 711
economic appeasement 302, 304, 305, 306, 307, 320
Egypt 709
estimate of German air strength 607, 608
Ethiopian crisis 82, 103, 108, 115
Far East 433, 479–80, 499–501, 503–5, 508–9, 531–2, 535–6, 809–12, 814
fear of German action before 1939 293
Franco-Soviet mutual assistance pact (1935) 423
Greece 379, 709, 961
Italy 235, 240, 570
Munich conference 639, 640, 641, 711
Nazi-Soviet Pact (1939) 894
Netherlands 809
Norway 935–6
opposes Halifax's visit to Hitler 336, 337
opposition to appeasement 340
opposition to 'Italy first' strategy 742
pessimism over agreement with Germany 322
Poland 1003, 1004, 1007, 1009
Polish guarantee 737
Portugal 200
prevention of war on three fronts 293
priority list for arms exports 400
rearmament 50, 297, 684
relative dangers of Communism and Fascism 437–8
response to German economic offensive in northern Europe 390
Rhineland reoccupation 142, 148, 159
Rumbold's '*Mein Kampf*' despatch 23
Soviet Union 415, 425, 426, 428, 431, 432–3, 435, 888–9, 895, 1033–4
Spanish Civil War 202, 203, 205, 206, 217, 235
tasked with securing agreement with Germany 297–8
'Tilea affair' 734–5
treatment of Jews in Germany 972
Turkey 709
warned of invasion of Poland 822
warned of Nazi-Soviet pact 822
World Disarmament Conference (1932-34) 42, 46
Yugoslavia 369
and France:
Anglo-French plan for war 784–6
asserts solidarity with 724
avoidance of continental commitment 296, 344
blindness towards 1053
closer partnership between 697
Czechoslovak policy criticised by 565
differences over Italy 564, 794–5
differences over Spain 235
economic coordination 777–8

Great Britain: (*cont.*)
Ethiopian crisis 109, 113, 116–17
failure to consult over German naval agreement 91–3
failure to give military guarantee 603
follows British lead 340–1
Franco-Little Entente alliance proposals 397–8
Franco-Soviet pact (1935) 430
Hitler-Halifax meeting (1937) 341
implications of Popular Front government 298
joint staff planning (1939) 723, 725
lack of concern over military weakness of 344
lack of confidence in 128
limited staff talks between 564, 603
London Declaration (1935) 83
military commitment to 723
mutual dependence of 97
opposition to Franco-Soviet military collaboration 416, 419, 420
Polish guarantee raised 737
refusal to give security guarantee 54
staff talks (1936) 149, 151, 160–1
staff talks (1938) 719
staff talks (1939) 725, 784–7, 791–2
support for Franco-Italian *rapprochement* 81–2
suspicion between 92, 98, 116, 136
talks on Czechoslovakia 341–3, 564–5
talks on Czechoslovakia (15 Sept 1938) 611–12
three-power London meeting (1936) 299
and Germany:
Anglo-German Naval Agreement (1935) 87, 90–3, 391, 513, 833
Anglo-German naval arms limitation treaty (1937) 873
Anglo-German Payments Agreement (1934) 96–7, 373, 701–2, 704–5
Berlin talks between (1935) 86–7
cartel arrangements 390–1, 706–8
change in attitude towards 765
Churchill urges warning over Czechoslovakia 591
coal cartel agreement 706
concerns over air power 50, 87–8
conciliatory approach to 141–2, 153–4, 155
confusion over policy towards 292–3
declaration of war 1018
desire to reach agreement with 159, 161
exaggerated respect for totalitarian efficiency 312–13
Halifax-Wiedemann talks on Czechoslovakia 579–80
Hitler-Chamberlain meeting at Berchtesgaden 610
Hitler-Chamberlain talks at Godesberg 616–17
Hitler-Halifax meeting (1937) 336–9
Hitler offers bilateral talks (1935) 84
Hitler's campaign for friendship 152–3, 259–60, 317
Hitler's 'last offer' of understanding with 998–9
Hudson-Wohlthat talks 858–9
informal attempts to reach agreement on Poland 856–60

last-minute attempts at agreement with 1003–9
negotiations with 153–4
opposition to agreement with 340
policy towards 300, 310
private diplomacy 857–8
propaganda campaign by 861
reaction to *Kristallnacht* 679–80, 973, 978–9
reaction to Polish invasion 1009, 1011–12, 1013, 1014–17
rejects Henderson's proposals 556–7
rejects negotiated peace with 1062
response to Czech *coup* 733
seeks economic cooperation with 700–1, 702–8
tells of determination to stand by Poland 996
trade talks 702–4
trade with 302, 701–2, 703
ultimatum to 1016–17
uncertainty over Hitler's intentions 313, 721–2, 822, 1045
unlikelihood of German-Soviet agreement 893–5
warnings from 'opposition' Germans 589–90, 820–2
warnings of Nazi-Soviet *rapprochement* 886
and Greece:
arms credits to 961
assurances from 377–8
closer ties sought by 743
decline of influence in 960
economic ties with 378–9
expectations of 961
guarantee to 744, 746, 960
strategic importance of 709
ties between 959
unequal relationship between 961
and Hitler:
awareness of ideology in *Mein Kampf* 22–4
reaction to appointment as Chancellor 22
and Hungary 399–400, 956
and intelligence services:
Anglo-American cooperation 533
application and use of intelligence 1049
assessment system 822
Axis military advantage 774
disparity of forces 771
divisions among Hitler's advisers 311–12
estimate of German air strength 772
estimate of German army strength 772
exaggerated view of German air power 607–8
expects German attack in East 721
German air strength 301, 312
German dissident sources 721
German economic weaknesses 771
German military preparedness 609
German military strength 312, 608–9
German naval construction plans 90
German-Soviet *rapprochement* 893–4
German weaknesses 608
Italian weaknesses 792–3
Japan 504
reports German troop concentrations on Czech borders 592
rumours of attack on Poland 738
rumours of German attack in West 721–2

Great Britain: (*cont.*)
warns of German attack on Czechoslovakia 572
and Ireland 926–7
and Italy:
agreement sought by 562
Anglo-French differences over 564, 794–5
anti-British propaganda by 235
avoidance of confrontation over Ethiopia 105
Chamberlain-Mussolini meeting (1939) 697–8
Chamberlain seeks agreement with 235–6, 240–1, 562, 693–4
Chamberlain's misjudgement of Mussolini 685, 694–5, 698
debate over strategy towards 741–2
Easter Accords (1938) 562–3, 693–4
Eden and Chamberlain clash over approach to 236
Mediterranean Declaration (1937) 222–3
reaction to invasion of Albania by 743–4
reaction to Mussolini's proposed Four-Power Pact 33
refusal to sanction attack on Ethiopia by 89
report into impact of invasion of Ethiopia by 104–5
scepticism over intentions in East Africa 82
seeks detachment from Germany 794–5, 1053
'Zeila' plan for Ethiopia 105
and Japan:
anti-British feeling in 487
apprehensions about 84
awareness of ambitions of 478
Chamberlain favours settlement with 426, 479, 499, 508, 509
Craigie-Arita agreement 811
evaluation of army 487
FBI mission to Manchukuo 509
Leith-Ross mission 500–1
monitoring of Russo-Japanese relations 433
as most immediate threat 50–1
naval strategy 91
obstacles to agreement between 505
passive policy towards 499
policy options towards 499
preference for Soviet-Japanese hostility 482
seeks to work with America over 479–80
Tientsin crisis 809–12, 896–7
see also China; Far East; Sino-Japanese conflict
and Jewish refugees 860
Chamberlain's action on 978–9
children 982
increased intake of 982
public opinion 984
visa qualifications introduced 976
and Latvia 387, **388–9**
and Lithuania 387, **388–9**
and Luxembourg 933
and Memel, response to German occupation 733–4
and military planning and strategy:
abandonment of Eastern Europe 299–300
air deterrent 295–6
Anglo-American naval cooperation in Far East 532–3
Anglo-French defence of Belgium 785
Anglo-French plan for war (1939) 784–6, 1058–9
Anglo-French staff planning (1939) 723
Anglo-French staff talks (1936) 151
Anglo-French staff talks (1938) 719
Anglo-French staff talks (1939) 784–7, 791–2

assumption of attack in east 786
avoidance of continental commitment 296, 344, 605
blockade of Germany 777
Chamberlain's influence 295, 297
changed attitude in (1939) 770–1
continental commitment 724–5
defence priorities of chiefs of staff 400
defensive strategy 605–6, 777
deployment of expeditionary force 785–6
disparity of forces 771, 772
distribution of troops (1938) **801**
economic warfare 777–8
estimate of German army strength 772
European strategic appreciation (1939) 771
exaggerated view of German air power 607–8
expectations of long war 777
Far East 808–9
'fleet to Singapore' strategy 742, 749
German economic weaknesses 771
imperial obligations 800, 802, 803–5
intelligence on eve of Munich 630
Italian offensive dismissed 791, 792–3
'Italy first' strategy 741–2
lack of preparation for land war 345
little thought to Soviet Union 787
need to ensure French military support 293
no defence of Poland 786–7
preparation of two armies 725
relative dangers of Communism and Fascism 437–8
role of army 344–5
rumour of German attack on Holland 722–4
Salonika campaign suggested by French 791–2
Soviet role 749–50
support for France 723
threat assessment 426
threatening Hitler with two-front war 736
worst case scenario 649–50
and mobilization 630, 1011
and Munich conference:
Anglo-German statement 640–1
approach to settlement of international disputes 647–8
Chamberlain's triumphant return from 643
opposition to agreement 683–4
terms of agreement 639–40
and Nazi-Soviet Pact, warnings of 820, 822
and Netherlands 722–4, 931
and Nordic states 387, **388**, 390, 391
and Norway **388**, 935–6
and pacifist organizations 168–9
and peace ballot (1935) 106
as peace-keeper of Europe 605
and Poland:
Anglo-Polish alliance (1939) 998
calls for restraint by 842–3
Danzig 842
decision for war entrusted to 739
distrust of Beck 366
guarantee to 738–9, 740–1, 1032
informal attempts to reach agreement with Germany 856–60
keeps door open for negotiations with Germany 856–7, 858–9
last-minute attempts to avoid war over 1003–9
loan talks with 790

Great Britain: (*cont.*)
military mission to 788
military strength overstated by 789
no military effort to defend 786–7
promise of support for 738
reaction to German invasion 1009, 1011–12, 1013, 1014–17
reciprocal guarantee 738
secret agreement proposed by 737–8
staff talks (1939) 788–9
and Portugal 199, 200, 201, 944, 945
and press control 766
and public opinion:
change in 765–7
Ethiopian crisis 106, 108
on eve of war 767–8
expectation of victory 1025, 1035
hostility towards Germany 765
Jewish refugees 984
mood on outbreak of war 1023–5
opinion polls 766
opponents of war 1023–4
and rearmament:
acceleration of 606
aircraft production 606, 699, 773
air deficiencies 607
air vs army debate 295–6
army expansion 699–700, 724–5, 736
assumptions behind 605
Chain Home system (radar) 606
Chamberlain's interventions 51, 52, 294, 295–6, 313, 426, 507–8, 605, 606, 684–5, 698, 700
Churchill's criticism of air programme 606
conscription 736, 772
defence co-ordination minister appointed 293
Defence Requirements Committee's planning 51, 52, 293–5
defensive strategy 605–6
dependence upon imported raw materials 778
desire to avoid arms race 84
dilution of labour 780
domestic determinants of 297
doubts over financing of 780–1
economy as 'fourth arm of defence' 297, 700, 782, 1045
fears of economic effects 700, 1045
fears of inflationary effects 294, 302, 780, 1045
Labour Party support for 221
maintenance of economic and financial stability 297, 313, 700, 1045
military expenditure (1933-39) **345, 779**
military expenditure (1933-41) **676**
military expenditure (1935-40) **779**
military expenditure (1938) 1045
military expenditure on Indian Army 803
Ministry of Supply 685, 698
naval expansion 294, 507, 513, 514, 698–9, 773
post-Munich reconsideration 684–5
Royal Air Force expansion 87–8
shadow factory scheme 294
Third Deficiency Programme (1936) 293–5
White Paper on defence estimates (1935) 84
see also individual armed services

and Rhineland reoccupation:
attitude towards demilitarized zone 141, 142
muted reaction to 152
prepared to negotiate over 142, 146–7
public opinion 159
and Romania:
French pressure for guarantee 746
guarantee to 746, 1032
oil supplies 747
promise of support for 738
refuses request for unconditional guarantee 745
rumour of German action against 734–5
trade agreement 747
trade with 399, 709–10
and settlement of international disputes, approach to 647–8
and Sino-Japanese conflict 477
Anglo-American naval cooperation 532–3
Anglo-American talks 522–3
attack on British ships by Japanese 530
building of Burma Road 530, 537, 542
clarifies position on (1937) 525
considers naval demonstration (1937) 530
hesitancy in assisting Nationalists 536–7
Japanese naval blockade 518
mediation attempts over Shanghai 517
opposes economic boycott 521
rejects American blockade proposal 530–1
support for China 542–3
talks with Japan 538
and Soviet Union:
alliance negotiations 893, 895–900, 901–2
Anglo-Soviet naval arms limitation treaty (1937) 873
anticipates retreat into isolation 885
attitude towards 914–15
barriers to agreement between 914–15, 1055
Chamberlain's attitude towards 736–7, 750, 777
Churchill's hope for alliance between 431
considers tripartite alliance offer by 880–1
credit extended to 432
cross-party support for alliance with 1033
different aims in negotiations 888, 910–12
difficulties in way of *rapprochement* 431, 752
dilatoriness in securing cooperation of 749–51
divided opinion over relations with 428–9, 432–3, 886–7
doubts over alliance with 818
Eden's visit to (1935) 429–30
evaluation of armed forces (1935) 434–5
fear of alienating Germany 436
guaranteed loan proposal 432
impact of purges on relations 414–15, 435–6, 459
impact of Spanish Civil War on relations 414, 433–4
Metropolitan-Vickers affair 36, 425, 888
military alliance against Germany proposed by 751
military talks between (1939) 901–2, 906–7, 908, 909
monitoring of Russo-Japanese relations 433
mutual distrust 425, 430–2, 435, 1055
need for participation in deterrent strategy 749–50, 1032–3

Great Britain: (*cont.*)
preference for Soviet-Japanese hostility 482
response to Polish guarantee 739, 876, 877–8
revised alliance proposals from 888
seeks unilateral guarantee from 879, 886
significance for Far Eastern strategy 426
talks with (1939) 879
tripartite alliance offer 880, 882
unlikelihood of German-Soviet agreement 893–5
and Spain 201–2, 944
and Spanish Civil War, *see* Spanish Civil War
and Stresa talks (1935) 88–90
and Sweden, trade with **388**, 937
and trade policy 386–7
Anglo-German cartel arrangements 390–1, 706–8
Anglo-German coal cartel agreement 706
Anglo-German Payments Agreement (1934) 96–7, 373, 701–2, 704–5
Anglo-German talks 702–4
arms priority list 400
balance of trade 387, 392, 700
Baltic states 387, **388**, **389**
imports by value **799**
Japan 505
Ottawa agreements (1934) (imperial preference) 304, 305, 386, 387, 798, 815
pressures on British exporters 700–1
response to German domination of south-eastern Europe 709–10
response to German economic offensive in northern Europe 390, 391
Romania 399, 709–10, 747
Scandinavia 387, **388**
south-east Europe 398–9
Soviet Union 432
Turkey 709
United States 534, 816
and the Treasury:
assessment of German rearmament expenditure (1939) 781
concern over cost of RAF programme (1938) 699
coolness over guaranteed loan to Soviet Union (1935) 432
economy as 'fourth arm of defence' 297, 782, 1045
favours agreement with Japan 479, 499, 508, 509
fears of inflation 294, 780, 1045
influence over defence spending 698
Leith-Ross mission 500–1
maintenance of exchange rate 780, 782
opposes political use of clearings 390
pessimism over Britain's financial strength (1939) 781
rearmament 294
reluctance to make economic concessions to Germany 304
supports Anglo-American trade talks (1937) 534
warning over gold losses (1939) 780
and Turkey:
Anglo-French financial support for 964
Anglo-French-Turkish alliance (1939) 965
Anglo-French-Turkish military convention 963
Anglo-Turkish declaration (1939) 748, 962, 963
closer ties sought by 743
credit agreement 962
different aims in negotiations 963
guarantee to 744, 748

lack of financial assistance to 748–9
reluctance to provide assistance to 963–4
strategic importance of 709, 962
and United States:
Anglo-American trade agreement (1938) 534, 816
attempts to secure support of 1053
awareness of isolationist opinion 814
'Destroyers for Bases' deal (1940) 817
difficulties in relations between 480, 812–13
drain of gold to (1939) 781–2
economic rivalry 815
expectations of 634, 777
Far East 479–80
George VI's visit to 818
information campaign in 814
intelligence sharing 816
lack of cooperation in Far East 481–2
Lend-Lease (1941) 1062
naval appeal to 742
naval cooperation 340, 532–3, 808
naval talks 340, 808
rejects Roosevelt's peace plan 534
reluctance to involve in Europe 634
tripartite exchange rate agreement (1936) 174–5, 278
and Western Pact policy 260, 299, 300–1, 319
and World Disarmament Conference 31–2, 36–7
Anglo-French disagreements 41–2
'MacDonald plan' (1933) 32, 36–7
reaction to German withdrawal 43
reaction to Hitler's intervention 38
and Yugoslavia 369, 399, 951, 952
see also British Army; British Empire; Defence Requirements Committee (DRC); Dominions; Royal Air Force (RAF); Royal Navy
Great Depression 1
and causes of 1041
and impact of 2, 9, 1040, 1041
and political repercussions of 9, 1041–3
Great War, *see* First World War (Great War)
Greece 359
and arms exports 960
and Balkan Pact (1934) 68
and economic and financial policies 377
and Germany:
arms supplies from 960
intervention by 1062
maintenance of relations with 960–1
neutrality assurance to 961
presence established by 959
trade with 377, 378, 709, 710, 731, 960
and Great Britain 709
arms credits from 961
assurances to 377–8
decline of influence of 960
expectations of 961
guarantee by 744, 746, 960
reluctance to alienate 378–9
response to four-power declaration proposal by 735
seeks closer ties with 743
ties between 959
unequal relationship between 961
and Italy 850, 852, 853, 960, 1062

Greece (*cont.*)
- and neutrality 959–61
- and Rhineland reoccupation 152
- *see also* Metaxas, General Ioannis

Greek Powder and Cartridge Company 378, 960, 961
Greenwood, Arthur 738, 1016
Greiser, Arthur 365
Grew, Joseph 477, 810
Grynszpan, Herschel 677
Guadalajara, battle of 224–5
Guderian, General Heinz 253, 1060
Guernica 184, 225–6
Guisan, Henri 941

Haavara transfer 974–6
Hácha, Emil 727–8
Haile Selassie, Emperor of Ethiopia 100–1, 124, 130, 131
Halder, General Franz 578, 629, 638, 838, 897, 1005, 1030–31
Halifax, Lord (E F L Wood) 300
- and *Anschluss* 557
- and Austria 362
- and becomes foreign secretary 562
- and Belgium 723
- and colonial appeasement 306
- and Czechoslovakia:
  - considers Sudeten plebiscite 592
  - Halifax-Wiedemann talks 579–80
  - opposes further concessions 623
  - overruled on warning to Hitler 592
  - pledge of support to 626
  - policy towards 563, 564–5
  - proposes to admonish Czechs and warn Germans 591
  - Runciman mission 580–1
  - timetable for hand-over of territories 630–1
  - warning to Ribbentrop 572
- and France, visits Paris (1938) 712–13
- and Germany:
  - meets with Blomberg (1937) 339
  - meets with Goebbels (1937) 339
  - meets with Göring (1937) 338–9
  - meets with Hitler (1937) 336–9, 341
  - meets with Schacht (1937) 339
  - policy towards 711
  - ultimatum to 1017
- and Japan, Tientsin crisis 810
- and Poland:
  - Danzig 842
  - guarantee offered to 738–9
  - last-minute attempts at agreement with Germany 1004–5, 1006–7
  - reaction to German invasion 1009, 1011
  - reciprocal guarantee 738
- and rearmament 700, 711
- and Rhineland reoccupation 147
- and Romania 745
- and Sino-Japanese conflict 536
- and Soviet Union:
  - alliance negotiations 897, 898, 899, 901
  - attitude towards 750
  - considers tripartite alliance offer by 881
  - favours alliance talks 886, 887, 895
  - lack of urgency in negotiations with 902
  - participation in peace coalition 750–1
  - seeks unilateral guarantee from 879, 886
  - talks with Maisky (1939) 879
- and United States 781, 815
- and Yugoslavia 951–2

Hampton, Commander T C 808
Hankey, Sir Maurice 50, 202, 297, 310
Harrison, Tom 1024

Hassell, Ulrich von 137, 1000
and discussions with Mussolini 128–9, 261
and recalled by Hitler 335
on Ribbentrop's influence 316
Haushofer, Albrecht 267–8
Hawaii 481
Hayashi Senjuro, General 502, 503
Hayes, Major E C 435–6
Health Organization (HO) 173
Heimwehr 156
Henderson, Arthur 39, 40, 171
Henderson, Sir Neville 893
and assessment of 1008–9
and concessionary approach to Germany 337, 858
and Czechoslovakia 572
advocates negotiated settlement 590
antipathy towards 591
disapproves of warning to Hitler 592
warning to Czech minister 336
Wilson's meeting with Hitler 628
and Hitler:
conveys Britain's determination to stand by Poland 996
intentions of 328
'last offer' of understanding 998–9
meets with 556–7
and illness 721
and Poland 842, 1007
and ultimatum to Germany 1017
Henlein, Konrad 266–7, 364
and demands plebiscite 593–4
and *Freikorps* raids across Czech border 616
and instructions on tactics from Hitler 560, 585
and Karlovy Vary (Carlsbad) speech 560–1
and meets Vansittart 267, 561
Henry, Jules 611
Herriot, Édouard 601, 627
and Ethiopian crisis 107, 124
and Rhineland reoccupation 149
and visits Soviet Union (1933) 36
Hershelmann, E E 884
Herwarth, Hans von 589–90, 849, 894
Herzog, General James 1018
Hess, Alfred 187
Hess, Rudolf 187
Hesse, Prince Philipp of 554, 586
Hewel, Walther 686–7, 857
Heydrich, Reinhard 680, 978, 979
Heye, Hellmuth 574
Heywood, Major-General T G G 902
Hideki Tōjō, General 1065
Hierl, Konstantin 576
Hildebrand, Klaus 314
Hilger, Gustav 889, 893
Himmler, Heinrich 73, 156–7, 268, 680, 979
Hindenburg, Oskar 19
Hindenburg, Paul von 74
Hiranuma, Baron 695, 1001
Hirota Koki 488
and Amau declaration 488–9
and China, peace efforts 490
and Sino-Japanese conflict 516
apologises to America 532
expansion of aims 535–6
outlines peace terms 524–5
HISMA (Compañía Hispano-Marroquí de Transportes Limitada) 196
Hitler, Adolf 17–18
and anti-Bolshevism 15, 445
and anti-Semitism 14–16, 1043–4
America's role 15–16, 680, 989
disguises obsession with 16
implied genocide 680–1
international Jewish conspiracy 989
Kristallnacht 16–17, 677, 680
threatens annihilation of Jews 17, 973
and appointed Chancellor (1933) 10, 19–20
British reactions to 21–4

Hitler, Adolf (*cont.*)
domestic reactions to 20, 29–30
élite reaction 30
French reactions to 21, 22, 24–6
Italian reactions to 26–7
Soviet Union's reaction to 27–9
and architectural projects 311
and armed services:
enhanced authority over 334–5, 682
forces changes in leadership 334
and Austria:
Anschluss 552, 554, 555
attempted Nazi putsch 75
cautious approach to 264–5, 362–3
denies intention to annex 104
entry into 554
invasion of 553
meets with Schuschnigg 364
reassures Mussolini over 554
reveals intentions towards 314
ultimatum to Schuschnigg 552–3
unlikelihood of foreign intervention over *Anschluss* 360–2
visa tax imposed on 39
and authority over foreign policy 13
and Baltic states 392
and Bulgaria 958
and centrality of war for 823, 862–3, 1057
and Chamberlain:
animosity towards 672
Berchtesgaden meeting 610
convinced of Jewish influence over 860
differences between 651
duel between 647
expectations of 321
Godesberg meeting 616–17
low opinion of 644–5
misread by 650–1, 655–6, 683
and China 485–6
and colonial demands, as tactical weapon 260, 325
and concentration on domestic politics 29, 30
and confidence of 150, 157
and constraints on 13
and contingent nature of successes of 1051
and Czechoslovakia:
agrees to conference over 638
calms British anxieties over 579–80
diplomatic and economic doubts over plans for 578–9
diplomatic preparations for attack 585
elimination of 727–8
explains intentions to junior generals 578
Hungarian policy 588–9
invasion planning 365, 560, 571, 572–3, 584
meeting with Wilson 628
Munich agreement 639–40
non-aggression pact talks 268
Nuremberg speech 593
opposes Hungarian claims to Ruthenia 689
Polish policy 587–8
post-Munich bullying of 687
predicts no Anglo-French intervention 332–3
reassures army over 578
reply to Chamberlain's proposals 630
reply to Roosevelt's peace appeal 635
reveals intentions towards 314, 332, 333
seeks Italian support over 568
staging of incidents 585
uncertainty over British intentions 583–4, 630
and diplomatic service, forces changes in leadership 335

and disarmament, proposals for 45, 50
and economic and financial policies 335
'export, or die' speech 673, 675, 706
relations with *Reichsbank* 579, 674
and Enabling Law ratified (1933) 21
and expansionary intentions 314
Hossbach memorandum (1937) 242, 331–3
Soviet Union 18
western Europe 573, 682–3
and Far East 485–6
and France:
attitude towards 18–19
confident of no intervention over Poland 855–6
Daladier's proposed meeting with 40–1
invasion of 1060
peace overtures to (1933-34) 47
rejects Laval's approaches (1935) 117–18
and German minorities abroad 264
Danzig 265–6
Memel Germans 265
Sudeten Germans 560
and Great Britain 252
believes in possibility of friendship 17–18
Berlin talks with Simon (1935) 86–7
campaign for friendship with 152–3, 259–60, 317
confident of no intervention over Poland 855–6, 858
considers invasion plans 1063
expects war with 1029
frustration with 318
Hitler-Halifax meeting (1937) 336–8, 339
Hitler-Vansittart meeting (1936) 298
hopes for agreement after Polish campaign 900, 901
last-minute attempts at agreement with 998–9, 1003–6
as most dangerous adversary 831
offers bilateral talks (1935) 84
offers naval talks 87
rejects Henderson's proposals 556–7
seeks to separate from France 87
timing of war with 834
ultimatum from 1017
warned over war with 579
worry over possible Anglo-Soviet alliance 900–1
and Hungary 372–3, 954
and Italy 17, 561
and Japan 262–3, 488, 540
and *Lebensraum* 14, 332, 1048
dealing with West first 682–3
economic factors 384–5
expansion in the East 18
showdown with Soviet Union 18
and *Mein Kampf* (1925) 14, 22–4
anti-Semitism 15
foreign awareness of 22–4, 28
and Memel 728
and Munich conference:
considers his greatest error 672
as defeat for 672
dissatisfaction with 644–5, 656
impatience with settlement 681
terms of agreement 639–40
and Mussolini:
absolves from Pact of Steel responsibilities 1010–11
alerted to attack on Czechoslovakia 585
cancels meeting with (1939) 851
Danzig conference proposed by 851

Hitler, Adolf (*cont.*)
does not consult about Poland 849, 851
gains support over Austria 554
loyalty of 654
makes promise of support to 554
meeting between (1934) 75
meeting between (1938) 568
military alliance with 848–9, 850
pays tribute to 672
restores relations with 844
tensions over Austria 75–6
and 'Night of the Long Knives' 73–4
and non-aggression pact proposals (1935) 90
and non-aggression pact proposals (1936) 150
and non-aggression pact proposals (1937) 319, 320
and Nordic states 392
and northern Europe 392
and objectives of 12–14, 252, 863, 1043–4
as omnipotent leader 311
and opposition to 589–90, 629, 638, 653
intelligence from 721
warnings to Britain 820–2
and patience of 311
and peace offensive (1933) 44
and peace offer following Rhineland reoccupation 144, 150
and 'peace speech' (1936) 260
and personal oath to 74
and Poland:
assurances to (1933) 35
breaks off diplomatic relations 839
cancels attack on 999
confident of no Anglo-French intervention 855–6, 858, 860, 1030
Danzig 365, 733, 844
decides on military solution 833
denounces Non-Aggression Pact 833
diplomatic isolation of 1005
fear of foreign mediation over 995
intent on war over 1031, 1035
non-aggression pact with (1934) 62–4
orders attack on 999, 1004, 1005
orders invasion planning 833, 863
orders occupation of Danzig 691
readiness for invasion of 995
reassurance of Nazi-Soviet Pact 917
rejects Italian mediation over 1010
tells Italy of intentions 852
and *Political Testament* 15
and 'propaganda march' in Berlin 629
and rearmament 44, 96
armaments position 836–7
army expansion 85
awareness of problems 838
balance of payments problems 255, 556, 675
introduction of conscription 84–5
priority of 255–7, 1044
settles raw material allocations 331
steel allocations 335
see also individual armed services
and re-education of German people 673
and rejects western attempts at cooperation 314
and return of Saar territory 83, 84
and Rhineland reoccupation 130, 136–7, 142–4
motives for timing of 137
peace offer over 144, 150

rejection of British 'Text of Proposals' 150
secures Italian support for 137
and rise of, explanation of 10–12
and Romania 367, 948
and Schacht, relations with 258, 259, 304, 325
and self-portrayal as man of peace 144
and Sino-Japanese conflict 519, 524
and Soviet Union:
agrees to negotiations in Moscow 905
attacks Bolshevik-Jewish conspiracy 454
considers negotiating with 834, 863, 882
considers short-term agreement with 892
decides on war with 1063
enmity towards 414, 415, 445
initiates contacts with 889–90
invasion of 1064–5
Lebensraum 18
Nazi-Soviet Pact (1939) 889–90, 893, 900–1, 903, 905, 908–9, 917, 1030, 1052, 1055–6
rejects political talks proposal by (1937) 456
temporarily suspends approaches to 893
urgency over reaching agreement with 903, 908–9
worry over possible Anglo-Soviet alliance 900–1
and Spanish Civil War:
desire to prolong 242
German-Italian cooperation 190–1
impact on 185
limits involvement in 191
military assistance 187–8, 191
reasons for intervention 195–6
use of 184
and strategic thinking:
intent on war 1031–2, 1035
war in the East, *see Lebensraum*; Poland; Soviet Union
war in the West 682–3, 832–3, 834, 1019, 1029
and strengthening of domestic position 44
and takes title of Führer and Reich Chancellor (1934) 74
and talents of 12, 311, 1044
and Turkey 962
and uncertainty over intentions of 721–2
and United States 635, 1002, 1065–6
and War Directive No 1 1005, 1006, 1019
and West Wall 573, 576, 578, 673
and World Disarmament Conference 38, 40, 42–3
and Yugoslavia 367
conciliatory approach to 730, 949–50
encourages Mussolini against 952
Stojadinović's visit 404
uncertainty over neutrality of 952
and *Zweites Buch* (1928) 14, 15
Hlinka populist party (Slovakia) 66
Hoare, Sir Samuel (later Lord Templewood) 92, 106, 726
and becomes foreign secretary 105
and colonial appeasement 306
and Ethiopian crisis 115, 122
addresses League of Nations Assembly 111
Anglo-French talks on sanctions 109
Hoare-Laval plan 122–5
seeks naval assurance from France 113
warning to Mussolini 108
and Mediterranean Declaration (1937) 222

Hoare, Sir Samuel (*cont.*)
and opposition to army expenditure 700
and resignation of 125–6
and returns to cabinet 222
and Soviet Union 431, 898
and Spanish Civil War 202, 223–4
Hobsbawm, Eric 183
Hodgson, Sir Robert 244
Hodža, Milan 266, 615
and Sudeten Germans 267, 560, 585
and tariff preference proposals 403
Hoesch, Leopold von 142, 144
Hong Kong 539, 805
Hore-Belisha, Leslie 344, 725, 769, 792
Horst, W 1023
Horthy, Admiral Miklós 372, 954, 955
and Czechoslovakia 588–9
seizure of Ruthenia 728
and lack of sympathy for Hitler 371
Hossbach, Colonel Friedrich 331, 332
Hotchkiss (French munitions manufacturer) 402
Howard, Roy 452
Hudson, Robert 750, 859, 900–1
Hugenberg, Alfred 24, 29, 386
Hull, Cordell 97, 385
and Ethiopian crisis 110
and independence of 815
and Japan 481
Tientsin crisis 810
and Reciprocal Trade Agreements Act 97
and Sino-Japanese conflict 518, 533
and Spanish Civil War 207, 208
l'Humanité 417
human trafficking, and League of Nations 174
Hungarian Communist Party, and purges of 464
Hungary 359
and *Anschluss* 363
and anti-Semitism 372, 373, 981
and Arrow Cross movements 372, 373
and Czechoslovakia:
agrees to action with Germany against 372–3, 589
demand cession of territory 688–9
German-Italian arbitration of territorial demands (Vienna award, 1938) 689–90
policy towards 588–9
seize Ruthenia 728
seizes territory in 690
territorial claims against 614–15
and Germany:
agrees to joint action against Czechoslovakia 372–3, 589
alliance sought by officer corps 371
army contacts with 372
discussions over Czechoslovakia 588–9
economic relations with 955
lack of sympathy towards amongst older politicians 371
loyalty demanded by 955
non-belligerency in Polish campaign 954, 955–6
tensions between 371
trade agreement 269, 386
trade with 379–80, 731
and Great Britain 399, 956
and Italy 370–1, 853, 955
and Jewish refugees 976, 981
and Little Entente 588
and neutrality 954–6
and Poland, no participation in war against 954, 955–6
and rearmament 371–2, 373
and return of lost territories 373
and Romania 370, 588, 956
and Rome Protocols (1934) 69
and Slovakia 954
and territorial claims 954–5
and Yugoslavia 372, 404, 588, 950

Huntzinger, General Charles 963
Huxley, Aldous 168
Hymans, Paul 47, 53, 54, 70

ICI (Imperial Chemical Industries) 390–1
ideology:
as divisive factor 1047
and European divisions 359, 1047
and Great Britain, anti-Bolshevism 914–15
and Hitler 13, 1048
centrality of war 823, 862–3
and ideological assumptions of statesmen 1048–9
barrier to understanding 1050
democratic leaders 1050–51
and relative dangers of Communism and Fascism 437–8
and role of 4
and Soviet Union 439–40
deviations from 442–3
distinctions between capitalist states 443
fear of capitalist encirclement 439
inevitability of war with capitalist powers 439–40
response to Nazi challenge 1047
Stalin's foreign policy 913–14
and Spanish Civil War 181–3, 193, 1047–8
I G Farbenindustrie A G 390–1
L'Illustration 1026
Imperial Conference (1937) 515, 802
imperialism (general concept):
and impact of Second World War 1064
and Italy 100
and Lenin's theory of 439
Imperial Tobacco Company 710, 961
Imrédy, Béla 588, 614–15, 954
India 799, 805, 1018
Indian Army 800, 803
Indochina, and Japanese threat to 482–3, 526–7, 807
Industrial Intelligence Centre (IIC) 609, 705, 708, 778
Ingersoll, Captain Royal E 532
Inönü, Ismet 743, 947
Inskip, Sir Thomas 293, 302, 344–5, 802
intelligence services:
and application and use of intelligence 1049
and contribution to decision-making 1049
and democratic/reactive countries 1049
shortcomings in 1049
and formulation of national policy 1049
see also code-breaking; *Deuxième Bureau* (French military intelligence agency); entries under individual countries
inter-governmental committee on refugees (IGCR) 977, 978
international brigades, and Spanish Civil War 190, 206, 213–14, 218–19, 220, 246
International Court of Justice 929
International Exhibition (Paris, 1937) 241, 395
International Labour Organization (ILO) 173
International Peace Campaign (IPC) 169
International Whaling Conference 859
Iraq 798, 800, 983
Ireland 799
and neutrality 926–7, 1018
Iron Guard 405
Ironside, General Edmund 'Tiny' 789, 902
Ismay, General Hastings Lionel 'Pug' 592, 795
Italian Air Force, and unpreparedness of 854

Italian Army:
and Germans' negative opinion of 844
and military planning 317
and optimism over prospects in war 845
and unpreparedness of 845–6, 853, 854, 999, 1059
Italian Navy:
and Axis naval policy 315
and expansion of 508
and lack of naval strategy 853
and Mediterranean, strength in 792
and optimism over prospects in war 846
and unpreparedness of 854
Italy:
and Albania 368, 569
invasion of 742–3
occupation plans 693
and Anti-Comintern Pact 240, 241, 316–17, 486, 524
and anti-Semitism 570–1
and Austria 155
Anglo-French-Italian declaration on (1934) 76
concerns over *Anschluss* 27, 69
German-Italian tensions over 75–6
offers to defend independence of 78
reaction to failed Nazi putsch (1934) 75
reduced interest in 157
seeks German reassurance over 104
supports Hitler over 554
and Bulgaria 261
and Chiefs of Staff 69, 108–9, 194, 570, 844, 846
and China 486
and Corsica 851
and Croatia 850, 853
and Czechoslovakia:
asks Hitler for delay in mobilization 638
Britain seeks assistance over 636–8
Hitler seeks support over 568
planning for consequences of German attack 586–7
sides with Germany 586
warned by Germany of attack on 585–6
and declaration of war (1940) 1061
and Egypt 696, 793, 853
and Ethiopian crisis, *see* Ethiopian crisis
and expansionary programme 694, 696
'March to the Sea' 696
and Far East 484, 486
and Four-Power Pact proposal 28, 32
foreign reactions to 33–4
motives 32–3
provisions of 33
and France:
agreement over Ethiopia 78–9
anti-French campaign 569–70, 694
breaks off conversations with 567–8
disarmament proposals 41
Franco-Italian agreement (1935) 78–80
increasing distance between 282–3
Mediterranean Locarno project 75
military agreement between (1935) 80
military talks between 108–9
reaction to Anglo-Italian Easter Accords 563
reaction to invasion of Albania 745–6
recognises sovereignty over Ethiopia 693
refusal to accept ambassador from 283
talks between 31, 76, 78

territorial claims against 694
tougher stance adopted by 719
unhappiness with Italy's Austrian policy 69
unwillingness to make concessions 745, 846, 851
and Germany 155
absence of formal alliance 317
alliance negotiations 847–8
alliance proposals 695
alliance proposals (1938) 692–3
attitude towards rearmament of 53
caution over military alliance with 569
Ciano-Ribbentrop meeting (1939) 852
conflicting interests 261–2
cooperation between 561
discussions about Austria 314, 315, 316
fears over attack on Poland 851–2
German-Italian protocol (1936) 261
growing closeness between 314–16
impact of Spanish Civil War 185
inability to honour alliance with 999
mediation over Poland rejected by 1010
military pact conversations 568–9
military talks between 846–7
naval talks 696
not consulted by about Poland 849, 851
opts for partnership with 262
'Pact of Steel' (1939) 794, 846, 847, 848–50
presses for military alliance with 697
proposes conference on Danzig 851
rapprochement between 129, 261
reaction to Polish invasion 1009, 1013
recognition of Ethiopian annexation 261
responsibilities absolved by 1010–11
Rome-Berlin Axis proclaimed (1936) 157, 194
rumours of Nazi-Soviet pact 849
staff talks 697
support for Rhineland reoccupation 137
talks over non-aggression pact 128–9
tell of intentions in Poland 852
tensions over Austria 75–6
undelivered statement of neutrality to 855
vacillates in support of 855
and Great Britain:
anti-British propaganda 235
Chamberlain-Mussolini meeting (1939) 697–8
Chamberlain seeks agreement 235–6, 240–1, 562, 693–4
Chamberlain seeks to detach from Germany 794–5, 1053
Easter Accords (1938) 562–3, 693–4
hostility towards 850–1
Mediterranean Declaration (1937) 222–3
opposition to attack on Ethiopia 103
raises Ethiopia with 82, 89
reaction to Anglo-German Naval Agreement 93
reaction to invasion of Albania 743–4
seeks agreement with 562
'Zeila' plan for Ethiopia 105
and Greece 850, 852, 853, 960
invasion of 1062
and Hungary 370–1, 853, 955

Italy: (*cont.*)
and impact of Nazi-Soviet Pact 999
and imperial expansion 100
and intelligence services:
assassination of Barthou 78
break British code 698
pandering to leader's views 1049
spy in British embassy 698
and Japan 316, 486
and League of Nations:
departure from 316
sanctions imposed by 112
sanctions lifted by 131
and Libya, doubles troop numbers in 570, 697
and Little Entente, rivalry between 69
and 'Manifesto of the Race' 570–1
and military expenditure 853–4
and military planning:
German attack on Czechoslovakia 586–7
Mussolini's plans 850, 852–3
optimism of service chiefs 845–6
war against Germany and Britain 90, 103–4
war with Germany against Britain and France 317
Yugoslavia 852–3
and military weakness 845–6, 853, 854, 999, 1059
and non-belligerency (1939) 1011, 1059
and Poland 261–2, 1009, 1010, 1013
and post-First World War decade 1038
and raw material shortages 854
and reaction to Hitler's appointment as Chancellor 26–7
and rearmament 39
and Rhineland reoccupation 137, 149, 155
and Romania 261, 850
and Rome Protocols (1934) 69
and Sino-Japanese conflict 486
and Soviet Union, non-aggression pact (1933) 36
and Spanish Civil War, *see* Spanish Civil War
and Stresa talks (1935) 88–90
and Switzerland 940
and Tunisia 697, 851, 853
and unpreparedness for war 853–4, 999
and Yugoslavia 78, 261, 853
threat to 949
trade agreement 290
treaty between (1937) 367–9
see also Italian Air Force; Italian Army; Italian Navy
Iwaszkiewicz, Jarosław 1028–9
Izvestia 29, 212, 421, 868

Jacobson, Per 175
Jamaica, and British forces in 805
Jameson, Storm 168
Japan:
and anti-western imperialism 488
and China:
Amau declaration 488–9
desire to create economic bloc in North China 501
establishment of autonomous provinces 490
relations between (1933–35) 489–91
relations between (1936–37) 491–2
Sato's revised policy towards 502–3
Tangku truce (1933) 488
and extension of state power 536
and France 482–3
and Germany 484, 539–40
Anti-Comintern Pact 262, 263, 476, 484–5, 538

divided views on
Anti-Comintern Pact 485
divisions over scope of alliance with 695
extension of Anti-Comintern Pact 540
Hitler sanctions new talks with 262–3
racial views 487–8
recognition of Manchukuo 540
refuse to join tripartite pact 863
talks between (1935) 262
tripartite alliance proposals rejected by 846
and Great Britain:
anti-British feeling 487
apprehensions of 84
Chamberlain favours settlement with 426, 479, 499, 508, 509
Craigie-Arita agreement 811
FBI (Federation of British Industries) mission to Manchukuo 509
Leith-Ross mission 500–1
monitoring of Russo-Japanese relations 433
obstacles to agreement between 505
passive policy of 499
Tientsin crisis 809–12, 896–7
trade policy 505
and Italy 316, 486
and League of Nations, departure from 95, 476
and militarization of 491
and military influence in 263, 489, 503, 505
attempted coup 491
and military planning:
Imperial Defence Plan (1936) 512–13
naval strategy 512–13
United States 506
and nationalist feeling 491
and naval expansion 512
abrogation of Washington Naval Treaty 476
London Naval Conference (1935-36) 506, 509–10, 511
ratios with Britain and America 506, 507, 509, 510
and Nazi-Soviet Pact (1939) 1001, 1059
and Netherlands 483
and New Order in East Asia 539
and oil imports **537**
and racial solidarity 488
as revisionist power 476
and Soviet Union:
border disputes 869–70, 888, 891, 903, 904
Changkufeng 538
deterioration of relations between 74
military clashes between 467, 538
Nomonhan 904
reasons for concern by 477
relations monitored by Britain 433
risk of war between 492
sale of Chinese Eastern Railway by 492–3
and total mobilization faction takes control 491
and United States 481, 543–4
attack on (Pearl Harbor) 1065
commercial treaty abrogated by 811
military planning against 506
miscalculations about 1065
suggests Anglo-American cooperation 503–4
trade with 481
and war enthusiasm 1062–3
and western assumptions about 487
see also Sino-Japanese conflict
Jebb, Gladwyn 302, 390, 437, 722
Jeschonneck, Hans 576

Jews:
- in Austria 973, 976, 987–8
- and boycott of German goods 975
- and Co-ordinating Foundation 978
- in Czechoslovakia, refugees from 980
- and Evian conference (1938) 977
- in Germany:
  - American fundraising for resettlement 978
  - calls for immediate removal of 978
  - concentration camps 973
  - Council for German Jewry 982
  - deprived of citizenship 973
  - destination of emigrants **974**, **975**, **976**, 982–3
  - emigration of **678**, 679, 973–4, **977**, 982–3
  - exchange for foreign currency 974–6
  - exclusion from public life 678, 976
  - expropriation of 677–8
  - expulsion from 980, 987
  - genocide 1066
  - German people's acceptance of treatment of 980–1, 1045
  - Haavara transfer 974–6
  - Hitler threatens annihilation of 17, 680–1, 973, 1066
  - international knowledge of treatment of 972–3
  - *Kristallnacht* 16–17, 671, 677, 679–80, 973, 978
  - League of Nations inaction 979–80
  - Nuremberg Laws 678, 973
  - response to Hitler becoming Chancellor 20
  - Rublee-Wohlthat agreement 977–8
- and Joint Distribution Committee 980
- and Palestine 793, 974, 983–4
- and papal policy 985
- and reluctance of countries to admit refugees 976, 978, 981–2, 984–5, 987, 988–9
- and Wannsee conference 1066
- *see also* anti-Semitism; refugees

Jodl, General Alfred 334
Johnson Act (USA, 1934) 780, 783, 816, 1054
Jouvenal, Bertrand de 143
Jouvenel, Senator Henry de 31, 33–4

Kaganovich, Lazar 445, 880
Kamenev, Lev 210, 211
Kandelaki, David 444, 458
- and Soviet-German trade negotiations 447–9, 451, 454, 455–6

Kánya, Kálmán 371, 372–3, 589
Kehl 30
Keitel, General Wilhelm 552, 682
- and becomes head of OKW 334
- and Czechoslovakia, invasion planning 572, 573
- and forbids criticism of Hitler 584
- and Italy, talks with Pariani 846–7

Keller, General Pierre 419
Kemsley, Lord 857–8
Kennard, Sir H 738–9
Kennedy, Joseph 633, 810, 813, 818, 1002
Kenya 800
Keppler, Wilhelm 157, 255, 265, 315, 363
Kershaw, Ian 10, 150
Kessel, Albrecht von 589–90
Khalkhin-Gol (Nomonhan), battle of 812, 904
King, John Herbert 897–8
Kintomo Mushakoji 262
Kiosseivanov, George 950, 956, 957–8
Kirov, Sergie 460
Kleist, Peter 882, 889, 891, 908
Kleist-Schmenzin, Ewald von 589
Klemperer, Victor 861, 988
Knatchbull-Hugessen, Sir Hugh 517

Koch, Erich 882
Konoe Fumimaro, Prince 503
  and New Order in East Asia 539
  and resignation of 695
  and Sino-Japanese conflict 516, 528
    expansion of aims 535–6
Koo, Dr Wellington 520, 521
Koppenberg, Heinrich 574
Kordt, Erich 589–90, 638, 822
Kordt, Theodore 589–90, 591, 822
Koster, Roland 117
Krauch, Carl 574
Krejci, Ludwik 641
Krestinsky, Nikolai 74, 454, 559
Kristallnacht (10 Nov, 1938) 16–17, 671, 677, 679
  and domestic disapproval of 679
  and foreign reaction to 679–80, 973, 978–9
  and stifling of post-Munich euphoria 679
Krivitsky, Walter 211
Krofta, Kamil 268, 336–7, 395, 614, 642
Krupp (German arms manufacturer) 376, 380
Kun, Béla 464
Kung, H H 485
Kuomintang:
  and army modernization 490
  and arrest of Chiang Kai-shek 496–7
  and Chinese Communist Party 494, 495, 497, 498
  and currency reform 501
  and German military assistance 262, 485, 519
  and internationalist strategy 489
  and Japan, seeks agreement with 489–91
  and opposition to Chiang's policies 491, 492
  and Soviet Union 230–1, 496, 520
  see also China; Sino-Japanese conflict
Labour Party (Great Britain):
  and criticism of cartel arrangements with Germany 707
  and Czechoslovakia 592, 633
  and East Fulham by-election (1933) 45
  and rearmament, support for 221
  and Soviet purges 436
  and Spanish Civil War 221, 233
Lacroix, Victor de 595, 614
laissez-faire 705, 1042
  and Reynaud 717n56
Lamont, Thomas 340
Lampson, Sir Miles 133, 793
Lange, Christian 172
Langenheim, Adolf 187
La Pasionaria (Dolores Ibarruri Gomes) 218
Largo Caballero, Francisco 190, 207, 211, 214, 218
  and reliance on Soviets 228
  and resignation of 228
  and Stalin's advice to 220–1
Latin America 374–5, 974, 982
Latvia 359
  and Baltic states' mutual defence bloc 925
  and Germany:
    naval and intelligence contacts 393
    non-aggression treaty 893, 934, 939
    trade with 270, 388–9, 731
  and Great Britain 387, 388–9
  and League of Nations, impact of Ethiopian crisis 131
  and neutrality 939
  and Soviet Union 393, 910, 939
Laurent, Colonel Edmond 322
Laval, Pierre:
  and becomes foreign minister 77
  and breakdown of relations with Léger 77
  and Ethiopian crisis 107, 109, 136
    Anglo-French discussions 122

Laval, Pierre (*cont.*)
attempts to reach agreement with Italy 120
British seek naval assurance from 113
domestic criticism of 119
Hoare-Laval plan 122–5
pledges military support of Britain 116–17
and Germany:
overtures to Hitler (1935) 117–18
reconciliation with 52, 77, 81, 83–4, 94
return of Saar territory 83–4
and Great Britain, Anglo-French talks(1935) 82–3
and Italy:
agreement with Mussolini over Ethiopia 78–9, 102
seeks agreement with 77–8
and opposes Eastern Locarno Pact 72
and personality 77
and resignation of 128
and Soviet Union 80–1, 93–4, 415
and Stresa talks (1935) 88–9
League of Nations:
and arms trade publications 171
and Bruce Report (1939) 175
and Covenant of, sanctions clause 108
and Danzig 265
and disarmament, attempts to renew efforts on 172–3
and Economic and Financial Organization (EFO) 174–5
and Ethiopian crisis 100
appeals for intervention 101, 102
damaged by 134–5
delayed action over 105
Hoare's speech on collective security 111
impact on smaller countries 131–2
Mussolini rejects compromise solution 112
rebuked by Haile Selassie 131
response to Italian invasion 112
sanctions 108, 109, 112, 120–1, 126, 129–30, 131
and failure of 95, 135, 178, 1039–40
and German departure from 42–3
and German Jews, lack of action over 979
and Great Britain, public opinion 106, 108
and Health Organization (HO) 173
and human trafficking 174
and International Labour Organization (ILO) 173
and Italian departure from 316
and Japan's departure from 95, 476
and loss of confidence in 167
and minority rights 175
Minority Commission 176–7
and Permanent Mandates Commission (PMC) 175–6
and refugee regime 177–8
and Rhineland reoccupation:
condemns 149
French appeal over 144–5
inaction over 150–1, 152
and Sino-Japanese conflict 520–1, 522
and Social Section 174
and Soviet Union:
becomes member 74
expelled 1059–60
and Swiss departure from 131–2, 940
and technical and functional sections 173–5
and weakness of 3–4, 9
see also World Disarmament Conference (1932-34)
League of Nations Union (LNU) 106, 168, 169
Leahy, Admiral William D 808

Lebensraum, see Hitler, Adolf
Lebrun, Albert 736, 1010
Léger, Alexis 67, 74, 350, 1001
  and breakdown of relations with Laval 77
  and Czechoslovakia 611, 612
  and Ethiopian crisis 119, 120
  and Franco-Soviet pact (1935) 93
  and Laval-Mussolini agreement over Ethiopia 79
  and Munich conference 641, 713
  and Poland 283
  and Rhineland reoccupation 145, 146
  and Soviet Union, anxiety over military talks with 416
  and Spanish Civil War, Non-Intervention Agreement 204
Leipzig incident (1937) 233–4
Leith-Ross, Sir Frederick:
  and economic appeasement 302–3, 305, 307, 324, 702
    cartel arrangements 390
    talks with Schacht 308–9, 310
  and Far East mission 500–1
Lenin, Vladimir Ilyich 439
Leopold, Josef 265, 362, 363
Leopold III, King of Belgium 70, 151–2
  and dismisses rumour of German attack 723–4
  and peace appeal by 926, 929, 1003
  and policy of independence 279, 280, 927, 928
Lester, Sean 265
liberalism, and attack on 1042
Libya 570, 697, 720
Liddell Hart, Basil 296
Ligue internationale des combatants de la paix (LICP) 170
Lindbergh, Colonel Charles 597
Lindsay, Sir Ronald 503, 522–3, 525, 634, 812, 814
Lipski, Józef 63–4, 266, 587, 615, 1007–8
Lithuania 359
  and Baltic states' mutual defence bloc 925
  and Germany:
    invasion of Poland 839
    Memel handed over to 728
    Nazi-Soviet Pact provisions 910
    non-aggression treaty 939
    trade with **388–9, 731**
  and Great Britain 387, **388–9**
  and Memel Germans 265
  and Soviet Union, revision of Nazi-Soviet Pact terms 915
Little, Admiral Charles 517
Little Entente:
  and France 288
    failure of alliance talks with 395–8
    lack of enthusiasm for alliance with 288, 290
    pact desired by 290, 291
    suspicion of 35, 75, 93, 132
  and German weakening of 397
  and Hungary 588
  and Italy, rivalry between 69
  and League of Nations, impact of Ethiopian crisis 132
  and limitations of 407
  and Rhineland reoccupation 151
  see also Czechoslovakia; Romania; Yugoslavia
Litvinov, Maxim 28
  and Anglo-Soviet relations 36
  and anti-Fascist coalition strategy 443
    failure of 443–4
  and Austria, response to German invasion 559
  and Czechoslovakia 582, 583, 618, 875–6
  and declining influence of 463–4
  and deterrence 439, 443
  and disarmament proposals 39
  and dismissal of 884
  and distinctions between capitalist states 443, 875
  and Eastern Locarno Pact 74–5

Litvinov, Maxim (*cont.*)
and Ethiopian crisis 134
and Finland 938
and France 36, 93, 291, 421–2, 877, 879–80
and Germany 449
attempts to block political discussions with 450
relations with 459–60
trade negotiations (1935) 447
and Great Britain:
response to four-power declaration proposal by 735–6, 737, 876, 877–8
response to Polish guarantee 739, 876, 877–8
sets out conditions for agreement 879–80
tripartite political agreement proposal 751
and isolation of 875
and limited success of 1054
and loss of confidence in western powers 869
and Molotov, relations with 883–4
and Poland, conversations with (1934) 66
and purges 463
and Rhineland reoccupation 452
and Romania 288–9, 370
and satirises British and French policy 459
and Spanish Civil War 210, 212
and United States, visit to 36
and World Disarmament Conference 55
Lloyd, Lord 435n39
Lloyd George, David 260, 888, 900
Locarno consensus 1038
Locock, Guy 707
London Declaration (1935) 83
London Naval Conference (1935–36) 254, 511
and failure of naval arms control 512
and Japanese withdrawal from 511
and pre-conference talks 506–11
London Naval Treaty (1930) 511–12
and expiration of 506
Second London Naval Treaty (1936), and terms of 511
Loraine, Sir Percy 425, 794–5, 850–1
Lothian, Lord 303, 812
Lozovsky, Semen 885
Luce, Henry (editor of *Time Magazine*) 523
Lueger, Karl 980
Luftwaffe:
and bombers 86
and expansion of 86, 254, 673
aircraft production **835**, 1069–70
Junkers-88 bomber 574, 834
production difficulties 598–9, 674, 834
steel shortage 330–1
and Göring's announcement of existence of 84
and Great Britain:
inability to attack 608
unpreparedness for war with 834–5
and inability to mount strategic bombing campaign 653
and invasion of Low Countries and France 1060–61
and Spanish Civil War, testing of weapons and tactics 196, 219
and strength of 85–6, **598**, 772, 1069–70
foreign estimates of 597–9, 607–8, 772, 775
Lungu, Dov 405
Luxembourg 932–4
Lyons, Joseph 742, 808

Macaulay, Rose 168
MacDonald, James G 177–8, 979
MacDonald, Ramsay 31–2, 33, 37–8, 89
Maček, Vladko 953

MacKenzie King, William L 802, 818n82
Maclean, Donald 898
Madrid, and Spanish Civil War 184, 218–19
Maffey, Sir John 104
Maghreb, and French forces in 806
Maginot Line 138, 281, 344, 776
Magowan, John 704
Maisky, Ivan 212, 750, 869, 880
  and agreement offered to Britain and France 881
  and Anglo-Soviet alliance negotiations 895, 897, 900
  and Churchill 431
  and friendship with Vansittart 427
  and negotiations with Halifax (1939) 879
  and Spanish Civil War 221
    Non-Intervention Committee 215, 216
    reassures Eden over Soviet intentions 228–9
Makins, Ralph 856
Málaga, Italian attack on 224
Malaxa, Nicolae 734n5
Malaya 798
Malcolm, Sir Neil 979
Malenkov, Georgy 884
Malraux, André 209
Malta, and British forces in 805
Manchukuo 488
  and British mission to 509
  and German recognition of 540
  and German refusal to recognise 263
  and Italian recognition of 316
mandate system, and League of Nations 175–6
Mandel, Georges 146, 567, 627, 777, 996
Mannerheim, Field Marshal Carl Gustaf Emil 392
Manstein, Field Marshal Erich von 577
Mao Tse-tung 493, 529
  and arrest of Chiang Kai-shek 497
  and relations with Soviet Union 493–4
  see also Chinese Communist Party (CCP)
Marchendeau, Paul 777
Margerie, Roland de 565
Marx, Karl 8
Masařik, Hubert 641
Masaryk, Jan 364–5, 406, 622–3, 641
Mason-Macfarlane, Noel 630, 704
Massigli, René 350–1
  and appeasement, alarm at 319
  and Czechoslovakia 613
  and dialogue with Germany 278
  and Ethiopian crisis 119
  on German strategy in Eastern Europe 287
  and need for active policy in south-eastern Europe 395
  and Rhineland reoccupation 145
  and sent as ambassador to Turkey 713
Mass Observation 1024
Mastny, Vojtech 336, 641
Mauthausen concentration camp 248
Mediterranean Declaration (1937) (Anglo-Italian 'Gentlemen's Agreement') 222–3
Mediterranean Locarno, and French policy 75
Memel:
  and German occupation of 728
    British response to 733–4
    planning for 682
    Polish concern over 732
    Soviet concern over 739
  and Memel Germans 265
Menelik, Emperor of Ethiopia 100
Merekalov, Alexei 458, 877, 880
  and Merekalov-Weizsäcker meeting 882–3
  and predicts future German actions 881
Méric, Victor 170

Metaxas, General Ioannis 957
 and economic and financial policies 377
 and Germany 377, 709, 959–60, 961
 and Great Britain 377–8, 743
Metropolitan-Vickers affair 36, 425, 888
Mexico, and Spanish Civil War 181, 208
Miaja, General José 218
Middle East, and exposed British position 793
Miedzinski, Colonel Bogusław 29
Mikoyan, Anastas 880, 893
Milch, Erhard 450
Milward, Alan 383
minority rights, and League of Nations 175, 176–7
Moch, Jules 206
Mokanov, Stoica 958
Mola, General Emilio 181, 186, 187, 189, 218, 226
Molotov, Vyacheslav 81, 231, 445, 880
 and appointed commissar for foreign affairs 884
 and characteristics of 884
 and criticism of collective security 464
 and Finland, warning to 888
 and France, revised alliance proposals 888
 and Germany:
  agreement offered by 903
  Far East in negotiations with 904
  meeting with Schulenburg 890, 892–3
  Nazi-Soviet Pact (1939) 890, 892–3, 903, 904–6, 908
  negotiations with 905–6, 908
  positive signals to 888
  presents draft pact to 908
  Soviet relations with 27, 444, 452–3
 and Great Britain:
  alliance negotiations 893, 895, 896, 898–900, 901
  demands tripartite alliance 886
  doubts over sincerity of 887–8
  rejects proposal from 887
  revised alliance proposals 888
 and isolationism 451
 and Japan 492, 888, 891
 and Litvinov 883–4
 and reviews negotiations with Allied powers 888
 and Rhineland reoccupation 452
 and Stalin's trust in 884
Monnet, Jean 175, 717, 783
Montreaux Convention (1936) 132, 133, 288, 289, 962
Monzie, Anatole de 777, 996–7, 1014
Moravia 625, 690, 727, 821
Morgenthau, Henry 349, 500, 504, 543, 633
Morocco, and French forces in 806
Morton, Desmond 705, 708
Motta, Giuseppe 940
Munich conference:
 and Anglo-German statement 640–1
 and appeasement 645–6
 and Beneš accepts agreement 641–3
 and British approach to settlement of international disputes 647–8
 and Chamberlain's triumphant return from 643
 and divergent opinions on 646
 and exclusion of Soviet Union 645, 1054
 and French motives for accepting British leadership 712
 and Hitler agrees to 638
 and Hitler issues invitations to 639
 and Hitler's dissatisfaction with 644–5, 656, 672, 681
 and impact of 646–7, 656–7, 1052

and lessons of 656
and opposition to agreement, Britain 683–4
and terms of agreement 639–40
and United States, Roosevelt congratulates Chamberlain 643
see also under participants
Murray, Arthur 636
Mussolini, Benito:
and Albania 569, 693
invasion of 742–3
and Austria 155
accepts German dominance over 315, 316
attitude towards 75–6, 554
concerns over *Anschluss* 27, 69
offers to defend independence of 78
reaction to failed Nazi putsch (1934) 75
reduced interest in 157
seeks German reassurance over 104
supports Hitler over 554
talks with Göring 314
and awareness of military unpreparedness 854
and Ciano attempts to dissuade from war 852, 853, 855
and Czechoslovakia 586, 636–8, 845
and declaration of war 1061
and Ethiopian crisis:
agreement with Laval over Ethiopia 78–9, 102
ambitions in 100
attempts to divide Britain and France 120
determined on military solution 101–2
Hoare-Laval plan 124
increasing British hostility 108
military success 130
objectives in 101
prepared to risk conflict with Britain over 108
rallies support for campaign 116
rejects British 'Zeila' plan 105
rejects compromise solution 112
response to threat of oil sanctions 121
seeks clarification of French position 107
and foreign policy goals 316
expansionary programme 694, 696, 850, 852–3
'March to the Sea' 696
and Four-Power Pact suggested by (1933) 28, 32
motives 32–3
provisions of 33
reactions to 33–4
and France:
agreement with Laval over Ethiopia 78–9
anti-French campaign 569–70, 694
breaks off conversations with 567–8
disarmament proposals 41
talks with 31, 76
territorial claims against 694
and Germany:
attitude towards rearmament of 53
caution over military alliance with 569
commits to military alliance 695
discussions with Göring (1939) 847
fears over attack on Poland 851–2
inability to honour alliance with 999
irreversible commitment to 317
opts for partnership with 262
'Pact of Steel' (1939) 794, 846, 847, 848–50
presses for military alliance 697
proclaims Rome-Berlin Axis (1936) 157, 194

Mussolini, Benito (*cont.*)
seeks reassurance from about Austria 104
talks over non-aggression pact 128–9
visits Hitler (1937) 315
and Great Britain:
Chamberlain-Mussolini meeting (1939) 697–8
hostility towards 850–1
publishes newspaper attack on 235
reaction to Anglo-German Naval Agreement 93
and Greece 845
and Hitler:
attitude towards 693
encourages negotiations over Poland 1004
hurt by Czech *coup* 845
loyalty to 654
makes no effort to restrain 849–50
meeting between (1934) 75
meeting between (1938) 568
meeting cancelled by (1939) 851
mixed feelings over success of 26–7
not consulted by about Poland 849, 851
Pact of Steel responsibilities absolved by 1010–11
proposes conference on Danzig 851
reaction to appointment as Chancellor 27
undelivered statement of neutrality to 855
vacillates in support of 855
warns against anti-Semitism of 27
and Hungary 371
and ideological assumptions 1048
and impact of Nazi-Soviet Pact 999
on inevitability of war 849, 850
and 'Manifesto of the Race' 570–1
and Munich conference 654, 656
and non-belligerency (1939) 1011, 1059
and plans for possible war with Germany and Britain 90, 103–4
and post-First World War decade 1038
and proclaims establishment of Fascist Empire 130
and Rhineland reoccupation 155
and Spanish Civil War:
committed to 224, 225
defeat at Guadalajara 225
economic cost of 942
meaning of 183–4
military assistance 187, 191–3, 239, 696
naval blockade 236–7
reasons for intervention 193–5, 241
and Stresa talks (1935) 88–9
and Yugoslavia 845
Mussolini, Vittorio 124

Nadolny, Rudolf von 37, 43, 447
Naggiar, Paul-Emile 880, 889, 899, 900, 907
Nałkowska, Zofia 1027
Nanetti, Nino 209
Nanking, and attack on (1937–38) 528–9
Nansen, Fridtjof 177, 987
Nansen International Office for Refugees 177
nationalism:
and anti-Semitism 981
and Austen Chamberlain on German nationalism 33
and Catalan nationalism 214, 229
and Japan 1050
and Sino-Japanese conflict 516, 544
and Slovakia 66
National Salvation Association 491

naval disarmament:
and failure of naval arms control 512
and first London Naval Treaty (1930) 506, 511–12
and Japan, demand for parity 506
and preparations for new conference 506
and second London Naval Treaty (1936) 511–12
and United States, opposes changes in ratios 506–7
see also London Naval Conference (1935-36)
Naval Intelligence Division (NID), and German naval construction plans 90
navies, *see* French Navy; German Navy; Italian Navy; Red Navy; Royal Navy; United States Navy
Nazarov, Pavel 884
Nazi Party:
and Reichstag elections (1932) 19
and Reichstag elections (1933) 21
Nazi-Soviet Pact (1939)
and American awareness of talks 894
and economic and strategic consequences of 915–17
and France, believes agreement unlikely 893–5
and German-Soviet negotiations 890, 903, 904–6, 908
Far East in 904
Molotov presents draft pact 908
Ribbentrop authorises approach to Molotov 889–90, 892–3
Ribbentrop offers agreement 903
and Great Britain:
believes agreement unlikely 893–5
warnings from 'opposition' Germans 820, 822
and Hitler 1030
advantages for 1055–6
agrees to negotiations in Moscow 905
concerns over possible Anglo-Soviet alliance 900–1
initiates contact with Soviet Union 889–90
provides reassurance to 917
temporary suspension of approaches to Soviet Union 893
urgency over reaching agreement 903, 908–9
and Japan 1001, 1059
and Stalin:
dangers of agreement 903
motives for making agreement 910, 912–13, 1055
in negotiations 909
not prelude to world revolution 913
and terms of 909–10, 911
secret protocol 909–10
Neccas, Jaromir 611
Negrín, Juan 228, 230, 243, 245, 246
Netherlands:
and anti-Communism 930
and Belgium 930
and Dutch East Indies 483, 809, 929–30
and Dutch National Socialist Movement (NSB) 930–1
and economic and financial policies 930
and Far East 483
and Germany:
conciliatory approach to 930
economic importance 931
invaded by 1060
trade agreement 386
and Great Britain 722–4, 931
and Japan 483, 930
and Jewish refugees 976, 981–2
and League of Nations 929
criticism of 359, 923

Netherlands: (*cont.*)
impact of Ethiopian crisis 131
and limited defence forces 931
as 'middle power' 930
and mobilization 932
and neutrality 809, 923, 929, 930, 931, 932, 966–7
and strategic importance of 722
Neurath, Konstantin von 22, 28
and aims of 30
and China 262
and Czechoslovakia 268, 638
and dismissal of 335
and Far East 484
and Italy 261, 314–15
and questions Hitler's plans 333
and rearmament 37
and Soviet Union 458
and Spanish Civil War 233
and Sudeten Germans 267
and visit to London cancelled 234
and World Disarmament Conference 42
neutrality 924, 926, 934, 967, 1059
and Belgium 141, 279–81, 927, 928–9
and Bulgaria 956–9
and Central and Eastern Europe 407
and Churchill on 924
and compromise 967
and Denmark 923, 935
and Estonia 938, 939
and experience of First World War 966–7
and Franco 629
and Great Power failure 925
and Greece 959–61
and Hungary 954–6
and Ireland 926–7, 1018
and Latvia 939
and League of Nations, failure of 923–4, 925
and Luxembourg 934
and Nazi-Soviet Pact (1939) 909
and Netherlands 809, 923, 929, 930, 931, 932, 966–7
and Nordic states 393, 935
and Norway 131, 923, 936
and Poland 737–8
and Portugal 201, 944–6
and Romania 289, 369, 370, 745, 747, 947–9
and Spain 923, 941–4
and Sweden 923, 936–7
and Switzerland 132, 923, 939–41
and Turkey 961–5
and United States 1059
attempts to revise Neutrality Acts 777, 813–14, 818
declaration of 818–19
Neutrality Act (1935) 110
Neutrality Act (1937) 421n7, 518, 783, 811, 818
and Yugoslavia 407, 735, 949–54
News Chronicle 766
and favours Soviet alliance 887
newspapers:
and France:
controls over 770
Soviet subsidies 415
and Great Britain 887
attempts to control 766
New Statesman and Nation 1024
Newton, Basil 364, 580, 613, 614
New Zealand 515, 799, 800–2, 1018
Nicolson, Harold 607, 632, 1011
'Night of the Long Knives' (30 June, 1934) 73–4
Nin, Andreas 229, 464
NKVD (Soviet secret police) 185, 211, 215, 228, 445, 457, 460, 462, 463, 464, 465, 849, 880, 882, 884, 916
Noble, Admiral Sir Percy 807
Noël, Léon 283–5, 286, 394
Nomonhan (Khalkhin-Gol), battle of 812, 904
non-aggression pacts and treaties:
and Chinese-Soviet non-aggression pact (1937) 520
and Danish-German non-aggression pact 934, 935

and Estonian-German non-aggression pact 893, 934, 939
and German-Latvian non-aggression pact 893, 934, 939
and German-Lithuanian non-aggression pact 939
and German-Polish non-aggression treaty (1934) 62–4, 65–6, 833
and Italian-Soviet non-aggression pact (1933) 36
and Latvian-Soviet non-aggression pact 939
and Polish-Soviet non-aggression pact (1933) 65, 691
and Portuguese-Spanish Treaty of Friendship and Non-Aggression (1939) 201
as Soviet treaty formula 443
see also Nazi-Soviet Pact (1939)

Nordic states:
and defence spending 934
and Germany 386, 387, **388**, 392
and Great Britain 387, **388**, 390, 391
and League of Nations 167
impact of Ethiopian crisis 131
and limited cooperation among 935
and limits of regional solidarity 934
and Nazi sympathisers 392–3
and neutrality 393, 935
and Oslo meeting (1939) 934–5
and Ouchy Agreement (1932) 930
and Sweden urges military cooperation 935, 936
see also Denmark; Finland; Norway; Sweden

Norman, Montagu 702, 704

Norway:
and defence spending 936
and Germany:
little fear of 935
occupied by 1060
rejects non-aggression pact with 934
trade with **388**
and Great Britain **388**, 935–6
and League of Nations 359
criticism of 923
and neutrality 131, 393, 923, 936
and reluctant to engage in regional organizations 925

Nuremberg Laws 678, 973

Nye, Senator Gerald, and Spanish Civil War 208

Nye Committee (USA, 1934–36) 110, 172

Nyon Conference (1937) 237–8

Oberkommando der Wehrmacht (OKW)
and Czechoslovakia, invasion planning 334
and Keitel forbids criticism of Hitler 584
and Poland, invasion planning 833

Oberkommando des Heeres (OKH)
and Czechoslovakia, invasion planning 572
and opposition to war 577

Ogilvie-Forbes, George 203

Olympic Games (Germany, 1936) 137, 155, 260, 310

O'Malley, Owen 23

opinion polls:
and France 769
and Great Britain 766
and United States 814, 817

Ormsby-Gore, William 324

Orwell, George 183

Osborne, d'Arcy Godolphin 437

Oshima Hiroshi, Lt Col 262, 263, 484

Oslo Convention (1932) 930

Oslo group 393, 925, 926, 1003
see also Belgium; Luxembourg; Netherlands; Norway; Sweden

Oster, Colonel Hans 722, 820

Ouchy Agreement (1932) 930

Pacelli, Cardinal (later Pius XII), and Nazi-Catholic relations 985, 986
see also Pius XII, Pope
pacifism, and France 602
pacifist organizations:
and France:
Association pour la paix par le droit (APD) 168
Ligue internationale des combatants de la paix 170
Rassemblement universel pour la paix 169, 171
support for 170
and Great Britain:
divisions over attitude toward Germany 169
International Peace Campaign 169
League of Nations Union 168, 169
Peace Pledge Union 168–9
and influence of 168
and Spanish Civil War 184
and United States, 'Keep America Out of War' campaign 523
'Pact of Steel' (1939) 794, 846, 847, 848–50
Palestine:
and Arab rebellion 570, 793, 983
and British forces in 805
and civil disobedience 222
and Jewish immigration 974, 977, 983
Haavara transfer 974–6
restrictions on 793, 983–4
and partition proposed (Peel Commission, 1937) 983
Panay, USS 340, 530, 532
Pankhurst, Sylvia 106
papacy 985
and Concordat with Nazi regime (1933) 985
and condemnation of Communism (*Divini redemptoris*) 986
and Jewish policy 985
and *Mit brennender Sorge* (With Burning Anxiety) 315, 985–6
and Nazi-Catholic relations, détente in (1939) 986–7
and peace initiative (1939) 987, 1002–3
and Poland, fails to respond to German attack 1003
and silence on Jews 987
and suppresses criticism of treatment of Jews 986
Papen, Franz von 76, 326
and Austria 156, 362
and Hitler's appointment as Chancellor 19–20
and recalled by Hitler 335
Pariani, General Alberto 194, 569, 585, 586–7, 845, 955
and talks with Keitel 846–7
and warns of inability to launch offensive 853
Paris, and evacuations of 626, 1026
Parker, R. A. C. 236
Partido Obrero Unificación Marxista (Workers' Party of Marxist Unification, POUM) 185, 215, 227, 228, 229
Partido Socialista Unificado de Cataluña (Unified Socialist Party of Catalonia, PSUC) 214, 228
Paul, Prince of Yugoslavia 206, 290, 729–30
and Serbo-Croat talks 950–1, 953
and visits Hitler (1939) 730, 949–50
and visits London (1939) 951
Paul-Boncour, Joseph 46–7, 601
and Austria 557
and British assessment of 558
and Czechoslovakia 557–8
and disarmament 25, 172
and Four-Power Pact proposal 33
and Poland, failure to reassure 64
and Soviet Union, cautious approach to 67

and World Disarmament Conference 37, 43
Payart, Jean 583
Peace Ballot (1935) 106, 169
peace organizations, *see* pacifist organizations
Peace Pledge Union (PPU) 168, 184
Pearl Harbor 1065
Peden, George 804
Pedersen, Susan 176
Peel Commission 983
Persia 800
Perth, Lord, *see* Drummond, James Eric
'Pertinax' (French journalist), *see* Geraud, André ('Pertinax')
Pešić, General Petar 951
Pétain, Marshal Henri-Philippe 48, 52, 944
Peterson, Sir Maurice 120, 122
Philippines 481, 507
Phipps, Eric 153–4, 306, 558, 580, 1013, 1015
  and Czechoslovakia 623–4
  on dealing with Hitler 24
  on Hitler's diplomatic objectives 259
  and Hitler's disarmament proposals 45
  and Hitler's lack of interest in concessions 325
  and Rhineland reoccupation 432
  and sent as ambassador to Berlin (1933) 24
  and sent as ambassador to Paris (1937) 259
Picasso, Pablo 241
Piétri, François 769
Piggott, Major-General Francis 536
Piłsudska, Aleksandra 1028
Pitsudski, Józef 35, 366, 367
  and balancing Berlin and Moscow 65
  and France 63, 71
  and Germany 63, 65
  and Soviet Union, suspicion of 71
Pitmann, Senator Key 208
Pius XI, Pope:
  and acclaims Italian victory in Ethiopia 130
  and condemnation of Communism (*Divini redemptoris*) 986
  and death of 986
  and *Mit brennender Sorge* (With Burning Anxiety) 985–6
  and suppresses criticism of treatment of Jews 986
Pius XII, Pope:
  and Nazi-Catholic relations, détente in (1939) 986–7
  and peace initiative (1939) 987, 1002–3
  and Poland, fails to respond to German attack 1003
  and silence on Jews 987
  see also Pacelli, Cardinal
Pleven, René 783
Plotkin, Mikhail 884
Plymouth, Lord 215–16, 217, 305–6, 391
Poland 359
  and anti-Semitism 367, 981
  and Czechoslovakia:
    antagonism between 65, 95, 587–8
    anti-Czech campaign 66
    backs Hungarian claims to Ruthenia 689
    demand cession of territory 688
    reaction to German-Polish declaration (1934) 66
    territorial claims against 614, 615
    troops move into Ruthenia 732
    understanding sought by (1934) 64–5
  and Eastern Locarno Pact, opposition to 72–3
  and Enigma machine, shares information about 790
  and France:
    accord between (1939) 787
    air agreement talks 394

Poland (*cont.*)
attempts to re-define alliance by 713
Danzig 841
failure to monitor war planning 393–4
guarantee by 741, 777
limited value of alliance with 63
military mission from 788
misled by over military intentions 788
overstate military strength to 789
Rambouillet loan and arms agreement 283–6, 393, 394
reaction to German invasion 1010, 1012–14, 1015
reaction to German-Polish declaration (1934) 65–6
security guarantee refused by 63
seeks support from 64
slowness in supplying equipment by 394
suspicion between 71, 407
talks with (1934) 71
visit by Delbos (1937) 405
and Germany:
assurances from (1933) 35
assurances from (1938) 366
Danzig 265, 266, 365, 366, 690–2, 732–3, 787, 839, 840, 841–4
diplomatic relations broken off by 839
German-Polish non-aggression treaty (1934) 62–4, 65
Hitler orders attack 999, 1004, 1005
Hitler orders occupation of Danzig 691
invaded by 1009, 1012, 1020, 1058
invasion planning by 733, 833, 839, 863, 905
losses in war against 1029
Nazi-Soviet Pact provisions 910
negotiations between 690–1
policy over Czechoslovakia 587–8
press campaign by 843, 861
provoked by 839
rapprochement with 62
relaxation of tension over Danzig 842
revision of Nazi-Soviet Pact terms 915
simulated attack 995, 1009
trade with 379, 731
Upper Silesia 365–6
Westerplatte affair (Danzig) 30–1
and Great Britain:
Anglo-Polish alliance (1939) 998
Beck distrusted by 366
Danzig 842
guarantee by 738–9, 740–1, 1032
informal attempts to reach agreement with Germany 856–60
last-minute attempts to avoid war 1003–9
loan talks with 790
military mission from 788
promise of support by 738
proposes secret agreement with 737–8
reaction to German invasion 1009, 1011–12, 1013, 1014–17
reciprocal guarantee 738
staff talks (1939) 788–9
and Hungary 954, 955
and impact of Nazi-Soviet Pact 998
and Italy 261–2, 851–2, 1009, 1013
and Jewish refugees 981
and League of Nations, impact of Ethiopian crisis 132

and Memel, concern over 732
and military planning 787–8
strength of forces 1020
and mobilization 998, 1027
and neutrality 737–8
and post-First World War decade 1038
and public mood on outbreak of war 1027–9
and refugees from 956
and Rhineland reoccupation 151, 152
and Romania 394
and Soviet Union 29
assurances to (1933) 35
conversations between (1934) 66
invaded by 915, 1020, 1058
Nazi-Soviet Pact provisions 910
non-aggression pact (1933) 65, 691
passage of troops refused 907, 1033
Polish-Soviet agreement (1938) 878
response to British guarantee 739, 876, 877–8
response to French guarantee 877
revision of Nazi-Soviet Pact terms 915
suspicion of 71
troops deployed by during Czech crisis 619–22
and United States, offers mediation with Germany 1001–2
and Westerplatte affair (Danzig) 31
Portugal:
and encourages Franco to remain neutral 201
and Germany 199, 944–5
and Great Britain:
alliance with 945
military mission from 200, 945
promotion of relations by 200
tensions between 199, 944
and neutrality 944–6
and New State ('Estado Novo') 198
and Portuguese-Spanish Treaty of Friendship and Non-Aggression (1939) 201
and preservation of neutrality 201
and Sino-Japanese conflict 539
and Spanish Civil War 198, 199, 216
Posse, Hans Ernst 386
Potemkin, Vladimir Petrovich 231, 418, 424–5, 445, 453–4, 618, 880, 884–5
Pravda, and Radek's 'Revision of Versailles' 29
Prieto, Horacio 229
Primikov, Vitaly Markovich 464
Profintern 885
propaganda:
and Anglo-Portuguese relations 200
and France:
film 768
imperial sentiment 798
and German-Portuguese relations 199
and Germany, anti-Semitism 989
and Great Britain:
imperial sentiment 795–7
leaflet drops on Germany 1019–20
in United States 814
prostitution, and control of 174

Quakers 982, 985
Quiroga, Santiago Casares 186
Quisling, Vidkun 392

racism:
and Germany 264
and Italy 570–1
and Western assumptions about Japanese and Chinese 486–8
see also anti-Semitism
Raczynski, Count Edward 737–8

Radek, Karl:
and Germany, offers Baltic pact 66
and Japan, opposes appeasement of 492
and Poland, visit to (1933) 35–6
and 'Revision of Versailles' 29
and tried for treason 457, 462
Raeder, Admiral Erich 90, 333
and Italian navy 844
and lack of enthusiasm for Italian alliance 569
and offers resignation 835
and planning for naval war with Britain 574
Rajchman, Ludwik 173
Rassemblement universel pour la paix (RUP) 169, 171
Rath, Ernst von 677
realism, and international relations 1049–50
rearmament, *see* entries under individual countries
Reciprocal Trade Agreements Act (USA, 1934) 97
Red Army:
and British evaluation of 434–5
and expansion of 870, 871
technological and industrial backwardness 872–3
and Far East, reorganization in 904
and forward defence 912
and French evaluation of 417, 422
and officer shortages 870–1
and Poland, invasion of 1020
and political officers 870
and purges of 415, 420, 422, 435–6, 462, 464–5, 870
impact of 465–6
and Red Air Force:
British evaluation of 434, 435
new aircraft designs 870
and tanks 870
Red Navy:
and expansion of 871, 872
and purges of 465
and submarines 871–2
refugees:
and Co-ordinating Foundation 978
and Czechoslovakia 687
and Evian conference (1938) 976–7
and German Jews 679
and Great Britain 860
and inter-governmental committee on refugees (IGCR) 977, 978
and League of Nations 177–8
and liberalization by destination countries 982–3
and Luxembourg 933
and Poland 956
and reluctance of countries to admit Jews 976, 977, 978, 981–2, 984–5, 987, 988–9
and Spanish Civil War, flee to France 207, 247, 944
and United States 860, 976–7
Reichgruppe Industrie (RI) 389, 702–4
and Düsseldorf agreement (FBI-RI) 707
Reichstag fire 20–1, 29
Reichswehr:
and expansion of 44
and 'Night of the Long Knives' 73
and reaction to Hitler's appointment as Chancellor 30
and rearmament 30
and rejection of Versailles 29–30
see also Wehrmacht
Reichswerke Hermann Göring 331, 378
and seizure of Alpine (Austrian steel producer) 556
Renault 138
Renoir, Jean 769
Renondeau, General Gaston-Ernest 24–5
Renzetti, Guiseppe 26
reparations 1040
Reynaud, Paul 121, 567, 627, 770

and economic reform 716
and *laissez-faire* 717n56
and Polish guarantee 777, 996
and rearmament 277
and United States, offers French possessions to 783
and warning over military expenditure 782
Rheinmetall-Borsig (German company) 378, 960
Rhineland remilitarization/reoccupation 143
and Belgium 147, 148–9
and France:
diplomatic planning for 139–40
lack of military planning for 138–9
loss of prestige over 160
public opinion 158
response to 144–5, 146
seeks British agreement on sanctions 147–8
unwillingness to respond militarily 145–6, 158
and Germany 130, 136–7, 142–4
Hitler's peace offer 144, 150
motives for timing of 137
rejection of British 'Text of Proposals' 150
secures Italian support for 137
and Great Britain:
attitude towards 141, 142
muted reaction to 152
prepared to negotiate over 142
public opinion 159
response to 146–7
'Text of Proposals' 148–9
and Italy 137, 149, 155
and League of Nations:
condemned by 149
French appeal to 144–5
inaction over 150–1, 152
and muted reaction to 152
and Soviet Union, impact on 452
Ribbentrop, Joachim von 40, 301, 557
and Anti-Comintern Pact 263, 524
and assessment of British policy 317–18
and Austria, ultimatum to Schuschnigg 552
and becomes foreign minister (1938) 335
and Bulgaria 958
and colonial demands 260, 324
and Czechoslovakia 638
and France:
Danzig 841–2
Franco-German pact (1938) 714
ultimatum from 1019
and Great Britain:
as ambassador to 91–2, 153, 254, 263–4
convinced will not fight 859, 860
naval talks (1935) 90–1, 92
ultimatum from 1017–18
and Italy:
alliance negotiations 847–8
alliance proposals (1938) 692–3
discussions with Mussolini 316
'Pact of Steel' (1939) 848–9
promises to recognise rights of 845
proposes pact with 568, 569
staff talks 697
and Japan 484, 539–40, 846
and *Kristallnacht* 680, 979
and Non-Intervention Committee 216, 233
and Poland 841–2
convinced Britain will not fight over 859, 860
Danzig 691–2, 732
meeting with Henderson 1007
and reputation of 686
and Rhineland reoccupation 148, 153
and Soviet Union:
agreement offered to 903
authorises approach to Molotov 892–3
clandestine contacts with 882

Ribbentrop, Joachim von (*cont.*)
Far East in negotiations with 904
initiates contacts with 889–90
signs Nazi-Soviet Pact 910
Ribes, Champetier de 644
Riefenstahl, Leni 74
right-wing movements:
and Eastern Europe 9, 270, 371, 372, 373, 1041–2
and France, exploitation of Stavisky affair 48
Rimma (Romanian company) 376–7, 381
Rio Tinto Company 201, 244
Ritschl, A O 383
Ritter, Gerhard 1022
Ritter, Karl 377
Roatta, General Mario 190, 192
Roberts, Frank 894
Rochat, Charles 611
Röhm, Ernst 44, 73
Rohstoffe- und Waren-Einkaufsgesellschaft (ROWAK) 196
Romania 359
and *Anschluss* 363
and anti-Semitism 405, 981
and Balkan Pact (1934) 68
and Czechoslovakia 401, 689
and elections (1937) 405
and France:
air assistance pact talks 401
attempts to improve military cooperation by 400–1
failure to reach trade agreement 287
Franco-Little Entente alliance talks 396, 397
guarantee by 746
inability to supply arms by 401–4
lobbies for Little Entente alliance 288
oil supplies 402, 747
sabotage of oil fields explored by 747
suspicion between 407
trade agreement 715, 747
traditional links between 369–70
visit by Delbos (1937) 405
and Germany:
alliance offered by 370
arms supplies from 402
economic treaty (1939) 729
oil supplies 380–1, 382, 715, 747, 948
rumour of action by 734–5, 947
trade agreement 270, 376–7, 382, 581, 748
trade with 380–3, 731, 948, 1046
and Great Britain:
guarantee by 746, 1032
oil supplies 747
promise of support by 738
requests unconditional guarantee from 745
seeks assistance from 399–400
trade agreement 747
trade with 399, 709–10
and Hungary 370, 588, 956
and impact of Nazi-Soviet Pact 947
and Iron Guard 405
and Italy 261, 850
and Jewish refugees 981
and King Carol establishes personal dictatorship 405
and League of Nations, impact of Ethiopian crisis 132
and National Christian party 405
and neutrality 947–9
and non-alignment policy 289, 369, 370, 745, 747, 946
and Poland 394
and political divisions 288
and rearmament 401–2
and Rhineland reoccupation 151, 152
and Soviet Union:
Bessarabia 370, 910
minister withdrawn by 405

Nazi-Soviet Pact provisions 910
offer non-aggression treaty to 370
rapprochement between (1938) 581
talks over mutual assistance pact 288–9
and Turkey 68, 947
see also Little Entente
Romanian National Bank 381
Rome Protocols (1934) 69
Romilly, Esmond 220
Roosevelt, Franklin D:
and administrative style 815
and Axis threat to American security 813
and cautious approach to foreign policy 814–15, 817, 1053–4
and Czechoslovakia 633, 634–5, 635–6, 655
and declaration of war 1066
and enigmatic nature of 814
and Ethiopian crisis 110
and Far East:
Anglo-American naval talks 808
suggests Anglo-American cooperation 503–4
suggests peace conference (1936) 503
and France, sale of aircraft to 813
and Great Britain:
advice on fighting Germany 634
approves Chamberlain's diplomatic initiative 534
congratulates Chamberlain over Munich agreement 643
criticism of 813, 814
'Destroyers for Bases' deal (1940) 817
invites George VI to America 818
Lend-Lease (1941) 1062
naval talks 340, 808
refuses British request for warning to Hitler 723
suspicion of 633–4, 813
and Hitler's view as tool of 'Jewish conspiracy' 16, 680, 989
and intends keeping America out of war 818–19, 1054, 1062
and intervention in World Disarmament Conference 37–8
and Japan 481, 544
abrogates commercial treaty 811
means of pressuring 812
stronger line towards 1065
suggests Anglo-American cooperation 503–4
suspicion of 507
and Jewish refugees 976–7, 988
and London Naval Conference 510
and naval expansion 506–7, 514
and neutrality, declaration of 818–19
and Neutrality Acts 110, 421n7, 777, 813–14, 818
and offers mediation between Germany and Poland 1001–2
and peace-plan proposal (1937) 533–4
and peace-plan proposal (1939) 817–18
and pragmatism of 481
and rearmament 817
and Rhineland reoccupation 151
and Second World War, declaration of neutrality 818–19
and sensitivity to Washington opinion 814
and Silver Purchase Act (1934) 500
and Sino-Japanese conflict 527
considers and drops blockade idea 530, 532

Roosevelt, Franklin D (*cont.*)
proposes 'quarantining' Japan 531–2
'quarantine' speech in Chicago (1937) 521–2
and Spanish Civil War 207, 208
Rosenberg, Alfred 24, 264, 392
Rothermere, 1st Viscount (Harold Sidney Harmsworth) 1023–4
Royal Air Force (RAF):
and Bomber Command 607
and Chain Home system (radar) 606, 772
and deficiencies in 607
and expansion of 87–8
abandonment of bomber parity 606
aircraft production 606, 699, 773
cut in bomber programme 699
fighter forces 606, 699, 772
Hurricanes and Spitfires 772
Third Deficiency Programme (1936) 294–5
and Fighter Command 607
monoplane fighters 772
and imperial obligations 805
and planned expenditure 51, 52
Royal Commission on the Manufacture of and Trade in Armaments (1935-36) 172
Royal Navy:
and Anglo-German Naval Agreement (1935) 91–3, 391, 513
and Anglo-German naval talks 91
and anti-submarine warfare 773
and Ethiopian crisis 111–12, 113–14
and expansion of 513, 514, 698–9
'King George V' building programme 773
replacement programme 507
Third Deficiency Programme (1936) 294
and Far East, Anglo-American naval cooperation 340, 532–3, 808
and 'fleet to Singapore' strategy 742, 791
and imperial obligations 804
and 'Italy first' strategy 741–2
rejection of 791
and Japan 504–5
and Mediterranean, strength in 792
and naval arms race 513, 514
and planned expenditure 51, 52
disagreements over 507–8
and Spanish Civil War 205
and two-ocean fleet 774
Rozenberg, Marcel 210, 229
Rublee, George 977, 979
Rüdiger, Ernst 156
Rumbold, Horace 21
on Laval 136
and *Mein Kampf* despatch 23
and reaction to Hitler's appointment as Chancellor 20, 22, 23
and warns Hitler against anti-Jewish activities 22
Runciman, Walter, 1st Viscount Runciman of Doxford 386–7, 390, 503–4
and Czechoslovakian mission 580–1, 594, 595, 610
Russell, Bertrand 168
Russia, *see* Soviet Union
Ruthenia:
and clandestine German organizations 689
and Hungarian claims to 688–9
German-Italian arbitration of (1938, first Vienna award) 689–90
Hitler opposes 689
seized by 728
Rydz-Śmigły, Marshal Edward 284, 285–6, 739, 1004
Rykov, Alexei 27, 211

SA (*Sturmabteilung* - Storm-troopers) 44

and incorporation into German police 30
and *Kristallnacht* 677
and 'Night of the Long Knives' 73–4
Saar plebiscite (1935), and return to Germany 83–4
Sackville-West, Vita 632
Sadoul, Georges 1026
St Louis (Jewish refugee ship) 980
St Lucia 817
Saint-Quentin, René de 120, 122, 283
Salazar, António de Oliveira 198, 199, 944, 945–6
Salengro, Robert 272
Salonika, and French proposals for occupation of 791–2
Sanjurjo, General José 181, 187
Saraçoglu, Şükrü 964, 965
Sargent, Orme 23
and Austria 328
and Czechoslovakia 615
and economic appeasement 309
and Franco-Little Entente alliance proposals 397–8
on Hitler's diplomatic objectives 298–9
and Soviet Union, distrust of 428–9, 433
and undermining French government 558
Sarraut, Albert 46, 128, 145, 146, 777
Sato Naotake 502, 503
Saudi Arabia 798, 983
Saxe-Coburg-Gotha, Duke of 152
Scandinavian states:
and defence spending 934
and occupation of 934
see also Denmark; Nordic states; Norway; Sweden
Schacht, Hjalmar 977
and Anglo-German economic talks 704
and Blomberg, relations with 254–5
and British expectations of 702
and colonial demands 306–7, 309
and discussions with Blum 258, 291
and discussions with Leith-Ross 309
and economic crisis (1934) 96–7
and Göring, relations with 255, 257, 376
and Hitler, relations with 258, 259, 304, 325
and Italy 129
and meets with Halifax (1937) 339
and Montagu Norman, relations with 702, 704
and 'New Plan' 96–7, 269
and rearmament programme 254–5
and resigns as Economics Minister 674
and resigns as president of *Reichsbank* 705
and securing raw materials 269, 376–7
and Soviet Union:
trade negotiations (1935) 447–9
trade negotiations (1936) 454, 455–6
and support for army expansions 96
and visits London (1938) 704
Schleicher, Kurt von 19, 73
Schleswig Holstein (German battleship) 839, 1009
Schmidt, Guido 362
Schmidt, Paul 338, 649, 1017
Schmundt, Rudolf 576
Schneider-Creusot (French munitions manufacturer) 378, 402
Schnurre, Julius 869, 882, 885, 889, 893, 901, 903, 904
Schulenburg, Count Werner von 868, 903
and German-Soviet agreement talks 905–6, 908

Schulenburg (*cont.*)
and German-Soviet credit talks 882, 890
and German-Soviet friendship 449
and instructed to see Molotov 889–90, 892–3
and suggests German-Soviet trade pact 75
Schuller, Richard 403
Schuschnigg, Kurt von:
and attempts to strengthen government 155–6
and Austro-German agreement (1936) 157
and brings Seyss-Inquart into cabinet 363
and dismisses Rüdiger 156
and Habsburg restoration 362
and Hitler's ultimatum to 552–3
and meets with Hitler 364
and Mussolini's warnings to 314
and plans plebiscite on Austrian independence 553
and rejects customs and currency union proposals 364
and resignation of 553
and seeks *détente* with Germany 363
Schweisguth, General Victor-Henri 292, 417, 418
Schwerin, Lt Col Gerhard von 820–1, 886
Schwerin von Krosigk, Johann Ludwig Graf 579, 653
Second World War:
and British declaration of war 1018
and British Empire 1064
and different starting dates for 545
and ending of European predominance 2, 1066
and expansion into global conflict 1063
and fall of Chamberlain 1062
and fall of Low Countries and France 1060–61
and Finnish-Soviet war 1059–60
and French declaration of war 1019
and German-British stalemate 1062
and German declaration of war on United States 1065–6
and German invasion of Soviet Union ('Operation Barbarossa') 1064–5
and German-Soviet cooperation 1061–2
as Hitler's war 1029, 1035, 1037, 1057
and imperialism 1064
and Italian declaration of war (1940) 1061–2
and Japan 1062–3
and Japanese attack on America (Pearl Harbor) 1065
and political repercussions of 1063–4, 1066–7
and public mood on outbreak of:
France 1025–7, 1057
Germany 1021–3
Great Britain 1023–5
Poland 1027–9
and United States 1062
declaration of neutrality 818–19
declaration of war 1066
'Destroyers for Bases' deal (1940) 817
Lend-Lease (1941) 1062
Secrétariat Général de la Défense Nationale (SGDN) 566
Secret Intelligence Service (SIS) (Great Britain) 572, 721, 771
see also intelligence services
Seeckt, General Hans von 490
Seeds, Sir William 750, 876, 877–8
and Soviet alliance negotiations 888, 889, 896, 899, 901
and warns of Soviet neutrality pact 879

self-determination 2, 264, 560, 586, 588, 611, 642, 733, 752, 1039
Semenov, General A S 292, 417, 418, 420
Serbia, and Serbo-Croat talks 950–1, 953
Service de Renseignement (French military intelligence) 721
Seyss-Inquart, Artur 156, 265, 362, 363, 553
shadow factory scheme, and British rearmament 294
Shanghai:
  and battle for 516–17
  and bombing of 478
  and British forces in 805
Shaposhnikov, Marshal Boris M 907
Sheppard, Canon Dick 168, 184
Shigemitsu Mamoru 904
Shimomura, Captain (Japanese naval negotiator) 510
Shirer, William L 85, 1022
Shtein, Boris 463, 880
Silver Purchase Act (1934, USA) 500
Simon, John, 1st Viscount Simon 31, 32, 41
  and Anglo-German naval talks 91
  and economic appeasement 403
  and France, support for Laval's approach 81–2
  and Germany, Berlin talks with Hitler (1935) 86–7
  and rearmament (as Chancellor of the Exchequer) 698, 699
  and recognition of German rearmament 81
  and Stresa talks (1935) 89–90
  and United States 480, 781
  and World Disarmament Conference 42–3, 70
Simpson, Sir John Hope 979
Simpson, Wallis 169, 302n46
Singapore:
  and British base opened 515
  and British forces in 805
  and construction of British base 479, 507
  and doubts over defensibility of 808
  and fall of 1064
  and French doubts over defence of 807
  and Indian Army 800
Sino-Japanese conflict:
  and France 526–7, 539
  and Germany 518–19, 539–40
    arms supplies to China 519
    ends arms deliveries to China 524, 540
    mediation efforts 529
    neutrality 519
    support for Japan 524
  and Great Britain 477
    Anglo-American naval cooperation 532–3
    Anglo-American talks 522–3
    building of Burma Road 530, 537, 542
    clarifies position 525
    considers naval demonstration 530
    hesitancy in assisting Nationalists 536–7
    Japanese attack British ships 530
    Japanese naval blockade 518
    mediation attempts over Shanghai 517
    opposes economic boycott 521
    reasons for concern over 477–8
    rejects American blockade proposal 530–1
    support for China 542–3
    talks with Japan 538
    Tientsin crisis 896–7
  and inter-connection with global crisis 541, 544–5
  and Italy 486
  and Japan:
    all-out offensive (Oct, 1938) 539
    announce war of annihilation against Nationalists (Jan, 1938) 535

Sino-Japanese conflict: (*cont.*)
attack on Nanking (1937–38) 528–9
expansion of territorial aims 535–6
expeditionary force to central China 517
financial and economic strain on 537
military clashes with Soviet Union 869–70, 888, 891, 903, 904
naval blockade of China 518
negotiations with Wang Ching-wei 541
peace terms (Nov, 1937) 524–5
seek negotiations with Chiang Kai-shek 538
talks with Britain (July, 1938) 538
toughening of peace terms 528, 529
and League of Nations 520–1
calls for Nine Power Conference 522
denounces Japanese actions 522
and Marco Polo Bridge incident 515–16
and Nine Power (Brussels) Conference (1937)
called for by League of Nations 522
failure of 527–8
Japanese refusal to attend 524
United States 525–6
and Portugal 539
and Shanghai campaign 516–17
and Soviet Union 477, 520, 541–2
arms supplies to China 520, 541
concern over possible Anglo-Japanese agreement 536–7
military assistance to Kuomintang 230–1, 529
military clashes with Japan 869–70, 888, 891, 903, 904
and stalemate in 540–1
and Tangku truce (1933) 488
and unexpectedness of initial military engagement 516
and United States 527
Anglo-American talks 522–3
blockade idea considered and abandoned 530, 532
Brussels Conference (1937) 525–6
freeze on trade with Japan 1065
Japanese attack on American ships 530
Japanese naval blockade 518
oil embargo 1065
proposes 'quarantining' Japan 531–2
public sympathy for China 523
Roosevelt's 'quarantine' speech 521–2
see also China; Japan
Slovakia:
and German economic control 729
and German occupation of 727
and German support for independence 687
and Hungarian claims to 688
German-Italian arbitration of (1938, Vienna award) 689–90
and Poland, invasion of 839
smaller powers, and neutrality 923–67
see also individual countries
Śmigły-Rydz, *see* Rydz-Śmigły, Marshal Edward
Smith, F E 106
Smuts, Field Marshal Jan Christiaan 1018
social Darwinism 14, 27, 1048
Social Democratic Party (SPD, Germany) 19, 20
Sokolnikov, G Y 457, 462
Soong, T V 489, 500
Sorge, Richard 262, 477, 891, 903
South Africa 159, 798, 799–800, 802, 1018

Soviet Union:
and anti-Fascist coalition strategy:
failure of 443–4
Litvinov's policies 443
and appeasement 1064
Japan 492
and Austria, response to German invasion 559
and Baltic states 878
Anglo-Soviet alliance negotiations 895
Nazi-Soviet Pact provisions 910, 939
pressures to surrender sovereignty 916
revision of Nazi-Soviet Pact terms 915
and Bulgaria 959
and centralization 445
and China:
arrest of Chiang Kai-shek 496–7
Chinese Communist Party (CCP) 493–5
military assistance to Kuomintang 230–1, 520
negotiations with Kuomintang 496
non-aggression pact (1937) 520
and collective security 134, 245, 414, 439, 442, 451, 452, 878
and Czechoslovakia:
arms supplies to 581
backs Hungarian claims to Ruthenia 689
Beneš seeks to ascertain attitude of 613–14
Czech-Soviet mutual assistance pact (1935) 94–5, 581
inability to directly assist 581–2
Litvinov advocates tougher action against Germany 618
military assistance proposals 417–18
offers Anglo-French-Soviet consultations 583
preparatory military measures to assist (1938) 619–22
response to German invasion 875–6
response to invasion rumour 572
'wait and see' policy towards 582–3
and deterrence:
anti-Fascist coalition 443
mutual assistance pacts 439
and Eastern Locarno Pact 72–3, 74–5
Franco-Soviet negotiations (1935) 80–1
and Estonia 910, 938, 939
and Ethiopian crisis, impact of 134
and exposed position of 869
and Far East 541–2
Changkufeng 538
concern over 903–4
fear of war in 891
German-Soviet negotiations 904
high priority of 477
Nomonhan (Khalkhin-Gol) 904
and fears of capitalist attack 439–41
and Finland 878, 938–9
Anglo-Soviet alliance negotiations 895
Nazi-Soviet Pact provisions 910
pressure on 938
warning to 888
winter war between 1059–60
and foreign policy:
anti-Fascist coalition strategy 443–4
arrangement with Germany strategy 444
isolation strategy 446
Stalin's control of 444–5, 880, 881, 885, 913–14

Soviet Union: (*cont.*)
and Foreign Trade Commissariat 444
and France:
air mission to from 419
alliance negotiations 889, 893, 895–900, 901–2
assessment of policy of 424
barriers to agreement between 1054–5
British opposition to military collaboration 416, 419, 420
closer cooperation pressed by 751–2
conditions for agreement with 881
deterioration of relations between 424–5
different aims in negotiations 888, 910–12
difficulties in way of talks with (1939) 752
divided opinions over value of alliance 713
fear of German-Soviet *rapprochement* 420–1
Franco-Soviet mutual assistance pact (1935) 93–4, 415, 421, 430
Franco-Soviet talks (1933) 36, 67
Franco-Soviet talks (1935) 80–1
impact of purges on relations 415, 459
impact of Spanish Civil War on relations 414
military assistance proposals 417–18
military talks between (1936-37) 416–21, 422
military talks between (1939) 901–2, 906–7, 908, 909
mutual distrust 415, 456–7, 652
opposition to military talks 416–17, 419–20, 422
pressure for military staff talks 291
response to military proposals to 418
response to Polish guarantee 877
revised alliance proposals to 888
staff talks 326
trade agreement 424
tripartite alliance offered to 880
and Germany 863
agreement offered by 903
agrees to negotiations in Moscow 905
approaches towards (1935) 450–1
arguments in favour of arrangement with 444
awareness of intentions of 889, 891
Berlin Pact of Non-Aggression and Neutrality (1926), extension of (1933) 28
clandestine contacts between (1939) 882
contacts initiated by 889–90
credit talks 882
credit treaty (1935) 447
deterioration of relations between 454
difficulties in approaching 445
economic agreements (1939) 1058
Far East in negotiations between 904
Hitler considers negotiations 834, 863, 891
Hitler rejects political talks proposal (1937) 456
Hitler's urgency over reaching agreement 903, 908–9
impact of Litvinov's dismissal 885
increased cooperation with 1061–2
invaded by (1941) 1064–5

Litvinov contests policy towards 450
Litvinov on possible understanding between 459–60
Merekalov-Weizsäcker meeting 882–3
military contacts 27–8
Molotov on relations between 452–3
negotiations between (1939) 904–6, 908
offer of Baltic pact rejected by 66–7
positive signals to 888
presents draft pact to 908
provides naval base to 917
reaction to Hitler's appointment as Chancellor 27–9
re-appraisal of relations with (1933) 35–6
response to Hitler's Nuremberg speech (1936) 454
Ribbentrop authorises approach to Molotov 892–3
Stalin's motives for reaching agreement 910, 912–13
Surits' assessment of German policy 449–50
temporary suspension of approaches by 893
terms of Nazi-Soviet Pact 909–10, 911
trade agreement (1934) 447
trade agreement (1936) 454
trade agreement (1939) 908
trade negotiations (1935) 447–9, 451
trade negotiations (1936) 454, 455–6
trade negotiations (1938) 458–9
trade talks resumed (1939) 901
trade with 448, 892, 916–17
war decided by 1063
see also Nazi-Soviet Pact (1939)

and Great Britain:
alliance negotiations 893, 895–900, 901–2
Anglo-Soviet naval arms limitation treaty (1937) 873
barriers to agreement between 914–15, 1055
change in attitude by 427–8
Churchill's hope for alliance between 431
credit extended by 432
different aims in negotiations 888, 910–12
difficulties in way of *rapprochement* 431
difficulties in way of talks with 752
dilatoriness in securing cooperation by 749–51
guaranteed loan proposal 432
impact of purges on relations 414–15, 435–6, 459
impact of Spanish Civil War on relations 414, 433–4
Metropolitan-Vickers affair 36, 425, 888
military alliance against Germany proposed to 751
military talks between (1939) 901–2, 906–7, 908, 909
mutual distrust 425, 430–1, 432, 456–7, 1055
response to four-power declaration proposal by 735–6, 737
response to Polish guarantee 739, 876, 877–8
revised alliance proposals to 888
significance for Far Eastern strategy of 426
spy in Foreign Office 897–8
talks with (1939) 879
tripartite alliance offered to 880–1

Soviet Union: (*cont.*)
tripartite alliance offer rejected by 882
unilateral guarantee sought by 879, 886
visit by Eden (1935) 429–30
weakness of negotiating position 896–7
and ideology:
deviations from 442–3
distinctions between capitalist states 443
fear of capitalist encirclement 439
inevitability of war with capitalist powers 439–40
response to Nazi challenge 1047
and industrialization 441
and intelligence services:
German military plans 907–8
impact of purges 907
pandering to Stalin's views 1049
and isolationism 231, 446, 451, 458, 459
and Italy, non-aggression pact (1933) 36
and Japan:
appeasement of 492
border disputes 467, 538, 869–70, 888, 891, 903, 904
Changkufeng 538
deterioration of relations between 74
Nomonhan (Khalkhin-Gol) 904
reasons for concern with 477
relations monitored by Britain 433
risk of war between 492
sale of Chinese Eastern Railway 492–3
and Latvia 393, 910, 939
and League of Nations:
becomes member 74
expelled from 1059–60
and Lithuania, revision of Nazi-Soviet Pact terms 915
and mass deportations of Poles 916
and Memel, anxiety over German occupation 739
and military expenditure **441**, **446**
armament industries production **442**
increase in 873–5
weapons procurement **442**
and mobilization 619–22
and multilateral assistance pact proposed by (1933) 67
and Munich conference, exclusion from 645, 1054
and Narkomindel:
loss of influence 444
proposes pact with France and Poland 67
purges of 445, 460, 461–2, 463
and non-aggression treaties 443
and Poland 29
assurances from (1933) 35
conversations between (1934) 66
invasion of 915, 1020, 1058
losses in invasion of **1029**
Nazi-Soviet Pact provisions 910
non-aggression pact (1933) 65, 691
passage of troops refused by (1939) 907, 1033
Polish-Soviet agreement (1938) 878
response to British guarantee to 739, 876, 877–8
response to French guarantee to 877
revision of Nazi-Soviet Pact terms 915
troops deployed against during Czech crisis 619–22
and Politburo:
foreign affairs committee 880

reaction to Hitler's appointment as Chancellor 27
and post-First World War decade 1038–9
as pariah state 1039
and purges 185, 211, 230, 459
Comintern 464
economic effects of 466–7
explanation of 460–1
impact on relations with Britain and France 414–15
institutions targeted 461–2
Narkomindel (foreign ministry) 445, 460, 461–2, 463
national and ethnic groups 462
national communist parties 464
Red Army 415, 420, 422, 462, 464–6, 870
Red Navy 465
show trials 210–11, 453, 457, 559
'Trotskyists' in Spain 219, 227, 229, 464
and rearmament:
armament industries production 442
army expansion 870, 871
increased budget for 873–5
military expenditure 441, 446, 676
mobilization planning 875
naval expansion 871, 872
production increases 873, 874
Second Five-Year Plan (1933–1937) 441, 442, 446, 870, 871, 872, 874, 875
technological and industrial weakness 872–3
weapons procurement 442
and Rhineland reoccupation, impact of 452
and Romania:
Bessarabia 370, 910
Nazi-Soviet Pact provisions 910
non-aggression treaty offered by 370
rapprochement between (1938) 581
talks over mutual assistance pact 288–9
withdraws minister from 405
and show trials 210–11
and Sino-Japanese conflict 467, 477, 520, 541–2
arms supplies to China 520, 541
concern over possible Anglo-Japanese agreement 536–7
military assistance to Kuomintang 230–1, 529
and 'socialism in one country' 442
and Spanish Civil War, *see* Spanish Civil War
and trade policy, Germany 447–9, 451, 454, 455–6, 458–9, 916–17
and Turkey 748, 963, 964–5
and United States 36
see also Comintern; Nazi-Soviet Pact (1939); Red Army; Red Navy
Spaak, Paul Henri 279, 320
Spain:
and Anti-Comintern Pact 942
and France, Bérard-Jordana agreement 944
and Germany 196–8, 942, 943
and Great Britain 201–2, 244–5, 944
and League of Nations:
criticism of 359, 923
impact of Ethiopian crisis 131
and military forces 943
and national elections (1936) 186, 201
and neutrality 629, 923, 941–4
and Portuguese-Spanish Treaty of Friendship and Non-Aggression (1939) 201

Spanish Civil War 182
and aftermath of 247–8
and air power:
Guernica 225–6
increasing fear of bombing 184
siege of Madrid 219
and anarchists 214–15
and anti-Communism 184
and Basque campaign 225–7, 232–3
and beginning of 181
and Brunete 226
and Communist Party of Spain 209, 214, 215, 218, 219, 228
and divisions on left 214–15
and emotional response to 183
and France 203, 234, 414, 558
arms supplies to government 204
calls for prohibition of foreign volunteers 216, 217
clandestine military aid 206–7, 243
containment of conflict 221, 232
divisive impact on left 205–6, 243
frontier supervision proposal 216–17
impact on 185
non-intervention policy 181, 204, 205, 242–3
Nyon Conference (1937) 237–8
refugees flee to 207, 247–8, 944
and Germany 181
desire to prolong 242
economic benefits of intervention 196–8
German-Italian cooperation 190–1, 192
Guernica 225–6
limited involvement in 191
military assistance 187–8, 191, 219, 242
naval confrontations 233
organization of supplies 196
reasons for intervention 195–6
recognition of Nationalist government 190
testing of weapons and tactics 196, 219
use by 184
and Great Britain:
Attlee's view of policy 221
Cabinet divisions over 223–4
calls for prohibition of foreign volunteers 216, 217
containment of conflict 203, 221, 232
criticism of non-intervention policy 221
domestic political divisions over 232–3
fears of Communist Spain 202–3
frontier supervision proposal 216–17
impact on 185
impact on Anglo-Soviet relations 414, 433–4
initial reaction of 202
Labour Party's view of non-intervention 221, 233
naval confrontations 232–3
non-intervention policy 181, 202, 203, 205, 221–2, 243–4
Nyon Conference (1937) 237–8
policy preparation for Franco victory 244–5
public opinion 245
threat to Anglo-Portuguese alliance 199–200
and Guernica 225–6
as ideological struggle 181–3, 1047–8
and impact of 185–6
and international brigades 190, 206, 213–14, 218–19, 220, 246
and Italy 181
attack on Málaga 224

committed to 225
cost of intervention 195, 942
defeat at Guadalajara 224–5
disregard of non-intervention policy 223
German-Italian cooperation 185, 190–1, 192
impact on German-Italian relations 185
meaning for Mussolini 183–4
military assistance 187, 192–3, 219, 220, 239, 696
naval blockade 236–7
naval confrontations 233
Nyon Conference (1937) 237–9
reasons for intervention 193–5, 241
recognition of Nationalist government 190
Spanish-Italian trade 195
and Madrid campaign 189–90, 218–19
and media coverage of 183
and Mexico 181, 208
and Nationalist appeals for foreign assistance 187
and Nationalist military victory 246
and naval confrontations 232–4
Italian naval blockade 236–7
Nyon Conference (1937) 237–9
and negotiated peace, talks about 229
and Non-Intervention Agreement 204, 205, 233
and Non-Intervention Committee 199, 211, 212, 215–16, 217–18
and origins of 186–7
and Partido Obrero Unificación Marxista (POUM) 215, 227, 228, 229
and Partido Socialista Unificado de Cataluña (Unified Socialist Party of Catalonia, PSUC) 214, 228
and Popular Front 186
and Portugal 198, 199, 216
and Republican divisions 214–15
Communists tighten control 227–9
and Soviet Union 181, 208–9
accepts French non-intervention proposal 209–10
arms shipments 211, 212, 220, 230, 231, 245
attacks on 'Trotskyists' 215, 219, 227, 229, 464
cautious policy of 210, 221
change in attitude of 230, 245
decides to intervene 211–12
gold shipments to 213
impact on 185
impact on relations with Britain and France 212, 414, 433–4
instructions to Spanish Communists 209
international brigades 213–14
military delegation 210
military lessons learned by 870
money raised by 209
participation in Non-Intervention Committee 211, 212
and United States 207–8
Spanish Socialist Workers' Party (PSOE) 228
Speer, Albert 241, 256, 679, 972
SS (*Schutzstaffel* - Protective Squads):
and Jewish Affairs Division 975
and *Kristallnacht* 677
and 'Night of the Long Knives' 73
and simulation of Polish attack on Germany 995, 1009
Stahlhelm, and incorporation into German police 30
Stalin, Joseph 882
and anti-Semitism 989
and appeasement 1064

Stalin, Joseph (*cont.*)
and China:
Chinese Communist Party (CCP) 493–4
relations with Mao Tse-tung 493–4
response to Chiang Kai-shek's arrest 497
urges offensive by Chiang Kai-shek 904
and collective security 429–30
and control of foreign policy 444, 445, 880, 885
considers options 881
ideological framework 913–14
and Czechoslovakia 618, 619, 622
and Ethiopian crisis 134, 452
and Far East, reorganization of Red Army 904
and fears of capitalist attack 439–40
and France:
Franco-Soviet pact (1935) 94
military talks with (1939) 902
seeks military alliance with 94
and Germany:
awareness of intentions of 889, 891
dangers of agreement with 903
disregards warnings of attack by 1064
Hitler's urgency over reaching agreement 908–9
increased cooperation with 1061–2
intelligence on Hitler's plans 907–8
motives for reaching agreement with 910, 912–13
Nazi-Soviet Pact (1939) 909, 910, 1055
negotiations with 905, 908, 909
trade negotiations (1935) 447
trade with 916
and Great Britain:
meets Eden (1935) 429–30
negotiations with (1939) 902, 910–12
suspicion of 897, 900, 908, 912
and isolationism 446, 452
and Japan, danger from 477, 493
and Litvinov's dismissal 884
and newspaper interview (1936) 452
and non-alignment policy 881, 885
as pallbearer for German communist 35
and Poland:
invasion of 915
lack of confidence in Beck 878
and Popular Front strategy 443
and pragmatism of 443
and purges 185, 211, 229, 230, 457
economic effects of 466–7
explanation of 460–1
foreign and diplomatic services 462–3
institutions targeted 461–2, 464
national and ethnic groups 462
national Communist parties 464
Red Army 415, 420, 422, 462, 464–6
Red Navy 465
show trials 559
'Trotskyists' in Spain 464
and Soviet strength 868
and Spanish Civil War 209, 245
advice to Caballero 220–1
cautious policy towards 210, 221
decides to intervene 211, 212
international brigades 213
Republican divisions 215
and speech to XVIIIth party congress 867–8
ambiguities in 868–9
attack on 'non-aggressive' powers 868, 869
and suspicion of western plots 867–8, 869

and uncertainty of 66
and unity of country 446
Stanley, Oliver 704, 708, 781, 898
Stavisky, Serge 48
Stimson, Henry L 480
Stojadinović, Milan 290
and France 404
Franco-Little Entente alliance talks 396
and Germany:
trade with 380
visits Hitler 404
and Hungary 372
and Italy 404
treaty with (1937) 367–9
Straits Convention (1923), and revision of (1936) 132–3
Strang, William 329
and Eastern European policy 327–8
and Munich conference 639, 640
on Russo-German relations 23–4
and Soviet Union 750
alliance negotiations 888–9, 893
Metropolitan-Vickers affair 888
Strasser, Gregor 19
Stresa talks (1935) 88–90, 103
Stresemann, Gustav 1037, 1038
strikes, and France 348–9, 594, 716
Stumm, Baron von 889
Subotić, Ivan 368
Sudan, and British forces in 805
Sudeten German Home Front 266–7
Sudeten German Legion 594
Sudeten German Party (SdP) 267, 364, 585, 593–4
Sudeten Germans 266–7
and Anglo-French discussions 342–3, 365
and Beneŝ 406
concessions made by 584–5
grants all demands to ('Fourth Plan') 585
rejects Anglo-French demands 614
rejects Hitler's terms 622–3
secret offer to cede territory 611
and France:
Anglo-French demand to transfer territory 612–13
Anglo-French ultimatum 612–13
rejects Hitler's terms 624
and Germany 560
press campaign by 364
staging of incidents 585, 593
transfer of territory 681
and Great Britain:
accepts Henlein's view of problem 561
Anglo-French demand to transfer territory 612–13
Anglo-French ultimatum 612–13
presses for concessions to Sudeten leaders 581
Runciman mission 580–1, 594, 595, 610
sympathy for complaints of 364
and Henlein's demands 560–1
Suez Canal, and strategic importance for Britain 800
summit meetings, and Chamberlain 648–9
Surits, Yakov 75, 737, 751, 752, 869, 900
and France 424, 879
and Germany 449–50, 451, 455
Suvich, Fulvio 155
Sweden:
and Anglo-French-Soviet talks 936–7
and Finland 936, 937–8
and Germany 388, 389, 934, 937
and Great Britain, trade with 388, 937
and League of Nations 359
criticism of 923
and Nazi-Soviet Pact (1939) 937

Sweden: (*cont.*)
and neutrality 393, 923, 936–7
and trade policy 937
and urges Nordic military cooperation 935, 936
Swinton, 1st Earl of (Philip Cunliffe-Lister, Baron Masham) 296, 606
Switzerland:
and civil defence 941
and foreign policy objectives 940
and France, military talks with 785, 941
and Germany 941
and Italy 940
and Jewish refugees 976, 981–2
and League of Nations 167, 940
criticism of 359, 923
departure from 131–2, 940
impact of Ethiopian crisis 131–2, 940
and neutrality 132, 923, 939–41
and pro-Allied sentiment 941
Syria, and French reinforcement of 793
Syrovy, General Jan 615, 641
Sztojay, Dome 372

Tabouis, Geneviève ('Cassandra') 125, 1027
Tanganyika 306
tanks:
and Czechoslovakia 64
and France 138, 275, 344, 600, 776, 1060
and Germany 253
and Great Britain 435n39, 786
and Soviet Union 196, 219, 435, 441, 870
Tardieu, André 41, 52
'Tardieu plan' 34–5
TASS (Telegraph Agency of the Soviet Union), and journalists arrested in Germany 29
Tattarescu, Gheorghe 382–3
Taylor, A J P 647–8
Teichova, Alice 384
Teleki, Count Pál 954, 955, 956
Temperley, General A C 31
Tennant, E W 857
territorial acquisitions 11
Teruel, battle of (1937-38) 245–6
The Times:
and Czechoslovakia 591–2
and opposes Soviet alliance 887
Thomas, Colonel (later General) George 775, 837–8
Thorez, Maurice 213
Thummel, Paul 336
Tientsin crisis 809–12, 896–7
Tilea, Vergil 734, 735, 745
Timoshenko, Marshal Semyon Konstantinovich 466
Tiso, Father Jozef 727, 954
Titulescu, Nicolae 132, 151, 152, 289
Tocqueville, Alexis de 1063–4
Todt, Fritz 256, 576
Togoland 306, 310, 324, 325
Tooze, Adam 674, 838, 1031–2
totalitarianism, and exaggerated respect for efficiency of 312–13
trade policy, *see* under individual countries
Transylvania 370
Trautmann, Oskar 476–7, 484, 524, 528
Trauttmansdorff, Count zu 268
Treaty of Friendship and Arbitration (Turkey and Romania) (1932) 68
Trinidad 817
Tripartite Stabilization Agreement (1936) 174–5, 278
Trott, Adam von 821–2
Trujillo, Generalissimo Rafael 977
Truth 821
Tukhachevsky, Mikhail 27, 28, 420–1, 457, 462, 464, 465
and execution of 870
and Germany 449
Tunisia:
and Daladier visits 719

and Franco-Italian agreement (1935) 78–9
and French forces in 806
and Italy 697, 851, 853
Turkey 359
and Balkan Pact (1934) 68
and Bulgaria 957
and France 749
Anglo-French financial support 964
Anglo-French-Turkish alliance (1939) 965
Anglo-French-Turkish military convention 963
Franco-Turkish declaration (1939) 963
and Germany 377, 961–2
and Great Britain 709
Anglo-French financial support 964
Anglo-French-Turkish alliance (1939) 965
Anglo-French-Turkish military convention 963
Anglo-Turkish declaration (1939) 748, 962, 963
credit agreement 962
different aims in negotiations 963
guarantee by 744, 748
lack of financial assistance from 748–9
reluctant to provide assistance 963–4
response to four-power declaration proposal by 735
seeks closer ties with 743
strategic importance to 962
trade relations 709
and Italy, threat from 963
and Montreaux Convention (1936) 132, 133, 288, 289, 962
and neutrality 961–5
and revision of Straits Convention 132–3
and Rhineland reoccupation 152
and Romania 68, 947
and Soviet Union 748, 963, 964–5
and strategic importance of 744
and vulnerability of 963
and Yugoslavia, military convention with 68
Twardowsky, Fritz von 449
Tydings-McDuffie Act (USA, 1934) 507
Tyrrell, Sir William 41

Ugaki Kazushige, General 538
Ukraine:
and *Lebensraum* 414
and Soviet Union 915–16
Stalin on 867–8
Ulbricht, Walter 214
Uldricks, Teddy J 439
United States:
and anti-Semitism 860
and anti-war feeling 110
and China:
open door policy 480–1
public sympathy for 523
Silver Purchase Act (1934, USA) 500
support for Nationalists 487
trade with 481
and Czechoslovakia 655
criticism of Anglo-French policy 633
proposes international conference on 635–6
Roosevelt's appeal over 635
wait and see policy 634
and disarmament, Roosevelt's intervention in Geneva talks 37–8
and economic and financial policies:
abandonment of gold standard 9, 1042
impact on post-First World War Europe 1039, 1040–41
return to gold standard 1040

United States: (*cont.*)
tripartite exchange rate agreement (1936) 174–5, 278
and Ethiopian crisis 110
and Far East:
Anglo-American naval cooperation 532–3
Britain seeks to work with 479–80
as difficult partner to Britain 480
investments in 481
lack of cooperation with Britain 481–2
neutralization proposal 504
open door policy 480–1
suggests Anglo-American cooperation 503–4
and France:
public support for 814, 817
sale of aircraft to 717, 782–3, 813, 816–17
seeks access to money market 783
support expected by 777
and Germany:
debt default 96
declaration of war 1066
knowledge of German-Soviet talks 894
offers mediation over Poland 1001–2
reaction to *Kristallnacht* 679, 973
trade with 97, 815–16
war declared by 1065–6
and Great Britain:
Anglo-American trade agreement (1938) 534, 816
criticism of cartel arrangements with Germany 707
'Destroyers for Bases' deal (1940) 817
difficulties in relations between 812–13
difficult partner to in Far East 480, 481–2
economic rivalry 815
Far East 479–80, 481
George VI's visit 818
gold shipments 781–2
intelligence cooperation 533, 816
Lend-Lease (1941) 1062
naval appeal from 742
naval cooperation 532–3
naval talks (1938) 340
naval talks (1939) 808
proposes European peace plan 533–4
public support for 814, 817
response to Munich 534, 643
support expected by 634, 777
suspicion of 633–4
trade talks 534
tripartite exchange rate agreement (1936) 174–5, 278
and Hitler's view as tool of 'Jewish conspiracy' 16, 680, 989
and isolationism 110, 655, 814, 1039
and Japan 481, 543–4
abrogates commercial treaty with (1939) 811
attacked by 1065
freeze on trade with 1065
means of pressuring 812
miscalculations about 1065
oil embargo 1065
Pearl Harbor 1065
'Plan Orange' 506, 514
stronger line towards (early 1941) 1065
suggests Anglo-American cooperation 503–4
Tientsin crisis 810, 896–7
and Jewish refugees 860, 974
Evian conference (1938) 976–7
increased intake of 982–3
private funds raised for 978

public opinion 984
and neutrality 818–19, 1059
and Neutrality Act (1935) 110
and Neutrality Act (1937) 421n7, 518, 783, 811, 818
and pacifist organizations 523
and post-First World War decade 1039
economic impact on Europe 1039, 1040–41
and pro-China lobby 476
and public opinion 814, 817
support for Allied powers 814, 817, 1054
and rearmament 817
military expenditure 676
naval expansion 506–7, 513, 514
and retreat from Europe 95
and Silver Purchase Act (1934) 500
and Sino-Japanese conflict 527
American ships attacked by Japanese 530
Anglo-American naval cooperation 532–3
Brussels Conference (1937) 525–6
considers and drops blockade idea 530, 532
Japanese naval blockade 518
Panay affair 340, 530, 532
and Soviet Union 36
knowledge of German-Soviet talks 894
and Spanish Civil War 207–8
and trade policy:
Germany 815–16
Great Britain 534
United States Army Air Forces, and rearmament 817
United States Navy:
and Anglo-American naval talks 340, 808
and expansion of 506–7, 513, 514
Ustaša (Croatia) 78, 368
Van den Bergen, General Édouard 281, 322, 785, 928, 929
Van der Lubbe, Marinus 20
Van Langenhove, Fernand 279
Vansittart, Sir Robert 260, 300
and appeasement 298, 433
and Czechoslovakia, Plan Z 592
and Defence Requirements Committee 50
and demoted by Eden 328–9
and diminished influence of 126
and Ethiopian crisis 115, 116, 117, 122–3
anxiety to end crisis 119
Hoare-Laval plan 123, 124
and Far East, advocates working with America 479–80
and France 82, 420
and Germany:
meets Hitler (1936) 298
reaction to Hitler's appointment as Chancellor 23
and intelligence network 324, 329, 721, 820, 893
and meets Henlein 267
and rearmament 297
and Soviet Union 426–7, 427–8, 429, 750, 893
and Spanish Civil War 433
and United States 816
and World Disarmament Conference 41
Van Zeeland, Paul 140, 141
and increase in military expenditure 320
and policy of independence 279, 280
and Rhineland reoccupation 147, 148, 149
and Zeeland Plan 403, 404
Van Zuylen, Baron Pierre 279
Versailles, Treaty of (1919):
and Foch's verdict on 1037
and Germany, unilateral revision of 84–5

Versailles, Treaty of (1919) (*cont.*)
and Great Britain, unilateral revision of (Anglo-German naval agreement) 91–2
Victor Emmanuel III, King of Italy 108, 853, 1001
Vinson-Trammell Naval Bill (USA, 1934) 507, 514
Vivian, Captain Guy 487
Völkischer Beobachter 989
Voroshilov, Marshal Kliment E 27, 445, 465, 880
and Anglo-French-Soviet military talks 906, 908, 909
and Czechoslovakia 622
and France 74, 419
Vuillemin, General Joseph 417, 997
and Czechoslovakia 558
and German air superiority 597
and Poland 788

Wahls, Karl 1022
Wal Wal incident 101
Wandycz, Piotr 65
Wang Ching-wei 529, 536, 541
war debts 1040
Washington Naval Treaty (1922) 506
and Japanese abrogation of 476
Watt, D C 843, 1057
Wavell, General Archibald 434–5
Wehrmacht:
and acceptance of Hitler's strategic control 682
and British estimates of strength of 772
and Czechoslovakia:
Hitler's reassurances over 578
invasion planning 334, 365, 560, 571, 572–3, 584, 616, 681
and equipment shortages 834
and expansion of 252–3, 673, 835
acceleration of 574
conscription 84–5, 195, 736
Hitler announces expansion of (1935) 85
pessimism over future production 837–8
problems with 85
programme for (1936) 253
raw material shortages 330, 836–7
and France, invasion of 1060
and Hitler's purge of leadership 334–5
and Hitler takes personal command of 334
and Italy, negative opinion of forces of 844
and loyalty to Hitler 590
and mobile warfare 253
and opposition to war 577
and Poland:
invasion of 1009
invasion planning 833, 905
and position in Hitler state 577
and Rhineland demilitarized zone 85
and unpreparedness for war in 1938 652–3
and views Italy as burden 317
and weaknesses of 776
Weimar Republic 1038
and collapse of 10, 1043
Weir, William Douglas, 1st Viscount 296
Weizmann, Chaim 990
Weizsäcker, Ernst von 30, 327, 333, 681, 842
and Czechoslovakia 578, 638, 821
and German-Soviet relations 458
and Great Britain:
advises 'menacing silence' 856
Anglo-Soviet talks 890
warnings to 822
and opposition to war with Britain and France 820
and Poland 839, 1000
and Soviet Union 903
Anglo-Soviet talks 890
Merekalov-Weizsäcker meeting 882–3

proposes normal political relations with 890
Welczek, Johannes von 308, 593
Welles, Sumner 522–3, 525, 533, 808, 812, 815, 1059
Wells, H G 184
Wenner-Gren, Axel 820, 858
Werth, Alexander 407
Westerplatte (Danzig), and Polish reinforcement of 31
Weygand, General Maxime 40
and defensive strategy of 70
and disagreements with government 47
and opposition to disarmament 52
and Salonika campaign 791–2
and warns against German rearmament 25
Wiedemann, Fritz 573, 579–80
Wigram, Ralph 426
Wilhelmina, Queen of the Netherlands 929, 932, 1003
Wilson, Sir Horace 590, 591, 624, 649, 724, 858, 859, 887, 1016
and mission to Germany 626, 628, 630
and prepares 'capitulation' telegram to Beneŝ 631
Wilson, Woodrow 173, 1039
Witzleben, Erwin von 629
Wohlthat, Helmuth 380–1, 382, 706, 710, 734n5, 858–9, 900–1, 978
Wood, Sir Kingsley 606, 699, 781
World Disarmament Conference (1932-34) 1040
and adjournment of 39, 44, 167
and failure of 9, 55–6, 1043
and France 36–42
and Germany 36, 37
departure of 42–3
Hitler's intervention 38
reaction to withdrawal of 43–4
support for MacDonald plan (1933) 40
and Great Britain:
Anglo-French disagreements 41–2
'MacDonald plan' (1933) 31–2, 36–7
reaction to Hitler's intervention 38
and United States, Roosevelt's intervention 37–8
see also disarmament
World Economic Conference (1933) 9, 39

Yang Hu-ch'en, General 495, 496–7
Yeats, W B 1067
Yezhov, Nikolai 445, 880
Yoshida Shigeru 502, 503
Yugoslavia 359
and anti-Bolshevism 290
and army's poor state 400
and Balkan Pact (1934) 68, 950
and Bulgaria 367, 950, 958
and Czechoslovakia 588
and exposed position of 949
and France:
arms supplies from 401, 952
assurances to 404
attempts to improve military cooperation by 400–1
Franco-Little Entente alliance talks 396, 397
inability to supply arms by 402–3
increasing distance between 289–90
loss of influence by 395
military consultations between 951
reaction to Italian-Yugoslav treaty (1937) 369
refuses to abandon 404–5
suspicion between 407
trade agreement 287, 715
and Germany 367
arms credits from 950, 953
assurances of neutrality to 953

Yugoslavia (*cont.*)
conciliatory approach of 730, 949
Hitler-Stojadinović talks (1938) 404
trade agreement 269, 270, 376, 380, 386, 953, 954
trade with 380, 383, 729–30, 731, 1046
and Great Britain:
arms credits from 952
military consultations between 951
Prince Paul visits London (1939) 951–2
reaction to Italian-Yugoslav treaty (1937) 369
response to Anglo-Turkish declaration 950
restriction on arms supplies from 399
trade with 399
and Hungary 372, 404, 588, 950
and impact of Nazi-Soviet Pact 953
and Italy 78, 261, 853
threat from 949
trade agreement 290
treaty between (1937) 367–9
and Jewish refugees, closes door to 976
and neutrality 407, 735, 949–54
and non-alignment policy 946, 949
and Rhineland reoccupation 152
and Serbo-Croat talks 950–1, 953
and Soviet Union, fears of 290
and Turkey 68, 950
see also Little Entente
Yurenev, Konstantin 458

Zay, Jean 272, 601, 627, 777
Zetkin, Klara 35
Zhdanov, Andrei 231, 444, 464, 881, 897, 913
Zhukov, General (later Marshal) Georgii 904
Zinoviev, Grigorii 210
Zog, King of Albania 693, 742